THE PUBLIC GENERAL ACTS

AND CHURCH ASSEMBLY MEASURES

1969

with
Lists of the Public General Acts
and Local Acts
and a Table of the Effect of Legislation
and an Index

[IN TWO PARTS]

PART I

LONDON
HER MAJESTY'S STATIONERY OFFICE
1970
PRICE £10 10s. 0d. [£10·50] NET
(for both parts)

Printed by C. H. Baylis.
Controller of Her Majesty's Stationery Office and
Queen's Printer of Acts of Parliament

SBN 11 840044 4

The Public General Acts
and Church Assembly Measures
which received the Royal Assent in 1969
in which year ended the SEVENTEENTH
and began the EIGHTEENTH YEAR
of the Reign of HER MAJESTY
QUEEN ELIZABETH THE SECOND
and
ended the Third Session
and began the Fourth Session
of the Forty-Fourth Parliament of the
United Kingdom of Great Britain
and Northern Ireland

CONTENTS

PART I

PART II

TABLE I

Alphabetical List of the Public General Acts of 1969

TABLE II

Chronological List of the Public General Acts of 1969

* Consolidation Act.

Chapter		Part	Page
31	Appropriation Act	I	409
32	Finance Act	I	467
33	Housing Act	I	683
34	Housing (Scotland) Act	I	755
35	Transport (London) Act	I	819
36	Overseas Resources Development Act	I	904
37	Employer's Liability (Defective Equipment) Act ...	I	907
38	Sharing of Church Buildings Act	I	909
39	Age of Majority (Scotland) Act	I	925
40	Medical Act	I	931
41	National Mod (Scotland) Act	I	955
42	Architects Registration (Amendment) Act	I	957
43	Air Corporations Act	I	959
44	National Insurance Act	I	967
45	Iron and Steel Act	I	987
46	Family Law Reform Act	I	997
47	Nurses Act	II	1023
48	Post Office Act	II	1037
49	Education (Scotland) Act	II	1301
***50**	Trustee Savings Banks Act	II	1355
51	Development of Tourism Act	II	1421
52	Statute Law (Repeals) Act	II	1445
***53**	Late Night Refreshment Houses Act	II	1469
54	Children and Young Persons Act	II	1477
55	Divorce Reform Act	II	1603
56	Auctions (Bidding Agreements) Act	II	1611
57	Employers' Liability (Compulsory Insurance) Act ...	II	1615
58	Administration of Justice Act	II	1619
59	Law of Property Act	II	1645
60	Transport (London) Amendment Act	II	1683
61	Expiring Laws Act	II	1685
62	Rent (Control of Increases) Act	II	1687
63	Police Act	II	1696
64	Customs (Import Deposits) Act	II	1703
65	Ulster Defence Regiment Act	II	1705

* Consolidation Act.

TABLE III

Alphabetical List of the Local and Personal Acts of 1969

	Chapter No.
Aberdeen Corporation (Fish Market) Order Confirmation Act ...	xix
Barclays Bank Act	xiii
Barnsley Corporation Act	xi
Bedford Corporation Act	xlvi
Blackpool Corporation Act	lvii
Bradford Corporation Act	xlviii
Bristol Clifton and West of England Zoological Society Act	xxix
British Railways Act	xliii
British Transport Docks Act	xxiii
Bournemouth Corporation Act	vi
Cardiff Corporation Act	xlvii
Chelsea College, University of London Act	ix
City of London (Various Powers) Act	xxxix
Clyde Port Authority Order Confirmation Act	xxxi
Corn Exchange Act	xxvi
Covent Garden Market Act	ii
Coventry Corporation Act	vii
Derby Corporation Act	v
Derbyshire County Council Act	iii
Dudley Corporation Act	lii
Dundee Corporation Order Confirmation Act	xxxii
East Green, Aberdeen Order Confirmation Act	xxxiii
Edinburgh Corporation Order Confirmation Act	lxii
Edinburgh Trades Maiden Fund Order Confirmation Act	xx
Essex River and South Essex Water Act	xlix
Farmer & Company, Limited (Transfer of Registration) Act ...	xxvii
Foreman and Staff Mutual Benefit Society (Application of Rules) etc. Act	xii
Forth Ports Authority Order Confirmation Act	xxxiv
Glasgow Corporation Order Confirmation Act...	lxi
Glasgow Corporation (Superannuation etc.) Order Confirmation Act	x
Greater London Council (General Powers) Act	lii
Greater London Council (Money) Act	xli
Kidderminster Corporation Act	xliv
Lands Improvement Company's Amendment Act	xxv

TABLE IV

Chronological List of

the Church Assembly Measures of 1969

Measures passed by the National Assembly of the Church of England which received the Royal Assent during the year 1969

No. 1. Clergy Pensions (Amendment) Measure 1969.
No. 2. Synodical Government Measure 1969.

THE PUBLIC GENERAL ACTS OF 1969

Electricity (Scotland) Act 1969

1969 CHAPTER 1

An Act to increase the statutory limits imposed on the amounts outstanding in respect of borrowings by the Scottish Electricity Boards and to amend the law with respect to the authentication of the seals of the said Boards. [30th January 1969]

BE IT ENACTED by the Queen's most Excellent Majesty, by and with the advice and consent of the Lords Spiritual and Temporal, and Commons, in this present Parliament assembled, and by the authority of the same, as follows:—

Extension of borrowing powers of Scottish Electricity Boards.
1947 c. 54.
1963 c. 59.

1.—(1) In subsection (7) of section 47 of the Electricity Act 1947 as set out in Schedule 3 to the Electricity and Gas Act 1963 (which limits the borrowing powers of the North of Scotland Hydro-Electric Board and the South of Scotland Electricity Board) for the words " £500 million or such greater sum, not exceeding £580 million, as the Secretary of State may by order specify ", there shall be substituted the words " £700 million, or such greater sum, not exceeding £800 million, as the Secretary of State may by order specify ".

(2) Any power to make an order which is exercisable by virtue of this section includes power to revoke or vary any such order by a subsequent order.

(3) Any such power shall be exercisable by statutory instrument, and no order shall be made in the exercise of any such power unless a draft of the order has been laid before the Commons House of Parliament and has been approved by a resolution of that House.

(4) In consequence of subsection (1) of this section—

(*a*) section 1(3) of the Electricity and Gas Act 1963 shall cease to have effect; and

(*b*) in section 2(2) of the said Act of 1963 (which specifies enactments which limit the amount of the Government advances authorised to be made to the Scottish Electricity Boards and other bodies under that section) at the end there shall be added the words " or the Electricity (Scotland) Act 1969 ".

Authentication of seals of Boards.

2. It shall no longer be necessary for the seal of the North of Scotland Hydro-Electric Board or the South of Scotland Electricity Board to be authenticated by the signature of the chairman of the Board or by some other member of the Board authorised by the Board to act in his stead in that behalf; and accordingly paragraph 11 of Schedule 1 to the Hydro-Electric Development (Scotland) Act 1943 (which among other things provides for the authentication of the seals of the Scottish Electricity Boards) shall have effect as if for the words from " signatures " to " and " there were substituted the word " signature ".

1943 c. 32.

Short title and interpretation.

1963 c. 59.
1968 c. 39.

3.—(1) This Act may be cited as the Electricity (Scotland) Act 1969; and the Electricity (Scotland) Acts 1943 to 1957, the Electricity and Gas Act 1963 and the Gas and Electricity Act 1968 so far as they relate to Scotland, and this Act may be cited together as the Electricity (Scotland) Acts 1943 to 1969.

(2) Except where the context otherwise requires, any reference in this Act to any other enactment is a reference to that enactment as amended by any subsequent enactment, and includes a reference to it as applied by any subsequent enactment.

Local Government Grants (Social Need) Act 1969

1969 CHAPTER 2

An Act to authorise the payment to local authorities in Great Britain of grants towards expenditure incurred by reason of special social need in urban areas.

[30th January 1969]

BE IT ENACTED by the Queen's most Excellent Majesty, by and with the advice and consent of the Lords Spiritual and Temporal, and Commons, in this present Parliament assembled, and by the authority of the same, as follows:—

Provision for grants.

1.—(1) The Secretary of State may out of moneys provided by Parliament pay grants, of such amounts as he may with the consent of the Treasury determine, to local authorities who in his opinion are required in the exercise of any of their functions to incur expenditure by reason of the existence in any urban area of special social need.

(2) Grants under this section may be paid at such times, subject to such conditions and on account of such expenditure (for the year 1968–69 or any later year) as the Secretary of State may determine.

(3) The expressions " local authority " and " year " have the same meaning in this section, in its application to England and Wales, as they have for purposes of the Local Government Act 1966 by virtue of section 41 of that Act and, in its application to Scotland, as they have for purposes of the Local Government (Scotland) Act 1966 by virtue of section 46 of that Act.

1966 c. 42.
1966 c. 51.

Short title, and extent.

2.—(1) This Act may be cited as the Local Government Grants (Social Need) Act 1969.

(2) This Act does not extend to Northern Ireland.

Consolidated Fund Act 1969

1969 CHAPTER 3

An Act to apply a sum out of the Consolidated Fund to the service of the year ending on 31st March 1969.

[12th February, 1969]

Most Gracious Sovereign,

WE, Your Majesty's most dutiful and loyal subjects, the Commons of the United Kingdom in Parliament assembled, towards making good the supply which we have cheerfully granted to Your Majesty in this Session of Parliament, have resolved to grant unto Your Majesty the sum hereinafter mentioned; and do therefore most humbly beseech Your Majesty that it may be enacted, and be it enacted by the Queen's most Excellent Majesty, by and with the advice and consent of the Lords Spiritual and Temporal, and Commons, in this present Parliament assembled, and by the authority of the same, as follows:—

Issue out of the Consolidated Fund for the year ending 31st March 1969.

1. The Treasury may issue out of the Consolidated Fund of the United Kingdom and apply towards making good the supply granted to Her Majesty for the service of the year ending on 31st March 1969 the sum of £187,493,000.

Short title.

2. This Act may be cited as the Consolidated Fund Act 1969.

National Insurance &c. Act 1969

1969 CHAPTER 4

An Act to postpone the coming into force of the provision made by section 3(1) of the National Insurance Act 1966 with respect to the entitlement of suspended workers to unemployment benefit; and to make further provision with respect to periods of limitation governing the payment of benefit under the enactments relating to social security. [6th March 1969]

BE IT ENACTED by the Queen's most Excellent Majesty, by and with the advice and consent of the Lords Spiritual and Temporal, and Commons, in this present Parliament assembled, and by the authority of the same, as follows:—

Postponement of 1966 provisions restricting entitlement of suspended workers to unemployment benefit.

1.—(1) In section 3(1) of the Act of 1966 (which amends provisions of the Insurance Act so as, in effect, to provide that as from 10th March 1969 suspended workers are not to be entitled to flat-rate unemployment benefit for the first six days of suspension), for the words " as from the expiration of the period of three years beginning with the date of the passing of this Act " there shall be substituted the words " as from the appointed day ".

(2) The said section 3(1), so far as it operates for the purpose of provisions of the Insurance Act relating to unemployment benefit or to a day or period of interruption of employment, shall be deemed not to have come into force under the National Insurance Act 1966 (Commencement) (No. 2) Order 1966 (without prejudice, however, to its operation in relation to earnings-related supplement). S.I. 1966/633.

(3) An order under section 14(4) of the Act of 1966 appointing a day for the purpose of section 3(1) of that Act, in its application to provisions of the Insurance Act mentioned in subsection (2) of this section, shall not be made unless a draft of the order has

been laid before Parliament and approved by resolution of each House of Parliament; and section 14(6) of that Act shall not apply so as to require a statutory instrument containing such an order to be laid before Parliament after being made.

Amendments of Social Security Acts as to time-limit for payment of benefit.

2.—(1) In section 52 of the Insurance Act and section 27 of the Industrial Injuries Act (regulations respecting time and manner of payment of benefit), the following shall in each case be substituted for paragraph (*b*) of subsection (2):—

"(*b*) for extinguishing the right to payment of any sum by way of benefit if payment is not obtained within a prescribed period, not being less than twelve months, from the date on which the right is to be treated under the regulations as having arisen".

1966 c. 20. (2) In section 17(1) of the Ministry of Social Security Act 1966 (regulations for administering non-contributory benefit), the following shall be substituted for paragraph (*e*):—

"(*e*) for extinguishing the right to payment of any sum by way of benefit if payment is not obtained within a prescribed period, not being less than twelve months, from the date on which the right is to be treated under the regulations as having arisen".

(3) Section 52(2) of the Insurance Act (as amended by this section), so far as it authorises the making of regulations for the purpose mentioned in paragraph (*b*) thereof, shall apply to allow-
1965 c. 53. ances under the Family Allowances Act 1965 as it applies to benefit under the Insurance Act; and section 7(2) of the said Act of 1965 (extinguishment of right to payment of allowance when unclaimed for six months) shall cease to have effect.

(4) Regulations made by virtue of any of the following enactments (as amended or applied by this section)—

section 52(2)(*b*) of the Insurance Act,

section 27(2)(*b*) of the Industrial Injuries Act, or

section 17(1)(*e*) of the Ministry of Social Security Act 1966,

may relate to rights accruing before the passing of this Act.

Exclusion of requirement to submit regulations to advisory bodies.

3.—(1) Section 108 of the Insurance Act (which requires a preliminary draft of regulations to be submitted to the National Insurance Advisory Committee before the regulations are made or, in certain cases, before a draft is laid before Parliament) and section 62(2) of the Industrial Injuries Act (which requires a proposal to make regulations to be referred to the Industrial Injuries Advisory Council for consideration and advice) shall not apply to regulations made, or to a draft of regulations laid, before the expiration of six months beginning with the date of the passing of this Act if the instrument containing the regulations or, as the case may be, the draft states that the regulations are, by virtue of the following subsection, exempt from the requirements of the said sections 108 and 62(2).

(2) Regulations are exempt from the said requirements if they contain no provisions other than such as—

(*a*) are made in consequence of this Act; or

(*b*) amend the Insurance Act or the Act of 1966, or regulations made under the Insurance Act or the Industrial Injuries Act, by extending from six months to twelve months a period of limitation governing the payment of benefit.

(3) In section 108(9)(*d*) of the Insurance Act (exemption of regulations relating to family allowances from requirement of prior submission to National Insurance Advisory Committee), for the words " under Part IV " there shall be substituted the words " under Part II or Part IV "; and there shall be added at the end of sub-paragraph (ii) the words " or section 2(3) of the National Insurance &c. Act 1969 ".

Citation, construction, interpretation, repeal and extent.

4.—(1) This Act may be cited as the National Insurance &c. Act 1969, and—

(*a*) the National Insurance Acts 1965 to 1968 and this Act may be cited together as the National Insurance Acts 1965 to 1969;

(*b*) the National Insurance (Industrial Injuries) Acts 1965 to 1968 and section 2 of this Act may be cited together as the National Insurance (Industrial Injuries) Acts 1965 to 1969; and

(*c*) the Family Allowances Acts 1965 to 1968 and section 2 of this Act may be cited together as the Family Allowances Acts 1965 to 1969.

(2) This Act—

(*a*) so far as it relates to the subject matter of the Insurance Act, shall be construed as one with that Act; and

(*b*) so far as it relates to the subject matter of the Industrial Injuries Act, shall be construed as one with that Act.

(3) In this Act, " the Insurance Act " means the National Insurance Act 1965; " the Industrial Injuries Act " means the National Insurance (Industrial Injuries) Act 1965; and " the Act of 1966 " means the National Insurance Act 1966. 1965 c. 51. 1965 c. 52. 1966 c. 6.

(4) The following enactments in the Family Allowances Act 1965 are hereby repealed:— 1965 c. 53.

(*a*) section 7(2); and

(*b*) in section 13(1)(*e*), the words " for extending the period limited by section 7 of this Act for obtaining payment of such sums ".

(5) Without prejudice to the operation in relation to Northern Ireland of any such provision of the Insurance Act as is referred to in section 118(2) thereof, and of sections 83(5) and 87 of the Industrial Injuries Act, this Act shall not extend to Northern Ireland.

New Towns Act 1969

1969 CHAPTER 5

An Act to raise the limit on advances imposed by section 43 of the New Towns Act 1965, as amended by subsequent enactments. [6th March 1969]

BE IT ENACTED by the Queen's most Excellent Majesty, by and with the advice and consent of the Lords Spiritual and Temporal, and Commons, in this present Parliament assembled, and by the authority of the same, as follows:—

1.—(1) In section 43 of the New Towns Act 1965 as amended by the New Towns Act 1966 and the New Towns (Scotland) Act 1968 (which limits to £800,000,000 the aggregate amount of the advances made to development corporations and the Commission for the New Towns under the enactments therein mentioned) for the words " £800,000,000 " there shall be substituted the words " £1,100,000,000 ". Raising of limit on advances. 1965 c. 59. 1966 c. 44. 1968 c. 16.

(2) In consequence of subsection (1) of this section, section 1 of the New Towns Act 1966 is hereby repealed.

2.—(1) This Act may be cited as the New Towns Act 1969. Short title and extent.

(2) This Act does not extend to Northern Ireland.

Shipbuilding Industry Act 1969

1969 CHAPTER 6

An Act to amend section 7 of the Shipbuilding Industry Act 1967 by increasing the amount up to which the Minister of Technology may assume liability by giving guarantees under the section. [6th March 1969]

BE IT ENACTED by the Queen's most Excellent Majesty, by and with the advice and consent of the Lords Spiritual and Temporal, and Commons, in this present Parliament assembled, and by the authority of the same, as follows:—

Increase of limit on guarantees. 1967 c. 40.

1. In section 7 of the Shipbuilding Industry Act 1967 (under which the Minister of Technology may enter into guarantees to aid the financing of shipbuilding in the United Kingdom, but under subsection (5) his aggregate liability at any time exclusive of any liability in respect of interest is to be limited to £200 million) for the words " £200 million " in subsection (5) there shall be substituted the words " £400 million less the amount of any sums which have been paid by the Minister to meet a liability falling within this subsection and have not been repaid to him ".

Short title, citation and extent.

2.—(1) This Act may be cited as the Shipbuilding Industry Act 1969, and the Shipbuilding Industry Act 1967 and this Act may be cited together as the Shipbuilding Industry Acts 1967 and 1969.

(2) It is hereby declared that this Act extends to Northern Ireland.

Pensions (Increase) Act 1969

1969 CHAPTER 7

An Act to provide for increases or supplements in respect of certain pensions.

[6th March 1969]

BE IT ENACTED by the Queen's most Excellent Majesty, by and with the advice and consent of the Lords Spiritual and Temporal, and Commons, in this present Parliament assembled, and by the authority of the same, as follows:—

General increase of public service pensions.

1.—(1) Subject to the provisions of this Act, the annual rate of a pension specified in Part I, II or III of Schedule 1 to this Act which began not later than 1st July 1967 may, in respect of any period beginning on or after 1st April 1969, be increased by the pension authority by an amount equal to a percentage of the adjusted rate of the pension.

(2) The said percentage shall, in the case of a pension which began at a time specified in the first column of Part IV of Schedule 1 to this Act, be that specified in relation thereto in the second column of that Part of the Schedule.

(3) In the case of a pension specified in Part II of Schedule 1 to this Act, it shall be the duty of the pension authority to increase the pension in accordance with this section, except that this does not apply to the gratuities specified in section 6 of the Act of 1962 (being gratuities payable in respect of local government service and granted by way of periodical payments or an annuity).

(4) The provisions of Schedule 2 to this Act shall have effect, being provisions for the interpretation of this section and otherwise consequential thereon or supplementary thereto, including provisions corresponding to, or extending or applying, provisions of former Pensions (Increase) Acts with respect to increases or supplements under those Acts.

Extension and amendment of previous Pensions (Increase) Acts.

2.—(1) As from 1st April 1969, and in respect of any period beginning on or after that date, the Pensions (Increase) Acts specified in Schedule 3 to this Act shall have the extended application provided for by that Schedule.

(2) There shall be included among the pensions to which section 3 of the Act of 1962 applies (power of Minister of Overseas Development to make regulations authorising supplements to certain colonial and overseas pensions, corresponding to the increases provided by that Act and former Pensions (Increase) Acts) a pension payable by that Minister under section 5(1) of the Superannuation (Miscellaneous Provisions) Act 1967 (former officers of Government of Palestine).

1967 c. 28.

(3) Section 3(4) of the Act of 1962 (entitlement to supplement to be conditional on certain qualifications by reference to residence) is hereby repealed.

(4) In section 2(2) of the Act of 1965 (computation of pension increase where retirement is followed by further service), after the words " Schedule 1 " there shall be inserted the words " or is a pension specified in paragraph 10 or 11 of Part I of that Schedule and computed under the Superannuation Acts 1834 to 1949, or is a pension payable under section 15 of the Superannuation (Miscellaneous Provisions) Act 1967 (metropolitan civil staffs) ".

(5) In section 3(2) of the Act of 1965 (power to provide pension increases by regulations in case of persons pensionable under approved superannuation schemes) the following shall be inserted after sub-paragraph (ii) of paragraph (*a*):—

" or

(iii) have been employed by the Wheat Commission ; or

(iv) are members of the metropolitan civil staffs within the meaning of section 15 of the Superannuation (Miscellaneous Provisions) Act 1967 or have been so, whether before or after the appointed day for the purposes of that section."

(6) Section 2(1) of the Act of 1947 (obsolete power of pension authority to adjust amount of 1947 increase for benefit of pensioner under Old Age Pensions Act 1936) is hereby repealed.

1936 c. 31.

Expenses.

3. There shall be defrayed out of moneys provided by Parliament—

(*a*) any expenditure incurred by a government department under or by virtue of this Act ;

(*b*) any increase attributable to any provision of this Act in the sums payable out of moneys so provided under any other enactment.

4.—(1) In this Act, unless the context otherwise requires— Interpretation.

" the Act of " a specified year means the Pensions (Increase) Act of that year;

" enactment " includes an enactment in a local Act and a provisional order confirmed by Parliament;

" local authority " has the meaning assigned to it by section 40 of the Local Government Superannuation Act 1937 or, in Scotland, by section 34 of the Local Government Superannuation (Scotland) Act 1937; 1937 c. 68. 1937 c. 69.

" the Minister " means the Minister for the Civil Service;

" pension " has the same meaning as in the Act of 1959, as extended by section 6 of the Act of 1962 (local authority gratuities);

" pension authority " means, in relation to a pension specified in paragraph 2 of Part III of Schedule 1 to this Act, the Minister and, in relation to any other pension, the authority by whom the pension is payable;

" relevant increase " means an increase by virtue of, or by reference to increases under, any of the following enactments, that is to say, the Acts of 1920 and 1924, the Acts of 1944 and 1947, the Act of 1952, the Act of 1954, section 1 of the Act of 1956, section 1 of the Act of 1959, section 7(1) of the Judicial Pensions Act 1959, sections 1 and 2 of the Act of 1962, section 1 of the Act of 1965, and this Act; 1959 c. 9 (8 & 9 Eliz. 2).

and references to the increase of a specified year are to a relevant increase attributable to the Pensions (Increase) Act of that year.

(2) Unless the context otherwise requires, any reference in this Act to an enactment shall be construed as a reference to that enactment as amended, extended or applied by or under any other enactment, including an enactment in this Act.

5.—(1) This Act may be cited as the Pensions (Increase) Act 1969. Citation and extent.

(2) The Pensions (Increase) Acts 1920 to 1965, sections 48(1) to (4) and 62(3) of the Superannuation Act 1949, section 3 of, and Schedule 2 to, the Pensions (India, Pakistan & Burma) Act 1955, section 7(1) of the Judicial Pensions Act 1959, section 17 of the Ministerial Salaries and Members' Pensions Act 1965 and this Act may be cited together as the Pensions (Increase) Acts 1920 to 1969. 1949 c. 44. 1955 c. 22. 1965 c. 11.

(3) This Act extends to Great Britain only, except that—

(*a*) it extends to Northern Ireland for the purpose of the 1969 increase of pensions payable under Schdeule 8 to

1920 c. 67. the Government of Ireland Act 1920 (former Irish civil servants) or payable to or in respect of an existing Irish officer within the meaning of that Act under the Superannuation Acts 1834 to 1965, or payable under or by virtue of any other Act extending to Northern Ireland out of the Consolidated Fund of the United Kingdom or out of moneys provided by the Parliament of the United Kingdom ; and

(*b*) it extends to Northern Ireland, the Isle of Man and the Channel Islands, for the purpose of the increase of pensions payable by the trustees of a trustee savings bank or by the Inspection Committee of trustee savings banks.

SCHEDULES

SCHEDULE 1

Section 1.

PENSIONS QUALIFYING FOR INCREASE UNDER SECTION 1 ; TABLE OF PERCENTAGE INCREASES.

PART I

STATE PENSIONS

Past Prime Ministers

1. A pension payable under section 3 of the Ministerial Salaries Consolidation Act 1965. 1965 c. 58.

Civil Service

2. A pension payable under the Superannuation Acts 1965 and 1967.

Administration of Justice

3. A pension payable under the Lord Chancellor's Pension Act 1832. 1832 c. 111.

4. A pension payable, out of the Consolidated Fund or out of moneys provided by Parliament, under Part I of the Administration of Justice (Pensions) Act 1950 (widows and children of judges and senior officials in the legal system, including the Chairman and Deputy Chairman of the Monopolies Commission). 1950 c. 11 (14 & 15 Geo. 6).

5. A pension payable under section 9 of the County Courts Act 1934 (county court judges). 1934 c. 53.

6. A pension payable under section 20 of the Sheriff Courts (Scotland) Act 1907 or section 1 of the Sheriffs' Pensions (Scotland) Act 1961 (sheriffs and salaried sheriffs-substitute). 1907 c. 51. 1961 c. 42.

7. A pension payable under section 34(1) of the Courts-Martial (Appeals) Act 1951 (Judge Advocate General). 1951 c. 46.

8. A pension payable under a relevant pension enactment as defined in the Judicial Pensions Act 1959 (Lords of Appeal, Lords Justices of Appeal and High Court judges ; senior judges in Scotland and Northern Ireland). 1959 c. 9 (8 & 9 Eliz. 2).

9. A pension payable under section 4(5) of the Criminal Justice Administration Act 1956 (Recorder of Manchester or Liverpool). 1956 c. 34.

10. A pension payable under the Superannuation (President of the Industrial Court) Act 1954. 1954 c. 37.

11. A pension payable under section 2(6) of the Lands Tribunal Act 1949 to a former member of the Lands Tribunal. 1949 c. 42.

12. A pension payable under the Police Magistrates (Superannuation) Acts 1915 and 1929.

SCH. 1

Teachers

13. A pension payable under the Elementary School Teachers (Superannuation) Acts 1898 to 1912.

14. A pension payable under the Teachers (Superannuation) Acts 1918 to 1956.

This heading does not include—

(*a*) a pension specified in paragraph 7 of Part II of this Schedule ; or

1956 c. 53. (*b*) so much of any pension payable under the said Acts of 1918 to 1956 as would not have been payable apart from an election under section 10(1) of the Teachers (Superannuation) Act 1956.

15. A pension payable under the Education (Scotland) Acts 1939 to 1967.

S.I. 1957/356. This heading does not include a pension granted under Regulation 45 of the Teachers (Superannuation) (Scotland) Regulations 1957.

1967 c. 12. 16. A pension payable under regulations made under section 1 or section 7 of the Teachers' Superannuation Act 1967.

1968 c. 12. 17. A pension payable under the Teachers Superannuation (Scotland) Act 1968.

Police

1945 c. 17 (9 & 10 Geo. 6). 1948 c. 24. 18. A pension payable by a Secretary of State or the Minister of Overseas Development, under the Police (Overseas Service) Act 1945 or the Police Pensions Act 1948, to a person who at the time of his retirement was engaged as mentioned in section 1(1) of the said Act of 1945 (overseas service of police officers).

This heading includes a pension granted in consideration of the surrender of part of a pension so payable.

1958 c. 14. 19. A pension payable by a Secretary of State or the Minister of Overseas Development under the Police Pensions Act 1948 to a person who at the time of his retirement was engaged in service in respect of which the provisions of section 5 of the Overseas Service Act 1958 had effect (overseas service of police officers).

This heading includes a pension granted in consideration of the surrender of part of a pension so payable.

20. A pension payable by a Secretary of State under the Police Pensions Act 1948 to a person who at the time of his retirement either—

1964 c. 48. 1967 c. 77. (*a*) was serving as an inspector or assistant inspector of constabulary under the Police Act 1964 or the Police (Scotland) Act 1967 ; or

(*b*) was engaged in central service pursuant to section 43 of the Police Act 1964 or section 38 of the Police (Scotland) Act 1967.

This heading includes a pension granted in consideration of the surrender of part of a pension so payable.

SCH. 1

Metropolitan civil staffs

21. A pension payable under section 15 of the Superannuation (Miscellaneous Provisions) Act 1967. 1967 c. 28.

Fire Service

22. A pension payable by a Secretary of State or the Minister of Overseas Development in accordance with a scheme in force under section 26 of the Fire Services Act 1947. 1947 c. 41.

Revenue

23. A pension payable under section 29 of the Finance Act 1932, section 60 of the Finance (No. 2) Act 1945, or section 62 of the Finance Act 1946 (compensation to tax collectors and assessors for loss of employment). 1932 c. 25. 1945 c. 13 (9 & 10 Geo. 6). 1946 c. 64.

National Health Service

24. A pension payable by the Secretary of State under section 6 of the National Health Service Act 1946 (former officers of voluntary hospitals). 1946 c. 81.

25. A pension payable by the Secretary of State in pursuance of regulations made under section 67 or 68 of the National Health Service Act 1946 (former officers of hospital authorities and others engaged in health services).

26. A pension payable by the Secretary of State under section 6 of the National Health Service (Scotland) Act 1947 (former officers of voluntary hospitals). 1947 c. 27.

27. A pension payable by the Secretary of State in pursuance of regulations made under section 66 or 67 of the National Health Service (Scotland) Act 1947 (former officers of hospital authorities and others engaged in health services).

28. A pension payable by the Secretary of State under regulations made under section 60(2) of the Local Government Act 1958 or section 85(4) of the London Government Act 1963 (compensation for loss of office etc. due to reorganisation in National Health Service). 1958 c. 55. 1963 c. 33.

29. A pension payable by the Secretary of State by way of such compensation as is mentioned in section 7(1)(*b*) of the Pensions (Increase) Act 1959 (compensation for redundancy or loss of emoluments due to re-allocation of functions in government) in pursuance of an order under section 11(9) of the National Health Service Act 1946 (compensation of officers following reorganisation of hospital service). 1959 c. 50.

National Insurance

30. A pension payable by the Secretary of State in pursuance of regulations made under section 67 of the National Insurance Act 1946 (loss of employment or diminution of emoluments attributable to passing of that Act) or of rules made under section 3 of the Superannuation (Miscellaneous Provisions) Act 1948 (former employees of Approved Societies, etc.). 1946 c. 67. 1948 c. 33.

SCH. 1 This heading does not include a pension payable under the Superannuation Acts 1965 and 1967.

S.I. 1948/2434. 31. A pension payable under Rule 7 or 10 of the National Insurance and Civil Service (Superannuation) Rules 1948 (former employees of Approved Societies, etc.).

1965 c. 51. 32. A pension payable under section 79 of the National Insurance Act 1965 (National Insurance Commissioners).

Diplomatic, Colonial and Overseas Service

33. A pension payable under the Governors Pensions Acts 1957 and 1967.

1948 c. 4 (12, 13 & 14 Geo. 6). 34. A pension payable under the Judges Pensions (India and Burma) Act 1948.

1869 c. 43. 35. A pension payable under the Diplomatic Salaries &c. Act 1869.

Service in Ireland

1920 c. 67. 36. A pension payable under Schedule 8 to the Government of Ireland Act 1920 (former Irish civil servants).

37. A pension payable to or in respect of an existing Irish officer within the meaning of the Government of Ireland Act 1920, under the Superannuation Acts 1834 to 1965.

38. A pension payable under the enactments relating to pensions of the Royal Irish Constabulary.

1954 c. 17. This heading does not include a pension payable under regulations made under section 1 of the Royal Irish Constabulary (Widows' Pensions) Act 1954.

Miscellaneous

1959 c. 1 (8 & 9 Eliz. 2). 39. A pension payable under Mr. Speaker Morrison's Retirement Act 1959.

1963 c. 33. 40. A pension payable by the Minister of Housing and Local Government under regulations made under section 85(4) of the London Government Act 1963 (compensation to valuation panel staff for loss of employment etc., following reorganisation of London government).

S.I. 1949/2289. S.I. 1951/1327. 41. A pension payable by way of residual compensation under Part IV of the Gas (Staff Compensation) Regulations 1949 as amended by the Gas (Staff Compensation) (Amendment) Regulations 1951 (gas meter examiners and others employed by local authorities before nationalisation).

1914 c. 18 (5 & 6 Geo. 5). 42. A widow's pension payable by the Secretary of State in accordance with a scheme framed by the then Army Council under the Injuries in War (Compensation) Act 1914 (Session 2) for established civil servants employed abroad within the sphere of military operations.

1915 c. 24. 43. A pension payable by the Postmaster General in accordance with a scheme made under the Injuries in War (Compensation) Act 1915.

PART II SCH. 1

LOCAL AUTHORITY PENSIONS

Local government service

1. A pension payable by a local authority solely in respect of local government service.

This heading does not include a pension specified in paragraph 9, 10, 11 or 12 of this Part of this Schedule ; but subject to this, " local government service " means—

(*a*) service under any local authority ; or

(*b*) service which by virtue of any of the following enactments is, for superannuation purposes, treated as service under a local authority:—

Local Government (Emergency Provisions) Act 1916, section 2 or 3 (local government officers on war service) ; 1916 c. 12.

Local Government Superannuation Act 1937, section 12(3) (reckoning of former war service) ; 1937 c. 68.

Local Government Superannuation (Scotland) Act 1937, section 12(3) (reckoning of former war service) ; 1937 c. 69.

Local Government Staffs (War Service) Act 1939, section 3 (war service of local government officers and others) ; 1939 c. 94.

London County Council (General Powers) Act 1949, section 51(4) (firemen employed in training institution) ; 1949 c. lv.

(*c*) service which, by virtue of section 1(1) or (2) of the Local Government Superannuation Act 1939, is to be treated as service for the purposes of the Local Government Superannuation Act 1937, or the Local Government Superannuation (Scotland) Act 1937. 1939 c. 18.

This heading includes any such service as is mentioned above, notwithstanding that the local authority concerned have ceased to exist.

Administration of Justice

2. A pension payable under section 33 of the Justices of the Peace Act 1949 (stipendiary magistrates). 1949 c. 101.

3. A pension payable by a local authority under Part I of the Administration of Justice (Pensions) Act 1950 (widows and children of stipendiary magistrates and of chairmen and deputy chairmen of London Sessions). 1950 c. 11 (14 & 15 Geo. 6).

4. A pension payable under section 22 of the Administration of Justice (Pensions) Act 1950 (chairmen and deputy chairmen of London Sessions).

5. A pension payable by the Greater London Council in respect of service ending with employment by the committee of magistrates for the inner London area.

SCH. 1

1958 c. 55. 1963 c. 33. 6. A pension payable by a probation committee under regulations made under section 60(2) of the Local Government Act 1958 or section 85(4) of the London Government Act 1963 (compensation to probation staffs for loss of employment or emoluments due to reorganisation of local government).

Teachers

1925 c. 59. 7. A pension payable by a local authority under section 14(3)(*b*) of the Teachers (Superannuation) Act 1925.

Police and Fire services

8. A pension payable under any of the following enactments:—

1948 c. 24. 1921 c. 31. Police Pensions Act 1948, or any enactment repealed by that Act or the Police Pensions Act 1921;

1964 c. 48. Police Act 1964, section 34;

1967 c. 77. Police (Scotland) Act 1967, section 26;

This heading does not include—

(*a*) a pension specified in paragraph 18, 19 or 20 of Part I of this Schedule; or

(*b*) a pension payable to the widow or a child of the person in respect of whom it is granted, unless it is granted in consideration of the surrender of part of another pension.

9. A pension payable by a police authority under regulations made under section 60(2) of the Local Government Act 1958 or section 85(4) of the London Government Act 1963 (compensation to civilian employees and others for loss of employment or emoluments due to reorganisation of local government or amalgamation of police areas).

10. A pension payable under any enactment by a local authority, or by a police authority in England or Wales other than a local authority, in respect of service ending with—

(*a*) service as a civilian employed under section 10 of the Police Act 1964 by such a police authority; or

1960 c. 63. 1967 c. 76. (*b*) service as a traffic warden employed by such a police authority under section 2 of the Road Traffic and Roads Improvement Act 1960 or section 81(9) of the Road Traffic Regulation Act 1967.

This heading does not include a pension specified in paragraph 21 of Part I of this Schedule.

1947 c. 41. 11. A pension payable by a local authority in respect of service as a member of a fire brigade, in accordance with a scheme in force under section 26 of the Fire Services Act 1947.

12. A pension payable by a local authority, otherwise than as mentioned in paragraph 11 above, in respect of—

1925 c. 47. (*a*) service as a professional fireman (as defined by the Fire Brigade Pensions Act 1925); or (*b*) service which, by or under any enactment, is treated as approved service in a fire brigade. Sch. 1

13. A pension payable under the Police Pensions Act 1921 to the widow or a child of a person to whom the National Fire Service (Preservation of Pensions) (Police Firemen) Regulations 1941 applied at the time of that person's death or retirement. 1921 c. 31. S.R. & O. 1941/1271.

Miscellaneous

14. A pension payable by a local authority by way of such compensation as is mentioned in section 7(1)(*b*) of the Pensions (Increase) Act 1959 (retirement, redundancy or loss of emoluments due to reorganisation or transfer of local government functions, changes in the administration of justice or amalgamation of police areas). 1959 c. 50.

15. A pension specified in an Order in Council in force at the passing of this Act under section 4 of the Pensions (Increase) Act 1944 (extension of 1944 increase to local authority pensions not specified in Schedule 1 to that Act). 1944 c. 21.

This heading does not include a pension specified in paragraph 21 of Part I of this Schedule.

16. A pension payable under section 6 of the Coroners (Amendment) Act 1926 (county and borough coroners). 1926 c. 59.

17. A pension payable by a local authority in respect of service ending with service as a clerk, officer or servant employed under section 47 of the Local Government Act 1948 or section 92 of the General Rate Act 1967 by a local valuation panel. 1948 c. 26. 1967 c. 9.

18. A pension payable by a local authority in respect of service ending with service as a rent officer or deputy rent officer under section 22 or 24 of the Rent Act 1965 or section 40 of the Rent Act 1968. 1965 c. 75. 1968 c. 23.

Part III

Other Pensions

1. A pension payable by the trustees of a trustee savings bank or by the Inspection Committee of trustee savings banks.

2. A pension payable—

(*a*) under section 5(8) of the Cotton (Centralised Buying) Act 1947 (staff of Raw Cotton Commission); or 1947 c. 26.

(*b*) in pursuance of directions given under section 4(2) of the Cotton Act 1954 (compensation for loss of employment on winding up of Raw Cotton Commission). 1954 c. 24.

SCH. 1

PART IV

PERCENTAGE INCREASES TO BE APPLIED UNDER SECTION 1

Date of beginning of pension	*Percentage increase*
Not later than 1st July 1955	18 per cent.
After 1st July 1955 but not later than 1st July 1956 ...	17 per cent.
After 1st July 1956 but not later than 1st July 1957 ...	16 per cent.
After 1st July 1957 but not later than 1st July 1958 ...	15 per cent.
After 1st July 1958 but not later than 1st July 1959 ...	14 per cent.
After 1st July 1959 but not later than 1st July 1960 ...	13 per cent.
After 1st July 1960 but not later than 1st July 1961 ...	12 per cent.
After 1st July 1961 but not later than 1st July 1962 ...	11 per cent.
After 1st July 1962 but not later than 1st July 1963 ...	10 per cent.
After 1st July 1963 but not later than 1st July 1964 ...	8 per cent.
After 1st July 1964 but not later than 1st July 1965 ...	6 per cent.
After 1st July 1965 but not later than 1st July 1966 ...	4 per cent.
After 1st July 1966 but not later than 1st July 1967 ...	2 per cent.

Section 1(4).

SCHEDULE 2

INTERPRETATIVE, CONSEQUENTIAL AND SUPPLEMENTARY PROVISIONS

Date from which pension " begins "

1. For the purposes of this Act, a pension shall be deemed to begin on the day hereinafter specified, whether or not the pension accrues from that day, that is to say—

(*a*) where the amount of the pension is computed by reference to emoluments received for any period of service, or would be so computed apart from any provision specifying a fixed sum as the minimum rate of the pension, on the day following the last day of that service ;

(*b*) where the pension is granted under an enactment in consideration of the surrender of part of another pension, on the day from which the surrender takes effect or the day on which that other pension began, whichever is the earlier ;

(*c*) in any other case, on the day following the last day of the service in respect of which the pension is payable.

Meaning of " adjusted rate "

2. In section 1(1) of this Act, the expression " adjusted rate ", in relation to a pension, means the aggregate annual rate of the pension after any relevant increase (other than the 1969 increase), any fraction of a pound in that aggregate being treated as a whole pound.

Avoidance of double increase

3. In calculating the amount of a pension for the purposes of a relevant increase, the 1969 increase shall be disregarded ; and, in ascertaining the rate of a pension granted to a person by reference to the rate of some other person's pension, the 1969 increase of that other's pension shall be disregarded.

SCH. 2

Qualification for increase by reference to age etc.

4. Subsections (2) to (6) of section 1 of the Act of 1959 (which impose conditions of entitlement to a pension increase, including conditions that the pensioner must be of a certain age or physically or mentally infirm or, in the case of a woman, have at least one dependant) shall apply to the 1969 increase as they apply to the 1959, 1962 and 1965 increases.

Fire service pension granted at higher of two different rates

5.—(1) This paragraph applies to a pension specified in paragraph 22 of Part I, or in paragraphs 11, 12 or 13 of Part II, of Schedule 1 to this Act.

(2) Where such a pension has been granted at the higher of two different rates, the pensioner shall be entitled, in respect of any period beginning on or after 1st April 1969, to a pension at the higher of those rates after taking into account any relevant increase of each respectively of those rates.

Police pension regulations

6.—(1) This paragraph applies to regulations under section 1 of the Police Pensions Act 1948, section 34 of the Police Act 1964, or section 26 of the Police (Scotland) Act 1967, with respect to pensions payable to widows or children of the persons in respect of whom those pensions are granted, being pensions granted otherwise than in consideration of the surrender of part of another pension. 1948 c. 42. 1964 c. 48. 1967 c. 77.

(2) Any regulations to which this paragraph applies, being regulations for the grant of increases of any pension, may, if made within one year after the passing of this Act, be made so as to take effect from such date, whether before or after the making of the regulations, as may be specified therein, not being earlier than 1st April 1969.

Re-employed teachers

7. In the following regulations that is to say—

(*a*) the Teachers' Superannuation Regulations 1967, as amended by the Teachers' Superannuation (Amending) Regulations 1967; S.I. 1967/489. S.I. 1967/948.

(*b*) the Teachers (Superannuation) (Scotland) Regulations 1957, as amended by the Teachers Superannuation (Scotland) (Amendment) Regulations 1967; S.I. 1957/356. S.I. 1967/1736.

(*c*) the Teachers Superannuation (Scotland) Regulations 1969, S.I. 1969/77.

(which include provisions for the suspension or reduction of a retired teacher's superannuation allowance on re-employment), references to the Pensions (Increase) Acts 1920 to 1965 shall be construed as including references to this Act; but this paragraph shall not affect any power to vary or revoke any of the said regulations.

Officers re-employed after retirement

8. In relation to any period beginning on or after 1st April 1969, section 2 of the Act of 1965 (computation of pension increase where retirement is followed by further service) shall have effect with the following amendments:—

SCH. 2

(*a*) in subsection (1)(*b*), for the words " Schedule 1 to this Act " there shall be substituted the words " Schedule 1 to the Act of 1969 " ; and

(*b*) for so much of subsection (2) as precedes paragraph (*a*) there shall be substituted the following—

" Where any such pension as is referred to in subsection (1)(*b*) of this section is a pension specified in paragraphs 2, 14, 15, 16, or 17 of Part I of Schedule 1 to the Act of 1969, or is a pension specified in paragraph 25, 27, 28, or 29 of that Part of that Schedule and computed under the Superannuation Acts 1834 to 1949, or is a pension specified in paragraph 21 of that Part of that Schedule, and the reassessment falls to be made by reference to ".

Supplements to certain colonial and overseas pensions

9. In section 3(3) of the Act of 1962 (scale of supplements which may be allowed by regulations), and in section 3(5)(*b*) of that Act (scope of regulation-making power), references to previous Pensions (Increase) Acts or that Act shall, in relation to any period beginning on or after 1st April 1969, include a reference to this Act.

Persons subject to approved superannuation schemes

10. In section 3 of the Act of 1965 (which enables the Minister and certain other authorities to apply the 1965 and previous increases to persons with benefits under approved superannuation schemes), " the authorised increases " shall, in relation to any period beginning on or after 1st April 1969, include the benefits conferred by section 1 of this Act.

Extension of 1969 increase to other local authority pensions

11.—(1) Her Majesty may by Order in Council direct that, in relation to any pension specified in the Order, being a pension which is payable under any enactment by a local authority, whether out of superannuation funds or otherwise, but which is not specified in Part II of Schedule 1 to this Act, this Act shall have effect as if that pension were specified in the said Part II.

(2) An Order in Council under this paragraph—

(*a*) may include such incidental, consequential and supplemental provisions as appear to Her Majesty to be expedient ;

(*b*) may in particular make provision for securing that the cost of increasing any pension to which the Order relates is borne by the appropriate local authority ; and

(*c*) may be varied or revoked by a further Order in Council under this paragraph.

Power to modify increases by regulations

12.—(1) Where, in the case of a pension which is specified in Part I, II or III of Schedule 1 to this Act, or with respect to which an Order in Council under the foregoing paragraph is for the time being in force, an appropriate authority is satisfied that it is proper to do so, that authority or, where the authority is not the Minister, that authority with the consent of the Minister, may by regulations direct that section 1(1) or (2) of this Act, or paragraph 2 of this Schedule, shall apply in relation to that pension subject to such modifications, adaptations and exceptions as may be specified in the regulations. Sch. 2

(2) In this paragraph the expression "appropriate authority" means the Minister, the Lord Chancellor, a Secretary of State or the Minister of Housing and Local Government.

Power of Minister to authorise other increases by regulations

13. The Minister may make regulations—

(*a*) empowering any person specified in the regulations to pay increases of pensions payable by that person, or in respect of pensions payable by some other person wholly or partly by reference to service with the first-mentioned person, not exceeding the increases which would be payable if those pensions were specified in Part I, II or III of Schedule 1 to this Act;

(*b*) directing that, subject to such modifications, adaptations and exceptions as may be specified in the regulations, this Act shall apply in relation to a pension specified in Part I or Part II of Schedule 2 to the Pensions (India, Pakistan and Burma) Act 1955, as if it were specified in Part I of Schedule 1 to this Act. 1955 c. 22.

Provisions supplementary to paragraphs 11 to 13 above

14. An Order in Council under paragraph 11, or regulations under paragraph 12 or 13, of this Schedule may provide for any increases authorised thereby to take effect as from such date (whether before or after the making of the Order or regulations) as may be specified therein, not being earlier than 1st April 1969.

15. No recommendation to make an Order under paragraph 11 of this Schedule shall be made to Her Majesty in Council unless a draft of the Order has been laid before, and approved by a resolution of, each House of Parliament.

16. The power to make regulations under paragraph 12 or 13 of this Schedule shall be exercisable by statutory instrument, which shall be subject to annulment in pursuance of a resolution of either House of Parliament.

Administrative and financial provisions

17.—(1) The Minister may by regulations provide that, in relation to any class of pensions specified in the regulations, all or any of the functions of the pension authority under this Act shall be performed on behalf of the pension authority by such other authority as may be so specified.

Sch. 2

(2) Regulations under this paragraph shall be made by statutory instrument, which shall be subject to annulment in pursuance of a resolution of either House of Parliament.

18. Subject to the provisions of this Act and of any Order in Council under paragraph 11 of this Schedule, any provision made by or under any enactment shall, in so far as it relates to the apportionment of the cost of a pension between two or more authorities, or to the manner in which a pension is to be paid, or to the proof of title to sums payable on account of a pension, or in so far as it prohibits or restricts the assignment or charging of a pension or its application towards the payment of debts, have effect in relation to any increase of the pension under this Act as it has effect in relation to the pension; but save as aforesaid, and subject to paragraph 7 of this Schedule, any such increase shall not be treated as part of the pension for the purposes of any such provision as aforesaid.

19. In the case of a pension specified in an Order in Council in force at the passing of this Act under section 4 of the Act of 1944 (extension of 1944 increase to local authority pensions not specified in Schedule 1 to that Act), any provisions of the Order as to the manner in which the cost of any relevant increase to which the Order relates is to be borne shall apply in relation to the 1969 increase, and the provisions of this Act shall have effect subject to any such provisions of the Order.

20.—(1) Where a pension specified in paragraph 1, 7, 10, 11, 12, 15, 17 or 18 of Part II of Schedule 1 to this Act is increased under this Act, the cost of the increase shall be defrayed by the pension authority; but where the pension authority are not the last employing authority, the last employing authority shall reimburse the cost of the increase to the pension authority.

(2) In so far as the foregoing sub-paragraph applies to a pension specified in paragraph 15 of Part II of Schedule 1 to this Act, it shall have effect subject to any provision made by Order in Council under section 4 of the Act of 1944.

(3) For the purposes of this paragraph, the expression "the last employing authority" means, in relation to a pension, the local authority to whom the latest services in respect of which the pension is payable were rendered, so however that where the functions in connection with which those latest services were rendered have been transferred to some other local authority, the said expression shall mean the local authority by whom those functions are for the time being exercisable.

(4) Any question as to who are the last employing authority for the purposes of this paragraph shall, in default of agreement, be determined by the Minister of Housing and Local Government or, in Scotland, by the Secretary of State.

(5) Nothing in this paragraph shall affect the operation, in relation to the 1969 increase, of the provisions of section 14 of the
1890 c. 45. Police Act 1890 and section 10 of the Police Pensions Act 1921
1921 c. 31. as to the payment of pensions partly out of the Police Fund and partly out of moneys provided by Parliament.

Schedule 3

Section 2.

Extension of Past Increases to Certain Pensions specified in Schedule 1

1. The Acts of 1962 and 1965 shall apply to a pension specified in paragraph 9 of Part I of Schedule 1 to this Act (Recorder of Manchester or Liverpool) as if it were specified in Part I of the relevant Schedule to each of those Acts.

2. The Acts of 1944, 1947, 1952, 1956, 1959, 1962 and 1965 shall apply to a pension specified in paragraph 42 of Part I of Schedule 1 to this Act (widows of established civil servants employed abroad within the sphere of military operations in the First World War) as if it were specified in Part I of the relevant Schedule to each of those Acts.

3. The Acts of 1959, 1962 and 1965 shall apply to a pension specified in paragraph 3 of Part II of Schedule 1 to this Act (widows and children of stipendiary magistrates and of chairman and deputy chairmen of London Sessions) as if it were specified in Part II of the relevant Schedule to each of those Acts.

4. The Acts of 1962 and 1965 shall apply to a pension specified in paragraph 10 of Part II of Schedule 1 to this Act (civilians and traffic wardens employed with police) as if it were specified in Part II of the relevant Schedule to each of those Acts.

5. The Acts of 1952, 1956, 1959, 1962 and 1965 shall apply to a pension specified in paragraph 17 of Part II of Schedule 1 to this Act (employees of local valuation panel) as if it were specified in Part II of the relevant Schedule to each of those Acts.

6. In the foregoing paragraphs, " the relevant Schedule ", in relation to the Pensions (Increase) Act of any year, means the Schedule to that Act which lists the pensions qualifying for increase under section 1 of the Act.

Redundancy Rebates Act 1969

1969 CHAPTER 8

An Act to reduce the rebates payable under section 30 of the Redundancy Payments Act 1965.

[6th March 1969]

BE IT ENACTED by the Queen's most Excellent Majesty, by and with the advice and consent of the Lords Spiritual and Temporal, and Commons, in this present Parliament assembled, and by the authority of the same, as follows:—

Reduction of rebates.

1.—(1) Schedule 5 to the principal Act (calculation of rebates) shall, subject to the following provisions of this section, be amended as follows, that is to say, for the words " one and one-sixth weeks' ", " two-thirds " and " one-third ", where they occur in paragraphs 2 and 9 of that Schedule, there shall be substituted respectively the words " three-quarters of one week's ", " one-half " and " one-quarter ", and for the words " seven-ninths ", where they occur in paragraphs 3 and 12 of that Schedule, there shall be substituted the words " one-half ".

(2) Subsection (1) of this section shall not have effect in relation to a rebate payable in respect of the whole or part of a redundancy payment, if in the case of that redundancy payment the relevant date (in accordance with section 3(4), section 4(2) or section 6(2) of the principal Act, as the case may be) is a date earlier than the operative date of this Act.

(3) Subsection (1) of this section shall not have effect—

(*a*) in relation to a rebate payable in respect of a payment made by an employer under such an agreement as is mentioned in paragraph (*b*) of subsection (1) of section 30 of the principal Act, or (*b*) in relation to a rebate payable in respect of a payment made by an employer by virtue of an award made in relation to an agreement as mentioned in paragraph (*c*) of that subsection,

if in either case the date of termination (that is to say, the date on which the termination of the employee's contract of employment is treated for the purposes of the agreement in question as having taken effect) is a date earlier than the operative date of this Act.

(4) In this section " the principal Act " means the Redundancy Payments Act 1965, " redundancy payment " has the meaning assigned to it by section 1 of that Act, " rebate ", " employer " and " employee " have the same meanings as in section 30 of that Act, and " the operative date of this Act " means the second Monday after the date on which this Act is passed. 1965 c. 62.

2.—(1) This Act may be cited as the Redundancy Rebates Act 1969; and the Redundancy Payments Act 1965 and this Act may be cited together as the Redundancy Payments Acts 1965 and 1969. **Short title, citation and extent.**

(2) This Act shall not form part of the law of Northern Ireland.

Consolidated Fund (No. 2) Act 1969

1969 CHAPTER 9

An Act to apply certain sums out of the Consolidated Fund to the service of the years ending on 31st March 1968, 1969 and 1970. [27th March 1969]

Most Gracious Sovereign,

WE, Your Majesty's most dutiful and loyal subjects, the Commons of the United Kingdom in Parliament assembled, towards making good the supply which we have cheerfully granted to Your Majesty in this session of Parliament, have resolved to grant unto Your Majesty the sums hereinafter mentioned; and do therefore most humbly beseech Your Majesty that it may be enacted, and be it enacted by the Queen's most Excellent Majesty, by and with the advice and consent of the Lords Spiritual and Temporal, and Commons, in this present Parliament assembled, and by the authority of the same, as follows:—

Issue out of the Consolidated Fund for the years ending 31st March 1968 and 1969.

1. The Treasury may issue out of the Consolidated Fund of the United Kingdom and apply towards making good the supply granted to Her Majesty for the service of the years ending on 31st March 1968 and 1969, the sum of £187,516,499 12s. 4d.

Issue out of the Consolidated Fund for the year ending 31st March 1970.

2. The Treasury may issue out of the Consolidated Fund of the United Kingdom and apply towards making good the supply granted to Her Majesty for the service of the year ending on 31st March 1970, the sum of £4,499,227,800.

Short title.

3. This Act may be cited as the Consolidated Fund (No. 2) Act 1969.

Mines and Quarries (Tips) Act 1969

CHAPTER 10

An Act to make further provision in relation to tips associated with mines and quarries ; to prevent disused tips constituting a danger to members of the public ; and for purposes connected with those matters.

[27th March 1969]

BE IT ENACTED by the Queen's most Excellent Majesty, by and with the advice and consent of the Lords Spiritual and Temporal, and Commons, in this present Parliament assembled, and by the authority of the same, as follows:—

PART I

SECURITY OF TIPS ASSOCIATED WITH MINES AND QUARRIES

Security of certain tips and application of Mines and Quarries Act 1954.

1.—(1) Every tip to which this Part of this Act applies shall be made and kept secure.

(2) Provision may be made by regulations with respect to any matter or thing with respect to which it appears to the Minister requisite or expedient to make provision for the purpose of ensuring the security of tips to which this Part of this Act applies, for securing that land on which tipping operations are to be carried out is satisfactory for the purpose and otherwise for carrying this Part of this Act into effect.

(3) This Part of this Act shall be construed as one with the Mines and Quarries Act 1954 (in this Part of this Act referred to as "the principal Act") and, without prejudice to the generality of this provision,— 1954 c. 70.

(*a*) except where the context otherwise requires, any reference in the principal Act to that Act includes a reference to this Part of this Act and expressions

PART I

used in that Act have the same meaning in this Part of this Act as in that Act ; and

(*b*) the principal Act shall have effect subject to the modifications in Schedule 1 to this Act.

Tips to which Part I applies.

2.—(1) In this Act, the expression " tip " means an accumulation or deposit of refuse from a mine or quarry (whether in a solid state or in solution or suspension) other than an accumulation or deposit situated underground, and where any wall or other structure retains or confines a tip then, whether or not that wall or structure is itself composed of refuse, it shall be deemed to form part of the tip for the purposes of this Act.

(2) Subject to subsections (3) and (4) below, a tip is one to which this Part of this Act applies if either—

(*a*) the tip is on premises which are deemed to form part of a mine or quarry for the purposes of the principal Act by virtue of section 180(4) of that Act (which relates to premises for the time being used for the deposit of refuse) ; or

(*b*) the tip is not on such premises but the mine or quarry with which it is associated has not been abandoned and the premises on which the tip is situated continue to be occupied exclusively by the owner of that mine or quarry ;

and for the purposes of this Part of this Act a tip is an " active tip " if it falls within paragraph (*a*) above and a " closed tip " if it falls within paragraph (*b*) above.

(3) If part, but not the whole, of any premises on which a tip is situated is occupied exclusively by the owner of a mine or quarry and, by reason only that the whole of those premises is not occupied exclusively by the owner, the tip is not, apart from this subsection, one to which this Part of this Act applies (whether as an active tip or a closed tip) then,—

(*a*) subject to any direction under paragraph (*b*) below, the tip shall be deemed to be an active tip or a closed tip, as the case may be, and if an active tip, the premises on which it is situated shall be treated, for the purposes of the principal Act and this Part of this Act, as forming part of the mine or quarry with which it is associated ; and

(*b*) the Minister may by order direct that, as from such day as may be specified in the order, the whole or such part of the tip as may be so specified shall cease to be a tip to which this Part of this Act applies.

(4) If the whole or any part of a tip which, apart from this subsection, would be a tip to which this Part of this Act applies is appropriated to some use which, in the opinion of the Minister,

PART I

is inconsistent with the resumption of tipping operations on the tip, or on a particular part of it, the Minister may by order direct that, as from such day as may be specified in the order, the whole or such part of the tip as may be so specified shall cease to be a tip to which this Part of this Act applies.

(5) Notwithstanding anything in subsection (3)(a) above or in section 180(4) of the principal Act, where an order is made under subsection (3)(*b*) or subsection (4) above in relation to a tip which, apart from the order, would be an active tip, then, for the purposes of the principal Act and this Part of this Act, the premises on which the tip, or the part thereof which is specified in the order, is situated shall cease to form part of a mine or quarry as from the day specified in the order; but where such an order relates to part only of the tip, then (subject to any subsequent order) the remainder of the tip shall, of itself, be treated as an active tip and accordingly the premises on which the remainder of the tip is situated shall continue to form part of the mine or quarry with which the tip is associated.

Duties of owners and managers and powers of inspectors.

3.—(1) It shall be the duty of the owner and of the manager of every mine and of the owner and of any manager of every quarry to take such steps as may be necessary for securing that he is at all material times in possession of all information relevant for determining the nature and extent of any steps which it is requisite for him to take in order to discharge efficiently the duties imposed on him by or by virtue of this Part of this Act.

(2) Neither the manager of a mine as such, nor a manager of a quarry as such shall be guilty of an offence, by virtue of subsection (1) or subsection (2) of section 152 of the principal Act (which provides among other things that managers may be guilty of an offence where some other person contravenes a particular statutory provision) by reason of a contravention, in relation to a closed tip which is associated with the mine or quarry, of—

(*a*) any provision of this Part of this Act, of the principal Act, of any order made thereunder or of regulations; or

(*b*) a direction, prohibition, restriction or requirement given or imposed by a notice served under or by virtue of this Part of this Act or the principal Act by an inspector;

(*c*) a condition attached to an exemption, consent, approval or authority granted or given under or by virtue of this Part of this Act or the principal Act by the Minister or an inspector.

(3) In subsection (2) above, the expression " the manager ", in relation to a mine, includes an under-manager of the mine

PART I

and any person who is for the time being treated for the purposes of the principal Act as the manager or an under-manager of the mine, and the expression " manager ", in relation to a quarry, includes any person who is for the time being treated for the purposes of that Act as a manager of the quarry.

(4) For the purpose of determining whether a tip to which this Part of this Act applies is, or is likely to become, insecure an inspector shall have power to require the owner of the mine or quarry with which it is associated to furnish such information as the inspector may specify and may by notice served on the owner require him to carry out such procedures or conduct such tests as may be specified in the notice.

(5) In relation to an active tip, the powers of an inspector under subsection (4) above shall include power to require information from, or to serve a notice requiring the carrying out of procedures or the conduct of tests by, the manager of the mine or, as the case may be, a manager of the quarry, instead of, or as well as, the owner.

(6) The provisions of Part XV of the principal Act with respect to references upon notices served by inspectors shall apply to a notice served by an inspector under this section.

Notification of beginning and ending of tipping operations.

4.—(1) If at any time tipping operations from a mine or quarry of a prescribed class or description—

(*a*) are to be begun on premises which at that time are not the site of a tip to which this Part of this Act applies, or

(*b*) are to be resumed at a tip which at that time is a closed tip,

the owner of the mine or quarry shall give notice to the inspector for the district of the intention to begin or resume the tipping operations not less than thirty days, or such shorter period as the inspector may permit, before the beginning or resumption of the operations.

(2) Not more than two months after the date on which tipping operations from a mine or quarry of a prescribed class or description cease at an active tip, the owner of the mine or quarry shall give notice to the inspector for the district that tipping operations have ceased at that tip.

Tipping rules.

5.—(1) Regulations may require that, in the case of any mine or quarry with which is associated an active tip of such class or description as may be prescribed, the manager of the mine or, as the case may be, the owner of the quarry shall make rules (in this Part of this Act referred to as " tipping rules ") with respect to tipping operations on any active tip of a prescribed class or description and the nature of the refuse to be deposited on such a tip.

PART I

(2) Tipping rules shall comply with such requirements with respect to the form thereof and the matters to be specified therein as may be prescribed and may impose upon persons employed at the mine or quarry such duties and prohibitions as it appears to the manager of the mine or the owner of the quarry requisite or expedient to impose on them for securing compliance with any requirement imposed by or by virtue of this Part of this Act.

(3) If, with respect to any tipping rules for the time being in force, an inspector is of opinion that the rules require modification in any particular, he may serve on the manager of the mine concerned or, as the case may be, the owner of the quarry concerned, a notice specifying the particular in which, in his opinion, the rules require modification and the nature of the modification which, in his opinion, ought to be made, and requiring the manager or owner, before the expiry of such period beginning with the date on which the notice becomes operative as may be specified therein, to modify the tipping rules in accordance with the tenor of the notice.

(4) The provisions of Part XV of the principal Act with respect to references upon notices served by inspectors shall apply to a notice served by an inspector under this section.

(5) Any provision of tipping rules which is inconsistent with the provisions of any regulation shall, to the extent of the inconsistency, be of no effect.

(6) A copy of all tipping rules for the time being in force with respect to a mine or quarry shall be kept at the office at the mine or quarry or at such other place as may be approved by an inspector, and it shall be the duty of the manager of every mine and the owner of every quarry with respect to which tipping rules are for the time being in force to supply to every person employed at the mine or quarry whose duties consist of or include the carrying out of tipping operations a document explaining the effect of the tipping rules so far as they concern him.

(7) A document purporting to be certified by the manager of a mine or the owner of a quarry to be a true copy of any tipping rules for the time being in force with respect to that mine or quarry shall be receivable in evidence and shall, unless the contrary is proved, be deemed to be such a copy.

Plans and sections of tips.

6.—(1) Provision may be made by regulations for requiring that, in the case of every active or closed tip of a prescribed class or description, the person having responsibility for the tip shall keep at the office at the mine or quarry with which the tip is associated or at such other place as may be approved by an inspector accurate plans and sections of the tip and of the strata underlying it, being plans or, as the case may be,

PART I

sections complying with such requirements as are imposed by or by virtue of subsection (2) below; and regulations made by virtue of this subsection may require that plans and sections be so kept as at any time to disclose the extent of the tip delineated thereon both up to a day not earlier than such previous day as may be prescribed and up to a distance from its position at that time not greater than such as may be prescribed.

(2) Plans and sections required to be kept by virtue of subsection (1) above shall be of durable material and be prepared in such form and manner as may be specified by rules made by the Minister and on a scale not less than such as may be so specified and any such plans and sections shall record such information as may be so specified with respect to situation, contours, boundaries, the nature of the refuse deposited and any such other matters (whether similar to those specially mentioned in this subsection or not) as may be so specified.

(3) If it appears to an inspector that any information which, by virtue of the preceding provisions of this section, is required to be recorded on a plan or section required to be kept by the person having responsibility for an active or closed tip cannot be recorded thereon fully and clearly, he may serve on that person a notice requiring him to keep at the office at the mine or quarry with which the tip is associated or at such other place as may be approved by an inspector such supplementary plan, section or drawing specified in the notice as appears to the inspector by whom the notice is served to be requisite for the purpose of recording that information fully and clearly.

(4) For the purposes of this section the person having responsibility for a tip is—

(*a*) in the case of a tip which is associated with a quarry, the owner of the quarry; and

(*b*) in the case of an active tip which is associated with a mine, the manager of the mine; and

(*c*) in the case of a closed tip which is associated with a mine, the owner of the mine.

Transmission and preservation of plans, etc. relating to tips at abandoned mines and quarries.

7.—(1) Provision may be made by regulations for requiring that, in the event of the abandonment of a mine or quarry, the owner of the mine or quarry shall, within the prescribed period, send to the inspector for the district—

(*a*) all such plans, drawings and sections relating to tips associated with the mine or quarry as were required to be kept by virtue of section 6 above; and

(*b*) such other information as may be prescribed with respect to the nature and quantity of the refuse deposited on, and any other prescribed matters relating to, any tip associated with the mine or quarry.

PART I

(2) Subject to subsection (3) below, plans, drawings, sections and other information sent to an inspector in pursuance of subsection (1) above shall be preserved by the Minister or by some other person under arrangements made or approved by the Minister.

(3) Where, at the time at which the working of a mine or quarry is resumed, any plans, drawings, sections or other information relating to a tip associated, or formerly associated, with the mine or quarry are, by virtue of subsection (2) above, preserved by the Minister or by some other person (not being the owner of the mine or quarry), the owner shall, on giving not less than fourteen days' notice to the person by whom they are preserved and (where that person is not the Minister) to the Minister, be entitled to have the plans, drawings, sections and other information delivered to him.

(4) If required to do so before the expiry of a notice given by him under subsection (3) above, the owner of a mine or quarry shall afford to the Minister a reasonable opportunity of making copies of the whole, or such part as the Minister thinks fit, of any plans, drawings, sections and other information to which the notice relates.

Geological map to be kept of district in which certain tips are situated.

8.—(1) Regulations may require that the person having responsibility for a tip of a prescribed class or description, being a tip to which this Part of this Act applies, shall keep at the office at the mine or quarry with which the tip is associated or at such other place as may be approved by an inspector a geological map of the district in which the tip is situated, being a map conforming to such requirements (if any) as may be prescribed.

(2) Subsection (4) of section 6 above shall apply for the purposes of this section as it applies for the purposes of that section.

Penalty for offences relating to tips to which Part I applies.

9.—(1) Where any person is convicted of an offence under the principal Act by virtue of—

(*a*) a contravention of any provision of this Part of this Act, or

(*b*) an act or omission which, by virtue only of a provision of this Part of this Act, constitutes a contravention of any provision of the principal Act or of regulations,

and the act or omission which constituted the contravention was of such a nature that it impaired, or might in the opinion of the court have been expected to impair, the security of the tip, the court by which that person is convicted may impose upon him either in addition to, or in substitution for, any fine authorised by section 155(1) of the principal Act, imprisonment for a term not exceeding three months.

Part I

(2) In relation to any contravention falling within subsection (1) above, that subsection shall have effect in place of subsection (2) of section 155 of the principal Act (which restricts the penalty of imprisonment to offences where there was a risk of death, serious injury or danger to a person employed at a mine or quarry).

Interpretation of Part I.

10.—(1) In this Part of this Act (and in any provision of the principal Act where these expressions occur),—

(*a*) " tip ", " active tip " and " closed tip " shall be construed in accordance with section 2 above ;

(*b*) " tipping operations " means the depositing of refuse from a mine or quarry and the carrying out of any operations necessary for, or incidental to, the depositing of the refuse ; and

(*c*) " tipping rules " shall be construed in accordance with section 5(1) above.

(2) For the purposes of this Part of this Act and of the principal Act the mine or quarry with which a tip is associated shall be determined as follows,—

(*a*) in the case of a tip on premises which are deemed to form part of a mine or quarry for the purposes of the principal Act, the tip is associated with that mine or quarry ;

(*b*) in the case of a tip not falling within paragraph (*a*) above but on premises which, at any time after the commencement of the principal Act, were deemed to form part of a mine or quarry for the purposes of that Act, the tip is associated with that mine or quarry (or, as the case may be, the last such mine or quarry) ; and

(*c*) in any other case, the tip is associated with the mine or quarry from which refuse was deposited on the tip, or, in the case of a tip which was used for the deposit of refuse from two or more mines or quarries, such one of those mines or quarries as the Minister may direct.

(3) Any reference in this Part of this Act to any other enactment shall be taken as referring to that enactment as amended by or under any other enactment, including this Part of this Act.

Part II

Prevention of Public Danger from Disused Tips

Local authorities having functions under Part II.

11.—(1) For the purpose of ensuring that disused tips do not, by reason of instability, constitute a danger to members of the public, local authorities shall have the functions conferred on them by this Part of this Act.

PART II

(2) For the purposes of this Part of this Act a disused tip is a tip, as defined in section 2(1), which is neither an active nor a closed tip within the meaning of Part I of this Act.

(3) In this Part of this Act " local authority ", subject to subsection (4), means—

(*a*) in England and Wales, the council of a county, county borough or London borough, the Common Council of the City of London or the Council of the Isles of Scilly, and

(*b*) in Scotland, the council of a county or of a large burgh within the meaning of the Local Government (Scotland) Act 1947. 1947 c. 43

(4) A county council in England and Wales may, with the agreement of the council of the county district in question, delegate all or any of its functions under this Part of this Act to the council of a county district within its area, and any such delegation—

(*a*) may relate to the whole or only a part of the area of the county district; and

(*b*) may be subject to such financial and other terms and arrangements as may be agreed;

and in relation to any functions so delegated to the council of a county district, the expression " local authority " in this Part of this Act includes that council.

Information relating to disused tips.

12.—(1) For the purpose of enabling a local authority to assess whether a disused tip which is situated wholly or partly within its area is stable and whether any instability of the tip is or is likely to constitute a danger to members of the public, the local authority may, by notice served on the owner of the tip or on any other person who the authority has reason to believe may be able to assist it, require him, within such time, not being less than fourteen days, as may be specified in the notice, to produce to the authority such documents in his possession or control (whether in the form of maps, surveys, plans, records of work or otherwise and whether relating to the tip itself or the land on which it is situated) as may be so specified.

(2) Any person who without reasonable excuse fails to comply with a notice under this section shall be liable on summary conviction to a fine not exceeding £100, and any person who, in pursuance of such a notice,—

(*a*) with intent to deceive, produces any document or gives any information which is false in a material particular, or,

(*b*) knowingly or recklessly makes a statement which is false in a material particular,

shall be liable on summary conviction to a fine not exceeding

PART II

£400 or, on conviction on indictment, to imprisonment for a term not exceeding two years or to a fine or to both.

Right of entry to carry out exploratory tests, etc.

13.—(1) Subject to the following provisions of this section, a person duly authorised in writing by a local authority may at any reasonable time enter upon the land on which a disused tip is situated or upon any neighbouring land—

(*a*) for the purpose of investigating whether any instability of the tip might constitute a danger to members of the public;

(*b*) for the purpose of carrying out any operations (in this Part of this Act referred to as " exploratory tests ") which, in the opinion of the local authority, are necessary to determine whether the tip is unstable; and

(*c*) for the purpose of inspecting any operations which are being carried out on that land where those operations may affect the stability of the tip;

but, subject to the following provisions of this section, a person so authorised shall not demand admission as of right to any land which is occupied unless at least forty-eight hours' notice in writing of the intended entry has been given to the occupier.

(2) If it is shown to the satisfaction of a justice of the peace on sworn information in writing—

(*a*) that admission to any land which any person is entitled to enter under this section has been refused to that person, or that a refusal is apprehended, or that the occupier is temporarily absent, and

(*b*) that there is reasonable ground for entry on to the land for the purpose for which entry is required,

the justice may by warrant under his hand authorise that person to enter the land, if need be by force; but such a warrant shall not be issued on the ground that entry has been refused or that a refusal of entry is apprehended unless the justice is satisfied that notice in writing of the intention to apply for a warrant has been given to the occupier.

(3) Every warrant granted under this section shall continue in force until the purpose for which the entry is required has been satisfied.

(4) If a local authority has reasonable ground for believing that a disused tip is unstable and that possible danger to members of the public requires an immediate entry on to any such land as is referred to in subsection (1) for one or more of the purposes specified in that subsection, a person duly authorised in writing by the local authority may, at any time and without giving notice or obtaining a warrant under this section, enter upon the land for that purpose (or those purposes).

(5) A person duly authorised to enter on any land by virtue of this section shall, if so required, produce evidence of his

authority before so entering and may take with him on to the land such other persons and such equipment as may be necessary.

(6) Any person who wilfully obstructs a person entitled to enter land by virtue of this section shall be liable on summary conviction to a fine not exceeding £50 or, on a second or subsequent conviction, to a fine not exceeding £100.

(7) In the application of this section to Scotland—

(*a*) for any reference to a justice of the peace there shall be substituted a reference to the sheriff, or a magistrate or justice of the peace, having jurisdiction in the place where the land is situated;

(*b*) for the reference to sworn information in writing there shall be substituted a reference to evidence on oath.

Notice requiring owner of disused tip to carry out remedial operations.

14.—(1) If it appears to a local authority that a disused tip situated wholly or partly within its area is unstable and, by reason of that instability, constitutes or is likely to constitute a danger to members of the public, the authority may by notice in the prescribed form served on the owner thereof require him to carry out, within such period as may be specified in the notice, being a period beginning not earlier than twenty-one days after the date of service of the notice, such remedial operations as may be so specified.

(2) In this Part of this Act " remedial operations ", in relation to a disused tip, means operations which, in the opinion of the local authority concerned, are necessary to ensure the stability of the tip.

(3) A notice under this section may require the carrying out of remedial operations on the tip itself, on the land on which it is situated or on any neighbouring land which is in the occupation of the owner of the tip or in which he has, otherwise than as a mortgagee, an estate or interest superior to that of the occupier.

(4) Where a local authority serves a notice under this section on the owner of a disused tip, then, within the period of seven days beginning with the day on which the notice was served, the authority shall serve a copy of the notice on—

(*a*) any other person who is in occupation of the whole or part of the land on which any remedial operations specified in the notice are required to be carried out and any other person who, to the knowledge of the local authority, has an estate or interest, otherwise than as a mortgagee, in that land; and

(*b*) any other person who, to the knowledge of the local authority, either has an estate or interest, otherwise than as a mortgagee, in the land on which the tip is

Part II

situated, or had such an estate or interest at any time within the period of twelve years immediately preceding the date of the service of the notice on the owner of the tip; and

(*c*) any other person who, to the knowledge of the local authority, has an interest in (including a right to acquire) all or any of the material comprised in the tip; and

(*d*) any other person who, to the knowledge of the local authority, has at any time within the period referred to in paragraph (*b*) above used the tip for the purpose of the deposit of refuse from a mine or quarry; and

(*e*) any other person who the local authority has reason to believe has, at any time within that period, caused or contributed to the instability of the tip by the carrying out of any operations on the tip, on the land on which it is situated or on neighbouring land or by failing to take any steps which he might reasonably have taken to prevent the tip from becoming unstable.

(5) Where a local authority serves a notice under this section on the owner of a disused tip, then, within the period of twenty-one days beginning with the day on which the notice was served, the owner may serve a counter-notice under this subsection in the prescribed form requiring the local authority to exercise its powers under section 17; and where such a counter-notice is served—

(*a*) the local authority shall serve a copy of the counter-notice on every person on whom, under subsection (4), it served a copy of the notice under this section;

(*b*) the notice under this section and any copy thereof served under subsection (4) shall be deemed for the purposes of the following provisions of this Part of this Act never to have been served; and

(*c*) the local authority shall, as soon as reasonably practicable, exercise its powers under section 17 in relation to the disused tip in question.

(6) Where the owner of a disused tip is required by a notice under this section to carry out remedial operations on any land which is not in his occupation but in which he has an estate or interest superior to that of the occupier, then, as against the occupier and any other person having an estate or interest in the land in question, the owner of the disused tip shall have the right to enter on to the land in order to carry out the remedial operations and any consequential works of reinstatement and to take with him on to the land such other persons and such equipment as may be necessary.

PART II

(7) Where, in the course of carrying out remedial operations specified in a notice under this section, material which is not the property of the owner of the disused tip is removed from the tip, the owner may sell the material but shall account to the owner thereof for the proceeds of sale; but nothing in this subsection shall prevent the owner of a disused tip from setting off the proceeds of sale or any part thereof against any sum which he is entitled to recover from the owner of the material under the following provisions of this Part of this Act.

(8) If, without reasonable excuse, the owner of a disused tip on whom a notice is served under this section fails to carry out the remedial operations specified in the notice within the period specified therein or, if that period is extended on an application under subsection (3) or subsection (4) of section 15, within that period as so extended, he shall be liable on summary conviction to a fine not exceeding £400.

Appeals against notices under s. 14.

15.—(1) A person on whom is served a notice or a copy of a notice under section 14 may, within the period of twenty-one days beginning with the date of service of the notice on the owner, apply to the court for an order varying or cancelling the notice on any one or more of the following grounds, namely,—

(*a*) that there is no reasonable ground for believing that the tip is unstable or that, by reason of instability, the tip constitutes or is likely to constitute a danger to members of the public;

(*b*) that the remedial operations specified in the notice are more extensive than is necessary to secure the safety of members of the public;

(*c*) that the stability of the tip could be ensured by the carrying out of operations different, in whole or in part, from the remedial operations specified in the notice and that the owner is prepared to undertake those alternative operations;

(*d*) that the owner or some other person has already begun, or has entered into a contract with a third party to begin, operations different, in whole or in part, from the remedial operations specified in the notice and those alternative operations will ensure the stability of the tip;

(*e*) that the time within which the remedial operations are to be carried out is not reasonably sufficient for the purpose;

(*f*) that there is some defect or error in, or in connection with the notice.

(2) If and so far as an application under this section is based on the ground of some defect or error in or in connection with

PART II

the notice, the court shall dismiss the application if it is satisfied that the defect or error was not material.

(3) Subject to subsection (2), if the court is satisfied on an application under this section that the ground, or any of the grounds, of the application is made out, the court may make an order varying or, if the court thinks fit, cancelling the notice; and where a notice is varied under this section the notice and any copy thereof which has been served under section 14(4) shall be deemed always to have had effect as so varied.

(4) Where an application is made under this section and is not withdrawn, the period specified in the notice in question as the period within which the remedial operations are to be carried out shall not expire before the application is finally determined; and where on an application under this section the court is not satisfied that the ground, or any of the grounds, of the application is made out, the court may nevertheless by order extend the period specified in the notice as the period within which the remedial operations are to be carried out.

Cancellation by local authority of notice under s. 14.

16.—(1) Where a local authority has served on the owner of a disused tip a notice under section 14 requiring the carrying out of remedial operations then, notwithstanding that an application may have been made under section 15 in respect of the notice or that the owner may have begun to carry out the operations (and whether or not the period specified for the carrying out of the operations has expired) the local authority may at any time before the completion of the remedial operations cancel the notice under section 14 by a notice under this section in the prescribed form served on the owner.

(2) Where a notice is served under this section in respect of a notice under section 14, the local authority shall serve a copy of the notice so served on every person on whom it served a copy of the notice under section 14.

(3) Where a notice under section 14 is cancelled under this section then, without prejudice to any penalty already incurred by the owner of the tip under section 14(8), the owner shall no longer be required to carry out the remedial operations specified in the notice which is cancelled; but the service of a notice under this section shall not affect the right of the local authority to serve a further notice under section 14 in relation to the disused tip in question.

(4) Where a local authority has cancelled a notice under section 14 and the owner of the disused tip has incurred expenditure in compliance with the notice, the owner may apply to the court for an order directing the local authority to reimburse to him the whole, or such part as the court thinks fit, of—

(*a*) any expenditure incurred by him in consequence of the service of the notice under section 14; and

Part II

(*b*) any expenditure incurred by him which is attributable to the cancellation of that notice (whether relating to the reinstatement of any land, the cancellation of any contract or otherwise).

(5) In determining whether to make an order under subsection (4) or to what extent the local authority is to be required by such an order to reimburse the owner, the court shall have regard to all the circumstances of the case and, in particular, to the grounds on which the local authority cancelled the notice under section 14 and to whether the local authority has served or intends to serve a further notice on the owner under section 14 or whether the local authority intends to carry out remedial operations itself.

Carrying out of remedial operations and works of reinstatement by local authority.

17.—(1) Where a local authority considers that such circumstances exist as are specified in section 14(1) then, instead of serving a notice under that section requiring the owner of the disused tip in question to carry out remedial operations, the authority may itself carry out remedial operations and any works of reinstatement reasonably necessary in consequence of the carrying out of those remedial operations.

(2) Subject to subsection (3), where a local authority proposes to carry out remedial operations under subsection (1) in relation to a disused tip it shall, not less than twenty-one days before the operations are begun, serve notice on the owner of the tip of its intention to carry out the operations, specifying the nature and extent of the operations and of any consequential works of reinstatement which it proposes to carry out.

(3) If a local authority has reasonable ground for believing that a disused tip is unstable and that possible danger to members of the public requires the immediate carrying out of remedial operations, it may begin operations under subsection (1) forthwith, notwithstanding that no notice under subsection (2) has been served or that less than twenty-one days has elapsed since the service of such a notice; but if no such notice has been served at the time the remedial operations are begun, then, as soon thereafter as is reasonably practicable, the local authority shall serve notice on the owner of the tip of the commencement of the operations, specifying the nature and extent of the operations and of any consequential works of reinstatement which it proposes to carry out.

(4) A notice under subsection (2) or subsection (3) shall be in the prescribed form.

(5) Concurrently with the service of a notice under subsection (2) or subsection (3) on the owner of a disused tip, or as soon thereafter as is reasonably practicable a copy of that notice shall be served on every person falling within paragraphs (*a*) to (*e*) of section 14(4) (and for the purposes

PART II

of this subsection, any reference in those paragraphs to the notice shall be construed as a reference to the notice served on the owner of the disused tip under subsection (2) or subsection (3)).

(6) A local authority may sell any material removed from a disused tip in the course of remedial operations carried out by it under subsection (1) and shall account to the owner of the material for the proceeds of sale thereof; but nothing in this subsection shall prevent the local authority from setting off the proceeds of sale or any part thereof against any sum which the local authority is entitled to recover from the owner of the material under the following provisions of this Part of this Act.

(7) Where a local authority is the owner of a disused tip situated wholly or partly within its area, Schedule 2 to this Act shall apply in relation to the carrying out by the local authority of remedial operations relating to that tip.

Right of entry to carry out remedial operations and works of reinstatement.

18.—(1) Where a local authority has served a notice under section 17(2) of its intention to carry out remedial operations in relation to a disused tip or where no such notice has been served but section 17(3) applies, a person duly authorised in writing by the local authority may at any reasonable time enter upon the land on which the disused tip is situated or upon any neighbouring land for any purpose connected with the carrying out of remedial operations or consequential works of reinstatement; but, subject to the following provisions of this section, a person so authorised shall not demand admission as of right to any land which is occupied unless twenty-four hours' notice in writing of the intended entry has been given to the occupier.

(2) If it is shown to the satisfaction of a justice of the peace on sworn information in writing—

(*a*) that admission to any land which any person is entitled to enter under this section has been refused to that person, or that a refusal is apprehended, or that the occupier is temporarily absent, and

(*b*) that there is reasonable ground for entry on to the land for the purpose for which entry is required,

the justice may by warrant under his hand authorise that person to enter the land, if need be by force; but such a warrant shall not be issued on the ground that entry has been refused or that a refusal of entry is apprehended unless the justice is satisfied that notice in writing of the intention to apply for a warrant has been given to the occupier.

(3) Every warrant granted under this section shall continue in force until the purpose for which the entry is required has been satisfied.

PART II

(4) Notwithstanding anything in subsection (1), in a case falling within section 17(3), a person duly authorised in writing by the local authority concerned may exercise the right of entry conferred by subsection (1) without giving notice or obtaining a warrant under this section.

(5) A person duly authorised to enter on any land by virtue of this section shall, if so required, produce evidence of his authority before so entering and may take with him on to the land such other persons and such equipment as may be necessary.

(6) Any person who wilfully obstructs a person entitled to enter land by virtue of this section shall be liable on summary conviction to a fine not exceeding £50 or, on a second or subsequent conviction, to a fine not exceeding £100.

(7) In the application of this section to Scotland—

(*a*) for any reference to a justice of the peace there shall be substituted a reference to the sheriff, or a magistrate or justice of the peace, having jurisdiction in the place where the land is situated ;

(*b*) for the reference to sworn information in writing there shall be substituted a reference to evidence on oath.

Contribution orders.

19.—(1) Where a notice relating to remedial operations at a disused tip has been served on the owner of the tip under section 14 or section 17 and an application is made to the court under this section, the court may order that a contribution towards the expenses otherwise falling to be borne by the owner of the disused tip as a result of the carrying out of the remedial operations shall be made by any one or more of the following persons on whom notice of the application has been served, namely,—

(*a*) any person who at the date of the service of the notice under section 14 or section 17 had an estate or interest, otherwise than as a mortgagee, in the land on which the tip is situated and any person who had such an estate or interest at any time within the period of twelve years immediately preceding that date ;

(*b*) any other person who has, at any time within that period, used the tip for the purpose of the deposit of refuse from a mine or quarry ; and

(*c*) any other person who, in the opinion of the court, has at any time within that period caused or contributed to the instability of the tip by the carrying out of any operations on the tip, on the land on which it is situated or on neighbouring land or by failing to take any steps which he might reasonably have taken to prevent the tip from becoming unstable.

PART II

(2) An application under this section may be made by the owner of the disused tip on whom has been served the notice referred to in subsection (1) and, in the case of a notice under section 17, such an application may also be made by the local authority which served the notice.

(3) An application under this section shall be of no effect unless it is made within the following period namely,—

(*a*) where the application relates to a notice under section 14 and no application is made in respect of the notice under section 15, the period of three months beginning with the date of service of that notice on the owner; and

(*b*) where the application relates to a notice under section 14 in respect of which an application is made under section 15, the period beginning with the date of service of that notice on the owner and ending three months after the date on which the application under section 15 is withdrawn or finally determined; and

(*c*) where the application relates to a notice served under section 17, the period of three months beginning with the date of service of that notice on the owner of the disused tip.

(4) In determining whether to make an order under this section requiring any person to make a contribution or what is to be the amount of any such contribution the court shall have regard to all the circumstances of the case and, in particular,—

(*a*) to the extent to which it appears to the court that that person has, by any act or omission, caused or contributed to the instability of the tip;

(*b*) to the extent to which that person has used the tip for the deposit of refuse;

(*c*) to the nature and extent of any estate or interest which that person had, at the date of the service of the notice under section 14 or section 17, in the land on which the tip is situated;

(*d*) in the case of a person who had an estate or interest in that land but disposed of it before that date, to whether, in the opinion of the court, he disposed of his estate or interest for the purpose of evading any liability (whether under this Part of this Act or otherwise) in connection with the disused tip; and

(*e*) to the terms of any covenant, agreement or statutory provision affecting the rights and obligations in relation to the tip of that person and the owner thereof.

PART II

(5) An order under this section shall specify the amount of the contribution to be made by the person to whom it relates as a percentage (which, if the court thinks appropriate in any case, may be 100 per cent) of the total amount in respect of which a contribution can be claimed under the following provisions of this Part of this Act.

(6) In this Part of this Act—

"contributory" means the person to whom an order under this section relates;

"covenant", in relation to Scotland, means an obligation or agreement, and includes a real burden *ad factum praestandum*; and

"the specified percentage", in relation to a contributory, means the percentage specified, in accordance with subsection (5), in the order under this section relating to the contributory.

Compensation for damage or disturbance.

20.—(1) Subject to the following provisions of this section, where, as a result of remedial operations carried out by the owner of a disused tip in pursuance of a notice under section 14 or of exploratory tests or remedial operations carried out by a local authority under section 17(1),—

(*a*) any land on which entry is made for the purpose of carrying out those operations or tests is damaged, or

(*b*) any person is disturbed in his enjoyment of any land,

any person interested in the land which is damaged or, as the case may be, the person whose enjoyment of land is disturbed shall be entitled to recover compensation under this section in respect of that damage or disturbance.

(2) Subject to the following provisions of this Part of this Act,—

(*a*) compensation for damage or disturbance resulting from the carrying out of exploratory tests shall be recoverable from the local authority which carried out the tests; and

(*b*) compensation for damage or disturbance resulting from the carrying out of remedial operations shall be recoverable from the owner of the disused tip by whom, or, as the case may be, the local authority by which, the operations were carried out.

(3) Nothing in this section shall entitle the owner of a disused tip to compensation in respect of damage or disturbance resulting from remedial operations carried out by him or by any other person who was the owner of the disused tip at the time the remedial operations were carried out.

PART II

(4) Subsections (1) to (3) shall apply in relation to damage or disturbance resulting from the carrying out of works of reinstatement consequential upon any remedial operations and accordingly any reference in those subsections to remedial operations includes a reference to consequential works of reinstatement.

(5) Any dispute arising on a claim for compensation under this section shall be determined by the court.

(6) The provisions of Schedule 3 to this Act shall have effect in relation to any claim for compensation under this section by the owner of a disused tip or by a contributory.

Recovery from contributories of expenses of owner carrying out remedial operations.

21.—(1) Subject to the following provisions of this section, where—

(*a*) remedial operations have been carried out by the owner of a disused tip in compliance with a notice under section 14, and

(*b*) an order for contribution towards the expenses otherwise falling to be borne by the owner as a result of the carrying out of those operations has been made under section 19,

the owner of the disused tip shall be entitled to recover from the contributory the specified percentage of the total amount determined in accordance with subsection (2).

(2) Subject to subsection (4), the total amount in respect of which a contribution may be claimed by the owner of a disused tip in a case falling within subsection (1) is the aggregate of—

(*a*) the expenses reasonably incurred by the owner in carrying out the remedial operations referred to in subsection (1) and any works of reinstatement reasonably necessary in consequence of the carrying out of those operations ;

(*b*) the amount of any such compensation as is mentioned in paragraph (*b*) of section 20(2) (being compensation referable to those remedial operations or consequential works of reinstatement) which is recoverable (or has been recovered) from the owner in pursuance of a claim under section 20 ; and

(*c*) the amount of any such compensation as is referred to in paragraph (*b*) of section 20(2) in respect of which the owner could himself have made a claim under section 20 if the remedial operations (and any consequential works of reinstatement) had been carried out by the local authority.

PART II

(3) No contribution shall be recoverable under this section unless a demand therefor is served on the contributory specifying, in addition to the sum claimed by way of contribution,—

(*a*) the total amount in respect of which the contribution is claimed ; and

(*b*) the separate amounts which comprise that total, distinguished by reference to paragraphs (*a*), (*b*) and (*c*) of subsection (2).

(4) In any case where remedial operations have been carried out by the owner of a disused tip in compliance with a notice under section 14 and that notice was cancelled under section 16, this section and section 22 shall have effect subject to the modifications in Schedule 4 to this Act.

Appeals against demands under s. 21.

22.—(1) Within the period of six weeks beginning with the date of service on a contributory of a demand under section 21(3), the contributory may apply to the court for an order varying the demand on any one or more of the following grounds, namely,—

(*a*) that the amount of the expenses incurred by the owner of the disused tip in carrying out the remedial operations was greater than was reasonable ;

(*b*) that the amount of the expenses incurred by the owner in carrying out works of reinstatement was greater than was reasonably necessary to reinstate the land in consequence of the remedial operations ;

(*c*) that, because the time taken by the owner to carry out the remedial operations or any consequential works of reinstatement was unreasonably long, the compensation paid or payable to any person in pursuance of a claim under section 20 in respect of damage or disturbance is greater than it would otherwise have been ;

(*d*) that the amount of the compensation paid or payable to any person in pursuance of a claim under section 20 is greater than is necessary to compensate him in respect of any damage or disturbance suffered ;

(*e*) that the amount specified in the demand as being referable to paragraph (*c*) of section 21(2) is greater than the compensation which could have been claimed by the owner in the circumstances specified in that paragraph ;

(*f*) that the amount claimed in the demand is greater than the specified percentage of the amount determined under section 21(2).

(2) If on an application under subsection (1) the court is satisfied that the ground, or any of the grounds, of the application

PART II

is made out, the court may make an order reducing the amount recoverable by the owner of the disused tip from the contributory to such amount as the court thinks fit.

(3) Subject to the right to make an application under subsection (1) and to Schedule 4 to this Act a demand under section 21(3) shall be final and conclusive.

Right of local authority to recover certain expenses.

23.—(1) Subject to the following provisions of this section and to sections 24 and 25, where a local authority has carried out remedial operations in relation to a disused tip under section 17(1), the authority shall be entitled to recover from the owner of the tip—

(*a*) the expenses reasonably incurred by the authority in carrying out any exploratory tests which gave rise to the remedial operations;

(*b*) the expenses reasonably incurred by the authority in carrying out the remedial operations and any works of reinstatement reasonably necessary in consequence of the carrying out of those operations;

(*c*) such sum, not exceeding 5 per cent. of the expenses referred to in paragraphs (*a*) and (*b*) above, as the authority thinks fit in respect of its establishment charges; and

(*d*) the amount of any such compensation as is mentioned in section 20(2) (being compensation referable to the carrying out of the exploratory tests, remedial operations or works of reinstatement referred to in paragraphs (*a*) and (*b*) above) which is recoverable (or has been recovered) from the local authority in pursuance of a claim under section 20.

(2) Subject to the following provisions of this section and to section 24, where a local authority has carried out, in relation to a disused tip, exploratory tests which resulted in the service of a notice under section 14 requiring the owner of the tip to carry out remedial operations, the local authority shall be entitled to recover from the owner—

(*a*) the expenses reasonably incurred by the authority in carrying out those exploratory tests;

(*b*) such sum, not exceeding 5 per cent. of the expenses referred to in paragraph (*a*) above, as the authority thinks fit in respect of its establishment charges; and

(*c*) the amount of any such compensation as is mentioned in paragraph (*a*) of section 20(2) (being compensation referable to the carrying out of the exploratory tests referred to in paragraph (*a*) above) which is recoverable (or has been recovered) from the local authority in pursuance of a claim under section 20.

(3) Where an order has been made under section 19 requiring any person to make a contribution towards the expenses otherwise falling to be borne by the owner of a disused tip as a result of the carrying out of the remedial operations referred to in subsection (1), or, as the case may be, subsection (2),—

(*a*) the local authority referred to in that subsection shall be entitled to recover from the contributory the specified percentage of the amount recoverable (disregarding paragraph (*b*) below) from the owner of the disused tip under that subsection ; and

(*b*) the amount recoverable from the owner of the disused tip under that subsection shall be reduced by any sum or sums which the local authority is entitled to recover from any contributory or contributories by virtue of paragraph (*a*) above.

(4) No sum shall be recoverable under this section by a local authority from the owner of a disused tip or from any contributory unless a demand therefor is served on the owner or, as the case may be, the contributory specifying, in addition to the sum claimed by the local authority,—

(*a*) in the case of a demand served on a contributory, the total amount in respect of which the contribution is claimed ;

(*b*) in the case of a demand served on the owner of a disused tip, the sums (if any) which the local authority is entitled to recover from any contributory or contributories ; and

(*c*) in either case, the separate amounts which comprise the total amount recoverable by the local authority, distinguished by reference to each of paragraphs (*a*) to (*d*) of subsection (1) or, as the case may be, paragraphs (*a*) to (*c*) of subsection (2).

(5) Together with any sum recoverable by a local authority under this section from the owner of a disused tip or from a contributory, the local authority shall be entitled to recover interest from the date of service on him of the demand therefor under subsection (4) until the total amount recoverable from that person is paid, at such rate as may be specified by order made by the Ministers ; and, with the agreement of the authority, any sum so recoverable may be paid by such instalments as may be agreed.

PART II

(6) For the purposes of this section,—

(*a*) the owner of the disused tip, in a case falling within subsection (1), is the person who was the owner at the date of the commencement of the remedial operations referred to in that subsection and, in a case falling within subsection (2), is the person on whom was served the notice under section 14 referred to in that subsection; and

(*b*) exploratory tests relating to a disused tip shall be deemed to give rise to remedial operations in relation to that tip or, as the case may be, to result in the service of a notice under section 14 if, within the period of six months after the completion of the tests, the local authority began those operations or served the notice under section 14 on the owner of the tip.

Appeals against demands under s. 23.

24.—(1) Within the period of six weeks beginning with the date of the service on the owner of a disused tip or on a contributory of a demand under section 23(4), the person on whom the demand was served may apply to the court for an order varying or cancelling the demand on any one or more of the grounds specified in subsection (2) or subsection (3), whichever is appropriate to the case in question.

(2) Where the demand referred to in subsection (1) is made in a case falling within section 23(1), the grounds on which an application may be made under this section are—

(*a*) that the amount of the expenses incurred by the local authority in carrying out exploratory tests or remedial operations was greater than was reasonable;

(*b*) that the amount of the expenses incurred by the local authority in carrying out works of reinstatement was greater than was reasonably necessary to reinstate the land in consequence of the remedial operations;

(*c*) that, at the time the remedial operations were begun, there was no reasonable ground for believing that the disused tip concerned was unstable or that, by reason of instability, the tip constituted or was likely to constitute a danger to members of the public;

(*d*) that the remedial operations carried out by the local authority were more extensive than was necessary to secure the safety of members of the public;

(*e*) that, because the time taken by the local authority to carry out the exploratory tests or the remedial operations or any consequential works of reinstatement was unreasonably long, the compensation paid or payable to any person in pursuance of a claim under section 20 in respect of damage or disturbance is greater than it would otherwise have been;

(*f*) that the amount of the compensation paid or payable to any person in pursuance of a claim under section 20 is greater than is necessary to compensate him in respect of any damage or disturbance suffered;

(*g*) that, in the case of a demand served on a contributory, the amount claimed in the demand is greater than the specified percentage of the total amount recoverable by the local authority under section 23(1);

(*h*) that, in the case of a demand served on the owner of the disused tip concerned, the amount claimed in the demand does not give proper allowance for any sum or sums which the local authority is entitled to recover from any contributory or contributories.

(3) Where the demand referred to in subsection (1) is made in a case falling within section 23(2), the grounds on which an application may be made under this section are—

(*a*) that the amount of the expenses incurred by the local authority in carrying out the exploratory tests in question was greater than was reasonable;

(*b*) that, because the time taken by the local authority to carry out the exploratory tests was unreasonably long, the compensation paid or payable to any person in pursuance of a claim under section 20 in respect of damage or disturbance is greater than it would otherwise have been;

(*c*) that the amount of the compensation paid or payable to any person in pursuance of a claim under section 20 is greater than is necessary to compensate him in respect of any damage or disturbance suffered;

(*d*) that, in the case of a demand served on a contributory, the amount claimed in the demand is greater than the specified percentage of the total amount recoverable by the local authority under section 23(2);

(*e*) that, in the case of a demand served on the owner of the disused tip concerned, the amount claimed in the demand does not give proper allowance for any sum or sums which the local authority is entitled to recover from any contributory or contributories.

(4) If on an application under this section the court is satisfied that the ground, or any of the grounds, of the application is made out, the court may make an order either cancelling the demands in respect of which the application was made or reducing the amount recoverable from the person on whom that demand was served to such amount as the court thinks fit.

PART II

(5) Subject to the right to make an application under this section, a demand under section 23(4) shall be final and conclusive.

Grants towards local authority expenditure.

25.—(1) Where remedial operations are being or have been carried out in relation to a disused tip by a local authority, the appropriate Minister may, with the consent of the Treasury, make grants to the local authority towards the expenditure incurred by the authority in or in connection with the carrying out of the remedial operations, any previous exploratory tests and any consequential works of reinstatement.

(2) Grants made by the appropriate Minister under this section shall be of such amounts and payable at such times and subject to such conditions as he may from time to time determine either generally or in the case of any particular local authority or grant.

(3) Grants under this section may be made either as periodical grants in respect of the costs from time to time incurred or treated as incurred by a local authority in respect of the borrowing of money to defray expenditure qualifying for such grants, or as capital grants in respect of such expenditure or in substitution for such periodical grants.

(4) Where a grant is made to a local authority under this section the appropriate Minister may, after consultation with the local authority, give a direction that, having regard to the amount of the grant, the total amount recoverable from the owner of the disused tip concerned and any contributories under section 23, in respect of the expenditure referred to in paragraphs (*a*) to (*d*) of section 23(1), shall be limited to such amount as may be specified in the direction.

(5) Where a direction is given under subsection (4) limiting the amount recoverable from the owner of the disused tip and any contributories under section 23 to the amount specified in the direction then, in relation to the recovery of that amount by the local authority,—

(*a*) in a case where there are no contributories, the amount recoverable under that section from the owner by the local authority shall be reduced to the amount specified in the direction.

(*b*) any reference in section 23(3) to the amount recoverable from the owner of the disused tip shall be construed as a reference to the amount specified in the direction;

(*c*) a demand under section 23(4) shall state that the direction has been given and shall state the amount specified in the direction;

(*d*) in section 23(4), the reference in paragraph (*a*) to the total amount in respect of which the contribution is claimed and the reference in paragraph (*c*) to the total amount recoverable by the local authority shall each be construed as a reference to the total amount which would have been recoverable by the authority if no direction had been given ; and

(*e*) in paragraph (*g*) of section 24(2), for the reference to the total amount recoverable by the authority under section 23(1) there shall be substituted a reference to the amount specified in the direction.

Penalty for obstructing remedial operations and damaging completed works.

26.—(1) Any person who wilfully prevents or interferes with the carrying out of exploratory tests or remedial operations shall be liable on summary conviction to a fine not exceeding £100.

(2) Any person who wilfully damages or otherwise interferes with any works completed in the course of remedial operations for the purpose of ensuring the stability of a disused tip shall be liable on summary conviction to a fine not exceeding £400.

Offences under Part II.

27.—(1) Proceedings in respect of an offence under this Part of this Act shall not, in England and Wales, be instituted except by a local authority or by or with the consent of the Director of Public Prosecutions.

(2) Where an offence under this Part of this Act which has been committed by a body corporate is proved to have been committed with the consent or connivance of, or to be attributable to any neglect on the part of, a director, manager, secretary or other similar officer of the body corporate, or any person who was purporting to act in any such capacity, he, as well as the body corporate, shall be guilty of that offence and shall be liable to be proceeded against and punished accordingly.

(3) In this section " director ", in relation to a body corporate established by or under any enactment for the purpose of carrying on under national ownership any industry or part of an industry or undertaking, being a body corporate whose affairs are managed by its members, means a member of that body corporate.

" The court " in England and Wales.

28.—(1) Subject to the following provisions of this section, in the application of this Part of this Act in England and Wales, " the court " means the High Court.

(2) With the consent of the local authority which served a notice or copy of a notice under section 14, an application for the variation or cancellation of the notice under section 15 may be brought in the county court ; and with the consent of the person on whom notice of an application under section 19 is served, an application under that section may be made in the county court.

PART II

(3) Where, in any proceedings to which this subsection applies, the amount relevant to those proceedings does not exceed the limit for the time being imposed on the jurisdiction of a county court under paragraph (*b*) of section 40(1) of the County Courts Act 1959 (money recoverable by statute), proceedings to which this subsection applies may be begun in the county court instead of in the High Court.

1959 c. 22.

(4) The proceedings to which subsection (3) applies are those specified in paragraphs (*a*) to (*e*) below and the amounts relevant to any such proceedings are as follows:—

(*a*) in proceedings under section 16(4), the amount claimed by the owner of the disused tip from the local authority under that section;

(*b*) in proceedings to determine the amount of any compensation under section 20, the amount claimed by way of compensation;

(*c*) in proceedings for the variation of a demand served on a contributory under section 21, the amount claimed by way of contribution;

(*d*) in proceedings for the variation or cancellation of a demand served on the owner of a disused tip or a contributory under section 23, the amount claimed by the local authority from the owner or the contributory, as the case may be; and

(*e*) in proceedings for the variation or cancellation of a demand served on a contributory under paragraph 6(2) of Schedule 2 to this Act, the amount claimed by way of contribution.

Regulations and orders.

29.—(1) Any power conferred by this Part of this Act to make regulations and the power to make an order under section 23(5) shall be exercisable by statutory instrument.

(2) A statutory instrument containing regulations under this Part of this Act shall be subject to annulment in pursuance of a resolution of either House of Parliament.

(3) A statutory instrument containing an order under section 23(5) shall be laid before Parliament after being made.

(4) The power to make an order under section 23(5) includes power to vary or revoke such an order by a further order under that section.

Service of documents.

30.—(1) Any document which is required or authorised under this Part of this Act to be given to or served on any person may be given to or served on him—

(*a*) by delivering it to him or by leaving it at his proper address; or (*b*) by sending it to him by post.

PART II

(2) Any document required or authorised under this Part of this Act to be given to or served on a body corporate shall be duly given or served if it is given to or served on the secretary or clerk of that body.

(3) For the purposes of this section and of section 26 of the Interpretation Act 1889 (service of documents by post) in its application to this section, the proper address of any person to or on whom any document is to be given or served shall, in the case of the secretary or clerk of a body corporate, be that of the registered or principal office of that body, and in any other case shall be the last known address of the person to be served: 1889 c. 63.

Provided that, if the person to or on whom the document to be given or served has, in accordance with arrangements agreed, given an address in the United Kingdom for the giving or service of the document, his proper address for those purposes shall be that address.

(4) If the name or the address of any owner, lessee or occupier of land to or on whom any document is to be given or served under this Part of this Act cannot after reasonable inquiry be ascertained by the local authority or person seeking to give or serve the document, but there is on that land a building occupied by some person, the document may be given or served by addressing it to the person to or on whom it is to be given or served by the description of " owner ", " lessee " or " occupier " of the land (describing it) and either delivering it to some responsible person in the building or sending it by post to that building in a letter addressed to " the owner ", " the lessee ", or " the occupier ", as the case may be.

(5) In relation to any document required or authorised under this Part of this Act to be given or served by a local authority, the preceding provisions of this section shall have effect in place of section 287A of the Local Government Act 1933 or section 349 of the Local Government (Scotland) Act 1947 (service of notices by local authority) but nothing in this section shall affect the operation in relation to such a document of section 287B of the said Act of 1933 or, as the case may be, section 347 of the said Act of 1947 (authentication of documents). 1933 c. 51. 1947 c. 43.

Ecclesiastical property.

31.—(1) No notice under section 14 may be served in respect of a disused tip if the land on which the tip is situated is ecclesiastical property, but nothing in this subsection affects the powers of a local authority under section 17.

(2) Where under this Part of this Act a document is required or authorised to be given to, or served on, any person as

PART II

occupier of, or owner of an estate or interest in, any land which is ecclesiastical property, a copy of the document shall be given to or served on the Church Commissioners.

(3) Any compensation payable under section 20 to a person by virtue of his having an estate in fee simple in any land shall, if that land is ecclesiastical property, be paid (where the fee simple is vested in any person other than the Church Commissioners) to them instead of that person.

(4) Any sums paid under subsection (3) to the Church Commissioners with reference to any land shall, if the land is not consecrated, be applied by them for the purposes for which the proceeds of a sale by agreement of the fee simple in the land would be applicable under any enactment or Measure authorising such a sale, and, if the land is consecrated, be applied by them in such a manner as they may determine.

(5) Where the fee simple in any ecclesiastical property is in abeyance—

(*a*) it shall be treated for the purposes of this Part of this Act as being vested in the Church Commissioners; and

(*b*) where, by virtue of paragraph (*a*) above, the Church Commissioners are owners of land belonging to a benefice and, by virtue of their ownership of that land, are under a liability to pay any sum under this Part of this Act, either as owner of a disused tip or as a contributory, their liability shall be met from, and shall not exceed the total of, the sums held by them for that benefice.

(6) Where subsection (5) does not apply but a liability to pay any sum under this Part of this Act falls on any person, either as owner of a disused tip or as a contributory, by virtue of there being vested in him the fee simple in land belonging to a benefice, the Church Commissioners may apply any sums held by them for that benefice in discharging the whole or any part of that liability.

(7) In the foregoing provisions of this section "benefice" means an ecclesiastical benefice of the Church of England and "ecclesiastical property" means land belonging to a benefice or being or forming part of a church subject to the jurisdiction of the bishop of any diocese of the Church of England or the site of a church so subject, or being or forming part of a burial ground so subject.

(8) Subsection (1) applies in relation to Scottish church land as it applies to ecclesiastical property within the meaning of subsection (7).

In this subsection, "Scottish church land" means any land being or forming part of a church of the Church of Scotland, or the site of such a church, or the manse, glebe, churchyard or burial ground appertaining to such a church.

Raising of money in special cases to meet expenditure under Part II.

32.—(1) The provisions of this section shall have effect with respect to the raising of money in particular cases for the payment—

(*a*) of any expenses incurred in carrying out remedial operations in pursuance of a notice under section 14 and in carrying out any consequential works of reinstatement;

(*b*) of any compensation recoverable under section 20 and referable to any such remedial operations or works of reinstatement; and

(*c*) of any sums recoverable under section 21 or section 23 or paragraph 6 of Schedule 2 to this Act;

and in the following provisions of this section the expression "relevant expenditure" means any such expenses, compensation or sums as are referred to in paragraphs (*a*), (*b*) and (*c*) above.

(2) In relation to England and Wales—

(*a*) the purposes authorised for the application of capital moneys by section 73 of the Settled Land Act 1925, by that section as applied by section 28 of the Law of Property Act 1925 in relation to trusts for sale and by section 26 of the Universities and College Estates Act 1925 shall include the payment of any relevant expenditure; 1925 c. 18. 1925 c. 20. 1925 c. 24.

(*b*) the purposes authorised by section 71 of the Settled Land Act 1925, by that section as applied by section 28 of the Law of Property Act 1925 in relation to trusts for sale and by section 30 of the Universities and College Estates Act 1925 as purposes for which moneys may be raised by mortgage shall include the payment of any relevant expenditure;

(*c*) the purposes authorised by section 25 of the Act of the fifty-seventh year of King George the Third, chapter 97, for the application of moneys arising by any such sale of annuities standing in the name or to the account of the Duchy of Lancaster as is therein mentioned shall include the payment of any relevant expenditure arising by virtue of the application of any provision of this Part of this Act to property belonging to Her Majesty in right of that Duchy; and

(*d*) the purposes authorised by section 8 of the Duchy of Cornwall Management Act 1863 for the advancement of parts of such gross sums as are therein mentioned 1863 c. 49.

PART II

shall include the payment of any relevant expenditure arising by virtue of the application of any provision of this Part of this Act to property belonging to the Duchy of Cornwall.

(3) In relation to Scotland, for the purpose of paying any relevant expenditure, a trustee, a liferenter or an heir of entail in possession shall have power to expend capital money and to sell, or to borrow money on the security of, the estate or any part thereof, heritable as well as moveable.

Application of provisions of Public Health Act 1936.
1936 c. 49.

33. In the application of this Part of this Act in England and Wales, the following provisions of Part XII of the Public Health Act 1936 shall apply as if this Part of this Act were contained in that Act and as if any reference in that Act to a local authority were a reference to a local authority within the meaning of this Part of this Act, that is to say,—

(*a*) section 272 (power of councils to combine for purposes of Act);

(*b*) section 274 (power of councils to execute works outside their area);

(*c*) section 275 (power of local authority to execute work on behalf of owners);

(*d*) section 277 (power of councils to require information as to ownership of premises);

(*e*) section 304 (judges and justices not to be disqualified by liability to rates);

(*f*) section 305 (protection of members and officers of local authorities from personal liability); and

(*g*) section 341 (power to apply provisions of Act to Crown property).

Miscellaneous provisions relating to local authorities, etc. in Scotland.

34.—(1) A local authority in Scotland may execute outside their area any works which under this Part of this Act they may execute within their area, subject to entering into an agreement with the local authority of the area in which the works are being carried out as to the terms and conditions on which any such works are to be executed.

(2) A local authority in Scotland may by agreement with the owner of a disused tip themselves execute at his expense any works which they have under this Part of this Act required him to execute, and for that purpose they shall have all such rights as he would have.

(3) In the application of this Part of this Act to Scotland, the provisions of the following enactments shall apply for any purpose of this Part of this Act as they apply for the purposes of the respective enactments, and as if any reference in these enactments to any local authority were a reference to a local

authority within the meaning of this Part of this Act, that is to say,— PART II

(*a*) section 25(2) and (3) of the Building (Scotland) Act 1959 (power of councils to require information as to ownership of premises); 1959 c. 24.

(*b*) section 166 of the Public Health (Scotland) Act 1897 (protection of members and officers of local authorities from personal liability); 1897 c. 38.

(*c*) section 16 of the Land Drainage (Scotland) Act 1958 (Crown rights). 1958 c. 24.

Application to Scotland.

35. In the application of this Part of this Act in Scotland—

(*a*) " the court " means the sheriff, and any application to the sheriff under this Part of this Act shall be disposed of in a summary manner; and

(*b*) " mortgagee " means creditor in a heritable security, and " heritable security " has the same meaning as in the Conveyancing (Scotland) Act 1924 except that it includes a security constituted by ex facie absolute disposition or assignation. 1924 c. 27.

Interpretation of Part II.

36.—(1) In this Part of this Act—

" appropriate Minister " shall be construed in accordance with subsection (4);

" contributory " has the meaning assigned to it by section 19(6);

" disused tip " has the meaning assigned to it by section 11(2);

" exploratory tests " has the meaning assigned to it by section 13(1)(*b*);

" local authority " shall be construed in accordance with subsections (3) and (4) of section 11;

" the Ministers " means the Minister of Housing and Local Government, the Secretary of State for Wales and the Secretary of State for Scotland acting jointly;

" operations " includes surveys and tests as well as tipping operations (within the meaning of Part I of this Act) and building, engineering, mining and other operations;

" prescribed " means prescribed by regulations made by the appropriate Minister;

" remedial operations " has the meaning assigned to it by section 14(2); and

" the specified percentage " has the meaning assigned to it by section 19(6).

PART II

(2) For the purposes of this Part of this Act a disused tip shall be treated as unstable if and only if there is, or there is reasonable ground for believing that there is likely to be, such a movement of the refuse which makes up the tip as to cause a significant increase in the area of land covered by the tip.

(3) In this Part of this Act the expression " owner " in relation to a disused tip means—

(*a*) with respect to England and Wales, the person who has a legal estate in the land on which the tip is situated which—

(i) is either the fee simple or a tenancy for a specific term which has not less than one year unexpired and is not a mortgage term ; and

(ii) is not in reversion expectant on the termination of such a tenancy ; and

(*b*) with respect to Scotland,

(i) except in a case to which sub-paragraph (ii) of this paragraph applies, the proprietor of the dominium utile or, in the case of land not held on feudal tenure, the proprietor, of the land on which the tip is situated ;

(ii) in any case where the land on which the tip is situated is subject to a lease, not being an excluded lease, the tenant who is in possession of the land under the lease or who would, but for the existence of a sub-lease which is an excluded lease, be entitled to such possession.

In this sub-paragraph " excluded lease " means a lease for a year or from year to year or for a lesser period, or any other lease the unexpired period of which does not exceed a year ; " lease " includes sub-lease ; and " tenant " includes sub-tenant :

Provided that, in the case of land in Scotland subject to a heritable security constituted by ex facie absolute disposition or assignation, the debtor shall, for the purposes of this Part of this Act, be treated as the proprietor or, as the case may be, as the tenant except where the creditor is in possession of the land.

(4) Any reference in this Part of this Act to the appropriate Minister shall be construed—

(*a*) in the application of this Part of this Act to England, except Monmouthshire, as a reference to the Minister of Housing and Local Government ;

PART II

(*b*) in its application to Wales and Monmouthshire, as a reference to the Secretary of State for Wales; and

(*c*) in its application to Scotland, as a reference to the Secretary of State for Scotland.

(5) Any reference in this Part of this Act to a section or subsection which is not otherwise identified is a reference to that section of this Act or to that subsection of the section in which the reference occurs, as the case may be.

(6) Any reference in this Part of this Act to any other enactment shall be taken as referring to that enactment as amended by or under any other enactment.

PART III

GENERAL PROVISIONS

Financial provisions.

37. There shall be defrayed out of moneys provided by Parliament—

(*a*) any sums required for the payment of grants under section 25 of this Act; and

(*b*) any increase attributable to this Act in the sums payable out of moneys so provided under any other enactment.

Short title, citation, commencement and extent.

38.—(1) This Act may be cited as the Mines and Quarries (Tips) Act 1969.

1954 c. 70.

(2) Part I of this Act and the Mines and Quarries Act 1954 may be cited together as the Mines and Quarries Acts 1954 and 1969.

(3) Part I of this Act shall come into operation on such day as the Minister of Power may by order made by statutory instrument appoint and Part II of this Act, in its application to England and Wales, shall come into operation on such day as the Minister of Housing and Local Government and the Secretary of State for Wales may by order made by statutory instrument jointly appoint, and in its application to Scotland on such day as the Secretary of State for Scotland may by order so made appoint.

(4) Sections 28 and 33 of this Act do not extend to Scotland and sections 34 and 35 extend to Scotland only.

(5) This Act does not extend to Northern Ireland.

SCHEDULES

Section 1.

SCHEDULE 1

1954 c. 70.

MODIFICATIONS OF MINES AND QUARRIES ACT 1954

1. In paragraph (*b*) of section 1(1) of the principal Act (which imposes a general duty on the owner of every mine and quarry to secure compliance with the provisions of that Act, so far as applicable to the mine or quarry) and in the words following that paragraph, after the words " the mine or quarry " there shall be inserted the words " and any closed tip associated with the mine or quarry ".

2. In subsection (2) of section 2 of the principal Act (general duties and powers of mine managers), subsection (2) of section 11 of that Act (responsibilities of surveyors) and section 99 of that Act (general powers and duties of quarry managers) the expression " the following provisions of this Act " shall be deemed to include the provisions of Part I of this Act.

3. In section 89 of the principal Act (penalisation of failure to observe safety directions, etc.) after the word " support " in paragraph (*a*) and paragraph (*b*) there shall be inserted the words " or tipping ", and, notwithstanding that in the application of section 89 of the principal Act to quarries by section 115 of that Act, so much of section 89 as relates to transport or support rules is excluded, so much of section 89 as relates to tipping rules shall not be excluded.

4.—(1) For the purposes of Part VI of the principal Act (notification and investigation of accidents and diseases) a closed tip shall be deemed to form part of the mine or quarry with which it is associated.

(2) In relation to accidents or dangerous occurrences which happen at a closed tip, any reference in section 116 of that Act to the responsible person shall be construed as a reference to the owner of the mine.

5. In section 135 of the principal Act (which requires that copies of the principal Act and of other instruments shall be provided at mines and quarries) after the words " this Act ", in the first place where they occur, there shall be inserted the words " and of Part I of the Mines and Quarries (Tips) Act 1969 " and after the words " support rules " there shall be inserted the words " tipping rules ".

6.—(1) For the purposes of sections 145 and 146 of the principal Act (general powers of inspectors and power of an inspector to require remedy for immediate or apprehended danger) a closed tip shall be deemed to form part of the mine or quarry with which it is associated.

(2) In section 145(2) of the principal Act (penalties relating to powers of inspectors) after the words " this section " in paragraph (*a*) and the words " the foregoing subsection " in paragraph (*b*) there shall be inserted the words " or subsections (4) and (5) of section 3 of the Mines and Quarries (Tips) Act 1969 ".

(3) In so far as a notice under section 146 of the principal Act relates to, or to any matter, thing or practice at, a closed tip, any reference in that section to the responsible person shall be construed as a reference to the owner of the mine. SCH. 1

7. For the purposes of Part XIV of the principal Act (offences, penalties and legal proceedings) a closed tip shall be deemed to form part of the mine or quarry with which it is associated.

SCHEDULE 2

Section 17(7).

PROVISIONS APPLICABLE WHERE LOCAL AUTHORITY CARRIES OUT REMEDIAL OPERATIONS ON DISUSED TIP OF WHICH IT IS OWNER

1. The provisions of this Schedule apply where a local authority is the owner of a disused tip situated wholly or partly within its area and the local authority—

(*a*) considers that the disused tip is unstable and, by reason of that instability, constitutes or is likely to constitute a danger to members of the public ; and

(*b*) determines accordingly to carry out remedial operations in relation to that tip ; and

(*c*) requires to enter on to any land which is not in its occupation in order to carry out those remedial operations or consequential works of reinstatement or considers that it may be entitled to claim a contribution from any person under Part II of this Act.

2. Before commencing remedial operations, or as soon thereafter as is reasonably practicable, the local authority shall serve a notice in the prescribed form, specifying the nature and extent of the remedial operations and of any consequential works of reinstatement which it proposes to carry out, on every person falling within paragraphs (*a*) to (*e*) of section 14(4) and, for this purpose, for the words " service of the notice on the owner of the tip " in paragraph (*b*) of section 14(4) there shall be substituted the words " commencement of the remedial operations ".

3. Where a local authority has served a notice under paragraph 2 above on any person,—

(*a*) section 14(7) shall apply as if the reference therein to a notice under section 14 were a reference to the notice under paragraph 2 above ; and

(*b*) in so far as the local authority requires to enter on to any land which is not in its occupation, section 18 shall apply as it applies where a local authority has served a notice under section 17(2).

4. Where a local authority has served a notice under paragraph 2 above on any person then, at any time within the period of three months beginning with the date of the commencement of the remedial operations specified in that notice, the local authority may make an

SCH. 2 application under section 19 and, for this purpose, that section shall have effect subject to the following modifications, namely,—

(*a*) in subsection (1), the words from " a notice " to " section 17 and " shall be omitted, and in paragraph (*a*), for the words " service of the notice under section 14 or section 17 " there shall be substituted the words " commencement of the remedial operations " ; and

(*b*) subsections (2) and (3) shall be omitted.

5. Where remedial operations are carried out by a local authority in the circumstances referred to in paragraph 1 above, section 20 shall apply as it applies where remedial operations are carried out by a local authority under section 17(1).

6.—(1) Subject to the following provisions of this paragraph, where a local authority has carried out remedial operations in the circumstances referred to in paragraph 1 above and an order has been made under section 19 requiring any person to make a contribution towards the expenses otherwise falling to be borne by the local authority, as owner of the disused tip, the local authority shall be entitled to recover from the contributory the specified percentage of—

(*a*) the expenditure reasonably incurred by the authority in carrying out those remedial operations and any works of reinstatement reasonably necessary in consequence of the carrying out of those operations ; and

(*b*) the amount of any such compensation as is mentioned in paragraph (*b*) of section 20(2) (being compensation referable to those remedial operations or consequential works of reinstatement) which is recoverable (or has been recovered) from the local authority in pursuance of a claim under section 20 ; and

(*c*) the amount of any such compensation as is referred to in paragraph (*b*) of section 20(2) in respect of which the local authority could itself have made a claim under section 20 if the disused tip had been situated in the area of another local authority and that other authority had carried out those remedial operations (and any consequential works of reinstatement).

(2) No sum shall be recoverable under this paragraph by a local authority from a contributory unless a demand therefor is served on the contributory specifying, in addition to the sum claimed by way of contribution,—

(*a*) the total amount in respect of which the contribution is claimed ; and

(*b*) the separate amounts which comprise that total, distinguished by reference to paragraphs (*a*), (*b*) and (*c*) of sub-paragraph (1) above.

(3) Section 23(5) shall apply to any sum recoverable under this paragraph as it applies to sums recoverable under section 23.

Sch. 2

(4) Within the period of six weeks beginning with the date of the service on a contributory of a demand under sub-paragraph (2) above, the contributory may apply to the court for an order varying or cancelling the demand—

(*a*) on any one or more of the grounds specified in paragraphs (*b*) to (*f*) of section 24(2) ; or

(*b*) on the ground that the amount of the expenses incurred by the local authority in carrying out the remedial operations was greater than was reasonable ; or

(*c*) on the ground that the amount claimed in the demand is greater than the specified percentage of the aggregate of the expenditure referred to in paragraphs (*a*) to (*c*) of sub-paragraph (1) above.

(5) Section 24(4) shall apply in relation to an application under sub-paragraph (4) above as it applies in relation to an application under section 24 and, subject to the right to make an application under that sub-paragraph, a demand under sub-paragraph (2) above shall be final and conclusive.

7.—(1) In any case where—

(*a*) a local authority has carried out remedial operations in the circumstances referred to in paragraph 1 above, and

(*b*) an order has been made under section 19 requiring any person to make a contribution towards the expenses otherwise falling to be borne by the local authority, as owner of the disused tip, and

(*c*) a grant has been made under section 25 and the Minister proposes to give a direction under section 25(4),

section 25(4) shall have effect as if, for the words from " recoverable " to " section 23(1) " there were substituted the words " recoverable from any contributories under paragraph 6 of Schedule 2 to this Act in respect of the expenditure referred to in paragraphs (*a*) to (*c*) of sub-paragraph (1) of that paragraph ", and section 25(5) shall not apply.

(2) Where sub-paragraph (1) above applies, then, in relation to the recovery of any sum from a contributory under paragraph 6 above, that paragraph shall have effect subject to the following modifications—

(*a*) the amount recoverable under sub-paragraph (1) thereof shall be limited to the specified percentage of the amount specified in the direction ;

(*b*) a demand under sub-paragraph (2) shall state that the direction has been given and shall state the amount specified in the direction ;

(*c*) in sub-paragraph (2), paragraph (*a*) shall be construed as applying to the total amount which would have been recoverable by the local authority under paragraph 6 if no direction had been given ; and

(*d*) in paragraph (*c*) of sub-paragraph (4), for the words from " aggregate " onwards there shall be substituted the words " amount specified in the direction ".

Section 20.

SCHEDULE 3

CLAIMS FOR COMPENSATION BY OWNERS AND CONTRIBUTORIES

1.—(1) This Schedule applies to the owner of a disused tip if—

(*a*) a local authority has carried out remedial operations in relation to that tip or has carried out any such exploratory tests as are referred to in section 23(1)(*a*) ; and

(*b*) the owner has served on the local authority a claim for compensation under section 20 in respect of damage or disturbance resulting from the carrying out of those exploratory tests or remedial operations ; and

(*c*) either no order for contribution has been made under section 19 in respect of the expenses otherwise falling to be borne by the owner in respect of the carrying out of those exploratory tests or remedial operations or one or more such orders have been made but the specified percentage or, as the case may be, the aggregate of the specified percentages is less than 100.

(2) This Schedule applies to a contributory if—

(*a*) the expenses in respect of which a contribution may be claimed under section 21 or section 23 include expenses incurred in carrying out remedial operations or any such exploratory tests as are referred to in subsection (1) or subsection (2) of section 23 ; and

(*b*) the contributory has served on the owner of the disused tip or, as the case may be, the local authority concerned a claim for compensation under section 20 in respect of damage or disturbance resulting from the carrying out of those exploratory tests or remedial operations.

2.—(1) Where this Schedule applies to the owner of a disused tip then, subject to sub-paragraph (2) below, until the expiry of the period of twelve months beginning with the date on which the remedial operations referred to in paragraph 1(1)(*a*) above were completed, the owner shall not be entitled to enforce his claim for compensation otherwise than by way of set-off against any sum demanded from him by the local authority under section 23.

(2) Where a demand under subsection (4) of section 23 in respect of the expenditure referred to in subsection (1) or subsection (2) of that section is served by the local authority concerned on the owner of a disused tip to whom this Schedule applies and the amount recoverable by virtue of that demand (having regard to any application made by the owner under section 24) is less than the amount of the owner's claim for compensation against the local authority, sub-paragraph (1) above shall not apply to any proceedings brought by the owner to recover the balance of that compensation from the local authority.

3.—(1) Where this Schedule applies to a contributory then, subject to sub-paragraph (2) below, until the expiry of the relevant period, the contributory shall not be entitled to enforce his claim

Sch. 3

for compensation otherwise than by way of set-off against any sum demanded from him by way of contribution under section 21 or, as the case may be, section 23.

(2) Where a demand for contribution under section 21 or section 23 in respect of the expenses referred to in paragraph 1(2)(*a*) above is served on a contributory to whom this Schedule applies and the amount recoverable by virtue of that demand (having regard to any application made by the contributory under section 22 or section 24) is less than the amount of the contributory's claim for compensation against the person or local authority making the demand, sub-paragraph (1) above shall not apply to any proceedings brought by the contributory to recover the balance of that compensation from that person or local authority.

(3) For the purposes of this paragraph, the relevant period shall be determined as follows,—

(*a*) in relation to a claim by a contributory for compensation recoverable from the owner of a disused tip, the period of twelve months beginning with the date of the completion by the owner of the remedial operations referred to in paragraph 1(2)(*a*) above ;

(*b*) in relation to a claim by a contributory for compensation recoverable from a local authority in a case where the expenses in respect of which a contribution may be claimed from him by the local authority are such as are mentioned in section 23(1), the period of twelve months beginning with the date of the completion of the remedial operations referred to in that section ; and

(*c*) in relation to a claim by a contributory for compensation recoverable from a local authority in a case where the expenses in respect of which a contribution may be claimed from him by the local authority are such as are mentioned in section 23(2), the period of twelve months beginning with the date of the completion of the exploratory tests referred to in that section.

4. Any reference in this Schedule to remedial operations includes a reference to works of reinstatement consequential on those remedial operations.

5. Where Schedule 2 to this Act applies, the preceding provisions of this Schedule shall apply as if—

(*a*) any reference in paragraph 1(2), paragraph 3(1) or paragraph 3(2) to section 23 included a reference to paragraph 6 of Schedule 2 to this Act ;

(*b*) the reference in paragraph 3(2) to section 24 included a reference to paragraph 6(4) of that Schedule ; and

(*c*) the reference in paragraph 3(3)(*b*) to section 23(1) included a reference to paragraph 6(1) of that Schedule.

6.—(1) The time within which the owner of a disused tip or contributory to whom this Schedule applies may bring proceedings

SCH. 3 to recover the whole or any part of the compensation to which his claim under section 20 refers shall be six years from—

(*a*) the expiry of the period referred to in sub-paragraph (1) of paragraph 2 or, as the case may be, of paragraph 3 above; or

(*b*) where sub-paragraph (2) of paragraph 2 or of paragraph 3 above applies, the date of the service of the demand referred to in that sub-paragraph.

(2) In relation to England and Wales, sub-paragraph (1) above
1939 c. 21. shall be construed as one with Part I of the Limitation Act 1939.

(3) In relation to Scotland, in reckoning the period of six years mentioned in sub-paragraph (1) above, no account shall be taken of any period during which the owner or, as the case may be, the contributory was in minority or less age or was under legal disability.

Sections 21, 22.

SCHEDULE 4

MODIFICATIONS OF SECTIONS 21 AND 22 WHERE NOTICE UNDER SECTION 14 IS CANCELLED

1. In any case where—

(*a*) a local authority has served a notice on the owner of a disused tip under section 14, and

(*b*) the owner has carried out remedial operations in compliance with the notice, and

(*c*) the local authority has cancelled the notice by a notice under section 16,

sections 21 and 22 shall have effect subject to the modifications specified in the following provisions of this Schedule.

2. Any reference in those sections to remedial operations carried out in compliance with the notice under section 14 shall be construed as a reference to remedial operations so carried out before the notice was cancelled.

3.—(1) In determining, for the purpose of sections 21 and 22, the amount of the expenses reasonably incurred by the owner in carrying out remedial operations, there shall be deducted any sum which—

(*a*) is recoverable (or has been recovered) by the owner from the local authority by virtue of an order under section 16(4); and

(*b*) is referable to expenditure incurred by the owner in consequence of the service of the notice under section 14.

(2) No sum shall be recoverable by the owner under section 21 in respect of expenses incurred by him in carrying out works of reinstatement.

SCH. 4

4. Where, by virtue of an order under section 16(4), the owner is entitled to recover (or has recovered) from the local authority any sum in respect of expenditure incurred by him in consequence of the service of a notice under section 14—

(*a*) a demand under section 21(3) shall specify the total sum recoverable (or recovered) by virtue of the order, distinguishing between the part which is referable to expenditure incurred in consequence of the service of the notice under section 14 and the part which is referable to expenditure incurred by the owner which is attributable to the cancellation of the notice ; and

(*b*) any reference in section 21(3) to the total amount in respect of which the contribution is claimed shall be construed as a reference to the amount in respect of which the contribution could have been claimed if no such order had been made ; and

(*c*) an application may be made under section 22 on the ground that the amount claimed in the demand does not give proper allowance for any sum which is required to be deducted by virtue of paragraph 3 above.

National Theatre Act 1969

1969 CHAPTER 11

An Act to raise the limit imposed by section 1 of the National Theatre Act 1949 on the contributions which may be made under that section. [27th March 1969]

BE IT ENACTED by the Queen's most Excellent Majesty, by and with the advice and consent of the Lords Spiritual and Temporal, and Commons, in this present Parliament assembled, and by the authority of the same, as follows:—

Revised limit on contributions. 1949 c. 16. 1946 c. 31.

1. In section 1 of the National Theatre Act 1949 (which, as modified by Order in Council under the Ministers of the Crown (Transfer of Functions) Act 1946, authorises the Secretary of State to make contributions not exceeding one million pounds in respect of the cost of erecting and equipping a national theatre) for the words " (not exceeding one million pounds) " there shall be substituted the words " (not exceeding £3,750,000) ".

Short title and citation.

2. This Act may be cited as the National Theatre Act 1969; and the National Theatre Act 1949 and this Act may be cited together as the National Theatre Acts 1949 and 1969.

Genocide Act 1969

1969 CHAPTER 12

An Act to give effect to the Convention on the Prevention and Punishment of the Crime of Genocide. [27th March 1969]

BE IT ENACTED by the Queen's most Excellent Majesty, by and with the advice and consent of the Lords Spiritual and Temporal, and Commons, in this present Parliament assembled, and by the authority of the same, as follows:—

1.—(1) A person commits an offence of genocide if he commits any act falling within the definition of " genocide " in Article II of the Genocide Convention as set out in the Schedule to this Act. **Genocide.**

(2) A person guilty of an offence of genocide shall on conviction on indictment—

(*a*) if the offence consists of the killing of any person, be sentenced to imprisonment for life;

(*b*) in any other case, be liable to imprisonment for a term not exceeding fourteen years.

(3) Proceedings for an offence of genocide shall not be instituted in England or Wales except by or with the consent of the Attorney General and shall not be instituted in Northern Ireland except by or with the consent of the Attorney General for Northern Ireland.

(4) In Schedule 1 to the Criminal Law Act 1967 the following paragraph shall be added at the end of List B (offences outside the jurisdiction of quarter sessions):— 1967 c. 58.

" 20. Offences of genocide and any attempt, conspiracy or incitement to commit such an offence."

1959 c. 25. (N.I.). 1967 c. 18 (N.I.).

(5) At the end of section 40(1) of the County Courts Act (Northern Ireland) 1959 as amended by section 8 of the Criminal Law Act (Northern Ireland) 1967 (original criminal jurisdiction of county courts in Northern Ireland) the following paragraph shall be added:—

" (*h*) any offence of genocide and any attempt, conspiracy or incitement to commit such an offence ".

1955 c. 18. 1955 c. 19.

(6) Section 70 of the Army Act 1955 and section 70 of the Air Force Act 1955 (civil offences) shall each be amended by inserting:—

(*a*) in subsection (3), the following paragraph (before paragraph (*b*)):—

" (*ab*) if the corresponding civil offence is an offence of genocide consisting of the killing of any person, be liable to imprisonment for life; "

(*b*) in subsection (4), after the words " or rape " the words " or an offence of genocide "; and

(*c*) in subsection (5), after the words " or manslaughter " the words " or an offence of genocide consisting of the killing of any person ".

1957 c. 53.

(7) In the Naval Discipline Act 1957:—

(*a*) in section 42(1)(*b*) (punishment of murder) after the words " offence of murder " there shall be inserted the words " or of genocide consisting of the killing of any person "; and

(*b*) in section 48(2) (exclusion of jurisdiction of courts-martial) after the words " or rape " there shall be inserted the words " or genocide " and after the words " or manslaughter " there shall be inserted the words " or an offence of genocide consisting of the killing of any person ".

Extradition and evidence for foreign courts. 1870 c. 52. 1967 c. 68.

2.—(1) There shall be deemed to be included—

(*a*) in the list of extradition crimes contained in Schedule 1 to the Extradition Act 1870; and

(*b*) among the descriptions of offences set out in Schedule 1 to the Fugitive Offenders Act 1967,

any offence of genocide and (so far as not so included by virtue of the foregoing) any attempt or conspiracy to commit such an offence and any direct and public incitement to commit such an offence.

(2) For the purposes of the Acts mentioned in subsection (1) of this section, the Extradition Act 1873 and the Backing of Warrants (Republic of Ireland) Act 1965, no offence which, if committed in the United Kingdom, would be punishable as an offence of genocide or as an attempt, conspiracy or incitement to commit such an offence shall be regarded as an offence of a political character, and no proceedings in respect of such an offence shall be regarded as a criminal matter of a political character.

1873 c. 60.
1965 c. 45.

(3) It shall not be an objection to any proceedings taken against a person by virtue of the preceding provisions of this section that under the law in force at the time when and in the place where he is alleged to have committed the act of which he is accused or of which he was convicted he could not have been punished therefor.

Application to Channel Islands, Isle of Man and colonies.

3.—(1) Sections 17 and 22 of the Extradition Act 1870 (which also apply to the Extradition Act 1873), section 12 of the Backing of Warrants (Republic of Ireland) Act 1965 and sections 16 and 17 of the Fugitive Offenders Act 1967 (application to Channel Islands, Isle of Man and United Kingdom dependencies) shall extend respectively to the provisions of this Act amending those Acts.

1870 c. 52.
1967 c. 68.

(2) Her Majesty may by Order in Council make provision for extending the other provisions of this Act, with such exceptions, adaptations or modifications as may be specified in the Order, to any of the Channel Islands, the Isle of Man or any colony, other than a colony for whose external relations a country other than the United Kingdom is responsible.

(3) An Order in Council under this section may be varied or revoked by a subsequent Order in Council.

Short title and interpretation.

4.—(1) This Act may be cited as the Genocide Act 1969.

(2) In this Act "the Genocide Convention" means the Convention on the Prevention and Punishment of the Crime of Genocide approved by the General Assembly of the United Nations on 9th December 1948.

Section 1.

SCHEDULE

ARTICLE II OF GENOCIDE CONVENTION

In the present Convention, genocide means any of the following acts committed with intent to destroy, in whole or in part, a national, ethnical, racial or religious group, as such:

(*a*) Killing members of the group;

(*b*) Causing serious bodily or mental harm to members of the group;

(*c*) Deliberately inflicting on the group conditions of life calculated to bring about its physical destruction in whole or in part;

(*d*) Imposing measures intended to prevent births within the group;

(*e*) Forcibly transferring children of the group to another group.

Licensing (Scotland) Act 1969

1969 CHAPTER 13

An Act to amend the Licensing (Scotland) Act 1959 so as to make provision for the establishment of licensing courts for new small burghs formed under section 133 of the Local Government (Scotland) Act 1947; and for purposes connected therewith. [27th March 1969]

BE IT ENACTED by the Queen's most Excellent Majesty, by and with the advice and consent of the Lords Spiritual and Temporal, and Commons, in this present Parliament assembled, and by the authority of the same, as follows:—

Amendment of s. 31 of Licensing (Scotland) Act 1959. 1947 c. 43. 1959 c. 51.

1.—(1) For the purpose of making provision for the establishment of a licensing court for any new small burgh formed under section 133 of the Local Government (Scotland) Act 1947 and for the effecting of alterations in licensing courts and courts of appeal consequential on such establishment, section 31 of the Licensing (Scotland) Act 1959 (which among other things makes provision for the effecting of alterations in licensing courts and courts of appeal consequential on any increase or decrease in population) shall have effect subject to the amendments specified in the following provisions of this section.

(2) In subsection (1), in paragraph (*d*), at the end there shall be inserted the words " or, in the case of a new small burgh formed under section 133 of the Local Government (Scotland) Act 1947 after the said date, the boundaries thereof as fixed under that section.".

(3) In subsection (2), at the beginning there shall be inserted the words " Subject to subsections (2A) and (2B) of this section ".

(4) After subsection (2) there shall be inserted the following subsections:—

" (2A) The Secretary of State shall—

(*a*) in the case of any new small burgh formed under section 133 of the Local Government (Scotland) Act

1947 after 23rd April 1961 (being the date of the census taken in 1961) and before the commencement of the Licensing (Scotland) Act 1969;

(*b*) where any new small burgh is formed under the said section 133 after that commencement,

obtain from the Registrar General of Births, Deaths and Marriages for Scotland an estimate (made by reference to the estimates prepared by the Registrar General relating to 30th June in the latest year for which such estimates are available) of the population of the new burgh and of the county or, where the county is divided into licensing districts, the licensing district of which the new burgh forms part, and if the Secretary of State is satisfied, having regard to that estimate, that the new burgh contains a population of or exceeding 7,000 he shall make an order—

(i) declaring the population, according to the said estimate, of the new burgh and of the county or, as the case may be, the licensing district in which it is situated; and

(ii) unless the population of the new burgh as so declared is 20,000 or more, altering Part II of the First Schedule to this Act so that the new burgh is included therein and so as to provide for due representation on the court of appeal constituted under the said Part II for the county in which the new burgh is situated of every burgh situated in that county and included in the said Part II; and

(iii) prescribing the date or dates on which a licensing court shall be established for the new burgh and alterations in licensing courts and courts of appeal consequential on such establishment shall take effect.

(2B) Where—

(*a*) an order is made under subsection (2A) of this section declaring the population of any area, and

(*b*) that declaration is made according to an estimate relating to a date which fell after the census for the time being last taken, and

(*c*) after the making of that order an order falls to be made under subsection (2) of this section consequent on the said census,

then for the purposes of the last-mentioned order, so far as it relates to an area whose population has been declared as aforesaid, references (however expressed) in the said subsection (2) to population calculated according to a census shall be construed as references to population as so declared.".

2.—(1) This Act may be cited as the Licensing (Scotland) Act 1969, and the Licensing (Scotland) Acts 1959 and 1962 and this Act may be cited together as the Licensing (Scotland) Acts 1959 to 1969. Short title and extent.

(2) This Act shall extend to Scotland only.

Horserace Betting Levy Act 1969

1969 CHAPTER 14

An Act to make further provision with respect to the contributions to be made, under Part I of the Betting, Gaming and Lotteries Act 1963, by bookmakers and the Totalisator Board to the Horserace Betting Levy Board; and to amend section 24 of the said Act of 1963 with respect to the appointment and removal of members of the last-mentioned Board.

[27th March 1969]

BE IT ENACTED by the Queen's most Excellent Majesty, by and with the advice and consent of the Lords Spiritual and Temporal, and Commons, in this present Parliament assembled, and by the authority of the same, as follows:—

Determination of annual scheme for bookmakers' levy.

1.—(1) In section 27 of the Act of 1963 (settlement of annual scheme for levy to be paid by bookmakers to the Horserace Betting Levy Board), the provisions of subsection (5) (which requires a scheme to be settled, in the absence of agreement between the Bookmakers' Committee and the Board, by the members of the Board appointed by the Secretary of State) shall, in relation to the levy period beginning with 1st April 1970 and any subsequent levy period, be replaced by those of the following subsection.

(2) If six months before the beginning of a levy period the Levy Board have not approved recommendations or revised recommendations of the Bookmakers' Committee with respect to the scheme to have effect under section 27 for that period (or if no such recommendations have been received by the Levy Board), then—

(*a*) the Levy Board shall forthwith report the circumstances to the Secretary of State; and

(*b*) the Secretary of State shall determine the scheme to have effect as aforesaid.

(3) The Secretary of State may under subsection (2) of this section either—

(*a*) determine a new scheme for the said period ; or

(*b*) direct that the current scheme shall continue to have effect for that period also, subject to such modifications (if any) as he may specify.

(4) A scheme determined by members of the Levy Board for the levy period beginning with 1st April 1969 shall not have effect unless confirmed by the Secretary of State, who may in confirming it direct that it shall have effect with such modifications as he may specify.

(5) Before determining a scheme under subsection (2) of this section, or confirming a scheme under subsection (4) thereof, the Secretary of State may appoint one or more persons to enquire into, and report to him their opinion on, any matter appearing to him to be relevant to the form or content of the scheme.

(6) The Secretary of State may require the Levy Board to pay to a person appointed by him under subsection (5) of this section such remuneration as the Secretary of State may specify and any travelling and other expenses reasonably incurred by that person in doing that which he was appointed by the Secretary of State to do.

(7) The period of months specified in subsection (2) of this section may be varied by order of the Secretary of State substituting, in relation to any levy period beginning after the date on which the order comes into force, a different period, whether longer or shorter, but not longer than fifteen months:

Provided that where the effect of an order is to increase the said period of months, the order shall not be made so as to come into force later than three months before the beginning of the increased period.

(8) The power of the Secretary of State to make an order under subsection (7) of this section shall be exercisable by statutory instrument and include power to vary or revoke the order by a subsequent order.

Assessment to levy of individual bookmakers.

2.—(1) Subsections (1) to (4) of section 28 of the Act of 1963 (bookmaker's assessment to levy to be in accordance with his declaration as to the category into which he falls, subject to alteration by the Bookmakers' Committee, or, failing a declaration by him, to be determined by the Committee, subject in either case to appeal to an appeal tribunal) shall not have effect in relation to the levy period beginning with 1st April 1969 or any subsequent levy period.

(2) A bookmaker shall, whether or not he submits a declaration in accordance with the scheme having effect for any such

period, be assessed to, or exempted from, levy in accordance with such opinion as the Government-appointed members of the Levy Board may form as to the category into which he falls for the purposes of the scheme.

(3) In this section, references to the Government-appointed members of the Levy Board are to the three persons for the time being appointed to be members of the Board by the Secretary of State.

(4) In considering the category into which a bookmaker falls for the purposes of a scheme, the said members of the Board may consult the Bookmakers' Committee and such other persons, if any, as those members of the Board think proper.

(5) In subsection (10) of the said section 28 (penalty for unauthorised disclosure of information concerning an individual bookmaker),—

(*a*) after the words " this section ", where first occurring, there shall be inserted the words " or section 2 of the Horserace Betting Levy Act 1969 " ;

(*b*) after those words where they occur for the second time there shall be inserted the words " or by members of the Levy Board in pursuance of section 2(4) of the said Act of 1969 " ; and

(*c*) after those words where they occur for the third time there shall be inserted the words " or under section 2 of the said Act of 1969 ".

Levy Board's costs on appeal by bookmaker against assessment of levy.

3.—(1) The following subsection shall have effect where, under section 28 of the Act of 1963 (assessment of individual bookmakers to levy), a bookmaker appeals in respect of an assessment notice issued by the Levy Board in his case, and the appeal, having been referred to a tribunal established under section 29 of that Act, is either dismissed by the tribunal or abandoned by the bookmaker.

(2) If the tribunal thinks it just that the bookmaker should make a payment towards expenses appearing to it to have been reasonably incurred by the Levy Board in connection with the appeal, the tribunal may certify accordingly and the Board shall be entitled to recover from the bookmaker as a debt due to them the amount specified in the certificate.

Non-renewal of bookmaker's permit in case of failure to pay levy.

4.—(1) Subject to this section, where an application is made to the appropriate authority under Schedule 1 to the Act of 1963 for the renewal of a bookmaker's permit and the authority, at the time when they determine the application, are satisfied—

(*a*) that the applicant is in default in respect of bookmakers' levy and has been so for at least three months ; and (*b*) that on a previous occasion (not before the passing of this Act, nor before the period of five years ending with the date of the application), being an occasion on which the permit was renewed (whether by the same or another authority), he was so in default and had been so for at least three months,

the authority shall refuse the application.

(2) Subsection (1) of this section shall apply only where the Levy Board appear, by counsel or a solicitor, at the hearing of the application and maintain an objection duly made by them in accordance with Schedule 1 to the Act of 1963, being an objection to the renewal of the permit on the ground (either alone or among other grounds) that the applicant has failed to discharge his liabilities by way of the bookmakers' levy.

(3) For the purposes of subsection (1) of this section, a person is in default in respect of bookmakers' levy if—

(*a*) there has become due from him under section 28(7) of the Act of 1963 an amount assessed as payable by him by way of levy ; and

(*b*) the whole or any part of that amount remains unpaid.

(4) In paragraph 15 of Schedule 1 to the Act of 1963 (which specifies the grounds on which the grant or renewal of a bookmaker's permit or betting agency permit must be refused by the appropriate authority), the following shall be inserted after sub-paragraph (*e*):—

" (*ee*) has within the immediately preceding twelve months been refused the renewal of a bookmaker's permit under section 4 of the Horserace Betting Levy Act 1969 and has not obtained the approval of the Levy Board to his application ".

(5) Nothing in this section shall be taken as prejudicing paragraph 16(2) of Schedule 1 to the Act of 1963 (under which an authority dealing with an application for the renewal of a bookmaker's permit have a discretion to refuse the application on the ground of the character or conduct of the applicant, including his failure to pay levy).

Annual contribution by Totalisator Board.

5.—(1) If, in the case of the levy period beginning with 1st April 1970 or any subsequent levy period, the Totalisator Board object to the contribution determined by the Levy Board under section 30(1) of the Act of 1963, the contribution payable by the Totalisator Board in respect of that period shall instead be determined by the Secretary of State.

(2) If the contribution payable by the Totalisator Board in respect of the levy period beginning with 1st April 1969 falls,

or has before the passing of this Act fallen, to be determined under section 30(2) of the Act of 1963 by the three members of the Levy Board referred to in that subsection, their determination shall not have effect unless confirmed by the Secretary of State; and if the Secretary of State decides not to confirm it, he shall himself determine the contribution.

(3) Before determining a contribution under this section, or confirming a determination under subsection (2) thereof, the Secretary of State may appoint one or more persons to enquire into, and report to him their opinion on, any matter appearing to him to be relevant to the subject matter of his determination.

(4) The Secretary of State may require the Levy Board to pay to a person appointed by him under subsection (3) of this section such remuneration as the Secretary of State may specify and any travelling and other expenses reasonably incurred by that person in doing that which he was appointed by the Secretary of State to do.

Amendment of s. 24 of Act of 1963 as to appointment of members of Levy Board

6.—(1) In consequence of the amalgamation of the Jockey Club and the National Hunt Committee, section 24 of the Act of 1963 (constitution and membership of Levy Board) shall be amended in accordance with this section.

(2) In section 24(2), for paragraphs (*b*) and (*c*) (which provide for two members of the Board to be appointed by the Jockey Club and one by the National Hunt Committee) there shall be substituted the following:—

" (*b*) three members shall be appointed by the Jockey Club (incorporating the National Hunt Committee) ".

(3) In section 24(3) (duration and terms of membership and removal of members) for the words " subsection (2)(*b*) or (*c*) " there shall be substituted the words " subsection (2)(*b*) ".

(4) In section 24(4) (temporary substitute members)—

(*a*) for the words " the National Hunt Committee " there shall be substituted the words " (incorporating the National Hunt Committee) "; and

(*b*) for the words " subsection (2)(*b*), (*c*), (*d*) or (*e*) " there shall be substituted the words " subsection (2)(*b*), (*d*) or (*e*) ".

(5) Any person who at the passing of this Act is, or acts as, a member of the Levy Board by virtue of appointment under section 24(2) or (4) of the Act of 1963 by the Jockey Club or the National Hunt Committee shall be deemed to have been appointed by the Jockey Club (incorporating the National Hunt Committee).

Citation, interpretation, repeal and extent.

7.—(1) This Act may be cited as the Horserace Betting Levy Act 1969.

1963 c. 2.

(2) In this Act " the Act of 1963 " means the Betting, Gaming and Lotteries Act 1963 ; and the expressions " bookmaker ", " Bookmakers' Committee ", " bookmaker's permit ", " Levy Board ", " levy period " and " Totalisator Board " have the same meanings as in that Act.

(3) In section 25(2)(*a*) of the Act of 1963 (application of moneys in the hands of the Levy Board), for the words " section 26 or 29 of this Act or section 9 of the Betting Levy Act 1961 " there shall be substituted the words " any enactment ".

(4) The following enactments in the Act of 1963 are hereby repealed:—

section 27(5), except in relation to a levy period beginning with or before 1st April 1969 ;

section 28(1) to (4), except in relation to a levy period beginning before that date ; and

section 30(2), except in relation to a levy period beginning with or before that date.

(5) This Act shall not extend to Northern Ireland.

Representation of the People Act 1969

1969 CHAPTER 15

An Act to amend the law about the qualification of electors at elections to the Parliament of the United Kingdom or at local government elections in Great Britain, and the qualification for election to and membership of local authorities in England and Wales, about the conduct of and manner of voting at those elections and about candidates' election expenses thereat, and otherwise to make provision about matters incidental to those elections, and for purposes connected therewith. [17th April 1969]

BE IT ENACTED by the Queen's most Excellent Majesty, by and with the advice and consent of the Lords Spiritual and Temporal, and Commons, in this present Parliament assembled, and by the authority of the same, as follows:—

The franchise and its exercise

1.—(1) For purposes of the Representation of the People Acts a person shall be of voting age if he is of the age of eighteen years or over; and, if otherwise qualified, a person who is of voting age on the date of the poll at a parliamentary or local government election shall be entitled to vote as an elector, whether or not he is of voting age on the qualifying date. Voting age.

(2) A person, if otherwise qualified, shall accordingly be entitled to be registered in a register of parliamentary electors or a register of local government electors if he will attain voting age before the end of the twelve months following the day by which the register is required to be published; but, if he will not be of voting age on the first day of those twelve months—

(*a*) his entry in the register shall give the date on which he will attain that age; and (*b*) until the date given in the entry he shall not by virtue of the entry be treated as an elector for any purposes other than purposes of an election at which the day fixed for the poll is that or a later date.

(3) A person, if otherwise qualified, shall be capable of voting as proxy at parliamentary or local government elections at which he is of voting age on the date of the poll, and of being appointed proxy for that purpose before he is of voting age.

(4) A person shall be qualified under the parliamentary or local elections rules to assist a blind voter to vote if that person is one of the relatives specified in the relevant rule and is of voting age.

(5) For purposes of the Representation of the People Acts a person shall be deemed, according to the law in Northern Ireland as well as according to the law in other parts of the United Kingdom, not to have attained a given age until the commencement of the relevant anniversary of the day of his birth.

Service declarations and qualification.

2.—(1) A service declaration shall be made with a view to registration in the register of electors for a particular year, and with reference to the qualifying date to which that register looks, and shall not have effect to enable the declarant to be registered in any other register.

(2) A service declaration made with reference to any qualifying date shall be made during the twelve months ending with that date, but shall not have effect if after it is made and before that date the declarant ceases to have a service qualification or, in so far as regulations so provide, if after it is made and before that date there is a change in the circumstances giving the service qualification.

(3) Persons who are employed by the British Council in posts outside the United Kingdom and their wives shall be included among the persons having a service qualification in like manner as members of the forces and their wives are included by section
1949 c. 68. 10(1) of the Representation of the People Act 1949.

(4) Where a married woman has a service qualification, her husband shall have one in circumstances corresponding to those in which a wife does.

Merchant seamen.

3.—(1) At any time when a merchant seaman is not resident in the United Kingdom and would have been resident there but for the nature of his occupation, he shall be entitled to be treated for purposes of sections 1 and 2 of the Representation of the People Act 1949 as resident—

(*a*) at any place at which he would have been resident but for the nature of his occupation; or (*b*) at any hostel or club providing accommodation for merchant seamen at which he commonly stays in the course of his occupation.

For this purpose " merchant seaman " means any person not having a service qualification whose employment or the greater part of it is carried out on board seagoing ships, and includes any such person while temporarily without employment.

(2) Regulations made with respect to the matters mentioned in section 42 of the Representation of the People Act 1949 (form of register etc.) may contain provisions as to marking the register so as to distinguish those who are registered by virtue of the special provision about residence applying to merchant seamen or who, though not so registered, are merchant seamen within the meaning of that provision. 1949 c. 68.

4.—(1) A convicted person during the time that he is detained in a penal institution in pursuance of his sentence shall be legally incapable of voting at any parliamentary or local government election. Disfranchisement of offenders in prison, etc.

(2) For this purpose—

(*a*) " convicted person " means any person found guilty of an offence (whether under the law of the United Kingdom or not), including a person found guilty by a court-martial under the Army Act 1955, the Air Force Act 1955 or the Naval Discipline Act 1957 or on a summary trial under section 49 of the Naval Discipline Act 1957, but not including a person dealt with by committal or other summary process for contempt of court; and 1955 c. 18. 1955 c. 19. 1957 c. 53.

(*b*) " penal institution " means an institution to which the Prison Act 1952, the Prisons (Scotland) Act 1952 or the Prison Act (Northern Ireland) 1953 applies; and 1952 c. 52. 1952 c. 61.

(*c*) a person detained for default in complying with his sentence shall not be treated as detained in pursuance of the sentence, whether or not the sentence provided for detention in the event of default, but a person detained by virtue of a conditional pardon in respect of an offence shall be treated as detained in pursuance of his sentence for the offence. 1953 c. 18 (N.I.).

(3) It is immaterial for purposes of this section whether a conviction or sentence was before or after the passing of this Act.

5.—(1) The persons excepted under section 12 or 23 of the Representation of the People Act 1949 from the requirement of subsection (1) of the section that all persons voting as electors at a parliamentary election or at a local government election shall do so in person at the appropriate polling station shall Extension for married persons of right to vote by proxy or by post.

include, where they are entitled to vote by proxy or by post in accordance with subsection (2) below,—

(*a*) those who have a service qualification depending on marriage to, and residence outside the United Kingdom to be with, a person having a service qualification; and

(*b*) those unable or likely to be unable to go in person to the polling station by reason of the general nature of the occupation, service or employment of, and their resulting absence from their qualifying address to be with, their husband or wife.

(2) At parliamentary elections and at local government elections at which postal voting is allowed, a person who is not registered as a service voter but who either—

(*a*) has made a service declaration in respect of a qualification depending on marriage as described in subsection (1) above; or

(*b*) is as a married person unable or likely to be unable to go to the poll by reason of absence in the circumstances there described;

shall have the like right to vote by proxy and, in the case dealt with by paragraph (*b*) above, the like right to vote by post as a person unable or likely to be unable to go to the poll by reason of the general nature of his occupation, service or employment.

(3) An application to be treated as an absent voter in pursuance of this section shall be for an indefinite period, and accordingly section 13 of the Representation of the People Act 1949 shall apply to an application based on either of the grounds related to the applicant's marriage as it applies to an application based on the general nature of the applicant's occupation, service or employment.

1949 c. 68.

amendments as to proxy and postal voting.

6.—(1) For section 12(7)(*a*) and for section 15(3)(*a*) of the Representation of the People Act 1949 (under which two addresses within the area of the same borough or urban district are to be treated as in the same area so as to exclude a right to vote by post on a change of address) there shall in each case be substituted—

" (*a*) both are within the area of the same borough and in the same constituency or are within the area of the same urban district ".

(2) The provisions of the Representation of the People Act 1949 as to postal voting at parliamentary or local government elections by persons who are unable or likely to be unable, by reason of physical incapacity, to go in person to the polling

station or if able to go, to vote unaided shall apply in like manner to persons who are unable or likely to be unable by reason of religious observance, except that any application to be treated as an absent voter, if it is based on the ground of religious observance, shall be for a particular election only.

(3) At any parliamentary or local government election a person, whether registered as a service voter or not,—

(*a*) may vote in person as an elector notwithstanding any appointment of a proxy to vote for him, if he applies for a ballot paper for the purpose before a ballot paper has been issued for him to vote by proxy; but

(*b*) shall not be entitled to vote in person as an elector—

(i) where he may vote by proxy by virtue of an appointment for the time being in force and he does not so apply; or

(ii) where he has applied to be treated as an absent voter and is entitled in pursuance of the application to vote by post.

(4) The provisions of sections 15 and 25 of the Representation of the People Act 1949 so far as they relate to postal voting by proxies shall apply to proxies for an elector who is not registered as a service voter as they apply to proxies for an elector who is so registered. **1949 c. 68.**

(5) In section 23(7) of the Representation of the People Act 1949, as amended by paragraph 7(2) of the Seventh Schedule to the Local Government Act 1958, the words " rural district " shall be omitted. **1958 c. 55.**

(6) At parliamentary elections the notice of election shall state the date by which applications to be treated as an absent voter and other applications and notices about postal or proxy voting must reach the registration officer in order that they may be effective for the election; and in addition the registration officer shall give notice of that date in the constituency by such means as he thinks best calculated to bring the information to the notice of those concerned.

(7) At local government elections at which postal voting is allowed, subsection (6) above shall apply with the substitution of a reference to the electoral area for the reference to the constituency.

Preparation and corr ection of registers of electors.

7.—(1) It shall be the general duty of a registration officer to prepare and publish registers of electors in conformity with the Representation of the People Act 1949, and (without prejudice to any specific requirement of the Act or regulations under it) to take reasonable steps to obtain information required by him for the purpose.

(2) Where a register of electors as published does not carry out the intention of the registration officer—

(*a*) to include the name of any person shown in the electors lists as a person entitled to be registered; or

(*b*) to give or not to give in a person's entry a date as that on which he will attain voting age, or as to the date to be given; or

(*c*) to give effect to a decision on a claim or objection made with respect to the electors lists;

then (subject to the decision on any appeal from a decision on a claim or objection) the registration officer on becoming aware of the fact shall make the necessary correction in the register; but an alteration made in a register of electors under this subsection on or after the date on which notice of an election is given shall not have effect for purposes of that election.

1949 c. 68. (3) In Schedule 4 to the Representation of the People Act 1949 (provisions which may be contained in regulations as to registration etc.) there shall be omitted so much of paragraph 5(2) as relates to obtaining birth certificates for a fee of 6d. or less or to exempting statutory declarations from stamp duty.

Candidates, their expenses and agents etc.

Limit on, and declaration and publication of, election expenses.

8.—(1) The amount to which a candidate's election expenses are limited by section 64(1) of the Representation of the People Act 1949 shall be—

(*a*) for a candidate at a parliamentary election—

(i) in a county constituency, £750 together with an additional 1s. 0d. for every six entries in the register of electors to be used at the election (as first published) and for any less number of entries above a multiple of six; and

(ii) in a borough constituency, £750 together with an additional 1s. 0d. for every eight entries in the register of electors to be used at the election (as first published) and for any less number of entries above a multiple of eight;

(*b*) for a candidate at a local government election—

(i) at an election to the Greater London Council (other than an election to which paragraph 5 of
1963 c. 33. Schedule 2 to the London Government Act 1963 does not apply to determine the electoral areas), £200 together with an additional 1s. 0d. for every four entries in the register of electors to be used at the election (as first published) and for any less number of entries above a multiple of four; and

(ii) at any other local government election, £30 together with an additional 1s. 0d. for every six entries in the register of electors to be used at the election (as first published) and for any less number of entries above a multiple of six:

Provided that the provision made by section 64(3) for taking entries in the electors lists instead of entries in a register not published by the time there mentioned shall apply to this subsection as it is expressed to apply to section 64(2).

(2) Where at an election a poll is countermanded or abandoned by reason of the death of a candidate, the maximum amount of election expenses shall, for any of the other candidates who then remain validly nominated, be twice or, if there has been a previous increase under this subsection, three times what it would have been but for any increase under this subsection; but the maximum amount shall not be affected for any candidate by the change in the timing of the election or of any step in the proceedings thereat.

(3) For a candidate at a ward election in the City of London the maximum amount of election expenses shall be £30 together with an additional 1s. 0d. for every six electors (taken according to the enumeration of the ward list to be used at the election) and for any less number above a multiple of six; but the provision made for increasing the maximum amount of election expenses in the event of the death of a candidate shall apply to the maximum amount under this subsection.

(4) An election agent's or candidate's declaration as to election expenses under section 70 of the Representation of the People Act 1949 may be made either before a justice of the peace or before any person who is— 1949 c. 68.

(*a*) in England or Wales chairman or clerk of the Greater London Council, a county council or a district council or mayor or town clerk of a borough or rural borough; or

(*b*) in Scotland a county clerk or town clerk; or

(*c*) in Northern Ireland the secretary of a county council or a town clerk.

(5) At a parliamentary election the returning officer shall, within ten days after the end of the time allowed for transmitting to him returns as to election expenses, publish in not less than two newspapers circulating in the constituency for which the election was held, and shall send to each of the election agents, a notice of the time and place at which the returns and declarations (including the accompanying documents) can be inspected; but if any return or declaration has not been received by the returning officer before the notice is despatched for publication.

the notice shall so state, and a like notice about that return or declaration, if afterwards received, shall within ten days after the receipt be published in like manner and sent to each of the election agents other than the agent who is in default or is agent for the candidate in default.

1949 c. 68. The foregoing provisions of this subsection shall be substituted for section 76 of the Representation of the People Act 1949 (which requires a summary of each return to be published within ten days of receipt of that return), and shall have effect accordingly.

(6) In section 77(1) of the Representation of the People Act 1949 and in paragraph 8(1) of Schedule 6 (under which returns and declarations as to election expenses must be open to inspection on payment of a fee of 1s. 0d., and copies must be supplied at the price there mentioned) for the words " fee of one shilling " there shall be substituted the words " prescribed fee " and for the words " at the price of twopence for every seventy-two words " there shall be substituted the words " at the prescribed price ".

Broadcasting during elections.

9.—(1) Pending a parliamentary or local government election it shall not be lawful for any item about the constituency or electoral area to be broadcast from a television or other wireless transmitting station in the United Kingdom if any of the persons who are for the time being candidates at the election takes part in the item and the broadcast is not made with his consent; and where an item about a constituency or electoral area is so broadcast pending a parliamentary or local government election there, then if the broadcast either is made before the latest time for delivery of nomination papers, or is made after that time but without the consent of any candidate remaining validly nominated, any person taking part in the item for the purpose of promoting or procuring his election shall be guilty of an illegal practice, unless the broadcast is so made without his consent.

(2) For purposes of subsection (1) above—

(*a*) a parliamentary election shall be deemed to be pending during the period ending with the close of the poll and beginning—

(i) at a general election, with the date of the dissolution of Parliament or any earlier time at which Her Majesty's intention to dissolve Parliament is announced; or

(ii) at a by-election, with the date of the issue of the writ for the election or any earlier date on which a certificate of the vacancy is notified in the Gazette

1784 c. 26. in accordance with the Recess Elections Act 1784, the Election of Members during Recess Act 1858, the Bankruptcy (Ireland) Amendment Act 1872 or the Bankruptcy Act 1883; and 1858 c. 110. 1872 c. 58. 1883 c. 52.

(*b*) a local government election shall be deemed to be pending during the period ending with the close of the poll and beginning—

(i) at an ordinary election, five weeks before the day fixed as the day of election in accordance with section 57 of the Representation of the People Act 1948 or, in Scotland, by or under the Local Government (Scotland) Act 1947; or 1948 c. 65. 1947 c. 43.

(ii) at an election to fill a casual vacancy, with the date of publication of notice of the election.

(3) Subsections (1) and (2) above shall be construed and have effect as if contained in Part II of the Representation of the People Act 1949. 1949 c. 68.

(4) Section 63(1) of the Representation of the People Act 1949 (which, subject to the exceptions in the proviso, makes illegal certain expenses when incurred without authority from a candidate's election agent) shall be amended by inserting in paragraph (i) of the proviso, after the words " a newspaper or other periodical ", the words " or in a broadcast made by the British Broadcasting Corporation or the Independent Television Authority ".

(5) Section 80(1) of the Representation of the People Act 1949 (which, in connection with parliamentary elections, makes illegal the use of wireless transmitting stations outside the United Kingdom otherwise than under arrangements for a broadcast by the British Broadcasting Corporation) shall be amended as follows:—

(*a*) for the words " parliamentary election " there shall be substituted the words " parliamentary or local government election "; and

(*b*) for the words " any wireless transmitting station " there shall be substituted the words " any television or other wireless transmitting station "; and

(*c*) at the end of the subsection there shall be added the words " or of arrangements made with the Independent Television Authority or a programme contractor (within the meaning of the Television Act 1964) for it to be received by the Authority or contractor and retransmitted by the Authority ". 1964 c. 21.

(6) Neither section 80 of the Representation of the People Act 1949 nor subsection (1) above shall, by virtue of section 167 of that Act, apply to municipal elections in the City of London

other than ward elections but for purposes of subsection (1) above a ward election shall be deemed to be pending during the period beginning in the case of an annual election three weeks before the day fixed for the election and in other cases with the day on which the precept is issued, and ending in all cases with the day of the poll (or, if no poll is taken, with the day fixed for the election).

Bands of music, torches, flags and banners.
1949 c. 68.

10. Section 97 of the Representation of the People Act 1949 (which makes it illegal to incur election expenses on account of bands of music, torches, flags and banners) shall cease to have effect.

Election agents and polling agents.

11.—(1) The declaration as a candidate's election agent of a person other than the candidate shall be of no effect under section 55 of the Representation of the People Act 1949 unless it is made and signed by that person or is accompanied by a written declaration of acceptance signed by him.

(2) An election agent's right, at a parliamentary election for a county constituency, to appoint sub-agents shall be a right to appoint one such agent for any part of the constituency (and not only for each polling district as provided by section 56(1) of the Representation of the People Act 1949).

(3) The office of the election agent for a parliamentary election shall be within the constituency or an adjoining constituency or in a borough which is partly comprised in or adjoins the constituency, and that of a sub-agent shall be in the area within which he is appointed to act; and the office of an election agent for a local government election shall be within the local government area or in the constituency or one of the constituencies in which the area is comprised, or in a borough which adjoins the area, or in an urban or rural district or, in Scotland, an electoral division which adjoins it.

(4) The following provisions shall have effect as regards the appointment of polling agents:—

(*a*) at parliamentary elections and at local government elections the appointment may be made by the election agent on behalf of the candidate, whether the polling agent is paid or unpaid;

(*b*) at local government elections in Scotland (as in England and Wales) a candidate may appoint more than one polling agent to attend at a polling station, but neither at parliamentary elections nor at local government elections (in whatever part of Great Britain) shall more than one polling agent be admitted at the same time to a polling station on behalf of the same candidate;

(c) at parliamentary elections the notice to be given to the returning officer of the appointment of a polling agent (otherwise than to replace an agent who dies or becomes incapable of acting) shall be given not later than the time by which notice must be given of the appointment of a counting agent, that is to say, in general not later than the second day before the day of the poll.

(5) A candidate's election agent may do or assist in doing anything which a polling or counting agent of his is authorised to do ; and anything required or authorised by the parliamentary elections rules or the local elections rules to be done in the presence of the polling or counting agents may be done in the presence of a candidate's election agent instead of his polling agent or counting agents.

(6) Subsections (1) to (3) above shall have effect as if contained in Part II of the Representation of the People Act 1949. 1949 c. 68.

Conduct of elections

Description of candidate in nomination paper and on ballot paper.

12.—(1) In rule 7 of the parliamentary elections rules (which relates to the nomination of candidates at parliamentary elections, and of which paragraphs (2), (3) and (4) are applied to local government elections in England and Wales)—

(a) in paragraph (2) (contents of nomination paper) before the words " description of the candidate " there shall be inserted the words " (if desired) " ; and

(b) in paragraph (3) for the words " The description shall not refer to the candidate's political activities " there shall be substituted the words " The description (if any) shall not exceed six words in length " ; and

(c) paragraph (4) (which authorises a returning officer to shorten or replace a description if it is unduly long) shall be omitted.

(2) In rule 5 of the local elections rules in Schedule 3 to the Representation of the People Act 1949, after paragraph (4), there shall be inserted as a new paragraph (4A) :—

" (4A) The particulars of a candidate given in a nomination paper may, if desired, include a description in addition to the particulars required by paragraph (3) or (4) of this rule ; but a description included by virtue of this paragraph shall not exceed six words in length " ;

and in rule 12(2)(a) of those rules (under which the particulars on a ballot paper are to be taken from the nomination papers) after the word " residence " there shall be inserted the words " and description (if any) ".

Countermand or abandonment of poll on death of candidate.

13.—(1) If at a contested election proof is given to the satisfaction of the returning officer before the result of the election is declared that one of the persons named or to be named as candidate in the ballot papers has died, then—

(*a*) at a parliamentary election the returning officer shall countermand notice of the poll or, if polling has begun, direct that the poll be abandoned, and all proceedings with reference to the election shall be commenced afresh in all respects as if the writ had been received twenty-eight days after the day on which proof was given to the returning officer of the death except that—

(i) no fresh nomination shall be necessary in the case of a person shown in the statement of persons nominated as standing nominated; and

(ii) in the case of a general election, as in the case of a by-election, the time for delivery of nomination papers and the time for polling shall be determined in accordance with the third column in the timetable in rule 1 of the parliamentary elections rules (with the necessary modification of any reference to the date on which the writ is received);

(*b*) at a local government election, the returning officer shall countermand the poll or, if polling has begun, direct that the poll be abandoned, and the provisions of
1949 c. 68. section 36(2) of the Representation of the People Act 1949 shall apply.

(2) Where the poll is abandoned by reason of the death of a candidate, the proceedings at or consequent on that poll shall be interrupted, and the presiding officer at any polling station shall take the like steps (so far as not already taken) for the delivery to the returning officer of ballot boxes and of ballot papers and other documents as he is required to take on the close of the poll in due course, and the returning officer shall dispose of ballot papers and other documents in his possession as he is required to do on the completion in due course of the counting of the votes; but—

(*a*) it shall not be necessary for any ballot paper account to be prepared or verified; and

(*b*) the returning officer, without taking any step or further step for the counting of the ballot papers or of the votes, shall seal up all the ballot papers, whether the votes on them have been counted or not, and it shall not be necessary to seal up counted and rejected ballot papers in separate packets.

(3) The provisions of Schedules 2 and 3 to the Representation of the People Act 1949 as to the inspection, production, retention and destruction of ballot papers and other documents relating to a poll at an election shall apply to any such documents relating to a poll abandoned by reason of the death of a candidate, with the following modifications:— 1949 c. 68.

(*a*) ballot papers on which the votes were neither counted nor rejected shall be treated as counted ballot papers; and

(*b*) no order shall be made for the production or inspection of any ballot papers or for the opening of a sealed packet of counterfoils or certificates as to employment on duty on the day of the poll unless the order is made by a court with reference to a prosecution.

(4) Accordingly in section 72(1)(*a*) of the Local Government Act 1933 and in section 63 of the Local Government (Scotland) Act 1947 (which provide for the holding of a new election where at a local government election the poll is countermanded by reason of the death of a candidate before its commencement) after the words " the poll ", where they first occur, there shall in each case be inserted the words " is abandoned by reason of the death of a candidate or ". 1933 c. 51. 1947 c. 43.

(5) This section shall have effect in place of rule 24 of the parliamentary elections rules, rule 20 of the local elections rules in Schedule 2 to the Representation of the People Act 1949 and rule 18 of those in Schedule 3.

Miscellaneous amendments of elections rules.

14. In Schedules 2 and 3 to the Representation of the People Act 1949 the provisions specified in Part I of Schedule 1 to this Act (of which the subject matter is indicated in column 2 of the Schedule) shall cease to have effect and are hereby repealed; and the provisions of Part II of Schedule 1 to this Act shall have effect to modify the operation of the parliamentary elections rules and the local elections rules.

Provisions relating wholly or mainly to local government elections

Non-resident and property qualifications in local government.

15. The non-resident qualification for voting at local government elections, and the property qualification under section 57(*b*) of the Local Government Act 1933 for election to or membership of a local authority, are hereby abolished:

Provided that any member of a local authority who is qualified for membership either as a local government elector with a non-resident qualification or by virtue of section 57(*b*) of the Local Government Act 1933, but ceases to have the qualification by the operation of this section shall, until his then current term of office comes to an end continue to be qualified for membership of the authority (but without prejudice to any disqualification).

Date of qualification of candidate at local government election.

1933 c. 51.

16. A person shall not be qualified under section 57 of the Local Government Act 1933 to be elected a member of a local authority unless he is qualified in accordance with that section at the time of his nomination as a candidate and, if there is a poll, remains so qualified on the day of election; and in section 57(*c*) and (*d*) (under which twelve months' continuous residence up to the day of election qualifies for election to or membership of a local authority) for the words " the day of election " there shall in each case be substituted " the day on which he is nominated as a candidate ".

Filling of regular and casual vacancies at uncontested ordinary election.

17.—(1) Where an election to fill one or more casual vacancies in the office of councillor of a borough or urban or rural district in which the council do not regularly retire simultaneously is combined with an ordinary election of councillors, and the election is not contested, then the following provisions shall apply (instead of the provision in section 67(5)(*b*) of the Local Government Act 1933 that the persons deemed to be elected to fill the casual vacancies shall be determined by lot):—

(*a*) those declared elected (if fewer than the vacancies to be filled) shall be deemed elected to fill the vacancies in which they will hold office for the longest periods;

(*b*) those declared elected as remaining validly nominated shall be deemed elected to fill the vacancies with the longer terms in office in preference to those declared elected as retiring councillors though not remaining validly nominated;

(*c*) where there are two or more persons declared elected as remaining validly nominated and they are to fill vacancies in which they will hold office for different periods, the question which of them is to be deemed to fill any vacancy with a longer or shorter period in office shall be determined by lot, and so also where there are two or more persons declared elected as retiring councillors though not remaining validly nominated and they are to fill vacancies in which they will hold office for different periods.

1949 c. 68.

(2) In the local elections rules in Schedule 2 to the Representation of the People Act 1949, in rule 13(5) (which provides that vacancies not filled by persons remaining validly nominated shall be filled by such of the retiring councillors as are designated by the rules there set out) for the words " such of the retiring

councillors for the electoral area " there shall be substituted the words " the retiring councillors for the electoral area who, if duly nominated, would have been qualified for election or, if their number is more than that of the vacancies not filled under paragraph (3) of this rule, such of those councillors ".

18.—(1) In section 57(3) of the Representation of the People Act 1948, there shall be omitted the proviso (under which in England and Wales the ordinary day of election of councillors other than county councillors, if it would by the ordinary rule fall in the week before Whit Sunday, is to be a day in the week ending on the Thursday before Whit Sunday) ; and in place of that proviso there shall be inserted— Timing of elections, and of steps at elections. 1948 c. 65.

> " Provided that if the said week is the week including Ascension Day, the week ending with the day before Ascension Day shall be substituted therefor ".

(2) In rule 2 of the parliamentary elections rules (which provides that certain days are to be disregarded in computing time for purposes of the rules) for the words " Christmas Day, Good Friday, bank holiday " there shall be substituted the words " day of the Christmas break, of the Easter break or of a bank holiday break ", and at the end of the rule there shall be added as a new paragraph (3):—

> " (3) In this rule ' the Christmas break ' means the period beginning with the last week day before Christmas Day and ending with the first week day after Christmas Day which is not a bank holiday, ' the Easter break ' means the period beginning with the Thursday before and ending with the Tuesday after Easter Day, and ' a bank holiday break ' means any bank holiday not included in the Christmas break or the Easter break and the period beginning with the last week day before that bank holiday and ending with the next week day which is not a bank holiday:
>
> Provided that so much of this paragraph as includes in a bank holiday break a period before and after a bank holiday shall not apply to bank holidays, other than New Year's Day, which are not bank holidays in England and Wales ".

(3) In the local elections rules in Schedule 2 to the Representation of the People Act 1949, in rule 2 there shall be made the same amendments as are under subsection (2) above to be made in rule 2 of the parliamentary elections rules (except that the new paragraph shall be paragraph (2) and shall not include the proviso), and in addition— 1949 c. 68.

(*a*) the words " and the Saturday before and the Tuesday after Easter Day or Whit Sunday " shall be omitted ; and (*b*) in the proviso (which provides for the preparation of special lists and issue of postal ballot papers to proceed on those Saturdays and Tuesdays) for the words from " on the said Saturday " to " Whit Sunday " there shall be substituted the words " on the first or last days of the Christmas break, the Easter break or a bank holiday break or on the Saturday in the Easter break ".

1956 c. 43. (4) In section 6 of the Local Government Elections Act 1956 (which makes similar provision for computing the time limit of thirty days for holding certain elections in England and Wales to fill casual vacancies) there shall be made the same amendments as are under subsection (3) above to be made in rule 2 of the local elections rules, except that subsection (3)(*b*) does not apply and there shall be a new subsection (1A) instead of a new paragraph (2).

(5) In relation to the period within which any local government election is to be held, and in relation to the day of election at any local government election, section 295 of the Local Government Act 1933 shall have effect as if the days mentioned in section 295(1) included any day of the Christmas break, the Easter break or a bank holiday break within the meaning of rule 2 of the local elections rules as amended by subsection (3) above; and in section 295(2) (under which, if an election is postponed, the day on which it is held is to be treated as the day of election for all purposes of that Act) the reference to the purposes of that Act shall include the purposes of the Representation of the People Acts.

1933 c. 51.

This subsection shall apply to elections of elective auditors as it applies to local government elections.

Expenses of returning officers etc. at or in connection with local government elections.

19.—(1) The council which is required to pay the expenses properly incurred by a returning officer in relation to any local government election may treat those expenses as including all costs properly incurred by the returning officer in connection with or in contemplation of any legal proceedings arising out of the election (including any criminal proceedings against the returning officer), whether or not the proceedings are in fact instituted.

(2) In relation to elections of borough councillors in England (outside Greater London) or in Wales subsection (1) above shall apply to expenses of the mayor or town clerk as it applies to expenses of the returning officer, and in relation to elections in Scotland subsection (1) shall so apply to expenses of a county clerk or town clerk.

(3) Subsection (1) above shall apply to elections of elective auditors as it applies to local government elections.

(4) In section 26(7) of the Representation of the People Act 1949 (which enables returning officers at contested elections of county councillors in England and Wales to obtain from the council advances up to £10 for every 1,000 electors), and in section 30(5) of that Act (which makes the like provision for Scotland), for the words " such sum not exceeding ten pounds for every one thousand electors at the election as he may require " there shall be substituted the words " such reasonable sum in respect of his expenses at the election as he may require ". 1949 c. 68.

Other incidental matters

Refunds to local authorities of additional superannuation contributions for returning officers.

20. Where the superannuation contributions required to be paid by a local authority in respect of any person are increased by any fee paid under section 20 of the Representation of the People Act 1949 as part of a returning officer's charges at a parliamentary election, then on an account being submitted to the Treasury a sum equal to the increase shall be charged on and paid out of the Consolidated Fund of the United Kingdom to the authority.

Summary prosecutions of offences at local elections.

21.—(1) In section 155 of the Representation of the People Act 1949 (which, in relation to parliamentary elections, makes provision as to the prosecution of offences committed outside the United Kingdom by British subjects or citizens of the Republic of Ireland) in subsection (1) the words " so far as it relates to parliamentary elections," shall be omitted.

(2) In section 159(5) of the Representation of People Act 1949 (under which summary prosecutions for offences at elections under the local government Act may be brought outside the local government area by the Director of Public Prosecutions or his assistant) there shall be omitted the words " by the Director of Public Prosecutions or his assistant ", and there shall also be omitted the words from " For the purposes of this subsection " onwards (which have ceased to be relevant in consequence of changes in the law relating to commissions of the peace).

References, in connection with election petitions, to offices of profit under the Crown.

22.—(1) In section 115(2) of the Representation of the People Act 1949 (under which a barrister is not qualified to constitute an election court for a local election in England or Wales if he holds an office or place of profit under the Crown other than that of recorder) there shall be omitted the words from " or holds " onwards.

(2) In section 122(3) of the Representation of the People Act 1949 (which provides for the trial of a parliamentary election petition to proceed notwithstanding the acceptance by the

respondent of an office of profit under the Crown) for the words " an office of profit under the Crown " there shall be substituted the words " an office vacating his seat in Parliament ".

Supplementary

Consequential provisions as to ward elections in City of London.
1949 c. 68.
1957 c. x.

23.—(1) Without prejudice to the application of any provisions of this Act to elections in the City of London by virtue of section 167 of the Representation of the People Act 1949, the following provisions of this section shall have effect as regards the operation, in connection with matters affected by the passing of this Act, of Part II (ward elections) of the City of London (Various Powers) Act 1957 (referred to below in this section as " the City Act ").

(2) Notwithstanding anything in section 6(1) of the City Act—

(*a*) a person qualified apart from age to vote as an elector at a ward election shall, subject to paragraph (*b*) below, be entitled to do so if he is of the age of eighteen years or over on the date of the poll ; but

(*b*) a person registered in the ward list to be used at a ward election shall not be entitled to vote as an elector at the election if his entry in the ward list gives a date later than the date of the poll as the date on which he will attain the age of eighteen years ;

and the ward lists and provisional ward lists shall give for any elector the date on which it appears to the secondary that the elector will attain the age of eighteen, if that date is after the 16th November in the year in which the ward lists are to be published, and claims and objections asking for the omission, insertion or alteration of a date in a ward list as that on which an elector will attain that age may be made as in the case of claims and objections relating to the inclusion of a person's name in the list, and sections 7(4) and 9 of the City Act shall with any necessary modifications apply accordingly.

(3) In section 8 of the City Act (which applies with adaptations certain provisions of the Representation of the People Act 1949) any reference to a provision of the Representation of the People Act 1949 which is amended by this Act shall have effect as a reference to that provision as so amended ; and that section shall apply to the following provisions of this Act, that is to say, sections 1(3), 2(1) and (2), 3(1), 4, 5 and 6(3) as if they were provisions of the Representation of the People Act 1949 mentioned in and applied by subsection (1) of that section.

Accordingly any power under the Representation of the People Act 1949 to prescribe the form of service declaration may be exercised so as to take account of the difference between the qualifying date under that Act and the qualifying date under the City Act.

(4) The repeal by this Act of section 5 of the Representation of the People Act 1949 shall not affect the operation of any provision of that section as applied by section 4(2) of the City Act. 1949 c. 68.

24.—(1) In the provisions of the Representation of the People Act 1949 mentioned in Schedule 2 to this Act there shall be made the amendments provided for by that Schedule, being amendments which bring the text of that Act into conformity with the foregoing provisions of this Act or are otherwise consequential on or supplementary to those provisions. Other consequential and supplementary amendments, and repeals.

(2) The amendments made by Schedule 2 to this Act in section 48 of the Representation of the People Act 1949, and any amendment made by Schedule 1 or 2 in any of the local elections rules which are applied by section 67 of the Licensing Act 1964 (polls about Sunday closing in Wales and Monmouthshire), shall have effect also in the section or rule as so applied; and in Schedule 8 to that Act— 1964 c. 26.

(*a*) in paragraphs 4 and 5(1)(*c*) (which refer to a person making a declaration of secrecy) after the words " read to " there shall be inserted the words " or by "; and

(*b*) in the Appendix, in the form of declaration to be made by the companion of a blind person, for the words " twenty-one years " there shall be substituted the words " eighteen years ".

(3) In Part VI of Schedule 3 to the Local Government Act 1933, in paragraph 5(5) (which was substituted for the previous paragraph 5(5) by section 5 of the Local Government Elections Act 1956 and applies certain provisions to polls consequent on a parish meeting)— 1933 c. 51. 1956 c. 43.

(*a*) after the words " A poll consequent on a parish meeting " there shall be inserted the words " shall be a poll of those entitled to attend the meeting as local government electors, and "; and

(*b*) any reference to a provision of the Representation of the People Act 1949 which is amended by this Act shall have effect as a reference to that provision as so amended, and the reference to the local elections rules shall apply also to paragraph 11 of Schedule 1 to this Act.

(4) The enactments mentioned in Schedule 3 to this Act (which includes in Part I certain enactments already spent or

otherwise out of date) are hereby repealed to the extent specified in column 3 of the Schedule, in addition to the enactments repealed by Part I of Schedule 1 to this Act.

1933 c. 51. 1949 c. 68. (5) The amendments and repeals made by this Act in section 57 of the Local Government Act 1933 and sections 2 and 5 of the Representation of the People Act 1949 shall have effect subject to the same saving as is contained in section 15 of this Act.

Expenses.

25. In so far as any provision of this Act relating to the parliamentary or local government franchise, the place or manner of voting at parliamentary or local government elections or the conduct of those elections increases the registration expenses of registration officers, there shall be paid out of moneys provided by Parliament—

(*a*) in the case of expenses of registration officers in Great Britain, any additional sums payable by way of rate support grant because of the increase; and

(*b*) in the case of expenses of registration officers in Northern Ireland, the addition to the sums which under section 43(2) of the Representation of the People Act 1949 are to be paid out of moneys provided by Parliament on account of those expenses;

and in so far as any such provision of this Act increases the amount of the sums to be charged on and paid out of the Consolidated Fund of the United Kingdom under section 20 of the Representation of the People Act 1949 on account of the charges of returning officers at parliamentary elections, the increase shall be so charged and paid.

Construction with Representation of the People Act 1949, and printing of that Act with insertions.

26.—(1) Expressions to which, for purposes of the Representation of the People Act 1949, a meaning is assigned by that Act or any Act amending it shall have the same meaning for purposes of this Act.

(2) The powers conferred—

1958 c. 55. (*a*) in relation to elections of district, rural borough or parish councillors by section 29 of the Representation of the People Act 1949, as amended by the Local Government Act 1958; and

1963 c. 33. (*b*) in relation to elections of London borough councillors or Greater London councillors by paragraphs 13 and 14 of Schedule 3 to the London Government Act 1963;

to modify the local elections rules shall apply to those rules as amended by this Act, and to the provisions of this Act amending them, and also to sections 1(4), 6(7), 11(4) and (5), 13(1) to (3) and 14 (with Schedule 1) of this Act.

(3) Without prejudice to any specific direction in this Act that a provision is to have effect as part of the Representation of the People Act 1949, any provision made by that Act with respect to its operation in special cases, and in particular— 1949 c. 68.

(*a*) section 36(4) as amended by the Local Government Act 1958 (modifications in the event of omission to hold rural borough or parish election); 1958 c. 55.

(*b*) section 165(2) and (4) (elections of elective auditors, and elections otherwise than by local government electors to borough council of Oxford or Cambridge); and

(*c*) section 172(4) (application to Council of Isles of Scilly);

shall apply in like manner to any relevant provisions of this Act.

(4) Section 174(2) and (3) of the Representation of the People Act 1949 (which relate to the operation of the Act as regards Northern Ireland) shall apply to this Act as they apply to that.

(5) In any revised edition of the statutes published by authority the enactments mentioned in column 1 in Schedule 4 to this Act may be inserted in the Representation of the People Act 1949 as indicated in column 2 of that Schedule, with any adjustment which may be required of references in those enactments to that Act, and such further adaptations as are so indicated.

Commencement.

27.—(1) Subject to subsection (2) below, the following provisions of this Act, that is to say, sections 1, 2 and 3 and, so far as it relates to the qualification for voting at local government elections, section 15, shall come into force so as to have effect with respect to the registers of electors to be published in the year 1970 and the elections for which those registers are used; and to the extent to which it has effect for the purpose of those provisions any other provision of this Act (including any provision of Schedule 2 making an amendment consequential on or supplementary to those provisions) shall come into force in like manner.

(2) Section 23 of this Act, in so far as it relates to the age for voting at ward elections, or applies any provision of sections 1 to 3 of this Act or, to the extent to which it is consequential on or supplementary to any provision of those sections, any amendment made by Schedule 2 to this Act shall come into force so as to have effect with respect to the ward lists to be published in the year 1970 and elections for which those ward lists are used.

(3) Subject to subsections (1) and (2) above, the provisions of this Act shall come into force on such day as may be appointed by order of the Secretary of State, and different days may be appointed for different provisions and for different purposes of the same provision.

(4) The power of the Secretary of State to make orders under subsection (3) above shall be exercisable by statutory instrument, which shall be laid before Parliament after being made.

Citation.

28. This Act may be cited as the Representation of the People Act 1969, and shall be included among the Acts that may be cited as the Representation of the People Acts.

SCHEDULES

SCHEDULE 1

Sections 14 and 24(2).

MISCELLANEOUS AMENDMENTS OF PARLIAMENTARY AND LOCAL ELECTIONS RULES

PART I

REPEALS IN SCHEDULES 2 AND 3 TO REPRESENTATION OF THE PEOPLE ACT 1949

1949 c. 68.

In Schedule 2, in the parliamentary elections rules,—	
Rule 5	Telegraphic information of issue of writ.
Rule 23(3) and (4) ...	Telegraphic notice of poll and of nominations.
In rule 26(5), the words from " so that " onwards.	Voting compartments at polling station to number at least one for every 150 electors.
In Schedule 2, in the local elections rules,—	
Rule 8(2)(*c*), together with the preceding " and ".	At county council elections place for delivery of nomination papers to be in the electoral division or an adjoining electoral division if the division is not wholly within a borough or urban district.
Rule 18(4)	Prohibition on holding election in place of worship.
Rule 19(3) from " but " onwards.	Candidate's right to require notice of poll to include names of those signing a second and third nomination paper.
In Schedule 3 (Scottish local elections rules)—	
Rule 5(7)	Restriction on nomination of town councillors.
Rule 17(2), from " and, in the case of " onwards.	Candidate's right to require notice of poll to include names of those signing a second and third nomination paper.

PART II

OTHER AMENDMENTS

Preliminary

1.—(1) In this Part of this Schedule " the English and Welsh rules " means the local elections rules in Schedule 2 to the Representation of the People Act 1949 and " the Scottish rules " means the local elections rules in Schedule 3 to that Act.

SCH. 1 (2) Except in so far as the contrary intention appears, the following provisions of this Schedule apply to parliamentary elections, to local government elections in England and Wales, and to local government elections in Scotland.

Polling hours at parliamentary elections

2. In the time-table in rule 1 of the parliamentary elections rules, in the entry relating to polling, for the words " nine in the evening " in the second column and in the third there shall be substituted the words " ten at night ".

Time-table at local government elections in Scotland

3. In rule 1 of the Scottish rules, in the entry in the time-table relating to the delivery of notice of withdrawal of nomination, for the words " second Tuesday " there shall be substituted the words " third Friday ".

The official mark

4. In rule 20 of the parliamentary elections rules, rule 16 of the English and Welsh rules and rule 13 of the Scottish rules (which deal with the official mark on ballot papers)—

(*a*) in paragraph (1) for the words " which shall be either embossed or perforated " there shall be substituted the words " which shall perforate the ballot paper " ; and

(*b*) at the end of the rule there shall be added as a new paragraph (3)—

" (3) The official mark used for ballot papers issued for the purpose of voting by post shall not be used at the same election for ballot papers issued for the purpose of voting in person."

Nomination at parliamentary elections

5.—(1) At a parliamentary election—

(*a*) notwithstanding rule 7(1) of the parliamentary elections rules a candidate's nomination paper may be delivered to the returning officer on behalf of the candidate by his election agent if the agent's name and address have been previously given to the returning officer as required by section 55 of
1949 c. 68. the Representation of the People Act 1949 or are so given at the time the nomination paper is delivered ; and

(*b*) notwithstanding rule 12(1) of the parliamentary elections rules, a candidate's wife or husband shall be entitled to be present at the delivery of the candidate's nomination paper, and thereafter may, so long as the candidate stands nominated, attend the proceedings during the time for delivery of nomination papers or making objections thereto, but while attending as the candidate's wife or husband shall not have the right conferred by rule 12(3) of inspecting, or objecting to the validity of, nomination papers.

SCH. 1

(2) In the Appendix to Schedule 2 to the Representation of the People Act 1949, in the form of nomination paper for a parliamentary election— 1949 c. 68.

(*a*) the third column relating to the candidate shall be headed " Home address in full " (instead of " Place of Residence ") and the third and fourth columns shall be transposed so that the description is in the third and the address in the fourth column ;

(*b*) in the first column relating to persons subscribing the nomination paper the heading shall be " Signatures " (instead of " Signature "), and the column for their electoral numbers shall be sub-divided into two columns by a sub-heading " Distinctive letter " and a sub-heading " Number ".

Nomination at local government elections

6.—(1) The following provisions shall apply to nominations at local government elections in England and Wales:—

(*a*) the nomination paper shall give for each person subscribing it his electoral number (meaning thereby his number as an elector for the electoral area as defined in rule 6(6) of the English and Welsh rules) ;

(*b*) at an ordinary election a telegram consenting to a nomination shall be admissible in place of the candidate's written consent, as it is at an election to fill a casual vacancy ;

(*c*) in rule 9(2) of the English and Welsh rules (examination and decision on validity of nomination papers) there shall be omitted the words " As soon as practicable after the latest time for delivery of nomination papers ", and there shall be added at the end of the paragraph the words " and shall do so as soon as practicable after each paper is delivered ".

(2) In the Scottish rules—

(*a*) in rule 5 there shall be added at the end of paragraph (3) and at the end of paragraph (4) the words " and shall give for each person subscribing it his number in the relevant register of local government electors " ;

(*b*) at the end of rule 7 there shall be added the following paragraph:—

" (2) It shall be the duty of the returning officer or the town clerk, as the case may be, to reach his decision on the validity of a nomination paper, as required by the foregoing paragraph, as soon as practicable after each paper is received ".

Ballot papers at local government elections in Scotland

7.—(1) In rule 12(2)(*a*) of the Scottish rules there shall be added at the end the words " and (where such a surname or address has been changed between the qualifying date and the last day for the submission of nomination papers) shall also, if so required by the candidate, give the present surname and the current address ".

Sch. 1

(2) In Form F in the Appendix to the Scottish rules—

(*a*) in the Form of Front of Ballot Paper, for the designation under SMITH there shall be substituted the following designation—

" (Mary Smith, now Mary Wilson of 72, High Street, Rutherglen, formerly of 24, Young Street, Rutherglen) " ; and

(*b*) in the directions as to printing the ballot paper, in paragraph 3, after the words " full name " there shall be inserted the words " (including if required by the candidate present name where there has been a change of name) ", and after the word " address ", in both places where that word occurs, there shall be inserted the words " (including if so required current address) ".

Declaration of secrecy

8.—(1) The constables on duty at polling stations or at the counting of the votes shall not be required to make the declaration of secrecy, and a clerk making it in order to attend at the counting of the votes need not make it before the opening of the poll but shall do so before he is permitted to attend the counting.

1919 c. 68. (2) The provisions of the Representation of the People Act 1949 referred to in the declaration may be read by the declarant in the presence of the person taking it, instead of being read to the declarant by that person.

(3) A person other than the returning officer, instead of making the declaration before a justice of the peace (or person having the same powers as to the taking of declarations) or before the returning officer, may make it in England or Wales before the clerk of the Greater London Council, a county council or a district council or the town clerk of a borough or rural borough, in Scotland before a county clerk or town clerk, and in Northern Ireland before the secretary of a county council or a town clerk.

Delivery to returning officer of ballot boxes etc.

9. In rule 44(1) of the parliamentary elections rules and in rule 37(1) of the Scottish rules (which provide that on the close of the poll the presiding officer at a polling station is to make into sealed packets the ballot boxes, the marked copies of the register etc., and is to deliver the packets to the returning officer) after the words " deliver the packets " there shall be inserted the words " or cause them to be delivered "and at the end of the paragraph there shall be added—

" Provided that if the packets are not delivered by the presiding officer personally to the returning officer, the arrangements for their delivery shall require the approval of the returning officer ".

Ballot paper account

SCH. 1

10.—(1) In rule 44(3) of the parliamentary elections rules and in rule 37(3) of the Scottish rules (under which the presiding officer at a polling station is required in accounting for the ballot papers entrusted to him to state the number of ballot papers in the ballot box) for the words " in the ballot box " there shall be substituted the words " issued and not otherwise accounted for ".

(2) The ballot paper accounts, instead of being verified in the presence of counting agents after the completion of the counting, shall be verified in the presence of election agents after the ballot papers in the ballot boxes have been counted and the number recorded, and before the ballot papers are mixed up.

Attendance at counting of votes

11. A person not entitled to attend at the counting of the votes shall not be permitted to do so by the returning officer unless the returning officer is satisfied that the efficient counting of the votes will not be impeded, and the returning officer has either consulted the election agents or thought it impracticable to consult them.

Information as to polling districts

12.—(1) The returning officer shall, as soon as practicable after publication of a notice of poll, give to each of the election agents a description in writing of the polling districts, if any:

Provided that where it is for the mayor or town clerk to give notice of the poll, the description required by this sub-paragraph shall also be given by him instead of by the returning officer.

(2) In the English and Welsh rules there shall be omitted rule 19(2)(*e*) (which requires a notice of poll to include a description of polling districts).

Publication and contents of certain notices

13.—(1) In rule 4 of the English and Welsh rules—

(*a*) in paragraph (2) (publication of notice of election at county council elections) for the words from " in addition " onwards there shall be substituted the words " in addition by causing it to be exhibited at such conspicuous places in the electoral division as the officer giving the notice shall determine " ; and

(*b*) in paragraphs (3) and (4), as amended by paragraph 34 of Schedule 3 to the London Government Act 1963 (publication of notice of election at other elections) for the words " such places " there shall be substituted the words " such conspicuous places ". 1963 c. 33.

(2) Rule 30 of the parliamentary elections rules and, in the Appendix to Schedule 2, the form of directions for the guidance of voters in voting shall be amended as follows:—

(*a*) in rule 30(4) (which requires the directions to be exhibited outside every polling station and in every compartment of every polling station) for the words from " outside every polling station " onwards there shall be substituted the words " inside and outside every polling station " ;

SCH. 1

(*b*) at the end of rule 30 there shall be added as a new paragraph (5):—

"(5) In every compartment of every polling station there shall be exhibited a notice as follows—"The voter may vote for not more than one candidate";

(*c*) in the form of directions for the guidance of voters in voting there shall be omitted paragraph 1 (which states that a voter may vote for not more than one candidate) and the note requiring the directions to be illustrated by examples of the ballot paper, and paragraphs 2 to 7 shall be renumbered as paragraphs 1 to 6;

and accordingly in rule 25 of the English and Welsh rules (which applies and adapts rule 30 of the parliamentary elections rules) after the words "electoral area" there shall be inserted the words "the notice to be exhibited in the compartments shall be modified as necessary where there is more than one vacancy".

(3) In rule 23 of the Scottish rules there shall be made the same amendments as are made by sub-paragraph (2)(*a*) and (*b*) above in rule 30 of the parliamentary elections rules, except that the notice to be exhibited in the compartments shall be given as—

"The voter may vote for candidate[s]";

and those words shall be omitted from Form G in the Appendix to the Scottish rules.

(4) At the end of rule 51(1)(*c*) of the parliamentary elections rules, and at the end of rule 46(1) of the English and Welsh rules (which provide for publishing the result of a contested election and the total number of votes given for each candidate) there shall be added the words "together with the number of rejected ballot papers under each head shown in the statement of rejected ballot papers".

(5) At the end of rule 44 of the Scottish rules, there shall be added the words "and the statements referred to in the foregoing sub-paragraphs shall show the total number of votes given for each candidate at the poll, whether elected or not, together with the number of rejected ballot papers under each head shown in the statement of rejected ballot papers".

Section 24(1), (2).

SCHEDULE 2

1949 c. 68.

CONSEQUENTIAL AND SUPPLEMENTARY AMENDMENTS OF REPRESENTATION OF THE PEOPLE ACT 1949

1. In section 1(1) (parliamentary electors) and in section 2(1) (local government electors) for the words from "those" to "Ireland" there shall in each case be substituted the words—

"those who—

(*a*) are resident there on the qualifying date; and

(*b*) (age apart) are on that date and on the date of the poll not subject to any legal incapacity to vote and either British subjects or citizens of the Republic of Ireland; and (*c*) are on the date of the poll of voting age (that is to say, of the age of eighteen years or over) ". SCH. 2

2.—(1) In section 8(1) proviso and in section 8(2) proviso (*c*) (under which a person having a service qualification on the qualifying date is to be registered only in pursuance of a service declaration in force on that date) for the words " and in force on that date " there shall in each case be substituted the words " with reference to that date ".

(2) In section 8(2) proviso there shall be omitted paragraphs (*a*) and (*b*) (which make provision against a person being registered as a local government elector more than once in any area or being registered as a non-resident if entitled to be registered as a resident).

3. At the end of section 9(1)(*c*) (determination by registration officer of claims and objections) there shall be added the words " including claims and objections asking for the omission, insertion or alteration of a date as that on which a person will become of voting age and entitled to be treated as an elector ".

4.—(1) In section 10(1) after paragraph (*b*) there shall be inserted as a new paragraph (*bb*)—

" (*bb*) any person who is employed by the British Council in a post outside the United Kingdom " ;

and at the end of paragraph (*c*) there shall be added the words " and any man who is the husband of such a person and is residing outside the United Kingdom to be with his wife ".

(2) In section 10(5) (particulars to be given in service declarations) there shall be substituted for paragraphs (*a*) to (*d*)—

" (*a*) the date of the declaration ;

(*b*) that on that date and, unless it is a qualifying date, on the qualifying date next following the declarant is or will be, or but for the circumstances entitling him to make the declaration would have been, residing in the United Kingdom ;

(*c*) the address of that residence or, if the declarant cannot give any such address, an address at which he has resided in the United Kingdom ;

(*d*) that on the date of the declaration the declarant is a British subject or a citizen of the Republic of Ireland ;

(*e*) whether the declarant had on the date of the declaration attained the age of eighteen years, and, if he had not, the date of his birth ; and

(*f*) such particulars (if any) as may be prescribed of the declarant's identity and service qualification ".

(3) In section 10(6) (which deals with the effect to be given to a service declaration) for the words " A person whose service declaration is in force on the qualifying date " there shall be substituted the words " Where a service declaration is made with reference to the qualifying date for any register, then in relation to that register the declarant ".

(4) In section 10(9) (under which a new service declaration automatically cancels a declaration bearing an earlier date) after the

SCH. 2

words " bearing an earlier date " there shall be inserted the words " and made with reference to the same qualifying date ".

5. In section 12 (place and manner of voting as elector at parliamentary elections) after the word " incapacity " in subsection (1)(*c*) there shall be inserted the words " or of religious observance ".

6.—(1) In section 14(2) (qualification for voting or appointment as proxy at parliamentary elections) for the words " of full age, not subject to any legal incapacity " there shall be substituted the words " not subject (age apart) to any legal incapacity ", and after the next " and " there shall be inserted the word " is ".

(2) In section 14(5)(*a*) (which deals with the period of validity of a proxy appointment for a service voter) for the words " for all elections for which he is registered in pursuance of the same service declaration " there shall be substituted the words " for all elections for which he remains registered as a service voter at the same qualifying address ".

7. Section 15 (place and manner of voting as proxy) shall be amended as follows:—

(*a*) in subsection (1) there shall be omitted the words from " of a person " to " service voter's proxy) ";

(*b*) the words " service voter's " shall be omitted where they first occur in subsection (2) and in subsection (4);

(*c*) in any other place for the words " service voter's " or " service voter " there shall be substituted the word " elector's " or " elector ".

8.—(1) In section 23 (place and manner of voting as local government elector) after the word " incapacity " in subsection (1)(*c*) there shall be inserted the words " or of religious observance ".

(2) In section 23(4) (postal voting by local government electors other than service voters) for the words " Subject to the last foregoing subsection " there shall be substituted the words " Unless treated as an absent voter under the last foregoing subsection ".

9. In section 24(2) (absent voting applications which are for a particular local government election only) there shall be added at the end of the subsection—

" or

(*d*) religious observance ".

10. In section 25(3) (qualification for voting or appointment as peer's proxy at local government elections) for the words " of full age, not subject to any legal incapacity " there shall be substituted the words " not subject (age apart) to any legal incapacity ", and after the word " and " there shall be inserted the word " is ".

11.—(1) In section 39(2) (conclusive effect of register of local government electors) there shall be substituted for paragraph (*a*)—

" (*a*) whether or not a person registered therein was on the qualifying date resident at the address shown ".

(2) In section 39 there shall be inserted after subsection (3) as a new subsection (3A)—

"(3A) Any entry in the register of parliamentary or local government electors, if it gives a date as that on which the person named will attain voting age, shall for any purpose of this Part of this Act relating to him as elector be conclusive that until the date given in the entry he is not of voting age nor entitled to be treated as an elector except for purposes of an election at which the day fixed for the poll is that or a later date".

(3) In section 39(4) (under which a person registered as an elector or entered in the list of proxies is not to be excluded from voting on the ground of legal incapacity) for the words "full age", where first occurring, there shall be substituted the words "voting age", and the words "or was not of full age" shall be omitted.

12.—(1) In section 46(4) (arrangements to be made for securing to members of the forces and Crown servants opportunities for exercising, and instructions as to, their rights in connection with service declarations etc.) there shall be made the following amendments—

(*a*) in paragraph (*b*) for the words "by him and, in the case of a man, by his wife" there shall be substituted the words "by him and any wife of his or, as the case may be, by her and any husband of hers"; and

(*b*) the proviso (which excludes from the requirements of the subsection certain members of the forces below the age of twenty years and three months) shall be omitted.

(2) In section 46 there shall be inserted after subsection (4) as a new subsection (4A)—

"(4A) In relation to persons having a service qualification by virtue of section 10(1)(*bb*) of this Act the British Council shall be under a corresponding obligation to that imposed by subsection (4) above on the appropriate government department."

13.—(1) In section 48(1) (offences, of voting, applying to be an absent voter or to appoint a proxy, etc., while subject to legal incapacity) there shall be added at the end of the subsection—

"For the purposes of this subsection references to a person being subject to a legal incapacity to vote do not, in relation to things done before polling day at the election or first election at or for which they are done, include his being below voting age if he will be of voting age on that day";

and accordingly the proviso to section 48(1) shall be omitted.

(2) Section 48(2) and (3) (plural voting and similar offences) shall be amended as follows:—

(*a*) in section 48(2)(*b*) (voting as elector in person when entitled to vote as absent voter) for the words "as an absent voter" there shall be substituted the words "by post; or", and in section 48(2)(*c*) (service voter voting as elector in person when his proxy has voted in person or is entitled to vote by post) there shall be omitted the words "for which he is registered as a service voter";

SCH. 2 (*b*) in section 48(3)(*c*) (voting in person as proxy for service voter who has already voted in person or is entitled to vote by post) the words " has already voted in person thereat or " shall be omitted, and at the end of the subsection there shall be added—

" or

(*d*) he votes in person as proxy for an elector at a parliamentary or local government election knowing that the elector has already voted in person thereat ".

14. Section 56 (nomination of sub-agent at parliamentary elections) shall be amended as follows:—

(*a*) in subsection (1) for the words following the word " appoint " there shall be substituted the words " to act in any part of the constituency one, but not more than one, deputy election agent (in this Act referred to as a sub-agent) " ;

(*b*) in subsection (2) for the words " in a polling district " there shall be substituted the words " in a part of the constituency for which there is a sub-agent ", the words " for that district " shall be omitted and for the words " in his district " there shall be substituted " in his part of the constituency " ;

(*c*) at the end of the section there shall be added as a new subsection (5):—

" (5) The declaration to be made to the appropriate officer, and the notice to be given by him, under subsection (3) or (4) above shall specify the part of the constituency within which any sub-agent is appointed to act."

15. In section 58(4) (address to be taken as election agent's office where no appointment of election agent is made) for the words " if that address is not in the constituency or local government area or in a county of a city or town adjoining thereto ", and in section 58(6) for the words " if that address is not in the local government area or in a county of a city or town adjoining thereto ", there shall be substituted the words " if that address is outside the permitted area for the office ".

16. In section 64(2) for paragraphs (*a*) to (*d*) there shall be substituted paragraphs (*a*) and (*b*) in terms of section 8(1)(*a*) and (*b*) of this Act, and after section 64(4) there shall be inserted as a new subsection (4A) a subsection in terms of section 8(2) of this Act.

17. At the end of section 79(4) (definition of " elector " as recipient of election address sent post free) there shall be added the words " (and accordingly includes a person shown in the register or electors lists as below voting age if it appears therefrom that he will be of voting age on the day fixed for the poll, but not otherwise) ".

18. In section 106 (computation of time for purposes of Part II of the Act) in subsection (2) for the words " Christmas Day, Good
1871 c. 17. Friday, any bank holiday under the Bank Holidays Act 1871 ", there shall be substituted the words " any day of the Christmas break, of the Easter break or of a bank holiday break " ; and at

the end of the section there shall be added as a new subsection (3):— SCH. 2

"(3) In this section 'the Christmas break' means the period beginning with the last week day before Christmas Day and ending with the first week day after Christmas Day which is not a bank holiday, 'the Easter break' means the period beginning with the Thursday before and ending with the Tuesday after Easter Day, and 'a bank holiday break' means any bank holiday under the Bank Holidays Act 1871 (in England 1871 c. 17. and Wales, in Scotland or in Northern Ireland, as the case may be) which is not included in the Christmas break or the Easter break and the period beginning with the last weekday before that bank holiday and ending with the next weekday which is not a bank holiday under that Act:

Provided that so much of this subsection as includes in a bank holiday break a period before and after a bank holiday shall not apply in Scotland or Northern Ireland to a bank holiday which is not also a bank holiday in England and Wales, except in Scotland New Year's Day".

19. Section 109 (time for presentation of parliamentary election petition) shall be amended as follows:—

(*a*) in subsection (3)(*a*) (under which a petition with reference to an illegal practice must, in general, be presented within fourteen days after the day specified in subsection (4)) for the words "fourteen days" there shall be substituted the words "twenty-one days"; and

(*b*) in subsection (4) (under which the time limit runs from receipt by the returning officer of the return and declaration as to the member's election expenses or from allowance of an authorised excuse) after the words "The said day is" there shall be inserted the words "the tenth day after the end of the time allowed for transmitting to the returning officer returns as to election expenses at the election or, if later."

20. In section 167 for subsection (4) there shall be substituted a new subsection in terms of section 8(3) of this Act, but omitting the words "in the City of London".

21. In section 171(1)—

(*a*) in the definition of "elector" there shall be added at the end the words "but does not include those shown in the register as below voting age on the day fixed for the poll"; and

(*b*) for the definition of "service voter" there shall be substituted—

"'service voter' means a person who has made a service declaration and is registered or entitled to be registered in pursuance of it".

22. In rule 5 of the local elections rules in Schedule 2 there shall be substituted for paragraph (2) (which applies the provisions in the

SCH. 2

parliamentary elections rules as to the matters to be stated with respect to the candidate in a nomination paper) the following paragraph:—

"(2) Paragraphs (2) and (3) of rule 7 of the parliamentary elections rules shall apply."

23.—(1) Rule 8(6) of the parliamentary elections rules and in rule 6(6) of the local elections rules in Schedule 2 (which relate to the subscription of nomination papers) the definitions of "elector" and "elector for the electoral area" shall be amended by adding at the end the words "(and accordingly includes a person shown in the register or electors lists as below voting age if it appears therefrom that he will be of voting age on the day fixed for the poll, but not otherwise)".

(2) In rule 7(*c*) of the local elections rules in Schedule 3 after the word "appear" there shall be inserted the words "as those of electors for purposes of the election" and in rule 7(*e*) after the words "provisions of" there shall be inserted the words "rule 5(4A), or".

24. In rule 7(2) of the local elections rules in Schedule 2 (candidate's consent to nomination to include statement that he is qualified for election) for the words "statement that he is qualified" there shall be substituted the words "statement declaring, with reference to the date of his nomination, that to the best of his belief he will be or is qualified".

25.—(1) In rule 24(1) of the local elections rules in Schedule 3 for the words "one polling agent to attend at each polling station" there shall be substituted the words "polling agents to attend at polling stations".

(2) Rule 31 of the parliamentary elections rules and rule 24 of the local elections rules in Schedule 3 shall be amended as follows:

(*a*) in paragraph (2) in rule 31 of the parliamentary elections rules there shall be omitted the words "in the case of counting agents";

(*b*) in paragraph (4) of each of those rules for the words "counting agents may be appointed" there shall be substituted the words "any appointment authorised by this rule may be made".

26.—(1) Rule 32 of the parliamentary elections rules shall be amended as follows:—

(*a*) at the end of paragraph (1)(*a*) there shall be added the words "and the presiding officers", and in paragraph (1)(*b*) the words "officer or" shall be omitted;

(*b*) in paragraph (2) after sub-paragraph (*c*) there shall be inserted as a new paragraph (*d*):—

"(*d*) any clerk making the declaration in order to attend at the counting of the votes";

(*c*) at the end of paragraph (3) there shall be added the proviso: —

"Provided that—

(*a*) in England and Wales the declaration may be made by the returning officer or any other person before a person who is chairman of the Greater London Council, a county council or a district council or mayor of a borough or rural borough, and may be made by a person other than the returning officer before a person who is clerk of any such council or town clerk of a borough or rural borough ; and

(*b*) in Scotland the declaration may be made by a person other than the returning officer before a county clerk or town clerk ; and

(*c*) in Northern Ireland the declaration may be made by a person other than the returning officer before the secretary of a county council or a town clerk " ;

(*d*) in paragraph (3), before the proviso so added, there shall be inserted the words " or shall be read by the declarant in the presence of that person ", and in paragraph (4) in the form of declaration for the words " read to me " there shall be substituted the words " read to [*by*] me ".

(2) At the end of rule 27 of the local elections rules in Schedule 2 there shall be added the words " with the omission in the proviso to paragraph (3) of the words ' in England or Wales ' in paragraph (*a*) and of paragraphs (*b*) and (*c*) ".

(3) In rule 25 of the local elections rules in Schedule 3—

(*a*) in paragraph (2) after sub-paragraph (*c*) there shall be inserted as a new paragraph (*d*): —

" (*d*) any clerk making the declaration in order to attend at the counting of the votes " ;

(*b*) in paragraph (3) after the words " or of the returning officer " there shall be inserted the words " or of a county clerk or town clerk " ;

(*c*) at the end of paragraph (3) there shall be added the words " or shall be read by the declarant in the presence of that person " ;

and in the Appendix to those rules, in the form of declaration of secrecy (Form H), for the words " read to me " there shall be substituted the words " read to [*by*] me ".

27. In rule 33 of the parliamentary elections rules and in rule 26 of the local elections rules in Schedule 3, after paragraph (1), there shall be inserted as a new paragraph (1A)—

" (1A) Not more than one polling agent shall be admitted at the same time to a polling station on behalf of the same candidate ".

28. In rule 40(3)(*b*) of the parliamentary elections rules and in rule 33(3)(*b*) of the local elections rules in Schedule 3 (persons

SCH. 2 entitled to assist blind voters) for the words " twenty-one years " there shall be substituted the words " eighteen years ".

29.—(1) Rule 46 of the parliamentary elections rules shall be amended as follows:—

(*a*) at the end of paragraph (1)(*a*) there shall be inserted the words " and in the presence of the election agents verify each ballot paper account "; and

(*b*) after paragraph (4) there shall be inserted as paragraph (4A) a paragraph in terms of the rule 55(2) repealed by this Act, but omitting the words " then in the presence of the counting agents " and substituting for the words " any counting agent " the words " any election agent ".

(2) Rule 39 of the local elections rules in Schedule 3 shall be amended as follows :—

(*a*) at the end of paragraph (1)(*a*) there shall be added " and, if required by a candidate or an election agent, in the presence of the election agents verify each ballot paper account "; and

(*b*) after paragraph (4) there shall be inserted as paragraph (4A) a paragraph in terms of rule 46(2) omitting the words " If required by a candidate or a counting agent " and the words " in the presence of the counting agents " and substituting for the words " any counting agent " the words " any election agent ".

30. In rule 48(4) of the parliamentary elections rules and rule 43(5) of the local elections rules in Schedule 2 and rule 41(4) of the local election rules in Schedule 3 the words " and any counting agent may copy the statement " shall be omitted.

31. In rule 54(3) of the parliamentary elections rules (which requires a candidate's deposit to be returned as soon as practicable if the poll is countermanded by reason of his death) after the word " countermanded " there shall be inserted the words " or abandoned ".

32. In the Appendix to Schedule 2, in the form of notice of a parliamentary election, there shall be added at the end as paragraph 3 of the Note:—

" 3. Electors and their proxies should take note that applications to be treated as an absent voter and other applications and notices about postal or proxy voting must reach the registration officer by the day of next if they are to be effective for this election ";

and a Note in the same terms shall be added at the end of each of the forms of notice of election in the Appendix to Schedule 3.

33. In the Appendix to Schedule 2, in the form of nomination paper for a parliamentary election, there shall be added at the end as paragraph 5 of the Note:—

" A person whose name is entered in the register or electors lists may not subscribe a nomination paper if the entry gives as the date on which he will become of voting age a date later than the day fixed for the poll ";

and a note in the same terms shall be added after the Note required to be printed on the back of a nomination paper for a local government election by each of the forms of nomination paper in the Appendix to Schedule 3. SCH. 2

34. In the Appendix to Schedule 3, in Form A.1, in paragraph 3, and in Forms A.II and A.III, in paragraphs 2 of both those forms, for the word " Tuesday ", where second occurring, there shall be substituted the word " Friday ".

35. In the Appendix to Schedule 3—

(a) in Forms B1, B2 and B3, after the words " preceding this date) ", there shall be inserted the words " and in either case the candidates description, if any " ;

(b) in Forms D1, D2 and D3, after the column headed " Addresses or Places of Residence " there shall be inserted a new column headed
" Description
(if any) " ;

(c) in Forms E1, E2 and E3, after the column headed " Addresses or Places of Residence of Candidates " there shall be inserted a new column headed
" Description
(if any) " ;

(d) in Form F, the second column shall include the description of the candidate, if any, and accordingly in that column there shall be made the following insertions—

(i) after the word " Hamilton ", of the words " , salesman, Labour " ;

(ii) after the word " Lanarkshire ", where that word first occurs, of the words " , schoolteacher, Progressive " ;

(iii) after the word " Lanarkshire ", where that word second occurs, of the words " National Independent Teenage Party " ;

and in Note 3, after the word "residence ", where that word first occurs, there shall be inserted the words " and his description, if any ", and for the words " unless it " there shall be substituted the words " and description except where his address, place of residence or description ".

36. In the Appendix to Schedule 3 in each of the forms of Notice of Poll there shall be added to the concluding paragraph the words " , but a person whose name is so registered may not vote if the entry in the register of electors gives as the date on which he will become of voting age a date later than the day fixed for the poll."

37. The three forms of declaration to be made by the companion of a blind voter which are contained in the Appendix to Schedule 2 and in that to Schedule 3 shall each be amended by substituting for the words " twenty-one years " the words " eighteen years ".

38.—(1) In Schedule 4, in paragraph 2, for the words from " any householder " to " the agent or factor of any such person " there shall be substituted the word " persons ".

SCH. 2

(2) In Schedule 4, in paragraph 5(2)(*b*), for the words " of any such declaration " there shall be substituted the words " for the purpose of the regulations of any statutory declaration ".

(3) In Schedule 4, in paragraph 5(3) (matters about which, in connection with absent voting, regulations may prescribe the required, sufficient or conclusive evidence) after the words " of his being subject to any physical incapacity and as to its probable duration " there shall be inserted the words " or of his being bound to any religious observance and of the nature and times of the observance ".

39. In Schedule 5, in the form of declarations as to election expenses, after the words " Justice of the Peace . . ." (below the space for the signature of the person taking the declaration) there shall be inserted the words " *or as the case may be* ".

40. In Schedule 8, paragraph 1(1) (which contains provision for the interpretation of statutory references to the register of parliamentary and local government electors, and to a parliamentary or local government elector, and other terms) after the words " elector shall be construed accordingly " there shall be inserted the words " (but so that in relation to a person shown in a register or electors list as attaining voting age on a specified date these references shall not apply except for the purposes of an election at which the day fixed for the poll falls on or after that date) " ; and at the end of paragraph 7(2) there shall be added the words " but where paragraph 1(1) applies to an Act passed before the Representation of the People Act 1969, this provision shall not prevent it applying with the amendment made by the Representation of the People Act 1969 ".

Section 24(4).

SCHEDULE 3

REPEALS

PART I

SPENT OR UNNECESSARY ENACTMENTS

Chapter	Short Title	Extent of Repeal
9 & 10 Geo. 6. c. 3.	The Coatbridge and Springburn Elections (Validation) Act 1945.	The whole Act.
9 & 10 Geo. 6. c. 43.	The Camberwell, Bristol and Nottingham Elections (Validation) Act 1946.	The whole Act.
12, 13 & 14 Geo. 6. c. 46.	The House of Commons (Indemnification of Certain Members) Act 1949.	The whole Act.
12, 13 & 14 Geo. 6. c. 68.	The Representation of the People Act 1949.	Section 1(2) proviso. Section 29(4). Section 66(6) from the words " The reference " onwards. Section 73(3) from " or if " to " two years after the offence was committed ".

SCH. 3

Chapter	Short Title	Extent of repeal
12, 13 & 14 Geo. 6. c. 68. —*cont.*	The Representation of the People Act 1949—*cont.*	Section 74(9) from the words " The reference " onwards. Section 87(2). Section 91(6) from the words " The reference " onwards. Section 102. Section 109(8) from the words " The reference " onwards. Section 116(2) from the words " and if " onwards. Section 128(6) from the words " The reference " onwards. Section 145(4) from the words " The reference " onwards. Section 146(7). In section 152(1) the words " or of election commissioners ". Section 152(6) from the words " The reference " onwards. Section 154(1) from " or if " to " two years after the offence was committed ". In section 171(1) the definition of " election commissioners ". In section 172(3) proviso the words " or section 22 ".
12, 13 & 14 Geo. 6. c. 86.	The Electoral Registers Act 1949.	In section 1(6) the words " (whether prepared before or after the passing of this Act)." Section 1(7).
12, 13 & 14 Geo. 6. c. 90.	The Election Commissioners Act 1949.	The whole Act.
14 & 15 Geo. 6. c. 39.	The Common Informers Act 1951.	In the Schedule, the entry for the Representation of the People Act 1949.
2 & 3 Eliz. 2. c. 8.	The Electoral Registers Act 1953.	Section 1(4).
2 & 3 Eliz. 2. c. 29.	The Niall Macpherson Indemnity Act 1954.	The whole Act.
4 & 5 Eliz. 2. c. 10.	The Validation of Elections Act 1955.	The whole Act.
4 & 5 Eliz. 2. c. 12.	The Validation of Elections (No. 2) Act 1955.	The whole Act.
4 & 5 Eliz. 2. c. 13.	The Validation of Elections (No. 3) Act 1955.	The whole Act.
4 & 5 Eliz. 2. c. 27.	The Charles Beattie Indemnity Act 1956.	The whole Act.
4 & 5 Eliz. 2. c. 43.	The Local Government Elections Act 1956.	In section 1, in subsection (1) the words " After the year nineteen hundred and fifty-seven ", and subsection (2) from the words " and paragraph (*c*) " onwards. In section 2, in subsection (1) the words preceding paragraph (*a*), and subsection (2).

SCH. 3

Chapter	Title or Short Title	Extent of Repeal
4 & 5 Eliz. 2 c. 43—*cont.*	The Local Government Elections Act 1956—*cont.*	In section 3 the words " first ordinary ", the words " held after the year nineteen hundred and fifty-seven " and the words " or any subsequent election of such councillors ". Section 4(4). Section 5(2). Section 6(2).
5 & 6 Eliz. 2. c. 43.	The Representation of the People (Amendment) Act 1957.	The whole Act.
7 & 8 Eliz. 2. c. 9.	The Representation of the People (Amendment) Act 1958.	The whole Act.
1963 c. 33.	The London Government Act 1963.	In Schedule 3, in paragraph 2 the words " On and after 1st April 1965 " in sub-paragraph (1) and sub-paragraph (2); in paragraph 3 the words " On and after 1st April 1965 " in sub-paragraph (1) and sub-paragraph (2); paragraphs 4 to 12 (but not so as to affect the term of office of any county aldermen); in paragraph 13(2), paragraphs (*a*) and (*b*) except the words " the town clerk of the borough "; in paragraph 14(2), paragraph (*a*) and the words " if the election is held on or after that date " in paragraph (*b*); in paragraph 21 the words from " until " to " that date "; in paragraphs 26, 31 and 32 the words " As from 1st April 1965 "; paragraph 36.

PART II

CONSEQUENTIAL REPEALS

Chapter	Short Title	Extent of Repeal
23 & 24 Geo. 5. c. 51.	The Local Government Act 1933.	Section 57(*b*). Section 67(5)(*b*).
12, 13 & 14 Geo. 6. c. 68.	The Representation of the People Act 1949.	Section 5. In section 8(2) proviso, paragraphs (*a*) and (*b*), and in paragraph (*c*) the words " as resident in any local government area ". In section 10, in subsection (3) the words " to be registered or " and subsection (10).

SCH. 3

Chapter	Short Title	Extent of Repeal
12, 13 & 14 Geo. 6. c. 68 —*cont.*	The Representation of the People Act 1949—*cont.*	In section 12, in subsection (2) the word " either " and the words from " or " at the end of paragraph (*a*) onwards, and subsection (5). In section 23, in subsection (2) from the word " unless " onwards, in subsection (3) the words " and not otherwise ", and subsection (5). In section 24(3)(*b*) the words from " as a resident " to " versa, or ". In section 25, in subsection (4) the words " for a service voter " and the words " for an elector ", and in subsection (6) the words " In relation to service voters and their proxies ". Section 38. In section 39, in subsection (2) (*c*) the words " as a resident ", subsection (2)(*d*), and in subsection (4) the words " or was not of full age ". In section 45(1)(*c*) the words " or as a non-resident " and the following words. Section 46(4) proviso. Section 48(1) proviso. Section 57(2). In section 65(2) in paragraph (*a*) the words " polling agents ", and in paragraph (i) of the proviso the words " polling agent ". In section 70, in subsection (1) and in subsection (2), the words " before a justice of the peace ". Section 97. Section 115(2) from the words " or holds " onwards. In section 159(5) the words " by the Director of Public Prosecutions or his assistant ", and the words from " For the purposes " onwards. In section 165(3) the words " thirty-eight ". In Schedule 2, in the parliamentary elections rules, in rule 1 the note at the end of the time-table; rule 7(4); rule 24; in rule 38(1)(*a*) the words " either embossed or perforated "; and rule 55(2).

E

SCH. 3

Chapter	Short Title	Extent of Repeal
12, 13 & 14 Geo. 6. c. 68 —*cont.*	The Representation of the People Act 1949—*cont.*	In Schedule 2, in the local elections rules, in rule 7(1) proviso the words " in the case of an election to fill a casual vacancy "; rule 19(2) (*e*); and rule 20. In Schedule 3, in rule 7, the words " paragraph 7 of rule 5, or "; rule 18; in rule 31(1)(*a*) the words " either embossed or perforated "; and rule 46(2). In Schedule 4, paragraph 5(2) from the beginning of paragraph (*a*) to the words " duty, and " in paragraph (*b*).
12, 13 & 14 Geo. 6. c. 86.	The Electoral Registers Act 1949.	Section 2. Schedule 1.
2 & 3 Eliz. 2. c. 8.	The Electoral Registers Act 1953.	Section 1(2) and (3). The Schedule.
4 & 5 Eliz. 2. c. 60.	The Valuation and Rating (Scotland) Act 1956.	Section 35.
7 & 8 Eliz. 2. c. 51.	The Licensing (Scotland) Act 1959.	In section 120, in the definition of " elector " the words " or of occupation of lands and heritages ".
1963 c. 33.	The London Government Act 1963.	In Schedule 3, paragraph 25.
	Act of Parliament of Scotland	
1707 c. 8.	The Election Act 1707.	The words " Elect or ".

Section 26.

SCHEDULE 4

INSERTIONS AUTHORISED IN REPRESENTATION OF THE PEOPLE ACT 1949 IN REVISED EDITION OF STATUTES

Enactment	*Place and manner of insertion*
The Electoral Registers Act 1949 (12, 13 & 14 Geo. 6. c. 86).	
Section 1(2) (as set out in section 1(1) of the Electoral Registers Act 1953).	As section 7A(1), but omitting the words " or, in Northern Ireland, registers of parliamentary electors ".
Section 1(3) and (4) (as so set out).	As section 3(1) and (2).
Section 1(5) and (6) ...	As section 7A(2) and (3).

Enactment	*Place and manner of insertion*
The Local Government Elections Act 1956 (4 & 5 Eliz. 2. c. 43).	
Section 4(1) to (3) (as amended by the Local Government Act 1958).	As section 29(4), (4A) and (4B).
The Local Government Act 1958 (6 & 7 Eliz. 2. c. 55).	
Paragraph 31(1) of Schedule 8.	As an additional paragraph of section 29(3), but omitting the words describing the effect of section 29(3).
The Elections (Welsh Forms) Act 1964 (c. 31).	
Section 1	As section 174A, but substituting for the words " this Act " in subsection (3) the words " this section ".
This Act.	
Section 1(2)	As section 8(3).
Section 1(3)	Both as section 14(2A) (omitting the words " or local government ") and as an additional paragraph in section 25(3) (omitting the words " parliamentary or ").
Section 1(5)	As section 174(1A).
Section 2(1) and (2) ...	As section 10(3A) and (3B).
Section 3(1)	As section 4(2A).
Section 3(2)	As paragraph 8A in Schedule 4, but omitting the words preceding the word " provisions ".
Section 4	As section 2A.
Section 5(1)(*a*) and (*b*) ...	Both as section 12(1)(*f*) and (*g*) and as section 23(1)(*e*) and (*f*).
Section 5(2)	Both as section 12(4A) and as section 23(4A), but beginning with the words " a person who is not registered as a service voter " and omitting the preceding words.
Section 5(3)	As section 13(3A), but omitting the word " accordingly " and the preceding words.
Section 6(3)	Both as section 12(4B) and as section 23(4B), but beginning with the words " a person ".
Section 6(6)	Both as rule 6A in the parliamentary elections rules and as rule 4(1A) in the Scottish local elections rules, but omitting the words " at parliamentary elections " and, in the Scottish local elections rules, substituting for the word " constituency " the words " electoral area ".

SCH. 4

Enactment	*Place and manner of insertion*
Section 6(7)	As rule 4A of the local elections rules, but substituting for the words " subsection (6) above " the words " rule 6A of the parliamentary elections rules ", and omitting the preceding words.
Section 7(1)	As section 7(2A).
Section 7(2)	As section 9(3).
Section 8(4)	As section 70(2A).
Section 9(1) and (2) ...	As section 80A.
Section 9(6)	As section 167(5A), but substituting for the words " subsection (1) above " the words " section 80A".
Section 11(1)	As section 55(4A).
Section 11(3)	As section 57(2).
Section 11(5)	Both as rule 31(7A) in the parliamentary elections rules and as rule 24(7A) in the local elections rules in Schedule 3, but omitting in each case any reference to any other set of rules.
Section 13(1) to (3) ...	Both as rule 61 (in a new Part VI) in the parliamentary elections rules, but omitting in subsection (1)(*a*) the words " at a parliamentary election " and subsection (1)(*b*): and as rule 52A (in Part VI) in the local elections rules in Schedule 2 and rule 55A (in a new Part VII) in the local elections rules in Schedule 3, but omitting subsection (1)(*a*) and in subsection (1)(*b*) the words " at a local government election ".
Section 19(1) and (2) ...	As section 38.
Section 19(3)	As an additional paragraph in section 165(3), but substituting for the words " Subsection (1) " the words " Section 38 ".
Section 20	As section 20(4A).
In Part II of Schedule 1—	
paragraph 5(1)(*a*) and (*b*).	As rule 7(1A) and rule 12(4) respectively in the parliamentary elections rules.
paragraph 6(1)(*a*) ...	As rule 6(2A) in the local elections rules.
paragraph 11... ...	Both as rule 45(2A) in the parliamentary elections rules and as rule 38(2A) in the local elections rules in Schedule 3.

Enactment	*Place and manner of insertion*
paragraph 12(1) ...	Both as rule 23(3) in the parliamentary elections rules, and as rule 19(4) in the local elections rules in Schedule 2, and as rule 17(4) in the local elections rules in Schedule 3, but omitting in the parliamentary elections rules the words " if any " and the proviso, and in the local elections rules in Schedule 2 the words " or town clerk ", and in the rules in Schedule 3 the words " mayor or ".

Customs Duties (Dumping and Subsidies) Act 1969

1969 CHAPTER 16

An Act to consolidate the Customs Duties (Dumping and Subsidies) Acts 1957 and 1968 and related enactments. [24th April 1969]

BE IT ENACTED by the Queen's most Excellent Majesty, by and with the advice and consent of the Lords Spiritual and Temporal, and Commons, in this present Parliament assembled, and by the authority of the same, as follows:—

Principal provisions as to anti-dumping duties

Charge of anti-dumping duties.

1.—(1) Where it appears to the Board of Trade—

(*a*) that goods of any description are being or have been imported into the United Kingdom in circumstances in which they are under the provisions of this Act to be regarded as having been dumped ; and

(*b*) that, having regard to all the circumstances, it would be in the national interest ;

they may exercise in such manner as they think necessary to meet the dumping the power described in subsection (3) below, subject however to the restriction imposed by subsection (3)(*b*) on the exercise of the power as regards treaty countries.

(2) For the purposes of this Act imported goods shall be regarded as having been dumped—

(*a*) if the export price from the country of origin is less than the fair market price there (whether the country of exportation is the same or a different country) ; or

(*b*) if the export price from the country of exportation (if a different country) is less than the fair market price there.

(3) The power which the Board of Trade may exercise where this subsection applies is a power by order to impose on goods of a description specified in the order a duty of customs chargeable on the importation of the goods into the United Kingdom at a rate specified in the order; but an order made in the exercise of the power—

(*a*) shall include in the matters by reference to which the description of goods is framed either the country of origin or the country of exportation; and

(*b*) shall not impose a duty on any goods as goods of which the country of origin, or country of exportation, is a treaty country (that is to say, a country in relation to which Her Majesty's Government in the United Kingdom is for the time being bound under the provisions of the General Agreement on Tariffs and Trade concluded at Geneva in the year 1947), unless the Board of Trade are satisfied that the case is within subsection (4) below.

(4) For a case to be within this subsection the effect of the dumping must be such as either—

(*a*) to cause or threaten material injury to an established industry in the United Kingdom, or materially retard the establishment of an industry in the United Kingdom; or

(*b*) to cause or threaten material injury to an established industry in another treaty country which is the country of origin of any like goods (that is, any identical or comparable goods) imported into the United Kingdom.

(5) Subject to subsection (3)(*a*) above, an order made in the exercise of the power described in that subsection may include such provisions with respect to the description of the goods chargeable with duty and with respect to the cases in which duty is chargeable as may appear to the Board of Trade to be required for the purposes of this Act, including provisions limiting the description of the goods by reference to the particular persons or organisations by whom the goods were produced or who were concerned with the production of the goods in some specified manner.

Relief by reference to actual margin of dumping.

2.—(1) Where it appears to the Board of Trade that relief under this section should be available as respects a duty imposed by an order under section 1 above they may, if they think fit, by the same or another order apply the provisions of this section in relation to the duty.

(2) Where this section applies in relation to any duty, the importer of any goods chargeable with the duty as being goods of which a specified country is the country of origin or, as the

case may be, country of exportation may apply to the Board of Trade for relief from the duty on those goods.

(3) If on an application so made the Board of Trade are satisfied that the export price of the goods from that country with the amount of the duty added to it exceeds the fair market price of the goods in that country, the Board shall notify the Commissioners of Customs and Excise of the amount of the excess, and the Commissioners shall remit or repay the duty up to that amount.

(4) An application under this section as respects any goods shall not be made more than six months after the duty has been paid on the goods, and in connection with any such application the applicant shall furnish such information and evidence as the Board of Trade may require from him for ascertaining the export price or fair market price in the country in question.

(5) If a person for the purposes of an application under this section—

(*a*) makes any statement which is false in a material particular; or

(*b*) produces any account, estimate, return or other document which is false in a material particular;

the amount of any duty remitted or repaid under this section on the application shall be recoverable as a debt due to the Crown; and if the statement was made or the document was produced knowingly or recklessly, that person shall be liable on summary conviction to imprisonment for a term not exceeding three months or to a fine not exceeding £100 or to both.

Ascertainment of export price from country of origin (basic rules).

3.—(1) In relation to goods imported into the United Kingdom the export price from the country of origin, if the goods were wholly produced in that country, shall for the purposes of this Act be determined in accordance with subsection (2) or (3) below.

(2) If goods are imported under a contract of sale which is a sale in the open market between buyer and seller independent of each other, and the Board of Trade are satisfied as to that fact, as to the price on that sale and as to such other facts as are material for this purpose, the export price shall be the price on that sale subject to a deduction for the cost of insurance and freight from the port or place of exportation in the country to the port or place of importation, and for any other costs, charges or expenses incurred in respect of the goods after they left the port or place of exportation, except so far as any such costs, charges or expenses have to be met separately by the purchaser.

(3) If subsection (2) above does not apply, the Board of Trade shall determine the export price by reference to such sale of the goods (or of any goods in which they were incorporated) as the Board may select with such adjustments as may appear to the Board to be proper.

(4) In referring to a sale in the open market between buyer and seller independent of each other subsection (2) above presupposes—

(*a*) that the price is the sole consideration; and

(*b*) that the price made is not influenced by any commercial, financial or other relationship, whether by contract or otherwise, between the seller or any person associated in business with him and the buyer or any person associated in business with him (other than the relationship created by the sale of the goods in question); and

(*c*) that no part of the proceeds of the subsequent resale, use or disposal of the goods will accrue either directly or indirectly to the seller or any person associated in business with him.

Two persons shall for this purpose be deemed to be associated in business with one another if, whether directly or indirectly, either of them has any interest in the business or property of the other, or both have a common interest in any business or property, or some third person has an interest in the business or property of both of them.

Ascertainment of fair market price in country of origin (basic rules).

4.—(1) For the purposes of this Act relating to dumping the fair market price of goods in the country of origin, if the goods were wholly produced in that country, shall be determined as follows.

(2) Subject to subsections (3) and (4) below, the fair market price shall be taken to be the price at which goods of the description in question (that is to say, any identical or comparable goods) are being sold in the ordinary course of trade in the country for consumption or use there, but subject to any necessary adjustments, whether for differences in conditions and terms of sale, for differences in taxation or otherwise, which may be required to ensure comparability.

(3) Subject to subsection (4) below, if it appears to the Board of Trade that goods of that description are not being sold in the country, or not in such circumstances that the fair market price can be determined in accordance with subsection (2) above, the fair market price shall be determined by the Board either—

(*a*) by reference to any price obtained for goods of that description when exported from that country, with adjustments made to ensure comparability; or (*b*) if the Board think fit, by reference to the cost or estimated cost of production of the goods the dumping of which is in question, with such additions in respect of administrative, selling or other costs and profit as may appear to the Board of Trade to be proper.

The price by reference to which a determination is made under paragraph (*a*) above may be the highest admissible price, but should be a representative price.

(4) If it appears to the Board of Trade that the system of trading in the country is such, as a result of government monopoly and control, that the fair market price there cannot appropriately be determined in accordance either with subsection (2) or with subsection (3) above, then there shall be taken as representing the fair market price such price as the Board may determine by reference to any price obtained for goods of that description when exported to the United Kingdom from another country, with adjustments made to ensure comparability.

(5) References in this section to adjustments required or made to ensure comparability are references to adjustments required or made to ensure that the comparison between the fair market price and the export price is effectively a comparison between the prices on two similar sales.

(6) No account shall be taken under this section of any application of restrictions or charges on the exportation of materials from any country so as to favour producers in that country who use those materials in goods produced by them.

Meaning of " country of origin ", and adjustments of rules as to export price and fair market price.

5.—(1) For the purposes of this Act " country of origin ", in relation to goods which were wholly produced in any country, means that country.

(2) For goods not wholly produced in one country, a country shall be regarded for the purposes of this Act as their country of origin—

(*a*) if some stage in the production of the goods was carried out in that country and the cost of carrying out such stages, if any, in the production of the goods as were carried out after those goods last left that country (but before the importation of the goods into the United Kingdom) was less than 25 per cent. of the cost of production of the goods as so imported ; or

(*b*) if some stage in the production of any components or materials incorporated in the goods was carried out in that country and the cost of carrying out such stages in production as were carried out after those components or materials last left that country to convert those components or materials into the goods as imported into the United Kingdom was less than 25 per cent. of the cost of production of the goods as so imported;

and any reference in this Act to the country of origin shall be taken, in a case where there are two or more countries which answer to that description, as a reference to any of those countries.

(3) Where a country is to be regarded under subsection (2) above as the country of origin of any goods, and some stage in the production of the goods, or of any components or materials incorporated in the goods, was carried out after they last left the country, then the export price of the goods from that country, or their fair market price in it, shall be determined as (in accordance with section 3 or 4 above) the corresponding price is to be determined in the case of goods wholly produced in a country except that—

(*a*) the deductions to be made by the Board of Trade in the price by reference to which the export price from that country is to be ascertained shall include a deduction for the cost of carrying out any such stage in the production of the goods and in the production of any components or materials incorporated in the goods; and

(*b*) the fair market price in that country shall be the fair market price of those goods or, as the case may be, of those components or materials in the state in which they left the country.

Meaning of "country of exportation," and export price and fair market price there.

6.—(1) For the purposes of this Act " country of exportation ", in relation to any goods, means the country from which they were consigned to the United Kingdom; and where goods, in the course of consignment from any country to the United Kingdom, pass through or are transhipped in any third country, that third country shall not on that account be regarded for purposes of this Act as the country of exportation.

(2) The export price of goods from a country as the country of exportation, or the fair market price of goods in a country as the country of exportation, shall be determined as (in accordance with section 3 or 4 above) the corresponding price from or in the country of origin is to be determined in the case of goods wholly produced in one country.

Principal provisions as to countervailing duties

Charge of, and relief from, duties to offset subsidies.

7.—(1) Where it appears to the Board of Trade—

(*a*) that some government or other authority outside the United Kingdom has been giving a subsidy affecting goods of any description which are being or have been imported into the United Kingdom; and (*b*) that, having regard to all the circumstances, it would be in the national interest;

they may exercise in such manner as they think necessary to meet the giving of the subsidy the power described in section 1(3) above, subject however to the restriction imposed by section 1(3)(*b*) on the exercise of the power as regards treaty countries (the reference in section 1(4) to the effect of the dumping being replaced for this purpose by a reference to the effect of the giving of the subsidy).

(2) References in this Act to giving a subsidy are references to giving, directly or indirectly, a bounty or subsidy on the production or exportation of goods (whether by grant, loan, tax relief or in any other way and whether related directly to the goods themselves, to materials of the goods or to something else), and include—

(*a*) the giving of any special subsidy on the transport of a particular product; and

(*b*) the giving of favourable treatment to producers or exporters in the course of administering any governmental control over the exchange of currencies where such treatment has the effect of assisting a reduction of the prices of goods offered for export;

but do not include the application of restrictions or charges on the exportation of materials from any country so as to favour producers in that country who use those materials in goods produced by them.

(3) Section 2 above may be applied to a duty imposed by an order under this section as it may be applied to a duty imposed by an order under section 1; but, where it is applied by virtue of this subsection, references to the fair market price in a country shall be replaced in it by references to the export price from that country increased by such amount (if any) as may be necessary to offset the effect of the giving of the subsidy.

Provisional and retrospective charges to duty

Power to impose retrospective duties after provisional charge.

8.—(1) Subject to subsection (5) below, an order under section 1 or 7 above may impose a duty on goods of any description for a period before the making of the order if, by a preliminary order made under subsection (2) below and remaining in force, a provisional charge to the duty (or a greater duty) was imposed during that period on goods of that description.

(2) Subject to subsections (4) and (5) below, the Board of Trade may by an order under this subsection (in this Act referred to as a " preliminary order ") impose a provisional charge to duty under section 1 or 7 above on goods of any description if at any time it appears to the Board, on the facts so far before

them, that the conditions of subsection (1)(*a*) of the section as to the dumping or subsidisation of imports into the United Kingdom are fulfilled and that in the circumstances it is expedient to impose such a charge.

(3) A preliminary order, if not previously revoked, shall cease to have effect at the expiration of three months beginning with the date it comes into force, except in so far as it is extended by a further order made within that period, and in so far as it is so extended, shall cease to have effect at the expiration of six months beginning with that date.

(4) Section 1(3)(*a*) and (5) above shall apply to a preliminary order as they apply to orders made in the exercise of the power described in section 1(3).

(5) The powers conferred by this section shall be subject to the following restrictions on their exercise in respect of the dumping or subsidisation of goods of any description as being goods of which the country of origin, or country of exportation, is a treaty country, that is to say:—

(*a*) a preliminary order shall not be made unless the facts so far before the Board of Trade indicate that the effect of the dumping or of the giving of the subsidy is such as to cause or threaten material injury to an established industry in the United Kingdom ; and

(*b*) an order shall not be made imposing a duty retrospectively unless the Board of Trade are satisfied, as regards importations made during or before the period of the provisional charge, that the effect of the dumping or of the giving of the subsidy has been such as to cause material injury to an established industry in the United Kingdom.

Effect of preliminary order.

9.—(1) No duty shall be leviable by virtue only of a provisional charge imposed by a preliminary order ; but, subject to that and to the following provisions of this section, a preliminary order shall, as regards the period for which it is in force, have the same operation as if the charge to duty had not been provisional.

(2) Where any imported goods which are or may be subject to a provisional charge are entered for home use, whether on importation or from warehouse, then notwithstanding anything in subsection (1) above or in the Customs and Excise Act 1952— 1952 c. 44.

(*a*) delivery of the goods without payment of duty shall not be refused by reason of the provisional charge if the importer gives security to the satisfaction of the Commissioners of Customs and Excise for the payment of any duty which may be retrospectively charged on the goods by reference to that provisional charge;

(*b*) security shall be so given where payment of the duty provisionally charged would, if the duty were leviable, be required;

(*c*) where security is given by virtue of this subsection the customs Acts as they apply by virtue of subsection (1) above shall have effect as if the security were one given under section 255 of the Customs and Excise Act 1952 (security for duty not immediately ascertainable).

1952 c. 44.

(3) Without prejudice to the generality of subsection (1) above, the like relief in respect of a provisional charge to duty may be given by way of remission of the charge as if the charge were not provisional (and section 2 above may be applied accordingly); and the amount of any relief given in respect of a provisional charge on any goods shall, if a duty is retrospectively charged on the goods by reference to that provisional charge,—

(*a*) be set off against the amount of the retrospective duty; and

(*b*) be treated as given on account of any corresponding relief from the retrospective duty.

(4) The lapsing of a provisional charge to duty on the revocation or expiration of the preliminary order shall not affect the liability to any penalty, forfeiture or prosecution in respect of things done during the period of the provisional charge.

Miscellaneous provisions as to duties and reliefs from duty

Additional provisions as to charge of duties, and relief at commencement etc. of charge.

10.—(1) Any duty chargeable under this Act on any goods shall be chargeable in addition to any other duty of customs for the time being chargeable thereon and, notwithstanding any other enactment (including, unless the contrary is expressly provided, any future enactment), the charge of duty under this Act shall not affect liability to customs duty chargeable under any other Act or the amount of any such duty.

1957 c. 49.

(2) Section 259 of the Customs and Excise Act 1952 and section 5 of the Finance Act 1957 (which make provision as to duties and drawbacks in respect of dutiable parts or ingredients) shall not have effect in relation to duties under this Act.

(3) A duty under this Act—

(*a*) may be made chargeable by reference to value or to weight or other measure of quantity;

(*b*) may be imposed, varied or removed for any period or periods, whether continuous or not, or without limit of period;

(*c*) may be made chargeable at different rates for different periods.

(4) In connection with the commencement, variation or termination of a duty under this Act, the order relating to the duty may include provisions authorising repayments in respect of duty where it is shown that the prescribed conditions are fulfilled.

(5) In section 3(1) of the Import Duties Act 1958 (which provides that in general import duties are not chargeable on goods chargeable with other customs duties) for the words " subsection (4) of section 2 of the Customs Duties (Dumping and Subsidies) Act 1957 " there shall be substituted the words " subsection (1) of section 10 of the Customs Duties (Dumping and Subsidies) Act 1969 ". 1958 c. 6. 1957 c. 18.

Drawback on exportations from U.K.

11.—(1) The Board of Trade may by order provide for the allowance of drawback in respect of all or any duties under this Act on the exportation of goods in such circumstances and subject to such conditions as they may specify.

(2) The drawback may be in respect of duty paid on the goods or in respect of duty paid on materials used in the manufacture of the goods, and the rate of the drawback may be determined in such manner and by reference to such matters as the Board of Trade may specify.

(3) An order under this section may provide—

(*a*) for drawback in respect of a provisional charge to duty to be allowed by way of remission of the charge as if duty secured were duty paid ; and

(*b*) for drawback of retrospective duty to be allowed on the exportation of goods at any time after the coming into force of the preliminary order by reference to which the duty is charged.

Other reliefs relating to exportations from U.K.

12.—(1) The following enactments providing for relief from import duties chargeable under section 1 of the Import Duties Act 1958, that is to say—

(*a*) section 7 of that Act (which applies where the intention is to re-export the imported goods or goods incorporating them or manufactured or produced from them) ; and

(*b*) section 1 of the Finance Act 1966 (which applies where the relief would conduce to the exportation of other goods) ; 1966 c. 18.

shall apply in relation to duties under this Act as they apply in relation to duties under section 1 of the Import Duties Act 1958.

(2) The reference in subsection (1)(*a*) above to section 7 of the Import Duties Act 1958 is a reference to that section as amended by section 2(1) to (3) of the Finance Act 1965.

1958 c. 6.
1965 c. 25.

(3) Accordingly for section 7(4) of the Import Duties Act 1958 there shall be substituted ;—

> " (4) This section shall apply in relation to duties under the Customs Duties (Dumping and Subsidies) Act 1969 as it applies in relation to import duties " ;

and in section 1(1) of the Finance Act 1966 for the words " the Customs Duties (Dumping and Subsidies) Act 1957 " there shall be substituted the words " the Customs Duties (Dumping and Subsidies) Act 1969 ".

1966 c. 18.
1957 c. 18.

Supplementary

Construction of references to production of goods, and ascertainment of cost of production.

13.—(1) In this Act, references to producing goods include references to growing or manufacturing goods and to the application of any process in the course of producing goods.

(2) The Board of Trade may by regulations prescribe for the purposes of this Act—

(*a*) the costs, charges and expenses to be taken into account in ascertaining costs of production or the cost of any stage in production ;

(*b*) the manner in which cost of production is to be ascertained in cases where different stages are carried out by different persons ;

(*c*) the manner in which the cost of different stages of production is to be ascertained.

(3) The power of the Board of Trade to make regulations under subsection (2) above shall be exercisable by statutory instrument.

Power to require information from importers.

14.—(1) The Commissioners of Customs and Excise may require the importer of any goods to state such facts concerning the goods and their history as the Commissioners may think necessary to determine whether the country of origin is a country specified in an order under this Act or what is the country of exportation.

(2) Where an order under this Act limits the description of goods in respect of which a charge is imposed under this Act or the cases in which it is imposed so that the question whether goods are subject to any and, if so, what charge depends on other matters besides the country of origin or country of exportation, the Commissioners may also require the importer to state such facts as they may think necessary to determine that question so far as regards those other matters.

(3) Where under this section an importer is required to state any facts, the Commissioners may require him to furnish them in such form as they may require with proof of any statements made, except that proof of the country of origin of any goods shall be required in relation to any charge under this Act only if the country of exportation is one to which this subsection is by direction of the Board of Trade to apply for the purpose.

(4) Where under this section an importer is required to state any facts or to furnish proof of any statement, and the required facts are not stated, or the proof is not furnished to the satisfaction of the Commissioners, the country of origin or country of exportation (if the requirement relates to that) or the other facts referred to in subsection (2) above (if the requirement is imposed under that subsection) shall be deemed for the purposes of this Act to be such as the Commissioners may determine.

Parliamentary procedure on orders, and power of revocation etc.

15.—(1) Any power of the Board of Trade to make orders under this Act shall be exercisable by statutory instrument, which in any case not falling within subsection (2) below shall be subject to annulment in pursuance of a resolution of the Commons House of Parliament.

(2) Where an order under section 1 or 7 of this Act imposes or increases any duty, and does not do so only by the total or partial revocation of a previous order so as to annul the suspension of a duty removed for a period or periods by the previous order, the statutory instrument shall be laid before the Commons House of Parliament after being made, and the order shall cease to have effect at the end of twenty-eight days after that on which it is made (but without prejudice to anything previously done under the order or to the making of a new order) unless at some time before the end of those twenty-eight days the order is approved by resolution of that House.

In reckoning for the purposes of this subsection any period of twenty-eight days, no account shall be taken of any time during which Parliament is dissolved or prorogued or during which the Commons House is adjourned for more than four days.

(3) Where an order has the effect of altering the rate of duty on any goods in such a way that the new rate is not directly comparable with the old, it shall not be treated for the purposes of subsection (2) above as increasing the duty on those goods if it declares the opinion of the Board of Trade to be that, in the circumstances existing at the date of the order, the alteration is not calculated to raise the general level of duty on the goods.

(4) Any power of making orders conferred on the Board of Trade by this Act shall include a power to vary or revoke an order made under the power.

Annual report to Parliament.

16.—(1) As soon as may be after the end of each financial year the Board of Trade shall lay before each House of Parliament a report as to the orders (including preliminary orders) under which during that year there has been a charge to duty under this Act, indicating the contents of those orders and their operation in that year in relation to goods which have been imported into the United Kingdom.

(2) The report for any year shall deal also with any retrospective operation in relation to the preceding year of orders made during the year.

Miscellaneous definitions.

17. In this Act—

"country" includes any territory;

"importer" in relation to any goods at any time between their importation and the time when they are delivered out of customs charge, includes any owner or other person for the time being possessed of or beneficially interested in the goods;

"preliminary order" means an order under section 8(2) of this Act;

"treaty country" means a country in relation to which Her Majesty's Government in the United Kingdom is for the time being bound under the provisions of the General Agreement on Tariffs and Trade concluded at Geneva in the year 1947.

Repeal and transitional provisions.

1958 c. 6.

18.—(1) The Customs Duties (Dumping and Subsidies) Acts 1957 and 1968 and section 13(6) of the Import Duties Act 1958 are hereby repealed.

(2) The repeal by this Act of the Customs Duties (Dumping and Subsidies) Acts 1957 and 1968 shall not invalidate any order or regulations made or other thing done under or in connection with those Acts; and as from the commencement of this Act, this Act and any other relevant enactment shall have the like effect in relation to any orders or regulations made or other things done under or in connection with those Acts as it would have in relation to a like thing done under or in connection with this Act.

(3) Without prejudice to subsection (2) above so much of any document as refers expressly or by implication to any enactment repealed by this Act shall, if and so far as the context

permits, be construed as referring to this Act or the corresponding enactment therein.

(4) Nothing in subsection (2) or (3) above shall be taken to exclude the general application to this Act of section 38 of the Interpretation Act 1889 (which relates to repeals). 1889 c. 63.

Short title, extent and commencement.

19.—(1) This Act may be cited as the Customs Duties (Dumping and Subsidies) Act 1969.

(2) It is hereby declared that this Act extends to Northern Ireland.

(3) This Act shall come into force at the beginning of May 1969.

Betting, Gaming and Lotteries (Amendment) Act 1969

1969 CHAPTER 17

An Act to amend the provisions of the Betting, Gaming and Lotteries Act 1963 in relation to the maximum percentage which may be deducted by the operator from amounts staked on the totalisator.

[16th May 1969]

BE IT ENACTED by the Queen's most Excellent Majesty, by and with the advice and consent of the Lords Spiritual and Temporal, and Commons, in this present Parliament assembled, and by the authority of the same, as follows:—

Amendment of Act of 1963 c. 2.

1. The Betting, Gaming and Lotteries Act 1963 shall have effect as if in paragraph 3(*a*) of Schedule 5, after the words " six per cent " there were inserted the words " or such other percentage as may be specified in an order made by the Secretary of State by statutory instrument " and as if at the end of paragraph 3 of that Schedule there were inserted the following:—

" Any power conferred by this paragraph to make an order shall include power to vary or revoke the order by subsequent order."

Short title and citation.

2. This Act may be cited as the Betting, Gaming and Lotteries (Amendment) Act 1969 and this Act and the Betting, Gaming and Lotteries Act 1963 may be cited together as the Betting, Gaming and Lotteries Acts 1963 and 1969.

Nuclear Installations Act 1969

1969 CHAPTER 18

An Act to make in the Nuclear Installations Act 1965 certain amendments necessary to bring that Act into conformity with international agreements.

[16th May 1969]

BE IT ENACTED by the Queen's most Excellent Majesty, by and with the advice and consent of the Lords Spiritual and Temporal, and Commons, in this present Parliament assembled, and by the authority of the same, as follows:—

Restriction of liability for certain damage. 1965 c. 57.

1. In the Nuclear Installations Act 1965 (hereafter in this Act referred to as " the principal Act "), in section 12 (which relates to the right to compensation in respect of certain injury or damage) after subsection (3) there shall be inserted the following subsection:—

" (3A) Subject to subsection (4) of this section, where damage to any property has been caused which was not caused in breach of a duty imposed by section 7, 8, 9 or 10 of this Act but which would have been caused in breach of such a duty if in subsection (1)(*a*) or (*b*) of the said section 7 the words ' other than the licensee ' or in subsection (1) of the said section 10 the words ' other than that operator ' had not been enacted, no liability which, apart from this subsection, would have been incurred by any person in respect of that damage shall be so incurred except—

(*a*) in pursuance of an agreement to incur liability in respect of such damage entered into in writing before the occurrence of the damage; or

(*b*) where the damage was caused by an act or omission of that person done with intent to cause injury or damage ";

and in subsection (4) of the said section 12 (which provides that nothing in subsection (1)(*b*) of that section shall affect certain enactments giving effect to international agreements with respect to the carriage of goods) after the words " subsection (1)(*b*) " there shall be inserted the words " or in subsection (3A) ".

Adjustment of certain amounts.

2.—(1) In sections 17(3)(*b*)(ii) and 21(1) of the principal Act (which relate to the amount available for meeting certain claims under that Act) for the words " one and three-quarter million pounds " there shall in each case be substituted the words " £2,100,000 ".

(2) In subsections (1) and (4) of section 18 of the principal Act (which relate to the amount of compensation for which cover is to be provided) for the words " forty-three million pounds " wherever those words occur there shall be substituted the words " £50 million ".

Extension of compensation in certain cases.

3. In section 13(5)(*b*) of the principal Act (under which, where in the case of an occurrence which constitutes a breach of a duty imposed by section 7, 8, 9 or 10 of that Act a person other than the person subject to that duty makes any payment in respect of injury or damage caused by that occurrence, the person making the payment is entitled to make a claim for compensation under that Act if the occurrence took place within the territorial limits of a country which is not a relevant territory within the meaning of that Act and certain other conditions are satisfied), after the words " took place " there shall be inserted the words " or the injury or damage was incurred ".

Expenses.

4. There shall be paid out of moneys provided by Parliament any increase attributable to any of the provisions of this Act in the sums so payable under the principal Act.

Citation.

5.—(1) This Act may be cited as the Nuclear Installations Act 1969.

1965 c. 57.

(2) The Nuclear Installations Act 1965 and this Act may be cited together as the Nuclear Installations Acts 1965 and 1969.

Decimal Currency Act 1969

1969 CHAPTER 19

An Act to make further provision in connection with the introduction of a decimal currency, and to impose restrictions on the melting or breaking of metal coins. [16th May 1969]

BE IT ENACTED by the Queen's most Excellent Majesty, by and with the advice and consent of the Lords Spiritual and Temporal, and Commons, in this present Parliament assembled, and by the authority of the same, as follows:—

1.—(1) Coins made by the Mint in accordance with section 2 of the Decimal Currency Act 1967 or in accordance with the Coinage Acts 1870 to 1946 and not called in by proclamation under paragraph (5) of section 11 of the Coinage Act 1870 shall be legal tender as follows, that is to say— Legal tender. 1967 c. 47. 1870 c. 10.

(*a*) coins of cupro-nickel or silver of denominations of more than ten new pence or two shillings, for payment of any amount not exceeding ten pounds;

(*b*) coins of cupro-nickel or silver of denominations of not more than ten new pence or two shillings, for payment of any amount not exceeding five pounds;

(*c*) coins of bronze, for payment of any amount not exceeding twenty new pence or four shillings.

(2) In the foregoing subsection " coins of bronze " includes threepences of mixed metal.

(3) Subject to subsection (6) of this section and to any direction given by virtue of section 15(5) of this Act, coins of the old currency other than gold coins shall not be legal tender after the end of the transitional period.

(4) For the purpose of being used for any payment in accordance with the foregoing provisions of this section a coin of either the old or the new currency may be treated as being a current coin of the other currency of equal value.

1870 c. 10. 1967 c. 47.

(5) The powers exercisable by proclamation by virtue of section 11 of the Coinage Act 1870 shall include power to direct that any coins of the new currency made by the Mint in accordance with section 2 of the Decimal Currency Act 1967 other than coins of cupro-nickel, silver or bronze shall be current and be legal tender for payment of any amount not exceeding such amount (not greater than ten pounds) as may be specified in the proclamation.

(6) For the purposes of this section silver coins of the Queen's Maundy money made in accordance with section 3 of the Coinage Act 1870 shall be treated as made in accordance with section 2 of the Decimal Currency Act 1967 and, if issued before the appointed day, shall be treated as denominated in the same number of new pence as the number of pence in which they were denominated.

Bills of exchange and promissory notes.

2.—(1) A bill of exchange or promissory note drawn or made on or after the appointed day shall be invalid if the sum payable is an amount of money wholly or partly in shillings or pence.

(2) A bill of exchange or promissory note for an amount wholly or partly in shillings or pence dated 15th February 1971 or later shall be deemed to have been drawn or made before 15th February 1971 if it bears a certificate in writing by a banker that it was so drawn or made.

Conversion of references to shillings and pence in certain instruments.

3.—(1) On and after the appointed day any reference to an amount of money in the old currency contained in an instrument to which this section applies shall, in so far as it refers to an amount in shillings or pence, be read as referring to the corresponding amount in the new currency calculated in accordance with the provisions of Schedule 1 to this Act.

(2) If a reference to an amount of money in the old currency contained in an instrument to which this section applies is altered so as to make it read as it would otherwise fall to be read in accordance with subsection (1) of this section, the alteration shall not affect the validity of the instrument and, in the case of a bill of exchange or promissory note, shall not be treated as a material alteration for the purposes of section 64 of the Bills of Exchange Act 1882.

1882 c. 61.

(3) This section applies to instruments of any of the following descriptions drawn, made or issued before the appointed day, namely—

(a) cheques and other instruments to which section 4 of the Cheques Act 1957 applies; 1957 c. 36.

(b) bills of exchange other than cheques;

(c) promissory notes;

(d) money orders and postal orders;

(e) any warrant issued by or on behalf of the Director of Savings for the payment of a sum of money;

(f) any document issued under the authority of the Secretary of State for Social Services or the Ministry of Health and Social Services for Northern Ireland which is intended to enable a person to obtain payment of the sum mentioned in the document but is not a bill of exchange;

(g) any document not mentioned in the foregoing paragraphs which is intended to enable a person to obtain through a banker payment of any sum mentioned in the document.

Conversion of bank balances.

4.—(1) Where the amount of the balance standing to the credit or debit of an account at a bank on or after the appointed day is not a whole number of pounds, so much of that amount as is in shillings or pence may be treated as the corresponding amount in the new currency calculated in accordance with the provisions of Schedule 1 to this Act.

(2) In this section " bank " includes the National Savings Bank and any savings bank as defined in section 7(6) of the Payment of Wages Act 1960. 1960 c. 37.

Payment of certain periodical payments.

5.—(1) This section applies to any amount of money in the old currency payable on or after the appointed day as one of a series of payments of the same amount payable periodically, whether pursuant to an instrument or otherwise, not being an amount mentioned in subsection (3) of this section.

(2) Subject to the provisions of this Act, where an amount of money to which this section applies is not a whole number of pounds, so much of it as is in shillings or pence may be paid by paying the corresponding amount in the new currency calculated in accordance with the provisions of Schedule 1 to this Act.

(3) This section does not apply to—

(a) an amount payable to an employee or the holder of any office by way of wages, salary or other remuneration; or (*b*) the amount of any payment to which section 6 of this Act applies.

Payments under friendly society and industrial assurance company contracts.

6.—(1) This section applies to all payments payable to or by a registered friendly society or industrial assurance company under any friendly society or industrial assurance company contract made before the appointed day.

(2) The appropriate authority may make regulations with respect to the methods to be applied for the purpose of determining the amounts in the new currency payable in respect of payments to which this section applies that fall due on or after the appointed day.

(3) Without prejudice to the generality of subsection (2) of this section, regulations under that subsection may, subject to subsection (4) of this section, authorise—

(*a*) the adoption by registered friendly societies and industrial assurance companies of any prescribed scheme for securing that under contracts to which the scheme applies no amount other than a new halfpenny or a multiple thereof will be payable in respect of any payment to which this section applies that falls due as aforesaid ; or

(*b*) the adoption by any such society or company of any special scheme for that purpose which may, in such circumstances as may be prescribed, be approved by the appropriate authority.

(4) A scheme prescribed or approved in pursuance of subsection (3) of this section may include provision for securing that where any payments that are payable to the society or company under a friendly society or industrial assurance company contract to which the scheme applies are increased by virtue of the scheme, any benefits payable by the society or company under that contract which are referable to those payments are appropriately increased ; but in relation to any scheme so prescribed that includes such provision, provision shall be made by regulations under subsection (2) of this section—

(*a*) for securing that any person by whom any payments so increased are payable will, if he so requests, be notified of any corresponding increase in any such benefits ; and

(*b*) for affording to any such person who considers that the increase in the benefits is not fair in relation to the increase in the payments an opportunity of appealing to the appropriate authority ; and

(*c*) for enabling the appropriate authority on any such appeal to direct the society or company concerned to effect in the benefits to which the appeal relates and the like benefits payable under other like contracts an increase of such amount as may be specified in the direction instead of the increase complained of.

(5) Regulations made under subsection (2) of this section may provide for the making of alterations in the rules of registered friendly societies in connection with the adoption of schemes prescribed or approved in pursuance of subsection (3) of this section.

(6) The appropriate authority may make regulations for securing that, if at any time before the appointed day the half-penny ceases to be legal tender, any payment payable to the society or company under a friendly society or industrial assurance company contract which is one of a series of payments payable periodically thereunder of an amount which, apart from the regulations, would be or include a halfpenny, shall be reduced or increased by a halfpenny in such a way that successive payments in the series are reduced and increased alternately.

(7) Regulations made under subsection (2) or subsection (6) of this section may—

(*a*) make different provision for payments payable at different intervals, for payments payable under different classes of contracts and for other different circumstances; and

(*b*) contain such transitional, incidental and supplementary provisions as the appropriate authority thinks necessary or expedient for the purpose of the regulations.

(8) Any regulations under this section shall be made by statutory instrument, which shall be subject to annulment in pursuance of a resolution of either House of Parliament.

(9) The following expressions, where used in this or the next following section, have the following meanings respectively, that is to say—

" the appropriate authority "—

(*a*) in relation to payments payable under an industrial assurance company contract or under a friendly society contract made by a collecting society, means the Industrial Assurance Commissioner;

(*b*) in relation to payments payable under any other friendly society contract, means the Chief Registrar of Friendly Societies;

" friendly society contract " means a contract made by a registered friendly society with a member of the society in the course of its business in Great Britain, whether contained in the rules of the society or not;

"industrial assurance company", "industrial assurance business" and "collecting society" have the meanings assigned by section 1 of the Industrial Assurance Act 1923;

1923 c. 8.

"industrial assurance company contract" means a contract of assurance made by an industrial assurance company in the course of its industrial assurance business in Great Britain;

"prescribed" means prescribed by regulations made under subsection (2) of this section;

"registered friendly society" or "society" means a friendly society registered in any part of the United Kingdom under the Friendly Societies Act 1896 or a branch so registered under that Act of a friendly society so registered.

1896 c. 25.

1946 c. 36. (10) The Statutory Instruments Act 1946 shall apply to any power to make statutory instruments conferred by this section as if the Industrial Assurance Commissioner and the Chief Registrar of Friendly Societies were Ministers of the Crown.

(11) In the application of this section to Northern Ireland—

(*a*) for subsection (8) there shall be substituted—

"(8) Any regulations under this section shall be subject to negative resolution within the meaning of section 41(6) of the Interpretation Act (Northern Ireland) 1954.";

1954 c. 33 (N.I.).

(*b*) in subsection (9)—

(i) for the references to the Industrial Assurance Commissioner and the Chief Registrar of Friendly Societies there shall be substituted references to the Ministry of Commerce for Northern Ireland;

(ii) for the references to Great Britain there shall be substituted references to Northern Ireland; and

(iii) for the reference to the Industrial Assurance Act 1923 there shall be substituted a reference to the Industrial Assurance Act (Northern Ireland) 1924;

1924 c. 21 (N.I.).

(*c*) subsection (10) shall be omitted.

Provisions supplementary to s. 6.

1966 c. 18.

7.—(1) In applying the limits imposed by paragraph 5 of Schedule 8 to the Finance Act 1966 (limits on amounts which a member, or person claiming through a member, of a registered friendly society is entitled to receive from any one or more such societies), any increase in any benefit under a friendly society contract resulting from the adoption of a scheme prescribed or approved in pursuance of subsection (3) of the last foregoing section shall be disregarded.

(2) For the purposes of subsection (2) of section 2 of the Industrial Assurance and Friendly Societies Act 1948 (power to insure life of parent or grandparent for not more than thirty pounds) there shall be excluded so much of any sum insured to be paid, or paid, on the death of any one of a person's parents or grandparents as represents any increase in any benefit payable by the society or company under a friendly society or industrial assurance company contract resulting from the adoption of a scheme prescribed or approved as aforesaid. 1948 c. 39.

(3) Where a nomination made, whether before or after the appointed day, under section 56 of the Friendly Societies Act 1896 (which enables members of certain registered societies to dispose of sums payable on their death by nomination) does not specify the maximum sum of money which is to be payable by virtue of the nomination, and the sum to which the nomination relates exceeds five hundred pounds but would not exceed that amount if any such increase as is mentioned in subsection (1) of this section were disregarded, the nomination shall not be invalidated by reason only of the excess, and the sum payable to the nominee under section 57 of that Act shall include the excess. 1896 c. 25.

(4) Where at the time of his death a member of a registered friendly society is entitled from the funds thereof to a sum which exceeds five hundred pounds but would not exceed that amount if any such increase as is mentioned in subsection (1) of this section were disregarded, the power of distribution on death conferred on the society by subsection (1) of section 58 of the Friendly Societies Act 1896 shall apply to the whole of that sum, and for the purposes of subsection (2) of that section the whole of that sum shall be taken to be the sum which he might have nominated.

(5) The power of the Industrial Assurance Commissioner to make regulations under subsection (2) of section 8 of the Industrial Assurance and Friendly Societies Act 1948 shall, without prejudice to the generality of that subsection, include power by any such regulations—

(*a*) to provide for the insertion in premium receipt books provided under that section of statements approved by him explaining the effect of any regulations made under the last foregoing section;

(*b*) to prescribe the information to be entered in such books for the purpose of explaining the effect of the adoption by a collecting society or industrial assurance company of a scheme prescribed or approved in pursuance of subsection (3) of the last foregoing section.

(6) In the application of this section to Northern Ireland—

1948 c. 39.

1948 c. 22 (N.I.).

(*a*) for the references to the Industrial Assurance and Friendly Societies Act 1948 there shall be substituted references to the Industrial Assurance and Friendly Societies Act (Northern Ireland) 1948; and

(*b*) for the references to the Industrial Assurance Commissioner in subsection (5) there shall be substituted references to the Ministry of Commerce for Northern Ireland.

Registered stock transferable in multiples of one penny.

8.—(1) Any registered stock which immediately before the appointed day is transferable in multiples of one penny shall on and after the appointed day be transferable instead in multiples of one new penny except in so far as, in the exercise of any power in that behalf, other provision is or has been made as to the amounts in which that stock is to be transferable as from that or any later day.

(2) In any prospectus or other document issued before the appointed day that sets out the terms on which any such registered stock is to be issued or held, any reference to one penny as the amount in multiples of which that stock is to be transferable shall on and after that day be read as a reference to one new penny.

(3) Where the amount of the balance of any such registered stock standing in the name of any person immediately before the appointed day in an account in the register is not a whole number of pounds, so much of that amount as is in shillings or pence shall on and after that day be treated as the corresponding amount in the new currency calculated in accordance with the provisions of Schedule 1 to this Act.

(4) In this section " registered stock " includes inscribed stock, and " the register ", in relation to any registered stock, means any register or book in which that stock is registered or inscribed.

Payments after end of transitional period.

9. Where an amount of money in the old currency which is not a whole number of pounds falls to be paid after the end of the transitional period, the amount payable in respect of so much of it as is in shillings or pence shall be the corresponding amount in the new currency calculated in accordance with the provisions of Schedule 1 to this Act.

10.—(1) Subject to the provisions of this section and of any order made under section 11 of this Act, where an enactment or subordinate instrument passed or made before the appointed day contains a reference to an amount of money in the old currency which is not a whole number of pounds, that reference shall, in so far as it refers to an amount in shillings or pence, be read on and after that day as referring to the equivalent of that amount in the new currency.

Amendment of references to shillings and pence in enactments and subordinate instruments.

(2) Subsection (1) of this section—

(*a*) does not apply to any reference contained in this Act or any instrument made thereunder or in any other enactment or subordinate instrument relating to coinage or currency, whenever passed or made ; and

(*b*) in the case of an enactment or subordinate instrument passed or made after the passing of the Decimal Currency Act 1967 does not apply if a contrary intention appears.

1967 c. 47.

(3) On and after the appointed day the enactments mentioned in Schedule 2 to this Act (which contain references to amounts of money in the old currency of which the equivalent in the new currency is neither a new penny nor a multiple thereof) shall have effect subject to the amendments provided for by that Schedule.

(4) Where the expenses of any body established by a local instrument fall to be defrayed out of a common fund (however described) to which under any local instrument two or more authorities may be required to contribute in proportions determined by reference to the estimated or actual product of a rate of a penny in the pound, then in any local instrument that provides (in whatever terms) for the fixing or subsequent adjustment of the contributions of those authorities, references to the estimated or actual product of such a rate shall, in relation to contributions of those authorities for any period beginning after 31st March 1971, be read as references to the estimated or actual product of a rate of a new penny in the pound.

(5) In this section " local instrument " means a local Act, any instrument made under a local Act, or any instrument of a local nature made under a public Act.

11.—(1) Where an enactment or subordinate instrument passed or made before the appointed day contains a reference to an amount of money in the old currency which is not a whole number of pounds, the Treasury, or any Minister of the Crown with the consent of the Treasury, may by order—

Supplementary power to amend enactments etc. referring to shillings and pence.

(*a*) if the equivalent of that amount in the new currency is not a new penny or a multiple thereof, substitute for that reference a reference to such amount in the new currency as in the opinion of the authority making the order is the appropriate multiple of a new halfpenny (or if the case so requires a reference to a new halfpenny);

(*b*) make such other amendment in that enactment or instrument as in the opinion of that authority is appropriate for securing either that any amount payable thereunder will be a new halfpenny or a multiple thereof or that any amount payable thereunder will be a new penny or a multiple thereof;

(*c*) if that reference is part of a rate, percentage, proportion, formula or other basis of calculation, make such amendment in the enactment or instrument as in the opinion of that authority is appropriate for securing that the basis of calculation is expressed in the new currency and in convenient terms.

(2) An order under this section—

(*a*) may include such consequential, supplementary or transitional provisions as the authority making the order thinks fit; and

(*b*) may be revoked or varied by a subsequent order.

(3) An order under this section shall not come into operation before the appointed day.

(4) No order altering the rate of any tax shall be made under this section.

(5) Any order under this section shall be made by statutory instrument, which shall be subject to annulment in pursuance of a resolution of either House of Parliament.

(6) The amendment of any provision by an order under this section shall not prejudice any power to amend or vary that provision conferred by any other enactment.

(7) In this section "Minister of the Crown" includes the Board of Trade.

(8) In the application of this section to Northern Ireland—

(*a*) for any reference to the Treasury or to any Minister of the Crown there shall, in relation to any enactment which the Parliament of Northern Ireland has power to amend or any subordinate instrument made under such an enactment, be substituted respectively a reference to the Ministry of Finance for Northern Ireland or to any other Ministry of Northern Ireland; and (*b*) in relation to an order made by the Ministry of Finance for Northern Ireland or any other Ministry of Northern Ireland with its consent, for subsection (5) there shall be substituted—

"(5) Any order under this section shall be subject to negative resolution within the meaning of section 41(6) of the Interpretation Act (Northern Ireland) 1954." 1954 c. 33 (N.I.).

Modification of forms.

12.—(1) Where any form set out in an enactment or subordinate instrument passed or made before the appointed day is designed to accommodate references to sums of money wholly or partly in shillings or pence, the form may be used with such modifications as are necessary to enable it to accommodate references to sums of money wholly or partly in new pence.

(2) The foregoing subsection is without prejudice to any other provision authorising the modification of any such form.

Special modifications of Bills of Exchange Act 1882.

13.—(1) The following days, namely 11th, 12th and 13th February 1971, shall be non-business days for the purposes of the Bills of Exchange Act 1882; but on those days— 1882 c. 61.

(*a*) a cheque or other instrument to which section 4 of the Cheques Act 1957 applies may be presented by a banker (whether or not he is the person on whom it is drawn) to a banker for payment; and 1957 c. 36.

(*b*) a banker to whom such a cheque or other instrument has at any time been so presented for payment may pay it and may debit the account of his customer with the amount thereof,

as if those days were business days.

(2) Notwithstanding anything in section 14 of the Bills of Exchange Act 1882, a bill of exchange or promissory note—

(*a*) shall be due and payable on 10th February 1971 if the last day of grace for it under that section falls on 11th or 12th February 1971; and

(*b*) shall be due and payable on 15th February 1971 if that last day of grace falls on 13th or 14th February 1971.

Restrictions on melting or breaking of metal coins.

14.—(1) No person shall, except under the authority of a licence granted by the Treasury, melt down or break up any metal coin which is for the time being current in the United Kingdom or which, having been current there, has at any time after the passing of this Act ceased to be so.

(2) Any person who contravenes subsection (1) of this section shall be liable—

(*a*) on summary conviction, to a fine not exceeding £400;

(*b*) on conviction on indictment, to a fine or to imprisonment for a term not exceeding two years, or both.

(3) If any condition attached to a licence granted under subsection (1) of this section is contravened or not complied with, the person to whom the licence was granted shall be liable on summary conviction to a fine not exceeding £400:

Provided that where a person is charged with an offence under this subsection it shall be a defence to prove that the contravention or non-compliance occurred without his consent or connivance and that he exercised all due diligence to prevent it.

(4) The court by or before which any person is convicted of an offence under this section may, whether or not it imposes any other punishment, order the articles in respect of which the offence was committed to be forfeited to Her Majesty.

(5) Where an offence under this section committed by a body corporate is proved to have been committed with the consent or connivance of, or to be attributable to any neglect on the part of, any director, manager, secretary or other similar officer of the body corporate or any person who was purporting to act in any such capacity, he as well as the body corporate shall be guilty of that offence and shall be liable to be proceeded against and punished accordingly.

Minor and consequential amendments of enactments.

15.—(1) Section 3 of the Coinage Act 1870 (standard of coins) shall apply only to gold coins and to silver coins of the Queen's Maundy money, and accordingly—

1870 c. 10.

(*a*) in that section, after the word " Act " (where it first occurs) there shall be inserted the words " being gold coins or coins of silver of the Queen's Maundy money ", and for the words " silver or bronze " there shall be substituted the words " or any silver coin of the Queen's Maundy money " ; and

(*b*) for the entries in Schedule 1 to that Act relating to silver and bronze coins there shall be substituted the entries relating to silver coins of the Queen's Maundy money set out in Schedule 3 to this Act (which reproduce the effect of the existing provisions as to the standard weight, standard fineness and remedy allowance for such silver coins contained in the said Schedule 1, as amended, and in section 6 of the Coinage Act 1946).

1946 c. 74.

(2) Section 4 of the Coinage Act 1870 (legal tender) shall apply only to gold coins, and accordingly in that section the word " gold " shall be inserted after the words " if made in ", and the words " In the case of gold coins " and the words from " In the case of silver " onwards shall be omitted.

(3) Paragraph (4) of section 11 of the Coinage Act 1870 (power by proclamation to determine the weight below which a coin is not to be current) shall cease to have effect. 1870 c. 10.

(4) In paragraph (9) of section 11 of the Coinage Act 1870 (application to British possessions) the reference to that Act shall include a reference to this Act.

(5) The powers exercisable by proclamation by virtue of section 11 of the Coinage Act 1870 shall include power to direct that cupro-nickel or silver coins issued by the Mint before the appointed day in accordance with the Coinage Acts 1870 to 1946, being coins of any denomination specified in the proclamation, shall on and after such day (not earlier than the appointed day) as may be so specified be treated as coins of the new currency made by the Mint in accordance with section 2 of the Decimal Currency Act 1967 and as being of such denomination of that currency as may be so specified. 1967 c. 47.

(6) In Schedule 1 to the Coinage Act 1870, the paragraph beginning " The weight and fineness of the coins specified in this Schedule " (which explains the origin of certain provisions in that Schedule but is of no legal effect) shall be omitted.

(7) In the case of cupro-nickel coins of the denomination of fifty new pence issued for use before the appointed day as current coins of the denomination of ten shillings by virtue of section 2(4) of the Decimal Currency Act 1967, section 1 of the Coinage Act 1946 (cupro-nickel coins to be legal tender for payments up to forty shillings) shall apply as if the reference to an amount not exceeding forty shillings were a reference to an amount not exceeding ten pounds. 1946 c. 74.

(8) In section 4(1) of the Coinage Act 1946, for the words " under the power conferred by paragraph (*c*) of section three of this Act " there shall be substituted the words " by virtue of section 2(3) of the Decimal Currency Act 1967 ".

Interpretation.

16.—(1) In this Act—

" the appointed day " means 15th February 1971 (the day appointed under section 1 of the Decimal Currency Act 1967);

" enactment " includes an enactment contained in a local Act;

" local Act " includes a provisional order confirmed by an Act of Parliament;

" the new currency " means the new currency of the United Kingdom provided for by the Decimal Currency Act 1967;

"the old currency" means the currency of the United Kingdom in force before the appointed day;

"subordinate instrument" means an instrument of a legislative and not an executive character made under an enactment;

"the transitional period" means the period beginning with the appointed day and ending with such day as the Treasury may appoint by order made by statutory instrument subject to annulment in pursuance of a resolution of either House of Parliament.

(2) In this Act—

(*a*) references to coins made by the Mint include references to coins made at any place with the authority of the Mint; and

(*b*) references to coins of the new currency made in accordance
1967 c. 47. with section 2 of the Decimal Currency Act 1967 include references to coins made in accordance with any
1870 c. 10. proclamation made under section 11 of the Coinage Act 1870 by virtue of section 2(3) of the said Act of 1967.

(3) Except in so far as the context otherwise requires, any reference in this Act to any enactment or instrument is a reference to it as amended, and includes a reference to it as applied, by or under any other enactment or instrument, including this Act.

Repeal of s. 5(1)(*d*) of Decimal Currency Act 1967, and other repeals.

17.—(1) Section 5(1)(*d*) of the Decimal Currency Act 1967 (which makes it a function of the Decimal Currency Board to consider representations with respect to expenditure or loss incurred or to be incurred by particular persons or classes of persons in consequence of the change to the new currency) is hereby repealed.

(2) The enactments specified in Schedule 4 to this Act are hereby repealed, as from the appointed day, to the extent specified in the third column of that Schedule; but the repeal by this Act of an enactment contained in the Coinage Acts 1870 to 1946 shall not affect any power to apply that enactment to a British possession by proclamation under section 11 of the Coinage Act 1870.

1920 c. 70. (3) Section 2 of the Gold and Silver (Export Control, &c.) Act 1920 (which is superseded by section 14 of this Act) is hereby repealed, but any licence in force under that section immediately before the date of the passing of this Act shall not be invalidated by the repeal of that section but shall have effect as from that date as if granted under subsection (1) of the said section 14.

18.—(1) This Act extends to Northern Ireland. Northern Ireland.

(2) Nothing in this Act shall be taken to restrict the power of the Parliament of Northern Ireland to make laws, and any laws made by that Parliament in the exercise of that power shall have effect notwithstanding anything in this Act.

(3) In this Act " enactment " includes an enactment of the Parliament of Northern Ireland and " Act " or " Act of Parliament " includes an Act of that Parliament; and in this Act as it applies to Northern Ireland, except in Schedule 2, any reference to an enactment of that Parliament or to an enactment which that Parliament has power to amend shall include a reference to any enactment of that Parliament passed after this Act which re-enacts the said enactment with or without modifications.

19.—(1) This Act may be cited as the Decimal Currency Act 1969, and the Decimal Currency Act 1967 and this Act may be cited together as the Decimal Currency Acts 1967 and 1969. Short title, citation and commencement. 1967 c. 47.

(2) Section 1 of this Act, and section 15 of this Act, except subsections (4), (5) and (7), shall not come into force until the appointed day.

SCHEDULES

Sections 3, 4, 5, 8, 9.

SCHEDULE 1

METHOD OF CALCULATING IN CERTAIN CASES THE AMOUNT IN NEW PENCE CORRESPONDING TO AN AMOUNT IN SHILLINGS AND PENCE

The amount in the new currency corresponding to an amount in shillings, shillings and pence or pence shall be calculated as follows—

(*a*) for any whole two shillings or multiple thereof the corresponding amount in the new currency shall be taken to be ten new pence or that multiple thereof; and

(*b*) for any amount or remaining amount of less than two shillings shown in column 1 of the following Table the corresponding amount in the new currency shall be taken to be the amount (if any) in new pence shown opposite that amount in column 2 of that Table (and accordingly an amount or remaining amount of one penny shall be disregarded).

TABLE

Amount in old currency	*Corresponding amount in new pence*
1d.	—
2d.	1p
3d.	1p
4d.	2p
5d.	2p
6d.	3p
7d.	3p
8d.	3p
9d.	4p
10d.	4p
11d.	5p
1s. 0d.	5p
1s. 1d.	5p
1s. 2d.	6p
1s. 3d.	6p
1s. 4d.	7p
1s. 5d.	7p
1s. 6d.	7p
1s. 7d.	8p
1s. 8d.	8p
1s. 9d.	9p
1s. 10d.	9p
1s. 11d.	10p

SCHEDULE 2

Section 10.

AMENDMENTS OF PROVISIONS REFERRING TO AMOUNTS IN SHILLINGS AND PENCE

The Militia (City of London) Act 1820

1820 c. 100.

1. In section 35 of the Militia (City of London) Act 1820, for the words " thirteen shillings and fourpence " there shall be substituted the words " and sixty-seven new pence ".

The Pawnbrokers Act 1872

1872 c. 93.

2.—(1) The Pawnbrokers Act 1872 shall be amended in accordance with the following provisions of this paragraph.

(2) In Schedule 3, in the provisions relating to the forms of pawn ticket (as amended by section 6 of the Pawnbrokers Act 1960)— 1960 c. 24.

(*a*) in forms A, B and C, in the item specifying the charge for the pawn ticket, for the word " twopence " there shall be substituted the words " one new penny ";

(*b*) in forms A and B, for the item specifying the valuation fee there shall be substituted—

" for valuation fee on receipt of the pledge, on each thirty new pence or part of thirty new pence lent ... ... one new penny "

and, in the item specifying the amount which may be charged for profit, for the words " two shillings or part of two shillings " and " one halfpenny " there shall be substituted respectively the words " twenty-five new pence or part of twenty-five new pence " and " one new halfpenny ";

(*c*) in form C, in the item specifying the amount which may be charged for profit, for the words " two shillings and sixpence or part of two shillings and sixpence " and " one halfpenny " there shall be substituted respectively the words " thirty new pence or part of thirty new pence " and " one new halfpenny ".

(3) In Schedule 4—

(*a*) in Part I, for the words " two shillings or fraction of two shillings lent ... one halfpenny ", in both places where they occur, there shall be substituted the words " twenty-five new pence or fraction of twenty-five new pence lent ... one new halfpenny ", and for the words " two shillings and sixpence or fraction of a sum of two shillings and sixpence ... one halfpenny " there shall be substituted the words "thirty new pence or fraction of a sum of thirty new pence ... one new halfpenny ";

(*b*) in the provisions substituted for Parts II to IV by section 4 of the Pawnbrokers Act 1960 (including those provisions as set out in the Schedule to that Act), for the word " twopence ", in both places where it occurs, there shall be substituted the words " one new penny ".

(4) Nothing in the foregoing provisions of this paragraph shall apply to a loan made before the appointed day.

SCH. 2

The Revenue, Friendly Societies and National Debt Act 1882

1882 c. 72. 3. In section 18 of the Revenue, Friendly Societies and National Debt Act 1882, for the word " penny " there shall be substituted the words " new penny ".

1882 c. 77.

The Citation Amendment (Scotland) Act 1882

4. In Schedule 2 to the Citation Amendment (Scotland) Act 1882, in the provisions relating to inferior courts—

(*a*) in paragraph 1, for the words from " the above-mentioned fees " to the end there shall be substituted the words " the first-mentioned fee shall be allowed for the first party only, and for every other party there shall be allowed a reduced fee of 3½p (instead of 5p) "; and

(*b*) in paragraph 2(1), the item specifying the fee for citing every witness after the first for the same diet shall have effect as if the amount specified were 3½p instead of 8d.

1899 c. 44.

The Small Dwellings Acquisition Act 1899

5. In subsection (4) of section 9 of the Small Dwellings Acquisition Act 1899, as originally enacted, for the words " one halfpenny ", in both places where they occur, there shall be substituted the words " 0·3p " and for the words " one penny ", in both places where they occur, there shall be substituted the words " 0·6p "; and
1929 c. 17. section 75 of the Local Government Act 1929 (increase of certain statutory limits) shall not apply to the said section 9 as amended by this paragraph.

1922 c. 51.

The Allotments Act 1922

6. In subsection (1) of section 16 of the Allotments Act 1922, for the words from " taken " onwards there shall be substituted the words " taken, to exceed the receipts of the council under those provisions by no greater amount than would be produced by a rate of 0·8p in the pound "; and section 75 of the Local Government Act 1929 (increase of certain statutory limits) shall not apply to the said section 16 as amended by this paragraph.

1923 c. 18.

The War Memorials (Local Authorities' Powers) Act 1923

7. In section 2 of the War Memorials (Local Authorities' Powers) Act 1923, as originally enacted, for the words " a penny " there shall be substituted the words " 0·6p ", and section 75 of the Local Government Act 1929 (increase of certain statutory limits) shall not apply to that section as amended by this paragraph.

1931 c. 17.

The Local Authorities (Publicity) Act 1931

8. In section 1(1) of the Local Authorities (Publicity) Act 1931, for the words " one halfpenny " there shall be substituted the words " 0·2p ".

1933 c. 51.

The Local Government Act 1933

9. In section 193(3) of the Local Government Act 1933, for the words " fourpence " and " eightpence " there shall be substituted respectively the words " 1·7p " and " 3·3p ", and in section 193(5) of that Act, for the word " eightpence " there shall be substituted the words " 3·3p ".

SCH. 2

The Health Resorts and Watering Places Act 1936

10. In section 1(1)(*b*) of the Health Resorts and Watering Places Act 1936, for the words " three pence " there shall be substituted the words " 1·3p ". 1936 c. 48.

The Local Government (Scotland) Act 1947 1947 c. 43.

11.—(1) The Local Government (Scotland) Act 1947 shall be amended in accordance with the following provisions of this paragraph.

(2) In section 191(2), for the words " one penny " there shall be substituted the words " 0·4p ".

(3) In section 191(3)(*c*), for the words " three pence " there shall be substituted the words " 1·3p ".

(4) In section 191(3)(*f*), for the words " one halfpenny " there shall be substituted the words " 0·2p ".

(5) In section 191(3)(*g*), for the words " three pence " there shall be substituted the words " 1·3p ".

(6) In section 236, for the words " penny " and " halfpenny ", wherever they occur, there shall be substituted respectively the words " new penny " and " new halfpenny ".

(7) In proviso (*a*) to section 339(1), for the words " two pence " there shall be substituted the words " 0·8p ".

The Local Government (Miscellaneous Provisions) Act 1953 1953 c. 26.

12. In section 2(2) of the Local Government (Miscellaneous Provisions) Act 1953, for the words " fourpence ", " threepence " and " twopence " there shall be substituted respectively the words " 1·7p ", " 1·3p " and " 0·8p ".

The Maintenance Orders Act 1958 1958 c. 39.

13. In section 13(3) of the Maintenance Orders Act 1958, for the word " sixpence ", in both places where it occurs, there shall be substituted the words " three new pence ".

The Town and Country Planning Act 1959 1959 c. 53.

14. In section 27(3)(*b*) of the Town and Country Planning Act 1959, for the words " one penny " there shall be substituted the words " 0·4p ".

The Housing Act 1961 1961 c. 65.

15. Paragraph 2(3) of Schedule 1 to the Housing Act 1961, in its application by virtue of paragraph 3 of that Schedule to a dwelling to which the said paragraph 3 applies, shall have effect in relation to any financial year beginning after the appointed day as if for the references to the product of a penny rate there were substituted references to the product of a new penny rate.

The Public Health and Local Government (Miscellaneous Provisions) Act (Northern Ireland) 1962 1962 c. 12 (N.I.).

16. In section 16(2) of the Public Health and Local Government (Miscellaneous Provisions) Act (Northern Ireland) 1962—

(*a*) in paragraphs (*a*) and (*b*), for the words " one halfpenny " there shall be substituted the words " 0·2p "; and

SCH. 2 (*b*) in paragraph (*c*), for the words " one penny " there shall be substituted the words " 0·4p ".

1963 c. 2. *The Betting, Gaming and Lotteries Act 1963*

17. In Schedule 5 to the Betting, Gaming and Lotteries Act 1963, there shall be substituted for paragraph 5 the following paragraph—

" 5. Where the amount payable in respect of each betting unit staked by a person winning a bet is or includes a fraction of a new penny, then—

(*a*) if that fraction does not exceed one-half, it may be retained by the operator; but

(*b*) if that fraction exceeds one-half, the amount payable in respect of each betting unit staked by the said person shall be deemed to be increased to the nearest multiple of a new penny."

1963 c. 12. *The Local Government (Financial Provisions) (Scotland) Act 1963*

18.—(1) In relation to the year 1971–72 and subsequent years the Local Government (Financial Provisions) (Scotland) Act 1963 shall have effect subject to the amendments specified in sub-paragraph (2) of this paragraph.

(2) In section 7(1) and section 9(1), for the words " one penny " there shall be substituted the words " one new penny ".

1963 c. 38. *The Water Resources Act 1963*

19.—(1) In relation to the financial year beginning with 1st April 1971 and subsequent financial years the Water Resources Act 1963 shall have effect subject to the amendments specified in the following provisions of this paragraph.

(2) In section 87(6) and (7), for the words " four times " there shall be substituted the words " 1·7 times ".

(3) In section 87(9), for the word " penny " there shall be substituted the words " new penny ".

(4) In section 121(2) and (3), for the words " one penny " there shall be substituted the words " one new penny ".

1963 c. 46. *The Local Government (Financial Provisions) Act 1963*

20. Section 6 of the Local Government (Financial Provisions) Act 1963 shall be amended as follows—

(*a*) in subsections (2) and (6), for the words " one penny " and " one-fifth of a penny " respectively, wherever they occur, there shall be substituted the words " 0·4p " and " 0·1p "; and

(*b*) in subsection (5), for the words " a penny " there shall be substituted the words " any amount ".

1964 c. 26. *The Licensing Act 1964*

21. In section 30 of the Licensing Act 1964, in subsection (5) (including that subsection as set out in paragraph 4 of Schedule 7 to the
1967 c. 54. Finance Act 1967), for the word " threepence " there shall be substituted the words " one new penny ".

SCH. 2

The Trading Stamps Act 1964

22. In section 3(3) of the Trading Stamps Act 1964, for the word "penny", in both places where it occurs, there shall be substituted the words "new penny". 1964 c. 71.

The Public Libraries and Museums Act 1964 1964 c. 75.

23. In paragraph 2(1) of Schedule 2 to the Public Libraries and Museums Act 1964, for the words "one-fifth of a penny" and "one penny" respectively there shall be substituted the words "0·1p" and "0·4p".

The Trading Stamps Act (Northern Ireland) 1965 1965 c. 6 (N.I.).

24. In section 3(3) of the Trading Stamps Act (Northern Ireland) 1965, for the word "penny", in both places where it occurs, there shall be substituted the words "new penny".

The Rating Act 1966 1966 c. 9

25. In section 10(1) of the Rating Act 1966, for the words "one penny" there shall be substituted the words "any amount".

The Local Government Act 1966 1966 c. 42.

26.—(1) In relation to the year 1971–72 and subsequent years the Local Government Act 1966 shall have effect subject to the amendments specified in sub-paragraph (2) of this paragraph.

(2) In paragraphs 1 and 3(1) of Part II of Schedule 1, for the words "one penny" there shall be substituted the words "one new penny".

The Local Government (Scotland) Act 1966 1966 c. 51.

27.—(1) In relation to the year 1971–72 and subsequent years the Local Government (Scotland) Act 1966 shall have effect subject to the amendments specified in sub-paragraph (2) of this paragraph.

(2) In sections 12, 14(1) and 46(1), and in paragraph 2 of Part I, and paragraph 1 of Part II of Schedule 1, for the words "one penny", wherever they occur, there shall be substituted the words "one new penny", and in paragraph 3 of Part III of that Schedule for the word "penny", in both places where it occurs, there shall be substituted the words "new penny".

The General Rate Act 1967 1967 c. 9.

28.—(1) In relation to the year beginning with 1st April 1971 and subsequent years the General Rate Act 1967 shall have effect subject to the amendments specified in the following provisions of this paragraph.

(2) In section 12(4), for the words "a penny" there shall be substituted the words "a new penny".

(3) In section 48, in subsection (1)(*b*) the words "(disregarding any halfpenny)" shall be omitted, and after subsection (1) there shall be inserted as a new subsection (1A)—

> "(1A) If the amount mentioned in paragraph (*b*) of subsection (1) of this section includes a fraction of a new penny other than one-half, that fraction, if less than one-half, shall be disregarded and, if greater than one-half, shall be treated as one-half."

SCH. 2 (4) In section 113(1)(*c*), for the word " penny " there shall be substituted the words " new penny ".

(5) In paragraph 4(1) of Schedule 5, for the word " penny " there shall be substituted the words " new penny ".

1967 c. 2. (N.I.).

The Local Government (Finance) Act (Northern Ireland) 1967

29.—(1) In relation to the year beginning with 1st April 1971 and subsequent years the Local Government (Finance) Act (Northern Ireland) 1967 shall have effect subject to the amendments specified in sub-paragraph (2) of this paragraph.

(2) In section 1, in subsections (1) and (4) the words " (disregarding any halfpenny) " shall be omitted, and after subsection (7) there shall be inserted the following subsection—

> " (7A) For the purposes of subsections (1) and (4), if one-half of the amount prescribed under subsection (1) includes a fraction of a new penny other than one-half, that fraction, if less than one-half, shall be disregarded and, if greater than one-half, shall be treated as one-half."

1968 c. 34.

The Agriculture (Miscellaneous Provisions) Act 1968

30.—(1) In relation to the year beginning with 1st April 1971 and subsequent years the Agriculture (Miscellaneous Provisions) Act 1968 shall have effect subject to the amendments specified in sub-paragraph (2) of this paragraph.

(2) In section 22, in subsection (2) for the words " one penny ", in both places where they occur, there shall be substituted the words " one new penny ", and subsection (3) shall be omitted.

1968 c. 73.

The Transport Act 1968

31.—(1) In relation to anything falling to be done after 31st March 1971 the Transport Act 1968 shall have effect subject to the amendments specified in sub-paragraph (2) of this paragraph.

(2) In section 13(2) and in paragraph 2 of Part I of Schedule 5, for the words " one penny " there shall be substituted the words " one new penny ".

SCHEDULE 3

Section 15.

ENTRIES TO BE SUBSTITUTED IN SCHEDULE 1 TO COINAGE ACT 1870

1870 c. 10.

Denomination of Coin	Standard Weight		Least Current Weight		Standard Fineness	Remedy Allowance		
	Imperial Weight	Metric Weight	Imperial Weight	Metric Weight		Weight per piece		Millesimal Fineness
	Grains	Grams	Grains	Grams		Imperial Grains	Metric Grams	
SILVER:								
Four new pence	29·09090	1·88506	—	—	Thirty-seven-fortieths fine silver, three-fortieths alloy; or millesimal fineness 925.	0·262	0·0170	5
Three new pence	21·81818	1·41379	—	—		0·212	0·0138	
Two new pence	14·54545	0·94253	—	—		0·144	0·0093	
New penny ...	7·27272	0·47126	—	—		0·087	0·0056	

Section 17.

SCHEDULE 4

REPEALS

Chapter	Short Title	Extent of Repeal
1870 c. 10.	The Coinage Act 1870.	In section 4, the words from " or less " to " Act " (where it last occurs), the words " In the case of gold coins " and the words from " In the case of silver " onwards. Section 6. In section 11, paragraphs (4) and (6). In Schedule 1, the paragraph beginning " The weight and fineness of the coins ".
1891 c. 72.	The Coinage Act 1891.	In the Schedule, the entries relating to silver and bronze coins.
1920 c. 3.	The Coinage Act 1920.	Section 1(1).
1920 c. 70.	The Gold and Silver (Export Control, &c.) Act 1920.	The whole Act, so far as unrepealed.
1946 c. 74.	The Coinage Act 1946.	Sections 1 to 3. In section 5(1), the words from the beginning to " 1920, and " and the words from " and to " to " this Act ". Section 6. The Schedule.
1948 c. 26.	The Local Government Act 1948.	Section 137.
1950 c. 31.	The Allotments Act 1950.	Section 11(1).
1960 c. 24.	The Pawnbrokers Act 1960.	Section 6(1)(*c*).
1967 c. 9.	The General Rate Act 1967.	In section 48(1)(*b*), the words " (disregarding any halfpenny) ", except in relation to any period ending before 1st April 1971.
1967 c. 47.	The Decimal Currency Act 1967.	In section 2, the words from " and so much " onwards in subsection (3), and subsection (4). In section 3(3), the words from " and in section 4 " onwards. In Schedule 2, the words " Section 2 of the Gold and Silver (Export Control, &c.) Act 1920 ".
1967 c. 2 (N.I.).	The Local Government (Finance) Act (Northern Ireland) 1967.	In section 1(1) and (4), the words " (disregarding any halfpenny) ", except in relation to any period ending before 1st April 1971.
1968 c. 34.	The Agriculture (Miscellaneous Provisions) Act 1968.	Section 22(3), except in relation to any period ending before 1st April 1971.

Foreign Compensation Act 1969

1969 CHAPTER 20

An Act to make provision with respect to certain property (including the proceeds thereof and any income or other property accruing therefrom) of persons formerly resident or carrying on business in Estonia, Latvia, Lithuania or a part of Czechoslovakia, Finland, Poland or Rumania which has been ceded to the Union of Soviet Socialist Republics, and to amend the Foreign Compensation Act 1950. [16th May 1969]

WHEREAS by an agreement entered into on 5th January 1968 between Her Majesty's Government in the United Kingdom and the Government of the Union of Soviet Socialist Republics each of those Governments undertook not to pursue with the other on its own behalf or on behalf of other persons, or to support, the claims described in Articles 1 and 2 of the agreement and the former Government undertook to make a settlement of claims against the latter Government by the holders of the unredeemed notes mentioned in Article 4 of the agreement and agreed to pay to the latter Government the sum of £500,000 out of the property or proceeds of property claimed by the latter:

And whereas it is expedient to make provision for carrying out such of those undertakings as were given by Her Majesty's Government in the United Kingdom;

Be it therefore enacted by the Queen's most Excellent Majesty, by and with the advice and consent of the Lords Spiritual and Temporal, and Commons, in this present Parliament assembled, and by the authority of the same, as follows:—

Extension of power to deal with property of Baltic States and ceded territories. 1939 c. 89.

1.—(1) The purposes for which the Board of Trade may make orders under section 7 of the Trading with the Enemy Act 1939 (collection of enemy debts and custody of enemy property), and for which powers or duties conferred or imposed by that section or any such order on a custodian of enemy property may be exercised or are to be performed, shall include the disposal of or other dealing with former property of a Baltic State or ceded territory to enable a custodian of enemy property to perform his functions under subsections (3) and (5) below.

(2) Any order made by the Board of Trade under that section may make the like provision in relation to former property of a Baltic State or ceded territory as might be made by such an order in relation to enemy property if a state of war existed:

Provided that an order made by virtue of this subsection shall not provide for the payment to, or the vesting in, a custodian of enemy property of any money or other property unless an order had been made under or by virtue of that section before the passing of this Act purporting to require it to be paid to a custodian or to vest it or the right to transfer it in a custodian.

(3) Notwithstanding anything in that section or any order thereunder, a custodian of enemy property shall, if the Treasury so directs—

(*a*) pay to the Foreign Compensation Commission, for the purpose of enabling them to make payments in respect of any of the claims mentioned in Articles 1 and 4 of the agreement recited above or other similar claims, any money held by the custodian, being former property of a Baltic State or ceded territory, and any income arising therefrom which has not before the giving of the direction been paid into the Exchequer;

(*b*) pay to any other person specified in the direction any of that money;

(*c*) transfer to any person so specified any such property which, or the right to transfer which, is vested in the custodian;

1953 c. 52. and section 4(1) of the Enemy Property Act 1953 (payment into Exchequer of income from money invested by a custodian) shall not apply to income with respect to which a direction has been given under paragraph (*a*) above.

(4) The Board of Trade may out of moneys provided by Parliament pay to the Foreign Compensation Commission sums not exceeding in the aggregate the amount of any income which has accrued since 12th February 1967 from former property of a Baltic State or ceded territory and has been paid into the Exchequer in pursuance of the said section 4(1).

(5) When so directed by the Treasury, the custodian of enemy property shall, by way of repaying a payment of £500,000 made out of moneys provided by Parliament for the purpose of implementing the provisions of the agreement recited above for the payment of that sum to the Government of the Union of

Soviet Socialist Republics, pay the like sum into the Consolidated Fund out of money held by him, being former property of a Baltic State or ceded territory.

(6) Section 3(4) and (5) of the Enemy Property Act 1953 (saving for right to recover property dealt with under the Trading with the Enemy Act 1939 as enemy property) shall not operate so as to authorise the recovery after 5th January 1968 of any former property of a Baltic State or ceded territory, except property which on any of the relevant dates belonged to or was held or managed on behalf of an individual, or of any proceeds of such property, and any such property or proceeds (except as aforesaid) recovered by virtue of those subsections between that date and the passing of this Act shall be re-transferred or repaid, as the case may require.

1953 c. 52.
1939 c. 89.

Amendments of Foreign Compensation Act 1950.
1950 c. 12.

2.—(1) The powers conferred by section 3 of the Foreign Compensation Act 1950 (claims to, and distribution of, compensation paid by foreign governments) shall be exercisable if Her Majesty's Government in the United Kingdom enter into or contemplate an agreement with the government of any other country (whether foreign or not) providing for the payment of compensation by the latter government; and accordingly in that section for the words " any foreign country " there shall be substituted the words " any other country ".

(2) An Order in Council under the said section 3 may make the like provision with respect to money paid to the Foreign Compensation Commission by virtue of section 1(3) or (4) above as may be made by any such Order in relation to sums paid to Her Majesty's Government in the United Kingdom by way of compensation by the government of any other country under an agreement between the two governments.

(3) An Order in Council may be made under the said section 3 not only in the circumstances therein mentioned, but also if it appears to Her Majesty expedient to provide, in case agreement is reached between Her Majesty's Government in the United Kingdom and the government of any other country for the payment of compensation by the latter, for the registration, investigation and determination of claims to such compensation.

(4) Section 2(3) of the Foreign Compensation Act 1950 (appointment by Commonwealth governments of additional members of the Foreign Compensation Commission for the purpose of determining claims to compensation paid by the Governments of Yugoslavia and Czechoslovakia) shall cease to have effect.

Determinations of the Foreign Compensation Commission and appeals against such determinations.

3.—(1) The Foreign Compensation Commission shall have power to determine any question as to the construction or interpretation of any provision of an Order in Council under section 3 of the Foreign Compensation Act 1950 with respect to claims falling to be determined by them.

1950 c. 12.

(2) Subject to subsection (4) below, the Commission shall, if so required by a person mentioned in subsection (6) below who is aggrieved by any determination of the Commission on any question of law relating to the jurisdiction of the Commission or on any question mentioned in subsection (1) above, state and sign a case for the decision of the Court of Appeal.

(3) In this section " determination " includes a determination which under rules under section 4(2) of the Foreign Compensation Act 1950 (rules of procedure) is a provisional determination, and anything which purports to be a determination.

(4) Where the Court of Appeal decide a question on a case stated and signed by the Commission on a provisional determination in any proceedings, subsection (2) above shall not require the Commission to state and sign a case on a final determination by them of that question in those proceedings.

(5) Any person mentioned in subsection (6) below may, with a view to requiring the Commission to state and sign a case under this section, request the Commission to furnish a written statement of the reasons for any determination of theirs, but the Commission shall not be obliged to state the reasons for any determination unless it is given on a claim in which a question mentioned in subsection (2) above arises.

(6) The persons who may make a request under subsection (5) above or a requirement under subsection (2) above in relation to any claim are the claimant and any person appointed by the Commission to represent the interests of any fund out of which the claim would, if allowed, be met.

(7) Any such request or requirement must be in writing, and—

(*a*) any such request may be disregarded unless it is received by the Commission within the period of four weeks beginning with the date on which the Commission send notice of the determination in question or such other period as may be provided for by or under rules under section 4(2) of the Foreign Compensation Act 1950; and

(*b*) any such requirement may be disregarded unless it is received by the Commission within the period of eight weeks beginning with that date or the period of four weeks beginning with the date on which the Commission send a statement of reasons for the determination in question, whichever expires last, or within such other period as may be provided for by or under rules of court.

(8) Notwithstanding anything in section 3 of the Appellate Jurisdiction Act 1876 (right of appeal to the House of Lords from decisions of the Court of Appeal), no appeal shall lie to the House of Lords from a decision of the Court of Appeal on an appeal under this section. 1876 c. 59.

(9) Except as provided by subsection (2) above and subsection (10) below, no determination by the Commission on any claim made to them under the Foreign Compensation Act 1950 shall be called in question in any court of law. 1950 c. 12.

(10) Subsection (9) above shall not affect any right of any person to bring proceedings questioning any determination of the Commission on the ground that it is contrary to natural justice.

(11) Subsections (2) to (10) above shall not apply to a determination of the Commission of which notice was sent by them before the passing of this Act.

(12) Section 4(4) of the Foreign Compensation Act 1950 (which makes provision corresponding to subsection (9) above) shall not apply to a determination of the Commission of which notice is sent by them after the passing of this Act.

Interpretation.

4.—(1) In this Act, except so far as the context otherwise requires,—

"Baltic State" means Estonia, Latvia or Lithuania (including Memel and the city and territory of Vilna);

"ceded territory" means a part of Czechoslovakia, Finland, Poland or Rumania which has been ceded to the Union of Soviet Socialist Republics;

"former property", in relation to a Baltic State or ceded territory, means—

(*a*) any property which on any of the relevant dates belonged to or was held or managed on behalf of an individual resident or carrying on business on that date in any such State or territory;

(*b*) any property which during the period beginning with 3rd September 1939 and ending with 8th May 1945 belonged to or was held or managed on behalf of a body of persons (whether corporate or unincorporate) carrying on business at any time during that period in any such State or territory; and

(*c*) without prejudice to paragraph (*b*) above, any gold, securities, or credit balance at a bank with respect to which a direction was given on 24th July

S.R. & O. 1939/1620; 1940/1329. 1940 under Regulation 2A of the Defence (Finance) Regulations 1939;

and any proceeds of, any income arising from, and any other payments in respect of, any such property and any other property accruing therefrom;

" property " includes all rights or interests of any kind in property;

" relevant date ", in relation to any property, means any of the following dates, that is to say—

(*a*) the date on which the right to dispose of the property was first regulated by an order under section 7 of the Trading with the Enemy Act 1939; 1939 c. 89.

(*b*) the date on which the property or the right to transfer it was vested by virtue of such an order in a custodian of enemy property;

(*c*) in the case of a sum of money, the date on which the sum was first required by such an order to be paid, or was in fact paid in pursuance of such an order, to a custodian of enemy property.

(2) Any reference in this Act to any enactment or regulation is a reference thereto as amended, and includes a reference thereto as extended or applied, by or under any other enactment, including this Act.

Short title. **5.** This Act may be cited as the Foreign Compensation Act 1969.

Immigration Appeals Act 1969

1969 CHAPTER 21

An Act to confer rights of appeal against the exercise by the Secretary of State and officers acting under his instructions of their powers in respect of the admission into and removal from the United Kingdom of persons to whom section 1 or 6 of the Commonwealth Immigrants Act 1962 applies, and to enable provision to be made by Order in Council for conferring corresponding rights of appeal on aliens; to enable deportation orders to be made without the recommendation of a court in the case of persons to whom the said section 6 applies who fail to comply with conditions subject to which they have been admitted into the United Kingdom; to make provision as respects the holding of entry certificates by certain persons to whom the said section 1 applies who seek admission into the United Kingdom; to make the owners or agents of ships and aircraft liable for certain expenses incurred in respect of persons to whom the said section 1 applies who are directed to be removed from the United Kingdom; and for purposes connected with the matters aforesaid. [16th May 1969]

BE IT ENACTED by the Queen's most Excellent Majesty, by and with the advice and consent of the Lords Spiritual and Temporal, and Commons, in this present Parliament assembled, and by the authority of the same, as follows:—

PART I

IMMIGRATION APPEALS

The appellate authorities

The adjudicators and the Tribunal.

1.—(1) For the purposes of this Part of this Act there shall be—

(*a*) adjudicators appointed by the Secretary of State ; and

PART I

(*b*) an Immigration Appeal Tribunal (hereafter in this Act referred to as " the Tribunal ") whose members shall be appointed by the Lord Chancellor.

(2) Schedule 1 to this Act shall have effect in relation to the adjudicators and the Tribunal.

Rights of appeal

Appeal against exclusion from United Kingdom.

2.—(1) Subject to the provisions of this Part of this Act, a person may appeal to an adjudicator against—

(*a*) a refusal under section 2(1) of the Act of 1962 to admit him into the United Kingdom;

(*b*) a prohibition on his landing imposed under paragraph 8(1) of Schedule 1 to that Act (prohibition on member of ship's crew landing without authority);

(*c*) a refusal of an application for the grant to him of an entry certificate, being an application duly made to a person having authority to grant such a certificate on behalf of the Government of the United Kingdom.

(2) The adjudicator shall dismiss any appeal under subsection (1) of this section if it appears to him that, at the time of the refusal or prohibition, a deportation order was in force in respect of the appellant; and he shall dismiss any appeal under paragraph (*a*) of that subsection if it appears to him that the appellant has landed in the United Kingdom in contravention of section 4A of the Act of 1962 (landing without fulfilling conditions as to examination).

(3) Schedule 2 to this Act shall have effect for suspending the enforcement of any such refusal as is mentioned in subsection (1)(*a*) of this section while an appeal against it is pending under this Part of this Act.

Appeal against conditions of admission.

3.—(1) Subject to the provisions of this Part of this Act, a person may appeal to an adjudicator against—

(*a*) the imposition in his case of any condition of admission restricting the period for which he may remain in the United Kingdom to less than seven or such other number of days as may be prescribed for the purposes of this paragraph by an order made by the Secretary of State;

(*b*) the variation by a notice under paragraph 2(5) of Schedule 1 to the Act of 1962 of any condition of admission which has been imposed in his case;

(*c*) a refusal to revoke or vary, by such a notice as aforesaid, any condition of admission which has been imposed in his case.

PART I

(2) The power to make orders for the purposes of subsection (1)(*a*) of this section shall be exercisable by statutory instrument and shall include power to revoke or vary any previous order so made.

(3) Where an appeal is duly brought under subsection (1)(*a*) or (*c*) of this section the appellant shall not, so long as the appeal is pending, be required to leave the United Kingdom by reason of any condition restricting the period for which he may remain there; and where an appeal is duly brought under subsection (1)(*b*) of this section the variation which is the subject of the appeal shall not take effect so long as the appeal is pending.

(4) In this section "condition of admission" means a condition subject to which a person is admitted into the United Kingdom under section 2(1) of the Act of 1962, and in subsection (1)(*b*) and (*c*) includes any condition so far as it has effect in the United Kingdom by virtue of paragraph 2 of Schedule 3 to that Act (conditions imposed in the Channel Islands or Isle of Man).

Appeal against deportation orders.

4.—(1) Subject to subsection (2) of this section and to the other provisions of this Part of this Act, a person may appeal to an adjudicator against—

(*a*) a decision of the Secretary of State to make a deportation order in respect of him under Part II of this Act;

(*b*) a refusal by the Secretary of State to revoke a deportation order made in respect of him under the said Part II or under Part II of the Act of 1962.

(2) A person shall not be entitled to appeal under subsection (1)(*b*) of this section until he has complied with the requirement in the order in question that he should leave the United Kingdom or while he is in breach of the prohibition in it against returning there.

(3) A deportation order shall not be made under Part II of this Act so long as an appeal may be brought against the decision to make that order and, if such an appeal is duly brought, so long as the appeal is pending.

Appeal against directions for removal from United Kingdom.

5.—(1) Subject to the provisions of this Part of this Act, a person may appeal to an adjudicator against the giving of directions for his removal from the United Kingdom in any case where the directions are given—

(*a*) on the ground that he is to be treated by virtue of paragraph 8(2) or 9 of Schedule 1 to the Act of 1962 as having been refused admission into the United Kingdom (member of ship's crew landing or remaining illegally and person arriving as stowaway); or

PART I

(*b*) on the ground that he has returned to the United Kingdom in breach of a deportation order.

(2) In any appeal under subsection (1) of this section against the giving of any directions, the only question for the determination of the adjudicator shall be whether the facts of the case are such that there was in law power to give the directions on the ground on which they were given or, in the case of an appeal under paragraph (*a*) of that subsection, either on that ground or on the ground that a deportation order was in force in respect of the appellant; and if the adjudicator determines that question in the affirmative he shall dismiss the appeal.

(3) Subject to subsection (4) of this section and to the other provisions of this Part of this Act, where directions are given for the removal of a person from the United Kingdom he may appeal to an adjudicator against the giving of the directions on the ground that he ought not to be removed to the country or territory to which he would be removed if the directions were carried out.

(4) Where a person appeals against the giving of any directions both under subsection (1) and under subsection (3) of this section the appeals shall be heard together; and where a person appeals under section 2(1)(*a*) or section 4 of this Act, then, if the Secretary of State or an immigration officer has served on him (whether before or after the appeal is brought) a notice stating that any directions for his removal from the United Kingdom which may be given by virtue of the refusal or deportation order which is the subject of the appeal will be such as to effect his removal to a country or territory, or one of several countries or territories, specified in the notice—

(*a*) the appellant shall be entitled in that appeal to object that he ought not to be removed to the country or territory, or to any of the countries or territories, specified in the notice; and

(*b*) no appeal shall lie under subsection (3) of this section against any directions which are subsequently given by virtue of the refusal or deportation order in question if their effect would be his removal to a country or territory to which he has not objected as aforesaid or as respects which his objection has not been sustained.

(5) Where before a person appeals under section 2(1)(*a*) of this Act directions have been given for his removal and those directions cease to have effect in consequence of the bringing of the appeal, the appellant shall be treated as having been served with a notice under subsection (4) of this section specifying the country or territory to which he would have been removed if those directions had been carried out.

PART I

(6) Schedule 2 to this Act shall have effect as respects the suspension of any directions while an appeal in respect of them is pending under this Part of this Act.

Notice of matters in respect of which there are rights of appeal.

6.—(1) The Secretary of State may by regulations provide—

(*a*) for a notice in writing of any decision or action against which an appeal can be brought under this Part of this Act to be given to the person by whom such an appeal can be brought;

(*b*) for any such notice to include a statement of the reasons for the decision or action and, where the action is the giving of directions for the removal of any person from the United Kingdom, of the country or territory to which he is to be removed;

(*c*) for any such notice to be accompanied by a statement containing particulars of the rights of appeal available under this Part of this Act and of the procedure by which those rights may be exercised;

(*d*) for the form of any such notice or statement.

(2) The power to make regulations under this section shall be exercisable by statutory instrument, and any statutory instrument containing such regulations shall be subject to annulment in pursuance of a resolution of either House of Parliament.

Further appeal from adjudicator to Tribunal

Review by Tribunal of determination of adjudicator.

7.—(1) Subject to subsection (2) of this section, any party to an appeal to an adjudicator may, if dissatisfied with his determination thereon, appeal to the Tribunal.

(2) Rules of procedure may provide that, in such cases as may be specified in the rules, an appeal shall lie under this section only with the leave of the adjudicator or the Tribunal, or only with the leave of the Tribunal; but—

(*a*) an appeal shall lie under this section without leave where the adjudicator has allowed an appeal under section 2(1)(*a*) of this Act and the Secretary of State certifies that he considers it desirable in the public interest that the case should be decided by the Tribunal; and

(*b*) if leave to appeal under this section is by virtue of the rules required in a case where the adjudicator has dismissed an appeal under the said section 2(1)(*a*) the authority having power under the rules to grant leave shall grant it if satisfied that the person who was the appellant before the adjudicator held an entry certificate at the time of the refusal which was the subject of the appeal.

Part I

Proceedings on appeal

Determination of appeals.

8.—(1) Subject to sections 2(2) and 5(2) of this Act, an adjudicator who hears an appeal under this Part of this Act—

(*a*) shall allow the appeal if he considers—

(i) that the decision or action against which the appeal is brought was not in accordance with the law or with any immigration rules applicable to the case ; or

(ii) where the decision or action involved the exercise of a discretion by the Secretary of State or an officer, that the discretion should have been exercised differently ; and

(*b*) in any other case, shall dismiss the appeal.

(2) For the purposes of paragraph (*a*) of the foregoing subsection the adjudicator may review any determination of a question of fact on which the decision or action was based ; and for the purposes of paragraph (*a*)(ii) of that subsection no decision or action which is in accordance with the immigration rules shall be treated as having involved the exercise of a discretion by the Secretary of State by reason only of the fact that he has been requested by or on behalf of the appellant to depart, or to authorise an officer to depart, from the rules and has refused to do so.

(3) In relation to an appeal which under section 9 of this Act is heard at first instance by the Tribunal, the foregoing provisions of this section shall apply to the Tribunal as they apply to an adjudicator.

(4) On an appeal under this Part of this Act to the Tribunal from the determination of an adjudicator, the Tribunal may affirm the determination or make any other determination which could have been made by the adjudicator.

(5) Where an adjudicator or the Tribunal allows an appeal, the adjudicator or Tribunal shall give such directions for giving effect to the determination as the adjudicator or Tribunal thinks requisite, and may also make recommendations with respect to any other action which the adjudicator or Tribunal considers should be taken in the case under the Act of 1962.

(6) Subject to section 9(2) of this Act, it shall be the duty of the Secretary of State and of any officer to whom directions are given under subsection (5) of this section to comply therewith, except that directions given by an adjudicator need not be complied with so long as an appeal can be brought against his determination and, if such an appeal is duly brought, so long as the appeal is pending.

PART I

Special procedure in cases involving national security or forgery of documents.

9.—(1) Where a person appeals to an adjudicator against any decision or action and it appears to the Secretary of State that the decision or action was taken in the interests of national security, the Secretary of State may direct that the appeal shall be referred to and heard by the Tribunal instead of by an adjudicator; and for the purpose of hearing appeals referred to it under this section the Tribunal shall be constituted by a special panel of its members nominated by the Lord Chancellor and the Secretary of State acting jointly.

(2) Section 8(6) of this Act shall not apply to a case which is dealt with in accordance with directions given under subsection (1) of this section.

(3) If—

(*a*) in the case of an appeal which is dealt with in accordance with directions given under subsection (1) of this section, the Secretary of State certifies that the disclosure to the appellant of any matters relevant to the case would be contrary to the interests of national security; or

(*b*) in the case of any appeal under this Part of this Act in which it is alleged that a passport, entry certificate or employment voucher (or any part thereof or entry therein) on which a party relies is a forgery, the adjudicator or Tribunal hearing the appeal determines that the disclosure to that party of any matters relating to the method of detection would be contrary to the public interest,

those matters shall be presented to the adjudicator or Tribunal without being disclosed as aforesaid; and for the purposes of this subsection any part of the proceedings may take place in the absence of the appellant or that party, as the case may be, and of his representatives.

Reference of cases for further consideration.

10.—(1) Where in any case—

(*a*) an appeal to an adjudicator (or an appeal referred to the Tribunal under section 9 of this Act) has been dismissed; or

(*b*) the Tribunal has affirmed the determination of an adjudicator dismissing an appeal,

the Secretary of State may at any time refer for consideration under this section any matter relating to the case which was not before the adjudicator or Tribunal.

(2) Any reference under this section shall be to an adjudicator or to the Tribunal, and the adjudicator or Tribunal shall consider the matter which is the subject of the reference and report to the Secretary of State the opinion of the adjudicator or Tribunal thereon.

PART I

Rules of procedure.

11.—(1) The Secretary of State may make rules (in this Act referred to as " rules of procedure ") with respect to the bringing of appeals and the making of applications under this Part of this Act to appellate authorities, that is to say adjudicators and the Tribunal, and with respect to the proceedings of such authorities and matters incidental to or consequential on such proceedings.

(2) Rules made under this section may in particular make provision—

(*a*) as to the manner in which and the time within which appeals are to be brought and applications made for leave to appeal ;

(*b*) as to the persons who are to be parties to proceedings before an appellate authority and for treating the Secretary of State (either generally or in such circumstances as may be prescribed by the rules) as a party to such proceedings where he would not otherwise be a party to them, and enabling him to appear and to be heard accordingly ;

(*c*) for enabling any party to be represented before an appellate authority by any person whether having professional qualifications or not ;

(*d*) for requiring persons to attend to give evidence and produce documents, and for authorising the administration of oaths to witnesses ;

(*e*) with respect to the mode and burden of proof and admissibility of evidence ;

(*f*) in the case of an appeal to the Tribunal under section 7 of this Act, for enabling evidence to be given otherwise than orally and for an appeal to be remitted to an adjudicator for further evidence to be obtained ;

(*g*) for enabling an appellate authority to exclude members of the public from proceedings of such an authority ;

(*h*) for enabling an appeal to be heard in the absence of the appellant in cases where the appellant is outside the United Kingdom ;

(*i*) for enabling an appellate authority to dispose of an appeal without a formal hearing where the appellant is outside the United Kingdom or does not request such a hearing or the authority has decided to allow the appeal ;

(*j*) for enabling an appellate authority to determine an appeal in a summary way where it appears that the issues raised on the appeal have been determined in previous proceedings under this Part of this Act and the circumstances do not materially differ from those subsisting at the time of the previous proceedings ;

PART I

(*k*) for requiring the matters put forward in support of an appeal under section 5(3) of this Act to be submitted in writing and for enabling an appellate authority to dismiss the appeal without a formal hearing if of opinion that those matters do not warrant one;

(*l*) as to the procedure to be followed under section 5(4) of this Act;

(*m*) as to the procedure to be followed in cases where the Secretary of State has given a direction or certificate under section 9 of this Act;

(*n*) for any functions of the Tribunal which relate to matters ancillary or antecedent to an appeal, or which are conferred by Schedule 3 to this Act, to be performed by a single member of the Tribunal;

(*o*) conferring on appellate authorities such ancillary powers as the Secretary of State thinks necessary for the purposes of the exercise of their functions;

(*p*) for the recording and proof of decisions of the appellate authorities.

(3) A person who without reasonable excuse fails to comply with any requirement imposed by rules under subsection (2)(*d*) of this section shall be guilty of an offence and liable on summary conviction to a fine not exceeding £100.

(4) The power to make rules under this section shall be exercisable by statutory instrument, and any statutory instrument containing such rules shall be subject to annulment in pursuance of a resolution of either House of Parliament.

Release of appellants pending hearing.

12. Schedule 3 to this Act shall have effect as respects the release on bail of appellants who are in detention.

Members of ships' crews.

13.—(1) If a person who has appealed under section 2(1)(*b*) of this Act is authorised by an immigration officer to land for the purpose of prosecuting his appeal he may, while on shore for that purpose, be detained under the authority of an immigration officer or constable: and section 13(1) and (4) of the Act of 1962 (provisions as to detained persons) shall have effect as if this subsection were contained in that Act.

(2) If while an appeal under the said section 2(1)(*b*) is pending the appellant's ship leaves the port in question but the appellant remains on shore with the authority of an immigration officer, the appellant shall thereafter be treated for the purposes of the Act of 1962 as if he had been refused admission into the United Kingdom and the appeal shall thereafter be treated for the purposes of this Act as if it were an appeal under section 2(1)(*a*) of this Act.

PART I

Provision of corresponding rights of appeal for aliens

Rights of appeal for aliens.
1914 c. 12.

14.—(1) Her Majesty may by Order in Council under section 1 of the Aliens Restriction Act 1914 make such provision for appeals in connection with the powers for the time being exercisable in respect of the admission into and removal from the United Kingdom of aliens as appears to Her Majesty to be appropriate having regard to the provision made by this Part of this Act for appeals in connection with the powers conferred by the Act of 1962.

(2) Any Order made under section 1 of the said Act of 1914 by virtue of this section may provide for appeals under the Order to lie to the appellate authorities constituted for the purposes of this Part of this Act, and may apply any of the provisions of this Act for the purposes of the Order subject to such modifications as may be specified therein.

Advice and assistance for persons with rights of appeal

Financial support for organisations providing advice and assistance for persons with rights of appeal.

15. The Secretary of State may with the consent of the Treasury make grants to any voluntary organisation which provides advice or assistance for, or other services for the welfare of, persons who have rights of appeal under this Part of this Act or any Order made in pursuance of section 14 thereof.

PART II

DEPORTATION OF COMMONWEALTH CITIZENS FOR BREACH OF CONDITIONS OF ADMISSION

Power to deport Commonwealth citizens for breach of conditions of admission.

16.—(1) If the Secretary of State is satisfied that a Commonwealth citizen to whom section 6 of the Act of 1962 applies has failed to comply with a condition imposed on him under section 2(1) of that Act or Schedule 1 thereto he may, subject to the provisions of this section, make an order requiring him to leave the United Kingdom and prohibiting him from returning there so long as the order is in force.

(2) An order shall not be made under this section in respect of a person who—

(*a*) was ordinarily resident in the United Kingdom on the date on which, in accordance with regulations under section 6 of this Act, he was given notice of the decision to make the order; and

(*b*) had been continuously so resident for a period of at least five years ending with that date;

and for the purpose of calculating the period for which a person had been so resident (but not of determining whether he had been continuously so resident) no account shall be taken of any continuous period of six months or more during which he was detained under a sentence or order passed or made by any court on a conviction of an offence.

(3) Subsections (3) and (4) of section 6 of the Act of 1962 (application to British protected persons and citizens of Republic of Ireland and onus of proof) shall have effect in relation to this section, and to the said section 6 as applied for the purposes of this section, as they have effect in relation to Part II of that Act and to that section as originally enacted.

Revocation and enforcement of orders.

17.—(1) The following provisions of the Act of 1962, that is to say—

section 9(3) (revocation of deportation orders);

section 10 and Schedule 2 (removal and detention of persons subject to deportation orders) except paragraph 2(1) of that Schedule;

section 11(1), (3) and (4) (offences in connection with deportation orders),

shall have effect in relation to a deportation order under this Part of this Act as they have effect in relation to a deportation order under Part II of that Act; and in section 2(5) of that Act (refusal of admission to person in respect of whom a deportation order under Part II of that Act is in force) the reference to a deportation order under the said Part II shall include a reference to a deportation order under this Part of this Act.

(2) Where a person who, in accordance with regulations under section 6 of this Act, has been given notice of a decision to make a deportation order in respect of him under this Part of this Act is neither detained in pursuance of the sentence or order of any court nor for the time being released on bail by any court having power so to release him, he may be detained under the authority of the Secretary of State until the deportation order—

(*a*) is made; or

(*b*) by reason of the final determination of an appeal under Part I of this Act in favour of that person, cannot be made.

(3) Instead of detaining or continuing to detain a person under subsection (2) of this section, the Secretary of State may by order impose on him such restrictions as to his place of residence, and such requirements as to reporting to the police, as the Secretary of State thinks fit.

(4) Section 11(2) of the Act of 1962 (offence of failing to comply with restrictions or requirements imposed under paragraph 2 of Schedule 2 to that Act) shall have effect as if the

PART II reference therein to that paragraph included a reference to subsection (3) of this section; and section 13 of that Act (provisions as to detained persons) shall have effect as if subsection (2) of this section were contained in that Act.

(5) If a justice of the peace is satisfied by written information substantiated on oath that there is reasonable ground for suspecting that a person who is liable to be arrested under section 13 of the Act of 1962 by reason of his being liable to detention—

(*a*) under paragraph 2(2) of Schedule 2 to that Act as applied by subsection (1) of this section; or

(*b*) under subsection (2) of this section,

is to be found on any premises, he may grant a warrant authorising any constable acting for the police area in which the premises are situated, at any time or times within one month from the date of the warrant, to enter, if need be by force, the premises named in the warrant for the purpose of searching for and arresting that person.

(6) Subsection (5) of this section shall, in its application to premises in Scotland, have effect subject to the following modifications, namely—

(*a*) for the reference to a justice of the peace there shall be substituted a reference to the sheriff, or a magistrate or justice of the peace, having jurisdiction in the place where the premises are situated;

(*b*) for the reference to written information substantiated on oath there shall be substituted a reference to evidence on oath;

and that subsection shall, in its application to premises in Northern Ireland, have effect with the omission of the words "acting for the police area in which the premises are situated".

Disqualification for citizenship by registration.
1948 c. 56.

18.—(1) A person in respect of whom a deportation order is in force under this Part of this Act shall not be entitled to be registered as a citizen of the United Kingdom and Colonies under section 6(1) of the British Nationality Act 1948 (registration of certain Commonwealth citizens and citizens of the Republic of Ireland).

(2) Where, in accordance with regulations under section 6 of this Act, a person has been given notice of a decision to make a deportation order in respect of him under this Part of this Act, he shall not be entitled to be registered as a citizen of the United Kingdom and Colonies under the said section 6(1) unless and until an appeal by him under Part I of this Act against the decision has been finally determined in his favour or the Secretary of State notifies him that the order will not be made.

Part II

Application to Channel Islands and Isle of Man.

19.—(1) In subsection (1) of section 16 of this Act the reference to a condition imposed under section 2(1) of the Act of 1962 includes a reference to a condition imposed under the said section 2(1) as extended under section 18 of that Act so far as the condition has effect in the United Kingdom by virtue of paragraph 2 of Schedule 3 to that Act (conditions imposed in the Channel Islands or Isle of Man).

(2) Subsection (2) of the said section 16 shall have effect as if the Channel Islands and the Isle of Man (in this section collectively referred to as the Islands) were included in the United Kingdom.

(3) Her Majesty may by Order in Council direct that all or any of the provisions of this Part of this Act shall extend, with such exceptions, adaptations and modifications, if any, as may be specified in the Order, to any of the Islands.

(4) The power to make an Order in Council under subsection (3) of this section shall include power to revoke or vary a previous Order so made.

(5) Subject to subsection (6) of this section, a deportation order made in any of the Islands under this Part of this Act as extended under this section shall have effect, in the United Kingdom, as if it were a deportation order made by the Secretary of State under this Part of this Act requiring the person to whom it relates to leave the United Kingdom and prohibiting him from returning there; and section 10 of the Act of 1962 and Schedule 2 thereto, as applied by section 17 of this Act, shall apply accordingly with the necessary modifications.

(6) The Secretary of State may in any particular case direct that subsection (5) of this section shall not apply in relation to a deportation order made in any of the Islands; and nothing in that subsection shall render it unlawful for a person in respect of whom a deportation order made in any of the Islands is in force to enter the United Kingdom on his way from that Island to a place outside the United Kingdom.

(7) The Secretary of State may defray or contribute towards expenses incurred by the governments of the Islands in connection with the removal of persons under this Part of this Act as extended under this section.

Part III

Miscellaneous and Supplementary Provisions

Power to refuse admission to wives and children under 16 if they do not hold entry certificates.

20.—(1) In subsection (2)(*b*) of section 2 of the Act of 1962 (under which a woman may not be refused admission into the United Kingdom if she satisfies an immigration officer as to the matters there specified) after the words " satisfies an immigration officer " there shall be inserted the words " that she holds

PART III

a current entry certificate granted for the purposes of this paragraph and ".

(2) In subsection (2A) of the said section 2 (under which a person under the age of 16 may not be refused admission into the United Kingdom if he satisfies an immigration officer as to the matters there specified) after the words " satisfies an immigration officer " there shall be inserted the words " that he holds a current entry certificate granted for the purposes of this subsection and ".

(3) The Secretary of State shall make arrangements for securing that the persons having authority to grant entry certificates on behalf of the Government of the United Kingdom shall, on due application, grant such a certificate for the purposes of the said subsection (2)(*b*) or (2A) on being satisfied that, apart from the foregoing provisions of this section, the applicant would be entitled to admission into the United Kingdom under the said subsection (2)(*b*) or (2A) or would be so entitled if the applicant's husband, parent or parents were admitted with the applicant.

Liability of owners or agents of ships and aircraft for expenses incurred in respect of persons directed to be removed from the United Kingdom.

21.—(1) Subject to the provisions of this section, where directions are given under paragraph 3 of Schedule 1 to the Act of 1962 for the removal of a person from the United Kingdom the owners or agents of the ship or aircraft in which he arrived shall be liable to pay to the Secretary of State, on demand, any expenses incurred by the latter in respect of the custody, accommodation or maintenance of that person at any time after his arrival while he was detained or liable to be detained under paragraph 4(1) of that Schedule.

(2) The foregoing subsection shall not apply to expenses in respect of a person who, when he arrived in the United Kingdom, held a current entry certificate or was the person described in a current employment voucher; and for the purposes of this subsection a document purporting to be such a certificate or voucher shall be treated as genuine unless its falsity is reasonably apparent.

(3) If a person is admitted into the United Kingdom before the directions for his removal have been carried out, or he is so admitted thereafter in consequence of the determination in his favour of an appeal under Part I of this Act (being an appeal against a refusal of admission by virtue of which the directions were given or against the directions themselves), no sum shall be demanded under subsection (1) of this section for expenses incurred in respect of that person and any such sum already demanded and paid shall be refunded.

(4) In subsection (1) of this section " directions " does not include directions which by virtue of Schedule 2 to this Act have

ceased to have effect or are for the time being of no effect; and the expenses to which that subsection applies include expenses in conveying the person in question to and from the place where he is detained or accommodated unless the journey is made for the purpose of attending an appeal by him under Part I of this Act.

(5) Her Majesty may by Order in Council under section 1 of the Aliens Restriction Act 1914 make provision in relation to aliens for purposes corresponding to the purposes of this section. 1914 c. 12

Proof of certificates etc.

22.—(1) Any document purporting to be a notice, certificate or direction given by the Secretary of State for the purposes of any provision of Part I of this Act or an order or direction made or given by him under Part II thereof, and to be signed by him or on his behalf, shall be received in evidence, and shall, until the contrary is proved, be deemed to be made or given by him.

(2) Prima facie evidence of any such notice, certificate, direction or order as aforesaid may, in any legal proceedings or in any proceedings under this Act, be given by the production of a document bearing a certificate purporting to be signed by or on behalf of the Secretary of State and stating that the document is a true copy of the notice, certificate, direction or order.

(3) In section 15(3) of the Act of 1962 (proof of orders etc. under that Act) the reference to legal proceedings shall include a reference to proceedings under this Act.

Expenses.

23. There shall be defrayed out of moneys provided by Parliament any expenditure of the Secretary of State under or in consequence of any provision of this Act.

Short title, interpretation and commencement.

24.—(1) This Act may be cited as the Immigration Appeals Act 1969.

(2) In this Act—

"the Act of 1962" means the Commonwealth Immigrants Act 1962; 1962 c. 21.

"deportation order" means, except where the context otherwise requires, an order under Part II of the Act of 1962 or Part II of this Act;

"employment voucher" means a voucher of the kind described in section 2(3)(*a*) of the Act of 1962;

"entry certificate" means a certificate which, in accordance with immigration rules, is to be taken as evidence of eligibility for admission into the United Kingdom;

PART III

" immigration officer " has the same meaning as in the Act of 1962;

" immigration rules " means rules made by the Secretary of State for the administration of—

(*a*) the control of entry into the United Kingdom of persons to whom the Act of 1962 applies; and

(*b*) the control of such persons after entry,

being rules which have been published and laid before Parliament;

" rules of procedure " means rules made under section 11 of this Act;

" ship " includes every description of vessel used in navigation and a hovercraft as defined in section 4(1) of the Hovercraft Act 1968.

1968 c. 59.

(3) For the purposes of this Act an appeal under Part I of this Act shall be treated as pending during the period beginning when notice of appeal is duly given and ending when the appeal is finally determined or withdrawn; and in the case of an appeal to an adjudicator, the appeal shall not be treated as finally determined so long as a further appeal can be brought by virtue of section 7 of this Act and, if such an appeal is duly brought, until it is determined or withdrawn.

(4) Any reference in this Act to any other enactment is a reference thereto as amended, and includes a reference thereto as extended or applied, by or under any other enactment, including this Act.

(5) Sections 20 and 21 shall come into operation on the passing of this Act and the other provisions of this Act shall come into operation on such date as the Secretary of State may by order made by statutory instrument appoint; and different dates may be appointed by order under this subsection for different purposes of this Act.

(6) No provision of Part I of this Act shall be construed as conferring a right of appeal against any decision or action which was taken before the coming into operation of that provision.

SCHEDULES

SCHEDULE 1

Section 1.

The Adjudicators and the Tribunal

Part I

The Adjudicators

1. There shall be such number of adjudicators as the Secretary of State may with the consent of the Treasury determine, and the Secretary of State shall appoint one of them as chief adjudicator.

2.—(1) An adjudicator shall hold and vacate his office in accordance with the terms of his appointment and shall, on ceasing to hold office, be eligible for re-appointment.

(2) An adjudicator may at any time by notice in writing to the Secretary of State resign his office.

3. The Secretary of State shall pay—

(*a*) to the adjudicators, such remuneration and allowances as he may, with the approval of the Treasury, determine ;

(*b*) as regards any of the adjudicators in whose case he may so determine with the approval of the Minister for the Civil Service, such pension, allowance or gratuity to or in respect of him, or such sums towards the provision of such pension, allowance or gratuity, as may be so determined ;

and, if a person ceases to be an adjudicator and it appears to the Secretary of State that there are special circumstances which make it right that that person should receive compensation, the Secretary of State may, with the approval of the said Minister, pay to that person a sum of such amount as the Secretary of State may, with the approval of that Minister, determine.

4. In Part III of Schedule 1 to the House of Commons Disqualification Act 1957 (which lists offices the holders of which are disqualified for membership of the House of Commons), and in the said Part III as it applies by virtue of Schedule 3 to that Act in relation to the Senate and House of Commons of Northern Ireland, there shall be inserted at the appropriate point the words " Adjudicator appointed for the purposes of Part I of the Immigration Appeals Act 1969 ". 1957 c. 20.

5. The adjudicators shall sit at such times and in such places as the Secretary of State may direct ; and the chief adjudicator shall allocate duties among the adjudicators and have such other functions as may be conferred on him by the Secretary of State.

Part II

The Tribunal

Members

6. The Tribunal shall consist of such number of members as the Lord Chancellor may determine, and the Lord Chancellor shall appoint one of them to be president.

SCH. 1

7. The president and such number of the other members of the Tribunal as the Lord Chancellor may determine shall be barristers, advocates or solicitors, in each case of not less than seven years' standing.

8.—(1) A member of the Tribunal shall hold and vacate his office in accordance with the terms of his appointment and shall, on ceasing to hold office, be eligible for re-appointment.

(2) Any member of the Tribunal may at any time by notice in writing to the Lord Chancellor resign his office.

9. The Secretary of State shall pay—

(*a*) to the members of the Tribunal, such remuneration and allowances as he may, with the approval of the Treasury, determine ;

(*b*) as regards any member in whose case he may so determine with the approval of the Minister for the Civil Service, such pension, allowance or gratuity to or in respect of him, or such sums towards the provision of such pension, allowance or gratuity, as may be so determined ;

and, if a person ceases to be a member of the Tribunal and it appears to the Secretary of State that there are special circumstances which make it right that that person should receive compensation, the Secretary of State may, with the approval of the said Minister, pay to that person a sum of such amount as the Secretary of State may, with the approval of that Minister, determine.

1957 c. 20.

10. In Part II of Schedule 1 to the House of Commons Disqualification Act 1957 (which lists bodies of which all members are disqualified for membership of the House of Commons), and in the said Part II as it applies by virtue of Schedule 3 to that Act in relation to the Senate and House of Commons of Northern Ireland, there shall be inserted at the appropriate point the words " The Immigration Appeal Tribunal ".

Proceedings

11. For the purpose of hearing and determining appeals under Part I of this Act or any matter preliminary or incidental to any such appeal, the Tribunal shall sit at such times and in such place or places as the Lord Chancellor may direct, and may sit in two or more divisions.

12. Subject to section 9 of this Act and to rules of procedure, the Tribunal shall be deemed to be duly constituted if it consists of three members (or a greater uneven number of members) of whom at least one is qualified as mentioned in paragraph 7 of this Schedule ; and the determination of any question before the Tribunal shall be according to the opinion of the majority of the members hearing the case.

13. The Lord Chancellor may appoint members of the Tribunal who are qualified as mentioned in paragraph 7 of this Schedule to act on behalf of the president in his temporary absence or inability to act.

14. The president or, in his absence, the member qualified as mentioned in paragraph 7 of this Schedule (or, if there is more than one such member present, the senior of them) shall preside at a sitting of the Tribunal. SCH. 1

PART III

STAFF AND EXPENSES

15. The Secretary of State may appoint such officers and servants for the adjudicators and the Tribunal as he may, with the approval of the Treasury as to remuneration and numbers, determine.

16. The remuneration of officers and servants appointed as aforesaid, and such expenses of the adjudicators and the Tribunal as the Secretary of State may with the approval of the Treasury determine, shall be defrayed by the Secretary of State.

SCHEDULE 2

Sections 2 and 5.

SUSPENSION OF DIRECTIONS FOR REMOVAL PENDING APPEAL

Directions following a refusal of admission which is under appeal

1. Subject to the provisions of this Schedule, where an appeal is duly brought under section 2(1)(*a*) of this Act—

(*a*) no directions for the removal of the appellant from the United Kingdom shall, so long as the appeal is pending, be given by virtue of the refusal which is the subject of the appeal ; and

(*b*) except so far as already carried out, any directions which have been so given before the appeal was brought shall cease to have effect.

Directions which are under appeal

2. Subject to the provisions of this Schedule, where an appeal is duly brought under section 5 of this Act against the giving of any directions, those directions, except so far as already carried out, shall be of no effect so long as the appeal is pending.

Members of ship's crew and stowaways

3.—(1) The foregoing provisions of this Schedule shall not prevent—

(*a*) the giving of directions for the removal of an appellant who has arrived in the United Kingdom as a member of the crew of a ship or as a stowaway ; or

(*b*) the continuance in force of directions for the removal of any such person which have already been given.

(2) In this paragraph "member of the crew" has the same meaning as in Schedule 1 to the Act of 1962.

SCH. 2

Removal where adjudicator dismisses appeal

4.—(1) Where an appeal under section 2(1)(*a*) or section 5 of this Act has been dismissed by an adjudicator, then, unless forthwith after the appeal has been dismissed—

(*a*) the appellant duly gives notice of appeal against the determination of the adjudicator ; or

(*b*) in a case in which leave to appeal against that determination is required and the adjudicator has power to grant leave, the appellant duly applies for and obtains the leave of the adjudicator,

paragraph 1 of this Schedule shall not prevent the giving of directions for the removal of the appellant, and for the purposes of paragraph 2 of this Schedule the appeal shall be treated as if it were no longer pending.

(2) Where a person who has been removed from the United Kingdom under directions given or in force by virtue of sub-paragraph (1) of this paragraph subsequently appeals successfully to the Tribunal against the determination of the adjudicator, the Tribunal may order the Secretary of State to pay to that person such sum as the Tribunal may direct in respect of any expenses incurred by that person in consequence of his having been removed as aforesaid.

Detention

5. The foregoing provisions of this Schedule shall not affect the powers of detention conferred by paragraph 4 of Schedule 1 to the Act of 1962 except that a person shall not be detained on board a ship or aircraft so as to compel him to leave the United Kingdom in it at a time when by virtue of those provisions no directions for his removal can be given or any such directions have ceased to have effect or are for the time being of no effect.

Time limit for giving of directions

6. In calculating the period of two months referred to in paragraph 3(3) of Schedule 1 to the Act of 1962 (being the time limit for giving directions for the removal of a person from the United Kingdom) there shall be disregarded, in the case of a person who duly brings an appeal under Part I of this Act, the period during which the appeal is pending.

Section 12.

SCHEDULE 3

RELEASE OF APPELLANTS PENDING APPEAL

Preliminary

1. This Schedule applies to any person (in this Schedule referred to as an appellant) who has an appeal pending under Part I of this Act and is for the time being detained under paragraph 4 of Schedule 1 to the Act of 1962 or Part II of this Act.

Bail by immigration officer or police officer

2. An immigration officer not below the rank of chief immigration officer or a police officer not below the rank of inspector may release an appellant on his entering into a recognizance, with or without sureties, conditioned for his appearance before an adjudicator or the Tribunal at a time and place named in the recognizance.

Bail by adjudicator Sch. 3

3.—(1) An adjudicator may release an appellant on his entering into a recognizance, with or without sureties, conditioned for his appearance before that or any other adjudicator or the Tribunal at a time and place named in the recognizance.

(2) Where an adjudicator dismisses an appeal but—

(*a*) grants leave to the appellant to appeal to the Tribunal ; or

(*b*) in a case in which leave to appeal is not required, the appellant has duly given notice of appeal to the Tribunal,

the adjudicator shall, if the appellant so requests, exercise his powers under this paragraph.

Bail by Tribunal

4.—(1) Where an appellant has duly applied for leave to appeal to the Tribunal, the Tribunal may release him on his entering into a recognizance, with or without sureties, conditioned for his appearance before the Tribunal at a time and place named in the recognizance.

(2) Where—

(*a*) the Tribunal grants leave to an appellant to appeal to the Tribunal ; or

(*b*) in a case in which leave to appeal is not required, the appellant has duly given notice of appeal to the Tribunal,

the Tribunal shall, if the appellant so requests, release him as aforesaid.

Restrictions on grant of bail

5.—(1) Notwithstanding the foregoing provisions of this Schedule, an appellant shall not be released under this Schedule without the consent of the Secretary of State—

(*a*) if directions for the removal of the appellant from the United Kingdom are for the time being in force, or the power to give such directions is for the time being exercisable ; or

(*b*) if the Secretary of State has given a certificate under section 7(2)(*a*) of this Act in relation to the case of the appellant.

(2) Notwithstanding paragraph 3(2) or 4(2) of this Schedule, an adjudicator and the Tribunal shall not be obliged to release an appellant unless the appellant enters into a proper recognizance and produces sufficient and satisfactory sureties, if required to do so ; and an adjudicator and the Tribunal shall not be obliged to release an appellant if it appears to the adjudicator or the Tribunal, as the case may be—

(*a*) that the appellant, having on any previous occasion been released on bail (whether under this Schedule or under any other provision), has failed to comply with the conditions of any recognizance entered into by him on that occasion ;

(*b*) that the appellant is likely to commit an offence unless he is retained in detention ;

SCH. 3

(*c*) that the release of the appellant is likely to cause danger to public health ;

(*d*) that the decision or action which is the subject of the appeal was based on the ground that the presence of the appellant in the United Kingdom would be contrary to the interests of national security ;

(*e*) that the appellant is suffering from mental disorder and that his continued detention is necessary in his own interests or for the protection of any other person ; or

(*f*) that the appellant is under the age of seventeen, that arrangements ought to be made for his care in the event of his release and that no satisfactory arrangements for that purpose have been made.

Postponement of taking recognizance

6. In any case in which an adjudicator or the Tribunal has power or is required by the foregoing provisions of this Schedule to release an appellant on his entering into a recognizance, the adjudicator or Tribunal may, instead of taking a recognizance, fix the amount of the recognizance in which the appellant and his sureties, if any, are to be bound, with a view to its being taken subsequently by any such person as may be specified by the adjudicator or the Tribunal, and on the recognizance being so taken the appellant shall be released.

Conditions

7. The conditions of a recognizance taken under this Schedule may include conditions appearing to the person taking the recognizance (or, where the taking of the recognizance is postponed under paragraph 6 of this Schedule, to the adjudicator or the Tribunal) to be likely to result in the appearance of the appellant at the time and place named in the recognizance.

Forfeiture of recognizances

8.—(1) Where a recognizance entered into under this Schedule conditioned for the appearance of an appellant before an adjudicator or the Tribunal appears to the adjudicator or the Tribunal, as the case may be, to be forfeited, the adjudicator or Tribunal may by order declare it to be forfeited and adjudge the persons bound thereby, whether as principal or sureties, or any of them, to pay the sum in which they are respectively bound or such part of it, if any, as the adjudicator or Tribunal thinks fit.

(2) An order under this paragraph shall, for the purposes of this sub-paragraph, specify a magistrates' court ; and the recognizance shall be treated for the purposes of collection, enforcement and remission of the sum forfeited as having been forfeited by the court so specified.

(3) Where an adjudicator or the Tribunal makes an order under this paragraph the adjudicator or Tribunal shall, as soon as practicable, give particulars of the recognizance to the clerk of the court

specified in the order in pursuance of the last foregoing sub-paragraph. SCH. 3

(4) Any sum the payment of which is enforceable by a magistrates' court by virtue of this paragraph shall be treated for the purposes of the Justices of the Peace Act 1949 and, in particular, section 27 thereof as being due under a recognizance forfeited by such a court and as being Exchequer moneys. 1949 c. 101.

Arrest of appellants released on bail

9.—(1) An immigration officer or constable may arrest without warrant a person who has been released by virtue of this Schedule—

(*a*) if he has reasonable grounds for believing that that person is likely to break the condition that he will appear at the time and place required or any other condition on which he was so released, or has reasonable cause to suspect that that person is breaking or has broken any such other condition ; or

(*b*) on being notified in writing by any surety for that person that the surety believes that that person is likely to break the first-mentioned condition and for that reason the surety wishes to be relieved of his obligations as a surety.

(2) If a justice of the peace is satisfied by written information substantiated on oath that there is reasonable ground for suspecting that a person who is liable to be arrested under this paragraph is to be found on any premises, he may grant a warrant authorising any constable acting for the police area in which the premises are situated, at any time or times within one month from the date of the warrant, to enter, if need be by force, the premises named in the warrant for the purpose of searching for and arresting that person.

(3) A person arrested under this paragraph shall—

(*a*) except where he was so arrested within the period of twenty-four hours immediately preceding an occasion on which he is required by virtue of a condition on which he was released to appear before an adjudicator or the Tribunal, be brought as soon as practicable and, in any event, within twenty-four hours after his arrest before an adjudicator, or, if that is not practicable, before a justice of the peace acting for the petty sessions area in which he was arrested ; and

(*b*) in the said excepted case, if he is required to appear as aforesaid before an adjudicator, shall be brought before that adjudicator, or, if he is required as aforesaid to appear before the Tribunal, shall be brought before the Tribunal.

(4) An adjudicator or justice of the peace before whom a person is brought by virtue of paragraph (*a*) of the last foregoing sub-paragraph may, if of the opinion that that person has broken or is likely to break any condition on which he was released, direct that he be detained under the authority of the person by whom he

SCH. 3 was arrested or alternatively release him on his original recognizance or on a new recognizance, with or without sureties, and, if not of that opinion, shall release him on his original recognizance.

Application to Scotland

10. This Schedule shall apply to Scotland with the following modifications—

(*a*) in paragraphs 2, 3 and 4, for the words " on his entering into a recognizance, with or without sureties " there shall be substituted the words " on bail, the bail bond being " and for the word " recognizance " (where second occurring) there shall be substituted the words " bail bond " ;

(*b*) in paragraph 5(2), for the words from " unless the appellant " to " to do so " there shall be substituted the words " unless sufficient and satisfactory bail is found, if so required ", and in paragraph 5(2)(*a*) for the word " recognizance " there shall be substituted the words " bail bond " ;

(*c*) for paragraphs 6 to 8 there shall be substituted the following—

" *Postponement of taking bail*

6. In any case in which an adjudicator or the Tribunal has power or is required by the foregoing provisions of this Schedule to release any person on bail, the adjudicator or Tribunal may, instead of taking the bail, fix the amount of the bail with a view to its being taken subsequently by any such person as may be specified by the adjudicator or the Tribunal, and on the bail being so taken the appellant shall be released.

Conditions

7. The conditions of a bail bond taken under this Schedule may include conditions appearing to the person granting bail (or, where the taking of the bail is postponed under paragraph 6 of this Schedule, to the adjudicator or the Tribunal) to be likely to result in the appearance of the appellant at the time and place named in the bail bond.

Forfeiture of bail

8. Where a person released on bail fails to comply with the terms of a bail bond conditioned for his appearance before an adjudicator or the Tribunal, the adjudicator or Tribunal may declare the bail to be forfeited, and any bail so forfeited shall be transmitted by the adjudicator or the Tribunal to the sheriff court having jurisdiction in the area where the proceedings took place, and shall be treated as having been forfeited by that court." ;

(*d*) in paragraph 9—

(i) sub-paragraph (1)(*b*) shall not apply ;

(ii) in the application of sub-paragraph (2) to premises in Scotland, for the reference to a justice of the peace there shall be substituted a reference to the sheriff, or a magistrate or justice of the peace, having jurisdiction in the place where the premises are situated, and for the reference to written information substantiated on oath there shall be substituted a reference to evidence on oath ;

(iii) in sub-paragraph (3)(*a*), for the words from " a justice of the peace " to " arrested " there shall be substituted the words " the sheriff " ;

(iv) in sub-paragraph (4), for the words " justice of the peace " there shall be substituted the word " sheriff " and for the words from " alternatively " to the end there shall be substituted the words " alternatively release him on his original bail or on new bail, and, if not of that opinion, shall release him on his original bail.".

Application to Northern Ireland

11. In the application of this Schedule to Northern Ireland—

(*a*) for the reference in paragraph 2 to a police officer not below the rank of inspector there shall be substituted a reference to an officer of the Royal Ulster Constabulary not below the rank of head-constable ;

(*b*) for the reference in sub-paragraph (2) of paragraph 8 to a magistrates' court there shall be substituted a reference to a court of summary jurisdiction and for sub-paragraph (4) of that paragraph there shall be substituted the following—

" (4) Any sum the payment of which is enforceable by virtue of this paragraph by a court of summary jurisdiction shall, for the purposes of section 20(5) of the Administration of Justice Act (Northern Ireland) 1954, be treated as a forfeited recognizance." ; 1954 c. 9 (N.I.).

(*c*) in paragraph 9(2) the words " acting for the police area in which the premises are situated " shall be omitted.

Redundant Churches and other Religious Buildings Act 1969

1969 CHAPTER 22

An Act to authorise the making of grants to the Redundant Churches Fund; to exclude section 40 of the Town and Country Planning Act 1968 in relation to the demolition, in certain cases, of redundant places of public worship; to provide for, and make provision in connection with, the transfer to the Minister of Housing and Local Government or the Secretary of State of certain such places; and to make other provision relating to the acquisition and maintenance by that Minister and the Secretary of State of redundant churches and other religious buildings.

[16th May 1969]

BE IT ENACTED by the Queen's most Excellent Majesty, by and with the advice and consent of the Lords Spiritual and Temporal, and Commons, in this present Parliament assembled, and by the authority of the same, as follows:—

Grants to Redundant Churches Fund.

1968 No. 1.

1.—(1) Subject to the provisions of this section, in the period beginning with the passing of this Act and expiring with the day preceding the fifth anniversary of the coming into operation of the Pastoral Measure 1968 (hereafter in this section referred to as " the initial period ") and in such later periods as may be specified by the Minister of Housing and Local Government by order made with the approval of the Treasury, that Minister may, with the like approval, out of moneys provided by Parliament, make, in respect of expenditure incurred or to be incurred by the Redundant Churches Fund established by that Measure, grants to that Fund of such amounts, payable at such times and subject to such conditions, if any, as he may from time to time determine.

(2) The aggregate amount of the grants that may be paid under the foregoing subsection in the initial period shall not exceed £200,000 and the aggregate amount of the grants that may be so paid in a period specified in an order made under that subsection shall not exceed such sum as may, in relation to that period, be specified in the order.

(3) The power to make an order under subsection (1) above shall include power to vary or revoke that order by a subsequent order thereunder.

(4) The power to make an order under subsection (1) above shall be exercisable by statutory instrument, but a statutory instrument containing such an order shall not be made unless a draft of the instrument has been approved by a resolution of the Commons House of Parliament.

Section 40 of Town and Country Planning Act 1968 not to prevent demolition of buildings in pursuance of schemes under Pastoral Measure 1968.

2. Section 40 of the Town and Country Planning Act 1968 (which restricts the execution of works for the demolition, alteration or extension of a building for the time being included in a list compiled or approved under section 32 of the Town and Country Planning Act 1962) shall not apply to the execution of works for the demolition, in pursuance of a pastoral or redundancy scheme (within the meaning of the Pastoral Measure 1968), of a redundant building (within the meaning of that Measure) or a part of such a building.

1968 c. 72.
1962 c. 38.
1968 No. 1.

Substitution, in section 66 of Pastoral Measure 1968, of Minister of Housing and Local Government for Minister of Public Building and Works.

3. Section 66 of the Pastoral Measure 1968 (which authorises a Diocesan Board of Finance and the Redundant Churches Fund to make agreements with the Minister of Public Building and Works for the acquisition and preservation by him of redundant buildings vested in that Board or that Fund) shall have effect with the substitution, for any reference to the Minister of Public Building and Works, of a reference to the Minister of Housing and Local Government.

Power of court to authorise the transfer of certain redundant places of public religious worship to the Minister of Housing and Local Government or the Secretary of State.

4.—(1) If, in the case of a building which is a place of public religious worship and held by or in trust for a charity but is not a church subject to the provisions of the Pastoral Measure 1968, the court is satisfied that the building, or a part thereof, is no longer required for use as a place of public religious worship and that the Minister is willing to enter into an agreement for the acquisition by him, under the powers conferred on him by section 5 of the Historic Buildings and Ancient Monuments Act 1953, of the building or part by way of gift or for a consideration other than a full consideration, but that it is not within the powers of the persons in whom the building is vested to carry out the agreement except by virtue of this section, the court may, under its jurisdiction with respect to charities,

1953 c. 49.

establish a scheme for the making and carrying out of the agreement, and, if it appears to the court proper to do so, the scheme may provide for the acquisition by the Minister under the said section 5, whether or not by way of gift or for such a consideration, of other land, if any, held by or in trust for the charity and comprising, or contiguous or adjacent to, the building, and of objects, if any, which are, or have been, ordinarily kept in the building.

(2) A scheme under this section may provide for conferring on the Minister such rights of way over any land held by or in trust for the charity as appear to the court to be necessary for the purpose of the performance of his functions in relation to the building or any land acquired by him under the scheme or for giving to the public reasonable access to the building or land and, so far as so necessary, such rights of way, if any, as are, before the making of the scheme, enjoyed by persons attending services at the building.

(3) A scheme made under subsection (1) above may provide for the making of an application to the Minister, by a person specified in, or appointed in pursuance of, the scheme, for the restoration, if the Minister thinks fit, of the building or part to use as a place of public religious worship; and if the Minister, whether or not such an application is made to him, requests the Charity Commissioners to make provision for restoration of the building or part to such use, they may do so by a scheme under their jurisdiction under section 18 of the Charities Act 1960 (which confers on the Charity Commissioners and the Secretary of State for Education and Science concurrent jurisdiction with the High Court for certain purposes) notwithstanding anything in subsection (4) of that section or that the charity by or in trust for whom the building was held before the establishment of the scheme mentioned in subsection (1) above has ceased to exist; and if it has ceased to exist, the scheme may provide for the constitution of a charity by or in trust for whom the building on its restoration is to be held.

1960 c. 58.

(4) Sections 18 (except subsections (6) and (13)) and 21 (publicity) of the Charities Act 1960 shall have effect in relation to a scheme made under subsection (1) above as they do in relation to a scheme for the administration of a charity.

(5) In this and the next following section " the Minister ", except in the case of the application of either of those sections to Wales and Monmouthshire, means the Minister of Housing and Local Government, and in the said excepted case means the Secretary of State; and expressions to which a meaning is assigned by the Charities Act 1960 for the purposes of that Act have that meaning also for the purposes of this and the next following section.

5.—(1) Where a building is acquired by the Minister in pursuance of the last foregoing section, then, so long as it remains vested in him, any property of a charity the purposes of which include the repair and maintenance of the building or the provision of objects for keeping in the building or the maintenance of objects ordinarily kept there, shall continue to be applicable for that purpose.

Trusts for repair, &c., of a building to continue after its transfer under section 4.

(2) Where a part of a building is so acquired by the Minister, then, so long as it remains vested in him, any such property as aforesaid shall be applicable for the repair and maintenance of that part of the building, or the provision of objects for keeping in that part or the maintenance of objects ordinarily kept there, to such extent, if any, as may be provided by the scheme under which the agreement for the acquisition by the Minister of the part of the building is made.

6. So much of section 7 of the Historic Buildings and Ancient Monuments Act 1953 as requires the payment to the Minister of Housing and Local Government and the Secretary of State out of the National Land Fund of sums equal to the amount of the expenses incurred by them under section 5 of that Act shall not apply to expenses incurred by that Minister in the exercise, in relation to redundant buildings within the meaning of the Pastoral Measure 1968, of powers conferred by the said section 5, or by that Minister or the Secretary of State in the exercise, in relation to buildings falling within section 4 of this Act, of powers so conferred.

Expenses of Ministers in relation to redundant religious buildings not to be reimbursed out of the National Land Fund.
1953 c. 49.
1968 No. 1.

7.—(1) This Act may be cited as the Redundant Churches and other Religious Buildings Act 1969.

Short title, saving, repeal and extent.

(2) Nothing in this Act shall be taken to prejudice any power of the court (within the meaning of the Charities Act 1960) or the Charity Commissioners to establish a scheme for the administration of a charity or the power of the Charity Commissioners under section 23 of that Act to authorise dealings with trust property.

1960 c. 58.

(3) The proviso to section 91 of the Pastoral Measure 1968 is hereby repealed.

(4) This Act does not extend to Scotland or Northern Ireland.

Army Reserve Act 1969

1969 CHAPTER 23

An Act to extend the period during which certain national servicemen or national service volunteers are liable to serve in the army reserve.

[16th May 1969]

BE IT ENACTED by the Queen's most Excellent Majesty, by and with the advice and consent of the Lords Spiritual and Temporal, and Commons, in this present Parliament assembled, and by the authority of the same, as follows:—

Extension of reserve liability after military service.

1.—(1) In relation to a national serviceman or national service volunteer within the meaning of the Act of 1954—

(*a*) whose whole-time and part-time service within the meaning of the National Service Acts 1948 to 1950 or service treated under those Acts as performed in lieu thereof or as equivalent thereto was completed after 31st December 1962; and

(*b*) whose last service in the armed forces of the Crown (within the meaning of the Act of 1954) was military service;

section 1 of the Act of 1954 (under which, as amended by section 1 of the Act of 1964, such a person becomes a member of the army reserve until the last day of June 1969) shall have effect as if for references to 1969 there were substituted references to 1974.

(2) Section 1 of the Act of 1964 is hereby repealed; and the following provisions of the Act of 1954 (which have no application after the end of June 1969) are hereby repealed as from 1st July 1969:

in section 2, subsections (1) and (5)

in section 3, subsections (1) and (4) and, in subsection (5), the words " and section 1 of the Air Force Reserve Act 1950 " and the words " and men of the air force reserve respectively "

in section 6, subsection (5) and paragraphs (*a*) and (*c*) of subsection (6).

Interpretation and short title.

2.—(1) In this Act " the Act of 1954 " means the Navy, Army and Air Force Reserves Act 1954 and " the Act of 1964 " means the Navy, Army and Air Force Reserves Act 1964. 1954 c. 10. 1964 c. 11.

(2) This Act may be cited as the Army Reserve Act 1969.

Tattooing of Minors Act 1969

1969 CHAPTER 24

An Act to prohibit the tattooing of persons under the age of eighteen years. [16th May 1969]

BE IT ENACTED by the Queen's most Excellent Majesty, by and with the advice and consent of the Lords Spiritual and Temporal, and Commons, in this present Parliament assembled, and by the authority of the same, as follows:—

Prohibition of tattooing of minors.

1. It shall be an offence to tattoo a person under the age of eighteen except when the tattoo is performed for medical reasons by a duly qualified medical practitioner or by a person working under his direction, but it shall be a defence for a person charged to show that at the time the tattoo was performed he had reasonable cause to believe that the person tattooed was of or over the age of eighteen and did in fact so believe.

Penalties.

2. Any person committing such an offence shall be liable on summary conviction to a fine not exceeding fifty pounds, or, in the case of a second or subsequent conviction, to a fine not exceeding one hundred pounds.

Definition.

3. For the purposes of this Act " tattoo " shall mean the insertion into the skin of any colouring material designed to leave a permanent mark.

Short title, commencement and extent.

4.—(1) This Act may be cited as the Tattooing of Minors Act 1969.

(2) This Act shall come into force at the expiration of one month beginning with the date it is passed.

(3) This Act shall not extend to Northern Ireland.

Public Health (Recurring Nuisances) Act 1969

1969 CHAPTER 25

An Act to enable local authorities to deal more effectively with recurring nuisances. [25th June 1969]

BE IT ENACTED by the Queen's most Excellent Majesty, by and with the advice and consent of the Lords Spiritual and Temporal, and Commons, in this present Parliament assembled, and by the authority of the same, as follows:—

Notices prohibiting recurrence of nuisances, etc.

1.—(1) Where a local authority are satisfied that a statutory nuisance has occurred on any premises and is likely to recur on the same premises, they may serve a notice (in this Act referred to as a prohibition notice)—

(*a*) in the case of a nuisance arising from any defect of a structural character, on the owner of the premises, and

(*b*) in any other case, on the person by whose act, default or sufferance the nuisance arose or, if that person cannot be found, on the owner or occupier of the premises,

prohibiting a recurrence of the nuisance and requiring him to take such steps as may be necessary to prevent a recurrence.

(2) A local authority may if they think fit specify in a prohibition notice any works necessary to prevent a recurrence of the nuisance to which the notice relates and require the execution of those works.

(3) A prohibition notice may be served whether the nuisance to which it relates is in existence at the time of service of the notice or not and whether or not an abatement notice has previously been served with respect to that nuisance.

(4) A prohibition notice and an abatement notice may be contained in the same document.

Power of court to make nuisance order if prohibition notice disregarded.

2.—(1) Where a local authority have served a prohibition notice with respect to a nuisance and the nuisance recurs or the person on whom the notice was served fails to comply with any of the requirements of the notice, the authority may cause a complaint to be made to a justice of the peace.

(2) If on the hearing of a complaint under this section it is proved—

(*a*) that the nuisance has recurred (whether or not it still exists at the date of the hearing) or that the defendant has failed to comply with any of the requirements of the prohibition notice, and

(*b*) that the nuisance is likely to recur,

1936 c. 49.

the magistrates' court hearing the complaint shall have the like power to make a nuisance order under section 94 of the Public Health Act 1936 in relation to the nuisance, the requirements of the prohibition notice or both as they have to make such an order under that section in relation to a nuisance to which an abatement notice relates, the requirements of an abatement notice or both; and the court may also exercise any other power exercisable by a court on proceedings under that section.

Application of Part III of Public Health Act 1936 to proceedings under section 2 of this Act.

3.—(1) Subject to subsection (2) of this section, the provisions of Part III of the Public Health Act 1936 (other than section 99) shall, with the necessary adaptations and modifications, apply in relation to proceedings under section 2 of this Act as they apply in relation to proceedings under section 94 of that Act.

(2) Section 94(3) of the Act of 1936 shall not apply in relation to proceedings under section 2 of this Act, but where on the hearing of a complaint under section 2 it is proved that at the date of the making of the complaint the nuisance to which the prohibition relates had recurred or that the defendant had failed to comply with any of the requirements of the notice and, in either case, that the nuisance was likely to recur, then, whether or not at the date of the hearing the failure continues or the nuisance is likely to recur, the court shall order the defendant to pay to the local authority such reasonable sum as the court may determine in respect of the expenses incurred by the authority in, or in connection with, the making of the complaint and the proceedings before the court.

Short title, construction, commencement and extent.

4.—(1) This Act may be cited as the Public Health (Recurring Nuisances) Act 1969.

(2) This Act shall be construed as one with Part III of the Public Health Act 1936.

(3) Subject to subsection (4) of this section, any reference in any enactment to Part III of that Act shall be construed as including a reference to this Act.

(4) Subsection (3) of this section shall not apply to the references to Part III of the Public Health Act 1936 in section 16 of the Clean Air Act 1956 (which deems certain smoke nuisances to be statutory nuisances for the purposes of Part III of the Act of 1936 and provides a special procedure for preventing recurrence of such nuisances).

1936 c. 49.
1956 c. 52.

(5) The reference in section 268(3) of the Public Health Act 1936 to an abatement notice shall be construed as including a reference to a prohibition notice.

(6) Any reference in this Act to any enactment is a reference to that enactment as amended by or under any other enactment.

(7) This Act shall come into force at the expiration of the period of one month beginning with the date on which it is passed.

(8) This Act does not extend to Scotland or to Northern Ireland.

Agriculture (Spring Traps) (Scotland) Act 1969

1969 CHAPTER 26

An Act to make provision with respect to the termination of the power to authorise by order under section 50(4) of the Agriculture (Scotland) Act 1948 the use of spring traps other than approved traps in Scotland.

[25th June 1969]

BE IT ENACTED by the Queen's most Excellent Majesty, by and with the advice and consent of the Lords Spiritual and Temporal, and Commons, in this present Parliament assembled, and by the authority of the same, as follows:—

Use of spring traps other than approved traps no longer to be authorised. 1948 c. 45.

1. Subject to section 2 of this Act, after the appointed day it shall no longer be competent for the Secretary of State to make an order under subsection (4) of section 50 of the Agriculture (Scotland) Act 1948 authorising the use of a spring trap other than an approved trap as defined in subsection (3) of that section; and, accordingly, on that day the said subsection (4), and subsection (5) of that section (which empowers the Secretary of State by order to withdraw an authority granted under subsection (4)), shall cease to have effect.

Killing or taking of otters by spring traps.

2. After 1st July 1969 it shall no longer be competent for the Secretary of State to make an order under subsection (4) of section 50 of the Agriculture (Scotland) Act 1948 authorising the use of a spring trap other than an approved trap as defined by subsection (3) of that section for the purpose of killing or taking otters; and as from the said date any order authorising the killing or taking of otters by spring traps shall cease to have effect.

Meaning of appointed day.

3.—(1) The appointed day for the purposes of section 1 of this Act shall be 1st April 1973:

Provided that, subject to the next following subsection, the Secretary of State may by order appoint a day earlier than 1st April 1973 but not earlier than two years after the passing of this Act.

(2) The day appointed in an order made under this section shall not be earlier than one year after the day on which the order is made.

(3) The power of the Secretary of State to make an order under this section shall be exercisable by statutory instrument, and such an order shall be subject to annulment by resolution of either House of Parliament.

Short title and extent.

4.—(1) This Act may be cited as the Agriculture (Spring Traps) (Scotland) Act 1969.

(2) This Act shall extend to Scotland only.

Vehicle and Driving Licences Act 1969

1969 CHAPTER 27

An Act to make further provision, in relation to mechanically propelled vehicles, about the licensing, registration and marking of vehicles, the payment of excise duty, the licensing of drivers, offences and the provision of copies of test certificates; and for purposes connected with those matters. [25th June 1969]

BE IT ENACTED by the Queen's most Excellent Majesty, by and with the advice and consent of the Lords Spiritual and Temporal, and Commons, in this present Parliament assembled, and by the authority of the same, as follows:—

Transfer of functions

1.—(1) The functions conferred on local authorities by the Vehicles (Excise) Act 1962 and Part II of the Road Traffic Act 1960 (which provide for the levying of excise duty on vehicles, the licensing and registration of vehicles and the licensing of drivers) shall be transferred to the Minister of Transport by virtue of this section on the transfer date.

Transfer to Minister of local authorities' functions relating to vehicle and driving licences etc.

1962 c. 13.
1960 c. 16.

(2) In this Act—

" the transfer date " means such date as the Minister may by order appoint for the purposes of the foregoing subsection ; and

" relevant functions " means functions which will be or were transferred to the Minister by virtue of this section on the transfer date.

2.—(1) The Minister may by order make such provision as he considers appropriate for the purposes of section 1 of this Act—

Provisions supplementary to s. 1.

(*a*) with respect to the transfer and management and the custody of property which is held by local authorities for the purposes of any relevant functions and the transfer of rights acquired and liabilities incurred by local authorities in connection with any relevant functions ;

(*b*) with respect to the payment by the Minister of compensation in respect of any transfer of property or rights in pursuance of paragraph (*a*) above and in respect of liabilities of local authorities which are not transferred in pursuance of that paragraph ; and

(*c*) for securing that anything done by or in relation to a local authority before the transfer date in connection with any relevant functions is deemed on and after that date to have been done by or in relation to the Minister and, without prejudice to the foregoing provisions of this paragraph, that anything begun before that date by a local authority in the exercise of any relevant functions may be carried on and completed on and after that date by the Minister ;

and an order under this subsection may be made to take effect before the transfer date in so far as the Minister considers that it should so take effect for the purpose of facilitating the exercise by him of any relevant functions.

(2) The Minister shall not make an order under the foregoing subsection with respect to the transfer of premises appearing to him to form part of premises held by a local authority for the purposes of relevant and other functions unless he has given notice to the authority of his proposal to make the order and has specified in the notice the time within which the authority may request that the order shall be in accordance with the following provisions of this subsection ; and where the authority does so request and the Minister decides to make the order, then—

(*a*) the order shall secure that the transfer is for such period only as the Minister may determine, being a period ending not later than the end of the period of seven years beginning with the transfer date ; and

(*b*) without prejudice to the generality of the foregoing subsection, the other terms of the transfer shall be such as may be specified in the order.

(3) The Minister shall make regulations providing for the payment by him, subject to such exceptions or conditions as may be prescribed, of compensation to or in respect of persons who are or were, or but for any national service of theirs would be or would have been, the holders of any such place, situation or employment as may be prescribed and who suffer or have suffered loss of employment or loss or diminution of emoluments which is attributable to the provisions of section 1 of this Act ; and any such regulations may include provision for the determination of questions arising under the regulations.

In this subsection " national service " means any such service in any of Her Majesty's forces or other employment (whether or not in the service of Her Majesty) as may be prescribed.

(4) If a person employed by a local authority for the purposes of any relevant functions ceases to be employed by that authority in consequence of the provisions of section 1 of this Act and as soon as practicable after so ceasing enters an employment of a class specified in section 2(2) of the Superannuation (Miscellaneous Provisions) Act 1948, the latter employment and his employment by the authority aforesaid shall be deemed to be one continuous employment for the purposes of the National Insurance (Modification of Local Government Superannuation Schemes) Regulations 1961 and the National Insurance (Modification of Local Government Superannuation Schemes) (Scotland) Regulations 1961 and any certificate specifying non-participating employments in pursuance of the National Insurance Act 1965; and in section 6(5) of the Local Government Superannuation Act 1937 and section 6(5) of the Local Government Superannuation (Scotland) Act 1937 (under which a contributory employee whose remuneration is reduced in consequence, among other things, of such an incapacity as is there mentioned may make the same superannuation contributions as if the reduction had not occurred) and in any corresponding provision of a local Act scheme within the meaning of the latter Act the references to such an incapacity shall be construed as including references to the provisions of the said section 1.

1948 c. 33.
S.I. 1961 No. 21.
S.I. 1961 No. 206.
1965 c. 51.
1937 c. 68.
1937 c. 69.

Any question arising under this subsection or either of the said sections 6(5) or such a scheme as to whether a person was employed by a local authority for the purposes of any relevant functions or entered another employment as soon as practicable after ceasing to be employed by a local authority or as to whether an employment ceased or a reduction of remuneration occurred in consequence of the provisions of the said section 1 shall be determined by the Minister.

(5) Without prejudice to the powers of local authorities apart from this subsection, any local authority shall have power to enter into an agreement with the Minister providing for the exercise of any relevant functions on and after the transfer date by the authority on behalf of the Minister on such terms as may be provided by the agreement; and it is hereby declared that, in relation to any period before the transfer date, a local authority have and always had power to make arrangements with the Postmaster General for him to issue licences and collect duty under the Act of 1962 on their behalf, and subsection (1) of this section shall be construed accordingly.

(6) The functions mentioned in section 1(1) of this Act include the functions relating to the licensing of drivers which are conferred on the Council of the Isles of Scilly by virtue of the Isles of Scilly Order 1937, and in relation to the functions so conferred the said Council shall be deemed to be a local

S.R. & O. 1937 No. 783.

authority for the purposes of this section; and it is hereby declared that after the transfer date the Minister's functions under the Act of 1962 extend to the Isles of Scilly, and references to local authorities and relevant functions in subsection (5) of this section shall include respectively references to the said Council and the Minister's said functions in relation to the Isles.

(7) Nothing in this Act shall relieve a local authority from the obligation to pay into the Consolidated Fund any fees for licences received by the authority before the transfer date under Part II of the Act of 1960 and any sums received by the authority before that date by way of duty or penalties under the Act of 1962.

(8) The enactments mentioned in Part I of Schedule 1 to this Act shall have effect subject to the amendments specified in that Part (which are consequential upon the provisions of section 1 of this Act).

Interim provisions with respect to functions of local authorities.

3.—(1) The Minister may, at any time before the transfer date, by order provide that any relevant functions shall, as respects any area specified in the order, be exercisable by a local authority so specified instead of by the authority by whom they would be exercisable apart from the order.

(2) Where at any time before the transfer date a local authority is to cease to be a local authority and it appears to the Minister that, having regard to the provisions of section 1 of this Act, it is expedient to prevent that event from affecting the exercise of any of the relevant functions, he may by order direct that the relevant functions shall, except so far as the order otherwise provides, be exercised after that event as if it had not occurred.

(3) An order under the foregoing provisions of this section may contain such provisions, if any, as the Minister considers appropriate with respect to the transfer of persons employed by a local authority and shall contain provisions for safeguarding the interests of such persons; and section 2(3) of this Act shall have effect for the purposes of this section as if for the reference to section 1 of this Act there were substituted a reference to this section.

(4) If an authority exercising functions by virtue of an order under subsection (2) of this section is not a local authority, it shall be deemed to be a local authority for the purposes of those functions and references to a local authority in any enactment (including this Act) shall be construed accordingly; and the reference in section 1(1) of this Act to functions conferred by the enactments there mentioned shall be construed as including a reference to functions conferred by virtue of the foregoing provisions of this section.

Vehicle licences

Commencement and duration of licences.

4.—(1) Subject to the provisions of section 5 of this Act, a licence shall first have effect on the day specified by the applicant in the application for the licence.

(2) Any trade licence may be taken out for a period of twelve months, and a general trade licence may be taken out for a period of four months.

(3) A licence for a period of four months shall expire with such day in the fourth month after that in which the licence first has effect as corresponds to the day preceding that on which it first has effect, so however that a licence for that period shall—

(*a*) if it first has effect on the first day of a month, expire with the last day of the third month after that month; and

(*b*) if it first has effect on 30th or 31st October, expire with the last day of the following February.

(4) The enactments mentioned in Part II of Schedule 1 to this Act shall have effect subject to the amendments specified in that Part (which are consequential upon the foregoing provisions of this section).

(5) Section 3 of the Act of 1962 (which provides for the making of orders authorising the issue of licences for the periods and on payment of duty at the rates mentioned in that section) shall cease to have effect.

(6) Nothing in any of the foregoing provisions of this section affects any licence taken out before that provision comes into force.

(7) A licence which first has effect before the day on which it is issued shall not affect any criminal liability incurred before that day.

(8) Notwithstanding anything in the Act of 1962 or the foregoing provisions of this section, the Minister may, during the period of two years beginning with the day when this section comes into force, provide by regulations that, in such cases as may be determined by or under the regulations, the duration of a licence taken out after the coming into force of the regulations shall be longer or shorter, by such period not exceeding thirty days as may be so determined, than its duration would have been apart from the regulations; and where the duration of a licence is altered by virtue of this subsection the duty payable upon the licence shall be increased or reduced proportionately.

(9) At the expiration of the period of two years mentioned in subsection (8) of this section that subsection shall cease to have effect, but without prejudice to any licence issued or any

payment made or falling to be made by virtue of any regulations in force under that subsection immediately before the expiration of that period.

(10) In this section " licence " means a vehicle licence.

Temporary licences.

5.—(1) Where an application is made for a vehicle licence for any period (except a trade licence and a seven day licence), the Minister may if he thinks fit, instead of issuing forthwith a licence for that period—

(*a*) issue a licence (in this Act referred to as a " temporary licence ") for fourteen days or such other period as may be prescribed and having effect from such day as may be prescribed ; and

(*b*) issue from time to time a further temporary licence in respect of the vehicle to which a previous temporary licence relates.

(2) A temporary licence shall be deemed to be a vehicle licence, and except where the context otherwise requires references to a vehicle licence in any enactment (including this Act) shall be construed accordingly ; but nothing in this section shall affect the amount of any duty payable in connection with an application for a vehicle licence.

(3) Where an application is made for a vehicle licence for any period and a temporary licence is issued in pursuance of the application, section 11(2) of the Finance Act 1967 (under which a vehicle licence ceases to be in force for certain purposes on the transfer of the vehicle unless it is delivered with the vehicle to the transferee) shall not apply to that vehicle licence if on a transfer of the relevant vehicle during the currency of the temporary licence the temporary licence is delivered with the vehicle to the transferee.

1967 c. 54.

Issue etc. of temporary licences by motor dealers.

6.—(1) The Minister may by regulations make such provision as he considers appropriate with respect to the allocation of temporary licences to motor dealers who apply for such allocations and appear to the Minister suitable to receive them and with respect to the issue of the licences by motor dealers.

(2) Without prejudice to the generality of subsection (1) of this section, regulations under this section may include provision—

(*a*) as to the mode of application for the allocation of licences and as to the fees payable in respect of allocations ;

(*b*) specifying the categories of vehicles for which allocations of licences may be made ;

(*c*) prohibiting the issue of temporary licences in pursuance of applications for trade licences or seven day licences ;

(*d*) for requiring a motor dealer to pay to the Minister, in respect of each licence allocated to the dealer, the excise duty chargeable in respect of the licence which will be specified in the application in consequence of which the allocated licence can be issued ;

(*e*) as to the replacement of allocated licences which are lost, damaged or destroyed and as to the fees payable in connection with their replacement ; and

(*f*) as to the transfer of licences allocated to a motor dealer in cases where the dealer dies or becomes incapacitated or bankrupt and in such other cases as may be prescribed.

(3) Without prejudice to the generality of subsection (1) of this section, regulations under this section may also include provision for—

(*a*) requiring a motor dealer to whom an allocation of licences is made to keep a record in the prescribed form of the licences allocated to him and of the licences issued by him, and to permit the record to be inspected at all reasonable times by any officer of the Minister and any constable ;

(*b*) restricting the circumstances in which a motor dealer may issue licences ;

(*c*) requiring a motor dealer, before he issues a licence in respect of a vehicle—

(i) to obtain from the proposed holder of the licence an application for a vehicle licence in the prescribed form,

(ii) to ascertain that the prescribed requirements as to test certificates and insurance are satisfied in respect of the vehicle,

(iii) to ensure that the licence is appropriate for the vehicle and takes effect on the prescribed date, and

(iv) to make on the licence, and on any copy of it specified in the regulations, such entries as the Minister may determine ;

(*d*) requiring a motor dealer by whom a licence is issued to deliver or despatch to the Minister, within the prescribed period beginning with the day on which the dealer issues the licence, the prescribed particulars and documents relating to the licence and the vehicle for which it is issued ;

(*e*) securing that after any change takes effect in the rate of excise duty chargeable in respect of a vehicle licence of any description, a licence previously allocated to a dealer is not issued by him in consequence of an application for a vehicle licence of that description, but that a licence issued in contravention of regulations made in pursuance of the foregoing provisions of this paragraph shall not be invalid by reason only of the contravention; and

(*f*) providing that a person who contravenes or fails to comply with any specified provision of the regulations shall be guilty of an offence under this Act.

Provisions supplementary to s. 6.

7.—(1) Any unissued licence allocated to a motor dealer in pursuance of the foregoing section may at any time be surrendered in the prescribed manner to the Minister by the dealer or by any person to whom the licence has been transferred under regulations made in pursuance of subsection (2)(*f*) of that section.

(2) A motor dealer and any other person having the custody of any unissued licence allocated to the dealer in pursuance of the foregoing section shall, if required to do so by the Minister and subject to section 21(2) of this Act, forthwith surrender any such licence to the Minister in such manner as the Minister may direct; and a person who knowingly fails to comply with a requirement made by the Minister under this subsection shall be guilty of an offence under this Act.

(3) On the surrender of a licence in pursuance of this section the dealer or other person in question shall be entitled to be paid by the Minister the amount paid by the dealer in respect of the licence under regulations made in pursuance of subsection (2)(*d*) of the foregoing section.

(4) Where a licence is issued by a motor dealer in contravention of regulations made in pursuance of subsection (3)(*e*) of the foregoing section, the dealer shall be liable to pay to the Minister a sum equal to the amount (if any) by which the amount paid by the dealer as mentioned in subsection (3) of this section is exceeded by the amount which would have been so paid if the allocation of the licence to the dealer had taken place at the time when the licence was issued.

(5) In section 13(1) of the Act of 1962 (which provides for the registration of a vehicle on the first issue of a licence for it) after the words " first issue " there shall be inserted the words " by the Minister ".

Surrender of licences.

8.—(1) The holder of a vehicle licence (other than a licence for a tramcar)—

(*a*) may at any time surrender the licence to the Minister in the prescribed manner; and

(*b*) shall on so surrendering the licence be entitled, if he satisfies the prescribed requirements and subject to the following provisions of this section, to receive from the Minister, by way of rebate of duty paid upon the surrendered licence, a sum equal to the relevant amount multiplied by the number of days in the relevant period.

(2) In this section " the relevant amount ", in relation to a surrendered licence, means one three-hundred-and-sixty-fifth of the annual rate by reference to which duty was charged upon the licence and " the relevant period ", in relation to a surrendered licence, means the period beginning with the day following that on which the licence is received by the Minister in pursuance of paragraph (*a*) of subsection (1) of this section and ending with the day on which the licence would have expired by the effluxion of time.

(3) No sum shall be payable under subsection (1) of this section in a case where the relevant period is less than thirty days, and in making any payment under that subsection a fraction of a penny shall be disregarded; and the Minister may, for the purposes of subsection (2) of this section, treat a surrendered licence delivered to him by post as received by him on the day on which it was posted.

(4) If during the currency of a temporary licence issued in pursuance of an application for a vehicle licence for any period, the temporary licence is surrendered under this section, it shall be treated for the purposes of this section as issued for that period or, if the Minister so directs, for any other period specified in the direction, being a period for which by virtue of subsection (5) of section 11 of this Act a licence could be issued in pursuance of the application; and where a further licence issued in pursuance of the application is held by any person at the time of the surrender of the temporary licence or is received by him thereafter—

(*a*) the further licence shall cease to be in force and he shall forthwith return it to the Minister and shall, if he knowingly fails to do so, be guilty of an offence under this Act; and

(*b*) if the Minister considers that there has been undue delay in complying with paragraph (*a*) of this subsection he may, without prejudice to any liability under that paragraph, reduce the relevant period by such number of days as he thinks fit for the purpose of calculating the sum payable in pursuance of subsection (1) of this section in respect of the surrendered temporary licence.

(5) Subsection (4) of this section shall have effect, during any period when section 9 of the Act of 1962 is in force, with the substitution of references to that section for references

to this section and with the omission of paragraph (*b*) and the words from " or if " to " application " in the second place where it occurs.

Duty on vehicles placed on roads.

9. For the purposes of sections 4 and 7 of the Act of 1962 and of any other provision of that Act and any subsequent enactment relating to the keeping of mechanically propelled vehicles on public roads (including such an enactment contained in this Act and in particular section 11(3) of this Act), a person keeps such a vehicle on a public road if he causes it to be on such a road for any period, however short, when it is not in use there.

Exemptions. 1967 c. 30.

10. It is hereby declared that in section 6(5) of the Act of 1962 and section 27 of the Road Safety Act 1967 (by virtue of paragraphs (*a*) to (*c*) of which a vehicle is not chargeable with duty under the Act of 1962 by reason of its use for the purpose of taking it by previous arrangement to, or bringing it from, such a test or examination as is there mentioned or a place where such work as is there mentioned is to be or has been done) any reference to the use of a vehicle for a purpose mentioned in any of those paragraphs is to its use solely for that purpose and any reference in any of those paragraphs to a previous arrangement is a reference to such an arrangement for a specified time on a specified date.

Continuous liability for vehicle excise duty

Continuous liability for vehicle excise duty.

11.—(1) Subject to the provisions of this and the following section, a person who for any period keeps a vehicle in respect of which duty under the Act of 1962 has at any time become chargeable shall, whether or not it is still a mechanically propelled vehicle, be liable to pay duty under that Act in respect of the vehicle for that period.

(2) Subject to the provisions of this and the following section, a person shall not be liable by virtue of subsection (1) of this section to pay duty under the Act of 1962 in respect of a vehicle—

(*a*) for any period for which duty under that Act in respect of the vehicle has been paid and has not been repaid in consequence of the surrender of a licence ;

(*b*) for any period in respect of which he has, in accordance with regulations under the following section, given notice to the Minister that the vehicle will not be used or kept on a public road ;

(*c*) for any period when the vehicle is not a mechanically propelled vehicle and a notice stating that it has ceased to be such a vehicle has, in accordance with regulations under the following section, been given to the Minister and not revoked in pursuance of subsection (2) of that section ;

(*d*) for any period when the vehicle is exempt from duty by virtue of section 6 of the Act of 1962 (except subsection (2) or subsection (5) of that section) or section 11 of the Finance Act 1964 ; 1964 c. 49.

(*e*) for any period when he keeps the vehicle solely for the purpose of selling or supplying it in the course of his business as a motor dealer or using it under the authority of a trade licence in the course of his business as a motor trader within the meaning of section 12 of the Act of 1962 ;

(*f*) in the case of such a vehicle as is mentioned in paragraph (*d*) of section 2(1) of the Act of 1962 (which relates to seven day licences for certain heavy goods vehicles), for any period as respects which the Minister is satisfied that the vehicle has not been used or kept on a public road otherwise than as authorised by a seven day licence ;

(*g*) for any period by reference to which there was calculated an amount ordered to be paid by him in respect of the vehicle in pursuance of section 12(1) of the Finance Act 1967 (under which an amount related to 1967 c. 54. the period during which a vehicle was unlicensed is required to be paid by the keeper of the vehicle who is convicted of using it during that period).

(3) A person shall not by virtue of paragraph (*b*) of subsection (2) of this section be exempt from his liability for any period under subsection (1) of this section in respect of a vehicle if—

(*a*) at any time during that period he or any other person with his consent uses or keeps the vehicle on a public road and no vehicle licence is in force for the vehicle at that time ; or

(*b*) after he has given notice under that paragraph in relation to the vehicle in respect of that period he applies for a vehicle licence for the vehicle to have effect on any day included in the first thirty days of that period ;

and for the purposes of paragraph (*a*) of this subsection the consent there mentioned shall be presumed to have been given unless the contrary is shown but any use or keeping of the vehicle in question as respects which the vehicle is exempt by virtue of any enactment for the time being in force from duty under the Act of 1962 shall be disregarded.

(4) Sums payable in pursuance of this section by way of duty in respect of a vehicle shall accrue due from day to day at one three-hundred-and-sixty-fifth of the annual rate of duty applicable to the vehicle on that day.

(5) Without prejudice to any other mode of recovering sums payable by virtue of this section, where an application for a vehicle licence for twelve months or four months for a vehicle is made by a person by whom such sums are payable in respect of the vehicle and a licence other than a temporary licence is to be issued in pursuance of the application, the licence shall, if the Minister so directs, be made to have effect for a shorter period specified in the direction, being a period which is not less than thirty days and is such that the difference between the amount tendered in connection with the application and the amount chargeable upon the licence for the specified period does not exceed the aggregate amount of the sums aforesaid; and the amount so chargeable shall be equal to the number of days in the specified period multiplied by—

(*a*) where the application is for a licence for twelve months, one three-hundred-and-sixty-fifth of the annual rate of duty under the Act of 1962 payable in respect of the vehicle on the date of the application; and

(*b*) where the application is for a licence for four months, eleven three-thousand-six-hundred and fiftieths of that rate;

and where a licence is made to have effect for a specified period in pursuance of this subsection the aggregate amount of the sums aforesaid shall be treated as reduced by the difference aforesaid.

Provisions supplementary to s. 11.

12.—(1) For the purposes of the foregoing section, a vehicle in respect of which a licence has been issued under the Act of 1962 and sums are payable by virtue of that section for any period shall, except so far as it is shown to have been a mechanically propelled vehicle of some other class or description during that period, be deemed to have belonged throughout that period to the class or description to which it belonged on the date when the last such licence was issued in respect of it.

(2) When a vehicle in respect of which a notice has been given in pursuance of paragraph (*c*) of subsection (2) of the foregoing section becomes a mechanically propelled vehicle, its keeper for the time being shall forthwith give to the Minister a further notice revoking the first-mentioned notice; and where a person required to give such a further notice does not do so, then—

(*a*) if he knowingly fails to give it he shall be guilty of an offence under this Act; and (*b*) in a case where he became the keeper of the vehicle after the first-mentioned notice was given it shall be deemed to have been revoked on the date when he became the keeper of the vehicle, and in any other case the first-mentioned notice shall be deemed not to have been given.

(3) The Minister may by regulations make such provision as he considers appropriate for the purposes of paragraph (*b*) or (*c*) of subsection (2) of the foregoing section or the foregoing subsection including, without prejudice to the generality of the power conferred by this subsection, provision—

(*a*) as to the form of and the particulars to be included in a notice under those provisions, the manner of giving such a notice and the time at which it is to be treated as being given;

(*b*) for securing that notice under the said paragraph (*b*) is not given in respect of a period of less than thirty days or more than twelve months;

(*c*) as to the mode of calculating the period in respect of which notice under the said paragraph (*b*) is to be treated as given;

(*d*) with respect to the mode of proving the giving of notice;

(*e*) for deeming notice to have been given in relation to a vehicle in respect of any period or at any time if in the circumstances of any particular case the Minister considers it reasonable to do so.

(4) In calculating any amount for the purposes of section 12(1) of the Finance Act 1967 (of which the effect is mentioned in subsection (2)(*g*) of the foregoing section), no day shall be omitted from the relevant period within the meaning of the said section 12 in consequence of proof that the vehicle in question was neither kept nor used by the convicted person on a public road on that day unless it is also proved that he was exempt by virtue of subsection (2)(*b*) or (*c*) of the foregoing section from liability under subsection (1) of that section in respect of that day. 1967 c. 54.

Drivers and driving licences

Alteration of provisions as to physical fitness of drivers.

13. For section 100 of the Act of 1960 (which imposes requirements as to the physical fitness of drivers) there shall be substituted the following section:—

Requirements as to physical fitness of drivers.

100.—(1) An application for the grant of a licence shall include a declaration by the applicant, in such form as the Minister may require, stating whether he is suffering or has at any time (or, if a period is prescribed for the purposes of this subsection, has during that period) suffered from any prescribed disability or from any other disability likely to cause the driving of a vehicle by him in pursuance of the licence to be a source of danger to the public.

(2) If it appears from the declaration aforesaid, or if on enquiry the licensing authority are satisfied from other information, that the applicant is suffering from a relevant disability, then, subject to the following provisions of this section, the authority shall refuse to grant the licence.

(3) The licensing authority shall not by virtue of subsection (2) of this section refuse to grant a licence—

(*a*) on account of any relevant disability, if the applicant has at any time passed a relevant test and it does not appear to the licensing authority that the disability has arisen or become more acute since that time or was, for whatever reason, not disclosed to the appropriate licensing authority at that time ;

(*b*) on account of any relevant disability which is prescribed for the purposes of this paragraph, if the applicant satisfies such conditions as may be prescribed with a view to authorising the grant of a licence to a person in whose case the disability is appropriately controlled ;

(*c*) on account of any relevant disability other than a disability prescribed for the purposes of this paragraph, if the application is for a provisional licence.

(4) If as a result of a test of competence to drive the licensing authority are satisfied that the person who took the test is suffering from a disability such that there is likely to be danger to the public—

(*a*) if he drives any vehicle ; or

(*b*) if he drives a vehicle other than a vehicle of a particular construction or design,

the licensing authority shall serve notice in writing to that effect on that person and shall include in the notice a description of the disability ; and where a notice is served in pursuance of this subsection, then—

(i) if the notice is in pursuance of paragraph (*a*) of this subsection and the disability is not prescribed for the purposes of subsection

(3)(*c*) of this section, it shall be deemed to be so prescribed in relation to the person aforesaid; and

(ii) if the notice is in pursuance of paragraph (*b*) of this subsection, any licence granted to that person shall be limited to vehicles of the particular construction or design specified in the notice.

(5) If the licensing authority by whom a current licence was granted are at any time satisfied on inquiry—

(*a*) that the licence holder is suffering from a relevant disability; and

(*b*) that the authority would be required by virtue of subsection (2) or subsection (4)(ii) of this section to refuse an application for the licence made by him at that time,

the authority may serve notice in writing on the licence holder revoking the licence at the expiration of a period specified in the notice which shall not be less than seven nor more than thirty days and shall begin with the date of service of the notice; and it shall be the duty of a person whose licence is revoked under this subsection to deliver up the licence to the licensing authority forthwith after the revocation.

(6) In this section—

"disability" includes disease;

"relevant disability" means such a disability as is mentioned in subsection (1) of this section; and

"relevant test", in relation to an application for a licence, means any such test of competence as is mentioned in section 99(1)(*a*) of this Act or a test as to fitness or ability in pursuance of section 100 of this Act as originally enacted, being a test authorising the grant of a licence in respect of vehicles of the classes or descriptions to which the application relates;

and for the purposes of subsection (3)(*a*) of this section a person to whom a licence was granted after the making of a declaration under paragraph (*c*) of the proviso to section 5(2) of the Road Traffic Act 1930 (which contained transitional provisions **1930 c. 43.**

with respect to certain disabilities) shall be treated as having passed, at the time of the declaration, a relevant test in respect of vehicles of the classes or descriptions to which the licence related.

Alteration of provisions as to grant and duration etc. of licences.

14.—(1) For sections 101 and 102 of the Act of 1960 (which among other things relate to the grant and duration of driving licences) there shall be substituted the following sections:—

Grant of licences.

101.—(1) Subject to the last foregoing section, the licensing authority shall, on payment of the prescribed fee, grant a licence to a person who—

(*a*) makes an application for it in such manner and containing such particulars as the Minister may specify; and

(*b*) furnishes the authority with such evidence or further evidence in support of the application as the authority may require; and

(*c*) surrenders to the authority any previous licence granted to him after this subsection comes into force or furnishes the authority with an explanation for not surrendering it which the authority consider adequate; and

(*d*) is not disqualified by reason of age or otherwise for obtaining the licence for which he makes the application and is not prevented from obtaining it by the provisions of section 99 of this Act.

(2) If the application aforesaid states that it is made for the purpose of enabling the applicant to drive a motor vehicle with a view to passing a test of competence to drive, any licence granted in pursuance of the application shall be a provisional licence for that purpose, and nothing in section 99 of this Act shall apply to such a licence; but a provisional licence shall—

(*a*) be granted subject to prescribed conditions; and

(*b*) in any cases prescribed for the purposes of this paragraph, be restricted so as to authorise only the driving of vehicles of the classes or descriptions so prescribed.

(3) A licence shall be in such form as the Minister may determine and shall—

(*a*) state whether, apart from subsection (4) of this section, it authorises its holder to drive motor vehicles of all classes and descriptions or of certain classes or descriptions only and, in the latter case, specify those classes or descriptions ;

(*b*) specify any restrictions to which, under the provisions of this Part of this Act, its holder is subject as respects the driving of vehicles of any class or description in pursuance of the licence ;

(*c*) in the case of a provisional licence, specify the conditions subject to which it is granted ; and

(*d*) where by virtue of subsection (4) of this section the licence authorises its holder to drive vehicles of classes or descriptions other than those specified in the licence in pursuance of paragraph (*a*) of this subsection, contain such statements as the Minister considers appropriate for indicating the effect of that subsection.

(4) A licence which, apart from this subsection, authorises its holder to drive motor vehicles of certain classes or descriptions only shall also authorise him to drive motor vehicles of all other classes and descriptions subject to the same conditions as if he were authorised by a provisional licence to drive the last-mentioned vehicles ; but a licence shall not by virtue of this subsection authorise a person to drive—

(*a*) a vehicle which he is prohibited from driving by section 97 of this Act ; or

(*b*) such a motor cycle as is mentioned in section 2 of the Road Traffic (Driving of Motor Cycles) Act 1960 (under which a provisional licence does not authorise the driving of heavy motor cycles) unless he has passed the test there mentioned. 1960 c. 69.

(5) In subsection (4) of this section the first reference to a licence does not include a reference to a licence granted before that subsection came into force or a provisional licence granted thereafter or any other licence of a description prescribed for the purposes of this subsection.

(6) A person who fails to comply with any condition applicable to him by virtue of subsection (2) or subsection (4) of this section shall be liable on summary conviction to a fine not exceeding fifty pounds.

Duration of licences.

102.—(1) A licence shall, unless previously revoked or surrendered, remain in force—

(*a*) except in a case falling within paragraph (*b*) or (*c*) of this subsection, for a period of three years or, if the licensing authority so determine in the case of a licence to be granted to a person appearing to the authority to be suffering from a relevant disability within the meaning of section 100 of this Act, for such shorter period, not less than one year, as the authority may determine;

(*b*) in the case of a licence granted in exchange for a subsisting licence and in pursuance of an application requesting a licence for the period authorised by this paragraph, for a period equal to the remainder of that for which the subsisting licence was granted;

(*c*) in the case of a provisional licence, for a period of one year;

and any such period shall begin with the date on which the licence in question is expressed to come into force.

(2) Where it appears to the licensing authority that a licence granted by them to any person is required to be endorsed in pursuance of any enactment or was granted in error or with an error or omission in the particulars specified in the licence or required to be so endorsed on it, the authority may serve notice in writing on that person revoking the licence and requiring him to deliver up the licence forthwith to the authority.

(3) Where the name or address of the licence holder as specified in a licence ceases to be correct, its holder shall forthwith surrender the licence to the licensing authority and furnish to the authority particulars of the alterations falling to be made in the name or address and, in the case of a provisional licence as respects which the prescribed conditions are satisfied, with a statement of his sex and date of birth.

(4) On the surrender of a licence by any person in pursuance of subsection (2) or subsection (3) of this section, the licensing authority—

(*a*) shall, except where the licence was granted in error or is surrendered in pursuance of the said subsection (2) in consequence of an error or omission appearing to the authority to be attributable to that person's fault or in consequence of a current disqualification ; and

(*b*) may in such an excepted case which does not involve a current disqualification,

grant to that person free of charge a new licence for the period for which the surrendered licence was granted.

(5) A person who fails to comply with the provisions of subsection (3) of this section shall be liable on summary conviction to a fine not exceeding twenty pounds.

(2) A licence in force by virtue of section 101 or section 102 of the Act of 1960 immediately before subsection (1) of this section comes into force shall have effect thereafter as if duly granted in pursuance of section 101 of that Act (as replaced by that subsection) on the day on which it was actually granted ; but nothing in this section shall extend the duration of a provisional licence granted before that subsection comes into force or the duration of a licence so granted to a person as resident outside the United Kingdom.

Alteration of provisions about appeals in respect of licences.

15. For section 103 of the Act of 1960 (which provides for an appeal against the refusal or revocation of a driving licence) there shall be substituted the following section:—

Appeals relating to licences.

103. A person who is aggrieved by the licensing authority's—

(*a*) refusal to grant or revocation of a licence in pursuance of section 100 of this Act ; or

(*b*) grant of a licence for less than three years in pursuance of section 102(1)(*a*) of this Act ; or

(*c*) revocation of a licence in pursuance of section 102(2) of this Act,

or by a notice served on him in pursuance of section 100(4) of this Act may, after giving to the licensing authority notice of his intention to do so, appeal to a magistrates' court acting for the petty sessions area in which he resides or, if he resides in Scotland, to the sheriff within whose jurisdiction he resides ; and on any such appeal the court or sheriff may make such order as it or he thinks fit and the order shall be binding on the licensing authority.

Other amendments of enactments relating to drivers etc.

16.—(1) At the end of section 98 of the Act of 1960 (under which it is an offence to drive or to employ a person to drive a vehicle unless the driver holds an appropriate driving licence) there shall be added the following subsections:—

(5) Notwithstanding the foregoing provisions of this section, a person may at any time drive or employ another person to drive a vehicle of any class or description if—

(*a*) the driver has held and is entitled to obtain a licence to drive vehicles of that class or description; and

(*b*) an application by the driver for the grant of such a licence for a period which includes that time has been received by the licensing authority or such a licence granted to him has been revoked or surrendered in pursuance of section 102 of this Act; and

(*c*) any conditions which by virtue of section 101(2) or (4) of this Act apply to the driving under the authority of the licence of vehicles of that class or description are complied with;

but the benefit of the foregoing provisions of this subsection shall not extend beyond the date when a licence is granted in pursuance of the application mentioned in paragraph (*b*) above or, as the case may be, in pursuance of subsection (4) of the said section 102 in consequence of the revocation or surrender so mentioned nor (in a case where a licence is not in fact so granted) beyond the expiration of the period for which it fell to be granted.

(6) Regulations may provide that a person who becomes resident in Great Britain shall, during the prescribed period after he becomes so resident, be treated for the purposes of subsections (1) and (2) of this section as the holder of a licence authorising him to drive motor vehicles of the prescribed classes or descriptions if he satisfies the prescribed conditions and is the holder of a permit of the prescribed description authorising him to drive vehicles under the law of a country outside the United Kingdom; and the regulations may provide for the application of any enactment relating to licences or licence holders, with or without modifications, in relation to any such permit and its holder respectively.

(2) The Act of 1960 shall have effect subject to the further amendments specified in Schedule 2 to this Act.

(3) In section 7(4) of the Road Traffic Act 1962 (under which a court must in certain circumstances require a driving licence to be produced for endorsement) after the words " as required " there shall be inserted the words " then, unless he satisfies the court that he has applied for a new licence and has not received it ". 1962 c. 59.

(4) In section 7(7) of the Road Traffic Act 1962 (which provides for the issue of driving licences free from endorsements) for the words from " either " to " time " there shall be substituted the words " on applying for the grant of a licence in pursuance of paragraph (*a*) of subsection (1) of section 101 of the principal Act and satisfying the other requirements of that subsection ".

(5) In section 19(2) of the Road Safety Act 1967 (which prohibits the grant of a full licence to drive heavy goods vehicles of any class unless the applicant satisfies the licensing authority that during the preceding ten years he has passed the driving test or held a full licence for vehicles of that class) and in section 19(7) of that Act (which enables such a licence to be granted to a person who has held a corresponding Northern Ireland licence during that period) for the words " ten years " there shall be substituted the words " five years ". 1967 c. 30.

(6) In section 85(2)(*a*) of the Road Traffic Regulation Act 1967 (under which the owner of a vehicle may be required to identify the driver of it who is alleged to have committed an offence to which that section applies) for the words " owner of " there shall be substituted the words " person keeping ". 1967 c. 76.

(7) A notice sent by a court to the licensing authority or the Minister in pursuance of section 112 of the Act of 1960, section 4 of the Road Traffic Act 1962 or section 56(10) of the Criminal Justice Act 1967 shall be sent in such manner and to such address and contain such particulars as the Minister may determine, and a licence so sent in pursuance of the said section 112 shall be sent to such address as the Minister may determine. 1967 c. 80.

Miscellaneous

Regulations with respect to the transfer and identification of vehicles.

17. For section 16 of the Act of 1962 (which enables regulations to be made with respect to the registration etc. of vehicles) there shall be substituted the following section:—

Regulations with respect to the transfer and identification of vehicles.

16. Regulations under this Act may—

(*a*) require a person who becomes or ceases to be the keeper of a mechanically propelled vehicle, or who acts as the auctioneer at the sale of such a vehicle by auction, to furnish the prescribed information to the Minister in the prescribed manner;

(*b*) specify the size, shape and character of the registration marks or the signs to be affixed to any such vehicle (including a vehicle used by virtue of a trade licence) and the manner in which the marks or signs are to be displayed and rendered easily distinguishable by day and by night;

(*c*) make provision with respect to the furnishing of information and production of certificates of insurance or security and test certificates relating to mechanically propelled vehicles in respect of which duty is not chargeable under this Act and with respect to the registration and identification of such vehicles (including vehicles belonging to the Crown);

(*d*) make provision with respect to the inspection and surrender of any registration document issued in respect of a vehicle and provide that, in a case where the surrender of such a document is required in connection with an application for a licence under this Act, the licence shall not be issued if the document is not surrendered;

(*e*) make provision with respect to the replacement of any such document and as to the fee payable in prescribed circumstances in respect of any replacement; and

(*f*) provide for information contained in any records maintained by the Minister with respect to the marking, registration or keeping of vehicles to be made public or to be made available, either without payment or on payment of the prescribed fee, to such persons as may be determined by or under the regulations.

Copies of test certificates.

18.—(1) The power to make regulations conferred by section 65(6) of the Act of 1960 (which relates to vehicle tests) shall include power to make provision as to the issue of copies of test certificates within the meaning of that section and as to the fees to be paid for the issue of copies; and in section 66(6) of that Act (which among other things enables regulations to provide that a licence for a vehicle shall be refused unless an effective test certificate for the vehicle is produced) at the end of paragraph (*a*) there shall be inserted the words " the furnishing to the Minister of a copy of such a certificate, or ".

(2) Regulations under subsection (9) of section 14 of the Road Safety Act 1967 (which enables regulations to provide that licences under the Act of 1962 shall not be granted for goods vehicles to which subsection (2) or subsection (3) of that section applies unless evidence is produced that test certificates are in force for the vehicles or that they comply with the relevant type approval requirements) may be made so as to apply to such classes only of those vehicles as may be specified in the regulations. 1967 c. 30.

Marking of engines and bodies.

19.—(1) The Minister may by regulations make such provision as he thinks appropriate with respect to the marking of the engines and bodies of mechanically propelled vehicles.

(2) Without prejudice to the generality of subsection (1) of this section, regulations under this section may include provision—

(*a*) as to the persons by whom and the times at which engines and bodies of vehicles are to be marked;

(*b*) as to the form of any mark and the manner and position in which it is to be made;

(*c*) for requiring particulars of marks made in pursuance of the regulations to be furnished to the Minister; and

(*d*) providing that a person who contravenes or fails to comply with any specified provision of the regulations shall be guilty of an offence under this Act.

Issue etc. of vehicle registration marks by motor dealers.

20.—(1) The Minister may by regulations make such provision as he considers appropriate with respect to the allocation of registration marks for vehicles to motor dealers who apply for such allocations and appear to the Minister suitable to receive them and with respect to the assigning of the marks to vehicles by motor dealers.

(2) Without prejudice to the generality of subsection (1) of this section, regulations under this section may include provision—

(*a*) as to the mode of application for the allocation of registration marks;

(*b*) as to the transfer of registration marks allocated to a motor dealer in cases where the dealer dies or becomes incapacitated or bankrupt and in such other cases as may be prescribed; and

(*c*) subject to section 21(2) of this Act, as to the cancellation of allocations of registration marks.

(3) Without prejudice to the generality of subsection (1) of this section, regulations under this section may also include provision for—

(*a*) restricting the circumstances in which a motor dealer may assign a registration mark to a vehicle;

(*b*) securing that registration marks allocated to a dealer are assigned by him in such sequence as the Minister considers appropriate and that no registration mark is assigned to a vehicle to which such a mark has already been assigned;

(*c*) requiring a motor dealer to furnish the Minister within the prescribed period with the prescribed particulars in respect of each vehicle to which the dealer assigns a registration mark; and

(*d*) providing that a person who contravenes or fails to comply with any specified provision of the regulations shall be guilty of an offence under this Act.

(4) A registration mark assigned to a vehicle in pursuance of this section shall be deemed to be assigned to it under section 13 of the Act of 1962.

(5) Where particulars in respect of a vehicle are furnished to the Minister in pursuance of this section before the Minister first issues a vehicle licence for the vehicle, the Minister shall register the vehicle in accordance with the said section 13 on receiving the particulars instead of on the first issue of a licence and shall not be required to assign a registration mark to the vehicle; and for the purposes of section 4(1) of the Road Traffic (Amendment) Act 1967 (under which the period after which a test certificate is required for a vehicle used before being registered in accordance with the said section 13 is calculated by reference to the vehicle's date of manufacture) any use of a vehicle before it is so registered and after a mark is assigned to it in pursuance of this section shall be disregarded.

1967 c. 70.

Review of decisions relating to motor traders etc.

21.—(1) If the Minister—

(*a*) rejects an application by a motor dealer for an allocation of temporary licences or registration marks in pursuance of this Act; or

(*b*) requires a motor dealer or any other person to surrender any unissued licences allocated to the dealer in pursuance of this Act or cancels an allocation of registration marks made to a dealer in pursuance of this Act; or (*c*) refuses an application for a trade licence made by a motor trader or vehicle tester within the meaning of section 12 of the Act of 1962,

and the dealer, trader, tester or other person in question requests the Minister within the prescribed period to review his decision, it shall be the duty of the Minister to comply with the request and, in doing so, to consider any representations made to him in writing within the period aforesaid by the person who made the request.

(2) Such a requirement or cancellation as is mentioned in paragraph (*b*) of subsection (1) of this section shall not take effect before the expiration of the period aforesaid and, where during that period a request is made in pursuance of that subsection in respect of the requirement or cancellation, shall not take effect before the Minister gives notice in writing of the result of the review to the person who made the request.

(3) Where in pursuance of subsection (7) of the said section 12 (which relates to appeals to the Minister from refusals of local authorities to issue trade licences) an appeal is pending immediately before the date when the repeal of that subsection by this Act takes effect, the making of the appeal shall be treated as a request in pursuance of subsection (1) of this section in respect of such a refusal as is mentioned in paragraph (*c*) of that subsection.

Information as to date of birth and sex.

22.—(1) If on convicting a person of an offence specified in Part I or Part II of Schedule 1 to the Road Traffic Act 1962 (which relates to offences involving endorsements of driving licences and disqualifications) or of an offence treated as so specified by virtue of section 5 of the Road Safety Act 1967 or of such other offence as may be prescribed, the court orders his driving licence to be endorsed or orders him to be temporarily disqualified and does not know his date of birth, the court shall order him to state that date in writing.

1962 c. 59.
1967 c. 30.

(2) It shall be the duty of a person giving a notification to the clerk of a court in pursuance of section 1(2) of the Magistrates' Courts Act 1957 (which relates to pleas of guilty in the absence of the accused) in respect of an offence mentioned in subsection (1) of this section to include in the notification a statement of the date of birth and the sex of the accused ; and in a case where the foregoing provisions of this subsection are not complied with the court shall, if on convicting the accused it orders his driving licence to be endorsed or orders him to be temporarily disqualified and does not know his date of birth or sex, order him to furnish that information in writing to the court.

1957 c. 29.

(3) References in this section to temporary disqualification are references to disqualification in pursuance of subsection (8) of

1967 c. 80. section 56 of the Criminal Justice Act 1967; and nothing in subsection (5) of that section (which provides that where a magistrates' court commits a person to another court under subsection (1) of that section, certain of its powers and duties are transferred to that other court) shall apply to any duty imposed upon a magistrates' court by the foregoing provisions of this section in consequence of an order for temporary disqualification.

(4) A person who knowingly fails to comply with an order under subsection (1) or subsection (2) of this section shall be guilty of an offence under this Act.

(5) In section 225 of the Act of 1960, at the end of subsection (1) (which enables a constable to require the production of a driving licence in certain circumstances) there shall be inserted the words " and shall in prescribed circumstances, on being so required by the constable, state his date of birth "; and in subsection (4) (which penalises a failure to produce a licence to a constable in pursuance of that section) after the words " to produce a licence " there shall be inserted the words " or state his date of birth ".

(6) Where in accordance with this section a person has stated his date of birth to a court or a constable or in such a notification as aforesaid, the Minister may serve on that person a notice in writing requiring him to furnish the Minister—

(*a*) with such evidence in that person's possession or obtainable by him as the Minister may specify for the purpose of verifying that date; and

(*b*) if his name differs from his name at the time of his birth, with a statement in writing specifying his name at that time;

and a person who knowingly fails to comply with a notice under this subsection shall be guilty of an offence under this Act.

(7) In the application of this section to Scotland—

(*a*) for subsection (2) there shall be substituted the following subsection:—

(2) Where, in pursuance of section 26(3) of the
1954 c. 48. Summary Jurisdiction (Scotland) Act 1954 (pleas in absence of accused), a person gives written intimation of a plea of guilty in respect of an offence mentioned in subsection (1) of this section, he shall include in that written intimation a statement of the accused's date of birth and sex, and in a case where the foregoing provisions of this subsection are not

complied with the court, if on convicting the accused it orders his licence to be endorsed and does not know his date of birth or sex, shall order him to furnish that information in writing to the court;

(*b*) in subsection (6) for the word " notification " there shall be substituted the words " written intimation ".

Powers to prescribe fees.

23.—(1) The amount of the fees payable under the following enactments, that is to say—

(*a*) section 99(2)(*b*) of the Act of 1960 (driving tests);

(*b*) sections 101 and 102 of that Act, as replaced by section 14 of this Act (new driving licences);

(*c*) section 113(*g*) of that Act (replacement of lost or defaced driving licences);

(*d*) section 8(4) of the Act of 1962 (replacement of lost or destroyed vehicle licences);

(*e*) section 16(1)(*b*) and (*e*) or, after the coming into force of section 17 of this Act, section 16(*e*) and (*f*) of the Act of 1962 (replacement of documents and furnishing of information); and

(*f*) section 6 of this Act,

shall be such as may be approved by the Treasury.

(2) Accordingly the following enactments shall have effect subject to the following amendments—

in section 113(*g*) of the Act of 1960 the words " not exceeding two shillings and sixpence " shall cease to have effect, and at the end of that section there shall be inserted the following paragraph:—

Any fee prescribed under this Part of this Act shall be of an amount approved by the Treasury, and different fees may be prescribed for different circumstances.;

in section 8(4) of the Act of 1962 the words " (not exceeding five shillings) " shall cease to have effect;

in section 16(1) of the Act of 1962 the words " (which shall not exceed five shillings) " in paragraph (*b*) and " (not exceeding five shillings) " in paragraph (*e*) shall cease to have effect;

at the end of section 23(2) of the Act of 1962 there shall be inserted the words " but any fee prescribed under this Act shall be of an amount approved by the Treasury ".

Legal proceedings etc.

Appeal to county court or sheriff from direction under s. 8(4) or s. 11(5).

24. A person who, in pursuance of section 8 of this Act, is paid a sum which was calculated by reference to a period specified in a direction under subsection (4) of that section, or to whom a vehicle licence is issued for a period specified in a direction under subsection (5) of section 11 of this Act, may appeal to the county court, or in Scotland by way of summary application to the sheriff, on the ground that the Minister was not authorised by that subsection to give the direction.

Institution and conduct of proceedings in England and Wales.

25.—(1) Subject to the provisions of this section, proceedings for any offence under the Act of 1962 may be instituted in England and Wales by a local authority.

(2) Subject to the provisions of this section, summary proceedings for an offence under section 7, 10(4), 12(9) or 17(1) or (2) of the Act of 1962 or section 12(2) of this Act or regulations made in pursuance of that Act or in pursuance of section 6, 19 or 20 of this Act may be instituted in England and Wales by the Minister, a local authority or a constable (in this section severally referred to as " the authorised prosecutor ") at any time within six months from the date on which evidence sufficient in the opinion of the authorised prosecutor to warrant the proceedings came to his knowledge ; but no proceedings for any offence shall be instituted by virtue of this subsection more than three years after the commission of the offence.

(3) No proceedings for an offence under section 7, 10(4) or 12(9) of the Act of 1962 shall be instituted in England and Wales except by the authorised prosecutor ; and no proceedings for such an offence shall be so instituted by a constable except with the approval of the Minister or a local authority.

(4) A certificate stating—

(*a*) the date on which such evidence as is mentioned in subsection (2) of this section came to the knowledge of the authorised prosecutor ; or

(*b*) that the Minister's or a local authority's approval is given for the institution by a constable of any proceedings specified in the certificate,

and signed by or on behalf of the authorised prosecutor or, as the case may be, the Minister or the local authority shall for the purposes of this section be conclusive evidence of the date or approval in question ; and a certificate purporting to be given in pursuance of this subsection and to be signed as aforesaid shall be deemed to be so signed unless the contrary is proved.

(5) No proceedings for an offence shall be instituted or approved by virtue of the foregoing provisions of this section by

the Minister before the transfer date or by a local authority on or after that date.

(6) In a magistrates' court or before the registrar of a county court any proceedings by or against the Minister under this Act, the Act of 1962 or Part II of the Act of 1960 may be conducted on behalf of the Minister by a person authorised by him for the purposes of this subsection.

(7) Section 19(1) of the Act of 1962 (which relates to the institution of proceedings in England and Wales) shall cease to have effect.

Institution and conduct of proceedings in Scotland.

26.—(1) Subject to the provisions of this section, summary proceedings for an offence under the Act of 1962 except under section 17(1) or (2) thereof, or for an offence under this Act, except under section 22 thereof, may be instituted in Scotland by the Minister or, within their area, by a local authority.

(2) Notwithstanding the provisions of any enactment, the Minister or a local authority may institute proceedings by virtue of subsection (1) of this section in any court of summary jurisdiction in Scotland.

(3) Any proceedings in any court in Scotland, other than the High Court of Justiciary or the Court of Session, by or against the Minister under this Act, the Act of 1962 or Part II of the Act of 1960 may be conducted on behalf of the Minister by any person authorised by him for the purposes of this subsection.

(4) Summary proceedings in Scotland in respect of an offence under section 7, 10(4), 12(9) or 17(1) or (2) of the Act of 1962 or section 12(2) of this Act or under regulations made in pursuance of that Act or in pursuance of section 6, 19 or 20 of this Act, shall not be commenced more than three years after the commission of the offence, but subject to the foregoing limitation and notwithstanding anything in section 23 of the Summary Jurisdiction (Scotland) Act 1954 (limitation of time for proceedings in statutory offences) any such proceedings may be commenced— 1954 c. 48.

(*a*) in the case of proceedings instituted by the procurator fiscal as a result of information supplied to him by the Minister or a local authority, at any time within six months from the date on which such information came to the knowledge of the Minister or the local authority;

(*b*) in any other case, at any time within six months from the date on which evidence sufficient in the opinion of the person instituting the proceedings to justify proceedings came to his knowledge,

and subsection (2) of the said section 23 shall apply for the purposes of this subsection as it applies for the purposes of that section.

(5) For the purposes of subsection (4) of this section a certificate signed—

(*a*) in the case of any such proceedings as are mentioned in paragraph (*a*) of that subsection, by or on behalf of the Minister or the local authority;

(*b*) in any other case, by or on behalf of the person instituting the proceedings,

and stating the date on which such information or, as the case may be, such evidence as aforesaid came to his or their knowledge shall be conclusive evidence of that fact; and a certificate stating that matter and purporting to be signed by or on behalf of the Minister or the local authority or that person shall be deemed to be so signed unless the contrary is proved.

(6) No proceedings for an offence shall be instituted by virtue of the foregoing provisions of this section by the Minister before the transfer date or by a local authority on or after that date.

(7) Section 19(2) of the Act of 1962 (under which certain provisions of the Customs and Excise Act 1952 are not to apply to offences under the Act of 1962) shall not extend to Scotland except so far as it relates to section 287 of the said Act of 1952.

1952 c. 44.

(8) Section 19(3) of the Act of 1962 (which relates to the institution of proceedings in Scotland) shall cease to have effect.

Admissibility of records as evidence.

27.—(1) A statement contained in a document purporting to be—

(*a*) a part of the records maintained by the Minister or a local authority in connection with the relevant functions or any other functions exercisable by the Minister by virtue of this Act or a part of any other records maintained by the Minister with respect to vehicles; or

(*b*) a copy of a document forming part of those records; or

(*c*) a note of any information contained in those records,

and to be authenticated by a person authorised in that behalf by the Minister or, in the case of records maintained by a local authority, by the authority shall be admissible in any proceedings as evidence of any fact stated therein to the same extent as oral evidence of that fact is admissible in those proceedings.

(2) In subsection (1) of this section " document " and " statement " have the same meanings as in subsection (1) of section 10 of the Civil Evidence Act 1968, and the reference to a copy of a document shall be construed in accordance with subsection (2) of that section; but nothing in this subsection shall be

1968 c. 64.

construed as limiting to civil proceedings the references to proceedings in subsection (1) of this section.

(3) Nothing in the foregoing provisions of this section shall enable evidence to be given with respect to any matter other than a matter of the prescribed description.

(4) In its application to Scotland this section shall have effect as if—

(*a*) in subsection (1), for the words from " as evidence " onwards there were substituted the words " as sufficient evidence of any fact stated therein, so however that nothing in this subsection shall be deemed to make such a statement evidence in any proceedings except where oral evidence to the like effect would have been admissible in those proceedings " ; and

(*b*) in subsection (2), for the references to subsections (1) and (2) of section 10 of the Civil Evidence Act 1968 there were substituted references to subsections (3) and (4) respectively of section 17 of the Law Reform (Miscellaneous Provisions) (Scotland) Act 1968.

1968 c. 64.
1968 c. 70.

Alteration of penalties and offences and the application of sums under 1962 c. 13 ss. 17, 18 and 21 etc.

28.—(1) In section 17(1) and (2) of the Act of 1962 (under which a fine of £50 or imprisonment for six months may be imposed on summary conviction for offences under those subsections) for the words from " fifty pounds " onwards there shall be substituted the words " two hundred pounds or on conviction on indictment to imprisonment for a term not exceeding two years ".

(2) The said section 17(1) and (2) shall have effect subject to the following further amendments, that is to say—

(*a*) in subsection (1)(*b*) for the word " book " there shall be substituted the word " document " ;

(*b*) in subsection (2)(*a*) (which penalises a false declaration in connection with an application for a licence under the Act of 1962 for a vehicle) the reference to such an application shall include a reference to an application for an allocation in pursuance of section 6 or section 20 of this Act ; and

(*c*) in subsection (2)(*b*) (which penalises the furnishing of false particulars in connection with a change of registration of a vehicle) the reference to the Act of 1962 shall be construed as including a reference to this Act and for the words " in connection with a change of registration " there shall be substituted the words " relating to, or to the keeper ".

(3) For section 17(3) of the Act of 1962 (under which a fine of £20 may be imposed for any infringement of regulations under that Act) there shall be substituted the following subsection:—

(3) Regulations under this Act may provide that a person who contravenes or fails to comply with any specified provision of the regulations shall be guilty of an offence and liable on summary conviction to a fine of an amount not exceeding—

(*a*) in the case of a contravention or failure to comply with requirements imposed in pursuance of section 16(*a*) of this Act, fifty pounds;

(*b*) in any other case, twenty pounds.

(4) In section 18 of the Act of 1962 (under which information may be required as to the identity of persons alleged to be concerned in an offence under section 7 or section 12(9) of that Act)—

(*a*) after the words " section seven " in subsections (1) and (2)(*a*) there shall be inserted the words " subsection (4) of section ten ";

(*b*) for the word " owner " in subsection (1)(*a*) there shall be substituted the words " person keeping "; and

(*c*) in subsection (3) for the words " twenty pounds " there shall be substituted the words " fifty pounds ";

1967 c. 54. and in section 12(8) of the Finance Act 1967 (under which information may be required as to the identity of the keeper of a vehicle alleged to have been used in contravention of the said section 7) for the words " twenty pounds " there shall be substituted the words " fifty pounds ".

(5) Nothing in any of the foregoing provisions of this section shall apply to an offence committed before that provision comes into force.

(6) In section 21 of the Act of 1962 (which provides for the application of fines imposed and penalties recovered by virtue of that Act), the references to that Act shall include references to this Act, excluding sections 14 and 22; and in section 21(2) of the Act of 1962, after the word " and " where it first occurs there shall be inserted the words " penalties and ".

Defence to charge of using or keeping vehicle where new licence pending.

29.—(1) In any proceedings for an offence under section 7 or section 8(3) of the Act of 1962 of using or keeping at any time on a public road a mechanically propelled vehicle for which no licence was then in force or, as the case may be, without a current licence being then fixed to and exhibited on the vehicle, it shall be a defence to prove that—

(*a*) while an expired licence for the vehicle was in force an application was duly made for a further licence for the vehicle to take effect from or before the expiration of the expired licence and for a period including the time in question ; and

(*b*) the expired licence was at that time fixed to and exhibited on the vehicle in the manner prescribed in pursuance of the said section 8(3) ; and

(*c*) the period between the expiration of the expired licence and that time did not exceed fourteen days.

(2) In subsection (1) of this section " licence " means a vehicle licence other than a trade licence, and for the purposes of paragraph (*a*) of that subsection an application for a further licence is made when the application is received by the Minister.

(3) Accordingly, in subsection (1) of section 21 of the Civic Amenities Act 1967 (which relates to the disposal of abandoned vehicles)— 1967 c. 69.

(*a*) any reference in paragraphs (*a*) and (*b*) to a current licence shall be construed as including a reference to a licence which was current during any part of the period of fourteen days ending with the day preceding that on which the removal of the vehicle in question took placc ; and

(*b*) the reference in paragraph (*b*) to the expiration of a licence shall be construed as a reference to the expiration of the period of fourteen days beginning with the day following that on which the licence expired,

and for the purposes of paragraph (*c*) of that subsection an expired licence shall be treated as still in force during the period of fourteen days beginning with the day following that on which it expired, and the reference in that paragraph to the expiration of the licence shall be construed accordingly.

Fixing of amount payable under 1967 c. 54 s. 12 on plea of guilty by absent accused.

30. Where in pursuance of section 1(2) of the Magistrates' Courts Act 1957 a person is convicted in his absence of an offence under section 7 of the Act of 1962 (which penalises the using or keeping of an unlicensed vehicle) and it is proved to the satisfaction of the court, on oath or in the manner prescribed by rules made under section 15 of the Justices of the Peace Act 1949, that there was served on the accused with the summons a notice stating that, in the event of his being convicted of the offence, it will be alleged that an order requiring him to pay an amount specified in the notice falls to be made by the court in pursuance of subsection (1) of section 12 of the Finance Act 1967 (under which an amount related to the period during which a vehicle was unlicensed is required to be paid by the keeper of the vehicle who is convicted of using it during that period) then, unless in the notification purporting to be given by or on behalf of the accused in pursuance of

1957 c. 29.
1949 c. 101.

the said section 1(2) it is stated that the amount so specified is inappropriate, the court shall proceed in pursuance of the said subsection (1) as if that amount had been calculated as required by that subsection.

Jurisdiction under 1960 c. 16 s. 103.

31. It is hereby declared that, without prejudice to section 99(3) of the Act of 1960 (under which a magistrates' court or the sheriff may, on the application of a person who has taken a test of competence to drive, determine that the test was improperly carried out and authorise the applicant to take a further test without payment), in any proceedings under section 103 of that Act (which among other things provides for an appeal against the refusal or revocation of a driving licence) the court or sheriff is not entitled to entertain any question as to whether the appellant passed such a test if he was declared by the person who conducted it to have failed it.

Offences under this Act.

32. A person guilty of an offence under this Act shall be liable on summary conviction to a fine of an amount not exceeding—

(*a*) in the case of an offence under section 7(2), 8(4), 12(2) or 22 or regulations made in pursuance of section 19 of this Act, fifty pounds;

(*b*) in any other case, twenty pounds.

Supplemental

Interpretation.

33.—(1) In this Act the following expressions have the following meanings unless the contrary intention appears, that is to say—

1960 c. 16.

" the Act of 1960 " means the Road Traffic Act 1960;

1962 c. 13.

" the Act of 1962 " means the Vehicles (Excise) Act 1962;

1947 c. 43.

" local authority " means the council of a county, the Greater London Council, the council of a county borough and the council of a burgh within the meaning of the Local Government (Scotland) Act 1947 containing a population, according to the census for the time being last taken, of or exceeding fifty thousand, and for the purposes of this definition every other burgh shall be deemed to form part of the county in which it is situated;

" the Minister " means the Minister of Transport;

" motor dealer " means a person carrying on the business of selling or supplying mechanically propelled vehicles;

" prescribed " means prescribed by regulations made by the Minister;

"public road", "trade licence" and "general trade licence" have the same meanings as in the Act of 1962;

"relevant functions" and "the transfer date" have the meanings assigned to them by section 1(2) of this Act;

"seven day licence" means a licence for which provision is made by section 2(1)(*d*) of the Act of 1962;

"temporary licence" has the meaning assigned to it by section 5(1) of this Act; and

"vehicle licence" means a licence under the Act of 1962.

(2) Unless the contrary intention appears, any reference in this Act to any enactment is a reference to it as amended by or under any other enactment including this Act.

34.—(1) Any power to make orders or regulations conferred on the Minister by this Act shall be exercisable by statutory instrument; and any statutory instrument made by virtue of this Act shall be subject to annulment in pursuance of a resolution of either House of Parliament. Orders and regulations.

(2) Any order under this Act made by the Minister and any regulations so made under this Act, Part II of the Act of 1960 or the Act of 1962 may—

(*a*) make different provision for different circumstances;

(*b*) provide for exemptions from any provisions of the order or regulations; and

(*c*) contain such incidental and supplemental provisions as the Minister considers expedient for the purposes of the order or regulations,

and nothing in any other provision of this Act or those enactments shall be construed as prejudicing the generality of the foregoing provisions of this subsection.

(3) Any power to make an order or regulations which is exercisable by the Minister by virtue of this Act includes power to provide by the order or regulations that any document for which provision is made by the order or regulations shall be in such form and contain such particulars as may be specified by a person specified in the order or regulations.

(4) An order made by the Minister under any provision of this Act (except an order under section 2(1) in so far as the order transfers any property, rights or liabilities, an order appointing the transfer date and an order under section 38(2) of this Act) may be revoked or varied by a subsequent order under that provision.

(5) In section 23(1) of the Act of 1962 (which among other things confers power to make regulations for the purpose of carrying that Act into effect), the second reference to that Act and the reference to any other provision of that Act shall be construed as including a reference to this Act, except so far as it relates to driving licences and test certificates and except section 27.

Service of notices.

35. A notice authorised to be served on any person by section 100 or section 102(2) of the Act of 1960 or section 21(2) or section 22(6) of this Act may be served on him by delivering it to him or by leaving it at his proper address or by sending it to him by post; and for the purposes of this section and section 26 of the Interpretation Act 1889 in its application to this section the proper address of any person shall be his latest address as known to the person giving the notice.

1889 c. 63.

Financial provisions.

36.—(1) There shall be defrayed out of moneys provided by Parliament—

(*a*) any expenses incurred by the Minister by virtue of this Act; and

(*b*) any increase attributable to the provisions of this Act in the sums payable under any other enactment out of moneys so provided.

(2) Any sums received by the Minister by virtue of this Act by way of fees shall be paid into the Consolidated Fund.

Repeals.

37. The enactments mentioned in the first and second columns of Schedule 3 to this Act are hereby repealed to the extent specified in the third column of that Schedule.

Short title, commencement and extent.

38.—(1) This Act may be cited as the Vehicle and Driving Licences Act 1969.

(2) This Act shall come into force on such day as the Minister may by order appoint; and different days may be appointed under this subsection for different provisions of this Act, or for different provisions of this Act so far as they apply to such cases only as may be specified in the order.

(3) This Act does not extend to Northern Ireland.

SCHEDULES

SCHEDULE 1

CONSEQUENTIAL AMENDMENTS OF ENACTMENTS

PART I

Section 2 (8).

AMENDMENTS CONSEQUENTIAL ON S.1

The Road Traffic Act 1960

1960 c. 16.

1. At the end of section 115 of the Act of 1960 there shall be inserted the following subsection:—

(2) For the purposes of this Part of this Act the licensing authority is—

(*a*) on and after the transfer date within the meaning of the Vehicle and Driving Licences Act 1969, the Minister; and

(*b*) before that date, the relevant council specified in section 101(1) of this Act as in force immediately before the coming into force of section 14 of that Act,

and accordingly the said section 115 as originally enacted shall be subsection (1) of that section.

2. Any reference in Part II of the Act of 1960 to a licensing authority shall be construed as a reference to the licensing authority.

3. The following provisions of the Act of 1960 shall cease to have effect, that is to say—

in section 109(3) the words from " to be granted " to " was granted) ";

in section 112(1) the words from " by which the " to " resides " and the words " by which it was granted ", and in section 112(2) the words from " in whose area " onwards;

in section 113, paragraphs (*b*) and (*c*);

in section 114(1) the words from " in the same manner " onwards.

The Vehicles (Excise) Act 1962

1962 c. 13.

4. Subject to paragraphs 5 and 8 below, for any reference in the Act of 1962 to a county council within the meaning of that Act there shall be substituted a reference to the Minister.

5. In section 5(2) of the Act of 1962, for the words from " and of any " to " their county " there shall be substituted the words " the Minister and his officers (including any body or person authorised by the Minister to act as his agent for the purposes of this Act) shall have ".

6. In section 13(1) of the Act of 1962, for the words " the prescribed manner " there shall be substituted the words " such manner as the Minister thinks fit."

SCH. 1

7. At the end of section 19(2) of the Act of 1962 there shall be inserted the words " and section 287 of that Act (which relates to the application of penalties) shall not apply to penalties recovered under or in pursuance of this Act ".

8. The following provisions of the Act of 1962 shall cease to have effect, that is to say—

in section 5(1) the words from " in accordance " onwards, in section 5(3) the words from " and subject " to " this section ", in section 5(4) the words from " in such manner " onwards, and section 5(5) and (6);

in section 6(6) the words " if authorised so to do by the Minister ";

in section 9(1) the words from " with which " onwards;

in section 11(1), paragraph (*a*);

in section 12(1) the words " in which his business premises are situated " and section 12(7) and (8);

in section 13(1) the words " issuing the licence " and " and the council which has registered it ";

in section 21(2) the words from " in such manner " onwards;

sections 22, 23(4) and 24(5) and in section 24(1) the definition of " county " (including the provision relating to references to the council of a county).

1966 c. 42.

The Local Government Act 1966

9. In section 33 of the Local Government Act 1966 the reference to the functions relating to highways shall include a reference to the relevant functions, and any reference in that section to a council or the Minister within the meaning of that section shall respectively be construed, in relation to the relevant functions, as a reference to a local authority or the Minister within the meaning of this Act.

In this paragraph " relevant functions " includes the Minister's functions under the Act of 1962 in relation to the Isles of Scilly and " local authority " includes the Council of the said Isles.

1966 c. 51.

The Local Government (Scotland) Act 1966

10. In section 35 of the Local Government (Scotland) Act 1966—

(*a*) in subsection (1), after the words " A local authority " there shall be inserted the words " within the meaning of section 113(1) of the Town and Country Planning (Scotland) Act 1947 ";

1947 c. 53.

(*b*) after subsection (1) there shall be inserted the following subsection:—

(1A) A local authority within the meaning of section 33 of the Vehicle and Driving Licences Act 1969 may enter into an agreement with the Minister of Transport for the placing at his disposal, for the purpose of any of the relevant functions within the meaning of the said Act of 1969, on such terms as may be provided by the agreement, of the services of persons employed by the local authority and of any premises, equipment and other facilities under their control. ; SCH. I

(*c*) in subsection (2), after the words " Secretary of State " there shall be inserted the words " or the Minister of Transport " ;

(*d*) in subsection (3) the words from " 'local authority' " to " and " in the second place where it occurs shall cease to have effect.

The Finance Act 1967 1967 c. 54.

11. For the references to a county council in section 12(2)(*a*) and (8) of the Finance Act 1967 there shall be substituted references to the Minister.

The Criminal Justice Act 1967 1967 c. 80.

12. In section 56(10) of the Criminal Justice Act 1967, for paragraphs (*a*) and (*b*) there shall be substituted the words " send notice of the order to the Minister of Transport ", and for the words from " any such " onwards there shall be substituted the words " the Minister of Transport ".

PART II Section 4 (4).

AMENDMENTS CONSEQUENTIAL ON S. 4

The Vehicles (Excise) Act 1962 1962 c. 13.

13. The following provisions of the Act of 1962 shall cease to have effect, that is to say—

section 2(1)(*a*), and in section 2(1)(*b*) and (*c*) the words from " running " onwards ;

in section 2(2)(*a*) the words " one calendar year or " and " other " ;

section 12(4).

14. In section 10(3) of the Act of 1962 for the word " months " in both places there shall be substituted the word " days " and for the words from " any " onwards there shall be substituted the words " that period being treated as 365 days in the case of a licence for twelve months and 120 days in the case of a licence for four months ".

15. In section 12(5) of the Act of 1962 for the words " calendar year " there shall be substituted the words " period of twelve

SCH. I months " and for the words " three months shall be eleven fortieths " there shall be substituted the words " four months shall be eleven thirtieths ".

1967 c. 54.

The Finance Act 1967

16. In section 12(2) of the Finance Act 1967, for the words " one twelfth " there shall be substituted the words " one three-hundred-and-sixty-fifth ", for the words " calendar month or part of a calendar month " there shall be substituted the word " day " and for the words " calendar month immediately following that in " there shall be substituted the words " day following that on ".

17. In section 12(3) and (4) of the Finance Act 1967, for the words " month or part of a month " and the words " month or part " wherever else they occur there shall be substituted the word " day ".

18. In section 12(4) of the Finance Act 1967, for the words " at the beginning of " there shall be substituted the word " on ".

Section 16 (2).

SCHEDULE 2

AMENDMENTS OF PROVISIONS OF ACT OF 1960 RELATING TO DRIVERS ETC.

1. Section 99(4) (under which the requirements as to tests imposed by subsection (1) of that section may be dispensed with for persons not resident in Great Britain) shall cease to have effect; but the repeal of section 99(4) by this Act, shall not affect—

(*a*) a licence granted by virtue of section 99(4) before the repeal takes effect; or

(*b*) the references in section 99(1) to licences granted by virtue of section 99(4) or of a provision for the time being corresponding thereto.

2. For subsection (5) of section 99 (which provides that certain tests of competence are sufficient to authorise the granting of a driving licence) there shall be substituted the following subsection:—

(5) For the purposes of paragraph (*a*) of subsection (1) of this section a test of competence shall be sufficient for the granting of a licence authorising the driving of—

(*a*) vehicles of any class or description, if at the time the test was passed (whether before or after the passing of this Act) it authorised the granting of a licence to drive vehicles of that class or description;

(*b*) vehicles of any classes or descriptions which are designated by regulations as a group for the purposes of the said paragraph (*a*), if at the said time the test authorised the granting of a licence to drive vehicles of any class or description included in the group ; Sch. 2

and if vehicles of any classes or descriptions are designated by regulations as a group for the purposes of paragraph (*b*) of subsection (1) of this section, a licence authorising the driving of vehicles of a class or description included in the group shall be deemed for the purposes of the said paragraph (*b*) to authorise the driving of vehicles of all classes or descriptions included in the group.

The last foregoing reference to a licence and the first reference to a licence in the said paragraph (*b*) do not include a licence which has been revoked in pursuance of section 102(2) of this Act.

3. In section 110 (which among other things penalises a person who applies for or obtains a licence while he is disqualified for holding or obtaining it) the words " applies for or " in paragraph (*a*) shall cease to have effect.

4. In section 112(1) (which requires the licence of a disqualified person to be retained by the licensing authority until the disqualification expires or is removed and he demands the return of the licence) for the words from " shall keep " onwards there shall be substituted the words " may dispose of it as the authority think fit ; but where the disqualification expires or is removed before the expiration of the period for which the licence was granted and the person to whom it was granted makes to the authority during that period, in such form and containing such particulars supported by such evidence or further evidence as the Minister may specify, a demand for the grant of a new licence for the period for which the licence aforesaid was granted, the authority shall comply with the demand ", and in section 112(3) the words from " on the return " to " him or " shall cease to have effect.

5. In section 115, in the definition of " provisional licence ", for the words " section one hundred and two " there shall be substituted the words " section 101(2) ".

6. In section 225(1)(*d*) and section 226(2) (under which a constable may require a person to produce his licence for examination or to state his name and address if he is accompanying or has accompanied a person driving a vehicle under a provisional licence) for the words " accompanies " and " to have accompanied " there shall be substituted respectively the words " supervises " and " was supervising ".

7. In section 225(2) (which enables a constable to seize a licence which is not delivered up as required by section 100(6) of the Act of 1960) for the words " subsection (6) of section one hundred thereof " there shall be substituted the words " section 100 or section 102 of this Act " and for the words " for cancellation as required by that subsection " there shall be substituted the words " in pursuance of that section ", and the words " for cancellation " in the second place where they occur shall cease to have effect.

SCH. 2

8. In section 232(2)(*a*) (under which the owner of a vehicle may be required to identify the driver of it who is alleged to have committed an offence to which that section applies) for the words " owner of " there shall be substituted the words " person keeping ".

9. At the end of section 233(1) (which specifies the documents of which, among other things, the forgery or misuse is an offence under that section) there shall be inserted the following paragraph:—

1967 c. 30.

(*h*) any document which, in pursuance of section 99(2) of this Act or section 20(1) of the Road Safety Act 1967, is issued as evidence of the result of a test of competence to drive.

10. In section 241(2)(*c*)(ii) and (4)(*a*) (which among other things relate to the service of a notice on the owner of a vehicle) for the word " owner " there shall be substituted the word " keeper ".

11. In section 244 (which specifies the time for beginning summary proceedings for certain offences), for the words from " from " where it first occurs onwards there shall be substituted the words " from the date on which evidence sufficient in the opinion of the prosecutor to warrant the proceedings came to his knowledge ; but no such proceedings shall be brought by virtue of this section more than three years after the commission of the offence.

For the purposes of this section a certificate signed by or on behalf of the prosecutor and stating the date on which such evidence as aforesaid came to his knowledge shall be conclusive evidence of that fact ; and a certificate stating that matter and purporting to be so signed shall be deemed to be so signed unless the contrary is proved."

12. In section 247 (which relates to the destination of fines)—

(*a*) in subsection (1), after the words " forty-eight) " there shall be inserted the words " or a fine imposed in respect of an offence under section 22 of the Vehicle and Driving Licences Act 1969 " ;

(*b*) in subsection (2), after the words " Twelfth Schedule) " in the second place where they occur there shall be inserted the words " or a fine imposed in respect of an offence under section 22 of the Vehicle and Driving Licences Act 1969 ".

13. At the end of paragraph 1 of Schedule 15 (which contains transitional provisions for the grant of drivers' licences for heavy goods vehicles to persons in the habit of driving such vehicles) there shall be inserted the following:—

The reference in the foregoing provisions of this paragraph to the driving of a heavy goods vehicle does not include a reference to the driving of such a vehicle of a prescribed class or of such a vehicle while it is being used in prescribed circumstances.

SCHEDULE 3

Section 37.

REPEALS

Chapter	Short title	Extent of repeal
1920 c. 72.	The Roads Act 1920.	Section 3(4). In section 17, the definitions of " county " and " county council ". Section 18.
1955 c. 6. (4 & 5 Eliz. 2)	The Miscellaneous Financial Provisions Act 1955.	In Schedule 1, the entry relating to the Roads Act 1920.
1960 c. 16.	The Road Traffic Act 1960.	Section 99(4). In section 109(3), the words from " to be granted " to " Act ". In section 110(*a*), the words " applies for or ". In section 112, in subsection (1) the words from " by which the " to " resides " and the words " by which it was granted ", in subsection (2) the words from " in whose area " onwards, and in subsection (3) the words from " on the return " to " him or ". In section 113, paragraphs (*b*) and (*c*) and in paragraph (*g*) the words " not exceeding two shillings and sixpence ". In section 114(1), the words from " in the same manner " onwards. In section 115, the definition of " test of fitness to drive ". In section 225, in subsection (1)(*d*) the words " section one hundred and two of ", and in subsection (2) the words " for cancellation " in the second place where they occur. In section 226(2), the words " section one hundred and two of ". In section 247(2), the words from " in the manner " to " mentioned ".
1962 c. 13.	The Vehicles (Excise) Act 1962.	In section 2, in subsections (1) and (2) the words " Subject to the provisions of the following section ", subsection (1)(*a*), in subsection (1)(*b*) and (*c*) the words from " running "

SCH. 3

Chapter	Short title	Extent of repeal
1962 c. 13 —*cont.*	The Vehicles (Excise) Act 1962—*cont.*	onwards, and in subsection (2)(*a*) the words " one calendar year or " and " other ". Section 3. In section 5, in subsection (1) the words from " in accordance " onwards, in subsection (3) the words from " and subject " to " this section ", in subsection (4) the words from " in such manner " onwards, and subsections (5) and (6). In section 6(6), the words " if authorised so to do by the Minister ". In section 8(4), the words " (not exceeding five shillings) ". Section 9. In section 11(1), paragraph (*a*). In section 12, in subsection (1) the words " in which his business premises are situated ", and subsections (4), (7) and (8). In section 13(1), the words " issuing the licence " and " and the council which has registered it ". In section 16(1), the words " (which shall not exceed five shillings) " in paragraph (*b*) and " (not exceeding five shillings) " in paragraph (*e*). Section 19(1) and (3). In section 21(2), the words from " in such manner " onwards. Sections 22 and 23(4). In section 24, the definition of " county " (including the provision relating to references to the council of a county) and subsection (5). In Schedule 7, the entry relating to the Road Traffic Act 1960.
1962 c. 59.	The Road Traffic Act 1962.	In section 4(1), the words from " in whose area " onwards. Section 46.
1963 c. 33.	The London Government Act 1963.	Section 20. In Part I of Schedule 5, paragraph 24.
1964 c. 92.	The Finance (No. 2) Act 1964.	In section 9(6), the words " or in any Order in Council under that section ".

SCH. 3

Chapter	Short title	Extent of repeal
1966 c. 18.	The Finance Act 1966.	In section 2(13)(*a*), the words " or in any Order in Council under that section ".
1966 c. 51.	The Local Government (Scotland) Act 1966.	In section 35(3), the words from " 'local authority' " to " and " in the second place where it occurs.

Ponies Act 1969

1969 CHAPTER 28

An Act to improve the conditions under which ponies are exported; to prohibit or restrict the export of certain ponies; and for purposes connected therewith. [25th June 1969]

BE IT ENACTED by the Queen's most Excellent Majesty, by and with the advice and consent of the Lords Spiritual and Temporal, and Commons, in this present Parliament assembled, and by the authority of the same, as follows:—

Restriction on export of ponies. 1950 c. 36.

1. The Diseases of Animals Act 1950 shall be amended as follows:—

(*a*) after subsection (4) of section 37 thereof (which relates to restrictions on the export of horses) there shall be inserted the following subsection:—

"(4A) Subsections (1) and (2) of this section shall not apply to ponies, but, subject to the following provisions of this Act, it shall not be lawful to ship, or attempt to ship, any pony in any vessel from any port in Great Britain to any port outside the United Kingdom, the Channel Islands and the Isle of Man unless—

(*a*) the Minister or, in Scotland, the Secretary of State is satisfied that the pony is intended for breeding, riding or exhibition and is of not less value than £100 or, in the case of a pony not exceeding 12 hands in height other than a pony of the Shetland breed not exceeding 10½ hands in height, £70, or in the case of such a pony of the Shetland breed, £40, or such other value in any of those cases as may be prescribed by order of the Minister and the Secretary of State acting jointly; and

(*b*) immediately before shipment the pony has been individually inspected by a veterinary inspector and has been certified in writing by the inspector to be capable of being conveyed to the port to which it is to be shipped, and disembarked, without unnecessary suffering;

and, without prejudice to paragraph (*b*) of this subsection, a veterinary inspector shall not certify a pony to be capable of being conveyed and disembarked as aforesaid if, being a mare, it is in his opinion heavy in foal, showing fullness of udder or too old to travel or, being a foal, it is in his opinion too young to travel."

(*b*) in subsection (5) of section 37 thereof, after the word " examined " there shall be inserted the words " or inspected ".

(*c*) in section 84(4) thereof, after the definition of " police area " there shall be inserted the following definition, namely:—

" pony " means any horse not more than 14½ hands in height, except a foal travelling with its dam if the dam is over 14½ hands.

2.—(1) The Minister of Agriculture, Fisheries and Food and the Secretary of State acting jointly shall by order make such provision as they think necessary or expedient for the following purposes— Regulation of export of ponies.

(*a*) for prohibiting the export of ponies by sea or air from any place in Great Britain to any place outside the United Kingdom, the Channel Islands and the Isle of Man unless such ponies are rested immediately before being loaded in the vessel or aircraft in which they are to be carried;

(*b*) for regulating and prescribing the premises at which and the periods during which ponies are to be so rested;

(*c*) for prescribing and regulating the cleansing and supervision of such premises and the provision thereat of clean and sufficient bedding and adequate supplies of fodder and water.

(2) This section shall be construed as one with the Diseases of Animals Act 1950. 1950 c. 36.

Further amendment of Diseases of Animals Act 1950.
1950 c. 36.

3.—(1) In the Diseases of Animals Act 1950 there shall be inserted after section 40 the following section:—

"Restriction on export of registered ponies.

40A.—(1) It shall not be lawful to ship, or attempt to ship, a registered pony in any vessel from any port in Great Britain to any port outside the United Kingdom, the Channel Islands and the Isle of Man unless there has first been obtained from the secretary of a society in whose stud book the pony is registered a certificate (hereinafter called an 'export certificate') that the pony is registered with that society.

(2) The export certificate in respect of a registered pony shall be delivered at the time of shipment to the master of the vessel on which the pony is shipped, who shall on demand produce the export certificate to any constable or any inspector or other officer of the Minister or the local authority and allow such constable, inspector or other officer to take a copy of or extract from the export certificate.

(3) For the purposes of this section the expression 'registered pony' means a pony registered in the Arab Horse Society Stud Book, the National Pony Society Stud Book, the British Palomino Society Stud Book or the British Spotted Horse and Pony Society Stud Book, or in the stud book of any of the following native breed societies, namely, English Connemara, Dales, Dartmoor, Exmoor, Fell, Highland, New Forest, Shetland and Welsh."

(2) In section 41 of the said Act of 1950 (enforcement of provisions as to shipment of horses) for the words "four last foregoing sections", wherever they occur, there shall be substituted the words "five last foregoing sections".

Short title, commencement, and adaptation to air transport.
1954 c. 39.

4.—(1) This Act may be cited as the Ponies Act 1969.

(2) This Act shall come into force on 1st January 1970.

(3) In section 11 of the Agriculture (Miscellaneous Provisions) Act 1954 and in Schedule 2 to that Act (which provide for the adaptation to air transport of the Diseases of Animals Act 1950) any reference to the said Act of 1950 shall include a reference to that Act as amended by this Act.

Tanzania Act 1969

1969 CHAPTER 29

An Act to make provision for modifying the law in consequence of the union of Tanganyika and Zanzibar to form the United Republic of Tanganyika and Zanzibar as a republic within the Commonwealth and the subsequent adoption by that republic of the name of Tanzania; to make provision as to the operation of the Colonial and Other Territories (Divorce Jurisdiction) Acts 1926 to 1950 in relation to the courts of Tanganyika and of the united republic; and for purposes connected therewith. [25th June 1969]

BE IT ENACTED by the Queen's most Excellent Majesty, by and with the advice and consent of the Lords Spiritual and Temporal, and Commons, in this present Parliament assembled, and by the authority of the same, as follows:—

Modifications of British Nationality Acts.

1.—(1) The British Nationality Acts shall have effect, and shall be deemed to have had effect as from 29th October 1964, as if in section 1(3) of the British Nationality Act 1948 (Commonwealth countries having separate citizenship)— 1948 c. 56.

(*a*) the words " and Zanzibar " were omitted, and

(*b*) for the word " Tanganyika " there were substituted the word " Tanzania ".

(2) In relation to the period beginning on 26th April 1964 and ending with 28th October 1964 those Acts shall be deemed to have had effect as if in the said section 1(3)—

(*a*) the words " and Zanzibar " were omitted, and

(*b*) for the word " Tanganyika " there were substituted the words " the United Republic of Tanganyika and Zanzibar ".

(3) A person who, for the purposes of the British Nationality Acts 1948 and 1958 and of the British Protectorates, Protected States and Protected Persons Order in Council 1949, was S.I. 1949 No. 140.

immediately before 9th December 1961 a British protected person by virtue of his connection with Tanganyika, but never became a citizen of Tanganyika,—

(*a*) if he became a citizen of the United Republic of Tanganyika and Zanzibar, shall be deemed, on becoming such a citizen, to have ceased to be a British protected person for the purposes of the British Nationality Acts and of that Order in Council;

(*b*) if he became, or after the passing of this Act becomes, a citizen of Tanzania, shall be deemed, on becoming such a citizen, to have ceased, or (as the case may be) to cease, to be a British protected person for the purposes of those Acts and for the purposes of that Order in Council or of the British Protectorates, Protected States and Protected Persons Order in Council 1965.

S.I. 1965 No. 1864.

1967 c. 4.

(4) In accordance with section 3(3) of the West Indies Act 1967, it is hereby declared that this section extends to all associated states.

Divorce jurisdiction.

1961 c. 1 (10 & 11 Eliz. 2.).

2.—(1) Notwithstanding anything in section 3(4) of, and paragraph 15 of Schedule 2 to, the Tanganyika Independence Act 1961, and notwithstanding the union of Tanganyika with Zanzibar to form the united republic and the adoption by that republic of the name of Tanzania, all courts having jurisdiction under the laws of Tanganyika or of the united republic—

(*a*) shall be deemed to have had during the period beginning on 9th December 1961 and ending with 17th May 1965, and

(*b*) in relation to proceedings instituted before 18th May 1965, shall be deemed to have had, and to continue to have,

the same jurisdiction under the Divorce Jurisdiction Acts as courts having jurisdiction under the laws of Tanganyika would have had if the Tanganyika Independence Act 1961 had not been passed.

(2) Where subsection (1) of this section has effect in relation to a decree or order made by any such court as is mentioned in that subsection, the production (whether before or after the passing of this Act) of a copy of the decree or order purporting to be certified and signed by the appropriate registrar shall have the like effect for the purposes of the Divorce Jurisdiction Acts as if that copy—

(*a*) had been certified and transmitted, by the proper officer of the court by which the decree or order was made, for registration in the court of the domicile, and

(*b*) had been received on the date on which it is or was so produced.

(3) For the avoidance of doubt it is hereby declared that—

(a) except as provided by subsection (1) of this section, no court having jurisdiction under the laws of the united republic has any jurisdiction under the Divorce Jurisdiction Acts to make a decree for the dissolution of a marriage, or as incidental thereto to make any order as to any matter ; and

(b) nothing in this section shall be construed as extending to the united republic as part of its law.

(4) In this section any reference to registration in the court of the domicile shall be construed in accordance with section 6(3) of the Colonial and Other Territories (Divorce Jurisdiction) Act 1950. 1950 c. 20.

(5) In this section " the appropriate registrar "—

(a) in relation to a decree or order made by a court having jurisdiction under the laws of Tanganyika, means the registrar of that court or of any court having (apart from the Divorce Jurisdiction Acts) the like general jurisdiction under the laws of the united republic, and

(b) in relation to a decree or order made by a court having jurisdiction under the laws of the united republic, means the registrar of that court ;

and in this subsection " registrar " includes any officer performing functions similar to those of a registrar.

(6) In this section " the united republic "—

(a) in relation to any time on or after 26th April 1964 and before 29th October 1964, means the United Republic of Tanganyika and Zanzibar, and

(b) in relation to any time on or after 29th October 1964, means the United Republic of Tanzania.

3.—(1) The Ships and Aircraft (Transfer Restriction) Act 1939 shall not apply to any ship by reason only of its being registered in, or licensed under the law of, Tanzania ; and the penal provisions of that Act shall not apply to persons in Tanzania (but without prejudice to the operation with respect to any ship to which that Act does apply of the provisions thereof relating to the forfeiture of ships). Ships. 1939 c. 70.

(2) In the Whaling Industry (Regulation) Act 1934, the expression " British ship to which this Act applies " shall not include a British ship registered in Tanzania. 1934 c. 49.

(3) This section shall be deemed to have come into operation on 26th April 1964 ; and, in relation to any time within the

period beginning on that date and ending with 28th October 1964, any reference in this section to Tanzania shall be construed as a reference to the United Republic of Tanganyika and Zanzibar.

Power to apply other statutory provisions to Tanzania.

4.—(1) Subject to the following provisions of this section, Her Majesty may by Order in Council specify any enactment of the Parliament of the United Kingdom for the time being in force, or any instrument for the time being in force and having effect by virtue of such an enactment, and make such provision as may appear to Her Majesty to be appropriate for securing that, to such extent and subject to such exceptions and modifications (if any) as Her Majesty thinks fit, that enactment or instrument has the like operation in relation to Tanzania, and persons and things belonging to or connected with Tanzania, as it has in relation to territories to which the enactment or instrument is applicable and in relation to persons and things belonging to or connected with such territories.

(2) No Order in Council shall be made under this section in respect of an enactment or instrument unless it is an enactment or instrument which either—

(*a*) specifies Tanganyika by name, or

(*b*) is an enactment or instrument which would have had effect in relation to Tanganyika, or to persons or things belonging to or connected with Tanganyika, if Tanganyika had continued to be a separate territory and had continued to be part of Her Majesty's dominions.

(3) No Order in Council shall be made under this section in respect of the British Nationality Acts or the Divorce Jurisdiction Acts.

(4) An Order in Council under this section may make provision in accordance with subsection (1) of this section in such manner as appears to Her Majesty to be appropriate in relation to any enactment or instrument specified in the Order, and in particular (but without prejudice to the generality of this subsection)—

(*a*) may amend the enactment or instrument by inserting in it one or more references to Tanzania by name, or

(*b*) if the enactment or instrument refers to Tanganyika by name, may amend it by substituting a reference to Tanzania for any such reference ;

and, where any enactment or instrument specified in the Order refers to Zanzibar by name, the Order in Council may include provision amending it so as to omit any reference to Zanzibar.

(5) Where an Order in Council under this section specifies an enactment which confers a power to make Orders in Council, any power which in consequence of the Order is exercisable by virtue of that enactment in relation to Tanzania, or persons or things belonging to or connected with Tanzania, may be so exercised either by the same Order in Council or by a subsequent Order in Council.

(6) Any Order in Council made under this section, and any other Order in Council which exercises in relation to Tanzania, or persons or things belonging to or connected with Tanzania, a power which is so exercisable in the circumstances specified in subsection (5) of this section,—

(*a*) may be made with retrospective effect as from 26th April 1964 or any later date, and

(*b*) in so far as it is made so as to have effect in respect of any time before 29th October 1964, may be made as if in this section any reference to Tanzania were a reference to the United Republic of Tanganyika and Zanzibar.

(7) For the purpose of making an Order in Council under this section, any referencc in subsection (1) of this section to any enactment or instrument for the time being in force shall be construed as a reference to any enactment or instrument in force immediately before the Order is made, whether the enactment or instrument was passed or made before or after the passing of this Act.

(8) Any reference in this section to a territory to which an enactment or instrument is applicable shall be construed as a reference to a territory which either—

(*a*) is specified by name in the enactment or instrument, or

(*b*) falls within a general description specified in a provision contained in the enactment or instrument whereby the enactment or instrument has effect in relation to territories falling within that description or in relation to persons or things of a class so specified which belong to or are connected with such territories.

Power to repeal certain enactments relating to Tanganyika and Zanzibar.

5.—(1) Where it appears to Her Majesty in Council that an enactment to which this section applies has (whether in consequence of the exercise of any power conferred by section 4 of this Act or otherwise) become obsolete, spent or unnecessary, Her Majesty may by Order in Council provide that that enactment shall cease to have effect.

(2) This section applies to all enactments contained in the Tanganyika Independence Act 1961, the Tanganyika Republic Act 1962 and the Zanzibar Act 1963, except section 1 of the Tanganyika Independence Act 1961.

1961 c. 1 (10 & 11 Eliz. 2).
1962 c. 1 (11 & 12 Eliz. 2).
1963 c. 55.
1889 c. 63.

(3) Section 38(2) of the Interpretation Act 1889 (which relates to the effect of repeals) shall have effect in relation to any repeal effected by an Order in Council under this section as if the Order were an Act of Parliament.

Supplementary provisions.

6.—(1) Any Order in Council under this Act—

(*a*) may contain such transitional or other incidental or supplemental provisions as appear to Her Majesty to be necessary or expedient;

(*b*) may be varied or revoked by a subsequent Order in Council; and

(*c*) shall be subject to annulment in pursuance of a resolution of either House of Parliament.

(2) Subject to the next following subsection, any provision made by an Order in Council under this Act with respect to an enactment of the Parliament of the United Kingdom, or with respect to an instrument having effect by virtue of such an enactment, shall, except in so far as the Order otherwise provides, have effect as part of the law of every territory outside the United Kingdom to which the enactment or instrument in question extends, as well as having effect as part of the law of the United Kingdom.

(3) Any provision made by an Order in Council as mentioned in subsection (2) of this section—

(*a*) shall not have effect as part of the law of any associated state unless either the Order in Council is made at the request and with the consent of that state or the provision so made is one which (in accordance with Schedule 1 to the West Indies Act 1967) the legislature of that state has no power to make at the date on which the Order is made, and

1967 c. 4.

(*b*) shall not have effect as part of the law of any territory if it is a territory for whose government Her Majesty's Government in the United Kingdom have no responsibility at that date, and accordingly shall not have effect as part of the law of Tanzania.

(4) In subsection (3)(*a*) of this section the reference to the request and consent of an associated state shall be construed in accordance with section 19(5) of the West Indies Act 1967.

(5) Nothing in section 4 or section 5 of this Act shall affect the exercise (whether before or after the passing of this Act) of any power exercisable apart from those sections.

7.—(1) In this Act— Interpretation.

(*a*) subject to the next following subsection, " the British Nationality Acts " means the British Nationality Acts 1948 to 1965; and

(*b*) the Divorce Jurisdiction Acts mean the Colonial and Other Territories (Divorce Jurisdiction) Acts 1926 to 1950.

(2) In so far as, by virtue of section 1 of this Act, the British Nationality Acts are deemed to have had effect as mentioned in that section in relation to a time before the commencement of the British Nationality Act 1965, " the British Nationality Acts " shall be taken to mean such of the British Nationality Acts 1948 to 1964 as were in force at that time. 1965 c. 34.

(3) References in this Act to any enactment are references to that enactment as amended or extended by or under any other enactment.

8. This Act may be cited as the Tanzania Act 1969. Short title.

Town and Country Planning (Scotland) Act 1969

1969 CHAPTER 30

An Act to amend the law of Scotland relating to town and country planning, the compulsory acquisition of land and the disposal of land by public authorities; to make provision for Planning Inquiry Commissions; to make provision for grants for research relating to, and education with respect to, the planning and design of the physical environment; to extend the purposes for which Exchequer contributions may be made under the Housing and Town Development (Scotland) Act 1957; and for connected purposes. [25th June 1969]

BE IT ENACTED by the Queen's most Excellent Majesty, by and with the advice and consent of the Lords Spiritual and Temporal, and Commons, in this present Parliament assembled, and by the authority of the same, as follows:—

PART I

NEW PROVISIONS AS TO DEVELOPMENT PLANS

Survey and structure plan

Survey of planning districts.

1.—(1) It shall be the duty of the local planning authority to institute a survey of their district, in so far as they have not already done so, examining the matters which may be expected to affect the development of that district or the planning of its development and to keep all such matters under review.

(2) Notwithstanding that the local planning authority have carried out their duty under subsection (1) above, the authority may, if they think fit, and shall, if directed to do so by the Secretary of State, institute a fresh survey of their district examining the matters mentioned in that subsection.

PART I

(3) Without prejudice to the generality of the foregoing provisions of this section, the matters to be examined and kept under review thereunder shall include the following, that is to say—

(*a*) the principal physical and economic characteristics of the district of the authority (including the principal purposes for which land is used) and, so far as they may be expected to affect that district, of any neighbouring districts;

(*b*) the size, composition and distribution of the population of that district (whether resident or otherwise);

(*c*) without prejudice to paragraph (*a*) above, the communications, transport system and traffic of that district and, so far as they may be expected to affect that district, of any neighbouring districts;

(*d*) any considerations not mentioned in any of the foregoing paragraphs which may be expected to affect any matters so mentioned;

(*e*) such other matters as may be prescribed or as the Secretary of State may in a particular case direct;

(*f*) any changes already projected in any of the matters mentioned in any of the foregoing paragraphs and the effect which those changes are likely to have on the development of that district or the planning of such development.

(4) A local planning authority shall, for the purpose of discharging their functions under this section of examining and keeping under review any matters relating to the district of another such authority, consult with that other authority about those matters.

(5) Subsection (1) above shall, as respects any period during which this section is in operation in part only of the district of a local planning authority, be construed as requiring a local planning authority to institute a survey of that part of that district and to keep under review matters affecting only that part of that district; and subsection (2) above shall, whether or not this section is in operation in the whole of such a district, have effect as if the power thereby conferred included power for a local planning authority to institute, and for the Secretary of State to direct them to institute, a fresh survey of part only of their district; and references in subsection (3) above to the district of a local planning authority or any neighbouring districts shall be construed accordingly.

Preparation of structure plans.

2.—(1) The local planning authority shall, within such period from the commencement of this section within their district as the Secretary of State may direct, prepare and send the Secretary of State a report of their survey under section 1 above and at the same time prepare and submit to him for his approval a structure plan for their district complying with the provisions of subsection (3) below.

(2) The said report shall include an estimate of any changes likely to occur during such period as the Secretary of State may direct in the matters mentioned in section 1(3) above; and different periods may be specified by any such direction in relation to different matters.

(3) The structure plan for any district shall be a written statement—

(*a*) formulating the local planning authority's policy and general proposals in respect of the development and other use of land in that district (including measures for the improvement of the physical environment and the management of traffic);

(*b*) stating the relationship of those proposals to general proposals for the development and other use of land in neighbouring districts which may be expected to affect that district; and

(*c*) containing such other matters as may be prescribed or as the Secretary of State may in any particular case direct.

(4) In formulating their policy and general proposals under subsection (3)(*a*) above the local planning authority shall secure that the policy and proposals are justified by the results of their survey under section 1 above and by any other information which they may obtain, and shall have regard—

(*a*) to current policies with respect to the economic planning and development of the region as a whole;

(*b*) to the resources likely to be available for the carrying out of the proposals of the structure plan; and

(*c*) to such other matters as the Secretary of State may direct them to take into account.

(5) A local planning authority's general proposals under this section with respect to land in their district shall indicate any area of that district (in this Act referred to as an " action area ") which they have selected for the commencement during a prescribed period of comprehensive treatment, in accordance with a local plan prepared for the selected area as a whole, by development, redevelopment or improvement of the whole or part of the area selected, or partly by one and partly by another method, and the nature of the treatment selected.

(6) A structure plan for any district shall contain or be accompanied by such diagrams, illustrations and descriptive matter as

PART I

the local planning authority think appropriate for the purpose of explaining or illustrating the proposals in the plan or as may be prescribed or as may in any particular case be specified in directions given by the Secretary of State; and any such diagrams, illustrations and descriptive matter shall be treated as forming part of the plan.

(7) At any time before the Secretary of State has, under section 4 below, approved a structure plan with respect to the whole of the district of a local planning authority, the authority may with his consent, and shall, if so directed by him, prepare and submit to him for his approval a structure plan relating to part of that district; and where the Secretary of State has given a consent or direction for the preparation of a structure plan for part of such a district, references in this Part of this Act to such a district shall, in relation to a structure plan, be construed as including references to part of that district.

Publicity in connection with preparation of structure plan.

3.—(1) When preparing a structure plan for their district and before finally determining its content for submission to the Secretary of State, the local planning authority shall take such steps as will in their opinion secure—

(*a*) that adequate publicity is given in their district to the report of the survey under section 1 above and to the matters which they propose to include in the plan;

(*b*) that persons who may be expected to desire an opportunity of making representations to the authority with respect to those matters are made aware that they are entitled to an opportunity of doing so; and

(*c*) that such persons are given an adequate opportunity of making such representations;

and the authority shall consider any representations made to them within the prescribed period.

(2) Not later than the submission of a structure plan to the Secretary of State, the local planning authority shall make copies of the plan as submitted to the Secretary of State available for inspection at their office and at such other places as may be prescribed; and each copy shall be accompanied by a statement of the time within which objections to the plan may be made to the Secretary of State.

(3) A structure plan submitted by the local planning authority to the Secretary of State for his approval shall be accompanied by a statement containing such particulars, if any, as may be prescribed—

(*a*) of the steps which the authority have taken to comply with subsection (1) above; and (*b*) of the authority's consultations with, and consideration of the views of, other persons with respect to those matters.

(4) If after considering the statement submitted with, and the matters included in, the structure plan and any other information provided by the local planning authority, the Secretary of State is satisfied that the purposes of paragraphs (*a*) to (*c*) of subsection (1) above have been adequately achieved by the steps taken by the authority in compliance with that subsection, he shall proceed to consider whether to approve the structure plan; and if he is not so satisfied he shall return the plan to the authority and direct them—

(*a*) to take such further action as he may specify in order better to achieve those purposes; and

(*b*) after doing so, to resubmit the plan with such modifications, if any, as they then consider appropriate and, if so required by the direction, to do so within a specified period.

(5) Where the Secretary of State returns the structure plan to the local planning authority under subsection (4) above, he shall inform the authority of his reasons for doing so and, if any person has made to him an objection to the plan, shall also inform that person that he has returned the plan.

(6) A local planning authority who are given directions by the Secretary of State under subsection (4) above shall forthwith withdraw the copies of the plan made available for inspection as required by subsection (2) above.

(7) Subsections (2) to (6) of this section shall apply, with the necessary modifications, in relation to a structure plan resubmitted to the Secretary of State in accordance with directions given by him under subsection (4) as they apply in relation to the plan as originally submitted.

Approval or rejection of structure plan by Secretary of State.

4.—(1) The Secretary of State may, after considering a structure plan submitted (or resubmitted) to him, either approve it (in whole or in part and with or without modifications or reservations) or reject it.

(2) In considering any such plan the Secretary of State may take into account any matters which he thinks are relevant, whether or not they were taken into account in the plan as submitted to him.

PART I

(3) Where on taking any such plan into consideration the Secretary of State does not determine then to reject it, he shall, before determining whether or not to approve it—

(*a*) consider any objections to the plan, so far as they are made in accordance with regulations under this Part of this Act;

(*b*) afford to any persons whose objections so made are not withdrawn an opportunity of appearing before, and being heard by, a person appointed by him for the purpose; and

(*c*) if a local inquiry or other hearing is held, also afford the like opportunity to the local planning authority and such other persons as he thinks fit.

(4) Without prejudice to subsection (3) above, on considering a structure plan the Secretary of State may consult with, or consider the views of, any local planning authority or other persons, but shall not be under an obligation to consult with, or consider the views of, any other authority or persons or, except as provided by that subsection, to afford an opportunity for the making of any objections or other representations, or to cause any local inquiry or other hearing to be held.

Alteration of structure plans.

5.—(1) At any time after the approval of a structure plan for their district a local planning authority may submit to the Secretary of State and shall, if so directed by the Secretary of State, submit to him within a period specified in the direction, proposals for such alterations to that plan as appear to them to be expedient or as the Secretary of State may direct, as the case may be, and any such proposals may relate to the whole or to part of that district.

(2) The local planning authority shall send with the proposals submitted by them under this section a report of the results of their review of the relevant matters under section 1 above together with any other information on which the proposals are based, and sections 3 and 4 above shall apply with any necessary modifications in relation to the proposals as they apply in relation to a structure plan.

Local plans

Preparation of local plans.

6.—(1) A local planning authority who are in course of preparing a structure plan for their district, or have prepared for their district a structure plan which has not been approved or rejected by the Secretary of State, may prepare a local plan for any part of that district.

(2) Where a structure plan for their district has been approved by the Secretary of State, the local planning authority shall as

soon as practicable consider, and thereafter keep under review, the desirability of preparing and, if they consider it desirable and they have not already done so, shall prepare a local plan for any part of the district. PART I

(3) A local plan shall consist of a map and a written statement and shall—

(*a*) formulate in such detail as the authority think appropriate the authority's proposals for the development and other use of land in that part of their district or for any description of development or other use of such land (including in either case such measures as the authority think fit for the improvement of the physical environment and the management of traffic); and

(*b*) contain such matters as may be prescribed or as the Secretary of State may in any particular case direct.

(4) Different local plans may be prepared for different purposes for the same part of any district.

(5) A local plan shall contain or be accompanied by such diagrams, illustrations and descriptive matter as the local planning authority think appropriate for the purpose of explaining or illustrating the proposals in the plan or as may be prescribed or as may in any particular case be specified in directions given by the Secretary of State; and any such diagrams, illustrations and descriptive matter shall be treated as forming part of the plan.

(6) Where an area is indicated as an action area in a structure plan which has been approved by the Secretary of State, the local planning authority shall (if they have not already done so) as soon as practicable after the approval of the plan prepare a local plan for that area.

(7) Without prejudice to the foregoing provisions of this section, the local planning authority shall, if the Secretary of State gives them a direction in that behalf with respect to a part of a district for which a structure plan has been, or is in course of being, prepared, as soon as practicable prepare for that part a local plan of such nature as may be specified in the direction.

(8) Directions under subsection (7) above may be given by the Secretary of State either before or after he approves the structure plan, but no such directions shall require a local planning authority to take any steps to comply therewith until the structure plan has been approved by him.

(9) In formulating their proposals in a local plan the local planning authority shall secure that the proposals conform generally to the structure plan as it stands for the time being

PART I

(whether or not it has been approved by the Secretary of State) and shall have regard to any information and any other considerations which appear to them to be relevant or which may be prescribed, or which the Secretary of State may in any particular case direct them to take into account.

(10) Before giving a direction under the foregoing provisions of this section to a local planning authority, the Secretary of State shall consult the authority with respect to the proposed direction.

(11) Where a local planning authority are required by this section to prepare a local plan, they shall take steps for the adoption of the plan.

Publicity for preparation of local plans.

7.—(1) A local planning authority who propose to prepare a local plan shall take such steps as will in their opinion secure—

(*a*) that adequate publicity is given in their district to any relevant matter arising out of a survey of the district carried out by them under section 1 of this Act and to the matters proposed to be included in the plan;

(*b*) that persons who may be expected to desire an opportunity of making representations to the authority with respect to those matters are made aware that they are entitled to an opportunity of doing so; and

(*c*) that such persons are given an adequate opportunity of making such representations;

and the authority shall consider any representations made to them within the prescribed period.

(2) When the local planning authority have prepared a local plan, they shall, before adopting it or submitting it for approval under section 9(4) of this Act (but not before the Secretary of State has approved the structure plan so far as it applies to the area of that local plan), make copies of the local plan available for inspection at their office and at such other places as may be prescribed and send a copy to the Secretary of State; and each copy made available for inspection shall be accompanied by a statement of the time within which objections to the local plan may be made to the authority.

(3) A copy of a local plan sent to the Secretary of State under subsection (2) above shall be accompanied by a statement containing such particulars, if any, as may be prescribed—

(*a*) of the steps which the authority has taken to comply with subsection (1) above; and

(*b*) of the authority's consultations with, and their consideration of the views of, other persons.

(4) If, on considering the statement submitted with, and the matters included in, the local plan and any other information

provided by the local planning authority, the Secretary of State is not satisfied that the purposes of paragraphs (*a*) to (*c*) of subsection (1) above have been adequately achieved by the steps taken by the authority in compliance with that subsection, he may, within twenty-one days of the receipt of the statement, direct the authority not to take any further steps for the adoption of the plan without taking such further action as he may specify in order better to achieve those purposes and satisfying him that they have done so. Part I

(5) A local planning authority who are given directions by the Secretary of State under subsection (4) above shall—

(*a*) forthwith withdraw the copies of the local plan made available for inspection as required by subsection (2) above, and

(*b*) notify any person bv whom objections to the local plan have been made to the authority that the Secretary of State has given such directions as aforesaid.

8.—(1) For the purpose of considering objections made to a local plan the local planning authority may, and shall in the case of objections so made in accordance with regulations under this Part of this Act, cause a local inquiry or other hearing to be held by a person appointed by the Secretary of State or, in such cases as may be prescribed by regulations under this Part of this Act, by the authority themselves, and— Inquiries, etc. with respect to local plans.

(*a*) subsections (4) to (6) of section 50 of the Act of 1945 (power to summon and examine witnesses) shall apply to an inquiry held under this section as it applies to an inquiry held under that section ;

(*b*) the Tribunals and Inquiries Act 1958 shall apply to a local inquiry or other hearing held under this section as it applies to a statutory inquiry held by the Secretary of State, but as if in section 12(1) of that Act (statement of reasons for decisions) the reference to any decision taken by a Minister were a reference to a decision taken by a local authority. 1958 c. 66.

(2) Regulations made for the purposes of subsection (1) above may—

(*a*) make provision with respect to the appointment and qualifications for appointment of persons to hold a local inquiry or other hearing under that subsection, including provision enabling the Secretary of State to direct a local planning authority to appoint a particular person, or one of a specified list or class of persons ;

(*b*) make provision with respect to the remuneration and allowances of a person appointed for the said purpose.

PART I

Adoption and approval of local plans.

9.—(1) After the expiry of the period afforded for making objections to a local plan or, if such objections have been duly made during that period, after considering the objections so made, the local planning authority may, subject to section 7 above and subsections (2) and (3) below, by resolution adopt the plan either as originally prepared or as modified so as to take account of any such objections or of any matters arising out of such objections.

(2) The local planning authority shall not adopt a local plan unless it conforms generally to the structure plan as approved by the Secretary of State.

(3) After copies of a local plan have been sent to the Secretary of State and before the plan has been adopted by the local planning authority, the Secretary of State may direct that the plan shall not have effect unless approved by him.

(4) Where the Secretary of State gives a direction under subsection (3) above, the local planning authority shall submit the plan accordingly to him for his approval, and—

(*a*) section 4 above shall, subject to paragraph (*b*) below, apply in relation to the plan as it applies in relation to a structure plan;

(*b*) before deciding whether or not to approve the plan, the Secretary of State shall consider any objections thereto which have been considered by the authority, but he shall not be obliged to cause an inquiry or other hearing to be held into the plan if any such inquiry or hearing has already been held at the instance of the authority; and

(*c*) after the giving of the direction the authority shall have no further power or duty to hold a local inquiry or other hearing under section 8 above in connection with the plan.

Alteration to local plans.

10.—(1) A local planning authority may at any time make proposals for the alteration, repeal or replacement of a local plan adopted by them and may at any time, with the consent of the Secretary of State, make proposals for the alteration, repeal or replacement of a local plan approved by him.

(2) Without prejudice to subsection (1) above, a local planning authority shall, if the Secretary of State gives them a direction in that behalf with respect to a local plan adopted by them or approved by him, as soon as practicable prepare proposals of a kind specified in the direction, being proposals for the alteration, repeal or replacement of the plan.

PART I

(3) The provisions of sections 6(9) to (11), 7, 8, and 9 above shall apply in relation to the making of proposals for the alteration, repeal or replacement of a local plan under this section and to alterations to a local plan so proposed as they apply in relation to the preparation of a local plan under the said section 6 and to a local plan prepared thereunder, but as if the reference in section 9(4)(*a*) to section 4 above were a reference to section 5 above.

Supplementary provisions

Disregarding of representations with respect to development authorised by or under other enactments.

11. Notwithstanding anything in the foregoing provisions of this Act, neither the Secretary of State nor a local planning authority shall be required to consider representations or objections with respect to a structure plan, a local plan or any proposal to alter, repeal or replace any such plan if it appears to the Secretary of State or the authority, as the case may be, that those representations or objections are in substance representations or objections with respect to things done or proposed to be done in pursuance of—

(*a*) an order or scheme under section 1 of the Trunk Roads Act 1936, sections 1 and 4 of the Trunk Roads Act 1946 or section 1, 3 or 14 of the Special Roads Act 1949 (trunk road orders, special road schemes and ancillary orders);

1936 c. 5. (1 Edw. 8 & 1 Geo. 6). 1946 c. 30. 1949 c. 32.

(*b*) an order under section 1 of the New Towns Act 1946 or section 1 of the New Towns (Scotland) Act 1968 (designation of sites of new towns).

1946 c. 68. 1968 c. 16.

Default powers of Secretary of State.

12.—(1) Where, by virtue of any of the foregoing provisions of this Part of this Act, any survey is required to be carried out or any structure or local plan or proposals for the alteration, repeal or replacement thereof are required to be prepared or submitted to the Secretary of State, or steps are required to be taken for the adoption of any such plan or proposals, then—

(*a*) if at any time the Secretary of State is satisfied after holding a local inquiry or other hearing that the local planning authority are not carrying out the survey or are not taking the steps necessary to enable them to submit or adopt such a plan or proposals within a reasonable period; or

(*b*) in a case where a period is specified for the submission or adoption of any such plan or proposals, if no such plan or proposals have been submitted or adopted within that period;

the Secretary of State may carry out the survey or prepare and make a structure plan or local plan or, as the case may be, alter, repeal or replace it, as he thinks fit.

PART I

(2) Where under subsection (1) above the Secretary of State has power to do anything which should have been done by a local planning authority, he may, if he thinks fit, authorise any other local planning authority who appear to the Secretary of State to have an interest in the proper planning of the district of the first-mentioned authority to do that thing.

(3) Where under this section anything which ought to have been done by a local planning authority is done by the Secretary of State or another such authority, the foregoing provisions of this Part of this Act shall, so far as applicable, apply with any necessary modifications in relation to the doing of that thing by the Secretary of State and the latter authority and the thing so done.

(4) Where the Secretary of State incurs expenses under this section in connection with the doing of anything which should have been done by a local planning authority, so much of those expenses as may be certified by the Secretary of State to have been incurred in the performance of functions of that authority shall on demand be repaid by that authority to him.

(5) Where under this section anything which should have been done by one local planning authority is done by another such authority, any expenses reasonably incurred in connection with the doing of that thing by the latter authority, as certified by the Secretary of State, shall be repaid to the latter authority by the former authority.

Supplementary provisions as to structure and local plans.

13.—(1) Without prejudice to the powers conferred on him by the foregoing provisions of this Part of this Act, the Secretary of State may make regulations with respect to the form and content of structure and local plans and with respect to the procedure to be followed in connection with their preparation, submission, withdrawal, approval, adoption, making, alteration, repeal and replacement; and in particular any such regulations may—

(*a*) provide for the publicity to be given to the report of any survey carried out by a local planning authority under section 1 of this Act;

(*b*) provide for the notice to be given of, or the publicity to be given to, matters included or proposed to be included in any such plan, and the approval, adoption or making of any such plan or any alteration, repeal or replacement thereof or to any other prescribed procedural step, and for publicity to be given to the procedure to be followed as aforesaid;

(*c*) make provision with respect to the making and consideration of representations with respect to matters to be included in, or objections to, any such plan or proposals for its alteration, repeal or replacement;

(*d*) without prejudice to paragraph (*b*) above, provide for notice to be given to particular persons of the approval, adoption or alteration of any plan, if they have objected to the plan and have notified the local planning authority of their wish to receive notice, subject (if the regulations so provide) to the payment of a reasonable charge for receiving it;

(*e*) require or authorise a local planning authority to consult with or consider the views of other persons before taking any prescribed procedural step;

(*f*) require a local planning authority, in such cases as may be prescribed or in such particular cases as the Secretary of State may direct, to provide persons making a request in that behalf with copies of any plan or document which has been made public for the purpose mentioned in section 3(1)(*a*) or 7(1)(*a*) of this Act or has been made available for inspection under section 3(2) or 7(2) of this Act, subject (if the regulations so provide) to the payment of a reasonable charge therefor;

(*g*) provide for the publication and inspection of any structure plan or local plan which has been approved, adopted or made, or any document approved, adopted or made altering, repealing or replacing any such plan, and for copies of any such plan or document to be made available on sale.

(2) Regulations under this section may extend throughout Scotland or to specified areas only and may make different provisions for different cases.

(3) Subject to the foregoing provisions of this Part of this Act and to any regulations under this section, the Secretary of State may give directions to any local planning authority, or to local planning authorities generally—

(*a*) for formulating the procedure for the carrying out of their functions under this Part of this Act;

(*b*) for requiring them to give him such information as he may require for carrying out any of his functions under this Part of this Act.

(4) Subject to the provisions of section 14 below and section 31 of the Act of 1959 (proceedings for challenging validity of certain orders etc.), a structure plan or local plan or any alteration, repeal or replacement thereof shall become operative on a date appointed for the purpose in the relevant notice of approval,

PART I

resolution of adoption or notice of the making, alteration, repeal or replacement of the plan.

Proceedings for questioning validity of structure plans, etc.

14.—(1) If any person aggrieved by a structure plan or local plan, or by any alteration, repeal or replacement of any such plan, desires to question the validity of the plan, alteration, repeal or replacement on the ground that it is not within the powers conferred by this Part of this Act, or that any requirement of that Part or of any regulations made thereunder has not been complied with in relation to the approval or adoption of the plan, alteration, repeal or replacement, he may, within six weeks from the date of the publication of the first notice of the approval or adoption of the plan, alteration, repeal or replacement required by regulations under section 13(1) above, make an application to the Court of Session under this section.

(2) On any application under this section, the Court of Session—

(*a*) may by interim order, wholly or in part, suspend the operation of the plan, alteration, repeal or replacement, either generally or in so far as it effects any property of the applicant, until the final determination of the proceedings;

(*b*) if satisfied that the plan, alteration, repeal or replacement is wholly or to any extent outside the powers conferred by this Part of this Act, or that the interests of the applicant have been substantially prejudiced by the failure to comply with any requirement of that Part or of any regulations made thereunder, may wholly or in part quash the plan, alteration, repeal or replacement, as the case may be, either generally or in so far as it affects any property of the applicant.

(3) Subject to subsection (2) above, a structure plan, local plan or any alteration, repeal or replacement of any such plan shall not be questioned in any legal proceedings whatsoever.

PART II

ENFORCEMENT OF PLANNING CONTROL

Enforcement notices

New provision as to enforcement notices.

15.—(1) Where it appears to the local planning authority that there has been a breach of planning control after the end of 1964, then, subject to any directions given by the Secretary of State and to the following provisions of this section, the authority, if they consider it expedient to do so having regard to the provisions of the development plan and to any other material considerations, may serve a notice under this section (in this Act and the Act of 1947 referred to as an " enforcement notice ") requiring the breach to be remedied.

(2) There is a breach of planning control if development has been carried out, whether before or after the commencement of this Part of this Act, without the grant of planning permission required in that behalf in accordance with Part II of the Act of 1947 or if any conditions or limitations subject to which planning permission was granted have not been complied with.

(3) Where an enforcement notice relates to a breach of planning control consisting in—

(*a*) the carrying out without planning permission of building, engineering, mining or other operations in, on, over or under land ; or

(*b*) the failure to comply with any condition or limitation which relates to the carrying out of such operations and subject to which planning permission was granted for the development of that land ; or

(*c*) the making without planning permission of a change of use of any building to use as a single dwelling-house,

it may be served only within the period of four years from the date of the breach.

(4) If any dispute arises under the last foregoing subsection as to the date on which the breach of planning control occurred, the onus of proof as to that date shall rest on the person claiming the benefit of that subsection.

(5) An enforcement notice shall be served on the owner, lessee and occupier of the land to which it relates and on any other person having an interest in that land, being an interest which in the opinion of the authority is materially affected by the notice.

(6) An enforcement notice shall specify—

(*a*) the matters alleged to constitute a breach of planning control ;

(*b*) the steps required by the authority to be taken in order to remedy the breach, that is to say steps for the purpose of restoring the land to its condition before the development took place or (according to the particular circumstances of the breach) of securing compliance with the conditions or limitations subject to which planning permission was granted ; and

(*c*) the period for compliance with the notice, that is to say the period (beginning with the date when the notice

PART II

takes effect) within which those steps are required to be taken.

(7) The steps which may be required by an enforcement notice to be taken include the demolition or alteration of any buildings or works, the discontinuance of any use of land, or the carrying out on land of any building or other operations.

(8) Subject to section 16 below, an enforcement notice shall take effect at the end of such period, not less than twenty-eight days after the service of the notice, as may be specified in the notice.

(9) The local planning authority may withdraw an enforcement notice (without prejudice to their power to serve another) at any time before it takes effect; and, if they do so, they shall forthwith give notice of the withdrawal to every person who was served with the notice.

Appeal against enforcement notice.

16.—(1) A person on whom an enforcement notice is served, or any other person having an interest in the land, may, at any time within the period specified in the notice as the period at the end of which it is to take effect, appeal to the Secretary of State against the notice on any of the following grounds:—

(*a*) that planning permission ought to be granted for the development to which the notice relates or, as the case may be, that a condition or limitation alleged in the enforcement notice not to have been complied with ought to be discharged;

(*b*) that the matters alleged in the notice do not constitute a breach of planning control;

(*c*) in the case of a notice which, by virtue of section 15(3) above, may be served only within the period of four years from the date of the breach of planning control to which the notice relates, that that period has elapsed at the date of service;

(*d*) in the case of a notice not falling within paragraph (*c*) above, that the breach of planning control alleged by the notice occurred before the beginning of 1965;

(*e*) that the enforcement notice was not served as required by section 15(5) of this Act;

(*f*) that the steps required by the notice to be taken exceed what is necessary to remedy any breach of planning control;

(*g*) that the specified period for compliance with the notice falls short of what should reasonably be allowed.

(2) An appeal under this section shall be made by notice in writing to the Secretary of State, which shall indicate the

grounds of the appeal and state the facts on which it is based; and on any such appeal the Secretary of State shall, if either the appellant or the local planning authority so desire, afford to each of them an opportunity of appearing before, and being heard by, a person appointed by the Secretary of State for the purpose.

(3) Where an appeal is brought under this section, the enforcement notice shall be of no effect pending the final determination or the withdrawal of the appeal.

(4) On an appeal under this section—

(*a*) the Secretary of State may correct any informality, defect or error in the enforcement notice if he is satisfied that the informality, defect or error is not material;

(*b*) in a case where it would otherwise be a ground for determining the appeal in favour of the appellant that a person required by section 15(5) of this Act to be served with the notice was not served, the Secretary of State may disregard that fact if neither the appellant nor that person has been substantially prejudiced by the failure to serve him.

(5) On the determination of an appeal under this section, the Secretary of State shall give directions for giving effect to his determination, including, where appropriate, directions for quashing the enforcement notice or for varying the terms of the notice in favour of the appellant; and the Secretary of State may—

(*a*) grant planning permission for the development to which the enforcement notice relates or, as the case may be, discharge any condition or limitation subject to which planning permission for that development was granted;

(*b*) determine any purpose for which the land may, in the circumstances obtaining at the time of the determination, be lawfully used, having regard to any past use thereof and to any planning permission relating to the land.

(6) In considering whether to grant planning permission under subsection (5) above, the Secretary of State shall have regard to the provisions of the development plan, so far as material to the subject-matter of the enforcement notice, and to any other material considerations, and any planning permission granted by him under that subsection may—

(*a*) include permission to retain or complete any buildings or works on the land, or to do so without complying

Part II

with some condition attached to a previous planning permission;

(*b*) be granted subject to such conditions as the Secretary of State thinks fit;

and where under that subsection he discharges a condition or limitation, he may substitute for it any other condition or limitation.

(7) Where an appeal against an enforcement notice is brought under this section, the appellant shall be deemed to have made an application for planning permission for the development to which the notice relates and, in relation to any exercise by the Secretary of State of his powers under subsection (5) above, the following provisions shall have effect:—

(*a*) any planning permission granted thereunder shall be treated as granted on the said application;

(*b*) in relation to a grant of planning permission or a determination under that subsection, the Secretary of State's decision shall be final; and

(*c*) for the purposes of section 12(5) of the Act of 1947 (local planning authority's register of planning applications) the decision shall be treated as having been given by the Secretary of State in dealing with an application for planning permission made to the local planning authority.

(8) The validity of an enforcement notice shall not, except by way of an appeal under this section, be questioned in any proceedings whatsoever on any of the grounds specified in paragraphs (*b*) to (*e*) of subsection (1) above.

(9) Subsection (8) above shall not apply to proceedings brought under section 22(3) of the Act of 1947 against a person who—

(*a*) has held an interest in the land since before the enforcement notice was served under section 15 above; and

(*b*) did not have the enforcement notice served on him thereunder; and

(*c*) satisfies the court that—

(i) he did not know and could not reasonably have been expected to know that the enforcement notice had been served; and

(ii) his interests have been substantially prejudiced by the failure to serve him.

Enforcement notice to have effect against subsequent development.

17.—(1) Compliance with an enforcement notice, whether in respect of—

(*a*) the demolition or alteration of any buildings or works, or (*b*) the discontinuance of any use of land,

or in respect of any other requirements contained in the enforcement notice, shall not discharge the enforcement notice.

(2) Without prejudice to the preceding subsection, any provision of an enforcement notice requiring a use of land to be discontinued shall operate as a requirement that it shall be discontinued permanently, to the extent that it is in contravention of Part II of the Act of 1947; and accordingly the resumption of that use at any time after it has been discontinued in compliance with the enforcement notice shall to that extent be in contravention of the enforcement notice.

(3) Without prejudice to subsection (1) of this section, if any development is carried out on land by way of reinstating or restoring buildings or works which have been demolished or altered in compliance with an enforcement notice, the notice shall, notwithstanding that its terms are not apt for the purpose be deemed to apply in relation to the buildings or works as reinstated or restored as it applied in relation to the buildings or works before they were demolished or altered.

(4) A person who, without the grant of planning permission in that behalf, carries out any development on land by way of reinstating or restoring buildings or works which have been demolished or altered in compliance with an enforcement notice shall be guilty of an offence, and shall be liable on summary conviction to a fine not exceeding £100.

Established use

18.—(1) For the purposes of this Part of this Act, a use of land is established if— Certification of established use.

(*a*) it was begun before the beginning of 1965 without planning permission in that behalf and has continued since the end of 1964; or

(*b*) it was begun before the beginning of 1965 under a planning permission in that behalf granted subject to conditions or limitations, which either have never been complied with or have not been complied with since the end of 1964; or

(*c*) it was begun after the end of 1964 as the result of a change of use not requiring planning permission and there has been since the end of 1964 no change of use requiring planning permission.

(2) Where a person having an interest in land claims that a particular use of it has become established, he may apply to the local planning authority for a certificate (in this Act referred to as an " established use certificate ") to that effect:

PART II

Provided that no such application may be made in respect of the use of land as a single dwelling-house, or of any use not subsisting at the time of the application.

(3) An established use certificate may be granted (either by the local planning authority, or under section 19 below by the Secretary of State)—

(*a*) either for the whole of the land specified in the application, or for a part of it; or

(*b*) in the case of an application specifying two or more uses, either for all those uses or for some one or more of them.

(4) On an application to them under this section, the local planning authority shall, if and so far as they are satisfied that the applicant's claim is made out, grant to him an established use certificate accordingly; and if and so far as they are not so satisfied, they shall refuse the application.

(5) Where an application is made to a local planning authority for an established use certificate, then unless within such period as may be prescribed by a development order, or within such extended period as may at any time be agreed upon in writing between the applicant and the local planning authority, the authority give notice to the applicant of their decision on the application, then, for the purposes of section 19(2) below, the application shall be deemed to be refused.

(6) Schedule 1 to this Act shall have effect with respect to established use certificates and applications therefor and to appeals under section 19 below.

(7) An established use certificate shall, as respects any matters stated therein, be conclusive for the purposes of an appeal to the Secretary of State against an enforcement notice served in respect of any land to which the certificate relates, but only where the notice is served after the date of the application on which the certificate was granted.

(8) If any person, for the purpose of procuring a particular decision on an application (whether by himself or another) for an established use certificate or on an appeal arising out of such an application—

(*a*) knowingly or recklessly makes a statement which is false in a material particular; or

(*b*) with intent to deceive, produces, furnishes, sends or otherwise makes use of any document which is false in a material particular; or

(*c*) with intent to deceive, withholds any material information, he shall be guilty of an offence and liable on summary conviction to a fine not exceeding £400 or, on conviction on indictment, to imprisonment for a term not exceeding two years or a fine, or both.

PART II

Grant of certificate by Secretary of State on referred application or appeal against refusal.

19.—(1) The Secretary of State may give directions requiring applications for established use certificates to be referred to him instead of being dealt with by local planning authorities; and, on any such application being referred to him in accordance with such directions, section 18(4) above shall apply in relation to the Secretary of State as it applies in relation to the local planning authority in the case of an application determined by them.

(2) Where an application is made to a local planning authority for an established use certificate and is refused, or is refused in part, the applicant may by notice under this subsection appeal to the Secretary of State; and on any such appeal the Secretary of State shall—

(*a*) if and so far as he is satisfied that the authority's refusal is not well-founded, grant to the appellant an established use certificate accordingly or, as the case may be, modify the certificate granted by the authority on the application; and

(*b*) if and so far as he is satisfied that the authority's refusal is well-founded, dismiss the appeal.

(3) On an application referred to him under subsection (1) above or on an appeal to him under subsection (2) above, the Secretary of State may, in respect of any use of land for which an established use certificate is not granted (either by him or by the local planning authority), grant planning permission for that use or, as the case may be, for the continuance of that use without complying with some condition subject to which a previous planning permission was granted.

(4) Before determining an application or appeal under this section, the Secretary of State shall, if either the applicant or appellant (as the case may be) or the local planning authority so desire, afford to each of them an opportunity of appearing before, and being heard by, a person appointed by the Secretary of State for the purpose.

(5) In the case of any use of land for which the Secretary of State has power to grant planning permission under this section, the applicant or appellant shall be deemed to have made an application for such planning permission; and any planning permission so granted shall be treated as granted on the said application.

PART II

Stop notices

Power to stop further development pending proceedings on enforcement notice.

20.—(1) Where in respect of any land the local planning authority have served an enforcement notice, they may at any time before the notice takes effect serve a further notice (in this Act referred to as a " stop notice ") referring to, and having annexed to it a copy of, the enforcement notice and prohibiting any person on whom the stop notice is served from carrying out or continuing any specified operations on the land, being operations either alleged in the enforcement notice to constitute a breach of planning control or so closely associated therewith as to constitute substantially the same operations.

(2) The operations which may be the subject of a stop notice shall include the deposit of refuse or waste materials on land where that is a breach of planning control alleged in the enforcement notice.

(3) A stop notice may be served by the local planning authority on any person who appears to them to have an interest in the land or to be concerned with the carrying out or continuance of any operations thereon.

(4) A stop notice—

(*a*) shall specify the date (not earlier than three nor later than fourteen days from the day on which the notice is first served on any person) when it is to take effect;

(*b*) in relation to any person served with it, shall have effect as from that date or the third day after the date of service on him, whichever is the later; and

(*c*) shall, without prejudice to subsection (7) below, cease to have effect when the enforcement notice takes effect or is withdrawn or quashed.

(5) If while a stop notice has effect in relation to him a person carries out, or causes or permits to be carried out, any operations prohibited by the notice, he shall be guilty of an offence and liable on summary conviction to a fine not exceeding £400, or on conviction on indictment to a fine; and if the offence is continued after conviction he shall be liable on summary conviction to a further fine not exceeding £50 for every day on which it is continued, or on conviction on indictment to a further fine.

(6) A stop notice shall not be invalid by reason that the enforcement notice to which it relates was not served as required by section 15(5) above if it is shown that the local planning authority took all such steps as were reasonably practicable to effect proper service.

(7) The local planning authority may at any time withdraw a stop notice (without prejudice to their power to serve another)

by serving notice to that effect on persons who were served with the stop notice, which shall cease to have effect as from the date of service of the notice under this subsection.

(8) Where a person (in this subsection called " the contractor ") is under contract to another person (in this subsection called " the developer ") to carry out any operations on land and—

(*a*) a stop notice takes effect (whether in relation to the developer or the contractor, or both) prohibiting the carrying out or continuance of those operations; and

(*b*) the operations are countermanded or discontinued by the contractor accordingly,

then, unless and in so far as the contract makes provision explicitly to the contrary of this subsection, the developer shall be under the same liability in contract as if the operations had been countermanded or discontinued on instructions given by him in breach of the contract.

This subsection applies only to contracts entered into before the end of 1969, whether before or after the commencement of this section.

Compensation for loss due to stop notice.

21.—(1) Where a stop notice ceases to have effect, a person who, at the time when it was first served, had an interest in the land to which it relates shall, in any of the circumstances mentioned in subsection (2) below, be entitled to be compensated by the local planning authority in respect of any loss or damage directly attributable to the prohibition contained in the notice.

(2) A person shall be entitled to compensation under subsection (1) above in respect of a prohibition contained in a stop notice in any of the following circumstances:—

(*a*) the enforcement notice is quashed on any of the grounds mentioned in paragraph (*b*), (*c*), (*d*) or (*e*) of section 16(1) above;

(*b*) the allegation in the enforcement notice on which the prohibition in the stop notice is dependent is not upheld by reason that the enforcement notice is varied on one of those grounds;

(*c*) the enforcement notice is withdrawn by the local planning authority otherwise than in consequence of the grant by them of planning permission for the development to which the notice relates or for its retention or continuance without compliance with a condition or limitation subject to which a previous planning permission was granted;

(*d*) the stop notice is withdrawn.

PART II

(3) A prohibition in a stop notice shall be treated for the purposes of subsection (2) above as dependent on an allegation in an enforcement notice if and to the extent that the operations to which the prohibition in the stop notice relates are the same as those alleged in the enforcement notice to constitute a breach of planning control or are so closely associated therewith as to constitute substantially the same operations.

(4) A claim for compensation under this section shall be made to the local planning authority within the time and in the manner prescribed by regulations under the Act of 1947.

(5) The loss or damage in respect of which compensation is payable under this section in respect of a prohibition shall include a sum payable in respect of a breach of contract caused by the taking of action necessary to comply with the prohibition or of any liability arising by virtue of section 20(8) of this Act.

PART III

APPEALS

Determination of planning and similar appeals by persons appointed by the Secretary of State.

22.—(1) An appeal to which this section applies, being an appeal of a prescribed class, shall, except in such classes of case as may for the time being be prescribed or as may be specified in directions given by the Secretary of State, be determined by a person appointed by the Secretary of State for the purpose instead of by the Secretary of State.

(2) This section applies to—

(*a*) appeals under section 14 of the Act of 1947 (planning decisions), or under that section as applied by or under any other provision of that Act;

1967 c. 69.

(*b*) appeals under section 14 of the Civic Amenities Act 1967 (default powers and appeals in connection with tree preservation orders);

(c) appeals under section 16 of this Act, or under that section as applied by regulations under any provision of the Act of 1947;

(*d*) appeals under section 19(2) of this Act;

(*e*) appeals under Schedule 4 to this Act.

(3) Regulations made for the purpose of this section may provide for the giving of publicity to any directions given by the Secretary of State under subsection (1) above.

(4) Subsection (1) above shall not affect any provision contained in this Act or the Act of 1947 or any instrument thereunder that an appeal shall lie to, or a notice of appeal shall be served on, the Secretary of State.

(5) A person appointed under this section to determine an appeal shall have the like powers and duties in relation to the appeal as the Secretary of State under whichever are relevant of the following provisions, that is to say— PART III

(*a*) in relation to appeals under section 14 of the Act of 1947, subsection (2) of that section, subsections (1) and (2) of section 12 of that Act, and section 36 of the Act of 1959;

(*b*) in relation to appeals under section 14 of the Civic Amenities Act 1967, section 16(4) and (5) above; 1967 c. 69.

(*c*) in relation to appeals under section 16 of this Act, subsections (4) to (6) of that section;

(*d*) in relation to appeals under section 19 of this Act, subsections (2) and (3) of that section;

(*e*) in relation to appeals under paragraph 6 of Schedule 4 to this Act, sub-paragraph (3) of that paragraph;

(*f*) in relation to appeals under paragraph 17 of that Schedule, sub-paragraphs (4) and (5) of that paragraph;

and those relevant provisions, subsection (3) and, where relevant, subsection (7) of section 16 above or paragraph 6(5) or 17(6) of the said Schedule, as the case may be, shall apply accordingly.

(6) The provisions of section 13(2) of the Act of 1947 as applied by section 14(2) of that Act, sections 16(2) and 19(4) above and paragraphs 6(4) and 17(2) of the said Schedule 4, relating to the affording of an opportunity of appearing before, and being heard by, a person appointed by the Secretary of State, shall not apply to an appeal which falls to be determined by a person appointed under this section, but before the determination of any such appeal the Secretary of State shall ask the applicant or appellant, as the case may require, and the local planning authority whether they wish to appear before and be heard by the person so appointed, and—

(*a*) the appeal may be determined without a hearing of the parties if both of them express a wish not to appear and be heard as aforesaid; and

(*b*) the person so appointed shall, if either of the parties expresses a wish to appear and be heard, afford to both of them an opportunity of so doing.

(7) Subject to subsection (8) below, the decision of a person appointed under this section on any appeal to which this section applies shall be final.

(8) An appeal determined by any such person by virtue of this section shall be treated for the purposes of Part II of the Act of 1947, Part IV of the Act of 1954 and sections 31 and 32

Part III

of the Act of 1959 as having been determined by the Secretary of State.

Determination of appeals by the Secretary of State.

23.—(1) The Secretary of State may, if he thinks fit, direct that an appeal which, by virtue of section 22 above and apart from this subsection, falls to be determined by a person appointed by the Secretary of State shall instead be determined by the Secretary of State.

(2) A direction under this section shall state the reasons for which it is given and shall be served on the person, if any, so appointed, the applicant or appellant, the local planning authority and any person who has made representations relating to the subject matter of the appeal which the authority are required to take into account under section 36(4)(*b*) of the Act of 1959 (representations by owners and agricultural tenants).

(3) Where in consequence of a direction under this section an appeal to which section 22 above applies falls to be determined by the Secretary of State, whichever of the following provisions are relevant, that is to say those of—

the Act of 1947;

section 16 of this Act;

section 19(2) to (5) of this Act;

Part I of Schedule 4 to this Act; and

1967 c. 69. section 14 of the Civic Amenities Act 1967,

shall, subject to the following provisions of this section, apply to the appeal as if section 22 above had never applied thereto.

(4) Where in consequence of a direction under this section the Secretary of State determines an appeal himself, he shall afford to the applicant or appellant, the local planning authority and any person who has made any such representations as aforesaid an opportunity of appearing before, and being heard by, a person appointed by the Secretary of State for that purpose either—

(*a*) if the reasons for the direction raise matters with respect to which either the applicant or appellant, or the local planning authority or any such person have not made representations; or

(*b*) if the applicant or appellant or the local planning authority had not been asked in pursuance of section 22(6) above whether they wished to appear before and be heard by a person appointed to hear the appeal, or had been asked that question and had expressed no wish in answer thereto, or had expressed a wish to appear and be heard as aforesaid, but had not been afforded an opportunity of doing so.

PART III

(5) Except as provided by subsection (4) above, where the Secretary of State determines an appeal in consequence of a direction under this section he shall not be obliged to afford any person an opportunity of appearing before, and being heard by, a person appointed for the purpose, or of making fresh representations or making or withdrawing any representations already made, and in determining the appeal the Secretary of State may take into account any report made to him by the person previously appointed to determine it.

Appointment of another person to determine an appeal.

24.—(1) Where the Secretary of State has appointed a person to determine an appeal under section 22 above, the Secretary of State may, at any time before the determination of the appeal, appoint another person to determine it instead of the first-mentioned person.

(2) Subsections (5) to (8) of the said section 22 shall, subject to subsection (3) below, apply in relation to an appeal which falls to be determined by a person appointed under this section as they apply in relation to an appeal which falls to be determined by a person appointed under that section.

(3) If before the appointment of a person under this section to determine an appeal the Secretary of State had, with reference to the person previously appointed, asked the question referred to in section 22(6) above, the question need not be asked again with reference to the person appointed under this section, and any answers to the question shall be treated as given with reference to him, but—

(*a*) the consideration of the appeal or any inquiry or other hearing in connection therewith, if already begun, shall be begun afresh; and

(*b*) it shall not be necessary to afford any person an opportunity of making fresh representations or modifying or withdrawing any representations already made.

Local inquiries and hearings.

25.—(1) A person appointed under section 22 or 24 above to determine an appeal may (whether or not the parties have asked for an opportunity to appear and be heard) hold a local inquiry in connection with the appeal and shall hold such an inquiry if the Secretary of State directs him to do so.

(2) Subject to subsection (3) below, the expenses—

(*a*) of any hearing held by virtue of section 22(6)(*b*) above; and

(*b*) of any inquiry held by virtue of this section,

shall be defrayed by the Secretary of State.

(3) Subsections (4) to (9) of section 50 of the Act of 1945 (power to summon and examine witnesses, and expenses at

PART III

inquiries) shall apply to an inquiry held under this section as they apply to an inquiry held under that section.

Stopping of appeals.

26. If before or during the determination, whether by the Secretary of State or otherwise, of an appeal under section 14 of the Act of 1947 (appeals against planning decisions) in respect of an application for planning permission to develop land, the Secretary of State forms the opinion that, having regard to the provisions of subsections (1), (2) and (4) of section 12 of the Act of 1947 (planning permission and industrial development certificates), of section 1(3) of the Control of Office and Industrial Development Act 1965 (office development permits) and of the development order and to any directions given under that order, planning permission for that development—

1965 c. 33.

(*a*) could not have been granted by the local planning authority, or

(*b*) could not have been granted by them otherwise than subject to the conditions imposed by them,

he may decline to determine the appeal or to proceed with the determination, or, as the case may be, may direct that the determination shall not be begun or proceeded with.

Supplementary.
1858 c. 66.

27.—(1) The Tribunals and Inquiries Act 1958 shall apply to a local inquiry or other hearing held in pursuance of this Part of this Act as it applies to a statutory inquiry held by the Secretary of State, but as if in section 12(1) of that Act (statement of reasons for decisions) the reference to any decision taken by a Minister were a reference to a decision taken by a person appointed to determine the relevant appeal under section 22 or 24 above.

(2) The functions of determining an appeal and doing anything in connection therewith conferred by this Part of this Act on a person appointed to determine an appeal thereunder who is an officer of the Scottish Office shall be treated for the purposes of the Parliamentary Commissioner Act 1967 as functions of that Office.

1967 c. 13.

PART IV

ACQUISITION AND DISPOSAL OF LAND

Land acquisition by government departments and local authorities

Repeal of existing provisions for compulsory acquisition of land.
1953 c. 36.

28. Section 34 of the Act of 1947 (compulsory acquisition of designated land by Ministers, local authorities and statutory undertakers) and section 35 of that Act (compulsory acquisition by local authorities of land for development) shall cease to have effect, and section 47 of the Post Office Act 1953 shall cease to have effect so far as it authorises the Postmaster General to acquire land compulsorily; and—

(*a*) sections 29 and 30 below shall have effect instead of those sections; and

(*b*) references in any other enactment to the designation in a development plan of land as land subject to compulsory acquisition and to land so designated shall cease to have effect.

Compulsory acquisition of land in connection with development and for other planning purposes.

29.—(1) The Secretary of State may authorise a local authority to whom this section applies to acquire compulsorily any land within their area if he is satisfied—

(*a*) that the land is required in order to secure or assist the treatment as a whole, by development, redevelopment or improvement, or partly by one and partly by another method, of the land or of any area in which the land is situated; or

(*b*) that it is expedient in the public interest that the land should be held together with land so required; or

(*c*) that the land is required for development or redevelopment, or both, as a whole for the purpose of providing for the relocation of population or industry or the replacement of open space in the course of the redevelopment or improvement, or both, of another area as a whole; or

(*d*) that it is expedient to acquire the land immediately for a purpose which it is necessary to achieve in the interests of the proper planning of an area in which the land is situated.

(2) Where under subsection (1) above the Secretary of State has power to authorise a local authority to whom this section applies to acquire any land compulsorily, he may, after the requisite consultation, authorise the land to be so acquired by another authority, being a local authority within the meaning of the Act of 1947.

(3) Before giving an authorisation under subsection (2) above, the Secretary of State shall—

(*a*) where the land is in a county, consult with the county council;

(*b*) where the land is in a large burgh, consult with the town council;

(*c*) where the land is in a small burgh, consult with the town council and with the county council within whose area the burgh is situated.

PART IV

(4) The Acquisition Act 1947 shall apply to the compulsory acquisition of land under this section and accordingly shall have effect as if this section had been in force immediately before the commencement of that Act.

(5) The local authorities to whom this section applies are the councils of counties, large burghs and small burghs.

Compulsory acquisition of land by certain Ministers.

1953 c. 36.

30.—(1) The Minister of Public Building and Works may acquire compulsorily any land necessary for the public service.

(2) The Postmaster General may acquire compulsorily any land required for the purposes of the Post Office as defined in section 87 of the Post Office Act 1953.

(3) The power of acquiring land compulsorily under this section shall include power to acquire a servitude or other right over land by the grant of a new right:

Provided that this subsection shall not apply to a servitude or other right over any land which would, for the purposes of the Acquisition Act 1947, form part of a common or open space.

(4) The Acquisition Act 1947 shall apply to any compulsory acquisition by the Minister of Public Building and Works or the Postmaster General under this section as it applies to a compulsory acquisition by another Minister in a case falling within section 1(1) of that Act.

Power of authorities possessing compulsory purchase powers to make general vesting declarations.

31.—(1) Schedule 2 to this Act shall have effect for the purpose of enabling any authority to whom this section applies to vest in themselves by a declaration land which they are authorised by a compulsory purchase order to acquire and, with respect to the effect of such a declaration, the payment and recovery of sums in respect of compensation for the acquisition of land so vested and other matters connected therewith.

(2) This section applies to any Minister or local or other public authority authorised to acquire land by means of a compulsory purchase order, and any such authority is in the said Schedule 2 referred to as an acquiring authority.

Compulsory purchase or appropriation of open spaces.

32.—(1) In paragraph 11 of Schedule 1 to the Acquisition Act 1947 (which applies special parliamentary procedure in the case of compulsory purchase of land forming part of a common or open space, and is applied by section 39 of the Act of 1947 to appropriation of land by local authorities under that section), in sub-paragraph (1)(*b*) (exemption where land is required for widening of an existing highway and the Secretary of State certifies that it is unnecessary to give land in exchange), for the words " that the land is " there shall be substituted the words " that the land does not exceed 250 square yards in extent or is ".

(2) Nothing in this section applies to or affects an order made before the commencement of this section.

Grounds on which Secretary of State may refuse to confirm purchase notice.

33.—(1) This section shall have effect where, on an application for planning permission to develop any land which has a restricted use by virtue of a previous planning permission, permission is refused or granted subject to conditions and an owner of the land serves a purchase notice under section 17 of the Act of 1947.

(2) For the purposes of this section, land is to be treated as having a restricted use by virtue of a previous planning permission if it is part of a larger area in respect of which planning permission was previously granted (and has not been revoked) and either—

(*a*) it remains a condition of the planning permission (however expressed) that that part shall remain undeveloped or be preserved or laid out in a particular way as amenity land in relation to the remainder; or

(*b*) the planning permission was granted on an application which contemplated (expressly or by necessary implication) that the part should not be comprised in the development for which planning permission was sought, or should be preserved or laid out as aforesaid.

(3) If a copy of the purchase notice is transmitted to the Secretary of State under section 17(2) of the Act of 1947 (action to be taken by authority on whom a purchase notice is served, when they are unwilling to comply with the notice) the Secretary of State, although satisfied that the land has become incapable of reasonably beneficial use in its existing state, shall nevertheless not be required under that subsection to confirm the notice if it appears to him that the land ought, in accordance with the previous planning permission, to remain undeveloped or, as the case may be, remain or be preserved or laid out as amenity land in relation to the remainder of the larger area for which that planning permission was granted.

Planning blight

New descriptions of land qualifying for protection.

34.—(1) Section 38(1) of the Act of 1959 (land affected by planning proposals and qualifying for protection under Part IV of that Act) shall have effect as if the land specified therein included land which—

(*a*) is land indicated in a structure plan in force either as land which may be required for the purposes of any functions of a government department, local authority

PART IV

or statutory undertakers, or of the National Coal Board, or as land which may be included in an action area; or

(*b*) is land allocated for the purposes of any such functions by a local plan in force, or is land defined in such a plan as the site of proposed development for the purposes of any such functions; or

(*c*) is land in respect of which a compulsory purchase order is in force, where the appropriate authority have power to serve, but have not served, notice to treat in respect of the land; or

(*d*) is land on which the Secretary of State proposes to provide a trunk road or a special road and has given to the local planning authority written notice of his intention to provide the road, together with maps or plans sufficient to identify the proposed route of the road.

(2) Subsection (1)(*a*) above shall not apply to land situated in an area for which a local plan is in force, where that plan—

(*a*) allocates any land in the area for the purposes of such functions as are mentioned in that paragraph; or

(*b*) defines any land in the area as the site of proposed development for the purposes of any such functions.

(3) In section 38(2) of the Act of 1959 (notice requiring purchase of claimant's interest on ground of planning blight), and for the purposes of that subsection as applied by section 38(3) of that Act, " the relevant date "—

(*a*) in relation to land mentioned in subsection (1)(*c*) above, means the date when the order for its compulsory purchase was confirmed or made by the Secretary of State; and

(*b*) in relation to land mentioned in subsection (1)(*d*) above means the date on which the Secretary of State gave to the local planning authority the written notice specified in that paragraph.

(4) Paragraphs (*a*) and (*b*) of subsection (1) above shall have effect instead of paragraphs (*a*) and (*b*) of the said section 38(1).

Power of heritable creditor to serve blight notice.

35.—(1) The provisions of this section shall have effect for enabling heritable creditors to take advantage of the provisions of Part IV of the Act of 1959 (notice requiring purchase by local planning authority on grounds of planning blight).

(2) Where the whole or part of a hereditament or agricultural unit is comprised in land of any of the descriptions contained in

paragraphs (*b*) to (*f*) of section 38(1) of the Act of 1959 or paragraphs (*a*) to (*d*) of section 34(1) of this Act and a person claims that—

(*a*) he is entitled as heritable creditor (by virtue of a power which has become exercisable) to sell an interest in the hereditament or unit, giving immediate vacant possession of the land; and

(*b*) since the relevant date (within the meaning of section 42 of the Act of 1959 or, as the case may be, section 34(3) above) he has made reasonable endeavours to sell that interest; and

(*c*) he has been unable to sell it except at a price substantially lower than that for which it might reasonably have been expected to sell if no part of the hereditament or unit were comprised in land of any of the said descriptions,

then, subject to the provisions of this section, he may serve on the appropriate authority a notice in the prescribed form requiring that authority to purchase that interest to the extent specified in, and otherwise in accordance with, Part IV of the Act of 1959.

(3) Subsection (2) above shall apply in relation to an interest in part of a hereditament or agricultural unit as it applies in relation to an interest in the entirety of a hereditament or agricultural unit:

Provided that this subsection shall not enable a person—

(*a*) if his interest as heritable creditor is in the entirety of a hereditament or agricultural unit, to make any claim or serve any notice under this section in respect of any interest in part of the hereditament or unit; or

(*b*) if his interest as heritable creditor is only in part of a hereditament or agricultural unit, to make or serve any such notice or claim in respect of any interest in less than the entirety of that part.

(4) Notice under this section shall not be served unless one or other of the following conditions is satisfied with regard to the interest which the heritable creditor claims he has the power to sell:—

(*a*) the interest could be the subject of a notice under section 38 of the Act of 1959 served by the person entitled thereto on the date of service of the notice under this section; or

(*b*) the interest could have been the subject of such a notice served by that person on a date not more than six months before the date of service of the notice under this section.

PART IV

(5) If any question arises which authority are the appropriate authority for the purposes of subsection (2) above, subsection (4)(b) above shall then apply with the substitution for the period of six months of a reference to that period extended by so long as it takes to obtain a determination of the question.

(6) No notice under this section shall be served in respect of a hereditament or agricultural unit, or any part of a hereditament or agricultural unit, at a time when a notice already served under section 38 of the Act of 1959 is outstanding with respect to the hereditament, unit or part; and no notice shall be so served under section 38 of that Act at a time when a notice already served under this section is so outstanding.

(7) For the purposes of subsection (6) above, a notice served under this section or section 38 of the Act of 1959 shall be treated as outstanding with respect to a hereditament or agricultural unit, or to part of a hereditament or agricultural unit, until—

(*a*) it is withdrawn in relation to the hereditament, unit or part; or

(*b*) an objection to the notice having been made by a counter-notice under section 39 of the Act of 1959, either—

(i) the period of two months specified in section 40(1) of the Act of 1959 elapses without the claimant having required the objection to be referred to the Lands Tribunal under that section; or

(ii) the objection, having been so referred to the Lands Tribunal, is upheld by the Tribunal with respect to the hereditament, unit or part.

(8) The grounds on which objection may be made in a counter-notice under section 39 of the Act of 1959 to a notice under this section are those specified in paragraphs (*a*) to (*c*) of subsection (2) of that section and, in a case to which section 36(1) below applies, the ground specified in that subsection and also the following grounds:—

(*a*) that, on the date of service of the notice under this section, the claimant had no interest as heritable creditor in any part of the hereditament or agricultural unit to which the notice relates;

(*b*) that (for reasons specified in the counter-notice) the claimant had not on that date the power referred to in subsection (2)(*a*) above;

(*c*) that the conditions specified in subsection (2)(*b*) and (*c*) above are not fulfilled;

(*d*) that (for reasons specified in the counter-notice) neither of the conditions specified in subsection (4) above was, on the date of service of the notice under this section, satisfied with regard to the interest referred to in that subsection.

(9) The provisions of the Act of 1959 specified in Schedule 3 to this Act (being provisions relating to blight notices and to proceedings arising out of such notices) shall be amended in accordance with that Schedule.

Extension of grounds of objection to blight notice.

36.—(1) Where a blight notice is served under section 38 of the Act of 1959 or section 35 above, then in the case of land—

(*a*) falling within section 38(1)(*c*) of the Act of 1959 or section 34(1)(*a*) of this Act, and

(*b*) not falling within section 38(1)(*e*) or (*f*) of that Act or section 34(1)(*d*) of this Act,

the grounds on which an objection may be made in a counter-notice under section 39 of the Act of 1959 shall include the grounds that the appropriate authority (unless compelled to do so by virtue of Part IV of that Act and section 35 above) do not propose to acquire in the exercise of any relevant powers any part of the hereditament or (in the case of an agricultural unit) any part of the affected area during the period of fifteen years from the date of the counter-notice or such longer period from that date as may be specified in the counter-notice.

(2) An objection may not be made as aforesaid on the grounds mentioned in subsection (1) above if it may be made on the grounds mentioned in section 39(2)(*b*) of the Act of 1959 (objection on the grounds that the appropriate authority do not propose to acquire any part of the hereditament or affected area in question).

(3) An objection on the grounds mentioned in subsection (1) above which is referred to the Lands Tribunal shall not be upheld by the Tribunal unless it is shown to the satisfaction of the Tribunal that the objection is well-founded.

(4) Paragraph 11(1) and (2) of Schedule 5 to the Act of 1959 (lapsing of compulsory purchase powers when objection under section 39 of that Act is successful) shall apply in relation to an objection on the said grounds as they apply in relation to an objection on the grounds mentioned in section 39(2)(*b*) of that Act.

(5) A county council or a town council may, subject to such conditions as may be approved by the Secretary of State, advance money to any person for the purpose of enabling him to acquire a hereditament or agricultural unit in respect of which a counter-notice has been served under section 39 of the Act of 1959 specifying the grounds mentioned in subsection (1) above as, or as one of, the grounds of objection, if, in the case of a

PART IV

hereditament, its annual value does not exceed such amount as may be prescribed for the purposes of section 38(4)(*a*) of that Act (interests qualifying for protection under that Act).

(6) Paragraph (*c*) of section 39(2) of the Act of 1959 (objection on the grounds that the appropriate authority propose to acquire part only of the affected area of an agricultural unit) and the following provisions of that Act, that is to say, sections 40(5) and 41(3) (subsequent proceedings where such an objection made) and paragraph 12(1) and (2) of Schedule 5 to that Act (lapsing of compulsory purchase powers when objection under section 39 is successful) shall apply to hereditaments as they apply to any such area, references in those provisions to the affected area being construed as references to the hereditament.

1845 c. 19.

(7) Subsection (6) above shall not affect the right of a claimant under section 90 of the Lands Clauses Consolidation (Scotland) Act 1845 to sell the whole of the hereditament, or (in the case of an agricultural unit) the whole of the affected area, which he has required the authority to purchase.

(8) Subsection (6) above shall not affect the right of a claimant under paragraph 4 of Schedule 2 to the Acquisition Act 1947 to sell (unless the Lands Tribunal otherwise determines) the whole of the hereditament, or (in the case of an agricultural unit) the whole of the affected area, which he has required the authority to purchase; and accordingly, in determining whether or not to uphold an objection relating to a hereditament on the grounds mentioned in paragraph (*c*) of section 39(2) of the Act of 1959, the Tribunal shall consider (in addition to the other matters which they are required to consider) whether—

(*a*) in the case of a house, building or manufactory, the part proposed to be acquired can be taken without material detriment to the house, building or manufactory; or

(*b*) in the case of a park or garden belonging to a house the part proposed to be acquired can be taken without seriously affecting the amenity or convenience of the house.

Compensation for compulsory purchase of land in clearance areas and of historic buildings.

37. Where an interest in land is acquired in pursuance of a blight notice and the interest is one—

(*a*) in respect of which a compulsory purchase order is in force under section 1 of the Acquisition Act 1947 (as applied by section 50 of this Act) containing a direction for minimum compensation under section 53 of this Act; or

1966 c. 49.

(*b*) in respect of which a compulsory purchase order is in force under Part III of the Housing (Scotland) Act 1966, the compensation payable for the acquisition shall, in a case falling within paragraph (*a*) above, be assessed in accordance with the direction mentioned in that paragraph and, in a case falling within paragraph (*b*) above, be assessed in accordance with Part III of the said Act of 1966, in either case as if the notice to treat deemed to have been served in respect of the interest under section 41 of the Act of 1959 had been served in pursuance of the compulsory purchase order.

Miscellaneous amendments of Act of 1959.

38.—(1) Paragraphs 6 and 7 of Schedule 5 to the Act of 1959 (exclusion of compensation for severance and disturbance) shall cease to have effect.

(2) For a person to be treated under section 42(2) or (4) of the Act of 1959 (definitions for purposes of blight notice provisions) as owner-occupier or resident owner-occupier of a hereditament, his occupation thereof at a relevant time or during a relevant period, if not occupation of the whole of the hereditament, must be or, as the case may be, have been occupation of a substantial part of it.

(3) In subsections (2)(*b*), (3)(*b*) and (4)(*b*) of the said section 42, the period of six months ending not more than six months before the date of service shall in each case be replaced by a period of six months ending not more than twelve months before that date.

(4) If any question arises which authority is the appropriate authority for the purposes of the said Part IV or section 35 of this Act—

(*a*) section 39(1) of the Act of 1959 (objection to blight notice) shall have effect as if the reference to the date of service of that notice were a reference to that date or the date on which that question is determined, whichever is the later ; and

(*b*) subsections (2)(*b*), (3)(*b*) and (4)(*b*) of section 42 of that Act shall apply with the substitution for the reference to twelve months before the date of service of a reference to that period extended by so long as it takes to obtain a determination of the question.

Disposal of land by public authorities

Restriction on exercise by public authorities of power of disposing of land.

39. Section 27(1) of the Act of 1959 (power of local and other public authorities to dispose of land without consent of a Minister) shall not apply to the exercise of a power to dispose of land conferred by any enactment if the power is exercised in respect of

(*a*) an approved house within the meaning of section 1 of the Housing (Financial Provisions) (Scotland) Act 1968 ; or

1968 c. 31.

PART IV

(*b*) housing accommodation in respect of which there has been made to a local authority (whether before or after the commencement of the Act of 1959) an Exchequer contribution within the meaning of section 67(2) of the said Act of 1968.

PART V

BUILDINGS OF ARCHITECTURAL OR HISTORIC INTEREST

Restrictions on demolition and other works

New provisions restricting demolition etc. of listed buildings.

40.—(1) In this Part of this Act the expression " listed building " means a building which is for the time being included in a list compiled or approved by the Secretary of State under section 28 of the Act of 1947 (buildings of special architectural or historic interest).

(2) Subject to this Part of this Act, if a person executes or causes to be executed any works for the demolition of a listed building or for its alteration or extension in any manner which would affect its character as a building of special architectural or historic interest, and the works are not authorised under this Part of this Act, he shall be guilty of an offence.

(3) For the purposes of this Part of this Act, any object or structure fixed to a building or forming part of the land and comprised within the curtilage of a building shall be treated as part of the building.

(4) Works for the demolition of a listed building, or for its alteration or extension, are authorised under this Part of this Act only if—

(*a*) the local planning authority or the Secretary of State have granted written consent (hereafter in this Act referred to as " listed building consent ") for the execution of the works and the works are executed in accordance with the terms of the consent and of any conditions attached to the consent under section 41 below; and

(*b*) in the case of demolition, notice of the proposal to execute the works has been given to the Royal Commission and thereafter either—

(i) for a period of at least three months following the grant of listed building consent and before the commencement of the works, reasonable access to the building has been made available to members or officers of the Commission for the purpose of recording it; or

(ii) the Commission have, by their Secretary or other officer of theirs with authority to act on the Commission's behalf for the purposes of this section, stated in writing that they have completed their recording of the building or that they do not wish to record it.

(5) In subsection (4) above " the Royal Commission " means the Royal Commission on the Ancient and Historical Monuments of Scotland; but the Secretary of State may, by order made by statutory instrument, provide that the said subsection shall, in the case of works executed or to be executed on or after such date as may be specified in the order, have effect with the substitution for the reference to the Royal Commission of a reference to such other body as may be so specified.

(6) Without prejudice to subsection (2) above, if a person executing or causing to be executed any works in relation to a listed building under a listed building consent fails to comply with any condition attached to the consent under section 41 below, he shall be guilty of an offence.

(7) A person guilty of an offence under this section shall be liable—

(*a*) on summary conviction to imprisonment for a term of not more than three months or a fine of not more than £250, or both; or

(*b*) on conviction on indictment to imprisonment for a term not exceeding twelve months or a fine, or both;

and in determining the amount of any fine to be imposed on a person convicted on indictment the court shall in particular have regard to any financial benefit which has accrued or appears likely to accrue to him in consequence of the offence.

(8) In proceedings for an offence under this section it shall be a defence to prove that the works were urgently necessary in the interests of safety or health, or for the preservation of the building, and that notice in writing of the need for the works was given to the local planning authority as soon as reasonably practicable.

(9) Section 27 of the Act of 1947 (building preservation orders) and subsections (5) to (8) of section 28 of that Act (recording of list and effect of inclusion of building in a list under that section of the Act) shall cease to have effect.

(10) Every building which, before the commencement of this Part of this Act, was subject to a building preservation order under section 27 of the Act of 1947, but was not then included in a list compiled or approved under section 28 of that Act, shall be deemed to be a listed building; but the Secretary of State

PART V

may at any time direct, in the case of any building, that this subsection shall no longer apply to it and the local planning authority in whose district the building is situated, on being notified of the Secretary of State's direction, shall give notice of it to the owner, lessee and occupier of the building.

(11) Before giving a direction under subsection (10) above in relation to a building, the Secretary of State shall consult with the local planning authority and with the owner, lessee and occupier of the building.

Provisions supplementary to s. 40.

41.—(1) Section 40 above shall not apply to works for the demolition, alteration or extension of—

(*a*) an ecclesiastical building which is for the time being used for ecclesiastical purposes or would be so used but for the works; or

(*b*) a building which is the subject of a scheme or order under the enactments for the time being in force with respect to ancient monuments; or

(*c*) a building for the time being included in a list of monuments published by the Secretary of State under any such enactment.

For the purposes of this subsection, a building used or available for use by a minister of religion wholly or mainly as a residence from which to perform the duties of his office shall be treated as not being an ecclesiastical building.

(2) Where, on an application in that behalf, planning permission is granted after the commencement of this Part of this Act and—

(*a*) the development for which the permission is granted includes the carrying out of any works for the alteration or extension of a listed building; and

(*b*) the planning permission or any condition subject to which it is granted is so framed as expressly to authorise the execution of the works (describing them),

the planning permission shall operate as listed building consent in respect of those works; but, except as provided by this subsection, the grant of planning permission for any development shall not make it unnecessary for such consent to be obtained in respect of any works to which section 40 above applies.

(3) In considering whether to grant planning permission for development which consists in or includes works for the alteration or extension of a listed building, and in considering whether to grant listed building consent for any works, the local planning authority or the Secretary of State, as the case may be, shall have special regard to the desirability of preserving

the building or any features of special architectural or historic interest which it possesses.

(4) Without prejudice to section 12(1) of the Act of 1947 (grant of planning permission unconditionally or subject to conditions), the conditions which may under that subsection be attached to a grant of planning permission shall, in the case of such development as is referred to in subsection (2) above, include conditions with respect to—

(*a*) the preservation of particular features of the building, either as part of it or after severance therefrom;

(*b*) the making good, after the works are completed, of any damage caused to the building by the works;

(*c*) the reconstruction of the building or any part of it following the execution of any works, with the use of original materials so far as practicable and with such alterations of the interior of the building as may be specified in the conditions.

(5) Listed building consent may be granted either unconditionally or subject to conditions, which may include such conditions as are mentioned in subsection (4) above.

(6) Part I of Schedule 4 to this Act shall have effect with respect to applications to local planning authorities for listed building consent, the reference of such applications to the Secretary of State and appeals against decisions on such applications; and Part II of that Schedule shall have effect with respect to the revocation of listed building consent by a local planning authority or the Secretary of State and to the compensation payable in the case of revocation.

Owner's and lessee's rights on refusal of consent to works

Purchase notice on refusal or conditional grant of listed building consent.

42.—(1) Where, on an application for listed building consent in respect of a building, consent is refused or is granted subject to conditions or, by an order under Part II of Schedule 4 to this Act, listed building consent is revoked or modified, then if any owner or lessee of the land claims—

(*a*) that the land has become incapable of reasonably beneficial use in its existing state; and

(*b*) in a case where consent was granted subject to conditions with respect to the execution of the works, or, as the case may be, was modified by the imposition of such conditions, that the land cannot be rendered capable of reasonably beneficial use by the carrying out of the works in accordance with those conditions; and

(*c*) in any case that the land cannot be rendered capable of reasonably beneficial use by the carrying out of

Part V

any other works for which listed building consent has been granted or for which the local planning authority or the Secretary of State have undertaken to grant such consent,

he may, within the prescribed time and manner, serve on the local planning authority in whose district the land is situated a notice requiring that authority to purchase his interest in the land in accordance with Part III of Schedule 4 to this Act.

(2) A notice under this section is in this Act referred to as a " listed building purchase notice ".

(3) In this section and in Part III of Schedule 4 to this Act, " the land " means the building in respect of which listed building consent has been refused, or granted subject to conditions, or modified by the imposition of conditions, and in respect of which its owner or lessee serves a notice under this section, together with any land comprising the building, or contiguous or adjacent to it, and owned or occupied with it, being land as to which the owner or lessee claims that its use is substantially inseparable from that of the building and that it ought to be treated, together with the building, as a single holding.

(4) Where, for the purpose of determining whether the conditions specified in paragraphs (*a*) to (*c*) of subsection (1) above are satisfied in relation to the land, any question arises as to what is or would in any particular circumstances be a reasonably beneficial use of that land, then, in determining that question for that purpose, no account shall be taken of any prospective use of that land which would involve the carrying out of new development or of any works requiring listed building consent which might be executed to the building, other than works for which the local planning authority or the Secretary of State have undertaken to grant such consent.

Compensation for refusal of consent to alterations etc.

43.—(1) The provisions of this section shall have effect where an application is made for listed building consent for the alteration or extension of a listed building and—

(*a*) either the works do not constitute development or they do so but the development is such that planning permission therefor is granted by a development order; and

(*b*) the Secretary of State, either on appeal or on the reference of the application to him, refuses such consent or grants it subject to conditions.

(2) If, on a claim made to the local planning authority within the prescribed time and manner, it is shown that the value of the interest of any person in the land is less than it would

have been if listed building consent had been granted, or had been granted unconditionally, as the case may be, the local planning authority shall pay to that person compensation of an amount equal to the difference.

(3) In determining, for the purposes of subsection (2) above, whether or to what extent the value of an interest in land is less than it would have been if the permission had been granted, or had been granted unconditionally—

(*a*) it shall be assumed that any subsequent application for the like consent would be determined in the same way; but

(*b*) if, in the case of a refusal of listed building consent, the Secretary of State, on refusing that consent, undertook to grant such consent for some other works to the building in the event of an application being made in that behalf, regard shall be had to that undertaking.

(4) No compensation shall be payable under this section in respect of an interest in land in respect of which a purchase notice is served, whether under section 17, or under that section as applied by section 20(4), of the Act of 1947 or under section 42 above, being a purchase notice which takes effect.

Enforcement

Notice to enforce s. 40 control.

44.—(1) Where it appears to the local planning authority that any works have been, or are being, executed to a listed building in their area and are such as to involve a contravention of section 40(2) or (6) of this Act, then, subject to any directions given by the Secretary of State, they may, if they consider it expedient to do so having regard to the effect of the works on the character of the building as one of special architectural or historic interest, serve a notice—

(*a*) specifying the alleged contravention; and

(*b*) requiring such steps as may be specified in the notice for restoring that building to its former state, or, as the case may be, for bringing it to the state it would have been in if the terms and conditions of any listed building consent for the works had been complied with, to be taken within such period as may be so specified.

(2) A notice under this section is hereafter in this Act referred to as a " listed building enforcement notice ".

(3) Every local planning authority shall keep available for public inspection free of charge at reasonable hours and at a convenient place a list containing particulars of any building in

Part V

their district in respect of which a listed building enforcement notice has been served.

(4) Part IV of Schedule 4 to this Act shall have effect with respect to listed building enforcement notices and appeals against such notices.

Penalties for non-compliance with notice under s. 44.

45.—(1) Where a listed building enforcement notice has been served in respect of any building and any steps required by the notice to be taken have not been taken within the period allowed for compliance with the notice, the person responsible for the contravention mentioned in section 44(1) above shall be guilty of an offence and liable on summary conviction to a fine not exceeding £400, or on conviction on indictment to a fine.

(2) If, after a person has been convicted under the foregoing provisions of this section, he does not as soon as practicable do everything in his power to secure compliance with the notice, he shall be guilty of a further offence and be liable—

(*a*) on summary conviction to a fine of not more than £50 for each day following his first conviction on which any of the requirements of the notice remain unfulfilled ; or

(*b*) on conviction on indictment to a fine.

(3) Any reference in this section or section 46 below to the period allowed for compliance with a listed building enforcement notice is a reference to the period specified in the notice as that within which the steps specified in the notice are required thereby to be taken, or such extended period as the local planning authority may allow for taking them.

Execution and cost of works required under enforcement procedure.

46.—(1) If, within the period allowed for compliance with a listed building enforcement notice, any steps required by the notice to be taken have not been taken, the authority may enter on the land and take those steps and may recover from the person who is then the owner or lessee of the land any expenses reasonably incurred by them in doing so.

(2) Any expenses incurred by the owner, lessee or occupier of a building for the purpose of complying with a listed building enforcement notice and any sums paid by the owner or lessee of a building under subsection (1) of this section in respect of expenses incurred by the local planning authority in taking steps required by such a notice to be taken, shall be deemed to be incurred or paid for the use and at the request of the person who carried out the works to which the notice relates.

1946 c. 42.

(3) Section 22(5) of the Act of 1947 (application by regulations of certain provisions of the Water (Scotland) Act 1946 in

relation to enforcement) shall apply in relation to a listed building enforcement notice as they apply in relation to an enforcement notice; and any regulations made by virtue of this subsection may provide for the charging on the land on which the building stands of any expenses recoverable by a local planning authority under subsection (1) of this section.

Enforcement by, or by direction of, the Secretary of State.

47.—(1) If it appears to the Secretary of State, after consultation with the local planning authority, to be expedient that a listed building enforcement notice should be served in respect of any land, he may give directions to the local planning authority requiring them to serve such a notice, or may himself serve such a notice; and any notice so served by the Secretary of State shall have the like effect as a notice served by the local planning authority.

(2) In relation to a listed building enforcement notice served by the Secretary of State, the provisions of sections 45(3) and 46 of this Act shall apply as if for any reference therein to the local planning authority there were substituted a reference to the Secretary of State.

Other measures open to local planning authority and the Secretary of State

Building preservation notice in respect of building not listed.

48.—(1) If it appears to the local planning authority, in the case of a building in their district which is not a listed building, that it is of special architectural or historic interest and is in danger of demolition or of alteration in such a way as to affect its character as such, they may (subject to subsection (2) below) serve on the owner, lessee and occupier of the building a notice (referred to in this section as a " building preservation notice ")—

(*a*) stating that the building appears to them to be of special architectural or historic interest and that they have requested the Secretary of State to consider including it in a list compiled or approved under section 28 of the Act of 1947; and

(*b*) explaining the effect of subsections (3) and (4) of this section.

(2) A building preservation notice shall not be served in respect of—

(*a*) an ecclesiastical building which is for the time being used for ecclesiastical purposes; or

(*b*) a building which is the subject of a scheme or order under the enactments for the time being in force with respect to ancient monuments; or

PART V

(*c*) a building for the time being included in a list of monuments published by the Secretary of State under any such enactment.

For the purposes of this subsection, a building used or available for use by a minister of religion wholly or mainly as a residence from which to perform the duties of his office shall be treated as not being an ecclesiastical building.

(3) A building preservation notice shall come into force as soon as it has been served on the owner, lessee and occupier of the building to which it relates and shall remain in force for six months from the date when it is served or, as the case may be, last served; but it shall cease to be in force if, before the expiration of that period, the Secretary of State either includes the building in a list compiled or approved under section 28 of the Act of 1947 or notifies the local planning authority in writing that he does not intend to do so.

(4) While a building preservation notice is in force with respect to a building, the provisions of this Part of this Act shall have effect in relation to it as if the building were a listed building; and if the notice ceases to be in force (otherwise than by reason of the building being included in a list compiled or approved under the said section 28), the provisions of Part V of Schedule 4 to this Act shall have effect with respect to things done or occurring under the notice or with reference to the building being treated as listed.

(5) If, following the service of a building preservation notice, the Secretary of State notifies the local planning authority that he does not propose to include the building in a list compiled or approved under section 28 of the Act of 1947, the authority—

(*a*) shall forthwith give notice of the Secretary of State's decision to the owner, lessee and occupier of the building; and

(*b*) shall not, within the period of twelve months beginning with the date of the Secretary of State's notification, serve another such notice in respect of the said building.

Compensation for loss or damage caused by service of building preservation notice.

49.—(1) The following provisions of this section shall have effect as respects compensation where a building preservation notice is served.

(2) The local planning authority shall not be under any obligation to pay compensation under section 43 of this Act in respect of any refusal of listed building consent or its grant subject to conditions, unless and until the building is included in a list compiled or approved by the Secretary of State under section 28 of the Act of 1947; but this subsection shall not

prevent a claim for such compensation being made before the building is so included. PART V

(3) If the building preservation notice ceases to have effect without the building having been included in a list so compiled or approved, then, subject to a claim in that behalf being made to the local planning authority within the prescribed time and in the prescribed manner, any person who at the time when the notice was served had an interest in the building shall be entitled to be paid compensation by the authority in respect of any loss or damage directly attributable to the effect of the notice.

(4) The loss or damage in respect of which compensation is payable under subsection (3) above shall include a sum payable in respect of a breach of contract caused by the necessity of discontinuing or countermanding any works to the building on account of the building preservation notice being in force with respect thereto.

Compulsory acquisition of listed building in need of repair.

50.—(1) Where it appears to the Secretary of State, in the case of a building to which this section applies, that reasonable steps are not being taken for properly preserving it, the Secretary of State may authorise the local planning authority for the district in which the building is situated to acquire compulsorily under this section the building and any land comprising or contiguous or adjacent to it which appears to the Secretary of State to be required for preserving the building or its amenities, or for affording access to it, or for its proper control or management.

(2) Where it appears to the Secretary of State, in the case of a building to which this section applies, that reasonable steps are not being taken for properly preserving it, he may be authorised under this section to acquire compulsorily the building and any land comprising or contiguous or adjacent to it which appears to him to be required for the purpose mentioned in subsection (1) of this section.

(3) This section applies to any listed building, not being—

(*a*) an ecclesiastical building which is for the time being used for ecclesiastical purposes; or

(*b*) a building which is the subject of a scheme or order under the enactments for the time being in force with respect to ancient monuments; or

(*c*) a building for the time being included in a list of monuments published by the Secretary of State under any such enactment.

For the purposes of this subsection, a building used or available for use by a minister of religion wholly or mainly as

PART V

a residence from which to perform the duties of his office shall be treated as not being an ecclesiastical building.

(4) The Secretary of State shall not make or confirm a compulsory purchase order for the acquisition of any building by virtue of this section unless he is satisfied that it is expedient to make provision for the preservation of the building and to authorise its compulsory acquisition for that purpose.

(5) The Acquisition Act 1947 shall apply to the compulsory acquisition of land under this section and accordingly shall have effect—

(*a*) as if this section had been in force immediately before the commencement of that Act; and

(*b*) as if references therein to the Minister of Transport and to the enactments specified in section 1(1)(*b*) of that Act included respectively references to the Secretary of State and to the provisions of this section.

(6) Any person having an interest in a building which it is proposed to acquire compulsorily under this section may, within twenty-eight days after the service of the notice required to be served under paragraph 3 of Schedule 1 to the Acquisition Act 1947, apply to the sheriff for an order prohibiting further proceedings on the compulsory purchase order; and, if the sheriff is satisfied that reasonable steps have been taken for properly preserving the building, he shall make an order accordingly.

(7) A person aggrieved by a decision of the sheriff on an application under subsection (6) above may appeal against the decision to the Court of Session, but on a question of law only.

Repairs notice as preliminary to compulsory acquisition.

51.—(1) Neither a local planning authority nor the Secretary of State shall start the compulsory purchase of a building under section 50 above unless at least two months previously they have served on the owner of the building, and not withdrawn, a notice under this section (referred to in this section as a " repairs notice ")—

(*a*) specifying the works which they consider reasonably necessary for the proper preservation of the building; and

(*b*) explaining the effect of sections 50 to 53 of this Act.

(2) Where a local planning authority or the Secretary of State have served a repairs notice, the demolition of the building thereafter shall not prevent them from being authorised under section 50 above to acquire compulsorily the site of the building, if the Secretary of State is satisfied that he would have confirmed or, as the case may be, would have made a compulsory purchase order in respect of the building had it not been demolished.

PART V

(3) An authority or the Secretary of State may at any time withdraw a repairs notice served by them; and if they do so, they shall forthwith give notice of the withdrawal to the person who was served with the notice.

(4) A person on whom there has been served a repairs notice shall not in any case be entitled to serve a purchase notice under section 17 of the Act of 1947 or section 42 of this Act until the expiration of three months beginning with the date of the service of the repairs notice; and if during the said period of three months the local planning authority or the Secretary of State start the compulsory acquisition of the building in the exercise of their powers under section 50 above, the person shall not be so entitled unless and until the compulsory acquisition is discontinued.

(5) For the purposes of this section a compulsory acquisition—

(*a*) is started when the local planning authority or the Secretary of State, as the case may be, serve the notice required by paragraph 3(*b*) of Schedule 1 to the Acquisition Act 1947; and

(*b*) is discontinued, in the case of acquisition by a local planning authority, when they withdraw the compulsory purchase order or the Secretary of State decides not to confirm it and, in the case of acquisition by the Secretary of State, when he decides not to make the compulsory purchase order.

Compensation on compulsory acquisition.

52. Subject to section 53 below, for the purpose of assessing compensation in respect of any compulsory acquisition of land including a building which, immediately before the date of the compulsory purchase order, was listed, it shall be assumed that listed building consent would be granted for any works for the alteration or extension of the building, or for its demolition, other than works in respect of which such consent has been applied for before the date of the order and refused by the Secretary of State, or granted by him subject to conditions, the circumstances having been such that compensation thereupon became payable under section 43 of this Act.

Minimum compensation in case of building deliberately left derelict.

53.—(1) A local planning authority proposing to acquire a building compulsorily under section 50 above, if they are satisfied that the building has been deliberately allowed to fall into disrepair for the purpose of justifying its demolition and the development or re-development of the site or any adjoining site, may include in the compulsory purchase order as submitted to the Secretary of State for confirmation an application for a direction for minimum compensation; and the Secretary of State, if he is so satisfied, may include such a direction in the order as confirmed by him.

PART V

(2) Subject to the provisions of this section, where the Secretary of State acquires a building compulsorily under section 50 of this Act, he may, if he is satisfied as mentioned in subsection (1) above, include a direction for minimum compensation in the compulsory purchase order.

(3) The notice required to be served in accordance with paragraph 3(*b*) of Schedule 1 to the Acquisition Act 1947 (notices stating effect of compulsory purchase order, or, as the case may be, draft order) shall, without prejudice to so much of that paragraph as requires the notice to state the effect of the order, include a statement that the authority have made application for a direction for minimum compensation or, as the case may be, that the Secretary of State has included such a direction in the draft order prepared by him in accordance with paragraph 7 of that Schedule and shall in either case explain the meaning of the expression " direction for minimum compensation ".

(4) A direction for minimum compensation, in relation to a building compulsorily acquired, is a direction that for the purpose of assessing compensation it is to be assumed, notwith-
1963 c. 51. standing anything to the contrary in the Land Compensation (Scotland) Act 1963 or this Act, that planning permission would not be granted for any development or re-development of the site of the building and that listed building consent would not be granted for any works for the demolition, alteration or extension of the building other than development or works necessary for restoring it to, and maintaining it in, a proper state of repair; and if a compulsory purchase order is confirmed or made with the inclusion of such a direction, the compensation in respect of the compulsory acquisition shall be assessed in accordance with the direction.

(5) Where a local planning authority include in a compulsory purchase order made by them an application for a direction for minimum compensation, or the Secretary of State includes such a direction in a draft compulsory purchase order prepared by him, any person having an interest in the building may, within twenty-eight days after the service of the notice required by paragraph 3(*b*) of Schedule 1 to the Acquisition Act 1947, apply to the sheriff for an order that the local planning authority's application for a direction for minimum compensation be refused or, as the case may be, that such a direction be not included in the compulsory purchase order as made by the Secretary of State; and if the sheriff is satisfied that the building has not been deliberately allowed to fall into disrepair for the purpose mentioned in subsection (1) of this section, he shall make the order applied for.

(6) A person aggrieved by a decision of the sheriff on an application under subsection (5) above may appeal against

the decision to the Court of Session, but on a question of law only.

PART V

(7) The rights conferred by subsections (5) and (6) of this section shall not prejudice those conferred by section 50(6) and (7) of this Act.

Miscellaneous

Matters which may be taken into account by the Secretary of State in listing buildings under s. 28 of Act of 1947.

54. In considering whether to include a building in a list compiled or approved under section 28 of the Act of 1947, the Secretary of State may take into account not only the building itself but also—

(*a*) any respect in which its exterior contributes to the architectural or historic interest of any group of buildings of which it forms part; and

(*b*) the desirability of preserving, on the ground of its architectural or historic interest, any feature of the building consisting of a man-made object or structure fixed to the building or forming part of the land and comprised within the curtilage of the building.

Application of control to local planning authorities.

55.—(1) In relation to buildings of local planning authorities which are listed, and to the execution of works for their demolition, alteration or extension, this Part of this Act shall have effect subject to such exceptions and modifications as may be prescribed.

(2) Regulations made under this section may in particular provide for securing—

(*a*) that any application by a local planning authority for listed building consent shall be made to the Secretary of State; and

(*b*) that any notice authorised to be served under this Part of this Act in relation to a listed building belonging to a local planning authority shall be served by the Secretary of State.

Directions by Secretary of State to local planning authorities with respect to development affecting Conservation Areas.

56.—(1) The Secretary of State may give directions to local planning authorities with respect to the matters which they are to take into consideration in determining an application—

(*a*) for planning permission for any such development as is referred to in section 1(6) of the Civic Amenities Act 1967 (special provisions as to publicity for applications affecting Conservation Areas); or

1967 c. 69.

(*b*) for listed building consent for any works for the demolition, alteration or extension of a building in a Conservation Area.

PART V

and with respect to the consultations which such authorities are to undertake before determining any such application.

(2) Different directions may under this section be given to different local planning authorities; and any such directions may require an authority—

(*a*) before determining an application, to consult such persons or bodies of persons as the Secretary of State may specify, being persons or bodies appearing to him to be competent to give advice in relation to the development or description of development to which the directions have reference;

(*b*) to supply to any person or body, whom they are required by the directions to consult, specified documents or information enabling that person or body to form an opinion on which to base their advice;

(*c*) to establish committees, consisting either of members of the authority or of other persons, or of both, to advise the authority in relation to the determination of such applications as are referred to in subsection (1) above.

Additional requirement of notice for development affecting Conservation Areas.
1967 c. 69.

57.—(1) Where an application for planning permission for any development of land is made to a local planning authority and the case is one where the authority are required to comply with section 1(6) of the Civic Amenities Act 1967 (special publicity for planning applications affecting Conservation Areas) the authority shall also comply with the following subsection.

(2) The authority shall, for not less than seven days, display a notice on or near the land to which the application relates, containing the same particulars as are required by section 1(6)(*a*) of the Civic Amenities Act 1967 to be contained in the notice to be published by the authority in a local newspaper.

(3) An application for planning permission to which section 1(6) of the said Act of 1967 applies shall not be determined by the local planning authority before both of the following periods have elapsed, namely:—

(*a*) the period of twenty-one days referred to in paragraph (*a*) of that subsection; and

(*b*) the period of twenty-one days beginning with the date on which the notice required by subsection (2) of this section was first displayed;

and in determining the application the authority shall take into account any representations relating to the application which are received by them before both those periods have elapsed.

(4) In the said section 1(6), paragraphs (*b*) and (*c*) shall cease to have effect.

58. The power of a local authority under section 1(1)(*b*) of the Local Authorities (Historic Buildings) Act 1962 to contribute towards expenses incurred or to be incurred in the repair or maintenance of a building in their area appearing to them to be of architectural or historic interest shall be exercisable without the consent of the Secretary of State.

Removal of need for Secretary of State's consent to certain local authority grants.
1962 c. 36.

59. In paragraph 12 of Schedule 1 to the Acquisition Act 1947 (application of special parliamentary procedure to compulsory purchase order affecting ancient monument etc. subject to certificate by Secretary of State that undertakings have been given as to its preservation), the reference to land being, or being the site of, an ancient monument or other object of archaeological interest shall be construed as not including a reference to a listed building or any land or object comprised within the curtilage of such a building unless the building or object is specified in the Schedule to the Ancient Monuments Protection Act 1882 or is for the time being specified in a list published under section 12 of the Ancient Monuments Consolidation and Amendment Act 1913

Compulsory purchase affecting ancient monuments, etc.
1882 c. 73.
1913 c. 32.

60.—(1) A building may be included in a list compiled or approved by the Secretary of State under section 28 of the Act of 1947 notwithstanding that it is Crown land.

Crown land.

(2) Notwithstanding any interest of the Crown in Crown land, but subject to the provisions of section 83 of the Act of 1947 (exercise of powers under that Act in relation to Crown land) any restrictions or powers imposed or conferred by this Part of this Act shall apply and be exercisable in relation to Crown land to the extent of any interest therein for the time being held otherwise than by or on behalf of the Crown.

(3) In this section the expression " Crown land " has the same meaning as in the said section 83.

PART VI

MISCELLANEOUS CHANGES IN PLANNING LAW

Planning Inquiry Commissions

61.—(1) The Secretary of State may constitute a Planning Inquiry Commission to inquire into and report on any matter referred to them under section 62 below.

Constitution of Planning Inquiry Commissions.

PART VI (2) Any such commission shall consist of a chairman and not less than two nor more than four other members appointed by the Secretary of State.

(3) The Secretary of State may pay to the members of any such commission such remuneration and allowances as he may with the consent of the Minister for the Civil Service determine, and may provide for each such commission such officers or servants, and such accommodation, as appears to him expedient to provide for the purpose of assisting the commission in the discharge of their functions.

(4) The validity of any proceedings of any such commission shall not be affected by any vacancy among the members of the commission or by any defect in the appointment of any member.

(5) In Part II of Schedule 1 to the House of Commons Disqualification Act 1957 (commissions, tribunals and other bodies all members of which are disqualified under that Act), in its application to the House of Commons of the Parliament of the United Kingdom, the following entry shall be inserted at the appropriate place in alphabetical order:—

1957 c. 20.

> " A Planning Inquiry Commission constituted under Part VI of the Town and Country Planning (Scotland) Act 1969 ".

References to a Planning Inquiry Commission.

62.—(1) The following matters may, in the circumstances mentioned in subsection (2) below, be referred to a Planning Inquiry Commission, that is to say—

- (*a*) an application for planning permission which the Secretary of State has, under section 13 of the Act of 1947, directed to be referred to him instead of being dealt with by a local planning authority;
- (*b*) an appeal under section 14 of that Act (appeals to the Secretary of State against planning decisions) as originally enacted or as applied by or under any other provision of that Act;
- (*c*) a proposal that a government department should give a direction under section 32 of that Act that planning permission shall be deemed to be granted for development by a local authority or by statutory undertakers which is required by any enactment to be authorised by that department;
- (*d*) a proposal that development should be carried out by or on behalf of a government department.

(2) Any of the matters mentioned in subsection (1) above may be referred to any such commission under this section if it appears expedient to the responsible Minister or Ministers

that the question whether the proposed development should be permitted to be carried out should be the subject of a special inquiry on either or both of the following grounds:—

(*a*) there are considerations of national or regional importance which are relevant to the determination of that question and require evaluation, but a proper evaluation thereof cannot be made unless there is a special inquiry for the purpose;

(*b*) the technical or scientific aspects of the proposed development are of so unfamiliar a character as to jeopardise a proper determination of that question unless there is a special inquiry for the purpose.

(3) Two or more of the matters mentioned in subsection (1) above may be referred to the same commission under this section if it appears to the responsible Minister or Ministers that they relate to proposals to carry out development for similar purposes on different sites.

(4) Where a matter referred to a commission under this section relates to a proposal to carry out development for any purpose at a particular site, the responsible Minister or Ministers may also refer to the commission the question whether development for that purpose should instead be carried out at an alternative site.

(5) The responsible Minister or Ministers shall, on referring a matter to a commission under this section, state in the reference the reasons therefor and may draw the attention of the commission to any points which seem to him or them to be relevant to their inquiry.

(6) A commission inquiring into a matter referred to them under this section shall—

(*a*) identify and investigate the considerations relevant to, or the technical or scientific aspects of, that matter which in their opinion are relevant to the question whether the proposed development should be permitted to be carried out and assess the importance to be attached to those considerations or aspects;

(*b*) thereafter, if the applicant, in the case of a matter mentioned in subsection (1)(*a*), (*b*) or (*c*) above, or the local planning authority in any case so desire, afford to each of them, and, in the case of an application or appeal mentioned in the said subsection (1)(*a*) or (*b*), to any person who has made representations relating to the subject matter of the application or appeal which the authority are required to take into account under section 35(4) or 36(4) of the Act of

Part VI

1959, an opportunity of appearing before and being heard by one or more members of the commission;

(*c*) report to the responsible Minister or Ministers on the matter referred to them.

(7) Any such commission may, with the approval of the Secretary of State and at his expense, arrange for the carrying out (whether by the commission themselves or by others) of research of any kind appearing to them to be relevant to a matter referred to them for inquiry and report.

(8) The provisions of section 13(2) of the Act of 1947, and of that subsection as applied by section 14(2) of that Act, and of sections 22(6) and 23(4) of this Act, relating to the affording of an opportunity of appearing before, and being heard by, a person appointed by the Secretary of State, shall not apply to an application for planning permission or an appeal referred to a commission under subsection (1) above.

(9) Schedule 5 to this Act shall have effect for the construction of references in this section and section 63 below to " the responsible Minister or Ministers "

Procedure on reference to a Planning Inquiry Commission.

63.—(1) A reference to a Planning Inquiry Commission of a proposal that development should be carried out by or on behalf of a government department may be made at any time, and a reference of any other matter mentioned in section 62 above may be made at any time before, but not after, the determination of the relevant application for planning permission under section 13 of the Act of 1947 or the relevant appeal under section 14 of that Act or, as the case may be, the giving of the relevant direction under section 32 of that Act, notwithstanding that an inquiry or other hearing has been held into the proposal by a person appointed by any Minister for the purpose.

(2) Notice of the making of a reference to any such commission shall be published in the prescribed manner, and a copy of the notice shall be served on the local planning authority for the area in which it is proposed that the relevant development shall be carried out, and—

(*a*) in the case of an application for planning permission or an appeal under section 13 or 14 of the Act of 1947, on the applicant and any person who has made representations relating to the subject matter of the application or appeal which the authority are required to take into account under section 35(4) or 36(4) of the Act of 1959;

(*b*) in the case of a proposal that a direction should be given under section 32 of the Act of 1947 with respect to any development, on the local authority or statutory undertakers applying for authorisation to carry out that development. PART VI

(3) A Planning Inquiry Commission shall, for the purpose of complying with section 62(6)(*b*) above, hold a local inquiry; and they may hold such an inquiry, if they think it necessary for the proper discharge of their functions, notwithstanding that neither the applicant nor the local planning authority desire an opportunity of appearing and being heard.

(4) Where a Planning Inquiry Commission are to hold a local inquiry under subsection (3) above in connection with a matter referred to them, and it appears to the responsible Minister or Ministers, in the case of some other matter falling to be determined by a Minister of the Crown and required or authorised by an enactment other than this section to be the subject of a local inquiry, that the two matters are so far cognate that they should be considered together, he or, as the case may be, they may direct that the two inquiries be held concurrently or combined as one inquiry.

(5) An inquiry held by such a commission under this section shall be treated for the purposes of the Tribunals and Inquiries Act 1958 as one held by a Minister in pursuance of a duty imposed by a statutory provision. 1958 c. 66.

(6) Subsections (4) to (9) of section 50 of the Act of 1945 (power to summon and examine witnesses, and expenses at inquiries) shall apply to an inquiry held under subsection (3) above as they apply to an inquiry held under that section.

(7) Subject to the provisions of this section and to any directions given to them by the responsible Minister or Ministers, a Planning Inquiry Commission shall have power to regulate their own procedure.

Commissions to inquire into planning matters affecting Scotland and England.

64.—(1) The Ministers may constitute a Joint Planning Inquiry Commission to inquire into and report on any matter referred to them under this section; and the matters which may be so referred are those which may, under section 62 of this Act or section 62 of the Town and Country Planning Act 1968, be referred to a Planning Inquiry Commission but which appear to the Ministers to involve considerations affecting both Scotland and England. 1968 c. 72.

(2) A Joint Planning Inquiry Commission shall consist of a chairman and not less than two nor more than four other members appointed by the Ministers.

(3) The Ministers may pay to the members of any such commission such remuneration and allowances as they may with the consent of the Minister for the Civil Service determine, and

PART VI

may provide for each such commission such officers or servants, and such accommodation, as appears to them expedient to provide for the purpose of assisting the commission in the discharge of their functions.

(4) The validity of any proceedings of any such commission shall not be affected by any vacancy among the members of the commission or by any defect in the appointment of any member.

1957 c. 20.

(5) In Part II of Schedule 1 to the House of Commons Disqualification Act 1957 (commissions, tribunals and other bodies all members of which are disqualified under that Act), in its application to the House of Commons of the Parliament of the United Kingdom, the following entry shall be inserted at the appropriate place in alphabetical order:—

> " A Joint Planning Inquiry Commission constituted under Part VI of the Town and Country Planning (Scotland) Act 1969 ".

(6) In this section " the Ministers " means the Secretary of State and the Minister of Housing and Local Government, acting jointly; but their functions under subsection (3) of this section may, by arrangements made between them, be exercised by either acting on behalf of both.

(7) Schedule 6 to this Act shall have effect with respect to the Joint Planning Inquiry Commissions and references to them under this section, and with respect to the proceedings of a commission on any such reference.

Delegation of planning functions

Delegation of planning functions to officers of local authorities.

65.—(1) A local planning authority may delegate to any officer of the authority who in their opinion is suitably qualified or experienced for the purpose the function of determining all or any, or a specified class, of the following applications, that is to say—

(*a*) an application for planning permission under section 12 of the Act of 1947;

(*b*) an application for a determination under section 15 of that Act of the questions whether the carrying out of operations on land or the making of any change in the use of land constitutes or involves development of the land and, if so, whether an application for planning permission in respect thereof is required, having regard to the provisions of the development order;

(*c*) an application for consent under an order under section 26 of that Act to the cutting down, topping, lopping or destruction of trees;

PART VI

(d) an application for consent under regulations under section 29 of that Act to the display of advertisements;

(e) an application for an established use certificate under section 18 of this Act;

(f) an application for an approval required by a development order or by a condition imposed on the grant of planning permission;

(2) A delegation made by a local authority under this section to an officer of theirs—

(a) shall be made to the officer by name;

(b) may be made with or without restrictions or conditions; and

(c) may be withdrawn at any time by the delegating authority (either generally or in respect of a particular application), without prejudice to anything previously done by the officer thereunder.

(3) Where a local authority have under this section delegated to an officer of theirs the function of determining applications, and the officer so requests in the case of any application specified by him, the delegating authority shall themselves, instead of him, determine the application.

(4) Where any functions have under this section been delegated to an officer of a local authority, any determination by him of such an application as is referred to in subsection (1) of this section shall, if it is notified in writing to the applicant, be treated for all purposes as a determination of the delegating authority.

(5) Where an action has been brought against an officer of a local authority in respect of an act done by him in the discharge or purported discharge of functions delegated to him under this section, and the circumstances are such that he is not legally entitled to require that authority to indemnify him, the authority may nevertheless indemnify him against the whole or part of any damages and expenses which he may have been ordered to pay or may have incurred, if they are satisfied that he honestly believed both that the act complained of was done in the discharge of those functions and that his duty required or entitled him to do it.

(6) In relation to any functions delegated under this section by a local authority to an officer of theirs, any reference to the local planning authority in any enactment relating to those functions shall (subject to the terms of the delegation and so far as the context does not otherwise require) be construed as including a reference to that officer.

PART VI

Duration of planning permission

Limit of duration of planning permissions past and future.

66.—(1) Subject to the provisions of this section, every planning permission granted or deemed to have been granted before the commencement of this section shall, if the development to which it relates has not been begun before the beginning of 1969, be deemed to have been granted subject to a condition that the development must be begun not later than the expiration of five years beginning with the said commencement.

(2) Subject to the provisions of this section, every planning permission granted or deemed to be granted after the commencement of this section shall be granted or, as the case may be, be deemed to be granted, subject to the condition that the development to which it relates must be begun not later than the expiration of—

(*a*) five years beginning with the date on which the permission is granted or, as the case may be, deemed to be granted ; or

(*b*) such other period (whether longer or shorter) beginning with the said date as the authority concerned with the terms of the planning permission may direct, being a period which the authority consider appropriate having regard to the provisions of the development plan and to any other material considerations.

(3) If after the commencement of this section planning permission is granted without the condition required by subsection (2) above, it shall be deemed to have been granted subject to the condition that the development to which it relates must be begun not later than the expiration of five years beginning with the date of the grant.

(4) Nothing in this section applies—

(*a*) to any outline planning permission, as defined by section 67 below ;

(*b*) to any planning permission granted by a development order ;

(*c*) to any planning permission which was granted or deemed to be granted before the commencement of this section, subject to an express condition that the development to which it relates should be begun, or be completed, not later than a specified date or within a specified period ;

(*d*) to any planning permission granted for a limited period (within the meaning of section 12(2) of the Act of 1947) ; or (*e*) to any planning permission granted under section 16 of the Act of 1947 on an application relating to buildings or works completed, or a use of land instituted, before the date of the application.

Outline planning permissions.

67.—(1) In this section and section 66 above, " outline planning permission " means planning permission granted, in accordance with the provisions of a development order, with the reservation for subsequent approval by the local planning authority or the Secretary of State of matters (referred to in this section as " reserved matters ") not particularised in the application.

(2) Subject to the provisions of this section, where before the commencement of this section outline planning permission has been granted for development consisting in or including the carrying out of building or other operations, and the development has not been begun before the beginning of 1969, that planning permission shall be deemed to have been granted subject to conditions to the following effect:—

(*a*) that, in the case of any reserved matter, application for approval must be made not later than the expiration of three years beginning with the date of the commencement of this section; and

(*b*) that the development to which the permission relates must be begun not later than whichever is the later of the following dates—

(i) the expiration of five years from the date of the commencement of this section; or

(ii) the expiration of two years from the final approval of the reserved matters, or in the case of approval on different dates, the final approval of the last such matter to be approved.

(3) Subsection (2) above shall not apply to a planning permission granted before the commencement of this section subject to an express condition that the development to which it relates should be begun, or be completed, or that application for approval of any reserved matter should be made, not later than a specified date or within a specified period.

(4) Subject to the provisions of this section, where outline planning permission is granted after the commencement of this section for such development as is referred to in subsection (2) above, it shall be granted subject to conditions to the following effect:—

(*a*) that, in the case of any reserved matter, application for approval must be made not later than the expiration of three years beginning with the date of the grant of outline planning permission; and

PART VI

(*b*) that the development to which the permission relates must be begun not later than whichever is the later of the following dates—

(i) the expiration of five years from the date of the grant of outline planning permission; or

(ii) the expiration of two years from the final approval of the reserved matters or, in the case of approval on different dates, the final approval of the last such matter to be approved.

(5) If after the commencement of this section outline planning permission is granted without the conditions required by subsection (4) above, it shall be deemed to have been granted subject to those conditions.

(6) The authority concerned with the terms of an outline planning permission may, in applying subsection (4) above, substitute, or direct that there be substituted, for the periods of three years, five years or two years referred to in that subsection such other periods respectively (whether longer or shorter) as they consider appropriate.

(7) The said authority may, in applying the said subsection, specify, or direct that there be specified, separate periods under paragraph (*a*) of the subsection in relation to separate parts of the development to which the planning permission relates; and, if they do so, the condition required by paragraph (*b*) of the subsection shall then be framed correspondingly by reference to those parts, instead of by reference to the development as a whole.

(8) In considering whether to exercise their powers under subsections (6) and (7) above, the said authority shall have regard to the provisions of the development plan and to any other material considerations.

Provisions supplementary to ss. 66 and 67.

1967 c. 1.

68.—(1) For the purposes of sections 66 and 67 above, development shall be taken to be begun on the earliest date on which any specified operation (as defined in section 64(3) of the Land Commission Act 1967) comprised in the development begins to be carried out.

(2) The authority referred to in section 66(2)(*b*) and section 67(6) above is the local planning authority or the Secretary of State, in the case of planning permission granted by them, and—

(*a*) in the case of planning permission granted by an order under section 24 of the Act of 1947 (authorised uses of land) is the local planning authority making the order;

(*b*) in the case of planning permission under section 32 of the Act of 1947 (grant by direction of a government department) is the department on whose direction planning permission is deemed to be granted; and

(*c*) in the case of planning permission granted on an appeal determined, under section 22 or 24 of this Act, by a person appointed by the Secretary of State to determine the appeal, is that person.

(3) For the purposes of section 67(2) and (4) above, a reserved matter shall be treated as finally approved when an application for approval is granted or, in a case where the application is made to the local planning authority and there is an appeal to the Secretary of State against the authority's decision on the application and the Secretary of State or a person appointed by him under section 22 or 24 of this Act to determine the appeal grants the approval, on the date of the determination of the appeal by the Secretary of State or that person.

(4) Where after the commencement of sections 66 and 67 above a local planning authority grant planning permission, the fact that any of the conditions of the permission are required by this Act to be imposed, or are deemed by this Act to be imposed, shall not prevent the conditions being the subject of an appeal under section 14 of the Act of 1947 against the decision of the authority.

(5) In the case of planning permission having conditions attached to it by or under section 66(1), (2) or (3) or section 67(2), (4) or (5) above (whether outline or other)—

(*a*) development carried out after the date by which the conditions of the permission require it to be carried out shall be treated as not authorised by the permission; and

(*b*) an application for approval of a reserved matter, if it is made after the date by which the conditions require it to be made, shall be treated as not made in accordance with the terms of the permission.

(6) Compensation under Part II of the Act of 1954 shall not be payable in respect of the application to any planning permission of any of the conditions referred to in sections 66 and 67 of this Act.

(7) The said conditions shall be disregarded for the purposes—

(*a*) of section 17 of the Act of 1947 (right of landowner to serve purchase notice, where he claims that the land has become incapable of reasonably beneficial use on account of the refusal of planning permission or the imposition of conditions) ;

(*b*) of section 18 of that Act (compensation for planning decisions restricting development) ; and

(*c*) of Schedule 4 to the Act of 1945 (compensation of statutory undertakers in respect of certain planning decisions).

Termination of planning permission by reference to time limit.

69.—(1) The following provisions of this section shall have effect where, by virtue of section 66 or 67 above, a planning permission (whether granted before or after the commencement of those sections) is subject to a condition that the development to which the permission relates must be begun before the expiration of a particular period and that development has been begun within that period but the period has elapsed without the development having been completed.

(2) If the local planning authority are of opinion that the development will not be completed within a reasonable period they may serve a notice (hereafter in this section referred to as a " completion notice ") stating that the planning permission will cease to have effect at the expiration of a further period specified in the notice, being a period of not less than twelve months after the notice takes effect.

(3) A completion notice—

(*a*) shall be served on the owner and occupier of the land and on any other person who, in the opinion of the local planning authority, will be affected by the notice ; and

(*b*) shall take effect only if and when it is confirmed by the Secretary of State, who may in confirming it substitute some longer period for that specified in the notice as the period at the expiration of which the planning permission is to cease to have effect.

(4) If within such period as may be specified in a completion notice (not being less than twenty-eight days from the service thereof) any person on whom the notice is served so requires, the Secretary of State, before confirming the notice, shall afford to that person and to the local planning authority an opportunity of appearing before, and being heard by, a person appointed by the Secretary of State for the purpose.

(5) If a completion notice takes effect, the planning permission therein referred to shall, at the expiration of the period specified in the notice, whether the original period specified under subsection (2) above or a longer period substituted by the Secretary of State under subsection (3) above, be invalid except

so far as it authorises any development carried out thereunder up to the end of that period.

(6) The local planning authority may withdraw a completion notice at any time before the expiration of the period specified therein as the period at the expiration of which the planning permission is to cease to have effect; and if they do so they shall forthwith give notice of the withdrawal to every person who was served with the completion notice.

Statutory undertakers

New provision as to what is "operational land" of statutory undertakers.

70.—(1) Where an interest in land is held by statutory undertakers for the purpose of the carrying on of their undertaking and—

(*a*) the interest was acquired by them after the commencement of this section; or

(*b*) it was held by them immediately before that commencement, but the circumstances were then such that the land did not fall to be treated as operational land for the purposes of the Act of 1947,

then the following subsection shall have effect for the purpose of determining whether the land is to be so treated and shall so have effect notwithstanding the definition of "operational land" in section 113(1) of the Act of 1947.

(2) The land shall not be treated as operational land for the purposes of the Act of 1947 unless one or both of the following conditions are satisfied with respect to it, namely—

(*a*) there is, or at some time has been, in force with respect to the land a specific planning permission for its development and that development, if carried out, would involve, or have involved, the use of the land for the purpose of the carrying on of the statutory undertakers' undertaking; or

(*b*) the undertakers' interest in the land was acquired by them as the result of a transfer under provisions of the Transport Act 1968 from other statutory undertakers and the land was, immediately before the transfer, operational land of those other undertakers. 1968 c. 73.

(3) A specific planning permission for the purpose of subsection (2)(*a*) above is a planning permission—

(*a*) granted on an application in that behalf under Part II of the Act of 1947; or

(*b*) granted by provisions of a development order granting planning permission generally for development which has received specific parliamentary approval; or

PART VI

(*c*) granted by a special development order in respect of development specifically described in the order; or

(*d*) deemed to be granted by virtue of a direction of a government department under section 32 of the Act of 1947;

and the reference in paragraph (*b*) of this subsection to development which has received specific parliamentary approval shall be construed as referring to development authorised by a local or private Act of Parliament or by an order approved by both Houses of Parliament or by an order which has been brought into operation in accordance with the provisions of the Statutory Orders (Special Procedure) Act 1945, being an Act or order which designates specifically both the nature of the development thereby authorised and the land upon which it may be carried out.

1945 c. 18, (9 & 10 Geo. 6).

Planning applications and appeals by statutory undertakers.

71.—(1) In the circumstances mentioned in subsection (2) below, paragraph 1(1) of Schedule 5 to the Act of 1947 (statutory undertakers' planning applications and appeals, if in respect of operational land, to be dealt with by Ministers) shall apply to an application or appeal by statutory undertakers in respect of land which is not operational land as it applies to an application or appeal in respect of land which is.

(2) The said circumstances are that—

(*a*) an interest in the land in question is held by the undertakers with a view to its being used for the purpose of carrying on their undertaking; or

(*b*) it is land in which they propose to acquire an interest with a view to its being so used,

and (in either case) the planning permission, if granted on the application or appeal, would be for development involving the use of the land for that purpose.

(3) The following provisions (being provisions which require certain planning decisions and orders affecting statutory undertakers to be subject to special parliamentary procedure) shall cease to have effect:—

(*a*) section 24(7) of the Act of 1945 (order extinguishing a right of way or rights of statutory undertakers in respect of apparatus under certain land), except as respects an order made before the commencement of this section;

(*b*) section 42(4)(*b*) of the Act of 1947 (compulsory purchase order with respect to land acquired by statutory undertakers for the purpose of their undertaking), except as respects an order made or confirmed before that commencement;

PART VI

(c) paragraph 1(2) of Schedule 5 to the Act of 1947 (decision on planning application in respect of operational land or appeal thereon), except as respects an application for planning permission made before that commencement or an appeal from the decision on an application so made;

(d) paragraph 2(1)(a) of that Schedule (decision of a government department refusing, or attaching conditions to, statutory authorisation for development), except as respects a decision made before that commencement;

(e) paragraph 3(2) of that Schedule (order revoking or modifying planning permission in respect of operational land), except as respects an order of which notice has been given under that subsection before that commencement; and

(f) paragraph 4(2) of that Schedule (order requiring discontinuance of use etc. of operational land), except as respects an order of which notice has been given under that subsection before that commencement.

Restrictions on entitlement of statutory undertakers to compensation for adverse planning decisions.

72.—(1) Except as provided by subsection (2) below, statutory undertakers shall not be entitled to compensation in respect of a decision mentioned in paragraph 1(a) or (b) of Schedule 4 to the Act of 1945 (right to compensation in respect of certain decisions and orders) where that decision is made after the commencement of this section.

(2) Subsection (1) above shall not apply to compensation in respect of a decision made in accordance with paragraph 1 of Schedule 5 to the Act of 1947 refusing planning permission for the development of operational land, or granting such permission subject to conditions, where—

(a) planning permission for that development would have been granted by a development order but for a direction given under such an order that planning permission so granted should not apply to the development; and

(b) it is not development which has received specific parliamentary approval (within the meaning given to that expression by section 70(3) of this Act).

(3) Section 20(3) of the Act of 1947 (compensation on refusal of planning permission or its grant subject to conditions) shall not apply in relation to planning permission for the development of operational land of statutory undertakers.

Modifications of s. 24 of Act of 1945.

73.—(1) Section 24 of the Act of 1945 (power of Secretary of State, local planning authority or statutory undertakers, on acquisition or appropriation of land for development, by service

PART VI

of notice to secure extinguishment of statutory undertakers' rights over the land or the removal of their apparatus) shall be amended in accordance with this section.

(2) A notice under that section shall not be served by the acquiring or appropriating authority unless they are satisfied that the extinguishment of the statutory undertakers' right or, as the case may be, the removal of their apparatus, is necessary for the purposes of carrying out any development with a view to which the land was acquired or appropriated.

(3) The period referred to in subsection (1) of the said section (that is to say the period to be specified in a notice under the section as the period at the end of which the statutory undertakers' right will be extinguished or, as the case may be, before the end of which their apparatus shall be removed) shall be a period of not less than twenty-eight days from the date of service of the notice.

Notice for same purposes as s. 24 of Act of 1945, but given by statutory undertakers to developing authority.

74.—(1) Subject to the provisions of this section, where land has been acquired or appropriated as mentioned in section 24(1) of the Act of 1945, and—

(*a*) there is on, under or over the land any apparatus vested in or belonging to statutory undertakers; and

(*b*) the undertakers claim that development to be carried out on the land is such as to require, on technical or other grounds connected with the carrying on of their undertaking, the removal or re-siting of the apparatus affected by the development,

the undertakers may serve on the acquiring or appropriating authority a notice claiming the right to enter on the land and carry out such works for the removal or re-siting of the apparatus or any part of it as may be specified in the notice.

(2) Where, after the land has been acquired or appropriated as aforesaid, development of the land is begun to be carried out, no notice under this section shall be served later than twenty-one days after the beginning of the development.

(3) Where a notice is served under this section, the authority on whom it is served may, before the end of the period of twenty-eight days from the date of service, serve on the statutory undertakers a counter-notice stating that they object to all or any of the provisions of the notice and specifying the grounds of their objection.

(4) If no counter-notice is served under subsection (3) above, the statutory undertakers shall, after the end of the period of twenty-eight days therein mentioned, have the rights claimed in their notice.

(5) If a counter-notice is served under subsection (3) above, the statutory undertakers who served the notice under this section may either withdraw it or may apply to the Secretary of State and the appropriate Minister for an order under this section conferring on the undertakers the rights claimed in the notice or such modified rights as the Secretary of State and the appropriate Minister think it expedient to confer on them.

(6) Where, by virtue of this section or of an order of Ministers thereunder, statutory undertakers have the right to execute works for the removal or re-siting of apparatus, they may arrange with the acquiring or appropriating authority for the works to be carried out by that authority, under the superintendence of the undertakers, instead of by the undertakers themselves.

(7) Where works are carried out for the removal or re-siting of statutory undertakers' apparatus, being works which the undertakers have the right to carry out by virtue of this section or an order of Ministers thereunder, the undertakers shall be entitled to compensation from the acquiring or appropriating authority and the amount of the compensation shall be an amount calculated in accordance with paragraph 2 of Schedule 4 to the Act of 1945, but reduced, in a case where the authority carry out the works, by the actual cost to the authority of doing so.

(8) In the said paragraph 2, as it applies for the purposes of this section, any reference to " the proceeding giving rise to compensation " shall, instead of being construed in accordance with sub-paragraph (4) of that paragraph, be construed as a reference to the circumstances making it necessary for the apparatus in question to be removed or re-sited.

General planning control

Expansion of building below ground to constitute development.

75. Notwithstanding anything in section 10(2)(*a*) of the Act of 1947 (carrying out of works for the maintenance, improvement or other alteration of a building not to constitute development if it is wholly internal or does not materially affect the building's external appearance), the carrying out of works for the alteration of any building by providing additional space therein below ground shall, if begun after the commencement of this section, be treated for the purposes of the Act of 1947 as involving development.

Modification of transitory exemptions based on pre-1948 use.

76.—(1) Section 10(5)(*a*) of the Act of 1947 (exemption from requirement of planning permission for resumption of normal use before the original appointed day) and section 10(5)(*c*) of that Act (the same as to resumption of use of land which on that day was unoccupied) shall not have effect as respects any use of land begun or resumed after the commencement of this section.

PART VI

(2) In the case of land which on the original appointed day was normally used for one purpose and was also used on occasions for another purpose, section 10(5)(*b*) of the Act of 1947 (exemption from requirement of planning permission for resumption of previous occasional use) shall, as respects any use of the land for the other purpose after the commencement of this section, apply only if the land has, since the original appointed day, been used for the other purpose on at least one similar occasion before the beginning of 1969.

(3) In applying sections 10(5), 16(5) and 16(6) of the Act of 1947 (factors relevant for determining whether planning permission is required for resumption of use), no account shall be taken of any contravention of planning control other than contravention of the provisions of Part II of the Act of 1947; and accordingly—

(*a*) in proviso (i) to section 10(5), for the words "previous planning control within the meaning of section 72 of this Act" there shall be substituted the words "the provisions of this Part of this Act";

(*b*) in the proviso to section 16(5), the words from "or begun" to the end shall cease to have effect;

(*c*) in section 16(6), the words from "or was begun" to the end shall cease to have effect; and

(*d*) section 72(9) shall cease to have effect.

(4) Section 22(4) of the Act of 1947 (planning permission not required, where land has been developed without such permission, for a use of the land which would have been lawful apart from the development) shall not apply to any use of land which, by the operation of this section, has become unlawful without planning permission.

(5) In this section "the original appointed day" means the appointed day for the purposes of the Act of 1947, that is to say, 1st July 1948.

Posting of site notice prior to planning application.

77.—(1) An application for planning permission for development of any class to which section 35 of the Act of 1959 (certain classes of planning application, prescribed by development order, to be supported by evidence of prior publicity) applies shall not be entertained by the local planning authority unless it is accompanied by one or other of the following certificates, signed by or on behalf of the applicant, that is to say—

(*a*) a certificate stating that he has complied with subsection (2) of this section and when he did so; or (*b*) a certificate stating that he has been unable to comply with it because he has not such rights of access or other rights in respect of the land as would enable him to do so, but that he has taken such reasonable steps as are open to him (specifying them) to acquire those rights and has been unable to acquire them.

(2) In order to comply with this subsection a person must—

(*a*) post on the land a notice, in such form as may be prescribed by a development order, stating that the application for planning permission is to be made; and

(*b*) leave the notice in position for not less than seven days in a period of not more than one month immediately preceding the making of the application to the local planning authority.

(3) The said notice must be posted by affixing it firmly to some object on the land, and must be sited and displayed in such a way as to be easily visible and legible by members of the public without going on the land.

(4) The applicant shall not be treated as unable to comply with subsection (2) of this section if the notice is, without any fault or intention of his, removed, obscured or defaced before the seven days referred to in subsection (2)(*b*) above have elapsed, so long as he has taken reasonable steps for its protection and, if need be, replacement; and, if he has cause to rely on this subsection, his certificate under subsection (1) above shall state the relevant circumstances.

(5) The notice required by subsection (2) of this section shall (in addition to any other matters required to be contained therein) name a place within the locality where a copy of the application for planning permission, and of all plans and other documents submitted therewith, will be open to inspection by the public at all reasonable hours during such period as may be specified in the notice, not being a period of less than twenty-one days beginning with the date on which the notice is first posted.

(6) If any person issues a certificate which purports to comply with the requirements of this section and which contains a statement which he knows to be false and misleading in a material particular, or recklessly issues a certificate which purports to comply with those requirements and which contains a statement which is false or misleading in a material particular, he shall be guilty of an offence and liable on summary conviction to a fine not exceeding £100.

PART VI

(7) Any certificate issued for the purpose of this section shall be in such form as may be prescribed by a development order.

Extension of s. 12 of Act of 1947 with respect to development affecting trunk and special roads.

78. In section 12(3) of the Act of 1947 (power to provide by a development order for regulating the manner in which applications for planning permission are to be dealt with by local planning authorities), the reference in paragraph (*a*) to development shall include, and be deemed always to have included, a reference to development of or affecting land on which the Secretary of State proposes to provide a trunk road or a special road, being a road the route of which is shown as such in the development plan or in the case of which the Secretary of State has given to the local planning authority written notice of his intention to provide the road, together with maps or plans sufficient to identify the proposed route of the road.

Information regarding and local register of planning applications.

79.—(1) A development order may make provision for requiring applicants for planning permission for development or for any class of development prescribed by or under the order to furnish at such time and to such persons as may be so prescribed such information with respect to the application as may be so prescribed.

(2) A development order may make provision for the register of planning applications kept by a local planning authority under section 12(5) of the Act of 1947 to be kept in two or more parts, each part containing such information relating to applications for planning permission made to the authority as may be prescribed by the order, and may also make provison—

(*a*) for a specified part of the register to contain copies of applications and of any plans or drawings submitted therewith ; and

(*b*) for the entry relating to any application, and every thing relating thereto, to be removed from that part of the register when the application (including any appeal arising out of it) has been finally disposed of, without prejudice to the inclusion of any different entry relating thereto in another part of the register.

Reference to Secretary of State of application for approval under outline planning permission.

80. The power of the Secretary of State to give directions under section 13 of the Act of 1947, requiring applications for planning permission to be referred to him instead of being dealt with by the local planning authority, shall be exercisable also in relation to applications for any approval of an authority required under a development order, and references to applications in subsections (1) and (3) and in the proviso to subsection (2) of that section shall be construed accordingly.

PART VI

Unopposed revocation or modification of planning permission.

81.—(1) The following provisions shall have effect where the local planning authority have made an order under section 19 of the Act of 1947 (revocation or modification of planning permission) but have not submitted the order to the Secretary of State for confirmation by him, and—

(*a*) the owner, the lessee and the occupier of the land and all persons who in the authority's opinion will be affected by the order have notified the authority in writing that they do not object to the order; and

(*b*) it appears to the authority that no claim for compensation is likely to arise under section 20 of the Act of 1947 on account of the order.

(2) The authority shall advertise in the prescribed manner the fact that the order has been made, and the advertisement shall specify—

(*a*) the period (not less than twenty-eight days from the date on which the advertisement first appears) within which persons affected by the order may give notice to the Secretary of State that they wish for an opportunity of appearing before, and being heard by, a person appointed by the Secretary of State for the purpose; and

(*b*) the period (not less than fourteen days from the expiration of the period referred to in paragraph (*a*) above) at the expiration of which, if no such notice is given to the Secretary of State, the order may take effect by virtue of this section and without being confirmed by the Secretary of State.

(3) The authority shall also serve notice to the same effect on the persons mentioned in subsection (1)(*a*) above, and the notice shall include a statement of the effect of subsection (7) of this section.

(4) The authority shall send a copy of any advertisement published under subsection (2) above to the Secretary of State not more than three days after the publication.

(5) If within the period referred to in subsection (2)(*a*) above no person claiming to be affected by the order has given notice to the Secretary of State as aforesaid, and the Secretary of State has not directed that the order be submitted to him for confirmation, the order shall, at the expiration of the period referred to in subsection (2)(*b*) of this section, take effect by virtue of this section and without being confirmed by the Secretary of State as required by section 19(1) of the Act of 1947.

(6) This section does not apply to an order revoking or modifying a planning permission granted, or deemed to have been granted, by the Secretary of State under Part II of the Act of

PART VI

1947 or under Part II or Part V of this Act; nor does it apply to an order modifying any conditions to which a planning permission is subject by virtue of section 66 or 67 of this Act.

(7) No compensation shall be payable under section 20 of the Act of 1947 in respect of an order under section 19 of that Act which takes effect by virtue of this section and without being confirmed by the Secretary of State.

Procedure in connection with making and confirmation of tree preservation orders.

82.—(1) The provisions which may, by virtue of subsection (1)(*c*) of section 26 of the Act of 1947 (tree preservation orders), be applied by such an order in relation to any consent thereunder shall include section 81 of this Act.

(2) Regulations made by virtue of section 26(5) of the Act of 1947 may (without prejudice to the generality of that subsection) make provision as follows:—

(*a*) that, before a tree preservation order is submitted to the Secretary of State for confirmation, notice of the making of the order shall be given to the owners, lessees and occupiers of land affected by the order and to such other persons, if any, as may be specified in the regulations;

(*b*) that objections and representations with respect to the order, if duly made in accordance with the regulations, shall be considered before the order is confirmed by the Secretary of State;

(*c*) that, if no objections or representations are so made, or if any so made are withdrawn, the order, instead of requiring the confirmation of the Secretary of State in accordance with section 26(4) of the Act of 1947, may be confirmed (but without any modification), as an unopposed order, by the authority who made it; and

(*d*) that copies of the order, when confirmed by the Secretary of State or the authority, shall be served on such persons as may be specified in the regulations.

Notice by Secretary of State to planning authority when exercising default powers.

83.—(1) The Secretary of State, where he proposes under section 96 of the Act of 1947 (default powers) to make an order—

(*a*) under section 19 of that Act (revocation or modification of planning permission), or under the provisions of that section as applied by any order or regulations made under Part II of that Act; or

(*b*) under section 24 of that Act (discontinuance of specified use of land or alteration or removal of buildings or works), shall serve a notice of the proposal on the local planning authority; and if within such period as may be specified in the notice (not less than twenty-eight days from the date of service) the authority so require, the Secretary of State, before making the order, shall afford to the authority an opportunity of appearing before, and being heard by, a person appointed by him for the purpose.

(2) The obligation of the Secretary of State to serve a notice under this section shall be without prejudice to any requirements of Part II of the Act of 1947, or regulations made thereunder, having effect by virtue of section 96(3) of that Act (requirements as to notice etc., where Secretary of State acts in place of local planning authority).

Control of office development

Partial abrogation of dual control of office development. 1966 c. 34.

84.—(1) Without prejudice to section 23 of the Industrial Development Act 1966 (restrictions or conditions which may be attached to industrial development certificates issued by the Board of Trade under section 12(4) of the Act of 1947) the conditions which the Board of Trade may under that section attach to an industrial development certificate shall include conditions restricting the amount of office floor space to be contained in any building which is the subject of the development or precluding it from containing any office floor space; and the conditions may be framed so as to apply (either or both) to the building as originally erected or as subsequently extended or altered.

(2) Notwithstanding section 5(1) of the Act of 1965 (of which the effect is that an industrial development certificate under section 12(4) of the Act of 1947 as well as an office development permit under section 1(3) of the Act of 1965 is required in support of an application for planning permission for development which is not only industrial but involves the provision of office premises), compliance with the said section 1(3) shall not be required in respect of an application for planning permission for industrial development to which this section applies, where there has been issued by the Board of Trade and furnished to the local planning authority with the application a copy of an industrial development certificate with conditions attached thereto by virtue of subsection (1) above.

(3) In this section, " industrial development " means the development of land in any manner specified in section 12(4) of the Act of 1947 (requirement of Board of Trade industrial development certificate to support application for planning permission for development involving provision of industrial building or change in the use of premises so that a building becomes industrial); and this section applies to industrial

PART VI

development only if there will result therefrom no office premises except such as are comprised within the curtilage of an industrial building and are used or designed for use for providing services or facilities ancillary to the use of other premises in the same building or curtilage.

(4) Development in respect of which there has been issued by the Board of Trade an industrial development certificate with conditions attached thereto by virtue of subsection (1) of this section shall be treated as not included in any reference to " related development " in section 2 of the Act of 1965 (which makes an office development permit unnecessary if the amount of office floor space to be created is below the prescribed exemption limit, but for this purpose requires that space to be aggregated with office floor space created, or to be created, in the course of other development affecting the same building or site).

Modifications of s. 7 of 1965 Act.

85.—(1) Section 7 of the Act of 1965 (attachment to certain planning permissions of conditions restricting office floor space, where the permission can be granted without an office development permit) shall not apply to a planning permission granted after the commencement of this section for the erection of a building on any land, unless it is in an area to which Part I of that Act applied at the time when the application for the planning permission was made.

(2) Section 7 of the Act of 1965 shall not apply to a planning permission granted after the said commencement for the erection of a building with a floor space less than twice the prescribed exemption limit; nor shall it apply to a planning permission so granted for the erection of a building (of whatever floor space) which is wholly residential.

(3) Section 7 of the Act of 1965 shall not apply to a planning permission which is subject to conditions by virtue of section 23(5) or (6) of the Industrial Development Act 1966 (attachment to planning permission of conditions subject to which an industrial development certificate was issued by the Board of Trade) and those conditions either restrict the office floor space which the building may contain or preclude it from containing any office floor space.

1966 c. 34.

Restriction on creation of office premises in building altered or extended.

86.—(1) The provisions of this section shall, subject to subsection (4) below, have effect with respect to a planning permission granted after the commencement of this section for the alteration or extension of a building in an area to which Part I of the Act of 1965 applies at the time of the grant and also applied when the application for planning permission was made, but shall have effect only in the case of a building erected under a planning permission granted after the said commencement. PART VI

(2) If the case is the following, that is to say:—

(*a*) either the erection of the building was not development to which Part I of the Act of 1965 applied or it was so but no office development permit was required therefor; and

(*b*) either the proposed alteration or extension is not development to which the said Part I applies or it is so but no office development permit is required therefor; and

(*c*) there will result from the proposed alteration or extension a building with an aggregate floor space of twice, or more than twice, the prescribed exemption limit,

the planning permission for the alteration or extension shall be granted subject to the condition specified in subsection (3) of this section (in addition to any other conditions imposed by the authority granting the permission).

(3) The said condition is that the use of the building as altered or extended, or as subsequently further altered or extended, shall be restricted so that (whether in consequence of a change of use or otherwise) it does not at any time contain office premises having an aggregate office floor space which exceeds the prescribed exemption limit.

(4) In the following two cases this section shall not apply:—

(*a*) where the planning permission is in respect of a building which, after its alteration or extension, will be wholly residential; and

(*b*) where the planning permission is subject to conditions by virtue of section 23(5) or (6) of the Industrial Development Act 1966 and those conditions either restrict the office floor space which the building as extended or altered may contain or preclude it from containing any office floor space. 1966 c. 34.

Corresponding restriction on planning permission for erection of several buildings.

87.—(1) The provisions of this section shall have effect with respect to a planning permission granted after the commencement of this section for development involving the erection of two or more buildings in an area to which Part I of the Act of 1965 applies at the time of the grant and also applied when the application for planning permission was made, except in a case where all the buildings are exempt from this section.

(2) Any one of the said buildings shall be exempt from this section if—

(*a*) it is wholly residential; or

PART VI

1966 c. 34.

(*b*) the planning permission is subject to conditions by virtue of section 23(5) or (6) of the Industrial Development Act 1966 and those conditions either restrict the office floor space which the building may contain or preclude it from containing any office floor space.

(3) If the aggregate floor space of the buildings proposed to be erected (leaving out of account any which are exempt from this section) is twice, or more than twice, the prescribed exemption limit and either the erection of the buildings is not development to which Part I of the Act of 1965 applies or it is so, but no office development permit is required therefor, the planning permission shall be granted subject to the condition specified in subsection (4) below (in addition to any other conditions imposed by the authority granting the permission).

(4) The said condition is that the use of each one of the buildings (excluding any which are exempt from this section) shall be restricted so that (whether in consequence of a change of use or otherwise) it does not at any time contain office premises having an aggregate floor space which exceeds the limit for that building specified in the condition, which limit shall (subject to subsection (5) below) be a floor space bearing such proportion to the building's total floor space as the prescribed exemption limit bears to the aggregate floor space of all the buildings (excluding any which are exempt from this section) for whose erection the planning permission is granted.

(5) The authority granting the planning permission may in doing so specify in the said condition, as it applies to any building, a limit different from the one provided by subsection (4) above, but not so that the total of the limits for all the buildings to which the condition applies exceeds the prescribed exemption limit.

(6) If after the grant of the planning permission a further application for planning permission is made in respect of all or any of the buildings to which the condition specified in subsection (4) of this section applies, and the further application involves a departure from the terms of the said condition as applying to any building, the application shall be subject to section 1(3) of the Act of 1965 (requirement of office development permit), notwithstanding any provision of that Act exempting development from the requirements of that section in particular cases.

Provisions supplementary to ss. 84 to 87.

88.—(1) A planning permission with respect to which section 86 or 87 above has effect shall not be invalid by reason only that the requirements of section 86(2) or 87(3), as the case may be, are not complied with; but in that case the planning permission shall be deemed to have been granted subject to the

PART VI

condition specified in section 86(3) or 87(4), as the case may be, or (if any other conditions are imposed by the authority granting the permission) to have been granted subject to the conditions so specified in addition to the other conditions; and references in those sections to a condition imposed thereunder shall be construed accordingly as including references to a condition deemed to be imposed.

(2) In sections 84 to 87 of this Act—

(*a*) " industrial building " has the meaning given to it by section 21 of the Local Employment Act 1960, as amended by section 25 of the Industrial Development Act 1966; 1960 c. 18. 1966 c. 34.

(*b*) " office development permit ", " office premises " and " office floor space " have the same meanings as they have for the purposes of the Act of 1965;

(*c*) " the prescribed exemption limit ", in relation to a planning permission, has the meaning given to it by section 7(5) of the Act of 1965 in relation to planning permission granted as mentioned in subsection (1)(*b*) of that section (restrictions on office development to be attached to planning permission not requiring office development permit); and

(*d*) " wholly residential " in relation to a building, means for use exclusively as a dwelling-house or comprising only units of accommodation for such use.

Stopping-up and diversion of highways

Procedure for making orders for stopping-up and diverting highways.

89.—(1) Where the Secretary of State would, if planning permission for any development had been granted under Part II of the Act of 1947, have power to make an order under section 46(1) of that Act authorising the stopping-up or diversion of a highway in order to enable that development to be carried out, then, notwithstanding that such permission has not been granted, the Secretary of State may, in the circumstances specified in subsections (2) to (4) below, publish notice of the draft of such an order in accordance with Schedule 6 to that Act (procedure in relation to orders under section 46).

(2) The Secretary of State may publish such a notice as aforesaid where the relevant development is the subject of an application for planning permission and—

(*a*) that application is made by a local authority or statutory undertakers or the National Coal Board; or

(*b*) that application stands referred to the Secretary of State in pursuance of a direction under section 13 of the Act of 1947; or

PART VI

(*c*) the applicant has appealed to the Secretary of State under section 14 of that Act against a refusal of planning permission or of approval required under a development order, or against a condition of any such permission or approval.

(3) The Secretary of State may publish such a notice as aforesaid where—

(*a*) the relevant development is to be carried out by a local authority, statutory undertakers or the National Coal Board and requires, by virtue of an enactment, the authorisation of a government department; and

1958 c. 69.

(*b*) the developers have made application to the department for that authorisation and also requested a direction under section 32 of the Act of 1947 or, in the case of the National Coal Board, under section 2 of the Opencast Coal Act 1958, that planning permission be deemed to be granted for that development.

(4) The Secretary of State may publish such a notice as aforesaid where the local planning authority certify that they have begun to take such steps, in accordance with regulations made by virtue of section 32 of the Act of 1947 (application of planning control to local planning authorities), as are requisite in order to enable them to obtain planning permission for the relevant development.

(5) Paragraph 5 of Schedule 6 to that Act (power of Secretary of State to make an order under section 46 after considering any relevant objections and report) shall not be construed as authorising the Secretary of State to make an order under section 46(1) of that Act, of which notice has been published by virtue of subsection (1) above, until planning permission is granted for the development which occasions the making of the order.

New powers to authorise stopping-up and diversion of highways.

90.—(1) If planning permission is granted under Part II of the Act of 1947 for constructing or improving, or the Secretary of State proposes to construct or improve, a highway (hereafter in this section referred to as " the main highway "), he may by order authorise the stopping-up or diversion of any other highway which crosses or enters the route of the main highway or which is, or will be, otherwise affected by the construction or improvement of the main highway, if it appears to him expedient to do so—

(*a*) in the interests of the safety of users of the main highway; or

(*b*) to facilitate the movement of traffic on the main highway.

PART VI

(2) Subsections (3) to (5) of section 22 of the Act of 1945, subsections (2) to (7) of section 46, subsections (2) to (4) of section 111 of the Act of 1947 and Schedule 6 to that Act (ancillary provisions, provisions as to compulsory acquisition of land in connection with highways and provisions as to telegraph lines) and section 89 above shall apply in relation to an order under this section as they apply in relation to an order under section 46(1) of the Act of 1947.

(3) In section 32(3) of the Mineral Workings Act 1951 (rights of statutory undertakers in respect of their apparatus where order made under section 46 of the Act of 1947), after the reference to the said section 46 there shall be inserted an alternative reference to this section. 1951 c. 60.

Conversion of highway into footpath or bridleway.

91.—(1) The provisions of this section shall have effect where a competent authority by resolution adopt a proposal for improving the amenity of part of their area, being a proposal which involves a highway in that area (being a highway over which the public have a right of way with vehicles, but not a trunk road or a road classified as a principal road for the purpose of advances under section 8 of the Development and Road Improvement Funds Act 1909) being changed to a footpath or bridleway. 1909 c. 47.

(2) The Secretary of State may, on an application made by a competent authority, by order provide for the extinguishment of any right which persons may have to use vehicles on that highway.

(3) An order made under subsection (2) of this section may include such provision as the Secretary of State (after consultation with the local planning authority and the highway authority, if different from the competent authority) thinks fit for permitting the use on the highway of vehicles (whether mechanically propelled or not), in such cases as may be specified in the order, notwithstanding the extinguishment of any such right as is mentioned in that subsection; and any such provision may be framed by reference to particular descriptions of vehicles, or to particular persons by whom, or on whose authority, vehicles may be used, or to the circumstances in which, or the times at which, vehicles may be used for particular purposes.

(4) No statutory provision prohibiting or restricting the use of footpaths or bridleways shall affect any use of a vehicle on a highway in relation to which an order made under subsection (2) above has effect, where the use is permitted in accordance with provisions of the order included by virtue of subsection (3) above.

(5) Any person who, at the time of an order under subsection (2) of this section coming into force, has an interest in land having

PART VI

lawful access to a highway to which the order relates shall be entitled to be compensated by the competent authority in respect of any depreciation in the value of his interest which is directly attributable to the order and of any other loss or damage which is so attributable.

In this subsection " lawful access " means access authorised by planning permission granted under the Act of 1947, or access in respect of which no such permission is necessary.

(6) A claim for compensation under subsection (5) above shall be made to the competent authority within the time and in the manner prescribed by regulations under the Act of 1947.

(7) Subsections (3) to (5) of section 22 of the Act of 1945, subsections (2) to (5) of section 46, subsections (2) to (4) of section 111 of the Act of 1947 and Schedule 6 to that Act (ancillary provisions, provisions as to compulsory acquisition of land in connection with highways and provisions as to telegraph lines) shall apply in relation to an order under this section as they apply in relation to an order under section 46(1) of the Act of 1947.

(8) The Secretary of State may, on an application made by a competent authority, by order revoke an order made by him in relation to a highway under subsection (2) above ; and the effect of the order shall be to reinstate any right to use vehicles on the highway, being a right which was extinguished by virtue of the order under the said subsection.

(9) Subsection (8) above shall not be taken as prejudicing any provision of the Act of 1947 enabling orders to be varied or revoked.

(10) The competent authorities for the purposes of this section are county councils and town councils, and before making an application under subsection (2) or (8) above a competent authority shall consult with the local planning authority and the highway authority (in a case where they are themselves not that authority).

(11) In this section " statutory provision " means a provision contained in, or having effect under, any enactment.

Provision of amenity for highway reserved for pedestrians.

92.—(1) Where in relation to a highway an order has been made under section 91(2) above, a competent authority may carry out and maintain any such works on or in the highway, or place on or in it any such objects or structures, as appear to them to be expedient for the purposes of giving effect to the order or of enhancing the amenity of the highway and its immediate surroundings or to be otherwise desirable for a purpose beneficial to the public.

PART VI

(2) The powers exercisable by a competent authority under this section shall extend to laying out any part of the highway with lawns, trees, shrubs and flower-beds and to providing facilities for recreation or refreshment.

(3) A competent authority may so exercise their powers under this section as to restrict the access of the public to any part of the highway, but shall not so exercise them as—

(*a*) to prevent persons from entering the highway at any place where they could enter it before the order under section 91 was made; or

(*b*) to prevent the passage of the public along the highway; or

(*c*) to prevent normal access by pedestrians to premises adjoining the highway; or

(*d*) to prevent any use of vehicles which is permitted by an order made under the said section 91 and applying to the highway; or

(*e*) to prevent statutory undertakers from having access to any work of theirs under, in, on, over, along or across the highway.

(4) An order under section 91(8) above may make provision requiring the removal of any obstruction of the highway resulting from the exercise by a competent authority of their powers under this section.

(5) The competent authorities for the purposes of this section are county councils and town councils, but such an authority shall not exercise any powers conferred by this section unless they have obtained the consent of the local planning authority and the highway authority (in a case where they are themselves not that authority).

Powers for local planning authorities analogous to s. 46 of the Act of 1947.

93.—(1) Subject to section 95 below, a local planning authority may by order authorise the stopping up or diversion of any footpath or bridleway if they are satisfied that it is necessary to do so in order to enable development to be carried out—

(*a*) in accordance with planning permission granted under Part II of the Act of 1947 or the enactments replaced by that Part of the Act; or

(*b*) by a government department.

(2) An order under this section may, if the local planning authority are satisfied that it should do so, provide—

(*a*) for the creation of an alternative footpath or bridleway for use as a replacement for the one authorised

PART VI

by the order to be stopped up or diverted, or for the improvement of an existing path or way for such use;

(*b*) for authorising or requiring works to be carried out in relation to any footpath or bridleway for whose stopping-up or diversion, creation or improvement, provision is made by the order;

(*c*) for the preservation of any rights of statutory undertakers in respect of apparatus of theirs which immediately before the date of the order is under, in, on, over, along or across any such footpath or bridleway;

(*d*) for requiring any person named in the order to pay, or make contributions in respect of, the cost of carrying out any such works.

(3) The powers of a local planning authority under this section shall include power to make an order authorising the stopping-up or diversion of a footpath or bridleway which is temporarily stopped up or diverted under any other enactment.

1951 c. 60.

(4) Section 32(1) and (2) of the Mineral Workings Act 1951 (temporary order for stopping-up or diversion of highway) shall apply to an order made by a local planning authority under this section as it applies to an order made by the Secretary of State under section 46 of the Act of 1947, with the substitution—

(*a*) for references to the Secretary of State of references to a local planning authority; and

(*b*) for the reference in subsection (2) to section 46(4) of the Act of 1947 of a reference to subsection (2) of this section.

Extinguishment of footpaths etc. over land held for planning purposes.

94.—(1) Subject to section 95 below, where any land has been acquired or appropriated for planning purposes and is for the time being held by a local authority for the purposes for which it was acquired or appropriated, the authority may by order extinguish any public right of way over the land, being a footpath or bridleway, if they are satisfied that an alternative right of way has been or will be provided, or that the provision of an alternative right of way is not required.

(2) Any reference in subsection (1) above to the acquisition of land for planning purposes is a reference to the acquisition thereof under section 35 or 37 of the Act of 1947 or section 29 of this Act; and any reference to the appropriation of land for planning purposes is a reference to the appropriation thereof for purposes for which land can, or could have been, acquired under those sections.

95.—(1) An order under section 93 or 94 of this Act shall not take effect unless confirmed by the Secretary of State, or unless confirmed, as an unopposed order, by the authority who made it.

PART VI

Confirmation, validity, etc. of orders under ss. 93 and 94.

(2) The Secretary of State shall not confirm any such order unless satisfied as to every matter of which the authority making the order are required under section 93 or 94 (as the case may be) to be satisfied.

(3) The time specified—

(*a*) in an order under section 93 above as the time from which a footpath or bridleway is to be stopped up or diverted ; or

(*b*) in an order under section 94 above as the time from which a right of way is to be extinguished,

shall not be earlier than confirmation of the order.

(4) Schedule 7 to this Act shall have effect with respect to the confirmation of orders under section 93 or 94 of this Act and the publicity for such orders after they are confirmed.

Amendments of s. 46 of and Schedule 6 to Act of 1947.

96.—(1) It is hereby declared for the avoidance of doubt that the incidental and consequential provisions which may be included in an order under section 46 of the Act of 1947 or section 90 or 91 above by virtue of section 46(4) of that Act shall include provisions providing for the preservation of any rights of statutory undertakers in respect of any apparatus of theirs which immediately before the date of the order is under, in, on, over, along or across the highway to which the order relates.

(2) In paragraphs 1(*b*) and 4 of Schedule 6 to the Act of 1947 (periods for inspecting and objecting to a draft order under section 46), for the words " three months " there shall be substituted the words " twenty-eight days ".

Exchequer and Treasury matters

Grants for research, etc.

97. The Secretary of State may, with the consent of the Treasury, make grants for assisting establishments engaged in promoting or assisting research relating to, and education with respect to, the planning and design of the physical environment.

Exchequer contributions in connection with town development.

1957 c. 38.

98. In section 14(1) of the Housing and Town Development (Scotland) Act 1957 (Exchequer contributions towards specified expenses incurred by a local authority in connection with town development), after paragraph (*b*) there shall be inserted the following paragraph:—

(*c*) expenses of providing buildings and other works for social, cultural or recreational purposes ".

PART VI

Agreements of Crown Estate Commissioners.

99. An agreement made by the Crown Estate Commissioners under section 84 of the Act of 1947 (whereby a government department may agree with local planning authorities to secure the use of Crown land in conformity with the development plan) shall not require the approval of the Treasury; and accordingly, in paragraph (*a*) of the proviso to that section, the words " the Commissioners of Crown Lands or by " shall cease to have effect.

Punishment of offences

Increase of certain penalties under Acts of 1947 and 1959.

100. In the sections of the Act of 1947 and the Act of 1959 specified in Schedule 8 to this Act, the amendments shown in that Schedule shall be made (being amendments to increase the penalties to which persons may be subject under those sections and in certain cases to provide for punishment on indictment as well as summarily).

Offences by corporations.

101.—(1) Where an offence under the Town and Country Planning (Scotland) Acts 1947 to 1966 or this Act, which has been committed by a body corporate, is proved to have been committed with the consent or connivance of, or to be attributable to any neglect on the part of, a director, manager, secretary or other similar officer of the body corporate, or any person who was purporting to act in any such capacity, he, as well as the body corporate, shall be guilty of that offence and be liable to be proceeded against accordingly.

(2) In subsection (1) above, the expression " director ", in relation to any body corporate established by or under an enactment for the purpose of carrying on under national ownership an industry or part of an industry or undertaking, being a body corporate whose affairs are managed by the members thereof, means a member of that body corporate.

PART VII

GENERAL

Expenses.

102. There shall be defrayed out of moneys provided by Parliament—

(*a*) any sums required for the payment of grants under section 97 above;

(*b*) any other expenses of a Minister under this Act; and

(*c*) any increase attributable to the provisions of this Act in the sums payable out of moneys so provided under any other enactment.

PART VII

Interpretation.

103.—(1) In this Act, unless the context otherwise requires—

" the Act of 1945 " means the Town and Country Planning (Scotland) Act 1945; 1945 c. 33.

" the Acquisition Act 1947 " means the Acquisition of Land (Authorisation Procedure) (Scotland) Act 1947; 1947 c. 42.

" the Act of 1947 " means the Town and Country Planning (Scotland) Act 1947; 1947 c. 53.

" the Act of 1954 " means the Town and Country Planning (Scotland) Act 1954; 1954 c. 73.

" the Act of 1959 " means the Town and Country Planning (Scotland) Act 1959; 1959 c. 70.

" the Act of 1965 " means the Control of Office and Industrial Development Act 1965; 1965 c. 33.

" bridleway " and " footpath " have the same meanings as in section 47 of the Countryside (Scotland) Act 1967; 1967 c. 86.

" the Lands Tribunal " means the Lands Tribunal for Scotland;

" new development " has the same meaning as in section 16(5) of the Act of 1954;

" prescribed " means prescribed by regulations made by the Secretary of State under this Act.

(2) This Act and the Act of 1947 shall have effect as if this Act were part of that Act.

(3) Until sections 1 to 3 of the Lands Tribunal Act 1949 come into force as regards Scotland, for any reference in this Act to the Lands Tribunal there shall be substituted a reference to an official arbiter appointed under Part I of the Land Compensation (Scotland) Act 1963, and sections 3 and 5 of that Act shall apply, subject to any necessary modifications, in relation to the determination of any question under this Act by an arbiter so appointed.

1949 c. 42.
1963 c. 51.

(4) Any reference in this Act to any other enactment is a reference thereto as amended, and includes a reference thereto as extended or applied, by or under any other enactment, including this Act.

Commencement.

104.—(1) This Act shall come into operation on a day appointed by an order made by statutory instrument by the Secretary of State, and different days may be appointed under this section for different purposes and, in particular, different days may be so appointed for the coming into operation of the same provision in different areas.

PART VII

(2) No order under this section relating to Part III of this Act shall be made unless a draft of the order has been approved by both Houses of Parliament.

(3) Any reference in this Act to the commencement of any provision thereof shall be construed as a reference to the day appointed for the coming into operation of that provision or, in the case of a provision which comes into operation on different days in different areas, shall, in relation to any area, be construed as a reference to the day appointed for the coming into operation of that provision in that area.

(4) An order under this section may make such transitional provision as appears to the Secretary of State to be necessary or expedient in connection with the provisions thereby brought into force, including such adaptation of those provisions or any provision of this Act then in force as appear to him to be necessary or expedient in consequence of the partial operation of this Act (whether before or after the day appointed by the order).

(5) The Secretary of State shall maintain and keep up to date a register showing the effect of orders made under this section in such a way as enables members of the public to inform themselves—

(*a*) as to the provisions of this Act which have come, or are to be brought, into operation, and on which dates and in relation to which areas; and

(*b*) as to whether, in the case of a particular area, any transitional provision has been made by such an order.

(6) The register maintained by the Secretary of State under this section shall be kept at his principal offices in Edinburgh; and the register shall be available for inspection by the public at all reasonable hours.

Adaptation, amendment and modification of enactments.

105. Schedule 9 to this Act shall have effect for adapting and interpreting Acts other than this Act and for making amendments and modifications to such Acts, being minor amendments and amendments consequential on the foregoing provisions of this Act.

Transitional provisions and savings.

106. Schedule 10 to this Act shall have effect for the purpose of the transition to the provisions of this Act from the law in force before the commencement of those provisions and with respect to the application of this Act to things done before the commencement of those provisions.

Repeals.

107. The enactments specified in Schedule 11 to this Act are hereby repealed to the extent specified in the third column of that Schedule.

Part VII

Short title, citation and extent.

108.—(1) This Act may be cited as the Town and Country Planning (Scotland) Act 1969.

(2) The Town and Country Planning (Scotland) Acts 1947 to 1966 and this Act may be cited as the Town and Country Planning (Scotland) Acts 1947 to 1969.

(3) This Act, except so far as it provides for Joint Planning Inquiry Commissions and except so far as it amends the House of Commons Disqualification Act 1957, shall extend to Scotland only.

1957 c. 20.

SCHEDULES

Section 18.

SCHEDULE 1

Provisions as to Established use Certificates

Application for certificate and appeal against refusal thereof

1. An application for an established use certificate shall be made in such manner as may be prescribed by a development order, and shall include such particulars, and be verified by such evidence, as may be required by such an order or by any directions given thereunder, or by the local planning authority or, in the case of an application referred to the Secretary of State, by him.

2. Provision may be made by a development order for regulating the manner in which applications for established use certificates are to be dealt with by local planning authorities, and, in particular—

(*a*) for requiring the authority to give to any applicant for such a certificate, within such time as may be prescribed by the order, such notice as may be so prescribed as to the manner in which his application has been dealt with ;

(*b*) for requiring the authority to give to the Secretary of State, and to such other persons as may be prescribed by or under the order, such information as may be so prescribed with respect to applications for such certificates made to the authority, including information as to the manner in which any such application has been dealt with.

3.—(1) A development order may provide that an application for an established use certificate, or an appeal against the refusal of such an application, shall not be entertained unless it is accompanied by a certificate in such form as may be prescribed by the order and corresponding to one or other of those described in paragraphs (*a*) to (*d*) of section 36(1) of the Act of 1959 (requirement of certificate that the applicant is the owner of the land or has given notice to the owners of his intended application, or has tried to do so) and any such order may—

(*a*) include requirements corresponding to those contained in subsections (2) to (4) of that section ; and

(*b*) make provision as to who, in the case of any land, is to be treated as the owner for the purposes of any provision of the order made by virtue of this sub-paragraph.

(2) If any person issues a certificate which purports to comply with any provision of a development order made by virtue of sub-paragraph (1) above and which contains a statement which he knows to be false or misleading in a material particular, or recklessly issues a certificate which purports to comply with those

requirements and which contains a statement which is false or misleading in a material particular, he shall be guilty of an offence and liable on summary conviction to a fine not exceeding £100. SCH. 1

Provisions with respect to grant of certificate

4. An established use certificate shall be in such form as may be prescribed by a development order and shall specify—

(*a*) the land to which the certificate relates and any use thereof which is certified by the certificate as established ;

(*b*) by reference to the paragraphs of section 18(1) of this Act, the grounds on which that use is so certified ; and

(*c*) the date on which the application for the certificate was made, which shall be the date at which the use is certified as established.

5. Where the Secretary of State, or a person appointed by him under section 22 or 24 of this Act to determine an appeal, grants an established use certificate, the Secretary of State or that person shall give notice to the local planning authority of that fact.

6. In section 12(5) of the Act of 1947 (register of decisions on planning applications) references to applications for planning permission shall include references to applications for established use certificates ; and the information which may be prescribed as being required to be contained in a register kept under that subsection shall include information with respect to established use certificates granted by the Secretary of State or by a person appointed by him under section 22 or 24 of this Act to determine an appeal.

SCHEDULE 2

Section 31.

GENERAL VESTING DECLARATIONS FOR LAND COMPULSORILY ACQUIRED

Execution of general vesting declarations

1.—(1) Where a compulsory purchase order authorising an acquiring authority to acquire any land has come into operation, the authority may execute in respect of any of the land which they are authorised to acquire by the compulsory purchase order a declaration in the prescribed form (in this Schedule referred to as " a general vesting declaration ") vesting the land in themselves as from the end of such period as may be specified in the declaration (not being less than twenty-eight days) from the date on which the service of notices required by paragraph 4 below is completed.

(2) A general vesting declaration shall contain a particular description of the lands affected or a description by reference of those lands in the manner provided by section 61 of the Conveyancing (Scotland) Act 1874. 1874 c. 94.

2.—(1) Before making a general vesting declaration with respect to any land which is subject to a compulsory purchase order, the

SCH. 2 acquiring authority shall include in the notice of the making or confirmation of the order which is required to be published or served by paragraph 6 of Schedule 1 to the Acquisition Act 1947 or any other provision of the relevant enactments corresponding to that paragraph, or in a notice given subsequently and before the service of the notice to treat in respect of that land—

(*a*) such a statement of the effect of paragraphs 1 to 8 of this Schedule as may be prescribed ; and

(*b*) a notification to the effect that every person who, if a general vesting declaration were made in respect of all the land comprised in the order in respect of which notice to treat has not been given, would be entitled to claim compensation in respect of any such land is invited to give information to the authority making the declaration in the prescribed form with respect to his name and address and the land in question.

(2) The requirements of the relevant enactments with respect to the publication and service of a notice of the making or confirmation of a compulsory purchase order shall apply to a notice under this paragraph given subsequently to the first-mentioned notice.

3. A general vesting declaration shall not be executed before the end of the period of two months beginning with the date of the first publication of the notice complying with paragraph 2(1) above, or such longer period, if any, as may be specified in the notice:

Provided that, with the consent in writing of every occupier of any of the land specified in the declaration, the acquiring authority may execute a general vesting declaration before the end of that period of two months, or of the longer period so specified, as the case may be.

4. As soon as may be after executing a general vesting declaration, the acquiring authority shall serve—

(*a*) on every occupier of any of the land specified in the declaration (other than land in which there subsists a short tenancy or a long tenancy which is about to expire) ; and

(*b*) on every other person who has given information to the authority with respect to any of that land in pursuance of the invitation published and served under paragraph 2(1) above,

a notice in the prescribed form specifying the land and stating the effect of the declaration.

5. For the purposes of this Schedule, a certificate by the acquiring authority that the service of notices required by paragraph 4 above was completed on a date specified in the certificate shall be conclusive evidence of the fact so stated.

Effect of general vesting declaration

6. At the end of the period specified in a general vesting declaration, the provisions of the Lands Clauses Acts and of section 6 of
1845 c. 33. the Railways Clauses Consolidation (Scotland) Act 1845 (both as

incorporated by Schedule 2 to the Acquisition Act 1947) and of the Land Compensation (Scotland) Act 1963 shall apply as if, on the date on which the declaration was made, a notice to treat had been served on every person on whom, under section 17 of the Lands Clauses Consolidation (Scotland) Act 1845 (on the assumption that they required to take the whole of the land specified in the declaration and had knowledge of all the parties referred to in that section) the acquiring authority could have served such a notice, other than—

SCH. 2
1963 c. 51.
1845 c. 19.

(*a*) any person entitled to an interest in the land in respect of which such a notice had actually been served before the end of that period ; and

(*b*) any person entitled to a short tenancy or a long tenancy which is about to expire.

7. At the end of the period specified in a general vesting declaration, the land specified in the declaration, together with the right to enter upon and take possession of it, shall vest in the acquiring authority as if the circumstances in which under the said Act of 1845 an authority authorised to purchase land compulsorily have any power to expede a notarial instrument (whether for vesting land or any interest in land in themselves or for extinguishing the whole or part of any feu-duty, ground annual or rent, or other payment or incumbrance) had arisen in respect of all the land and all interests therein, and the acquiring authority had duly exercised that power accordingly at the end of that period.

8. Where any land specified in a general vesting declaration is land in which there subsists a short tenancy or a long tenancy which is about to expire—

(*a*) the right of entry conferred by paragraph 7 above shall not be exercisable in respect of that land unless, after serving a notice to treat in respect of that tenancy, the acquiring authority have served upon every occupier of any of the land in which the tenancy subsists a notice stating that, at the end of such period as is specified in the notice (not being less than fourteen days) from the date on which the notice is served, they intend to enter upon and take possession of such land as is specified in the notice, and that period has expired ; and

(*b*) the vesting of the land in the acquiring authority shall be subject to the tenancy until that period expires, or the tenancy comes to an end, whichever first occurs.

9.—(1) Subject to the following sub-paragraph, subsection (5) of section 10 of, and the supplementary provisions contained in Schedule 3 to the Land Commission Act 1967 (being provisions as to recording in the Register of Sasines, exclusion of power of entry, objections to severance, compensation and other miscellaneous matters arising on the making of a general vesting declaration under Part II of that Act) shall have effect for the purposes of paragraphs 6 to 8 above as they have effect for the purposes of section 10 of that Act.

1967 c. 1.

Sch. 2

(2) For the purpose of applying the said Schedule 3 to paragraphs 6 and 8 above, the following substitution of references shall be made therein—

1967 c. 1.

Original reference in Land Commission Act 1967, Schedule 3	*Substituted references for purposes of this Schedule*
The Land Commission	An acquiring authority
The Land Commission Act 1967...	This Act
The Land Commission Act 1967—	
Section 9(3)	Paragraph 4 of this Schedule
Section 10	Paragraphs 6 to 8 of this Schedule
Section 10(2)	Paragraph 7 of this Schedule.

(3) In the said Schedule 3 as so applied, " land " shall have the same meaning as in this Schedule.

Recovery of compensation overpaid

10. The provisions of paragraphs 11 to 15 below shall have effect where, after the acquiring authority have made a general vesting declaration in respect of any land, a person claims compensation in respect of the acquisition by the authority of an interest in any land by virtue of the declaration, and the authority pay compensation in respect of that interest.

11. If, in a case falling within paragraph 10 above, it is subsequently shown—

(*a*) that the land, or the claimant's interest in it, was subject to an incumbrance which was not disclosed in the particulars of his claim ; and

(*b*) that by reason of that incumbrance the compensation paid exceeded the compensation to which the claimant was entitled in respect of that interest,

the acquiring authority may recover the amount of the excess from the claimant.

12. If, in a case falling within paragraph 10 above, it is subsequently shown that the claimant was not entitled to the interest in question, either in the whole or in part of the land to which the claim related, the acquiring authority may recover from him an amount equal to the compensation paid, or to so much of that compensation as, on a proper apportionment thereof, is attributable to that part of the land, as the case may be.

13. Any question arising under paragraph 11 or 12 above—

(*a*) as to the amount of the compensation to which the claimant was entitled in respect of an interest in land ; or

(*b*) as to the apportionment of any compensation paid,

shall be referred to and determined by the Lands Tribunal ; and in relation to the determination of any such question, the provisions
1963 c. 51. of section 3 of the Land Compensation (Scotland) Act 1963 shall apply, subject to any necessary modifications.

SCH. 2

14. Subject to paragraph 13 above, any amount recoverable by the acquiring authority under paragraph 11 or 12 above shall be recoverable in any court of competent jurisdiction.

15. Any sum recovered under paragraph 11 or 12 above in respect of land by an acquiring authority who are a local authority shall be applied towards the repayment of any debt incurred in acquiring or redeveloping that land or if no debt was so incurred shall be paid into the account out of which the compensation in respect of the acquisition of that land was paid.

Penalty for false information in claiming compensation

16.—(1) If any person, for the purpose of obtaining for himself or for any other person any compensation in respect of the acquisition by the acquiring authority of an interest in land by virtue of a general vesting declaration—

(*a*) knowingly or recklessly makes a statement which is false in a material particular ; or

(*b*) with intent to deceive produces, furnishes, sends or otherwise makes use of any book, account, or other document which is false in a material particular ; or

(*c*) with intent to deceive withholds any material information,

he shall be guilty of an offence.

(2) Any person guilty of an offence under this paragraph shall (without prejudice to the recovery of any sum under paragraph 11 or 12 above) be liable—

(*a*) on summary conviction, to a fine not exceeding £400 ;

(*b*) on conviction on indictment, to imprisonment for a term not exceeding two years or a fine, or both.

Supplemental

17.—(1) In this Schedule " short tenancy " means a tenancy for a year or from year to year or any lesser interest, and " long tenancy which is about to expire ", in relation to a general vesting declaration, means a tenancy granted for an interest greater than a short tenancy, but having at the date of the declaration a period still to run which is not more than the specified period (that is to say, such period, longer than one year, as may for the purposes of this paragraph be specified in the declaration in relation to the land in which the tenancy subsists).

(2) In determining for the purposes of this paragraph what period a tenancy still has to run at the date of a general vesting declaration it shall be assumed—

(*a*) that the tenant will exercise any option to renew the tenancy, and will not exercise any option to terminate the tenancy, then or thereafter available to him, and

SCH. 2

(*b*) that the landlord will exercise any option to terminate the tenancy then or thereafter available to him.

18. In this Schedule—

" relevant enactments ", in relation to an acquiring authority, means the enactments under which that authority may acquire or be authorised to acquire land compulsorily and which prescribe a procedure for effecting the compulsory acquisition of land by them by means of a compulsory purchase order ;

" land ", in relation to compulsory acquisition by an acquiring authority, has the same meaning as in the relevant enactments.

Section 35.

SCHEDULE 3

CONSEQUENTIAL AMENDMENTS OF PLANNING BLIGHT PROVISIONS OF ACT OF 1959

Section 38

In subsection (1)—

(*a*) after the words " this Act " there shall be inserted the words " and of sections 34 to 38 of the Act of 1969 " ;

(*b*) paragraphs (*a*) and (*b*) shall be omitted ; and

(*c*) in paragraph (*c*), for the words in parenthesis there shall be substituted the words " (otherwise than by being dealt with in a manner mentioned in section 34(1)(*a*) or (*b*) of the Act of 1969) ".

In subsection (6), for the words " a notice served under this section " there shall be substituted the words " a blight notice ".

After subsection (6), there shall be added the following subsection—

" (7) In this Act and in Part IV of the Act of 1969, ' blight notice ' means a notice served under this section or under section 35 of the Act of 1969."

Section 39

In subsection (1), for the words " Where a notice has been served under the last preceding section " there shall be substituted the words " Where a blight notice has been served ".

For subsection (3) there shall be substituted the following subsection—

" (3) Any counter-notice served under this section in respect of a blight notice shall specify the grounds (being one or more of the grounds specified in subsection (2) above or, as relevant, section 35(8) or 36(1) of the Act of 1969) on which the appropriate authority object to the notice."

Section 40

In subsection (1), for the words " notice served under section thirty-eight of this Act " there shall be substituted the words " a blight notice ".

Section 41

In subsection (1), for the words " Where a notice has been served under section thirty-eight of this Act " there shall be substituted the words " Where a blight notice has been served ".

In subsection (2)(*b*), for the words " the notice under section thirty-eight of this Act " there shall be substituted the words " the blight notice ".

In subsection (3), for the words from the beginning to " that notice " there shall be substituted the words " Where the appropriate authority have served a counter-notice objecting to a blight notice ".

Section 42

In subsections (2)(*a*), (2)(*b*), (4)(*a*) and (4)(*b*), for the words " the whole or part " (wherever occurring) there shall be substituted the words " the whole or a substantial part ".

In subsections (2)(*b*), (3)(*b*) and (4)(*b*), for the words " six months before the date of service " there shall be substituted the words " twelve months before the date of service ".

In subsection (5)—

(*a*) in the definition of " the relevant date "—

(i) in paragraph (*a*), the word " designated " shall be omitted in both places ; and for the words " any of the paragraphs (*a*) to (*c*) of subsection (1) of section thirty-eight of this Act " there shall be substituted the words " paragraph (*c*) of section 38(1) above or paragraph (*a*) or (*b*) of section 34(1) of the Act of 1969 " ; and

(ii) in paragraphs (*b*), (*c*) and (*d*), for the words " that subsection " there shall be substituted, in each place, the words " section 38(1) above " ; and

(*b*) for the definition of " the specified descriptions " there shall be substituted the following definition—

" ' the specified descriptions " means the descriptions contained in paragraphs (*c*) to (*f*) of section 38(1) of this Act and paragraphs (*a*) to (*d*) of section 34(1) of the Act of 1969 ".

Section 54

In subsection (1), after the definition of the Act of 1954 there shall be inserted the following definition—

" ' the Act of 1969 ' means the Town and Country Planning (Scotland) Act 1969."

Schedule 5

In paragraph 8, for the words " a notice has been served under section thirty-eight of this Act " there shall be substituted the words " a blight notice has been served ".

Paragraphs 11(3) and 12(3) shall be omitted.

In paragraph 13, for the words " a notice under section thirty-eight of this Act " there shall be substituted the words " a blight notice ".

Sections 41, 42, 44 and 48.

SCHEDULE 4

Control of Works for Demolition, Alteration or Extension of Listed Buildings

Part I

Applications for Listed Building Consent

1.—(1) Provision may be made by regulations under this Act with respect to the form and manner in which applications for listed building consent are to be made, the manner in which such applications are to be advertised and the time within which they are to be dealt with by local planning authorities or, as the case may be, by the Secretary of State.

(2) Any listed building consent shall (except in so far as it otherwise provides) enure for the benefit of the building and of all persons for the time being interested therein.

2.—(1) Regulations under this Act may provide that an application for listed building consent, or an appeal against the refusal of such an application, shall not be entertained unless it is accompanied by a certificate in the prescribed form corresponding to one or other of those described in paragraphs (*a*) to (*d*) of section 36(1) of the Act of 1959 (requirement of certificate that the applicant is the owner of the land or has given notice to the owners of his intended application or has tried to do so) and any such regulations may—

(*a*) include requirements corresponding to those contained in subsections (2) to (4) of that section ; and

(*b*) make provision as to who, in the case of any building, is to be treated as the owner for the purposes of any provision of the regulations made by virtue of this sub-paragraph.

(2) If any person issues a certificate which purports to comply with the requirements of regulations made by virtue of this paragraph and which contains a statement which he knows to be false or misleading in a material particular, or recklessly issues a certificate which purports to comply with those requirements and which contains a statement which is false or misleading in a material particular, he shall be guilty of an offence and liable on summary conviction to a fine not exceeding £100.

3.—(1) The Secretary of State may give directions requiring applications for listed building consent to be referred to him instead of being dealt with by the local planning authority.

(2) A direction under this paragraph may relate either to a particular application, or to applications in respect of such buildings as may be specified in the direction.

(3) An application in respect of which a direction under this paragraph has effect shall be referred to the Secretary of State accordingly.

SCH. 4

(4) Before determining an application referred to him under this paragraph, the Secretary of State shall, if either the applicant or the authority so desire, afford to each of them an opportunity of appearing before, and being heard by, a person appointed by the Secretary of State.

(5) The decision of the Secretary of State on any application referred to him under this paragraph shall be final.

4.—(1) Subject to the following provisions, a local planning authority to whom application is made for listed building consent shall not grant such consent, unless they have notified the Secretary of State of the application (giving particulars of the works for which the consent is required) and either—

(*a*) a period of twenty-eight days has expired beginning with the date of the notification, without the Secretary of State having directed the reference of the application to him ; or

(*b*) the Secretary of State has notified the authority that he does not intend to require the reference of the application.

(2) The Secretary of State may, at any time before the said period expires, give notice to the authority that he requires further time in which to consider whether to require the reference of the application to him, and the foregoing sub-paragraph shall then have effect with the substitution for a period of twenty-eight days or such longer period as may be specified in the Secretary of State's notice.

5.—(1) The Secretary of State may give directions that, in the case of such descriptions of application for listed building consent as he may specify, other than such consent for the demolition of a building, paragraph 4 above shall not apply ; and accordingly, so long as the directions are in force, local planning authorities may determine applications of such descriptions in any manner they think fit, without notifying the Secretary of State.

(2) Without prejudice to the foregoing provisions of this Schedule, the Secretary of State may give directions to local planning authorities requiring them, in such cases or classes of case as may be specified in the directions, to notify to him and to such other persons as may be so specified any applications made to them for listed building consent, and the decisions taken by the authorities thereon.

6.—(1) Where an application is made to the local planning authority for listed building consent and the consent is refused by the authority or is granted by them subject to conditions, the applicant, if he is aggrieved by the decision, may, by notice served in the prescribed manner within such period as may be prescribed, not less than twenty-eight days from the receipt by him of notification of the decision, appeal to the Secretary of State.

(2) A person appealing under this paragraph may include in his notice thereunder, as the ground or one of the grounds of his appeal, a claim—

(*a*) that the building is not of special architectural or historic interest and ought to be removed from any list compiled or approved by the Secretary of State under section 28 of the Act of 1947 ; or

SCH. 4

(*b*) in the case of a building to which section 40(10) of this Act applies, that the Secretary of State should give a direction under that section with respect to the building; or

(*c*) in the case of a building subject to a building preservation notice under section 48 of this Act, that the building should not be included in a list compiled or approved under the said section 28.

(3) Subject to the following provisions of this paragraph, the Secretary of State may allow or dismiss an appeal thereunder, or may reverse or vary any part of the decision of the authority, whether the appeal relates to that part thereof or not, and—

(*a*) may deal with the application as if it had been made to him in the first instance; and

(*b*) may, if he thinks fit, exercise his power under section 28 of the Act of 1947 to amend any list compiled or approved thereunder by removing from it the building to which the appeal relates or his power under section 40(10) of this Act to direct that that subsection shall no longer apply to the building.

(4) Before determining an appeal under this paragraph, the Secretary of State shall, if either the applicant or the local planning authority so desire, afford to each of them an opportunity of appearing before, and being heard by, a person appointed by the Secretary of State for the purpose.

(5) The decision of the Secretary of State on any appeal under this paragraph shall be final.

7. Where an application is made to the local planning authority for listed building consent, then, unless within the prescribed period from the date of the receipt of the application, or within such extended period as may at any time be agreed upon in writing between the applicant and the authority, the authority either—

(*a*) give notice to the applicant of their decision on the application; or

(*b*) give notice to him that the application has been referred to the Secretary of State in accordance with directions given under paragraph 3 of this Schedule,

the provisions of paragraph 6 of this Schedule shall apply in relation to the application as if listed building consent had been refused by the authority and as if notification of their decision had been received by the applicant at the end of the prescribed period or at the end of the said extended period, as the case may be.

PART II

REVOCATION OF LISTED BUILDING CONSENT

8.—(1) If it appears to the local planning authority, having regard to the development plan and to any other material considerations, that it is expedient to revoke or modify listed building consent in respect of any works to a building, being consent granted on an application made under Part I of this Schedule, the authority, subject to the following provisions of this paragraph, may by order revoke or modify the consent to such extent as (having regard to these matters) they consider expedient.

(2) An order under this paragraph shall not take effect unless it is confirmed by the Secretary of State ; and the Secretary of State may confirm any such order submitted to him either without modification or subject to such modifications as he considers expedient.

(3) Where a local planning authority submit an order to the Secretary of State for confirmation under this paragraph, the authority shall serve notice on the owner, lessee and occupier of the building affected and on any other person who in their opinion will be affected by the order ; and if within such period as may be specified in that notice (not being less than twenty-eight days after the service thereof) any person on whom the notice is served so requires, the Secretary of State, before confirming the order, shall afford to that person and to the local planning authority an opportunity of appearing before, and being heard by, a person appointed by the Secretary of State for the purpose.

(4) The power conferred by this paragraph to revoke or modify listed building consent in respect of any works may be exercised at any time before those works have been completed, but the revocation or modification shall not affect so much of those works as has been previously carried out.

9.—(1) If it appears to the Secretary of State, after consultation with the local planning authority, to be expedient that an order under paragraph 8 above should be made, he may give directions to the authority requiring them to submit to him such an order for his confirmation, or may himself make such an order ; and any order so made by the Secretary of State shall have the like effect as if it had been made by the authority and confirmed by the Secretary of State under that paragraph.

(2) The provisions of paragraph 8 above shall have effect, subject to any necessary modifications, in relation to any proposal by the Secretary of State to make such an order by virtue of this paragraph, in relation to the making thereof by the Secretary of State, and in relation to the service of copies thereof as so made.

10.—(1) Where listed building consent is revoked or modified by an order under this Part of this Schedule, then if on a claim made to the local planning authority in the time and in the manner prescribed by regulations under this Act, it is shown that a person interested in the building—

(*a*) has incurred expenditure in carrying out works which are rendered abortive by the revocation or modification, or

(*b*) has otherwise sustained loss or damage which is directly attributable to the revocation or modification,

the authority shall pay to that person compensation in respect of that expenditure, loss or damage.

(2) For the purposes of this paragraph, any expenditure incurred in the preparation of plans for the purposes of any works, or upon

SCH. 4

other similar matters preparatory thereto, shall be taken to be included in the expenditure incurred in carrying out those works.

(3) Subject to sub-paragraph (2) above, no compensation shall be paid under this paragraph in respect of any works carried out before the grant of the listed building consent which is revoked or modified, or in respect of any other loss or damage (not being loss or damage consisting of depreciation of the value of an interest in land) arising out of anything done or omitted to be done before the grant of that consent.

11.—(1) The following provisions shall have effect where the local planning authority have made an order under paragraph 8 of this Schedule but have not submitted the order to the Secretary of State for confirmation by him, and—

(*a*) the owner, lessee and occupier of the land and all persons who in the authority's opinion will be affected by the order have notified the authority in writing that they do not object to the order ; and

(*b*) it appears to the authority that no claim for compensation is likely to arise under paragraph 10 above.

(2) The authority shall advertise in the prescribed manner the fact that the order has been made, and the advertisement shall specify—

(*a*) the period (not less than twenty-eight days from the date on which the advertisement first appears) within which persons affected by the order may give notice to the Secretary of State that they wish for an opportunity of appearing before, and being heard by, a person appointed by the Secretary of State for the purpose ; and

(*b*) the period (not less than fourteen days from the expiration of the period referred to in paragraph (*a*) above) at the expiration of which, if no such notice is given to the Secretary of State, the order may take effect by virtue of this paragraph and without being confirmed by the Secretary of State.

(3) The authority shall also serve notice to the same effect on the persons mentioned in sub-paragraph (1)(*a*) above, and the notice shall include a statement of the effect of sub-paragraph (7) below.

(4) The authority shall send a copy of any advertisement published under sub-paragraph (2) above to the Secretary of State, not more than three days after the publication.

(5) If within the period referred to in sub-paragraph (2)(*a*) above no person claiming to be affected by the order has given notice to the Secretary of State as aforesaid and the Secretary of State has not directed that the order be submitted to him for confirmation, the order shall, at the expiration of the period referred to in sub-paragraph (2)(*b*) above, take effect by virtue of this paragraph and without being confirmed by the Secretary of State as required by paragraph 8 of this Schedule.

(6) This paragraph does not apply to an order revoking or modifying a listed building consent granted by the Secretary of State under Part V of this Act or under this Schedule.

SCH. 4

(7) No compensation shall be payable under paragraph 10 of this Schedule in respect of an order under paragraph 8 thereof which takes effect by virtue of this paragraph and without being confirmed by the Secretary of State.

PART III

PROCEEDINGS ON LISTED BUILDING PURCHASE NOTICE

12.—(1) The local planning authority on whom a listed building purchase notice is served shall, before the end of the period of three months beginning with the date of service of that notice, serve on the owner or lessee by whom the purchase notice was served a notice stating either—

(*a*) that the authority are willing to comply with the purchase notice, or

(*b*) that another local planning authority or statutory undertakers specified in the notice under this sub-paragraph have agreed to comply with it in their place ; or

(*c*) that for reasons specified in the notice under this sub-paragraph, the authority are not willing to comply with the purchase notice and have not found any other local planning authority or statutory undertakers who will agree to comply with it in their place and that they have transmitted a copy of the purchase notice to the Secretary of State, on a date specified in the notice under this sub-paragraph, together with a statement of the reasons so specified.

(2) Where the local planning authority on whom a listed building purchase notice is served by an owner or lessee have served on him a notice in accordance with sub-paragraph (1)(*a*) or (*b*) above, the authority, or the other local planning authority or statutory undertakers specified in the notice, as the case may be, shall be deemed to be authorised to acquire the interest of the owner or lessee compulsorily in accordance with the provisions of section 50 of this Act, and to have served a notice to treat in respect thereof on the date of service of the notice under sub-paragraph (1) of this paragraph.

(3) Where the authority on whom a listed building purchase notice is served by an owner or lessee propose to serve on him a notice in accordance with sub-paragraph (1)(*c*) above, they shall transmit a copy of the purchase notice to the Secretary of State together with a statement of their reasons ; and subsections (5) and (7) of section 17 of the Act of 1947 (procedure on reference of purchase notice to the Secretary of State) shall then apply in relation to the purchase notice as it applies in relation to a purchase notice under that section, with the substitution for references therein to the Secretary of State taking action under that section of references to his taking action under paragraph 13 of this Schedule.

13.—(1) Subject to the following provisions of this paragraph, if the Secretary of State is satisfied that the conditions specified in paragraphs (*a*) to (*c*) of section 42(1) of this Act are fulfilled in relation to a listed building purchase notice, he shall confirm the notice:

SCH. 4

Provided that, if he is satisfied that the said conditions are fulfilled only in respect of part of the land, he shall confirm the notice only in respect of that part and the notice shall have effect accordingly.

(2) The Secretary of State shall not confirm the purchase notice unless he is satisfied that the land comprises such land contiguous or adjacent to the building as is in his opinion required for preserving the building or its amenities, or for affording access to it, or for its proper control or management.

(3) If it appears to the Secretary of State to be expedient to do so in the case of a listed building purchase notice served on account of listed building consent being refused or granted subject to conditions, he may, in lieu of confirming the purchase notice, grant listed building consent for the works in respect of which the application was made or, where such consent for those works was granted subject to conditions, revoke or amend those conditions so far as it appears to him to be required in order to enable the land to be rendered capable of reasonably beneficial use by the carrying out of those works.

(4) If it appears to the Secretary of State to be expedient to do so in the case of a listed building purchase notice served on account of listed building consent being revoked or modified by an order under Part II of this Schedule, he may, in lieu of confirming the notice, cancel the order revoking the consent or, where the order modified the consent by the imposition of conditions, revoke or amend those conditions so far as appears to him to be required in order to enable the land to be rendered capable of reasonably beneficial use by the carrying out of the works in respect of which the consent was granted.

(5) If it appears to the Secretary of State that the land, or any part of it, could be rendered capable of reasonably beneficial use within a reasonable time by the carrying out of any other works for which listed building consent ought to be granted, he may, in lieu of confirming the listed building purchase notice, or in lieu of confirming it so far as it relates to that part of the land, as the case may be, direct that listed building consent for those works shall be granted in the event of an application being made in that behalf.

(6) If it appears to the Secretary of State that the land, or any part of the land, could be rendered capable of reasonably beneficial use within a reasonable time by the carrying out of any development for which planning permission ought to be granted, he may, in lieu of confirming the listed building purchase notice, or in lieu of confirming it so far as it relates to that part of the land, as the case may be, direct that planning permission for that development shall be granted in the event of an application being made in that behalf.

(7) If it appears to the Secretary of State, having regard to the probable ultimate use of the building or the site thereof, that it is expedient to do so, he may, if he confirms the notice, modify it either in relation to the whole or in relation to any part of the land by substituting another local planning authority or statutory undertakers for the authority on whom the notice was served.

(8) In section 17 of the Act of 1947 as applied by paragraph 12(3) above, any reference to the taking of action by the Secretary of State under this paragraph is a reference to the taking by him of any such action as is mentioned in sub-paragraphs (1) or (3) to (7) of this paragraph, or to the taking by him of a decision not to confirm the purchase notice on the grounds that any of the conditions specified in paragraphs (*a*) to (*c*) of section 42(1) of this Act are not fulfilled. SCH. 4

14.—(1) Where the Secretary of State confirms a listed building purchase notice, the authority on whom the notice was served (or, if under paragraph 13(7) above the Secretary of State modified the notice by substituting another authority or statutory undertakers for that authority, that other authority or those undertakers) shall be deemed to be authorised to acquire the relevant interest compulsorily in accordance with the provisions of section 50 of this Act and to have served a notice to treat in respect thereof on such date as the Secretary of State may direct.

(2) If, before the end of the relevant period, the Secretary of State has neither confirmed the purchase notice nor taken any such action in respect thereof as is mentioned in sub-paragraphs (3) to (6) of paragraph 13 above, and has not notified the owner or lessee by whom the notice was served that he does not propose to confirm the notice, the notice shall be deemed to be confirmed at the end of that period and the authority on whom the notice was served shall be deemed to have been authorised to acquire the relevant interest compulsorily in accordance with the provisions of section 50 of this Act and to have served a notice to treat in respect thereof at the end of that period.

(3) In this paragraph—

(*a*) " the relevant interest " means the owner's or lessee's interest in the land or, if the purchase notice is confirmed by the Secretary of State in respect of only part of the land, the owner's or lessee's interest in that part ;

(*b*) " the relevant period " is whichever of the following periods first expires, that is to say—

(i) the period of nine months beginning with the date of the service of the purchase notice ; and

(ii) the period of six months beginning with the date on which a copy of the purchase notice was transmitted to the Secretary of State.

(4) Where the Secretary of State has notified the owner or lessee by whom a listed building purchase notice has been served of a decision on his part to confirm, or not to confirm, the notice (including any decision to confirm the notice only in respect of part of the land, or to give any direction as to the granting of listed building consent), and that decision of the Secretary of State is quashed under the provisions of section 31 of the Act of 1959, the purchase notice shall be treated as cancelled, but the owner or lessee may serve a further listed building purchase notice in its place.

SCH. 4

(5) For the purpose of any regulations made under this Act as to the time within which a listed building purchase notice may be served, the service of a purchase notice under sub-paragraph (4) above shall not be treated as out of time if the notice is served within the period which would be applicable in accordance with those regulations if the decision to refuse listed building consent or to grant it subject to conditions (being the decision in consequence of which the listed building purchase notice is served) had been made on the date on which the decision of the Secretary of State was quashed as mentioned in sub-paragraph (4) above.

15. Where in consequence of listed building consent being revoked or modified by an order under Part II of this Schedule, compensation is payable in respect of expenditure incurred in carrying out any works to the building in respect of which the consent was granted, then if a listed building purchase notice is served in respect of an interest in the land, any compensation payable in respect of the acquisition of that interest in pursuance of the purchase notice shall be reduced by an amount equal to the value of the works in respect of which compensation is payable by virtue of paragraph 10 above.

PART IV

PROVISIONS ABOUT ENFORCEMENT NOTICES UNDER SECTION 44

16.—(1) A listed building enforcement notice shall be served on the owner, lessee and occupier of the building to which it relates; and on any other person having an interest in the building, being an interest which in the opinion of the authority is materially affected by the notice.

(2) Subject to the following provisions of this Schedule, a listed building enforcement notice shall take effect at the end of such period, not less than twenty-eight days after the service of the notice, as may be specified therein.

(3) The local planning authority may withdraw a listed building enforcement notice (without prejudice to their power to serve another) at any time before it takes effect; and if they do so, they shall forthwith give notice of the withdrawal to every person who was served with the notice.

17.—(1) A person on whom a listed building enforcement notice is served, or any other person having an interest in the building to which it relates, may, at any time within the period specified in the notice as the period at the end of which it is to take effect, appeal to the Secretary of State against the notice on any of the following grounds:—

(*a*) that the building is not of special architectural or historic interest;

(*b*) that the matters alleged to constitute a contravention of section 40 of this Act do not involve such a contravention;

(*c*) that the works were urgently necessary in the interests of safety or health, or for the preservation of the building;

(*d*) that listed building consent ought to be granted for the works, or that any relevant condition of such consent which has been granted ought to be discharged, or different conditions substituted;

(*e*) that the notice was not served as required by paragraph 16 of this Schedule;

(*f*) that the requirements of the notice exceed what is necessary for restoring the building to its condition before the works were carried out;

(*g*) that the period specified in the notice as the period within which any steps required thereby are to be taken falls short of what should reasonably be allowed;

(*h*) that the steps required by the notice to be taken would not serve the purpose of restoring the character of the building in its former state.

(2) An appeal under this paragraph shall be made by notice in writing to the Secretary of State, which shall indicate the grounds of appeal and state the facts on which it is based; and on any such appeal the Secretary of State shall, if either the appellant or the local planning authority so desire, afford to each of them an opportunity of appearing before, and being heard by, a person appointed by the Secretary of State for the purpose.

(3) Where an appeal is brought under this paragraph, the notice shall be of no effect pending the final determination or withdrawal of the appeal.

(4) Where an appeal is brought under this paragraph—

(*a*) the Secretary of State may correct any informality, defect or error in the notice if he is satisfied that the informality, defect or error is not material;

(*b*) in a case where it would otherwise be a ground for determining the appeal in favour of the appellant that a person required by paragraph 16 of this Schedule to be served with the notice was not served, the Secretary of State may disregard that fact if he is satisfied that the person has not been substantially prejudiced by the failure to serve him.

(5) On the determination of an appeal under this paragraph, the Secretary of State shall give directions for giving effect to his determination, including, where appropriate, directions for quashing the listed building enforcement notice or for varying the terms of the notice in favour of the appellant, and the Secretary of State may—

(*a*) grant listed building consent for the works to which the notice relates or, as the case may be, discharge any condition subject to which such consent was granted and substitute any other condition, whether more or less onerous;

(*b*) in so far as any works already executed constitute development for which planning permission is required, grant such permission in respect of the works;

(*c*) if he thinks fit, exercise his power under section 28 of the Act of 1947 to amend any list compiled or approved thereunder by removing from it the building to which the appeal

SCH. 4

relates or his power under section 40(10) of this Act to direct that that subsection shall no longer apply to the building.

(6) Any planning permission granted by the Secretary of State under sub-paragraph (5) above shall be treated as granted on an application for the like permission under Part II of the Act of 1947, and any listed building consent granted by him thereunder shall be treated as granted on an application for the like consent under Part I of this Schedule ; and—

(*a*) in relation to the grant thereunder either of planning permission or of listed building consent, the Secretary of State's decision shall be final ;

(*b*) for the purposes of section 12(5) of the Act of 1947 (local planning authority's register of planning applications) a decision of the Secretary of State to grant planning permission shall be treated as having been given by him in dealing with an application for planning permission made to the local planning authority.

18. The validity of a listed building enforcement notice shall not, except by way of an appeal under this Part of this Schedule, be questioned in any proceedings whatsoever on any of the grounds specified in sub-paragraphs (*b*) or (*e*) of paragraph 17(1) of this Schedule.

PART V

PROVISIONS APPLICABLE ON LAPSE OF BUILDING PRESERVATION NOTICE

19. The provisions of this Part of this Schedule apply where a building preservation notice ceases to be in force by virtue of section 48(3) of this Act, otherwise than by reason of the building to which it relates being included in a list compiled or approved under section 28 of the Act of 1947.

20. The fact that the building preservation notice has ceased to be in force shall not affect the liability of any person to be prosecuted and punished for an offence under section 40 or 45 of this Act committed by him with respect to the said building while the notice was in force.

21. Any proceedings on or arising out of an application for listed building consent made while the building preservation notice was in force shall lapse and any listed building consent granted with respect to the building while the notice was in force shall also lapse.

22. Any listed building enforcement notice served by the local planning authority while the building preservation notice was in force shall cease to have effect and any proceedings thereon under Part IV of this Schedule shall lapse, but section 46(1) and (2) of this

Act shall continue to have effect as respects any expenses incurred by the local authority, owner, lessee or occupier as therein mentioned and with respect to any sums paid on account of such expenses. SCH. 4

SCHEDULE 5

Section 62.

CONSTRUCTION OF REFERENCES IN SECTIONS 62 AND 63 TO " THE RESPONSIBLE MINISTER OR MINISTERS "

1. In relation to matters specified in the first column of the Table below (being matters mentioned in section 62(1) above which may be referred to a Planning Inquiry Commission under that section) " the responsible Minister or Ministers " for the purposes of sections 62 and 63 of this Act are those specified opposite in the second column of the Table.

2. Where an entry in the second column of the Table specifies two or more Ministers, that entry shall be construed as referring to those Ministers acting jointly.

TABLE

Referred matter	Responsible Minister or Ministers
1. Application for planning permission or an appeal—	
(*a*) relating to operational land of statutory undertakers, or to land in the case of which the circumstances mentioned in section 71(2) of this Act are present,	The Secretary of State and the appropriate Minister (if different).
(*b*) relating to other land.	The Secretary of State.
2. Proposal that a government department should give a direction or that development should be carried out by or on behalf of a government department.	The Secretary of State and the Minister (if different) in charge of the government department concerned.

SCHEDULE 6

Section 64.

JOINT PLANNING INQUIRY COMMISSIONS

Interpretation

1. In relation to matters specified in the first column of the Table below (being matters which under section 64 of this Act may be referred to a Joint Planning Inquiry Commission), " the responsible

SCH. 6 Ministers ", for the purposes of this Schedule, are those specified opposite in the second column of the Table, acting jointly.

TABLE

Referred matter	Responsible Ministers
(1) Application for planning permission or appeal—	
(*a*) relating to operational land of statutory undertakers, or to land in the case of which there are present the circumstances mentioned in section 71(2) of this Act, or the corresponding provision of the Act of 1968,	The Secretary of State, the Minister of Housing and Local Government and the appropriate Minister (if different).
(*b*) relating to other land.	The Secretary of State and the Minister of Housing and Local Government.
(2) Proposal that a government department should give a direction under section 32 of the Act of 1947 or section 41 of the Act of 1962, or that development should be carried out by or on behalf of a government department.	The Secretary of State, the Minister of Housing and Local Government and the Minister (if different) in charge of the government department concerned.

2. In this Schedule—

(*a*) " the Act of 1962 " and " the Act of 1968 " mean respectively the Town and Country Planning Act 1962 and the Town and Country Planning Act 1968 ;

1962 c. 38.
1968 c. 72.

(*b*) " commission " means a Joint Planning Inquiry Commission constituted under section 64 of this Act ; and

(*c*) " referred matter " means a matter referred to a commission under that section.

3. Where this Schedule refers to the appropriate Minister, the local authority or the local planning authority, the reference shall be construed, according to its context, as if it were contained in the Act of 1947 or in the Act of 1962.

The reference

4. Two or more of the matters mentioned in subsection (1) of section 64 of this Act may be referred to the same commission if it appears to the responsible Ministers that they relate to proposals to carry out development for similar purposes on different sites.

SCH. 6

5. Where a referred matter relates to a proposal to carry out development for any purpose at a particular site, the responsible Ministers may also refer to the commission the question whether development for that purpose should be instead carried out at an alternative site, whether in Scotland or in England, or partly in one and partly in the other.

6. The responsible Ministers shall, on referring a matter to a commission, state in the reference the reasons therefor and may draw the attention of the commission to any points which seem to them to be relevant to their inquiry.

7.—(1) A reference to a commission of a proposal that development should be carried out by or on behalf of a government department may be made at any time.

(2) A reference of any other matter mentioned in subsection (1) of section 64 of this Act may be made at any time before, but not after, the determination of the relevant referred application or the relevant appeal or, as the case may be, the giving of the relevant direction, notwithstanding that an inquiry or other hearing has been held into the proposal by a person appointed by any Minister for the purpose.

Notice of reference to persons and authorities concerned

8.—(1) Notice of the making of a reference to a commission shall be published in the prescribed manner, and a copy of the notice shall be served on the local planning authority for the area in which it is proposed that the relevant development shall be carried out.

(2) In the case of an application for planning permission referred under section 13 of the Act of 1947 or section 22 of the Act of 1962, or an appeal under section 14 of the Act of 1947 or section 23 of the Act of 1962, notice shall also be served—

(*a*) on the applicant or appellant ; and

(*b*) on any person who has made representations, relating to the subject matter of the application or appeal, which the local planning authority are required to take into account under section 35(4) or 36(4) of the Act of 1959 or, as the case may be, section 17(2) or (3) of the Act of 1962.

(3) In the case of a proposal that a direction should be given by a government department under section 32 of the Act of 1947 or section 41 of the Act of 1962 with respect to any development, notice shall also be served on the local authority or statutory undertakers applying for authorisation to carry out that development.

(4) In this paragraph, " prescribed " means prescribed by regulations made by the Secretary of State and the Minister of Housing and Local Government jointly in the exercise of their respective powers under the Act of 1947 and the Act of 1962.

SCH. 6

Proceedings of commission on reference

9. A commission inquiring into a referred matter shall—

(*a*) identify and investigate the considerations relevant to, or the technical or scientific aspects of, that matter which in their opinion are relevant to the question whether the proposed development should be permitted to be carried out, and assess the importance to be attached to those considerations or aspects;

(*b*) thereafter, comply with paragraph 10 below in respect of affording to persons an opportunity of appearing before, and being heard by, one or more members of the commission;

(*c*) report to the responsible Ministers on the said matter.

10. A commission shall afford the following persons an opportunity of appearing and being heard as aforesaid:—

(*a*) in any case, the local planning authority, if the authority so desire;

(*b*) in the case of a matter mentioned in section 62(1)(*a*), (*b*) or (*c*) of this Act or section 62(1)(*a*), (*b*) or (*c*) of the Act of 1968, the applicant, if he so desires; and

(*c*) in the case of an application or appeal mentioned in either of the said sections 62(1)(*a*) or (*b*), any person who has made representations relating to the subject matter of the application or appeal which the local planning authority are required to take into account under section 35(4) or 36(4) of the Act of 1959 or section 17(2) or (3) of the Act of 1962.

11.—(1) The provisions of section 13(2) of the Act of 1947 and of that subsection as applied by section 14(2) of that Act, and of sections 22(6) and 23(4) of this Act, relating to the affording of an opportunity of appearing before, and being heard by, a person appointed by the Secretary of State, shall not apply to an application for planning permission, or an appeal, referred to a commission.

(2) Sections 22(5) and 23(5) of the Act of 1962 (duty of Minister of Housing and Local Government to afford parties a hearing in cases of called-in applications for planning permission and appeals), and sections 21(6) and 22(4) of the Act of 1968 (corresponding provision in relation to appeal determined by a person appointed by the Minister under Part III of that Act) shall not apply to an application for planning permission, or an appeal, referred to a commission.

Local inquiries

12. A commission shall, for the purpose of complying with paragraph 10 above, hold a local inquiry; and they may hold such an inquiry if they think it necessary for the proper discharge of

their functions, notwithstanding that neither the applicant nor the local planning authority desire the opportunity of appearing and being heard. SCH. 6

13. Where a commission are to hold a local inquiry in connection with a referred matter and it appears to the responsible Ministers, in the case of some other matter falling to be determined by a Minister of the Crown and required or authorised by an enactment other than this Schedule to be the subject of a local inquiry, that the two matters are so far cognate that they should be considered together, the responsible Ministers may direct that the two inquiries be held concurrently or combined as one inquiry.

14. For the purposes of the Tribunals and Inquiries Act 1958, a local inquiry held by a commission— 1958 c. 66.

(*a*) if held in Scotland, shall be treated as one held by the Secretary of State in pursuance of a duty imposed by a statutory provision ; and

(*b*) if held in England, shall be treated as one held by the Minister of Housing and Local Government in pursuance of a duty so imposed.

15.—(1) Subsections (4) to (9) of section 50 of the Act of 1945 (power to summon and examine witnesses, and expenses at inquiries) shall apply to a local inquiry held by a commission in Scotland as they apply to an inquiry held under that section.

(2) Subsections (2) to (5) of section 290 of the Local Government Act 1933 (evidence and costs at local inquiries) shall apply in relation to a local inquiry held by a commission in England as they apply in relation to an inquiry caused to be held by a department under subsection (1) of that section, with the substitution for references to a department (other than the first reference in subsection (4)) of references to the Minister of Housing and Local Government. 1933 c. 51

Supplementary

16.—(1) A commission may, with the approval of the Ministers and at their expense, arrange for the carrying out (whether by the commission themselves or by others) of research of any kind appearing to the commission to be relevant to a referred matter.

(2) In this paragraph " the Ministers " means the Secretary of State and the Minister of Housing and Local Government, acting jointly ; but their functions under this paragraph may, by arrangements made between them, be exercised by either acting on behalf of both.

17. Subject to the provisions of this Schedule, and to any directions given to them by the responsible Ministers, a commission shall have power to regulate their own procedure.

Section 95.

SCHEDULE 7

PROCEDURE IN CONNECTION WITH ORDERS RELATING TO FOOTPATHS AND BRIDLEWAYS

PART I

CONFIRMATION OF ORDERS

1.—(1) Before an order under section 93 or 94 of this Act is submitted to the Secretary of State for confirmation or confirmed as an unopposed order, the authority by whom the order was made shall give notice in the prescribed form—

(*a*) stating the general effect of the order and that it has been made and is about to be submitted for confirmation or to be confirmed as an unopposed order ;

(*b*) naming a place in the area in which the land to which the order relates is situated where a copy of the order may be inspected free of charge at all reasonable hours ; and

(*c*) specifying the time (not being less than twenty-eight days from the date of the first publication of the notice) within which, and the manner in which, representations or objections with respect to the order may be made.

(2) Subject to sub-paragraph (3) below, the notice to be given under sub-paragraph (1) above shall be given—

(*a*) by publication in the Edinburgh Gazette and in at least one local newspaper circulating in the area in which the land to which the order relates is situated ; and

(*b*) by serving a like notice on—

(i) every owner, occupier and lessee (except tenants for a month or a period less than a month and statutory tenants within the meaning of the Housing (Repairs and Rents) (Scotland) Act 1954) of any of that land ; 1954 c. 50.

(ii) every county or town council whose area includes any of that land ;

(iii) any statutory undertakers to whom there belongs, or by whom there is used, for the purposes of their undertaking, any apparatus under, in, on, over, along or across that land ; and

(iv) any person named in the order by virtue of section 93(2)(*d*) of this Act ; and

(*c*) by causing a copy of the notice to be displayed in a prominent position at the ends of so much of any footpath or bridleway as is to be stopped up, diverted or extinguished by virtue of the order.

(3) Except in the case of an owner, occupier or lessee being a local authority or statutory undertakers, the Secretary of State may in any particular case direct that it shall not be necessary to comply with sub-paragraph (2)(*b*)(i) above ; but if he so directs in the case of any land then in addition to publication the notice shall be addressed to " the owners and any occupiers " of the land

(describing it) and a copy or copies of the notice shall be affixed to some conspicuous object or objects on the land.

2. If no representations or objections are duly made, or if any so made are withdrawn, the authority by whom the order was made may, instead of submitting the order to the Secretary of State, themselves confirm the order (but without any modification).

3.—(1) If any representation duly made is not withdrawn, the Secretary of State shall, before confirming the order, if the objection is made by a local authority, cause a local inquiry to be held, and in any other case either—

(*a*) cause a local inquiry to be held ; or

(*b*) afford to any person by whom any representation or objection has been duly made and not withdrawn an opportunity of being heard by a person appointed by the Secretary of State for the purpose,

and, after considering the report of the person appointed to hold the inquiry or to hear representations or objections, may confirm the order, with or without modifications:

Provided that in the case of an order under section 93 of this Act, if objection is made by statutory undertakers on the ground that the order provides for the creation of a public right of way over land covered by works used for the purpose of their undertaking, or over the curtilage of such land, and the objection is not withdrawn, the order shall be subject to special parliamentary procedure.

(2) Notwithstanding anything in the foregoing provisions of this paragraph, the Secretary of State shall not confirm an order so as to affect land not affected by the order as submitted to him, except after—

(*a*) giving such notice as appears to him requisite of his proposal so to modify the order, specifying the time (not being less than twenty-eight days from the date of the first publication of the notice) within which, and the manner in which representations or objections with respect to the proposal may be made ;

(*b*) holding a local inquiry or affording to any person by whom any representation or objection has been duly made and not withdrawn an opportunity of being heard by a person appointed by the Secretary of State for the purpose ; and

(*c*) considering the report of the person appointed to hold the inquiry or to hear representations or objections as the case may be ;

and, in the case of an order under section 93 of this Act, if objection is made by statutory undertakers on the ground that the order as modified would provide for the creation of a public right of way over land covered by works used for the purposes of their undertaking, or over the curtilage of such land, and the objection is not withdrawn, the order shall be subject to special parliamentary procedure.

Sch. 7

4.—(1) The Secretary of State shall not confirm an order under section 93 of this Act which extinguishes a right of way over land under, in, on, over, along or across which there is any apparatus belonging to or used by statutory undertakers for the purpose of their undertaking, unless the undertakers have consented to the confirmation of the order ; and any such consent may be given subject to the condition that there are included in the order such provisions for the protection of the undertakers as they may reasonably require.

(2) The consent of statutory undertakers to any such order shall not be unreasonably withheld ; and any question arising under this paragraph whether the withholding of consent is unreasonable, or whether any requirement is reasonable, shall be determined by whichever Minister is the appropriate Minister in relation to the statutory undertakers concerned.

5. Regulations under this Act may, subject to this Part of this Schedule, make such provision as the Secretary of State thinks expedient as to the procedure on the making, submission and confirmation of orders under sections 93 and 94 of this Act.

Part II

Publicity for Orders after Confirmation

6. As soon as may be after an order under section 93 or 94 of this Act has been confirmed by the Secretary of State or confirmed as an unopposed order, the authority by whom the order was made shall publish, in the manner required by paragraph 1(2) of this Schedule, a notice in the prescribed form, describing the general effect of the order, stating that it has been confirmed, and naming a place where a copy thereof as confirmed may be inspected free of charge at all reasonable hours, and shall—

(*a*) serve a like notice and a copy of the order as confirmed on any persons on whom notices were required to be served under the said paragraph 1(2) ; and

(*b*) cause a like notice to be displayed in the like manner as the notice required to be displayed under the said paragraph 1(2):

Provided that no such notice or copy need be served on a person unless he has sent to the authority a request in that behalf, specifying an address for service.

Section 100.

SCHEDULE 8

Increase of Penalties under the Act of 1947 and the Act of 1959

The Act of 1947

Section 22 (*Supplementary provisions as to enforcement*)

In subsection (3) (penalty for use of land in contravention of enforcement notice), for the words " fifty pounds " there shall be substituted the words " £400, or on conviction on indictment to a

SCH. 8

fine ", for the words " not exceeding twenty pounds " there shall be substituted the words " not exceeding £50 " and at the end there shall be added the words " or on conviction on indictment to a fine ".

Section 24 (*Orders requiring discontinuance of use or alteration or removal of buildings or works*)

In subsection (4) (penalty for non-compliance with order), for the words " fifty pounds " there shall be substituted the words " £400, or on conviction on indictment to a fine ", for the words " not exceeding twenty pounds " there shall be substituted the words " not exceeding £50 " and at the end there shall be added the words " or on conviction on indictment to a fine ".

Section 30 (*Supplementary provisions regarding control of advertisements*)

In subsection (3) (penalty for displaying advertisements in contravention of regulations), for the words from " fifty pounds " to the end of the subsection there shall be substituted the words " £100 and, in the case of a continuing offence, £5 for each day during which the offence continues after conviction ".

Section 99 (*Powers of entry*)

In subsection (6) (penalty for disclosing trade secrets obtained on entry to a factory etc.), for the words from " one hundred pounds " to the end of the subsection there shall be substituted the words " £400 or on conviction on indictment to imprisonment for a term not exceeding two years or a fine, or both ".

Section 102 (*Power to require information as to ownership of land*)

For the words from " and any person who, having " to the end of the section there shall be substituted the following subsections—

" (2) Any person who, having been required in pursuance of this section to give any information, fails to give that information shall be liable on summary conviction to a fine not exceeding £100.

(3) Any person who, having been so required to give any information, knowingly makes any misstatement in respect thereof shall be liable on summary conviction to a fine not exceeding £400 or on conviction on indictment to imprisonment for a term not exceeding two years or to a fine, or both.".

The Act of 1959

Section 36 (*Notification of application for planning permission to owners of the land and others*)

In subsection (6) (penalty for false certificate under section 36(1)), for the words " not exceeding fifty pounds " there shall be substituted the words " not exceeding £100 ".

Section 105.

SCHEDULE 9

Adaptation and Interpretation of Enactments, etc.

Part I

General Provisions for Adaptation and Interpretation

1963 c. 51. 1967 c. 1.

1. For the purposes of the Act of 1947, this Act, any other enactment relating to town and country planning, the Land Compensation (Scotland) Act 1963 and Part II of the Land Commission Act 1967, the development plan for any area (whether the whole or part of the district of a local planning authority) shall be taken as consisting of—

(*a*) the provisions of the structure plan for the time being in force for that district or the relevant part of that district, together with the Secretary of State's notice of approval of the plan ;

(*b*) any alterations to that plan, together with the Secretary of State's notices of approval thereof ;

(*c*) any provisions of a local plan for the time being applicable to the area, together with a copy of the authority's resolution of adoption or, as the case may be, the Secretary of State's notice of approval of the local plan ; and

(*d*) any alterations to that local plan, together with a copy of the authority's resolutions of adoption or, as the case may be, the Secretary of State's notices of approval thereof.

2. References in paragraph 1 above to the provisions of any plan, notices of approval, alterations and resolutions of adoption shall, in relation to an area forming part of the district to which they are applicable, be respectively construed as references to so much of those provisions, notices, alterations and resolutions as is applicable to the area.

3. References in paragraphs 1 and 2 above to notices of approval shall, in relation to any plan or alteration made by the Secretary of State under section 12 of this Act, be construed as references to notices of the making of the plan or alteration.

4. Any reference in the Town and Country Planning (Scotland) Acts 1947 to 1966 to the carrying out of a survey or the preparation, approval, making or amendment of a development plan under Part II of the Act of 1947 or to a plan or amendment approved or made under the said Part II shall be construed as a reference to the carrying out of a survey or the preparation, approval, adoption, making or amendment of a structure plan or local plan under Part I of this Act or, as the case may be, to a plan or amendment approved, adopted or made thereunder.

5. References in any Act to the acquisition of land under Part III of the Act of 1947 or to land acquired thereunder shall be respectively construed as, or as including (according as the context

requires) references to the acquisition of land under any provision of this Act and to land acquired under any such provision, and— SCH. 9

(*a*) any such references in sections 24 to 28 of the Act of 1945 (ancillary provisions as to the acquisition of land) shall be respectively construed as also including references to the compulsory acquisition of land under any enactment other than the Act of 1947 and this Act and to land compulsorily acquired under any such enactment; and

(*b*) in section 17(1B) of the Act of 1947 (effect of purchase notice accepted by local planning authority or statutory undertakers), and section 17(2) of that Act (confirmation of purchase notice by Secretary of State), references to compulsory acquisition shall, in the case of statutory undertakers, be construed as references to any statutory provision (however expressed) under which the undertakers have power, or may be authorised, to purchase land compulsorily for the purposes of their undertaking.

6. Any reference in the Land Compensation (Scotland) Act 1963 to an area defined in the current development plan as an area of comprehensive development shall be construed as a reference to an action area for which a local plan is in force. 1963 c. 51.

7. The foregoing provisions of this Schedule shall have effect subject to any specific provision contained in Part II of this Schedule and to the provisions of Schedule 10 to this Act.

PART II

SPECIFIC ADAPTATIONS, AMENDMENTS AND MODIFICATIONS

The Town and Country Planning (Scotland) Act 1945 (*c*. 33)

8. In section 18(4) (consent of Secretary of State to disposal or appropriation of certain land) after the word " section " there shall be inserted the words " or of land acquired or appropriated for planning purposes for a reason mentioned in section 29(1)(*a*) to (*c*) of the Town and Country Planning (Scotland) Act 1969 ".

9. In section 18(5) (special provisions as to land comprised in an area of comprehensive development) for the words " comprised in an area defined by a development plan as an area of comprehensive development " there shall be substituted the words " acquired or appropriated for planning purposes for a reason mentioned in section 29(1)(*a*) to (*c*) of the Town and Country Planning (Scotland) Act 1969 ".

The Town and Country Planning (Scotland) Act 1947 (*c*. 53)

10. Any reference to section 35 of the Act shall be construed (according as the context may require) as including, or as being replaced by, a reference to section 29 of this Act.

Sch. 9

11. In section 12 (applications for planning permission)—

(*a*) in subsection (1), after the word " provisions " (where first occurring) there shall be inserted the words " of sections 66 and 67 of the Act of 1969 and " ;

(*b*) in subsection (3)(*a*), after the word " authority " there shall be inserted the words " either indefinitely or ".

12. In section 17 (obligation to purchase land on refusal of planning permission in certain cases), the following amendments shall be made:—

(*a*) after subsection (1A) of that subsection there shall be inserted the following subsection:—

" (1AA) Where the local planning authority upon whom a purchase notice is served under this section do not, within the period specified in subsection (1A) above, serve a notice under that subsection on the owner by whom the purchase notice was served, the purchase notice shall be deemed to be confirmed at the expiration of that period, and the authority shall be deemed to be authorised to acquire the interest of the owner compulsorily in accordance with the provisions of Part III of this Act, and to have served a notice to treat in respect thereof at the expiration of the said period." ;

(*b*) in subsection (1B), for the words " the last foregoing subsection " (in both places where they occur) there shall be substituted the words " subsection (1A) above " ;

(*c*) in subsection (3), the words " the end of the period specified in subsection (1A) of this section " and the words " whichever is the earlier " shall cease to have effect ;

(*d*) in subsection (7), after the word " purpose " there shall be inserted the words " or the persons, authorities and undertakers concerned have agreed to dispense with such a hearing ".

13. In section 22 (supplementary provisions as to enforcement)—

(*a*) in subsection (1), for the words " sheriff under the last foregoing section " there shall be substituted the words " Secretary of State " ;

(*b*) in subsection (2) for the words " any development " there shall be substituted the words " any breach of planning control (as defined by section 15 of the Act of 1969) " and for the words " by whom the development was carried out " there shall be substituted the words " by whom the breach of planning control was committed ".

14. In section 23(1) (agreements regulating development or use of land), the words " with the approval of the Secretary of State " shall be omitted.

15. In section 28(4) (duty of Secretary of State to notify owner etc. of building when it has become, or ceased to be, listed), for the words " the Secretary of State shall serve a notice " there shall be

substituted the words " the local planning authority concerned in whose district the building is situated, on being informed of the fact by the Secretary of State, shall serve a notice in the prescribed form ".

16. In section 29(1)(*d*) (enforcement of control of advertising), after the words " this Act " there shall be inserted the words " or Part II of the Act of 1969 ".

17. In section 29(4) (definition of areas of special control in connection with advertisements), the words from " either " to first " or " shall be omitted.

18. In section 30(2) (compensation for restrictions on advertising), for the words " the date on which the regulations come into force " there shall be substituted the words " 16th August 1948 ".

19. In section 32(3) (local authority land), after the words " this Part of this Act ", where they first occur, there shall be inserted the words " and Part II of the Act of 1969 ", and after the words " this Part of this Act ", where they subsequently occur, there shall be inserted the words " or Part II of the Act of 1969 ".

20. In section 38(5) (acquisition by agreement of buildings of architectural or historic interest), for the words from " any building " to the end of the subsection there shall be substituted the following paragraphs :—

" (*a*) any building appearing to them to be of special architectural or historic interest ; and

(*b*) any land comprising or contiguous or adjacent to it which appears to the Secretary of State to be required for preserving the building or its amenities, or for affording access to it, or for its proper control or management."

21. In section 39(1) (appropriation of land for planning purposes), the words " specified in a development plan (being a purpose " shall cease to have effect.

22. In section 42(1) (objections to compulsory purchase orders), for the words from the beginning to " purpose " there shall be substituted the words " Where it is proposed that land should be acquired compulsorily under section 29 or 30 of the Act of 1969 ".

23. In section 73(2) (authorisation of existing development), for the words " Part II of this Act " there shall be substituted the words " Part II of the Act of 1969 ".

24. In section 78(1) (power to modify Act in relation to minerals), after the words " of this Act " there shall be inserted the words " and of the Act of 1969 ".

25. In section 83 (Crown land), the following amendments shall be made :—

(*a*) in subsection (3)(*a*), for the words " twenty-one, twenty-four, twenty-six, twenty-seven or thirty-one of this Act " there

SCH. 9

shall be substituted the words "24, 26 or 31 of this Act or section 15 or 44 of the Act of 1969";

(*b*) in subsection (4), after the word "Act" there shall be inserted the words "or section 42 of the Act of 1969";

(*c*) for subsection (5) there shall be substituted the following subsections:—

"(5) No enforcement notice shall be served under section 15 of the Act of 1969 in respect of development carried out by or on behalf of the Crown after the appointed day on land which was Crown land at the time when the development was carried out.

(5A) No enforcement notice under section 44 of the Act of 1969 shall be served in respect of works executed by or on behalf of the Crown in respect of a building which was Crown land at the time when the works were executed."

26. In section 86(1) (application to National Coal Board of provisions of the Act of 1947 relating to statutory undertakers), after the words "of this Act" (where first occurring) there shall be inserted the words "or of the Act of 1969".

27. In section 93 (contributions by Ministers towards compensation paid by local authorities), after the words "section seventeen of this Act)" there shall be inserted the words "or Part II, III, or V of the Act of 1969".

28. In section 94(1)(*b*) (contribution by local authorities and statutory undertakers), at the end there shall be added the words "or Part II or Part V of the Act of 1969 or Schedule 4 to that Act".

29. In section 95(2) (expenses of local authorities), for the words "section thirty-four of this Act" there shall be substituted the words "the Act of 1969".

30. Section 96 (default powers of Secretary of State) shall be amended as follows:—

(*a*) in subsection (1), for the words from "an enforcement notice" to "section 31 of this Act" there shall be substituted the following words—

"(*a*) an enforcement notice under section 15 of the Act of 1969 or under the provisions of that section as applied by regulations made under section 29 of this Act; or

(*b*) a notice under section 31 of this Act; or

(*c*) a stop notice under section 20 of the Act of 1969; or

(*d*) an enforcement notice under section 44 of that Act; or

(*e*) a completion notice under section 69 of that Act;

should be served ", and for the words in the proviso from " an enforcement notice " to " this Act " there shall be substituted the words " an enforcement notice under section 15 or 44 of the Act of 1969 which is served by the Secretary of State, the provisions of section 22 of this Act or, as the case may be, sections 45 and 46 of that Act " ; SCH. 9

(*b*) for subsection (4)(*a*) there shall be substituted the following paragraph:—

" (*a*) that the council of a county or a burgh have failed to take steps for the acquisition of any land which, in the opinion of the Secretary of State, ought to be acquired by that council under section 29 of the Act of 1969 for a purpose which it is necessary to achieve in the interests of the proper planning of an area in which the land is situated, or ".

31. Section 99 (powers of entry) shall be amended as follows:—

(*a*) at the end of subsection (1)(*c*) there shall be added the words " or to serve any notice under Part II or Part V of the Act of 1969 " ;

(*b*) after that subsection there shall be inserted the following subsections:—

" (1A) Any person duly authorised in writing by the Secretary of State may at any reasonable time enter any land for the purpose of surveying any building thereon in connection with a proposal to include the building in, or exclude it from, a list compiled or approved under section 28 of this Act.

(1B) Any person duly authorised in writing by the Secretary of State or a local planning authority may at any reasonable time enter any land for the purpose of ascertaining whether, with respect to any building on the land, an offence has been, or is being, committed under Part V of the Act of 1969, or whether the building is being maintained in a proper state of repair " ;

(*c*) in subsection (2), for the words from " a Minister " to " so designated " there shall be substituted the words " a local authority or Minister authorised to acquire land under section 29 or 30 of the Act of 1969 " ;

(*d*) in subsection (3)(*a*), at the end there shall be added the words " or under the Act of 1969 ".

32. In section 105(1) (determination of disputes as to compensation), after the words " compulsory acquisition of land) " there shall be inserted the words " or under Part II or Part V or section 91 of the Act of 1969 ".

33. In section 113(1) (interpretation), after the definition of " Act of 1945 " there shall be inserted the following—

" ' Act of 1969 ' means the Town and Country Planning (Scotland) Act 1969 ; ".

SCH. 9 34. In paragraph 1 of Part III of Schedule 1 (joint advisory committees for advising constituent authorities as to preparation of development plans etc.), the reference to development plans shall be construed as a reference to structure plans and local plans.

35. In Schedule 4, in paragraph 1, after the words " of this Act " there shall be inserted the words " or under Part V or section 91 of the Act of 1969 ".

36. In Schedule 5 (development by statutory undertakers), the following amendments shall be made:—

(*a*) in paragraph 1(1), after the words " such an application " there shall be inserted the words " or such an application is deemed to be made under section 16(7) of the Act of 1969 on an appeal under that section by statutory undertakers " ;

(*b*) after paragraph 1(1) there shall be inserted the following sub-paragraph:—

" (1A) An application for planning permission which is deemed to have been made by virtue of section 19(5) of the Act of 1969 shall be determined by the Secretary of State and the appropriate Minister."

The Building (Scotland) Act 1959 (*c.* 24)

37. Section 17(2) (restriction on demolition requirement or on requirement as to operations to be carried out) shall be amended as follows:—

(*a*) for paragraph (*b*) there shall be substituted the following paragraph—

" (*b*) subject to a building preservation notice under section 48 of the Town and Country Planning (Scotland) Act 1969 " ;

(*b*) in paragraph (*c*) for the words " said Act of 1947 " there shall be substituted the words " Town and Country Planning (Scotland) Act 1947 " ;

(*c*) after the words " Act of 1931 " there shall be inserted the words " the said Act of 1969 ".

Town and Country Planning (Scotland) Act 1959 (*c.* 70)

38. In section 31 (proceedings for challenging validity of certain orders and decisions), the following amendments shall be made :—

(*a*) at the end of subsection (3) there shall be added the following paragraphs—

" (*f*) any order under section 22 of the Town and Country Planning (Scotland) Act 1945 (extinguishment of right of way) ;

1945 c. 33.

(*g*) any order under section 26 of the said Act of 1945 (relief for statutory undertakers) ;

(*h*) any order under section 46 of the Act of 1947 (stopping up and diversion of highways) ;

(*i*) any order under section 90 of the Act of 1969 (stopping up and diversion of highways); SCH. 9

(*j*) any order under section 91 of the Act of 1969 (conversion of highway into footpath or bridleway);

(*k*) any order under section 93 or 94 of the Act of 1969 (stopping up and extinguishment of footpaths etc.);

(*l*) any order under Part II of Schedule 4 to the Act of 1969 (revocation or modification of listed building consent).";

(*b*) at the end of subsection (4) there shall be added the following paragraphs—

"(*f*) any decision of the Secretary of State on an appeal to him under section 14 of the Civic Amenities Act 1967;" 1967 c. 69.

(*g*) any decision of the Secretary of State on an appeal to him under section 16(1)(*a*), (*f*) or (*g*) of the Act of 1969 against any enforcement notice;

(*h*) any decision of the Secretary of State on an application for an established use certificate referred to him under section 19(1) of the Act of 1969;

(*i*) any decision of the Secretary of State on an appeal under section 19(2) of the Act of 1969;

(*j*) any decision of the Secretary of State to confirm a purchase notice under section 42 of the Act of 1969 or not to confirm such a notice (including any decision not to confirm such a notice in respect of part of the land to which it relates, and including any decision to grant any permission, or give any direction, in lieu of confirming such a notice either wholly or in part);

(*k*) any decision of the Secretary of State to confirm a completion notice under section 69 of the Act of 1969;

(*l*) any decision of the Secretary of State on an application referred to him under paragraph 3 of Schedule 4 to the Act of 1969, being an application for listed building consent for any works;

(*m*) any decision of the Secretary of State on an appeal to him under paragraph 6 or Part IV of that Schedule;

(*n*) any decision of the Secretary of State under paragraph 17(5)(*a*) of that Schedule to grant listed building consent for any works or under paragraph 17(5)(*b*) of that Schedule to grant planning permission in respect of any works.";

(*c*) in subsection (5)(*b*), after the words "Act of 1954" there shall be inserted the words "of the Act of 1969".

39. In section 35(1)(*b*) (certain planning applications not to be determined before end of a specified period), for the words from "appearing from the evidence" onwards there shall be substituted the words "of the application".

SCH. 9

40. In section 36(1) (application for planning permission to be accompanied by certificate that applicant is proprietor or lessee of the land etc.)—

(*a*) in paragraph (*c*), for the words " and that " to the end of the paragraph there shall be substituted the words " that he has taken such steps as are reasonably open to him (specifying them) to ascertain the names and addresses of the remainder of those persons and that he has been unable to do so " ; and

(*b*) in paragraph (*d*), for the words " and that " to the end of the paragraph there shall be substituted the words " that he has taken such steps as are reasonably open to him (specifying them) to ascertain the names and addresses of the persons mentioned in paragraph (*b*) of this subsection and that he has been unable to do so ".

The Control of Office and Industrial Development Act 1965 (*c*. 33)

41. In section 17 (application to Scotland), after the words " Act of 1962 " there shall be inserted the words " or of the Town and Country Planning Act 1968 ".

1968 c. 72.

The Industrial Development Act 1966 (*c*. 34)

42. In section 24 (provisions as to conditions of industrial development certificates), in subsection (9)(*b*), for the words after the word " reference " where first occurring there shall be substituted the words " in subsection (3) to section 16 of the Town and Country Planning Act 1968 there shall be substituted a reference to section 16 of the Town and Country Planning (Scotland) Act 1969 ".

The Housing (*Scotland*) *Act* 1966 (*c*. 49)

43. In section 18 (provisions as to houses subject to building preservation orders etc.), in subsection (1), for paragraphs (*a*) and (*b*) there shall be substituted the following paragraphs—

" (*a*) in relation to which a building preservation notice served under section 48 of the Town and Country Planning (Scotland) Act 1969 is in force, or

(*b*) which is a listed building within the meaning of Part V of that Act ",

and, in subsection (2), for paragraphs (*a*) and (*b*) there shall be substituted the following paragraphs—

" (*a*) subject to a building preservation notice served under the said section 48, or

(*b*) a listed building within the meaning of the said Part V."

The Local Government (*Scotland*) *Act* 1966 (*c*. 51)

44. In section 25(3)(*c*) (exemption from rating of unoccupied property), for the words from " of a building " to " of that Act " there shall be substituted the words " of a building preservation

notice as defined by section 48 of the Town and Country Planning (Scotland) Act 1969 or are included in a list compiled or approved under section 28 of the Town and Country Planning (Scotland) Act 1947 ". SCH. 9 1947 c. 53.

The Land Commission Act 1967 (*c*. 1)

45. In section 6(3) (conditions precedent to the compulsory purchase of land by the Land Commission), the reference in paragraph (*b*) to the current development plan shall be construed as a reference to a local plan for the time being applicable to the district and any alterations thereto (including a plan or alterations made available for inspection in pursuance of section 7(2) of this Act, but not yet in force) and the authority's resolutions of adoption or, as the case may be, the Secretary of State's notices of approval or making of the plan or alterations.

The Civic Amenities Act 1967 (*c*. 69)

46. In section 1 (preservation of character of areas of special architectural or historic interest), at the end of subsection (5)(*b*) there shall be added the words " or the Scottish Planning Act of 1969 ".

47. In section 3 (acts causing or likely to result in damage to listed buildings), for subsection (4) there shall be substituted the following subsection—

" (4) In the application of this section to Scotland—

(*a*) in subsection (1), for the references to section 41(1) of the Planning Act of 1968 and section 32 of the Planning Act there shall be substituted respectively references to section 41(1) of the Scottish Planning Act of 1969 and section 28(1) of the Scottish Planning Act;

(*b*) in subsection (2), for the references to the Planning Act and to Part V of the Planning Act of 1968 there shall be substituted respectively references to the Scottish Planning Act and Part V of the Scottish Planning Act of 1969."

48. In section 6 (works to preserve listed buildings etc.), in subsection (2), for the words from " the proviso " to the end there shall be substituted the words " subsection (2) of section 48 of the Scottish Planning Act of 1969 ".

49. In section 8 (management of buildings acquired under section 38 of the Scottish Planning Act), in subsection (3)(*b*), for the words after the word " references " where first occurring there shall be substituted the words " to section 71(1)(*b*) of the Planning Act, sections 50(1) and 50(2) of the Planning Act of 1968 there shall be substituted respectively references to section 38(5) of the Scottish Planning Act, sections 50(1) and 50(2) of the Scottish Planning Act of 1969 ".

Sch. 9

50. In section 14 (default powers and appeals relating to notices in connection with tree preservation orders), for paragraph (*b*) of subsection (5) there shall be substituted the following paragraph—

"(*b*) in subsection (3), for the words from 'section 16(2)' onwards there shall be substituted the words 'section 16(2), (3) and (4)(*a*) of the Town and Country Planning (Scotland) Act 1969 and so much of section 16(5) of that Act as enables the Secretary of State to give directions shall apply in relation to any such appeal as they apply in relation to an appeal against an enforcement notice'".

51. In section 16 (power of local planning authority to make tree preservation order with immediate effect)—

(*a*) in subsection (1), the words "by the Minister" shall be omitted; and

(*b*) for subsections (2) and (3) there shall be substituted the following subsections:—

"(2) Notwithstanding section 26(4) of the Scottish Planning Act, an order which contains such a direction shall take effect provisionally on such date as may be specified therein and shall continue in force by virtue of this section until—

(*a*) the expiration of a period of six months beginning with the date on which the order was made; or

(*b*) the date on which the order is confirmed or, in the case of an order which can be confirmed only by the Minister, on which he notifies the authority who made the order that he does not propose to confirm it;

whichever first occurs.

(3) Provision shall be made by regulations under the Scottish Planning Act for securing—

(*a*) that the notices to be given of the making of a tree preservation order containing a direction under this section shall include a statement of the effect of the direction; and

(*b*) that where the Minister, in the case of an order which can be confirmed only by him, within the period of six months referred to in subsection (2) above, notifies the authority that he does not propose to confirm the order, copies of that notice shall be served on the owners, occupiers and lessees of the land to which the order related.".

52. In section 30 (interpretation), in subsection (1), after the definition of "the Scottish Planning Act" there shall be inserted the following—

"the Scottish Planning Act of 1969" means the Town and Country Planning (Scotland) Act 1969".

SCHEDULE 10

Section 106.

Transitional Provisions and Savings

Development plans

1. Until the repeal of the enactments in Part II of the Act of 1947 mentioned in Schedule 11 to this Act as respects any area (whether the whole or part of the district of a local planning authority), proposals for any alterations or additions to a development plan in force in the area shall not without the approval of the Secretary of State be submitted to him under section 4 of that Act.

2. On the repeal of the said enactments in the said Part II as respects any area, the development plan which was in force in the area immediately before the repeal takes effect (hereafter in this Schedule referred to as " the old development plan ") shall, subject to the following provisions of this Schedule, continue in force as respects that area and be treated for the purposes of the Act of 1947, this Act, any other enactment relating to town and country planning, the Land Compensation (Scotland) Act 1963 and the Land Commission Act 1967 as being comprised in, or as being, the development plan therefor.

1963 c. 51.
1967 c. 1.

3. Subject to the following provisions of this Schedule, where by virtue of paragraph 2 above the old development plan for any area is treated as being comprised in a development plan for that area and there is a conflict between any of its provisions and those of the structure plan for that area, the provisions of the structure plan shall be taken to prevail for the purposes of Parts II and III of the Act of 1947, Part II of the Act of 1954, Part IV of the Act of 1959, Parts II and VI of this Act and Schedule 4 to this Act.

4. Where a structure plan is in force in any area, but no local plan is in force in that area, a street authorisation map prepared in pursuance of the Town and Country Planning (Development Plans) (Scotland) Regulations 1966 for that area shall—

S.I. 1966/1385.

(*a*) if in force immediately before the structure plan comes into force, be treated for the purposes of this Act as having been adopted as a local plan by the local planning authority;

(*b*) if immediately before the structure plan comes into force it was under consideration by the Secretary of State, be treated for those purposes as having been so adopted on being approved by the Secretary of State.

5. Where a structure plan is in force in any area, but no local plan is in force in that area, then, for any of the purposes of the Land Compensation (Scotland) Act 1963—

(*a*) the development plan or current development plan shall, as respects that area, be taken as being whichever of the following plans gives rise to those assumptions as to the grant of planning permission which are more favourable to the owner of the land acquired, for that purpose, that is to say, the structure plan, so far as applicable to the

SCH. 10

area, and any alterations thereto, together with the Secretary of State's notice of approval of the plan and alterations, or the old development plan ;

(*b*) land situated in an area defined in the current development plan as an area of comprehensive development shall be taken to be situated in whichever of the following areas leads to such assumptions as aforesaid, that is to say, any area wholly or partly within the area first-mentioned in this paragraph selected by the structure plan as an action area or the area so defined in the old development plan.

6. Subject to paragraph 7 below, the Secretary of State may by order wholly or partly revoke a development plan continued in force under this Schedule whether in its application to the whole of the district of a local planning authority or in its application to part of that district and make such consequential amendments to the plan as appear to him to be necessary or expedient.

7. Before making an order with respect to a development plan under paragraph 6 above, the Secretary of State shall consult with the local planning authority for the district to which the plan relates.

8. Any reference in paragraphs 1 and 2 above to the repeal of Part II of the Act of 1947 shall, in a case where that repeal is brought by an order under section 104 of this Act into operation on different days, be construed as a reference to a repeal of such of the provisions of the said Part II as may be specified in the order.

Enforcement of planning control

9.—(1) References in this Act to an enforcement notice shall be construed as not including references to an enforcement notice served, before the commencement of Part II of this Act, under section 21 of the Act of 1947.

(2) In relation to an enforcement notice so served, the provisions of the Act of 1947, and of any other Act passed before this Act, shall continue to apply as if this Act had not been passed.

(3) Nothing in this paragraph shall prevent the withdrawal, after the said commencement, of an enforcement notice so served or the service thereafter of an enforcement notice under Part II of this Act.

1967 c. 69. 10. The amendment of section 14 of the Civic Amenities Act 1967 which is made by paragraph 50 of Schedule 9 to this Act shall not have effect in relation to a notice served under that section before the commencement of Part II of this Act.

Acquisition of land

11. Sections 28 to 30 of this Act shall not apply to any land the acquisition of which was, immediately before the commencement of those sections, authorised by a compulsory purchase order made by a local authority or statutory undertakers or by a Minister, or

was then proposed to be authorised by such an order which had not been confirmed by a Minister or, as the case may be, had been prepared in draft by a Minister, but with respect to which a notice had then been published in accordance with paragraph 3(*a*) of Schedule 1 to the Acquisition Act 1947.

12. Section 31 of this Act shall not apply to the compulsory acquisition of land with respect to which a compulsory purchase order was in force before the commencement of that section.

13. In relation to a notice served under section 38 of the Act of 1959 before the commencement of sections 34 and 35 of this Act, and to any hereditament or agricultural unit which is the subject of the notice, Part IV of and Schedule 5 to the Act of 1959 shall, after that commencement, have effect without any of the amendments made by Part IV of this Act.

14.—(1) Notwithstanding any amendment by this Act of sections 38 to 42 of, and Schedule 5 to, the Act of 1959, the description of land contained in section 38(1)(*b*) of that Act (land allocated by a development plan for the purposes of a government department, etc.) shall continue as one of the specified descriptions for the purposes of those sections and that Schedule in their application to any district to which this paragraph applies.

(2) This paragraph applies to any area for which no local plan is in force under Part I of this Act—

(*a*) allocating any land in the area for the purposes of such functions as are mentioned in section 34(1)(*a*) of this Act; or

(*b*) defining any land in the area as the site of proposed development for the purposes of any such functions.

(3) To the extent that section 38(1)(*b*) of the Act of 1959 survives by virtue of this paragraph, and for so long as it does so, the amendment by this Act of the definition of " the relevant date " in section 42(5) of that Act shall be treated as not displacing the reference in that definition to section 38(1)(*b*).

15. The validity of a compulsory purchase order made under section 34, 35 or 38 of the Act of 1947 shall not be affected by the repeal of that section; and a compulsory purchase order made (but not confirmed), or made in draft, before the repeal of that section took effect may be confirmed or made thereunder as if this Act had not been passed.

Buildings of architectural or historic interest

16.—(1) Where, before the commencement of Part V of this Act, consent under a building preservation order has been given, either by the local planning authority or by the Secretary of State on appeal, for the execution of any works, the consent shall operate in respect of those works as listed building consent, subject to the same

SCH. 10 conditions (if any) as were attached to the consent under the building preservation order.

(2) In the case of demolition works for which consent has been given under a building preservation order compliance with section 40(4)(*b*) of this Act shall not be required.

17. Where, before the commencement of Part V of this Act an application has been made for consent under a building preservation order for any works, any proceedings pending at the commencement of Part V of this Act and arising out of the application (including any appeal) may be continued and disposed of under and in accordance with the provisions of Part V of this Act corresponding to provisions of the building preservation order as to the making of applications, the decision of the local planning authority thereon and appeals to the Secretary of State against the said decision.

18. The repeal by this Act of section 27 of the Act of 1947 shall not prevent a local planning authority from taking such proceedings as could have been taken to enforce any building preservation order made under that section and for securing the restoration of a building to its former state as could have been taken but for the repeal ; and in relation to any such proceedings the provisions of the order and of any provisions of the Act of 1947 incorporated therewith, shall continue to have the same effect as if this Act had not been passed.

The National Coal Board

19. The provisions of the Act of 1947 applied by regulations under section 86(1) of that Act in relation to the National Coal Board and land of that Board shall, until the coming into operation of the first regulations made under that subsection after the commencement of sections 70 to 72 of this Act, continue to have effect as so applied as if those sections had not been enacted.

Section 107.

SCHEDULE 11

ENACTMENTS REPEALED

Chapter	Short Title	Extent of Repeal
8 & 9 Geo. 6. c. 33.	The Town and Country Planning (Scotland) Act 1945.	Section 24(7), (subject to the exception in section 71(3) of this Act). Schedule 6.
10 & 11 Geo. 6. c. 53.	The Town and Country Planning (Scotland) Act 1947.	Sections 3 to 9. In the proviso to section 10(5), sub-paragraph (i). In section 14(1), the proviso. In section 16(5), in the proviso, the words from " or begun " to the end. In section 16(6), the words from " or was begun " to the end.

Chapter	Short Title	Extent of Repeal
10 & 11 Geo. 6. c. 53—*cont.*	The Town and Country Planning (Scotland) Act 1947—*cont.*	In section 17(3), the words " the end of the period specified in subsection (1A) of this section " and the words " whichever is the earlier ". Section 21. In section 23(1), the words " with the approval of the Secretary of State ". In section 26(5), the words from " and such regulations " to " to which it relates ". Section 27. Section 28(5) to (8). In section 29(4), the words from " either " to " plans or ". In section 30(2), the proviso. Sections 33 to 36. In section 37(1), the words in parenthesis. Section 38, except subsection (5). In section 39(1), the words from " specified " to " a purpose ". In section 42, subsection (3), in subsection (4), the words in parenthesis, in the proviso to that subsection the words from " or the land " to " subsection " and paragraph (*b*), (subject to the exception in section 71(3) of this Act), and subsection (6). Section 72(9). In section 83, in subsection (2)(*a*), the words from " and may " to " acquisition ", and subsection (3)(*b*). In section 84, in paragraph (*a*) of the proviso, the words " the Commissioners of Crown Lands or by ". Section 96(2)(*e*). In section 107(4), the words " the foregoing provisions of ". In section 113(1), the definitions of " building preservation order " and " development plan ". In Schedule 5, paragraphs 1(2), 2(1)(*a*), 3(2) and 4(2), (subject to the exception in section 71(3) of this Act). In Schedule 6, paragraph 7. In Schedule 10, paragraph 17.

SCH. 11

Chapter	Short Title	Extent of Repeal
1 & 2 Eliz. 2. c. 36.	The Post Office Act 1953.	In section 47(5), the words " or the Town and Country Planning (Scotland) Act 1947 ". In Schedule 1, paragraphs 4 to 7.
5 & 6 Eliz. 2. c. 48.	The Electricity Act 1957.	Section 36.
6 & 7 Eliz. 2. c. 30.	The Land Powers (Defence) Act 1958.	Section 8(4).
7 & 8 Eliz. 2. c. 70.	The Town and Country Planning (Scotland) Act 1959.	In section 31, subsection (3)(*d*), in subsection (4)(*d*), the words " or section twenty-seven ", in subsection (5), in the proviso, the words " or section twenty-seven ", in subsection (9), the proviso and, in subsection (10), the words from " do not include " to " (with that exception) ". Section 38(1)(*a*) and (*b*). In section 42, in subsection (5), in the definition of " the relevant date ", the word " designated " wherever it occurs, and subsection (6). In Schedule 5, paragraphs 6, 7, 11(3) and 12(3).
9 & 10 Eliz. 2. c. 15.	The Post Office Act 1961.	In the Schedule, so much as amends paragraphs 5, 6 and 7 of Schedule 1 to the Post Office Act 1953.
1963 c. 51.	The Land Compensation (Scotland) Act 1963.	In section 16, the word " designation ". In section 45(1), the words " by the Secretary of State ".
1966 c. 49.	The Housing (Scotland) Act 1966.	Section 176.
1967 c. 1.	The Land Commission Act 1967.	Section 6(3)(*c*).
1967 c. 69.	The Civic Amenities Act 1967.	In section 1(6), paragraphs (*b*) and (*c*). Section 2. In section 6(2), the words " in respect of which a building preservation order is in force or ". Sections 7, 9 and 10. In section 16(1), the words " by the Minister ".
1968 c. 16.	The New Towns (Scotland) Act 1968.	Sections 15 to 17. Schedule 7.
1968 c. 72.	The Town and Country Planning Act 1968.	In Schedule 9, paragraphs 66(*b*) and 71(*c*).

ELIZABETH II

1969 CHAPTER 31

An Act to apply a sum out of the Consolidated Fund to the service of the year ending on 31st March 1970, and to appropriate the supplies granted in this Session of Parliament. [25th July 1969]

Most Gracious Sovereign,

WE, Your Majesty's most dutiful and loyal subjects the Commons of the United Kingdom in Parliament assembled, towards making good the supply which we have cheerfully granted to Your Majesty in this Session of Parliament, have resolved to grant unto Your Majesty the sum hereinafter mentioned; and do therefore most humbly beseech Your Majesty that it may be enacted, and be it enacted by the Queen's most Excellent Majesty, by and with the advice and consent of the Lords Spiritual and Temporal, and Commons, in this present Parliament assembled, and by the authority of the same, as follows:—

Grant out of Consolidated Fund

Issue out of the Consolidated Fund for the year ending 31st March 1970.

1. The Treasury may issue out of the Consolidated Fund of the United Kingdom and apply towards making good the supply granted to Her Majesty for the service of the year ending on 31st March 1970 the sum of £7,294,158,700.

Appropriation of Grants

Appropriation of sums voted for supply services.

2. All sums granted by this Act and the other Acts mentioned in Schedule (A) annexed to this Act out of the said Consolidated Fund towards making good the supply granted to Her Majesty amounting, as appears by the said schedule, in the aggregate, to the sum of £12,168,395,999 12s 4d are appropriated, and shall be deemed to have been appropriated as from the date of the passing of the Acts mentioned in the said Schedule (A), for the services and purposes expressed in Schedule (B) annexed hereto.

The abstract of schedules and schedules annexed hereto, with the notes (if any) to such schedules, shall be deemed to be part of this Act in the same manner as if they had been contained in the body thereof.

In addition to the said sums granted out of the Consolidated Fund, there may be applied out of any money directed, under section 2 of the Public Accounts and Charges Act 1891, to be applied as appropriations in aid of the grants for the services and purposes specified in Schedule (B) annexed hereto the sums respectively set forth in the last column of the said Schedule.

1891 c. 24.

Sanction of Treasury for temporary application of surpluses on certain votes for Navy, Army and Air Services, to meet deficiencies on other votes for the same service.

3.—(1) So long as the aggregate expenditure on Navy, Army and Air Services respectively is not made to exceed the aggregate sums appropriated by this Act for those services respectively, any surplus arising on any vote for those services either by an excess of the sum realised on account of appropriations in aid of the vote over the sum which may be applied under this Act as appropriations in aid of that vote, or by saving of expenditure on that vote, may, with the sanction of the Treasury, be temporarily applied either in making up any deficiency in the sums realised on account of appropriations in aid of any other vote in the same department, or in defraying expenditure in the same department which is not provided for in the sums appropriated to the service of the department by this Act, and which it may be detrimental to the public service to postpone until provision can be made for it by Parliament in the usual course.

(2) A statement showing all cases in which the sanction of the Treasury has been given to the temporary application of a surplus under this section, and showing the circumstances under which the sanction of the Treasury has been given, shall be laid before the House of Commons with the appropriation accounts of the Navy, Army and Air Services for the year, in order that any temporary application of any surplus sanctioned by the Treasury under this section may be submitted for the sanction of Parliament.

Sanction for application of surpluses on certain Navy, Army and Air Votes for 1967–68.
1967 c. 59.
1968 c. 43.

4. Whereas under the powers given for the purpose by the Appropriation Acts 1967 and 1968 surpluses arising on certain votes for Navy, Army and Air Services have been applied towards making good deficits on those services respectively as shown in the statements set out in Schedule (C) to this Act:

It is enacted that the application of those surpluses as shown in the said statements is hereby sanctioned.

Short title.

5. This Act may be cited as the Appropriation Act 1969.

ABSTRACT

OF

SCHEDULES (A) and (B) to which this Act refers

SCHEDULE (A)

Section 2.

Grants out of the Consolidated Fund ... £12,168,395,999 12s. 4d.

SCHEDULE (B)—APPROPRIATION OF GRANTS

Section 2.

	Supply Grants			Appropriations in Aid		
	£	s.	d.	£	s.	d.
1967–68 and 1968–69						
Part 1. Civil (Excesses), 1967–68	2,457,499	12	4	1,079,493	3	8
Part 2. Defence (Central) (Supplementary), 1968–69 -	1,000	0	0	1,328,000	0	0
Part 3. Defence (Navy) (Supplementary), 1968–69 -	27,700,000	0	0	750,000	0	0
Part 4. Defence (Air) (Supplementary), 1968–69 - -	9,501,000	0	0	4,970,000	0	0
Part 5. Civil Departments (Supplementary), 1968–69 -	335,350,000	0	0	32,757,300	0	0
	375,009,499	12	4	40,884,793	3	8

SCHEDULE (B).—APPROPRIATION OF GRANTS—*continued*

	Supply Grants			Appropriations in Aid		
	£	s.	d.	£	s.	d.
1969–70						
Part 6. Defence (Central) -	33,667,000	0	0	53,951,000	0	0
Part 7. Defence (Navy) -	645,624,000	0	0	40,173,000	0	0
Part 8. Defence (Army) -	598,000,000	0	0	63,300,000	0	0
Defence (Royal Ordnance Factories) - - - -	2,550,000	0	0	46,200,000	0	0
Defence (Army) Purchasing (Repayment) Services - -	1,000	0	0	—		
Part 9. Defence (Air) - -	592,000,000	0	0	46,235,000	0	0
TOTAL, DEFENCE - -£	1,871,842,000	0	0	249,859,000	0	0
Part 10. Civil, Class I - -	199,795,000	0	0	7,418,300	0	0
Part 11. Civil, Class II - -	296,536,500	0	0	8,787,927	0	0
Part 12. Civil, Class III -	256,454,000	0	0	26,802,000	0	0
Part 13. Civil, Class IV -	2,803,482,000	0	0	286,308,000	0	0
Part 14. Civil, Class V -	419,115,000	0	0	7,842,000	0	0
Part 15. Civil, Class VI -	4,962,266,000	0	0	334,246,570	0	0
Part 16. Civil, Class VII -	449,218,000	0	0	91,832,000	0	0
Part 17. Civil, Class VIII -	17,121,000	0	0	248,200	0	0
Part 18. Civil, Class IX -	471,289,000	0	0	91,599,040	0	0
Part 19. Civil, Class X -	17,085,000	0	0	84,594,300	0	0
Part 20. Civil, Class XI -	29,183,000	0	0	5,279,590	0	0
TOTAL, CIVIL - -£	9,921,544,500	0	0	944,957,927	0	0
GRAND TOTAL - -£	12,168,395,999	12	4	1,235,701,720	3	8

SCHEDULE (A)

GRANTS OUT OF THE CONSOLIDATED FUND

	£	s.	d.
For the service of the year ended 31st March 1968—			
Under Act 1969 c. 9	2,457,499	12	4
For the service of the year ended 31st March 1969—			
Under Act 1969 c. 3	187,493,000	0	0
Under Act 1969 c. 9	185,059,000	0	0
For the service of the year ending on 31st March 1970—			
Under Act 1969 c. 9	4,499,227,800	0	0
Under this Act	7,294,158,700	0	0
TOTAL	12,168,395,999	12	4

Civil (Excesses), 1967–68.

SCHEDULE (B).—PART 1

CIVIL (EXCESSES), 1967–68

SUMS granted, and sums which may be applied as appropriations in aid in addition thereto, to make good excesses on certain grants for Civil Services for the year ended 31st March 1968, viz.:—

Vote		Supply Grants			Appropriations in Aid		
		£	s.	d.	£	s.	d.
	CLASS IV						
1	MINISTRY OF TRANSPORT -	147,648	6	7	—		
5	ROADS, &C., SCOTLAND - -	1,091,695	19	6	16,127	18	5
18	MINISTRY OF TECHNOLOGY -	435,842	9	2	42,259	14	2
	CLASS VI						
2	SCOTTISH DEVELOPMENT DEPARTMENT - - - -	10	0	0	—		
20	NON-CONTRIBUTORY BENEFITS -	712,872	7	11	1,015,512	11	7
	CLASS VII						
5	UNIVERSITIES AND COLLEGES, &C., GREAT BRITAIN - -	10	0	0	—		
	CLASS IX						
8	WORKS AND BUILDINGS FOR ROYAL ORDNANCE FACTORIES	34,619	4	5	—		
11	ROYAL PALACES - - -	12,868	18	11	—		
12	ROYAL PARKS AND PLEASURE GARDENS - - - -	21,932	5	10	5,592	19	6
	TOTAL, CIVIL (EXCESSES), 1967–68 £	2,457,499	12	4	1,079,493	3	8

SCHEDULE (B).—PART 2

Defence (Central) (Supplementary), 1968–69.

DEFENCE (CENTRAL) (SUPPLEMENTARY), 1968–69

SUPPLEMENTARY SUM granted, and sum which may be applied as appropriations in aid in addition thereto, to defray the charge of Defence (Central) for the year ended 31st March 1969, viz.:—

	Supply Grant	Appropriations in Aid
	£	£
For the salaries and expenses of the Central Defence Staffs, the Defence Secretariat and the Central Defence Scientific Staff and certain Joint Service Establishments; purchases of defence equipment for sale abroad; expenses in connection with sales of defence equipment and International Defence Organisations, including international subscriptions; and sundry other services including certain grants in aid -	1,000	1,328,000

Defence (Navy) (Supplementary), 1968–69.

SCHEDULE (B).—PART 3

DEFENCE (NAVY) (SUPPLEMENTARY), 1968–69

SCHEDULE OF SUPPLEMENTARY SUMS granted, and of the sums which may be applied as appropriations in aid in addition thereto, to meet expenditure beyond the sum already provided in the grants for Navy Services for the year ended 31st March 1969, viz.:—

	Supply Grants	Appropriations in Aid
Vote	£	£
1. Pay, &c., of the Royal Navy and Royal Marines - - - - - - -	8,050,000	*−*100,000*
3. Navy Department Headquarters - -	500,000	—
4. Research and Development and Other Scientific Services - - - -	1,700,000	100,000
5. Medical Services, Education and Civilians on Fleet Services - - - - -	1,050,000	50,000
6. Naval Stores, Armament, Victualling and Other Material Supply Services - -	2,750,000	450,000
7. H.M. Ships, Aircraft and Weapons, New Construction and Repairs - - -	10,650,000	250,000
8. Miscellaneous Effective Services - -	1,100,000	—
9. Non-Effective Services - - - -	1,900,000	—
TOTAL, DEFENCE (NAVY) (SUPPLEMENTARY), 1968–69 - - - -£	27,700,000	750,000

* Deficit.

SCHEDULE (B).—PART 4

Defence (Air) (Supplementary), 1968–69.

DEFENCE (AIR) (SUPPLEMENTARY), 1968–69

SCHEDULE OF SUPPLEMENTARY SUMS granted, and of the sums which may be applied as appropriations in aid in addition thereto, to meet expenditure beyond the sum already provided in the grants for Air Services for the year ended on 31st March 1969, viz.:—

Vote	Supply Grants	Appropriations in Aid
	£	£
1. Pay, &c., of the Air Force	7,190,000	*—*90,000*
2. Reserve and Auxiliary Services	*Cr.* 85,000	*—*22,000*
3. Air Force Department Headquarters	300,000	*—*3,000*
4. Civilians at Outstations and the Meteorological Office	3,030,000	285,000
5. Movements	1,260,000	*—*480,000*
6. Supplies	3,900,000	490,000
7. Aircraft and Stores	*Cr.* 8,100,000	4,800,000
8. Miscellaneous Effective Services	310,000	*—*10,000*
9. Non-effective Services	1,696,000	—
TOTAL, DEFENCE (AIR) (SUPPLEMENTARY), 1968–69 £	9,501,000	4,970,000

* Deficit.

Civil Departments (Supplementary), 1968–69.

SCHEDULE (B).—PART 5

CIVIL DEPARTMENTS (SUPPLEMENTARY), 1968–69

SCHEDULE OF SUPPLEMENTARY SUMS granted, and of the sums which may be applied as appropriations in aid in addition thereto, to defray the charges for the Services herein particularly mentioned for the year ended 31st March 1969, viz.:—

	Supply Grants	Appropriations in Aid
	£	£
CLASS I		
Vote		
1. For the salaries and expenses of the House of Lords	23,000	3,000
2. For the salaries and expenses of the House of Commons, including certain grants in aid	82,000	3,000
3. For the salaries and expenses of the Department of Her Majesty's Treasury and subordinate departments and of the First Secretary of State, the Lord Privy Seal, the Chancellor of the Duchy of Lancaster, and the Minister without Portfolio	301,000	**−43,500*
3A. For the salaries and expenses of the Cabinet Office, of the Paymaster General and private office staff and of the co-ordinating staff of the Secretary of State for Social Services	27,000	458,000
4. For the salaries and expenses of the Department of Her Majesty's Secretary of State for Economic Affairs, the Chancellor of the Duchy of Lancaster and of the National Economic Development Council, and for certain grants in aid	1,000	—
7. For the salaries and expenses of the Customs and Excise Department, including a subscription to an international organisation	2,454,000	348,000
8. For the salaries and expenses of the Inland Revenue Department	8,812,000	259,000
9. For transitional relief under the Finance Act 1965 for companies with an overseas source of trading income	10,000,000	—

* Deficit

SCHEDULE (B).—PART 5—*continued*

Civil Departments (Supplementary), 1968–69.

	Supply Grants	Appropriations in Aid
	£	£
CLASS I—*continued*		
Vote		
10. For the salaries and expenses of the Department of the Comptroller and Auditor General - - - - -	87,000	24,000
11. For the salaries and expenses of the Civil Service Department and the Civil Service Commission, of the Office of the Parliamentary Counsel, and sundry other services including a subscription to an international organisation and grants in aid - - - - -	391,000	1,116,550
12. For the salaries and expenses of Royal Commissions, committees, special enquiries, &c., and for a grant in aid -	96,000	—
CLASS II		
1. For the salaries and expenses of the offices of Her Majesty's Secretary of State for Foreign Affairs, Her Majesty's Secretary of State for Commonwealth Affairs, Her Majesty's Secretary of State for Foreign and Commonwealth Affairs and the Minister without Portfolio; Her Majesty's Diplomatic Service; and sundry other services connected therewith - - - - - - -	1,676,000	*–*22,000*
2. For expenditure by the Foreign Office and Foreign and Commonwealth Office on sundry foreign grants and services, including subscriptions, &c. to certain international organisations and certain grants in aid - - - - -	1,648,000	102,000
4. For expenditure by the Commonwealth Office and Foreign and Commonwealth Office on sundry Commonwealth grants and services, including subscriptions to certain international organisations and certain grants in aid - - - -	6,958,000	719,000
5. For the salaries and expenses of the Ministry of Overseas Development, including refund of selective employment tax to the Commonwealth Development Corporation - - - - -	199,000	—

* Deficit.

Civil Departments (Supplementary), 1968–69.

SCHEDULE (B).—Part 5—*continued*

	Supply Grants	Appropriations in Aid
	£	£
Class II—*continued*		
Vote		
6. For expenditure by the Ministry of Overseas Development on grants and services connected with multilateral overseas aid, including subscriptions to certain international organisations and certain grants in aid - - - - - - -	11,315,000	—
7. For expenditure by the Ministry of Overseas Development on grants and services connected with bilateral overseas aid, including certain grants in aid -	8,173,000	63,000
8. For expenditure by the Ministry of Overseas Development on sundry services connected with overseas aid, including certain grants in aid - -	750,000	—
10. For a grant in aid of the Commonwealth War Graves Commission and certain other expenses - - - - -	9,000	—
Class III		
1. For the salaries and expenses of the office of Her Majesty's Secretary of State for the Home Department; expenses and grants in connection with certain law, fire and sundry other services; and certain grants in aid - - - -	1,345,000	*–*655,000*
2. For the salaries and expenses of the office of the Secretary of State for Scotland and of the Scottish Home and Health Department; for a grant to the Legal Aid (Scotland) Fund; for expenses in connection with fire, probation and sundry other services; and for grants in aid - - - - - - - -	313,000	5,000
5. For grants in respect of expenditure incurred by police authorities in England and Wales, expenses in connection with the police services and a subscription to an international organisation - -	3,690,000	492,000

* Deficit.

SCHEDULE (B).—PART 5—*continued*

Civil Departments (Supplementary), 1968–69.

	Supply Grants	Appropriations in Aid
	£	£
CLASS III—*continued*		
Vote		
6. For grants in respect of expenditure incurred by police authorites in Scotland, and expenses in connection with the police services - - - - -	1,047,000	**−18,000*
7. For the salaries and expenses of prison service establishments in England and Wales - - - - - - -	843,000	**−416,000*
8. For the salaries and expenses of prison service establishments in Scotland -	345,000	50,000
11. For such of the salaries and expenses of the Supreme Court of Judicature, Law Commission and Courts-Martial Appeal Court as are not charged on the Consolidated Fund ; the salaries and expenses of the Judge Advocate General and Judge Advocate of the Fleet, Pensions Appeal Tribunals, the Lands Tribunal, the Restrictive Practices Court and Council on Tribunals, and certain other expenses - - - -	465,000	**−175,000*
12. For the salaries and expenses of the County Courts - - - - - - -	403,000	202,000
14. For the salaries and expenses of the Law Officers' Department, the Department of Her Majesty's Procurator-General and Solicitor for the Affairs of Her Majesty's Treasury and the Department of the Director of Public Prosecutions; for the costs of prosecutions and other legal proceedings and of Parliamentary Agency - - - - - - -	128,000	**−6,000*
15. For the salaries and expenses of the Lord Advocate's Department, of the Courts of Law and Justice, of the Scottish Law Commission, and of the Courts, Tribunals, &c.; and for sundry services -	85,000	55,000
16. For such of the salaries and expenses of the Supreme Court of Judicature and Court of Criminal Appeal of Northern Ireland as are not charged on the Consolidated Fund; the salaries and expenses of Pensions Appeals in Northern Ireland and certain other expenses - - -	15,000	—

* Deficit.

Civil Departments (Supplementary), 1968–69.

SCHEDULE (B).—PART 5—*continued*

	Supply Grants	Appropriations in Aid
	£	£
CLASS IV		
Vote		
1. For salaries and expenses of the Ministry of Transport, and certain Tribunals and Committees - - - - -	3,330,000	**−3,015,000*
3. For services connected with inland transport, including repayments, &c., of selective employment tax to the nationalised transport undertakings; for expenditure on grants for the assistance of public passenger transport; ports, a Channel Tunnel, Governmental shipping services, and sundry other services, including subscriptions to certain international organisations - - - -	1,000	—
4. For expenditure, including grants and loans to highway, &c., authorities on the construction, improvement and maintenance of roads, &c., in England and sundry services connected therewith; for expenditure on the collection of motor vehicle duties, &c., and the registration of motor vehicles in Great Britain; for road research; and for sundry other services - - - - - -	1,000	—
5. For expenditure, including grants and loans to highway, &c., authorities, on the construction, improvement and maintenance of roads, &c., in Scotland and sundry services connected therewith; for expenditure on grants for the assistance of public passenger transport; and for sundry other transport services -	1,339,000	21,000
6. For expenditure, including grants to highway, &c., authorities on the construction, improvement and maintenance of roads, &c., in Wales and sundry services connected therewith; for expenditure on grants for the assistance of public passenger transport; and for sundry other transport services - - -	1,725,000	—

* Deficit.

SCHEDULE (B).—PART 5—*continued*

Civil Departments (Supplementary), 1968–69.

	Supply Grants	Appropriations in Aid
	£	£
CLASS IV—*continued*		
Vote		
7. For the salaries and expenses of the Department of Her Majesty's First Secretary of State and Secretary of State for Employment and Productivity, including those relating to the Employment Exchange service and the inspection of factories; for expenses, grants and loans in connection with employment, training, rehabilitation, &c.; for expenses of the National Board for Prices and Incomes, the Commission on Industrial Relations and the Industrial Court; for a subscription to the International Labour Organisation, a grant in aid and sundry other services - -	2,528,000	**–129,000*
8. For payments by the Department of Employment and Productivity to certain employers who have paid selective employment tax - - - - - -	20,000,000	—
9. For the salaries and expenses of the office of the Committee of Privy Council for Trade and subordinate departments and agencies - - - - - - -	1,528,000	**–71,000*
10. For the construction, maintenance and operation of civil aerodromes, for civil air navigational services, for loans and services connected with shipping, for contributions &c., to certain international organisations, certain repayments, &c., of selective employment tax, and for sundry other services - -	1,000	—
11. For the expenditure of the Board of Trade on the promotion of trade, exports and industrial efficiency, and on trading and other services, including loans, subscriptions to certain international organisations and grants in aid - -	19,301,000	—
12. For the promotion of local employment -	3,500,000	—
13. For the expenditure of the Board of Trade on grants for assisting investment in new business assets - - - -	93,000,000	—

* Deficit.

Civil Departments (Supplementary), 1968–69.

SCHEDULE (B).—PART 5—*continued*

	Supply Grants	Appropriations in Aid
	£	£
CLASS IV—*continued*		
Vote		
14. For the salaries and expenses of the Export Credits Guarantee Department, including a subscription to an international organisation, and for payments under guarantees given after consultation with the Export Guarantees Advisory Council	1,000	—
17. For the salaries and expenses of the Ministry of Power; for expenditure on oil storage and distribution; for assistance to the coal industry; for certain repayments, &c., of selective employment tax; for expenses in connection with the nationalisation of the Iron and Steel Industry; for payments to the Governments of Northern Ireland and the Isle of Man; and for sundry other services - - - - - - -	5,159,000	—
18. For the salaries and expenses of the Ministry of Technology, including the administration of research, development and inspection - - - - - -	3,700,000	48,000
19. For the expenditure of the Ministry of Technology on technological and industrial services, including certain subscriptions to international organisations and grants in aid - - - - -	1,000	—
20. For expenditure by the Ministry of Technology on supply services (including research, development and inspection), and in connection with the development and production of civil aircraft and associated safety equipment, on a contribution to an international organisation, loans, grants in aid, the purchase of the undertaking of a company and sundry other items - - - -	1,000	—
24. For payments towards meeting the expenses of the United Kingdom Atomic Energy Authority, for subscriptions, &c., to international projects and organisations, for the administration of a national stockpile of uranium ore, for a grant in aid, for repayment, &c., of selective employment tax to the Atomic Energy Authority Trading Fund, for the purchase of plutonium, for the purchase of shares and for associated guarantees -	1,128,000	9,143,000

SCHEDULE (B).—PART 5—*continued*

Civil Departments (Supplementary), 1968–69.

	Supply Grants	Appropriations in Aid
	£	£
CLASS V		
Vote 1. For the salaries and expenses of the Ministry of Agriculture, Fisheries and Food; of the Royal Botanic Gardens, Kew; of the White Fish Authority and Scottish Committee; of the Plant Variety Rights Office; and of the Meat and Livestock Commission - - - -	2,230,000	36,000
2. For the salaries and expenses of the Department of Agriculture and Fisheries for Scotland; for expenditure in connection with sundry agricultural, food and harbour services, the development of the Highlands and Islands and rural development elsewhere, including grants, loans and grants in aid; and for refunds of selective employment tax to agricultural, horticultural and forestry employers - - - - - -	1,000	24,000
3. For expenditure by the Ministry of Agriculture, Fisheries and Food on grants and subsidies for the encouragement of food production and the improvement of agriculture and for sundry other services - - - - - -	2,540,000	—
4. For expenditure by the Department of Agriculture and Fisheries for Scotland on grants and subsidies for the encouragement of food production and the improvement of agriculture - - -	200,000	—
7. For expenditure by the Ministry of Agriculture, Fisheries and Food in connection with sundry agricultural and food services, and rural development, including grants, loans, grants in aid, certain subscriptions to international organisations and for refunds of selective employment tax to agricultural, horticultural and forestry employers - -	2,012,000	250,000

Civil Departments (Supplementary), 1968–69.

SCHEDULE (B).—PART 5—*continued*

Vote	Supply Grants	Appropriations in Aid
	£	£
CLASS V—*continued*		
9. For grants, loans and expenses in connection with assistance to fishermen; grants and loans to the White Fish Authority; expenditure on research and development relating to fisheries and fish marketing and on the construction, improvement and maintenance of harbours and fishing facilities; subscriptions to certain international organisations and a grant in aid of the White Fish Marketing Fund - - - - -	1,690,000	—
10. In connection with Scottish fisheries and the United Kingdom herring industry for grants, loans and expenses in connection with assistance to fishermen, fishery protection, research and development relating to fisheries and fish marketing and the construction, improvement and maintenance of harbours and fishing facilities; and a grant in aid of the Herring Marketing Fund - -	250,000	—
11. For a grant in aid of the Forestry Fund -	350,000	—
CLASS VI		
1. For the salaries and expenses of the Ministry of Housing and Local Government and certain tribunals, commissions &c.; grants and expenses in connection with environmental services and civil defence; tax and rating payments including selective employment refunds; sundry other services; a subscription to an international organisation and grants in aid - - - - -	1,000	—
2. For the salaries and expenses of the Scottish Development Department and certain tribunals, &c.; for grants and payments including loans in connection with environmental services, selective employment refunds and rate rebates, assistance to the coal industry, storm damage relief and sundry other services, including a grant in aid to the Highlands and Islands Development Board and other grants in aid - - - -	6,417,000	—

SCHEDULE (B).—PART 5—*continued*

Civil Departments (Supplementary), 1968–69.

	Supply Grants	Appropriations in Aid
	£	£
CLASS VI—*continued*		
Vote		
3. For the salaries and expenses of the office of the Secretary of State for Wales and certain tribunals, &c.; grants and expenses in connection with environmental services and civil defence; expenses in connection with the investiture of the Prince of Wales; tax and rating payments including selective employment refunds; and sundry other services and grants in aid	198,000	—
8. For rate support grants, general grants and equalisation grants to local authorities in Scotland	2,402,000	—
10. For the salaries and expenses of the Ministry of Health; for the expenses of certain committees, &c.; and for sundry services	1,000	*—*3,197,000*
11. For the provision of hospital services, &c., under the National Health Service &c., in England and Wales; and other services	28,632,000	2,871,000
12. For the provision of Executive Councils' services, &c., under the National Health Service in England and Wales	11,242,000	1,106,000
13. For the provision in England and Wales of certain miscellaneous services under the National Health Service, &c.; and of certain welfare services; for a subscription to the World Health Organisation and for certain grants in aid; and for sundry services	711,000	788,000
14. For expenditure by the Department of Health and Social Security on pensions, allowances, gratuities, &c., payable under Section 6(6) of the National Health Service Act 1946, or under Regulations made under Section 67 of that Act; and certain payments to the National Insurance Fund	1,000	1,096,000

* Deficit

Civil Departments (Supplementary), 1968–69.

SCHEDULE (B).—PART 5—*continued*

	Supply Grants	Appropriations in Aid
	£	£
CLASS VI—*continued*		
Vote		
15. For the provision of services under the National Health Service in Scotland and other health and welfare services including a grant in aid - - - - -	8,426,000	199,000
17. For the salaries and expenses of Her Majesty's Secretary of State for Social Services, the Department of Health and Social Security, the Ministry of Health and the Ministry of Social Security including appellate, advisory and sundry other services, for certain selective employment refunds and a subscription to an international organisation - -	2,378,000	14,263,000
19. For payments in respect of family allowances - - - - - - - -	2,000,000	—
20. For supplementary pensions and allowances, &c. - - - - - - -	35,000,000	3,000,000
CLASS VII		
1. For the salaries and expenses of the Department of Her Majesty's Secretary of State for Education and Science; for grants and loans in connection with education, &c.; for sundry services; for a subscription to an international organisation and for certain grants in aid	1,000	—
2. For the salaries and expenses of the Scottish Education Department; for grants in connection with education &c.; for sundry services and for grants in aid -	1,000	—
3. For expenditure by the Department of Her Majesty's Secretary of State for Education and Science on superannuation allowances and gratuities, &c. in respect of teachers - - - - - - -	2,000	1,239,000
5. For the salaries and expenses of the University Grants Committee, for grants in aid and grants towards the expenses of, and for loans to, universities, colleges, the British Academy, &c. and for other services - - - - - -	1,765,000	—

SCHEDULE (B).—Part 5—*continued*

Civil Departments (Supplementary), 1968–69.

	Supply Grants	Appropriations in Aid
	£	£
Class VII—*continued*		
Vote		
8. For grants in aid of the Natural Environment Research Council including a subscription to an international organisation	199,000	—
10. For a grant in aid of the Agricultural Research Council - - - - -	311,000	—
11. For the salaries and expenses of the British Museum (Natural History), including a purchase grant in aid - -	66,000	—
Class VIII		
1. For the salaries and expenses of the British Museum, including a purchase grant in aid - - - - - - -	74,000	28,000
3. For the salaries and expenses of the Victoria and Albert Museum, including purchase grants in aid - - - -	23,000	—
4. For the salaries and expenses of the Imperial War Museum, including purchase grants in aid - - - -	1,000	4,000
5. For the salaries and expenses of the London Museum, including a purchase grant in aid - - - - - -	2,000	1,200
6. For the salaries and expenses of the National Gallery, including a purchase grant in aid - - - - - -	6,000	1,000
7. For the salaries and expenses of the National Maritime Museum, including a purchase grant in aid - - -	9,000	—
8. For the salaries and expenses of the National Portrait Gallery, including purchase grants in aid - - - -	1,000	8,000
9. For the salaries and expenses of the Tate Gallery, including purchase grants in aid	7,000	2,000
10. For the salaries and expenses of the Wallace Collection - - - -	3,000	—

Civil Departments (Supplementary), 1968–69.

SCHEDULE (B).—PART 5—*continued*

	Supply Grants	Appropriations in Aid
	£	£
CLASS VIII—*continued*		
Vote		
11. For the salaries and expenses of the Royal Scottish Museum, including purchase grants in aid, certain other grants in aid and a grant to the Scottish Council for Museums and Galleries - - -	2,000	600
12. For the salaries and expenses of the National Gallery of Scotland, the Scottish National Gallery of Modern Art and the Scottish National Portrait Gallery, including purchase grants in aid	6,000	—
13. For the salaries and expenses of the National Library of Scotland, including a purchase grant in aid - - -	5,000	—
14. For the salaries and expenses of the National Museum of Antiquities of Scotland, including a purchase grant in aid - - - - - - -	1,000	—
15. For grants in aid of the National Library of Wales and the National Museum of Wales and a grant to the Council of Museums in Wales - - - -	1,000	—
16. For grants to, and grants in aid of, certain institutions and bodies connected with the arts - - - - - -	10,000	—
CLASS IX		
1. For the salaries and expenses of the Ministry of Public Building and Works	400,000	1,300,000
2. For expenditure on public building and accommodation services, &c., in the United Kingdom, including grants in aid and sundry other services; on Ancient Monuments; and on Building Research and Development - - - - -	1,000	—
13. For the salaries and expenses of the Government Social Survey Department -	20,000	—
14. For civil superannuation and other pensions and non-recurrent payments; and for certain other expenditure in connection therewith - - - - - -	1,800,000	420,000

SCHEDULE (B).—PART 5—*continued*

Civil Departments (Supplementary), 1968–69.

	Supply Grants	Appropriations in Aid
	£	£
CLASS X		
Vote		
1. For the salaries and expenses of the Charity Commission for England and Wales	33,000	—
2. For the salaries and expenses of the Crown Estate Office	14,000	—
3. For the salaries and expenses of the Registry of Friendly Societies	9,000	—
5. For the salaries and expenses of the National Debt Office and Pensions Commutation Board	1,000	3,000
6. For the salaries and expenses of the establishment under the Public Works Loan Commission and the expenses of the Commission	1,000	2,000
7. For the salaries and expenses of the Office of the Public Trustee	1,000	60,000
8. For the salaries and expenses of the Land Registry	1,000	433,000
11. For the salaries and expenses of the Public Record Office	5,000	—
12. For the salaries and expenses of the Scottish Record Office	2,000	2,000
13. For the salaries and expenses of the Office of the Registrar General	129,000	46,000
14. For the salaries and expenses of the Department of the Registrar General of Births, Deaths and Marriages in Scotland	17,000	9,000
15. For the salaries and expenses of the Department of the Registers of Scotland	1,000	28,000
16. For the salaries and expenses, including publicity, of the National Savings Committee	55,000	—

Civil Departments (Supplementary), 1968–69.

SCHEDULE (B).—PART 5—*continued*

	Supply Grants	Appropriations in Aid
	£	£
CLASS XI		
Vote		
1. For grants to, and grants in aid of, the British Broadcasting Corporation and for payments to the Postmaster General	4,787,000	51,000
2. For the salaries and expenses of the Carlisle State Management District -	1,000	185,000
3. For the salaries and expenses of the State Management Districts in Scotland -	1,000	88,000
4. For pensions, &c., in respect of service in the former Indian and Burma Services and under the former Government of Palestine, and in respect of certain other service overseas; for supplements to certain colonial and other overseas pensions; for certain payments to the Governments of India and Pakistan in connection with pensions; and for sundry services and expenses - -	966,000	*−*108,000*
9. For certain miscellaneous expenses and grants in aid - - - - - -	2,000	*−*42,550*
TOTAL, CIVIL DEPARTMENTS (SUPPLEMENTARY), 1968–69 - - -£	335,350,000	32,757,300

* Deficit.

SCHEDULE (B).—PART 6

Defence (Central), 1969–70.

DEFENCE (CENTRAL)

SUM granted, and sum which may be applied as appropriations in aid in addition thereto, to defray the charge of Defence (Central) which will come in course of payment during the year ending on 31st March 1970, viz.:—

	Supply Grants	Appropriations in Aid
	£	£
For the salaries and expenses of the Central Defence Staffs, the Defence Secretariat and the Central Defence Scientific Staff and of certain Joint Service Establishments; purchases of defence equipment for sale abroad; expenses in connection with sales of defence equipment and International Defence Organisations, including international subscriptions; and sundry other services including certain grants in aid - - -	33,667,000	53,951,000

Defence (Navy), 1969–70.

SCHEDULE (B).—PART 7

DEFENCE (NAVY)

SCHEDULE OF SUMS granted, and of the sums which may be applied as appropriations in aid in addition thereto, to defray the charges of the Navy Services herein particularly mentioned, which will come in course of payment during the year ending on 31st March 1970, including provision for officers, seamen, juniors and Royal Marines, and members of the Women's Royal Naval Service and Queen Alexandra's Royal Naval Nursing Service, to a number not exceeding 95,500, in addition to reserve forces, viz.:—

	Supply Grants	Appropriations in Aid
	£	£
Vote		
1. For the pay, &c. of the Royal Navy and Royal Marines - - - - - -	102,882,000	3,730,000
2. For the pay and expenses of the Royal Naval Reserve, the Royal Fleet Reserve and Cadet Forces, &c. - - - -	1,584,000	2,000
3. For the salaries, wages and expenses of the Navy Department Headquarters - -	5,815,000	37,000
4. For scientific services, including a subscription to the International Hydrographic Bureau - - - - - -	37,501,000	1,146,000
5. For medical services, education and civilians on Fleet services - - -	20,025,000	567,000
6. For Naval Stores, Armament, Victualling and other Material Supply Services -	230,655,000	22,520,000
7. For the new construction, repair, &c., of H.M. Ships, Aircraft and Weapons -	202,363,000	6,772,000
8. For miscellaneous effective services, including a grant in aid - - - -	14,335,000	5,299,000
9. For non-effective services - - -	30,464,000	100,000
TOTAL, NAVY SERVICES - £	645,624,000	40,173,000

SCHEDULE (B).—PART 8

Defence (Army), 1969–70.

DEFENCE (ARMY)

SCHEDULE OF SUMS granted, and of the sums which may be applied as appropriations in aid in addition thereto, to defray the charges of the Army Services herein particularly mentioned, which will come in course of payment during the year ending on 31st March 1970, including provision for Land Forces to a number not exceeding 210,000, all ranks, in addition to the Regular Army Reserves, Territorial and Army Volunteer Reserve and Cadet Forces, viz.:—

	Supply Grants	Appropriations in Aid
	£	£
Vote		
1. For the pay, &c., of the Army - - -	187,500,000	12,740,000
2. For the Regular Army Reserves (including other ranks to a number not exceeding 50,000), Territorial and Army Volunteer Reserve (to a number not exceeding 80,000 all ranks) (including within these Reserves the Special Army Volunteer Reserve to a number not exceeding 2,400 all ranks) and Cadet Forces -	9,930,000	1,720,000
3. For salaries, wages, &c., of civilian staff of the Army Department Headquarters	4,830,000	20,000
4. For salaries, wages, &c., of civilians at outstations - - - - - - -	143,300,000	2,320,000
5. For movements - - - - - -	23,130,000	1,030,000
6. For supplies - - - - - - -	22,890,000	4,420,000
7. For stores and equipment (including stores and equipment for research, design and development projects and inspection; and certain capital and ancillary services)	128,000,000	15,000,000
8. For miscellaneous effective services, including grants in aid - - - - -	8,420,000	13,400,000
9. For non-effective services, including a grant in aid - - - - - - -	59,170,000	170,000
10. For lands and buildings and certain ancillary services - - - - -	10,830,000	12,480,000
TOTAL, ARMY SERVICES - -£	598,000,000	63,300,000

Defence (Army), 1969–70.

SCHEDULE (B).—PART 8—*continued*

	Supply Grants	Appropriations in Aid
	£	£
Defence (Royal Ordnance Factories): For operating the Royal Ordnance Factories	2,550,000	46,200,000
Defence (Army) Purchasing (Repayment) Services: For expenditure incurred by the Army Department on the supply of munitions, common-user and other articles for the Government service and on miscellaneous supply - - - - - - -	1,000	—

SCHEDULE (B).—Part 9

Defence (Air), 1969–70.

DEFENCE (AIR)

Schedule of Sums granted, and of the sums which may be applied as appropriations in aid in addition thereto, to defray the charges of the Air Services herein particularly mentioned, which will come in course of payment during the year ending on 31st March 1970, including provision for officers, airmen and airwomen for Air Force Service to a number not exceeding 118,000, all ranks, in addition to reserve and auxiliary services and cadet forces, viz.:—

	Supply Grants	Appropriations in Aid
	£	£
Vote		
1. For the pay, &c., of the Air Force	145,800,000	8,426,000
2. For Reserve and Auxiliary Services and Cadet Forces (to a number not exceeding 15,310, all ranks, for the Royal Air Force Reserve, and 435, all ranks, for the Royal Auxiliary Air Force)	690,000	281,000
3. For salaries, wages, &c., of civilian staff of the Air Force Department Headquarters	3,570,000	3,000
4. For salaries, wages, &c., of civilians at out-stations and the Meteorological Office	52,800,000	4,140,000
5. For movements	12,800,000	2,700,000
6. For supplies	37,000,000	5,860,000
7. For aircraft and stores	302,500,000	15,000,000
8. For miscellaneous effective services, including certain grants in aid and a subscription to the World Meteorological Organisation	4,840,000	9,660,000
9. For non-effective services	32,000,000	165,000
Total, Air Services £	592,000,000	46,235,000

Civil, Class I, 1969–70.

SCHEDULE (B).—PART 10

CIVIL.—CLASS I

SCHEDULE OF SUMS granted, and of the sums which may be applied as appropriations in aid in addition thereto, to defray the charges of the several Civil Services herein particularly mentioned, which will come in course of payment during the year ending on 31st March 1970, viz.:—

	Supply Grants	Appropriations in Aid
	£	£
Vote		
1. For the salaries and expenses of the House of Lords - - - - - - -	495,000	9,000
2. For the salaries and expenses of the House of Commons, including certain grants in aid - - - - - - - -	3,350,000	10,000
3. For the salaries and expenses of the Department of Her Majesty's Treasury and subordinate departments - -	3,415,000	195,000
4. For the salaries and expenses of the Civil Service Department, of the Office of the Parliamentary Counsel, and sundry other services including a subscription to an international organisation and grants in aid - - - - -	5,435,000	373,000
5. For the salaries and expenses of the Cabinet Office, the Minister without Portfolio, the Paymaster General and the co-ordinating staff of the Secretary of State for Social Services - - -	1,233,000	—
6. For the salaries and expenses of the Department of Her Majesty's Secretary of State for Economic Affairs, the Chancellor of the Duchy of Lancaster and of the National Economic Development Council, and for certain grants in aid - - - - - - - -	2,361,000	300
7. For the salaries and expenses of the Department of Her Majesty's Most Honourable Privy Council - - -	79,000	3,000
8. For the salaries and expenses of the Customs and Excise Department, including a subscription to an international organisation - - - - -	36,150,000	2,365,000

SCHEDULE (B).—PART 10—*continued*

Civil, Class I, 1969–70.

	Supply Grants	Appropriations in Aid
	£	£
Vote		
9. For the salaries and expenses of the Inland Revenue Department - - -	100,274,000	4,225,000
10. For transitional relief under the Finance Act 1965 for companies with an overseas source of trading income - - -	45,000,000	—
11. For the salaries and expenses of the Department of the Comptroller and Auditor General - - - - -	1,130,000	238,000
12. For the salaries and expenses of Royal Commissions, committees, special enquiries, &c., and for a grant in aid -	728,000	—
13. For the salaries and expenses of the Office of the Parliamentary Commissioner for Administration - - - - -	145,000	—
TOTAL, CIVIL, CLASS I - - -£	199,795,000	7,418,300

Civil, Class II, 1969–70.

SCHEDULE (B).—PART 11

CIVIL.—CLASS II

SCHEDULE OF SUMS granted, and of the sums which may be applied as appropriations in aid in addition thereto, to defray the charges of the several Civil Services herein particularly mentioned, which will come in course of payment during the year ending on 31st March 1970, viz.:—

Vote	Supply Grants	Appropriations in Aid
	£	£
1. For the salaries and expenses of the office of Her Majesty's Secretary of State for Foreign and Commonwealth Affairs; Her Majesty's Diplomatic Service; and sundry other services connected therewith - - - - - - -	48,952,000	4,769,000
2. For expenditure by the Foreign and Commonwealth Office on sundry grants and services, including subscriptions, &c., to certain international organisations and certain grants in aid (including a Supplementary sum of £1,742,000) -	33,511,000	2,009,000
3. For a grant in aid of the British Council -	8,049,000	—
4. For the salaries and expenses of the Ministry of Overseas Development, including refund of selective employment tax to the Commonwealth Development Corporation - - -	3,340,000	45,000
5. For expenditure by the Ministry of Overseas Development on grants and services connected with multilateral overseas aid, including subscriptions to certain international organisations and certain grants in aid (including a Supplementary sum of £113,000) - - - - -	22,793,000	—
6. For expenditure by the Ministry of Overseas Development on grants and services connected with bilateral overseas aid, including certain grants in aid - -	128,578,000	279,000
7. For expenditure by the Ministry of Overseas Development on sundry services connected with overseas aid, including certain grants in aid (including a Supplementary sum of £56,500) - - -	29,513,500	1,685,927

SCHEDULE (B).—Part 11—*continued*

Civil, Class II, 1969–70

Vote	Supply Grants	Appropriations in Aid
	£	£
8. For schemes and loans made under the Colonial Development and Welfare Acts 1959 to 1965 and for loans made to the Commonwealth Development Corporation under the Overseas Resources Development Acts 1959 and 1963 - -	20,000,000	—
9. For a grant in aid of the Commonwealth War Graves Commission and certain other expenses - - - - - -	1,800,000	—
Total, Civil, Class II - - - £	296,536,500	8,787,927

Civil, Class III, 1969–70.

SCHEDULE (B).—PART 12

CIVIL.—CLASS III

SCHEDULE OF SUMS granted, and of the sums which may be applied as appropriations in aid in addition thereto, to defray the charges of the several Civil Services herein particularly mentioned, which will come in course of payment during the year ending on 31st March 1970, viz.:—

	Supply Grants	Appropriations in Aid
	£	£
Vote		
1. For the salaries and expenses of the office of Her Majesty's Secretary of State for the Home Department; expenses and grants in connection with certain law, fire and sundry other services; and certain grants in aid - - - - -	33,809,000	6,055,000
2. For the salaries and expenses of the office of the Secretary of State for Scotland and of the Scottish Home and Health Department; for a grant to the Legal Aid (Scotland) Fund; for expenses in connection with fire and sundry other services; and for a grant in aid - -	4,293,000	269,000
3. For grants and expenses in connection with civil defence and certain remanet expenditure - - - - - - -	4,499,000	409,000
4. For grants and expenses in connection with civil defence in Scotland and certain remanet expenditure - - - -	539,000	28,000
5. For grants in respect of expenditure incurred by police authorities in England and Wales, expenses in connection with the police services and a subscription to an international organisation - -	134,521,000	2,559,000
6. For grants in respect of expenditure incurred by police authorities in Scotland, and expenses in connection with the police services - - - - - -	12,884,000	165,000
7. For the salaries and expenses of prison service establishments in England and Wales - - - - - - - -	42,018,000	4,249,000

SCHEDULE (B).—PART 12—*continued*

Civil, Class III, 1969–70.

Vote	Supply Grants	Appropriations in Aid
	£	£
8. For the salaries and expenses of prison service establishments in Scotland -	4,536,000	411,000
9. For grants and expenses in England and Wales in respect of approved schools, remand homes and voluntary homes, and for training in and research on child care - - - - - - -	7,435,000	165,000
10. For such of the salaries and expenses of the Supreme Court of Judicature, Law Commission and Courts-Martial Appeal Court as are not charged on the Consolidated Fund; the salaries and expenses of the Judge Advocate General and Judge Advocate of the Fleet, Pensions Appeal Tribunals, the Lands Tribunal, the Restrictive Practices Court and Council on Tribunals, and certain other expenses - - - - -	799,000	3,678,000
11. For the salaries and expenses of the County Courts - - - - - - -	552,000	7,400,000
12. For a grant to the Legal Aid Fund - -	8,171,000	—
13. For the salaries and expenses of the Law Officers' Department, the Department of Her Majesty's Procurator-General and Solicitor for the Affairs of Her Majesty's Treasury and the Department of the Director of Public Prosecutions; for the costs of prosecutions and other legal proceedings and of Parliamentary Agency - - - - - - -	1,373,000	509,000
14. For the salaries and expenses of the Lord Advocate's Department, of the Courts of Law and Justice, of the Scottish Law Commission, and of the Courts, Tribunals, &c.; and for sundry services, and a grant in aid - - - - -	893,000	850,000
15. For such of the salaries and expenses of the Supreme Court of Judicature and Court of Criminal Appeal of Northern Ireland as are not charged on the Consolidated Fund; the salaries and expenses of Pensions Appeals in Northern Ireland and certain other expenses -	132,000	55,000
TOTAL, CIVIL, CLASS III - - £	256,454,000	26,802,000

Civil, Class IV, 1969–70.

SCHEDULE (B).—PART 13

CIVIL.—CLASS IV

SCHEDULE OF SUMS granted, and of the sums which may be applied as appropriations in aid in addition thereto, to defray the charges of the several Civil Services herein particularly mentioned, which will come in course of payment during the year ending on 31st March 1970, viz.:—

	Supply Grants	Appropriations in Aid
	£	£
Vote		
1. For the salaries and expenses of the Ministry of Transport, and certain Tribunals and Committees - - -	4,550,000	9,955,000
2. For the expenditure of the Ministry of Transport in grant to the British Railways Board, the London Transport Board and the British Waterways Board in respect of deficits on their revenue accounts - - - - - - -	12,450,000	—
3. For services connected with inland transport, including grants for the assistance of public passenger and freight transport; other transport services connected with ports, inland waterways and a Channel Tunnel, including grants, loans, a grant in aid and subscriptions to certain international organisations; repayments &c., of selective employment tax to nationalised transport undertakings; and sundry other services (including a Supplementary sum of £6,900,000) - - - - - -	204,930,000	90,000
4. For expenditure, including grants and loans to highway, &c., authorities on the construction, improvement and maintenance of roads, &c., in England and sundry services connected therewith; for expenditure on the collection of motor vehicle duties, &c., and the registration of motor vehicles in Great Britain; for road research; and for sundry other services - - - - - - -	265,720,000	14,825,000
5. For expenditure, including grants and loans to highway, &c., authorities, on the construction, improvement and maintenance of roads, &c., in Scotland and sundry services connected therewith; for expenditure on grants for the assistance of public passenger transport; and for sundry other transport services -	39,130,000	120,000

SCHEDULE (B).—PART 13—*continued*

Civil, Class IV, 1969–70.

Vote	Supply Grants	Appropriations in Aid
	£	£
6. For expenditure, including grants to highway, &c., authorities on the construction, improvement and maintenance of roads, &c., in Wales and sundry services connected therewith; for expenditure on grants for the assistance of public passenger transport; and for sundry other transport services - - - -	15,172,000	16,000
7. For the salaries and expenses of the Department of Her Majesty's First Secretary of State and Secretary of State for Employment and Productivity including those relating to the Employment Exchange service and the inspection of factories; for expenses, grants and loans in connection with employment, training, rehabilitation, &c.; for expenses of the National Board for Prices and Incomes, the Commission on Industrial Relations and the Industrial Court; for a subscription to the International Labour Organisation, a grant in aid and sundry other services (including a Supplementary sum of £1,628,000)	66,553,000	14,814,000
8. For payments by the Department of Employment and Productivity to certain employers who have paid selective employment tax (including a Supplementary sum of £99,000,000) - -	894,000,000	5,000
9. For the salaries and expenses of the office of the Committee of Privy Council for Trade and subordinate departments and agencies, and for certain payments to the Foreign Compensation Commission -	15,252,000	7,358,000
10. For the construction, maintenance and operation of civil aerodromes, for civil air navigational services, for loans and services connected with shipping, for contributions &c., to certain international organisations, grants in aid, certain repayments, &c., of selective employment tax, and for sundry other services (including a Supplementary sum of £2,730,000) - - - - - -	24,329,000	13,229,000
11. For the expenditure of the Board of Trade on the promotion of trade, exports and industrial efficiency, and on trading and other services, including loans, subscriptions to certain international organisations and grants in aid (including a Supplementary sum of £1,000) - - -	23,893,000	158,000

Civil, Class IV, 1969–70.

SCHEDULE (B).—Part 13—*continued*

Vote	Supply Grants	Appropriations in Aid
	£	£
12. For the promotion of local employment -	69,000,000	450,000
13. For the expenditure of the Board of Trade on grants for assisting investment in new business assets - - - - - -	460,000,000	—
14. For the salaries and expenses of the Export Credits Guarantee Department, including a subscription to an international organisation, and for payments under guarantees given after consultation with the Export Guarantees Advisory Council	1,000	16,467,000
15. For payments under special guarantees given or arising from other arrangements made by the Board of Trade in the national interest and for advances to the Acquisition of Guaranteed Securities Fund - - - - - -	1,000	10,865,000
16. For expenditure by the Department of Economic Affairs on public investment in the Industrial Reorganisation Corporation - - - - - -	15,000,000	—
17. For the salaries and expenses of the Ministry of Power; for expenditure on oil storage and distribution; for assistance to the coal industry; for certain repayments, &c., of selective employment tax; for expenses in connection with the nationalisation of the Iron and Steel Industry; for payments to the Governments of Northern Ireland and the Isle of Man; for sundry other services and for a grant in aid (including a Supplementary sum of £13,000,000) -	108,307,000	2,907,000
18. For the salaries and expenses of the Headquarters and Establishments of the Ministry of Technology - - -	84,686,000	7,191,000
19. For the expenditure of the Ministry of Technology on technological and industrial services, including certain subscriptions to international organisations and grants in aid (including a Supplementary sum of £3,000) - - -	32,064,000	488,000

SCHEDULE (B).—PART 13—*continued*

Civil, Class IV, 1969–70.

Vote	Supply Grants	Appropriations in Aid
	£	£
20. For expenditure by the Ministry of Technology on supply services (including research and development) and in connection with the development and production of civil aircraft and associated safety equipment, on contributions to international organisations, loans, grants in aid and sundry other items - -	230,694,000	28,941,000
21. For expenditure by the Ministry of Technology on the supply of aircraft and other equipment for the Government service and on miscellaneous supply -	1,000	—
22. For certain expenditure by the Ministry of Technology on the purchase of U.S. aircraft and for research and development connected therewith - - -	1,000	89,999,000
23. For payments to the United Kingdom Atomic Energy Authority for outstanding liabilities in respect of the capital cost of plant being maintained as reserve capacity, and certain terminal expenses, and for payments to the Authority and to others for special materials and services - - - - - -	32,390,000	—
24. For payments towards meeting the expenses of the United Kingdom Atomic Energy Authority, for subscriptions, &c., to international projects and organisations, for the administration of a national stockpile of uranium ore, for a grant in aid, for repayment &c., of selective employment tax to the Atomic Energy Authority Trading Fund, for the purchase of shares and for associated guarantees - - - - - -	28,303,000	66,890,000
25. For loans to the United Kingdom Atomic Energy Authority Trading Fund - -	1,400,000	—

Civil, Class IV, 1969–70.

SCHEDULE (B).—PART 13—*continued*

Vote	Supply Grants	Appropriations in Aid
	£	£
26. For the salaries of Post Office Ministers; for the salaries and expenses of the Ministry of Posts and Telecommunications; for grants to, and grants in aid of, the British Broadcasting Corporation; for certain payments to the Post Office; for subscriptions to international organisations; and for sundry other services - - - - - -	135,304,000	1,540,000
27. For repayments of selective employment tax to the Post Office and to Cable and Wireless Ltd. (including a Supplementary sum of £4,968,000) - - - -	40,351,000	—
TOTAL, CIVIL, CLASS IV - - £	2,803,482,000	286,308,000

SCHEDULE (B).—PART 14

Civil, Class V, 1969–70.

CIVIL.—CLASS V

SCHEDULE OF SUMS granted, and of the sums which may be applied as appropriations in aid in addition thereto, to defray the charges of the several Civil Services herein particularly mentioned, which will come in course of payment during the year ending on 31st March 1970, viz.:—

	Supply Grants	Appropriations in Aid
	£	£
Vote		
1. For the salaries and expenses of the Ministry of Agriculture, Fisheries and Food; of the Royal Botanic Gardens, Kew; of the White Fish Authority and Scottish Committee; of the Plant Variety Rights Office; and of the Meat and Livestock Commission - - -	34,717,000	871,000
2. For the salaries and expenses of the Department of Agriculture and Fisheries for Scotland; for expenditure in connection with sundry agricultural, horticultural, food and harbour services including grants, loans and grants in aid; and for refunds of selective employment tax to agricultural, horticultural and forestry employers - - - - - - -	17,162,000	1,430,000
3. For expenditure by the Ministry of Agriculture, Fisheries and Food on grants and subsidies for the encouragement of food production and the improvement of agriculture and for sundry other services -	109,459,000	40,000
4. For expenditure by the Department of Agriculture and Fisheries for Scotland on grants and subsidies for the encouragement of food production and the improvement of agriculture - -	28,450,000	—
5. For expenditure by the Ministry of Agriculture, Fisheries and Food in implementation of agricultural price guarantees and for sundry other services	128,235,000	15,000
6. For expenditure by the Department of Agriculture and Fisheries for Scotland in implementation of agricultural price guarantees - - - - - - -	14,853,000	—

Civil, Class V, 1969–70.

SCHEDULE (B).—PART 14—*continued*

Vote	Supply Grants	Appropriations in Aid
	£	£
7. For expenditure by the Ministry of Agriculture, Fisheries and Food in connection with sundry agricultural and food services, and rural development, including grants, loans, grants in aid, certain subscriptions to international organisations and for refunds of selective employment tax to agricultural, horticultural and forestry employers (including a Supplementary sum of £5,787,000) -	58,729,000	4,322,000
8. For expenditure by the Ministry of Agriculture, Fisheries and Food in connection with the procurement and maintenance of strategic reserves - -	1,000	1,149,000
9. For grants, loans and expenses in connection with assistance to fishermen; grants and loans to the White Fish Authority; expenditure on research and development relating to fisheries and fish marketing and on the construction, improvement and maintenance of harbours and fishing facilities; subscriptions to certain international organisations and a grant in aid of the White Fish Marketing Fund - -	8,236,000	4,000
10. In connection with Scottish fisheries and the United Kingdom herring industry for grants, loans and expenses in connection with assistance to fishermen, fishery protection, research and development relating to fisheries and fish marketing and the construction, improvement and maintenance of harbours and fishing facilities; and a grant in aid of the Herring Marketing Fund - - -	3,523,000	11,000
11. For a grant in aid of the Forestry Fund -	15,750,000	—
TOTAL, CIVIL, CLASS V - -£	419,115,000	7,842,000

SCHEDULE (B).—PART 15

Civil, Class VI, 1969–70.

CIVIL.—CLASS VI

SCHEDULE OF SUMS granted, and of the sums which may be applied as appropriations in aid in addition thereto, to defray the charges of the several Civil Services herein particularly mentioned, which will come in course of payment during the year ending on 31st March 1970, viz.:—

	Supply Grants	Appropriations in Aid
	£	£
Vote		
1. For the salaries and expenses of the Ministry of Housing and Local Government and certain tribunals, commissions &c.; grants and expenses in connection with environmental services and civil defence; tax and rating payments including selective employment refunds; sundry other services, including loans; a subscription to an international organisation and grants in aid (including a Supplementary sum of £24,748,000)	200,594,000	1,831,000
2. For the salaries and expenses of the Scottish Development Department and certain tribunals, &c.; for grants and payments, including loans, in connection with environmental services, selective employment refunds and rate rebates, assistance to the coal industry, storm damage relief and sundry other services, including a grant in aid to the Highlands and Islands Development Board and other grants in aid (including a Supplementary sum of £3,987,000) - - -	36,400,000	24,870
3. For the salaries and expenses of the office of the Secretary of State for Wales and certain tribunals, &c.; grants and expenses in connection with health services, environmental services and civil defence; expenses in connection with the investiture of the Prince of Wales; tax and rating payments including selective employment refunds; sundry other services including loans; and grants in aid (including a Supplementary sum of £1,755,000) - - - - - -	14,951,000	254,700
4. For grants and other payments relating to the provision, improvement, repair and purchase of housing accommodation in England - - - - - -	147,629,000	858,000

Civil, Class VI, 1969–70.

SCHEDULE (B).—PART 15—*continued*

Vote	Supply Grants	Appropriations in Aid
	£	£
5. For grants and other payments relating to the provision, improvement, repair and purchase of housing accommodation in Scotland	36,105,000	186,000
6. For grants and other payments relating to the provision, improvement, repair and purchase of housing accommodation in Wales	8,477,000	80,000
7. For rate support grants and rate deficiency grants to local authorities in England and Wales	1,536,857,000	—
8. For rate support grants and equalisation grants to local authorities in Scotland	180,679,000	—
9. For the salaries and expenses of the Land Commission	1,145,000	812,000
10. For the salaries and expenses of Her Majesty's Secretary of State for Social Services and the Department of Health and Social Security including appellate, advisory and sundry other services, for certain selective employment refunds and a subscription to an international organisation (including a Supplementary sum of £3,000,000)	68,053,000	71,335,000
11. For the provision of hospital services, &c., under the National Health Service, &c., in England; and other services (including a Supplementary sum of £19,500,000)	819,137,000	123,950,000
12. For the provision of Executive Councils' services, &c., under the National Health Service in England (including a Supplementary sum of £12,800,000)	306,164,000	48,306,000
13. For the provision in England of certain miscellaneous services under the National Health Service, &c., and of certain welfare services; for a subscription to the World Health Organisation and for certain grants in aid; and for sundry services	51,607,000	2,272,000
14. For the provision of services under the National Health Service in Scotland and other health and welfare services including a grant in aid	158,303,000	17,722,000

SCHEDULE (B).—Part 15—*continued*

Civil, Class VI, 1969–70.

Vote	Supply Grants	Appropriations in Aid
	£	£
15. For the provision of services under the National Health Service in Wales and other health and welfare services - -	74,469,000	8,149,000
16. For expenditure by the Department of Health and Social Security on pensions, allowances, gratuities, &c., payable under section 6(6) of the National Health Service Act 1946, or under Regulations made under section 67 of that Act; and certain payments to the National Insurance Fund - - -	1,000	39,559,000
17. For expenditure by the Scottish Home and Health Department on pensions, allowances and gratuities, &c., payable under section 6(8) of the National Health Service (Scotland) Act 1947 or under Regulations made under section 66 of that Act; and certain payments to the National Insurance Fund - - -	1,000	4,841,000
18. For sums payable out of the Consolidated Fund to the National Insurance Fund and the Industrial Injuries Fund (including a Supplementary sum of £16,500,000)	374,200,000	—
19. For payments in respect of family allowances - - - - - - - -	341,960,000	40,000
20. For supplementary pensions and allowances, &c. - - - - - - -	478,000,000	14,000,000
21. For payments in respect of pensions, gratuities and allowances for disablement or death arising out of war, or service in the Armed Forces after 2 September 1939, and for sundry other services (including a Supplementary sum of £4,300,000) - - - - - - -	125,516,000	13,000
22. For grants and expenses in Scotland in connection with social work services, for certain expenditure on the probation service, and for a grant in aid - -	2,018,000	13,000
Total, Civil, Class VI - - £	4,962,266,000	334,246,570

Civil, Class VII, 1969–70.

SCHEDULE (B).—Part 16

CIVIL.—Class VII

Schedule of Sums granted, and of the sums which may be applied as appropriations in aid in addition thereto, to defray the charges of the several Civil Services herein particularly mentioned, which will come in course of payment during the year ending on 31st March 1970, viz.:—

	Supply Grants	Appropriations in Aid
	£	£
Vote		
1. For the salaries and expenses of the Department of Her Majesty's Secretary of State for Education and Science; for grants and loans in connection with education, &c.; for sundry services and for certain grants in aid - - - - -	69,464,000	670,000
2. For the salaries and expenses of the Scottish Education Department; for grants in connection with education, &c.; for sundry services and for grants in aid	35,875,000	51,000
3. For expenditure by the Department of Her Majesty's Secretary of State for Education and Science on superannuation allowances and gratuities, &c., in respect of teachers - - - - -	1,000	80,409,000
4. For expenditure by the Scottish Education Department on superannuation allowances and gratuities, &c., in respect of teachers - - - - - -	3,008,000	10,676,000
5. For the salaries and expenses of the University Grants Committee, for grants in aid and grants towards the expenses of, and for loans to, universities, colleges, the British Academy, &c., and for other services - - - - - -	246,558,000	—
6. For a grant in aid of the Social Science Research Council - - - -	2,380,000	—
7. For grants in aid of the Science Research Council including subscriptions to certain international organisations -	45,844,000	—
8. For grants in aid of the Natural Environment Research Council including a subscription to an international organisation	11,725,000	—

SCHEDULE (B).—PART 16—*continued*

Civil, Class VII, 1969–70.

	Supply Grants	Appropriations in Aid
	£	£
Vote		
9. For grants in aid of the Medical Research Council including a subscription to an international organisation - - -	17,141,000	—
10. For a grant in aid of the Agricultural Research Council - - - -	14,663,000	—
11. For the salaries and expenses of the British Museum (Natural History), including a purchase grant in aid - - - -	1,104,000	26,000
12. For grants in aid of certain institutions and bodies concerned with science, for services connected therewith and a subscription to an international organisation - - - - - - -	1,455,000	—
TOTAL, CIVIL, CLASS VII - £	449,218,000	91,832,000

Civil, Class VIII, 1969–70.

SCHEDULE (B).—PART 17

CIVIL.—CLASS VIII

SCHEDULE OF SUMS granted, and of the sums which may be applied as appropriations in aid in addition thereto, to defray the charges of the several Civil Services herein particularly mentioned, which will come in course of payment during the year ending on 31st March 1970, viz.:—

	Supply Grants	Appropriations in Aid
	£	£
Vote		
1. For the salaries and expenses of the British Museum, including a purchase grant in aid - - - - - - - -	2,864,000	150,000
2. For the salaries and expenses of the Science Museum, including a purchase grant in aid - - - - - - - -	641,000	3,000
3. For the salaries and expenses of the Victoria and Albert Museum, including purchase grants in aid - - - - - -	1,129,000	17,000
4. For the salaries and expenses of the Imperial War Museum, including a purchase grant in aid - - - - -	237,000	13,000
5. For the salaries and expenses of the London Museum, including a purchase grant in aid - - - - - - -	111,000	3,400
6. For the salaries and expenses of the National Gallery, including a purchase grant in aid - - - - - - -	503,000	5,000
7. For the salaries and expenses of the National Maritime Museum, including a purchase grant in aid - - -	275,000	2,000
8. For the salaries and expenses of the National Portrait Gallery, including purchase grants in aid - - - - -	111,000	16,000
9. For the salaries and expenses of the Tate Gallery, including purchase grants in aid (including a Supplementary sum of £20,000) - - - - - - -	349,000	20,000
10. For the salaries and expenses of the Wallace Collection - - - - -	88,000	7,500

SCHEDULE (B).—PART 17—*continued*

Civil, Class VIII, 1969–70.

Vote	Supply Grants	Appropriations in Aid
	£	£
11. For the salaries and expenses of the Royal Scottish Museum, including purchase grants in aid, certain other grants in aid and a grant to the Scottish Council for Museums and Galleries - - -	254,000	500
12. For the salaries and expenses of the National Gallery of Scotland, the Scottish National Gallery of Modern Art and the Scottish National Portrait Gallery, including purchase grants in aid	174,000	5,000
13. For the salaries and expenses of the National Library of Scotland, including a purchase grant in aid - - -	244,000	5,500
14. For the salaries and expenses of the National Museum of Antiquities of Scotland, including a purchase grant in aid - - - - - - - -	75,000	300
15. For grants in aid of the National Library of Wales and the National Museum of Wales and a grant to the Council of Museums in Wales - - - - -	780,000	—
16. For grants to, and grants in aid of, certain institutions and bodies connected with the arts - - - - - - -	9,286,000	—
TOTAL, CIVIL, CLASS VIII - - -£	17,121,000	248,200

Civil, Class IX, 1969–70.

SCHEDULE (B).—PART 18

CIVIL.—CLASS IX

SCHEDULE OF SUMS granted, and of the sums which may be applied as appropriations in aid in addition thereto, to defray the charges of the several Civil Services herein particularly mentioned, which will come in course of payment during the year ending on 31st March 1970, viz.:—

	Supply Grants	Appropriations in Aid
	£	£
Vote		
1. For the salaries and expenses of the Ministry of Public Building and Works	44,800,000	13,180,000
2. For expenditure on public building and accommodation services, &c., in the United Kingdom, including grants in aid and sundry other services; on ancient monuments; on building research and development; and on assistance to the Zoological Society of London (including a Supplementary sum of £1,000)	93,161,000	13,251,030
2A. To defray the cost of a memorial to the memory of the late Sir Winston Churchill - - - - - - -	3,000	—
3. For expenditure on public building and accommodation services, &c., overseas	8,545,000	725,000
4. For expenditure on works and buildings for the Ministry of Defence (Navy Department) - - - - - -	35,530,000	150,000
5. For expenditure on works and buildings for the Ministry of Defence (Army Department) - - - - - -	68,300,000	800,000
6. For expenditure on works and buildings for the Ministry of Defence (Air Force Department) - - - - - -	46,260,000	12,980,000
7. For expenditure on certain works and buildings for the Ministry of Technology and for civil aviation services - -	7,450,000	—
8. For the salaries and expenses of the Rating of Government Property Department, and for rates and contributions in lieu of rates for property occupied by the Crown and premises occupied by representatives of Commonwealth and foreign countries and international organisations	38,705,000	2,250,000

SCHEDULE (B).—PART 18—*continued*

Civil, Class IX, 1969–70.

Vote	Supply Grants	Appropriations in Aid
	£	£
9. For the salaries and expenses of the Stationery Office; for stationery, printing, books, office equipment, &c.; for official publications; and for sundry services -	38,243,000	18,682,010
10. For the salaries and expenses of the Central Office of Information - - - -	12,987,000	2,928,000
11. For the salaries and expenses of the Department of the Government Actuary -	73,000	56,000
12. For a grant in aid of the Government Hospitality Fund - - - - -	180,000	—
13. For the salaries and expenses of the Government Social Survey Department	981,000	3,000
14. For civil superannuation and other pensions and non-recurrent payments; and for certain other expenditure in connection therewith - - - - -	76,070,000	4,200,000
15. For non-effective annual allowances, gratuities and certain expenses in connection with superannuation in respect of Post Office employment - - - -	1,000	22,394,000
TOTAL, CIVIL, CLASS IX - - -£	471,289,000	91,599,040

Civil, Class X, 1969–70.

SCHEDULE (B).—PART 19

CIVIL.—CLASS X

SCHEDULE OF SUMS granted, and of the sums which may be applied as appropriations in aid in addition thereto, to defray the charges of the several Civil Services herein particularly mentioned, which will come in course of payment during the year ending on 31st March 1970, viz.:—

	Supply Grants	Appropriations in Aid
	£	£
Vote		
1. For the salaries and expenses of the Charity Commission for England and Wales -	537,000	200
2. For the salaries and expenses of the Crown Estate Office - - - - -	251,000	—
3. For the salaries and expenses of the Registry of Friendly Societies - - -	183,000	13,000
4. For the salaries and expenses of the Royal Mint in the production of coins, medals, badges, dies, seals, &c.; for the withdrawal of coin; and in preparation for the introduction of a decimal coinage -	1,000	56,487,000
5. For the salaries and expenses of the National Debt Office and Pensions Commutation Board - - - -	1,000	111,000
6. For the salaries and expenses of the establishment under the Public Works Loan Commission and the expenses of the Commission - - - - -	1,000	76,000
7. For the salaries and expenses of the office of the Public Trustee - - - -	1,000	916,000
8. For the salaries and expenses of the Land Registry - - - - - -	1,000	5,345,000
9. For the salaries and expenses of the Office of the Registrar of Restrictive Trading Agreements - - - - - -	166,000	100
10. For the survey of Great Britain and other mapping services - - - - -	5,132,000	2,368,000
11. For the salaries and expenses of the Public Record Office - - - - -	307,000	100,000

SCHEDULE (B).—PART 19—*continued*

Civil, Class X, 1969–70.

	Supply Grants	Appropriations in Aid
	£	£
Vote		
12. For the salaries and expenses of the Scottish Record Office - - - -	127,000	27,000
13. For the salaries and expenses of the Office of the Registrar General including a grant in aid - - - - - - -	1,719,000	739,000
14. For the salaries and expenses of the Department of the Registrar General of Births, Deaths and Marriages in Scotland -	250,000	82,000
15. For the salaries and expenses of the Department of the Registers of Scotland	1,000	397,000
16. For the salaries and expenses, including publicity, of the National Savings Committee - - - - - - - -	2,026,000	—
17. For the salaries and expenses of the Decimal Currency Board - - -	118,000	—
18. For the salaries and expenses of the Department for National Savings - -	6,263,000	17,933,000
TOTAL, CIVIL, CLASS X - - -£	17,085,000	84,594,300

Civil Class XI, 1969–70.

SCHEDULE (B).—PART 20

CIVIL.—CLASS XI

SCHEDULE OF SUMS granted, and of the sums which may be applied as appropriations in aid in addition thereto, to defray the charges of the several Civil Services herein particularly mentioned, which will come in course of payment during the year ending on 31st March 1970, viz.:—

	Supply Grants	Appropriations in Aid
Vote	£	£
1. For the salaries and expenses of the Carlisle State Management District - - -	1,000	3,464,000
2. For the salaries and expenses of the State Management Districts in Scotland -	1,000	900,000
3. For pensions, &c., in respect of service in the former Indian and Burma Services and under the former Government of Palestine, and in respect of certain other service overseas; for supplements to certain colonial and other overseas pensions; for certain payments to the Governments of India and Pakistan in connection with pensions; and for sundry services and expenses - - - -	14,240,000	812,000
4. For pensions, &c., and compensation allowances awarded to retired and disbanded members of the Royal Irish Constabulary, and to their widows, including annuities to the National Debt Commissioners in respect of commutation of compensation allowances - -	960,000	—
5. For charges in connection with land purchase in Northern Ireland, and the expenses of management of guaranteed stocks and bonds issued for the purpose of Irish land purchase - - - -	659,000	100
6. For a grant in aid of the Development Fund	2,495,000	—
7. For Her Majesty's foreign and other secret services - - - - - -	10,250,000	—
8. For certain miscellaneous expenses, and grants in aid (including a Supplementary sum of £12,000) - - - - -	520,000	103,490
9. To repay to the Civil Contingencies Fund certain miscellaneous advances - -	57,000	—
TOTAL, CIVIL, CLASS XI - - -£	29,183,000	5,279,590

SCHEDULE (C).—PART 1

Navy Services 1967–68, Votes	Deficits		Surpluses	
	Excesses of Actual over Estimated Gross Expenditure	Deficiencies of Actual as compared with Estimated Receipts	Surpluses of Estimated over Actual Gross Expenditure	Surpluses of Actual as compared with Estimated Receipts
	£ s. d.	£ s. d.	£ s. d.	£ s. d.
1. Pay, &c., of the Royal Navy and Royal Marines	248,498 8 11	—	—	97,781 10 6
2. Royal Naval Reserves	30,025 18 6	—	—	585 18 6
3. Navy Department Headquarters ...	—	4,713 19 6*	23,410 14 3	—
4. Research and Development and other Scientific Services ...	—	—	1,106,519 11 8	150,836 1 9
5. Medical Services, Education and Civilians on Fleet Services ...	—	—	688,177 13 7	16,111 3 4
6. Naval Stores, Armament, Victualling and other Material Supply Services ...	—	—	2,719,373 16 11	1,540 18 10
7. H.M. Ships, Aircraft and Weapons, New Construction and Repairs	2,090,163 6 6	—	—	1,505,514 19 6
8. Miscellaneous Effective Services	415,648 11 9	—	—	115,558 9 2
9. Non-Effective Services	5,155 16 1	—	—	33,855 11 11

* This deficiency of receipts was wholly offset by a surplus of estimated over actual gross expenditure.

SCHEDULE (C).—PART 2

Army Services 1967–68, Votes	Deficits		Surpluses	
	Excesses of Actual over Estimated Gross Expenditure	Deficiencies of Actual as compared with Estimated Receipts	Surpluses of Estimated over Actual Gross Expenditure	Surpluses of Actual as compared with Estimated Receipts
	£ s. d.	£ s. d.	£ s. d.	£ s. d.
1. Pay, &c., of the Army	—	—	58,260 11 6	112,928 11 1
2. Reserve and Cadet Forces	384,104 19 1	461,325 3 6	—	—
3. Army Department Headquarters ...	—	—	34,661 4 8	6,497 0 5
4. Civilians at Outstations	900,325 5 8	—	—	63,094 1 3
5. Movements	—	3,231 13 11*	681,926 3 9	—
6. Supplies	—	85,511 16 10*	474,570 7 9	—
7. Stores and Equipment	—	—	639,339 18 8	552,560 6 9
8. Miscellaneous Effective Services	—	—	398,009 5 2	1,113,681 0 8
9. Non-Effective Services	3,877 8 1	—	—	22,847 0 4
10. Defence Lands and Buildings	—	301,046 19 0*	1,770,658 11 7	—

* These deficiencies of receipts were wholly offset by surpluses of estimated over actual gross expenditure.

SCHEDULE (C).—PART 3

Air Services 1967–68, Votes	Deficits						Surpluses					
	Excesses of Actual over Estimated Gross Expenditure			Deficiencies of Actual as compared with Estimated Receipts			Surpluses of Estimated over Actual Gross Expenditure			Surpluses of Actual as compared with Estimated Receipts		
	£	*s.*	*d.*	£	*s.*	*d.*	£	*s.*	*d.*	£	*s.*	*d.*
1. Pay, &c., of the Air Force	1,411,742	9	9	12,037	3	5	—			—		
2. Reserve and Auxiliary Services	—			6,088	15	6*	60,879	2	5	—		
3. Air Force Department Headquarters ...	37,764	18	3	4,750	13	11	—			—		
4. Civilians at Outstations and the Meteorological Office	3,293,233	6	0	169,303	0	9	—			—		
5. Movements	2,685,167	1	10	678,706	1	6	—			—		
6. Supplies	2,370,734	15	6	—			—			447,344	15	4
7. Aircraft and Stores ...	—			2,440,548	14	9*	20,458,422	3	1	—		
8. Miscellaneous Effective Services	—			—			335,946	5	7	327,492	4	1
9. Non-Effective Services	—			—			1,345,512	10	4	26,852	7	1

* These deficiencies of receipts were wholly offset by surpluses of estimated over actual gross expenditure.

Finance Act 1969

1969 CHAPTER 32

An Act to grant certain duties, to alter other duties, and to amend the law relating to the National Debt and the Public Revenue, and to make further provision in connection with Finance. [25th July 1969]

Most Gracious Sovereign

WE, Your Majesty's most dutiful and loyal subjects, the Commons of the United Kingdom in Parliament assembled, towards raising the necessary supplies to defray Your Majesty's public expenses, and making an addition to the public revenue, have freely and voluntarily resolved to give and grant unto Your Majesty the several duties hereinafter mentioned; and do therefore most humbly beseech Your Majesty that it may be enacted, and be it enacted by the Queen's Most Excellent Majesty, by and with the advice and consent of the Lords Spiritual and Temporal, and Commons, in this present Parliament assembled, and by the authority of the same, as follows:—

PART I

CUSTOMS AND EXCISE

Termination of surcharge under Finance Act 1961 s. 9 and related increases in duties.

1961 c. 36.
S.I. 1968/1845.

1.—(1) As from 16th April 1969 or, in the case of the duties referred to in subsection (3) of this section, as from six o'clock in the evening on 15th April 1969, the adjustment of ten per cent. having effect under subsection (2) of section 9 of the Finance Act 1961 by virtue of the Surcharge on Revenue Duties Order 1968 shall no longer have effect in relation to the duties or taxes to which that order applies or any drawback, rebate, allowance or other payments in connection with any of those duties or taxes; but—

(*a*) the provisions of subsections (2) to (4)(*a*) of this section shall have effect with a view to making in the rates

PART I

of those duties and taxes increases which, taking into account international agreements and other relevant matters, are comparable to the amount of the adjustment aforesaid, together, in certain cases, with a further amount; and

(*b*) the period after which orders of the Treasury under the said section 9 may not be made or continue in force (which, by section 10(1) of the Finance Act 1968, was extended until the end of August 1969) shall extend until the end of August 1970 or such later date as Parliament may hereafter determine.

1968 c. 44.

(2) As from 16th April 1969, for the following provisions of the Finance Act 1964 setting out rates of customs and excise duties and of drawback, namely—

1964 c. 49.

(*a*) Table 1 in Schedule 1 (spirits other than imported perfumed spirits) as substituted by section 1(1) of the Finance Act 1968;

(*b*) Schedule 2 (beer) as substituted by section 1(2) of the Finance Act 1967;

1967 c. 54

(*c*) Schedule 3 (wine) as substituted by the said section 1(1);

(*d*) Schedule 4 (British wine) as substituted by the said section 1(1);

(*e*) Schedule 5 (tobacco) as amended by section 1(2) of the Finance Act 1965 and section 1(2) of the Finance Act 1968,

1965 c. 25.

there shall be substituted the provisions set out in Schedules 1, 2, 3, 4 and 5 respectively to this Act; but this subsection shall not affect the rates of drawback payable in the case of goods in respect of which duty has been paid otherwise than at the rates having effect by virtue of this subsection.

(3) As from six o'clock in the evening of 15th April 1969—

(*a*) section 2 of the Finance (No. 2) Act 1964 (which, as amended by section 2(1)(*a*) of the Finance Act 1968, provides for a duty of customs at the rate of three shillings and elevenpence a gallon to be charged on imported hydrocarbon oils and for a duty of excise at the same rate to be charged on hydrocarbon oils produced in the United Kingdom, on petrol substitutes and on spirits used for making power methylated spirits) shall have effect with the substitution for the words " three shillings and elevenpence " of the words " four shillings and sixpence ";

1964 c. 92.

(*b*) the rate at which rebate of the customs or excise duty on hydrocarbon oils is allowed under section 199 of the Customs and Excise Act 1952 for heavy oils

1954 c. 44.

PART I

delivered for home use shall in all cases be a rate 2·4 pence a gallon less than the rate at which the duty in question is for the time being chargeable;

(*c*) section 6(4) of the Finance Act 1964 (which, as amended 1964 c. 49.
by section 1(3)(*c*) of the Finance Act 1967, provides 1967 c. 54.
in certain cases where light oils charged with the customs or excise duty on hydrocarbon oils are delivered for home use as furnace fuel for a rebate of duty at a rate 2·2 pence a gallon less than the rate at which the duty is charged) shall have effect with the substitution for the words "2·2 pence" of the words "2·4 pence".

(4) Subject to any new order of the Treasury under section 2 of the Purchase Tax Act 1963, Part I of Schedule 1 to that 1963 c. 9.
Act (chargeable and exempt goods and rates of tax) as amended by section 5 of the Finance Act 1968 shall have effect— 1968 c. 44.

(*a*) as from 16th April 1969, with the substitution for any reference to 12½ per cent., 20 per cent., 33⅓ per cent. or 50 per cent. of a reference respectively to 13¾ per cent., 22 per cent., 36⅔ per cent. or 55 per cent.; and

(*b*) as from 27th May 1969, with the further amendments specified in Schedule 6 to this Act (being amendments adding further goods to those chargeable with purchase tax or amending the provisions as to exemptions).

(5) The provisions of Schedule 7 to this Act shall have effect for the purpose of—

(*a*) defining whisky for all purposes of customs and excise;

(*b*) relaxing the restrictions on the fortification of British wine;

(*c*) making in section 4(3) of the Finance Act 1964 amendments consequential on section 3(1)(*c*) of the Finance Act 1968 and subsection (2) of this section;

(*d*) revising the provisions as to relief from the duty of customs or excise on hydrocarbon oil.

Excise duty on use of premises for off-course betting.

2.—(1) There shall be charged a duty of excise on a licence (to be known as a betting premises licence) authorising the use of premises for off-course betting.

(2) Premises are used for off-course betting if, not being comprised in a track, they are used in the course of the business of a bookmaker or the Horserace Totalisator Board for the purpose of effecting betting transactions with or through a bookmaker or the Board, being transactions which result in bets chargeable under section 12 of the Finance Act 1966 with the 1966 c. 18.
general betting duty.

PART I

(3) Subject to paragraph 4 of Schedule 8 to this Act, the duty on a betting premises licence shall be—

(*a*) in the case of premises which for rating purposes constitute or are comprised in a hereditament having a rateable value, three times that value; and

(*b*) in any other case, £150.

(4) As from 1st October 1969, no premises in Great Britain shall be used for off-course betting unless the user holds a betting premises licence in respect thereof which is for the time being in force; and for this purpose " the user "—

(*a*) in the case of premises used in the course of the business of a bookmaker, means the bookmaker or a servant or agent of his responsible to him for effecting betting transactions on the premises; and

(*b*) in the case of premises used in the course of the business of the Horserace Totalisator Board, means the Board.

(5) Subsection (4) of this section shall not apply to the use of premises in circumstances where the user and all the persons with whom betting transactions are effected either reside or work on those premises, or on premises of which those premises form part.

(6) A betting premises licence in respect of any premises shall not be granted to a person other than the Horserace Totalisator Board unless either—

(*a*) he is the holder of a betting office licence under Part I of the Act of 1963 authorising him to use the premises as a betting office; or

(*b*) he is the holder of a bookmaker's permit under that Act and the Commissioners are satisfied that the premises are not, and will not during the currency of the licence be, used as a betting office;

and such a licence shall not be granted to the Board unless either they are the holders of a betting office licence under the said Part I authorising them to use the premises as a betting office or the Commissioners are, with respect to the premises, satisfied as mentioned in paragraph (*b*) of this subsection.

(7) Where a betting office licence under Part I of the Act of 1963, authorising the use of any premises as a betting office, ceases to be in force, any betting premises licence granted to the holder in respect of those premises shall become void; and where a person is the holder of a bookmaker's permit under that Act and the permit ceases to be in force, any betting premises licence of which he is the holder (in respect of any premises, wherever situated) shall become void.

PART I

(8) A betting premises licence shall expire at the end of 30th September next after the date on which it is expressed to take effect.

(9) The provisions of Schedule 8 to this Act (being provisions as to administration and enforcement) shall have effect with respect to betting premises licences and the duty thereon.

(10) For the avoidance of doubt, it is hereby declared that nothing contained in, or done under, this section or Schedule 8 to this Act shall make lawful anything which would be unlawful apart from those provisions.

(11) In this section and in Schedule 8 to this Act—

" the Act of 1963 " means the Betting, Gaming and Lotteries Act 1963 ; 1963 c. 2.

" betting transaction ", " bookmaker " and " track " have the same meaning as in the Act of 1963 ;

" Great Britain " includes the territorial waters of the United Kingdom adjacent to Great Britain ;

" hereditament ", in relation to Scotland, means lands and heritages ;

" premises " includes any place whatsoever and any means of transport ; and

" rateable value ", in relation to a hereditament, means (without prejudice to paragraph 6 of Schedule 8 to this Act) the rateable value shown in the valuation list (or, in Scotland, the valuation roll) as for the time being in force.

Bingo duty.

3.—(1) As from 1st October 1969, a duty of excise, to be known as bingo duty, shall be charged on the playing of bingo in Great Britain and be paid by the promoter of the bingo.

(2) Bingo duty shall be charged in respect of bingo played in a particular week ; and the amount of the duty shall be—

(*a*) two-and-a-half per cent. of the total of the money taken by or on behalf of the promoter in that week as payment by players for their cards, plus

(*b*) (subject to subsection (4) of this section) one-thirty-ninth of the amount (if any) by which that total, after deduction of the two-and-a-half per cent. chargeable under paragraph (*a*), is exceeded by the total value of the prizes won in that week's bingo.

(3) For the purposes of this section, a player's " cards " are the sets of numbers or symbols (in whatever form or lay-out) with which he plays bingo, matching them against calls made by the house ; and a player pays for a card when he gives money

PART I

in exchange for, or for the use of, a particular card, whether it is appropriated to a particular game or can be appropriated by the player to a game of his choice.

(4) Where bingo is promoted at one place and, for the purpose of a particular game, it is combined with bingo played at another place and promoted by another person, so that the players at both places share in the chance of winning a prize contributed partly by one promoter and partly by the other, then for the purposes of the charge to bingo duty under subsection (2)(*b*) of this section—

(*a*) as against the promoter of the bingo at the place where the prize is won there shall be counted so much only of the value of the prize as represents his contribution; and

(*b*) so much of the value of the prize as represents the contribution of the other promoter shall be counted as a prize won at bingo promoted by him;

and where in the case of bingo so combined the prize is provided wholly by or on behalf of one of the promoters concerned, its whole value shall be counted against him under the said subsection (2)(*b*), wherever it is won.

(5) It shall not be lawful for a game of bingo, being bingo which is chargeable with bingo duty and is promoted at a place in Great Britain, to be combined as mentioned in subsection (4) of this section with other bingo played elsewhere than in Great Britain, except where the other bingo is played in Northern Ireland or the Isle of Man and is chargeable, under an Act of the Parliament of Northern Ireland or, as the case may be, Tynwald with duty corresponding to bingo duty and at a rate not less than that which is chargeable under this section.

(6) Bingo duty shall be recoverable jointly and severally from all or any of the following persons—

(*a*) the promoter;

(*b*) any person who took money as payment by players for cards or paid prizes to players;

(*c*) any person who was responsible for the management of the premises on which bingo was played;

(*d*) where the promoter or any such person as is mentioned in paragraph (*b*) or (*c*) of this subsection is a company, any director of the company.

(7) The playing of bingo shall not be chargeable with bingo duty in any of the cases specified in Part I of Schedule 9 to this Act.

(8) In section 32(1)(*b*) of the Act of 1963 (which makes it a condition of lawful gaming that money or money's worth put down by players as stakes or paid by them as losses is not to

be disposed of otherwise than to a player as winnings) after the word " winnings " there shall be added the words " or by payment of bingo duty ". PART I

(9) The provisions of Part II of Schedule 9 to this Act (being provisions as to administration and enforcement) shall have effect with respect to bingo duty.

(10) In this section and in Schedule 9 to this Act—

" the Act of 1963 " means the Betting, Gaming and Lotteries Act 1963 ; 1963 c. 2.

" bingo " includes any version of that game, by whatever name called, except a version whose rules permit a player to withdraw any part of his initial stake after the game has begun ;

" Great Britain " includes the territorial waters of the United Kingdom adjacent to Great Britain ;

" money " includes any token, voucher or other object given by a player in exchange for cards and recognised for the purpose of the exchange to represent a particular sum of money ;

" prize " means anything won or to be won at bingo, whether money or something else having a value, and " value " and " paid ", in relation to prizes, shall be construed accordingly ;

" the promoter ", in relation to bingo, means the person to whom the players look for the payment of prizes, and " promote " and " promotion " shall be construed accordingly ; and

" week " means a period of seven days beginning with Monday and includes the period of five days beginning with 1st October 1969.

(11) In proceedings relating to bingo duty under the excise Acts an averment in any process that a particular game is a version of bingo shall, until the contrary is proved, be sufficient evidence that it is so.

(12) For the avoidance of doubt, it is hereby declared that nothing contained in or done under the provisions of this section or Schedule 9 to this Act shall make lawful anything which would be unlawful apart from those provisions.

Gaming licence duty. 1966 c. 18.

4.—(1) The amount of the duty under section 13 of the Finance Act 1966 on a gaming licence in respect of any premises granted so as to expire on a date later than 30th September 1969

Part I

shall be determined with the substitution for the Table set out in subsection (2) of that section (as amended by section 4(3) of the Finance Act 1968) of the Table set out in Part I of Schedule 10 to this Act.

1968 c. 44.

(2) As from 1st October 1969, a gaming licence under the said section 13 shall not be required for any gaming by way of bingo, and the power of the Treasury by order under subsection (6) of that section to add to the games mentioned in subsection (5) thereof shall not include power to add the game of bingo, except a version of that game not chargeable with bingo duty under section 3 of this Act.

(3) In accordance with subsection (2) of this section, section 13 of, and Schedule 3 to, the Finance Act 1966 shall be amended as shown in Part II of Schedule 10 to this Act.

1966 c. 18.

(4) Where, after 30th June 1969, a gaming licence authorising the use of premises for gaming by way of bingo only has been granted so as to expire at the end of 30th September 1970, and at any time after 1st October 1969 the holder of the licence surrenders it to the proper officer, he shall be entitled to repayment of three-quarters of the amount of the duty paid on the licence.

Gaming machines.

5.—(1) There shall be charged a duty of excise on a licence (to be called a gaming machine licence) authorising gaming machines to be provided for gaming on premises in respect of which the licence is granted.

(2) Part I of Schedule 11 to this Act shall have effect for defining what is a gaming machine for the purposes of this section and that Schedule: and for those purposes a " penny machine " is a gaming machine which, in order to be played once, requires the insertion of a single penny and which cannot be played in any other way.

(3) A gaming machine licence shall be either—

(*a*) an ordinary licence, being—

(i) a whole-year licence for the period from 1st October in any year to 30th September in the following year, or

(ii) a half-year licence for the period from 1st October in any year to 31st March in the following year or from 1st April in any year to 30th September in that year ; or (*b*) a holiday season licence (for penny machines only) for the period from 1st March in any year to 31st October in that year, **Part I**

(all dates inclusive); and where a licence of either description is granted so as to have effect for the remainder of a licence period which has partly expired, the charge to duty shall be unaffected by the circumstance that a licence of the other description has been in force in respect of the same premises for any part of that period.

(4) The duty on an ordinary licence shall be determined by reference—

(*a*) to whether the premises in question have, or have not, local authority approval under the Gaming Acts; and

(*b*) to whether the licence authorises the provision of machines chargeable at the lower, or the higher, rate and to the number of machines of either description which it authorises.

(5) Part II of Schedule 11 to this Act shall have effect with respect to the cases in which premises are to be treated as having local authority approval under the Gaming Acts; and for the purposes of an ordinary licence—

(*a*) a machine is chargeable at the lower rate if it can only be played by the insertion into the machine of a coin or coins of a denomination, or aggregate denomination, not exceeding threepence; and

(*b*) a machine is chargeable at the higher rate in any other case;

except that, where the game playable by means of a machine can be played more than once for the insertion of a coin or coins of a denomination, or aggregate denomination, exceeding threepence, the machine is to be treated as chargeable at the lower rate if in effect the amount payable to play the game once does not exceed threepence.

(6) The duty on an ordinary whole-year licence shall be in accordance with the following Tables and—

(*a*) Table A shall apply where the Commissioners are satisfied that the premises in question will, on the date on which the licence is first in force, have local authority approval under the Gaming Acts; and

(*b*) Table B shall apply in any other case.

PART I

TABLE A

Premises with local authority approval

Description of machines authorised by the licence	Number of machines of that description so authorised	Duty on whole-year licence
Chargeable at the lower rate.	One machine	£12 10s. 0d.
	Two or more machines	£12 10s. 0d. plus £75 per machine in excess of one.
Chargeable at the higher rate	One machine	£25.
	Two or more machines	£25 plus £150 per machine in excess of one.

TABLE B

Premises without local authority approval

Description of machines authorised by the licence	Number of machines of that description so authorised	Duty on whole-year licence
Chargeable at the lower rate	One machine	£50.
	Two or more machines	£50 plus £150 per machine in excess of one.
Chargeable at the higher rate	One machine	£100.
	Two or more machines	£100 plus £300 per machine in excess of one.

(7) The duty on an ordinary half-year licence shall be eleven-twentieths of that which it would have been if the licence were an ordinary whole-year, but otherwise identical, licence.

(8) A holiday season licence shall be granted only for premises as to which the Commissioners are satisfied that they will, on the date on which the licence is first in force, have local authority approval under the Gaming Acts by virtue of paragraph 5 or 6 of Schedule 11 to this Act ; and—

(*a*) the licence shall be one which authorises the provision only of penny machines up to a number specified in the licence ; and (*b*) the duty on the licence shall be £15 multiplied by that number.

(9) For the purposes of this section, a machine which two or more persons can play simultaneously (whether or not participating with one another in the same game) shall not be treated as one machine but—

(*a*) in the case of a penny machine, shall be treated for the purposes of a holiday season licence as a number of penny machines equal to the number of persons who can play the machine simultaneously;

(*b*) in the case of a penny machine or any other machine which no player can play except by the insertion into the machine of a coin or coins of a denomination, or aggregate denomination, not exceeding threepence, shall be treated for the purposes of an ordinary licence as a number of machines, all chargeable at the lower rate, equal to the number of persons who can play the machine simultaneously; and

(*c*) in a case not falling within paragraph (*b*) of this subsection, shall be treated for the purposes of an ordinary licence as a number of machines, all chargeable at the higher rate, equal to that number of persons;

and the number of persons who can play a particular machine simultaneously shall be determined by reference to the number of individual playing positions provided on the machine.

(10) Part III of Schedule 11 to this Act shall have effect for exempting from the requirement of a gaming machine licence the provision of gaming machines at certain charitable entertainments and pleasure fairs and for the temporary exemption of certain premises where only penny machines are provided.

(11) As from 1st October 1969—

(*a*) except where one of the exemptions in Part III of Schedule 11 to this Act applies, no gaming machine shall be provided for gaming on any premises situated in Great Britain unless there is a gaming machine licence for the time being in force in respect of the premises;

(*b*) at any time when an ordinary licence is in force in respect of any such premises and authorises the provision only of gaming machines chargeable at one of the two rates, no gaming machine chargeable at the other rate shall be provided for gaming on those premises;

(*c*) at any time when an ordinary licence is so in force and authorises the provision of a specified number of

PART I machines chargeable at a specified rate, gaming machines chargeable at that rate shall not be provided for gaming on those premises in excess of the number authorised by the licence for machines so chargeable; and

(*d*) at any time when a holiday season licence is in force in respect of any such premises, gaming machines shall not be provided for gaming on those premises except penny machines up to the number specified in the licence.

(12) A machine is provided for gaming on any premises if it is made available thereon in such a way that persons resorting to the premises can play it; and where on any premises one or more gaming machines are so made available, any such machine anywhere on the premises shall be treated as provided for gaming thereon, notwithstanding that it is not so made available or is not in a state in which it can be played.

(13) The provisions of Part IV of Schedule 11 to this Act (being provisions as to administration and enforcement) shall have effect with respect to gaming machine licences and the duty thereon.

(14) For the avoidance of doubt, it is hereby declared that nothing contained in, or done under, this section or Schedule 11 to this Act shall make lawful anything which would be unlawful apart from those provisions.

(15) In this section and in Schedule 11 to this Act—

1963 c. 2. "the Act of 1963" means the Betting, Gaming and Lotteries Act 1963;

1968 c. 65. "the Act of 1968" means the Gaming Act 1968;

"coin" means coin lawfully current in the United Kingdom;

"Great Britain" includes the territorial waters of the United Kingdom adjacent to Great Britain; and

"premises" includes any place whatsoever and any means of transport.

1966 c. 18. (16) As from 1st October 1969, section 14 of the Finance Act 1966 (which charges an excise licence duty in respect of gaming machines, but with an incidence different from that of this section) shall cease to have effect; and accordingly in section 15 of that Act (supplemental provisions as to duties on betting and gaming), in subsections (4) and (6), for the words "sections 12 to 14" (in both places) there shall be substituted the words "sections 12 and 13".

(17) Where, after 30th June 1969, a gaming machine licence under section 14 of the Finance Act 1966 has been granted so as to expire at the end of 30th September 1970, and at any time after 1st October 1969 the holder of the licence surrenders it to the proper officer, he shall be entitled to repayment of three-quarters of the amount of the duty paid on the licence. **PART I** **1966 c. 18.**

Vehicle licences.

6.—(1) As from 1st September 1969, the Vehicles (Excise) Act 1962 shall have effect as if in section 6 (which provides for certain exemptions from duty) after subsection (2) there were inserted the following subsections:— **1962 c. 13.**

" (2A) A mechanically propelled vehicle shall not be chargeable with any duty under this Act if purchase tax in respect of the vehicle is remitted under section 23 of the Purchase Tax Act 1963 on the ground that the vehicle has been acquired from its manufacturer by a person who is an overseas resident; but if at any time purchase tax becomes payable in respect of that vehicle under section 9 of the Finance Act 1967, or would have become so payable but for any authorisation or waiver under subsection (1) of the said section 9, then the provisions of subsection (2C) of this section shall apply in relation to that vehicle. **1963 c. 9.** **1967 c. 54.**

(2B) Where in the case of any mechanically propelled vehicle it is shown to the satisfaction of the authority with whom the vehicle is registered—

(*a*) that the vehicle is not chargeable with purchase tax ; and

(*b*) that the vehicle is being acquired from a person who is for the time being registered as a manufacturer of such vehicles by the Minister and who is the manufacturer of the vehicle for the purposes of that register ; and

(*c*) that the person so acquiring the vehicle would fall to be treated as an overseas resident for the purposes of the said section 23,

that authority may exempt the vehicle from duty under this Act for a period of twelve months subject to specified conditions, being such conditions as the Minister may from time to time think necessary for the protection of the revenue ; but if at any time during those twelve months any of the conditions subject to which the exemption is granted is not complied with, the provisions of subsection (2C) of this section shall apply in relation to the vehicle.

(2C) Where under subsection (2A) or (2B) of this section the provisions of this subsection are to apply in relation to a vehicle, the vehicle shall be deemed never to have been exempted from duty under the said subsection (2A) or

PART I

1967 c. 54. (2B) and, without prejudice to the provisions of section 12 of the Finance Act 1967 (under which an amount related to the period during which a vehicle was unlicensed is required to be paid by the keeper of the vehicle who is convicted of using it during that period), unless, or except to the extent that, the authority with whom the vehicle is registered sees fit to waive payment of the whole or part of the duty, there shall be recoverable by that authority as a debt due to that authority—

(*a*) from the person by whom the vehicle was acquired from its manufacturer, the duty in respect of the whole period since the registration of the vehicle; or

(*b*) from any other person who is for the time being the keeper of the vehicle, the duty in respect of the period since the vehicle was first kept by that other person,

other than any part of that period by reference to which there was calculated an amount ordered to be paid by the person in question in respect of the vehicle in pursuance of subsection (1) of the said section 12."

(2) As from 1st January 1970—

1962 c. 13. (*a*) for subsections (1) to (5) of section 12 of the Vehicles (Excise) Act 1962 (which relate to trade licences) there shall be substituted the new subsections (1) to (5) set out in Part I of Schedule 12 to this Act, being new subsections designed—

(i) to restrict the vehicles which may be used under a trade licence, in the case of a motor trader, to vehicles temporarily in his possession in the course of his business as a motor trader and recovery vehicles kept by him for the purpose of dealing with disabled vehicles in the course of that business or, in the case of a vehicle tester, to vehicles submitted for testing by him in the course of his business as a vehicle tester;

(ii) to restrict the purposes for which vehicles may be used under a trade licence;

(iii) to substitute for general trade licences and limited trade licences a single type of trade licence at the rate of duty applicable in accordance with those new subsections;

(iv) to make further consequential amendments to the existing subsections;

(*b*) the provisions of the said Act of 1962 or of the Vehicle and Driving Licences Act 1969 specified in Part II of the said Schedule 12 shall have effect with the supplementary or consequential amendments respectively so specified. PART I 1969 c. 27.

(3) Any reference in the Vehicle and Driving Licences Act 1969 to any provision of the Vehicles (Excise) Act 1962 which has been amended by this section shall be construed as a reference to that provision as so amended. 1962 c. 13.

(4) This section shall be construed as one with the Vehicles (Excise) Act 1962.

PART II

INCOME TAX AND CORPORATION TAX

Rates of Tax

Charge of income tax 1969–70.

7. Income tax for the year 1969-70 shall be charged at the standard rate of 41·25 per cent. (which is equivalent to 8s. 3d. in the pound) and, in the case of an individual whose total income exceeds £2,000, at such higher rates in respect of the excess as Parliament may hereafter determine.

Surtax rates for 1968–69.

8. Income tax for the year 1968-69 shall be charged, in the case of an individual whose total income exceeded £2,000, at the same higher rates in respect of the excess as were charged for the year 1967-68.

Charge of corporation tax for financial year 1968.

9. Corporation tax shall be charged for the financial year 1968 at the rate of 45 per cent.

Reliefs and deductions

Alterations of personal reliefs.

10.—(1) The provisions of this section shall have effect for the year 1969-70 and subsequent years of assessment.

(2) In section 210 of the Income Tax Act 1952 (personal reliefs), as amended by section 10(2) of the Finance Act 1965, in paragraph (*a*) of subsection (1) (married) for the reference to £340 there shall be substituted a reference to £375, in paragraph (*b*) of that subsection (single) for the reference to £220 there shall be substituted a reference to £255, and in subsection (2) of the said section 210 (wife's earned income relief) for the reference to £220 there shall be substituted a reference to £255. 1952 c. 10. 1965 c. 25.

PART II

1952 c. 10. (3) The following Table shall be substituted for the Table set out in section 220(1) of the Income Tax Act 1952 (reduced rate relief):—

TABLE

Where the relevant amount—

does not exceed £260 ...	a deduction equal to 11·25 per cent. of the relevant amount (which is equivalent to a deduction of 2s. 3d. for each pound of the relevant amount);
exceeds £260	the same deduction as if the relevant amount were £260.

(4) In subsections (2) and (3) of section 211 of the Income Tax Act 1952 (old age relief), as amended by section 12(2) of

1963 c. 25. the Finance Act 1963, for the references to £900 (maximum income qualifying for full relief) there shall be substituted references to £1,000.

(5) In section 216(1) of the Income Tax Act 1952 (relief for dependent relative), as amended by subsections (2) and (3) of

1967 c. 54. section 16 of the Finance Act 1967, for the reference to £235 (lower income limit of dependent relative) there shall be substituted a reference to £245, for the reference to £310 (the normal higher income limit) there shall be substituted a reference to £320 and for the references in the said section 216(1) and the said subsection (3) to £345 (the higher income limit where the claimant is a woman other than a married woman living with her husband) there shall be substituted references to £355.

1957 c. 49. (6) Section 13 of the Finance Act 1957 (relief for persons over sixty five with small incomes), as amended by section 14(1)

1968 c. 44. of the Finance Act 1968, shall be amended by substituting for the references to £415 and £665 (income limits for exemption) references to £425 and £680 and for the reference to £230 (the excess over those limits beyond which relief by reduction of tax is excluded) a reference to £265.

1952 c. 33. (7) In section 15(2) of the Finance Act 1952 (relief for small

1965 c. 25. incomes), as amended by section 10(5) of the Finance Act 1965, for the reference to £705 (income limit for marginal relief) there shall be substituted a reference to £710.

1960 c. 44. (8) In section 17(2) of the Finance Act 1960 (additional relief for widows and others in respect of children) for the reference to £75 (which was substituted by section 16(5) of the Finance Act 1967) there shall be substituted a reference to £100, and the reference to £75 in section 218(4) of the Income Tax Act 1952 (which is applied for the purposes of the said section 17) shall be construed accordingly.

(9) The amounts of tax deductible or repayable under section 157 of the Income Tax Act 1952 (pay as you earn) before 22nd June, 1969, shall be deemed not to have been affected by the preceding provisions of this section, but this subsection shall not prevent any necessary correction being made on or after that day by adjusting subsequent deductions or repayments under that section or, if need be, by an assessment. PART II 1952 c. 10.

Child relief, accumulation settlements and family allowances.

11.—(1) Section 212 of the Income Tax Act 1952 (which entitles the parent of a child who is under sixteen or receiving full-time education to relief or, if that relief is not due or claimed, entitles the individual maintaining the child to similar relief) shall be amended in accordance with subsections (2) and (3) below.

(2) In subsection (1) of the said section 212, for the words from " that he has living " to " educational establishment " there shall be substituted the words—

" (*a*) that there is living at any time within the year of assessment a child of his with respect to whom one of the conditions in subsection (2) of this section is fulfilled, or

(*b*) that for the year of assessment he has the custody of and maintains at his own expense a child (other than a child of his) with respect to whom one of those conditions is fulfilled " ;

and any reference in any enactment passed before the passing of this Act to relief under subsection (2) of the said section 212 shall be construed as a reference to relief under subsection (1)(*b*) of that section, as amended by this subsection.

(3) For subsection (2) of the said section 212 there shall be substituted the following subsection :—

" (2) The conditions referred to in subsection (1) of this section are—

(*a*) that the child is born in, or is under the age of sixteen years at the commencement of, the year of assessment referred to in that subsection ; or

(*b*) that the child is over the age of sixteen years at the commencement of that year of assessment but is receiving full-time instruction at any university, college, school or other educational establishment."

(4) At the end of the said section 212 there shall be added the following subsection: —

" (6) Notwithstanding anything in section 9 of the Family Law Reform Act 1969 or any corresponding enactment of 1969 c. 46.

PART II

the Parliament of Northern Ireland or any rule of law in Scotland, for the purposes of this section a child whose birthday falls on 6th April shall be taken to be over the age of eleven at the commencement of the year which begins with his eleventh birthday and over the age of sixteen at the commencement of the year which begins with his sixteenth birthday."

1952 c. 10

(5) For the purposes of section 228 of the Income Tax Act 1952 (relief in respect of income accumulated under trusts) no account shall be taken of any tax paid in respect of income for a year of assessment beginning after the year 1968-69 or of any relief to which a person would have been entitled for such a year of assessment in the circumstances mentioned in that section.

1968 c. 44.

(6) Subsection (4) of section 14 of the Finance Act 1968 (which for 1968-69 provided that an individual's total reliefs should be reduced in respect of each family allowance in respect of which he was assessable to income tax) shall be amended by substituting—

(*a*) for the words " 1968-69 " the words " 1969-70 or any subsequent year of assessment ", and

(*b*) for the words from " tax at the standard rate on £36 " to the end of the subsection the words " tax at the standard rate on £42 or, if the payments in question are payments for a part only of the year, by a proportionate part of that amount ",

and subsections (5) to (7) of that section (which contain ancillary provisions) shall have effect accordingly.

Albert and Edward medals.

12.—(1) Annuities paid to holders of the Albert Medal or of the Edward Medal by virtue of holding that award shall be disregarded for all the purposes of the Income Tax Acts.

(2) This section has effect as from 14th November 1968 (that is to say the date on which annuities became so payable).

Relief for painters, sculptors and other artists.

13.—(1) In section 471 of the Income Tax Act 1952 (copyright: relief by spreading lump sums over two or three years) after subsection (1) insert—

" (1A) Where the artist obtains any sum for the sale of a painting, sculpture or other work of art, or by way of commission or fee for the creation of the work of art, and—

(*a*) he was engaged on the making of the work of art for a period of more than twelve months, or

(*b*) he was engaged for a period of more than twelve months in making a number of works of art for an exhibition, and the work is one of them,

he shall be entitled to claim that effect shall be given to the following provisions of this section as respects that sum."

(2) Nothing in section 22 of the Finance Act 1953 (which amends the said section 471) shall be taken as affecting the relief given by this section. PART II 1953 c. 34.

(3) This section shall apply to sums falling to be included in computing profits or gains for the year 1969-70 or any subsequent year of assessment, and in relation to those sums shall authorise the making of assessments for years of assessment earlier than the year 1969-70.

Local authority borrowing in foreign currency.

14.—(1) If the Treasury direct that this section shall apply to any securities issued by a local authority and expressed in the currency of a country which at the time of the issue is outside the scheduled territories, interest on those securities—

(*a*) shall be paid without deduction of income tax, and

(*b*) so long as the beneficial owner is not resident in the United Kingdom, shall be exempt from income tax (but not from corporation tax).

(2) Where for repayment of the principal amount due under the securities there is an option between one or more currencies within subsection (1) above and one or more other currencies, that subsection shall be applicable to the securities if the option is exercisable only by the holder of the securities, and shall not be applicable to the securities in any other case.

(3) Section 429 of the Income Tax Act 1952 (treatment for tax, including corporation tax, of income of foreign life assurance funds) shall have effect as if references to securities in subsection (2) of that section included any securities to which this section applies. 1952 c. 10.

(4) Where any income of any person is by virtue of any provision of the Income Tax Acts to be deemed to be income of any other person, that income shall not be exempt from tax by virtue of this section by reason of the first-mentioned person not being resident in the United Kingdom.

(5) In this section—

" local authority " has the meaning given by section 66(2) of the Finance Act 1965, 1965 c. 25.

" the scheduled territories " means the territories specified in Schedule 1 to the Exchange Control Act 1947 as for the time being in force. 1947 c. 14.

Definitions of farm land and farming.

15. For the definition of " farm land " in section 526(1) of the Income Tax Act 1952 (which includes the farmhouse) and the related definition of " farming " substitute

' " farm land " means land in the United Kingdom wholly or mainly occupied for the purposes of husbandry,

PART II

but excluding any dwelling or domestic offices, and excluding market garden land, and " farming " shall be construed accordingly '.

Children

Reduction in age of majority for tax purposes.

1969 c. 46.
1969 c. 39.

16.—(1) Subject to the following provisions of this section, section 1 of the Family Law Reform Act 1969 and section 1 of the Age of Majority (Scotland) Act 1969 (which reduce the age of majority to eighteen except for the purposes of the statutory provisions referred to in Schedule 2 thereof) shall apply for the purposes of any statutory provision, as defined in those sections, relating to income tax (including surtax), capital gains tax, corporation tax or estate duty; and accordingly paragraph 3 of Schedule 2 to each of those Acts shall cease to have effect.

(2) At the end of section 13 of the Family Law Reform Act 1969 (powers of Parliament of Northern Ireland to make laws for purposes similar to purposes of Part I of that Act) there shall be added the words " as amended by the Finance Act 1969 ".

1952 c. 10.

(3) Notwithstanding anything in subsection (1) above, for the year 1969-70 and subsequent years of assessment any reference to an infant in Chapter II of Part XVIII of the Income Tax Act 1952 (settlements on children generally) shall be construed as a reference to a person who either—

(*a*) has not attained the age of eighteen ; or

(*b*) has attained that age but has not attained the age of twenty-one and is not working regularly, within the meaning of section 15(4) of the Finance Act 1968.

1968 c. 44.

(4) Section 15 of, and Schedule 8 to, the Finance Act 1968 (aggregation for 1969-70 and subsequent years of certain income of unmarried infants with income of their parents) shall have effect, and shall be deemed always to have had effect, as if any reference therein to an infant were a reference to a person who has not attained the age of eighteen.

(5) Without prejudice to subsection (3) of the said section 15 (which disapplies that section and provisions of the said Chapter II where for any year of assessment the aggregate income of an infant does not exceed £5) income paid to or for the benefit of a child of a settlor shall not be treated as provided in section 397(1) of the said Act of 1952 (income of child under settlement made by his parent treated as parent's income) for any year of assessment in which the child is over the age of eighteen if the aggregate amount of the income paid to or for the benefit of the child which, but for this subsection, would be so treated by virtue of the said Chapter II, does not exceed £5.

Part II

Exclusion from aggregation of certain income of infants. 1968 c. 44.

17. Section 15(2) of the Finance Act 1968 (which excludes certain income of an infant from aggregation with his or her parent's income) shall be amended—

(*a*) by adding, at the end of paragraph (*b*) (which relates to income from sums paid by way of damages for personal injuries) the words " or paid in respect of any such personal injury by a body established for charitable purposes only or by the Criminal Injuries Compensation Board or under any enactment of the Parliament of Northern Ireland providing for compensation in respect of criminal injuries " ; and

(*b*) by inserting after the said paragraph (*b*) the words " or

(*c*) income consisting of payments made to a female infant by the putative father of a child of the infant and for the benefit, maintenance or education of that child."

Disallowance of interest as a deduction

Disallowance of interest as a deduction. 1952 c. 10.

18.—(1) In section 169(1) of the Income Tax Act 1952 (allowable deductions from income in charging income tax at standard rate), and in section 2(2)(*a*) of that Act (corresponding provision for surtax), references to yearly interest or annual interest shall be omitted.

This subsection applies—

(*a*) to interest paid after 5th April 1970, and

(*b*) to interest paid earlier on any debt incurred after 15th April 1969.

(2) Section 200 of the Income Tax Act 1952 (relief for interest paid gross to banks etc. out of taxed income) shall cease to have effect.

This subsection applies to all interest paid after 5th April 1970, and to interest paid in the year 1969-70 in respect of any period beginning after 30th June 1969.

(3) Section 445(3)(*b*) of the Income Tax Act 1952 (relief for payments to building societies, etc.) shall cease to have effect

This subsection applies—

(*a*) to interest paid after 5th April 1970,

(*b*) to interest paid earlier on any debt incurred after 15th April 1969.

(4) In section 137(*l*) of the Income Tax Act 1952 (disallowance as business expenses of annual interest etc. paid out of taxed profits) the reference to annual interest shall be omitted.

PART II

This subsection applies—

(*a*) for the purposes of income tax for the year 1969-70 and earlier years of assessment, to interest paid on any debt incurred after 15th April 1969, and

(*b*) for the purposes of income tax for the year 1970-71 and subsequent years of assessment, to any payment of annual interest, whenever made.

1965 c. 25.

(5) No payment of interest made by a company which is such a payment as is mentioned in section 52(3) of the Finance Act 1965 (charges on income of companies) shall be treated as a charge on income unless—

(*a*) the company exists wholly or mainly for the purpose of carrying on a trade, or

(*b*) the payment of interest is wholly and exclusively laid out or expended for the purposes of a trade carried on by the company, or

(*c*) the company is an investment company (as defined by section 57(4) of the Finance Act 1965, and including an authorised unit trust scheme), or

(*d*) the payment of interest would be eligible for relief under the next following section, or section 24 of this Act, if it were made by an individual.

This subsection applies—

(i) to interest paid after 5th April 1970, and

(ii) to bank, discount house or stock exchange interest paid in the year 1969-70 in respect of any period beginning after 30th June 1969, and

(iii) to interest paid in the year 1969-70 on any debt incurred after 15th April 1969, not being bank, discount house or stock exchange interest,

and in this subsection " trade " has the meaning given by section 89(2)(*j*) of the Finance Act 1965.

1952 c. 10.

(6) In section 132(1)(*c*) of the Income Tax Act 1952 (allowable deductions in Cases IV and V of Schedule D) the reference to annual interest shall be omitted.

This subsection applies—

(*a*) to interest on any debt incurred after 15th April 1969, and

(*b*) to interest paid after 5th April 1975 on a debt incurred on or before 15th April 1969.

(7) Schedule 13 to this Act shall have effect for supplementing this and the nine next following sections which in that Schedule are referred to as " the principal sections ".

PART II

(8) Any payment made for the period ending on 15th May, 1970, in respect of yearly interest on a debt incurred on or before 15th April 1969, and secured on land in Scotland shall, if made on or before 15th August 1970, be deemed for the purposes of this section to have been paid and payable before 6th April 1970.

Loans for purchase or improvement of land.

19.—(1) Interest eligible for relief under this section shall, if the person paying the interest so claims, be deducted from or set off against his income for the year of assessment in which the interest is paid, and income tax shall be discharged or repaid accordingly.

(2) Subject to the provisions of this section, interest is eligible for relief under this section if it is paid by a person for the time being owning an estate or interest in land in the United Kingdom on a loan to defray money applied—

(*a*) in purchasing the estate or interest, or one absorbed into, or given up to obtain, the estate or interest, or

(*b*) in improving or developing the land, or buildings on the land, or

(*c*) in paying off another loan where the claimant could have obtained relief under this section for interest on that other loan if it had not been paid off (and, if free of interest, assuming it carried interest).

(3) Subsection (2) above shall not apply to a loan unless made in connection with the application of the money, and either on the occasion of its application, or within what is in the circumstances a reasonable time from the application of the money, and that subsection shall not apply to a loan the proceeds of which are applied for some other purpose before being applied as described in that subsection.

(4) If and so far as a loan made by allowing the debtor to overdraw an account is applied in improving land or buildings (otherwise than by the construction of a building or part of a building) no relief shall be given in respect of interest on the loan falling due more than three years after the end of the year of assessment in which the loan is so applied.

(5) References in this section to money applied in improving or developing land or buildings include references to payments in respect of maintenance or repairs incurred by reason of dilapidation attributable to a period before the estate or interest was acquired, but otherwise do not include references to payments in respect of maintenance or repairs, or any of the other payments mentioned in paragraph 1 of Schedule 4 to the Finance Act 1963 (payments deductible from rent). 1963 c. 25

PART II

(6) References in this section to money applied in improving or developing land include references to expenditure incurred or defrayed directly or indirectly in respect of street works, other than works of maintenance or repair, for any highway or road, or in Scotland any right of way, adjoining or serving the land.

(7) References in this section to an estate or interest in land include references to the property in any caravan but, unless it is a large caravan, no relief shall be given by virtue of this subsection in respect of the payment of any interest unless—

(*a*) the caravan, taken with the land on which it stands, is for the time being a rateable hereditament for the pur-
1967 c. 9. poses of the General Rate Act 1967 or any corresponding enactment in force in Scotland or Northern Ireland, and

(*b*) the owner, or his wife or her husband, has, as occupier of the caravan, duly paid rates under that Act or any such enactment for the period in which the interest was paid.

In this subsection " hereditament ", in relation to Scotland, means lands and heritages.

(8) References in this section to an estate or interest do not include references—

(*a*) to a rentcharge or, in Scotland, a superiority or the interest of a creditor in a contract of ground annual ; or

(*b*) to the interest of a chargee or mortgagee, or, in Scotland, the interest of a creditor in a charge or security of any kind over land.

(9) Where relief for any year of assessment is given under this section in respect of interest on any debt, then interest on that debt shall not be allowable as a deduction for any other purpose of the Income Tax Acts for that year or any subsequent year of assessment if and so far as this section applies to that interest ; and where interest on any debt is allowed as a deduction in computing profits or gains or losses for the purposes of income tax for any year of assessment (being the year 1970-71 or any later year of assessment), then this section shall not apply to interest on that debt in relation to that or any subsequent year of assessment.

In this subsection references to relief having been given or a deduction being allowed are references to its being given or allowed in a claim or assessment which has been finally determined.

(10) Subsection (2)(*a*) above shall not apply—

(*a*) where the seller and purchaser are a husband and his wife, and either sells to the other, or

PART II

(*b*) where the purchaser, or the wife or husband of the purchaser, has, since 15th April 1969, disposed of an estate or interest in the land in question and it appears that the main purpose of the disposal and purchase was to obtain relief in respect of interest on the loan, or

(*c*) where the purchasers are the trustees of a settlement, and the seller is the settlor, or the wife or husband of the settlor, and it appears that the main purpose of the purchase is to obtain relief in respect of interest on the loan, or

(*d*) where the purchaser is directly or indirectly purchasing from a person connected with him, and the price substantially exceeds the value of what is acquired,

and subsection (2)(*b*) above shall not apply where the person spending the money is connected with the person who, directly or indirectly, receives the money, and the money substantially exceeds the value of the work done.

For the purposes of this subsection—

(i) references to a husband and wife are references to a husband and his wife living with him,

(ii) any question whether a person is connected with another shall be determined in accordance with paragraph 21 of Schedule 7 to the Finance Act 1965. 1965 c. 25.

(11) In this section, as it applies throughout the United Kingdom—

" caravan " has the meaning given by section 29(1) of the Caravan Sites and Control of Development Act 1960, 1960 c. 62.

" large caravan " means one which has either or both of the following dimensions—

(*a*) an overall length (excluding any drawbar) exceeding 22 feet;

(*b*) an overall width, exceeding 7 feet 6 inches

where " overall length " and " overall width " have the meanings given in Regulation 3 of the Motor Vehicles (Construction and Use) Regulations 1966, S.I. 1966/1288.

" street works " means any works for the sewering, levelling, paving, metalling, flagging, channelling and making good of a road, and includes the provision of proper means for lighting a road.

20.—(1) This section applies to a loan to an individual to defray money applied— Loan applied in acquiring interest in close company.

(*a*) in acquiring any part of the ordinary share capital of a close company within subsection (2) below, or

PART II

(*b*) in lending money to such a close company which is used wholly and exclusively for the purposes of the business of the company or of any associated company (being a close company within subsection (2) below) of the company, or

(*c*) in paying off another loan where relief could have been obtained under this section for interest on that other loan if it had not been paid off (and, if free of interest, assuming it carried interest).

(2) Subsection (1) above applies to a close company—

(*a*) if it is a trading company, or

(*b*) if it is a member of a trading group, or

(*c*) if the whole, or substantially the whole, of its income is of one or more of the following descriptions, that is—

(i) estate or trading income, or

(ii) interest and dividends or other distributions received from a subsidiary which is itself within paragraph (*a*), (*b*) or (*c*) of this subsection.

(3) Relief shall be given in respect of any payment of the interest by the individual on the loan—

(*a*) if when the interest is paid he has a material interest in the company, and

(*b*) if, taking the period from the application of the proceeds of the loan until the interest was paid as a whole, he has worked for the greater part of his time in the actual management or conduct of the business of the company, or of any associated company of the company, and

(*c*) if he shows that in that period he has not recovered any capital from the close company, apart from any amount taken into account under the next following subsection.

(4) If at any time after the application of the proceeds of the loan the individual has recovered any amount of capital from the close company without using that amount in repayment of the loan, he shall be treated for the purposes of this section as if he had at that time repaid that amount out of the loan, and so that out of the interest otherwise eligible for relief and payable for any period after that time there shall be deducted an amount equal to interest on the amount of capital so recovered.

If under the following provisions of this Act this section applies to a loan part only of which fulfils the conditions in this section, so as to afford relief for interest on that part, the deduction to be made under this subsection shall be made wholly out of interest on that part.

PART II

(5) The individual shall be treated as having recovered an amount of capital from the close company if—

(*a*) he receives consideration of that amount or value for the sale of any part of the ordinary share capital of the company, or any consideration of that amount or value by way of repayment of any part of that ordinary share capital, or

(*b*) the close company repays that amount of a loan or advance from him, or

(*c*) he receives consideration of that amount or value for assigning any debt due to him from the close company.

In the case of a sale or assignment otherwise than by way of a bargain made at arm's length, the sale or assignment shall be deemed to be for consideration of an amount equal to the market value of what is disposed of.

(6) Subsections (3), (4) and (5) above shall apply to a loan within subsection (1)(*c*) above as if it, and any loan it replaces, were one loan, and so that—

(*a*) references to the application of the proceeds of the loan are references to the application of the proceeds of the original loan, and

(*b*) any restriction under subsection (4) above which applied to any loan which has been replaced shall apply also to the loan which replaces it.

(7) Subsection (1) above shall not apply to a loan unless made in connection with the application of the money, and either on the occasion of its application, or within what is in the circumstances a reasonable time from the application of the money, and that subsection shall not apply to a loan the proceeds of which are applied for some other purpose before being applied as described in that subsection.

(8) Interest eligible for relief under this section shall be deducted from or set off against the income of the individual for the year of assessment in which the interest is paid, and income tax shall be discharged or repaid accordingly.

(9) Expressions used in this section which are given a meaning by any provision in Schedule 18 to the Finance Act 1965 shall have that meaning in this section, and for the purposes of this section— 1965 c. 25.

(*a*) " distribution " has the same meaning as in Part IV of the Finance Act 1965,

(*b*) the question whether a company is the subsidiary of another company shall be determined in accordance with paragraph 9 of Schedule 12 to the Finance Act 1965,

PART II

(*c*) the question whether a person has a material interest in a company shall be determined in accordance with paragraph 7 of Schedule 14 to this Act.

Loan applied in acquiring interest in a partnership.

21.—(1) This section applies to a loan to an individual to defray money applied—

(*a*) in purchasing a share in a partnership, or

(*b*) in contributing money to a partnership by way of capital or a premium, or in advancing money to the partnership, where the money contributed or advanced is used wholly and exclusively for the purposes of the trade, profession or vocation carried on by the partnership, or

(*c*) in paying off another loan where relief could have been obtained under this section for interest on that other loan if it had not been paid off (and, if free of interest, asssuming it carried interest).

(2) Relief shall be given in respect of any payment of interest by the individual on the loan—

(*a*) if throughout the period from the application of the proceeds of the loan until the interest was paid he has personally acted in the conduct of the trade, profession or vocation carried on by the partnership, and

(*b*) if he shows that in that period he has not recovered any capital from the partnership, apart from any amount taken into account under the next following subsection.

(3) If at any time after the application of the proceeds of the loan the individual has recovered any amount of capital from the partnership without using that amount in repayment of the loan, he shall be treated for the purposes of this section as if he had at that time repaid that amount out of the loan, and so that out of the interest otherwise eligible for relief and payable for any period after that time there shall be deducted an amount equal to interest on the amount of capital so recovered.

If under the following provisions of this Act this section applies to a loan part only of which fulfils the conditions in this section, so as to afford relief for interest on that part the deduction to be made under this subsection shall be made wholly out of interest on that part.

(4) The individual shall be treated as having recovered an amount of capital from the partnership if—

(*a*) he receives a consideration of that amount or value for the sale of any part of his interest in the partnership, or (*b*) the partnership returns any amount of capital to him or repays any amount advanced by him, or

(*c*) he receives consideration of that amount or value for assigning any debt due to him from the partnership.

In the case of a sale or assignment otherwise than by way of a bargain made at arm's length, the sale or assignment shall be deemed to be for consideration of an amount equal to the market value of what is disposed of.

(5) Subsections (2), (3) and (4) above shall apply to a loan within subsection (1)(*c*) above as if it, and any loan it replaces, were one loan, and so that—

(*a*) references to the application of the proceeds of the loan are references to the application of the proceeds of the original loan, and

(*b*) any restriction under subsection (3) above which applied to any loan which has been replaced shall apply also as respects the loan which replaces it.

(6) Subsection (1) above shall not apply to a loan unless made in connection with the application of the money, and either on the occasion of its application, or within what is in the circumstances a reasonable time from the application of the money, and that subsection shall not apply to a loan the proceeds of which are applied for some other purpose before being applied as described in that subsection.

(7) Interest eligible for relief under this section shall be deducted from or set off against the income of the individual for the year of assessment in which the interest is paid, and income tax shall be discharged or repaid accordingly.

Loan to purchase machinery or plant used by a partnership. 1968 c. 44.

22.—(1) Where an individual is a member of a partnership which under section 44 of the Capital Allowances Act 1968 is entitled to a capital allowance or liable to a balancing charge for any year of assessment in respect of machinery or plant belonging to the individual, he shall be entitled to relief on any interest paid by him in that year on a loan to defray money applied as capital expenditure on the provision of that machinery or plant.

(2) No relief shall be given under this section in respect of interest falling due and payable more than three years after the end of the year of assessment in which the debt was incurred.

(3) Where the machinery or plant is in use partly for the purposes of the trade, profession or vocation carried on by the partnership and partly for other purposes section 28 of the said Act (part-time use) shall apply in relation to relief under this section as it applies in relation to writing-down allowances.

Part II

(4) Interest eligible for relief under this section shall be deducted from or set off against the income of the individual for the year of assessment in which the interest is paid, and income tax shall be discharged or repaid accordingly.

Loan to pay estate duty.

23.—(1) This section applies to any loan to the personal representatives of a deceased person the proceeds of which are applied—

1894 c. 30.

(*a*) in paying, before the grant of representation, estate duty in accordance with section 6(2) of the Finance Act 1894, being estate duty in respect of personal property of which the deceased was competent to dispose at his death payable on delivery of the Inland Revenue affidavit, or

(*b*) in paying off another loan where relief could have been obtained under this section for interest on that other loan if it had not been paid off.

(2) Interest paid on the loan in respect of any period ending within one year from the making of the loan within subsection (1)(*a*) above shall be deducted from or set off against the income of the personal representatives as such for the year in which the interest is paid:

1940 c. 29.

Provided that in relation to estate duty on property the principal value of which falls to be ascertained under section 55 of the Finance Act 1940 (shares and debentures of certain companies) this subsection shall have effect with the substitution for " one year " of " three years ".

(3) No relief shall be given under this section in respect of interest on so much of any loan as is applied in paying estate duty in respect of property situate in Great Britain which did not pass to the personal representatives as such, or in respect of property which, even if it had been situate in Great Britain, would not have passed to the personal representatives as such.

(4) Sufficient evidence of the amount of estate duty paid in accordance with the said section 6(2) in respect of any particular description of property, and of any statements relevant to its computation in the Inland Revenue affidavit, may be given by the production of a document purporting to be a certificate from the Board.

(5) For the purposes of this section—

(*a*) " estate duty " means estate duty leviable under the law in force in Great Britain or the law in force in Northern Ireland, together with any interest payable on the duty, (*b*) references to interest in respect of a period ending on or before a given time apply whether or not interest continues to run after that time. PART II

(6) This section shall apply to estate duty leviable under the law of Northern Ireland with the substitution for the estate duty enactments mentioned in this section of the corresponding enactments forming part of the law of Northern Ireland, and with the substitution of " Northern Ireland " for " Great Britain " in subsection (3) above, and the reference to the Board shall include a reference to the Ministry of Finance for Northern Ireland.

Loans made on or before 15th April 1969.

24.—(1) Relief shall be given in respect of any payment of interest falling due before 6th April 1975 on a debt incurred on or before 15th April 1969, being annual interest—

(*a*) on which the recipient is chargeable to tax under Case III of Schedule D, and

(*b*) which is not interest on a debt incurred by overdrawing an account with the creditor,

where both the date when the payment fell due and its amount were fixed by or under arrangements made when the debt was incurred, or subsequent arrangements in force on 15th April 1969.

(2) Relief shall be given in respect of any bank, discount or stock exchange interest paid after 5th April 1970 if, assuming that it had been paid without deduction of tax when it became due and payable, relief could have been given in respect of it under section 200 of the Income Tax Act 1952. 1952 c. 10.

(3) Interest eligible for relief under this section shall be deducted from or set off against the income of the person paying the interest for the year of assessment in which the interest is paid, and income tax shall be discharged or repaid accordingly.

Relief for payments of interest; further provisions.

25.—(1) This section has effect as respects relief under sections 19 to 24 of this Act (in this Act referred to, together with this section, as " the sections of this Act giving relief in respect of interest ").

(2) Where credit is given for any money due from the purchaser under any sale, that shall be treated for the purposes of the said sections as the making of a loan to defray money applied by the purchaser in making the purchase.

(3) If interest is paid at a rate in excess of a reasonable commercial rate, so much of any payment as represents such an excess shall not be eligible for relief under any of the said sections.

PART II

(4) Where the whole of a debt does not fulfil the conditions required by any one of the said sections, relief shall be given under the section only in respect of the proportion of any payment of interest equal to the proportion of the debt fulfilling those conditions at the time of the application of the money in question.

1964 c. 37.

(5) The relief shall only be given on the making of a claim to which section 9 of the Income Tax Management Act 1964 shall apply, and an appeal on the claim shall be to the General Commissioners unless the appellant elects that it shall lie instead to the Special Commissioners.

(6) If relief is given in respect of any interest under any of the said sections, the interest shall not be allowable as a deduction for any other purpose of the Income Tax Acts.

(7) No relief shall be given against income chargeable to corporation tax, or any other income of a company.

(8) No relief shall be given in respect of—

1952 c. 10.

(*a*) interest which is payable under deduction of tax by virtue of section 169 or section 170 of the Income Tax Act 1952, except where paid without deduction of tax to a bank carrying on a bona fide banking business in the United Kingdom, or

(*b*) interest in respect of which relief may be given under section 200 or section 445(3)(*b*) of that Act, or

(*c*) interest paid before 6th April, 1969.

Deduction of income tax from payment of interest.

26.—(1) Where any yearly interest of money chargeable to tax under Case III of Schedule D is paid—

(*a*) by a company, or by a local authority, or

(*b*) by or on behalf of a partnership of which a company is a member, or

(*c*) by any person to another person whose usual place of abode is outside the United Kingdom,

the person by or through whom the payment is made shall, on making the payment, deduct out of it a sum representing the amount of income tax thereon at the standard rate in force at the time of the payment.

(2) Subsection (1)(*a*) above shall not apply to a payment made in a fiduciary or representative capacity, and subsection (1) above shall not apply—

(*a*) to interest payable in the United Kingdom on an advance from a bank carrying on a bona fide banking business in the United Kingdom, or

(b) to interest paid by such a bank in the ordinary course of that business.

(3) In section 170(1)(a) of the Income Tax Act 1952 (payments not out of profits or gains charged to income tax) the words " interest of money " shall be omitted. 1952 c. 10.

(4) Subsections (2) and (4) of the said section 170, and section 50 of the Finance Act 1963 (certificates of deduction), shall apply to payments within subsection (1) above as they apply to payments within the said section 170(1). 1963 c. 25.

(5) Nothing in this section applies to the right of election under section 48(7) of the Finance Act 1965 (payments by one member of a group of companies to another member). 1965 c. 25.

(6) This section applies—

(a) to interest paid after 5th April 1970, and

(b) to interest paid after the passing of this Act on a debt incurred after 15th April 1969.

(7) So far as it relates to interest paid before the passing of this Act, the resolution of the Commons House of Parliament prohibiting in certain cases the deduction of tax from interest on a debt incurred after 15th April 1969 is hereby confirmed as if contained in this Act, and where that resolution did not apply to any payment of interest before the passing of this Act on a debt incurred after 15th April 1969, the deduction shall be treated as having been made under this section, and not under section 169 or section 170 of the Income Tax Act 1952.

Special provisions for certain close companies.

27.—(1) Subject to the provisions of this section, all interest paid by a close company in any accounting period shall be apportioned under section 78 of the Finance Act 1965 (apportionment for surtax) as if the interest were income of the close company for the accounting period.

(2) Subsection (1) of this section shall not apply to a company—

(a) if it is a trading company, or

(b) if it is a member of a trading group, or

(c) if the whole, or substantially the whole, of its income is of one or more of the following descriptions, that is—

(i) estate or trading income,

(ii) interest, and dividends or other distributions, received from a subsidiary which is itself within paragraphs (a), (b) or (c) of this subsection.

Part II

(3) Subsection (1) of this section shall not apply—

(*a*) to interest which would be eligible for relief under sections 19 or 24 above if paid by an individual, or

(*b*) to interest which is money wholly and exclusively laid out or expended for the purposes of a trade carried on by the company.

(4) If any amount of interest apportionable under subsection (1) above is interest paid to a participator in the close company, the amount apportionable to that participator by virtue of subsection (1) above shall be reduced by the first-mentioned amount (and without requiring the reduction to be reflected in the amount apportioned to any other person).

(5) Subsection (2) of the said section 78 (annual payments) shall not apply to any annual interest.

(6) Subsection (4) of the said section 78 (restrictions on the making of apportionments) has effect subject to the provisions of this section, and an amount apportionable by virtue of this section shall be in addition to amounts (if any) apportionable under the said section 78 without this section.

(7) In determining under the said section 78 and the enactments applying for the purposes of that section the person to whom any amount is to be apportionable by virtue of this section, any interest which any person possesses as a loan creditor shall be disregarded (but without prejudice to the making of an apportionment to him in any other capacity).

(8) Expressions used in this section which are given a meaning by any provision in Schedule 18 to the Finance Act 1965 shall have that meaning in this section and for the purposes of this section—

1965 c. 25.

(*a*) " distribution " has the same meaning as in Part IV of the Finance Act 1965,

(*b*) the question whether a company is a subsidiary of another company shall be determined in accordance with paragraph 9 of Schedule 12 to the Finance Act 1965.

(9) This section applies—

(*a*) to interest paid after 5th April 1970, and

(*b*) to bank, discount house or stock exchange interest paid in the year 1969-70 in respect of any period beginning after 30th June 1969, and

(*c*) to interest paid in the year 1969-70 on any debt incurred after 15th April 1969, not being bank, discount house or stock exchange interest.

Companies

Close companies: no restriction on deductions for directors' remuneration.

28.—(1) Section 74 of the Finance Act 1965 (restriction on deductions for remuneration of directors other than whole-time service directors) shall cease to have effect.

1965 c. 25.

(2) This section applies as respects accounting periods ending after the end of March 1969:

Provided that in the case of any such accounting period beginning before the end of March 1969 the said section 74 shall apply, but the decrease under that section in allowable deductions for the accounting period shall be the proportion of the decrease which would be made apart from this section which the part of the accounting period before the end of March 1969 bears to the whole accounting period.

(3) The following provisions of this section have effect where a close company has an accounting period of less than twelve months beginning or ending between 1st January 1968 and 31st March 1969 unless the terminal date of the accounting period (or of each such accounting period) was decided, or fixed by a decision, before 15th April 1969, and there is sufficient evidence of the decision in some document in existence before 15th April 1969.

(4) Where any accounting period of the close company falls wholly or partly within the nine months beginning on 1st April 1969 and ending with 31st December 1969, and the remuneration of its directors (other than whole-time service directors) for the accounting period, or, as the case may be, for the part falling within those nine months, exceeds the limit determined below, the deduction which may be made for the directors' remuneration in computing for corporation tax the close company's profits for the accounting period shall be diminished by an amount equal to the excess, and that shall be in addition to such diminution, if any, as is to be made under the said section 74 as modified by the proviso to subsection (2) above.

(5) The said limit is—

(*a*) for an accounting period comprising the whole of the said period of 9 months, 9/18ths of the remuneration of directors (other than whole-time service directors) for the eighteen months beginning on 1st July 1968 and ending on 31st December 1969,

(*b*) for an accounting period comprising part only of the said 9 months, a proportionately smaller fraction of the said remuneration.

(6) If any part of the 18 months or the 9 months does not fall within any accounting period of the close company, the

PART II

denominator, or as the case may be the numerator, of the fraction of 9/18ths shall be proportionately reduced.

For the purpose of this subsection an accounting period falling after the commencement of the winding up of the close company shall be treated as if it were not an accounting period.

(7) For the purposes of this section all necessary apportionments of remuneration to part of an accounting period shall be made on a time basis according to the respective lengths of the parts of the period.

(8) This section shall be construed as one with the said section 74.

Other amendments of Corporation Tax Acts.

29. Schedule 14 to this Act (which amends the provisions of the Corporation Tax Acts, including the provisions about close companies) shall have effect.

Avoidance of tax

Change in ownership of company: disallowance of trading losses.

30.—(1) If—

(*a*) within any period of three years there is both a change in the ownership of a company and (either earlier or later in that period, or at the same time) a major change in the nature or conduct of a trade carried on by the company, or

(*b*) at any time after the scale of the activities in a trade carried on by a company has become small or negligible, and before any considerable revival of the trade, there is a change in the ownership of the company,

1965 c. 25.

no relief shall be given under section 58 of the Finance Act 1965 (relief for trading losses against future trading profits or total profits) by setting a loss incurred by the company in an accounting period beginning before the change of ownership against any income or other profits of an accounting period ending after the change of ownership.

(2) In applying this section to the accounting period in which the change of ownership occurs, the part ending with the change of ownership, and the part after, shall be treated as two separate accounting periods, and the profits or losses of the accounting period shall be apportioned to the two parts.

The apportionment shall be on a time basis according to the respective lengths of those parts except that if it appears that that method would work unreasonably or unjustly such other method shall be used as appears just and reasonable.

(3) In subsection (1) above "major change in the nature or conduct of a trade" includes— PART II

(*a*) a major change in the type of property dealt in, or services or facilities provided, in the trade, or

(*b*) a major change in customers, outlets or markets of the trade,

and this section applies even if the change is the result of a gradual process which began outside the period of three years mentioned in subsection (1)(*a*) above.

(4) In relation to any relief available under section 61 of the Finance Act 1965 (company reconstructions) to a successor company, subsection (1) above shall apply as if any loss sustained by a predecessor company had been sustained by a successor company and as if the references to a trade included references to the trade as carried on by a predecessor company. 1965 c. 25.

(5) Schedule 15 to this Act shall have effect for supplementing this section, which is there referred to as the "principal section".

(6) This section and that Schedule shall be construed as one with Part IV of the Finance Act 1965.

(7) This section shall not apply if the change of ownership took place before 15th April 1969, and subsection (1)(*a*) above shall not apply if the major change in the nature or conduct of the trade was completed before that date.

In other respects this section has effect by reference to circumstances and events before that date, as well as by reference to later circumstances and events.

31.—(1) This section has effect where— Sale by individual of income derived from his personal activities.

(*a*) transactions or arrangements are effected or made to exploit the earning capacity of an individual in any occupation by putting some other person in a position to enjoy all or any part of the profits or gains or other income, or of the receipts, derived from the individual's activities in that occupation, or anything derived directly or indirectly from any such income or receipts, and

(*b*) as part of, or in connection with, or in consequence of, the transactions or arrangements any capital amount is obtained by the individual for himself or for any other person, and

(*c*) the main object, or one of the main objects, of the transactions or arrangements was the avoidance or reduction of liability to income tax.

Part II

(2) Any such capital amount shall for all the purposes of the Income Tax Acts be treated as being earned income of the individual which arises when the capital amount is receivable, and which is chargeable to tax under Case VI of Schedule D.

(3) In this section—

(*a*) references to any occupation are references to any activities of any of the kinds pursued in any profession or vocation, irrespective of whether the individual is engaged in a profession or vocation, or is employed by or holds office under some other person, and

(*b*) references in subsection (1) above to income or receipts include references to payments for any description of copyright or licence or franchise or other right deriving its value from the activities, including past activities, of the individual.

(4) This section shall not apply to a capital amount obtained from the disposal—

(*a*) of assets (including any goodwill) of a profession or vocation, or of a share in a partnership which is carrying on a profession or vocation, or

(*b*) of shares in a company,

so far as the value of what is disposed of, at the time of disposal, is attributable to the value of the profession or vocation as a going concern, or as the case may be to the value of the company's business as a going concern:

Provided that if the value of the profession, vocation or business as a going concern is derived to a material extent from prospective income or receipts derived directly or indirectly from the individual's activities in the occupation, and for which, when all capital amounts are disregarded, the individual will not have received full consideration, whether as a partner in a partnership or as an employee or otherwise, this subsection shall not exempt the part of the capital amount so derived.

In this subsection references to the company's business include references to the business of any other company in which it holds shares directly or indirectly.

(5) For the purposes of subsection (1)(*b*) above the cases where an individual obtains any capital amount for some other person include cases where the individual has put some other person in a position to receive the capital amount by providing that other person with something of value derived, directly or indirectly, from the individual's activities in the occupation.

PART II

(6) This section shall apply whether or not all or any of the relevant arrangements took place before the passing of this Act, but shall not apply as respects a capital amount receivable before 15th April 1969.

Artificial transactions in land.

32.—(1) This section is enacted to prevent the avoidance of tax by persons concerned with land or the development of land.

(2) This section applies wherever—

(*a*) land, or any property deriving its value from land, is acquired with the sole or main object of realising a gain from disposing of the land, or

(*b*) land is held as trading stock, or

(*c*) land is developed with the sole or main object of realising a gain from disposing of the land when developed,

and any gain of a capital nature is obtained from the disposal of the land—

(i) by the person acquiring, holding or developing the land, or by any connected person, or

(ii) where any arrangement or scheme is effected as respects the land which enables a gain to be realised by any indirect method, or by any series of transactions, by any person who is a party to, or concerned in, the arrangement or scheme;

and this subsection applies whether any such person obtains the gain for himself or for any other person.

(3) Where this section applies, the whole of any such gain shall for all the purposes of the Income Tax Acts and the Corporation Tax Acts be treated—

(*a*) as being income which arises when the gain is realised, and which constitutes profits or gains chargeable to tax under Case VI of Schedule D for the year of assessment or company's accounting period in which the gain is realised, and

(*b*) subject to the following provisions of this section, as being income of the person by whom the gain is realised.

(4) For the purposes of this section land is disposed of if, by any one or more transactions, or by any arrangement or scheme, whether concerning the land or property deriving its value from the land, the property in the land, or control over the land, is effectually disposed of, and references in subsection (2) above to the acquisition or development of property with a view to realising the gain from disposing of the land shall be construed accordingly.

PART II

(5) For the said purposes—

(*a*) where, whether by a premature sale or otherwise, a person directly or indirectly transmits the opportunity of making a gain to another person, that other person's gain is obtained for him by the first-mentioned person, and

(*b*) any number of transactions may be regarded as constituting a single arrangement or scheme if a common purpose can be discerned in them, or if there is other sufficient evidence of a common purpose.

(6) For the purposes of this section such method of computing a gain shall be adopted as is just and reasonable in the circumstances, taking into account the value of what is obtained for disposing of the land, and allowing only such expenses as are attributable to the land disposed of, and in applying this subsection—

(*a*) where a freehold is acquired and the reversion is retained on disposal, account may be taken of the way in which the profits or gains under Case I of Schedule D of a person dealing in land are computed in such a case, and

(*b*) account may be taken of the adjustments to be made in computing such profits or gains under subsections
1963 c. 25. (5), (6) and (7) of section 29 of the Finance Act 1963 (allowance for tax on premiums on leases).

In the application of this subsection to Scotland, " freehold " means the estate or interest of the proprietor of the *dominium utile* or, in the case of property other than feudal property, of the owner, and " reversion " means the interest of the landlord in property subject to a lease.

(7) Subsection (2)(*c*) of this section shall not apply to so much of any gain as is fairly attributable to the period, if any, before the intention to develop the land was formed, and which would not fall under paragraph (*a*) or paragraph (*b*) of that subsection; and in applying this subsection account shall be taken of the treatment under Case I of Schedule D of a person who appropriates land as trading stock.

(8) If all or any part of the gain accruing to any person is derived from value, or an opportunity of realising a gain, provided directly or indirectly by some other person, whether or not put at the disposal of the first-mentioned person, subsection (3)(*b*) of this section shall apply to the gain, or that part of it, with the substitution of that other person for the person by whom the gain was realised.

(9) This section shall not apply to a gain accruing to an individual which by virtue of section 29 of the Finance Act 1965 (private residences) is exempt from capital gains tax, or which would be so exempt but for the provisions of paragraph 2 of Schedule 12 to the Finance Act 1968 (residence acquired partly with a view to making a gain).

1965 c. 25.

1968 c. 44.

(10) Where there is a disposal of shares in—

(*a*) a company which holds land as trading stock, or

(*b*) a company which owns directly or indirectly 90 per cent. or more of the ordinary share capital of another company which holds land as trading stock,

and all the land so held is disposed of in the normal course of its trade by the company which held it, and so as to procure that all opportunity of profit in respect of the land arises to that company, then this section shall not by virtue of subsection (2)(i) apply to any gain to the holder of shares as being a gain on property deriving value from that land (but without prejudice to any liability under paragraph (ii) of the said subsection (2)).

(11) Where a person who considers that paragraph (*a*) or paragraph (*c*) of subsection (2) of this section may apply as respects a gain of a capital nature which that person has obtained from the disposal of land, or which he would obtain from a proposed disposal of land, supplies to the inspector to whom he makes his return of income written particulars showing how the gain has arisen or would arise—

(*a*) the inspector shall, within thirty days from his receipt of the particulars, notify that person whether or not he is satisfied that, in the circumstances as described in the particulars, the gain will not, or would not, be chargeable to tax on that person under this section, and

(*b*) if the inspector notifies that person that he is so satisfied, the gain shall not be chargeable on that person under this section:

Provided that if the particulars given under this section with respect to the gain are not such as to make full and accurate disclosure of all facts and considerations relating thereto which are material to be known to the inspector, any notification given by the inspector under this subsection shall be void.

(12) In this section—

(*a*) references to the land include references to all or any part of the land, and " land " includes buildings, and any estate or interest in land or buildings ;

PART II

(*b*) references to property deriving its value from land include—

(i) any shareholding in a company, or any partnership interest, or any interest in settled property, deriving its value directly or indirectly from land, and

(ii) any option, consent or embargo affecting the disposition of land,

and for the purposes of this section any question whether a person is connected with another shall be determined in accord-
1965 c. 25. ance with paragraph 21 of Schedule 7 to the Finance Act 1965.

(13) Schedule 16 to this Act shall have effect to supplement this and the last preceding section, and this and the last preceding section are in that Schedule referred to as the " principal sections ".

(14) This section shall apply whether or not all or any of the relevant transactions, or all or any part of any relevant arrangement or scheme, was effected before the passing of this Act, but shall not apply to any gain realised before 15th April 1969.

(15) The following provisions, enacted to prevent avoidance of tax by transactions in land and other property, shall cease to have effect as respects any transaction or event carried out or occurring on or after 15th April 1969.

The said provisions are—

1960 c. 44. (*a*) in the Finance Act 1960, sections 21 to 24, all of section 25 except subsection (4), and section 26, and

1962 c. 44. (*b*) in the Finance Act 1962, sections 23 and 24 and in section 25 subsection (1) except so far as it relates to section 28, and subsection (2).

Transfer of assets abroad. 1952 c. 10.

33.—(1) Section 412 of the Income Tax Act 1952 (avoidance of tax by transactions resulting in transfer of income to persons abroad) shall have effect subject to the following provisions of this section.

(2) In subsection (1) of that section (which deals with cases where, by means of a transfer of assets, either alone or in conjunction with associated operations, an individual acquires rights by virtue of which he has power to enjoy income of a person abroad) for the words from " such an individual " to " he has " there shall be substituted the words " by virtue or in consequence of any such transfer, either alone or in conjunction with associated operations, such an individual has ".

(3) In subsection (6) of that section (which provides that in determining whether an individual has power to enjoy income of a person abroad, account shall be taken of all benefits which accrue to him as a result of the relevant transfer and any associated operations) after the words "accrue to the individual" there shall be inserted the words "(whether or not he has rights at law or in equity in or to those benefits)". PART II

(4) After subsection (3) of section 413 of the Income Tax Act 1952 (which contains provisions supplemental to section 412) there shall be inserted the following subsection:— 1952 c. 10.

"(4) In any case where an individual has for the purposes of the last preceding section power to enjoy income of a person abroad by reason of his receiving any such benefit as is referred to in subsection (5)(*c*) of that section, then notwithstanding anything in subsection (1) of this section, the individual shall be chargeable to income tax by virtue of that section for the year of assessment in which the benefit is received on the whole of the amount or value of that benefit except in so far as it is shown that the benefit derives directly or indirectly from income on which he has already been charged to tax for that or a previous year of assessment."

(5) This section shall have effect for all the purposes of income tax for the year 1969-70 and subsequent years of assessment and also for estimating an individual's total income for the purposes of surtax for the year 1968-69.

Case VIII of Schedule D

34.—(1) In section 25(5)(*a*) of the Finance Act 1963 (ascertainment of duration of a lease) the words "either" and "or by the tenant" shall be repealed, and at the end of the said paragraph (*a*) add "by the landlord". Premiums on leases. 1963 c. 25.

(2) Paragraph (*b*) of the said section 25(5) (circumstances making it unlikely that the lease will continue until the expiration of its term) shall be applied by reference to the facts which were known or ascertainable at the time of the grant of the lease, and the proviso to the said section 25(5) shall be repealed:

Provided that in relation to tax under section 22(4) of the Finance Act 1963 (premium for variation or waiver of any of the terms of a lease) for the reference above to the time of the grant of the lease there shall be substituted a reference to the time when the contract providing for the variation or waiver is entered into.

(3) In applying the said paragraph (*b*) it shall be assumed that all parties concerned, whatever their relationship, act as they would act if they were at arm's length.

PART II

(4) After paragraph (*b*) of the said section 25(5) add:—

" (*c*) where the terms of the lease include provision for the extension of the lease beyond a given date by notice given by the tenant account may be taken of any circumstances making it likely that the lease will be so extended ".

(5) Subject to the next following subsection, this section has effect—

(*a*) as respects a lease granted after 12th June 1969, and

1963 c. 52. (*b*) so far as it relates to section 22(4) of the Finance Act 1963, as respects a variation or waiver the contract for which is entered into after that date.

(6) So far as relates to relief under—

1952 c. 10. 1965 c. 25. (*a*) section 342 of the Income Tax Act 1952 or section 58(1) of the Finance Act 1965 (carry forward of trading losses), or

1953 c. 34. (*b*) section 341 of the Income Tax Act 1952 as applied by section 15(3) of the Finance Act 1953 (set-off of trading loss against general income of succeeding year), or

(*c*) paragraph 1 of Schedule 4 to the Finance Act 1963 (sums deductible from rent),

given by setting a loss against, or making a deduction from, income of—

(i) the year 1969-70 or any subsequent year of assessment, or

(ii) a company's accounting period ending after 5th April 1969,

this section shall be deemed to have had effect as from the passing of the Finance Act 1963, and as respects leases granted at any time.

(7) In applying subsection (6) above it shall be assumed—

(*a*) that all relief which could not be affected by the operation of that subsection was given (for all years of assessment and accounting periods before or after the passing of this Act) before relief which could be affected by the operation of that subsection, and

(*b*) that, in particular, any loss which would not have been sustained if subsection (1) of this section had always had effect was postponed to any other loss in giving relief against income of a year of assessment before the year 1969-70, or a company's accounting period ending on or before 5th April 1969.

This subsection shall have effect notwithstanding the provisions of paragraph 17 of Schedule 4 to the Finance Act 1963, or any other enactment governing the order in which reliefs are given. PART II

(8) All such adjustments shall be made, whether by way of assessment or discharge or repayment of tax, as are required to give effect to this section.

PART III

ESTATE DUTY

Amount and estate rate of estate duty.

35.—(1) Estate duty shall no longer be levied and paid at graduated rates on the principal value of the property comprised in an estate but, subject to any enactment providing for the reduction of the amount payable on any particular property comprised in the estate, there shall be levied and paid by way of estate duty on the estate an amount determined in accordance with Part I of Schedule 17 to this Act by reference to the aggregate principal value of all the property comprised in the estate.

(2) Subject to any such enactment as aforesaid, the amount of estate duty payable on any particular property comprised in an estate shall be the amount produced by levying duty on the principal value of that property at the estate rate, that is to say, the rate per cent. representing the proportion which the amount determined in relation to the estate under subsection (1) of this section bears to the aggregate principal value of all the property comprised in the estate; and any reference in the enactments relating to estate duty (other than section 29 of the Finance Act 1949) to the rate or amount of duty on, or on the principal value of, property shall be construed as a reference to the estate rate, or, as the case may be, to the amount produced by levying duty on the principal value of the property at the estate rate. 1949 c. 47.

Changes as to property passing on death.

36.—(1) In section 2(1) of the Finance Act 1894 (which provides in relation to estate duty that property passing on a death shall be deemed to include property of the descriptions specified in the paragraphs of that subsection) for the words " shall be deemed to include " there shall be substituted the words " means for the purposes of estate duty ". 1894 c. 30.

(2) For paragraph (*b*) of the said section 2(1) (which specifies property in which the deceased or any other person had an interest ceasing on the death of the deceased to the extent to which a benefit accrues or arises by the cesser of that interest) there shall be substituted the following paragraph (hereafter in

PART III

this Part of this Act and in Part II of Schedule 17 thereto referred to as " the substituted section 2(1)(*b*) "):—

" (*b*) subject to section 37 of the Finance Act 1969, property in the case of which—

(i) at any time during the period of seven years ending with the date of the deceased's death the property was comprised in a settlement and the deceased was entitled to a beneficial interest in possession in that property as, or as successor to an interest of, a beneficiary under the settlement; or

(ii) the property being or having been comprised as aforesaid and the deceased having at a time before the period of seven years aforesaid been entitled to such an interest in that property as is mentioned in sub-paragraph (i) of this paragraph which determined or was disposed of at a date before the beginning of that period, the deceased was not at all times during that period entirely excluded from possession and enjoyment of the property and from any benefit to him by contract or otherwise; or

(iii) the property being, or having at a time after 15th April 1969 been, comprised in settled property subject to a trust conferring a discretion on the trustees or some other person as to the application of all or part of any of the combined income of all the property from time to time subject to that trust which is for the time being available for distribution (not being a discretion only as to the amount for the time being of an annuity under the settlement or as to the provision of maintenance for a person under the age which by virtue of the law which regulates the disposition constituting the settlement falls to be treated for the purposes of the trust as full age)—

(*aa*) the deceased having immediately before the date of his death been eligible to benefit as a result of the discretion aforesaid and the property in question having at that date been subject to the trust, the deceased has so benefited at any time during the material period (that is to say, so much of the period of seven years ending with that date as falls after 15th April 1963) at which the property was subject to the trust; or

PART III

(*bb*) the deceased having ceased to be eligible as aforesaid, or the property in question having ceased to be subject to the trust, at a time within the period of seven years ending with the date of his death, the deceased has so benefited at a time during the material period (that is to say, so much of the period of seven years ending with the date when the deceased or, as the case may be, that property so ceased as falls after 15th April 1963) at which that property was subject to the trust; or

(*cc*) the deceased or the property in question having ceased as aforesaid before the beginning of the period of seven years ending with the date of his death, but the deceased not having been entirely excluded from possession and enjoyment of that property and from any benefit to him by contract or otherwise at all times during that period, the deceased has so benefited at a time during the material period (that is to say, so much of the period of seven years ending with the date when the deceased or, as the case may be, that property so ceased as falls after 15th April 1963) at which that property was subject to the trust; or

(iv) the property was at the date of the deceased's death comprised in settled property held by trustees under a settlement made by the deceased whereby that settled property was held on trust to accumulate, or with a power for the trustees at the discretion of the trustees or some other person to accumulate, the whole or part of any income of that settled property, and that trust for, or power of, accumulation determined at the death."

(3) At the end of the said section 2(1) there shall be added the following paragraphs:—

"(*e*) without prejudice to section 3 of this Act, property consisting of an interest of the deceased as a partner under a partnership agreement, being an interest to which under the terms of that or some other agreement some person other than the deceased's executor as such becomes or will become entitled on or by reference to the deceased's death otherwise than by the exercise of an option to acquire that interest;

PART III

(*f*) subject to section 37(5) of the Finance Act 1969, property subject to an option to purchase granted otherwise than by the deceased's will to a person other than the deceased and exercisable on or by reference to the deceased's death, in a case where the property passes, or would if there had been no option to purchase it have passed, on the deceased's death apart from this paragraph;

(*g*) in the application of this Act to Scotland—

(i) property of which the deceased was not at the time of his death competent to dispose and which on his death devolves in accordance with the terms of a special destination contained in any deed;

(ii) property of which the deceased was at the time of his death a proper liferenter;

(iii) the interest of lessee under any lease, other than such a lease as is mentioned in section 36(5)(*a*)(ii) of the Finance Act 1969, being an interest held by the deceased at the time of his death but of which he was not at that time competent to dispose."

(4) Without prejudice to paragraph (*a*) of subsection (5) of
1894 c. 30. this section, in paragraph (*i*) of section 22(1) of the Finance Act 1894 (which provides that in that Act the expression " settlement " means any instrument, whether relating to real property or personal property, which is a settlement within the meaning
1882 c. 38. of section two of the Settled Land Act 1882, or if it related to real property would be a settlement within the meaning of that section, and includes a settlement effected by a parol trust)—

(*a*) for the words " section two of the Settled Land Act 1882 " there shall be substituted the words " the
1925 c. 18. Settled Land Act 1925 ";

(*b*) after the words " real property " in the second place where they occur there shall be inserted the words " in England or Wales ";

(*c*) for the words " that section " there shall be substituted the words " that Act ";

and in the application to Scotland of the said paragraph (*i*) as amended by the foregoing provisions of this subsection for the words from " any instrument " to " that Act " there shall be substituted the words " any deed by virtue of which any property, wherever situated, is for the time being held in trust for any purposes ".

(5) In the enactments relating to estate duty— PART III

(*a*) the expression " settlement "—

(i) for the avoidance of doubt is hereby declared to include—

(*aa*) any disposition whereby property is held by trustees on trust to accumulate the whole or part of any income of that property or with a power for the trustees to make payments out of that income at the discretion of the trustees or some other person with or without a power to accumulate surplus income ; and

(*bb*) any disposition regulated by the law of a territory outside Great Britain which would constitute a settlement within the meaning of section 22(1)(*i*) of the Finance Act 1894 if it had been regulated by the law of England or, as the case may require, of Scotland ; 1894 c. 30.

(ii) shall include a lease of property which is for a life or lives or for a period ascertainable only by reference to a death or which is terminable on, or at a date ascertainable only by reference to, a death, that property being treated as the property comprised in the settlement ;

(iii) in relation to Scotland, shall include an entail and any deed by virtue of which an annuity is charged on, or on the rents of, any property, that property being treated as the property comprised in the settlement ;

(*b*) notwithstanding anything in section 22(1)(*j*) of the Finance Act 1894, the expression " interest in expectancy " shall, except for the purposes of section 7(6) of that Act, include a reversion expectant upon the termination of such a lease as is referred to in paragraph (*a*)(ii) of this subsection ;

(*c*) an interest in settled property shall be treated as having determined on its ceasing to exist as a separate interest ;

(*d*) when part of any settled property is disposed of for the purpose of paying any tax or duty (including any tax or duty under the laws of any territory outside Great Britain) for which the trustees are accountable and which is properly payable out of the capital of the settled property or of paying any costs, expenses or fees of the trustees which are properly so payable, that

PART III

part shall not be treated as passing by reason of an interest under the settlement on any death occurring after the disposition;

(*e*) in the application of those enactments to Scotland, and subject to any provision thereof relating to the eligibility of a person to benefit under such a trust as is mentioned in sub-paragraph (iii) of the substituted section 2(1)(*b*), where a person is at any time entitled to an interest of any kind under a settlement that person shall be deemed to be entitled at that time to a corresponding interest in the property comprised in that settlement, and (notwithstanding the provisions of section 40(2) of this Act) this paragraph shall be deemed always to have had effect.

(6) For the purposes of the substituted section 2(1)(*b*)—

(*a*) the expression " successor " in relation to an interest in settled property of a beneficiary under the settlement means a successor, whether immediate or otherwise and whether by disposition or devolution, to that beneficiary's interest;

(*b*) where in the case of any property comprised in a settlement, the deceased was at any time beneficially entitled in possession to an interest which was not an interest as, or as successor to an interest of, a beneficiary under that settlement but which by one or more further settlements or other dispositions or devolutions had been created out of or derived from an interest of a beneficiary under that settlement, then, for the purposes of sub-paragraph (i) or (ii) of the substituted section 2(1)(*b*), the deceased shall be deemed to have been entitled at that time to a beneficial interest in possession in that property as successor to an interest of a beneficiary under that settlement;

(*c*) where any property subject to such a trust as is mentioned in sub-paragraph (iii) or (iv) of the substituted section 2(1)(*b*) was an interest in property comprised in another settlement or was an interest which by one or more further settlements or other dispositions or devolutions had been created out of or derived from an interest of a beneficiary under another settlement, then, for the purpose of charging estate duty by virtue of the said sub-paragraph (iii) or (iv), as the case may be, the property comprised in that other settlement, so far as it consists of property in which the interest subject to that trust subsists, shall be treated for the purposes of that sub-paragraph as being the property subject to that trust;

PART III

(*d*) references in this Part of this Act to the income of any property shall be construed as references to that income after the deduction of any costs, expenses or fees properly payable out of that income;

(*e*) in relation to Scotland, references in this Part of this Act to the disposition of an interest in settled property shall include references to the propulsion of the fee under any tailzied destination;

and, for the purposes of section 28(2) of the Finance Act 1949 (which relates to estate duty on property situated outside Great Britain), where in the case of any property passing on a death as being or having been property comprised in a settlement the deceased was or is deemed to have been entitled to an interest in that property as successor to an interest of a beneficiary under that settlement, or where in the case of any property so passing paragraph (*c*) of this subsection applies to that property, that property shall be deemed to pass on the death under or by reason of the disposition constituting that settlement or, as the case may be, the disposition constituting the other settlement referred to in the said paragraph (*c*). 1949 c. 37.

(7) Where a deceased person was immediately before his death beneficially entitled to a joint tenancy of any property, his severable share of that property shall be treated for the purposes of estate duty as property of which he was competent to dispose at his death.

(8) In the application to Scotland of sections 2 and 22 of the Finance Act 1894 as amended by the foregoing provisions of this section, and in subsection (5)(*a*)(iii) of this section, the expression " deed " shall include any disposition, arrangement, contract, resolution, instrument or writing. 1894 c. 30.

Part only of property to be treated as passing in certain cases.

37.—(1) Where on any death estate duty falls to be charged on any property by virtue of sub-paragraph (i) or (ii) of the substituted section 2(1)(*b*) by reason of an interest in that property—

(*a*) if that interest did not confer a right to receive the whole of any income of that property during the whole of the relevant period, that is to say, any period during which the deceased was entitled to that interest which falls within the period of seven years ending with the relevant date, namely—

(i) if the interest determined or was disposed of at a date before the death, that date, or

(ii) in any other case, the date of the death,

but conferred a right to receive a part of that income which varied in accordance with, or as the result of,

PART III

the exercise of any power in that behalf, there shall be treated as passing on the death by virtue of the said sub-paragraph (i) or (ii) part only of that property, being a part bearing to the whole of that property the same proportion as the aggregate amount received by the deceased during the relevant period out of that income by virtue of that interest bears to the aggregate amount of that income during that period;

(*b*) if paragraph (*a*) of this subsection does not apply but at the relevant date aforesaid that interest extended to part but not to the whole of any income of the property, there shall be treated as passing on the death by virtue of the said sub-paragraph (i) or (ii) part only of that property, being a part bearing to the whole of that property a proportion equal to the proportion of any income of the property to which the interest extended (or would if there had been any such income have extended) at that date.

(2) Where on any death estate duty falls to be charged on any property by virtue of the said sub-paragraph (i) or (ii) but the interest in question was an interest by virtue of which the deceased was entitled jointly or in common with one or more other persons to the use and enjoyment, but not to receive any income, of the property, there shall be treated as passing on the death by virtue of that sub-paragraph part only of that property, being a part bearing to the whole of that property the same proportion as at the relevant date, namely—

(*a*) if the deceased's interest determined or was disposed of at a date before the death, that date, or

(*b*) in any other case, the date of the death,

the annual value of the deceased's interest bore to the aggregate of the annual values of the interests of the deceased and the other person or persons in question.

(3) Where on any death estate duty falls to be charged by virtue of sub-paragraph (iii) of the substituted section 2(1)(*b*) on any property which is or has been comprised in settled property subject to such a trust as is mentioned in that sub-paragraph, but the whole of the combined income of all the property from time to time subject to that trust arising during the relevant period was not paid to or applied for the benefit of the deceased as a result of the discretion so mentioned, there shall be treated as passing on the death by virtue of that sub-paragraph part only of the property in question, being a part bearing to the whole of the property in question the same proportion as, subject to paragraph (*d*) of this subsection, the part of the combined

income of that property which was so paid or applied during that period bears to the whole of that income arising during that period; and for the purposes of this subsection—

(*a*) the expression "the relevant period" means such period during which the property in question was subject to the trust and the deceased was eligible to benefit as a result of the discretion aforesaid as falls within the material period for the purposes of head (*aa*), (*bb*) or (*cc*), as the case may require, of the said sub-paragraph (iii);

(*b*) subject to paragraph (*c*) of this subsection, any sum paid to or applied for the benefit of any person eligible to benefit as a result of the discretion aforesaid out of any of the property subject to the trust, whether purporting to be so paid or applied out of income or by way of a distribution of capital, being a sum paid or applied after 15th April 1963 and not being a sum paid as mentioned in section 36(5)(*d*) of this Act, shall be treated as having been paid or applied out of income as a result of that discretion if or to the extent that the sum in question does not exceed the amount, if any, by which the aggregate amount of all the income with respect to which that discretion was exercisable arising during the period beginning with 16th April 1963 and ending with the date when the sum in question was so paid or applied exceeds the aggregate amount of all sums previously paid or applied out of that property during that period to persons eligible as aforesaid and, if or to the extent that the sum in question does not fall to be treated under this paragraph as having been paid or applied out of income, it shall be treated as having been paid or applied by way of a distribution of capital;

(*c*) in determining, for the purposes of the application of paragraph (*b*) of this subsection to a particular sum paid or applied as therein mentioned, the aggregate amount of all sums previously so paid or applied, there shall be left out of account any sum so previously paid or applied if or to the extent that it falls to be treated under that paragraph as having been made by way of a distribution of capital; and if two or more sums were so paid or applied on the same date, that paragraph shall apply as if both or all of those sums had been a single sum of their aggregate amount, and, if part only of that aggregate amount falls to be treated under that paragraph as having been paid or applied out of income and both or all of those payments or

PART III

applications were not to or for the benefit of the same person, that part shall be apportioned between the different payments or applications in proportion to the sums respectively paid or applied ;

(*d*) if, in consequence of paragraphs (*b*) and (*c*) of this subsection, the aggregate amount which falls to be treated as having been paid or applied during the relevant period as a result of the discretion aforesaid out of income exceeds the amount of the income with respect to which that discretion applies which arose during that period, the combined income of all the property from time to time subject to the trust arising during that period shall be treated as increased by the amount of the excess ;

(*e*) the amount of the combined income of the property from time to time subject to the trust during any period shall be treated as increased by an amount equal to the value of any benefit by way of the use and enjoyment of any of that property during that period afforded to any person by the trustees in accordance with the trust, and the person to whom that benefit was afforded shall be treated as having received out of that income during that period an amount equal to that value.

(4) Where on any death estate duty falls to be charged on any property by virtue of sub-paragraph (iv) of the substituted section 2(1)(*b*) but at the date of the death the whole of the income of the settled property in which the property in question was comprised arising during the whole of the period during which the trust or power to accumulate has subsisted has not been accumulated, there shall be treated as passing on the death by virtue of the said sub-paragraph (iv) part only of the property in question, being a part bearing to the whole of the property in question the same proportion as the amount of that income less any payments by the trustees made out of that income (or which would by virtue of paragraphs (*b*) and (*c*) of subsection (3) of this section fall to be treated as so made) bears to the whole of that income ; but for the purposes of this subsection paragraph (*e*) of the said subsection (3) shall be disregarded.

(5) Where on any death estate duty falls to be charged on any property by virtue of paragraph (*f*) of section 2(1) of the
1894 c. 30. Finance Act 1894 as inserted by section 36(3) of this Act—

(*a*) the principal value of the property shall be determined as if there had been no option to purchase ;

(*b*) if the option is exercised, but the purchase price under the option is less than the principal value of the

PART III

property determined as aforesaid, there shall be treated as passing on the death as separate properties—

(i) a part of the property bearing to the whole thereof the same proportion as the purchase price bears to that principal value;

(ii) without prejudice to section 3 of the Finance Act 1894, a part equal to the remainder of the property, 1894 c. 30.

the principal values of those parts being taken to be the corresponding proportions of that principal value;

(*c*) where paragraph (*b*) of this subsection does not apply, there shall be treated as passing on the deceased's death the property freed from the option;

(*d*) the persons accountable for any duty on the property on a part thereof passing by virtue of paragraph (*b*)(i) or on the whole thereof passing in accordance with paragraph (*c*) of this subsection shall be the persons who would have been accountable for the duty on the property if there had been no option to purchase, and the person accountable for any duty on a part of the property passing by virtue of paragraph (*b*)(ii) of this subsection shall be the person by whom or for whose benefit the option was exercised.

Estate duty in respect of interests in expectancy.

38.—(1) If, in a case where estate duty falls, or would apart from paragraph 2 of Part II of Schedule 17 to this Act or section 7(10) of the Finance Act 1894 fall, to be charged on a death by virtue of any of the sub-paragraphs of the substituted section 2(1)(*b*) on property which has been settled property—

(*a*) the settlement has come to an end before the death; but

(*b*) while the settlement subsisted, one or more interests in expectancy in the settled property were purchased within the period of seven years ending with the date of the death either by the deceased or out of, or by means of, any property which would have passed for the purposes of estate duty on the deceased's death if he had died immediately before the purchase,

then, notwithstanding anything in the said paragraph 2 or section 7(10), in addition to any other charge of estate duty, estate duty shall be chargeable on the property passing on that death by virtue of the sub-paragraph in question of the substituted section 2(1)(*b*), but as if the principal value of that property were an amount equal to the amount or value of the consideration given for the purchase or purchases.

PART III

(2) Where on any death estate duty falls to be charged by virtue of the substituted section 2(1)(*b*) on settled property as respects which the settlement continues to subsist at the death, and the property passing on the death also includes any interest in expectancy in the settled property which was purchased as mentioned in subsection (1)(*b*) of this section, then, notwithstanding anything in section 7(10) of the Finance Act 1894, estate duty shall also be chargeable in respect of that interest; and for that purpose the principal value of that interest shall be taken to be—

1894 c. 30.

(*a*) the amount or value of the consideration given for the purchase; or

(*b*) if the persons accountable for the duty so elect by notice in writing given to the Board within twelve months of the death or such longer period as the Board may allow, the principal value of that interest determined in accordance with section 7(5) of the Finance Act 1894;

and section 7(6) of the Finance Act 1894 shall not apply to that interest unless notice of an election under paragraph (*b*) of this subsection has been given in relation to that interest.

(3) For the purposes of subsections (1) and (2) of this section, where a settlement has come to an end as respects part but not all of the property comprised in it, there shall be deemed to have been a separate settlement of that part; and for the purposes of the said subsection (2)—

(*a*) where at the death there are separate interests in or derived out of an interest purchased, the purchase of that interest shall be treated as having comprised a separate purchase of each of those interests;

(*b*) where a purchased interest has ceased to subsist as a separate interest before the death and before the time when it was originally limited to determine and has been absorbed or enlarged into another interest, that other interest shall be treated as if it had been the subject-matter of the purchase, so, however, that for the purposes of paragraph (*b*) of the said subsection (2), the value on which duty is charged shall, instead of being the principal value of that other interest, be such proportion of that principal value as is attributable to any purchased interest which that other interest is treated under this paragraph as representing.

(4) For the purposes of subsection (1) or (2)(*a*) of this section—

(*a*) any consideration for the purchase of an interest in settled property consisting of another interest under the settlement shall be disregarded except where there has been a prior purchase such as is mentioned in subsection (1)(*b*) of this section of that other interest, in which case the consideration for that prior purchase shall be treated (except for the purpose of determining the value of that consideration) as given not for that prior purchase but, in place of that other interest, for the first-mentioned purchase; PART III

(*b*) where under section 37 of this Act part only of the property in which the purchased interest subsisted would fall to be treated as passing on the death, the consideration for the purchase shall be treated as reduced to a corresponding extent.

(5) Where such a purchase as is mentioned in subsection (1)(*b*) of this section was made not less than four years before the death, the amount or value of the consideration for the purchase for the purposes of subsection (1) or (2)(*a*) of this section, or the principal value of the interest for the purposes of subsection (2)(*b*) of this section, shall (after any deduction therefrom by virtue of subsection (7) of this section) be treated as reduced—

(*a*) if the purchase was made less than five years before the death, by fifteen per cent.;

(*b*) if the purchase was made not less than five but less than six years before the death, by thirty per cent.;

(*c*) if the purchase was made not less than six years before the death, by sixty per cent.

(6) Where such a purchase as is mentioned in subsection (1)(*b*) of this section was made from a body of persons established for public or charitable purposes only or from the trustees of a trust so established, this section shall have effect in relation to that purchase as if in the said subsection (1)(*b*) for the reference to seven years there were substituted a reference to one year.

(7) Where duty is chargeable by virtue of subsection (1) or (2) of this section by reason of a purchase of an interest, and the deceased incurred any debt or created any incumbrance wholly or partly as consideration for that purchase, that consideration for the debt or incumbrance shall be left out of account for the purpose of section 31 of the Finance Act 1939 (which excludes 1939 c. 41. or limits the making for purposes of estate duty of an allowance for certain debts incurred or incumbrances created by the deceased for the purchase of property coming ultimately from himself); and where duty is chargeable by virtue of the said subsection (2) any allowance for a debt or incumbrance, to the extent to which it could not be made apart from this subsection, shall be made by deduction from the value on which the duty is charged by virtue of the said subsection (2) and not otherwise.

PART III

(8) For the purposes of this section—

(*a*) where such a trust in relation to any property as is mentioned in sub-paragraph (iii) of the substituted section 2(1)(*b*) is expectant on the determination of a prior interest in that property, eligibility to benefit under that trust shall be deemed to be an interest in expectancy in that property of all the persons so eligible;

(*b*) any transaction whereby a person for money or money's worth acquires an interest or secures its extinction for his benefit shall be deemed to be a purchase of that interest by him, and any interest extinguished shall be treated as absorbed into the interest benefiting from the extinction;

(*c*) any consideration for a purchase given otherwise than in cash shall be valued as at the date of the purchase;

(*d*) any consideration given for the purchase of more than one interest under a settlement or for the purchase of an interest under a settlement and for something else, shall be apportioned as may be just.

Objects of national, scientific, historic or artistic interest.
1930 c. 28.
1950 c. 15.
1965 c. 25.

39.—(1) Where on any death an object to which section 40 of the Finance Act 1930 (which relates to the exemption from estate duty of objects of national, scientific, historic or artistic interest) applies has been exempted under subsection (1) of that section in pursuance of an undertaking under section 48(1) of the Finance Act 1950 as amended by section 31(7) of the Finance Act 1965 from estate duty in respect of that death, the provisions of this section shall have effect if duty subsequently becomes chargeable in relation to that object under subsection (2) of the said section 40 by reason of a sale or other disposal of the object or under subsection (3) of the said section 48 by reason of a non-observance of the undertaking.

(2) If the event giving rise to the charge under the said subsection (2) or (3) occurred within the period of three years beginning with the date of the death, then, notwithstanding anything in the said section 40 or 48, the charge shall be on the principal value of the object at the date of the death, no allowance shall be made under section 31(8) of the Finance Act 1965 in determining that value, and that value shall, for all the purposes of estate duty, be aggregated with the principal value of the estate of which the object would but for the exemption have formed part as if the object had never been exempted.

(3) If the event giving rise to the charge under the said subsection (2) or (3) occurred after the expiration of the period aforesaid, then, notwithstanding anything in the said section

40 or 48, the rate at which estate duty becomes chargeable in relation to the object shall be the rate which would have been the estate rate of duty on the property comprised in the estate of which the object would have formed part on the death but for its exemption from duty if the aggregate principal value of that estate for the purposes of duty in respect of the death had been increased by the amount of the proceeds of sale or the value of the object at the time of the disposal otherwise than on sale or at the time of the non-observance of the undertaking, as the case may be. PART III

(4) Where two or more objects exempted as mentioned in subsection (1) of this section from estate duty in respect of the same death are objects which at the date of the death together formed a set, then if—

(*a*) there being a sale or other disposal of one of those objects, there is a sale or other disposal of another or others of them (whether by the same or by a different person) either—

(i) to the same person; or

(ii) to persons who are acting in concert or who are, in the terms of paragraph 21 of Schedule 7 to the Finance Act 1965, connected persons, 1965 c. 25.

whether on the same or a different occasion; or

(*b*) there being a non-observance of the undertaking referred to in the said subsection (1) in regard to one or more of those objects, there is a further non-observance of that undertaking in regard to another or others of them whether by the same or by a different person and whether on the same or a different occasion; or

(*c*) there being a non-observance of that undertaking in regard to one or more of those objects, the object or objects in question and another or others of the objects comprised in the set are sold or otherwise disposed of in such manner that paragraph (*a*) of this subsection applies,

then, notwithstanding anything in subsection (4) of the said section 48, for the purpose of charging duty in accordance with this section under the said subsection (2) or (3) all the sales or other disposals referred to in paragraph (*a*) of this subsection, or all the non-observances referred to in paragraph (*b*) of this subsection, or, in a case falling within paragraph (*c*) of this subsection, all the non-observances and sales or other disposals there referred to, as the case may be, shall be treated as having taken place at the date of the earliest of them and to have been a sale of all the objects affected by the sales or other disposals or non-observances in question as a single item at a price equal to the aggregate amount of the proceeds of sale of any of those

Part III

objects which has been sold since the death and the principal value at that earliest date of any of those objects which has not been sold since the death; and on each occasion on which this subsection operates in relation to any sale or other disposal or non-observance, any estate duty previously charged in relation to any of the objects affected by that or any previous relevant sale or other disposal or non-observance or, by virtue of subsection (2) of this section, on any estate of which any of those objects would have formed part but for their exemption from duty shall be adjusted accordingly.

Supplementary and transitional provisions as to estate duty.

40.—(1) There shall have effect with respect to estate duty the supplementary provisions contained in Part II of Schedule 17 to this Act; and the enactments specified in Part III of that Schedule shall have effect subject to the amendments respectively so specified, being amendments consequential on the provisions of this Part of this Act and the repeal by this Act of the enactments specified in Part V of Schedule 21 to this Act.

(2) The provisions of this Part of this Act shall apply in relation to any death occurring after 15th April 1969 but—

(*a*) where an interest in property comprised in a settlement has determined before that date, there shall not be charged on any death by way of estate duty on that property which is attributable to that interest a greater amount than would have fallen to be charged on that death by way of such duty on that property if the relevant provisions as defined by subsection (3) of this section had not been passed;

(*b*) the provisions of section 38(5) of this Act shall not have effect so as to give a lesser percentage reduction in the principal value of any property than the percentage reduction (if any) which, assuming that the deceased had died on 19th March 1968, would have fallen to be made as respects the property under sub-
1960 c. 44. section (1) of section 64 of the Finance Act 1960 if
1968 c. 44. section 35 of the Finance Act 1968 and the relevant provisions aforesaid had not been passed;

(*c*) for the purposes of aggregation, property passing on a death after 15th April 1969 as comprised in a gift of, or of rights under, either a policy of assurance on the life of the deceased issued in respect of an insurance made before 20th March 1968 or a contract for a deferred annuity becoming payable on the death of the deceased entered into before 20th March 1968 shall be treated in accordance with subsections (7) to (13) of section 38 of the Finance Act 1968 as if the repeal by this Act of those subsections, the proviso to section 4 of the Finance Act 1894 and section 33(2) and (3) of the Finance Act 1954 had not been made; PART III 1894 c. 30. 1954 c. 44.

(*d*) where an interest in expectancy in any property was before 15th April 1969 bona fide sold or mortgaged for full consideration in money or money's worth, then—

(i) no other duty on that property shall be payable by the purchaser or mortgagee when the interest falls into possession than would have been payable if the relevant provisions aforesaid had not been passed; and

(ii) in the case of a mortgage any higher duty payable by the mortgagor shall rank as a charge subsequent to that of the mortgagee,

and section 56(1) of the Finance Act 1940 (which relates to transactions with companies under the control of not more than five persons) shall apply for the purposes of this paragraph as it applies for the purposes of section 3 of the Finance Act 1894; 1940 c. 29

(*e*) the repeal by this Act of paragraph (16) of section 23 of the Finance Act 1894 shall not affect any relief which would otherwise have been due under that paragraph in a case where estate duty has been paid, whether before or after 15th April 1969, on the death on or before that date of one of the parties to a marriage, so far as respects the payment of estate duty on the death of the other party to the marriage.

(3) In subsection (2) of this section the expression " the relevant provisions " means the following provisions of this Act, namely—

(*a*) sections 36, 37 and 38;

(*b*) Schedule 17 other than Part I and other than paragraphs 7, 8, 13 and 19 of Part III;

(*c*) Part V of Schedule 21 other than so much thereof as is consequential only on the provisions of section 35.

PART IV

CAPITAL GAINS AND BETTERMENT LEVY

Capital gains

41.—(1) Subject to the following provisions of this section, a gain shall not be a chargeable gain for the purposes of capital gains tax or corporation tax on chargeable gains if it accrues on the disposal by any person of any specified securities, as defined in subsection (2) below. Gilt-edged securities exempt from tax on capital gains.

PART IV

(2) For the purposes of this section "specified securities" means the securities specified in Part I of Schedule 18 to this Act and such of the following securities, denominated in sterling and issued after 15th April 1969, as may be specified by order made by the Treasury by statutory instrument, namely,—

1968 c. 13.

(*a*) stocks and registered bonds issued under section 12 of the National Loans Act 1968; and

1948 c. 67.

(*b*) stocks and registered bonds guaranteed by the Treasury and issued under the Electricity (Scotland) Acts 1943 to 1954, the Electricity Acts 1947 and 1957 and the Gas Act 1948;

and the Treasury shall cause particulars of any order made under this subsection to be published in the London and Edinburgh Gazettes as soon as may be after the order is made.

1965 c. 25.

(3) Subsection (1) above applies to disposals of specified securities after 15th April 1969 and, except in the case of any disposal which is deemed to occur on that day by virtue of any provision of section 24 (deaths) or section 25 (settled property) of the Finance Act 1965, to any disposal of specified securities which occurred after 3.30 p.m. on that day.

(4) Subsection (1) above does not apply in the case of a disposal by a company, within the meaning of Part IV of the Finance Act 1965, unless the disposal of the securities occurs more than twelve months after their acquisition, and for the purposes of this subsection—

(*a*) if in consequence of a conversion on their redemption of any specified securities, those securities and a new holding of specified securities are, under paragraph 4(2) of Schedule 7 to the Finance Act 1965, as applied by paragraph 5 of that Schedule, to be treated as the same asset acquired as the converted securities were acquired, the date of acquisition of the new holding shall be deemed to be the date of the acquisition of the converted securities; and

1962 c. 44.

(*b*) the rules of identification in paragraph 8 of Schedule 9 to the Finance Act 1962 shall apply; and

(*c*) in relation to a disposal of specified securities to which, by virtue of this subsection, subsection (1) above does not apply, the expenditure allowable under paragraph 4 of Schedule 6 to the Finance Act 1965 (cost of acquisition, etc.) shall, notwithstanding the provisions as to the pooling of securities in Schedule 7 to that Act, be determined by reference to the acquisition of the securities identified in accordance with paragraph (*b*) above.

PART IV

(5) Where under Schedule 13 to the Finance Act 1965 (groups of companies) the persons disposing of and acquiring an asset are to be treated as if the consideration were of such an amount that neither a gain nor a loss accrues on the disposal, the person acquiring the asset shall be treated for the purposes of subsection (4) above (and of the enactments referred to in that subsection so far as applied for the purposes of that subsection) as acquiring it at the time when the other acquired it. 1965 c. 25.

(6) Part II of Schedule 18 to this Act shall have effect in relation to certain disposals and appropriations of specified securities by companies.

(7) Part III of Schedule 18 to this Act shall have effect in relation to certain disposals of 6½ per cent. Treasury Stock 1971 issued by way of compensation in accordance with section 10 of the Iron and Steel Act 1967. 1967 c. 17.

(8) Schedule 9 to the Finance Act 1965 (Government securities issued at a discount: neutral zone for chargeable gains) shall have effect after 15th April 1969 with the omission of all the entries except those relating to—

(*a*) Nyasaland Government 3% Guaranteed Stock 1954/74,

(*b*) Sudan Government 4% Guaranteed Stock 1974,

(*c*) Sudan Government 4½% Guaranteed Stock 1939/73, and

(*d*) Tanganyika Government 4% Guaranteed Stock 1952/72.

Long-term and short-term tax on capital gains.

42. Schedule 19 to this Act (which makes further provision for amending the enactments relating to long-term and short-term capital gains) shall have effect.

Betterment Levy

Exemption where top value is £1,500 or less.

43. After section 59 of the Land Commission Act 1967 insert— 1967 c. 1.

"59A.—(1) Subject to the provisions of this section, no levy shall be chargeable in respect of a chargeable act or event which occurs after 5th April 1969 if—

(*a*) the top value does not exceed £1,500, and

(*b*) relief under this section is not excluded by subsection (2) below.

In the following provisions of this section—

"the applicant for relief" means the person who under section 36 of this Act is liable for levy in respect of the chargeable act or event apart from this section, and any person on whose behalf he is acting,

PART IV

"the financial year" means the financial year in which that chargeable act or event took place, and "financial year" means a year ending on 31st March.

(2) No relief shall be given under subsection (1) above if, in relation to any other chargeable act or event in the financial year, the applicant for relief, or his or her wife or husband, is—

(*a*) the person, or one of the persons, liable for levy (apart from this section), or

(*b*) a person on whose behalf the person, or any of the persons, so liable for levy is acting,

unless the top value mentioned in subsection (1)(*a*) above, when added to the total of the top values for any such other chargeable acts or events, does not exceed £1,500.

(3) For the purposes of this section—

(*a*) the personal representatives of a deceased person shall be regarded as one person distinct from the persons who may from time to time be the personal representatives,

(*b*) the trustees of a settlement shall be treated as one person distinct from the persons who may from time to time be trustees, and from the trustees of any other settlement,

1925 c. 18.

(*c*) a person exercising the powers of a tenant for life under the Settled Land Act 1925 shall be treated as a trustee of the settlement.

(4) No account shall be taken under subsection (2) above of any chargeable act or event unless some amount of levy is chargeable in respect of it, or would be so chargeable apart from the provisions of this section.

(5) If, apart from the provisions of this section, levy in Case C in respect of the same chargeable act or event is chargeable on two or more different assessable interests, the chargeable act or event shall be treated for the purposes of this section as different chargeable acts or events related to those different assessable interests.

(6) For the purpose of determining whether this section applies to a chargeable act or event in any financial year the Commission may under section 43 of this Act serve a notice as respects any other chargeable act or event which in the opinion of the Commission has or may have occurred in that financial year, and the information which may be required under that section shall include information about

PART IV

any person on whose behalf the person served with the notice has been acting in relation to that act or event, and any other information which assists or may assist in establishing whether subsection (2) above applies to the other chargeable act or event.

(7) It is hereby declared that any information given to the Commission for the purpose of obtaining relief under this section is information which the person giving it is required to give under this Part of this Act, and section 81(5) of this Act shall apply accordingly.

(8) In this section " top value " means, in relation to any chargeable act or event, the " market value ", or as the case may be the amount of the " consideration for the disposition " or " compensation " taken into account in arriving at net development value under section 29(3), 30(3), 31(2), 33(3)(*a*) or 34(3)(*a*) of this Act or the relevant regulations under section 35 of this Act:

Provided that any amount to be added under regulation 3(4)(*c*) of the Case F General Regulations 1967 or the Case F General (Scotland) Regulations 1967, or under any corresponding regulation made after the passing of this Act, shall be included in the top value in Case F."

S.I. 1967/496
S.I. 1967/492.

Single dwelling-house built on land given or bequeathed.
1967 c. 1.

44.—(1) After section 60 of the Land Commission Act 1967 insert—

" 60A.—(1) This section has effect where a project of material development consisting exclusively of the building of a single dwelling-house is begun, and—

(*a*) the developing owner acquired his assessable interest in the land comprised in the project as a gift, or as a legacy, and intends to occupy the dwelling-house as his only or main residence, or

(*b*) the developing owner intends to give his assessable interest in that land to some other person who intends to occupy the dwelling-house as his only or main residence, or

(*c*) where section 32(5)(*b*) or (*c*) of this Act applies to the developing owner (so that he is a prospective purchaser under an enforceable contract), the contract is to acquire for less than full consideration (so as to be partly by way of gift) and the developing owner intends to occupy the dwelling-house as his only or main residence,

and the person so intending to occupy the dwelling-house is in fact the first occupier and continues in occupation for at least six months, or if earlier until his death.

Part IV

(2) No relief shall be given under subsection (1)(*b*) or (*c*) above unless the person intending to occupy the dwelling-house in fact acquires the assessable interest as a gift, or as a legacy, within twelve months, or such longer period as the Commission may allow, from the beginning of the project.

(3) No relief shall be given under this section as respects a gift made before 1st July 1948, or as respects a legacy on a death before that date.

(4) If the developing owner so elects, he shall be treated for the purposes of Case C levy in respect of the project as if he acquired the gift or legacy for capital consideration equal to its market value—

(*a*) where subsection (1)(*a*) above applies, at the time of the gift or death,

(*b*) where subsection (1)(*b*) or (*c*) above applies, at the beginning of the project,

and for the purposes of Schedule 5 to this Act he shall be deemed to have acquired the gift or legacy at that time by way of a disposition to him which was the last relevant disposition.

(5) In determining the market value of a gift or legacy at the time given by subsection (4) above, account shall be taken of the state of the land at that time, and of the incidents attaching to the assessable interest at that time, and of all other circumstances, including circumstances concerning planning permission, which would have been taken into account by a purchaser at that time.

(6) If the time given by subsection (4) above falls between 30th June 1948 and 6th April 1967, Part V of Schedule 4 to this Act shall have effect in relation to the project as if paragraph 49 of that Schedule were omitted, and if that time does not fall between those dates, the acquisition which took place, or is deemed to have taken place, at that time, shall be treated for the purposes of Schedule 5 to this Act as a disposition within paragraph 3(*b*) of that Schedule, that is to say a duly notified disposition after 6th April 1967.

(7) References in this section to an assessable interest in the land comprised in the project include references to an assessable interest in any part of the land, and where the gift or legacy relates only to part of that land, or in part to land not comprised in the project, this section shall apply with any necessary apportionments and computations.

(8) Where—

(*a*) part only of the developing owner's assessable interest is derived from a gift or legacy (that is to say it is a gift or legacy of a lesser or less valuable interest or one relating to part only of the land in which the assessable interest subsists), or

(*b*) part only of the developing owner's assessable interest is included in a gift or legacy from the developing owner,

paragraphs (*a*) and (*b*) of subsection (1) above, and the provisions of this Act applying for the purposes of those paragraphs, shall have effect as if the assessable interest were two separate interests one of which is the subject of the gift or legacy, and all such apportionments, computations and valuations shall be made as are necessary to give effect to this subsection.

(9) For the purposes of this section—

(*a*) property acquired by way of gift includes property acquired for less than market value if the Land Commission are satisfied that the grantor intended to give a benefit by accepting less than market value,

(*b*) property acquired as a legacy includes property appropriated in or towards satisfaction of any interest or share in property devolving under a testamentary disposition or on an intestacy,

(*c*) any reference to the building of a dwelling-house shall be construed as including a reference to the construction or laying out of any garage, outhouse, garden, yard, court, forecourt or other appurtenance for occupation with, and for the purposes of, the dwelling-house.

(10) This section shall not have effect unless notice is duly served under section 38 of this Act in respect of the project consisting of the building of the dwelling-house, but the Commission may for the purposes of this section accept such a notice although out of time under subsection (2) of that section.

(11) An election under this section shall be made within such time and in such form as the Commission direct.

(12) Relief shall be given under this section on proof of the relevant facts to the satisfaction of the Commission.

(13) It is hereby declared that any information given to the Commission for the purpose of obtaining relief

PART IV

under this section is information which the person giving it is required to give under this Part of this Act, and section 81(5) of this Act shall apply accordingly."

1967 c. 1.

(2) The Land Commission Act 1967 shall be deemed always to have had effect as amended by this section.

(3) The Commission shall make all such repayments of levy and interest received by them as are required to give effect to subsection (2) above, and shall deduct the amount so repaid from the sums falling to be paid into the Exchequer under section 4(2) of the said Act.

(4) Any objection to a notice of assessment of levy on the ground that the amendments made by this section affect the amount of the levy may be made under section 46 of the said Act at any time before 1st January 1970, although out of time under that section.

Base value of owner-occupied dwelling-house.

45.—(1) In Schedule 4 to the Land Commission Act 1967 after paragraph 5 (Case A: base value equal to eleven-tenths of current use value) insert—

"5A.—(1) In paragraph 5(*a*) above 'twelve-tenths' shall be substituted for 'eleven-tenths' if the relevant land—

(*a*) is the site of a single dwelling-house which is the grantor's sole or main residence, and

(*b*) does not exceed one quarter of an acre, and comprises no other building.

(2) Sub-paragraph (1) above shall not apply unless the market value of the relevant interest (determined under paragraph 1 above) is £10,000 or less.

(3) If the said market value exceeds £10,000 the amount of levy in respect of the disposition shall not exceed—

(*a*) what would be the amount of the levy if that market value had been £10,000 (and without sub-paragraph (2) above), plus

(*b*) the said excess over £10,000.

(4) This paragraph shall only apply if the grantor has occupied the dwelling-house as his only or main residence for at least six months (or for two or more periods adding up to at least six months) out of the eighteeen months ending with the date of the disposition.

(5) If the grantor is a trustee, and the dwelling-house has been the sole or main residence of a person who—

(*a*) is entitled to occupy it under the terms of the settlement, or (*b*) is a beneficiary under the settlement and allowed by the trustee to occupy it,

sub-paragraph (1)(*a*) and sub-paragraph (4) above shall have effect as if that person were the grantor.

(6) If the grantor is the personal representative of a deceased person, sub-paragraph (1)(*a*) above shall apply to a dwelling-house which was the deceased's sole or main residence and sub-paragraph (4) above shall not apply, but the deceased person must have occupied the dwelling-house as his only or main residence—

(*a*) for at least six months (or for two or more periods adding up to at least six months) out of the eighteen months ending with the date of the death, or

(*b*) if he acquired the dwelling-house within the said period of eighteen months, for the period between the acquisition and his death.

(7) In this paragraph any reference to a dwelling-house shall be construed as including a reference to any garage, outhouse, garden, yard, court, forecourt or other appurtenance for occupation with, and for the purposes of, the dwelling-house.

(8) This paragraph shall apply as respects a disposition after 5th April 1969."

(2) After paragraph 15 of the said Schedule 4 (corresponding provision for Case B) insert—

" 15A.—(1) In paragraph 15(*a*) above ' twelve-tenths ' shall be substituted for ' eleven-tenths ' if the relevant land—

(*a*) is the site of a single dwelling-house which is the grantor's sole or main residence, and

(*b*) does not exceed one quarter of an acre, and comprises no other building.

(2) Sub-paragraph (1) above shall not apply unless the consideration for the disposition (determined under paragraph 7 above) is £10,000 or less.

(3) If the said consideration exceeds £10,000 the amount of the levy in respect of the disposition shall not exceed—

(*a*) what would be the amount of the levy if the said consideration had been £10,000 (and without sub-paragraph (2) above), plus

(*b*) the said excess over £10,000.

(4) Sub-paragraphs (4), (5), (6) and (7) of paragraph 5A above shall apply for the purposes of this paragraph as for the purposes of that paragraph.

PART IV

(5) This paragraph shall apply as respects a disposition after 5th April 1969."

Allowance for costs of sale. 1967 c. 1.

46. In paragraph 19 of Schedule 6 to the Land Commission Act 1967 after sub-paragraph (2) insert—

" (2A) In relation to a chargeable act or event after 5th April 1969 and within Case A, B, E or F, this paragraph also applies to expenditure wholly and exclusively incurred by the appropriate person for the purposes of the disposition, being—

(*a*) fees, commission or remuneration paid for the professional services of any surveyor or valuer, or auctioneer, or agent or legal adviser or accountant, and costs of transfer or conveyance (including stamp duty), and

(*b*) costs of advertising to find a buyer,

unless and except to the extent that the person incurring the expenditure, having regard to the provisions of paragraph 4 of Schedule 14 to the Finance Act 1967, elects that this sub-paragraph shall not apply to the expenditure, or some part of it."

1967 c. 54.

Relief for land bought between 22nd September 1965 and 6th April 1967.

47.—(1) In Schedule 5 to the Land Commission Act 1967 insert the following paragraphs after paragraph 10 (which gives relief for acquisitions in the period between 22nd September 1965 and 6th April 1967)—

" *Plots for single houses*

10A.—(1) Paragraph 10(1) above shall apply if it is shown to the satisfaction of the Commission that at the time of the disposition the person becoming entitled to the chargeable interest in the land comprised in the disposition intended to erect a single dwelling-house on the land, and did not intend to erect any other building on the land or to dispose of any part of the land suitable for material development.

(2) If the disposition was made in pursuance of an enforceable contract made after 22nd September 1965 sub-paragraph (1) above shall apply with the substitution for the reference to the time of the disposition of a reference to either that time or to the time of the making of the contract.

(3) In this paragraph the reference to a dwelling-house includes a reference to any garage, out-house, garden, yard, court, forecourt or other appurtenance for occupation with, and for the purposes of, the dwelling-house.

(4) Section 81(5) of this Act (penalty for false information) shall apply as respects any statement given for the purposes of this paragraph as it applies to a statement giving information required under Part III of this Act. Part IV

Other purchases in interim period

10B.—(1) Paragraph 10(1) above shall apply if—

(*a*) the amount of the consideration given for the disposition does not exceed £2,500, and

(*b*) where that amount is the result of an apportionment under paragraph 14 of Schedule 6 to this Act, the amount before apportionment does not exceed £2,500.

(2) Subject to sub-paragraph (3) below, if the said amount of the consideration exceeds £2,500, the grantee may (if that would give him more relief than he could get otherwise under paragraph 10(1) above or paragraph 11 below) be treated for the purposes of sub-paragraph (1) above as if that amount were £2,500, but, if he is so treated, he shall also be so treated for the purposes of paragraph 7 above, and of all the other provisions of Part III of this Act.

(3) If the amount of the consideration given for the disposition is the result of such an apportionment, and the amount before apportionment exceeds £2,500, sub-paragraph (2) above shall not apply, but the grantee may (if that would give him relief) be treated as if the amount before apportionment were £2,500, so that the amount of the consideration given for the disposition is reduced to the relevant apportioned part of that £2,500 both for the purposes of sub-paragraph (1) above and for the purposes of all other provisions of Part III of this Act, including paragraph 7 above."

(2) At the end of the said paragraph 10(1) insert " or if paragraph 10A or 10B below applies:

Provided that the said paragraphs 10A and 10B shall not apply except where they afford relief."

(3) The Land Commission Act 1967 shall be deemed always to have had effect as amended by this section, and any regulations under that Act expressed to relate to relief corresponding to any relief conferred by this section may, notwithstanding anything in that Act, apply to chargeable acts or events at any time after 5th April 1967. 1967 c. 1.

(4) The Commission shall make all such repayments of levy and interest received by them as are required to give effect

Part IV

to subsection (3) above, and shall deduct the amount so repaid from the sums falling to be paid into the Exchequer under section 4(2) of the said Act.

(5) Any objection to a notice of assessment of levy on the ground that the amendments made by this section affect the amount of the levy may be made under section 46 of the said Act at any time before 1st January 1970, although out of time under that section.

Levy in Case C, and related provisions.

1967 c. 1.

48.—(1) In Part II of Schedule 5 to the Land Commission Act 1967 (Case C: base value derived from contract) at the end of paragraph 18 insert—

" but paragraph 20 below shall not apply to a project begun after 5th April 1969 unless the contract (to purchase the interest or take the tenancy)—

(i) is performed within a period of twelve months beginning with the beginning of the project, or such longer period as the Commission may in their discretion allow, and

(ii) is performed for the consideration, and in accordance with all the other terms, specified in or determined under the contract as subsisting on the relevant date.

18A.—(1) The power to serve notices of assessment under section 55 of this Act shall include power to serve notice of any assessment to give effect to the provisions of paragraph 18 above, or to recover any levy chargeable because paragraph 18(i) or (ii) above is not satisfied.

(2) If paragraph 18(ii) above would be satisfied but that, before the date specified in paragraph 20(2) below, the provisions of the contract have been varied, and the Commission are satisfied that it is just and reasonable so to do, the Commission may direct that this Part of this Schedule shall have effect as if the variation had been made before the relevant date.

(3) If paragraph 20 below does not apply to the relevant interest (or where there is more than one relevant interest, to one of them) because paragraph 18(i) or (ii) above is not satisfied, liability for levy (with any interest) in respect of that relevant interest shall be a joint and several liability of the developing owner and of the other party to the contract.

(4) Section 83(2)(*c*) of this Act shall not make it unlawful for any party to the contract to incur a liability to indemnify the developing owner for any amount or additional amount

of levy (with interest) payable only because the contract is not performed in accordance with paragraph 18(i) or (ii) above.

(5) This Part of this Schedule shall not have effect if, in consequence of paragraph 2 of Schedule 13 to this Act (groups of companies), the performance of the contract does not constitute a chargeable act or event."

(2) For paragraph 8(1) of Schedule 6 to the said Act (adjustment of current use value where prospective purchaser develops before purchase) substitute—

" 8.—(1) The provisions of this paragraph shall have effect for the purpose of assessing levy in Case A or Case B in respect of a disposition where—

(*a*) all or any part of the relevant land was comprised in a project of material development which constituted a chargeable act or event taking place before the disposition, and in relation to which there was a developing owner, and

(*b*) the grantor (or a person from whom he took otherwise than for valuable consideration) was, when the project was begun, entitled to the fee simple of the relevant land comprised in the project, or to a tenancy, other than a minor tenancy, in that land, but was not the developing owner ",

and in sub-paragraph (2)(*b*) of the said paragraph 8 for " the relevant land " substitute " the relevant land comprised in the project ".

(3) For paragraph 4 of Schedule 5 to the said Act (purchase price to be disregarded if purchaser has developed the land) substitute—

" 4.—(1) A previous disposition of the chargeable interest (whether made before, on or after the first appointed day) shall not be taken for the purposes of this Part of this Schedule to have been a relevant disposition of that interest if—

(*a*) a project of material development of the whole or part of the relevant land was begun after that disposition was made but before the relevant date, and

(*b*) the beginning of the carrying out of that project constituted a chargeable act or event,

except where, in relation to the project, some person was chargeable to Case C levy as a developing owner under contract to acquire the whole of the chargeable interest, or, where the chargeable act or event is the grant of a

PART IV tenancy, as a developing owner under contract to acquire an equivalent tenancy out of the chargeable interest.

(2) For the purposes of this paragraph—

(*a*) a person is chargeable to Case C levy as a developing owner under contract to acquire an interest if section 32(7)(*b*) or (*c*) applies to him, and the interest is the assessable interest, or one of the assessable interests, by virtue of which he is the developing owner, and

(*b*) a person is so chargeable as a developing owner under contract to acquire a tenancy out of an interest if the said section 32(7)(*b*) or (*c*) applies to him, and the assessable interest, or one of the assessable interests, by virtue of which he is the developing owner is such a tenancy as is mentioned in the said paragraph (*c*) to be granted out of the interest."

(4) At the end of paragraph 2 of Schedule 11 to the said Act (credit carried forward from Case C) insert—

"Provided that where the said paragraph 20 had effect, that is to say had effect as respects the liability of the developing owner as a party to a contract, the credit shall not be carried forward to any disposition by the other party to the contract, or by a person who takes from that other party otherwise than for valuable consideration."

1967 c. 1. (5) Paragraph 19 of Schedule 5 to the Land Commission Act 1967 (which is superseded by this section) is hereby repealed.

(6) Subsections (2), (3) and (4) above have effect where the project of material development is begun after 5th April 1969.

Minor amendments. **49.**—(1) At the end of section 47 of the Land Commission Act 1967 (reference of objections to Lands Tribunal) add—

"(5) It is hereby declared that where the amount of levy depends, under any provision contained in or made under this Part of this Act, on the Commission being satisfied of any fact or intention, the Lands Tribunal has jurisdiction under this section to review any relevant decision of the Commission under that provision"

(2) At the end of section 51(2) of the said Act (orders prescribing the rate of interest on levy, and the rate of interest under subsection (8) of the section on refunds of payments on account) add—

"Provided that an order under this section may for the purposes of subsection (8) below prescribe a rate of interest which is different from the rate prescribed for the other purposes of this section ". PART IV

(3) In Schedule 6 to the said Act after paragraph 1 (definition of consideration for a disposition) insert—

" 1A. It is hereby declared that under paragraph 1 above the amount of the consideration given or to be given for a disposition includes, where the grantee holds an option to acquire what he obtains by the disposition, any consideration in money or money's worth for the grant of the option.

This paragraph applies both where the option was granted to the grantee under the disposition and also where it was granted to some other person and assigned to the grantee under the disposition."

(4) In Part I of Schedule 13 to the said Act (groups of companies) after paragraph 3 insert—

" 3A.—(1) This paragraph has effect as respects a company which at any time after 5th April 1969 ceases to exist and which immediately before that time was a member of a group of companies.

(2) Any levy which would have been assessable and chargeable on the company if it had not ceased to exist shall be assessable and chargeable (in the name of that company) on any other company—

(*a*) which at that time was the principal company of the group, or

(*b*) which in any part of the period of two years ending with that time was a member of the group and was then entitled to the chargeable interest in respect of which the levy is assessed and charged."

PART V

SELECTIVE EMPLOYMENT TAX

50.—(1) In relation to any contribution week beginning on or after 7th July 1969, for paragraphs (*a*) to (*d*) of section 44(1) of the Finance Act 1966 as amended by section 51(1) of the Finance Act 1968 (which specify the weekly amount payable in respect of a person by way of selective employment tax) there shall be substituted the following paragraphs:— Selective employment tax. 1966 c. 18. 1968 c. 44.

" (*a*) if that person is a man over the age of 18, 48s.; or

(*b*) if that person is a woman over the age of 18, 24s. or

Part V

(*c*) if that person is a boy under the age of 18, 24s.; or

(*d*) if that person is a girl under the age of 18, 16s."

1967 c. 54. 1966 c. 18.

(2) In Schedule 12 to the Finance Act 1967, the references to Part VI of the Finance Act 1966 in paragraphs 8 and 10 shall be construed as including references to this section.

1920 c. 67.

(3) This section shall be construed as one with Part VI of the Finance Act 1966 and shall extend to Northern Ireland, but for the purposes of section 6 of the Government of Ireland Act 1920 shall be deemed to be contained in an Act passed before the appointed day.

Selective employment payments. 1968 c. 44.

51.—(1) Schedule 17 to the Finance Act 1968 (which relates to the areas in which refund under section 2 of the principal Act of selective employment tax in respect of persons employed in hotels or similar establishments is payable) shall have effect and be deemed always to have had effect as if in paragraph (1)(*b*) after the entry " Stranraer " there were inserted the entry " Strathaven Sub-Office ".

(2) With a view to enabling the same treatment for the purposes of the principal Act as is afforded to the printing and publishing of newspapers and periodicals to be afforded to other printing, publishing, bookbinding, engraving and similar activities, the definition of " non-qualifying activities " in section 10(1) of that Act shall have effect with the insertion in paragraph (*a*) of that definition, after the number " 486 ", of the words " under minimum list heading 489 ".

(3) Subject to subsections (4) to (7) of this section, in the said section 10(1), in the definition of " Standard Industrial Classification ", for the words " the consolidated edition published by Her Majesty's Stationery Office in 1963 " there shall be substituted the words " the revised edition published by Her Majesty's Stationery Office in 1968 ".

(4) In consequence of the provisions of subsection (3) of this section, the following provisions of the principal Act shall have effect with the amendments hereinafter respectively specified, being amendments designed to substitute for references in that Act to provisions of the 1963 edition of the Standard Industrial Classification references to the corresponding provisions of the 1968 edition thereof, that is to say—

(*a*) in section 1(2)(*a*)(i) and in section 10(4), for the words " Orders III to XVI " there shall be substituted the words " Orders III to XIX ";

(*b*) in section 2(3)(*a*)(iv)—

(i) for the words " Order XIX " there shall be substituted the words " Order XXII ";

(ii) for the words " heading 709 " there shall be substituted the words " headings 704 and 709 "; PART V

(c) in section 10(1), in paragraph (a) of the definition of " non-qualifying activities ", for the words " heading 486 " there shall be substituted the words " heading 485 or 486 ".

(5) For the purposes of the application of section 2 of the principal Act in relation to activities falling under minimum list heading 708 in the said 1968 edition, nothing in paragraph (a) of the definition of " non-qualifying activities " in section 10(1) of that Act shall cause activities falling within so much of that heading as relates to cable or telegraph services to be treated as non-qualifying activities.

(6) For the purposes of the principal Act, so much of the Note at the beginning of Order II in the said 1968 edition as relates to processing activities shall be disregarded.

(7) Nothing in Order XXI or XXII in the said 1968 edition shall be construed as bringing within the activities falling under any minimum list heading in either of those Orders the construction, installation, provision, maintenance or repair of the means of, or of anything required for, carrying on those activities.

(8) Subsections (2) to (7) of this section shall be deemed to have come into force on 7th July 1969 but nothing in those subsections shall affect any right which had accrued before the passing of this Act to receive a payment under the principal Act in respect of any period before the passing of this Act.

(9) If or so far as any decision of any tribunal or court on the interpretation for the purposes of the principal Act of any provision of the 1963 edition of the Standard Industrial Classification is inconsistent with the provisions of subsection (7) of this section or relates to a provision in that edition which differs from the corresponding provision in the 1968 edition, that decision shall not be binding in relation to any period after the passing of this Act.

(10) In subsection (1) of section 4 of the principal Act (which specifies the employers to whom that section applies) at the end there shall be added the following paragraph:—

" (i) a Passenger Transport Executive for a designated area within the meaning of section 9(1) of the Transport Act 1968 ". 1968 c. 73.

(11) In this section the expression " the principal Act " means the Selective Employment Payments Act 1966, and this section shall be construed as one with that Act. 1966 c 32.

PART VI

MISCELLANEOUS

Treasury borrowing through trustee savings banks.

1968 c. 13.

1954 c. 63.

1956 c. 54.

52.—(1) It is hereby declared that the power to raise money under section 12 of the National Loans Act 1968 includes power to raise money through trustee savings banks as defined in the Trustee Savings Banks Act 1954 or through any bank or department certified by the Treasury for the purposes of section 9 of the Finance Act 1956 (savings banks under local Acts).

(2) The Treasury may, by statutory instrument, make regulations with respect to the manner in which and the conditions under which money authorised to be raised under the National Loans Act 1968 may be raised through trustee savings banks as so defined or any bank or department so certified.

(3) Regulations under this section may—

(*a*) apply any provision of any Act relating to savings banks, or of any regulations made under any such Act, with such modifications as appear necessary or expedient,

(*b*) direct that all or any of the provisions of the regulations shall, with such modifications as appear necessary or expedient, apply and be deemed always to have applied, to money raised before the date on which the regulations came into force as they apply to money raised after that date.

(4) A statutory instrument containing regulations under this section shall be laid before the Commons House of Parliament.

(5) This section shall extend to the Channel Islands.

Contractual savings schemes.

53.—(1) Any terminal bonus, or interest or other sum, payable under a certified contractual savings scheme—

(*a*) in respect of money raised under section 12 of the National Loans Act 1968, or

(*b*) in respect of shares in a building society,

shall be disregarded for all the purposes of the Income Tax Acts and of the enactments relating to capital gains tax.

(2) In this section " certified contractual savings scheme " means, except in relation to a building society, a scheme—

1958 (7 & 8 Eliz. 2) c. 6.

(*a*) governed by regulations made under section 12 of the National Debt Act 1958 or the last preceding section, and

(*b*) providing for periodical contributions by individuals for a specified period, and the repayment in accordance with the regulations of contributions together with any additional sum by way of bonus or interest, and

PART VI

(*c*) certified by the Treasury as qualifying for exemption under this section.

(3) In this section "certified contractual savings scheme" means, in relation to a building society, a scheme—

(*a*) providing for periodical contributions by individuals for a specified period, being contributions by way of investment in shares in the building society, and

(*b*) certified by the Treasury as corresponding to a scheme certified under subsection (2) above, and as qualifying for exemption under this section.

(4) Nothing in this section shall be taken as affecting section 71(2)(*a*) of the Finance Act 1965 (allowance of dividends on society's shares in computing the society's profits for corporation tax), and that paragraph shall apply to any terminal bonus paid by the society under a certified contractual savings scheme as if it were a dividend on a share in the society. 1965 c. 25.

(5) In this section "building society" means a building society within the meaning of the Building Societies Act 1962 or the Building Societies Act (Northern Ireland) 1967. 1962 c. 37. 1967 c. 31. (N.I.).

Transfer of Treasury functions under Import Duties Act 1958 s. 6. 1958 c. 6.

54.—(1) The power under section 6 of the Import Duties Act 1958 (relief from duty in the case of goods qualifying under Schedule 4 to that Act) to direct that payment of duty shall not be required is hereby transferred from the Treasury to the Board of Trade.

(2) Accordingly, in that section—

(*a*) in subsections (1), (2), (3) and (6), for each reference to the Treasury (except the second reference in subsection (1)) there shall be substituted a reference to the Board of Trade;

(*b*) in subsection (1), for the words "if the Treasury on the recommendation of the Board of Trade are satisfied" there shall be substituted the words "if the Board of Trade are satisfied"; and

(*c*) in subsection (4), for the words "The Board of Trade shall not make a recommendation" there shall be substituted the words "The Board of Trade shall not give a direction".

(3) Any direction given by the Treasury under the said section 6 before the coming into force of this section shall have effect as if given by the Board of Trade; and where a direction so given is subject to a condition requiring any consent of the Treasury, that condition shall be construed as requiring instead the consent of the Board.

(4) This section shall come into force on 1st October 1969.

PART VI

Transfer of Treasury functions under Purchase Tax Act 1963, s. 21 and Finance Act 1967 s. 8.

1963 c. 9.

55.—(1) The power under section 21 of the Purchase Tax Act 1963 (relief from purchase tax on importation in the case of the particular categories of goods to which that section applies) to direct that tax shall not be payable or, if it has been paid, shall be repaid is hereby transferred from the Treasury to the Commissioners of Customs and Excise.

(2) Accordingly, in subsections (1), (3) and (4) of that section, for each reference to the Treasury there shall be substituted a reference to the Commissioners.

(3) Any direction given by the Treasury under the said section 21 before the coming into force of this section shall have effect as if given by the Commissioners; and where a direction so given is subject to a condition requiring any consent of the Treasury, that condition shall be construed as requiring instead the consent of the Commissioners.

1967 c. 54.

(4) In section 8 of the Finance Act 1967 (relief from purchase tax on chargeable transactions in the United Kingdom involving goods and articles such as are mentioned in section 21(4) of the Purchase Tax Act 1963), in subsection (2)—

(*a*) for each reference to the Treasury there shall be substituted a reference to the Commissioners; and

(*b*) in paragraph (*b*), after the word " they " there shall be inserted the words " or (before the coming into force of section 55 of the Finance Act 1969) the Treasury ".

(5) This section shall come into force on 1st October 1969.

Exemption from duty on loan capital of loans in foreign currencies.

1899 c. 9.
1947 c. 14.

56.—(1) Subject to subsection (2) of this section, duty under section 8 of the Finance Act 1899 (which relates to duty in respect of loan capital) shall not be chargeable in respect of loan capital issued on or after 1st August 1969 in the currency or currencies of one or more territories outside the territories specified in Schedule 1 to the Exchange Control Act 1947 as for the time being in force.

(2) The foregoing subsection shall not apply to loan capital for the repayment of which there is an option between one or more such currencies as aforesaid and one or more other currencies which is exercisable by any person other than the person to whom repayment for the time being falls to be made.

1891 c. 39.

(3) This section shall be construed as one with the Stamp Act 1891.

PART VI

57. In the proviso to section 2(1) of the Miscellaneous Financial Provisions Act 1950 (which, as amended by section 44 of the Finance Act 1967, restricts the total principal amounts outstanding in respect of advances to the Exchequer of Northern Ireland under the said section 2 to £120 million) for the words " one hundred and twenty million pounds " there shall be substituted the words " £170 million ".

Loans to Government of Northern Ireland. 1950 c. 21. 1967 c. 54.

58.—(1) For the purpose of any statistical survey conducted or to be conducted by the Department of Employment and Productivity or by the Business Statistics Office of the Board of Trade, the Board of Inland Revenue may disclose to an authorised officer of that Department or Office—

Disclosure of information for statistical purposes by Board of Inland Revenue.

(*a*) the names and addresses of persons (in this section referred to as " employers ") required under section 157 of the Income Tax Act 1952 (pay as you earn) to make deductions of tax from payments of, or on account of, emoluments to which that section applies; and 1952 c. 10.

(*b*) information concerning the number of persons (in this section referred to as " employees ") in receipt of emoluments paid by an employer.

(2) For the purpose of any statistical survey relating to earnings conducted or to be conducted by the Department of Employment and Productivity, the Board of Inland Revenue may disclose to an authorised officer of that Department the name and address of the employer of any person who is one of a number of employees selected (as a statistical sample) for the purpose of that survey.

(3) Subsections (1) and (2) above shall have effect notwithstanding any obligation as to secrecy imposed on the Board or any officer of the Board under the Income Tax Management Act 1964 or otherwise. 1964 c. 37.

(4) Subject to subsection (5) below, no information obtained by virtue of this section by an officer of the Department of Employment and Productivity or of the Business Statistics Office of the Board of Trade may be disclosed except—

(*a*) to another officer of that Department or Office for the purpose of the statistical survey concerned, or

(*b*) to another department (including a department of the Government of Northern Ireland) for the purpose of a statistical survey conducted or to be conducted by that department.

PART VI

(5) Subsection (4) above does not apply to the disclosure of any such information as is mentioned in subsection (1) or subsection (2) above—

(*a*) in the form of a summary so framed as not to enable particulars relating to an employer or employee to be ascertained from it, or

(*b*) in the case of such information as is mentioned in subsection (1) above, with the consent of the employer concerned and, in the case of such information as is mentioned in subsection (2) above, with the consent of the employee concerned.

(6) If any person who has obtained any information by virtue of any provision of this section discloses that information otherwise than in accordance with paragraph (*a*) or paragraph (*b*) of subsection (4) or subsection (5) above, he shall be liable on summary conviction to a fine not exceeding £400, or on conviction on indictment to imprisonment for a term not exceeding two years or to a fine or to both.

(7) References in this section to the Department of Employment and Productivity or the Business Statistics Office of the Board of Trade include references to any department of the Government of Northern Ireland carrying out similar functions.

Disclosure of information by Commissioners of Customs and Excise.

59. If the Horserace Betting Levy Board so request at any time with respect to a specified person and a specified period, and the Commissioners of Customs and Excise are satisfied that the Board require the information for the purpose of determining whether or not that person falls to be assessed by the Board to pay in respect of that period such a contribution as is mentioned in section 24(1) of the Betting, Gaming and Lotteries Act 1963 and that the Board will not use the information for any other purpose, the Commissioners may inform the Board whether that person has or has not made a payment to the Commissioners during or in respect of that period on account of the general betting duty.

1963 c. 2.

Amendments for purposes of tax consolidation.

60. The enactments specified in Schedule 20 to this Act shall have effect subject to the amendments specified in that Schedule, being amendments designed to facilitate, or otherwise desirable in connection with, the consolidation of the Income Tax Acts, the Corporation Tax Acts and certain enactments relating to capital gains tax.

Citation, interpretation, construction, extent and repeals.

61.—(1) This Act may be cited as the Finance Act 1969.

(2) In this Act, except where the context otherwise requires, " the Board " means the Commissioners of Inland Revenue.

(3) In this Act— PART VI

(a) Part I (except sections 1(1) and (4) and (6)) shall be construed as one with the Customs and Excise Act 1952; 1952 c. 44.

(b) sections 1(4) and 55 shall be construed as one with the Purchase Tax Act 1963; 1963 c. 9.

(c) Part II, so far as it relates to income tax, shall be construed as one with the Income Tax Acts and, so far as it relates to corporation tax shall be construed as one with the Corporation Tax Acts;

(d) Part III shall be construed as one with Part I of the Finance Act 1894; 1894 c. 30.

(e) Part IV, so far as it relates to chargeable gains, shall be construed as one with Part III of the Finance Act 1965. 1965 c. 25.

(4) Any reference in this Act to any other enactment shall, except so far as the context otherwise requires, be construed as a reference to that enactment as amended or applied by or under any other enactment, including this Act.

(5) Except as otherwise expressly provided, such of the provisions of this Act as relate to matters in respect of which the Parliament of Northern Ireland has power to make laws shall not extend to Northern Ireland.

(6) The enactments mentioned in Schedule 21 to this Act (which include enactments which are spent or otherwise unnecessary) are hereby repealed to the extent mentioned in the third column of that Schedule, but subject to any provision in relation thereto made at the end of any Part of that Schedule.

SCHEDULES

Section 1(2).

SCHEDULE 1

SPIRITS (RATES OF CUSTOMS AND EXCISE DUTIES)

TABLE 1: SPIRITS OTHER THAN IMPORTED PERFUMED SPIRITS

Description of spirits	Excise rate	Customs rates		
		Full	Common-wealth	Con-vention
	£ s. d.	£ s. d.	£ s. d.	£ s. d.
1. British spirits (per proof gallon)	18 17 0	—	—	—
2. Imported spirits other than perfumed spirits—				
(*a*) not comprised below in this paragraph (per proof gallon) ...	—	18 19 6	18 17 0	18 17 0
(*b*) liqueurs, cordials, mixtures and other preparations in bottle, entered in such manner as to indicate that the strength is not to be tested (per gallon) ...	—	25 12 0	25 8 6	25 8 6
	each of the above rates of duty being, in the case of spirits not warehoused or warehoused for less than three years, increased by 1s. 6d. per proof gallon or, for spirits within paragraph 2(*b*) of this Table, by 2s. 0d. per gallon.			

SCHEDULE 2

Section 1(2).

Beer (Rates of Customs and Excise Duties and Drawbacks)

	Excise rates (per 36 gallons)	Customs rates (per 36 gallons)		
		Full	Common-wealth	Con-vention
	£ s. d.	£ s. d.	£ s. d.	£ s. d.
1. Duty	10 7 6	11 7 6	10 7 6	10 7 6
2. Drawback	10 7 6	11 7 6	10 7 6	10 7 6
	each of the above rates of duty and drawback being, in the case of beer of an original gravity exceeding 1030 degrees, increased by 8s. 9·6d. for each additional degree.			

Supplementary provision as to drawback

As respects beer the worts whereof before fermentation were of a specific gravity of less than 1030 degrees the amount of drawback allowable shall not exceed the amount of the customs or excise duty shown to the satisfaction of the Commissioners to have been paid.

Section 1(2).

SCHEDULE 3

WINE (RATES OF CUSTOMS DUTIES)

Description of Wine	Rates of duty (per gallon)	
	Full	Common-wealth
	£ s. d.	£ s. d.
Light wine:—		
Still—		
not in bottle	1 12 3	1 10 3
in bottle	1 14 9	1 11 9
Sparkling	2 4 9	2 2 9
Other wine:—		
Still—		
not in bottle	2 14 3	2 4 3
in bottle	2 16 9	2 5 9
Sparkling	3 6 9	2 16 9
together, in the case of wine exceeding 42 degrees proof spirit, with an addition for each additional degree or fraction of a degree of	4 6	3 8

For the purposes of this Schedule, " light wine " means wine not exceeding 25 degrees or, in the case of wine qualifying for Commonwealth preference, 27 degrees of proof spirit.

Section 1(2).

SCHEDULE 4

BRITISH WINE (RATES OF EXCISE DUTIES)

Description of British wine	Rates of duty (per gallon)
	£ s. d.
Light British wine:—	
Still	1 9 9
Sparkling	1 15 9
Other British wine:—	
Still	1 14 9
Sparkling	2 0 9

For the purposes of this Schedule, " light British wine " means British wine not exceeding 27 degrees of proof spirit.

SCHEDULE 5

Section 1(2).

TOBACCO (RATES OF CUSTOMS AND EXCISE DUTIES AND DRAWBACKS)

TABLE 1

Customs	Rates of duty per pound			
	Full	Common-wealth	Con-vention	Republic of Ireland
	£ s. d.	£ s. d.	£ s. d.	£ s. d.
TOBACCO				
1. Unmanufactured:				
Containing 10 per cent. or more by weight of moisture	5 0 10	4 19 3½	5 0 10	4 19 3½
Other	5 1 10	5 0 1½	5 1 10	5 0 1½
2. Manufactured, viz.:				
Cigars	5 9 8½	5 6 9	5 6 9	5 6 9
Cigarettes	5 6 4	5 3 11½	5 1 11½	5 1 11½
Cavendish or negrohead:				
Manufactured in bond	5 3 4	5 1 4½	5 3 4	5 1 4½
Other	5 5 4	5 3 1	5 3 1	5 3 1
Other	5 3 7	5 1 7½	5 0 10	5 0 10
3. Snuff and snuff work (including tobacco dust or powder and ground tobacco)	5 4 1	5 2 0½	5 1 10	5 1 10

TABLE 2

Excise	Rates of duty per pound
	£ s. d.
TOBACCO	
1. Unmanufactured:	
Containing 10 per cent. or more by weight of moisture	4 19 1½
Other	4 19 11½
2. Manufactured:	
Cavendish or negrohead manufactured in bond	5 1 4½

SCH. 5

TABLE 3

Description of Tobacco	Rates of drawback (per pound)	
	In respect of tobacco on which customs duty at the full or Convention rate has been paid	In respect of tobacco on which customs duty at the Commonwealth or Republic of Ireland rate or excise duty has been paid
	£ s. d.	£ s. d.
Cigars	5 5 2	5 3 7½
Cigarettes	5 1 10	5 0 3½
Cut, roll, cake or other manufactured tobacco	5 1 7	5 0 0½
Snuff (not being offal snuff)	5 2 1	5 0 6½
Stalks and tobacco refuse	5 1 1	4 19 6½

Section 1(4).

SCHEDULE 6

1963 c. 9.

AMENDMENTS TO PART I OF SCHEDULE 1 TO PURCHASE TAX ACT 1963

1. In Group 2, paragraphs (1), (2) and (3) of the exemptions shall be omitted.

2. In Group 5, after the word " decorations " there shall be inserted the words " paper cups, paper plates and other paper tableware, paper handkerchiefs, paper tissues ".

3. In Group 6, for so much of that Group as precedes the word " Exempt " there shall be substituted the following:—

" Articles of textile, plastic, paper or similar material of a kind used for soft furnishings, bedding or other domestic purposes." 13¾%

4. In Group 7—

(*a*) after the words " otherwise treated " there shall be inserted the words " and plastic sheeting in the piece or in cut lengths, being sheeting of a kind suitable for making garments or curtains, tablecloths and similar soft furnishings ";

(*b*) for the words " Tissues and fabrics not exceeding 12 inches in width " there shall be substituted the words " Articles not comprised below in this Group ";

(*c*) the words " *Not chargeable under this Group* " and the words " Tissues and fabrics exceeding 12 inches in width " shall be omitted;

(*d*) in paragraph (10) of the exemptions, for the words " three inches " there shall be substituted the words " six inches ".

5. In Group 10, in paragraph (*a*), for the word " Wallpaper " there shall be substituted the words " Wallpaper, plastic wall coverings in rolls with or without paper backing, and any of the following made of material of a kind principally used for wall or ceiling decoration which is similar to the material of wallpaper or plastic wall covering, namely, panels, borders, friezes and cornerpieces ". Sch. 6

6. After Group 35, there shall be added the following new Groups:—

" Group 36

Any of the following when packaged for human consumption without further preparation, namely, potato crisps, potato sticks, potato puffs and similar products made from the potato, or from potato flour, or from potato starch, and savoury food products obtained by the swelling of cereals or cereal products; and salted or roasted nuts other than nuts in shell.	22%

Group 37

Pet foods, canned, packaged or prepared; packaged foods (not being pet foods) for birds other than poultry or game; and biscuits and meal for cats and dogs."	22%

SCHEDULE 7

Section 1(5).

Miscellaneous Provisions as to Customs and Excise

Definition of whisky

1. In relation to spirits distilled on or after 1st August 1969, section 243(1)(*b*) of the Customs and Excise Act 1952 (which defines Scotch whisky) shall cease to have effect, and for all purposes of customs and excise— 1952 c. 44.

(*a*) the expression " whisky " shall mean spirits which have been distilled from a mash of cereals which has been—

(i) saccharified by the diastase of malt contained therein with or without other natural diastases approved for the purpose by the Commissioners ; and

(ii) fermented by the action of yeast ; and

(iii) distilled at less than 166·4 degrees proof in such a way that the distillate has an aroma and flavour derived from the materials used,

and which have been matured in wooden casks in warehouse for a period of at least three years ;

(*b*) the expression " Scotch whisky " shall mean whisky which has been distilled in Scotland ;

(*c*) the expression " blended whisky " or " blended Scotch whisky " shall mean a blend of a number of distillates each of which separately is entitled to the description whisky or Scotch whisky as the case may be ;

SCH. 7 (*d*) the period for which any blended whisky or blended Scotch whisky shall be treated as having been matured as mentioned in sub-paragraph (*a*) of this paragraph shall be taken to be that applicable in the case of the most recently distilled of the spirits contained in the blend.

Fortification of British wine

1952 c. 44. 2. In section 142 of the Customs and Excise Act 1952 (under which the Commissioners may permit the addition of spirits to British wine in warehouse, subject to a limit of ten gallons of proof spirits to one hundred gallons of wine), for the words " ten gallons " there shall be substituted the words " twenty gallons ".

Consequential amendments to s. 4(3) *of Finance Act* 1964

1964 c. 49. 3. In section 4(3) of the Finance Act 1964—

(*a*) for the words " and fourth " in both places where they occur there shall be substituted the words " fourth and fifth " ;

(*b*) the word " and " in the second place where it occurs shall be omitted ;

(*c*) after the date " 1960 " there shall be inserted the words " and to goods of the Republic of Ireland consigned to the United Kingdom from that country ".

Hydrocarbon oils : reliefs

4.—(1) As from 1st September 1969, section 6(1) of the Finance Act 1964 (which authorises the delivery of hydrocarbon oil for home use to an approved person without payment of customs or excise duty chargeable thereon where the oil is to be used or supplied by that person for certain purposes) shall cease to have effect, and the provisions of this paragraph shall have effect in place thereof.

(2) The Commissioners may permit hydrocarbon oil to be delivered for home use to an approved person, without payment of customs or excise duty chargeable thereon, where the oil—

(*a*) is to be put by him to a use qualifying for relief under this paragraph ; or

(*b*) is to be supplied by him in the course of a trade of supplying oil for any such use.

(3) The uses of hydrocarbon oil qualifying for relief under this paragraph are—

(*a*) use in the manufacture or preparation of any article, not being hydrocarbon oil or an article which in the opinion of the Commissioners should, according to its use, be classed with hydrocarbon oil ; and

(*b*) use for cleaning plant, in connection with any use of the plant in the manufacture or preparation of such an article ;

but does not include the use of oil as fuel or, except as provided by sub-paragraph (4) of this paragraph, as a lubricant.

(4) Where, in the manufacture or preparation of an article described in sub-paragraph (3)(*a*) of this paragraph, hydrocarbon oil is used for preventing or reducing friction, adhesion or contact between parts or components of the article, or between the article or a part or component thereof and any plant used in the manufacture or preparation or any part or component of plant so used, that use of the oil is to be included among the uses qualifying for relief under this paragraph. SCH. 7

(5) In this paragraph " plant " means any machinery, apparatus, equipment or vessel.

5.—(1) In consequence of the provisions of paragraph 4 of this Schedule, as from 1st September 1969 section 6 of the Finance Act 1964 and Schedule 6 to that Act shall have effect with the amendments hereafter specified in this paragraph. 1964 c. 49.

(2) In subsection (2) of the said section 6—

(*a*) for the words " subsection (1) above " there shall be substituted the words " paragraph 4 of Schedule 7 to the Finance Act 1969 " ; and

(*b*) for the words " used by an approved person as mentioned in paragraph (*a*) of that subsection " there shall be substituted the words " put by an approved person to a use qualifying for relief under the said paragraph 4 ".

(3) In subsections (5) and (6) of the said section 6, and in paragraphs 1 and 2 of the said Schedule 6, references to subsection (1) of the said section 6 shall be construed as references to paragraph 4 of this Schedule.

(4) For paragraph 25 of the said Schedule 6 there shall be substituted the following paragraph:—

" 25. Except with the consent of the Commissioners, no oil in the case of which delivery without payment of duty has been permitted under paragraph 4 of Schedule 7 to the Finance Act 1969 shall be put to a use not qualifying for relief under that paragraph or be acquired or taken into any vehicle, appliance or storage tank in order to be put to such a use; and in giving their consent the Commissioners may impose such conditions as they think fit."

(5) In paragraph 26(1) of the said Schedule 6, for the words " that it will be used otherwise than as mentioned in section 6(1)(*a*) of this Act " there shall be substituted the words " that it will be put to a use not qualifying for relief under paragraph 4 of Schedule 7 to the Finance Act 1969 ".

(6) In paragraph 28 of the said Schedule 6, for sub-paragraph (*a*) there shall be substituted the following:—

" (*a*) references to delivery permitted under paragraph 4 of Schedule 7 to the Finance Act 1969 referred to rebate allowed under the said section 6(4), and references to a use not qualifying for relief under the said paragraph 4 referred to use otherwise than as mentioned in the said section 6(4)."

Section 2.

SCHEDULE 8

PROVISIONS RELATING TO BETTING PREMISES LICENCES AND DUTY THEREON

General administration

1.—(1) The duty on betting premises licences shall be under the care and management of the Commissioners, who may (without prejudice to any other provision of this Schedule) make regulations providing for any matter for which provision appears to them to be necessary for the administration or enforcement of the duty, or for the protection of the revenue in respect thereof.

(2) Regulations of the Commissioners under this Schedule shall be made by statutory instrument, which shall be subject to annulment in pursuance of a resolution of the Commons House of Parliament.

Provisions as to grant, transfer etc. of licences

2. An application for a betting premises licence in respect of any premises shall, in the case of a new licence, be made to the Commissioners not later than fourteen days before—

(*a*) 1st October 1969 ; or

(*b*) the first day after that date on which the premises are to be used for off-course betting,

and, in the case of a licence in continuation of one of which the applicant is the holder, be made not later than fourteen days before the date on which the licence applied for is to take effect.

3. The proper officer may, in such manner as the Commissioners may direct, and without any additional payment, transfer a betting premises licence in respect of any premises to a successor in title to the interest in those premises of the person to whom the licence was granted.

Payment and repayment of duty

1952 c. 44. 4. Section 237 of the Customs and Excise Act 1952 (reduced duty on beginner's part-year licence) shall apply to a betting premises licence.

5.—(1) Where a betting premises licence is granted so as to have effect from the beginning of the licence-year or from a date in that year not later than the end of February, and section 237 of the Customs and Excise Act 1952 does not apply for the reduction of the duty payable on the licence, the licence may at the option of the person liable for the duty be granted on payment of only half of the full duty ; and in that case the second half shall be paid not later than the following 1st March.

(2) If default is made in payment of the second half of the duty, the licence shall be of no effect so long as the default continues.

(3) If after 1st March any sum remains unpaid in respect of the second half of the duty, that sum may be recovered as a debt due to the Crown.

6. Provision may be made by regulations of the Commissioners under this Schedule for the adjustment (by way of repayment or a further charge of duty) of the duty charged on a betting premises licence in respect of any premises, where that duty is determined by reference to the rateable value of a hereditament and an alteration of the valuation list (or, in Scotland, the valuation roll) affecting that hereditament or that rateable value comes into effect as respects the whole of the period of validity of that licence. SCH. 8

7. Section 234 of the Customs and Excise Act 1952 (which relates to payment for excise licences by cheque) shall apply to the duty on a betting premises licence, but as if for the reference to a penalty of £50 there were substituted a reference to a penalty of £500. 1952 c. 44.

8.—(1) If while a betting premises licence is in force in respect of any premises (not being a licence on which a reduced duty was paid under section 237 of the Customs and Excise Act 1952), and not later than the end of June immediately preceding the date on which the licence is due to expire, the holder of the licence surrenders it to the proper officer and satisfies him that during the period between the date of surrender and the date when the licence would otherwise expire, he will not be concerned with any use of the premises for off-course betting, then, subject to and in accordance with the following provisions, the holder of the licence shall be entitled to a partial repayment of duty.

(2) If at the time of the surrender of the licence the whole of the duty has been paid, the repayment under this paragraph shall be—

(*a*) three-quarters of the duty paid, if the licence is surrendered before 1st January;

(*b*) one-half of the duty paid, if the licence is surrendered on or after 1st January and before 1st April; and

(*c*) one-quarter of the duty paid, if the licence is surrendered on or after 1st April.

(3) If, by virtue of the exercise of the option under paragraph 5 of this Schedule, only half of the full duty on the licence was paid at the time of the grant, and the second half has not been paid, there shall be no repayment under this paragraph unless the licence is surrendered before 1st January, and the repayment shall then be one-half of that which has been paid.

Enforcement

9. If any premises are used for the purpose of off-course betting in contravention of section 2(4) of this Act—

(*a*) the user of the premises (" user " for this purpose having the meaning given to it by the said section 2(4)) shall be liable—

(i) on summary conviction to a penalty of treble the amount of the duty on any licence which ought to have

Sch. 8

been taken out in respect of the premises, or to imprisonment for not more than twelve months, or to both;

(ii) on conviction on indictment to a like penalty or to imprisonment for not more than two years, or to both; and

(*b*) in addition and without prejudice to any liability under sub-paragraph (*a*) of this paragraph, unless and until a betting premises licence in respect of those premises is taken out during the period of twelve months beginning with 1st October during which the contravention occurred, an amount equal to the duty on the licence, together with interest thereon from the date of the contravention, shall become due and be recoverable as a debt due to the Crown jointly and severally from all or any of the persons liable under the said sub-paragraph (*a*).

10. If any person contravenes or fails to comply with any provision of this Schedule or regulations made thereunder, he shall be liable to a penalty of £500.

11. Where a person is convicted of an offence under paragraph 10 of this Schedule consisting in a failure to comply with a provision of this Schedule or regulations made thereunder, and the failure continues after conviction, he shall be guilty of a further offence under the said paragraph 10, and may on conviction be punished accordingly.

12. Where an offence under paragraph 9 or 10 of this Schedule has been committed by a body corporate, every person who at the time of the commission of the offence was a director, general manager, secretary or other similar officer of the body corporate, or was purporting to act in any such capacity, shall be deemed to be guilty of that offence unless he proves that the offence was committed without his consent or connivance and that he exercised all such diligence to prevent the commission of the offence as he ought to have exercised having regard to the nature of his functions in that capacity, and in all the circumstances.

13. Any officer may enter on any premises in respect of which a betting premises licence is in force, and on any other premises which he has reasonable cause to suspect are being, or have been, used for off-course betting, or are about to be so used, and inspect those premises and require any person concerned with the management of the premises—

(*a*) to produce, or secure the production of, any betting premises licence for the time being in force in respect thereof; and

(*b*) to provide information with respect to the use of the premises and any activities carried on there.

14.—(1) If a justice of the peace or, in Scotland, the sheriff or a magistrate is satisfied on information on oath that there is reasonable ground for suspecting that any premises are being, or have been, used for off-course betting, in contravention of section 2(4) of this Act, or are about to be so used, he may issue a warrant in writing authorising an officer to enter the premises, if necessary by force, at any time within fourteen days from the time of the issue of the warrant, and search them. Sch. 8

(2) An officer who enters any premises under the authority of such a warrant may—

(*a*) seize and remove any records, accounts or other documents, money or valuable thing, or other thing whatsoever, found on the premises which he has reasonable cause to believe may be required as evidence for the purposes of proceedings in respect of a contravention of section 2(4) of this Act ; and

(*b*) search any person found on the premises whom he has reasonable cause to believe to be concerned with the effecting of betting transactions.

Supplementary

15. In considering for the purposes of paragraph 16(1), 17(*b*) or 27(4)(*a*) of Schedule 1 to the Act of 1963 (which relate to the grant, renewal and cancellation of bookmakers' permits, betting agency permits and betting office licences) whether a person is or is not a fit and proper person to be the holder of a bookmaker's permit or, as the case may be, to hold a betting office licence, the appropriate authority shall have regard to any case in which that person has been concerned with any contravention of section 2(4) of this Act or with any contravention of, or failure to comply with, any provision of this Schedule or regulations made thereunder.

16. Paragraph 20(1) of Schedule 3 to the Finance Act 1966 (which enables a court, when convicting a person of certain offences in connection with the general betting duty, to order the forfeiture and cancellation of a betting office licence in respect of his premises) shall apply in relation to a conviction of an offence under paragraph 9 or 10 of this Schedule as it applies in relation to such a conviction as is referred to in the said paragraph 20(1). 1966 c. 18.

SCHEDULE 9

Section 3.

Provisions Relating to Bingo Duty

Part I

Exemptions from Duty

Domestic bingo

1. Bingo played both in a private dwelling and on a domestic occasion.

SCH. 9

Club bingo

2. Bingo played as an activity of a club, in compliance with the following conditions:—

(*a*) the subscription for membership of the club does not exceed two pounds a year; and

(*b*) not more than one payment by way of a charge for admission to any premises being or including the place at which bingo is played is payable by a person in order to enable him to play bingo, and that payment does not exceed one shilling; and

(*c*) no other payment is required to be or has been made, and no obligation to make any other payment is required to be incurred, in order to enable a person to play bingo.

Charitable and other similar entertainments

3. Bingo provided by way of an amusement at an entertainment (whether limited to one day or extending over two or more days) being a bazaar, sale of work, fête, dinner, dance, sporting or athletic event or other entertainment of a similar character, in compliance with the following conditions:—

(*a*) the whole proceeds of the entertainment (including the proceeds of bingo) after deducting the expenses of it (including any expenses incurred in connection with bingo and the provision of prizes) will be devoted to purposes other than private gain; and

(*b*) the opportunity to play bingo is not the only, or the only substantial, inducement to persons to attend the entertainment.

Section 54(1) and (3) of the Act of 1963 (construction of references in that Act to "private gain") shall apply for the construction of this paragraph as they apply for the construction of sections 33, 37, 43 and 48 of that Act.

4. Bingo played at an entertainment promoted otherwise than for purposes of private gain, in compliance with the following conditions:—

(*a*) not more than one payment (whether by way of entrance-fee, payment for cards or otherwise) is made by each player of bingo at the entertainment, and no such payment exceeds ten shillings;

(*b*) the total value of all prizes won at bingo played at the entertainment does not exceed fifty pounds;

(*c*) the whole of the proceeds of such payments as are mentioned in sub-paragraph (*a*) of this paragraph, after deducting sums lawfully appropriated on account of expenses or for the provision of prizes at bingo, is applied for purposes other than private gain;

(*d*) the sum appropriated out of the said proceeds in respect of expenses does not exceed the reasonable cost of the facilities provided for playing bingo.

For the purposes of this paragraph, two or more entertainments promoted on the same premises by the same person on the same day shall be treated as one single entertainment; and section 54(1) and (3) of the Act of 1963 (construction of references to private gain) shall apply for the construction of this paragraph as they apply for the construction of sections 33, 37, 43 and 48 of that Act. SCH. 9

Small-scale amusements provided commercially

5. Bingo played, in compliance with the conditions of this paragraph—

(*a*) on any premises in respect of which a permit under section 49 of the Act of 1963 (provision of amusements with prizes) has been granted in accordance with Schedule 6 to that Act and is for the time being in force;

(*b*) on any premises in respect of which there is for the time being in force a gaming machine licence under section 5 of this Act, and which have local authority approval under the Gaming Acts by virtue of paragraph 6 of Schedule 11 to this Act; or

(*c*) at any pleasure fair consisting wholly or mainly of amusements provided by travelling showmen, which is held on any day of a year on premises not previously used in that year for more than twenty-seven days for the holding of such a pleasure fair.

The conditions of this paragraph are that—

(i) the amount payable by any person for a card for any one game of bingo does not exceed one shilling;

(ii) the total amount taken as payment by players for their cards for any one game does not exceed fifty shillings;

(iii) no money prize exceeding one shilling is distributed or offered;

(iv) the winning of, or the purchase of a chance to win, a prize does not entitle any person (whether subject to a further payment by him or not) to any further opportunity to win money or money's worth by taking part in any gaming (within the meaning of the Gaming Act 1968) or in any lottery; and 1968 c. 65.

(v) in the case of such a pleasure fair as is described above, the opportunity to play bingo is not the only, or the only substantial, inducement to persons to attend the fair.

Machine bingo

6. Bingo played by means of a gaming machine the provision of which on premises requires the authority of an excise licence under section 5 of this Act.

SCH. 9

PART II

ADMINISTRATION AND ENFORCEMENT

Definitions

7. In this Part of this Schedule,—

(*a*) " bingo-promoter " means a person who promotes the playing of bingo chargeable with bingo duty ;

(*b*) " prescribed " means prescribed by regulations ; and

(*c*) " regulations " means regulations of the Commissioners under this Part of this Schedule, which shall be made by statutory instrument and be subject to annulment in pursuance of a resolution of the Commons House of Parliament.

General administration

8.—(1) Bingo duty shall be under the care and management of the Commissioners and shall be accounted for by such persons, and accounted for and paid at such times and in such manner, as may be required by or under regulations.

(2) Without prejudice to any other provision of this Schedule, regulations may provide for any matter for which provision appears to the Commissioners to be necessary for the administration or enforcement of bingo duty, or for the protection of the revenue in respect of that duty.

Notification to Commissioners by, and registration of, bingo-promoters

9.—(1) Any person who intends to promote the playing of bingo on or after 1st October 1969, being bingo which will, or may, be chargeable with bingo duty, shall, not less than fourteen days before the first day on which bingo is to be played, notify the Commissioners of his intention, specifying the premises on which the bingo is to be played, and applying to be registered as a bingo-promoter.

(2) Where a person notifies his intention as aforesaid, he shall be entitled to be registered by the Commissioners, except that the Commissioners may, where it appears to them to be requisite for the security of the revenue to do so, impose as a condition of a person's registration, or may subsequently impose as a condition of the continuance in force of his registration, a requirement that he shall give such security (or further security), by way of deposit or otherwise, for any bingo duty which he is, or may become, liable to pay as the Commissioners may from time to time require.

(3) Where, in the case of a person who is for the time being registered as a bingo-promoter, the Commissioners exercise their power under sub-paragraph (2) of this paragraph to impose, as a condition of the continuance in force of his registration, a requirement that he shall give security or further security, and he does not give it, the Commissioners may cancel his registration (without prejudice, however, to his right to apply again to be registered).

Announcement of prizes SCH. 9

10. A bingo-promoter shall ensure that, before the beginning of any game of bingo promoted by him, the value of any prize to be won in the game is made known to the players in accordance with such requirements as may be prescribed for the purposes of this paragraph.

Books, records, accounts, etc.

11.—(1) A bingo-promoter shall keep such books, records and accounts as may be prescribed, or as the Commissioners may direct either generally or in a particular case.

(2) Any such books, records and accounts—

(*a*) shall be preserved for at least two years or such shorter period as the Commissioners may in any particular case direct ; and

(*b*) shall be kept in such form as the Commissioners may direct either generally or in a particular case ;

and different directions under this sub-paragraph may be given by the Commissioners in relation to different cases or to different classes of books, records or accounts.

(3) A bingo-promoter shall, if so required by the Commissioners or an officer—

(*a*) produce, at a time and place specified in the requirement, such books, records, accounts or documents relating to the playing of bingo promoted by him as may be so specified ; and

(*b*) give such other information relating thereto as may be so specified.

(4) Without prejudice to the foregoing provisions of this paragraph, regulations may include provision requiring bingo-promoters to keep and, if required by the Commissioners or an officer, to produce for inspection records showing the value of prizes won at bingo.

Entry and inspection of premises

12.—(1) Any officer may, without paying, enter on any premises where bingo is played or on which he has reasonable cause to suspect that bingo has been or is about to be played, and inspect the premises and anything whatsoever which he finds there ; and he may further—

(*a*) require any person concerned with the management of the premises to provide him with information with respect to activities carried on there ;

(*b*) require any person on the premises who appears to him to be, or to have been, playing any game to provide him with information with respect to the game and, in particular, to produce to him any document or thing in

SCH. 9 his possession which is or was used in connection with the playing of the game.

(2) An officer who enters any premises in the exercise of powers conferred by this paragraph shall be permitted to remain there at any time when the premises are being used for any gaming (within
1968 c. 65. the meaning of the Gaming Act 1968), or when he has reasonable cause to suspect that they are about to be so used.

Power of Commissioners to estimate duty payable

13. Where an amount is due on account of bingo duty from any person, but by reason of his failure to keep, or to produce or furnish to the proper officer, any books, records, accounts or other documents which he is required or directed under this Schedule to keep, produce or furnish, or of his failure to take or permit to be taken any other step which he is so required to take or permit to be taken, or by reason of such books, records or accounts being materially incomplete or inaccurate, the Commissioners are unable to ascertain the amount of duty properly due from him, the Commissioners may estimate the amount due; and (without prejudice to the recovery of the full amount due or to the making of a further estimate in that behalf) the amount estimated shall be recoverable as duty properly due, unless in any action relating thereto the person liable proves the amount properly due and that amount is less than the amount estimated.

Settlement of disputed matters relevant to computation of duty

14.—(1) Without prejudice to paragraph 13 of this Schedule, if any dispute arises between the Commissioners and a bingo-promoter as to the amount taken by him or on his behalf, on a particular occasion, as payment by players for cards, or as to the value of any prize, then—

(*a*) the Commissioners shall by notice in writing to the bingo-promoter specify what in their opinion the amount or value is; and

(*b*) the amount of duty chargeable to, and recoverable from, the promoter shall be computed in accordance with that opinion.

(2) If the promoter disputes the Commissioners' opinion as to the said amount or value, he may at any time within three months of the date of the notice, and subject to his having paid the full amount of duty which in accordance with that opinion (as stated in the notice) is due from him, apply to the High Court or, in Scotland, the Court of Session for a declaration as to what the said amount or value is.

(3) If on an application under sub-paragraph (2) of this paragraph the court makes a declaration specifying a different amount or value from that specified in the Commissioners' notice, then—

(*a*) the notice shall be amended accordingly;

SCH. 9

(*b*) any amount by which duty is found to have been overpaid shall be repaid by the Commissioners together with interest thereon from the date of overpayment at such rate as the court may determine;

(*c*) any amount by which duty is found to have been underpaid shall be recoverable as duty properly due.

Recovery of amount due

15.—(1) If a person, on written demand by the proper officer, refuses or neglects to pay any amount recoverable from him by way of bingo duty, the amount recoverable may be levied by distress on his goods and chattels; and the proper officer may for that purpose by warrant signed by him authorise any person to distrain accordingly and to sell anything so distrained by public auction after giving six days' notice of the sale.

(2) Where an amount recoverable by virtue of this paragraph is determined (wholly or in part) by reference to the duty on the playing of bingo on any premises, the goods and chattels on which distress may be levied shall include any goods and chattels used for the purposes of the bingo and found on those premises; but distress shall not be levied on such goods or chattels unless a copy of the demand for the amount recoverable has been served on the bingo-promoter, or the person having the management of those premises, by sending it by post addressed to him at the premises or at an address at which he carries on any business.

(3) The proceeds of sale of anything distrained under this paragraph shall be applied in or towards payment of the costs and expenses of the distress and sale and the payment of the amount recoverable, and the surplus (if any) shall be paid to the person on whom the distress was levied.

(4) Where under this paragraph distress is levied for duty payable in accordance with an estimate by the Commissioners under paragraph 13 of this Schedule and it is afterwards proved that the amount properly due was less than the amount estimated, this shall not affect the legality of the distress or anything done under this paragraph in connection therewith; but the proceeds of sale shall be applied under sub-paragraph (3) of this paragraph in accordance with the amount properly due and not in accordance with the amount estimated.

(5) In the application of this paragaph to Scotland, any reference to distress shall be construed as a reference to diligence, any reference to distraining or to the levying of distress shall be construed as a reference to the doing of diligence, and the expression " chattels " means corporeal movables.

Duty payable by bankrupt, insolvent estate or company in liquidation

16.—(1) There shall be included among the debts which—

(*a*) under section 33 of the Bankruptcy Act 1914 are to be paid in priority to all other debts in the distribution of the property of a bankrupt or deceased debtor; or 1914 c. 59.

SCH. 9

1913 c. 20. (*b*) under section 118 of the Bankruptcy (Scotland) Act 1913 are to be paid in priority to all other debts in the division of a bankrupt's estate ; or

1948 c. 28. (*c*) under section 319 of the Companies Act 1948 are to be paid in priority to all other debts in the winding-up of a company, or under section 94 of that Act are on an appointment of a receiver on behalf of debenture holders, or taking of possession by or on behalf of debenture holders, to be paid in priority to any claim for principal or interest in respect of the debentures,

any amount which is due by way of bingo duty from the bankrupt, deceased debtor or company at the relevant date and which became due within twelve months next before that date.

(2) In the foregoing sub-paragraph, " the relevant date "—

1914 c. 59. (*a*) in relation to section 33 of the Bankruptcy Act 1914 means the date of the receiving order or of the death, as the case may be ;

(*b*) in relation to section 118 of the Bankruptcy (Scotland) Act 1913 means the date mentioned in subsection (4) of that section ; and

(*c*) in relation to section 319 of the Companies Act 1948 has the meaning assigned to it by that section, and in relation to section 94 of that Act means the date of the appointment of the receiver or taking of possession.

Enforcement

17.—(1) If any person is knowingly concerned in, or in the taking of steps with a view to, the fraudulent evasion (by him or any other person) of bingo duty, he shall be liable to a penalty of £500 or treble the amount of the duty payment of which is sought to be evaded, whichever is the greater.

(2) If any person—

(*a*) is knowingly concerned with the promotion of bingo (being bingo which is or may be chargeable with bingo duty), where the promoter is not registered by the Commissioners in accordance with paragraph 9 of this Schedule ; or

(*b*) is knowingly concerned with the combination of any game of bingo with other bingo contrary to section 3(5) of this Act ;

he shall be liable to a penalty of £500.

(3) Where a person is convicted of an offence under sub-paragraph (1) or (2) of this paragraph the court may, in lieu of or in addition to ordering him to pay the said penalty, order him to be imprisoned for a term not exceeding two years.

(4) If any person contravenes or fails to comply with any provision of this Part of this Schedule or of regulations, or fails to comply with any requirement made of him by or under any such provision, he shall be liable to a penalty of £500.

18. Where a person is convicted of an offence under paragraph 17(4) of this Schedule, consisting in a failure to comply with any provision of this Part of this Schedule or of regulations, and the failure continues after the conviction, he shall be guilty of a further offence under the said paragraph 17(4) and may on conviction be punished accordingly. SCH. 9

19. Where an offence under paragraph 17 of this Schedule has been committed by a body corporate, every person who at the time of the commission of the offence was a director, general manager, secretary or other similar officer of the body corporate, or was purporting to act in any such capacity, shall be deemed to be guilty of that offence unless he proves that the offence was committed without his consent or connivance and that he exercised all such diligence to prevent the commission of the offence as he ought to have exercised having regard to the nature of his functions in that capacity, and in all the circumstances.

20.—(1) If a justice of the peace or, in Scotland, the sheriff or a magistrate is satisfied on information on oath that there is reasonable ground for suspecting that an offence under paragraph 17 of this Schedule is being, has been, or is about to be committed on any premises, he may issue a warrant in writing authorising any officer to enter those premises, if necessary by force, at any time within fourteen days from the time of the issue of the warrant and search them.

(2) An officer who enters premises under the authority of such a warrant may—

(*a*) seize and remove any books, records, accounts, documents, money or valuable thing, and any instrument, device, apparatus or other thing whatsoever found on the premises, which he has reasonable cause to believe may be required as evidence for the purposes of proceedings in respect of such an offence ; and

(*b*) search any person found on the premises whom he has reasonable cause to believe to be concerned with the promotion of bingo or, as the case may be, with the management of any premises used for the purpose of playing bingo.

Supplementary

21. Where an officer takes any action in pursuance of instructions by the Commissioners or a Collector of Customs and Excise given in connection with the enactments relating to bingo duty and apart from this paragraph, would in taking that action be committing an offence under the enactments relating to gaming, he shall not be guilty of that offence.

22.—(1) In paragraph 20(1) of Schedule 2 to the Gaming Act 1968 (grounds on which the grant or renewal of a licence under that Act **1968 c. 65.**

SCH. 9 may be refused by the licensing authority), the following shall be added after sub-paragraph (*e*):—

"(*f*) that any bingo duty under section 3 of the Finance Act 1969 payable in respect of bingo played on the premises remains unpaid";

and at the end of the said paragraph 20 there shall be added the following:—

"(3) Where the licensing authority entertain an application for the grant or renewal of a licence under this Act in respect of any premises, and are satisfied that any bingo duty payable as mentioned in sub-paragraph (1)(*f*) of this paragraph remains unpaid, they shall refuse the application.".

(2) In paragraph 60 of the said Schedule 2 (grounds for refusal of transfer of licence), in sub-paragraph (*c*) (ground that the transferee has not paid duty under section 13 of the Finance Act 1966), after the word "1966" there shall be inserted the words "or any bingo duty payable by him under section 3 of the Finance Act 1969".

1966 c. 18.

1968 c. 65.

23. In paragraph 9 of Schedule 3 to the Gaming Act 1968 (grounds on which, in England or Wales, the licensing authority may refuse renewal of registration of club or institute under Part II of that Act), the following shall be added after sub-paragraph (*e*):—

"(*f*) that any bingo duty under section 3 of the Finance Act 1969 payable in respect of bingo played on the premises remains unpaid;

and where the authority entertain an application for the renewal of registration and are satisfied that any bingo duty payable as mentioned in sub-paragraph (*f*) above remains unpaid, they shall refuse the application."

24. In paragraph 11 of Schedule 4 to the Gaming Act 1968 (grounds on which, in Scotland, the sheriff may refuse renewal of registration of a club or institute under Part II of that Act) the following shall be added after sub-paragraph (*e*):—

"(*f*) that any bingo duty under section 3 of the Finance Act 1969 payable in respect of bingo played on the premises remains unpaid;

and where the sheriff entertains an application for the renewal of registration and is satisfied that any bingo duty payable as mentioned in sub-paragraph (*f*) above remains unpaid, he shall refuse the application."

SCHEDULE 10

Section 4.

PROVISIONS RELATING TO GAMING LICENCE DUTY

PART I

AMOUNT OF DUTY IN RESPECT OF PREMISES

TABLE

Description of premises	Amount of duty
	£
1. Premises other than— (*a*) premises which for rating purposes constitute or are comprised in a hereditament of a rateable value exceeding £1,000; (*b*) premises consisting of or comprised in a vessel.	750
2. Premises— (*a*) which for rating purposes constitute or are comprised in a hereditament of a rateable value exceeding £1,000 but not exceeding £1,500; or (*b*) which consist of or are comprised in a vessel.	7,500
3. Premises which for rating purposes constitute or are comprised in a hereditament of a rateable value exceeding £1,500 but not exceeding £2,250.	20,000
4. Premises which for rating purposes constitute or are comprised in a hereditament of a rateable value exceeding £2,250 but not exceeding £3,000.	40,000
5. Premises which for rating purposes constitute or are comprised in a hereditament of a rateable value exceeding £3,000.	100,000

PART II

CONSEQUENTIAL AMENDMENTS OF FINANCE ACT 1966, SECTION 13 AND SCHEDULE 3

Amendment of section 13

1. In section 13 of the Finance Act 1966— 1966 c. 18.

(*a*) in subsection (1), for paragraphs (*a*) and (*b*) there shall be substituted the words " by way of any game to which this section for the time being applies ";

(*b*) in subsection (4), paragraphs (*c*) and (*d*) shall be omitted; and

(*c*) in subsection (5), the words " in addition to bingo " shall be omitted.

SCH. 10

Amendments of Schedule 3

1966 c. 18.

2. In paragraph 7 of Schedule 3 to the Finance Act 1966, in sub-paragraph (*b*), for the words " bingo or any other game " there shall be substituted the words " any game ".

3. In paragraph 11 of the said Schedule, in sub-paragraph (*a*), the words " bingo or, as the case may be, by way of " shall be omitted.

Section 5.

SCHEDULE 11

PROVISIONS RELATING TO GAMING MACHINE LICENCE DUTY

PART I

MEANING OF " GAMING MACHINE "

1. Subject to paragraph 4 of this Schedule, any machine is a gaming machine for the purposes of section 5 of this Act if it is of the following description:—

(*a*) it is constructed or adapted for playing a game of chance by means of it ;

(*b*) a player pays to play the machine (except where he has an opportunity to play payment-free as the result of having previously played successfully), either by inserting a coin or token into the machine or in some other way ; and

(*c*) the outcome of the game is determined by the chances inherent in the action of the machine, whether or not provision is made for manipulation of the machine by a player.

2. In the foregoing paragraph, " game of chance " includes a game of chance and skill combined and a pretended game of chance or of chance and skill combined ; and the fact that a game contains an element of skill shall not prevent it being treated as a game of chance if nothing but superlative skill can overcome the element of chance.

3. For the purposes above-mentioned, it is immaterial whether a machine is capable of being played by only one person at a time, or is capable of being played by more than one person.

4. A machine shall not be treated as a gaming machine for the purposes of section 5 of this Act if either—

(*a*) it is constructed or adapted so that a person playing it once and successfully receives nothing except an opportunity, afforded by the automatic action of the machine, to play again (once or more often) without paying ; or

(*b*) it is constructed or adapted so that, where a person plays it once and successfully, that which he receives is determined by the automatic action of the machine and is either—

(i) a money prize not greater than the amount payable to play the machine once, or

(ii) a token which is, or two or more tokens which in the aggregate are, exchangeable only for such a money prize. SCH. 11

PART II

MEANING OF "LOCAL AUTHORITY APPROVAL UNDER THE GAMING ACTS"

5. Subject to paragraph 8 of this Schedule, premises are to be treated as having local authority approval under the Gaming Acts if there is for the time being in force in respect of the premises a permit granted under Schedule 6 to the Act of 1963 (permit for provision of amusements with prizes under section 49 of that Act).

6. Subject to paragraph 8 of this Schedule, premises are to be so treated if there is for the time being in force in respect of them a permit granted under section 34 of the Act of 1968 (conditions under which gaming may be carried on by means of machines).

7. Premises are to be so treated at any time when—

(*a*) there is for the time being in force in respect of them a licence under the Act of 1968 ; and

(*b*) by virtue of a direction of the licensing authority under section 32 of that Act (approval for provision of more than two machines) section 34 of that Act has effect in relation to the premises.

8. Premises are not to be so treated if a club or a miners' welfare institute within the meaning of the Act of 1968 is for the time being registered in respect of them under Part III of that Act (which regulates gaming by means of machines).

PART III

EXEMPTION FROM REQUIREMENT OF EXCISE LICENCE

Charitable entertainments, etc.

9.—(1) A gaming machine licence shall not be required in order to authorise the provision of a gaming machine at an entertainment (whether limited to one day or extending over two or more days), being a bazaar, sale of work, fête, dinner, dance, sporting or athletic event or other entertainment of a similar character, where the conditions of this paragraph are complied with in relation to the entertainment.

(2) The conditions of this paragraph are that—

(*a*) the whole proceeds of the entertainment (including the proceeds of gaming by means of any machine) after deducting the expenses of the entertainment, including any expenses incurred in connection with the provision of gaming

Sch. 11

machines and of prizes to successful players thereof, will be devoted to purposes other than private gain ; and

(*b*) the opportunity to win prizes by playing the machine (or that machine and any other provided for gaming at the entertainment) does not constitute the only, or the only substantial, inducement for persons to attend the entertainment.

(3) Section 54(1) and (3) of the Act of 1963 (construction of references in that Act to " private gain ") shall apply for the construction of sub-paragraph (2)(*a*) of this paragraph as they apply for the construction of sections 33, 37, 43 and 48 of that Act.

Pleasure fairs

10.—(1) A gaming machine licence shall not be required in order to authorise the provision of a gaming machine at a pleasure fair, consisting wholly or mainly of amusements provided by travelling showmen, which is held on any day of a year on premises not previously used in that year for more than twenty-seven days for the holding of such a pleasure fair, where the conditions of this paragraph are complied with in relation to the machine.

(2) The conditions of this paragraph are that—

(*a*) the amount payable to play the machine once does not exceed one shilling ;

(*b*) a person playing the machine once and successfully does not receive any thing other than one of the following prizes or combinations of prizes :—

(i) a money prize not exceeding two shillings or a token which is, or two or more tokens which in the aggregate are, exchangeable only for such a money prize ;

(ii) a non-monetary prize or prizes of a value or aggregate value not exceeding five shillings or a token exchangeable only for such a non-monetary prize or such non-monetary prizes ;

(iii) a money prize not exceeding two shillings together with a non-monetary prize of a value which does not exceed five shillings less the amount of the money prize ;

(iv) one or more tokens which can be exchanged for a non-monetary prize or non-monetary prizes at the appropriate rate ; and

(*c*) the opportunity to play the machine (or that machine and any other provided for gaming at the fair) does not constitute the only, or the only substantial, inducement for persons to attend the fair.

(3) In sub-paragraph (2)(*b*) of this paragraph, " non-monetary prize ", in relation to a machine, means a prize which does not consist of or include any money and does not consist of or include any token which can be exchanged for money or money's worth

or be used for playing the machine ; and, for the purposes of sub-paragraph (2)(*b*)(iv), a token or tokens shall be taken to be exchanged for a non-monetary prize or prizes at the appropriate rate if either—

(*a*) the value or aggregate value of the prize or prizes does not exceed five shillings and the token or tokens exchanged represent the maximum number of tokens which can be won by playing the machine once ; or

(*b*) in any other case, the value or aggregate value of the prize or prizes does not exceed five shillings and bears to five shillings a proportion not exceeding that which the number of tokens exchanged bears to the maximum number of tokens which can be won by playing the machine once.

(4) The condition specified in sub-paragraph (2)(*b*) of this paragraph shall not, in relation to a machine, be taken to be contravened by reason only that a successful player of the machine receives an opportunity to play again (once or more often) without paying, so long as the most which he can receive if he wins each time he plays again is a money prize or money prizes of an amount, or aggregate amount, of two shillings or less.

Temporary exemption for certain premises with only penny machines

11. During the month of October 1969, a gaming machine licence shall not be required in order to authorise the provision on premises of gaming machines at any time when there are on those premises no such machines other than penny machines ; but this exemption applies to premises only at a time when they have local authority approval under the Gaming Acts by virtue of paragraph 5 or 6 of this Schedule.

Part IV

Administration and Enforcement

General administration

12.—(1) The duty on gaming machine licences shall be under the care and management of the Commissioners, who may (without prejudice to any other provision of this Schedule) make regulations providing for any matter for which provision appears to them to be necessary for the administration or enforcement of the duty, or for the protection of the revenue in respect thereof ; and in this Part of this Schedule—

(*a*) " regulations " means regulations of the Commissioners made thereunder ; and

(*b*) " prescribed " means prescribed by regulations.

(2) Regulations shall be made by statutory instrument, which shall be subject to annulment in pursuance of a resolution of the Commons House of Parliament.

Sch. 11

Provisions as to grant, duration, transfer etc. of licences

13.—(1) An application for an ordinary licence in respect of any premises shall, in the case of a new licence, be made to the Commissioners not later than fourteen days before—

(*a*) 1st October 1969 ; or

(*b*) the date on which the licence is to be in force ;

and, in the case of an ordinary licence in continuation of one of which the applicant is the holder, be made not later than fourteen days before the date on which the licence held by him is due to expire.

(2) An application for a holiday season licence in respect of any premises shall be made not less than fourteen days before the date on which the licence is to be first in force.

14.—(1) A licence shall be expressed to take effect on the first day of the period for which it is granted or, if it is granted after the beginning of a licence-period to have effect for the remainder of that period, on the day following the date of the grant.

(2) An ordinary whole year licence shall expire at the end of 30th September next after the date on which it is expressed to take effect ; and an ordinary half-year licence shall expire at the end of 31st March or, as the case may be, 30th September next after that date.

(3) A holiday season licence shall expire at the end of 31st October next after the date on which it is expressed to take effect.

(4) If a holiday season licence is granted in respect of any premises, any ordinary licence in respect of those premises shall (if not surrendered under paragraph 19 of this Schedule) become void as from the day on which the holiday season licence is first in force.

(5) If an ordinary licence (whole-year or half-year) is granted in respect of any premises, any holiday season licence in respect of those premises shall become void as from the day on which the ordinary licence is first in force.

15.—(1) The proper officer may, in such manner as the Commissioners may direct, and without any additional payment, transfer a gaming machine licence in respect of any premises to a successor in title to the interest in those premises of the person to whom the licence was granted.

(2) Where the holder of a gaming machine licence in respect of any premises dies, the proper officer may transfer the licence, in such manner as the Commissioners may direct and without any additional payment, to some other person for the remainder of the period for which the licence was granted.

Amendment of licence

16.—(1) Where there is a gaming machine licence for the time being in force in respect of any premises, the holder may at any time apply to the Commissioners for the licence to be amended under this paragraph, and the proper officer shall, on payment of the additional duty (if any), amend the licence accordingly. Sch. 11

(2) An ordinary licence may be amended under this paragraph—

(*a*) so as to increase the number of machines which are authorised by the licence for the premises in question (whether chargeable at one or other, or at each, of the two rates respectively); or

(*b*) so as to increase the number of machines chargeable at one rate and reduce the number chargeable at the other rate; or

(*c*) in the case of a licence which authorises only machines chargeable at one rate, so as to authorise a specified number of machines chargeable at the other rate.

(3) A holiday season licence may be amended under this paragraph so as to increase the number of penny machines which are authorised by the licence for the premises in question.

(4) The additional duty referred to in sub-paragraph (1) of this paragraph shall be payable only where—

(*a*) the amount of the duty originally paid on the licence; or

(*b*) in the case of a licence previously amended under this paragraph, that amount plus any additional duty paid in respect of that amendment,

is exceeded by the amount of duty which would have been payable on the original licence if it had been granted as proposed to be amended; and the amount of the additional duty shall then be the difference between those two amounts, except that where an ordinary whole-year licence falls to be amended in pursuance of an application made after 31st March immediately preceding 30th September on which it is due to expire, the additional duty shall be eleven-twentieths of that difference.

(5) Regulations may make provision with respect to the procedure for amending licences under this paragraph, and any such regulations may include provision—

(*a*) as to the method of amendment (that is to say, whether it is to be effected by endorsement of the licence, or by the issue of an amended licence, or otherwise howsoever); and

(*b*) as to the time at which a licence is to have effect as amended.

Payment and repayment of duty

17. Section 234 of the Customs and Excise Act 1952 (which relates to payment for excise licences by cheque) shall apply to the duty on a gaming machine licence, but as if for the reference to a penalty of £50 there were substituted a reference to a penalty of £500. 1952 c. 44.

Existing supply agreements

18.—(1) The following provisions of this paragraph shall have effect where a person (called " the hirer ") has, before 1st October

SCH. 11 1969, entered into an agreement with another person (called " the supplier ") for the provision by the supplier on any premises of a gaming machine during a period beginning before, and extending beyond, that date.

(2) If the consideration for the provision of the gaming machine was determined on the assumption that someone other than the hirer would pay the duty on any gaming machine licence required for
1966 c. 18. the premises under section 14 of the Finance Act 1966, and the hirer has paid, or will be accountable for, the corresponding duty under section 5 of this Act, the hirer shall be entitled to recover from the supplier such amount, or to make such reduction in periodical payments due from him under the agreement, as may be agreed between them (or, in default of agreement, as may be determined by the appropriate court) to be fair in all the circumstances having regard in particular—

(*a*) to the period for which, under the agreement, the supplier is to provide a gaming machine as aforesaid on the premises in question ; and

(*b*) to the incidence of the duty under the said section 14 and section 5 as respects that period.

(3) In the last foregoing sub-paragraph, " the appropriate court " means—

(*a*) where the premises in question are in England or Wales, the county court ; and

(*b*) where the said premises are in Scotland, the sheriff.

19.—(1) The following provisions shall have effect where an ordinary whole-year licence is in force in respect of any premises and not later than 31st March immediately preceding 30th September on which the licence is due to expire, the holder of the licence surrenders it to the proper officer.

(2) Subject to the following sub-paragraph, the holder, if he satisfies the proper officer either—

(*a*) that, during the period between the date of the surrender and that on which the licence would otherwise expire, he will not be concerned with the provision of any gaming machines for gaming on the premises to which the licence relates ; or

(*b*) that as from the date of the surrender there will be in force in respect of those premises a holiday season licence,

shall be entitled to repayment of an amount equal to nine-twentieths of the duty paid on the licence.

(3) The last foregoing sub-paragraph shall not apply if any person has been convicted of an offence under paragraph 22 of this Schedule in respect of a contravention on the premises of section 5(11) of this Act, being a contravention which occurred between the grant of the licence and the date of surrender ; and where at the said date proceedings for such an offence are pending against any person, the right to repayment under this paragraph shall not arise until

the proceedings are terminated, nor unless every person charged in those proceedings with such an offence has been acquitted thereof. SCH. 11

Requirements to be observed by licence-holder

20. The holder of a gaming machine licence in respect of any premises shall secure that the licence is displayed on the premises at such times and in such manner as may be prescribed, and shall on demand by an officer at any time produce the licence for the officer's inspection.

21. Regulations may make provision with respect to the labelling or marking of gaming machines provided on any premises in respect of which a gaming machine licence is for the time being in force, with a view to enabling such machines to be identified as chargeable at the lower rate or at the higher rate or, as the case may be, as penny machines; and any such regulations may include provision as to the size and description of labels or marks to be applied to machines, as to the cases in which they are required to be, or are prohibited from being, applied, and as to the manner of their application.

Enforcement

22. If any gaming machine is provided for gaming on any premises in contravention of section 5(11) of this Act, any person who, at the time when it is so provided—

(*a*) is the owner, lessee or occupier of the premises; or

(*b*) is for the time being responsible to the owner, lessee or occupier for the management of the premises; or

(*c*) is a person responsible for issuing or exchanging coins or tokens for use in playing any gaming machine on the premises, or otherwise for controlling the use of any such machine; or

(*d*) is for the time being responsible for controlling the admission of persons to the premises or for providing persons resorting thereto with any goods or services; or

(*e*) is the owner or hirer of the machine; or

(*f*) is a party to any contract under which a gaming machine may, or is required to, be on the premises at that time,

shall be guilty of an offence and be liable to a penalty of £500 or, if he knowingly or recklessly brought about the relevant contravention of section 5(11) of this Act, or took any steps with a view to procuring it—

(i) on summary conviction to a penalty of £1,000 or to imprisonment for not more than twelve months, or to both; or

(ii) on conviction on indictment, to the like penalty or to imprisonment for not more than two years, or to both.

23.—(1) If any person contravenes or fails to comply with any provision of this Part of this Schedule or regulations, or fails or refuses to comply with any requirement lawfully made of him under this Part of this Schedule or regulations, he shall be guilty of an offence and be liable to a penalty of £500.

SCH. 11

(2) Where a person is convicted of an offence under this paragraph consisting in a failure to comply with any provision of this Part of this Schedule or regulations, and the failure continues after the conviction, he shall be guilty of a further offence under this paragraph and may on conviction be punished accordingly.

24. Where an offence under paragraph 22 or 23 of this Schedule has been committed by a body corporate, every person who at the time of the commission of the offence was a director, general manager, secretary or other similar officer of the body corporate, or was purporting to act in any such capacity, shall be deemed to be guilty of that offence unless he proves—

(*a*) in the case of an offence under paragraph 22, that he did not consent to, or connive at, the relevant contravention of section 5(11) of this Act ; or

(*b*) in the case of an offence under paragraph 23, that the offence was committed without his consent or connivance,

and that he exercised all such diligence to prevent the contravention or, as the case may be, the commission of the offence as he ought to have exercised having regard to the nature of his functions in that capacity and in all the circumstances.

25. Any officer may (without payment) enter on any premises on which he knows or has reasonable cause to suspect that gaming machines are or have been provided for gaming and inspect those premises and require any person who is concerned in the management of the premises, or who is on the premises and appears to the officer to have any responsibility whatsoever in respect of their management or of the control of the admission of persons thereto—

(*a*) to produce or secure the production of any gaming machine licence for the time being in force in respect of the premises ; or

(*b*) to provide information with respect to any use to which the premises are or have been put, or to any machine which is or has been on the premises and any game which may have been played by means of such a machine or to the way in which the machine works, or to the amount which is or has been payable to play it.

26.—(1) If a justice of the peace or, in Scotland, a sheriff or a magistrate is satisfied on information on oath that there is reasonable ground for suspecting that gaming machines are or have been, or are to be, provided for gaming on any premises in contravention of section 5(11) of this Act, he may issue a warrant in writing authorising an officer to enter the premises, if necessary by force, at any time within fourteen days of the issue of the warrant, and search the premises.

(2) An officer who enters premises under the authority of such a warrant may—

(*a*) seize and remove any records, accounts or other documents, or any gaming machine (including any machine appearing to the officer to be constructed or adapted, or to be capable of use, for playing a game of chance by means of it), or any tokens or other thing whatsoever, found on the premises which he has reasonable cause to believe may be required as evidence for the purposes of proceedings in respect of an offence under paragraph 22 or 23 of this Schedule: Sch. 11

(b) search any person found on the premises whom he has reasonable cause to believe to be or have been concerned with the provision of gaming machines on the premises, or with the management of the premises, or to be or have been responsible for controlling the admission of persons to the premises.

27. Where an officer finds gaming machines provided on any premises in such circumstances that a gaming machine licence is required so as to authorise them so to be provided and either—

(a) there is not produced to him on demand a valid gaming machine licence in respect of the premises ; or

(b) such a licence is produced, but the officer is satisfied that, having regard to the number of machines on the premises and their description, there is or has been a contravention of section 5(11) of this Act in respect of the premises,

all gaming machines found on the premises shall be liable to forfeiture.

Supplementary

28. Where an officer takes any action in pursuance of instructions of the Commissioners or a Collector of Customs and Excise given in connection with the enforcement of the enactments relating to the duty on gaming machine licences and, apart from the provisions of this paragraph, the officer would in taking that action be committing an offence under the enactments relating to betting or gaming, he shall not be guilty of that offence.

29.—(1) The clerk to the appropriate authority shall keep a register in the prescribed form and containing the prescribed particulars of—

(a) all permits issued by the authority for the purposes of section 49 of the Act of 1963 (permitted gaming in the form of amusements with prizes) ;

(b) all permits so issued for the purposes of section 34 of the Act of 1968 (conditions under which gaming may be carried on by means of machines) ; and

(c) all directions given by the authority under section 32 of the Act of 1968 (approval for provision of more than two gaming machines) ;

and any such register shall be open during reasonable hours for inspection by any officer.

(2) In the foregoing sub-paragraph, " the appropriate authority "—

(a) in relation to permits issued for the purposes of section 49 of the Act of 1963, means the local authority within the meaning of Schedule 6 to that Act ;

SCH. 11

(*b*) in relation to permits issued for the purposes of section 34 of the Act of 1968, has the same meaning as in Schedule 9 to that Act ; and

(*c*) in relation to directions under section 32 of the Act of 1968, means the licensing authority under that Act.

30. In paragraph 48(1) of Schedule 2 to the Act of 1968 (cancellation of licence under that Act on conviction of certain offences), for the words " or section 14 of that Act " there shall be substituted the words " of that Act, or of an offence under paragraph 22 or 23 of Schedule 11 to the Finance Act 1969 " ; and the like substitution shall be made for the words " or section 14 of that Act " in—

(*a*) paragraph 17(1) of Schedule 3 to the Act of 1968 (cancellation or registration of club or miners' welfare institute in England or Wales) ; and

(*b*) paragraph 15(1) of Schedule 4 to that Act (the same in relation to Scotland).

Section 6.

SCHEDULE 12

AMENDMENT OF ENACTMENTS RELATING TO TRADE LICENCES FOR VEHICLES

PART I

1962 c. 13.

Subsections to be substituted for subsections (1) *to* (5) *of section* 12 *of the Vehicles* (*Excise*) *Act* 1962

12.—(1) If a motor trader or a vehicle tester applies in the prescribed manner to the council of the county in which his business premises are situated to take out a licence under this section (in this Act referred to as a " trade licence ")—

(i) in the case of a motor trader, for all mechanically propelled vehicles which are from time to time temporarily in his possession in the course of his business as a motor trader and all recovery vehicles kept by him for the purpose of dealing with disabled vehicles in the course of that business ; or

(ii) in the case of a vehicle tester, for all mechanically propelled vehicles which are from time to time submitted to him for testing in the course of his business as a vehicle tester,

the county council may, subject to the prescribed conditions, issue to him a trade licence on payment of duty at the rate applicable to the licence in accordance with the following provisions of this section:

Provided that the holder of a trade licence shall not be entitled by virtue of that licence—

(*a*) to use more than one mechanically propelled vehicle at any one time, except in the case of a recovery vehicle drawing a disabled vehicle ; or (*b*) to use any vehicle for any purpose other than such purposes as may be prescribed; or

(*c*) to keep any vehicle on a road if it is not being used thereon.

(2) Regulations shall be made under this section prescribing the conditions subject to which trade licences are to be issued and the purposes for which the holder of a trade licence may use a vehicle under the licence.

(3) The purposes which may be prescribed as those for which the holder of a trade licence may use a vehicle under the licence shall not include the conveyance of goods or burden of any description other than—

(*a*) a load which is carried solely for the purpose of testing or demonstrating the vehicle or any of its accessories or equipment and which is returned to the place of loading without having been removed from the vehicle except for such purpose or in the case of accident; or

(*b*) in the case of a recovery vehicle, any such load as is referred to in the definition of such a vehicle contained in subsection (10) of this section or a load consisting of a disabled vehicle; or

(*c*) any load built in as part of the vehicle or permanently attached thereto; or

(*d*) a load consisting of parts, accessories or equipment designed to be fitted to the vehicle and of tools for so fitting them; or

(*e*) a load consisting of a trailer;

and, for the purposes of this subsection, where a vehicle is so constructed that a trailer may by partial superimposition be attached to the vehicle in such a manner as to cause a substantial part of the weight of the trailer to be borne by the vehicle, the vehicle and the trailer shall be deemed to constitute a single vehicle.

(4) A trade licence may be taken out either for one calendar year or, except in the case of a licence which is to be used only for vehicles to which Schedule 1 to this Act relates, for a period of three months beginning with the first day of January, of April, of July or of October.

(5) The rate of duty applicable to a trade licence taken out for a calendar year shall be £15 or, if the licence is to be used only for vehicles to which Schedule 1 to this Act relates, £2 10s.; and the rate of duty applicable to a licence taken out for a period of three months shall be eleven fortieths of the rate applicable to the corresponding trade licence taken out for a calendar year, any fraction of a shilling being treated as a whole shilling if it exceeds sixpence but otherwise being disregarded.

SCH. 12

PART II

Further supplementary or consequential amendments

1962 c. 13. 1. For subsection (9) of section 12 of the Vehicles (Excise) Act 1962 there shall be substituted the following subsection:—

"(9) If on or after 1st January 1970 any person holding a trade licence or trade licences issued under this Act uses on a public road by virtue of that licence or those licences—

(i) a greater number of vehicles at any one time than he is authorised to use by virtue of that licence or those licences; or

(ii) any vehicle for any purpose other than such purposes as may have been prescribed under subsection (2) of this section,

or if on or after that date that person uses that licence or any of those licences for the purpose of keeping on a road a vehicle which is not being used on that road, he shall be liable to the greater of the following penalties, namely—

(*a*) an excise penalty of £50; or

(*b*) an excise penalty equal to five times the amount of the duty chargeable in respect of the vehicle or vehicles determined in accordance with section 5(1) of

1962 c. 44. the Finance Act 1962."

2. In subsection (10) of the said section 12 as amended by

1968 c. 44. section 9(*b*) of the Finance Act 1968, at the end there shall be added the words " and 'recovery vehicle' means a vehicle on which there is mounted apparatus designed for wholly or partly raising or for drawing a disabled vehicle, and which is not designed primarily for the conveyance of goods other than a disabled vehicle wholly raised by that apparatus, and which carries no other load other than articles required for the operation of, or in connection with, that apparatus or otherwise for dealing with disabled vehicles."

3. Until the coming into force of the substitution made by

1969 c. 27. section 17 of the Vehicle and Driving Licences Act 1969, section 16(2) of the Vehicles (Excise) Act 1962 shall have effect with the addition at the end thereof of the words " and

(*c*) make provision for the issue of trade plates to holders of trade licences and for the charging of a fee for the replacement of such plates by reason of damage to them or of their loss or destruction."

4. In section 17(1) of the Vehicles (Excise) Act 1962, after paragraph (*a*) there shall be inserted the following paragraph:—

"(*aa*) any trade plates or replacements such as are mentioned in subsection (2)(*c*) (or, after the coming into force of the substitution made by section 17 of the Vehicle and Driving Licences Act 1969, in paragraph (*bb*)) of section 16 of this Act; or".

5. For section 4(2) of the Vehicle and Driving Licences Act 1969 there shall be substituted the following subsection:— SCH. 12 1969 c. 27.

"(2) A trade licence may be taken out either for a period of twelve months or, except in the case of a licence which is to be used only for vehicles to which Schedule 1 to the Act of 1962 relates, for a period of four months."

6. In section 17 of the Vehicle and Driving Licences Act 1969, in the new section to be substituted thereby for section 16 of the Vehicles (Excise) Act 1962, after paragraph (*b*) there shall be inserted the following paragraph:— 1962 c. 13.

"(*bb*) make provision for the issue of trade plates to holders of trade licences and for the charging of a fee for the replacement of such plates by reason of damage to them or of their loss or destruction ;".

SCHEDULE 13

Sections 18 to 27.

DISALLOWANCE OF INTEREST

PART I

SUPPLEMENTARY AND TRANSITIONAL

Overdrafts

1.—(1) This paragraph has effect for the purposes of the sections of this Act giving relief in respect of interest, and of paragraph 7 of this Schedule.

(2) If a person draws money from a bank account or other running account, and applies it, or any part of it, so as to fulfil the conditions in any of the said sections or the said paragraph 7, he shall be regarded as obtaining a loan of that money up to the amount of the highest debit balance in the account in the six months beginning with the date on which the money is drawn:

Provided that if that date fell before 6th April 1968 it shall be assumed that the said highest debit balance was not less than the amount of money drawn from the account.

(3) If the account has been in credit throughout a year of assessment (excluding any year before the year 1968-69) any loan so obtained before the year in which the account has been in credit shall be treated as having been repaid at the beginning of that year.

(4) The whole of the interest on debit balances in the account in any year of assessment shall be available for attribution to any outstanding loans so obtained:

Provided that the amount of interest attributable to a loan, or to the aggregate of any loans, made before the beginning of the year 1968-69 shall not exceed the amount of interest on debit balances in the account in the year 1968-69 with which the said person has been charged.

SCH. 13 (5) A loan so obtained shall be regarded as carrying interest in any year of assessment at the rate chargeable on the account on the last day of that year on which the account was in debit, but only so far as interest is available for attribution under sub-paragraph (4) above and, where part only of a loan is eligible for relief under the provisions mentioned in sub-paragraph (1) above, that interest is to be attributed rateably to the eligible and ineligible parts of the loan.

(6) Where the amount of interest paid on a loan for part only of a year of assessment is to be ascertained, this paragraph shall be applied to ascertain the amount of interest paid for the whole of the year, and that amount shall be apportioned between that part of the year and the remainder according to their respective lengths.

Interest ceasing to be, or becoming, payable subject to deduction of tax

1952 c. 10. 2. Section 131 of the Income Tax Act 1952 and section 18 of the
1952 c. 33. Finance Act 1952 (income tax: preceding year basis and related provisions) shall apply—

(*a*) if at any time interest on a debt ceases to be payable subject to deduction of income tax, as if the debt were a new source of income acquired by the creditor at that time, and

(*b*) if at any time interest on a debt begins to be payable subject to deduction of income tax, as if the debt were a source of income which the creditor ceased to possess at that time.

Allowance of interest as a business expense: transitory provision

3.—(1) In computing for the purposes of income tax for the year 1970-71 or any subsequent year of assessment the profits or gains arising from a trade, profession or vocation in a basis period falling wholly or partly before 6th April 1970, there may, subject to section 137 of the Income Tax Act 1952, and subsection (9) of section 19 of this Act, be deducted—

(*a*) the gross amount of any annual interest paid before that date under deduction of tax, and

(*b*) the amount of any interest paid to a bank, stockbroker or discount house relief for which was allowed under section 200 of the Income Tax Act 1952 for the year of assessment in which the payment was made, and

(*c*) the amount of any interest paid to a building society relief for which was allowed under section 445(3) of the Income Tax Act 1952 for the year of assessment in which the payment was made.

(2) It is hereby declared that, subject to sub-paragraph (1) above, relief in respect of any payment of interest cannot be given both under the said section 200 and in computing the profits or gains of a trade, profession or vocation.

Sch. 13

(3) In this paragraph " basis period ", in relation to any year of assessment, means the period the profits or gains of which are taken into account in charging income tax under Case I or Case II of Schedule D on the profits or gains of the trade, profession or vocation for that year of assessment.

Allowance of interest as a business expense

4.—(1) Section 137(*f*) of the Income Tax Act 1952 (disallowance of deductions in respect of capital employed) shall not be treated as disallowing the deduction of any interest. 1952 c. 10.

(2) After paragraph (*l*) of the said section 137 insert—

(*ll*) any annual or other interest paid to a person not resident in the United Kingdom if and so far as it is interest at more than a reasonable commercial rate '.

(3) This paragraph shall apply for income tax purposes for the year 1968-69 and subsequent years of assessment, and for corporation tax purposes to accounting periods ending on or after 6th April 1968.

Business expenses : interest paid to non-residents

5.—(1) In computing the profits or gains arising from a trade, profession or vocation no sum shall be deducted in respect of any annual interest paid to a person not resident in the United Kingdom, unless—

(*a*) the person making the payment has deducted income tax from the payment in accordance with section 26 of this Act, and accounts for the tax so deducted, or

(*b*) the conditions set out in section 138(1) of the Income Tax Act 1952 (interest payable abroad), as read with subsections (3) and (4) of that section, are satisfied.

(2) If interest paid under deduction of tax in accordance with section 26 of this Act is deductible in computing the profits or gains of a trade, profession or vocation, the amount so deductible shall be the gross amount.

(3) In the said section 138 references to a trade shall, for the year 1969-70 and subsequent years of assessment, include references to a profession or vocation.

(4) This paragraph shall not apply for the purposes of corporation tax.

(5) Sub-paragraphs (1) and (2) of this paragraph apply—

(*a*) for the purposes of income tax for the year 1969-70 and earlier years of assessment, to interest paid on any debt incurred after 15th April 1969, and

(*b*) for the purposes of income tax for the year 1970-71 and subsequent years of assessment, to any payment of interest, whenever made.

SCH. 13

Interest eligible for relief: treatment as trading loss

6.—(1) Where a payment to which this paragraph applies is money wholly and exclusively laid out or expended for the purposes of a trade, profession or vocation the profits of which are chargeable to tax under Case I or Case II of Schedule D, and full effect cannot be given to the relief specified in sub-paragraph (2) below as respects the payment by reason of a want or deficiency of income of the year of assessment in which the payment is made, the amount unallowed may be carried forward to succeeding years of assessment,
1952 c. 10. as if it were a loss carried forward under section 342 of the Income Tax Act 1952, or may be treated for the purposes of section 18 of the
1954 c. 44. Finance Act 1954 (terminal losses) as a loss sustained at the date of payment.

(2) This paragraph applies to—

(*a*) interest eligible for relief under section 19 of this Act,

(*b*) payments of interest eligible for relief under section 24 of this Act,

(*c*) payments in respect of tithe redemption annuities to which
1963 c. 25. section 31(2) of the Finance Act 1963 applies,

(*d*) payments of interest made to a building society to which section 445(3)(*b*) of the Income Tax Act 1952 applied,

and, so far as it relates to the carrying forward of payments mentioned in paragraphs (*c*) and (*d*) above, shall be deemed always to have had effect.

Interest on loans to purchase machinery or plant used in an office or employment

7.—(1) Subject to the provisions of this paragraph, where the holder of an office or employment—

1968 c. 3. (*a*) is under Chapter II of Part I of the Capital Allowances Act 1968 entitled to a capital allowance or liable to a balancing charge for any year of assessment in respect of machinery or plant belonging to him and in use for the purposes of the office or employment, and

(*b*) pays interest in that year on a loan to defray money applied as capital expenditure on the provision of that machinery or plant,

there may be deducted from the emoluments to be assessed for that year the amount of the interest so paid.

(2) No relief shall be given under this paragraph in respect of interest falling due and payable more than three years after the end of the year of assessment in which the debt was incurred, or in respect of interest at more than a reasonable commercial rate.

(3) Where the machinery or plant is in use partly for the purposes of the office or employment and partly for other purposes section 28 of the Capital Allowances Act 1968 (part-time use) shall apply in relation to relief under this paragraph as it applies in relation to writing-down allowances.

(4) Where credit is given for any money payable to defray any capital expenditure, that shall be treated for the purposes of this paragraph as the making of a loan to defray that capital expenditure. SCH. 13

(5) As regards the year 1969-70 this paragraph shall not apply

(*a*) to interest on a debt incurred on or before 15th April 1969 which is payable under deduction of tax to a person other than a bank carrying on a bona fide banking business in the United Kingdom, or

(*b*) to any amount of interest in respect of which relief may be claimed under section 200 of the Income Tax Act 1952. 1952 c. 10.

Arrangements for payment of interest less tax or of fixed net amount

8.—(1) It is hereby declared that any provision made before or after the passing of this Act, whether orally or in writing, for the payment of interest " less tax ", or using words to that effect, is to be construed, in relation to interest payable without deduction of tax, as if the words " less tax ", or the equivalent words, were not included.

(2) In relation to interest on which the recipient is chargeable to tax under Case III of Schedule D, and which is payable without deduction of tax, any provision, made before or after the passing of this Act, whether orally or in writing, and however worded, for the payment of interest at such a rate (referred to below in this sub-paragraph as the " gross rate ") as shall, after the deduction of the standard rate of income tax for the time being in force, be equal to a stated rate, shall be construed as if it were a provision requiring the payment of interest at the gross rate.

Settlements

9.—(1) Section 411(3)(*b*) of the Income Tax Act 1952 (expenses deductible in arriving at the amount of settlement income which has not been distributed) shall apply to any interest paid by the trustees of the settlement subject to the provisions of this paragraph.

(2) If no sums within paragraph (*a*) of the said subsection (3) (distributions to beneficiaries) were paid to any person other than the settlor, or the wife or husband of the settlor, the whole of the interest shall be excluded from the said paragraph (*b*).

(3) If any sum was so paid, there shall be excluded from the said paragraph (*b*) a fraction $\frac{A - B}{A}$ of the interest where—

A is the whole of the income arising under the settlement (as defined in the said section 411(1)) in the year of assessment, less the sums referred to in the said subsection (3)(*b*) apart from this paragraph, and

B is so much of the sums within subsection (3)(*a*) of the said section 411 as is paid to persons other than the settlor, or the wife or husband of the settlor.

SCH. 13 (4) This paragraph shall not apply to interest in respect of which relief from tax at the standard rate is allowable under any provision of the Income Tax Acts or to interest payable to the settlor or the wife or husband of the settlor (if living with the settlor).

(5) Nothing in this paragraph shall be construed as affecting the liability to tax of the person receiving or entitled to the interest.

(6) This paragraph shall be construed as one with the said section 411.

10. All payments of interest shall be excluded from subsection (3)(*a*) of the said section 411.

Children's settlements

11.—(1) Where interest is paid by the trustees of a settlement to
1952 c. 10. which Chapter II of Part XVIII of the Income Tax Act 1952 applies there shall be deemed for the purposes of the said Chapter II to be paid to or for the benefit of a child of the settlor who at the time of the payment is an infant and unmarried (in addition to any other amount deemed to be so paid) an amount equal to a fraction $\frac{A-B}{A}$ of the interest, where—

A is the whole of the income arising under the settlement (as defined in section 411(1) of the Income Tax Act 1952) in the year of assessment, less the sums referred to in subsection (3)(*b*) of the said section 411 as it applies apart from paragraph 9 above, and

B is such part of A as is not paid to or for the benefit of any child of the settlor who is an infant and unmarried.

(2) This paragraph shall not apply to interest in respect of which relief from tax at the standard rate is allowable under any provision of the Income Tax Acts or to interest payable to the settlor or the wife or husband of the settlor (if living with the settlor).

(3) Nothing in this paragraph shall be construed as affecting the liability to tax of the person receiving or entitled to the interest.

(4) This paragraph shall be construed as one with the said Chapter II, and for the purposes of this paragraph the said section 411 shall be deemed to apply in relation to settlements to which that Chapter applies as it applies in relation to settlements to which Chapter III of Part XVIII of the Income Tax Act 1952 applies.

Tax avoidance : transactions associated with loans or credit

12.—(1) This paragraph applies as respects any transaction effected with reference to the lending of money or the giving of credit, or the varying of the terms on which money is lent or credit is given, or which is effected with a view to enabling or facilitating any such arrangement concerning the lending of money or the giving of credit.

This sub-paragraph has effect whether the transaction is effected between the lender or creditor and the borrower or debtor, or between either of them and a person connected with the other or between a person connected with one and a person connected with the other. SCH. 13

(2) If the transaction provides for the payment of any annuity or other annual payment, not being interest, being a payment chargeable to tax under Case III of Schedule D, the payment shall be treated for all the purposes of the Income Tax Acts and the Corporation Tax Acts as if it were a payment of annual interest.

(3) If the transaction is one by which the owner of any securities or other property carrying a right to income agrees to sell or transfer the property, and by the same or any collateral agreement—

(*a*) the purchaser or transferee, or a person connected with him, agrees that at a later date he will sell or transfer the same or any other property to the first-mentioned person, or a person connected with him, or

(*b*) the first-mentioned person, or a person connected with him, acquires an option, which he subsequently exercises, to buy or acquire the same or any other property from the said purchaser or transferee or a person connected with him,

then, without prejudice to the liability of any other person, the first-mentioned person shall be chargeable to tax under Case VI of Schedule D on an amount equal to any income which arises from the first-mentioned property at any time before the repayment of the loan or the termination of the credit.

(4) If under the transaction a person assigns, surrenders or otherwise agrees to waive or forgo income arising from any property (without a sale or transfer of the property) then, without prejudice to the liability of any other person, he shall be chargeable to tax under Case VI of Schedule D on a sum equal to the amount of income assigned, surrendered, waived or forgone.

(5) If credit is given for the purchase price of any property, and the rights attaching to the property are such that, during the subsistence of the debt, the purchaser's rights to income from the property are suspended or restricted, he shall be treated for the purposes of sub-paragraph (4) above as if he had surrendered a right to income of an amount equivalent to the income which he has in effect forgone by obtaining the credit.

(6) The amount of any income payable subject to deduction of income tax at the standard rate shall be taken for the purposes of sub-paragraph (4) above as the amount before deduction of that tax.

(7) Section 203 of the Income Tax Act 1952 (sale and repurchase of securities) shall not apply to any income to which sub-paragraph (3) above applies. 1952 c. 10.

(8) Paragraph 21 of Schedule 7 to the Finance Act 1965 shall apply for the construction of references in this paragraph to connected persons. 1965 c. 25.

SCH. 13

Information

13.—(1) Any person by whom any interest is paid in the year 1969-70 or any subsequent year of assessment without deduction of income tax shall, on being so required by a notice given to him by an inspector, furnish to the inspector, within the time limited by the notice—

(*a*) the name and address of the person to whom the interest has been paid or on whose behalf the interest has been received, and

(*b*) the amount of the interest so paid or received,

and any person who receives any such interest on behalf of another person shall on being so required furnish to the inspector the name and address of the person on whose behalf the interest has been received, and its amount.

(2) The persons to whom this paragraph applies include any officer in any public office or in any department of the Crown.

(3) This paragraph shall not impose any obligation on a bank carrying on a bona fide business in the United Kingdom in respect of any interest paid by the bank in the ordinary course of that business.

1960 c. 44. (4) Part III of the Finance Act 1960 (penalties) shall have effect as if this paragraph were among the provisions specified in the second column of Schedule 6 to that Act.

14.—(1) Any person who claims relief under sections 19 to 25 of this Act in respect of any payment of interest shall furnish to the inspector a statement in writing by the person to whom the payment is made showing—

(*a*) the date when the debt was incurred,

(*b*) the amount of the debt when incurred,

(*c*) the interest paid in the year of assessment for which the claim is made, and

(*d*) the name and address of the debtor.

(2) If the claim relates to interest on an overdraft the statement shall show (instead of the particulars in paragraphs (*a*) to (*d*) above)—

(*a*) the date when the money was drawn out of the account, and, unless that date fell before 6th April 1968, the highest debit balance in the account in the six months beginning with that date,

(*b*) the rate of interest chargeable on the account for the last day of the year of assessment to which the claim relates on which the account was in debit,

(*c*) the amount of interest on debit balances in the account in the year of assessment, and

(*d*) the name and address of the claimant.

(3) A person to whom any interest is paid by another person shall if that other person so requests in writing, furnish that other person with a statement in writing conforming with the preceding provisions of this paragraph and dealing with that payment of interest. SCH. 13

The duty imposed by this sub-paragraph shall be enforceable at the suit or instance of the person making the request.

(4) This paragraph shall not apply to interest paid to a building society as defined in section 445(5) of the Income Tax Act 1952 or a local authority. 1952 c. 10.

Betterment levy

15. Interest payable to the Land Commission under section 51 of the Land Commission Act 1967 at the rate determined by the Betterment Levy (Rate of Interest) (No. 2) Order 1969 or by any subsequent Order made under section 51(2) of that Act— 1967 c. 1. S.I. 1969/536.

(*a*) shall be paid without deduction of income tax, and

(*b*) shall not be allowed as a deduction in computing any income, profits or losses for any of the purposes of income tax or corporation tax.

Co-operative housing associations

16. At the end of section 43(1) of the Finance Act 1963 there shall be added— 1963 c. 25.

" and

(*c*) each member of the association shall be treated for the purposes of section 19 of the Finance Act 1969 as if he were the owner of the association's estate or interest in the property of which he is the tenant ".

Tenant purchase schemes

17. Where interest is payable by the tenant occupier of any property to the landlord in pursuance of arrangements whereby money advanced at interest by the landlord is applied by the tenant in purchasing the landlord's estate or interest but that estate or interest is not to pass to the tenant until some time after the interest begins to be payable, section 19 of this Act shall have effect in relation to the tenant as if he were the owner of the landlord's estate or interest.

Capital gains

18.—(1) Except as provided by paragraph 19 of Schedule 19 to this Act no payment of interest shall be allowable under paragraph 4 of Schedule 6 to the Finance Act 1965 (deductions allowable in computations for long-term tax on capital gains). 1965 c. 25.

(2) No interest shall be allowable in computing the amount of a gain or loss under Case VII of Schedule D (short-term gains).

This sub-paragraph applies—

(*a*) to interest paid after 5th April 1970, and

SCH. 13 (*b*) to bank, discount house or stock exchange interest paid in the year 1969-70 in respect of any period beginning after 30th June 1969, and

(*c*) to interest paid in the year 1969-70 on any debt incurred after 15th April 1969, not being bank, discount house or stock exchange interest.

Republic of Ireland

1952 c. 10. 19.—(1) Part III of Schedule 18 to the Income Tax Act 1952 (double taxation relief) shall be amended as follows.

(2) In paragraph 2(1)(*b*) in the said Part III (Cases IV and V of Schedule D) the reference to annual interest shall be omitted.

This sub-paragraph applies—

(*a*) to interest on any debt incurred after 15th April 1969, and

(*b*) to interest paid after 5th April 1975 on a debt incurred on or before 15th April 1969.

(3) Section 19 of this Act shall have effect as if any reference to the United Kingdom included a reference to the Republic of Ireland
1967 c. 9. and as if references to provisions of the General Rate Act 1967 included references to the corresponding enactments in force in the Republic of Ireland.

Interpretation

20. In the principal sections and this Schedule—

"bank, discount house or stock exchange interest" means interest paid without deduction of tax in the United Kingdom on an advance from a bank carrying on a bona fide banking business in the United Kingdom, or from a person bona fide carrying on business as a member of a stock exchange in the United Kingdom, or bona fide carrying on the business of a discount house in the United Kingdom, and references to such interest in respect of a period beginning after 30th June 1969 apply whether or not interest begins to run on or before that date,

"building society" includes any company within section 445(6) of the Income Tax Act 1952,

"company" and "local authority" have the same meaning as
1965 c. 25. in Part IV of the Finance Act 1965 but so that a company shall not be regarded as the subsidiary of another company unless both are bodies corporate,

"interest", unless the context otherwise requires, means both annual or yearly interest and interest other than annual or yearly interest.

PART II

CONSEQUENTIAL AMENDMENTS

References to yearly interest, annuities and other annual payments

21. In the following provisions of the Income Tax Act 1952 for the words "annual interest, annuity or other annual sum", or words to that effect, substitute—

"annuity or other annual payment (not being interest)".

The said provisions are— Sch. 13

section 2(2)(*a*);

section 132(1)(*c*);

in section 169, in the opening words of subsection (1) and in the opening words of subsection (2), and in paragraphs (*a*) and (*b*) of subsection (1);

section 170(1)(*a*);

section 511(1)(*b*);

in Schedule 18, Part III, paragraph 2(1)(*b*);

in Schedule 24, in the third head (where the substituted phrase is to be in the plural).

The amendments made above by this Part of this Schedule apply—

(*a*) to interest paid after 5th April 1970, and

(*b*) to interest paid earlier on any debt incurred after 15th April 1969.

22. In section 137(*l*) of the Income Tax Act 1952 for "annual interest or any annuity or other annual payment" substitute "any annuity or other annual payment (other than interest)". 1952 c. 10.

This paragraph applies for 1970-71 and subsequent years of assessment, and, as respects interest on a debt incurred after 15th April 1969, also for the year 1969-70 and earlier years of assessment.

23. Section 26 of this Act has effect subject to the provisions of sections 442 and 445 of the Income Tax Act 1952 (industrial and provident societies and building societies).

24. Section 524(4) of the Income Tax Act 1952 (assessments at standard rate to be conclusive for surtax) shall, for the purpose of estimating total income for the purposes of surtax apply in relation to any relief under any of sections 19 to 22, 24 and 25 of this Act as it applies in relation to allowances or adjustments on the ground of diminution of income or loss.

25. In paragraph 7(1) of Schedule 2 to the Finance Act 1956 (emoluments for duties performed in the Republic of Ireland) for "any annual interest paid or other annual payment" substitute "any annuity or other annual payment (other than interest)". 1956 c. 54.

This paragraph applies—

(*a*) to interest paid after 5th April 1970, and

(*b*) to interest paid in the year 1969-70 on any debt incurred after 15th April 1969.

26. At the end of paragraph 1 of Schedule 4 to the Finance Act 1963 (allowable deductions in Case VIII of Schedule D) insert— 1963 c. 25.

"Provided that this paragraph shall not apply to any payment of interest".

27. In section 52(5)(*a*) of the Finance Act 1965 (charges on income) and in Regulation 6 of the Double Taxation Relief (Taxes on Income) (General) Regulations 1966, the references to section 170 of the Income Tax Act 1952 shall, as from 15th April 1969, include a reference to section 26 of this Act. 1965 c. 25. S.I. 1966/312.

SCHEDULE 14

Section 29.

AMENDMENTS OF CORPORATION TAX ACTS

PART I

CLOSE COMPANIES

Staff housing schemes

1965 c. 25. 1.—(1) Subject to the provisions of this paragraph, section 75 of the Finance Act 1965 (loans to shareholders and others) shall not apply to a loan made to a director or employee of the close company, or of an associated company of the close company, under a bona fide scheme for assisting the purchase of houses by members of the staff of the close company, or of any associated company of the close company.

(2) This paragraph applies only if—

(*a*) the loan is used for the purpose of purchasing a dwelling which is or will be the borrower's only or main residence, and

(*b*) neither the amount of the loan, nor that amount when taken with any other outstanding loans made for the same purpose, by the close company or any of its associated companies to the borrower, or to the wife or husband of the borrower, exceeds £10,000, and

(*c*) the borrower works full-time for the close company, or any of its associated companies, and

(*d*) the borrower does not have a material interest in the close company or in any associated company of the close company.

(3) This paragraph has effect as respects any loan made on or after 15th April 1969.

1965 c. 25. *Other amendments of section* 75 *of the Finance Act* 1965

2.—(1) For the purposes of section 75 of the Finance Act 1965 the cases in which a close company is to be regarded as making a loan to any person include a case where—

(*a*) that person incurs a debt to the close company, or

(*b*) a debt due from that person to a third party is assigned to the close company,

and then the close company shall be regarded as making a loan of an amount equal to the debt.

(2) Sub-paragraph (1)(*a*) above shall not apply to a debt incurred for the supply by the close company of goods or services in the ordinary course of its trade or business unless the credit given exceeds six months or is longer than that normally given to the company's customers.

(3) For subsection (6)(*a*) of the said section 75 substitute—

"(*a*) a close company makes a loan or advance which, apart from this subsection, does not give rise to any charge on the company under subsection (1) above, and".

(4) This paragraph has effect as respects any loan, advance or debt made or incurred on or after 15th April 1969. Sch. 14

Abatement of shortfall for small companies

3.—(1) The part of the proviso to section 77(2) of the Finance Act 1965 concerning a trading company without an associated company shall be amended as follows. 1965 c. 25.

(2) If the trading company has got an associated company in the accounting period, the proviso shall apply with the omission of the words " not having any associated company ", and both the proviso and subsection (3)(*c*) of the said section 77 shall apply as if for £9,000 and £1,500 there were substituted—

(*a*) £4,500 and £750 unless the trading company has got more than one associated company in the accounting period,

(*b*) £3,000 and £500 if the trading company has got just two associated companies in the accounting period,

and so on dividing the £9,000 and £1,500 by one plus the number of associated companies which the trading company has got in the accounting period.

(3) In applying the proviso, and this paragraph, to any accounting period of the trading company, an associated company which has not carried on any trade or business at any time in that accounting period (or, if an associated company during part only of that accounting period, at any time in that part of that accounting period) shall be disregarded.

(4) For the purposes of the proviso and this paragraph, a company is to be treated as another's " associated company " at a given time if at that time one of the two has control of the other or both are under the control of the same person or persons.

For the said purposes this sub-paragraph has effect instead of paragraph 2 of Schedule 18 to the Finance Act 1965.

(5) In determining how many associated companies a trading company has got in an accounting period, an associated company shall be counted even if it was an associated company for part only of the accounting period, and two or more associated companies shall be counted even if they were associated companies for different parts of the accounting period.

(6) In the proviso " not having any associated company " shall be construed in accordance with the last preceding sub-paragraph, and section 77(3)(*d*) of the Finance Act 1965 (trading company without an associated company for part only of an accounting period) shall cease to have effect.

(7) This paragraph has effect for any accounting period ending after 15th April 1969:

Provided that in the case of any such period beginning on or before that date the relief to be given under the proviso shall be the aggregate of—

(*a*) the relief, if any, which would have been given if this paragraph (and the consequential repeal of the said section

SCH. 14 77(3)(*d*)) had not had effect, reduced in the proportion which so much of the accounting period as has elapsed before 16th April 1969 bears to the whole,

(*b*) the relief which would have been given apart from this proviso, reduced in the proportion which the remainder of the accounting period bears to the whole.

Distributions : interest paid to directors and directors' associates

4.—(1) This paragraph has effect where in any accounting period any interest is paid by a close company to, or to an associate of, a person—

(*a*) who is a director of the close company, or of any company which controls, or is controlled by, the close company, and

(*b*) who has a material interest—

(i) in the close company, or

(ii) where the close company is controlled by another company, in that other company.

(2) If the total amount so paid to any person in the accounting period exceeds the limit imposed in his case, the excess shall be a distribution made by the close company to that person.

(3) The limit shall be worked out in the first instance as an overall limit applying to the aggregate of all interest which is within sub-paragraph (1) above and which was paid by the close company in the accounting period, and, where there are two or more different recipients, that overall limit shall be apportioned between them according to the amounts of interest paid to them respectively.

(4) The overall limit shall be a sum equal to interest at 8 per cent. per annum on whichever is the less of—

(*a*) the total of the loans, advances and credits on which the interest within sub-paragraph (1) above was paid by the close company in the accounting period, or if that total was different at different times in the accounting period, the average total over the accounting period, and

(*b*) the nominal amount of the issued share capital of the close company plus the amount of any share premium account (or other comparable account by whatever name called) of the company, taking both amounts as at the beginning of the accounting period.

(5) In this paragraph " interest " includes any other consideration paid or given by the close company for the use of money advanced, or credit given, by any person, and references to interest " paid " shall be construed accordingly.

1965 c. 25. (6) This paragraph has effect instead of paragraph (*a*) of paragraph 9(1) of Schedule 11 to the Finance Act 1965, and shall be construed as if contained in Part II of that Schedule and subject to paragraph 9(4) of that Schedule.

(7) This paragraph has effect as respects any accounting period ending after 15th April 1969: Sch. 14

Provided that for the purposes of this paragraph an accounting period beginning on or before the said date, and ending after that date, shall be treated as two separate accounting periods the first of which ends with that date.

Close company controlled by another company: meaning of "participator"

5.—(1) For the purposes of sections 75 and 76 of the Finance Act 1965, and Part II of Schedule 11 to that Act, any participator in a company which controls another company shall be treated as being also a participator in that other company. 1965 c. 25.

(2) This paragraph has effect—

(*a*) for the purposes of the said section 75, as respects any loan or advance made on or after 15th April 1969,

(*b*) for the purposes of the said section 76, in respect of any payment made or consideration given by a company on or after that date, and

(*c*) for the purposes of the said Part II, in determining what are distributions made on or after that date.

Stock exchanges outside the United Kingdom

6.—(1) At the end of the definition of "recognised stock exchange" in section 89(2) of the Finance Act 1965 (which affects the definition of "close company" in Schedule 18 to that Act) add—

"and any such stock exchange outside the United Kingdom as is for the time being designated for the purposes of this section as a recognised stock exchange by order made by the Board.".

(2) An order made by the Board under the said section 89(2) as amended by this paragraph—

(*a*) may designate a stock exchange by name, or by reference to any class or description of stock exchanges, including a class or description framed by reference to any authority or approval given in a country outside the United Kingdom,

(*b*) may contain such transitional and other supplemental provisions as appear to the Board to be necessary or expedient, and

(*c*) may be varied or revoked by a subsequent order so made.

Interpretation

7.—(1) For the purposes of this Part of this Schedule a person has a material interest in a company—

(*a*) if he, either on his own or with any one or more of his associates, or if any associate of his with or without any other such associates, is the beneficial owner of, or able,

SCH. 14 directly or through the medium of other companies or by any other indirect means, to control, more than 5 per cent. of the ordinary share capital of the company, or

(*b*) if, on an amount equal to the whole distributable income of the company falling under Part IV of the Finance Act 1965 to be apportioned for the purposes of surtax, more than 5 per cent. of that amount could be apportioned to him together with his associates (if any), or to any associate of his, or any such associates taken together.

1965 c. 25.

(2) In this Part of this Schedule—

"control" in references to control of a company shall be construed in accordance with paragraph 3 of Schedule 18 to the Finance Act 1965,

"ordinary share capital" means all the issued share capital, by whatever name called, other than capital the holders whereof have a right to a dividend at a fixed rate or a rate fluctuating in accordance with the standard rate of income tax, but have no other right to share in the profits of the company.

PART II

OTHER AMENDMENTS OF CORPORATION TAX ACTS

Non-resident life assurance companies: investment income and annuity business

8.—(1) The following provisions of this paragraph shall have effect with respect to accounting periods ending after 15th April 1969 of any assurance company having its head office outside the United Kingdom but carrying on life assurance business through a branch or agency in the United Kingdom.

1952 c. 10. (2) For subsection (2) of section 430 of the Income Tax Act 1952 (apportionment of world non-annuity investment income of companies by reference to the proportion of total premiums received from United Kingdom policy holders or on a basis prescribed by the Commissioners of Inland Revenue) there shall be substituted the following subsection—

"(2) A portion only of the income from the investments of the life assurance fund (excluding the annuity fund, if any) shall be so charged and for any accounting period that portion shall be determined by the formula $\frac{A \times B}{C}$

where—

A is the total income from those investments for that period,

B is the average of the liabilities for that period to policy holders resident in the United Kingdom and to policy holders resident abroad whose proposals were made to the company at or through its branch or agency in the United Kingdom, and Sch. 14

C is the average of the liabilities for that period to all the company's policy holders,

but any reference in this subsection to liabilities does not include liabilities in respect of annuity business."

(3) In subsection (4) of section 24 of the Finance Act 1956 (apportionment of profits arising to companies from pension annuity business and general annuity business by reference to the said section 430(2)) for the words from "from pension annuity business" to the end of the subsection there shall be substituted the words "from general annuity business shall extend only to a portion of the profits arising from that business and that portion shall be determined by the formula $\frac{A \times B}{C}$ 1956 c. 54.

where—

A is the total amount of those profits,

B is the average of the liabilities attributable to that business for the relevant accounting period in respect of contracts with persons resident in the United Kingdom or contracts with persons resident abroad whose proposals were made to the company at or through its branch or agency in the United Kingdom, and

C is the average of the liabilities attributable to that business for that accounting period in respect of all contracts".

(4) For the purposes of the said sections 430(2) and 24(4), as amended by sub-paragraphs (2) and (3) above, the average of any liabilities for an accounting period shall be taken as one half of the aggregate of the liabilities at the beginning and end of the valuation period which coincides with that accounting period or in which that accounting period falls.

(5) For the purposes of this paragraph the liabilities of an assurance company attributable to any business at any time shall be ascertained by reference to the net liabilities of the company as valued by an actuary for the purposes of the relevant periodical return, and for this purpose "periodical return" means a return deposited with the Board of Trade under the Insurance Companies Act 1958 or a return required to be made under the corresponding enactment in force in Northern Ireland. 1958 c. 27.

(6) The relief under section 69(1) of the Finance Act 1965 available to such a company as is referred to in sub-paragraph (1) above in respect of its expenses of management shall be limited to expenses attributable to the life assurance business carried on by the company at or through its branch or agency in the United Kingdom. 1965 c. 25.

(7) Subsections (4) and (5) of the said section 430 (which are superseded by the provisions of this paragraph and of the Finance Act 1965) shall cease to have effect.

SCH. 14

Non-resident life assurance companies : determination of profits and reliefs

9.—(1) Nothing in the Corporation Tax Acts shall prevent the distributions of companies resident in the United Kingdom from being taken into account as part of the profits in computing, under section 24 of the Finance Act 1956, the profits arising from pension annuity business and general annuity business to a life assurance company falling within paragraph 8(1) above.

1956 c. 54.

1965 c. 25.

(2) For the purposes of subsection (3) of section 50 of the Finance Act 1965 (which provides that if a company not resident in the United Kingdom receives any payment on which it bears income tax by deduction and that payment is taken into account in computing its income for corporation tax, the income tax so deducted may be set off against any corporation tax to which the company is assessed) as it applies to life assurance companies, the amount of the income tax referred to in that subsection which shall be available for set-off under that subsection in an accounting period shall be limited in accordance with paragraphs (*a*) and (*b*) below, that is to say,—

1952 c. 10.

(*a*) if the company is chargeable to corporation tax for an accounting period in accordance with section 430 of the Income Tax Act 1952 in respect of the income from the investments of its life assurance fund, the amount of income tax available for set-off against any corporation tax assessed for that period on that income shall not exceed an amount equal to income tax at the standard rate on the portion of income from investments which is chargeable to corporation tax by virtue of subsection (2) of the said section 430 ; and

(*b*) if the company is chargeable to corporation tax for an accounting period in accordance with subsection (4) of section 24 of the Finance Act 1956 on a proportion of the total amount of the profits arising from its general annuity business, the amount of income tax available for set-off against any corporation tax assessed for that period on those profits shall not exceed an amount equal to income tax at the standard rate on the like proportion of the income from investments included in computing those profits.

1952 c. 10.

(3) The provisions of sub-paragraph (4) below apply in relation to a life assurance company falling within paragraph 8(1) above if, by virtue of arrangements specified in an Order in Council under section 347 of the Income Tax Act 1952 (double taxation relief orders), no charge to corporation tax under Case III of Schedule D arises under section 430 of that Act (as applied by section 69(3)(*c*) of the Finance Act 1965) in respect of any income of the company from the investments of its life assurance fund (excluding the annuity fund, if any) ; and any reference in sub-paragraph (4) below to a " company not chargeable under section 430 " shall be construed accordingly.

(4) For the purposes of section 62 of the Finance Act 1965 (set-off of losses etc. against franked investment income), so much of

any distributions received in the year 1966-67 or any subsequent year of assessment from a company resident in the United Kingdom by a company not chargeable under section 430 as is received in respect of the portion of the investments of its life assurance fund (excluding the annuity fund, if any) attributable to the business of its branch or agency in the United Kingdom shall be deemed to be franked investment income of that company, and accordingly the company may make a claim under subsection (1) of that section for any of the purposes specified in subsection (2) thereof. SCH. 14

(5) This paragraph shall have effect as if it had been enacted at the same time as Part IV of the Finance Act 1965 was enacted. 1965 c. 25.

Distribution materially reducing value of a dealing company's holding

10.—(1) Sub-paragraph (2) below applies where a company has, as a dealing company, a holding in another company resident in the United Kingdom (being a body corporate), and—

(*a*) the holding amounts to, or is an ingredient in a holding amounting to, 10 per cent. of all holdings of the same class in that company, and

(*b*) after 29th April 1969 a distribution is, or two or more distributions are, made in respect of the holding, and

(*c*) the value (at any accounting date or immediately before realisation or appropriation) of any security comprised in the holding is materially reduced below the value of the security at the time when it was acquired, and the whole or any part of this reduction is attributable to any distribution falling within paragraph (*b*) above,

and in relation to any security comprised in the holding, the company having the holding is in sub-paragraph (2) below referred to as " the dealing company " and so much of any reduction in the value of the security as is attributable to any distribution falling within paragraph (*b*) above is in that sub-paragraph referred to as " the relevant reduction ".

(2) Where this sub-paragraph applies, an amount equal to the relevant reduction in the value of a security comprised in the holding—

(*a*) shall, if and so long as the security is not realised or appropriated as mentioned below, be added to the value of the security for the purposes of any valuation ;

(*b*) shall be treated, on any realisation of the security in the course of trade, as a trading receipt of the dealing company or, in the event of a partial realisation, shall be so treated to an appropriate extent ; and

(*c*) shall be treated as a trading receipt of the dealing company if the security is appropriated in such circumstances that a profit on the sale of the security would no longer form part of the dealing company's trading profits.

SCH. 14 (3) References in this paragraph to a holding in a company refer to a holding of securities by virtue of which the holder may receive distributions made by the company, but so that—

(*a*) a company's holdings of different classes in another company shall be treated as separate holdings, and

(*b*) holdings of securities which differ in the entitlements or obligations they confer or impose shall be regarded as holdings of different classes.

(4) For the purposes of sub-paragraph (2) above—

(*a*) all a company's holdings of the same class in another company are to be treated as ingredients constituting a single holding, and

(*b*) a company's holding of a particular class shall be treated as an ingredient in a holding amounting to 10 per cent. of all holdings of that class if the aggregate of that holding and other holdings of that class held by connected persons amounts to 10 per cent. of all holdings of that class,

1965 c. 25. and paragraph 21 of Schedule 7 to the Finance Act 1965 (which defines " connected persons " for the purposes of Part III of that Act) shall have effect in relation to paragraph (*b*) above as if, in sub-paragraph (7) of the said paragraph 21, after the words " or exercise control of " in each place where they occur there were inserted the words " or to acquire a holding in ".

(5) Where this paragraph applies in relation to a distribution which
1959 c. 58. consists of or includes interest to which section 24 of the Finance Act 1959 (purchase and sale of securities: dealers) applies, any reduction under that section in the price paid for the securities in respect of which the distribution is made shall be adjusted in such manner as seem appropriate to the Board to take account of sub-paragraph (2) above.

(6) In relation to any distribution made after 29th April 1969,
1966 c. 18. paragraph (*a*) of section 31(4) of the Finance Act 1966 (limitations under double taxation agreements included in references to exemptions from income tax in section 65(5) of the Finance Act 1965) shall be amended by substituting for the words from " exemption " to the end of the paragraph the words " exemption from tax in section
1960 c. 44. 28(2)(*a*) of the Finance Act 1960 (cancellation of tax advantages from certain transactions in securities) and ".

(7) For the purposes of this paragraph " security " includes a share or other right and a company is a " dealing company " in relation to a holding if a profit on a sale of the holding would be taken into account in computing the company's trading profits.

Bondwashing

11.—(1) Where in a case falling within section 23 of the Finance Act 1959 (purchase and sale of securities) the first buyer is a company which does not carry on a trade falling within section 24 of that Act (dealers), the appropriate amount in respect of the interest as determined in accordance with Schedule 6 to that Act and any tax paid in respect of or deducted from that amount shall be disregarded except that, for the purposes of corporation tax on chargeable gains— SCH. 14

(a) where that appropriate amount is determined in accordance with paragraph 2 of that Schedule, the appropriate proportion of the net interest receivable by the first buyer as mentioned in that paragraph, and

(b) where that appropriate amount is determined in accordance with paragraph 4 of that Schedule, the net amount of interest corresponding to the gross interest referred to in that paragraph,

shall be treated as if it were a capital distribution within the meaning of Part III of the Finance Act 1965 received in respect of the holding of the securities concerned. 1965 c. 25.

(2) This paragraph applies to any interest received after 29th April 1969.

SCHEDULE 15

Section 30.

DISALLOWANCE OF TRADING LOSSES

Change of ownership of company

1. For the purposes of the principal section there is a change in the ownership of a company—

(a) if a single person acquires more than half the ordinary share capital of the company, or

(b) if two or more persons each acquire a holding of 5 per cent. or more of the ordinary share capital of the company, and those holdings together amount to more than half the ordinary share capital of the company, or

(c) if two or more persons each acquire a holding of the ordinary share capital of the company, and the holdings together amount to more than half the ordinary share capital of the company, but disregarding a holding of less than 5 per cent. unless it is an addition to an existing holding and the two holdings together amount to 5 per cent. or more of the ordinary share capital of the company.

2. In applying paragraph 1 above—

(a) the circumstances at any two points of time with not more than three years between may be compared, and a holder at the later time may be regarded as having acquired whatever he did not hold at the earlier time, irrespective of what he has acquired or disposed of in between,

(b) to allow for any issue of shares or other reorganisation of capital, the comparison may be made in terms of percentage holdings of the total ordinary share capital at the respective times, so that a person whose percentage holding is greater at the later time may be regarded as having acquired a percentage holding equal to the increase,

SCH. 15

(*c*) to decide for the purposes of paragraph (1)(*b*) or (*c*) above if any person has acquired a holding of at least 5 per cent., or a holding which makes at least 5 per cent. when added to an existing holding, acquisitions by, and holdings of, two or more persons who are connected persons within the meaning of paragraph 21 of Schedule 7 to the Finance Act 1965 shall be aggregated as if they were acquisitions by, and holdings of, one and the same person,

1965 c. 25.

(*d*) any acquisition of shares under the will or on the intestacy of a deceased person and, if it is shown that the gift is unsolicited and made without regard to the provisions of the principal section, any gift of shares, shall be left out of account.

3. Where, because persons, whether company members or not, possess extraordinary rights or powers under the articles of association or under any other document regulating the company, ownership of ordinary share capital may not be an appropriate test of whether there has been a major change in the persons for whose benefit the losses may ultimately enure, then in considering whether there has been a change of ownership of the company for the purposes of the principal section, holdings of all kinds of share capital, including preference shares, or of any particular category of share capital, or voting power or any other special kind of power, may be taken into account instead of ordinary share capital.

4. Where the principal section has operated to restrict relief by reference to a change of ownership taking place at any time, no transaction or circumstances before that time shall be taken into account in determining whether there is any subsequent change of ownership.

Groups of companies

5.—(1) A change in the ownership of a company shall be disregarded for the purposes of the principal section if—

(*a*) immediately before the change the company is the 75 per cent. subsidiary of another company, and

(*b*) (although there is a change in the direct ownership of the company) that other company continues after the change to own the first-mentioned company as a 75 per cent. subsidiary.

(2) If there is a change in the ownership of a company which has a 75 per cent. subsidiary (whether owned directly or indirectly) then, unless under sub-paragraph (1) above that change in ownership is to be disregarded, the principal section shall apply as if there had also been a change in the ownership of that 75 per cent. subsidiary.

Provisions as to ownership

6. For the purposes of this Schedule—

(*a*) references to ownership shall be construed as references to beneficial ownership, and references to acquisition shall be construed accordingly,

(b) the expression "ordinary share capital" in relation to a company means all the issued share capital (by whatever name called) of the company, other than capital the holders whereof have a right to a dividend at a fixed rate or at a rate fluctuating in accordance with the standard rate of income tax, but have no other right to share in the profits of the company, SCH. 15

(c) a company shall be deemed to be a 75 per cent. subsidiary of another company if and so long as not less than three quarters of its ordinary share capital is owned by that other company, whether directly or through another company or other companies, or partly directly and partly through another company or other companies,

(d) the amount of ordinary share capital of one company owned by a second company through another company or other companies, or partly directly and partly through another company or other companies, shall be determined in accordance with the provisions of Part I of Schedule 4 to the Finance Act 1938, 1938 c. 46.

(e) "share" includes "stock".

Time of change of ownership

7. If any acquisition of ordinary share capital or other property or rights taken into account in determining that there has been a change of ownership of a company was made in pursuance of a contract of sale or option or other contract, or the acquisition was made by a person holding such a contract, and the contract was made on or after 15th April 1969, the time when the change in the ownership of the company took place shall be determined as if the acquisiton had been made when the contract was made with the holder or when the benefit of it was assigned to him so that, in the case of a person exercising an option to purchase shares, he shall be regarded as having purchased the shares when he acquired the option.

Capital allowances

8. Where relief in respect of a company's losses has been restricted under the principal section then, notwithstanding section 87(3) of the Capital Allowances Act 1968, in applying the provisions of that 1968 c. 3. Act about balancing charges to the company by reference to any event after the change of ownership of the company, any allowance or deduction falling to be made in taxing the company's trade for any chargeable period before the change of ownership shall be disregarded unless the profits or gains of that chargeable period or of any subsequent chargeable period before the change of ownership were sufficient to give effect to the allowance or deduction.

In applying this paragraph it shall be assumed that any profits or gains are applied in giving effect to any such allowance or deduction in preference to being set off against any loss which is not attributable to such an allowance or deduction.

SCH. 15

Time allowed for making assessments

9. Where the operation of the principal section depends on circumstances or events at a time after the change of ownership (but not more than three years after), an assessment to give effect to the provisions of that section shall not be out of time if made within six years from that time, or the latest of those times.

Information

10. Any person in whose name any shares, stock or securities of a company are registered shall, if required by notice in writing by an inspector given for the purposes of the principal section, state whether or not he is the beneficial owner of those shares or securities and, if not the beneficial owner of those shares or securities or any of them, shall furnish the name and address of the person or persons on whose behalf those shares, stock or securities are registered in his name.

1960 c. 44. Part III of the Finance Act 1960 (penalties) shall have effect as if this paragraph were among the provisions specified in column 2 of Schedule 6 to that Act.

Sections 31 and 32.

SCHEDULE 16

TAX AVOIDANCE: SUPPLEMENTAL PROVISIONS

Artificial transactions

1.—(1) In applying the principal sections and this Schedule account shall be taken of any method, however indirect, by which—

(*a*) any property or right is transferred or transmitted, or

(*b*) the value of any property or right is enhanced or diminished,

and accordingly the occasion of the transfer or transmission of any property or right, however indirect, and the occasion when the value of any property or right is enhanced, may be an occasion when, under the principal sections, tax becomes chargeable.

(2) This paragraph applies in particular—

(*a*) to sales, contracts and other transactions made otherwise than for full consideration or for more than full consideration, and

(*b*) to any method by which any property or right, or the control of any property or right, is transferred or transmitted by assigning share capital or other rights in a company or any partnership or interest in settled property, and

(*c*) to the creation of any option or consent or embargo affecting the disposition of any property or right, and to the consideration given for the option, or for the giving of the consent or the release of the embargo, and

(*d*) to the disposal of any property or right on the winding up, dissolution or termination of any company, partnership or trust.

(3) In ascertaining for the said purposes the intentions of any person, the objects and powers of any company, partners or trustees, as set out in any memorandum, articles of association or other document, shall not be conclusive. Sch. 16

Value derived from underlying assets

2. In order to ascertain whether and to what extent the value of any property or right is derived from any other property or right, value may be traced through any number of companies, partnerships and trusts, and the property held by any company, partnership or trust shall be attributed to the shareholders, partners or beneficiaries at each stage in such manner as is appropriate in the circumstances.

Apportionments and valuations

3. In applying the principal sections and this Schedule—

(*a*) any expenditure or receipt or consideration or other amount may be apportioned by such method as is just and reasonable in the circumstances,

(*b*) all such valuations shall be made as are appropriate to give effect to the principal sections.

Sale of income derived from personal activities

4.—(1) This paragraph has effect where on any occasion an individual obtains a capital amount consisting of any property or right which derives substantially the whole of its value from the activities of the individual, or (as in the case where the individual acquires a stock option and subsequently exercises the stock option) there are two or more occasions on which an individual obtains a capital amount consisting of any such property or right.

(2) Tax under section 31 of this Act shall not be charged on any such occasion, but, without prejudice to the generality of the provisions of that section or this Schedule, tax under that section shall be charged on the occasion when the capital amount, or any such capital amount, is sold or otherwise realised, and shall be so charged by reference to the proceeds of sale or the realised value.

Persons acting in different capacities

5. For the purposes of the principal sections and this Schedule, and in particular for the purpose of the reference in section 31 of this Act to an individual putting some other person in a position to enjoy income or receipts, partners, or the trustees of settled property, or personal representatives, may be regarded as persons distinct from the individuals or other persons who are for the time being partners or trustees or personal representatives.

SCH. 16

Person assessed to tax in respect of consideration received by another

6.—(1) Where a person is assessed to tax under either of the principal sections, with this Schedule, in respect of consideration receivable by another person—

(*a*) he shall be entitled to recover from that other person any part of that tax which he has paid, and

(*b*) if any part of that tax remains unpaid at the expiration of six months from the date when it became due and payable, it shall be recoverable from that other person as though he were the person assessed, but without prejudice to the right to recover it from the person actually assessed,

and for the purposes of paragraph (*a*) above the Board or an inspector shall on request furnish a certificate specifying the amount of income in respect of which tax has been paid, and the amount of tax so paid ; and the certificate shall be conclusive evidence of any facts stated therein.

(2) For the purposes of this paragraph any income which a person is treated as having by virtue of the principal sections shall be treated as the highest part of his income.

Persons resident outside the United Kingdom

7.—(1) Section 31 of this Act shall apply to all persons, whether resident in the United Kingdom or not, if the occupation of the individual is carried on wholly or partly in the United Kingdom.

(2) Section 32 of this Act shall apply to all persons, whether resident in the United Kingdom or not, if all or any part of the land in question is situated in the United Kingdom.

(3) If it appears to the Board that any person entitled to any consideration or other amount taxable under the principal sections is not resident in the United Kingdom, the Board may direct that
1952 c. 10. section 170 of the Income Tax Act 1952 (payments not made out of profits or gains brought into charge to income tax) shall apply to any payment forming part of that amount as if it were an annual payment charged with tax under Schedule D, but without prejudice to the final determination of the liability of that person, including any liability under paragraph 6(1)(*b*) above.

Power to obtain information

8.—(1) The Board or an inspector may by notice in writing require any person to furnish them within such time as the Board or the inspector may direct (not being less than thirty days) with such particulars as the Board or the inspector think necessary for the purposes of the principal sections.

(2) The particulars which a person must furnish under this paragraph, if he is required by a notice from the Board or the inspector so to do, include particulars—

(*a*) as to transactions or arrangements with respect to which he is or was acting on behalf of others, and

SCH. 16

(b) as to transactions or arrangements which in the opinion of the Board or the inspector should properly be investigated for the purposes of the principal sections notwithstanding that, in the opinion of the person to whom the notice is given, no liability to tax arises under the principal sections, and

(c) as to whether the person to whom the notice is given has taken or is taking any, and if so what, part in any, and if so what, transactions or arrangements of a description specified in the notice.

(3) Notwithstanding anything in sub-paragraph (2) above, a solicitor shall not be deemed for the purposes of sub-paragraph (2)(c) above to have taken part in any transaction or arrangements by reason only that he has given professional advice to a client in connection with the transaction or arrangements, and shall not, in relation to anything done by him on behalf of a client, be compellable under this paragraph, except with the consent of his client, to do more than state that he is or was acting on behalf of a client, and give the name and address of his client.

(4) Part III of the Finance Act 1960 (penalties) shall have effect as if this paragraph were included in column 2 of Schedule 6 to that Act. 1960 c. 44.

Settlements

9. The principal sections have effect subject to Part XVIII of the Income Tax Act 1952 (settlements) and to any other provision of the Income Tax Acts deeming income to belong to a particular person. 1952 c. 10.

Tax on capital gains

10.—(1) Where under subsection (2)(c) of section 32 of this Act any person is charged to tax on the realisation of a gain, and the computation of the gain proceeded on the footing that the land or some other property was appropriated at any time as trading stock that land or other property shall be treated on that footing also for the purposes of paragraph 1 of Schedule 7 to the Finance Act 1965 and paragraph 12 of Schedule 14 to the Finance Act 1967 (capital gains: property becoming or ceasing to be stock in trade). 1965 c. 25. 1967 c. 54.

(2) Where under subsection (1)(b) of section 31 or subsection (8) of section 32 of this Act the person charged to tax is a person other than the person for whom the capital amount was obtained or the person by whom the gain was realised, and the tax has been paid, then for the purposes of paragraphs 2 and 5 of Schedule 6 to the Finance Act 1965 (profits taxable as income to be excluded from tax on capital gains), the person for whom the capital amount was obtained or the person by whom the gain was realised shall be regarded as having been charged to that tax.

SCH. 16

Interpretation

11.—(1) For the purposes of the principal sections and this Schedule—

"capital amount" means any amount, in money or money's worth, which, apart from the principal sections, does not fall to be included in any computation of income for purposes of the Income Tax Acts or the Corporation Tax Acts, and other expressions including the word "capital" shall be construed accordingly,

"company" includes any body corporate,

"ordinary share capital" has the meaning given by section 42(3) of the Finance Act 1938, (1938 c. 46.)

"share" includes stock

(2) For the said purposes any amount in money or money's worth shall not be regarded as having become receivable by some person until that person can effectively enjoy or dispose of it.

Sections 35 and 40.

SCHEDULE 17

ESTATE DUTY

PART I

DETERMINATION OF AMOUNT OF ESTATE DUTY ON ESTATE

The amount of the estate duty on an estate—

(*a*) if the aggregate principal value of all property comprised in the estate does not exceed £10,000, shall be nil;

(*b*) in any other case, shall be an amount equal to the aggregate of—

(i) 25 per cent. of any amount by which that aggregate principal value exceeds £10,000 but does not exceed £17,500; and

(ii) 30 per cent. of any amount by which that aggregate principal value exceeds £17,500 but does not exceed £30,000; and

(iii) 45 per cent. of any amount by which that aggregate principal value exceeds £30,000 but does not exceed £40,000; and

(iv) 60 per cent. of any amount by which that aggregate principal value exceeds £40,000 but does not exceed £80,000; and

(v) 65 per cent. of any amount by which that aggregate principal value exceeds £80,000 but does not exceed £150,000; and

(vi) 70 per cent. of any amount by which that aggregate principal value exceeds £150,000 but does not exceed £300,000; and

(vii) 75 per cent. of any amount by which that aggregate principal value exceeds £300,000 but does not exceed £500,000; and

(viii) 80 per cent. of any amount by which that aggregate principal value exceeds £500,000 but does not exceed £750,000 ; and SCH. 17

(ix) 85 per cent. of any amount by which that aggregate principal value exceeds £750,000,

but not exceeding an amount equal to 80 per cent. of that aggregate principal value.

PART II

SUPPLEMENTARY PROVISIONS

Treatment of interest of controlled company as interest of members

1. Where a company such as is mentioned in section 58(1) of the Finance Act 1940 has been entitled to a beneficial interest in possession in any settled property, or where the whole or part of the income of any settled property has, under such a trust as is mentioned in sub-paragraph (iii) of the substituted section 2(1)(*b*), been paid to or applied for the benefit of such a company, then, for the purposes of the substituted section 2(1)(*b*), each of the persons who would in the circumstances mentioned in section 56(1) of the Finance Act 1940 have been a person on trust for whom the company held that interest or income shall, to the like extent as that to which the company's assets would in the said circumstances have been held on trust for him, be deemed to have been entitled to the like interest in that property or, as the case may be, to have been a person to whom or for whose benefit that income was paid or applied. 1940 c. 29.

Relief in respect of settlement which has come to an end

2.—(1) Except as provided by section 38(1) of this Act, estate duty shall not be chargeable on a death by virtue of any of the sub-paragraphs of the substituted section 2(1)(*b*) on any property which has been settled property if the duty would be chargeable by reason of an interest under the settlement and the settlement has come to an end before the death by reason of the deceased's having become absolutely and indefeasibly entitled to the property or having attained full age.

(2) For the purposes of the foregoing sub-paragraph, where a settlement has come to an end as respects part but not all of the property comprised in it, there shall be deemed to have been a separate settlement of that part.

Relief in respect of interest which has determined or been disposed of

3. Where on any death estate duty falls to be charged on any property by virtue of any of the sub-paragraphs of the substituted section 2(1)(*b*) by reason of an interest in that property which determined or was disposed of at a date before the death, and since that date the deceased was at all times during a period of not less

SCH. 17 than four years ending with the date of the death entirely excluded from possession and enjoyment of the property and from any benefit to him by contract or otherwise, the value on which the duty is chargeable shall be reduced—

(*a*) if that period was less than five years, by fifteen per cent.;

(*b*) if that period was not less than five but less than six years, by thirty per cent.;

(*c*) if that period was not less than six years, by sixty per cent.

Provisions as to exclusion from benefit

4. Where, in the case of any property which at the death of any person is or has been comprised in a settlement, the deceased was entitled to an interest in that property which determined before his death, he shall not be treated for the purposes of the substituted section 2(1)(*b*) as not having been entirely excluded from possession and enjoyment of the property and from any benefit to him by contract or otherwise at any time after the date of the determination by reason only of his having been entitled at that time to another interest in that property if estate duty would have been, or would
1949 c. 47. but for section 28(2) of the Finance Act 1949 have been, or would if he had received any benefit by virtue of that other interest have been, chargeable on the property by virtue of the substituted section 2(1)(*b*) by reason of that other interest on his death at that time.

5. For the purposes of estate duty, a person who has been entitled to a beneficial interest in possession in settled property which has determined or been disposed of shall not be treated as entirely excluded from possession and enjoyment of the property and any benefit to him by contract or otherwise at any time after the determination or disposition at which he has a benefit by virtue of any
1940 c. 29. associated operations as defined by section 59 of the Finance Act 1940 which include any disposition resulting in, or effected in contemplation of or with reference to, the determination or, as the case may be, which include the disposition; and, where a company such as is mentioned in section 58(1) of the Finance Act 1940 was concerned in the determination or disposition or in those associated operations, any condition as to that person's being excluded as aforesaid contained in any of the enactments relating to estate duty shall be treated as satisfied if and only if it would have been so treated in the circumstances mentioned in section 56(1) of that Act.

Relief for trusts in respect of death of surviving spouse

6.—(1) Where a part of the property comprised in a settlement has
1894 c. 30. been treated by virtue of section 2(1)(*b*) of the Finance Act 1894, whether before or after the substitution made by section 36(2) of this Act, as passing on the death of one of the parties to a marriage and a part of the same property falls to be treated as passing by virtue of the substituted section 2(1)(*b*) on the later death of the other party to the marriage, and in the case of either of those deaths the part in question was treated as passing on that death by virtue of sub-paragraph (iii) or (iv) of the substituted section (2)(1)(*b*), then,

for the purposes of section 5(2) of the Finance Act 1894 (which relates to relief on the death of the surviving party to a marriage), there shall be treated as property passing on the later death in respect of which estate duty was paid on the earlier death a proportion of the part of the property comprised in the settlement which is treated as passing on the later death equal to whichever is the less of— SCH. 17 1894 c. 30.

(*a*) the proportion of the property so comprised which was treated as passing on the earlier death ; or

(*b*) the proportion of the property so comprised which is treated as passing on the later death less the proportion of that property which would have been treated as passing on the later death if the later death had occurred at the same time as the earlier death.

(2) For the purposes of the foregoing sub-paragraph, where different parts of the property comprised in a settlement are held on different trusts, there shall be deemed to be a separate settlement of each of those parts.

Relief for trusts in cases of quick succession

7.—(1) For the purposes of section 30 of the Finance Act 1958 (which relates to quick successions), where a part of the property comprised in a settlement subsisting at the date of the earlier death was treated as passing on the earlier death by virtue of section 2(1)(*b*) of the Finance Act 1894, whether before or after the substitution made by section 36(2) of this Act, and a part of the same property is treated as passing on the later death by virtue of the substituted section 2(1)(*b*), and in either case the part in question was or is treated as passing by virtue of sub-paragraph (iii) or (iv) of the substituted section 2(1)(*b*), there shall be treated as the same property passing on each of the deaths a proportion of the part of the property comprised in that settlement which passed on the earlier death equal to the proportion which the part of the property so comprised passing on the later death bears to the whole of the property so comprised. 1958 c. 56.

(2) For the purposes of the foregoing sub-paragraph, where different parts of the property comprised in a settlement are held on different trusts, there shall be deemed to be a separate settlement of each of those parts.

Relief for trusts in respect of certain securities

8. Where on a death, apart from this paragraph, estate duty by virtue of sub-paragraph (iii) or (iv) of the substituted section 2(1)(*b*) would be chargeable on any such securities as are mentioned in section 41(1) of the Finance Act 1966 and the deceased was neither domiciled nor ordinarily resident in the United Kingdom, those securities shall be deemed to have been in the beneficial ownership of the deceased immediately before the death. 1966 c. 18.

Sch. 17

Relief for charities, corporations sole, and certain superannuation or benevolent funds

9. For the purposes of the application of any of the sub-paragraphs of the substituted section 2(1)(*b*) in relation to an interest which has determined in a case where the determination was suffered for public or charitable purposes, the substituted section 2(1)(*b*) shall have effect as if for any reference therein to seven years there were substituted a reference to one year.

10. Estate duty shall not be chargeable on any property on any death by virtue of any of the sub-paragraphs of the substituted section 2(1)(*b*)—

(*a*) where the property is held on trusts which make provision for charitable purposes only (including any reasonable remuneration which may be authorised by the trust instrument for the trustees thereunder) and under which no payment for any other purpose is authorised or has been made ; or

(*b*) by reason of any benefit to the deceased as a corporation sole ; or

(*c*) by reason of an interest of the deceased under such a scheme or in such a fund as is described in section 387(1) or (2)
1952 c. 10. of the Income Tax Act 1952, being an interest by way of a pension or annuity other than a pension or annuity under a trust, whether or not established by the instrument establishing that scheme or fund, with respect to the application of some benefit provided under that scheme or from that fund otherwise than by way of a pension or annuity.

11.—(1) Where, in the case of any property which is or has been comprised in settled property subject to such a trust as is mentioned in sub-paragraph (iii) of the substituted section 2(1)(*b*), estate duty would, apart from the provisions of this paragraph, be chargeable on that property on a death by virtue of that sub-paragraph, that duty shall not be so chargeable if—

(*a*) the discretion referred to in that sub-paragraph has not at any time been exercisable with respect to any person other than—

(i) persons of a class specified in the trust instrument by reference to employment in a particular trade, profession or statutory undertaking or by reference to employment by, or the holding of office in, a body carrying on a trade, profession or statutory undertaking ; or

(ii) persons of a class so specified by reference to marriage with, relationship to, or dependency on such persons as are mentioned in the foregoing sub-paragraph ; or

(iii) a body or trust established for charitable purposes only ; and

(*b*) the deceased was neither a person by whom, or at whose expense, or out of funds provided by whom, the settlement was made nor a relative of such a person ; and

SCH. 17

(c) the settlement was not made, and any benefit received by the deceased from the exercise of the discretion aforesaid was not received, as part of associated operations as defined by section 59 of the Finance Act 1940 the purposes of which included the provision of benefit for, or for a relative of, any such person as is referred to in paragraph (b) above. 1940 c. 29.

(2) Where any such person as is referred to in sub-paragraph (1)(b) of this paragraph was such a company as is mentioned in section 58(1) of the Finance Act 1940, each of the persons who at the date of the making of the settlement would in the circumstances mentioned in section 56(1) of that Act have been included among the persons on trust for whom the assets of the company were held shall be deemed to have been such a person as is referred to in the said sub-paragraph (1)(b).

(3) In this paragraph—

(a) the expression " relative " in relation to any person means—

(i) the wife or husband of that person ;

(ii) the father, mother, child, uncle or aunt of that person ; and

(iii) any issue of any person falling within paragraph (i) or (ii) of this sub-paragraph and the other party to a marriage with any person so falling or with any such issue ;

(b) references to " child " and " issue " include references to an illegitimate or adopted child ;

(c) references to benefit received by the deceased from the exercise of the discretion aforesaid include references to any such non-exclusion of the deceased as is referred to in sub-paragraph (iii) of the substituted section 2(1)(b).

Treatment of eligibility to benefit under discretionary trust as interest in property

12. For the purposes of the following enactments, namely—

(a) section 47 of the Finance Act 1938 (which relates to interests in undistributed residue) ; 1938 c. 46.

(b) section 51 of the Finance Act 1947 (which relates to relief from estate duty on certain bearer securities) ; 1947 c. 35.

(c) section 44 of the Finance Act 1950 (which relates to the collection of duty from trustees) ; 1950 c. 15.

(d) section 29(5) of the Finance Act 1954 (which relates to interests in certain securities) ; 1954 c. 44.

(e) section 38(12) and (13) of the Finance Act 1957 (which relate to the date by reference to which property is to be identified and valued) ; and 1957 c. 49.

(f) section 36(5)(d) of this Act and paragraphs 2, 3, 4, 5, 9 and 10(c) of this Part of this Schedule,

in the case of any property which is, or as the case may require was or is to be, held on such a trust as is mentioned in sub-paragraph (iii) of the substituted section 2(1)(b), the eligibility of a person to benefit under that trust shall be treated as if it were an interest of that

SCH. 17 person in that property which will determine on that person ceasing to be eligible to benefit under, or on that property ceasing to be subject to, that trust, and for the purposes of the said section 47 as if the executors were the trustees under that trust and the residue of the estate were property so held.

Allowance for capital gains tax

13. Where on any death estate duty falls to be charged on any settled property by virtue of the substituted section 2(1)(*b*) but subsection (4) of section 25 of the Finance Act 1965 does not apply and is not prevented from applying by reason only of subsection (6) of the said section 25, references in subsections (2) to (8) of section 26 of that Act to capital gains tax chargeable in consequence of a death shall include references to capital gains tax which would have been chargeable in consequence of the death if the said subsection (4) had applied on the death; but the allowance to be made under subsection (2) of the said section 26 by virtue of this paragraph shall be the amount of the capital gains tax which would have been so chargeable discounted at a yearly rate of interest of five per cent. for the period from the date of the death to the date when the said subsection (4) will next apply to the settled property by virtue of subsection (6) or (7) of the said section 25.

1965 c. 25.

Persons accountable for estate duty

1894 c. 30.

14. For the purposes of section 8(4) of the Finance Act 1894 (under which, where property passes on a death and the deceased's executor is not accountable for the estate duty in respect of that property, a person to whom the property passes on the death for a beneficial interest in possession is included among the persons accountable for the duty) any person who is not entitled to such a beneficial interest but to whom or for whose benefit the whole or part of the income of the property has been paid or applied at a time after the death under such a trust as is mentioned in subparagraph (iii) of the substituted section 2(1)(*b*) shall, to the extent of the income so paid or applied, be deemed to be a person to whom the property passed on the death for such a beneficial interest.

PART III

CONSEQUENTIAL AMENDMENTS

1. In section 2 of the Finance Act 1894, for subsection (3) there shall be substituted the following:—

"(3) Where in the case of any property the deceased was entitled to an estate or interest therein in a fiduciary or representative capacity or by way of security, that property shall not be treated as passing on his death by reason of that entitlement."

2. In section 3 of the Finance Act 1894, at the end there shall be added the following subsection:—

"(3) Nothing in this section shall operate to exempt any property which is or has been comprised in a settlement from being charged with estate duty by virtue of section 2(1)(*b*) of this Act on the death of the deceased or to reduce the value for the purposes of estate duty of the property charged where that property passes on the deceased's death— SCH. 17

(*a*) by reason of the deceased being or having been entitled to an interest in that property as successor for the purposes of the said section 2(1)(*b*) to an interest of a beneficiary under the settlement, or

(*b*) by reason of the operation of section 36(6)(*c*) of the Finance Act 1969 in relation to that property in a case where an interest of, or created out of, or derived from an interest of, a person who is, or is successor to an interest of, a beneficiary under a settlement is subject to such a trust as is mentioned in sub-paragraph (iii) or (iv) of the said section 2(1)(*b*).

unless that property would have been exempted under this section on the death of that beneficiary."

3. In section 16(3) of the Finance Act 1894 as substituted by section 33(1) of the Finance Act 1954— 1894 c. 30. 1954 c. 44.

(*a*) for the words " such settled property as is hereinafter mentioned " there shall be substituted the words " property which, not being or having been such settled property as is hereinafter mentioned, is chargeable with estate duty by virtue of section 2(1)(*b*) of this Act " ;

(*b*) in paragraph (*a*), for the words " that settled property " in both places where they occur there shall be substituted the words " the said property chargeable as aforesaid " ;

(*c*) in paragraph (*b*), the words from " together " onwards shall be omitted ;

(*d*) the words " any settled property other than " and the words " other than " where secondly occurring shall be omitted.

4. In section 22(2)(*a*) of the Finance Act 1894, the words " including a tenant in tail whether in possession or not " shall be omitted.

5. In section 15 of the Finance Act 1896— 1896 c. 28.

(*a*) in subsection (1) for the words from " after " to " reverter " there shall be substituted the words " the property shall not be treated for the purposes of the principal Act as passing on that person's death if it reverts " ;

(*b*) in subsection (3) at the end there shall be added the words " or where the disposition is of an interest of the disponer in settled property by reason of which, if it had been retained by the disponer, estate duty would fall to be charged by virtue of section 2(1)(*b*) of the principal Act on the death of the disponer."

6. In section 59 of the Finance (1909-10) Act 1910— 1910 c. 8.

(*a*) in subsection (2), for the words " is deemed to pass " there shall be substituted the word " passes " ;

SCH. 17 (*b*) for subsection (3) there shall be substituted the following:—

"(3) Where property taken under a disposition purporting to operate as an immediate gift inter vivos passes on the death of the deceased by reason only that the property was not, as from the date of the disposition, retained to the entire exclusion of the deceased and of any benefit to him by contract or otherwise, the property shall not be treated as passing on the deceased's death if subsequently, by means of the surrender of the benefit reserved or otherwise, it is enjoyed to the entire exclusion of the deceased and of any benefit to him by contract or otherwise for so much of the period of seven years preceding the deceased's death as falls after 19th March 1963 or, in the case of a gift for public or charitable purposes, for a period of twelve months preceding the deceased's death."

1910 c. 8. 1912 c. 8. 7. In section 61(5) of the Finance (1909-10) Act 1910 as amended by section 9 of the Finance Act 1912—

(*a*) for the word "rate" where first occurring there shall be substituted the word "amount";

(*b*) for the words "at the rate due to the principal value of the estate, be payable" there shall be substituted the words "be payable at the estate rate".

1925 c. 36. 8. In section 23(1) of the Finance Act 1925—

(*a*) for the words from "the appropriate rate" where secondly occurring to "1919" there shall be substituted the words "fifty-five per cent of the estate rate";

(*b*) for the words from "appropriate rate" where last occurring onwards there shall be substituted the words "estate rate".

1937 c. 54. 9. In section 31(3)(*b*) of the Finance Act 1937, for the words "deemed to that extent to pass" there shall be substituted the words "treated as to that extent passing".

1938 c. 46. 10. In section 47 of the Finance Act 1938—

(*a*) in subsection (1), for the words from "the death" to "cease, and" there shall be substituted the words "a death on which estate duty would fall to be charged by virtue of section 2(1)(*b*) of that Act by reason of an interest in the whole or part of the residue of the estate of a testator or intestate to which the deceased would have been, or would apart from any determination or disposition of that interest have been, entitled if the administration of the estate had been completed during the deceased's lifetime but";

(*b*) in subsections (2) to (6) for the words "such an interest" wherever they occur there shall be substituted the words "the said interest".

1940 c. 29. 11. In section 46(1) of the Finance Act 1940, for the words "on his death" in the first place where those words occur there shall be substituted the words "on the occurrence of any event, including the expiration of a fixed period".

SCH. 17

12. In section 51(2C) of the Finance Act 1940 as amended by section 38 of the Finance Act 1944, for the words "deemed to pass" there shall be substituted the words "treated as passing". 1940 c. 29. 1944 c. 23.

13. In section 17(1) of the Finance (No. 2) Act 1940— 1940 c. 48.

(*a*) for the words from "the rates" where first occurring to "mortgage" where first occurring there shall be substituted the words "by reason of an increase in the rates of duty, the amount of duty payable in the case of a person dying when the interest falls into possession is more than the amount which would have been payable if the rates had not been increased since the sale or mortgage";

(*b*) in paragraph (*a*), for the words from "if" to "mortgage" there shall be substituted the words "if the rates of duty had not been increased".

14. In section 26 of the Finance Act 1943— 1943 c. 28.

(*a*) in subsection (1), for the words from the beginning to "deceased; and" there shall be substituted the words "Section 31 of the Finance Act 1939 (which provides—"; 1939 c. 41.

(*b*) in subsection (2) for the words "those sections" in both places where they occur there shall be substituted the words "that section";

(*c*) in subsection (3), for the words "the said section 30" there shall be substituted the words "section 30 of the said Act of 1939".

15. In section 51 of the Finance Act 1947, in the proviso, for the words "or of the disposition or determination of an interest limited to cease on the death" there shall be substituted the words "or pass by virtue of section 2(1)(*b*) of the Finance Act 1894 by reason of an interest therein which has been disposed of or determined." 1947 c. 35. 1894 c. 30.

16. In section 29(5) of the Finance Act 1949, for the words "deemed to pass" there shall be substituted the words "treated as passing". 1949 c. 47.

17. In section 33(1) of the Finance Act 1949, for the words "is deemed to pass" there shall be substituted the word "passes".

18. In section 44 of the Finance Act 1950— 1950 c. 15.

(*a*) in subsection (1), for the words from "limited" to "partly" there shall be substituted the words "by reason of which estate duty is chargeable on a death by virtue of section 2(1)(*b*) of the Finance Act 1894 has wholly or partly determined or been disposed of";

(*b*) in subsections (2) to (5), for the words "the said section forty-three" wherever they occur there shall be substituted the words "the said section 2(1)(*b*)";

(*c*) in subsection (8), for the words from "as it applies" onwards there shall be substituted the words "or section 43 of the Finance Act 1940, as it applies to duty payable by virtue of section 2(1)(*b*) of the Finance Act 1894."

SCH. 17 19. In section 28 of the Finance Act 1954—

1954 c. 54. (*a*) in subsection (1) for the words from " in accordance " onwards there shall be substituted the words " at fifty-five per cent. of the estate rate ";

(*b*) in subsection (2)(*b*), for the words from " the reduced " to " said section twenty-three) " there shall be substituted the words " fifty-five per cent. of the estate rate on such proportion of that net value as is attributable to the agricultural value (within the meaning of section 23 of the

1925 c. 36. Finance Act 1925) ".

20. In section 29(5) of the Finance Act 1954, in the proviso, for the words from " a disposition " to " cease on the death " there

1894 c. 30. shall be substituted the words " section 2(1)(*b*) of the Finance Act 1894 by reason of an interest therein which has been disposed of or determined ".

1956 c. 55. 21. In section 19 of the Finance Act 1956, in subsection (3), for the words from " an amount " onwards there shall be substituted the words—

" (*a*) if the death occurred after 3rd June 1969—

(i) subject to sub-paragraph (ii) of this paragraph, the amount which would be produced by levying estate duty on the amount of that income at the estate rate applicable to the estate in question under the law in force in Great Britain or, as the case may be, in Northern Ireland or, if estate duty is payable both in Great Britain and in Northern Ireland, whichever is the higher of the respective amounts which would be so produced ;

(ii) where section 16(3)(*b*) of the Finance Act 1894 or any other provision for corresponding purposes of the law in force in Northern Ireland applies for the purpose of determining the amount of the estate duty payable in Great Britain or, as the case may be, in Northern Ireland in respect of property consisting of or including that income, the amount which would be produced as aforesaid shall be taken to be an amount equal to so much of that amount of estate duty as may reasonably be regarded as attributable to that income ;

(*b*) if the death occurred before 4th June 1969 but after 15th April 1969—

(i) in a case where estate duty is payable in Great Britain but not in Northern Ireland, the amount which would be applicable if in paragraph (*a*) of this subsection for the reference to 3rd June 1969 there were substituted a reference to 15th April 1969 ;

(ii) in a case where estate duty is payable in Northern Ireland but not in Great Britain, the amount which would be applicable under this section if the amendments and repeals made therein by the Finance Act 1969 had not been made ;

(iii) in a case where estate duty is payable both in Great Britain and in Northern Ireland, whichever is the higher of the amount which would be applicable under sub-paragraph (i) of this paragraph if estate duty were payable in Great Britain but not in Northern Ireland and the amount which would be applicable under sub-paragraph (ii) thereof if estate duty were payable in Northern Ireland but not Great Britain ; " SCH. 17

and subsection (4) and paragraph (*a*) of subsection (7) of the said section 19 shall be omitted.

22. In section 38 of the Finance Act 1957— 1957 c. 49.

(*a*) in subsections (1), (5) and (8), for the words " deemed for purposes of estate duty to pass " there shall in each case be substituted the words " treated for purposes of estate duty as passing " ;

(*b*) in subsection (5), for the words " deemed to pass " there shall be substituted the words " treated as passing " ;

(*c*) in subsection (12), for the words from " is deemed " to " that section " there shall be substituted the words " is treated as passing on a death by virtue of section 2(1)(*b*) of the Finance Act 1894 by reason of an interest therein which has been disposed of or determined before the death " ; 1894 c. 30.

(*d*) in subsection (13)(*b*), for the words from " limited " onwards there shall be substituted the words " to which section 2(1)(*b*) of the Finance Act 1894 applies " ;

(*e*) in subsection (16)—

(i) for the words " comprised in a gift being deemed to pass " there shall be substituted the words " being treated as passing " ;

(ii) for the words " so comprised is to be deemed to pass on the death " there shall be substituted the words " is to be so treated ".

23. In section 39(2) of the Finance Act 1957, for the words from " so approved " to " applies " there shall be substituted the words " approved by the Board under section 22 of the Finance Act 1956 there becomes payable on a person's death an annuity to any widow, widower or dependant of that person ". 1956 c. 54.

24. In section 29(2) of the Finance Act 1958, for the words from " deemed " to " have passed " there shall be substituted the words " treated for purposes of estate duty as passing or having passed ". 1958 c. 56.

25. In paragraph 3 of Schedule 8 to the Finance Act 1958—

(*a*) in sub-paragraph (3), after the word " settlement " there shall be inserted the words " then, except on or by reference to a death on which duty falls to be charged on the settled property by virtue of section 2(1)(*b*) of the Finance Act, 1894 by reason of the interest purchased " ;

SCH. 17
1940 c. 29.
1894 c. 30.

(*b*) in sub-paragraph (4), for the words " section forty-three of the Finance Act 1940 " there shall be substituted the words " section 2(1)(*b*) of the Finance Act 1894 ";

(*c*) in sub-paragraph (6), for the words from " by reason " to " such an interest) " there shall be substituted the words " by virtue of section 2(1)(*b*) of the Finance Act 1894 by reason of an interest therein ", and in paragraph (*a*) of that sub-paragraph for the words " the interest so limited " there shall be substituted the words " that interest ".

1963 c. 25. 26. In section 53(2) of the Finance Act 1963, for the words " deemed to pass " there shall be substituted the word " passing ".

1966 c. 18. 27. In section 42 of the Finance Act 1966—

(*a*) in subsection (1), for the words " deemed for the purposes of estate duty to pass " there shall be substituted the words " treated for purposes of estate duty as passing ";

(*b*) in subsection (2), for the words from " treated " to " subsisted " there shall be substituted the words " treated for the purposes of estate duty as property comprised in a gift inter vivos which passes on a death or, as the case may be, as comprised in property which by virtue of section 2(1)(*b*) of the Finance Act 1894 passes on a death "; and at the end of that subsection there shall be added the words " or paragraph 3 of Part II of Schedule 17 to the Finance Act 1969 ";

(*c*) in subsection (3)(*a*), for the word " deemed " there shall be substituted the word " treated " and for the words " to pass " there shall be substituted the words " as passing ".

1967 c. 54. 28. In paragraph 2 of Schedule 15 to the Finance Act 1967—

(*a*) in sub-paragraph (1), for the words " deemed for the purposes of estate duty to pass " there shall be substituted the words " treated for the purposes of estate duty as passing ";

(*b*) in sub-paragraph (2), for the words from " treated " to " subsisted " there shall be substituted the words " treated for the purposes of estate duty as property comprised in a gift inter vivos which passes on a death or, as the case may be, as comprised in property which by virtue of section 2(1)(*b*) of the Finance Act 1894 passes on a death "; and at the end of that sub-paragraph there shall be added the words " or paragraph 3 of Part II of Schedule 17 to the Finance Act 1969 ".

1968 c. 44. 29. In section 35(2) of the Finance Act 1968, for the words " is deemed to pass " there shall be substituted the word " passes ".

30. In section 36(8) of the Finance Act 1968, for the words " is deemed to pass " there shall be substituted the word " passes ".

SCHEDULE 18

Section 41.

GILT-EDGED SECURITIES EXEMPT FROM TAX ON CHARGEABLE GAINS

PART I

SPECIFIED SECURITIES

Stocks and registered bonds charged on the National Loans Fund

6½ per cent. Exchequer Loan 1969.
6 per cent. Exchequer Loan 1970.
3 per cent. British Overseas Airways Stock 1960-70.
3 per cent. Savings Bonds 1960-70.
6½ per cent. Treasury Stock 1971.
5 per cent. Conversion Stock 1971.
6¾ per cent. Exchequer Loan 1971.
6 per cent. Conversion Stock 1972.
3 per cent. British Transport Stock 1967-72.
6¼ per cent. Exchequer Loan 1972.
6¾ per cent. Exchequer Stock 1973.
3 per cent. British Transport Stock 1968-73.
5¼ per cent. Conversion Stock 1974.
3 per cent. Savings Bonds 1965-75.
2½ per cent. British Overseas Airways Stock 1971-76.
6½ per cent. Treasury Loan 1976.
4 per cent. Victory Bonds.
4 per cent. British Transport Stock 1972-77.
5 per cent. Exchequer Loan 1976-78.
4 per cent. British Overseas Airways Stock 1974-80.
5¼ per cent. Funding Loan 1978-80.
3½ per cent. Treasury Stock 1977-80.
3½ per cent. Treasury Stock 1979-81.
2½ per cent. British Overseas Airways Stock 1977-82.
3 per cent. British Overseas Airways Stock 1980-83.
5½ per cent. Funding Stock 1982-84.
6½ per cent. Funding Loan 1985-87.
3 per cent. British Transport Stock 1978-88.
5 per cent. Treasury Stock 1986-89.
4 per cent. Funding Loan 1960-90.
5¾ per cent. Funding Loan 1987-91.
6 per cent. Funding Loan 1993.
6¾ per cent. Treasury Loan 1995-98.
3½ per cent. Funding Stock 1999-2004.
5½ per cent. Treasury Stock 2008-12.
2½ per cent. Treasury Stock 1986-2016.
2½ per cent. Annuities 1905 or after.
2¾ per cent. Annuities 1905 or after.
2½ per cent. Consolidated Stock 1923 or after.
4 per cent. Consolidated Loan 1957 or after.

SCH. 18

3½ per cent. Conversion Loan 1961 or after.
2½ per cent. Treasury Stock 1975 or after.
3 per cent. Treasury Stock 1966 or after.
3½ per cent. War Loan 1952 or after.

Securities issued by the Treasury under Part II of the Tithe Act 1936

3 per cent. Redemption Stock 1986-96.

Securities issued by certain public corporations and guaranteed by the Treasury

4½ per cent. British Electricity Stock 1967-69.
4½ per cent. South of Scotland Electricity Stock 1967-69.
3 per cent. North of Scotland Electricity Stock 1968-70.
3½ per cent. British Gas Stock 1969-71.
4 per cent. British Gas Stock 1969-72.
2½ per cent. North of Scotland Electricity Stock 1967-72.
3 per cent. British Electricity Stock 1968-73.
3 per cent. North of Scotland Electricity Stock 1968-73.
3 per cent. British Electricity Stock 1974-77.
4¼ per cent. British European Airways Stock 1972-77.
4 per cent. North of Scotland Electricity Stock 1973-78.
4¼ per cent. North of Scotland Electricity Stock 1974-79.
4¼ per cent. British Electricity Stock 1974-79.
3½ per cent. British Electricity Stock 1976-79.
3½ per cent. North of Scotland Electricity Stock 1977-80.
3 per cent. British European Airways Stock 1980-83.
3 per cent. North of Scotland Electricity Stock 1989-92.
3 per cent. British Gas Stock 1990-95.

PART II

DISPOSALS AND APPROPRIATIONS OF SPECIFIED SECURITIES BY COMPANIES

1.—(1) The provisions of this paragraph apply in relation to any specified securities if at the relevant time or at any time thereafter (whether before or after the commencement of this Act) the securities were held by a company in such circumstances that any gain or loss on their disposal would, apart from section 41 of this Act and Schedule 9 to the Finance Act 1965, have been taken into account in determining the company's liability to corporation tax on chargeable gains.

1965 c. 25.

(2) If after the relevant time the specified securities are appropriated by the company in such circumstances that if they were disposed of after the appropriation, any profit accruing on their disposal would be brought into account in computing the company's profits for corporation tax, then for the purposes of corporation tax any loss incurred by the company on the disposal of those securities

shall not exceed the loss which would have been incurred on that disposal if the amount or value of the consideration for the acquisition of the securities had been equal to their market value at the time of the appropriation. SCH. 18

2.—(1) This paragraph applies if—

(*a*) at the relevant time or at any time thereafter (whether before or after the commencement of this Act) any specified securities were held by a company in such circumstances that any profit accruing on their disposal would be brought into account in computing the company's profits for corporation tax ; and

(*b*) those securities are subsequently appropriated by the company in such circumstances that any gain accruing on their disposal would by virtue of section 41 of this Act be exempt from corporation tax on chargeable gains.

(2) Where this paragraph applies, the company concerned shall be treated for the purposes of corporation tax as if, immediately before the appropriation, it had sold and repurchased the specified securities at their market value at the time of the appropriation.

3. In this Part of the Schedule—

" company " has the same meaning as in Part IV of the Finance Act 1965 ; 1965 c. 25.

" the relevant time " means 3.30 p.m. on 15th April 1969 ; and

" specified securities " has the same meaning as in section 41 of this Act.

PART III

DISPOSAL OF SECURITIES ISSUED IN EXCHANGE FOR STEEL SHARES

4.—(1) The provisions of this Part of this Schedule apply in relation to a disposal to which section 41(1) of this Act applies of 6½ per cent. Treasury Stock 1971 (in this Part of this Schedule referred to as " compensation stock ") in relation to which the conditions in sub-paragraph (2) below are fulfilled.

(2) The conditions referred to in sub-paragraph (1) above are—

(*a*) that the stock disposed of consisted or formed part of a holding of compensation stock held on 15th April 1969 by the person making the disposal, and

(*b*) that the stock disposed of was acquired by that person, by virtue of section 10 of the Iron and Steel Act 1967, by way of compensation for the vesting in the British Steel Corporation under section 9 of that Act of securities (in this Part of this Schedule referred to as " steel shares ") previously held by him. 1967 c. 17.

(3) For the purpose of determining whether a disposal of compensation stock is one to which this Part of this Schedule applies, the rules of identification in paragraph 8 of Schedule 9 to the Finance Act 1962 shall apply in place of the provisions of paragraph 2 of Schedule 7 to the Finance Act 1965. 1962 c. 44.

SCH. 18

5.—(1) Notwithstanding anything in section 41(1) of this Act, where this Part of this Schedule applies in relation to a disposal by any person of compensation stock then, subject to sub-paragraph (2) below, there shall accrue to him on the disposal an allowable loss calculated in accordance with the following provisions of this paragraph.

(2) For the purpose of determining the allowable loss referred to in sub-paragraph (1) above, it shall be assumed that the person making the disposal had on the vesting date, within the meaning of the Iron and Steel Act 1967, disposed of all the holdings of steel shares held by him on that date for a consideration equal to the value of those shares as determined for the purposes of section 10 of that Act, and if on the disposal of any such holding an allowable loss would have accrued to him, or would have accrued to him if the disposal had not been one chargeable to income tax under Case VII of Schedule D (tax on short-term gains) the aggregate of those allowable losses shall be determined for the purposes of this paragraph; but if no such losses would have accrued sub-paragraph (1) above shall not apply.

1967 c. 17.

(3) The allowable loss accruing to the person making the disposal referred to in sub-paragraph (1) above is equal to the appropriate proportion of the aggregate of allowable losses referred to in sub-paragraph (2) above, and for this purpose the appropriate proportion is that which the compensation stock disposed of by him bears to the total compensation stock received by him by virtue of section 10 of the Iron and Steel Act 1967.

Section 42.

SCHEDULE 19

CAPITAL GAINS

Devaluation of sterling: securities acquired with borrowed foreign currency

1.—(1) This paragraph applies where, in pursuance of permission granted under the Exchange Control Act 1947, currency other than sterling was borrowed before 19th November 1967 for the purpose of investing in foreign securities (and had not been repaid before that date), and it was a condition of the permission—

1947 c. 14.

(*a*) that repayment of the borrowed currency should be made from the proceeds of the sale in foreign currency of the foreign securities so acquired or out of investment currency, and

(*b*) that the foreign securities so acquired should be kept in separate accounts to distinguish them from others in the same ownership,

and securities held in such a separate account on 19th November 1967 are in this paragraph referred to as "designated securities".

(2) In computing the gain accruing to the borrower on the disposal of any designated securities or on the disposal of any currency or amount standing in a bank account on 19th November 1967 and

representing the loan the sums allowable as a deduction under paragraph 4(1)(*a*) of Schedule 6 to the Finance Act 1965 (cost of acquisition) shall be increased by multiplying by seven sixths: SCH. 19 1965 c. 25.

Provided that the total amount of the increases so made in computing all gains (and losses) which are referable to any one loan (made before 19th November 1967) shall not exceed one sixth of the sterling parity value of that loan at the time it was made.

(3) Paragraph 2 of Schedule 7 to the Finance Act 1965 (pooling securities) shall apply separately in relation to any designated securities held in a particular account until such time as a disposal takes place on the occurrence of which the proviso to sub-paragraph (2) above operates to limit the increases which would otherwise be made under that sub-paragraph in allowable deductions.

(4) In this and the next following paragraph "foreign securities" means securities expressed in a currency other than sterling, or shares having a nominal value expressed in a currency other than sterling, or the dividends on which are payable in a currency other than sterling.

(5) This paragraph applies to any disposal after 18th November 1967, and all such adjustments shall be made by discharge or repayment of tax as are required to give effect to the provisions of this paragraph.

Devaluation of sterling: foreign insurance funds

2.—(1) The sums allowable as a deduction under paragraph 4(1)(*a*) of Schedule 6 to the Finance Act 1965 in computing any gains to which this paragraph applies shall be increased by multiplying by seven-sixths.

(2) This paragraph applies to gains accruing—

(*a*) to any underwriting member of Lloyd's or to any other approved association of underwriters, or

(*b*) to any company engaged in the business of marine protection and indemnity insurance on a mutual basis,

on the disposal by that person after 18th November 1967 of any foreign securities which on that date formed part of a trust fund—

(i) established by that person in any country or territory outside the United Kingdom, and

(ii) representing premiums received in the course of that person's business, and

(iii) wholly or mainly used for the purpose of meeting liabilities arising in that country or territory in respect of that business.

(3) All such adjustments shall be made by way of discharge or repayment of tax as are required to give effect to this paragraph.

SCH. 19

Currency in foreign bank accounts held to meet personal expenditure

1965 c. 25.

3.—(1) In Schedule 7 to the Finance Act 1965 after paragraph 11 there shall be inserted the following paragraph—

" 11A.—(1) Subject to the provisions of this paragraph, paragraph 11(1) above shall not apply to a debt owed by a bank which is not in sterling and which is represented by a sum standing to the credit of a person in an account in the bank.

(2) Sub-paragraph (1) above shall not apply to a sum in an individual's bank account representing currency acquired by the holder for the personal expenditure outside the United Kingdom of himself or his family or dependants (including expenditure on the provision or maintenance of any residence outside the United Kingdom).

(3) This paragraph applies to debts disposed of after 18th November 1967, and all such adjustments shall be made by way of discharge or repayment of tax as are required to give effect to this paragraph."

1962 c. 44.

(2) In Schedule 9 to the Finance Act 1962 after paragraph 15 there shall be inserted the following paragraph—

" 15A.—(1) Subject to the provisions of this paragraph, paragraph 15(1) above shall not apply to a debt owed by a bank which is not in sterling and which is represented by a sum standing to the credit of a person in an account in the bank, and accordingly the satisfaction of the debt or part of it shall be treated as a disposal of the debt or of that part by the creditor (that is the bank's customer) made at the time when the debt or that part is satisfied.

(2) Sub-paragraph (1) above shall not apply to a sum in an individual's bank account representing currency acquired by the holder for the personal expenditure outside the United Kingdom of himself or his family or dependants (including expenditure on the provision or maintenance of any residence outside the United Kingdom).

(3) This paragraph applies to debts disposed of after 18th November 1967, and all such adjustments shall be made by way of discharge or repayment of tax as are required to give effect to this paragraph."

1967 c. 54.

(3) Paragraph 11 of Schedule 13 to the Finance Act 1967 (which is re-enacted in this paragraph) shall cease to have effect.

Foreign currency : chargeable gains accruing to non-resident companies

4. In section 41(5) of the Finance Act 1965 after paragraph (*b*) there shall be inserted the following paragraph—

" (*bb*) a chargeable gain accruing on the disposal after 18th November 1967 of currency or of a debt within paragraph 11A(1) of Schedule 7 to this Act (foreign bank accounts), where the currency or debt is or represents money in use for the purposes of a trade carried on by the company wholly outside the United Kingdom, or ". SCH. 19

All such adjustments shall be made by way of discharge or repayment of tax as are required to give effect to this paragraph.

Personal representatives: gains and losses in three years after death

5.—(1) After section 24 of the Finance Act 1965 there shall be inserted the following section— 1965 c. 25.

" 24A.—(1) No gain or loss which accrues to the personal representatives of a deceased person in the period of three years beginning with the death shall be a chargeable gain or allowable loss but, subject to the provisions of this section, the deceased person (and his personal representatives) shall be treated as if any chargeable gain or allowable loss which would, but for the preceding provisions, have accrued to the personal representatives had accrued under section 24(1) above to the deceased person on his death (as a gain or loss unrelated to any particular asset).

(2) In computing for the purposes of section 25(5) below (£5,000 relief for settled property) whether any relief is given under section 24(2) above (£5,000 relief for deceased's estate) or whether relief is so given in respect of an aggregate sum less than the amount available for relief under section 24(2) above,—

(*a*) if the total of chargeable gains treated as accruing under section 24(1) above by virtue only of subsection (1) above exceeds the total of allowable losses so treated, the aggregate sum (if any) in respect of which relief is given under section 24(2) above shall be computed without regard to the provisions of subsection (1) above; but

(*b*) if the total of those chargeable gains is less than the total of those allowable losses, subsection (1) above shall be taken into account in computing the aggregate sum (if any) in respect of which relief is given under section 24(2) above.

(3) Where paragraph (*a*) of subsection (2) above applies for the purpose of computing the amount available for relief under section 25(5) below—

(*a*) the relief given under section 25(5) shall be computed before computing the relief under section 24(2) above; and

(*b*) in determining the relief to be given under section 24(2) above, having regard to subsection (1) above, from the £5,000 otherwise available for relief under that section there shall be deducted the aggregate sum in respect of which relief has been given under section 25(5) below.

SCH. 19

(4) Subsection (1) above shall not affect the amount of relief under section 26(1) below (allowance of capital gains tax against estate duty).

(5) Capital gains tax for the year of assessment in which the deceased died shall be assessable, chargeable and recoverable in the first instance without regard to any gain or loss which may accrue to the personal representatives, and all such adjustments, whether by way of assessment or discharge or repayment of tax, as are required to give effect to this section by reference to any gain or loss accruing after the death shall be made at the expiration of the said period of three years, or when the personal representatives have completed administration of the deceased's assets, whichever is the earlier.

An assessment made in pursuance of this subsection shall not be out of time if made within six years from the end of the year of assessment in which the deceased died."

1965 c. 25. (2) In section 25(5) of the Finance Act 1965 for the words " subsection (2) of the last foregoing section " there shall be substituted " section 24(2) above " in both the places where those words appear.

(3) In paragraph 16(1) of Schedule 6 to the Finance Act 1965 (allowance of incidental costs of actual disposal by personal representatives in computing gains accruing on disposal of assets deemed to be made by an individual on his death) for the words " whether by way of sale or by way of disposition to legatees " there shall be substituted the words " by way of disposition to legatees in the period of three years beginning with the death ".

(4) Section 24(8) of the Finance Act 1965 (allowable losses accruing to personal representatives: deduction from chargeable gains accruing to the deceased) shall cease to have effect.

(5) In paragraph 12(2) of Schedule 10 to the Finance Act 1965 (gains of trustees and personal representatives not to be gains of any other person except where section 22(5) of that Act applies) after the words " section 22(5) ", there shall be inserted the words " and section 24A ".

(6) This paragraph applies in the case of deaths occurring after 5th April 1969.

Legatees: assets appropriated in satisfaction of legacies

6.—(1) In section 45(1) of the Finance Act 1965 and section 16(1)
1962 c. 44. of the Finance Act 1962 after the definition of " legatee " there shall be inserted the following words—

" for the purposes of the definition of ' legatee ' above, and of any reference to a person acquiring an asset ' as legatee ', property taken under a testamentary disposition or on an intestacy or partial intestacy includes any asset appropriated by the personal representatives in or towards satisfaction of a pecuniary legacy or any other interest or share in the property devolving under the disposition or intestacy ".

(2) This paragraph applies in the case of deaths occurring after 5th April 1969.

Exemption for private residence: disposal between man and wife SCH. 19

7.—(1) In section 29(8) of the Finance Act 1965 after paragraph (*b*) there shall be inserted the following paragraph— 1965 c. 25.

"(*bb*) if paragraph (*b*) above applies, but the dwelling-house or part of a dwelling-house was not the only or main residence of both throughout the period of ownership of the one making the disposal, account shall be taken of any part of that period during which it was his only or main residence as if it was also that of the other, and".

(2) This paragraph applies in relation to disposals after 5th April 1969.

Settlements

8.—(1) Section 25(5) of the Finance Act 1965 (£5,000 relief against gains accruing to trustees on a death) shall be amended with respect to deaths after 5th April 1969 as follows—

(*a*) paragraph (*b*) (relief by reference to postponed occasion of charge) shall cease to have effect,

(*b*) in paragraph (*d*) (apportionment between two or more settlements) for the words from "according" to the end of the paragraph there shall be substituted the words—

"according to the respective aggregates of the chargeable gains (less allowable losses) which accrue to those trustees respectively on the death".

(2) After the said section 25(5) there shall be inserted the following subsection—

"(5A) Subsection (5) above shall not apply on a death after 5th April 1969 unless the deceased was at the time of death either resident or ordinarily resident in the United Kingdom".

(3) At the end of the proviso to section 25(1) of the Finance Act 1965 and of the proviso to section 12(6) of the Finance Act 1962 (residence of trustees) there shall be added the words "and if in such a case the trustees or a majority of them are or are treated in relation to that trust as not resident in the United Kingdom, the general administration of the trust shall be treated as ordinarily carried on outside the United Kingdom". 1962 c. 44.

(4) Sub-paragraph (3) above applies in relation to disposals of assets after 5th April 1969.

Distinction between trustees of settled property and bare trustees

9. It is hereby declared that references in Part III of the Finance Act 1965, and in Chapter II of Part II of the Finance Act 1962, to any asset held by a person as trustee for another person absolutely entitled as against the trustee are references to a case where that other person has the exclusive right, subject only to satisfying any outstanding charge, lien or other right of the trustees to resort to the asset for payment of duty, taxes, costs or other outgoings, to direct how that asset shall be dealt with.

Sch. 19

Part disposal of land

10.—(1) This paragraph applies to a transfer after 5th April 1969 of land forming part only of a holding of land, where—

(*a*) the amount or value of the consideration for the transfer is small, as compared with the market value of the holding as it subsisted immediately before the transfer, and

1965 c. 25. (*b*) the transfer is not one which, by virtue of paragraph 20 of Schedule 7 to the Finance Act 1965 (transfers between husband and wife) or paragraph 2 of Schedule 13 to that Act (transfers within groups of companies), is treated as giving rise to neither a gain nor a loss.

(2) Subject to sub-paragraph (3) below, if the transferor so claims, the transfer shall not be treated for the purposes of Part III of the Finance Act 1965 as a disposal, but all sums which, if it had been so treated, would have been brought into account for consideration for that disposal in the computation under Schedule 6 to that Act of a gain accruing on the disposal shall be deducted from any expenditure allowable under that Schedule as a deduction in computing a gain on any subsequent disposal of the holding.

(3) This paragraph shall not apply—

(*a*) if the amount or value of the consideration for the transfer exceeds £2,500, or

(*b*) where in the year of assessment in which the transfer is made, the transferor made any other disposal of land, if the total amount or value of the consideration for all disposals of land made by the transferor in that year exceeds £2,500.

(4) No account shall be taken under sub-paragraph (3) above of any transfer of land to which paragraph 4 of Schedule 10 to the
1966 c. 18. Finance Act 1966 (part disposal to authority with compulsory powers) applies.

(5) Paragraph 9 of Schedule 10 to the Finance Act 1966 (which deals with cases where no expenditure is attributable to the asset or that expenditure is small) shall apply as if this paragraph were mentioned in the said paragraph 9(1).

(6) In relation to a transfer which is not for full consideration in money or money's worth, " the amount or value of the consideration " in this paragraph shall mean the market value of the land transferred.

(7) In the application of this paragraph to a transfer to which
1967 c. 54. section 33(1) of the Finance Act 1967 (current use value) applies, or would apply but for this paragraph, for references to the amount or value of the consideration for the transfer or to the market value of the holding there shall be substituted references to the current use value of the land, or as the case may be of the holding, at the relevant time.

(8) For the purposes of this paragraph the holding of land shall comprise only the land in respect of which the expenditure allowable under paragraphs (*a*) and (*b*) of paragraph 4(1) of Schedule 6 to the Finance Act 1965 would be apportioned under paragraph 7 of that Schedule if the transfer had been treated as a disposal (that is, as a part disposal of the holding).

(9) In this paragraph references to a holding of land include references to any estate or interest in a holding of land, not being an estate or interest which is a wasting asset, and references to part of a holding shall be construed accordingly. SCH. 19

Compensation paid on compulsory acquisition

11.—(1) Where land or an interest in or right over land is acquired after 29th April 1969 and the acquisition is, or could have been, made under compulsory powers, then in considering whether, under paragraph 21(4) of Schedule 6 to the Finance Act 1965, the purchase price or compensation or other consideration for the acquisition should be apportioned and treated in part as a capital sum within section 22(3)(*a*) of the said Act, whether as compensation for loss of goodwill or for disturbance or otherwise, or should be apportioned in any other way, the fact that the acquisition is or could have been made compulsorily, and any statutory provision treating the purchase price or compensation or other consideration as exclusively paid in respect of the land itself, shall be disregarded. 1965 c. 25.

(2) Sub-paragraph (1) above applies with respect to the apportionments to be made under section 13(3) of the Finance Act 1962 as it applies to the apportionments to be made for the purposes of Schedule 6 to the Finance Act 1965. 1962 c. 44.

(3) In any case where land or an interest in land is acquired as mentioned in sub-paragraph (1) above from any person and the compensation or purchase price includes an amount in respect of severance of the land comprised in the acquisition or sale from other land in which that person is entitled in the same capacity to an interest or in respect of that other land as being injuriously affected, there shall be deemed for the purposes of Part III of the Finance Act 1965 to be a part disposal of that other land.

(4) Unless the person receiving the compensation makes an election under section 33(3) of the Finance Act 1967, the amount of the consideration for such a part disposal as is referred to in sub-paragraph (3) above shall in the case of land in Great Britain be determined in accordance with paragraph 5(4) of Schedule 14 to the Finance Act 1967 as if the part disposal derived from such a chargeable act or event as is referred to in that paragraph. 1967 c. 54.

Gifts to charities, etc.

12. At the end of paragraph 17(3) of Schedule 7 to the Finance Act 1965 (transactions between connected persons) there shall be added the words—

" Provided that this sub-paragraph shall not apply to a disposal after 5th April 1969 by way of gift in settlement if—

(*a*) the gift is exclusively for charitable purposes, or

(*b*) the gift and the income from it is wholly or primarily applicable for educational, cultural or recreational purposes, and the persons benefiting from the application for those purposes are confined to members of an association of persons for whose benefit the gift was made, not being persons all or most of whom are, in the terms of paragraph 21 of this Schedule, connected persons ".

SCH. 19

Returns by share dealers

1965 c. 25. 13. In paragraph 7 of Schedule 10 to the Finance Act 1965 after sub-paragraph (4) there shall be inserted the following sub-paragraph—

" (4A) A person (other than a member of a stock exchange in the United Kingdom) who acts as an agent or broker in the United Kingdom in transactions in shares or securities may be required to make a return giving particulars of any such transactions effected by him after 5th April 1968 and in the period specified in the notice, and giving particulars of—

(*a*) the parties to the transactions,

(*b*) the number or amount of the shares or securities dealt with in the respective transactions, and

(*c*) the amount or value of the consideration."

Appropriation to and from trading stock

14.—(1) In sub-paragraphs (1) and (3) of paragraph 1 of Schedule 7 to the Finance Act 1965 for the word " gain " there shall be substituted the words " chargeable gain " and for the word " loss " there shall be substituted the words " allowable loss ".

(2) In sub-paragraph (2) of that paragraph for the word " Where " there shall be substituted the words " If at any time " and after the words " as having acquired it " there shall be inserted the words " at that time ".

(3) This paragraph applies in relation to any appropriation of an asset after 29th April 1969.

Transfer of business to a company

15.—(1) This paragraph shall apply for the purposes of Part III of the Finance Act 1965, and of Chapter II of Part II of the Finance
1962 c. 44. Act 1962, where a person who is not a company transfers to a company a business as a going concern, together with the whole assets of the business, or together with the whole of those assets other than cash, and the business is so transferred wholly or partly in exchange for shares issued by the company to the person transferring the business.

Any shares so received by the transferor in exchange for the business are referred to below as " the new assets ".

(2) The amount determined under sub-paragraph (4) below shall be deducted from the aggregate (referred to below as " the amount of the gain on the old assets ") of the net chargeable gains plus net short-term gains accruing to the transferor on his disposal of the assets included in the business ; and if the amount of the gain on the old assets includes both net chargeable gains and net short-term gains, the deduction under this sub-paragraph shall be apportioned rateably between the two kinds of gains.

(3) For the purpose of computing any chargeable gain or short-term gain accruing on the disposal of any new asset—

(*a*) the amount determined under sub-paragraph (4) below shall be apportioned between the new assets as a whole, and (*b*) the sums allowable as a deduction under paragraph 4(1)(*a*) of Schedule 6 to the Finance Act 1965 (cost of acquisition in relation to chargeable gains) or, as the case may be, the sums allowable in computing any short-term gain on the disposal, shall be reduced by the amount apportioned to the new asset under paragraph (*a*) above ; SCH. 19 1965 c. 25.

and if the shares which comprise the new assets are not all of the same class, the apportionment between the shares under paragraph (*a*) above shall be in accordance with their market values at the time they were acquired by the transferor.

(4) The amount referred to in sub-paragraphs (2) and (3)(*a*) above shall not exceed the cost of the new assets but, subject to that, the said amount shall be a fraction $\frac{A}{B}$ of the amount of the gain on the old assets where—

" A " is the cost of the new assets, and

" B " is the value of the whole of the consideration received by the transferor in exchange for the business ;

and for the purposes of this sub-paragraph " the cost of the new assets " means any sums which would be allowable as a deduction under paragraph 4(1)(*a*) of Schedule 6 to the Finance Act 1965 if the new assets were disposed of as a whole in circumstances giving rise to a chargeable gain.

(5) The provisions of section 33 of, and Schedule 14 to, the Finance Act 1967 (current use value of land in Great Britain) shall be applied, where relevant, in fixing the amount of the gain on the old assets before the provisions of this paragraph are applied. 1967 c. 54.

(6) Paragraph 8 of Schedule 7 to the Finance Act 1965 and paragraph 14 of Schedule 9 to the Finance Act 1962 (which are superseded by this paragraph) shall cease to have effect. 1962 c. 44.

(7) In this paragraph " net chargeable gains " means chargeable gains less allowable losses, " short term gains " means gains taxable under Chapter II of Part II of the Finance Act 1962, and " net short term gains " means short term gains less losses allowable against those gains.

(8) References in this paragraph to the business, in relation to shares or consideration received in exchange for the business, include references to such assets of the business as are referred to in sub-paragraph (1) above.

(9) This paragraph applies in relation to any transfer of a business on or after 6th April 1969 and also, for the purpose of computing the chargeable gains and short term gains accruing to any person who has not before that date disposed of any of the new assets received by him, in relation to any transfer before that date which did not give rise to a chargeable or short-term gain.

Replacement of business assets : depreciating assets

16.—(1) Section 33 of the Finance Act 1965 shall have effect subject to the provisions of this paragraph in which—

(*a*) the " held over gain " means the amount by which, under subsection (1) or subsection (2) of the said section 33, and

SCH. 19

apart from the provisions of this paragraph, any chargeable gain on one asset (called " asset No. 1 ") is reduced, with a corresponding reduction of the expenditure allowable in respect of another asset (called " asset No. 2 "),

(*b*) any reference to a gain of any amount being carried forward to any asset is a reference to a reduction of that amount in a chargeable gain coupled with a reduction of the same amount in expenditure allowable in respect of that asset.

(2) If asset No. 2 is a depreciating asset, the held over gain shall not be carried forward, but the claimant shall be treated for the purposes of long-term and short-term tax on capital gains as if so much of the chargeable gain on asset No. 1 as is equal to the held over gain did not accrue until—

(*a*) the claimant disposes of asset No. 2, or

(*b*) he ceases to use asset No. 2 for the purposes of a trade carried on by him, or

(*c*) the expiration of a period of ten years beginning with the acquisition of asset No. 2,

whichever event comes first.

(3) If, in the circumstances specified in sub-paragraph (4) below, the claimant acquires an asset (called " asset No. 3 ") which is not a depreciating asset, and so claims under the said section 33—

(*a*) the gain held over from asset No. 1 shall be carried forward to asset No. 3, and

(*b*) the claim which applies to asset No. 2 shall be treated as withdrawn (so that sub-paragraph (2) above does not apply).

(4) The circumstances are that asset No. 3 is acquired not later than the time when the chargeable gain postponed under sub-paragraph (2) above would accrue and, assuming—

(*a*) that the consideration for asset No. 1 was applied in acquiring asset No. 3, and

(*b*) that the time between the disposal of asset No. 1 and the acquisition of asset No. 3 was within the time limited by subsection (3) of the said section 33,

the whole amount of the postponed gain could be carried forward from asset No. 1 to asset No. 3 ; and the claim under sub-paragraph (3) above shall be accepted as if those assumptions were true.

(5) If part only of the postponed gain could be carried forward from asset No. 1 to asset No. 3, and the claimant so requires, that and the other part of the postponed gain shall be treated as derived from two separate assets, so that, on that claim—

(*a*) sub-paragraph (3) above applies to the first-mentioned part, and

(*b*) the other part remains subject to sub-paragraph (2) above.

(6) Sub-paragraph (2) above shall apply where the claimant is a member of a group of companies as if all members of the group

for the time being were the same person (and in accordance with paragraph 6 of Schedule 13 to the Finance Act 1965, as if all trades carried on by members were the same trade), and so that the gain shall accrue to the member of the group holding the asset on the occurrence of the event mentioned in that sub-paragraph. SCH. 19 1965 c. 25.

This sub-paragraph shall be read as if contained in Part I of the said Schedule 13.

(7) For the purposes of this paragraph an asset is a depreciating asset at any time if—

(*a*) at that time it is a wasting asset as defined in paragraph 9 of Schedule 6 to the Finance Act 1965, or

(*b*) within the period of ten years beginning at that time it will become a wasting asset (so defined).

(8) This paragraph does not apply where both the disposal of asset No. 1 and the acquisition of asset No. 2 fell before 6th April 1969.

(9) This paragraph shall be construed as one with the said section 33.

Replacement of business assets : hovercraft

17.—(1) Section 33 of the Finance Act 1965 shall be amended by the addition, at the end of subsection (6), of a further class of asset to which that section applies, namely:—

CLASS 5

Hovercraft (within the meaning of the Hovercraft Act 1968) 1968 c. 59.

(2) This paragraph has effect with respect to any disposal of assets after 5th April 1969.

Company transferring assets to non-resident company

18.—(1) This paragraph shall apply where a company resident in the United Kingdom which is carrying on a trade outside the United Kingdom through a branch or agency transfers the trade carried on through that branch or agency, together with the whole assets of the business used for the purposes of that trade, or together with the whole of those assets other than cash, to a company not resident in the United Kingdom, and the business is so transferred wholly or partly in exchange for shares or for shares and loan stock issued by the transferee company to the transferor company, and the shares so issued, either alone or taken together with any other shares in the transferee company already held by the transferor company, amount in all to not less than one quarter of the ordinary share capital of the transferee company.

(2) For the purposes of Part III of the Finance Act 1965 the transferor company shall be treated as if a fraction of any chargeable gain accruing to it on its disposal of any asset so transferred to the transferee company did not accrue to the transferor company until—

(*a*) the transferee company disposes or partly disposes of that asset, or ceases to use it, or the transferee company is wound up or dissolved, or

Sch. 19

(*b*) the transferor company disposes of all or any of the shares or loan stock issued in exchange by the transferee company, or

(*c*) the expiration of a period of ten years beginning with the transfer, or

(*d*) the passing of a resolution or the making of an order, or any other act, for the winding up of the transferor company (unless that company is not in fact wound up or dissolved),

whichever event comes first.

1965 c. 25.

(3) A disposal of shares or loan stock by the transferor company which, by virtue of Schedule 13 to the Finance Act 1965 (groups of companies), is treated as giving rise to neither a gain nor a loss shall be disregarded for the purposes of sub-paragraph (2)(*b*) above, but on the first occasion after such a disposal that there is a disposal which is not so treated of all or any of those shares or that loan stock, that sub-paragraph shall apply as if the disposal were a disposal by the transferor company.

(4) The fraction referred to in sub-paragraph (2) above is $\frac{A}{B}$ where—

A is the market value at the time of the transfer of the shares and of any loan stock received by the transferor company in exchange for the business (including any such assets as are referred to in sub-paragraph (1) above), and

B is the market value at the time of the transfer of the whole of the consideration so received by the transferor company.

(5) For the purposes of this paragraph the ordinary share capital of a company means all the issued share capital (by whatever name called) of the company, other than capital the holders of which have a right to a dividend at a fixed rate but have no other right to share in the profits of the company; and if all or part of the ordinary share capital of the transferee company consists of shares of no par value, the proportion of one quarter shall be determined according to the market value of the ordinary share capital at the time of the transfer.

(6) This paragraph applies in relation to any transfer of a trade and assets after 10th April 1968 and all such adjustments shall be made by discharge or repayment of tax as are required to give effect to the provisions of this paragraph.

(7) This paragraph shall be construed as if it formed part of Part IV of the Finance Act 1965 (company taxation).

Interest charged to capital by a company

19.—(1) Where—

(*a*) a company incurs expenditure on the construction of any building, structure or works, being expenditure allowable as a deduction under paragraph 4 of Schedule 6 to the Finance Act 1965 in computing a gain accruing to the company on the disposal of the building, structure or work, or of any asset comprising it, and

Sch. 19

(b) that expenditure was defrayed out of borrowed money, and

(c) the company charged to capital all or any of the interest on that borrowed money referable to a period or part of a period ending on or before the disposal, and

(d) the disposal occurred after 5th April 1969,

the sums so allowable under the said paragraph 4 shall include the amount of that interest charged to capital.

(2) Paragraph 3 of Schedule 14 to the Finance Act 1967 (restriction on deductions where gain computed by reference to current use value of land) shall not restrict the sums allowable under sub-paragraph (1) above. 1967 c. 54.

(3) This paragraph shall be construed as if it formed part of Part IV of the Finance Act 1965 (company taxation). 1965 c. 25.

Company ceasing to be a member of a group

20. References in paragraphs 18 and 19 of Schedule 12 to the Finance Act 1968 to a company ceasing to be a member of a group of companies do not apply to cases where, after 5th April 1969, a company ceases to be a member of a group of companies— 1968 c. 44.

(a) by being wound up or dissolved, or

(b) in consequence of another member of the group being wound up or dissolved.

Loss on disposal of shares etc. attributable to depreciatory transaction

21.—(1) For the purposes of paragraph 20 of Schedule 12 to the Finance Act 1968 (losses attributable to depreciatory transactions in a group) as it has effect in relation to disposals of shares in or securities of a company after 29th April 1969, any transaction effected on or after 6th April 1965 which materially reduced the value of those shares or securities and fulfils the conditions specified in sub-paragraph (2) below shall be a depreciatory transaction, notwithstanding that it does not consist of such a disposal of assets as is referred to in sub-paragraph (1) of the said paragraph 20.

(2) The conditions referred to in sub-paragraph (1) above are—

(a) that the company, the shares in which or securities of which are disposed of as mentioned in the said paragraph 20(1) or any subsidiary of that company was a party to the transaction, and

(b) that the parties to the transaction were or included two or more companies which at the time of the transaction were members of the same group of companies.

(3) Without prejudice to the generality of sub-paragraph (1) above (or of any reference to a disposal of assets in the said paragraph 20) the cancellation of any shares in or securities of one member of a group of companies under section 66 of the Companies Act 1948 shall, to the extent that immediately before the cancellation those shares or securities were the property of another member of the group, be taken to be a transaction fulfilling the conditions in sub-paragraph (2) above. 1948 c. 48.

SCH. 19 (4) Where the following conditions apply, namely,—

(*a*) that one company (in this sub-paragraph referred to as " the first company ") has a holding in another company (in this sub-paragraph referred to as " the second company ") and the holding amounts to, or is an ingredient in a holding amounting to, 10 per cent. of all holdings of the same class in the second company,

(*b*) that the first company is not a dealing company, as defined in paragraph 10(7) of Schedule 14 to this Act, in relation to the holding,

(*c*) that a distribution is or has been made after 29th April 1969 to the first company in respect of the holding, and

(*d*) that the effect of the distribution is that the value of the holding is or has been materially reduced,

then, subject to sub-paragraph (5) below, the said paragraph 20 shall apply in relation to any disposal of any shares or securities comprised in the holding, whether the disposal is by the first company or by any other company to which the holding is transferred by a
1965 c. 25. transfer to which paragraph 2 of Schedule 13 to the Finance Act 1965 applies, as if the distribution were a depreciatory transaction and, if the companies concerned are not members of a group of companies, as if they were.

(5) For the purposes of the said paragraph 20, neither a transaction (whether consisting of the disposal of assets or otherwise) nor a distribution falling within sub-paragraph (4) above shall be treated as a depreciatory transaction to the extent that it consists of a payment which is required to be or has been brought into account, for the purposes of corporation tax on chargeable gains, in computing a chargeable gain or allowable loss accruing to the person making the disposal referred to in sub-paragraph (1) of that paragraph.

(6) Except in so far as this paragraph extends the concept of a depreciatory transaction, expressions used in this paragraph have the same meaning as in the said paragraph 20 and in this paragraph—

" distribution " has the meaning assigned to it by Schedule 11 to the Finance Act 1965,

" subsidiary " has the same meaning as in Schedule 12 to the
1968 c. 44. Finance Act 1968, and

" holding " has the same meaning as in paragraph 10 of Schedule 14 to this Act and sub-paragraph (4) of that paragraph shall apply for the purpose of determining whether a holding is an ingredient in a holding amounting to 10 per cent. of all holdings of a particular class.

(7) Section 65 of the Finance Act 1965 (tax avoidance in relation to capital gains and other matters by dividend stripping and bond-washing) shall not apply in relation to a distribution made after 29th April 1969.

Company amalgamations and reconstructions

22.—(1) In relation to any transfer of the whole or part of a company's business taking effect after 19th June 1969, any reference to a company in paragraph 7(2) of Schedule 7 to the Finance Act 1965 (transfer of business on amalgamation or reconstruction to be on a no-gain, no-loss basis in certain cases) shall be construed as a reference to a company within the meaning of Part IV of the Finance Act 1965 and where, on or before that date— SCH. 19 1965 c. 25.

(*a*) the said paragraph 7(2) applied on the transfer of the whole or part of a business to a body which is not a company within the meaning of the said Part IV, but

(*b*) all or any of the assets included in the transfer were not disposed of by that body,

then any disposal by that body after that date of any of the assets referred to in paragraph (*b*) above shall be disregarded for the purposes of Chapter II of Part II of the Finance Act 1962 (tax on short-term gains). 1962 c. 44.

(2) The said paragraph 7(2) shall not apply in the case of a transfer on or after 29th April 1969 of the whole or part of a company's business to a unit trust scheme to which subsection (1) or subsection (2) of section 38 of the Finance Act 1965 (unit trusts for exempt unit holders) applies.

(3) Where the said paragraph 7(2) of Schedule 7 has applied on the transfer of a company's business (in whole or in part) to a unit trust scheme to which at the time of the transfer neither subsection (1) nor subsection (2) of section 38 of the Finance Act 1965 applied, then if—

(*a*) at any time after the transfer the unit trust scheme becomes in a year of assessment one to which either of those subsections does apply, and

(*b*) at the beginning of that year of assessment the unit trust scheme still owns any of the assets of the business transferred,

the unit trust scheme shall be treated for all the purposes of Part III of the Finance Act 1965 as if immediately after the transfer it had sold, and immediately re-acquired, the assets referred to in paragraph (*b*) above at their market value at that time.

(4) Notwithstanding any limitation on the time for making assessments, an assessment to corporation tax chargeable in consequence of sub-paragraph (3) above may be made at any time within six years after the end of the year of assessment referred to in that sub-paragraph and where under that sub-paragraph a unit trust scheme is to be treated as having disposed of, and re-acquired, an asset of a business, all such recomputations of liability in respect of other disposals and all such adjustments of tax, whether by way of assessment or by way of discharge or repayment of tax as may be required in consequence of the provisions of that sub-paragraph shall be carried out.

(5) At the end of paragraph 15(2) of Schedule 12 to the Finance Act 1968 (application of paragraph 7(1) of Schedule 7 to Finance Act 1965 to companies having no share capital) there shall be added, with effect from 6th April 1969, the words— 1968 c. 44.

" In this sub-paragraph ' company ' has the same meaning as in Part III of the Finance Act 1965 ".

SCH. 19

Betterment levy relief : consequential adjustments

1967 c. 54. 23.—(1) In section 33 of the Finance Act 1967 (exclusion of development value) after subsection (3) insert—

"(3A) If a disposal constitutes a chargeable act or event ex-
1967 c. 1. empted from levy by section 59A of the Land Commission Act 1967 this section shall apply as if an election had been made under this section as respects the disposal."

(2) At the end of paragraph 2 of Schedule 14 to the said Act (adjustment of current use value reflecting new development) insert—

"(3) Where the project of material development is exempt from levy by virtue of section 59A of the Land Commission Act 1967—

(*a*) this paragraph shall not apply unless some amount of the development value in the project was charged to levy on an occasion before the beginning of the project, and

(*b*) if some amount of that development value was so charged to levy, the relief under this paragraph (that is to say the notional expenditure credited to the owner of the land under sub-paragraph (1)(*a*) above) shall not exceed that amount.

For the purposes of this sub-paragraph an amount of development value in the project shall be regarded as having been charged to levy on such an earlier occasion if, in relation to the project, there is a base value under Schedule 5 to the said Act, and the said amount shall be that base value less the current use value of the land immediately before the project was begun.

(4) Where under section 60A of the said Act the net development value is reduced by any amount, the relief under this paragraph shall be reduced by that amount".

Section 60.

SCHEDULE 20

CONSOLIDATION AMENDMENTS

Conversion of Case VIII of Schedule D (rents etc.) into new Schedule A

1963 c. 25. 1.—(1) Sections 14(1)(*b*), 15(1) and 15(2) of the Finance Act 1963 shall, in relation to income tax and corporation tax for years of assessment and accounting periods ending after 5th April 1970, have effect as if, instead of imposing a charge to tax under Case VIII of Schedule D, they imposed the like charge under a new Schedule, to be known as Schedule A ; and accordingly, in relation to tax for any such year or period—

(*a*) in all other enactments, instruments and documents, any reference to the said Case VIII, whether a specific reference or one imported by more general words, shall be construed as a reference to Schedule A, and

(*b*) in paragraph 1(*b*) of Schedule D, as set out in section 122
1952 c. 10. of the Income Tax Act 1952, after "not charged under" insert "Schedule A".

(2) It is hereby declared that nothing in this paragraph affects the continuity of the operation of the Income Tax Acts or the Corporation Tax Acts. SCH. 20

Restatement of details of Schedule B charge

2.—(1) Sub-paragraphs (2) to (4) below shall have effect in substitution for paragraph 2 of Schedule B, as set out in section 83 of the Income Tax Act 1952, sections 115(1) and 222 of that Act, section 28(2) of the Finance Act 1963 and section 54(5) of the Finance Act 1965. 1952 c. 10. 1963 c. 25. 1965 c. 25.

(2) Tax under Schedule B shall be charged on the occupier of the woodlands on the assessable value of his occupation in the year of assessment or company's accounting period, and the amount on which he is chargeable shall be deemed for all tax purposes to be income arising from that occupation.

(3) For the purposes of tax under that Schedule—

(*a*) the assessable value of a person's occupation of woodlands is an amount equal to one-third of the woodlands' annual value, or a proportionate part of that amount if the period in respect of which he is chargeable is less than one year, and

(*b*) the annual value of any woodlands shall be determined in accordance with Schedule 5 to the Finance Act 1963, but as if the land, instead of being woodlands, were let in its natural and unimproved state.

(4) For the purposes of the said Schedule B and of sub-paragraphs (2) and (3) above, every person having the use of lands shall be deemed to be the occupier thereof, and references to occupation shall be construed accordingly.

(5) In consequence of the above provisions, in section 28(3) of the Finance Act 1963, for all the words after " assessable value " substitute " for the purposes of Schedule B of his occupation of the land in that year ".

Case VII of Schedule D

3. The following provisions (which exclude from the short term capital gains tax, or from particular rules relating thereto, transactions where the acquisition or disposal took place before a certain date) shall cease to have effect—

(*a*) in the Finance Act 1962, the proviso to section 10(1), 1962 c. 44.

(*b*) in the Finance Act 1965, in section 17(9), the paragraph beginning " This subsection ", section 17(14) and section 18(6), and

(*c*) in the Finance Act 1968, section 33(5) and, in Schedule 13, paragraphs 1(4) and 5(1). 1968 c. 44.

Receipts after cessation or change of basis

4.—(1) No amount shall be deducted under section 32(4) of the Finance Act 1960 if that amount has been allowed under any other provision of the Income Tax Acts or the Corporation Tax Acts. 1960 c. 44.

SCH. 20
1960 c. 44.
1968 c. 44.
(2) Section 33(3) of the Finance Act 1960 and paragraph 6(1) of Schedule 10 to the Finance Act 1968 (elections for carry-back) shall be amended as follows—

(*a*) in the said section 33(3)—

(i) for " that person " substitute " or his personal representatives, that person or (in either case) his personal representatives ",

(ii) for the words from " in lieu of " to " year in " substitute " be charged as if the sum or sums in question were received on the date on ", and

(iii) for the words from " upon him " to " case may be " substitute " accordingly ", and

(*b*) in the said paragraph 6(1)—

(i) for " the recipient " substitute " by the person by whom the trade, profession or vocation was carried on before the discontinuance or change of basis, or his personal representatives, that person or (in either case) his personal representatives ", and

(ii) omit " on him ".

(3) It is hereby declared that, by virtue of section 63(5) of the
1965 c. 25. Finance Act 1965, section 34 of the Finance Act 1960 (receipts and losses accruing after change treated as discontinuance under section
1953 c. 34. 19 of the Finance Act 1953) applies in the case of an event treated as a discontinuance by virtue of section 54(2) of the said Act of 1965 as it applies in the case of a change so treated under the said section 19.

(4) It is further declared—

(*a*) that so much of section 18(6) of the Finance Act 1968 as provides that a trade, profession or vocation carried on before a discontinuance is not to be treated as the same as any carried on after the discontinuance applies only for the purposes of section 19 of that Act, and

(*b*) that paragraph 4(1) of Schedule 10 to the said Act of 1968 (work in progress) is to be construed in accordance with section 43(5) of the Finance Act 1960.

Pensions

1952 c. 10. 5.—(1) For paragraph 2 of Schedule E in section 156 of the Income Tax Act 1952 (charging pensions by reference to the terms of Schedule D) substitute—

" 2. Tax under this Schedule shall also be charged in respect of any pension which is paid otherwise than by or on behalf of a person outside the United Kingdom.".

(2) For paragraph 3 of that Schedule (pensions and annuities payable by reason of service outside the United Kingdom) substitute—

" 3. Where—

(*a*) any pension or annuity is payable in the United Kingdom by or through any public department, officer or agent of the government of a territory to which this paragraph applies (but otherwise than out of the public revenue of the United Kingdom or the public revenue of Northern Ireland) to a person who has been employed in relevant service outside the United Kingdom in respect of that service, or SCH. 20

(*b*) any pension or annuity is so payable to the widow, child, relative or dependant of any such person as aforesaid,

and the person in receipt of the pension or annuity is chargeable to tax as a person resident in the United Kingdom, the pension or annuity shall be chargeable to tax under this Schedule.

The territories to which this paragraph applies are—

(i) any country forming part of Her Majesty's dominions,

(ii) any other country for the time being mentioned in section 1(3) of the British Nationality Act 1948, and

(iii) any territory under Her Majesty's protection,

and in this paragraph " relevant service " means the service of the Crown, or service under the government of a territory to which this paragraph applies.".

(3) A pension which—

(*a*) is paid by or on behalf of a person outside the United Kingdom, and

(*b*) is not charged under paragraph 3 of Schedule E

shall be charged to tax under Case V of Schedule D.

Close companies : surtax apportionments : loan creditors

6.—(1) In paragraph 11(1) of Schedule 5 to the Finance Act 1966 (rule for determining interests of loan creditors in the case of any company which is an investment company), for " which is an investment company " substitute " which is not a trading company as defined in paragraph 8(1) of Schedule 18 to the said Act of 1965 ". 1966 c. 18.

(2) Subsection (5)(*a*) of section 78 of the Finance Act 1965 (applying certain provisions of the Income Tax Act 1952 to apportionments under that section) shall not have effect so as to apply the provisos to section 258(3) of the said Act of 1952 (beneficial interests in loans) in the case of any trading company as defined in paragraph 8(1) of Schedule 18 to the said Act of 1965: and in the said provisos as they apply by virtue of the said subsection (5)(*a*) in the case of any other company, " participator " shall not be substituted for " loan creditor " (as required by the said subsection (5)(*a*)), but— 1965 c. 25. 1952 c. 10.

(*a*) for " this Chapter " (in both places) substitute " section 78 of the Finance Act 1965 ",

(*b*) for " the said subsection (1) " (in both places) substitute " subsection (5) of the said section 78 ",

(*c*) omit " the income of " (twice), and

(*d*) for " by virtue of the preceding provisions of this section " (in both places) substitute " in respect of that loan capital or debt ".

SCH. 20

Foreign income tax

7.—(1) For the purposes of the Income Tax Acts and the Corporation Tax Acts, the amount of any income arising in any place outside the United Kingdom shall, subject to the provisions of this paragraph, be treated as reduced by any sum which has been paid in respect of tax on that income in the place where the income has arisen (that is to say tax payable under the law of a country outside the United Kingdom).

(2) Sub-paragraph (1) of this paragraph—

(*a*) shall not apply to income the tax on which is to be computed by reference to the amount of income received in the United Kingdom, and

1952 c. 10. (*b*) shall not affect the proviso to section 227(2) of the Income Tax Act 1952 (personal relief for non-residents: computation by reference to amount of total income, including income not taxed in the United Kingdom),

and this paragraph has effect subject to paragraph 2(2) of Schedule 16
1965 c. 25. to the Finance Act 1965 (no deduction for foreign tax where credit is allowable for that tax against income tax or corporation tax).

Commonwealth Agents-General, and official agents, etc.

8.—(1) An Agent-General who is resident in the United Kingdom shall be entitled to the same immunity from income tax as that to which the head of a mission so resident is entitled under the
1964 c. 81. Diplomatic Privileges Act 1964.

(2) Any person having or exercising any employment to which this sub-paragraph applies (not being a person employed in any trade, business or other undertaking carried on for the purposes of profit) shall be entitled to the same immunity from income tax as that to which a member of the staff of a mission is entitled under the Diplomatic Privileges Act 1964.

The employments to which this sub-paragraph applies are the employment in the United Kingdom as—

(*a*) a member of the personal staff of any Agent-General, or

(*b*) an official agent for, or for any state or province of, any of the countries for the time being mentioned in section 1(3)
1948 c. 56. of the British Nationality Act 1948 or the Republic of Ireland, or

(*c*) an official agent for any self-governing colony.

of a person certified by the High Commissioner of the country in question or, as the case may be, by the Agent-General for the state, province or self-governing colony in question to be ordinarily resident outside the United Kingdom and to be resident in the United Kingdom solely for the purpose of the performance of his duties as such member or official agent.

(3) In this paragraph—

"Agent-General" means the Agent-General for any state or province of a country within sub-paragraph (2)(*b*) above or for any self-governing colony;

"High Commissioner" includes the head of the mission of a country within sub-paragraph (2)(*b*) above, by whatever name called; SCH. 20

"mission" has the same meaning as in the Diplomatic Privileges Act 1964, and references to the head of a mission and a member of the staff of a mission shall be construed in accordance with that Act; 1964 c. 81.

"self-governing colony" means any colony certified by a Secretary of State to be a self-governing colony.

(4) Section 461 of the Income Tax Act 1952 (which is superseded by this paragraph) shall cease to have effect, and— 1952 c. 10.

(*a*) in section 39(2) of the Finance Act 1960 (application of Tax Acts to public departments), for the reference to any country, state, province or colony specified in subsection (2) of the said section 461 substitute a reference to any country, state, province or colony within sub-paragraph (2)(*b*) or (2)(*c*) above, 1960 c. 44.

(*b*) in section 35(3) of the Finance Act 1965 (capital gains tax exemptions), for the reference to the said section 461 substitute a reference to this paragraph. 1965 c. 25.

Definition of "company"

9.—(1) In the following provisions of the Income Tax Act 1952 "company" shall mean a company as defined for the purposes of Part IV of the Finance Act 1965—

Section 27(2) (returns by employers of lists of employees).

Chapter III of Part IX as applied to close companies by Part IV of the Finance Act 1965.

Section 444 (mutual business).

(2) The said definition of company shall also apply for the purposes of the following provisions relating to double taxation relief—

In the Income Tax Act 1952, paragraph 10 of Schedule 16 and paragraph 3 of Schedule 17.

Section 16 of the Finance Act 1964. 1964 c. 49.

Section 30(2) of the Finance Act 1966. 1966 c. 18.

Section 30 of the Finance Act 1968. 1968 c. 44.

(3) The said definition shall also apply for the purposes of Chapter II of Part II of the Finance Act 1962 (short term capital gains), but this sub-paragraph shall not be taken as extending the exemption from tax under the said Chapter II which is conferred on companies by section 82(2) of the Finance Act 1965 to any unit trust scheme which is not an authorised unit trust scheme within the meaning of section 69 of the Finance Act 1960. 1962 c. 44.

Meaning of "connected person"

10. In sections 32(1) and 47(3) of the Finance Act 1963 and section 25(10)(*b*) of the Finance Act 1966, for references to paragraph 20 of Schedule 9 to the Finance Act 1962 (meaning of "con- 1963 c. 25.

SCH. 20

1965 c. 25. nected person") substitute references to paragraph 21 of Schedule 7 to the Finance Act 1965 (which defines that expression similarly, but, in sub-paragraph (3), with minor variations as respects trustees of settlements); and the said paragraph 21 shall also apply instead of the said paragraph 20 for the purposes of paragraph 12(2) of

1962 c. 44. Schedule 9 to the Finance Act 1962.

Discharge of functions of Commissioners of Inland Revenue

1890 c. 21. 11.—(1) The Inland Revenue Regulation Act 1890 (in which "the Commissioners" means the Commissioners of Inland Revenue) shall be amended as follows.

(2) After section 4 insert—

"Exercise of functions of Commissioners. 4A. Any function conferred by or under any enactment, including any future enactment, on the Commissioners may be exercised by any officer of the Commissioners acting under their authority:

Provided that this section shall not apply to the making of any statutory instrument."

(3) At the end of section 24 add—

"(4) Any notice or other document purporting to be issued in exercise of any function conferred on the Commissioners shall, until the contrary is proved, be deemed to be so issued."

Appeals against assessment

12.—(1) An appeal may be brought against an assessment to income tax (including surtax), capital gains tax, or corporation tax by a notice of appeal in writing given within thirty days after the date of the notice of assessment.

(2) The notice of appeal shall be given to the inspector or other officer of the Board by whom the notice of assessment was given.

(3) An appeal against an assessment to surtax, or any other assessment made by the Board, shall be to the Special Commissioners.

(4) Subject to sub-paragraph (3) above, the appeal shall be to the General Commissioners, except that the appellant may elect (in

1964 c. 37. accordance with section 12(2) of the Income Tax Management Act 1964) to bring the appeal before the Special Commissioners instead of the General Commissioners.

(5) The notice of appeal against any assessment shall specify the grounds of appeal, but on the hearing of the appeal the Commissioners may allow the appellant to put forward any ground not specified in the notice, and take it into consideration if satisfied that the omission was not wilful or unreasonable.

(6) This paragraph has effect instead of—

1952 c. 10. (*a*) sections 51, 62 and 63(1) of the Income Tax Act 1952, and (so far as it relates to a right of appeal) section 229(4) of that Act, with the entry relating thereto in Schedule 4 to the Income Tax Management Act 1964, (*b*) paragraph 1(2) of Schedule 10 to the Finance Act 1965, and Regulations 3 and 4 of the Capital Gains Tax Regulations 1967, and Sch. 20 1965 c. 25. S.I. 1967/149.

(*c*) sub-paragraphs (2) and (4) of paragraph 6, and paragraph 17(2), of Schedule 6 to the Finance Act 1966, 1966 c. 18.

but has effect subject to any other express provision relating to any of the taxes mentioned in sub-paragraph (1) above, including in particular any provision under which an appeal lies to the Special Commissioners to the exclusion of the General Commissioners, any provision transferring jurisdiction to some other tribunal, and any provision making one kind of assessment conclusive in an appeal against another kind of assessment.

Evidence and procedure in appeals and other proceedings before Commissioners

13.—(1) Sub-paragraphs (2) and (3) below shall have effect in substitution for section 59(1) of the Income Tax Act 1952 (evidence). 1952 c. 10.

(2) Any party to an appeal to the Commissioners shall be entitled to adduce any lawful evidence.

(3) The Commissioners may summon any person (other than the appellant) to appear before them and give evidence, and a witness before the Commissioners may be examined on oath:

Provided that any agent or servant of the appellant, and any other person confidentially employed in his affairs, may refuse to be sworn or to answer any question to which he objects.

(4) In section 59(3)(*b*) of that Act, the words " or to subscribe the oath " shall be omitted; and the proviso to that subsection shall be taken as referring to any such person as is within the proviso to sub-paragraph (3) above.

(5) In section 52(4) of the said Act of 1952 (right of appellant or officers to appear by barrister or solicitor) for " the appellant or officers " substitute " any party to the appeal ".

Interest on overdue tax

14.—(1) Sections 495 and 496 of the Income Tax Act 1952 and section 58 of the Finance Act 1960, as extended to capital gains tax and corporation tax by paragraph 1(1) of Schedule 10 and paragraph 8 of Schedule 15 to the Finance Act 1965, shall have effect subject to and in accordance with the following provisions. 1960 c. 44

(2) Subsection (1) of the said section 495 shall apply to any assessment to corporation tax as it applies to any assessment to surtax.

(3) The said section 496 shall not apply in consequence of any repayment of tax under section 75(2) of the said Act of 1965.

(4) For the purposes of the said section 496, a relief from corporation tax or capital gains tax shall not be treated as affecting tax charged by any assessment unless the assessment is to the same tax, and a relief from tax under section 75, 76 or 77 of the said Act

SCH. 20 of 1965 shall not be so treated unless the assessment is to tax under the same section.

(5) For the purposes of section 58 of the said Act of 1960 as applied for capital gains tax, the date when capital gains tax charged for any year of assessment ought to have been paid shall be 6th July in the next following year of assessment.

Form of returns

15. Any return, statement or declaration under the enactments relating to capital gains tax shall be in such form as the Board prescribe.

Service of documents

16.—(1) Any notice or other document to be given, sent, served or delivered under the Income Tax Acts, the enactments relating to capital gains tax or the Corporation Tax Acts may be served by post, and, if to be given, sent, served or delivered to or on any person by the Board, by any officer of the Board, or by or on behalf of any body of Commissioners, may be so served addressed to that person—

(*a*) at his usual or last known place of residence, or his place of business or employment, or

(*b*) in the case of a company, at any other prescribed place and, in the case of a liquidator of a company, at his address for the purposes of the liquidation or any other prescribed place.

(2) In sub-paragraph (1) above " prescribed " means prescribed by regulations made by the Board, and the power of making regulations for the purposes of that sub-paragraph shall be exercisable by statutory instrument subject to annulment in pursuance of a resolution of the House of Commons.

(3) In this paragraph " company " has the same meaning as in
1965 c. 25. Part IV of the Finance Act 1965.

The Income Tax Act 1952

1952 c. 10. 17.—(1) Section 12(4) of the Income Tax Act 1952 (Commissioners not to be concerned with their own tax cases) shall cease to have effect, but no General Commissioner or Special Commissioner shall act as such in relation to any matter in which he has a personal interest, or is interested on behalf of another person, except with the express consent of the parties to the proceedings.

(2) Section 65(2) of the said Act of 1952 (double assessments) shall apply in relation to corporation tax as it applies in relation to income tax, but with the substitution for " year " of " accounting period ".

(3) Section 66(1) of the said Act of 1952 (relief for error or mistake) shall apply to any assessment to income tax, and the words " under Schedule D or Schedule E " shall cease to have effect.

(4) In section 72(2) of the said Act of 1952, omit paragraph (*c*) (dates for payment of tax in respect of office or employment not covered by pay as you earn regulations). SCH. 20

(5) For section 120 of the said Act of 1952 (dividends of non-residents) substitute the following—

> " 120.—(1) No tax shall be chargeable in respect of dividends payable in the United Kingdom on the securities of any state or territory outside the United Kingdom, or in respect of any dividends or proceeds chargeable apart from this subsection under paragraph 3 or 4 of Schedule C, if it is proved, on a claim in that behalf made to the Commissioners of Inland Revenue, that the person owning the securities and entitled to the dividends or proceeds is not resident in the United Kingdom.
>
> (2) Where securities are held under a trust, and the person who is the beneficiary in possession under the trust is the sole beneficiary in possession and can, by means either of the revocation of the trust or of the exercise of any powers under the trust, call upon the trustees at any time to transfer the securities to him absolutely free from any trust, that person shall, for the purposes of subsection (1) above, be deemed to be the person owning the securities."

(6) In section 121 of the said Act of 1952, in the definition of " dividends "—

(*a*) omit " (except in the phrase ' stock, dividends or interest ') ", and

(*b*) before " annuities ", where it first occurs, insert " public ".

Accordingly—

(i) in section 117 of the said Act, omit paragraph 6 of Schedule C, and

(ii) in section 119(1) and (2) of that Act, for " dividends or interest " substitute " or dividends ".

(7) The appeal given by section 127(3) of the said Act of 1952 as amended by Schedule 4 to the Income Tax Management Act 1964 (decision by Board whether or not to give a direction as to basis period) shall lie to the General Commissioners unless the appellant elects in accordance with section 12(2) of the said Act of 1964 to bring the appeal before the Special Commissioners instead of the General Commissioners. 1964 c. 37.

(8) In section 129(3) of the said Act of 1952 (notice to revise basis of assessment: change in persons carrying on trade)—

(*a*) for " if given after the occurrence of the change " substitute " if given after the occurrence of the change, and after notice has been given under section 19(3) of the Finance Act 1953 as respects the change ", and

(*b*) in paragraphs (i) and (ii), for " the persons " substitute " the individuals ".

(9) It is hereby declared that Part IV of the Finance Act 1965 does not apply anything in section 132 of the Income Tax Act 1952 (allowable deductions and remittance basis) for the purposes of 1965 c. 25. 1952 c. 10.

SCH. 20 corporation tax, but that so much of section 429(1) of the said Act of 1952 (foreign life assurance funds) as requires tax or income to be computed by reference to the amount of income received in the United Kingdom as in the cases mentioned in subsection (2) of the said section 132 does apply for the purposes of corporation tax under Cases IV and V of Schedule D.

(10) In section 137 of the said Act of 1952 (as amended by
1964 c. 37. paragraph (1)(*c*) of Schedule 4 to the Income Tax Management Act 1964)—

(*a*) in paragraph (*c*) (rent of accommodation used partly for trade, profession or vocation), omit " shall be such as may be determined by an inspector and ", and, for " an inspector is of opinion ", substitute " it appears ", and

(*b*) in paragraph (*i*) (bad and doubtful debts) omit " to the satisfaction of an inspector ".

(11) In section 144(4) of the said Act of 1952 (partnership returns), for " the respective Commissioners may, if they think fit," substitute " an inspector may, if he thinks fit," and for " they are " substitute " he is ".

1965 c. 25. (12) It is hereby declared that Part IV of the Finance Act 1965
1952 c. 10. does not apply section 148 or 153 of the Income Tax Act 1952 for the purposes of corporation tax.

(13) For the purposes of section 155(1) of the said Act of 1952 as applied by section 53 of the Finance Act 1965, apportionments shall be made on a time basis in accordance with section 89(6) of the said Act of 1965, and section 155(2) of the said Act of 1952 (apportionment on a monthly basis) shall not apply.

(14) In section 169(1) of the said Act of 1952 (payments out of profits or gains brought into charge to income tax) as amended by Part II of Schedule 13 to this Act, after " payment ", where it first occurs, insert " charged with tax under Case III of Schedule D " ; and in section 170(1)(*a*) of that Act (payments not out of profits or gains brought into charge to income tax) as so amended, before " Schedule D ", insert " Case III of ".

In consequence of the amendments made by the preceding provision—

(*a*) omit subsections (2) and (4) of the said section 169, and subsection (5) of the said section 170 ;

1963 c. 25. (*b*) in section 16(6) of the Finance Act 1963, omit " other payments being " and, before " Schedule D ", insert " Case III of ", and

(*c*) in sections 52(3)(*a*) and 53(5)(*b*) of the Finance Act 1965, for " but not including sums falling within section 169(4) (rents, etc.) " substitute " but not including sums which are, or but for any exemption would be, chargeable under Schedule A ".

(15) For section 190 of the said Act of 1952 (dividends of non-residents) there shall be substituted the following section—

" 190.—(1) In the cases mentioned in sections 188 and 189 above, no tax shall be chargeable if it is proved, on a claim in that behalf made to the Commissioners of Inland Revenue, that the person owning the stocks, funds, shares or securities and entitled to the dividends or proceeds is not resident in the United Kingdom. Sch. 20

(2) Where stocks, funds, shares or securities are held under a trust, and the person who is the beneficiary in possession under the trust is the sole beneficiary in possession and can, by means either of the revocation of the trust or of the exercise of any powers under the trust, call upon the trustees at any time to transfer the stocks, funds, shares or securities to him absolutely free from any trust, that person shall, for the purposes of subsection (1) above, be deemed to be the person owning the stocks, funds, shares or securities."

(16) Section 193 of the said Act of 1952 (exemption for interest on certain savings certificates issued to local residents by the government of Northern Ireland, of Ceylon, or of any colony, protectorate, protected state, trust territory or mandated territory) shall apply only to certificates issued by the government of Northern Ireland.

(17) Sections 203(1)(ii) and 416(3) of the said Act of 1952 (sale and repurchase of, and transfers of income arising from, securities) shall apply in relation to corporation tax in accordance with paragraph 3 of Schedule 15 to the Finance Act 1965, and with the omission, in the said section 203(1)(ii), of the words " unless he shows that it has borne tax at the standard rate ", and, in the said section 416(3), of the words " that it has borne tax at the standard rate or ". 1965 c. 25.

(18) In section 207(1)(*b*) of the said Act of 1952 (information about court orders), for " vary an order " substitute " vary or revive an order ".

(19) In section 212(5) of the said Act of 1952 (child relief) for " Governor of Northern Ireland " substitute " Ministry of Education for Northern Ireland ".

(20) In section 214(1) of the said Act of 1952 (child-minder and housekeeper relief), omit " for the purpose of having the charge and care of any child of his or " and " take such charge or ", and, after " some other female person ", insert " to reside with him ".

(21) In section 219(2)(*a*)(i) of the said Act of 1952 (life insurance relief: insurances made after 22nd June 1916), for " India " substitute " any other country mentioned in section 1(3) of the British Nationality Act 1948 "; and in section 225(2)(*a*)(i) of that Act (relief for earlier insurances), for " Her Majesty's dominions, India or the Republic of Ireland " substitute " the Crown's dominions ". 1948 c. 56.

(22) In section 226(5) of the said Act of 1952 (life insurance relief: supplementary provisions), for " Commissioners to whom the claim for relief is made " substitute " inspector ".

(23) In section 227(2)(*b*) of the said Act of 1952 (personal reliefs for non-residents), for " native State " substitute " territory ".

SCH. 20

(24) In section 229(1) of the said Act of 1952 (dates for payment of surtax) for " signed and allowed " substitute " made " (twice).

(25) Subsections (6) and (7) of section 229 of the said Act of 1952 (surtax regulations) shall cease to have effect, together with the
S.I. 1965/433. Income Tax (Surtax, etc.) Regulations 1965, but, in section 232 of that Act (power of Board to require additional particulars for purposes of surtax), after " The Board may for the purpose of charging surtax " insert " by notice in writing ".

(26) In section 237 of the said Act of 1952 (surtax avoidance by sales cum dividend, etc.), in subsection (7)(*b*), for " duty has been paid at the rate of one or two pounds per cent " substitute " ad valorem duty has been paid ".

(27) In section 249(2) of the said Act of 1952 (surtax apportionments), omit paragraph (*a*) and, in paragraph (*b*), after " shall " insert " for the purposes of surtax ".

(28) It is hereby declared that, in section 342(4) of the said Act of 1952 (losses carried forward) the expression " this Act " includes the
1965 c. 25. provisions of Part IV of the Finance Act 1965 about income tax under Schedule F (which replace the provisions of the said Act of 1952 about the taxation of company dividends).

(29) It is hereby declared that, in section 347(1)(*b*) and section 347(4) of the said Act of 1952 (matters which may be included in double taxation agreements), references to income included, in relation to the profits tax, references to profits chargeable to that tax, so that, under section 64(1) of the Finance Act 1965, the said provisions apply to income chargeable to corporation tax as well as income chargeable to income tax.

(30) In section 352 of the said Act of 1952 (power to make special agreements for double taxation relief in respect of shipping, air transport and agency profits), for " any country to which this section applies " in subsections (1) and (2) substitute " any territory outside the United Kingdom ", and for " country ", wherever else occurring in those subsections, substitute " territory ".

(31) In sections 354(2) and 359(1)(2) of the said Act of 1952
1968 c. 44. (husband and wife) and section 15(7) of the Finance Act 1968 (parent and child), after " curator ", wherever it occurs, insert " receiver ".

(32) In section 355(1) of the said Act of 1952 (option for separate assessment) for " income tax " and " tax " substitute " income tax other than surtax ".

(33) Exemption under section 379(1) of the said Act of 1952 in respect of income derived from investments or deposits of a superannuation fund shall be given on a claim to which section 9
1964 c. 37. of the Income Tax Management Act 1964 shall apply.

(34) For the purposes of any charge to corporation tax under section 419 of the said Act of 1952 (estates of deceased persons: absolute interests in residue), the residuary income of a company shall be computed in the first instance by reference to years of

assessment, and the residuary income for any such year shall be apportioned between the accounting periods (if more than one) comprising that year. SCH. 20

(35) In section 425(6)(*b*) of the said Act of 1952, for the words—

"expenses of management in respect of which repayment of tax may be claimed under this section"

substitute—

"expenses of management deductible under section 69(1) of the Finance Act 1965". 1965 c. 25.

(36) In sections 434(1) and 435(1) of the said Act of 1952 (time limit for election) after "year of assessment" insert "or company's accounting period".

(37) In section 437 of the said Act of 1952—

(*a*) for the definition of "assurance company" substitute "'assurance company' means any company, as defined in Part IV of the Finance Act 1965, being a company to which the Insurance Companies Act 1958 or the Insurance Companies Act (Northern Ireland) 1968 applies,"

(*b*) in the definition of "life assurance business" for "annuities" substitute "annuities on human life".

(38) Sections 439(2), 440(1) and 440(2) of the said Act of 1952 (tax exemptions of savings banks, friendly societies and trade unions) shall be amended as follows—

(*a*) in each of those provisions, omit "under Schedules C and D",

(*b*) in the said section 440(1), for "one hundred and sixty pounds" substitute "£160 a year", and

(*c*) in the said section 440(2), for the words from "interest" to "solely" substitute "income which is not trading income, and which is applicable and applied".

(39) In section 442 of the said Act of 1952 (share interest and loan interest of industrial and provident societies)—

(*a*) at the end of the proviso to subsection (1), insert "and in any such case, section 26 of the Finance Act 1969 shall apply to the payment as it applies to a payment of yearly interest, and income tax shall be deducted accordingly",

(*b*) in subsection (2), omit "without deduction of income tax", and

(*c*) in subsection (3), omit "subsection (2) of " and "becomes chargeable as therein provided", and, after "on that person", insert "becomes so chargeable".

(40) In the proviso to section 445(1) of the said Act of 1952 (Board's duty to ensure that arrangements with building societies preserve as nearly as may be the total tax payable to the Crown) for "total tax" substitute "total income tax".

SCH. 20

1965 c. 25.

(41) In the said section 445 " dividend " shall include any distribution as defined for the purposes of Part IV of the Finance Act 1965 whether described as a dividend or otherwise.

1952 c. 10.

(42) It is hereby declared that the provisions of the Income Tax Acts applying for the purposes of corporation tax by virtue of Part IV of the Finance Act 1965 include section 472 of the Income Tax Act 1952 (patent royalties).

(43) Section 510 of the said Act of 1952 (settling of appeals by agreement) shall apply, subject to any necessary modifications, to any proceedings which are to be heard and determined in the same way as an appeal against an assessment.

(44) The definition of " relative " in section 526(1) of the said Act of 1952 shall apply only for the purposes of Part VIII of that Act (personal reliefs).

(45) Part III of Schedule 8 to the said Act of 1952 (paying agents) shall be amended as follows—

(*a*) in paragraph 1(1), omit from " within one month " to " shall also ",

(*b*) after paragraph 1(2), insert—

" (3) Every chargeable person shall, not later than twelve months after paying any dividends or effecting any other transaction in respect of which he is a chargeable person, and unless within that time he delivers an account with respect to the dividends or proceeds in question under sub-paragraph (1) above, deliver to the Commissioners of Inland Revenue a written statement specifying his name and address and describing those dividends or proceeds.", and

(*c*) in paragraph 4, for " income tax " substitute " income or corporation tax ".

(46) In Schedule 10 to the said Act of 1952, for items 4 to 9 substitute the following—

" 4. Member of Queen Alexandra's Royal Army Nursing Corps.

5. Member of Women's Royal Army Corps.

6. Woman employed with the Royal Army Medical Corps or the Royal Army Dental Corps with relative rank as an officer.

7. Member of the Princess Mary's Royal Air Force Nursing Service and Reserve.

8. Member of the Women's Royal Air Force.

9. Woman officer of the Medical and Dental Branch of the Royal Air Force.

10. Member of the Voluntary Aid Detachment Reserves employed under the Admiralty Board of the Defence Council."

(47) Paragraph 13 of Schedule 16 to the said Act of 1952 (claims to be made within six years of relevant year of assessment) shall have effect for the purposes of corporation tax as if it specified a period of six years from the end of the company's accounting period for which the income falls to be charged to corporation tax, or would fall so to be charged if any corporation tax were chargeable in respect thereof. SCH. 20

The Finance Act 1956

18.—(1) In section 22(8) of the Finance Act 1956— 1956 c. 54.

(*a*) for " as director of an investment company (as defined in section 257 of the Income Tax Act 1952) " substitute " as director of a company whose income consists wholly or mainly of investment income (construing investment income in accordance with paragraph 8(1) of Schedule 18 to the Finance Act 1965) being a company ", and 1952 c. 10.

(*b*) for " that Act " substitute " the said Act of 1952 ".

(2) Section 9 of the Income Tax Management Act 1964 shall apply to a claim under section 28(1) of the Finance Act 1956 for relief under section 23 of that Act. 1964 c. 37.

(3) Section 28(2) of the said Act of 1956 shall apply only for the purposes of section 27 of that Act, and of section 28(1) of that Act as it has effect in relation to questions arising under the said section 27, and the power to make regulations conferred by subsections (3) and (4) of the said section 28 shall be exercisable for those purposes only.

(4) In section 28(5) of the said Act of 1956 for " this Part of this Act " substitute " section 23 or 27 of this Act ", and for " penalty of five hundred pounds " substitute " penalty not exceeding five hundred pounds ".

The Finance Act 1960

19.—(1) In section 27 of the Finance Act 1960 (sale of securities cum dividend), in subsections (4) and (5), omit from " except " to " nineteen hundred and sixty ". 1960 c. 44.

(2) In section 28(6) of the said Act of 1960 (appeal against notice of adjustment to counteract tax advantage), for " the clerk to the Special Commissioners " substitute " the Commissioners of Inland Revenue " ; and, in section 28(8) of that Act (supplemental), the first reference to section 247 of the Income Tax Act 1952 shall not include a reference to subsection (1) of that section.

(3) In section 37(7) of the said Act of 1960 (time for delivery of particulars), for " fourteen days " substitute " thirty days ".

(4) Section 51 of the said Act of 1960 (time limit for recovery from taxpayer of tax lost through his fault), as extended to capital gains tax by paragraph 1(1) of Schedule 10 to the Finance 1965 c. 25.

SCH. 20 Act 1965, shall apply separately to income tax and to capital gains tax, so that the making of an assessment to one of those taxes shall not affect the time allowed for the making of an assessment to the other tax.

(5) Section 60 of the said Act of 1960 (evidence in penalty proceedings) shall apply in relation to corporation tax as if "income" included chargeable gains.

(6) In section 69(2)(*a*) of the said Act of 1960 (sums appropriated for managers' remuneration), after "income" insert "or chargeable gains".

The Finance Act 1963

1963 c. 25. 20.—(1) In section 15(4) of the Finance Act 1963 (election for Case VIII to apply to furnished lettings), and in paragraph 7(2) of Schedule 4 to that Act (election with respect to land managed as one estate), after "year of assessment" insert "or company's accounting period".

(2) Subsections (4) and (5) of section 16 of the said Act of 1963 (collection of Case VIII tax from derivative lessees and agents) shall apply for corporation tax as well as for income tax.

(3) It is hereby declared that the provisions of the Income Tax Acts applying for the purposes of corporation tax by virtue of Part
1965 c. 25. IV of the Finance Act 1965 include section 17 of the said Act of 1963.

(4) Sections 18 and 30 of the said Act of 1963 (returns, etc., for purposes of Case VIII, and supplemental provisions with respect to determination of annual value) shall apply for the purposes of corporation tax.

(5) In section 22(6) of the said Act of 1963 (election with respect to premiums payable by instalments) for "before the expiration of the year of assessment following that in which he becomes entitled to the first such instalment" substitute "not later than one year after the year of assessment or company's accounting period in which he becomes entitled to the first such instalment".

(6) So much of paragraph 19 of Schedule 4 to the said Act of 1963 as relates to the construction of references in that Schedule to a lease shall not apply for the purposes of paragraphs 8 to 10 of that Schedule (deductions from rents: premiums etc.); and the definition in the said paragraph 19 of "premises" shall, instead of applying for the purposes of that Schedule only, apply for all the purposes of Chapter II of Part II of the said Act of 1963.

The Income Tax Management Act 1964

1964 c. 37. 21.—(1) In section 7(8) of the Income Tax Management Act 1964 (limitation of penalty for failure to make return) the limit on the penalty shall not apply unless it is shown that there was neither any income nor any chargeable gains to be included in the return.

(2) Where under section 9(4)(*a*) of the said Act of 1964 (claims under Acts passed after that Act) an appeal lies to the General Commissioners the appellant may elect (in accordance with section 12(2) of that Act) to bring the appeal before the Special Commissioners instead of the General Commissioners: SCH. 20

Provided that if an appeal to either body of Commissioners is pending against an assessment on the appellant which relates to the same source of income as that to which the claim relates, the appeal on the claim shall lie to that body of Commissioners.

(3) Section 15(2)(*a*) of the said Act of 1964 (application of section 12 of that Act to county court in Northern Ireland)—

(*a*) shall have effect as if its exclusion of subsection (2) of the said section 12 were an exclusion of the first paragraph only of that subsection, and

(*b*) shall be taken as applying section 59 of the Finance Act 1960 (summary recovery of penalty for offence under the said section 12), but not sections 52, 59 or 64 of the Income Tax Act 1952 (which are referred to in the said section 12). 1960 c. 44. 1952 c. 10.

(4) Paragraph 1 of Schedule 10 to the Finance Act 1965 shall be read as applying for the purposes of capital gains tax rules 5 and 6 in Schedule 3 to the said Act of 1964, but no other rule in that Schedule, the reference in the said rule 5 to Cases I and II of Schedule D being for that purpose disregarded. 1965 c. 25.

(5) In Schedule 4 to the said Act of 1964, in paragraph 2 of the entry relating to section 507 of the Income Tax Act 1952, omit " to which section 9 of this Act applies ".

The Finance Act 1965

22.—(1) Section 17(3) of the Finance Act 1965 (which excludes certain vehicles from the short term capital gains tax, and is superseded by the more general exclusion of wasting assets in paragraph 1 of Schedule 13 to the Finance Act 1968) shall cease to have effect. 1968 c. 44.

(2) In section 44(8) of the said Act of 1965 (determination by General Commissioners of value of certain shares or securities) insert at the end " and those Commissioners shall hear and determine the question in the same way as an appeal ".

(3) In section 47(1) of the said Act of 1965 (charging under Schedule F dividends and other distributions not charged under Schedule D or Schedule E), for " Schedule D or Schedule E " substitute " any other Schedule ".

(4) In section 47(5) of the said Act of 1965 (distributions made in respect of share capital in a winding-up excluded from references to distributions, except references in any provision specially relating to a winding-up) omit " except references in any provision specially relating to a winding-up ".

SCH. 20 (5) In section 62(4) of the said Act of 1965 (set off of losses, etc. against franked investment income), for "after", in both places where it occurs, substitute "within", and for "income" (in paragraph (*a*)) substitute "profits".

(6) If a claim under section 62(7) of the said Act of 1965 relates to section 59 of that Act (terminal losses), and an accounting period of the company falls partly outside the three years mentioned in subsection (1) of the said section 59, then—

(*a*) the restriction imposed by subsection (2) of the said section 59 on the amount of the reduction that may be made in the trading income of that period shall be applied only to any relief to be given apart from the said section 62, and shall be applied without regard to any amount treated as trading income of the period by virtue of that section, but

(*b*) relief under the said section 62 shall be given only against so much (if any) of the amount so treated as would, under subsection (3)(*a*) of that section, be apportioned to the part of the period falling within the three years in question if that part were a separate accounting period.

This sub-paragraph has effect in substitution for subsection (4) of the said section 62 as applied by subsection (7)(*b*) of that section.

(7) In sections 67 and 68 of the said Act of 1965 "unit trust" shall mean an authorised unit trust scheme as defined in section
1960 c. 44. 71(1) of the Finance Act 1960, and section 37 of the said Act of 1965 (relief for unit holders in respect of gains of unit trusts) shall have effect accordingly.

(8) In section 70(7) of the said Act of 1965 (amalgamations and transfers of engagements), references to industrial and provident societies shall be taken as references to registered industrial and provident societies.

(9) In section 71 of the said Act of 1965, "dividend" shall include any distribution as defined for the purposes of Part IV of that Act whether described as a dividend or otherwise.

(10) Subsections (2) and (5) of the said section 71 shall apply to
1952 c. 10. a company described in section 445(6) of the Income Tax Act 1952 (business similar to that of a building society) as they apply to a building society, except that in the said subsection (2) references to dividends and shares shall be deemed to be omitted.

1965 c. 25. (11) Section 77(3)(*a*) of the Finance Act 1965 shall not have effect so as to apply section 258(1) of the Income Tax Act 1952 (sums expended in or available for redemption of loan capital to be treated for purposes of shortfall charge as not applied to requirements of company's business) to any company which is either a trading company as defined in paragraph 8(1) of Schedule 18 to the said Act of 1965 or, under paragraph 8(2) of that Schedule, a member of a trading group.

(12) In paragraph 4(3) of Schedule 16 to the said Act of 1965 (dividends paid by companies resident in Commonwealth territories

to United Kingdom companies which control them: meaning of "control") the reference to the Commonwealth territories shall be construed as a reference to Her Majesty's dominions, any other country for the time being mentioned in section 1(3) of the British Nationality Act 1948, the British protectorates and protected states, and any trust territory administered by the government of any part of Her Majesty's dominions. SCH. 20 1948 c. 56.

(13) In paragraph 4(1)(*c*) of Schedule 18 to the said Act of 1965, "loan creditors" shall have the meaning given by section 258(4) of the Income Tax Act 1952, instead of that given by sub-paragraph (2) of the said paragraph 4 (so as to exclude loan creditors in respect of money lent in the ordinary course of banking business). 1952 c. 10.

(14) In paragraph 8(1) of Schedule 18 to the said Act of 1965 ("trading company" to include any company whose income does not consist mainly of investment income), for "consist mainly" substitute "consist wholly or mainly".

The Finance Act 1966

23.—(1) At the end of paragraph 18(1) of Schedule 6 to the Finance Act 1966 (which applies section 9 of the Income Tax Management Act 1964 to claims under section 62 of the Finance Act 1965 to set off losses etc., against franked investment income), insert "but paragraph 6(3) of this Schedule (Special Commissioners to determine appeals against assessments so far as relating to management expenses relief) shall apply to an appeal on any such claim as if it were an appeal against an assessment to corporation tax." 1966 c. 18. 1964 c. 37. 1965 c. 25.

(2) In paragraph 21(2)(*a*) of the said Schedule 6 (relief under section 75(2) of the Finance Act 1965 to be claimed within six years from end of year of assessment to which the claim relates), for "to which the claim relates" substitute "in which the repayment is made".

(3) Paragraph 24(1) of the said Schedule 6 (responsibility of company officers) shall apply to all provisions of the Income Tax Acts, and all the enactments relating to capital gains tax, as it applies to the Corporation Tax Acts, and section 20(3) of the Finance Act 1956 (responsibility for returns under that section in case of unincorporated bodies) shall not apply in the case of any body which is a company within the meaning of Part IV of the Finance Act 1965. 1956 c. 54.

The Finance Act 1967

24.—(1) It is hereby declared that, in paragraph 6 of Schedule 11 to the Finance Act 1967, "shares" includes, as in the provisions amended by that paragraph, stock. 1967 c. 54.

(2) In paragraph 8(3) of Schedule 11 to the said Act of 1967, for "for an accounting period after that event" substitute "for an accounting period ending after that event".

The Finance Act 1968

25.—(1) In section 55(6) of the Finance Act 1965 (application of Part I of Schedule 13 to that Act to nationalised bodies), and in

Sch. 20 1968 c. 73. 1968 c. 44. section 161(2) of the Transport Act 1968 (application of the said Part I to Executive for designated area), the references to the said Part I shall include references to Part II of Schedule 12 to the Finance Act 1968 except paragraphs 17 and 22.

1965 c. 25. (2) Sub-paragraphs (2) and (3) of paragraph 23 of Schedule 12 to the Finance Act 1968 (continuity of groups for the purposes of Part II of that Schedule) shall apply for the purposes of Part I of Schedule 13 to the Finance Act 1965 as they apply for the purposes of the said Part II.

Gas Act 1948

1948 c. 67. 26. In section 48(1) of the Gas Act 1948 (contributions by Boards to expenses of Gas Council) after " Council " insert " (including corporation tax) ".

Atomic Energy Authority Act 1954

1954 c. 32. 27. For paragraphs (*a*) to (*e*) of section 6(2) of the Atomic Energy Authority Act 1954 as amended by paragraph 12 of Schedule 15 to the Finance Act 1965 substitute—

" (*a*) from tax under Schedules A, B and C,

(*b*) from tax under Schedule D in respect of any yearly interest or other annual payment received by the Authority,

(*c*) from tax under Schedule F in respect of distributions received by the Authority, and

(*d*) from tax in respect of chargeable gains,

and section 48(1) of the Finance Act 1965 (franked investment income) shall not apply to such distributions as are mentioned in paragraph (*c*) above."

Electricity Act 1957

1952 c. 10. 1957 c. 48. 28.—(1) Paragraph 6 of Schedule 15 to the Finance Act 1965, in applying section 483 of the Income Tax Act 1952, shall be taken also to apply all the provisions of section 24 of the Electricity Act 1957.

(2) For section 21(2)(*c*) of the Electricity Act 1957 (contributions by Boards to expenses of Electricity Council) substitute—

" (*c*) corporation tax ".

National Loans Act 1968

1889 c. 13. 1939 c. 117. 1968 c. 13. 29. Without prejudice to the provisions of section 38(1) of the Interpretation Act 1889 (references to provisions repealed and re-enacted), references in the Income Tax Acts and the Corporation Tax Acts to section 2 of the National Loans Act 1939 shall include references to section 14 of the National Loans Act 1968.

Sch. 20

Commencement of amendments

30.—(1) Subject to sub-paragraphs (2) to (4) below, the preceding provisions of this Schedule, except provisions declaratory of the law, shall have effect only in relation to tax for years of assessment and companies' accounting periods ending after 5th April 1970.

(2) Paragraph 7 of this Schedule shall have effect as respects income tax for the year 1969-70 and subsequent years of assessment, and as respects corporation tax for the financial year 1969 and subsequent financial years.

(3) Paragraph 23(1) of this Schedule shall apply to any appeal notice of which is given after the passing of this Act.

(4) The following provisions shall come into force for all purposes on 6th April 1970, that is to say, paragraph 9(1) so far as it relates to section 27(2) of the Income Tax Act 1952, paragraphs 11 to 16, in paragraph 17, sub-paragraphs (1) to (3), (7), (11), (25), (31), (36), (43), (45) and (47), paragraph 19 except sub-paragraphs (1) and (6), in paragraph 20, sub-paragraphs (1), (4) and (5), paragraph 21, paragraph 22(2), and sub-paragraphs (2) and (3) of paragraph 23.

SCHEDULE 21

Section 61.

Repeals

Part I

Customs and Excise Repeals

Chapter	Short Title	Extent of Repeal
10 & 11 Eliz. 2. c. 13.	The Vehicles (Excise) Act 1962.	As from 1st January 1970— in section 9(1) the words " a limited trade licence or " and the word " general "; in section 9(2)(*a*) the word " general "; in section 24(1), the words " ' general trade licence ', and ' limited trade licence ' ".
1963 c. 25.	The Purchase Tax Act 1963.	In Part I of Schedule 1— in Group 2, paragraphs (1), (2) and (3) of the exemptions; in Group 7, the words " *Not chargeable under this Group* " and the words " Tissue and fabrics exceeding 12 inches in width ".
1964 c. 49.	The Finance Act 1964.	In section 4(3), the word " and " in the second place where it occurs. As from 1st September 1969, section 6(1).
1965 c. 25.	The Finance Act 1965.	Section 1.
1966 c. 18.	The Finance Act 1966.	As from 1st October 1969— in section 13, paragraphs (*c*)

SCH. 21

Chapter	Short Title	Extent of Repeal
1966 c. 18—*cont.*	The Finance Act 1966—*cont.*	and (*d*) of subsection (4) and in subsection (5) the words "in addition to bingo"; section 14; in section 15(6), the definitions of "gaming machine" and "supplier"; in Schedule 3— in paragraph 7, the words "or a gaming machine licence", the words "in the case of a gaming licence" and sub-paragraph (*c*); in paragraph 9, the words "or a gaming machine licence"; in paragraph 10, sub-paragraph (*b*); in paragraph 11, the words "or gaming machine licence", the words "in the case of a gaming licence", the words "bingo or, as the case may be, by way of", and sub-paragraph (*b*); in paragraph 13, the words "or gaming machine licence" and "or, as the case may be, 14(5)"; in paragraph 14, the words "or a gaming machine licence"; paragraphs 15 and 16; in paragraph 17(1), the words "or gaming machine licence", the words from "or, as the case may be, whereby" to "that date", and the words from "or, as the case may be to" onwards; in paragraph 18(1), the words "or on gaming machine licences" and the words "any of"; in paragraph 19, in sub-paragraph (*c*), the words "15, 16", and in sub-paragraph (*d*) the words "or gaming machines"; paragraph 22; and in paragraph 23(1), the words "or 14(1)" and "gaming machine".

SCH. 21

Chapter	Short Title	Extent of Repeal
1967 c. 54.	The Finance Act 1967.	Section 1(1) to (4). As from 1st January 1970, section 11(1)(*c*). Schedule 2.
1968 c. 44.	The Finance Act 1968.	Section 1(1), (2) and (4). Section 2(1). Section 3(1)(*c*). As from 1st October 1969, section 4(3). As from 1st January 1970, sections 8(2) and 9(*a*). Section 10(1). Schedules 1 to 3. As from 1st October 1969, Schedule 4 and, in paragraph 1 of Schedule 5, the words " or on gaming machine licences ". In Schedule 6, paragraphs 1 to 3.
1968 c. 65.	The Gaming Act 1968.	In Schedule 2, in paragraphs 20(1)(*e*) and 60(*c*), the words " or section 14 ". In Schedule 3, in paragraph 9(*e*), the words " or section 14 ". In Schedule 4, in paragraph 11(*e*), the words " or section 14 ". In Part III of Schedule 11, so much as amends section 13(4)(*c*) and section 14(2) of the Finance Act 1966, and so much as amends section 15(6) of that Act with respect to the definition of " gaming machine ".
1969 c. 27.	The Vehicle and Driving Licences Act 1969.	As from 1st January 1970, in section 33(1) the words " and ' general trade licence ' ".
1969 c. 32.	The Finance Act 1969.	As from 1st September 1969, paragraph 4(1) of Schedule 7.

PART II

DISALLOWANCE OF INTEREST

Chapter	Short Title	Extent of Repeal
15 & 16 Geo. 6. & 1 Eliz. 2. c. 10.	Income Tax Act 1952.	In section 138, for 1970–71 and subsequent years of assessment— in subsection (1)(*e*) the words " and without any

Sch. 21

Chapter	Short Title	Extent of Repeal
15 & 16 Geo. 6. & 1 Eliz. 2. c. 10—*cont.*	Income Tax Act 1952—*cont.*	deduction of United Kingdom income tax "; at the end of subsection (1) the words " notwithstanding anything in the last preceding section ", and subsection (2).
		Section 169(5) as respects interest paid after 15th August 1970.
		Section 200 as respects interest paid in 1970–71 or any subsequent year of assessment.
		Section 445(3)(*b*) for 1970-71 and subsequent years of assessment.
		Section 524(5)(*c*) for 1970–71 and subsequent years of assessment.
1963 c. 25.	The Finance Act 1963.	Section 43(4)(*a*) for 1970–71 and subsequent years of assessment.
1965 c. 25.	The Finance Act 1965.	In section 54(3) the words " nor section 137(*l*) of the Income Tax Act 1952 " for accounting periods ending in 1970-71 or any subsequent year of assessment.
		Section 71(1)(*b*) for 1970-71 and subsequent years of assessment.

Part III
Close Companies

Chapter	Short Title	Extent of Repeal
1965 c. 25.	The Finance Act 1965.	Section 74.
		In section 77 subsection (3)(*d*) and in the proviso to subsection (6) the words from " or below the amount " to the end of the section.
		In section 78(3) the words " (or amounts treated as such for purposes of section 77 above) ".
		Section 89(5).
		In Schedule 11, paragraph 9(1)(*a*).
		In Schedule 18, in paragraph 6(1), the words ' and " whole-time service director " ', paragraph 6(3) and paragraph 9(1)(*b*).

SCH. 21

Chapter	Short Title	Extent of Repeal
1966 c. 18.	The Finance Act 1966.	In Schedule 5, in paragraph 18(1)(*b*), the words from " is not in receipt " to " per annum and ", and in paragraph 18(3) the definition of " remuneration ".
1965 c. 54.	The Finance Act 1967.	In Schedule 11, in paragraph 9, the words " and paragraph 6(3) " and paragraph (*a*).

The repeals of section 77(3)(*d*) of, and paragraph 9(1)(*a*) of Schedule 11 to the Finance Act 1965 have effect as respects accounting periods beginning after 15th April 1969, and the repeals in paragraph 18 of Schedule 5 to the Finance Act 1966 have effect from that date.

The other repeals made by this Part of this Schedule apply as respects accounting periods ending after the end of March 1969 except so far as section 28 of this Act applies to any such accounting period.

PART IV

OTHER INCOME TAX AND CORPORATION TAX REPEALS

Chapter	Short Title	Extent of Repeal
15 & 16 Geo. 6. & 1 Eliz. 2. c. 10.	The Income Tax Act 1952	In subsection (1) of section 220, the words from " Where the relevant amount " to the end of the subsection. In section 430, subsections (4) and (5).
8 & 9 Eliz. 2. c. 44.	The Finance Act 1960.	In section 28(11), the proviso, except with respect to dividends received before 30th April 1969.
1963 c. 25.	The Finance Act 1963.	In section 12, subsections (2) and (5).
1964 c. 92.	The Finance (No. 2) Act 1964.	In section 1(2), the words from " and by the substitution " onwards.
1965 c. 25.	The Finance Act 1965.	Section 10(5). Section 65, except with respect to distributions made before 30th April 1969. Schedule 9, except the last four entries. In Schedule 15, paragraph 15(*b*), except with respect to distributions made before 30th April 1969. Schedule 17, except with respect to distributions made before 30th April 1969.
1966 c. 18.	The Finance Act 1966.	In Schedule 5, paragraph 17, except with respect to distributions made before 30th April 1969.

SCH. 21

Chapter	Short Title	Extent of Repeal
1967 c. 54.	The Finance Act 1967.	In section 16, subsection (2), in subsection (3) the words from " for the year " to " assessment " and subsection (5), except in so far as it preserves the effect of any provision of section 218 of the Income Tax Act 1952. In Schedule 11, except with respect to distributions made before 30th April 1969, sub-paragraphs (4) and (5) of paragraph 3 and paragraph 4.
1968 c. 44.	The Finance Act 1968.	Section 14(1). Section 27, except with respect to distributions made before 30th April 1969.
1969 c. 46.	The Family Law Reform Act 1969.	In Schedule 2, paragraph 3.
1969 c. 39.	The Age of Majority (Scotland) Act 1969.	In Schedule 2, paragraph 3.

PART V

ESTATE DUTY REPEALS

Chapter	Short Title	Extent
44 & 45 Vict. c. 12.	The Customs and Inland Revenue Act 1881.	Section 38(2)(*c*).
52 & 53 Vict. c. 7.	The Customs and Inland Revenue Act 1889.	In section 11(1), the paragraph beginning " The description of property marked (*c*) ".
57 & 58 Vict. c. 30.	The Finance Act 1894.	In section 1, the words " at the graduated rates hereinafter mentioned ". Section 2(1)(*d*). In section 4, the words " rate of " and " at the proper graduated rate " and the words from " Provided " onwards. Section 5(3). In section 7(6), the words " rate of " in both places where they occur. Section 7(7). In section 8(7), the words " at the appropriate rate ". In section 11(2), the words " the rate of " and " at that rate ". In section 11(3), the words " rate of " and " at " and the word " rate " where secondly occurring.

Sch. 21

Chapter	Short Title	Extent
57 & 58 Vict. c. 30—*cont.*	The Finance Act 1894—*cont.*	Section 15(1) and (3). In section 16(3) as substituted by section 33(1) of the Finance Act 1954, paragraph (*b*) from " together " onwards, the words " any settled property other than " and the words " other than " where secondly occurring. Section 22(1)(*l*). In section 22(2)(*a*), the words from " including " to " or not ". Section 23(12), (14), (15) and (16).
59 & 60 Vict. c. 28.	The Finance Act 1896.	Sections 14, 15(4) and 16.
63 & 64 Vict. c. 7.	The Finance Act 1900.	Section 12.
10 Edw. 7 & 1 Geo. 5. c. 8.	The Finance (1909–10) Act 1910.	Section 57.
4 & 5 Geo. 5. c. 10.	The Finance Act 1914.	Section 13(1).
15 & 16 Geo. 5. c. 36.	The Finance Act 1925.	In section 23(1), the words from " instead " to " Act " where next occurring. Section 23(4) from " and " onwards.
24 & 25 Geo. 5. c. 32.	The Finance Act 1934.	Section 28.
25 & 26 Geo. 5. c. 24.	The Finance Act 1935.	Section 33.
1 Edw. 8 and 1 Geo. 6. c. 54.	The Finance Act 1937.	In section 31(3), the words " or a benefit accrues therefrom " wherever those words occur, the words " or the benefit accruing on the death, as the case may be " and the words " or a benefit accruing ".
1 & 2 Geo. 6. c. 46.	The Finance Act 1938.	Sections 47(7) and 48.
2 & 3 Geo. 6. c. 41.	The Finance Act 1939.	In section 30, subsection (1) (except for the purposes of the reference thereto in section 31(1)) and subsections (2) and (4). In section 31(2), the words " property deemed to be included in the ".
3 & 4 Geo. 6. c. 29.	The Finance Act 1940.	Section 43. Section 45(3). In section 51(2A) as inserted by section 38 of the Finance Act 1944, the words from " (not being " to " office) ". Section 52.

Sch. 21

Chapter	Short Title	Extent
3 & 4 Geo. 6. c. 29—*cont.*	The Finance Act 1940—*cont.*	In section 56(2), the words from " in " where first occurring to "Act, or " where first occurring, the words " disposition or determination or ", the words " of the person who had the interest or ", the words " and of any benefit to him ", the words " in the said subsection (2) or " and the words " as the case may be ".
7 & 8 Geo. 6. c. 23.	The Finance Act 1944.	In section 38, in the subsection (2A) inserted thereby, the words from " (not being " to " office) ". In Part II of Schedule 4, paragraph 4.
12, 13 & 14 Geo. 6. c. 47.	The Finance Act 1949.	Section 28(1) from " and " onwards.
14 Geo. 6. c. 15.	The Finance Act 1950.	Section 43. Section 45. Schedule 7.
2 & 3 Eliz. 2 c. 44.	The Finance Act 1954.	In section 33(1), the words from " together " to " on that settled property) ", the words " any settled property other than " and the words " other than " where secondly occurring. Section 33(2) and (3).
4 & 5 Eliz. 2. c. 45.	The Finance Act 1956.	In section 19, subsection (4) and paragraph (*a*) of subsection (7). Sections 32 and 35.
5 & 6 Eliz. 2. c. 49.	The Finance Act 1957.	Section 38(10). In section 38(11), the words " or under section thirteen of the Finance Act 1914 ". In section 38(12), in paragraph (*a*) the word " and ", and paragraph (*b*). Section 38(16) from " and " onwards. Section 39(1).
6 & 7 Eliz. 2. c. 56.	The Finance Act 1958.	Section 28.
7 & 8 Eliz. 2. c. 58.	The Finance Act 1959.	In section 34(3), the words " be deemed to " and the words " so deemed to have passed ".
8 & 9 Eliz. 2. c. 44.	The Finance Act 1960.	In section 64(2), paragraphs (*b*), (*c*) and (*d*). In section 64(4), the word " or " at the end of paragraph (*b*), and paragraph (*c*).

Chapter	Short Title	Extent
1966 c. 18.	The Finance Act 1966.	Section 40. In section 41(2)(*b*), the words " of aggregation and ".
1968 c. 44.	The Finance Act 1968.	Sections 38 and 39. In Schedule 14, so much of paragraph 1 as amends the Finance Act 1894, section 43(2) of the Finance Act 1940, the Finance Act 1950, or the Finance Act 1958, and paragraph 2(2) and (3).

Subject to section 40(2) of this Act, this Part of this Schedule has effect in relation to any death occurring after 15th April 1969.

PART VI

CAPITAL GAINS REPEALS

Chapter	Short Title	Extent of Repeal
10 & 11 Eliz. 2. c. 44.	The Finance Act 1962.	In Schedule 9, paragraph 14.
1965 c. 25.	The Finance Act 1965.	Section 24(8). Section 25(5)(*b*). In Schedule 7, paragraph 8.
1967 c. 54.	The Finance Act 1967.	In Schedule 13, paragraph 11. In Schedule 14, paragraph 11.
1968 c. 44.	The Finance Act 1968.	In Schedule 12, paragraph 16 and, except with respect to distributions made before 30th April 1969, paragraph 17 and the proviso to paragraph 20(1).

The repeals of sections 24(8) and 25(5)(*b*) of the Finance Act 1965 do not have effect in the case of deaths occurring before 6th April 1969.

PART VII

SELECTIVE EMPLOYMENT TAX REPEALS

Chapter	Short Title	Extent of Repeal
1968 c. 44.	The Finance Act 1968.	Section 51(1) and (3). In section 51(4), the words from " shall be " to " and ".

SCH. 21

PART VIII

CONSOLIDATION REPEALS HAVING EFFECT FROM 6TH APRIL 1970

Chapter or Number	Short Title	Extent of Repeal
15 & 16 Geo. 6 & 1 Eliz. 2. c. 10.	The Income Tax Act 1952.	Section 12(4). Section 51. Section 52(2)(*b*). Section 59(1). In section 59(3)(*b*), the words " or to subscribe the oath ". Section 62. Section 63(1). In section 66(1), the words " under Schedule D or Schedule E ". In section 165(1), the words from " the references " to " body corporate and ". In section 229, in subsection (4), from the beginning to " determined and ", and subsections (6) and (7). Section 233(3). In section 244(6), from the beginning to " abode, and ". In section 247, subsections (1) and (4) as applied by section 28(8) of the Finance Act 1960. In section 359(5), the words " or other proper officer of the Crown ". Section 359(6). Section 360(3). In section 362(2), the words following " payment of tax " to the end of the subsection (including the proviso). In section 367(1)(2), the words from " unless the Commissioners " to the end. Section 515(2)(3)(4)(6)(7). In Schedule 8, in paragraph 1(1) of Part III, the words from " within one month " to " shall also ".
8 & 9 Eliz. 2. c. 44.	The Finance Act 1960.	In section 28(8), the words " and (4) ". In section 51(7), the words " any person nominated for that purpose by ". In section 58(6), the words " a person nominated for that purpose by ".
1964 c. 37.	The Income Tax Management Act 1964.	Section 5(8). Section 9(12). In section 12(1), the words " other officer of " (twice).

Chapter	Short Title	Extent of Repeal
1964 c. 37—*cont.*	The Income Tax Management Act 1964—*cont.*	In section 12(6), the words from " and in the application " to the end of the subsection. In Schedule 4, paragraph (2). In Schedule 4, the amendments of sections 51, 62(1) and 229(4) of the Income Tax Act 1952, in the amendments of sections 413 and 430 of that Act, and of section 24 of the Finance Act 1962, the words " under section 51 of the Income Tax Act 1952 ", and in the entry relating to section 507 of the Income Tax Act 1952, the words " to which section 9 of this Act applies ".
1965 c. 25.	The Finance Act 1965.	In Schedule 10, paragraph 1(2), and, in paragraph 8(1), the words " or other officer of the Board ". In Schedule 12, paragraph 5(2), so far as it relates to section 63(1) of the Income Tax Act 1952.
1966 c. 18.	The Finance Act 1966.	In Schedule 6, sub-paragraphs (2) and (4) of paragraph 6, in paragraph 9(7), the words " any person nominated for that purpose by ", paragraphs 11(7) and 17(2), paragraph 20(4) so far as it relates to sections 62 and 63(1) of the Income Tax Act 1952, and paragraph 26.
S.I. 1952 No. 653.	The Income Tax (Service of Notices) Regulations 1952.	The whole instrument.
S.I. 1965 No. 433.	The Income Tax (Surtax etc.) Regulations 1965.	The whole instrument.
S.I. 1967 No. 149.	The Capital Gains Tax Regulations 1967.	Regulations 3, 4, 5 and 10(2).
S.I. 1967 No. 150.	The Capital Gains Tax (Service of Notices) Regulations 1967.	The whole instrument.

This Part of this Schedule comes into force on 6th April 1970.

SCH. 21

PART IX

OTHER CONSOLIDATION REPEALS

Chapter	Short Title	Extent of Repeal
15 & 16 Geo. 6. & 1 Eliz. 2. c. 10.	The Income Tax Act 1952.	Section 72(2)(*c*). In section 83, paragraph 2 of Schedule B. Section 115(1). In section 117, paragraph 6 of Schedule C. In section 121, in the definition of " dividends " the words " (except in the phrase ' stock dividends or interest ') ". In section 122, the proviso to paragraph 1 of Schedule D. Section 132(1)(*b*). In section 137, in paragraph (*c*), the words " shall be such as may be determined by an inspector and ", and in paragraph (*i*), the words " to the satisfaction of an inspector ". Section 169(2)(4). Section 170(5). In section 193, in subsection (2), the words " of Ceylon or of any colony ", paragraphs (*b*) and (*c*) of subsection (3), and, in subsection (5), from the beginning to " colony; and ". In section 214, in subsection (1), the words " for the purpose of having the charge and care of any child of his or ", and the words " take such charge or ", and subsection (2). Section 222. Section 249(2)(*a*). In provisos (i) and (ii) to section 258(3), the words " the income of ". Section 348(5). Section 352(3). In section 379(4)(*c*) the words " in which claims for relief under this section are to be made and approved and ". In section 439(2) the words " under Schedules C and D ". In section 440, in subsections (1) and (2), the words " under Schedules C and D ".

SCH. 21

Chapter	Short Title	Extent of Repeal
15 & 16 Geo. 6. & 1 Eliz. 2. c. 10—*cont.*	The Income Tax Act 1952—*cont.*	In section 442, in subsection (2), the words " without deduction of income tax ", and, in subsection (3), the words " subsection (2) of " and " becomes chargeable as therein provided ". In section 444, in subsections (1) and (2), the words " or society " wherever they occur and subsection (4). In section 445(5), the definition of " dividend ". Section 461.
4 & 5 Eliz. 2. c. 54.	The Finance Act 1956.	In the proviso to section 28(1), the words from the first " any person " to " Special Commissioners, and ".
5 & 6 Eliz. 2. c. 6.	The Ghana Independence Act 1957.	In Schedule 2, paragraph 1.
5 & 6 Eliz. 2. c. 60.	The Federation of Malaya Independence Act 1957.	In Schedule 1, paragraph 5.
8 & 9 Eliz. 2. c. 44.	The Finance Act 1960.	In section 17(2)(*b*), the word " fourteen ". In section 27, in subsections (4) and (5), the words from " except " to " nineteen hundred and sixty ".
8 & 9 Eliz. 2. c. 52.	The Cyprus Act 1960.	In the Schedule, paragraph 7.
8 & 9 Eliz. 2. c. 55.	The Nigeria Independence Act 1960.	In Schedule 2, paragraph 1.
9 & 10 Eliz. 2. c. 16.	The Sierra Leone Independence Act 1961.	In Schedule 3, paragraph 1.
10 & 11 Eliz. 2. c. 1.	The Tanganyika Independence Act 1961.	In Schedule 2, paragraph 1.
10 & 11 Eliz. 2. c. 40.	The Jamaica Independence Act 1962.	In Schedule 2, paragraph 1.
10 & 11 Eliz. 2. c. 44.	The Finance Act 1962.	The proviso to section 10(1). In section 16(1), the definition of " company ". Section 22(4). In Schedule 9, paragraph 20.
10 & 11 Eliz. 2. c. 54.	The Trinidad and Tobago Independence Act 1962.	In Schedule 2, paragraph 1.
10 & 11 Eliz. 2. c. 57.	The Uganda Independence Act 1962.	In Schedule 3, paragraph 1.
1963 c. 25.	The Finance Act 1963.	In section 16(6), the words " other payments being ". Section 28(2).
1963 c. 54.	The Kenya Independence Act 1963.	In Schedule 2, paragraph 1.
1963 c. 55.	The Zanzibar Act 1963.	In Part I of Schedule 1, paragraph 1.
1964 c. 46.	The Malawi Independence Act 1964.	In Schedule 2, paragraph 1.

SCH. 21

Chapter	Short Title	Extent
1964 c. 65.	The Zambia Independence Act 1964.	In Schedule 1, paragraph 1.
1964 c. 86.	The Malta Independence Act 1964.	In Schedule 2, paragraph 1.
1964 c. 93.	The Gambia Independence Act 1964.	In Schedule 2, paragraph 1.
1965 c. 25.	The Finance Act 1965.	Section 17(3). In section 17(9), the paragraph beginning " This subsection ". Section 17(14). Section 18(6). In section 47(5), the words " except references in any provision specially relating to a winding up ". Section 54(5)(7). In section 62(7)(*b*), the words " and (4) ", and from " and with the substitution " to the end of the paragraph. In section 78(5)(*a*) the words " or to a loan creditor ". In Schedule 15, in paragraph 12, the words from " inserted " to " there shall be ".
1966 c. 14.	The Guyana Independence Act 1966.	In Schedule 2, paragraph 1.
1966 c. 18.	The Finance Act 1966.	In Schedule 5, in paragraph 3(1), the words " and the exemption conferred by section 6(2) of the Atomic Energy Authority Act 1954 ", and paragraph 11(2).
1966 c. 23.	The Botswana Independence Act 1966.	In Part I of the Schedule, paragraph 1.
1966 c. 24.	The Lesotho Independence Act 1966.	In Part I of the Schedule, paragraph 1.
1966 c. 29.	The Singapore Act 1966.	In the Schedule, paragraph 6.
1966 c. 37.	The Barbados Independence Act 1966.	In Schedule 2, paragraph 1.
1968 c. 8.	The Mauritius Independence Act 1968.	In Schedule 2, paragraph 1.
1968 c. 44.	The Finance Act 1968.	In section 17(6), the words " and (3) ". Section 33(5). In Schedule 10, in paragraph 6(1), the words " on him ". In Schedule 13, paragraphs 1(4) and 5(1).
1968 c. 56.	The Swaziland Independence Act 1968.	In the Schedule, paragraph 1.
S.R. & O. 1921 No. 1699.	Regulations dated 10th November 1921 made by Commissioners of Inland Revenue under Finance Act 1921, s. 32.	In Regulation 12, from " and all the provisions " to second " those claims ".

Sch. 21

Chapter	Short Title	Extent
S.I. 1956 No. 715.	The Ulster and Colonial Savings Certificates (Income Tax Exemption) Regulations 1956.	In Regulation 1, from " Certificates issued under " to the end, and Regulation 2, and the Schedule.

The above repeals of section 132(1)(*b*) of the Income Tax Act 1952 and section 54(7) of the Finance Act 1965 have effect as respects income tax for the year 1969–70 and subsequent years of assessment, and as respects corporation tax for the financial year 1969 and subsequent financial years.

Subject to that, this Part of this Schedule has effect only in relation to tax for years of assessment and companies' accounting periods ending after 5th April 1970.

Part X

Obsolete or Unnecessary Provisions in Tax Acts

Chapter	Short Title	Extent of Repeal
53 & 54 Vict. c. 21.	The Inland Revenue Regulation Act 1890.	Sections 21, 22 and 35(2) so far as they relate to capital gains tax and corporation tax.
5 & 6 Geo. 5. c. 89.	The Finance (No. 2) Act 1915.	Section 51(1).
15 & 16 Geo. 6. & 1 Eliz. 2. c. 10.	The Income Tax Act 1952.	Section 5(2). In section 12(1), the words " under this Act ". In section 17, the words " in the execution of this Act ", and the whole section except as respects General Commissioners or Special Commissioners. In section 31(1), the words (after paragraph (*b*)) from " Where " to the end of the subsection. Section 32. In section 74, in subsection (2) the words " or other peace officer" and "or officer", and in subsection (5) the words " or his deputy " (twice). In section 117, paragraph 7 of Schedule C. In section 122, in paragraph 1 of Schedule D, the words " in each case for every twenty shillings of the annual amount of the profits or gains ". Section 124(3). Section 126.

SCH. 21

Chapter	Short Title	Extent of Repeal
15 & 16 Geo. 6. & 1 Eliz. 2. c. 10—*cont.*	The Income Tax Act 1952 —*cont.*	In section 132(1), the words (after paragraph (*c*)) from " and the provisions " to the end of the subsection. In section 156, in paragraph 1A of Schedule E, the words " for every twenty shillings of the amount thereof for the year ". Section 157(4). Section 187(1)(*b*). Section 202(5). In section 223, proviso (i). In section 249, in subsection (3), the words " and any regulations made thereunder", in proviso (*b*) to subsection (4), the words " or the liquidator of a company ", and, in subsection (5), the words from " and where " to the end of the subsection. In section 316, in subsections (1) and (2)(*c*), the words " on or after the appointed day ". In section 317, in subsections (1) to (4), the words " on or after the appointed day ". In section 318, in subsections (1) and (2), the words " on or after the appointed day ". Section 319. In section 368, the words " (save as herein is excepted)". Section 373(1)(*b*). In section 392, the words " after the first day of May, nineteen hundred and twenty-two ". In section 439(2), proviso (*b*). In section 442(4), the words from " in such form " to " prescribe ". Section 444(3). In section 457(1), the words " bounty at the commencement or ". Section 457(5)(*b*). Section 463(5). In section 469, in subsections (1) and (2), the words " on or after the tenth day of April, nineteen hundred and fifty-one ". Section 473(2)(*b*). Section 479(2).

SCH. 21

Chapter	Short Title	Extent of Repeal
15 & 16 Geo. 6. & 1 Eliz. 2. c. 10—*cont.*	The Income Tax Act 1952 —*cont.*	In section 495(5), the words from " In this subsection 'collector' " to the end of the subsection. In section 498(1), proviso (*b*). In section 514, in subsections (1) and (2) the word " charge," and, in subsection (3), the words " or charge made upon an assessment " and " certificate of charge or " and the proviso. Section 525(2)(*e*). Section 528(3)(*b*). Section 529(3)(4). Section 530(1)(2). In Schedule 9, paragraphs and 2. In paragraph 1 of Schedule 16, in sub-paragraph (1) the definition of " foreign income tax ", sub-paragraph (2) and in sub-paragraph (3) the words " or foreign income tax ". In Part III of Schedule 18, in paragraph 2(1), the words (after (*b*)) from " and the provisions " to the end, and paragraph 2(3). In paragraph 1(1) of Schedule 19, in the definition of " payment ", the words " on or after the sixth day of April, nineteen hundred and forty-five ", and, in the definition of " contribution ", the words from " but does not " to " forty-five ". In Schedule 20, in paragraph 2(3), the proviso. Schedule 22, so far as not repealed. In Part II of Schedule 23, paragraphs 4 and 5. In Schedule 24, in the first paragraph, the words " value of property or ".
15 & 16 Geo. 6. & 1 Eliz. 2. c. 33.	The Finance Act 1952.	Section 17. Section 18(6)(*c*). In section 18(7), the words from " and notwithstanding " to the end of the subsection. In section 67(1), the proviso.
1 & 2 Eliz. 2. c. 34.	The Finance Act 1953.	Section 25(8).
2 & 3 Eliz. 2. c. 44.	The Finance Act 1954.	Section 25.

SCH. 21

Chapter	Short Title	Extent of Repeal
4 & 5 Eliz. 2. c. 17.	The Finance (No. 2) Act 1955.	In section 3(1), the proviso.
4 & 5 Eliz. 2. c. 54.	The Finance Act 1956.	In section 24(2)(*b*), the words from " (and without " to the end of paragraph (*b*). Section 27(6).
7 & 8 Eliz. 2. c. 58.	The Finance Act 1959.	In section 23(1), the words " on or after the eighth day of April, nineteen hundred and fifty-nine ".
8 & 9 Eliz. 2. c. 44.	The Finance Act 1960.	Section 33(4)(5). In section 63(1), the definitions of " assessment " and " Summary Jurisdiction Acts (Northern Ireland) ". In section 69(1), the words " (including the regulations made thereunder) ". In section 72, the proviso to subsection (1) and subsection (10).
9 & 10 Eliz. 2. c. 36.	The Finance Act 1961.	In section 28(2), the words " and may, if not final, be amended ".
10 & 11 Eliz. 2. c. 44.	The Finance Act 1962.	In section 12(9), the words from " and without prejudice " to the end of the subsection. In section 16(4), the words " whose business consists mainly in the making of investments ", and the words from " and in the case " to the end of the subsection. Section 17.
1963 c. 25.	The Finance Act 1963.	In section 29(1), from the beginning to " vocation; and ".
1965 c. 25.	The Finance Act 1965.	Section 17(12). In section 49(7), the words from " and the Board " to the end of the subsection. Section 55(4). Section 69(4). Section 78(7)(*c*). Section 80(5). In Schedule 15, paragraph 16.
1966 c. 18.	The Finance Act 1966.	Section 29(12)(*d*).
1967 c. 54.	The Finance Act 1967.	In section 39(2), the words " on a claim being made to them for the purpose ". In paragraph 5(7) of Schedule 11, the words " the Committee of Ways and Means of the House of Commons, or of ".
1968 c. 3.	The Capital Allowances Act 1968.	In Schedule 12, paragraph 3(4).
1968 c. 44.	The Finance Act 1968.	In Schedule 10, paragraph 7.

Housing Act 1969

1969 CHAPTER 33

An Act to make further provision for grants by local authorities and contributions out of moneys provided by Parliament towards the cost of providing dwellings by conversion or of improving dwellings and houses; to confer powers on local authorities to improve living conditions by improving the amenities of areas or of dwellings therein; to amend the law with regard to rents payable for certain dwellings in good repair and provided with certain amenities or improved with the assistance of local authorities; to make further provision with regard to houses in multiple occupation; to make further provision for payments in respect of unfit houses subject to compulsory purchase, clearance, demolition or closing orders; to alter the legal standard of fitness for human habitation and confer additional powers on local authorities to require the repair of houses; to amend the law relating to long tenancies and modify section 9(1) of the Leasehold Reform Act 1967; to amend Part II of the Housing Subsidies Act 1967; to amend section 46 of the Rent Act 1968; to increase the fine which may be imposed under section 170 of the Housing Act 1957; and for purposes connected with those matters. [25th July 1969]

BE IT ENACTED by the Queen's most Excellent Majesty, by and with the advice and consent of the Lords Spiritual and Temporal, and Commons, in this present Parliament assembled, and by the authority of the same, as follows:—

Part I

Financial assistance towards cost of improvements and conversions

Grants by local authorities

Improvement grants, standard grants and special grants.

1.—(1) Grants shall be payable by local authorities in accordance with the following provisions of this Part of this Act towards the cost of works required for—

(*a*) the provision of dwellings by the conversion of houses or other buildings;

(*b*) the improvement of dwellings; or

(*c*) the improvement of houses in multiple occupation by the provision of standard amenities;

where the provision or improvement is by a person other than a housing authority.

(2) A grant under this Part of this Act is in this Act referred to as—

(*a*) an improvement grant, if the works are required for the provision of a dwelling or for the improvement of a dwelling not consisting or not wholly consisting of the provision of standard amenities which the dwelling lacks;

(*b*) a standard grant, if the works are required for the improvement of a dwelling by the provision of standard amenities which it lacks;

(*c*) a special grant if the works are required for the improvement of a house in multiple occupation by the provision of standard amenities.

Improvement grants

Improvement grants.

2.—(1) A local authority may pay an improvement grant if an application therefor is made in accordance with this section and approved by them.

(2) Such an application must contain particulars of the works and an estimate of their cost, and such other particulars as the Minister may specify.

(3) Subject to subsection (4) of this section, a local authority shall not entertain an application for an improvement grant if the cost of the works as estimated in the application is less than £100 or such other amount as may for the time being be prescribed.

(4) Where, not more than three years before the making of the application, a standard grant was made in respect of the dwelling (or one of the dwellings) to which the application

relates and the application contains a statement of the cost towards which the standard grant was made, that cost shall be deemed, for the purposes of the preceding subsection, to be added to that estimated in the application.

(5) Where an application for an improvement grant relates to more than one dwelling then—

(*a*) if the dwellings are to be provided by the conversion of a house or other building, the cost referred to in subsection (3) of this section is the cost of the works divided by the number of dwellings ; and

(*b*) if the dwellings are to be improved, the cost referred to in subsection (3) of this section is so much of the cost of the works as is in the opinion of the local authority attributable to any one dwelling.

(6) Subject to section 25 of this Act, a local authority shall not entertain an application for an improvement grant unless they are satisfied that the applicant has, in every parcel of land on which the works specified in the application are to be or have been carried out, an interest which is either an estate in fee simple absolute in possession or a term of years absolute of which not less than five years remain unexpired at the date of the application.

Conditions for approval of application for improvement grant.

3.—(1) A local authority shall not approve an application for an improvement grant if the works specified therein have been begun unless they are satisfied that there were good reasons for beginning the works before the application was approved.

(2) A local authority shall not approve an application for an improvement grant unless they are satisfied that the dwelling or dwellings to which the application relates will provide satisfactory housing accommodation for such period and conform with such requirements with respect to construction and physical conditions and the provision of services and amenities as may for the time being be specified for the purposes of this section by the Minister.

Approval of application for improvement grant.

4.—(1) Where a local authority approve an application for an improvement grant they shall determine the amount of the expenses which, in their opinion, are proper to be incurred for the execution of the works specified in the application and shall notify the applicant of that amount; and the amount so notified is in this Part of this Act referred to as the approved expense of the works.

(2) The approved expense of any works shall not allow for works of repair and replacement more than one-half of that expense or such other part thereof as may for the time being be prescribed.

Part I

(3) Where the applicant satisfies the local authority that the works specified in the application cannot be or could not have been carried out without the carrying out of additional works and that this could not have been reasonably foreseen at the time the application was made the local authority may substitute a higher amount as the amount of the approved expense.

(4) In approving an application for an improvement grant a local authority may require as a condition of paying the grant that the works specified in the application are carried out within such time (which must not be less than twelve months) as the local authority may specify or such further time as the local authority may allow.

Amount of improvement grant.

5.—(1) The amount of an improvement grant shall be such amount as may be fixed by the local authority when they approve the application for the grant, but shall not exceed—

(*a*) one half of the approved expense of the works, nor

(*b*) subject to subsection (3) of this section, the limit imposed by or under subsection (2) of this section.

(2) The limit is the amount or, if the application relates to more than one dwelling, the aggregate of the amounts, applicable under the following paragraphs, that is to say,—

(*a*) £1,000, or such other amount as may be prescribed, if the dwelling is improved by the works or is provided by them otherwise than mentioned in paragraph (*b*) of this subsection ; and

(*b*) £1,200, or such other amount as may be prescribed, if the dwelling is provided by the conversion of a house or other building consisting of three or more storeys.

(3) The limit imposed by or under subsection (2) of this section may be exceeded by such amount as the Minister may approve, if the local authority are satisfied in a particular case that there are good reasons for fixing a higher amount ; and the approval of the Minister may be given either with respect to a particular case or with respect to a class of case.

(4) For the purposes of this section, where an improvement grant is to be paid towards the cost of works required for the provision of a dwelling all or part of which is in the basement of a building the basement shall count as a storey.

Payment of improvement grant.

6.—(1) An improvement grant may be paid after the completion of the works towards the cost of which it is payable or part of it may be paid in instalments as the works progress and the balance after the completion of the works.

(2) Where part of an improvement grant is paid in instalments the aggregate of the instalments paid shall not at any time before the completion of the works exceed one half of the aggregate cost of the works executed up to that time.

(3) The payment of an improvement grant or of any part thereof shall be conditional upon the works or the corresponding part of the works being executed to the satisfaction of the local authority.

(4) If an instalment of an improvement grant is paid before the completion of the works and the works are not completed within the time specified in subsection (5) of this section, that instalment and any further sums paid by the local authority as part of the grant shall, on being demanded by the local authority, forthwith become repayable to them by the person to whom the instalment was paid and shall carry interest at such rate as may be prescribed from the date on which it was paid by the local authority until repayment.

(5) Where the local authority have specified no time under section 4(4) of this Act for the completion of the works the time referred to in subsection (4) of this section is twelve months from the date on which the instalment is paid or such further time as the local authority may allow; and where they have specified a time or allowed further time under section 4(4) of this Act the time referred to in subsection (4) of this section is the time so specified or allowed.

Standard grants

Standard amenities.

7.—(1) Subject to subsection (2) of this section the standard amenities for the purposes of this Act shall be the amenities which are described in the Table set out in Part I of Schedule 1 to this Act and conform to such of the provisions of Part II of that Schedule as are applicable.

(2) The Minister may by order vary the provisions of Schedule 1 to this Act and any such order may contain such transitional or other supplemental provisions as appear to the Minister to be expedient.

Standard grants.

8.—(1) A local authority shall pay a standard grant if an application therefor is made in accordance with this section and approved by them and the works are executed to the satisfaction of the local authority.

(2) Such an application must specify the dwelling and the works, and, where the works are for the provision of some only of the standard amenities, must also state whether the dwelling is already provided with the remainder.

Part I

(3) A local authority shall not entertain an application for a standard grant with respect to a dwelling provided after 2nd October 1961.

(4) Subject to section 25 of this Act a local authority shall not entertain an application for a standard grant unless they are satisfied that the applicant has, in every parcel of land on which the works specified in the application are to be or have been carried out, an interest which is either an estate in fee simple absolute in possession or a term of years absolute of which not less than five years remain unexpired at the date of the application.

Conditions for approval of application for standard grant.

9.—(1) Subject to the following provisions of this section, a local authority shall approve an application for a standard grant if they are satisfied, and shall not approve it unless they are satisfied that, when the works specified in the application have been carried out,—

(*a*) the dwelling will be provided with all the standard amenities for the exclusive use of its occupants; and

(*b*) the dwelling will be in good repair, having regard to its age, character and locality, and disregarding internal decorative repair, and will in all other respects be fit for human habitation;

and that the dwelling is likely to remain fit for human habitation and available for use as a dwelling for a period of not less than fifteen years.

(2) A local authority shall not approve an application for a standard grant if the works specified therein have been begun unless they are satisfied that there were good reasons for beginning the works before the application was approved.

(3) Where the works specified in the application include works for the provision of a fixed bath or shower elsewhere than in a bathroom the local authority are not required to approve the application but may do so if otherwise they would be required or authorised to do so under this section.

(4) Where, under the preceding provisions of this section, a local authority would be required to approve an application for a standard grant if satisfied that, after the works specified in the application have been carried out, the dwelling will be provided with all the standard amenities, then, if—

(*a*) the application contains a statement, and the local authority are satisfied, that it is not practicable at reasonable expense to provide the dwelling with all the standard amenities, and

(*b*) the local authority are satisfied that after the works specified in the application have been carried out the

PART I

dwelling will be provided with the amenities included in the Table in Part I of Schedule 1 to this Act as items 5, 6 and 7 and that item 7 will conform to the provisions of paragraph 3 of Part II of that Schedule,

the local authority shall approve the application notwithstanding that the dwelling will not be provided with all the standard amenities, unless they are satisfied that the dwelling is or forms part of a house or building in respect of which they have power to serve a notice under section 15 of the Housing Act 1961 or that section as extended by section 21 of that Act (power to require execution of works). 1961 c. 65.

(5) In considering for the purposes of the preceding subsection whether it would be practicable at reasonable expense to provide the dwelling with all the standard amenities, the local authority shall have regard to the estimated cost of the works which would be required for that purpose and the value which it is estimated the dwelling (or the building of which it forms part) would have if works to provide the dwelling with all the standard amenities were carried out.

(6) Where the works specified in the application are to be carried out in compliance with an improvement notice served, or undertaking accepted, under Part II of the Housing Act 1964 and comprise the provision of a fixed bath or shower, then,— 1964 c. 56.

(*a*) if the fixed bath or shower is to be provided in a bathroom, the conditions stated in subsection (1) of this section shall, if otherwise satisfied, be deemed to be satisfied notwithstanding that the bath or shower is for the use of the occupants of more than one dwelling in a tenement block (within the meaning of Part II of that Act); and

(*b*) if the fixed bath or shower is to be provided elsewhere than in a bathroom, this section shall apply as if subsection (3) thereof were omitted.

(7) Subject to such general or special directions as may from time to time be given by the Minister, a local authority may approve an application for a standard grant notwithstanding that the conditions stated in subsection (1) of this section are not satisfied.

(8) An order under section 7(2) of this Act may vary the provisions of subsection (4) of this section.

Approval of application for standard grant.

10. In approving an application for a standard grant a local authority may require as a condition of paying the grant that the works specified in the application are carried out within such time (which must not be less than twelve months) as the local authority may specify or such further time as the local authority may allow.

PART I

Amount of standard grant.

11.—(1) The amount of a standard grant made towards the cost of any works shall, subject to the following provisions of this section, be one half of that cost.

(2) If any of the works are not exclusively for the purpose of providing one or more of the standard amenities, only so much of the cost of carrying out those works as is, in the opinion of the local authority, attributable to the provision of the standard amenity or standard amenities shall be taken into account under the preceding subsection.

(3) There shall be a limit on the amount of a standard grant, which shall be determined in accordance with Part III of Schedule 1 to this Act.

Effect of standard grant on amount of improvement grant

Effect of standard grant on amount of improvement grant.

12. Where after the making of a standard grant in respect of a dwelling an improvement grant is made in respect of that dwelling, section 5(2) of this Act shall have effect, in relation to that dwelling, as if the sum specified in or prescribed under paragraph (*a*) thereof were reduced by the amount of the standard grant.

Special grants

Special grants.

13.—(1) A local authority may pay a special grant if an application therefor is made in accordance with this section and approved by them and the works are executed to the satisfaction of the local authority.

(2) Such an application must specify the house and the works, and must state by how many households and individuals the house is occupied and with what standard amenities it is already provided.

(3) A local authority shall not entertain an application for a special grant unless they are satisfied that the applicant has, in every parcel of land on which the works specified in the application are to be or have been carried out, an interest which is either an estate in fee simple absolute in possession or a term of years absolute of which not less than five years remain unexpired at the date of the application.

(4) Part II of Schedule 1 to this Act shall apply for the purposes of the provisions of this Act relating to special grants as if paragraphs 2 and 3 and, in paragraph 1, the words from " except " onwards, were omitted.

PART I

Approval of application for special grant.

14.—(1) Subject to subsection (2) of this section and to any general or special directions which may be given by the Minister for the purposes of this section, a local authority may approve an application for a special grant in such circumstances as they think fit.

(2) A local authority shall not approve an application for a special grant if the works specified therein have been begun, unless they are satisfied that there were good reasons for beginning the works before the application was approved.

(3) In approving an application for a special grant a local authority may require as a condition of paying the grant that the works specified in the application are carried out within such time (which must not be less than twelve months) as the local authority may specify or such further time as the local authority may allow.

Amount of special grant.

15.—(1) The amount of a special grant made towards the cost of any works shall, subject to the following provisions of this section, be one half of that cost.

(2) If any of the works are not exclusively for the purpose of providing one or more of the standard amenities, only so much of the cost of carrying out those works as is, in the opinion of the local authority, attributable to the provision of the standard amenity or standard amenities shall be taken into account under the preceding subsection.

(3) The amount of a special grant shall not exceed the sum arrived at by allowing for each of the standard amenities provided the amount specified for an amenity of that description in the third column of the Table set out in Part I of Schedule 1 to this Act.

Contributions towards grants

Contributions towards grants.

16.—(1) The Minister may make a contribution towards the expense incurred by a local authority in making a grant under this Part of this Act.

(2) The contribution shall be a sum payable annually for a period of twenty years beginning with the financial year in which the works towards the cost of which the grant was made were completed, equal to three-quarters of the annual loan charges referable to the amount of the grant.

PART I

Contributions towards cost of improvements and conversions carried out by or under arrangements with housing authorities

Contributions to local authorities and other bodies for dwellings improved by them or provided by them by conversion.

17.—(1) The Minister may pay contributions to housing authorities towards the cost incurred by them in—

(*a*) the provision of dwellings by the conversion of houses or other buildings; or

(*b*) the improvement of dwellings;

in such circumstances as appear to the Minister to be sufficiently similar to those in which a grant under this Part of this Act might be paid by a local authority had the provision or improvement been by a person other than a housing authority.

(2) Such a contribution is in the following provisions of this Part of this Act referred to as—

(*a*) a standard contribution, if the cost is incurred only in the improvement of dwellings by the provision of standard amenities which they lack; and

(*b*) as an improvement contribution in any other case.

Improvement contributions.

18.—(1) The Minister may pay an improvement contribution with respect to any dwellings if an application therefor containing such estimates and particulars as he may require is made by a housing authority and approved by him.

(2) When approving the application the Minister shall determine an amount as the allowable cost and that amount shall, subject to the limit imposed by or under the following provisions of this section, be one-half of the aggregate of—

(*a*) the amount appearing to him to be the cost proper to be incurred by the housing authority for the purpose of carrying out any works required for the provision or improvement of the dwellings; and

(*b*) the cost (if any) incurred by the housing authority in acquiring an estate or interest in any building for the purpose of converting it into any of the dwellings or acquiring any estate or interest in any of the dwellings for the purpose of improving it.

(3) Subject to subsection (4) of this section, the allowable cost shall not exceed the amount arrived at by taking for each dwelling provided or improved £1,000 or such other sum as the Minister may by order specify, unless the case belongs to a class with respect to which the Minister, on being satisfied that there is good reason for doing so, has determined a higher amount or the Minister is satisfied that in the circumstances of the particular case there is good reason for determining a higher amount.

(4) Where the dwelling is one in which the housing authority have acquired an estate or interest for the purpose of improving it or is a dwelling provided by the conversion of a house or other building in which the housing authority have acquired an estate or interest for the purpose of converting it into dwellings, subsection (3) of this section shall have effect, with respect to the dwelling, as if £1,250 or such other sum as the Minister may by order specify were substituted for that specified by or under that subsection.

(5) The improvement contribution shall be a sum payable annually for a period of twenty years beginning with the financial year in which the works required for the provision or improvement of the dwellings are completed, equal to three-quarters of the annual loan charges referable to the allowable cost.

Standard contributions.

19.—(1) The Minister may pay a standard contribution with respect to any dwelling if an application therefor containing such estimates and particulars as he may require is made by a housing authority and approved by him.

(2) A standard contribution shall be a sum payable annually for a period of twenty years beginning with the financial year in which the works required for the provision of the standard amenities are completed, equal to three-quarters of the annual loan charges referable to the allowable cost.

(3) Subject to the following provisions of this section, the allowable cost with respect to any standard amenities shall be one-half of the cost shown to have been incurred in carrying out the works required for providing them.

(4) If any of the works are not exclusively for the purpose of providing one or more of the standard amenities, only so much of the cost of carrying out those works as is, in the opinion of the Minister, attributable to the provision of the standard amenity or standard amenities shall be taken into account under subsection (3) of this section.

(5) There shall be a limit on the allowable cost, which shall be determined in accordance with Part III of Schedule 1 to this Act.

Effect of standard contribution on amount of improvement contribution.

20. Where an application for an improvement contribution with respect to any dwelling is approved after the approval of an application for a standard contribution with respect to the same dwelling section 18 of this Act shall apply in relation to that dwelling as if the limit imposed by or under subsections (3) and (4) of that section were reduced by the amount of the allowable cost determined under section 19 of this Act.

PART I

Contributions for dwellings provided or improved by housing associations under arrangements with local authorities.

1958 c. 42.
1967 c. 29.

21.—(1) Where any arrangements between a local authority and a housing association under section 121 of the Act of 1957 (arrangements for provision of dwellings by conversion or for improvement of dwellings) are made after the passing of this Act the following provisions of this section shall apply (and accordingly section 12 of the Housing (Financial Provisions) Act 1958 and section 12 of the Housing Subsidies Act 1967 shall not apply).

(2) The approval of the Minister, both to the making of the arrangements and to the terms thereof, may be given either generally to local authorities or to any local authority or class of local authority or in any particular case and may be given unconditionally or subject to any conditions.

(3) The Minister shall pay a contribution towards the cost of carrying out the arrangements if an application therefor containing such particulars and estimates as the Minister may require is made by the local authority and the local authority certify, in such form as the Minister may direct, that the arrangements and the terms thereof comply with any conditions subject to which his approval was given, and that in their opinion the dwellings will provide satisfactory housing accommodation for such period and conform with such requirements with respect to construction and physical conditions and the provision of services and amenities as may for the time being be specified for the purposes of this section by the Minister.

(4) The Minister shall determine an amount as the allowable cost for the purposes of the contribution and that amount shall, subject to the limit imposed by or under the following provisions of this section, be one-half of the aggregate of—

(*a*) the amount certified by the local authority as appearing to them to be the cost proper to be incurred by the housing association for the purpose of executing any work required under the arrangements ; and

(*b*) the amount certified by the local authority as being the cost incurred by the housing association in acquiring any estate or interest in any building or dwelling with a view to entering into or for the purpose of carrying out the arrangements.

(5) Subject to subsection (6) of this section, the allowable cost shall not exceed the amount arrived at by taking for each dwelling provided or improved £1,000 or such other sum as the Minister may by order specify, unless the case belongs to a class with respect to which the Minister, on being satisfied that there is good reason for doing so, has determined a higher amount or the Minister is satisfied that in the circumstances of

the particular case there is good reason for determining a higher amount. PART I

(6) Where the dwelling is one in which the housing association have acquired an estate or interest with a view to entering into the arrangements or for the purpose of carrying them out or is a dwelling provided by the conversion of a house or other building in which the housing association have acquired an estate or interest with that view or for that purpose, subsection (5) of this section shall have effect, with respect to that dwelling, as if £1,250 or such other sum as the Minister may by order specify were substituted for that specified by or under that subsection.

(7) The contribution shall be a sum payable annually for a period of twenty years beginning with the financial year in which the works carried out in pursuance of the arrangements are completed, equal to three-quarters of the annual loan charges referable to the allowable cost; and for the purposes of this subsection the definition of "annual loan charges" in section 86(5) of this Act shall have effect as if the reference to a housing authority were a reference to a housing association.

(8) A contribution under this section shall be paid to the local authority, who shall pay to the housing association by way of annual grant an amount not less than the contribution.

(9) Where a dwelling is provided or improved by a housing association in pursuance of arrangements in respect of which a contribution is paid under this section, no grant under this Part of this Act shall be made to the housing association towards the cost of improving the dwelling.

(10) The Greater London Council shall be a local authority for the purposes of this section.

Power to vary contributions

22.—(1) The Minister may by order vary, with respect to grants, improvement contributions or standard contributions made in pursuance of applications approved after such date as may be specified in the order, or with respect to contributions made under the preceding section in pursuance of arrangements made after a date so specified, the sum payable annually under section 16, or as the case may be, section 18, 19 or 21 of this Act. Power to vary contributions.

(2) An order under this section—

(*a*) shall not be made unless a draft thereof has been approved by a resolution of the Commons House of Parliament; and

PART I

(*b*) shall not specify a date earlier than the date of the laying of the draft;

and before laying such a draft the Minister shall consult with such associations of local authorities as appear to him to be concerned and with any housing authority with whom consultation appears to him to be desirable.

(3) The council of a county shall be a local authority for the purposes of this section.

Supplemental

Statement of reasons for not approving application for grant or fixing less than maximum for improvement grant.

23. Where a local authority do not approve an application for a grant under this Part of this Act or fix the amount of an improvement grant at less than the maximum authorised by section 5 of this Act they shall state to the applicant in writing their reasons for doing so.

Assistance for works specified in applications for grants under former enactments.
1958 c. 42.
1959 c. 33.

24. For the purpose of allowing an application for an improvement grant or standard grant to be made notwithstanding that all or some of the works to be specified therein were specified in an application (made before the commencement of this Act) for an improvement grant under section 30 of the Housing (Financial Provisions) Act 1958 or a standard grant under section 4 of the House Purchase and Housing Act 1959, the local authority shall allow that application to be withdrawn, whether or not it has been approved, unless they are satisfied that the works specified in the application have been begun.

Special provisions as to parsonages, almshouses, etc.

25. Sections 2(6) and 8(4) of this Act do not apply in relation to—

(*a*) an application for a grant under this Part of this Act in respect of glebe land or the residence house of an ecclesiastical benefice made, during a period when the benefice is vacant, by a sequestrator of the profits thereof; or

(*b*) an application for such a grant in respect of a building held upon trust for use as an almshouse or as the residence of a minister of any religious denomination made by the trustees exercising the powers of management of the trust estate; or

(*c*) an application for such a grant made on behalf of a charity where land to which the application relates is land which, or an interest in which, is vested in the official custodian for charities or any other custodian trustee in trust for the charity;

and do not apply in relation to any land which is proposed to be sold or leased to the applicant under section 105(2) of the Act of 1957 (power to dispose of land for the purpose of carrying out works in connection with work on an adjoining house).

Local authorities for purposes of Part I.

26. The local authorities for the purposes of this Part of this Act are the councils of boroughs, urban districts and rural districts and the Common Council of the City of London.

Interpretation.

27. In this Part of this Act—

"house in multiple occupation" means a house which is occupied by persons who do not form a single household;

"housing authority" means the council of a county, county borough, London borough or county district, the Greater London Council, the Common Council of the City of London, the Commission for the New Towns or a development corporation within the meaning of the New Towns Act 1965; 1965 c. 59.

"improvement" includes alteration and enlargement and such repairs and replacements as are either incidental to some other improvement or needed (in the opinion of the person paying any grant or contribution) for the purpose of making the other improvement fully effective;

"improvement grant" has the meaning assigned to it by section 1(2) of this Act;

"prescribed", except where the context otherwise requires, means prescribed by regulations made by the Minister;

"special grant" and "standard grant" have the meanings assigned to them by section 1(2) of this Act.

PART II

GENERAL IMPROVEMENT AREAS

General improvement areas.

28.—(1) Where a report with respect to a predominantly residential area within the district of a local authority is submitted to them by a person or persons appearing to the authority to be suitably qualified (whether or not that person is or those persons include an officer of the authority) and it appears to the authority, upon consideration of the report and of any other

PART II

information in their possession, that living conditions in the area ought to be improved by the improvement of the amenities of the area or of dwellings therein or both and that such an improvement may be effected or assisted by the exercise of their powers under this Act, the authority may cause the area to be defined on a map and by resolution declare it to be a general improvement area.

(2) As soon as may be after passing a resolution declaring an area to be a general improvement area the local authority shall—

(*a*) publish in two or more newspapers circulating in the locality (of which one at least shall, if practicable, be a local newspaper) a notice of the resolution identifying the area and naming a place or places where a copy of the resolution, of the map on which the area is defined and of the report mentioned in subsection (1) of this section may be inspected at all reasonable times ;

(*b*) take such further steps as may appear to them best designed to secure that the resolution is brought to the attention of persons residing in the area or owning property therein and that those persons are informed of the name and address of the person to whom any enquiries and representations concerning any action to be taken in the exercise of the local authority's powers under this Part of this Act should be addressed ; and

(*c*) send to the Minister a copy of the resolution, of the report and of the map and a statement of the number of dwellings in the area.

Mutual exclusion of general improvement areas and clearance areas.

29.—(1) A general improvement area shall not be so defined as to include (but may be so defined as to surround)—

(*a*) any land comprised in an area declared to be a clearance area under Part III of the Act of 1957,

(*b*) any land purchased under section 43(3) of that Act as being land surrounded by or adjoining a clearance area, or

(*c*) any land included in a clearance area in accordance with section 49 of that Act,

unless the land has been cleared of buildings.

(2) Where the Minister on confirming a compulsory purchase order under Schedule 3 to the Act of 1957 or a clearance order under Schedule 5 to that Act modifies the order by excluding from a clearance area any land adjoining a general improvement

area, that land shall, unless the Minister otherwise directs, be deemed to be included in the general improvement area.

(3) A clearance area under Part III of the Act of 1957 shall not be so defined as to include any land which is for the time being included in a general improvement area.

Changes with respect to general improvement area.

30.—(1) A local authority may by resolution—

(*a*) exclude from a general improvement area any land for the time being included therein ; or

(*b*) declare an area to be no longer a general improvement area ;

but such a resolution shall be of no effect unless approved by the Minister.

(2) Where it appears to a local authority desirable in the interests of the improvement of the amenities of an area which has been declared a general improvement area that any land adjoining the area should be included in the general improvement area, they may by resolution include the land in the general improvement area and cause the general improvement area to be re-defined accordingly.

(3) As soon as may be after passing a resolution in pursuance of subsection (2) of this section the local authority shall—

(*a*) publish in two or more newspapers circulating in the locality (of which one at least shall, if practicable, be a local newspaper) a notice of the resolution identifying the land included in the area by the resolution and naming a place or places where a copy of the resolution, and of the map on which the general improvement area is re-defined, may be inspected at all reasonable times ; and

(*b*) send to the Minister a copy of the resolution and of the map and a statement of the number of dwellings on the land.

Duty to publish information.

31. Where a local authority have declared an area to be a general improvement area it shall be their duty to bring to the attention of persons residing in the area or owning property therein the action they propose to take in the exercise of their powers under this Part of this Act and the assistance available for the improvement of the amenities of the area or of the dwellings therein by publishing from time to time, in such manner as appears to them appropriate, such information as is in their opinion best designed to further the objects of this Part of this Act.

PART II

General powers exercisable by local authority in general improvement area.

32.—(1) Where a local authority have declared an area to be a general improvement area they may, for the purpose of effecting or assisting any such improvement as is mentioned in section 28(1) of this Act—

(*a*) carry out any works on land owned by them and assist (whether by grants or loans or otherwise) in the carrying out of any works on land not owned by them ;

(*b*) acquire any land by agreement ;

(*c*) let or otherwise dispose of any land for the time being owned by them ;

and may be authorised by the Minister to acquire compulsorily any land within the general improvement area or adjoining that area.

1946 c. 49.

(2) The Acquisition of Land (Authorisation Procedure) Act 1946 shall apply to a compulsory acquisition of land under this section as if this section had been in force immediately before the commencement of that Act.

(3) Where a local authority acquire land in pursuance of this section it shall be their duty to secure that any persons who may be displaced from residential accommodation on the land and for whom no suitable accommodation is otherwise available on reasonable terms will be provided with such accommodation before the displacement.

(4) Section 144 of the Act of 1957 (obligation to rehouse in certain circumstances) shall not apply to any acquisition of land under this section.

(5) Nothing in this section shall enable a local authority to improve any dwelling which has not been acquired or provided by them in pursuance of this section or to make any grant towards the cost of any works in any case where such a grant might be made under Part I of this Act.

Conversion of highway into footpath or bridle-way.

1968 c. 72.

33.—(1) A local authority may, with respect to any such highway in a general improvement area declared by them as is mentioned in subsection (1) of section 92 of the Town and Country Planning Act 1968 (conversion of highway into footpath or bridle-way) exercise the powers of a local planning authority under that section, whether or not they are the local planning authority ; but where they are not the local planning authority they shall not make an application under subsection (2) or subsection (8) of that section except with the consent of the local planning authority ; and where they are neither the local planning authority nor the highway authority any such application made by them shall in the first place be sent to the highway authority, who shall transmit it to the responsible Minister (within the meaning of that section).

(2) Where an order under subsection (2) of section 92 of that Act has been made on the application, by virtue of this section, of a local authority who are not the local planning authority,— PART II

(*a*) any compensation under subsection (5) of that section shall be payable by them instead of by the local planning authority ; and

(*b*) the local authority may exercise the powers exercisable by them under section 93 of that Act as the competent authority for the purposes of that section without the consent of the local planning authority.

Protection against blight.

34. Where, in pursuance of section 31 of this Act, a local authority have published information indicating that they propose to acquire any land in the exercise of their powers under this Part of this Act, sections 139 to 151 of the Town and Country Planning Act 1962 (protection of interests in land affected by planning proposals) shall have effect as if— 1962 c. 38.

(*a*) the land were included in that specified in subsection (1) of section 138 of that Act and its description in the definition of " the specified descriptions " in subsection (5) of that section ; and

(*b*) in section 139(3) of that Act " the relevant date " were defined, in relation to the land, as the date on which the information was first published ;

and section 152 of that Act (no withdrawal of constructive notice to treat) shall have effect accordingly ; and section 34 of the Town and Country Planning Act 1968 (power of mortgagee to serve blight notice) shall apply in relation to the land as it applies in relation to land of the description mentioned in subsection (2) of that section. 1968 c. 72.

Disposal and appropriation of land.

35.—(1) Where any land for the time being vested in a local authority for the purposes of this Part of this Act—

(*a*) consists of or forms part of an open space ; or

(*b*) has been compulsorily acquired under this Part of this Act ;

the local authority shall not dispose of it except with the consent of the Minister.

(2) Where the disposal of any land vested in a local authority for the purposes of this Part of this Act is not subject to the consent of the Minister in pursuance of subsection (1) of this section they shall not, without his consent, sell, exchange or, subject to subsection (4) of this section, let it for a price, consideration or rent less than the best that can reasonably be

PART II

obtained, having regard to any restrictions or conditions (including conditions as to payment or the giving of security for payment) subject to which the land is sold, exchanged or let.

(3) For the purposes of this section land shall be taken to have been acquired by an authority compulsorily if it was acquired by agreement at a time when they were authorised to acquire it compulsorily.

(4) The consent of the Minister under the preceding provisions of this section may be given either generally to local authorities or to any local authority or class of local authority or in any particular case and may be given either unconditionally or subject to any conditions; and the consent of the Minister under subsection (2) of this section shall not be required to any letting for a term not exceeding seven years.

(5) Where a local authority acquire any land in pursuance of this Part of this Act they shall comply with such general or special directions as may be given by the Minister as to the exercise of their power to appropriate the land for the purposes of Part V of the Act of 1957 (provision of housing accommodation).

(6) The power of a local authority under section 32(1)(*a*) of this Act to carry out works on land owned by them may, with the approval of the Minister given (with or without limitation) either generally or in a particular case, be exercised notwithstanding that they have not appropriated the land for the purposes of this Part of this Act.

(7) In this section "open space" means any land laid out as a public garden or used for the purposes of public recreation, and any disused burial ground; and section 29 of the Town and Country Planning Act 1959 (protection of persons deriving title to land under transactions requiring consent) applies to any transaction requiring consent under this section.

1959 c. 53.

Standard grants in general improvement area.

36. Where an application for a standard grant under Part I of this Act is made with respect to a dwelling in a general improvement area the local authority shall not be required to approve it but may approve it if they would otherwise be required or authorised to do so.

Contributions to local authorities towards expenditure incurred under this Part of this Act.

37.—(1) The Minister may, subject to any directions of the Treasury, pay a contribution to a local authority towards such expenditure incurred by them under this Part of this Act—

(*a*) in carrying out works or providing any land; or

(*b*) in making contributions to any other authority or person towards expenses which might be so incurred by the local authority;

as he may approve for the purposes of this section on an application by the local authority made, where the expenditure is incurred in carrying out any works, before the works are begun.

PART II

(2) For the purposes of this section—

(*a*) the cost of any works shall be taken to be the amount certified by the local authority as appearing to them to be the cost likely to be incurred by them in carrying out those works; and

(*b*) the cost of any land acquired by a local authority under this Part of this Act shall be taken to be the expenses incurred by the authority in connection with the acquisition, and the cost of any land appropriated by a local authority for the purposes of this Part of this Act shall be taken to be such amount as the Minister may determine.

(3) A contribution under this section shall be a sum payable annually for a period of twenty years beginning with the financial year in which the relevant works are completed, equal to one-half of the annual loan charges referable to the expenditure approved for the purposes of this section.

(4) The aggregate of any expenditure approved for the purposes of this section (whether on one or more applications) in respect of any general improvement area shall not exceed the sum arrived at by multiplying £100 by the number of dwellings stated by the local authority under the preceding provisions of this Part of this Act to be in the area or, if it appears to the Minister that there will be an increased number of dwellings in the area, by that increased number; but the Minister may, for the purposes of this subsection—

(*a*) treat two adjoining general improvement areas as one; or

(*b*) treat the addition, in pursuance of section 30 of this Act, of land to a general improvement area as the declaration of a separate general improvement area.

(5) The Minister may, with the consent of the Treasury, by order substitute another amount for the amount of £100 mentioned in subsection (4) of this section, and a statutory instrument containing such an order shall be subject to annulment in pursuance of a resolution of the Commons House of Parliament.

(6) For the purposes of this section the relevant works, in relation to any expenditure, are—

(*a*) if the expenditure is incurred in carrying out any works, those works; and

(*b*) if the expenditure is incurred in providing any land on which works are to be carried out, those works.

Part II

(7) Where any arrangement made between a local authority and a housing association so provides, any expenditure incurred by the housing association in pursuance of the arrangement which might have been incurred by the local authority under this Part of this Act shall be treated for the purposes of subsection (1) of this section as if it were expenditure so incurred by the local authority; and where any such expenditure is approved by the Minister for the purposes of this section—

(*a*) subsection (3) of this section shall have effect, in relation to it, as if in the definition of " annual loan charges " in section 86(5) of this Act the reference to a housing authority were a reference to a housing association; and

(*b*) the local authority shall pay to the housing association by way of annual grant an amount not less than so much of the contribution paid to the local authority under this section as is referable to that expenditure.

Effect of contribution under section 37 on Housing Revenue Account.

1958 c. 42.

38. Where any expenditure incurred by a local authority in relation to any houses or other land for the time being vested in them for the purposes of Part V of the Act of 1957 has been approved for the purposes of section 37 of this Act, then, notwithstanding section 50 of the Housing (Financial Provisions) Act 1958, neither the expenditure nor the contribution under section 37 shall be carried to the Housing Revenue Account, except with the consent of the Minister.

Local authorities for purposes of Part II.

39. Subject to section 40 of this Act, the local authorities for the purposes of this Part of this Act are the councils of boroughs, urban districts and rural districts and the Common Council of the City of London.

Special provisions as to Greater London.

40.—(1) The Greater London Council may exercise the powers of a local authority under sections 28 and 30 of this Act with respect to any area in Greater London, but only with the agreement of any local authority in whose district the area or any part of the area is situated.

(2) In relation to any house or other land in a general improvement area declared by the Greater London Council—

(*a*) the Greater London Council shall be deemed to be a local authority for the purposes of sections 17 to 22 and 74 of this Act and shall be deemed to be the local authority, to the exclusion of any other authority, for the purposes of the provisions of Part I of this Act other than sections 17 to 22, this Part, Part III and section 75 of this Act, and Part II of the Act of 1957; and

(b) any functions exercisable by the council of a London borough or the Common Council of the City of London under Part IV of the Act of 1957, Part II of the Housing Act 1961, section 19, 20 or 21 of the Housing Act 1964 or Part IV of that Act shall be so exercisable only after consultation with the Greater London Council.

PART II

1961 c. 65.

1964 c. 56.

Discontinuance of power to declare improvement area.

41. No further area shall be declared an improvement area under section 13 of the Housing Act 1964; and (without prejudice to the power of a local authority to take such action under Part II of that Act as appears to them appropriate with respect to dwellings in an area declared an improvement area before the commencement of this Act) subsection (4) of that section (which imposes an express duty to take action) shall not apply in a general improvement area.

Repeal of provisions relating to re-development areas.

42. Sections 55 to 57 of the Act of 1957 (which make provision for the declaration of re-development areas and the purchase of land for purposes of re-development) shall cease to have effect.

PART III

RENT OF DWELLINGS IN GOOD REPAIR AND PROVIDED WITH STANDARD AMENITIES

Conversion of controlled tenancies

Conversion of controlled tenancies of dwellings provided with standard amenities and in good repair.

43.—(1) The following provisions of this section shall have effect with respect to a controlled tenancy of a dwelling which is certified by the local authority, on the application of the landlord, to satisfy the following conditions, that is to say, that it is provided with all the standard amenities for the exclusive use of its occupants, that it is in good repair, having regard to its age, character and locality and disregarding internal decorative repair, and that it is in all other respects fit for human habitation.

(2) Except in the case mentioned in subsection (3) of this section the tenancy shall become a regulated tenancy on the issue of the certificate or (unless the tenancy has then become a regulated tenancy apart from this Act or has ceased to exist) on such later date as is specified in section 50 of this Act or an order made thereunder.

(3) If the controlled tenancy is one to which Part II of the Act of 1954 would apply, apart from section 9(3) of the Rent Act 1968, or would so apply if the controlled tenancy were a tenancy within the meaning of the Act of 1954, it shall,

1968 c. 23.

PART III on the issue of the certificate, cease to be a controlled tenancy and shall then be treated as a tenancy continuing by virtue of section 24 of the Act of 1954 after the expiry of a term of years certain.

1968 c. 23. (4) Section 46 of the Rent Act 1968 (determination of fair rent) shall apply in relation to a controlled tenancy which becomes a regulated tenancy by virtue of this Part of this Act as if the references in subsection (3) thereof to the tenant under the regulated tenancy included references to the tenant under the controlled tenancy.

(5) The conditions mentioned in subsection (1) of this section are in this Part of this Act referred to as the qualifying conditions and a certificate issued in accordance with this section as a qualification certificate.

1954 c. 56. (6) In this section " the Act of 1954 " means the Landlord and Tenant Act 1954.

Application for qualification certificate.

44.—(1) Except where an application for a qualification certificate is made under subsection (2) of this section it shall not be entertained unless either—

(*a*) the dwelling has at all times since the commencement of this Act been provided with all the standard amenities ; or

(*b*) any of the standard amenities previously lacking were provided by means of works begun before the commencement of this Act ;

1958 c. 42. and shall not be entertained while the conditions of Schedule 4 to the Housing (Financial Provisions) Act 1958 fall to be observed with respect to the dwelling.

(2) An application for a qualification certificate may be made with respect to a dwelling notwithstanding that at the time of the making of the application the dwelling lacks one or more of the standard amenities, if the application is made (whether or not as part of or in conjunction with an application for a grant under Part I of this Act) before any works are begun for providing the dwelling with the standard amenities which it lacks.

(3) An application for a qualification certificate must state the name of the tenant under the controlled tenancy and, if the application is made at a time when the dwelling does not satisfy the qualifying conditions, must state what works are required for those conditions to be satisfied and must be accompanied by plans and specifications of those works.

(4) Before considering an application for a qualification certificate a local authority shall send a copy of the application to the person named in the application as the tenant.

PART III

Procedure on applications under section 44(1).

45.—(1) Where an application for a qualification certificate is made under section 44(1) of this Act the local authority shall, before considering it, serve on the person named in the application as the tenant a notice in the prescribed form—

(*a*) informing him that he may, within twenty-eight days from the service of the notice or such other time as may be prescribed, make representations to the authority that the dwelling does not satisfy the qualifying conditions ; and

(*b*) containing such other information or explanation of the effect of this Part of this Act as may be prescribed.

(2) Where the local authority are satisfied, after considering any representations made in pursuance of subsection (1) of this section, that the dwelling satisfies the qualifying conditions, they shall issue to the applicant a qualification certificate, but if they are not so satisfied they shall give notice to the applicant of their refusal of his application ; and they shall send a copy of the certificate or of the notice to the tenant.

Procedure on applications under section 44(2).

46.—(1) Subject to subsection (5) of this section, where an application for a qualification certificate in respect of any dwelling is made under section 44(2) of this Act and it appears to the local authority that the dwelling will satisfy the qualifying conditions when the works specified in the application have been carried out, the local authority shall approve the application provisionally and shall issue to the applicant a certificate of provisional approval and send a copy thereof to the tenant.

(2) The provisions of Part I of Schedule 2 to this Act shall have effect for enabling a person who has obtained a certificate of provisional approval to apply for a certificate of fair rent.

(3) On the production by the applicant of a certificate of fair rent and on being satisfied that the dwelling satisfies the qualifying conditions the local authority shall issue the qualification certificate and shall send a copy of it to the tenant.

(4) If at the time the qualification certificate is issued the state of the dwelling differs in any respect from that which, at the time the application for the certificate was made, it could be expected to be in when the works specified in the application had been carried out, the local authority shall specify the differences in the certificate.

(5) In the case mentioned in section 43(3) of this Act the local authority shall not issue a certificate of provisional approval but shall, notwithstanding that the application is made under section 44(2) of this Act, issue the qualification certificate as

PART III

soon as they are satisfied that the dwelling satisfies the qualifying conditions and send a copy of the certificate to the tenant.

Registration of rent after issue of qualification certificate.
1968 c. 23.

47.—(1) Where a controlled tenancy of a dwelling has become a regulated tenancy by virtue of this Part of this Act an application by the landlord for the first registration of a rent for the dwelling under Part IV of the Rent Act 1968 must be accompanied by a copy of the qualification certificate and, if the certificate was issued under section 46(3) of this Act, also by a copy of the certificate of fair rent.

(2) Part II of Schedule 2 to this Act shall have effect, in lieu of Schedule 6 to the Rent Act 1968, with respect to an application made in pursuance of this section in a case where a qualification certificate has been issued under section 46(3) of this Act.

Statement of reasons for refusing certificate.

48. Where, on an application for a qualification certificate, a local authority refuse to issue the certificate or to issue a certificate of provisional approval, they shall give the applicant a written statement of their reasons for the refusal.

Appeal in certain cases against issue or refusal of qualification certificate.

49.—(1) Within twenty-eight days of the service on him under section 45(2) of this Act of a notice of refusal or such longer period as the county court may allow the applicant for a qualification certificate may appeal to the county court on the ground that the certificate ought to be issued; and on such an appeal the court may confirm the refusal or order the local authority to issue the certificate.

(2) Within twenty-eight days of the service on him under section 45(2) of this Act of a copy of a qualification certificate or such longer period as the county court may allow the tenant may appeal to the county court on either or both of the following grounds, that is to say—

(*a*) that the certificate ought not to have been issued;

(*b*) that the certificate is invalid by reason of a failure to comply with any requirement of this Part of this Act or of some informality, defect, or error;

and on any such appeal the court may confirm or quash the certificate, but if the appeal is on the ground mentioned in paragraph (*b*) of this subsection the court shall confirm the certificate unless satisfied that the interests of the appellant have been substantially prejudiced by the facts relied on by him.

(3) The following provisions shall apply on an appeal under this section, that is to say—

(*a*) the court shall have regard to the state of the dwelling at the time of the hearing as well as at the time of the issue or refusal of the certificate; and

PART III

(b) the court shall make no order for costs unless it appears to the court, having regard to the conduct of the parties and all other circumstances, that it would be equitable to do so.

(4) Any certificate issued in pursuance of an order made under subsection (1) of this section shall be deemed to be issued on the date of the order.

(5) Where a qualification certificate with respect to any dwelling is quashed by an order under this section after a rent for the dwelling has been registered in pursuance of this Part of this Act the registration shall be deemed never to have had effect and the rent officer shall delete it on being informed of the order.

Postponement in certain cases of effect of qualification certificate.

50.—(1) Where a qualification certificate with respect to a dwelling is issued under section 45(2) of this Act before the date applicable to the dwelling under the following provisions of this section, the controlled tenancy of the dwelling shall not become a regulated tenancy by virtue of this Part of this Act until that date; and in those provisions " value " means the rateable value on the appropriate day as ascertained for the purposes of Part I of the Rent Act 1968. 1968 c. 23.

(2) Subject to subsection (3) of this section—

(a) 1st January 1971 is the date applicable to a dwelling in Greater London of a value of £90 or more and a dwelling elsewhere of a value of £60 or more;

(b) 1st July 1971 is the date applicable to a dwelling in Greater London of a value of less than £90 but not less than £60 and a dwelling elsewhere of a value of less than £60 but not less than £40;

(c) 1st January 1972 is the date applicable to a dwelling in Greater London of a value of less than £60 and a dwelling elsewhere of a value of less than £40.

(3) The Minister may by order substitute as the date applicable to a dwelling of such value as may be specified in the order a date earlier than that which would be applicable to it under subsection (2) of this section; and an order under this section may make different provision with respect to different registration areas.

Modification of Rent Act 1968 in relation to tenancies converted under this Part of this Act.

51.—(1) Where an application for a qualification certificate has been made with respect to any dwelling any notice of increase under Part V of the Rent Act 1968 which is served after the date of the application shall be void so far as it relates to an increase authorised by section 56 of that Act (improvements) unless—

(a) the application was made under section 44(1) of this Act and the notice is served before the date applicable to the dwelling under section 50 of this Act; or

PART III

(*b*) the application has been withdrawn ; or

(*c*) the certificate has been refused and either the time for appealing against the refusal has expired or the refusal has been confirmed on appeal or the appeal has been abandoned ; or

(*d*) the certificate has been quashed on appeal.

(2) Where a controlled tenancy becomes a regulated tenancy by virtue of this Part of this Act—

1968 c. 23.

(*a*) it shall be disregarded for the purposes of section 20(3)(*a*) of the Rent Act 1968 (limit of rent during contractual periods) ;

(*b*) sections 22 to 24 of that Act (limit of rent during statutory periods) shall have effect in relation to the tenancy as if references therein to the last contractual period were references to the last rental period beginning before the tenancy becomes a regulated tenancy ; and

(*c*) sections 21(5) and 25(1) of that Act (effect of improvements on limit of rent before registration) shall not apply to any improvement effected before the tenancy becomes a regulated tenancy.

Recovery of rent increases due to provisions of this Part of this Act, etc.

52. Schedule 3 to this Act shall have effect for securing that where an increase in the rent payable under a regulated tenancy results from this Part of this Act or from works carried out with assistance provided under Part I of this Act it may be recovered only in such stages as are permitted under that Schedule.

Miscellaneous and supplementary provisions

Modification of Rent Act 1968 in relation to improvements assisted under Part I of this Act.
1968 c. 23.

53. Sections 21(5) and 25(1) of the Rent Act 1968 (effect of improvements on limit of rent before registration) shall not apply to any improvements with respect to which a grant under Part I of this Act is payable or has been paid.

Consent of tenant.

54.—(1) Where a dwelling which is subject to a controlled tenancy does not satisfy the qualifying conditions, and the works required for those conditions to be satisfied cannot be carried out without the consent of the tenant, then, if those works are specified in an application for a certificate of fair rent, his consent shall be of no effect unless given or confirmed in writing after the issue of the certificate.

(2) Where a dwelling which is subject to a statutory tenancy (whether a controlled or a regulated tenancy) does not satisfy

the qualifying conditions and the works required for those conditions to be satisfied cannot be carried out without the consent of the tenant but the tenant is unwilling to give or confirm his consent, then, if the conditions specified in subsection (3) of this section are satisfied, the county court may, on the application of the landlord, make an order empowering him to enter and carry out the works.

(3) The said conditions are—

(*a*) that the works were specified in an application for a certificate of fair rent and the certificate has been issued; and

(*b*) that, if the statutory tenancy is a regulated tenancy, the works were also specified in an application for a grant under Part I of this Act and the application has been approved; and

(*c*) that the court is not precluded from making the order by section 55 of this Act.

(4) An order under subsection (2) of this section may be made subject to such conditions as to the time at which the works are to be carried out and as to any provision to be made for the accommodation of the tenant and his household whilst they are carried out as the court may think fit; and where such an order is made subject to any condition as to time, compliance with that condition shall be deemed to be also compliance with any condition imposed by the local authority under section 4(4) or section 10 of this Act.

(5) In determining whether to make such an order and, if it is made, subject to what, if any, conditions, the court shall have regard to all the circumstances and, in particular, to any disadvantage to the tenant that might be expected to result from the works, the accommodation that might be available for him whilst the works are carried out, his means in relation to the increase of rent that would result and the stages in which that increase would become recoverable under the provisions of this Part of this Act.

Restriction on powers of court under section 54.

55.—(1) On an application under section 54(2) of this Act with respect to any dwelling the court shall not make an order empowering the landlord to enter and carry out any works if, not earlier than six months before the hearing, the rating authority for the area in which the dwelling is situated have certified that the tenant's income is within the limits for rate relief.

PART III (2) The rating authority shall, on the application of the tenant, certify that his means are within the limits for rate relief if—

(*a*) he has been granted a rate rebate under section 49 of the General Rate Act 1967 for the rebate period in which his application for the certificate is made; or

1967 c. 9.

(*b*) he would, on an application duly made, be entitled to such a rebate for that period or would be so entitled but for section 16(2) of the Ministry of Social Security Act 1966; or

1966 c. 20.

(*c*) his reckonable rates for that period do not exceed £3 15s. 0d. and his reckonable income does not exceed the appropriate limit;

and for the purposes of this subsection a person's reckonable rates for any period and the question whether his reckonable income exceeds the appropriate limit shall be determined as on an application for a rate rebate.

(3) An application for a certificate under this section must state the name and address of the landlord; and if on such an application the rating authority issue a certificate they shall send a copy of it to the person named in the application in pursuance of this subsection.

(4) For the purposes of any proceedings under section 54(2) of this Act any document purporting to be a certificate issued by a rating authority under this section and to be signed by the clerk to that authority shall be deemed to be such a certificate unless the contrary is proved.

(5) Any person who, for the purpose of obtaining such a certificate—

(*a*) furnishes any information which he knows to be false in a material particular; or

(*b*) withholds any material information;

shall be liable on summary conviction to a fine not exceeding £20.

Supplemental.
1968 c. 23.

56.—(1) The power to make regulations under section 50 of the Rent Act 1968 for the purposes of Part IV of that Act shall extend to this Part of this Act and the power to modify by such regulations the provisions of Schedules 6 and 7 to that Act shall extend to the provisions of Schedule 2 to this Act.

(2) The power of the Lord Chancellor under section 106 of the Rent Act 1968 to make rules and give directions for the purpose of giving effect to the provisions specified in subsection (3) of that section shall extend to sections 49 and 54 of this Act.

Part III

Interpretation.

57. In this Part of this Act—

"local authority" has the same meaning as in Part I of this Act;

"qualification certificate" and "qualifying conditions" have the meanings assigned to them by section 43(5) of this Act;

"registration area" means a registration area for the purposes of Part IV of the Rent Act 1968; 1968 c. 23.

and other expressions shall be construed as in the Rent Act 1968.

Part IV

Houses in multiple occupation

New definition of houses in multiple occupation.

58.—(1) Any statutory provision referring (in whatever terms) to a house which, or a part of which, is let in lodgings or which is occupied by members of more than one family shall have effect as if it referred to a house which is occupied by persons who do not form a single household.

(2) In this section "statutory provision" means any provision contained in an Act of Parliament or in any order or other instrument made under an Act of Parliament.

(3) In accordance with the preceding provisions of this section, the enactments mentioned in Part I of Schedule 8 to this Act shall have effect subject to the amendments specified in that Part; and the Minister may by order make similar amendments in any local Act or Act confirming a provisional order which was passed before the commencement of this Act.

Orders applying management code.

59.—(1) Subsection (2) of section 12 of the Housing Act 1961 (which requires a local authority to serve notice of intention to make an order applying the management code to a house) shall cease to have effect. 1961 c. 65.

(2) In subsection (4) of that section (right of appeal) for the words from "within" to "served" there shall be substituted the words "within twenty-one days from the service or such longer period as the local authority may in writing allow".

(3) In subsection (5) of that section (improvements between service of the notice and making of the order) for the words from "at the time when" to "time of the making of the order" there shall be substituted the words "at the time of the making of the order as well as at the time the appeal was instituted".

PART IV

Means of escape from fire.

60.—(1) If it appears to a local authority—

(*a*) that a house which is occupied by persons who do not form a single household is not provided with such means of escape from fire as the local authority consider necessary ; and

(*b*) that it would not be practicable to provide it with such means at reasonable expense ;

but that, if part of the house were not used for human habitation,—

(i) the means of escape from fire with which the house is provided would be adequate ; or

(ii) adequate means of escape from fire could be provided at reasonable expense ;

the local authority may secure that that part is not used for human habitation and, in the case mentioned in paragraph (ii) of this subsection, serve a notice under section 16 of the Housing Act 1961 requiring the execution of such works as are in the opinion of the local authority required to provide such means of escape from fire as will be necessary if that part of the house is not used for human habitation.

1961 c. 65.

(2) For the purpose of securing that a part of the house is not used for human habitation the local authority may, if after consultation with any owner or mortgagee they think fit to do so, accept an undertaking from him that that part will not be used for human habitation without the permission of the local authority.

(3) Any person who, knowing that an undertaking has been accepted under subsection (2) of this section, uses the part of the house to which the undertaking relates in contravention of the undertaking, or permits that part of the house to be so used, shall be guilty of an offence and liable on summary conviction to a fine not exceeding £20 and to a further fine of £5 for every day, or part of a day, on which he so uses it or permits it to be so used after conviction.

(4) If the local authority do not accept an undertaking under subsection (2) of this section with respect to a part of the house, or if, in a case where they have accepted such an undertaking, that part of the house is at any time used in contravention of the undertaking, the local authority may make a closing order with respect to that part of the house.

1947 c. 41.

(5) A local authority who are not, under the Fire Services Act 1947, the fire authority for the area in which the house is situated, or who have, under section 12 of that Act, delegated all their functions in respect of that area to another fire authority, shall, before making a closing order under this section or accepting an undertaking under subsection (2) thereof, consult with the fire authority concerned.

PART IV

(6) Part II of the Act of 1957 shall apply to a closing order made under this section as it applies to a closing order under section 18(1) of that Act, but the ground on which, under section 27(2) of that Act, the local authority are required to determine the order shall be that they are satisfied that the means of escape from fire with which the house is provided would be adequate (owing to a change of circumstances) even if the part of the house with respect to which the order was made were used for human habitation.

(7) Nothing in the Rent Act 1968 shall prevent possession being obtained of any part of a house which, in accordance with such an undertaking as is mentioned in subsection (2) of this section, cannot for the time being be used for human habitation. 1968 c. 23.

Offences and penalties.

61.—(1) Any obligation to execute works in pursuance of a notice served under section 14, 15 or 16 of the Housing Act 1961 shall continue notwithstanding that the period specified in the notice (with any extension permitted by the authority) or the period specified in relation to an appeal by section 65(5) of the Housing Act 1964 has expired; and a person shall be guilty of an offence if he wilfully fails to comply with that obligation after being convicted under section 65 of the Housing Act 1964 of failing to comply with the notice or after being convicted under this section of failing to comply with the obligation. 1961 c. 65. 1964 c. 56.

(2) A person guilty of an offence under this section shall be liable on summary conviction to a fine not exceeding £100.

(3) Where an offence under this section committed by a body corporate is proved to have been committed with the consent or connivance of, or to be attributable to any neglect on the part of, any director, manager, secretary or other similar officer of the body corporate, or any person purporting to act in any such capacity, he as well as the body corporate shall be deemed to be guilty of that offence and shall be liable to be proceeded against and punished accordingly.

(4) The preceding provisions of this section shall be without prejudice to the exercise by the local authority of their powers of carrying out the works under section 18 of the Housing Act 1961. 1961 c. 65.

(5) Section 159 of the Act of 1957 (powers of entry) shall apply for the purpose of ascertaining whether there has been an offence under this section but so much of that section as requires notice to be given of the intended entry shall not apply; and that purpose shall be deemed to be among those mentioned in section 68(1)(*b*) of the Housing Act 1964 (warrant to authorise entry).

PART IV

(6) Sections 19(11)(*a*) and 20(1)(*a*) of the Housing Act 1961 (penalty on first conviction of an offence of failing to comply with a direction or notice against overcrowding) shall each have effect, with respect to offences committed after the commencement of this Act, as if for the words " twenty pounds " there were substituted the words " one hundred pounds ".

Directions to prevent or reduce overcrowding in houses in multiple occupation. 1961 c. 65.

62.—(1) In section 19 of the Housing Act 1961 (directions to prevent or reduce overcrowding in houses in multiple occupation)—

(*a*) in subsection (1), for the words " the highest number of individuals " there shall be substituted the words " the highest number of individuals or households or both " and for the words " live in the house " the words " occupy the house " ; and

(*b*) for paragraphs (*a*) and (*b*) of subsection (2) there shall be substituted the words " not to permit the number of individuals or households occupying the house to increase to a number above the limit specified in the direction and, if it is for the time being above that number, not to permit it to increase further ".

1964 c. 56.

(2) In subsection (3) of section 67 of the Housing Act 1964 (which allows a number specified in a notice under that section, or a number determined by reference to it, to be adopted in fixing a limit under section 19(1) of the Housing Act 1961) the words between " adopt that number " and " in fixing a limit " shall be omitted.

Control order followed by compulsory purchase order.

63.—(1) The following provisions of this section shall have effect where a local authority have made a control order (that is to say an order under section 73 of the Housing Act 1964) with respect to a house and within twenty-eight days of the making of the order the authority make a compulsory purchase order for the acquisition of the house under Part V of the Act of 1957.

(2) The local authority need not prepare a scheme under section 79 of the Housing Act 1964 or serve a copy of such a scheme in pursuance of that section until they are notified by the Minister of his decision to confirm or not to confirm the compulsory purchase order ; and the time within which copies of the scheme are to be served under that section shall be—

(*a*) if the Minister's decision is not to confirm the compulsory purchase order, eight weeks from the date on which the Minister's decision is notified to the authority ;

(*b*) if the Minister's decision is to confirm the compulsory purchase order, eight weeks from the time at which the compulsory purchase order becomes operative.

(3) Where the compulsory purchase order is confirmed by the Minister and the local authority— PART IV

(*a*) enter into a contract to purchase the house, or

(*b*) in pursuance of a notice served under section 11 of the Compulsory Purchase Act 1965, either enter and take possession of the house or serve a notice under section 98 of the Act of 1957 authorising a person in occupation of the house or part of the house to continue in occupation, 1965 c. 56.

the control order shall cease to have effect on the date when the contract is made or the notice under section 11 is served.

(4) Where a control order ceases to have effect by virtue of subsection (3) of this section the local authority shall, subject to the following provisions of this section, be liable to pay to the dispossessed proprietor the balances which, since the coming into force of the control order, from time to time accrued to the local authority out of the net amount of the rent and other payments received by them while the control order was in force from persons occupying the house, after deducting—

(*a*) compensation payable by the local authority under section 78 and section 81 of the Housing Act 1964; and 1964 c. 56.

(*b*) all expenditure, other than capital expenditure, incurred by the local authority in respect of the house while the control order was in force, together with the appropriate establishment charges.

(5) For the purpose of enabling the local authority to recover, under the following provisions of this section, capital expenditure incurred in carrying out works in the house in the period before the control order ceases to have effect, the local authority may, by a notice served on the dispossessed proprietor, specify those works as being works which, if the control order had not been in force, the local authority could have required some person to carry out under Part II of the Housing Act 1961, or under any other enactment relating to housing or public health, and which could not be postponed because they were urgently required for the sake of the safety, welfare or health of persons living in the house or other persons. 1961 c. 65.

(6) Where a notice under the preceding subsection is served on the proprietor he may within twenty-one days of the service of the notice or such longer period as the local authority may in writing allow appeal to the county court; and on any such appeal the court may confirm, quash or vary the notice.

(7) Any expenditure reasonably incurred by the local authority in carrying out the works specified in a notice under subsection (5) of this section (or specified in such a notice as varied by the court) may be deducted by the local authority

PART IV

from the balances which they are, under subsection (4) of this section, liable to pay to the dispossessed proprietor; and so far as that expenditure exceeds those balances it may, if the house is purchased compulsorily, be deducted from the amount payable as compensation, and accordingly any interest payable on that amount shall be calculated after allowing for the deduction.

(8) A local authority shall give notice to the dispossessed proprietor of the balances which they propose to pay to him under subsection (4) of this section and he may, within twenty-one days of the service of the notice or such longer period as the local authority may in writing allow, appeal to the county court; and on any such appeal the county court, if of opinion that those balances are unduly low for any reason within the control of the local authority, having regard to the desirability of observing the standards of management contained in regulations made under section 13 of the Housing Act 1961, and to the other standards which the local authority ought to observe as to the number of persons living in the house and the rents which they ought to charge, the court shall direct that, for the purposes of the local authority's liability to the dispossessed proprietor under this section, the balances under subsection (4) thereof shall be deemed to be such greater sums as the court may direct, but those sums shall not exceed the amount which, in the opinion of the court, the dispossessed proprietor may have lost by the making of the control order.

1961 c. 65.

(9) If different persons are dispossessed proprietors in relation to different parts of the house, sums payable under this section by the local authority shall be apportioned between them in the manner provided by section 78(6) of the Housing Act 1964.

1964 c. 56.

(10) Any notice served on any person under subsection (5) or subsection (8) of this section shall inform him of his right of appeal under this section.

(11) Section 91 of the Housing Act 1964 (interpretation and construction of Part IV) shall apply as if this section were contained in Part IV of that Act.

Registers of houses in multiple occupation.

64.—(1) A scheme under section 22 of the Housing Act 1961 may be so made or amended as to contain provisions, either in lieu of or in addition to the provisions authorised by that section, for preventing, subject to subsection (3) of this section, multiple occupation of a house to an extent greater than that mentioned in that subsection unless the house is registered in pursuance of those provisions and the number of households or persons occupying it does not exceed the number so registered for that house ; and such provisions may prohibit persons from permitting others to take up residence in a house or part of a house but shall not prohibit any person from taking up or remaining in residence.

(2) In the following provisions of this section such provisions of a scheme as are authorised by subsection (1) of this section are referred to as control provisions.

(3) Control provisions shall not affect the continued occupation of a house by the number of households or persons occupying it at the time the provisions come into force and shall not affect any occupation of a house which is such that—

(*a*) the persons occupying the house form two households ; or

(*b*) apart from one household (if any) the house is occupied by not more than four persons.

(4) Control provisions may enable the local authority—

(*a*) to refuse to register or to vary the registration of a house on the ground that the house is unsuitable and incapable of being made suitable for such occupation as would be permitted by virtue of the registration or variation ;

(*b*) to refuse to register a house on the ground that the person having control of the house, or the person intended to be the person managing the house, is not a fit and proper person ; and

(*c*) to require, as a condition of registering or of varying the registration of a house, that such works are executed as will make the house suitable for such occupation as will be permitted by virtue of the registration or variation.

(5) Control provisions shall provide that, where the local authority refuse to register or to vary the registration of a house or require the execution of any works as a condition of doing so, they shall give the applicant a written statement of their reasons for doing so.

(6) Where a local authority notify a person who has applied for the registration or the variation of a registration of a house in pursuance of control provisions that they refuse to register the house or vary the registration in accordance with his application or that they require the execution of any works as a condition of doing so, he may, within twenty-one days of being so notified or such longer period as the local authority may in writing allow, appeal to the county court, and on such an appeal the county court may confirm, reverse or vary the decision of the authority ; and where the decision of the authority

Part IV

was a refusal to register or vary the registration of a house, the county court may direct them to register or vary the registration either in accordance with the application as made or in accordance with that application as varied in such manner as the county court may direct.

For the purposes of this subsection, where a local authority fail to register or vary the registration of a house within a period of five weeks after receiving an application therefor or such longer period as may be agreed in writing between the authority and the applicant they shall be deemed to have refused the application and to have notified him of their refusal at the end of that period.

1961 c. 65.

(7) Any person contravening or failing to comply with any provision of a scheme under section 22 of the Housing Act 1961 shall be guilty of an offence and liable on summary conviction—

(*a*) if the offence is a contravention of so much of the control provisions as relates to occupation, to a greater extent than permitted thereunder, of a house not registered in pursuance of those provisions, to a fine not exceeding £100 or, if the offence is committed by a person previously convicted of an offence consisting of a contravention of the control provisions, to imprisonment for a term not exceeding three months or a fine not exceeding £100 or both;

(*b*) if it is a contravention of so much of the control provisions as relates to the occupation of a house registered in pursuance of those provisions by more households or persons than the registration permits, to a fine not exceeding £100;

(*c*) in any other case to a fine not exceeding £10.

(8) In section 22(10) of the Housing Act 1961 for the words from " and without proof " to the end there shall be substituted the words " and the production of any document purporting to be a copy of an entry in any register kept under the scheme and to be certified as a true copy by the clerk of the authority shall be prima facie evidence of the entry, without, in either case, proof of the handwriting or official position of the person by whom it purports to be signed ".

Part V

Payments in respect of Unfit Houses purchased or Demolished, etc.

Extension of payments for well maintained houses.

65.—(1) In subsection (2) of section 30 of the Act of 1957 (which includes certain closing orders among the circumstances which may lead to the making of payments for well maintained

PART V

houses purchased at site value) the words " the proviso to subsection (1) of " shall be omitted and at the end of the subsection there shall be added the words " and shall also apply where a compulsory purchase may be authorised under section 12(1) of this Act, but with the modification that the period during which representations may be made under subsection (1) of this section shall end three months after notice of a compulsory purchase order is served in accordance with paragraph 3(1)(*b*) of Schedule 1 to the Acquisition of Land (Authorisation Procedure) Act 1946 and Schedule 1 to this Act." 1946 c. 49.

(2) In subsection (3)(*a*) of that section after the words " in pursuance of the notice " there shall be inserted the words " or under section 12 of this Act ".

Amendments with respect to amount of payments made for well maintained houses.

66.—(1) Part I of Schedule 2 to the Act of 1957 (ascertainment of amount payable for well maintained houses) shall have effect as set out in Schedule 4 to this Act.

(2) Subsection (1) of this section applies in relation to any payment made under section 30 or section 60 of the Act of 1957 in a case where the relevant date (within the meaning of paragraph 3 of that Part of the Schedule so set out) is later than 23rd April 1968.

Payments in respect of partially well maintained houses or parts of buildings.

67.—(1) A house which, apart from this section, would not fall to be treated as well maintained for the purposes of sections 30 and 60 of the Act of 1957 (payments in respect of condemned houses which have been well maintained) shall be so treated if either the exterior or the interior of the house has been well maintained and—

(*a*) in the case of section 30, the representation mentioned therein was made after the commencement of this Act; and

(*b*) in the case of section 60, the house is in an area which was declared a clearance area after the commencement of this Act or, where the section applies because of an order under paragraph 2 of Schedule 2 to the Land Compensation Act 1961, the order was made after the commencement of this Act. 1961 c. 33.

(2) Where a house comprises more than one dwelling or is occupied partly for the purposes of a dwelling or dwellings and partly for other purposes, then,—

(*a*) for the purposes of the relevant provisions so far as they relate to the maintenance of the interior of a house; but

(*b*) not for the purposes of those provisions so far as they relate to the maintenance if the exterior of a house;

PART V

the dwelling or each of the dwellings shall be deemed to be a house; and in this section "exterior", in relation to such a house, includes any part of the house which is not included in the interior of a dwelling.

(3) Where a closing order under section 18(1) of the Act of 1957 is made with respect to a part of a building which is used, or is suitable for use, as a dwelling and the interior of which is well maintained, section 30 of that Act and Part I of Schedule 2 to that Act shall apply in relation to that part as if it were a well maintained house and as if the closing order were a closing order under section 17 of that Act.

(4) A payment under section 30 or section 60 of the Act of 1957 which is made by virtue of this section shall, instead of being the amount ascertained in accordance with Part I of Schedule 2 to that Act, be one-half of the amount so ascertained.

(5) In this section "the relevant provisions" means this section and, so far as applicable by virtue of this section, sections 30 and 60 of the Act of 1957 and Part I of Schedule 2 to that Act.

Payments to owner-occupiers and others in respect of unfit houses purchased or demolished.

68.—(1) The provisions of Schedule 5 to this Act shall have effect with respect to certain payments to be made in respect of owner-occupied houses in certain circumstances; and where a payment under that Schedule falls to be made with respect to a house no payment with respect thereto shall be made under paragraph 4 of Schedule 2 to the Act of 1957.

(2) Part II of Schedule 2 to the Act of 1957 (payments to owner-occupiers and others in respect of unfit houses purchased or demolished) shall have effect, in the case of a house where—

(*a*) the relevant proceedings leading to the purchase or vacation of the house were begun (within the meaning of paragraph 4(6) of that Schedule) after 23rd April 1968; or

1961 c. 33.

(*b*) an order under paragraph 2 of Schedule 2 to the Land Compensation Act 1961 was made after that date declaring the house unfit for human habitation;

subject to the amendments specified in paragraphs 1, 2 and 4 of Schedule 6 to this Act and, in the case of a house where—

(i) such an order as is mentioned in paragraph 6 (business premises) of the said Part II was made after the commencement of this Act or is treated (by virtue of paragraph 7(1) of that Part) as having then been made; or

(ii) such an order as is mentioned in paragraph (*b*) of this subsection was made after the commencement of this Act;

also subject to the amendment specified in paragraph 3 of the said Schedule 6.

Repayment of certain payments made under Act of 1957 or this Act.

69. Where a payment in respect of a house has been made by a local authority under section 30 or 60 of the Act of 1957, Schedule 2 to that Act or Schedule 5 to this Act in connection with a demolition order, closing order or clearance order and, at any time after the commencement of this Act—

(*a*) the demolition order is revoked under section 24 of the Act of 1957; or

(*b*) the closing order is determined under section 27(2) of the Act of 1957; or

(*c*) an order under section 24 of the Housing Act 1961 comes into operation excluding the house from the clearance area and modifying or revoking the clearance order accordingly; 1961 c. 65.

then, if at that time the person to whom the payment was made is entitled to an interest in the house (within the meaning of Schedule 5 to this Act) he shall on demand repay the payment to the authority.

PART VI

MISCELLANEOUS AND SUPPLEMENTAL PROVISIONS

Review of housing conditions by local authorities.

70. It shall be the duty of every local authority (within the meaning of the enactments mentioned in this section) to cause an inspection of their district to be made from time to time with a view to determining what action to take in the performance of their functions under Part II or III of the Act of 1957, Part II of the Housing Act 1961, section 20 or Part IV of the Housing Act 1964 or Part II of this Act, and for the purpose of carrying out that duty the authority and their officers shall comply with any directions the Minister may give and shall keep such records and supply him with such information as he may specify. 1964 c. 56.

Standard of fitness for human habitation.

71. In section 4(1) of the Act of 1957 (matters to be taken into account in determining unfitness for human habitation) the following shall be inserted after paragraph (*c*)—

" (*cc*) internal arrangement ",

and the word " storage " shall be omitted from paragraph (*h*).

PART VI

Power of local authority to require repair of house.

72. In section 9 of the Act of 1957 (power to require repair of unfit house) the following subsection shall be inserted after subsection (1):—

"(1A) Where a local authority, upon consideration of an official representation, or a report from any of their officers, or other information in their possession, are satisfied that a house is in such state of disrepair that, although it is not unfit for human habitation, substantial repairs are required to bring it up to a reasonable standard, having regard to its age, character and locality, they may serve upon the person having control of the house a notice requiring him, within such reasonable time, not being less than twenty-one days, as may be specified in the notice, to execute the works specified in the notice, not being works of internal decorative repair."

Increase of fine under s. 170 of Housing Act 1957. 1957 c. 56.

73. Section 170 of the Housing Act 1957 (power of local authority to require information as to ownership of premises) shall have effect, with respect to offences committed after the commencement of this Act, as if for the words " five pounds " there were substituted the words " fifty pounds ".

Power of local authority to make advances repayable on maturity.

74.—(1) A local authority may, subject to such conditions as may be approved by the Minister, advance money to any person for the alteration, enlargement, repair or improvement of any dwelling, and the following provisions of this section shall apply with respect to an advance made under this section.

(2) The principal of the advance, together with interest thereon, shall be secured by a mortgage of the borrower's interest in the dwelling, and the amount of the principal shall not exceed the value which, in accordance with a valuation duly made on behalf of the local authority, it is estimated that interest will bear when the alteration, enlargement, repair or improvement has been carried out.

(3) The advance may be made by instalments from time to time as the works of alteration, enlargement, repair or improvement progress.

(4) The advance shall be made on terms providing for the repayment of the principal at the end of a fixed period, with or without a provision allowing the authority to extend that period, and with a provision for repayment on the happening of a specified event before the end of that period or extended period, and on such other terms as the local authority may think fit, having regard to all the circumstances.

(5) While repayment of the principal of an advance made under this section is not required in accordance with the terms of the advance, the local authority may suspend, with respect

to so much of any sum borrowed by them as is referable to the advance or with respect to any sum paid in respect of the advance out of their Consolidated Loans Fund, any periodical provision for repayment that may be required by any enactment or by any scheme (whether made under section 55 of the Local Government Act 1958 or under any local enactment) by which the Fund was established.

PART VI

1958 c. 55.

(6) The power conferred on a local authority by the preceding provisions of this section is without prejudice to any power to advance money exercisable by the authority under any other enactment; but where money is advanced by a local authority under section 43 of the Housing (Financial Provisions) Act 1958 for the acquisition of a house or the conversion into houses of any building, no money shall, in connection therewith, be advanced under this section for the alteration, enlargement, repair or improvement of that house or any of those houses.

1958 c. 42.

(7) The local authorities for the purposes of this section are the councils of counties, boroughs, urban districts and rural districts and the Common Council of the City of London.

Power of local authority to carry out works of improvement by agreement with and at expense of owner, etc.

75.—(1) A local authority for the purposes of Part I of this Act may by agreement with any person having the requisite interest execute at his expense any work towards the cost of which a grant under Part I of this Act is payable or might be paid on an application duly made and approved and any further work which it is in their opinion necessary or desirable to execute together with it.

(2) The works with respect to which an agreement may be made under subsection (1) of this section include, if the works are to be carried out in a general improvement area, any works—

(*a*) the carrying out of which will or might be assisted under section 32(1)(*a*) of this Act; or

(*b*) towards the cost of which an improvement grant might be made under Part I of this Act if that cost were not below the limit imposed by section 2(3) of this Act; or

(*c*) which are works of external repair (including decorative repair) or replacement not included in the definition of " improvement " in section 27 of this Act.

(3) In this section " the requisite interest ", in relation to any works, means an interest in every parcel of land on which the works are to be carried out which is either an estate in fee simple absolute in possession or a term of years absolute of which not less than five years remain unexpired.

PART VI

Amendment of Housing Act 1964, s. 43(3).
1964 c. 56.

76. In relation to the exercise by a local authority of their powers under Part II of the Housing Act 1964 in pursuance of any representations under section 19 of that Act which are made, or any preliminary notice under section 20 of that Act which is served, after the commencement of this Act, section 43(3) of that Act (which requires a water closet to be, if reasonably practicable, in and readily accessible from the dwelling) shall have effect as if for the words " and readily accessible from " there were substituted the words " and accessible from within ".

Extension of powers under s. 14 of Housing Subsidies Act 1967 to contributions in respect of conversion or improvement of dwellings.
1967 c. 29.
1949 c. 60.
1958 c. 42.
1959 c. 33.

77.—(1) Section 14 of the Housing Subsidies Act 1967 (power to reduce, discontinue or transfer subsidies in certain circumstances) shall have effect as if the payments specified in subsection (2) of this section were annual subsidies within the meaning of that section.

(2) The payments referred to in subsection (1) of this section are payments by the Minister under—

(*a*) section 15, 19 or 31(3) of the Housing Act 1949;

(*b*) section 9, 11 or 12 of the Housing (Financial Provisions) Act 1958;

(*c*) section 13 of the House Purchase and Housing Act 1959;

(*d*) section 17, 18, 19 or 21 of this Act;

and so much of any payment made by the Minister under section 37 of this Act as is referable to any expenditure incurred by a housing association and treated for the purposes of subsection (1) of that section as incurred by a local authority.

(3) In its application, by virtue of this section, to any payment referable to expenditure incurred by a housing association or development corporation in pursuance of arrangements made with a local authority under section 121 of the Act of 1957 or that section as applied by section 125 of that Act, section 14(5)(*b*) of the Housing Subsidies Act 1967 shall have effect as if those arrangements were included in the definition of " authorised arrangements " in section 21 of that Act and any dwelling improved in pursuance of the arrangements had been provided in pursuance thereof.

Power to increase subsidy for option mortgages.

78. At the end of section 28 of the Housing Subsidies Act 1967 (aggregate amount of subsidy under Part II) there shall be added the following:—

" (3) The Minister of Housing and Local Government, the Secretary of State for Wales and the Secretary of State for Scotland acting jointly may, with the approval of the Treasury, by order made by statutory instrument provide that with respect to interest payable for any period beginning on or after such date as may be specified in the order the calculation required by subsection (1)(*b*) of this section shall be made as if such higher percentages as may be specified in the order were substituted respectively for the two per cent. mentioned in that subsection and the one and three-quarters per cent. mentioned in subsection (2) of this section.

(4) An order under this section—

(*a*) may make different provision with respect to different cases or different classes of case and, in particular, with respect to repayment contracts providing for different rates of interest;

(*b*) may except from its provisions repayment contracts providing for such rates of interest as may be specified in the order; and

(*c*) may include provision enabling the Minister to determine a rate of interest as representative of the rate applicable at any time under repayment contracts of any description made with a qualifying lender during any period and relating to loans not subsidised under this Part of this Act and, if that rate is different from that then applicable under any repayment contract made with that lender during that period but relating to a loan so subsidised, to treat that contract for the purposes of this section as if the rate so determined were then applicable thereunder.

(5) The power to make an order under this section includes power to vary or revoke such an order by a subsequent order; but no such order shall be made unless a draft thereof has been laid before and approved by the Commons House of Parliament ".

Right to terminate period for which option notice has effect.

79.—(1) In section 24(3) of the Housing Subsidies Act 1967 the following shall be inserted after paragraph (vi):—

" (vii) the taking effect of a notice under section 26A of this Act."

1967 c. 29.

(2) After section 26 of that Act there shall be inserted the following section:—

" 26A.—(1) Where an option notice has been given in respect of a loan the person or persons in whom the rights and obligations under the repayment contract are for the time being vested may by notice to the lender bring the period for which the option notice has effect to an end on

PART VI

31st March of any year not earlier than 1973, but only if not less than five years have then elapsed since the date of the repayment contract.

(2) A notice under this section must be in writing and in such form as the Minister may direct and must be given not less than three months before the date on which it is to take effect."

Long tenancies at a low rent.

80.—(1) In determining whether a long tenancy is, or at any time before the commencement of this Act was,—

1968 c. 23. 1954 c. 56.

(*a*) a tenancy at a low rent within the meaning of the Rent Act 1968 or Part I of the Landlord and Tenant Act 1954; or

(*b*) a tenancy to which, by virtue of section 12(7) of the Act of 1920, the Rent Acts did not apply;

there shall be disregarded such part (if any) of the sums payable by the tenant as is expressed (in whatever terms) to be payable in respect of rates, services, repairs, maintenance, or insurance, unless it could not have been regarded by the parties as a part so payable.

(2) Nothing in this section shall affect the amount of any payment which a tenant is or was liable to make for any rental period beginning before the commencement of this Act.

(3) In this section—

" long tenancy " means a tenancy granted for a term certain exceeding twenty-one years, other than a tenancy which is, or may become, terminable before the end of that term by notice given to the tenant;

1920 c. 17.

" the Act of 1920 " means the Increase of Rent and Mortgage Interest (Restrictions) Act 1920; and

" the Rent Acts " means the Rent and Mortgage Interest Restrictions Acts 1920 to 1939.

Other long tenancies. 1968 c. 23. 1954 c. 56.

81.—(1) Where a tenancy is both a protected tenancy within the meaning of the Rent Act 1968 and a long tenancy within the meaning of Part I of the Landlord and Tenant Act 1954, then,—

(*a*) if the conditions specified in subsection (2) of this section are satisfied with respect to it, nothing in Part VII of the Rent Act 1968 (premiums &c.) or the enactments replaced by it shall apply or be deemed ever to have applied to the tenancy;

(*b*) if any of those conditions are not satisfied with respect to it Schedule 7 to this Act shall apply and, if the tenancy was granted before the passing of this Act, be deemed always to have applied to it.

(2) The conditions mentioned in subsection (1)(*a*) of this section are— PART VI

(*a*) that the tenancy is not, and cannot become, terminable within twenty years of the date when it was granted by notice given to the tenant; and

(*b*) that, unless the tenancy was granted before the passing of this Act or was granted in pursuance of Part I of the Leasehold Reform Act 1967, the sums payable by the tenant otherwise than in respect of rates, services, repairs, maintenance or insurance are not, under the terms of the tenancy, varied or liable to be varied within twenty years of the date when it was granted nor, thereafter, more than once in any twenty-one years; and 1967 c. 88.

(*c*) that assignment or underletting of the whole of the premises comprised in the tenancy is not precluded by the terms of the tenancy and, if it is subject to any consent, there is neither a term excluding section 144 of the Law of Property Act 1925 (no payment in nature of fine) nor a term requiring in connection with a request for consent the making of an offer to surrender the tenancy. 1925 c. 20.

(3) Where the condition specified in subsection (2)(*b*) of this section would be satisfied with respect to a sub-tenancy but for a term providing for one variation, within twenty years of the date when the sub-tenancy was granted, of the sums payable by the sub-tenant, that condition shall be deemed to be satisfied notwithstanding that term, if it is satisfied with respect to a superior tenancy of the premises comprised in the sub-tenancy (or of those and other premises).

(4) Nothing in this section shall affect the recovery, in pursuance of any judgment given or order or agreement made before 20th May 1969, of any amount which it was not lawful to receive under the law in force at the time it was received.

(5) In this section and in Schedule 7 to this Act " grant " includes continuance and renewal and " premium " has the same meaning as in Part VII of the Rent Act 1968. 1968 c. 23.

Price payable on enfranchisement of leasehold house. 1967 c. 88.

82. The Leasehold Reform Act 1967 shall have effect, and be deemed always to have had effect, as if in section 9(1) (which provides for the price to be paid by a tenant on an enfranchisement under the Act to be calculated on certain assumptions, by reference to a sale of the reversion in the open market by a willing seller) there had been inserted after the words " a willing seller " the words " (with the tenant and members of his family who reside in the house not buying or seeking to buy) ", and as

PART VI

if at the end of section 9(1) there were added the words "The reference in this subsection to members of the tenant's family shall be construed in accordance with section 7(7) of this Act":

Provided that this section shall not have effect where the price has been determined (by agreement or otherwise) before the passing of this Act.

Amendment of Rent Act 1968 s. 46.

83. At the end of section 46 of the Rent Act 1968 (determination of fair rent) there shall be added the following subsection:—

"(4) In this section 'improvement' includes the replacement of any fixture or fitting."

Supplemental

Cost of acquisition involving periodical payments.

84. In ascertaining for the purposes of section 18, 21 or 37 of this Act the cost of acquiring an estate or interest in a case where periodical payments fall to be made in connection with the acquisition that cost shall be taken to include such sum as the Minister may determine to be the capital equivalent of those payments.

Orders and regulations.

85.—(1) Any order made by the Minister under any provision of this Act may be varied or revoked by a subsequent order made thereunder.

(2) Any order made by the Minister under this Act and any regulations made under this Act shall be made by statutory instrument.

(3) Any statutory instrument made under this Act, except one containing an order under section 22, 37, 50, 58 or 87 shall be subject to annulment in pursuance of a resolution of either House of Parliament.

Interpretation. 1957 c. 56.

86.—(1) In this Act—

"the Act of 1957" means the Housing Act 1957;

"housing association" has the meaning assigned to it for the purposes of the Act of 1957 by section 189(1) of that Act;

"land" includes any estate or interest in land;

"the Minister", except where it means the Secretary of State, means the Minister of Housing and Local Government and, in the application to Wales and Monmouthshire of any provision other than sections 18(3), 18(4), 21(5), 21(6) and 22 and other than the definition of "prescribed" in section 27 as it relates to section 2(3), 4(2), 5(2) or 6(4), means the Secretary of State;

"standard amenities" has the meaning assigned to it by section 7 of this Act. PART VI

(2) For the purposes of this Act a person is a member of another's family if that person is—

(*a*) the other's wife or husband; or

(*b*) a son or daughter or a son-in-law or daughter-in-law of the other, or of the other's wife or husband; or

(*c*) the father or mother of the other, or of the other's wife or husband.

In paragraph (*b*) of this subsection any reference to a person's son or daughter includes a reference to any step-son or step-daughter, any illegitimate son or daughter, and any adopted son or daughter of that person, and "son-in-law" and "daughter-in-law" shall be construed accordingly.

(3) Section 4 of the Act of 1957 (standard of fitness for human habitation) shall apply for the purposes of this Act.

(4) For the purposes of this Act the cost of any works shall be taken to include the cost of the employment in connection with the works of an architect, engineer, surveyor, land-agent or other person in an advisory or supervisory capacity.

(5) For the purposes of this Act the annual loan charges referable to any amount shall be, subject to sections 21(7) and 37(7) of this Act, the annual sum that, in the opinion of the Minister, would fall to be provided by a housing authority for the payment of interest on, and the repayment of, a loan of that amount repayable over a period of twenty years.

(6) References in this Act to any enactment shall be construed, except where the context otherwise requires, as references to that enactment as amended, and as including references thereto as applied, by any other enactment, including any enactment contained in this Act.

87. Section 115 of the Rent Act 1968 (application to Isles of Scilly) shall have effect as if the reference therein to Part IV of that Act included a reference to Part III of this Act; and the other provisions of this Act shall have effect, in their application to the Isles of Scilly, subject to such exceptions, adaptations and modifications as the Minister may by order direct.

Application to Scilly Isles. 1968 c. 23.

88.—(1) The Minister may by order repeal or amend any provision in any local Act passed before this Act where it appears to him that the provision is inconsistent with, or has become unnecessary in consequence of, any provision of Part I, Part II or section 64 of this Act.

Power to repeal or amend local Acts.

Part VI

(2) Before making an order under this section the Minister shall consult with any local authority which appears to him to be concerned.

(3) An order under this section may contain such transitional, supplementary or incidental provisions as appear to the Minister to be expedient.

Minor and consequential amendments, repeals and savings.

89.—(1) The enactments mentioned in Schedule 8 to this Act shall have effect subject to the minor and consequential amendments specified therein.

(2) The transitional provisions and savings contained in Schedule 9 to this Act shall have effect.

(3) Subject to the savings contained in Schedule 9 to this Act, the enactments mentioned in Schedule 10 to this Act are hereby repealed to the extent specified in the third column of that Schedule.

Expenses.

90. Any expenses of the Minister under this Act and any expenses of the Minister under any other enactment which are attributable to the provisions of this Act shall be defrayed out of moneys provided by Parliament.

Citation, construction, commencement and extent.

1967 c. 29.

91.—(1) This Act may be cited as the Housing Act 1969.

(2) This Act, the Housing Acts 1957 to 1965 and the Housing Subsidies Act 1967 may be cited together as the Housing Acts 1957 to 1969.

(3) Part IV of this Act shall be construed as one with the Act of 1957.

(4) This Act, except sections 80 to 82, shall not come into force until the expiration of the period of one month beginning with the date on which it is passed.

(5) This Act, except sections 78 and 79, does not extend to Scotland.

(6) This Act does not extend to Northern Ireland.

SCHEDULES

SCHEDULE 1

Sections 7, 11(3), 19(5).

Standard Amenities

Part I

Table of standard amenities

Item	Description	Amount allowed (subject to Part III of this Schedule)
1.	A fixed bath or shower	£30
2.	A hot and cold water supply at a fixed bath or shower	£45
3.	A wash-hand basin	£10
4.	A hot and cold water supply at a wash-hand basin	£20
5.	A sink	£15
6.	A hot and cold water supply at a sink... ...	£30
7.	A water closet	£50

Part II

Provisions Applicable to Certain Amenities

1. The fixed bath or shower must be in a bathroom, except in the case mentioned in paragraph 2 of this Schedule.

2. If it is not reasonably practicable for the fixed bath or shower to be in a bathroom but it is reasonably practicable for it to be provided with a hot and cold water supply it need not be in a bathroom but may be in any part of the dwelling which is not a bedroom.

3. The water closet must, if reasonably practicable, be in, and accessible from within, the dwelling or, if that is not reasonably practicable, in such a position in the curtilage of the dwelling or, where the dwelling is part of a larger building, in that building, as to be readily accessible from the dwelling.

Part III

Limit on Amount of Standard Grant or Standard Contribution

4. The amount of—

(a) a standard grant, or

(b) the allowable cost for the purposes of a standard contribution,

shall not exceed £450 and shall not exceed the sum of the amounts allowable under the following provisions of this Schedule.

Sch. 1

5. Subject to paragraph 10 of this Schedule, for each of the standard amenities provided there shall be allowed the amount specified for an amenity of that description in the third column of the Table set out in Part I of this Schedule or the amount substituted therefor under the following provisions of this Schedule.

6.—(1) If the works comprise, in connection with all or any of the amenities provided, the bringing of a piped supply of cold water into the dwelling for the first time there shall also be allowed an amount fixed, in the case of a standard grant, by the local authority and, in the case of a standard contribution, by the Minister.

(2) The amount to be fixed under this paragraph shall be the amount which in the opinion of the local authority or Minister is one half of such part of the cost proper to be incurred in carrying out the works as is attributable to the bringing of the piped supply into the dwelling.

7.—(1) If the works comprise the provision of a fixed bath or shower in a bathroom and the bathroom is being provided by the building of a new structure or the conversion of out-buildings attached or to be attached to the dwelling (or to the building of which the dwelling forms part) then, if before the application for the grant or contribution is approved the local authority have, or the Minister has, been satisfied that it is not reasonably practicable to provide the bathroom in any other way there shall be substituted as the amount allowed for that amenity an amount fixed by the local authority or Minister.

(2) The amount to be fixed under this paragraph shall be such amount, higher than that specified in the Table set out in Part I of this Schedule, as in the opinion of the local authority or Minister is one half of such part of the cost proper to be incurred in carrying out the works as is attributable to the provision of the fixed bath or shower in a bathroom.

8.—(1) If the works comprise the provision of a water closet and, in connection therewith, the installation of a septic tank or a cesspool then, if before the application for the grant or contribution is approved the local authority have or the Minister has been satisfied that the connection of the water closet with main drainage is not possible or reasonably practicable there shall be substituted as the amount allowed for that amenity an amount fixed by the local authority or Minister.

(2) The amount to be fixed under this paragraph shall be such amount, higher than that specified in the Table set out in Part I of this Schedule, as in the opinion of the local authority or Minister is one half of such part of the cost proper to be incurred in carrying out the works as is attributable to the provision of the water closet.

9. The amount to be fixed under paragraph 6, 7 or 8 of this Schedule shall be fixed by the local authority or Minister when approving the application for the grant or contribution; but if the applicant satisfies the local authority or Minister that the

works by reference to the cost of which the amount is fixed cannot be or could not have been carried out without the carrying out of works in addition to those specified in the application, they or he may substitute a higher amount for that fixed under that paragraph. SCH. 1

10. An amount shall not be allowed for more than one amenity of the same description; and no amount shall be allowed for an amenity of any description if at the time the works were begun the dwelling was provided with an amenity of that description, except where the works involved interference with or replacement of that amenity and the local authority are or the Minister is satisfied that it would not have been reasonably practicable to avoid the interference or replacement.

SCHEDULE 2

Sections 46, 47.

CERTIFICATES OF FAIR RENT AND REGISTRATION OF RENT FOR CONVERTED TENANCIES

PART I

APPLICATIONS FOR CERTIFICATES OF FAIR RENT BY LANDLORDS UNDER CONTROLLED TENANCIES

1. Where, on an application for a qualification certificate, a local authority have issued a certificate of provisional approval, the applicant may apply to the rent officer for a certificate of fair rent.

2. An application made under paragraph 1 of this Schedule must be accompanied by copies of the plans and specifications which accompanied the application for the qualification certificate and of the certificate of provisional approval.

3. A certificate of fair rent issued on an application under this Schedule shall specify the rent which would be a fair rent under the regulated tenancy that might arise by virtue of section 43 of this Act if the works shown in the plans and specifications were carried out.

4. Schedule 7 to the Rent Act 1968 shall have effect with respect to an application made under this Schedule as if—

(*a*) paragraphs 1(*c*) and 3 were omitted; and

(*b*) in paragraph 4(1) for the words from the beginning to " he shall serve " there were substituted the words " The rent officer shall serve ", and

(*c*) in paragraph 9 the words preceding sub-paragraph (*a*) were omitted.

PART II

APPLICATIONS FOR REGISTRATION

Procedure on application to rent officer

5. On receiving the application for registration the rent officer shall ascertain whether any differences are specified in the qualification certificate in accordance with section 46(4) of this Act.

6. If no differences are so specified and the application was made not later than three months after the issue of the qualification certificate, the rent officer shall register the rent in accordance with the certificate of fair rent.

SCH. 2

7. In any other case he shall serve a notice on the tenant informing him of the application and specifying a period of not less than seven days from the service of the notice during which representations in writing may be made to the rent officer against the registration of the rent specified in the certificate.

8. Where no such representations are made then, unless it appears to the rent officer that the rent specified in the certificate of fair rent is higher than a fair rent, he shall register that rent and notify the landlord and tenant accordingly.

9.—(1) Where representations are made as mentioned in paragraph 7 of this Schedule or the rent officer is of opinion that the rent specified in the certificate of fair rent is higher than a fair rent he shall serve notice on the landlord and on the tenant informing them that he proposes, at a time (which shall not be earlier than seven days after the service of the notice) and place specified in the notice to consider in consultation with the landlord and the tenant, or such of them as may appear at that time and place, what rent, not exceeding that specified in the certificate of fair rent, ought to be registered.

(2) At any such consultation the landlord and tenant may each be represented by a person authorised by him in that behalf, whether or not that person is of counsel or a solicitor.

10.—(1) The rent officer shall consider, in accordance with the preceding paragraph, what rent ought to be registered, and—

(*a*) if, after considering it, he is of opinion that the rent specified in the certificate is not higher than a fair rent he shall register it ; but

(*b*) if, after considering it, he is of opinion that the rent so specified is higher than a fair rent he shall determine a fair rent and register that rent,

as the rent for the dwelling, and shall give notice of the registration to the landlord and the tenant.

(2) The notice shall state that if, within twenty-eight days of the service of the notice or such longer period as the rent officer or a rent assessment committee may allow, an objection in writing is received by the rent officer from the landlord or the tenant the matter will be referred to a rent assessment committee.

11.—(1) If such an objection is received, then—

(*a*) if it is received within the period of twenty-eight days mentioned in the preceding paragraph or a rent assessment committee so direct, the rent officer shall refer the matter to a rent assessment committee ;

(*b*) if it is received after that period, the rent officer may either refer the matter to a rent assessment committee or seek the directions of a rent assessment committee whether so to refer it.

(2) The rent officer shall indicate in the register whether the matter has been referred to a rent assessment committee in pursuance of this paragraph.

Determination of fair rent by rent assessment committee

SCH. 2

12. The rent assessment committee to whom a matter is referred under paragraph 11 of this Schedule shall serve on the landlord and on the tenant a notice specifying a period of not less than fourteen days from the service of the notice during which either representations in writing or a request to make oral representations may be made by him to the committee.

13. Where, within the period specified under paragraph 12 of this Schedule or such further period as the committee may allow, the landlord or the tenant requests to make oral representations the committee shall give him an opportunity to be heard either in person or by a person authorised by him in that behalf, whether or not that person is of counsel or a solicitor.

14.—(1) The committee shall make such inquiry, if any, as they think fit and consider any representation made to them in pursuance of the preceding paragraphs and—

(*a*) if it appears to them that the rent registered by the rent officer has been rightly registered they shall confirm it;

(*b*) in any other case they shall designate as the rent for the dwelling-house either the rent specified in the certificate of fair rent or such lower rent as appears to them to be a fair rent, as the case may require;

and they shall notify the landlord, the tenant and the rent officer accordingly.

(2) On receiving the notification, the rent officer shall, as the case may require, either indicate in the register that the rent has been confirmed or register the rent designated by the committee as the rent for the dwelling.

SCHEDULE 3

Section 52.

RESTRICTION ON RENT INCREASES

Restriction on rent increases after first registration

1. Where a rent for a dwelling which is subject to a regulated tenancy is registered under Part IV of the Rent Act 1968 and the registration is the first— 1968 c. 23.

(*a*) after the tenancy has become a regulated tenancy by virtue of Part III of this Act; or

(*b*) after the completion, during the existence of the tenancy, of works towards the cost of which a grant was payable under Part I of this Act;

then if the rent payable under the tenancy for any statutory period beginning during the period of delay imposed by paragraph 2 of this Schedule is less than the rent so registered, it shall not be increased by a notice of increase under section 22(2) of the Rent Act 1968 except to the extent (if any) permitted under the following provisions of this Schedule; and any such notice which purports to increase it further shall have effect to increase it to the extent so permitted but no further. 1968 c. 23.

SCH. 3

Period of delay

2. There shall be a period of delay with respect to any rent registered as mentioned in paragraph 1 of this Schedule, which shall be—

(*a*) if the rent is registered as mentioned in sub-paragraph (*a*) of that paragraph, a period of four years ;

(*b*) if the rent is registered as mentioned in sub-paragraph (*b*) of that paragraph, a period of two years ;

beginning with the date of registration.

Permitted increase

3.—(1) The rent may be increased to the aggregate of the following:—

(*a*) the amount of the previous limit, calculated in accordance with paragraph 4 of this Schedule ;

(*b*) the amount (if any) apportioned to services in accordance with paragraph 5 of this Schedule ; and

(*c*) the appropriate proportion of the difference between the registered rent and the aggregate of the amounts specified in paragraphs (*a*) and (*b*) above.

(2) The appropriate proportion mentioned in sub-paragraph (1)(*c*) of this paragraph shall be ascertained for any rental period in accordance with the following Table, in which the year of the period of delay in which the rental period begins is shown in the first column and the appropriate proportion in the second or third column, according as the period of delay imposed by paragraph 2 of this Schedule is two years or four years.

TABLE

Year of period of delay	Appropriate Proportion	
	Where period of delay is two years	Where period of delay is four years
1st year	one-third	one-fifth
2nd year	two-thirds	two-fifths
3rd year	—	three-fifths
4th year	—	four-fifths

(3) Notwithstanding anything in the preceding provisions of this paragraph, the amount to which the rent may be increased for any rental period shall not in any case be less than seven shillings and sixpence a week above the following, that is to say—

(*a*) if the rental period begins in the first year of the period of delay, the aggregate of the amounts specified in sub-paragraphs (1)(*a*) and (1)(*b*) of this paragraph ;

(*b*) if the rental period begins in a subsequent year, the amount to which the rent could be increased for a rental period beginning in the previous year;

but nothing in this paragraph shall be taken to enable the rent to be increased above the amount registered.

Previous limit

4.—(1) For the purposes of this Schedule the previous limit of a rent shall be taken to be, subject to sub-paragraph (2) of this paragraph, the amount which at the date of registration was recoverable by way of the rent or would have been so recoverable if all notices of increase authorised by the Rent Act 1968 or by regulations under section 9 of the Prices and Incomes Act 1968 had been served. 1968 c. 23. 1968 c. 42.

(2) Where the rent includes an amount payable in respect of rates, the amount so payable, ascertained in accordance with Schedule 4 to the Rent Act, 1968, shall be deducted from the amount specified in sub-paragraph (1) of this paragraph in calculating the previous limit of the rent.

Amount to be apportioned to services

5.—(1) Where the registered rent includes a payment in respect of services provided by the landlord or a superior landlord, then if—

(*a*) the rent is not registered as a variable rent in accordance with section 47(4) of the Rent Act 1968; but

(*b*) not less than 10 per cent. of the amount of the registered rent is in the opinion of the rent officer or rent assessment committee fairly attributable to the provision of the services;

the amount so attributable shall be noted in the register.

(2) Where it appears to the rent officer or rent assessment committee that some amount was in the previous limit attributable to the provision of services by the landlord or a superior landlord and was less than the amount noted in pursuance of sub-paragraph (1) of this paragraph, then—

(*a*) if the amount so attributable can be ascertained the difference between it and the amount so noted shall be the amount apportioned to the services;

(*b*) if the amount so attributable cannot be ascertained it shall be taken to be an amount bearing to the previous limit the same proportion as the amount noted in pursuance of sub-paragraph (1) of this paragraph bears to the amount of the registered rent, and the difference between the amount so taken and the amount so noted shall be the amount apportioned to the services;

and the amount apportioned to the services in accordance with this sub-paragraph shall also be noted in the register.

(3) Where it appears to the rent officer or rent assessment committee that no amount was in the previous limit attributable to the provision of services by the landlord or a superior landlord, the amount noted in pursuance of sub-paragraph (1) of this paragraph shall be the amount apportioned to the services and shall be noted as such in the register.

Sch. 3

Restriction on rent increases in cases of further registration during period of delay

6.—(1) Where a rent (in this paragraph referred to as the first rent) for a dwelling which is subject to a regulated tenancy has been registered as mentioned in paragraph 1 of this Schedule and, in any year of the period of delay imposed by paragraph 2 of this Schedule, a new rent for the dwelling is registered under Part IV
1968 c. 23. of the Rent Act 1968, then, if the new rent exceeds the rent for the time being recoverable under the regulated tenancy the following provisions of this paragraph shall apply and the preceding provisions of this Schedule shall not apply.

(2) The rent for any statutory period beginning before the end of the period of delay shall not be increased by a notice of increase under section 22(2) of the Rent Act 1968 except to the extent permitted by the following provisions of this paragraph ; and any such notice which purports to increase it further shall have effect to increase it to the extent so permitted but no further.

(3) If the new rent is less than the first rent the rent payable under the regulated tenancy may be increased (up to the amount registered) to the same extent as if the first rent had remained registered.

(4) If the new rent exceeds the first rent the registration shall not affect the amount recoverable for any rental period beginning in the year mentioned in sub-paragraph (1) of this paragraph ; and the rent for any statutory period beginning after that year may be increased to an amount arrived at by adding the difference between the first rent and the new rent to the amount to which the rent for that period could have been increased had the first rent remained registered.

Successive tenancies

7. Where a rent for a dwelling which is subject to a regulated tenancy is registered as mentioned in paragraph 1 of this Schedule and, during the period of delay imposed by paragraph 2 of this Schedule with respect to the rent, the tenant, or any person who might succeed him as a statutory tenant, becomes the tenant under a new regulated tenancy of the dwelling—

(*a*) the rent limit for any contractual period of the new regulated tenancy beginning during that period of delay shall be the amount to which, if the first-mentioned tenancy had continued, the rent payable thereunder could have been increased in accordance with this Schedule for a statutory period beginning at the same time, and in relation to such a contractual period the reference in section 47(3)
1968 c. 23. of the Rent Act 1968 to section 20(2) of that Act shall be construed as a reference to this paragraph ; and

(*b*) in relation to any statutory period of the new tenancy beginning during that period of delay the preceding provisions of this Schedule shall have effect as if it were a statutory period of the first-mentioned tenancy.

SCH. 3

8. Where—

(*a*) a controlled tenancy of a dwelling becomes a regulated tenancy by virtue of Part III of this Act ; or

(*b*) a dwelling improved by works towards the cost of which a grant is payable under Part I of this Act is, at the time the works are completed, subject to a regulated tenancy ;

and the tenant, or any person who might succeed him as a statutory tenant, becomes the tenant under a new regulated tenancy of the dwelling, then, if during the continuance of the new regulated tenancy a rent for the dwelling is registered under Part IV of the Rent Act 1968 and the registration would be such a registration as is mentioned in paragraph 1 of this Schedule had the regulated tenancy mentioned in sub-paragraph (*a*) or (*b*) of this paragraph continued, paragraphs 1 to 6 of this Schedule shall apply as if it had continued, and paragraph 7(*a*) of this Schedule shall apply with the necessary modifications. 1968 c. 23.

Application to tenancies converted by order under s. 8 of Rent Act 1968

9. Where a regulated tenancy of a dwelling has become a regulated tenancy by virtue of an order under section 8 of the Rent Act 1968 and a rent for the dwelling is registered as mentioned in paragraph 1(*b*) of this Schedule section 27 of that Act (restriction on rent increases) shall thereupon cease to apply to the tenancy.

Supplemental

10. In ascertaining for the purposes of this Schedule whether there is any difference between amounts or what that difference is such adjustments shall be made as may be necessary to take account of periods of different lengths ; and for that purpose a month shall be treated as one-twelfth and a week as one fifty-second of a year.

11. Where the rent specified in a certificate of fair rent includes a payment in respect of services provided by the landlord or a superior landlord and the amount which in the opinion of the rent officer or rent assessment committee is fairly attributable to the provision of the services is not less than ten per cent. of the amount of the rent then, if the application for the certificate is made in pursuance of section 46(2) of this Act or the applicant so requests the amount so attributable shall be noted in the certificate together with the amount to be entered in the register under paragraph 5 of this Schedule as the amount to be apportioned to the services.

12. Any amount to be noted in the register or in a certificate of fair rent in pursuance of paragraph 5 or paragraph 11 of this Schedule as an amount fairly attributable to the provision of services shall be included among the matters to be specified in an application for the registration or for the certificate and any such amount and any amount to be so noted as an amount apportioned or to be apportioned to the services shall be included among the matters

SCH. 3 with respect to which representations may be made or consultations are to be held or notices to be given under Schedule 6 or Schedule 7 to the Rent Act 1968 or Schedule 2 to this Act.

1968 c. 23.

13. Where a rent designated or determined by a rent assessment committee is registered in substitution for a rent determined by the rent officer, the preceding provisions of this Schedule shall have effect as if only the rent designated or determined by the rent assessment committee had been registered ; but the date of registration shall be deemed for the purposes of this Schedule (but not for the purposes of section 22(3) of the Rent Act 1968) to be the date on which the rent determined by the rent officer was registered.

Section 66.

SCHEDULE 4

PART I OF SCHEDULE 2 TO THE HOUSING ACT 1957 AS IT HAS EFFECT BY VIRTUE OF SECTION 66 OF THIS ACT

PART I

ASCERTAINMENT OF AMOUNT PAYABLE FOR WELL MAINTAINED HOUSES

1.—(1) Subject to the following provisions of this Part of this Schedule, the amount of any payment made in respect of a house under section 30 or section 60 of this Act shall be an amount equal to the rateable value of the house multiplied by four or such other multiplier as the Minister may by order made by statutory instrument prescribe.

(2) The amount shall not in any case exceed the amount (if any) by which the full value of the house (that is to say the amount which would have been payable as compensation if it had been purchased compulsorily but not as being unfit for human habitation) exceeds the site value thereof (that is to say the amount which is payable as compensation by virtue of its being purchased compulsorily as being unfit for human habitation, or which would have been so payable if it had been so purchased) ; and any question as to such value shall be determined, in default of agreement, as if it had been a question of disputed compensation arising on such a purchase.

(3) Where a payment falls to be made in respect of any interest in the house under Part II of this Schedule or under Schedule 5 to the Housing Act 1969, no payment shall be made in respect of that house under this Part of this Schedule unless the other payment relates to part only of the house, and in that case such part only of the amount which would otherwise be payable in accordance with the preceding provisions of this Part of this Schedule shall be payable as may reasonably be attributed to the remainder of the house.

2. An order made by the Minister under this Part of this Schedule shall be of no effect unless it is approved by a resolution of each House of Parliament. SCH. 4

3.—(1) For the purposes of this Part of this Schedule the rateable value of a house shall be determined as follows :—

(*a*) if the house is a hereditament for which a rateable value is shown in the valuation list in force on the relevant date, it shall be that rateable value ;

(*b*) if the house forms part only of such a hereditament or consists of or forms part of more than one such hereditament, its rateable value shall be taken to be such value as is found by a proper apportionment or aggregation of the rateable value or values so shown.

(2) Any question arising under this paragraph as to the proper apportionment or aggregation of any value or values shall be referred to and determined by the valuation officer (within the meaning of the General Rate Act 1967). 1967 c. 9.

(3) In this paragraph " the relevant date ", in relation to any house, means—

(*a*) if the house was vacated in pursuance of a demolition order or closing order or was declared unfit for human habitation by an order under paragraph 2 of Schedule 2 to the Land Compensation Act 1961, the date when the order was made ; 1961 c. 33.

(*b*) if the house was purchased compulsorily in pursuance of a notice served under section 19 of this Act, the date when the notice was served ;

(*c*) if the house was comprised in an area declared a clearance area, the date on which the area was so declared ;

(*d*) if the house was purchased compulsorily under section 12 of this Act, the date on which the notice mentioned in that section was served ;

(*e*) if the house might have been the subject of a demolition order but was, without the making of such an order, vacated and demolished in pursuance of an undertaking for its demolition given to the local authority, the date on which the undertaking was given.

SCHEDULE 5

Section 68.

PAYMENTS TO OWNER-OCCUPIERS AND OTHERS IN RESPECT OF UNFIT HOUSES PURCHASED OR DEMOLISHED

Right to and amount of payments

1.—(1) Where a house has been purchased at site value in pursuance of a compulsory purchase order made by virtue of Part II or Part III of the Act of 1957 or in pursuance of an order under paragraph 2 of Schedule 2 to the Land Compensation Act 1961, or has 1961 c. 33.

SCH. 5 been vacated in pursuance of a demolition order under Part II of the Act of 1957, a closing order under section 17 of that Act or a clearance order, then, if—

(*a*) the relevant date is later than 23rd April 1968 ; and

(*b*) on the relevant date and throughout the qualifying period the house was wholly or partly occupied as a private dwelling and the person so occupying it (or, if during that period it was so occupied by two or more persons in succession, each of those persons) was a person entitled to an interest in that house or a member of the family of a person so entitled ;

the authority concerned shall make in respect of that interest a payment of an amount determined in accordance with paragraphs 2 and 3 of this Schedule.

(2) Where an interest in a house purchased or vacated as mentioned in sub-paragraph (1) of this paragraph was acquired by any person (in this sub-paragraph referred to as the first owner) after 23rd April 1968 and less than two years before the relevant date, and a payment under sub-paragraph (1) of this paragraph in respect of that interest would have fallen to be made by the authority concerned had the qualifying period been a period beginning with the acquisition and ending with the relevant date, the authority concerned shall make to the person who was entitled to the interest at the date the house was purchased or vacated a payment of the like amount, if—

(*a*) the authority are satisfied that before acquiring the interest the first owner had made all reasonable enquiries to ascertain whether it was likely that the order, notice or declaration by reference to which the relevant date is defined in paragraph 5(1) of this Schedule would be made or served within two years of the acquisition and that he had no reason to believe that it was likely ; and

(*b*) the person entitled to the interest at the date when the house was purchased or vacated was the first owner or a member of his family.

(3) Where during a part of the qualifying period amounting, or during parts thereof together amounting, to not more than one year a person previously in occupation of the whole or part of the house was not in occupation thereof by reason only of a posting in the course of his duties as a member of the armed forces of the Crown or of a change in the place of his employment or occupation he shall be deemed for the purposes of this paragraph to have continued in occupation during that part or those parts.

2. Subject to paragraph 3 of this Schedule, the amount of any payment made under the preceding paragraph in respect of an interest shall be an amount equal to its full compulsory purchase value less the compensation which was or would have been payable in respect of the interest in connection with the compulsory purchase of the house at site value.

3.—(1) The amount which would otherwise be payable under paragraph 1 of this Schedule shall be reduced by such part, if any, of that amount as may reasonably be attributed to any part of the house occupied for any purposes other than those of a private dwelling at the date of the making of the compulsory purchase order, demolition order, closing order, clearance order or order under paragraph 2 of Schedule 2 to the Land Compensation Act 1961. SCH. 5 1961 c. 33.

(2) Any question arising under this paragraph as to the purposes for which any part of a house was occupied shall be determined by the Minister, and subject thereto the amount of any payment under paragraph 1 of this Schedule in respect of an interest shall be determined (in default of agreement) as if it were compensation payable in respect of the compulsory purchase of the interest under Part III of the Act of 1957, and the payment shall, subject to sub-paragraph (3) of this paragraph, be dealt with as if it were such compensation.

(3) Any such payment in respect of an interest which, at the date when the house was purchased compulsorily or, as the case may be, vacated, was held by virtue of an agreement to purchase by instalments shall be made to the person entitled to the interest at that date.

Provisions as to mortgages and other charges

4. Paragraph 5 of Schedule 2 to the Act of 1957 (relief and adjustments) shall apply in relation to a payment under this Schedule as it applies in relation to a payment under paragraph 4 of that Schedule.

Interpretation

5.—(1) In this Schedule, in relation to any house purchased or vacated, " the relevant date " and " the authority concerned " mean respectively—

(*a*) if the house was vacated in pursuance of a demolition order or closing order, the date when and the authority by whom the order was made;

(*b*) if the house was declared unfit for human habitation by an order under paragraph 2 of Schedule 2 to the Land Compensation Act 1961, the date when the order was made and the acquiring authority within the meaning of that Act;

(*c*) if the house was purchased compulsorily under section 12 of the Act of 1957, the date when and the authority by whom the notice mentioned in that section was served;

(*d*) if the house was purchased compulsorily in pursuance of a notice served under section 19 of the Act of 1957, the date when and the authority by whom the notice was served;

(*e*) if the house was comprised in an area declared as a clearance area, the date when and the authority by whom the area was so declared;

and " the qualifying period " means the period of two years ending with the relevant date, except that where that date is earlier than 22nd April 1970, it means the period beginning with 23rd April 1968 and ending with the relevant date.

SCH. 5

(2) In this Schedule—

"full compulsory purchase value", in relation to any interest in a house, means the compensation which would be payable in respect of the compulsory purchase of that interest if that compensation fell to be assessed in accordance with subsections (1) and (4) of section 59 of the Act of 1957 and, in the case of a house subject to a clearance order, demolition order or closing order, the making of that order were a service of the notice to treat;

"house" includes any building constructed or adapted wholly or partly as, or for the purposes of, a dwelling;

1968 c. 23. "interest" in a house does not include the interest of a tenant for a year or any less period or of a statutory tenant within the meaning of the Rent Act 1968;

"site value", in relation to the compulsory purchase of a house, means compensation in respect thereof assessed in accordance with the provisions of section 59(2) of the Act of 1957 (or under the corresponding provisions applicable to any compulsory purchase under Part II of that Act).

(3) For the purposes of this Schedule, a house which might have been the subject of a demolition order but which has, without the making of such an order, been vacated and demolished in pursuance of an undertaking for its demolition given to the local authority having power to make the order shall be deemed to have been vacated in pursuance of a demolition order made and served by that authority at the date when the undertaking was given.

(4) In this Schedule references to a demolition order do not include such an order in respect of a house already subject to a closing order so far as it affects any part of the house in relation to which a payment under section 30 of the Act of 1957, Schedule 2 to that Act or this Schedule has fallen to be made in respect of the closing order.

(5) For the purposes of this Schedule a person who on the death of another became entitled to any interest of his shall be deemed to have been entitled to that interest as from the date of the death.

Section 68.

SCHEDULE 6

1957 c. 56.

AMENDMENTS OF HOUSING ACT 1957, SCHEDULE 2 PART II

1. In paragraph 4(1)(*b*) the words "the proviso to subsection (1) of" shall be omitted.

2. For sub-paragraph (7) of paragraph 4 there shall be substituted the following—

"(7) For the purposes of this paragraph a person is a member of another's family if that person is—

(*a*) the other's wife or husband; or

(*b*) a son or daughter or a son-in-law or daughter-in-law of the other, or of the other's wife or husband; or

(c) the father or mother of the other, or of the other's wife or husband. SCH. 6

In paragraph (b) of this sub-paragraph any reference to a person's son or daughter includes a reference to any stepson or stepdaughter, any illegitimate son or daughter, and any adopted son or daughter, of that person, and "son-in-law" and "daughter-in-law" shall be construed accordingly."

3. In the proviso to paragraph 6(2), for the word "ten" there shall be subsituted the word "two".

4. In paragraph 7(3), for the words "or under this Schedule" there shall be substituted the words "under this Schedule or under Schedule 5 to the Housing Act 1969".

SCHEDULE 7

Section 81.

AMOUNT OF PREMIUM PERMISSIBLE UNDER SECTION 81

1. Where this Schedule applies to any tenancy and a premium was lawfully required and paid on the grant or an assignment of the tenancy nothing in section 86 of the Rent Act 1968 shall prevent any person from requiring or receiving, on an assignment of the tenancy, such part of the premium or, if more than one, of the last of them as is determined in accordance with the following provisions of this Schedule as the permissible part (without prejudice, however, to his requiring or receiving a greater sum in a case where he may lawfully do so under Schedule 11 to that Act). 1968 c. 23.

2. The permissible part shall be such part of the premium as bears to the whole thereof the same proportion as the period referable to that part bears to the period referable to the premium; and there shall be taken, as the period referable to the premium—

(a) if it was paid on the grant of the tenancy, the term for which the tenancy was granted; and

(b) if it was paid on an assignment of the tenancy, the residue of that term at the date of the assignment;

and, as the period referable to the permissible part, the residue of that term at the date of the assignment in connection with which that part may be required and received in pursuance of this Schedule.

3. Where the tenancy to which this Schedule applies was granted on the surrender of a previous tenancy and a premium had been lawfully required and paid on the grant or an assignment of the previous tenancy, the surrender value of the previous tenancy shall be treated, for the purposes of this Schedule, as a premium or, as the case may be, part of the premium, paid on the grant of the tenancy to which this Schedule applies.

4. For the purposes of paragraph 3 of this Schedule the surrender value of the previous tenancy shall be taken to be the amount which, had the previous tenancy been assigned instead of being surrendered and had this Schedule applied to it, would have been the amount that could have been required and received on the assignment in pursuance of this Schedule.

Sch. 7

5. In determining for the purposes of this Schedule the amount which may be or could have been required and received on the assignment of a tenancy terminable, before the end of the term for which it was granted, by notice to the tenant, that term shall be taken to be a term expiring at the earliest date on which such a notice given after the date of the assignment would have been capable of taking effect.

Sections 58 and 89.

SCHEDULE 8

Minor and Consequential Amendments

Part I

Amendments Consequential on Section 58

1957 c. 56.

The Housing Act 1957

1. In section 90(1) of the Housing Act 1957, for the words from " or of part " to " family " there shall be substituted the words " which is occupied by persons who do not form a single household ".

1961 c. 65.

The Housing Act 1961

2. In sections 12, 13(1), 13(2), 15, 16 and 21(1) of the Housing Act 1961, for the words " a house which, or a part of which, is let in lodgings or which is occupied by members of more than one family " there shall be substituted the words " a house which is occupied by persons who do not form a single household ".

3. In section 21(1) of that Act, for the words " wholly or partly let in lodgings or occupied by members of more than one family " there shall be substituted the words " occupied by persons who do not form a single household ".

4. In section 22(1) of that Act, for paragraph (*a*) there shall be substituted:

" (*a*) of houses which are occupied by persons who do not form a single household, and ".

1964 c. 56.

The Housing Act 1964

5. In sections 67, 69, 72 and 73 of the Housing Act 1964, for the words " which, or a part of which, is let in lodgings, or which is occupied by members of more than one family " there shall be substituted the words " which is occupied by persons who do not form a single household ".

Part II

Other Amendments

1957 c. 56.

The Housing Act 1957

6. In section 11(3) of the Housing Act 1957, after the words " against a notice " there shall be inserted the words " under section 9(1) of this Act."

7. In section 30(7) of that Act, for the words " or under the Second Schedule to this Act " there shall be substituted the words " under Schedule 2 to this Act or under Schedule 5 to the Housing Act 1969 ". SCH. 8

8. In section 91 of that Act, for the words " Part I of this Act " there shall be substituted the words " section 70 of the Housing Act 1969 ".

9. In section 121 of that Act the following shall be substituted for subsection (3):

> " (3) In this section the reference to repair is a reference to such repair or replacement as either is incidental to the execution of works of improvement, alteration or enlargement or is in the opinion of the local authority needed for making such works fully effective."

10. Section 98 of that Act shall apply as if the reference therein to a purchase under Part V of that Act of a house to be used for housing purposes included a reference to a purchase under Part II of this Act of any house.

11. Sections 101, 159, 160, 169 and 170 of that Act shall apply as if the references therein to that Act or Part V thereof included references to Part II of this Act.

12. Sections 171 to 176 of that Act shall apply as if references therein to that Act included references to Parts I and II of this Act.

13. Section 179 of that Act shall apply as if the reference therein to that Act included a reference to this Act.

14. Section 181(1) of that Act shall apply as if the reference therein to that Act included a reference to Part II of this Act.

15. Section 187(1) of that Act shall apply as if the reference therein to that Act included a reference to this Act.

The Housing (Financial Provisions) Act 1958 1958 c. 42

16. In section 25 of the Housing (Financial Provisions) Act 1958 references to sections 1 to 9 of that Act shall include references to sections 17 to 21 of this Act.

17. Section 28 of that Act shall apply in relation to any payment made by the Minister to a local authority under this Act.

18. In section 50(1)(*f*) of that Act for the words " or are deemed " there shall be substituted the words " or were deemed ".

19. Section 54 of that Act shall apply as if the references therein to that Act included references to this Act.

20. In section 58(2) of that Act there shall be added at the end the words " section 18 or section 19 of the Housing Act 1969 ".

The Land Compensation Act 1961 **1961 c. 33.**

21. At the end of paragraph 2(1)(*g*) of Schedule 2 to the Land Compensation Act 1961 there shall be added the words " or

(*h*) an acquisition under Part II of the Housing Act 1969 ".

22. In paragraph 2(2) of that Schedule for the words " subsections (2) and (3) " there shall be substituted the words " subsection (2) " and for the words from " section fifty-seven " to " sub-paragraph

SCH. 8 (1) of this paragraph" there shall be substituted the words "Part III of that Act as being unfit for human habitation".

23. In paragraph 3(2) of that Schedule there shall be added at the end of paragraph (*b*) the words "or under Schedule 5 to the Housing Act 1969".

24. In paragraph 6(2) of that Schedule the following shall be substituted for paragraph (*c*):

"(*c*) subsection (2) of section 59 (which relates to the purchase of land comprised in a clearance area)".

1964 c. 56. *The Housing Act* 1964

25. In section 34(3) of the Housing Act 1964 for the words "the
1957 c. 25. Rent Act 1957" there shall be substituted the words "the Rent Act
1968 c. 23. 1968".

26. In section 43(1) of that Act the following shall be substituted for paragraph (*g*):—

"(*g*) a sink".

27. In section 43(7) of that Act for the words "section 4" there shall be substituted the words "section 7 of the Housing Act 1969".

28. In section 57(4) of that Act for the words from "section 4" to "1958" there shall be substituted the words "Part I of the Housing Act 1969".

29. Section 69 of that Act shall have effect, except in relation to anything done before the commencement of this Act, as if for the reference to 13th November 1963 there were substituted a reference to any date not earlier than the commencement of this Act and as if the standard amenities mentioned in that section were defined as in this Act.

1967 c. 9. *The General Rate Act* 1967

30. Paragraph 2 of Schedule 13 to the General Rate Act 1967 shall have effect—

(*a*) as if the reference in sub-paragraph (1)(*b*) of that paragraph
1958 c. 42. to proposals approved under section 9 of the Housing (Financial Provisions) Act 1958 included a reference to applications approved under section 18 of this Act; and

(*b*) as if the grants referred to in sub-paragraph (1)(*c*) of that paragraph included grants and contributions to a housing association under Part I of this Act.

1967 c. 29. *The Housing Subsidies Act 1967*

31. In section 14(5)(*a*) of the Housing Subsidies Act 1967 for the word "1965" there shall be substituted the word "1969".

1968 c. 23. *The Rent Act* 1968

32. In section 57 of the Rent Act 1968, in subsection (1)(*a*), after the words "(standard grants)" there shall be inserted the words "Part I of the Housing Act 1969 (improvement grants and standard

grants) ", and in subsection (2)(*b*) after the words " House Purchase and Housing Act 1959 " there shall be inserted the words " or Part I of the Housing Act 1969 ". SCH. 8 1959 c. 33.

33. At the end of paragraph 26(2) of Schedule 16 to that Act there shall be added the words " and a statutory tenancy so arising in relation to which the said section 39 does not have effect shall be deemed to be a controlled tenancy within the meaning of this Act ".

SCHEDULE 9

Section 89.

SAVINGS AND TRANSITIONAL PROVISIONS

1. The repeal by this Act of any enactment relating to any grant, contribution or subsidy shall not affect any power or duty to act on any application or arrangements made or proposals approved before the commencement of this Act, any power to reduce the rate at which any such grant, contribution or subsidy is to be paid, any obligation to observe any condition falling to be observed in pursuance of such an enactment, any obligation to make a payment in consequence of a breach of such a condition, any power to vary the rate of interest on such a payment or the imposition of such a condition by such an enactment in a case where a standard grant or improvement grant is paid by virtue of this paragraph.

2. The repeal by this Act of section 18 of the Housing (Financial Provisions) Act 1958 is without prejudice to the exercise, with respect to any event occurring before the commencement of this Act, of any power under that section. 1958 c. 42.

3. The repeal by this Act of references in any provision of the Rent Act 1968 to any enactment contained in the Housing (Financial Provisions) Act 1958 or the House Purchase and Housing Act 1959 does not affect the operation of that provision in relation to any grant paid in pursuance of an application made before the commencement of this Act. 1968 c. 23. 1959 c. 33.

4. The repeal by this Act of section 16 of the Rent Act 1968 does not affect the operation of that section in relation to the letting of any dwelling-house while the conditions mentioned in that section require to be observed.

5. The repeal by this Act of section 49 of the Rent Act 1968 does not affect the operation of that section in relation to any dwelling-house while such a condition relating to the rent of the dwelling-house as is mentioned in that section requires to be observed.

6. The references in sections 2(4) and 12 of this Act to a standard grant shall be construed as including references to a grant under section 4 of the House Purchase and Housing Act 1959.

7. The references in section 20 of this Act to a standard contribution and to the allowable cost determined under section 19 of this Act shall be construed respectively as including references to a contribution under section 13 of the House Purchase and Housing Act 1959 and one-half of the amount referred to in section 14(1) of that Act or, as the case may be, section 51 of the Housing Act 1964. 1964 c. 56.

Section 89.

SCHEDULE 10

ENACTMENTS REPEALED

Chapter	Short Title	Extent of repeal
5 & 6 Eliz. 2. c. 56.	The Housing Act 1957.	Section 3. In section 4(1)(*h*) the word " storage ". In section 30(2) the words " the proviso to subsection (1) of ". Sections 55 to 57. In section 59, subsection (3) and the words " or (3) " in subsection (4). In section 61 the words " or re-development area ". In section 63(1) paragraph (*c*) and the word " or " preceding that paragraph. In section 67, in subsection (1) the words " or in a re-development plan or a new plan " and the words " or the approval of the plan ", and in subsection (2) the words " or approval ". In section 70, in subsection (1) the words " or in the case of premises comprised in a re-development plan approved by him "; and in subsection (2) the words " or re-development plan", the words "or approved" the words " or as a proposed re-development area ", the words " or of the re-development plan " the words " or plan " (in both places) and the words " or the re-development area ". In Schedule 2, in paragraph 4(1)(*b*) the words " the proviso to subsection (1) of ", paragraph 4(6)(*b*), and, in paragraph 7(2) in the definition of " site value " the words " or (3) ". In Schedule 3, in Part I, the proviso to paragraph 2(1), paragraphs 5 and 6; and in Part III, in paragraph 4 the words from " (*a*) where the premises " to " in any other case ", and paragraph 5. In Schedule 4, in paragraph 2, the words from " or by the Minister's " to " new plan ", the words " or of the approval of the plan " and the words " or the approval of the plan ",

SCH. 10

Chapter	Short Title	Extent of repeal
5 & 6 Eliz. 2 c. 56—*cont.*	The Housing Act 1957 —*cont.*	wherever they occur; and in paragraph 3 the words " or the approval of the plan ", the words " or the approval is given, as the case may be " and the words " or of the approval of the plan ".
6 & 7 Eliz. 2. c. 42.	The Housing (Financial Provisions) Act 1958.	Section 9. Section 12. Section 18, except so far as it relates to payments other than those specified in section 77(2) of this Act. Sections 30 to 42. Schedule 4.
7 & 8 Eliz. 2. c. 33.	The House Purchase and Housing Act 1959.	Part II. Section 28(2). In section 29(1), in the definition of " improvement grant " the words " under section 30 of the Act of 1958 or " and, in the definition of " standard amenities ", the words from " in Part II " to "Act and ". In Schedule 1, paragraphs 1, 2 and 9.
9 & 10 Eliz. 2. c. 33.	The Land Compensation Act 1961.	In Schedule 2, in paragraph 1(2)(*b*) the words from " or which " to "Act " and the words from " or did not " to " may be ".
9 & 10 Eliz. 2. c. 65.	The Housing Act 1961.	Section 12(2). Section 22(5). In section 24(5) paragraph (*b*) and the word " and " preceding that paragraph. In Schedule 2, paragraph 9. In Schedule 3, paragraph 6(2).
1964 c. 56.	The Housing Act 1964.	In section 13, subsections (1) to (3) and (5). Section 20(4). Part III except sections 57 and 59. In section 67(3) the words from " of individuals or a number " to " households ".
1967 c. 29.	The Housing Subsidies Act 1967.	Section 12.
1968 c. 23.	The Rent Act 1968.	Section 16. In section 25(4)(*a*), the words from " section 30 " to " (standard grants) or ".

SCH. 10

Chapter	Short Title	Extent of repeal
1968 c. 23. —*cont.*	The Rent Act 1968. —*cont.*	In section 31(a) the words from " section 30 " to " (standard grants) or ". Section 49. In section 50(2) the words " or section 49 ".

Housing (Scotland) Act 1969

1969 CHAPTER 34

An Act to prescribe a tolerable standard for houses and to make provision for the treatment of houses and areas, and for payments in respect of houses purchased or vacated, which do not meet that standard; to make new provision with respect to the repair of houses; to make further provision for grants by local authorities and contributions out of moneys provided by Parliament towards the cost of providing dwellings by conversion, or of improving dwellings; to amend the law with regard to rents payable for certain dwellings in good repair and provided with certain amenities or improved; to confer powers on local authorities in respect of the improvement of the amenities of residential areas; to provide that the replacement by a tenant of fixtures and fittings is to be disregarded in determining a fair rent under a regulated tenancy; to provide for the increase of rents of houses belonging to certain authorities without notice of removal; to amend section 160(1)(*a*) of the Housing (Scotland) Act 1966; to amend the meaning of " financial year " for the purposes of subsections (2) and (3) of section 2 of the Housing (Financial Provisions) (Scotland) Act 1968; and for purposes connected with those matters. [25th July 1969]

Be it enacted by the Queen's most Excellent Majesty, by and with the advice and consent of the Lords Spiritual and Temporal, and Commons, in this present Parliament assembled, and by the authority of the same, as follows:—

PART I

HOUSES NOT MEETING TOLERABLE STANDARD

General

General duty of local authority in respect of houses not meeting tolerable standard.

1.—(1) It shall be the duty of every local authority to secure that all houses in their district which do not meet the tolerable standard as defined in section 2 of this Act are closed, demolished or brought up to the tolerable standard within such period as is reasonable in all the circumstances.

(2) In determining what period is reasonable for the purposes of the foregoing subsection, regard shall be had to alternative housing accommodation likely to be available for any persons who may be displaced from houses as a result of any action proposed by the local authority in pursuance of that subsection.

(3) Every local authority shall from time to time cause to be made such a survey or inspection of their district as may be necessary for the performance of the duty imposed on them by subsection (1) of this section or for the purpose of ascertaining the availability of alternative housing accommodation.

(4) Sections 3 and 4 of the principal Act (which impose a duty on a local authority to discharge certain functions under Parts II and III of that Act in accordance with proposals approved by the Secretary of State and to inspect their district respectively) shall cease to have effect.

Definition of house meeting tolerable standard.

2.—(1) Subject to subsection (2) of this section, a house shall be held to meet the tolerable standard for the purposes of this Act if the house—

(*a*) is structurally stable;

(*b*) is substantially free from rising or penetrating damp;

(*c*) has satisfactory provision for natural and artificial lighting, for ventilation and for heating;

(*d*) has an adequate piped supply of wholesome water available within the house;

(*e*) has a sink provided with a satisfactory supply of both hot and cold water within the house;

(*f*) has a water closet—

(i) available for the exclusive use of the occupants of the house within the house or, where the house forms part of a building, within that building, and

(ii) readily accessible from, and suitably located, within the house or building, as the case may be;

(*g*) has an effective system for the drainage and disposal of foul and surface water;

(*h*) has satisfactory facilities for the cooking of food within the house;

(*i*) has satisfactory access to all external doors and outbuildings;

and any reference in this Act to a house not meeting the tolerable standard or being brought up to the tolerable standard shall be construed accordingly.

(2) The Secretary of State may by order vary or extend the criteria set out in the foregoing subsection in such a way as to raise the tolerable standard either generally or, after consultation with a particular local authority, in relation to the district, or any part of the district, of that authority.

(3) Any order under this section shall be made by statutory instrument, which shall be subject to annulment in pursuance of a resolution of either House of Parliament.

(4) This section shall be without prejudice to section 17 of the principal Act (which provides that certain underground rooms shall be deemed to be houses not meeting the tolerable standard for the purposes of Part II of that Act).

(5) Section 5 of the principal Act (determination of unfitness for human habitation) shall cease to have effect.

Local authority no longer to proceed by clearance or compulsory improvement.

3. It shall no longer be competent for a local authority to deal with any area in their district as a clearance area in accordance with sections 34 to 55 of the principal Act, nor to provide for the compulsory improvement of dwellings in any area in their district in accordance with Part IV of that Act; and accordingly the said sections 34 to 55 and Part IV shall cease to have effect.

Housing Treatment Areas

Local authority may pass resolution declaring area to be housing treatment area.

4.—(1) Where a local authority are satisfied that the houses, or the greater part of the houses, in any area in their district do not meet the tolerable standard, they may pass a resolution defining the area and declaring the area so defined to be a housing treatment area, that is to say, an area which is to be dealt with in one or other of the ways set out in the next following subsection.

(2) A resolution passed under this section shall provide that a housing treatment area shall be dealt with—

(*a*) by securing the demolition of all the buildings in the area; or

(*b*) by securing the carrying out of such works on the houses in the area that on the completion of the works all the houses then in the area will meet or will have been brought up to at least the tolerable standard; or

PART I

(*c*) by securing the demolition of some of the buildings in the area and by securing the carrying out of such works on the houses in the area, other than the houses in those buildings, that on the completion of the works all the houses then in the area will meet or will have been brought up to at least the tolerable standard.

(3) A housing treatment area shall not include the site of a building unless at least part of the building consists of a house which does not meet the tolerable standard.

(4) For the purposes of this section, a house in respect of which a closing order has been made and not determined shall be deemed to be a house which does not meet the tolerable standard.

Provisions supplementary to s. 4.

5.—(1) Where the resolution passed under section 4 of this Act provides that the housing treatment area is to be dealt with in accordance with subsection (2)(*a*) of that section, the local authority may at any time purchase the land within the area and themselves undertake, or otherwise secure, the demolition of the buildings.

(2) Where the resolution provides that the housing treatment area is to be dealt with in accordance with subsection (2)(*b*) of the said section 4 the local authority shall proceed as follows—

(*a*) subject to the next following paragraph, the local authority may at any time purchase any house in the area if in their opinion it is unlikely that the necessary works will be carried out to bring the house up to the tolerable standard unless they purchase it, and may themselves carry out such works as may be necessary to bring the house up to at least that standard;

(*b*) in the case of a house not comprised in a tenement the authority shall not exercise their powers under the foregoing paragraph, otherwise than by agreement, unless—

(i) they have served a notice on the owner of the house informing him that in accordance with a resolution passed by them under the said section 4 it is proposed that his house should be brought up to at least the tolerable standard;

(ii) at least twelve months have elapsed since the service of the notice.

(3) Where under subsection (2)(*a*) of this section the local authority purchase a house comprised in a tenement, they may also purchase any other part of the tenement in which the house

is comprised if in their opinion it is necessary to purchase such other part in order to carry out the necessary works on the house to bring it up to the tolerable standard.

(4) Where the resolution provides that the housing treatment area is to be dealt with in accordance with subsection (2)(*c*) of the said section 4, then—

(*a*) in so far as the resolution provides for the demolition of the buildings in the area, subsection (1) of this section shall apply as it applies where the resolution provides that the housing treatment area is to be dealt with in accordance with subsection (2)(*a*) of the said section 4, and

(*b*) in so far as the resolution provides for the houses in that area being brought up to at least the tolerable standard, subsections (2) and (3) of this section shall apply as they apply where the resolution provides that the housing treatment area is to be dealt with in accordance with subsection (2)(*b*) of the said section 4.

(5) In this section, " tenement " means a building which contains two or more flats, and, for the purpose of the definition of " tenement ", " flat " means a separate set of premises, whether or not on the same floor, constructed for use for the purposes of a house and forming part of a building from some other part of which it is divided horizontally.

6. Where a local authority determine to acquire any land comprised in an area declared by them to be a housing treatment area they may acquire also—

Local authority may acquire land surrounded by or adjoining housing treatment area.

(*a*) any land which is surrounded by the housing treatment area and the acquisition of which is reasonably necessary for the purpose of securing an area of convenient shape and dimensions ; and

(*b*) any adjoining land the acquisition of which is reasonably necessary for the satisfactory development or use of the housing treatment area.

7.—(1) In so far as a resolution passed under section 4 of this Act provides that some or all of the buildings in a housing treatment area should be demolished, the powers of acquiring land comprised in or surrounded by or adjoining such an area conferred on a local authority by this Part of this Act shall not be restricted by the fact that buildings within that area have been demolished since the area was declared to be a housing treatment area.

Provisions regarding acquisition of land by local authority.

(2) Land for the purposes of this Part of this Act may be acquired by a local authority by agreement under section 156

Part I

1947 c. 43. of the Local Government (Scotland) Act 1947 (notwithstanding anything in section 173 of that Act) and section 158 of that Act shall apply accordingly.

(3) A local authority may be authorised by the Secretary of State to purchase land compulsorily for the purposes of this Part of this Act and the Acquisition of Land (Authorisation Procedure) (Scotland) Act 1947 shall apply in relation to any such compulsory purchase as if this Act had been in force immediately before the commencement of that Act, but subject to the following modifications— (1947 c. 42.)

(*a*) the compulsory purchase order shall not be in the form prescribed under paragraph 2 of Schedule 1 to that Act, but shall be in a form prescribed under this section ;

(*b*) the notices referred to in paragraphs 3 and 6 of the said Schedule 1 shall not be in the form prescribed under those paragraphs, but shall be in a form prescribed under this section ;

(*c*) the order shall show separately the houses in the housing treatment area which do not meet the tolerable standard and the land proposed to be purchased outside the area ;

(*d*) the order as confirmed by the Secretary of State shall not authorise the local authority to purchase any house on less favourable terms with respect to compensation than the terms on which the order would have authorised them to purchase the house if the order had been confirmed without modification ;

(*e*) if the Secretary of State is of opinion that any land included by a local authority in a housing treatment area ought not to have been so included he shall on confirming the order so modify it as to exclude that land for all purposes from that area ;

(*f*) in section 1 of that Act any reference to the said Schedule 1 shall be construed as a reference to that Schedule as modified by this subsection ;

(*g*) in Part IV of that Schedule any reference to that Act or that Schedule and any reference to any regulation made thereunder shall be construed respectively as a reference to that Act as modified by this subsection and as including a reference to any regulation made under this subsection ;

(*h*) section 3 of that Act (power to extinguish certain public rights of way over land acquired) shall be omitted.

PART I

Power of local authority to retain houses subject to demolition for temporary occupation.

8.—(1) A local authority, who in a resolution passed under section 4 of this Act have provided that some or all of the buildings in a housing treatment area should be demolished, may postpone the demolition of any such building on land purchased by or belonging to the authority within that area, being a building which is, or which contains, a house which in the opinion of the authority must be continued in use as housing accommodation for the time being.

(2) Where the demolition of a building is postponed under the foregoing subsection, the authority shall carry out such works as may in their opinion from time to time be required for rendering or keeping such house capable of being continued in use as housing accommodation pending its demolition.

(3) In respect of any house retained by a local authority under this section for use for housing purposes, the authority shall have the like powers and duties as they have in respect of houses provided under Part VII of the principal Act.

Provisions with respect to land belonging to local authority.

9. A local authority may include in a housing treatment area any land belonging to them which they might have included in such an area if the land had not belonged to them; and where any land belonging to a local authority is included in a housing treatment area, or where any land belonging to a local authority is surrounded by or adjoins a housing treatment area and might have been purchased by the authority under section 6 of this Act had it not been previously acquired by them, the provisions of this Part of this Act shall apply in relation to any such land as if it had been purchased compulsorily by the authority as being land comprised in the housing treatment area or, as the case may be, as being land surrounded by or adjoining the housing treatment area.

Compensation in respect of land acquired compulsorily.

10.—(1) Where land is purchased compulsorily by a local authority under this Part of this Act, the compensation payable in respect thereof shall, subject to the following provisions of this section, be assessed by the Lands Tribunal in accordance with the Land Compensation (Scotland) Act 1963. 1963 c. 51.

(2) In the case of the compulsory acquisition of a house which is specified in the compulsory purchase order as not meeting the tolerable standard such compensation shall not (except by virtue of paragraph 2 of Schedule 2 to the said Act of 1963) exceed the value, at the time when the valuation is made, of the site of the house as a cleared site available for development in accordance with the requirements of the building regulations for the time being in force in the district.

PART I

(3) The reference in the last foregoing subsection to compensation is a reference to the compensation payable in respect of the purchase exclusive of any compensation for disturbance or for severance or for injurious affection.

(4) In the case of land purchased as aforesaid, other than land in respect of which the provisions of subsections (2) and (3) of this section have effect, the rules specified in Schedule 4 to the principal Act shall be observed.

Payments in respect of well-maintained houses.

11.—(1) Where as respects a house which is made the subject of a compulsory purchase order under this Part of this Act as not meeting the tolerable standard, the Secretary of State is satisfied, after causing the house to be inspected by one of his officers, that it has been well maintained, the Secretary of State may give directions for the making by the local authority of a payment calculated in accordance with section 21 of this Act in respect of the house.

(2) A payment under this section shall be made—

(*a*) if the house is occupied by an owner thereof, to him, or

(*b*) if the house is not so occupied, to the person or persons liable to maintain and repair the house, and, if more than one person is so liable, in such shares as the local authority think equitable in the circumstances:

Provided that, if any other person satisfies the local authority that the good maintenance of the house is attributable to a material extent to work carried out by him or at his expense, the authority may, if it appears to them to be equitable in the circumstances, make the payment, in whole or in part, to him.

Local authority may take possession of land to be acquired by agreement or appropriated for purposes of Part I.

12. Section 144 of the principal Act (which provides that a local authority may take possession of land to be acquired by agreement or appropriated for purposes of Part VII of that Act) shall apply for the purposes of this Part of this Act as it applies for the purposes of the said Part VII.

Local authority may sell or lease land purchased under Part I.

13. A local authority who have under this Part of this Act purchased any land comprised in or surrounded by or adjoining a housing treatment area—

(*a*) may, where the land was purchased for the purpose of bringing the houses in the area up to the tolerable standard, sell or lease any such house to any person subject to the condition that that person will bring the house up to at least that standard and to any other restriction or condition that they may think fit; or

(*b*) may, in any other case, sell or lease the land subject to such restrictions and conditions, if any, as they think

PART I

fit, or may, in accordance with section 163 of the Local Government (Scotland) Act 1947, appropriate the land for any purpose for which they are authorised to acquire land. 1947 c. 43.

Extinction of rights of way, servitudes, etc.

14.—(1) A local authority may, with the approval of the Secretary of State, by order extinguish any public right of way over any land purchased by them under this Part of this Act or provide for the closing or diversion of any street in connection with the development of a housing treatment area.

(2) An order made by a local authority under subsection (1) of this section shall be published in the prescribed manner, and if any objection thereto is made to the Secretary of State before the expiration of two months from the publication thereof, the Secretary of State shall not approve the order until he has caused a public local inquiry to be held into the matter.

(3) Where a local authority have resolved to purchase under this Part of this Act land over which a public right of way exists, it shall be lawful under the foregoing provisions of this section for the authority to make and for the Secretary of State to approve, in advance of the purchase, an order extinguishing that right as from the date on which the buildings on the land are vacated, or at the expiration of such period after that date as may be specified in the order or as the Secretary of State in approving the order may direct.

(4) Upon the completion by a local authority of the purchase by them of any land under this Part of this Act, all private rights of way and all rights of laying down, erecting, continuing or maintaining any apparatus on, under or over that land, and all other rights or servitudes in or relating to that land, shall be extinguished, and any such apparatus shall vest in the authority; and any person who suffers loss by the extinction or vesting of any such right or apparatus as aforesaid shall be entitled to be paid by the authority compensation to be determined by the Lands Tribunal in accordance with the Land Compensation (Scotland) Act 1963: 1963 c. 51.

Provided that this subsection shall not apply to any right vested in public undertakers of laying down, erecting, continuing or maintaining any apparatus or to any apparatus belonging to public undertakers, and shall have effect as respects other matters subject to any agreement which may be made between the local authority and the person in or to whom the right or apparatus in question is vested or belongs.

Provisions as to apparatus of public undertakers.

15.—(1) Where the removal or alteration of apparatus belonging to public undertakers on, under or over land purchased by a local authority under this Part of this Act or on, under or over a street running over or through or adjoining any

Part I

such land is reasonably necessary for the purpose of enabling the authority to exercise any of the powers conferred upon them by this Part of this Act, the authority shall have power to execute works for the removal or alteration of the apparatus subject to and in accordance with the provisions of this section.

(2) A local authority who intend to remove or alter any apparatus under the powers conferred by subsection (1) of this section shall serve on the undertakers notice in writing of their intention, with particulars of the proposed works and of the manner in which they are to be executed and plans and sections thereof, and shall not commence any works until the expiration of a period of 28 days from the date of service of the notice, and the undertakers may within that period by notice in writing served on the authority—

(*a*) object to the execution of the works or any of them on the ground that they are not necessary for the purpose aforesaid; or

(*b*) state requirements to which in their opinion effect ought to be given as to the manner of, or the observance of conditions in, the execution of the works, as to the execution of other works for the protection of other apparatus belonging to the undertakers, or as to the execution of other works for the provision of substituted apparatus whether permanent or temporary;

and—

(i) if objection is so made to any works and not withdrawn, the local authority shall not execute the works unless they are determined by arbitration to be so necessary;

(ii) if any such requirement as aforesaid is so made and not withdrawn, the local authority shall give effect thereto unless it is determined by arbitration to be unreasonable.

(3) A local authority shall make to public undertakers reasonable compensation for any damage which is sustained by them by reason of the execution by the authority of any works under subsection (1) of this section and which is not made good by the provision of substituted apparatus.

Any question as to the right of undertakers to recover compensation under this subsection or as to the amount thereof shall be determined by arbitration.

(4) Where the removal or alteration of apparatus belonging to public undertakers or the execution of works for the provision of substituted apparatus whether permanent or temporary is reasonably necessary for the purposes of their undertaking by reason of the stopping up, diversion or alteration of the level

or width of a street by a local authority under powers exercisable by virtue of this Act, such undertakers may, by notice in writing served on the authority require them at the expense of the authority to remove or alter the apparatus or to execute the works, and where any such requirement is so made and not withdrawn, the authority shall give effect thereto unless they serve notice in writing on the undertakers of their objection to the requirement within 28 days from the date of service of the notice upon them and the requirement is determined by arbitration to be unreasonable.

PART I

(5) At least 7 days before commencing any works which they are authorised or required under the foregoing provisions of this section to execute, the local authority shall, except in case of emergency, serve on the undertakers notice in writing of their intention so to do, and the works shall be executed by the authority under the superintendence (at the expense of the authority) and to the reasonable satisfaction of the undertakers.

Provided that, if within 7 days from the date of service on them of notice under this subsection the undertakers so elect, they shall themselves execute the works in accordance with the reasonable directions and to the reasonable satisfaction of the local authority, and the reasonable costs thereof shall be repaid to the undertakers by the authority.

(6) Any difference arising between public undertakers and a local authority under subsection (5) of this section and any matter which is by virtue of the foregoing provisions of this section to be determined by arbitration shall—

(*a*) in the case of a question arising under subsection (3) of this section be referred to and determined by the Lands Tribunal;

(*b*) in any other case be referred to and determined by an arbiter to be appointed, in default of agreement, by the Secretary of State.

(7) In this section references to the alteration of apparatus include references to diversion and to alterations of position or level.

Local authority may control occupation of houses in housing treatment area.

16.—(1) Subject to subsection (3) of this section, a local authority may at the same time as they pass a resolution under section 4 of this Act declaring an area to be a housing treatment area, make an order prohibiting the occupation of the houses in the area except with the consent of the authority.

(2) Within 28 days of making an order under this section, the local authority shall serve a notice in respect of every house in the housing treatment area—

(*a*) upon the person having control of the house, and

PART I

(*b*) upon any other person who is an owner or occupier of the house,

stating that the order has been made and indicating the effect of the order.

(3) An order made under this section shall not prohibit the occupation of a house in the area by a person occupying it on the date of the service of the notice in respect of the house under the last foregoing subsection.

(4) If any person, knowing that an order has been made under this section, occupies or permits to be occupied a house after the date of the service of the notice in respect of the house under subsection (2) of this section in contravention of the order, he shall be guilty of an offence and shall be liable on summary conviction to a fine not exceeding £20 and to a further fine of £5 for every day or part of a day on which he occupies the house, or permits it to be occupied, after conviction.

(5) An order made under this section shall cease to have effect in relation to a house,

(*a*) which already meets the tolerable standard and which is not a building or part of a building to be demolished in accordance with the resolution passed under section 4 of this Act, or

(*b*) which in accordance with the resolution is to be brought up to at least the tolerable standard,

on the date when, upon an application by the owner or the person having control of the house for a certificate that the house already meets the tolerable standard, or, as the case may be, has been brought up to the tolerable standard, the authority issue the certificate applied for.

(6) Where an applicant for a certificate under the last foregoing subsection is aggrieved by the refusal of the local authority to issue the certificate, he may appeal to the sheriff by giving notice of appeal within 21 days of the date of the refusal.

Application of tolerable standard for certain purposes of Part II of principal Act

Tolerable standard to replace standard of fitness in deciding whether to make closing or demolition orders.

17. A local authority, in deciding in respect of any house in their district whether to make a closing order or demolition order under section 15 of the principal Act, shall no longer have to satisfy themselves that the house is unfit for human habitation in terms of section 5 of that Act and incapable at a reasonable expense of being rendered so fit, but may instead make a closing order or demolition order under the said section 15 if they are satisfied that the house does not meet the tolerable standard and ought to be demolished.

PART I

Payments to certain owner-occupiers and others in respect of houses not meeting tolerable standard which are purchased or demolished

Right to and amount of payments.

18.—(1) Where a house has been purchased at restricted value in pursuance of a compulsory purchase order made by virtue of section 20 of the principal Act or section 7 of this Act, or in pursuance of an order under paragraph 1(2) of Schedule 2 to the Land Compensation (Scotland) Act 1963, or has been vacated in pursuance of a demolition order under section 15 or a closing order under section 15 or 18 of the principal Act, then if—

1963 c. 51.

(*a*) on the relevant date and throughout the qualifying period the house was occupied as a private dwelling, and the person so occupying the house (or, if during that period it was so occupied by two or more persons in succession, each of those persons) was a person entitled to an interest in that house or a member of the family of a person so entitled, and

(*b*) the full compulsory purchase value of the interest is greater than its restricted value,

the authority concerned shall make in respect of that interest a payment of an amount equal to the difference between the full compulsory purchase value and the restricted value.

(2) Any question as to the values referred to in the foregoing subsection shall be determined, in default of agreement, as if it had been a question of disputed compensation arising on such a purchase.

(3) Where an interest in a house purchased or vacated as described in subsection (1) of this section was acquired by any person (in this subsection referred to as the first owner) on or after 1st August 1968 and less than two years before the relevant date, and a payment under the said subsection (1) in respect of that interest would have fallen to be made by the authority concerned had the qualifying period been a period beginning with the acquisition and ending with the relevant date, the authority concerned shall make to the person who was entitled to the interest at the date when the house was purchased or vacated a payment of the like amount, if—

(*a*) the authority are satisfied that before acquiring the interest the first owner had made all reasonable inquiries to ascertain whether it was likely that the notice, resolution or order, by reference to which the relevant date is defined in section 20(1) of this Act would be served, passed or made within two years of the acquisition and that he had no reason to believe that it was likely ; and

PART I

(*b*) the person entitled to the interest at the date when the house was purchased or vacated was the first owner or a member of his family.

Provisions as to house subject to heritable security or purchased by instalments.

1967 c. 20.

1963 c. 51.

19. Section 18 of the Housing (Financial Provisions, &c.) (Scotland) Act 1967 (right of parties to certain agreements secured on, or related to, unfit houses to apply to sheriff for adjustment of the agreements) shall apply, whether or not a payment falls to be made in respect of an interest in a house under section 18 of this Act, where the house not meeting the tolerable standard is purchased at restricted value in pursuance of a compulsory purchase order made by virtue of section 19 or 20 of the principal Act or section 7 of this Act, or in pursuance of an order under paragraph 1(2) of Schedule 2 to the Land Compensation (Scotland) Act 1963, or has been vacated in pursuance of a demolition order or a closing order as it applies where a house has been purchased or vacated before the commencement of this Act as described in section 18 of the said Act of 1967.

Interpretation of ss. 18 and 19.

20.—(1) In section 18 of this Act, in relation to any house purchased or vacated, " the relevant date " and " the authority concerned " mean respectively—

(*a*) if the house was purchased compulsorily in pursuance of a notice served under section 20 of the principal Act, the date when and the authority by whom the notice was served ;

(*b*) if the house was comprised in an area declared in a resolution passed under section 4 of this Act to be a housing treatment area, the date when and the authority by whom the resolution was passed ;

(*c*) if the house was declared not to meet the tolerable standard by an order under paragraph 1(2) of Schedule 2 to the Land Compensation (Scotland) Act 1963, the date when the order was made and the acquiring authority within the meaning of that Act ;

(*d*) if the house was vacated in pursuance of a demolition order or closing order, the date when and the authority by whom the order was made ;

and " the qualifying period " means the period of two years ending with the relevant date, except that where that date is earlier than 31st July 1970, it means the period beginning with 1st August 1968 and ending with the relevant date.

(2) In sections 18 and 19 of this Act—

" full compulsory purchase value ", in relation to any interest in a house, means the compensation which would be payable in respect of the compulsory purchase of that

PART I

interest if the house were not being dealt with under Part II of the principal Act or Part I of this Act as not meeting the tolerable standard, and, in the case of a house subject to a demolition order or closing order, the making of that order were a service of the notice to treat;

" interest " in a house does not include the interest of a tenant for a year or any less period or of a statutory tenant within the meaning of the Rent Acts;

" restricted value ", in relation to the compulsory purchase of a house, means compensation in respect thereof assessed under section 19(3) and (4) or 20(5) and (6) of the principal Act or section 10(2) and (3) of this Act.

(3) For the purposes of section 18 of this Act, a house which might have been the subject of a demolition order but which has, without the making of such an order, been vacated and demolished in pursuance of an undertaking for its demolition given to the local authority having power to make the order shall be deemed to have been vacated in pursuance of a demolition order made and served by that authority at the date when the undertaking was given.

Payments for well maintained houses

Calculation of amount payable for well maintained houses.

21.—(1) This section shall apply in relation to any payment in respect of a well maintained house under section 25 of the principal Act or section 11 of this Act.

(2) Subject to subsection (3) of this section, a payment to which this section applies shall be of an amount equal to the rateable value of the house multiplied by seven and one-fifth or such other multiplier as may from time to time be prescribed.

(3) A payment to which this section applies shall not in any case exceed the amount (if any) by which the full compulsory purchase value of the house exceeds the restricted value thereof; and any question as to such value shall be determined, in default of agreement, as if it had been a question of disputed compensation arising on such a purchase.

(4) Where a payment falls to be made in respect of any interest in a house under section 18 of this Act, no payment shall be made in respect of that house under section 25 of the principal Act or section 11 of this Act.

(5) In this section—

" full compulsory purchase value " has the same meaning as in section 20(2) of this Act;

" prescribed " means prescribed by an order made by the Secretary of State by statutory instrument which shall be of no effect unless it is approved by a resolution of each House of Parliament;

PART I

" rateable value " means the rateable value entered in the valuation roll last authenticated prior to the relevant date ;

" restricted value " has the same meaning as in the said section 20(2) ; and

" the relevant date " in relation to any payment made with respect to any house means—

(*a*) if the house was purchased compulsorily in pursuance of a notice served under section 20 of the principal Act, the date when the notice was served ;

(*b*) if the house was comprised in an area declared in a resolution passed under section 4 of this Act to be a housing treatment area, the date when the resolution was passed ;

1963 c. 51.

(*c*) if the house was vacated in pursuance of a demolition order or a closing order, or was declared not to meet the tolerable standard by an order under paragraph 1(2) of Schedule 2 to the Land Compensation (Scotland) Act 1963, the date when the order was made.

Transitional provisions for purposes of sections 18 *to* 21

Transitional provisions for purposes of ss. 18 to 21.

22. The transitional provisions set out in Schedule 1 to this Act shall have effect for the purposes of sections 18 to 21 of this Act.

Repayment of certain payments

Repayment of certain payments under principal Act or this Act.

23. Where a payment in respect of a house has been made by a local authority under section 25 of the principal Act or section 11 or 18 of this Act in connection with a demolition order or a closing order and, at any time after the commencement of this Act, the demolition order or the closing order is determined by an order under section 15(3) of the principal Act, then if at any time the person to whom the payment was made is entitled to an interest in the house (within the meaning of section 20(2) of this Act), he shall on demand repay the payment to the authority.

PART II

HOUSES IN DISREPAIR

Power of local authority to secure repair of house in state of serious disrepair.

24.—(1) Where a local authority are satisfied that any house in their district is in a state of serious disrepair, they may serve upon the person having control of the house a notice—

(*a*) requiring him, within such reasonable time, not being less than 21 days, as may be specified in the notice, to execute the works specified in the notice, and (*b*) stating that, in the opinion of the local authority, those works will bring the house up to such a standard of repair as is reasonable having regard to the age, character and location, and disregarding the internal decorative repair, of the house.

(2) If a notice under subsection (1) of this section is not complied with, then, after the expiration of the time specified in the notice or, if an appeal has been made against the notice and the sheriff upon that appeal has confirmed the notice with or without variation, after the expiration of 21 days from the determination of the appeal or of such longer period as the sheriff in determining the appeal may fix, the local authority—

(*a*) may themselves execute the works specified in the notice or in the notice as varied by the sheriff, as the case may be, and

(*b*) may in addition execute any further works which are found to be necessary for the purpose of bringing the house up to the standard of repair referred to in subsection (1)(*b*) of this section, but which could not reasonably have been ascertained to be required prior to the service of the notice.

Any question as to whether further works are necessary or could not have been reasonably ascertained as aforesaid shall be determined by the sheriff, whose decision shall be final.

(3) No action taken under this section or under section 25 of this Act shall prejudice or affect any other powers of the local authority or any remedy available to the tenant of a house against his landlord, either at common law or otherwise.

(4) Where a local authority are of the opinion that a house in their district is in need of repair although not in a state of serious disrepair and that it is likely to deteriorate rapidly, or to cause material damage to another house, if nothing is done to repair it, they may deem it to be in a state of serious disrepair for the purposes of this section.

(5) Section 11 of the principal Act (power of local authority to secure repair of unfit house) shall cease to have effect.

Recovery by local authority of expenses under s. 24.

25.—(1) Any expenses incurred by a local authority under section 24(2) of this Act, together with interest from the date when a demand for the expenses is served until payment, may, subject as hereinafter provided, be recovered by the authority from the person having control of the house or, if he receives the rent of the house as trustee, tutor, curator, factor or agent for or of some other person, then either from him or from that other person, or in part from him and as to the remainder from that other person.

PART II

(2) The local authority may by order declare any such expenses to be payable by weekly, monthly, half-yearly or annual instalments within a period not exceeding thirty years with interest from the date of the service of the demand until the whole amount is paid, and any such instalments and interest, or any part thereof, may be recovered from any owner or occupier of the house, and, if recovered from an occupier, may be deducted by him from the rent of the house.

(3) Any interest payable under subsection (1) or subsection (2) of this section shall be at such rate as the local authority may fix:

Provided that there may from time to time be prescribed by the Secretary of State a maximum rate of interest for the purposes of either or both of those subsections.

(4) The provisions of Schedule 2 to this Act shall have effect for the purpose of enabling a local authority to make a charging order in respect of any expenses incurred by them under section 24(2) of this Act in relation to a house or building.

Recovery by lessee of proportion of expenses incurred in repairing house.

26.—(1) Where any person who incurs expenditure in complying with a notice under section 24(1) of this Act requiring the execution of works for bringing a house up to the standard of repair referred to in paragraph (*b*) of that subsection, or in defraying expenses incurred by a local authority under subsection (2) of that section in carrying out such works, is a lessee of the house or the agent of such a lessee, the lessee may recover from the lessor under the lease such part (if any) of that expenditure as may, in default of agreement between the parties, be determined by the sheriff on the application of either of them to be just having regard—

(*a*) to the obligations of the lessor and the lessee under the lease with respect to the repair of the house;

(*b*) to the length of the unexpired term of the lease;

(*c*) to the rent payable under the lease; and

(*d*) to all other relevant circumstances:

Provided that no sum shall be recoverable under this subsection unless the lessee or his agent within fourteen days after the service of such notice as aforesaid gave written intimation to the lessor of the service of the notice and of the purport thereof.

(2) Where a person from whom any sum is recoverable under subsection (1) of this section is himself a lessee of the house, the provisions of that subsection shall apply as if any sum so recoverable from him were expenditure incurred as mentioned in that subsection.

PART II

(3) In this section " lease " includes a sublease and any tenancy, and the expressions " lessee " and " lessor " shall be construed accordingly.

Appeals under Part II.

27.—(1) Any person aggrieved by—

(*a*) a notice under section 24 of this Act requiring the execution of works,

(*b*) a demand for the recovery of expenses incurred by a local authority in executing such works,

(*c*) an order made by a local authority with respect to any such expenses,

(*d*) a charging order made under Schedule 2 to this Act,

may appeal to the sheriff by giving notice of appeal within 21 days after the date of the service of the notice, demand or order, as the case may be; and no proceedings shall be taken by the local authority to enforce any notice, demand or order while an appeal against it is pending.

(2) On an appeal under paragraph (*b*), (*c*) or (*d*) of the foregoing subsection no question shall be raised which might have been raised on an appeal against the original notice requiring the execution of the works.

Date of operation of notices, demands and orders subject to appeal.

28. Any notice, demand or order against which an appeal might be brought to the sheriff under section 27 of this Act shall, if no such appeal is brought, become operative on the expiration of 21 days after the date of the service of the notice, demand or order, as the case may be, and shall be final and conclusive as to any matters which could have been raised on such an appeal, and any such notice, demand or order against which an appeal is brought shall, if and so far as it is confirmed by the sheriff, become operative as from the date of the determination of the appeal.

Power of entry for survey and examination.

29.—(1) Subject to the provisions of this section, where a notice has been served under section 24 of this Act in respect of any house requiring the execution of works, any person authorised by the local authority or by the Secretary of State may at all reasonable times enter the house or, where the house forms part of a building, any part of the building for the purpose of survey and examination.

(2) Any person so authorised shall give 24 hours' notice of his intention to enter any house or part of a building to the occupier thereof and to the owner, if the owner is known.

(3) An authorisation under this section shall be in writing and shall state the particular purpose or purposes for which the entry is authorised.

PART II

Power of Secretary of State to repeal or amend local enactments.

30.—(1) The Secretary of State may by order repeal or amend any provision in any local Act passed before the commencement of this Act where it appears to him that the provision is inconsistent with, or has become unnecessary in consequence of, any provision in this Part of this Act.

(2) Before making an order under this section the Secretary of State shall consult with any local authority which appear to him to be concerned.

(3) An order under this section may contain such additional, supplemental or incidental provisions as appear to the Secretary of State to be expedient.

(4) Any order under this section shall be made by statutory instrument, which shall be subject to annulment in pursuance of a resolution of either House of Parliament.

PART III

FINANCIAL ASSISTANCE TOWARDS COST OF IMPROVEMENTS AND CONVERSIONS

Exchequer contributions towards improvement of housing accommodation

Amendment of s. 13 of Act of 1968.

31. Section 13 of the Act of 1968 (exchequer contributions for dwellings provided by conversion or improved by local authorities or development corporations) shall have effect as if—

(*a*) after subsection (1) there were inserted the following subsection—

" (1A) The Secretary of State shall not approve improvement proposals if the works of conversion or improvement required for carrying out the improvement proposals have been begun, unless he is satisfied that there were good reasons for beginning the works before the improvement proposals were submitted to him." ;

(*b*) subsection (2) were omitted.

Amount of Exchequer contributions under s. 13 of Act of 1968.

32. Section 14 of the Act of 1968 (amount of exchequer contributions under section 13) shall have effect as if—

(*a*) in subsection (2), at the end, there were inserted the following proviso—

" Provided that where the Secretary of State is subsequently satisfied that the works could not be carried out without the carrying out of additional works and that this could not have been reasonably foreseen at the time the improvement proposals

PART III

were submitted to him, he may, subject to subsection (3) of this section, increase the amount determined by him under this subsection.",

(b) in subsection (3) for the words " fourteen hundred pounds " there were substituted the words " twenty-five hundred pounds ".

Definition of improvement in ss. 13 to 17 of Act of 1968.

33. For subsection (2) of section 18 of the Act of 1968 (definition of improvement) there shall be substituted the following subsection—

" (2) In sections 13 to 17 of this Act ' improvement ' includes alteration and enlargement and such repairs and replacements as are either incidental to some other improvement or are needed, in the opinion of the Secretary of State, for the purpose of making the other improvement fully effective, and ' improved ' shall be construed accordingly.".

Grants by local authorities for improvements

Amendment of s. 27 of Act of 1968.

34. Section 27 of the Act of 1968 (power of local authorities to make improvement grants) shall have effect as if—

(a) in subsection (1), the words " before the improvement works are begun " were omitted;

(b) after subsection (1) there were inserted the following subsection—

"(1A) A local authority shall not approve an application for an improvement grant if the improvement works have been begun unless they are satisfied that there were good reasons for beginning the works before the application was approved.";

(c) after subsection (6) there were inserted the following subsection—

" (6A) In approving an application for an improvement grant a local authority may require as a condition of paying the grant that the improvement works are carried out within such time (which must not be less than twelve months) as the local authority may specify or such further time as the local authority may allow.".

Insertion of s. 27A in Act of 1968.

35. After section 27 of the Act of 1968 there shall be inserted the following section—

" Approved expense for purpose of determining amount of improvement grants.

27A.—(1) Where a local authority approve an application for an improvement grant they shall notify the applicant of the amount approved by them as being the amount of the expenses which, in their opinion, are properly ascribable to the execution of the improvement works and, where the application relates to the provision or improvement of more

Part III

than one dwelling, of the proportion of that amount approved by them as being attributable to each dwelling proposed to be provided or improved.

The said amount is hereafter in this Part of this Act referred to, in relation to improvement works, as the "approved expense" of executing those works, and the proportion of that amount approved under this subsection as being attributable to a dwelling is so referred to, in relation to that dwelling, as the "approved proportion" of the approved expense.

(2) The approved expense of the improvement works shall not be such as to allow for works of repair and replacement more than one-half of that expense or such other part thereof as may for the time being be prescribed.

(3) Notwithstanding the foregoing provisions of this section, where the applicant subsequent to the approval by the local authority of the application for an improvement grant satisfies the authority that the improvement works cannot be or could not have been carried out without the carrying out of additional works and that this could not have been reasonably foreseen at the time the application was made, the authority may substitute a higher amount as the amount of the approved expense.".

Amendment of s. 28 of Act of 1968.

36. For section 28 of the Act of 1968 there shall be substituted the following section—

"Requirements precedent to approval of application for improvement grant.

28. The requirements referred to in section 27(6) of this Act are as follows, that is to say—

(*a*) that the dwelling or dwellings to which the application for an improvement grant relates will provide satisfactory housing accommodation for such period and conform with such requirements with respect to construction and physical condition and the provision of services and amenities as may for the time being be specified for the purposes of this section by the Secretary of State;

(*b*) that the applicant is, in respect of every parcel of land on which the improvement works are to be or are being carried out (other than land proposed to be sold or leased to him under section 145(4) of the principal Act) either the owner or the

PART III

lessee under a lease of which the period remaining unexpired at the date of the application is not less than five years."

Increase in amount of improvement grants.

37. Section 29(1) of the Act of 1968 (amount of improvement grants) shall have effect as if after paragraph (*b*) there were inserted the following paragraph—

" (*bb*) if the said application was so made on or after the date of commencement of the Housing (Scotland) Act 1969, twelve hundred pounds or such other amount as may for the time being be prescribed, for each dwelling so provided or improved ; ".

Definition of improvement in ss. 27 to 38 of Act of 1968.

38. For subsection (2) of section 38 of the Act of 1968 (definition of improvement) there shall be substituted the following subsection—

" (2) In the foregoing provisions of this Part of this Act and in the following provisions of this section, ' improvement ' includes alteration and enlargement and such repairs and replacements as are either incidental to some other improvement or are needed, in the opinion of the local authority paying the improvement grant, for the purpose of making the other improvement fully effective, and ' improved ' shall be construed accordingly.".

Grants by local authorities for provision of standard amenities

Amendment of definition of standard amenities.

39. For the purposes of Part II of the Act of 1968, the definition of standard amenities set out in subsection (1) of section 39 of that Act shall include a sink provided for the exclusive use of the occupants of a dwelling but shall no longer include satisfactory facilities for storing food so provided ; and accordingly in the said subsection (1), after paragraph (*d*), there shall be inserted the following paragraph—

" (*dd*) a sink,"

and paragraph (*g*) shall cease to have effect.

Amendment of s. 40 of Act of 1968.

40. Section 40 of the Act of 1968 (duty of local authorities to make standard grants) shall have effect as if in subsection (1) the words " before the works are begun " were omitted.

Amendment of s. 41 of Act of 1968.

41. For section 41 of the Act of 1968 (approval of applications for standard grants) there shall be substituted the following section—

"Approval of applications for standard grants.

41.—(1) A local authority shall approve an application for a standard grant if—

(*a*) they are satisfied as to the matters mentioned in subsections (3) and (4) of this section, and

PART III

(*b*) in the case of an application made by virtue of section 40(2) of this Act, they are satisfied also as to the matters mentioned in paragraphs (*a*) and (*b*) of that subsection,

and, subject to subsection (7) of this section, shall not approve any application if not so satisfied.

(2) A local authority shall not approve an application for a standard grant if the works specified therein have been begun unless they are satisfied that there were good reasons for beginning the works before the application was approved.

(3) The local authority must be satisfied that after the execution of the works specified in the application the dwelling will meet the tolerable standard and will be available for use as a dwelling for a period of not less than fifteen years.

(4) The local authority must also be satisfied that the applicant is, in respect of every parcel of land on which the works are to be or are being carried out (other than land proposed to be sold or leased to him under section 145(4) of the principal Act), either the owner or the lessee under a lease of which the period remaining unexpired at the date of the application is not less than five years.

(5) In considering an application made by virtue of section 40(2) of this Act the local authority shall have regard to the estimated cost of the works which would be required to provide the dwelling with all of the standard amenities and the value which it is estimated that the dwelling (or the building of which the dwelling forms part) would have if works to provide the dwelling with all of the standard amenities were carried out.

(6) In approving an application for a standard grant a local authority may require as a condition of paying the grant that the works specified in the application are carried out within such time (which must not be less than twelve months) as the local authority may specify or such further time as the local authority may allow.

(7) Subject to such general or special directions as may from time to time be given by the Secretary of State, a local authority may approve an application for a standard grant notwithstanding that the conditions stated in subsection (3) of this section are not satisfied.

(8) Section 2 of the Housing (Scotland) Act 1969 shall have effect for determining whether a dwelling meets the tolerable standard for the purposes of subsection (3) of this section as it has effect for determining whether a house meets that standard for the purposes of that Act. PART III

(9) Where the local authority do not approve an application for a standard grant they shall give to the applicant a written statement of the ground or grounds on which they have not approved it, and if, in the case of an application made by virtue of section 40(2) of this Act, that ground is, or those grounds include, the fact that the authority are not satisfied as to the matters mentioned in paragraphs (*a*) and (*b*) of that subsection, the said statement shall set out the reasons why the authority are not so satisfied."

Increase in amount of standard grants.

42. Section 42 of the Act of 1968 (amount of standard grants) shall have effect as if—

(*a*) in subsection (3), for the word " £350 " there were substituted the word " £450 " and for the Table there were substituted the following Table—

" TABLE

List of amenities	*Amount allowed towards limit*
A fixed bath or shower in a bathroom or elsewhere.	£30 or, if the bathroom is being provided by the building of a new structure or the conversion of outbuildings attached to the dwelling (or to the building of which the dwelling forms part) and, before the time when the local authority approve the application, they have been satisfied that it is not reasonably practicable to provide the bathroom in any other way, such higher amount as the local authority shall fix at that time as being in their opinion one-half of the part of the cost to be reasonably incurred in executing the works, being the part of the cost attributable to the provision of the fixed bath or shower.
A wash-hand basin	£10.
A hot and cold water supply at a fixed bath or shower.	£45.
A hot and cold water supply at a wash-hand basin.	£20.

PART III

List of amenities	*Amount allowed towards limit*
A sink	£15.
A hot and cold water supply at a sink.	£30.
A water closet	£50 or, if the works comprise the installation of a septic tank and, before the time when the local authority approve the application, they have been satisfied that the connection of the water closet with main drainage is not possible or reasonably practicable, such higher amount as the local authority shall fix at that time as being in their opinion one-half of the part of the cost to be reasonably incurred in executing the works, being the part of the cost attributable to the provision of the water closet.
If the works comprise, in connection with all or any of the amenities provided, the bringing of a piped supply of cold water into the dwelling for the first time.	Such amount as the local authority shall fix at the time when they approve the application as being in their opinion one-half of the part of the cost to be reasonably incurred in executing the works, being the part of the cost attributable to the bringing of the piped supply into the dwelling.";

(*b*) in subsection (4), at the end, there were inserted the following proviso—

"Provided that if the applicant subsequently satisfies the local authority that the works by reference to the cost of which the amount in respect of any item in the Table is fixed cannot be or could not have been carried out without the carrying out of works in addition to those specified in the application, they may substitute a higher amount for that fixed under this section."

Conditions relating to improvement grants and standard grants

Amendment and partial repeal of Schedule 3 to Act of 1968.

43. In Schedule 3 to the Act of 1968 (conditions to be observed with respect to dwellings provided or improved with the help of improvement grants or standard grants),—

(*a*) for paragraph 2 there shall be substituted the following paragraph—

"2. All steps as are practicable shall be taken to secure the maintenance of the dwelling in a reasonable state of repair.";

(*b*) paragraphs 4 and 6 are hereby repealed.

PART IV

RENT OF DWELLINGS IN GOOD REPAIR AND PROVIDED WITH STANDARD AMENITIES

Conversion of existing controlled tenancies

44.—(1) The following provisions of this section shall have effect with respect to an existing controlled tenancy of a dwelling which is certified by the local authority, on the application of the landlord, to satisfy the following conditions, that is to say, that it is provided with all the standard amenities, that it is in good repair, having regard to its age, character and locality and disregarding internal decorative repair, and that it meets the tolerable standard.

Conversion of existing controlled tenancies of dwellings provided with standard amenities and in good repair.

(2) The tenancy shall become a regulated tenancy on the issue of the certificate or (unless the tenancy has then become a regulated tenancy apart from this Act or has ceased to exist) on such later date as is specified in section 51 of this Act or an order made thereunder.

(3) Section 27 of the Rent Act 1965 (determination of fair rent) shall apply in relation to an existing controlled tenancy which becomes a regulated tenancy by virtue of this Part of this Act as if the references in subsection (3) thereof to the tenant under the regulated tenancy included references to the tenant under the existing controlled tenancy.

1965 c. 75.

(4) The conditions mentioned in subsection (1) of this section are in this Part of this Act referred to as the qualifying conditions and a certificate issued in accordance with this section as a qualification certificate.

45.—(1) Except where an application for a qualification certificate is made under subsection (2) of this section it shall not be entertained unless either—

Application for qualification certificate.

(*a*) the dwelling has at all times since the commencement of this Act been provided with all the standard amenities; or

(*b*) any of the standard amenities previously lacking were provided by means of works begun before the commencement of this Act;

and shall not be entertained while the conditions of Schedule 3 to the Act of 1968 as originally enacted fall to be observed with respect to the dwelling.

(2) An application for a qualification certificate may be made with respect to a dwelling notwithstanding that at the time of the making of the application the dwelling lacks one or more of the standard amenities, if the application is made (whether

PART IV

or not as part of or in conjunction with an application for a grant under Part II of the Act of 1968) before any works are begun for providing the dwelling with the standard amenities which it lacks.

(3) An application for a qualification certificate must state the name of the tenant under the existing controlled tenancy and, if the application is made at a time when the dwelling does not satisfy the qualifying conditions, must state what works are required for those conditions to be satisfied and must be accompanied by plans and specifications of those works.

(4) As soon as a local authority have received an application for a qualification certificate they shall send a copy of the application to the person named in the application as the tenant.

Procedure on applications under s. 45(1).

46.—(1) Where an application for a qualification certificate is made under section 45(1) of this Act the local authority shall, at the same time as they send a copy of the application to the person named in the application as the tenant in pursuance of section 45(4) of this Act, serve on him a notice in the prescribed form—

(*a*) informing him that he may, within 28 days from the service of the notice or such other time as may be prescribed, make representations to the authority that the dwelling does not satisfy the qualifying conditions; and

(*b*) containing such other information or explanation of the effect of this Part of this Act as may be prescribed.

(2) Where the local authority are satisfied, after considering any representations made in pursuance of subsection (1) of this section, that the dwelling satisfies the qualifying conditions, they shall issue to the applicant a qualification certificate, but if they are not so satisfied they shall give notice to the applicant of their refusal of his application; and they shall send a copy of the certificate or of the notice to the tenant.

Procedure on applications under s. 45(2).

47.—(1) Where an application for a qualification certificate is made under section 45(2) of this Act and it appears to the local authority that the dwelling will satisfy the qualifying conditions when the works specified in the application have been carried out, the local authority shall approve the application provisionally and shall issue to the applicant a certificate of provisional approval and send a copy thereof to the tenant.

(2) The provisions of Part I of Schedule 3 to this Act shall have effect for enabling a person who has obtained a certificate of provisional approval to apply for a certificate of fair rent.

PART IV

(3) On the production by the applicant of a certificate of fair rent issued on an application under Part I of Schedule 3 to this Act and on being satisfied that the dwelling satisfies the qualifying conditions, the local authority shall issue the qualification certificate and shall send a copy of it to the tenant.

(4) If at the time the qualification certificate is issued the state of the dwelling differs in any respect from that which, at the time the application for the certificate was made, it could be expected to be in when the works specified in the application had been carried out, the local authority shall specify the differences in the certificate.

Registration of rent on issue of qualification certificate. 1965 c. 75.

48.—(1) Where an existing controlled tenancy of a dwelling has become a regulated tenancy by virtue of this Part of this Act, an application by the landlord for the first registration of a rent for the dwelling under Part II of the Rent Act 1965 must be accompanied by a copy of the qualification certificate and, if the certificate was issued under section 47(3) of this Act, also by a copy of the certificate of fair rent.

(2) Part II of Schedule 3 to this Act shall have effect, in lieu of sections 29 and 44 of, and paragraphs 4 to 12 and 16(2) to (6) of Schedule 3 to, the Rent Act 1965, with respect to an application made in pursuance of this section in a case where a qualification certificate has been issued under section 47(3) of this Act.

Statement of reasons for refusing certificate.

49. Where, on an application for a qualification certificate, a local authority refuse to issue the certificate or to issue a certificate of provisional approval, they shall give to the applicant a written statement of their reasons for the refusal.

Appeal in certain cases against issue or refusal of qualification certificate.

50.—(1) Within 28 days of the service on him under section 46(2) of this Act of a notice of refusal or such longer period as the sheriff may allow, the applicant for a qualification certificate may appeal to the sheriff on the ground that the certificate ought to be issued; and on such an appeal the sheriff may confirm the refusal or order the local authority to issue the certificate.

(2) Within 28 days of the service on him under section 46(2) of this Act of a copy of a qualification certificate or such longer period as the sheriff may allow the tenant may appeal to the sheriff on either or both of the following grounds, that is to say—

(*a*) that the certificate ought not to have been issued;

(*b*) that the certificate is invalid by reason of a failure to comply with any requirement of this Part of this Act or of some informality, defect, or error;

PART IV

and on any such appeal the sheriff may confirm or quash the certificate, but if the appeal is on the ground mentioned in paragraph (*b*) of this subsection the sheriff shall confirm the certificate unless satisfied that the interests of the appellant have been substantially prejudiced by the facts relied on by him.

(3) On any appeal under this section the sheriff shall have regard to any change in the state of the dwelling between the date of the issue or refusal of the certificate and the date of the hearing, and shall make no order for expenses unless it appears to the sheriff, having regard to the conduct of the parties and all other circumstances, that it would be equitable to do so.

(4) Any certificate issued in pursuance of an order made under subsection (1) of this section shall be deemed to be issued on the date of the order.

(5) Where a qualification certificate with respect to any dwelling is quashed by an order under this section after a rent for the dwelling has been registered in pursuance of this Part of this Act the registration shall be deemed never to have had effect and the rent officer shall delete it on being informed of the order.

Postponement in certain cases of effect of qualification certificate.

51.—(1) Where a qualification certificate with respect to a dwelling is issued under section 46(2) of this Act before the date applicable to the dwelling under the following provisions of this section, the existing controlled tenancy of the dwelling shall not become a regulated tenancy by virtue of this Part of this Act until that date.

(2) Subject to subsection (3) of this section—

(*a*) 1st January 1971 is the date applicable to a dwelling of a value of £45 or more ;

(*b*) 1st July 1971 is the date applicable to a dwelling of a value of less than £45 but not less than £30 ;

(*c*) 1st January 1972 is the date applicable to a dwelling of a value of less than £30.

(3) The Secretary of State may by order made by statutory instrument substitute as the date applicable to a dwelling of such value as may be specified in the order a date earlier than that which would be applicable to it under subsection (2) of this section ; and an order under this section may make different provision with respect to different registration areas.

(4) In this section " value " means the rateable value on the appropriate day ; and, for the purposes of the definition of " value ", " the appropriate day " means, in relation to a dwelling which on the date of the commencement of this Act was or formed part of lands and heritages for which a rateable

PART IV

value was shown on the valuation roll then in force, that day, and in relation to any other dwelling, the date on which such a value is first shown on the valuation roll.

Modification of Rent Acts in relation to tenancies converted under Part IV.

52.—(1) Where an application for a qualification certificate has been made with respect to any dwelling any notice of increase under the Rent Acts which is served after the date of the application shall be void so far as it relates to an increase in rent authorised by section 2(1)(*a*) of the Increase of Rent and Mortgage Interest (Restrictions) Act 1920, unless— 1920 c. 17.

(*a*) the application was made under section 45(1) of this Act and the notice is served before the date applicable to the dwelling under section 51 of this Act; or

(*b*) the application has been withdrawn; or

(*c*) the certificate has been refused and either the time for appealing against the refusal has expired or the refusal has been confirmed on appeal or the appeal has been abandoned; or

(*d*) the certificate has been quashed on appeal.

(2) Where an existing controlled tenancy becomes a regulated tenancy by virtue of this Part of this Act—

(*a*) it shall be disregarded for the purposes of section 3(3)(*a*) of the Rent Act 1965 (limit of rent during contractual periods); and 1965 c. 75.

(*b*) sections 5 to 7 of that Act (limit of rent during statutory periods) shall have effect in relation to the tenancy as if references therein to the last contractual period were references to the last rental period beginning before the tenancy becomes a regulated tenancy; and

(*c*) sections 4(5) and 6(6) of that Act (effect of improvements on limit of rent before registration) shall not apply to any improvement effected before the tenancy becomes a regulated tenancy.

Recovery of rent increases due to provisions of Part IV of this Act etc.

53. Schedule 4 to this Act shall have effect for securing that where an increase in the rent payable under a regulated tenancy results from this Part of this Act or from works carried out with assistance provided under Part II of the Act of 1968 it may be recovered only in such stages as are permitted under that Schedule.

Miscellaneous and supplementary provisions

Modification of Rent Act 1965 in relation to improvements assisted under Part II of the Act of 1968.

54. Sections 4(5) and 6(6) of the Rent Act 1965 (effect of improvements on limit of rent before registration) shall not apply to any improvements with respect to which a grant under Part II of the Act of 1968 is payable after the commencement of this Act.

PART IV

Consent of tenant.

55.—(1) Where a dwelling which is subject to an existing controlled tenancy does not satisfy the qualifying conditions, and the works required for those conditions to be satisfied cannot be carried out without the consent of the tenant, then, if those works are specified in an application for a certificate of fair rent, his consent shall be of no effect unless given or confirmed in writing after the issue of the certificate.

(2) Where a dwelling which does not satisfy the qualifying conditions is subject to a statutory tenancy and the tenant is unwilling to give or confirm his consent to the carrying out of the works required for those conditions to be satisfied, then, if—

(*a*) those works were specified in an application for a certificate of fair rent and the certificate has been issued; and

(*b*) if the tenancy is a regulated tenancy, they were also specified in an application for a grant under Part II of the Act of 1968 and the application has been approved;

the sheriff may, on the application of the landlord, make an order empowering him to enter and carry out the works.

(3) An order under the last foregoing subsection may be made subject to such conditions as to the time at which the works are to be carried out and as to any provision to be made for the accommodation of the tenant and his household while they are carried out as the sheriff may think fit; and where such an order is made subject to any condition as to time, compliance with that condition shall be deemed to be also compliance with any condition imposed by the local authority under section 27(6A) or section 41(6) of the Act of 1968.

(4) In determining whether to make such an order and, if it is made, subject to what, if any, conditions, the sheriff shall have regard to all the circumstances and, in particular, to any disadvantage to the tenant that might be expected to result from the works, the accommodation that might be available for him while the works are carried out, his means in relation to the increase of rent that would result and the stages in which that increase would become recoverable under the provisions of this Part of this Act.

Supplemental.

1965 c. 75.

56.—(1) The power to make regulations under section 46 of the Rent Act 1965 for the purposes of that Act shall extend to this Part of this Act and the power to modify by such regulations the provisions of Schedules 3 and 4 to that Act shall extend to the provisions of Schedules 3 and 4 to this Act.

1920 c. 17.

(2) The power of the Court of Session under section 17(1) as read with section 18 of the Increase of Rent and Mortgage Interest (Restrictions) Act 1920 to make an act of sederunt and

give directions for the purpose of giving effect to the provisions of that Act shall extend to sections 50 and 55 of this Act.

PART IV

Interpretation of Part IV.

57. In this Part of this Act—

" existing controlled tenancy " has the same meaning as in section 11(2) of the Rent Act 1965 ; 1965 c. 75.

" local authority " has the same meaning as in the principal Act ;

" qualification certificate " and " qualifying conditions " have the meanings assigned to them by section 44(4) of this Act ;

" registration area " has the same meaning as in section 24(1) of the Rent Act 1965 ;

" standard amenities " has the same meaning as in section 39(1) of the Act of 1968 ;

and other expressions shall be construed as in the Rent Act 1965.

PART V

MISCELLANEOUS AND SUPPLEMENTAL

Miscellaneous

Powers of local authority in respect of improvement of amenities of residential areas.

58.—(1) For the purpose of securing the improvement of the amenities of a predominantly residential area within their district a local authority may—

(*a*) carry out any works on land owned by them and assist (whether by grants or loans or otherwise) in the carrying out of any works on land not owned by them ;

(*b*) acquire any land by agreement ;

and may be authorised by the Secretary of State to purchase any land compulsorily.

(2) The Acquisition of Land (Authorisation Procedure) (Scotland) Act 1947 shall apply to a compulsory purchase of land under this section as if this section had been in force immediately before the commencement of that Act. 1947 c. 42.

Exchequer contributions to local authority towards expenditure incurred under s. 58.

59.—(1) The Secretary of State may, subject to any directions of the Treasury, pay an exchequer contribution to a local authority towards such expenditure incurred by them under section 58 of this Act—

(*a*) in carrying out works, or acquiring or appropriating land, or

(*b*) in making contributions to any other authority or person towards expenses which might be so incurred by the local authority,

as he may approve for the purposes of this section on an application by the local authority made, where the expenditure is incurred in carrying out any works, before the works are begun.

PART V

(2) For the purposes of this section—

(*a*) the cost of any works shall be taken to be the amount certified by the local authority as appearing to them to be the cost likely to be incurred by them in carrying out those works; and

(*b*) the cost of any land acquired by a local authority under the said section 58 shall be taken to be the expenses incurred by the authority in connection with the acquisition, and the cost of any land appropriated by a local authority for the purposes of that section shall be taken to be such amount as the Secretary of State may determine.

(3) An exchequer contribution under this section shall be a sum payable annually for a period of twenty years beginning with the financial year in which the works are completed and that sum shall be equal to the annual loan charges referable to one-half of the expenditure approved for the purposes of this section.

(4) The aggregate of any expenditure approved for the purposes of this section (whether on one or more applications) shall not exceed the sum arrived at by taking £100 for each of the dwellings in the area.

(5) The Secretary of State may, with the consent of the Treasury, by order substitute another amount for the amount of £100 mentioned in subsection (4) of this section, and any such order shall be made by statutory instrument, which shall be subject to annulment in pursuance of a resolution of the Commons House of Parliament.

(6) For the purposes of this section the annual loan charges referable to any amount shall be the annual sum which, in the opinion of the Secretary of State, would fall to be provided by a local authority for the payment of interest on, and the repayment of, an amount of borrowed money equal to the amount of the exchequer contribution, being money the period for the repayment of which is twenty years.

(7) Where any arrangements made between a local authority and a housing association so provide, any expenditure incurred by the housing association in pursuance of the arrangements which might have been incurred by the local authority under the said section 58 shall be treated for the purposes of subsection (1) of this section as if it were expenditure so incurred by the local authority; and where any such expenditure is approved by the Secretary of State for the purposes of this section—

(*a*) subsection (6) of this section shall have effect, in relation to it, as if the reference therein to a local authority were a reference to the housing association, and

PART V

(*b*) the local authority shall pay to the housing association by way of annual grant an amount not less than so much of the exchequer contribution paid to the local authority under this section as is referable to that expenditure.

(8) In this section, " exchequer contribution " and " loan charges " have the same meanings as they have in section 67(2) of the Act of 1968.

Power of local authority to make advances repayable on maturity.

60.—(1) A local authority may, subject to such conditions as may be approved by the Secretary of State, advance money to any person for the alteration, enlargement, repair or improvement of any house, and the following provisions of this section shall apply with respect to an advance made under this section.

(2) The principal of the advance, together with interest thereon, shall be secured to the local authority by a bond and disposition in security of the house, or by a bond and assignation in security of a lease of the house, or by a bond and such other deed of security over the borrower's interest in the house as may be agreed between the authority and the borrower.

(3) The amount of the principal of the advance shall not exceed the value which, in accordance with a valuation duly made on behalf of the local authority, it is estimated that interest will bear when the alteration, enlargement, repair or improvement has been carried out.

(4) The advance may be made by instalments from time to time as the works of alteration, enlargement, repair or improvement progress.

(5) The advance shall be made in terms providing for the repayment of the principal at the end of a fixed period of not more than twenty years, with or without a provision allowing the authority to extend that period, and with a provision for repayment on the happening of a specified event before the end of that period or extended period, and on such other terms as the local authority may think fit, having regard to all the circumstances.

(6) While repayment of the principal of an advance made under this section is not required in accordance with the terms of the advance, the local authority may suspend, with respect to so much of any sum borrowed by them as is referable to the advance or with respect to any sum paid in respect of the advance out of a loans fund established under section 275 of the Local Government (Scotland) Act 1947, any repayment by periodical instalments of principal or principal and interest combined that may be required by any enactment. 1947 c. 43.

PART V

(7) The power conferred on a local authority by the foregoing provisions of this section is without prejudice to any power to advance money exercisable by the authority under any other enactment; but where money is advanced by a local authority under section 49 of the Act of 1968 for the acquisition or construction of a house or the conversion into houses of any building, no money shall, in connection therewith, be advanced under this section for the alteration, enlargement, repair or improvement of that house or any of those houses.

Replacement by tenant of fixtures and fittings to be disregarded in determining a fair rent.
1965 c. 75.

61. In determining for the purposes of the Rent Act 1965 what is or would be a fair rent under a regulated tenancy of a dwellinghouse, there shall be disregarded the replacement of any fixture or fitting carried out, otherwise than in pursuance of the terms of the tenancy, by the tenant under the regulated tenancy or any predecessor in title of his; and accordingly section 27(3)(*b*) of the said Act shall have effect as if after the word " improvement " there were inserted the words " or the replacement of any fixture or fitting ".

Increase of rents of houses belonging to certain authorities without notice of removal.

62.—(1) Subject to subsections (2) and (3) of this section, where a house belonging to an authority to which this section applies is let for any period, the rent payable to the authority under the tenancy may, without the tenancy being terminated, be increased with effect from the beginning of any rental period (that is to say, a period in respect of which a payment of rent falls to be made) by a written notice of increase given by the authority to the tenant not less than four weeks before the beginning of the rental period (or any earlier day on which the payment of rent in respect of that period falls to be made).

(2) Where an authority to which this section applies gives under subsection (1) of this section a notice of increase which is to be operative as from the beginning of a rental period and the tenancy continues into that period, the notice shall nevertheless not have effect if the tenancy is terminated by a notice of removal given by the tenant in accordance with the provisions express or implied of the tenancy, and—

(*a*) the notice of removal is given before the end of the period of two weeks following the date on which the notice of increase is given, or such longer period as may be allowed by the notice of increase; and

(*b*) the date on which the tenancy is made to terminate is not later than the earliest day on which the tenancy could be terminated by a notice of removal given by the tenant on the last day of that period.

(3) A notice of increase given by an authority to which this section applies under subsection (1) of this section shall not be valid unless it informs the tenant of— PART V

(a) his right to terminate the tenancy and the steps to be taken by him if he wishes to do so, and

(b) the dates by which, if the increase is not to be effective, the notice of removal must be received by the authority and the tenancy be made to terminate.

(4) This section shall apply in relation to a tenancy of a house belonging to an authority to which this section applies notwithstanding that the letting took place before the date of the commencement of this Act.

(5) This section shall apply to any of the following authorities, that is to say—

(a) a local authority;

(b) a development corporation as defined in section 2 of the New Towns (Scotland) Act 1968; 1968 c. 16.

(c) the Scottish Special Housing Association;

(d) a regional water board or a water development board as respectively defined in section 34(1) of the Water (Scotland) Act 1967. 1967 c. 78.

(6) In this section "local authority" means a town council, county council, joint county council of a combined county, or a joint board or a joint committee; and for the purposes of the definition of local authority "joint board" and "joint committee" have the meanings respectively assigned to them by section 379(1) of the Local Government (Scotland) Act 1947. 1947 c. 43.

(7) Section 12 of the Prices and Incomes Act 1968 (increase of local authority rents without notice to quit) is hereby repealed. 1968 c. 42.

Amendment of s. 160(1) (a) of principal Act.

63. Section 160(1)(a) of the principal Act (power of local authority to pay removal allowances to certain persons displaced) shall have effect as if after sub-paragraph (iv) there were inserted the following—

"or,

(v) in respect of which the local authority in the exercise of their functions under section 149 of this Act consider that it is necessary that the person should be displaced,".

Disapplication of section 168 of principal Act for certain purposes.

64. Section 168 of the principal Act (rehousing obligations where land is acquired under statutory provisions) shall not apply to any acquisition of land under Part I or this Part of this Act.

PART V

Amendment of meaning of "financial year" for purposes of s. 2(2) and (3) of Act of 1968.

65. At the end of section 2 of the Act of 1968 (aggregate cost contributions) there shall be inserted the following subsection—

" (6) For the purposes of the construction of subsections (2) and (3) of this section after 31st March 1969, " financial year " means a period of twelve months beginning on 1st April ; and in any order made under this section which comes into operation after 31st March 1969, " financial year " shall be construed accordingly.".

Supplemental

Application of provisions of principal Act.

66. The following provisions of the principal Act shall apply as if references therein to that Act included references to this Act, that is to say—

section 1 (definition of local authority for the purposes of Act),

section 2 (power of local authority to appoint committee),

sections 177 to 179 (special provisions as to land),

section 183 (except paragraph (*b*) and paragraphs (*d*) to (*g*) of subsection (1) thereof) (power of entry for survey, etc.),

section 184 (penalty for obstructing execution of Act),

section 188 (power of sheriff to authorise superior to execute works etc.),

subsections (2) to (5) of section 190 (procedure on appeals to sheriff),

section 191 (authentication of orders etc. by local authority),

section 193(1) (default of local authority),

sections 196 to 199 (provisions regarding orders, forms, regulations and dispensation with advertisements and notices),

sections 200 to 202 (provisions regarding exercise of functions by Secretary of State).

section 203 (power of heir of entail to sell or feu land for housing purposes),

section 205 (Crown rights),

section 209(1) (construction of references to Lands Tribunal).

Interpretation.

67.—(1) Subject to subsection (2) of this section, and except where the context otherwise requires, the expressions used in this Act and in the principal Act have the same meaning in this Act as in that Act.

PART V

(2) In this Act—

"housing treatment area" has the meaning assigned to it by section 4(1) of this Act;

"the principal Act" means the Housing (Scotland) Act 1966; 1966 c. 49.

"the Act of 1968" means the Housing (Financial Provisions) (Scotland) Act 1968. 1968 c. 31.

(3) References in this Act to any enactment are references to that enactment as amended, and include references thereto as applied, by any other enactment including, except where the context otherwise requires, this Act.

Expenses.

68. Any expenses of the Secretary of State under this Act and any expenses of the Secretary of State under any other enactment which are attributable to the provisions of this Act shall be defrayed out of moneys provided by Parliament.

Savings, minor and consequential amendments and repeals.

69.—(1) The savings contained in Schedule 5 to this Act shall have effect.

(2) The enactments specified in Schedule 6 to this Act shall have effect subject to the amendments set out in that Schedule, being minor amendments and amendments consequential on the foregoing provisions of this Act.

(3) Subject to the savings contained in Schedule 5 to this Act, the enactments specified in Schedule 7 to this Act are hereby repealed to the extent specified in the third column of that Schedule.

Citation, commencement and extent.

70.—(1) This Act may be cited as the Housing (Scotland) Act 1969.

(2) This Act, the principal Act and the Act of 1968 may be cited together as the Housing (Scotland) Acts 1966 to 1969.

(3) This Act shall come into force at the expiration of the period of one month beginning with the date on which it is passed.

(4) This Act shall extend to Scotland only.

SCHEDULES

Section 22.

SCHEDULE 1

TRANSITIONAL PROVISIONS FOR PURPOSES OF SECTIONS 18 TO 21

Right to and amount of payments

1. Sections 18 and 20 of this Act shall apply where a house has been purchased at restricted value in pursuance of a compulsory purchase order made by virtue of Part II of the principal Act as originally enacted or Part III of that Act, or in pursuance of an order under paragraph 1(2) of Schedule 2 to the Land Compensation (Scotland) Act 1963 as amended by the principal Act, or vacated in pursuance of a demolition order under section 15 or closing order under section 15 or 18 of the principal Act as those sections were originally enacted or a clearance order, and where the relevant date is on or after 1st August 1968, as they apply where a house has been purchased or vacated as described in section 18 of this Act, but as if the references to the relevant date, the authority concerned, the qualifying period, full compulsory purchase value and restricted value were references to those expressions as defined in the next following paragraph.

1963 c. 51.

2. (*a*) In the foregoing paragraph, in relation to any house purchased or vacated, " the relevant date " and " the authority concerned " mean respectively—

(i) if the house was purchased compulsorily under section 14(1) of the principal Act, the date when and the authority by whom the notice mentioned in section 11(1) of that Act was served ;

(ii) if the house was purchased compulsorily in pursuance of a notice served under section 20 of the principal Act, the date when and the authority by whom the notice was served ;

(iii) if the house was comprised in an area declared as a clearance area, the date when and the authority by whom the area was so declared ;

(iv) if the house was declared unfit for human habitation by an order under paragraph 1(2) of Schedule 2 to the Land Compensation (Scotland) Act 1963, the date when the order was made and the acquiring authority within the meaning of that Act ;

(v) if the house was vacated in pursuance of a demolition order or closing order, the date when and the authority by whom the order was made ;

and " the qualifying period " means the period beginning with 1st August 1968 and ending with the relevant date.

(*b*) In the foregoing paragraph—

" full compulsory purchase value ", in relation to any interest in a house, means the compensation which would be payable in respect of the compulsory purchase of that interest if the house were not being dealt with under Part II or Part III of the principal Act as being unfit for human habitation and, in the case of a house subject to a clearance order, demolition order or closing order, the making of that order were a service of the notice to treat ; SCH. 1

" restricted value ", in relation to the compulsory purchase of a house, means compensation in respect thereof assessed under section 14(5) to (7), 19(3) to (5), 20(5) to (7) or 47(2) to (4) of the principal Act.

Provisions as to house subject to heritable security or purchased by instalments

3. Section 18 of the Housing (Financial Provisions, &c.) (Scotland) Act 1967 (right of parties to certain agreements secured on, or related to, unfit houses to apply to sheriff for adjustment of the agreements) shall apply in a case where a house is purchased or vacated as described in subsection (1) of that section before the commencement of this Act, but where no application has been made to the sheriff under subsection (2) of that section before the commencement of this Act, as if this Act had not commenced. 1967 c. 20.

Payments for well maintained houses

4. Subsections (2) to (5) of section 21 of this Act shall apply to any payment in respect of a well maintained house under section 25 of the principal Act as originally enacted or section 49 of that Act in substitution for subsections (2) and (3) of the said section 49 where the relevant date is on or after 1st August 1968 as they apply to such a payment under the said section 25 or section 11 of this Act as is referred to in the said section 21 but as if—

(*a*) in subsection (4), after the words " section 18 of this Act " there were inserted the words " as applied by paragraph 1 of Schedule 1 to this Act " and for the words " section 25 of the principal Act or section 11 of this Act " there were substituted the words " section 25 of the principal Act as originally enacted or section 49 of that Act " ;

(*b*) in subsection (5)—

(i) " full compulsory purchase value " were defined as having the same meaning as in paragraph 2(*b*) of this Schedule ;

(ii) in the definition of " rateable value " the reference to the relevant date were a reference to the relevant date as defined in the following paragraph ;

(iii) " restricted value " were defined as having the same meaning as in paragraph 2(*b*) of this Schedule but with the omission of the reference to section 19 of the principal Act ;

(iv) the definition of " the relevant date " were omitted.

SCH. 1

5. In the last foregoing paragraph, " the relevant date " in relation to any payment made with respect to any house means—

(*a*) if the house was purchased compulsorily under section 14(1) of the principal Act, the date when the notice mentioned in section 11(1) of that Act was served;

(*b*) if the house was purchased compulsorily in pursuance of a notice served under section 20 of the principal Act, the date when the notice was served;

(*c*) if the house was comprised in an area declared as a clearance area, the date on which the area was so declared;

(*d*) if the house was vacated in pursuance of a demolition order or closing order or was declared unfit for human habitation by an order under paragraph 1(2) of Schedule 2 to the Land Compensation (Scotland) Act 1963, the date when the order was made.

1963 c. 51.

6. Where by virtue of paragraph 1 of this Schedule a payment falls to be made in respect of any interest in a house which has been vacated in pursuance of a demolition order or closing order under section 15 of the principal Act as originally enacted, no payment shall be made in respect of that house under section 25 of the principal Act or section 11 of this Act.

Section 25(4).

SCHEDULE 2

RECOVERY OF EXPENSES BY CHARGING ORDER

1. Where under section 24(2) of this Act a local authority have themselves incurred expenses in relation to a house or building, they may make in favour of themselves an order (in this Schedule referred to as a " charging order ") providing and declaring that the house or building is thereby charged and burdened with an annuity to pay the amount of the expenses.

2. The annuity charged shall be such sum as may be prescribed for every one hundred pounds of the said amount and so in proportion for any less sum, and shall commence from the date of the order and be payable for a term of 30 years to the local authority.

3. A charging order shall be in such form as may be prescribed and shall be recorded in the General Register of Sasines.

4. Every annuity constituting a charge by a charging order duly recorded in the General Register of Sasines shall be a charge on the premises specified in the order and shall have priority over—

(*a*) all future burdens and incumbrances on the same premises, and

(*b*) all existing burdens and incumbrances thereon except—

(i) feuduties, teinds, ground annuals, stipends and standard charges in lieu of stipends;

(ii) any charges created or arising under any provision of the Public Health (Scotland) Act 1897 or any Act

1897 c. 38.

amending that Act, or any local Act authorising a charge for recovery of expenses incurred by a local authority, or under this Schedule; and SCH. 2

(iii) any charge created under any Act authorising advances of public money.

5. A charging order duly recorded in the General Register of Sasines shall be conclusive evidence that the charge specified therein has been duly created in respect of the premises specified in the order.

6. Every annuity charged by a charging order may be recovered by the person for the time being entitled to it by the same means and in the like manner in all respects as if it were a feuduty.

7. A charging order and all sums payable thereunder may be from time to time transferred in like manner as a bond and disposition in security and sums payable thereunder.

8. Any owner of, or other person interested in, premises on which an annuity has been charged by any such charging order shall at any time be at liberty to redeem the annuity on payment to the local authority or other person entitled thereto of such sum as may be agreed upon or, in default of agreement, determined by the Secretary of State.

SCHEDULE 3

Sections 47 and 48.

CERTIFICATES OF FAIR RENT AND REGISTRATION OF RENT FOR CONVERTED TENANCIES

PART I

APPLICATIONS FOR CERTIFICATES OF FAIR RENT BY LANDLORDS UNDER CONTROLLED TENANCIES

1. Where, on an application for a qualification certificate, a local authority have issued a certificate of provisional approval, the applicant may apply to the rent officer for a certificate of fair rent.

2. An application made under paragraph 1 of this Schedule must be accompanied by copies of the plans and specifications which accompanied the application for the qualification certificate and of the certificate of provisional approval.

3. A certificate of fair rent issued on an application under this Schedule shall specify the rent which would be a fair rent under the regulated tenancy that might arise by virtue of section 44 of this Act if the works shown in the plans and specifications were carried out.

4. Schedule 4 to the Rent Act 1965 shall have effect with respect to an application made under this Schedule as if— 1965 c. 75.

(*a*) in paragraph 3 after the word "form" there were inserted the word "and" and the words from "and (except" to the end, and paragraph 5, were omitted; and

Sch. 3

(*b*) in paragraph 6 for the words from the beginning to " he shall serve " there were substituted the words " The rent officer shall serve ", and

(*c*) in paragraph 13 the words preceding sub-paragraph (*a*) were omitted.

Part II

Applications for Registration

Procedure on application to rent officer

5. On receiving the application for registration the rent officer shall ascertain whether any differences are specified in the qualification certificate in accordance with section 47(4) of this Act.

6. If no differences are so specified and the application was made not later than three months after the issue of the qualification certificate, the rent officer shall register the rent in accordance with the certificate of fair rent.

7. In any other case he shall serve a notice on the tenant informing him of the application and specifying a period of not less than 7 days from the service of the notice during which representations in writing may be made to the rent officer against the registration of the rent specified in the certificate.

8. Where no such representations are made then, unless it appears to the rent officer that the rent specified in the certificate of fair rent is higher than a fair rent, he shall register that rent and notify the landlord and tenant accordingly.

9.—(1) Where representations are made as mentioned in paragraph 7 of this Schedule or the rent officer is of opinion that the rent specified in the certificate of fair rent is higher than a fair rent, he shall serve notice on the landlord and on the tenant informing them that he proposes, at a time (which shall not be earlier than 7 days after the service of the notice) and place specified in the notice to consider in consultatation with the landlord and the tenant, or such of them as may appear at that time and place, what rent, not exceeding that specified in the certificate of fair rent, ought to be registered.

(2) At any such consultation the landlord and tenant may each be represented by a person authorised by him in that behalf, whether or not that person is an advocate or a solicitor.

10.—(1) The rent officer shall consider, in accordance with the last foregoing paragraph, what rent ought to be registered, and—

(*a*) if, after considering it, he is of opinion that the rent specified in the certificate is not higher than a fair rent he shall register it as the rent for the dwelling ; but

(*b*) if, after considering it, he is of opinion that the rent so specified is higher than a fair rent he shall determine a fair rent and register that rent as the rent for the dwelling ;

and shall give notice of the registration to the landlord and the tenant.

(2) The notice shall state that if, within 28 days of the service of the notice or such longer period as the rent officer or a rent assessment committee may allow, an objection in writing is received by the rent officer from the landlord or the tenant the matter will be referred to a rent assessment committee. SCH. 3

11.—(1) If such an objection is received, then—

(*a*) if it is received within the period of twenty-eight days mentioned in the last foregoing paragraph or a rent assessment committee so direct, the rent officer shall refer the matter to a rent assessment committee ;

(*b*) if it is received after that period, the rent officer may either refer the matter to a rent assessment committee or seek the directions of a rent assessment committee whether so to refer it.

(2) The rent officer shall indicate in the register whether the matter has been referred to a rent assessment committee in pursuance of this paragraph.

Determination of fair rent by rent assessment committee

12. The rent assessment committee to whom a matter is referred under paragraph 11 of this Schedule shall serve on the landlord and on the tenant a notice specifying a period of not less than fourteen days from the service of the notice during which either representations in writing or a request to make oral representations may be made by him to the committee.

13. Where, within the period specified under paragraph 12 of this Schedule or such further period as the committee may allow, the landlord or the tenant requests to make oral representations the committee shall give him an opportunity to be heard either in person or by a person authorised by him in that behalf, whether or not that person is an advocate or a solicitor.

14.—(1) The committee shall make such inquiry, if any, as they think fit and consider any representation made to them in pursuance of the two last foregoing paragraphs and—

(*a*) if it appears to them that the rent registered by the rent officer has been rightly registered they shall confirm it ;

(*b*) in any other case they shall designate as the rent for the dwelling either the rent specified in the certificate of fair rent or such lower rent as appears to them to be a fair rent, as the case may require ;

and they shall notify the landlord, the tenant and the rent officer accordingly.

(2) On receiving the notification, the rent officer shall, as the case may require, either indicate in the register that the rent has been confirmed or register the rent designated by the committee as the rent for the dwelling.

Section 53.

SCHEDULE 4

RESTRICTION ON RENT INCREASES

Restriction on rent increases after first registration

1965 c. 75. 1. Where a rent for a dwelling which is subject to a regulated tenancy is registered under Part II of the Rent Act 1965 and the registration is the first—

(*a*) after the tenancy has become a regulated tenancy by virtue of Part IV of this Act ; or

(*b*) after the completion, during the existence of the tenancy, of works towards the cost of which a grant was payable under Part II of the Act of 1968 ;

then if the rent payable under the tenancy for any statutory period beginning during the period of delay imposed by paragraph 2 of this Schedule is less than the rent so registered, it shall not be increased by a notice of increase under section 7(*b*) of the Rent Act 1965 except to the extent (if any) permitted under the following provisions of this Schedule ; and any such notice which purports to increase it further shall have effect to increase it to the extent so permitted but no further.

Period of delay

2. There shall be a period of delay with respect to any rent registered as mentioned in paragraph 1 of this Schedule, which shall be—

(*a*) if the rent is registered as mentioned in sub-paragraph (*a*) of that paragraph, a period of four years,

(*b*) if the rent is registered as mentioned in sub-paragraph (*b*) of that paragraph, a period of two years,

beginning with the date of registration.

Permitted increase

3.—(1) The rent may be increased to the aggregate of the following:—

(*a*) the amount of the previous limit, calculated in accordance with paragraph 4 of this Schedule ;

(*b*) the amount (if any) apportioned to services in accordance with paragraph 5 of this Schedule ; and

(*c*) the appropriate proportion of the difference between the registered rent and the aggregate of the amounts specified in paragraphs (*a*) and (*b*) above.

(2) The appropriate proportion mentioned in sub-paragraph (1)(*c*) of this paragraph shall be ascertained for any rental period in accordance with the following Table, in which the year of the period of delay in which the rental period begins is shown in the first column

and the appropriate proportion in the second or third column, according as the period of delay imposed by paragraph 2 of this Schedule is two years or four years. SCH. 4

TABLE

Year of period of delay	Appropriate Proportion	
	Where period of delay is two years	Where period of delay is four years
1st year	one-third	one-fifth
2nd year	two-thirds	two-fifths
3rd year	—	three-fifths
4th year	—	four-fifths

(3) Notwithstanding anything in the foregoing provisions of this paragraph, the amount to which the rent may be increased for any rental period shall not in any case be less than seven shillings and sixpence a week above the following, that is to say—

(*a*) if the rental period begins in the first year of the period of delay, the aggregate of the amounts specified in sub-paragraphs (1)(*a*) and (1)(*b*) of this paragraph ;

(*b*) if the rental period begins in a subsequent year, the amount to which the rent could be increased for a rental period beginning in the previous year ;

but nothing in this paragraph shall be taken to enable the rent to be increased above the amount registered.

Previous limit

4.—(1) For the purposes of this Schedule the previous limit of a rent shall be taken to be, subject to sub-paragraph (2) of this paragraph, the amount which at the date of registration was recoverable by way of the rent or would have been so recoverable if all notices of increase authorised by the Rent Acts or by regulations under section 9 of the Prices and Incomes Act 1968 had been served. 1968 c. 42.

(2) Where the rent includes an amount payable in respect of rates, the amount so payable, ascertained in accordance with Schedule 2 to the Rent Act 1957 as applied by section 47(2) of the Rent Act 1965 shall be deducted from the amount specified in sub-paragraph (1) of this paragraph in calculating the previous limit of the rent. 1957 c. 25. 1965 c. 75.

Amount to be apportioned to services

5.—(1) Where the registered rent includes a payment in respect of services provided by the landlord, then if—

(*a*) the rent is not registered as a variable rent in accordance with section 28(3) of the Rent Act 1965, but

SCH. 4

(*b*) not less than 10 per cent. of the amount of the registered rent is in the opinion of the rent officer or, as the case may be, rent assessment committee fairly attributable to the provision of the services,

the amount so attributable shall be noted in the register.

(2) Where it appears to the rent officer or rent assessment committee that some amount was in the previous limit attributable to the provision of services by the landlord and was less than the amount noted in pursuance of sub-paragraph (1) of this paragraph, then—

(*a*) if the amount so attributable can be ascertained the difference between it and the amount so noted shall be the amount apportioned to the services ;

(*b*) if the amount so attributable cannot be ascertained it shall be taken to be an amount bearing to the previous limit the same proportion as the amount noted in pursuance of sub-paragraph (1) of this paragraph bears to the amount of the registered rent, and the difference between the amount so taken and the amount so noted shall be the amount apportioned to the services ;

and the amount apportioned to the services in accordance with this sub-paragraph shall also be noted in the register.

(3) Where it appears to the rent officer or rent assessment committee that no amount was in the previous limit attributable to the provision of services by the landlord, the amount noted in pursuance of sub-paragraph (1) of this paragraph shall be the amount apportioned to the services and shall be noted as such in the register.

Restriction on rent increases in cases of further registration during period of delay

6.—(1) Where a rent (in this paragraph referred to as the first rent) for a dwelling which is subject to a regulated tenancy has been registered as mentioned in paragraph 1 of this Schedule and, in any year of the period of delay imposed by paragraph 2 of this Schedule, a new rent for the dwelling is registered under Part II of the Rent Act 1965, then, if the new rent exceeds the rent for the time being recoverable under the regulated tenancy the following provisions of this paragraph shall apply and the foregoing provisions of this Schedule shall not apply.

1965 c. 75.

(2) The rent for any statutory period beginning before the end of the period of delay shall not be increased by a notice of increase under section 7(*b*) of the Rent Act 1965 except to the extent permitted by the following provisions of this paragraph ; and any such notice which purports to increase it further shall have effect to increase it to the extent so permitted but no further.

(3) If the new rent is less than the first rent the rent payable under the regulated tenancy may be increased (up to the amount registered) to the same extent as if the first rent had remained registered.

Sch. 4

(4) If the new rent exceeds the first rent the registration shall not affect the amount recoverable for any rental period beginning in the year mentioned in sub-paragraph (1) of this paragraph ; and the rent for any statutory period beginning after that year may be increased to an amount arrived at by adding the difference between the first rent and the new rent to the amount to which the rent for that period could have been increased had the first rent remained registered.

Successive tenancies

7. Where a rent for a dwelling which is subject to a regulated tenancy is registered as mentioned in paragraph 1 of this Schedule and, during the period of delay imposed by paragraph 2 of this Schedule with respect to the rent, the tenant, or any person who might succeed him as a statutory tenant, becomes the tenant under a new regulated tenancy of the dwelling—

(*a*) the rent limit for any contractual period of the new regulated tenancy beginning during that period of delay shall be the amount to which, if the first-mentioned tenancy had continued, the rent payable thereunder could have been increased in accordance with this Schedule for a statutory period beginning at the same time, and in relation to such a contractual period the reference in section 28(2) of the Rent Act 1965 to section 3(2) of that Act shall be construed as a reference to this paragraph ; and 1965 c. 75.

(*b*) in relation to any statutory period of the new tenancy beginning during that period of delay the foregoing provisions of this Schedule shall have effect as if it were a statutory period of the first-mentioned tenancy.

8. Where—

(*a*) an existing controlled tenancy of a dwelling becomes a regulated tenancy by virtue of Part IV of this Act, or

(*b*) a dwelling improved by works towards the cost of which a grant is payable under Part II of the Act of 1968 is, at the time the works are completed, subject to a regulated tenancy,

and the tenant, or any person who might succeed him as a statutory tenant becomes the tenant under a new regulated tenancy of the dwelling, then, if during the continuance of the new regulated tenancy a rent for the dwelling is registered under Part II of the Rent Act 1965 and the registration would be such a registration as is mentioned in paragraph 1 of this Schedule had the regulated tenancy mentioned in sub-paragraph (*a*) or (*b*) of this paragraph continued, paragraphs 1 to 6 of this Schedule shall apply as if it had continued and paragraph 7(*a*) of this Schedule shall apply with the necessary modifications.

Application to tenancies converted by order under s. 11(3) of Rent Act 1965

9. Where a regulated tenancy of a dwelling has become a regulated tenancy by virtue of an order under section 11(3) of the Rent Act

SCH. 4 1965 and a rent for the dwelling is registered as mentioned in paragraph 1(*b*) of this Schedule, section 11(5) and (6) of that Act (restriction on rent increases) shall thereupon cease to apply to the tenancy.

Supplemental

10. In ascertaining for the purposes of this Schedule whether there is any difference between amounts or what that difference is, such adjustments shall be made as may be necessary to take account of periods of different lengths ; and for that purpose a month shall be treated as one-twelfth and a week as one fifty-second of a year.

11. Where the rent specified in a certificate of fair rent includes a payment in respect of services provided by the landlord and the amount which in the opinion of the rent officer or rent assessment committee is fairly attributable to the provision of the services is not less than ten per cent. of the amount of the rent then, if the application for the certificate is made in pursuance of section 47(2) of this Act or the applicant so requests, the amount so attributable shall be noted in the certificate together with the amount to be entered in the register under paragraph 5 of this Schedule as the amount to be apportioned to the services.

12. Any amount to be noted in the register or in a certificate of fair rent in pursuance of paragraph 5 or paragraph 11 of this Schedule as an amount fairly attributable to the provision of services shall be included among the matters to be specified in an application for the registration or for the certificate and any such amount and any amount to be so noted as an amount apportioned or to be apportioned to the services shall be included among the matters with respect to which representations may be made or consultations are to be held or notices to be given under paragraphs 4 to 12 and 16(2)
1965 c. 75. to (6) of Schedule 3 to the Rent Act 1965 or paragraphs 3 to 13 of Schedule 4 to that Act or Schedule 3 to this Act.

13. Where a rent designated or determined by a rent assessment committee is registered in substitution for a rent determined by the rent officer, the foregoing provisions of this Schedule shall have effect as if only the rent designated or determined by the rent assessment committee had been registered ; but the date of registration shall be deemed for the purposes of this Schedule (but not for the purposes of section 7(*b*) of the Rent Act 1965) to be the date on which the rent determined by the rent officer was registered.

Section 69(1).

SCHEDULE 5

SAVINGS

1. Nothing in this Act shall affect a compulsory purchase order made in pursuance of section 14, 19 or 20 or Part III or Part IV of the principal Act, a clearance order or a charging order made under that Act, or a notice served under section 11 of that Act, before the commencement of this Act ; and any such order or notice may be proceeded with in accordance with the provisions of the principal Act as if this Act had not been passed.

2. Nothing in this Act shall preclude— SCH. 5

(*a*) the making of a compulsory purchase order in respect of land comprised in a clearance area, or a clearance order, after the commencement of this Act, in pursuance of a clearance resolution passed before the commencement of this Act;

(*b*) the making of a compulsory purchase order or a charging order or the service of an improvement notice (as defined in section 87(1) of the principal Act), after the commencement of this Act, in pursuance of a resolution passed under section 58 of the principal Act before the commencement of this Act;

(*c*) the making of an order under section 12(2) of the principal Act, a compulsory purchase order in pursuance of section 14 of that Act, an order under subsection (1) or subsection (2) of section 15 of that Act or a charging order under section 28 or 30 of that Act, after the commencement of this Act, where the making of any such order is consequent upon the service of a notice under section 11(1) of that Act before the commencement of this Act;

and any such order or improvement notice may be proceeded with in accordance with the provisions of the principal Act as if this Act had not been passed.

3.—(1) The repeal by this Act of section 49 of the principal Act is without prejudice to any payment in respect of a well maintained house under that section or section 25 of the principal Act after the commencement of this Act where the relevant date is before 1st August 1968.

(2) In this paragraph "the relevant date" has the same meaning as in paragraph 5 of Schedule 1 to this Act.

4. The repeal by this Act of sections 51 and 52 of the principal Act is without prejudice to the exercise of any power by a local authority under either of those sections after the commencement of this Act with respect to any land purchased by them under Part III of the principal Act.

5. The repeal by this Act of references in any provision of the Rent Act 1965 to any enactment contained in Part II of the Act of 1968 does not affect the operation of that provision in relation to any grant paid in pursuance of an application made before the commencement of this Act. 1965 c. 75.

SCHEDULE 6

Section 69(2).

MINOR AND CONSEQUENTIAL AMENDMENTS

THE HOUSING REPAIRS AND RENTS (SCOTLAND) ACT 1954 (c. 50)

1. For section 39(2) (interpretation of Part II) there shall be substituted the following subsections—

"(2) In determining for the purposes of this Part of this Act whether a dwelling-house is fit or unfit for human habitation,

SCH. 6 regard shall be had to the extent, if any, to which by reason of disrepair or sanitary defects the dwelling-house falls short of the provisions of any building regulations in operation in the district.

(2A) In the last foregoing subsection—

1966 c. 49. (*a*) " building regulations " and " district " have the same meanings as in the Housing (Scotland) Act 1966 ;

(*b*) " sanitary defects " includes lack of air space or of ventilation, darkness, dampness, absence of adequate and readily accessible water supply or of sanitary arrangements or of other conveniences, and inadequate paving or drainage of courts, yards or passages.".

THE LAND COMPENSATION (SCOTLAND) ACT 1963 (C. 51)

2. In Schedule 2 (acquisition of houses as being unfit for human habitation)—

(*a*) in paragraph 1(1), for the words from " is unfit " to the end there shall be substituted the words " does not meet the tolerable standard " ;

(*b*) in paragraph 1(2)—

(i) for the words from " declaring " to " sub-paragraph " where it first occurs there shall be substituted the words " declaring that the house does not meet the tolerable standard ",

(ii) for the words between " subsequently confirmed by the Secretary of State " and " and as if any reference " there shall be substituted the words " section 10(2) and (3) and section 11 of the Housing (Scotland) Act 1969 (which relate respectively to compensation and well maintained payments in respect of houses purchased under Part I of the said Act of 1969) shall apply as if the house had been purchased under the said Part I as not meeting the tolerable standard " ;

(*c*) for paragraph 1(5) there shall be substituted the following sub-paragraph—

" (5) Section 2 of the Housing (Scotland) Act 1969 shall have effect in determining for the purposes of this paragraph whether a house meets the tolerable standard as it has effect in so determining for the purposes of that Act." ;

(*d*) in paragraph 1(6) for the words from " the provisions " to " areas " there shall be substituted the words " the provisions of Part I of the Housing (Scotland) Act 1969 relating to housing treatment areas " ;

(*e*) in paragraphs 2(1) and 3(1), for the words from " any of the provisions " to " value " there shall be substituted the words " section 19(2) to (4) of the Housing (Scotland) Act 1966 or section 10(2) and (3) of the Housing (Scotland) Act 1969 (which relate respectively to the compensation to be paid on the compulsory acquisition of closed houses,

SCH. 6

and of houses not meeting the tolerable standard) ", and for the words " that Act " there shall be substituted the words " those Acts ";

(*f*) in paragraph 2(3), for the reference to section 49 of the principal Act there shall be substituted a reference to section 25 of the principal Act or section 11 of this Act.

THE HOUSING (SCOTLAND) ACT 1966 (c. 49)

3. In section 6 (conditions to be implied on letting certain small houses)—

(*a*) in subsection (1) for the words " or section 40 of this Act " there shall be substituted the words " of this Act or section 8 of the Housing (Scotland) Act 1969 ";

(*b*) after subsection (3) there shall be inserted the following subsection—

" (3A) In determining for the purposes of this section whether a house is fit for human habitation, regard shall be had to the extent, if any, to which by reason of disrepair or sanitary defects the house falls short of the provisions of any building regulations in operation in the district." ;

(*c*) in subsection (4) at the end there shall be inserted—

" and

(*c*) the expression " sanitary defects " includes lack of air space or of ventilation, darkness, dampness, absence of adequate and readily accessible water supply or of sanitary arrangements or of other conveniences, and inadequate paving or drainage of courts, yards or passages.".

4. In section 15 (power of local authority to make closing and demolition orders)—

(*a*) in subsection (1), for the words from " is unfit " to " so fit " where they first occur, in paragraph (*b*) for the words from " are unfit " to " so fit ", and for the word " shall " there shall be substituted respectively the words " does not meet the tolerable standard and that it ought to be demolished ", the words " do not meet the tolerable standard ", and the word " may ";

(*b*) in subsection (2) for the words from " is, or " to " fit " and for the word " shall " where it first occurs there shall be substituted respectively the words " does not meet, or houses which do not meet, the tolerable standard and that the house or, as the case may be, houses ought to be demolished " and the word " may ";

(*c*) in subsection (2)(*b*) for the words " three months " wherever they occur there shall be substituted the words " six weeks ";

(*d*) in subsections (3) and (4) for any reference to a house or houses being rendered fit for human habitation there shall be substituted a reference to a house or houses being brought up to the tolerable standard.

SCH. 6

5. In section 17 (power to make closing orders with respect to underground rooms), for any reference to a house being unfit for human habitation there shall be substituted a reference to a house not meeting the tolerable standard.

6. In section 18 (provisions as to houses subject to building preservation orders, etc.)—

(*a*) in subsection (1) for the words " under a duty " and for the word " shall " occurring immediately after the word " instead ", there shall be substituted respectively the word " empowered " and the word " may " ;

(*b*) in subsection (2) after the word " and " there shall be inserted the word " may ".

7. In section 19 (powers of local authority in relation to building consisting wholly of closed houses)—

(*a*) in subsection (1) for paragraph (*b*) there shall be substituted the following paragraph—

" (*b*) the local authority may purchase the land by agreement or may, subject to the provisions of this section, be authorised by the Secretary of State to purchase it compulsorily." ;

(*b*) after subsection (1) there shall be inserted the following subsection—

" (1A) The provisions of the Acquisition of Land (Authorisation Procedure) (Scotland) Act 1947 shall apply in relation to the compulsory purchase of land under subsection (1)(*b*) of this section as if that subsection had been in force immediately before the commencement of that Act." ;

1947 c. 42.

(*c*) in subsection (2) for the words " to (5) " there shall be substituted the words " and (4) " ;

(*d*) for subsections (3) to (5) there shall be substituted the following subsections—

" (3) The compensation payable under this section shall not (except by virtue of paragraph 2 or paragraph 3 of Schedule 2 to the said Act of 1963) exceed the value, at the time when the valuation is made, of the site as a cleared site available for development in accordance with the requirements of the building regulations for the time being in force in the district.

(4) The references in subsections (2) and (3) of this section to compensation are references to the compensation payable in respect of the purchase exclusive of any compensation for disturbance or for severance or for injurious affection." ;

(*e*) in subsection (6) for the words from " 39 " to the end there shall be substituted the words " 13(*b*) of the Housing (Scotland) Act 1969 shall apply as if the land were in a housing treatment area and had been purchased for the purpose of demolishing the buildings thereon.".

8. In section 20 (local authority may acquire and repair house or building liable to closing or demolition order)—

(*a*) in subsection (1)(*a*) for the word " required " there shall be substituted the word " empowered " ;

(*b*) in subsection (4) for the words " to (7) " there shall be substituted the words " and (6) " ;

(*c*) for subsections (5) to (7) there shall be substituted the following subsections—

" (5) The compensation payable under this section shall not (except by virtue of paragraph 2 or paragraph 3 of Schedule 2 to the said Act of 1963) exceed the value, at the time when the valuation is made, of the site as a cleared site available for development in accordance with the requirements of the building regulations for the time being in force in the district.

(6) The references in subsections (4) and (5) of this section to compensation are references to the compensation payable in respect of the purchase exclusive of any compensation for disturbance or for severance or for injurious affection.".

9. In section 23 (power of local authority to purchase site of demolished building where expenses of demolition cannot be recovered), in subsection (4) for the words " 39 of this Act " there shall be substituted the words " 13(*b*) of the Housing (Scotland) Act 1969."

10. Section 24 (power of local authority to cleanse from vermin house to which demolition order applies) shall cease to have effect.

11. In section 25 (payments in respect of unfit but well-maintained houses), in subsection (1), for the words " paragraphs (*b*) to (*k*) of section 5(1) of this Act " and for the words from " the like " to the end of the subsection there shall be substituted respectively the words " section 2(1) of the Housing (Scotland) Act 1969 " and the words " a payment calculated in accordance with section 21 of the said Act of 1969 ".

12. In section 30(1) (power of local authority to make charging order in favour of themselves), for the words " sections 28 and 29 of this Act " and the words " said section 28 " there shall be substituted respectively the words " Schedule 2 to the Housing (Scotland) Act 1969 " and the words " said Schedule ".

13. In section 33 (interpretation of Part II), subsection (1)(*a*) shall cease to have effect.

14. In section 109 (carrying out of works by local authority)—

(*a*) in subsection (3), for the words " 11(3) and 12 of this Act " there shall be substituted the words " 24(3) and 25 of the Housing (Scotland) Act 1969 " ;

(*b*) in subsections (3) and (4), for the words " on an insanitary house " there shall be substituted the words " under section 24(2) of the said Act of 1969 " ;

SCH. 6

(*c*) in subsection (4), for the words " Sections 26 and 27 of this Act " there shall be substituted the words " Sections 27 and 28 of the Housing (Scotland) Act 1969 " ;

(*d*) in subsection (5), for the words from " subsections " to " 29, of this Act ", the words " they apply " and the words from " said section 28 " to the end, there shall be substituted respectively the words " Schedule 2 to the Housing (Scotland) Act 1969 ", the words " it applies " and the words " said Schedule ".

15. In section 114 (management code to be available for dwellings in certain tenements), for subsection (4) there shall be substituted the following subsection—

" (4) In this section—

" dwelling " means a building or part of a building occupied or intended to be occupied as a separate dwelling ;

1968 c. 31. " the standard amenities " has the same meaning as in section 39(1) of the Housing (Financial Provisions) (Scotland) Act 1968 ;

" tenement " has the same meaning as in section 5 of the Housing (Scotland) Act 1969.".

16. In section 127 (recovery by local authority of capital expenditure incurred in carrying out works included in scheme)—

(*a*) in subsection (3), for the references to section 12(1) of the principal Act there shall be substituted references to section 25(1) of this Act ;

(*b*) in subsection (5), for the words " 11(3) and 12 of this Act " there shall be substituted the words " 24(3) and 25 of the Housing (Scotland) Act 1969 " ;

(*c*) in subsections (5) and (6), for the words " on an insanitary house " there shall be substituted the words " under section 24(2) of the said Act of 1969 " ;

(*d*) in subsection (6), for the words " Sections 26 and 27 of this Act " there shall be substituted the words " Sections 27 and 28 of the Housing (Scotland) Act 1969 " ;

(*e*) in subsection (7), for the words from " subsections " to " 29, of this Act ", the words " they apply " and the words from " said section 28 " to the end, there shall be substituted respectively the words " Schedule 2 to the Housing (Scotland) Act 1969 ", the words " it applies " and the words " said Schedule ".

17. In section 130 (provisions where control order revoked on appeal), in subsection (10) for the words " 12(1) of this Act " there shall be substituted the words " 25(1) of the Housing (Scotland) Act 1969 ".

18. In section 137 (duty of local authority to review housing conditions and to frame proposals), for the words " the inspections and surveys carried out under section 4(1) of this Act " there shall be substituted the words " a survey or inspection made under section 1(3)

of the Housing (Scotland) Act 1969 ", and for the words from " new houses " to the end there shall be substituted the words " housing accommodation ". SCH. 6

19. In section 151(2) (conditions to be observed in management of local authority's houses), for the words " insanitary houses " there shall be substituted the words " houses which do not meet the tolerable standard ".

20. In section 155 (power of local authority to make arrangements with housing association for improvement of housing accommodation), for subsection (4) there shall be substituted the following subsection—

" (4) In this section ' improvement ' includes alteration and enlargement and such repairs and replacements as are either incidental to some other improvement or are needed for the purpose of making the other improvement fully effective, and ' improved ' shall be construed accordingly.".

21. In section 160 (power of local authority to pay removal and other allowances to certain persons displaced)—

(*a*) in subsection (1)(*a*)(i), for the words from " 14 " to " thereof " there shall be substituted the words " 20 or Part VII of this Act or section 7 of the Housing (Scotland) Act 1969 " ;

(*b*) in subsection (4), for the words " Part III of this Act " there shall be substituted the words " Part I of the Housing (Scotland) Act 1969 ".

22. In section 169 (byelaws with respect to houses in multiple occupation)—

(*a*) in subsection (2) for the words " this Act " where they occur for the second time there shall be substituted the words " the Housing (Scotland) Act 1969 " ;

(*b*) in subsection (3), for the words " Part II of this Act " there shall be substituted the words " Part II of the Housing (Scotland) Act 1969 ".

23. In section 180 (official representations)—

(*a*) for any reference to any house being unfit for human habitation there shall be substituted a reference to any house not meeting the tolerable standard ;

(*b*) in subsection (2), for the word " shall " there shall be substituted the word " may " ;

(*c*) subsection (3) shall cease to have effect.

24. In section 182 (recovery of possession of house to which Rent Acts apply), after the words " closing order " there shall be inserted the word " or ".

25. In section 183(1)(*b*) (power of entry for survey etc.), after the words " closing order " there shall be inserted the word " or ".

26. In section 185(1)(*a*) (penalty for preventing execution of works, etc.), after the word " orders) " there shall be inserted the words " or any of the provisions of Part II of the Housing (Scotland) Act 1969 ".

SCH. 6

27. In section 190(1) (procedure on application to sheriff), for the words from " under any " to " Part VI " there shall be substituted the words " under section 10 or Part VI of this Act or section 26 of the Housing (Scotland) Act 1969 ".

28. In section 192 (provisions relating to service of documents)—

(*a*) in subsection (4)(*b*), after the word " Act " there shall be inserted the words " or the Housing (Scotland) Act 1969 " ;

(*b*) in subsection (6), after the word " Act " there shall be inserted the words " or the Housing (Scotland) Act 1969 " ;

(*c*) in subsection (7), after the word " Act " there shall be inserted the words " or Part I or Part II of the Housing (Scotland) Act 1969 ".

29. In section 208 (interpretation), after subsection (1) there shall be inserted the following subsection—

" (1A) Section 2 of the Housing (Scotland) Act 1969 shall have effect in determining for the purposes of this Act whether a house meets the tolerable standard as it has effect in so determining for the purposes of that Act ; and any reference in this Act to a house not meeting the tolerable standard or being brought up to the tolerable standard shall be construed accordingly.".

30. In section 209(2) (construction of references to Lands Tribunal), for the words " 52(3) of this Act " there shall be substituted the words " 15(3) of the Housing (Scotland) Act 1969 " and for the word " costs " there shall be substituted the word " expenses ".

31. In section 210(2) (construction of references to this Act etc.), for the words " sections 165(1) and 200(2) " there shall be substituted the words " section 165(1) ".

THE HOUSING (FINANCIAL PROVISIONS, &C.) (SCOTLAND) ACT 1967 (c. 20)

32. In section 18 (right of parties to certain agreements secured on, or related to, unfit houses to apply to sheriff for adjustment of the agreements)—

(*a*) in subsection (1)—

(i) after the word " apply " there shall be inserted the words " whether or not a payment falls to be made in respect of an interest in a house under section 18 of the Housing (Scotland) Act 1969 " ;

(ii) for the words from " in pursuance " where they first occur to " clearance order " there shall be substituted the words " at restricted value in pursuance of a compulsory purchase order made by virtue of section 19 or
1966 c. 49. 20 of the Housing (Scotland) Act 1966 or section 7 of the Housing (Scotland) Act 1969, or in pursuance of an
1963 c. 51. order under paragraph 1(2) of Schedule 2 to the Land Compensation (Scotland) Act 1963, or has been vacated in pursuance of a demolition order or a closing order " ;

(*b*) in subsection (2)(*b*) for the words " closing order or clearance order " there shall be substituted the words " or closing order " ;

(*c*) in subsection (7) at the end there shall be inserted the following words "'restricted value' has the same meaning as in section 20(2) of the Housing (Scotland) Act 1969". SCH. 6

THE HOUSING (FINANCIAL PROVISIONS) (SCOTLAND) ACT 1968 (c. 31)

33. In section 19(1) (exchequer contributions towards expenditure of local authorities in respect of unfit houses purchased or held by them), in paragraph (*c*) for the words "40 of the principal Act" there shall be substituted the words "8 of the Housing (Scotland) Act 1969".

34. In section 26 (exchequer contributions towards certain deficits of Scottish Special Housing Association)—

(*a*) at the end of paragraph (c) there shall be inserted the words:—

"and

(*d*) in improving the amenities of predominantly residential areas;"

(*b*) at the end of head (ii) there shall be inserted the words:—

"and

(iii) any annual grant paid to the Association under section 59(7)(*b*) of the Housing (Scotland) Act 1969,".

35. In section 27 (power of local authorities to make improvement grants)—

(*a*) in subsection (2) for the words "proposed to be" where they first occur there shall be substituted the words "which are proposed to be or are being" and after the words "proposed to be" where they subsequently occur there shall be inserted the words "or are being";

(*b*) in subsection (8) for the words "if the applicant so requests, notify him" there shall be substituted the words "notify the applicant".

36. In section 31(11) (enforcement of conditions), for the words "section 29 of the principal Act" and the words "section 28 of that Act" there shall be substituted respectively the words "Schedule 2 to the Housing (Scotland) Act 1969" and the words "the said Schedule".

37. In section 38(1) (provision supplementary to sections 27 to 37), for the word "28(1)(*c*)" there shall be substituted the word "28(*b*)".

38. In section 40 (duty of local authorities to make standard grants)—

(*a*) in subsection (2), for the word "proposing" there shall be substituted the words "in respect of", and in paragraph (*b*) for the words from "comprised" to the end of the paragraph there shall be substituted the words "mentioned in paragraphs (*dd*), (*e*) and (*f*) of section 39(1) of this Act";

SCH. 6

(*b*) in subsection (3), for the words " proposed to be " there shall be substituted the words " which are proposed to be or are being."

39. In section 49(2) (power of local authority to make advances for purpose of increasing housing accommodation), for the words from " is or are " where they first occur to " habitation " and for the words " be in all respects so fit " there shall be substituted respectively the words " meets, meet or will meet the tolerable standard " and the words " meet that standard ".

40. In section 58(3)(*a*) (power of Secretary of State to reduce, suspend, discontinue or transfer particular exchequer contributions), after the words " this Act " there shall be inserted the words " or the Housing (Scotland) Act 1969 ".

41. In section 59 (effect on certain payments of housing ceasing to be available as such), at the end there shall be inserted the following subsections—

" (4) In determining for the purposes of this section whether a dwelling is fit for human habitation, regard shall be had to the extent, if any, to which by reason of disrepair or sanitary defects the dwelling falls short of the provisions of any building regulations in operation in the district.

(5) In the last foregoing subsection the expression " sanitary defects " includes lack of air space or of ventilation, darkness, dampness, absence of adequate and readily accessible water supply or of sanitary arrangements or of other conveniences, and inadequate paving or drainage of courts, yards or passages.".

42. In section 64 (power of local authorities to borrow for purposes of certain enactments)—

(*a*) for the word " 32 " there shall be substituted the word " 31 " ;

(*b*) at the end there shall be added the following paragraph—

" (*c*) the following provisions of the Housing (Scotland) Act 1969, namely, sections 58 and 60.".

43. In section 67 (interpretation), in subsection (2) after the words " under this Act " there shall be inserted the words " or section 59 of the Housing (Scotland) Act 1969 ".

44. In Schedule 3 (conditions to be observed with respect to dwellings provided or improved with the help of improvement grants or standard grants), in paragraph 5 for the words " 3 and 4 " there shall be substituted the words " and 3 ".

45. In Schedule 5 (enactments referred to in section 57(1)), at the end there shall be inserted the following—

" The Housing (Scotland) Act 1969
(1969 c. 34)
Section 59.".

46. In Schedule 6 (enactments referred to in section 58(1)), at the end there shall be inserted the following—

" The Housing (Scotland) Act 1969
(1969 c. 34)
Section 59.".

THE TOWN AND COUNTRY PLANNING (SCOTLAND) ACT 1969 (c. 30)

SCH. 6

47. In section 37 (compensation for compulsory purchase of land in clearance areas and of historic buildings)—

(*a*) in paragraph (*b*) for the words " Part III of the Housing (Scotland) Act 1966 " there shall be substituted the words " the said section 1 as applied by section 7 of the Housing (Scotland) Act 1969 ; "

(*b*) for the words " Part III of the said Act of 1966 " there shall be substituted the words " section 10(2) and (3) of the said Act of 1969."

THE POST OFFICE ACT 1969 (c. 48)

48. In paragraph 83 of Schedule 4 (adaptation of enactments)—

(*a*) in sub-paragraph (1), after the word " 1966 " there shall be inserted the words " or Part I of the Housing (Scotland) Act 1969 " ;

(*b*) in sub-paragraph (2), for the words " 51 of the Housing (Scotland) Act 1966 " there shall be substituted the words " 14 of the Housing (Scotland) Act 1969 " ; 1966 c. 49.

(*c*) in sub-paragraph (3), for the words " 51(4) of the Housing (Scotland) Act 1966 " there shall be substituted the words " 14(4) of the Housing (Scotland) Act 1969 ", and for the words " that Act " there shall be substituted the words " the Housing (Scotland) Act 1966 ".

SCHEDULE 7

Section 69(3).

ENACTMENTS REPEALED

Chapter	Short Title	Extent of Repeal
10 & 11 Geo. 6. c. 42.	The Acquisition of Land (Authorisation Procedure) (Scotland) Act 1947.	In section 1(4), paragraphs (*d*) and (*e*).
14 Geo. 6. c. 34.	The Housing (Scotland) Act 1950.	In section 125, the proviso.
1963 c. 51.	The Land Compensation (Scotland) Act 1963.	In Schedule 2, paragraph 5(2).
1965 c. 75.	The Rent Act 1965.	In section 6(7)(*a*) the words from " section 111 " to " 1959 or ". In section 17(2) the words from " section 111 " to " 1959 or ". In Schedule 3, paragraph 17.
1966 c. 49.	The Housing (Scotland) Act 1966.	Sections 3 to 5. Sections 11 to 14. Section 16.

SCH. 7

Chapter	Short Title	Extent of Repeal
1966 c. 49—*cont.*	The Housing (Scotland) Act 1966—*cont.*	In section 20, in subsection (1)(*a*) the word " whether " and the words " or of " to " Act) ", and subsection (2)(*b*). Section 24. In section 25(1)(*a*), the words " section 14(1) or ". In section 26, in subsection (1), paragraphs (*a*), (*b*) and (*c*), and the word " demand " wherever it occurs, subsections (2) and (3). In section 27, the word " demand ". Sections 28 and 29. In section 30, in subsection (1) the words from " (*a*) " to " (*b*) ", in subsection (2) the words from " in a " to " that subsection ". In section 31(2) the words from " or a notice " to " served " and the words " or notice ". Section 32. In section 33, in subsection (1), the words " 28, 29 " and paragraph (*a*). Sections 34 to 55. Part IV. In section 137, the words from " distinguishing " to the end. In section 160(1)(*a*)(ii) the words " or a clearance order ". In section 180, in subsection (2) the words from " or that " to the end, subsections (3) and (4). In section 181, in subsection (1) the words " a clearance order ", in the proviso to subsection (3), paragraph (*a*) and in subsection (4) the words " or a clearance order ". In section 182, the words " or a clearance order ". In section 183, in subsection (1)(*b*), the words " or a clearance order ", and subsection (1)(*d*). In section 185(1)(*a*), the words from " Part II " to " provisions of ".

Chapter	Short Title	Extent of Repeal
1966 c. 49—*cont.*	The Housing (Scotland) Act 1966—*cont.*	In section 187(1), the words " a clearance order ". In section 190(5), the words " Part IV or ". In section 192, subsection (1), in subsection (2) the words " Part IV or ", and in subsection (7) the words " Part IV ". Section 200(2). In section 208, in subsection (1) the definitions of " clearance area ", " clearance order " and " clearance resolution " and in the definition of " flat " the words " (except in Part IV of this Act) ", and in subsection (2) the words " and without prejudice to section 87(2) thereof ". Schedules 1 to 3. In Schedule 9, the part relating to the Housing (Repairs and Rents) (Scotland) Act 1954 and in the part relating to the Land Compensation (Scotland) Act 1963, paragraph 4.
1967 c. 1.	The Land Commission Act 1967.	In section 6(3)(*e*) the words from " or under " to " 1966 ".
1967 c. 20.	The Housing (Financial Provisions, &c.) (Scotland) Act 1967.	In section 18, subsections (3)(*a*)(iii) and (4).
1968 c. 31.	The Housing (Financial Provisions) (Scotland) Act 1968.	Section 13(2). In section 19(1), paragraph (*a*). In section 27, in subsection (1) the words " before the improvement works are begun ", subsection (5), in subsection (6), the word " (1) " and the words from " subject " to the end. In section 30(2), the words " (other than paragraph 4 thereof) ". Sections 32 and 33. In section 36(2), the proviso. Section 38(3). In section 39, in subsection (1), the words " and (*g*) satisfactory facilities for storing food ", and in subsection (3) the words " or of section 41(5) of this Act ".

SCH. 7

Chapter	Short Title	Extent of Repeal
1968 c. 31—*cont.*	The Housing (Financial Provisions) (Scotland) Act 1968—*cont.*	In section 40, in subsection (1) the words " before the works are begun ", subsection (4), subsection (5). In section 54 the words from " other " to " 33(1) of this Act ". Section 66 so far as relating to section 5 of the principal Act. In Schedule 3, paragraphs 4 and 6. In Schedule 9, paragraphs 1 to 4.
1968 c. 42.	The Prices and Incomes Act 1968.	Section 12.

Transport (London) Act 1969

1969 CHAPTER 35

An Act to make provision with respect to transport in and around Greater London and for connected purposes. [25th July 1969]

BE IT ENACTED by the Queen's most Excellent Majesty, by and with the advice and consent of the Lords Spiritual and Temporal, and Commons, in this present Parliament assembled, and by the authority of the same, as follows:—

PART I

GENERAL FUNCTIONS OF GREATER LONDON COUNCIL AS TO TRANSPORT

General duty of Greater London Council with respect to transport.

1. Without prejudice to any other duty imposed on them under any other Act, and in particular to their duty under section 84(1) of the Act of 1967, it shall be the general duty of the Greater London Council (hereafter in this Act referred to as " the Council ") to develop policies, and to encourage, organise and, where appropriate, carry out measures, which will promote the provision of integrated, efficient and economic transport facilities and services for Greater London.

Transport plans for Greater London.

2.—(1) Without prejudice to their duties under the enactments relating to town and country planning, the Council shall from time to time prepare, and cause to be published in such manner as seems to the Council appropriate for informing persons appearing to the Council to be concerned, plans relating to transport in Greater London with due regard to the relationship and interaction between transport facilities and services within, and such facilities and services outside, Greater London; and the Council shall send to the Minister a copy of any plan prepared by them under this section.

PART I

(2) Plans under this section shall be in such form, and relate to such aspects of transport and such periods, as the Council and the Minister may from time to time agree; and in preparing any such plan the Council shall consult with the Minister, the Railways Board and the London Transport Executive established under section 4 of this Act (hereafter in this Act referred to as " the Executive "), with any other local authority (being the council of a London borough, the Common Council or a county council) any part of whose area appears to the Council to be affected to a significant degree by the plan, and with any other bodies who appear to the Council to be able to contribute substantially to the formulation of the plan, and shall have regard—

(*a*) to any considerations to which the Minister may from time to time draw their attention, including, in particular, considerations of national or regional transport policy;

(*b*) to such of the following as are for the time being appropriate, namely—

(i) the initial development plan for Greater London within the meaning of section 25(2) of the London Government Act 1963;

1963 c. 33.

(ii) any proposals for alterations or additions to that plan made under section 26(2) of that Act;

(iii) any proposals for the Greater London development plan;

(iv) the Greater London development plan and any proposals for any alteration or addition to that plan under Part III of the said Act of 1963 or Part I of the Town and Country Planning Act 1968;

1968 c. 72.

(*c*) to any proposals for a further survey of Greater London under the said Part III or the said Part I; and

(*d*) to any exercise or proposed exercise by a local planning authority of their functions in connection with the development of any part of Greater London or of any area in the vicinity of Greater London.

(3) The Minister and the Railways Board shall have regard to any plan prepared, and to any proposals for such a plan on which they have been consulted, under this section for the purposes of settling in accordance with section 27(2) of the Act of 1962 the lines on which that Board are to act in framing and carrying out proposals involving substantial outlay by that Board or a subsidiary of theirs on capital account and, in the case of that Board, when framing and carrying out any such proposals which are likely to affect substantially transport in Greater London.

PART I

Power of Council to make grants.

3.—(1) Without prejudice to any other power of the Council to make grants for transport purposes, the Council shall have power to make grants—

(*a*) to the Executive for any purpose; or

(*b*) to the Railways Board in respect of passenger transport services or other passenger transport amenities or facilities provided or to be provided by them which appear to the Council to be required to meet the needs of Greater London;

but any expenditure incurred by the Council in making grants under this section shall not be relevant expenditure of the Council for the purposes of section 1 of the Local Government Act 1966. 1966 c. 42.

(2) In section 83(4) of the Capital Allowances Act 1968 and, in relation to chargeable periods ending on or before 5th April 1968, in section 35(3) of the Finance Act 1966 (which specify certain grants the making of which in respect of any expenditure disentitles the grantee to investment allowances or initial allowances in respect of that expenditure) at the end of the paragraph (*c*) added by section 161(3) of the Act of 1968 there shall in each case be inserted the words " or

1968 c. 3. 1966 c. 18.

(*d*) a grant made under section 3 of the Transport (London) Act 1969 ".

PART II

THE LONDON TRANSPORT EXECUTIVE

London Transport Executive.

4.—(1) For the purpose of implementing the policies which it is the duty of the Council under section 1 of this Act to develop, there shall be constituted a public authority to be called the London Transport Executive who shall be a body corporate with perpetual succession and a common seal and shall consist of—

(*a*) a chairman appointed by the Council; and

(*b*) not less than four nor more than ten other members appointed by the Council after consultation with the chairman of the Executive.

(2) The chairman and other members of the Executive shall be appointed by the Council from among persons who appear to the Council to have had wide experience of, and shown capacity in, transport, industrial, commercial or financial matters, administration, applied science, or the organisation of workers.

(3) Before appointing a person to be a member of the Executive, the Council shall satisfy themselves that he will have no such financial or other interest as is likely to affect prejudicially the discharge by him of his functions as a member of the

PART II Executive, and the Council shall also satisfy themselves from time to time with respect to every member of the Executive that he has no such interest; and any person who is, or whom the Council propose to appoint to be, a member of the Executive shall, whenever requested by the Council so to do, furnish to the Council such information as the Council consider necessary for the performance by the Council of their duties under this subsection.

(4) The Executive—

(*a*) shall pay to the members thereof such salaries or fees, and such allowances, as the Council may from time to time determine, and

(*b*) as regards any of the members in whose case the Council determine that such provision should be made, shall pay such pensions to or in respect of those members, or enter into and carry into effect agreements or arrangements with some other person for securing or preserving such pension rights for those members, as the Council may determine;

and if a person ceases to be a member of the Executive, otherwise than on the expiration of his term of office, and it appears to the Council that there are special circumstances which make it right that that person should receive compensation, the Council may require the Executive to pay to or in respect of that person a sum of such amount as the Council may determine.

1953 c. 25. (5) Section 15 of the Local Government Superannuation Act 1953 (which enables local authorities to admit to their superannuation schemes employees of statutory undertakers) and section 6(1)(*k*) of this Act shall have effect as if members of the Executive were employees of the Executive; but where a member of the Executive is admitted to participate in the benefits of a superannuation fund maintained by a local authority or of a pension fund or scheme in which employees of the Executive or any subsidiary of theirs participate—

(*a*) subsection (4)(*b*) of this section shall not apply to him; and

(*b*) the Executive shall make any payments which are required to be made in respect of him to the superannuation fund by the employing authority or, as the case may be, to the pension fund or under the pension scheme by the employer, and may make from his remuneration any deductions which the employing authority or, as the case may be, the employer might make in respect of his contributions to that fund or under that scheme if he were an employee of the Executive.

(6) So much of subsection (4) of this section as requires that the pensions, if any, which are to be paid in the case of members of the Executive are to be determined by the Council shall not apply in relation to any pension payable apart from the provisions of that subsection.

(7) The provisions of Schedule 1 to this Act shall have effect as regards the Executive.

General duties of Executive and other bodies with respect to passenger transport services for Greater London.

5.—(1) Subject always to the requirements of section 7(3) of this Act, it shall be the general duty of the Executive to exercise and perform their functions, in accordance with principles from time to time laid down or approved by the Council, in such manner as, in conjunction with the Railways Board and the Bus Company, and with due regard to efficiency, economy and safety of operation, to provide or secure the provision of such public passenger transport services as best meet the needs for the time being of Greater London.

(2) It shall be the duty of the Executive, the Railways Board and the Bus Company, either acting directly, or acting indirectly through subsidiaries of theirs, to co-operate with one another in the exercise and performance of their respective functions for the purpose—

(*a*) of co-ordinating the passenger transport services provided by, or by subsidiaries of, those authorities respectively; and

(*b*) of securing or facilitating the proper discharge of the Executive's duty under subsection (1) of this section,

and to afford to one another such information as to their services as may be reasonably required for those purposes; and for the purposes of such co-operation those authorities shall have power to enter into such arrangements with one another with respect to the exercise and performance of their respective functions on such terms as may appear to them to be expedient.

(3) It shall be incumbent on the Executive to take such steps as appear to them to be practicable and desirable for promoting—

(*a*) research on lines settled from time to time with the approval of the Council into matters affecting, or arising out of, the exercise of the functions of the Executive or any subsidiary of theirs; and

(*b*) the doing of such work as is requisite to enable there to be turned to account—

(i) the results of any research into any such matter as aforesaid (whether or not promoted by the Executive); and

PART II

(ii) anything resulting from any idea affecting, or arising out of, the exercise of any of those functions.

(4) The Executive may take such steps as are referred to in subsection (3) of this section with respect to any matter either by themselves carrying out the necessary research or doing the necessary work or by arranging for that research to be carried out or that work to be done by some other person with or without assistance (including financial assistance) from the Executive; but nothing in this section shall authorise the Executive to do themselves, either directly or through a subsidiary, any work such as is mentioned in paragraph (*b*) of the said subsection (3) which the Executive would not have power to do apart from this section.

(5) The Council may give directions to the Executive with respect to the exercise and performance of the Executive's functions under subsections (3) and (4) of this section.

(6) Nothing in subsection (1), (2) or (3) of this section shall be construed as imposing, either directly or indirectly, any form of duty or liability enforceable by proceedings before any court to which the Executive, the Railways Board or the Bus Company, as the case may be, would not otherwise be subject.

General powers of Executive.

6.—(1) Subject to the provisions of this Act, the Executive shall have power—

(*a*) to carry passengers by any form of land or water transport (including in either case hovercraft) within, to or from Greater London;

(*b*) so far as the Executive consider requisite—

(i) in connection with the exercise of their powers under paragraph (*a*) of this subsection, or

(ii) in order to avoid an interruption of services formerly provided by the London Board,

to carry passengers as mentioned in the said paragraph (*a*) between places outside Greater London;

(*c*) in any vehicle or vessel used for the carriage of passengers in pursuance of paragraph (*a*) or (*b*) of this subsection, or in another vehicle drawn by or with, or propelled with, any vehicle so used, to carry also luggage and other goods;

(*d*) to let passenger vehicles on hire with or without other vehicles drawn by or with, or propelled with, those passenger vehicles for the carriage of goods;

(*e*) to store within Greater London or in any premises of the Executive outside Greater London goods which have been or are to be carried by the Executive or a subsidiary of theirs and, so far as any premises provided for the purposes of that or any other part of their business are not required for those purposes, to use them to provide facilities for the storage of other goods;

(*f*) to make arrangements with any person providing passenger transport services by air for the provision of such services between places in Greater London or between such places and places outside Greater London, and to include in such arrangements provision for the making of payments to that person by the Executive;

(*g*) to supply, maintain and repair anything required for the purposes of the business of, or of a subsidiary of, the Executive or any of the national transport authorities or for the purposes of the Council;

(*h*) to supply to any person spare parts and components for passenger road vehicles disposed of by the Executive in the exercise of their powers under section 14(1)(*e*) of the Act of 1962 as applied by subsection (2) of this section, or by a subsidiary of the Executive, as being no longer required for the purposes of their business, and, for the purpose of supplying such spare parts or components which the Executive are satisfied cannot be satisfactorily obtained for the purpose by any other means, to manufacture them;

(*i*) subject to any directions by the Council, to construct, manufacture and produce anything which is required for any of the purposes of, or of a subsidiary of, the Executive or any of the national transport authorities or for the purposes of the Council;

(*j*) subject to any directions by the Council, at any place where the Executive, in the exercise of their powers under section 14(1)(*d*) of the Act of 1962 as applied by subsection (2) of this section, provide a car park, to repair motor vehicles for any persons, and to sell to any persons petrol, oil and spare parts and accessories for motor vehicles, whether or not those persons are using the car park;

(*k*) subject to any directions by the Council, to establish and administer pension schemes and pension funds in the interest of persons who are or have been employed by, or by a subsidiary of, the Executive or the London Board or by any other person of whom the Council are satisfied that the Executive are a successor in title, and

Part II

to pay pensions to or in respect of such persons, or to enter into and carry into effect agreements or arrangements with any other person for securing or preserving pension rights for such persons;

(*l*) with the consent of the Council, to lend money to be applied for the purposes of a pension scheme under which the Executive or a subsidiary of theirs pay employer's contributions or are subject to any other obligations;

(*m*) to do anything necessary for the purpose of fulfilling a contract entered into by the London Board before the vesting date notwithstanding that apart from this paragraph the Executive would not have power to do that thing;

but if the Executive engage, either directly or through a subsidiary, in any activities authorised by paragraph (*d*) or (*j*) of this subsection, the Executive shall in carrying on those activities act as if they were a company engaged in a commercial enterprise or, as the case may be, shall exercise their control over that subsidiary so as to ensure that the subsidiary in carrying on those activities acts as a company so engaged.

(2) Subject to the provisions of this Act, the following provisions with respect to the powers of the Boards, namely—

(*a*) section 11 of the Act of 1962 and section 49(1) to (3) of the Act of 1968 (which relate to the development of land);

(*b*) section 12 of the Act of 1962 (which relates to pipelines) so far as it relates to the construction and operation of pipe-lines required for the purposes of the business of a Board other than the operation of pipelines;

(*c*) sections 14(1) to (4) and 16 of the Act of 1962 and section 50(7) to (9) of the Act of 1968 (which contain supplemental provisions relating to the powers of the Boards);

(*d*) section 15 of the Act of 1962 (which relates to the power of the Minister to authorise the compulsory purchase of land by a Board);

(*e*) section 17(1) and (2) of the Act of 1962 (which relate to powers to promote or oppose Bills and orders);

(*f*) section 25(1) and (2) of the Act of 1962 and section 51(2) and (4) to (6) of the Act of 1968 (which relate to subsidiaries);

PART II

(*g*) section 43 of the Act of 1962 and sections 50(10) and (so far as relating to the said section 43) 51(2) of the Act of 1968 (which contain general provisions as to charges and facilities of the Boards),

shall apply to the Executive as they applied, apart from any other provision of the Act of 1962 or of 1968, to the London Board and have effect accordingly as if the Executive were one of the Boards, except that in their application to the Executive those provisions other than section 15 of the Act of 1962 shall have effect as if for any reference to the Minister there were substituted a reference to the Council.

(3) Subsection (1)(*l*) of this section and subsections (3) and (4) of section 14 of the Act of 1962 as applied by subsection (2) of this section shall not affect the power of the Executive—

(*a*) to lend money by way of investment or to subscribe for or acquire securities by way of investment; or

(*b*) to leave outstanding any loan made or guarantee given, or to retain any securities acquired, before the vesting date by the Commission or the London Board.

(4) The Council, the Executive and any subsidiary of the Executive shall each have power to enter into and carry out agreements with one another for the giving of assistance to one another by making available to the assisted party any services or facilities provided by, or any property of, the assisting party on such terms as may be agreed between those parties; and in section 72(2) of the London Government Act 1963 (which sets out the authorities for whom the Council may purchase, store and supply goods) at the end there shall be added the following paragraph:— 1963 c. 33.

" (*h*) the London Transport Executive and any subsidiary within the meaning of the Transport (London) Act 1969 of that Executive."

(5) Each of the powers conferred on the Executive by the foregoing provisions of this section shall be deemed to be in addition to, and not in derogation of, any other powers so conferred; and it is hereby declared that those provisions relate only to the capacity of the Executive as a statutory corporation, and nothing in those provisions shall be construed as authorising the disregard by the Executive of any enactment or rule of law.

(6) If at the vesting date any action has been taken by the London Board for the purpose of promoting a Bill in Parliament in pursuance of the powers conferred by, and with the consent of the Minister under, section 17 of the Act of 1962, the Executive may proceed with the promotion of that Bill as if that action had been taken by them in pursuance of the powers

PART II

conferred by, and with the consent of the Council under, the said section 17 as applied by subsection (2) of this section.

Financial duty of Executive.

7.—(1) In respect of each accounting period of the Executive, the Executive shall charge to revenue account, and secure that any subsidiary of theirs so charges, all charges which are proper to be made to revenue account, including, in particular, proper provision for the depreciation or renewal of assets.

(2) Without prejudice to the power of the Executive to establish specific reserves, they shall establish and maintain a general reserve, and the Council may give to the Executive directions as to any matter relating to the establishment or management of that general reserve, or the carrying of sums to the credit thereof, or the application thereof; but no part of the moneys comprised in that general reserve shall be applied otherwise than for purposes of the Executive or a subsidiary of theirs.

(3) The Executive shall so perform their functions as to ensure so far as practicable—

(*a*) that at the end of each such period as may from time to time be agreed for the purpose of this paragraph between the Executive and the Council the aggregate of the net balance of the consolidated revenue account of the Executive and any subsidiaries of theirs and the net balance of the general reserve of the Executive is such (not being a deficit) as may be approved by the Council with respect to that period, and

(*b*) that, if at the end of any accounting period of the Executive the said aggregate shows a deficit, the amount properly available to meet charges to revenue account of the Executive and their subsidiaries in the next following accounting period of the Executive exceeds those charges by at least the amount of that deficit.

(4) The Executive may, with the consent of the Council, make charges to capital account representing interest on expenditure of a capital nature (including expenditure of a capital nature incurred by the London Board before the vesting date), being interest for any period which ends on or before the end of the accounting period of the Executive in which the project or scheme to which the expenditure relates is in the opinion of the Council completed.

(5) The Executive shall from time to time, at such times, in such form and manner, and as respects such periods, as the Minister may after consultation with the Council require, submit to the Minister a statement approved by the Council of the

Executive's proposals for expenditure on capital account by the Executive and any subsidiaries of theirs; and—

(*a*) the Minister from time to time by notice in writing to the Executive may impose a limit on such expenditure by the Executive and their subsidiaries; and

(*b*) the Executive shall secure that any such expenditure is restricted within that limit.

(6) The Council, in exercising or performing their functions under this Act, shall have regard—

(*a*) to the duty imposed on the Executive by subsection (3) of this section; and

(*b*) to the provisions of subsection (5) of this section; and

(*c*) to any limit on capital expenditure by the Executive and their subsidiaries imposed by the Minister under the said subsection (5);

and where the requirements of paragraph (*b*) of the said subsection (3) fall to be complied with by the Executive, the Council shall take such action in the exercise and performance of their functions under this Act as appears to the Council to be necessary and appropriate in order to enable the Executive to comply with those requirements.

(7) For the purposes of subsections (1) and (3) of this section, the provisions of section 51(5) of the Act of 1968 shall be disregarded.

Borrowing by and loans to Executive.

8.—(1) The Executive may borrow temporarily, by way of overdraft or otherwise, from any person such sums as they may require for meeting their obligations and discharging their functions; but the Executive shall ensure that the aggregate of the amount outstanding in respect of any temporary loans raised by the Executive under this subsection or raised by any subsidiary of the Executive does not at any time exceed such amount as the Council may for the time being have approved.

(2) The Executive may, with the approval of the Council, borrow otherwise than by way of temporary loan from any person and in any manner such sums as the Executive may require for all or any of the following purposes, namely—

(*a*) for meeting any expenses properly chargeable to capital, being expenses incurred in connection with the provision or improvement of assets in connection with their business;

(*b*) for the provision of working capital;

(*c*) for acquiring an undertaking or part of an unaertaking;

(*d*) for the making of any payment which they are required by or under this Act to make by way of compensation;

PART II

(*e*) for subscribing for or acquiring securities of a body corporate otherwise than by way of investment ;

(*f*) for the payment of interest charged to capital account under section 7(4) of this Act ;

(*g*) to pay off any debt incurred by the Executive or any liability (including the fulfilment of any guarantee given by the Commission or the London Board) assumed by or transferred to the Executive in pursuance of this Act ;

(*h*) for making any loan, or fulfilling any guarantee given, in pursuance of the powers conferred on the Executive by this Act ;

(*j*) for any purpose for which capital moneys are properly applicable, whether or not specified in the foregoing paragraphs of this subsection ;

and the Executive shall exercise their control over any subsidiary of theirs so as to ensure that the subsidiary does not borrow otherwise than by way of temporary loan from any person without the approval of the Council or for any purpose other than purposes of the subsidiary such as are specified in paragraphs (*a*) to (*e*) and (*j*) of this subsection or for paying off any debt incurred by the subsidiary.

(3) The approval of the Council to a borrowing by the Executive under subsection (1) or (2) of this section from a person other than the Council shall operate as a guarantee by the Council of the repayment of the principal of, and the payment of interest on, the sum borrowed.

1963 c. 33. (4) In Schedule 2 to the London Government Act 1963, in sub-paragraph (2) of paragraph 27 (which specifies the classes of persons to whom the Council may make loans under that paragraph) after paragraph (*b*) there shall be inserted the following paragraph:—

" (*bb*) the London Transport Executive ";

and notwithstanding anything in paragraphs 25 to 29 of that Schedule the Council shall have power to lend to the Executive any amount which the Executive desire to borrow under subsection (1) of this section and for that purpose may themselves borrow temporarily, by way of overdraft or otherwise, from any person such sums as they may require so to lend to the Executive.

(5) Any loan by the Council to the Executive shall be made at a rate of interest sufficient to ensure so far as reasonably practicable that having regard to all the circumstances existing at the time when the loan to the Executive is made no loss will be incurred by the Council in respect of that loan.

(6) All moneys borrowed by the Executive shall be charged indifferently on all their revenues, and all securities created by the Executive shall rank equally without any priority; but nothing in this subsection shall affect any right to priority conferred by a security for any liability assumed by or transferred to the Executive in pursuance of this Act. PART II

(7) The provisions of this section shall have effect subject to any order made under section 1 of the Borrowing (Control and Guarantees) Act 1946, and for the purposes of that Act and any such order the Executive shall be deemed to be a local authority within the meaning of that Act. 1946 c. 58.

(8) The Executive shall be deemed to be a local authority for the purposes of—

(*a*) the enactments relating to loans by or borrowing from the Public Works Loan Commissioners; and

(*b*) section 203 of the Local Government Act 1933 and section 278 of the Local Government (Scotland) Act 1947 (which relieve lenders from making certain inquiries); 1933 c. 51. 1947 c. 43.

and the Minister may, on the application of the Executive made with the approval of the Council, by order provide for the application with or without modifications to borrowing by the Executive of any specified statutory provision relating to borrowing by a local authority.

(9) References in this section to borrowing do not include—

(*a*) borrowing by the Executive from a subsidiary of theirs; or

(*b*) the receipt of money by the Executive in the course of the carrying on of a savings bank operated by the Executive or the use by the Executive of money so received; or

(*c*) the receipt or use by the Executive of money of a pension fund established for the purposes of a pension scheme in which employees of the Executive or a subsidiary of theirs participate.

Provisions as to insurance by Executive.

9.—(1) Section 130 of the Local Government Act 1948 (which relates to insurance by local authorities against accidents to members) shall apply to the Executive as it applies to a local authority. 1948 c. 26.

(2) In subsection (2) of section 202 of the Act of 1960 (which specifies certain vehicles to which the requirements of section 201 of that Act as to users of motor vehicles being insured or

Part II

secured against third-party risks are not to apply) at the end there shall be added the following paragraph:—

1968 c. 73.

"(*e*) to a vehicle owned by the London Transport Executive or by a body which is within the meaning of the Transport (London) Act 1969 (but disregarding section 51(5) of the Transport Act 1968) a wholly-owned subsidiary of that Executive, at a time when the vehicle is being driven under the owner's control."

Accounts of Executive.

10.—(1) The Executive shall—

(*a*) cause proper accounts and other records in relation to their business to be kept; and

(*b*) prepare an annual statement of accounts in respect of such accounting period, in such form, and containing such particulars, compiled in such manner, as the Council may from time to time direct.

(2) The accounts of the Executive shall be audited by an auditor or auditors to be appointed annually by the Council, and any person so appointed as auditor shall be either the district auditor or some other person who is a member, or is a firm in Scotland each of the partners wherein is a member, of one or more of the following bodies namely—

the Institute of Chartered Accountants in England and Wales;

the Institute of Chartered Accountants of Scotland;

the Association of Certified and Corporate Accountants;

the Institute of Chartered Accountants in Ireland;

the Institute of Municipal Treasurers and Accountants;

any other body established in the United Kingdom who are—

(*a*) a body of accountants, and

1948 c. 38.

(*b*) for the time being recognised for the purposes of section 161(1)(*a*) of the Companies Act 1948 by the Board of Trade;

and any auditor so appointed shall be entitled to require from any officer of the Executive or of any subsidiary of theirs such books, deeds, contracts, accounts, vouchers, receipts and other documents, and such information and explanations, as may be necessary for the performance of his duties.

Additional provisions as to control of Executive by Council.

11.—(1) In addition to any power of the Council under any other provision of this Act to give directions to the Executive as respects any matter, the Council may give to the Executive general directions as to the exercise and performance by the Executive of their functions (including the exercise of rights conferred by the holding of interests in companies) in relation to matters appearing to the Council to affect the policies and measures which it is the duty of the Council under section 1 of this Act to develop, organise or carry out.

(2) Without prejudice to any requirement as to the approval or consent of the Council in any other provision contained in or applied by this Act, the Executive shall submit to the Council and obtain the Council's approval of—

(*a*) such annual or other estimates of income or expenditure of the Executive and any subsidiaries of theirs as the Council may require to be so submitted;

(*b*) any major change proposed to be made in any of those estimates after their approval by the Council;

(*c*) any proposal for expenditure by the Executive or any subsidiary of theirs which involves a substantial outlay on capital account;

(*d*) the general level and structure of the fares to be charged for the time being for the carriage of passengers by the Executive or any subsidiary of theirs on railway services or London bus services;

(*e*) any proposal by the Executive to form, promote or assist, or to join with any other person in forming, promoting or assisting, a company for carrying on any activities which the Executive have power to carry on.

(3) Unless the Council are of opinion that in all the circumstances it is unnecessary so to do, they shall cause particulars of the general level and structure of the fares referred to in subsection (2)(*d*) of this section as for the time being approved by the Council to be published in such manner as the Council may determine, and the Executive shall comply with any directions of the Council as to that publication; and the Council may direct the Executive to submit proposals for an alteration in the Executive's fare arrangements to achieve any object of general policy specified by the Council in the direction.

(4) The Executive shall provide the Council at such times or intervals and in such form and manner as the Council may require with information with respect to the operations and the expenditure on capital and revenue account respectively which are planned or under consideration by the Executive, and shall furnish the Council with such returns, accounts and other information with respect to the property and activities of the Executive or any subsidiary of theirs as the Council may from time to time require.

(5) In connection with the discharge of their functions under subsections (2)(*d*) and (3) of this section with respect to fares

Part II

for the carriage of passengers by the Executive's railways, the Council—

(*a*) shall in each year consult with the council of any county within which any of those railways are situated as to the general level and structure of such fares or journeys within, to or from that county ; and

(*b*) before approving any proposal for a change of substance in that general level and structure submitted to them for that purpose by the Executive shall inform the council of that county of that proposal and consider any offer by that council to make a financial contribution to the Executive in respect of the provision of services for the carriage of passengers by the Executive's railways within, to or from that county ;

and the Council shall so exercise their powers under subsection (4) of this section as to enable them to inform the council of that county in advance of any proposal by the Executive for a change of substance in the level of the provision made for such journeys.

(6) The Council may from time to time cause a review to be made of the organisation of the Executive's undertaking and may give to the Executive such directions as appear to the Council from any such review to be requisite to secure that the Executive's undertaking is organised in the most efficient manner ; and the Executive shall not make, or permit to be made, any substantial change in the manner in which their undertaking is organised except in pursuance of a direction given by the Council under this subsection or with the approval of the Council.

Minister's power to prevent improper conduct of subsidiary activities.

12.—(1) Where the activities of the Executive or any subsidiary of theirs include the carrying on—

(*a*) of the business of providing services for the carriage of passengers by road which both do not, and if section 23(2)(*a*) of this Act had not been passed would not, require authorisation by a road service licence ; or

(*b*) of any business of a description which the Executive are authorised to carry on by section 6(1)(*i*) of this Act,

subsection (2) of this section shall apply to that business.

(2) In the case of any business to which this subsection applies the annual report of the Executive under section 15 of this Act for any accounting period shall include a statement of—

(*a*) the amount, as determined by the Executive, of the turnover of the Executive or subsidiary for that period in respect of that business ;

PART II

(*b*) the extent or approximate extent (expressed in either case in monetary terms) to which, as so determined, the carrying on of that business contributed to, or restricted, the profit or loss of the Executive or subsidiary for that period before taxation;

(*c*) the method by which any determination for the purposes of paragraph (*a*) or (*b*) of this subsection was arrived at; and

(*d*) such further information, if any, relating to the carrying on by the Executive or subsidiary of that business as the Minister may from time to time direct.

(3) If, where the Executive or any subsidiary of theirs carry on any business to which subsection (2) of this section applies, it appears at any time to the Minister that, having regard to all the circumstances appearing to the Minister to be relevant, the charges made by the Executive or subsidiary in the course of that business are unduly low having regard to the cost of carrying on that business, the Minister shall, after consultation with the Council and with the Executive, either—

(*a*) direct the Executive to make, or, as the case may be, to ensure that the subsidiary makes, such modifications in their or its method of conducting that business as may be specified in the direction; or

(*b*) direct the Executive to discontinue, or, as the case may be, to ensure that the subsidiary discontinues, that business.

(4) The Minister may by order provide that subsection (2) of this section shall apply with or without modifications of that subsection and subsection (3) of this section—

(*a*) to any specified business carried on by the Executive or a subsidiary of theirs, being business of a description which the Executive are authorised by section 6(1)(*d*), (*g*), (*h*) or (*j*) of this Act to carry on; or

(*b*) to any other specified business of the Executive or any subsidiary of theirs, being business which appears to the Minister to be of a character only subsidiary or incidental to the discharge of the Executive's duty under section 5(1) of this Act and to be carried on on a substantial scale.

(5) The Executive shall secure that no subsidiary of theirs carries on any business with respect to which the Minister has given the Executive a direction under subsection (3)(*b*) of this section.

PART II

Machinery for negotiation and consultation with staff.

13. Section 137 of the Act of 1968 (which relates to machiner for negotiation and consultation with staff) shall apply to th Executive as if they were the Executive for a designated are within the meaning of section 9(1) of that Act and as i the Council were the Authority for that designated area, excep that a copy of any such agreement as is referred to in subsectio (2) of the said section 137 entered into by the Executive and o any instrument varying the terms of any such agreement shal be sent to the Secretary of State for Employment and Produc tivity as well as to the Council.

Users' consultative body.

14.—(1) As soon as may be after the vesting date, the Council shall establish a consultative body for the purpose of considering, and, where it appears to that body to be desirable, making recommendations with respect to, any matter affecting the services and facilities provided by the Executive which, not being concerned with the charges made for any service or facility or with a proposal for such a closure as is referred to in section 25(1) of this Act of a station or line on their railways—

(*a*) has been the subject of representations (other than representations appearing to that body to be frivolous) made to that body by or on behalf of users of those services or facilities; or

(*b*) has been referred to that body by the Council or by the Executive; or

(*c*) appears to that body to be a matter to which consideration ought to be given;

and copies of the minutes, conclusions and recommendations of that body shall be sent to the Council and to the Executive.

(2) Before the Council appoint any person to be a member of the body aforesaid they shall consult with such as they consider appropriate of any bodies appearing to them to be representative of the interests of persons likely to be significantly concerned with matters within the competence of the body aforesaid.

(3) The Council may give to the Executive any directions which, after consultation with the Executive and having regard to the provisions of section 7(6) of this Act, the Council think fit with respect to the matters dealt with in any recommendation of the body aforesaid.

(4) The Council shall provide the body aforesaid with such officers and servants, and such office accommodation, as appear to the Council to be requisite for the proper discharge of that body's functions.

(5) The Council may pay to the members of the body aforesaid such allowances as the Council may determine, being

allowances of such description and not exceeding such amount as might have been paid by that body if that body had been a body to which Part VI of the Local Government Act 1948 applies. Part II 1948 c. 26.

15.—(1) The Executive shall as soon as may be after the end of each of their accounting periods make to the Council a report on the exercise and performance of the Executive's functions during that period and shall send a copy of that report to the Minister; and the Council shall cause that report to be published in such manner as the Council think fit. Annual report by Executive.

(2) In addition to including the statement required by section 12(2) of this Act, the report of the Executive for any accounting period shall also set out—

(*a*) the statement of accounts for that period referred to in section 10(1)(*b*) of this Act, together with the report on that statement made by the auditor or auditors by whom the Executive's accounts for that period were audited; and

(*b*) any direction given in pursuance of this Act to the Executive during that period by the Council or by the Minister.

Part III

Transfers of Property, Rights, Liabilities and Functions

16.—(1) Subject to the provisions of this Act, on the appointed day for the purposes of this section (in this Act referred to as "the vesting date") all property, rights and liabilities of the London Board shall be transferred to, and by virtue of this Act vest in, the Executive. Transfer of property etc. of London Board.

(2) In the case of the following property, rights and liabilities of the London Board, that is to say—

(*a*) property which immediately before the vesting date was used or appropriated for use for the purposes of the part of the Board's undertaking commonly known as country buses and coaches and not for any other purposes of the Board;

(*b*) property situated outside Greater London which immediately before that date was provided for the convenience or information both of passengers on road services forming part of the activities of the said part of the Board's undertaking and of passengers on other road services of the Board;

PART III

(*c*) rights and liabilities subsisting immediately before that date for the purposes of the activities of the said part of the Board's undertaking,

subsection (1) of this section shall not apply but, subject to the provisions of this Act, the property, rights and liabilities in question shall on the vesting date be transferred to, and by virtue of this Act vest in, such company, being a wholly-owned subsidiary of the Bus Company, as the Bus Company may by notice published in the London Gazette designate for the purpose (hereafter in this Act referred to as " the designated company ").

(3) Schedule 2 to this Act shall apply to any transfer under this section, and subsections (1) and (2) of this section shall have effect subject to the provisions of that Schedule.

Disposal of London Board's statutory functions.

17.—(1) As from the vesting date the statutory provisions referred to in Schedule 3 to this Act shall have effect in accordance with the provisions of that Schedule.

(2) Subject to the said Schedule 3 and to any other provision in this Act, as from the vesting date the functions of the London Board under any statutory provision other than the Act of 1962, the Act of 1968 and this Act, including any such provision passed or made between the passing of this Act and the vesting date, shall be transferred in accordance with the subsequent provisions of this section.

(3) If and so far as the statutory provision—

(*a*) relates to that part of the London Board's undertaking, or to property, transferred by this Act to the Executive or, as the case may be, to the designated company ; or

(*b*) authorises the carrying out of works designed to be used in connection with the part of the London Board's undertaking so transferred or the acquisition of land for the purpose of carrying out such works,

the functions of the London Board under that statutory provision shall be transferred to the Executive or, as the case may be, to the designated company.

(4) If the statutory provision authorises the London Board to appoint, nominate, or concur in or approve the appointment or nomination of, a member of some body or the holder of some other office—

(*a*) this Act shall not affect the tenure of office of any person appointed or nominated under that statutory provision before the vesting date ; and

PART III

(b) subject to paragraph (a) of this subsection, the functions of the London Board under that statutory provision shall be transferred to the Executive, or to the designated company, or to both the Executive and the designated company acting either jointly or separately, as the Minister may by order direct.

(5) Subject to the foregoing provisions of this section, the functions of the London Board under any such statutory provision as is mentioned in subsection (2) of this section shall be transferred to the Executive.

Provisions as to pensions functions.

18.—(1) Subject to subsection (3) of this section, the provisions of subsections (2) to (9) of section 74 of the Act of 1962 (which relate to the Minister's power to make orders about pensions) shall have effect as if—

(a) the expression "Board" included the Executive; and

(b) the references in subsection (1)(a)(ii) of that section to the Commission included references to the London Board; and

(c) the reference in subsection (2)(a) of that section to a pension scheme in which employees of the Commission or a subsidiary of the Commission participated before the date there mentioned included a reference to a pension scheme in which employees of, or of a subsidiary of, the London Board participated before the vesting date.

(2) The Minister shall by order under the said section 74 as applied by subsection (1) of this section provide for the rights, liabilities and functions of the London Board relating to pensions or pension schemes, and any property held by that Board on trust for a pension scheme, to be divided between the Executive and the designated company, and on the vesting date transferred to them respectively, in such manner as he considers appropriate; and—

(a) that order may apply to the transfer under the order such of the provisions of Schedule 2 to this Act subject to such modifications as the Minister may consider appropriate; and

(b) save as may be provided by that order, the provisions of sections 16 and 17 of this Act shall not apply in relation to the property, rights, liabilities or functions to which the order relates.

(3) Nothing in the provisions of the said section 74 as applied by subsection (1) of this section shall prejudice the powers con-

PART III ferred on the Executive by section 6(1)(*k*) of this Act, and the powers conferred on the Minister by the said section 74—

(*a*) except on the application of the Executive made with the approval of the Council—

(i) shall not be exercisable in relation to any pension scheme established in pursuance of the powers conferred on the Executive as aforesaid; or

(ii) in the case of any Executive-transferred scheme which is a London transport scheme, shall not be exercisable in relation to participants in that scheme who are or have been employees of, or of a subsidiary of, the Executive; and

(*b*) except as aforesaid, and except where the Minister is satisfied that the exercise proposed of those powers will not result in any increase in the obligations or liabilities of the Executive, shall not be exercisable in the case of any other Executive-transferred scheme in relation to participants in that scheme who are or have been such employees as aforesaid;

and nothing in, or in any order made under, the said section 74 as applied as aforesaid shall require the consent or approval of the Minister to any action by the Executive with respect to such only of the participants in any pension scheme as are or have been such employees as aforesaid.

In this subsection, the expression "Executive-transferred scheme" means a pension scheme in connection with which rights, liabilities and functions of, or property held by, the London Board have been transferred to the Executive under subsection (2) of this section, and the expression "London transport scheme" means a pension scheme specified in Part 2 of the Schedule to the British Transport Reorganisation (Pensions of Employees) (No. 3) Order 1962, or established by or for the former London Transport Executive set up under the Transport Act 1947 or by or for the London Board.

S.I. 1962/2758.

1947 c. 49.

(4) Any person who—

(*a*) on or before the vesting date, ceases to be employed by one, and becomes employed by another, of the following bodies, namely, the London Board, the Executive, any of the national transport authorities and any subsidiary of that Board, the Executive or any of those authorities; or

(*b*) on the transfer date for the purposes of any transfer under section 21(3) or 22(2) of this Act is employed by a company which immediately before that date was a subsidiary of one body but on that date becomes a subsidiary of another body,

shall not in consequence cease to be eligible to participate in any pension scheme in which he was a participant immediately before so ceasing to be employed or, as the case may be, immediately before that transfer date.

(5) In the application of subsection (3) or (4) of this section to a pension scheme the benefits under which are or will be receivable as of right, persons who have obtained pension rights under the scheme without having contributed under the scheme shall be regarded as participants in the scheme; and the reference in the said subsection (4) to being eligible to participate in a pension scheme shall be construed accordingly.

(6) Subsections (4) and (5) of this section shall have effect subject to any order under the said section 74 made by virtue of subsection (1) of this section, being an order taking effect on or at any time after the vesting date.

Transfer or extinguishment of London Board's debts to Minister and power to make deficit grants to Board.

19.—(1) On the vesting date—

(*a*) there shall be extinguished—

(i) the commencing capital debt of the London Board under section 39 of the Act of 1962; and

(ii) the liability of the London Board in respect of the principal of all sums lent to that Board by the Minister under section 20 of that Act;

(*b*) the Council shall assume a debt due to the Minister (hereafter in this section referred to as the Council's "transferred capital debt") on such terms as may be imposed by the Minister under subsection (3) of this section;

(*c*) the Executive shall assume a debt due to the Council (hereafter in this section referred to as the Executive's "commencing capital debt") of an amount equal to the Council's transferred capital debt on the terms described in subsection (7) of this section; and

(*d*) the commencing capital debt of the Bus Company under Schedule 2 to the Act of 1968 shall be increased in accordance with the provisions of this section.

(2) The amount of the Council's transferred capital debt and of the increase of the Bus Company's commencing capital debt taken together shall be equal to one-tenth of the aggregate amount extinguished under subsection (1)(*a*) of this section; and the respective amounts of that debt and that increase shall be equal to such proportions respectively of the amount of that one-tenth as the Minister may by order prescribe having regard to the manner in which the property, rights and liabilities of the

PART III

London Board to which section 16 of this Act applies are divided under that section between the Executive and the designated company.

(3) Subject to subsection (4) of this section, the rate of interest payable on the transferred capital debt of the Council, the time when the principal is to be paid off and the other terms of the debt shall be such as the Minister may with the approval of the Treasury from time to time direct; and—

(*a*) any sums received by the Minister by way of interest on, or repayment of, that debt shall be paid into the National Loans Fund; and

(*b*) in section 44(1) of the Act of 1968 (which requires an account by the Minister of the receipt and disposal of certain sums) at the end there shall be added the following paragraph:—

"(*c*) any sums which, being received by the Minister by way of interest on, or the repayment of, the transferred capital debt of the Greater London Council under section 19 of the Transport (London) Act 1969, are required by subsection (3)(*a*) of that section to be paid by the Minister into the National Loans Fund."

(4) For the purposes of any period between the vesting date and the date of the making of the order under subsection (2) of this section the Minister may estimate what the transferred capital debt of the Council and the increase in the commencing capital debt of the Bus Company are likely to be and require the Council and the Bus Company to make to him provisional payments by way of interest on the appropriate estimated amount; and those provisional payments shall be on account of the payments of interest becoming due—

(*a*) in the case of the Council, under subsection (3) of this section;

(*b*) in the case of the Bus Company, under section 39(6) of the Act of 1962 as applied by paragraph 1 of Schedule 2 to the Act of 1968.

(5) The Minister may from time to time, but not later than the expiration of the period of five years beginning with the vesting date, by order vary the amounts prescribed under subsection (2) of this section where that appears to him expedient to take account of any adjustments in pursuance of provisions of this Act in the property, rights and liabilities of the London Board transferred respectively to the Executive and to the designated company, and any such order may contain such transitional provisions as appear to the Minister expedient to

PART III

ake account of any interest underpaid or overpaid on the transferred capital debt of the Council or, as the case may be, on the commencing capital debt of the Bus Company.

(6) The Minister's power to make an order under subsection (2) or (5) of this section shall be subject to the approval of the Treasury; and any such order shall be subject to annulment in pursuance of a resolution of the Commons House of Parliament.

(7) In the case of the commencing capital debt of the Executive, the rate of interest payable, the time when the principal is to be paid off, and the other terms of that debt, shall be the same (subject to the necessary adaptations) as those for the time being applicable under subsection (3) of this section in the case of the transferred capital debt of the Council; and—

(*a*) if any variation is made by an order under subsection (5) of this section in the transferred capital debt of the Council, the like variation shall be made in the commencing capital debt of the Executive and the Council may by directions to the Executive make such transitional provision as appears to the Council expedient to take account of any interest underpaid or overpaid on the commencing capital debt of the Executive;

(*b*) for the purposes of the period referred to in subsection (4) of this section the Council may require the Executive to make to them provisional payments of the like amount as are required to be made by the Council to the Minister and those provisional payments shall be on account of the payments of interest becoming due under this subsection.

(8) The Minister may, with the approval of the Treasury, make grants to the London Board or, after the vesting date, to the Executive to meet any deficit arising on the revenue account of the London Board in respect of the period beginning with 1st January 1969 and ending with the vesting date.

Power of Council to direct preparation of proposals for transfers of functions etc.

20.—(1) Subject to subsection (2) of this section, the Council may direct the Executive to prepare and submit to the Council proposals for arrangements whereby—

(*a*) specified transport services or facilities for the time being provided by, or by a subsidiary of, the Executive will instead be provided by some other person or will be discontinued; or

(*b*) specified transport services or facilities which the Executive have power to provide but which are for the time being provided by some person other than the

PART III

Executive or a subsidiary of theirs will instead be provided by, or by a subsidiary of, the Executive;

and, subject to any directions of the Council, any such proposals may include arrangements agreed between the Executive, any subsidiary of theirs and the other person concerned for the transfer between the Executive or that subsidiary and that other person of property, rights and liabilities; and on receiving any such proposals, the Council may direct the Executive to give effect to those proposals either without modification or with such modifications as may be specified by the Council, or not to proceed with the proposals, as the Council may think fit.

(2) The Council shall give to the Minister not less than eight weeks notice of their intention to give any direction to the Executive under subsection (1) of this section and shall furnish the Minister with all such information appearing to him to be relevant in connection with the direction as he may require; and if it appears to the Minister that the implementation of arrangements such as are required by the direction to be proposed or, as the case may be, the giving of effect to the proposals in accordance with the direction would be likely to result in the Executive and their subsidiaries ceasing to be the main providers, apart from the Railways Board, the Bus Company and their subsidiaries, of the passenger transport services required to meet the needs of Greater London, he may at any time before the expiry of that notice direct the Council to modify their proposed direction to the Executive in such manner as the Minister may specify, or not to proceed with the giving of their direction to the Executive, as the Minister may think fit.

Schemes for transfers between Executive and Railways Board or Bus Company.

21.—(1) Subject to subsection (2) of this section, the Executive and the Railways Board, or the Executive and the Bus Company, acting jointly, may as occasion seems to them to require it make schemes for the transfer from one to another of the Executive, that Board or, as the case may be, that Company, and any wholly-owned subsidiary of the Executive or that Board or, as the case may be, Company of any specified property, rights and liabilities, or of all property, rights and liabilities comprised in a specified part of the transferor's undertaking; and any such scheme may contain such supplementary, incidental and consequential provision as may appear to the Executive and the Railways Board or, as the case may be, to the Executive and the Bus Company to be necessary or expedient.

(2) A scheme under this section shall not come into force unless it has been approved by the Minister after consultation with the Council or until such date as the Minister may in giving his approval specify; and the Minister may approve a scheme either without modification or with such modification as,

after consultation with the Council, with the Executive and with the Railways Board or, as the case may be, the Bus Company, he thinks fit; but, without prejudice to his powers under section 22 of this Act, the Minister shall not approve any such scheme which makes provision for a transfer of any property, rights or liabilities which it appears to him would materially prejudice the proper discharge by the Executive, the Railways Board or the Bus Company of their respective functions.

(3) Subject to subsection (4) of this section, the property, rights and liabilities to which any such scheme relates shall on the date of the coming into force of the scheme be transferred, and by virtue of the scheme vest, in accordance with the scheme.

(4) Schedule 4 to the Act of 1968 shall apply to any transfer under subsection (3) of this section subject to any reference in that Schedule to a vesting by virtue of that Act being construed as a reference to a vesting by virtue of the scheme in question, and as if any other reference in that Schedule to that Act (otherwise than in a reference to a particular provision of that Act) were a reference to this Act; and that subsection shall have effect subject to the provisions of that Schedule.

Orders by Minister for transfers between Executive and Railways Board or Bus Company.

22.—(1) Subject to subsection (4) of this section, the Minister may by order—

(*a*) transfer from one to another of the Executive and their wholly-owned subsidiaries, or from, or from a wholly-owned subsidiary of, one to, or to such a subsidiary of, the other of—

(i) the Executive and the Railways Board; or

(ii) the Executive and the Bus Company,

any functions of, or of that subsidiary of, the Executive, that Board or that Company, as the case may be, being functions in connection with the carriage of passengers, and for that purpose amend any of the enactments relating to those functions;

(*b*) make any such provision with respect to, or to any wholly-owned subsidiary of, the authority or either of the authorities in question as is mentioned in section 21(1) of this Act,

and any such order shall make provision for the protection of the interests of persons transferred by or under the order from one employment to another and may contain such supplementary, incidental and consequential provision as may appear to the Minister to be necessary or expedient.

(2) Subject to subsection (3) of this section, in the case of an order under subsection (1) of this section making such provision as is mentioned in section 21(1) of this Act, the property, rights

PART III

and liabilities in question shall on such date as may be appointed for the purpose by the order be transferred, and by virtue of this Act vest, in accordance with the order.

(3) Schedule 4 to the Act of 1968 shall apply to any transfer under subsection (2) of this section and shall so apply as if for any reference in that Schedule to that Act (otherwise than in a reference to a particular provision of that Act) there were substituted a reference to this Act, and that subsection shall have effect subject to the provisions of that Schedule.

(4) The power to make orders under this section shall not be exercisable so as to cause all or substantially all of the functions of the Executive to become functions of, or of wholly-owned subsidiaries of, the Railways Board and the Bus Company; and before making any order under this section the Minister shall consult with the Council, the Executive, the Railways Board or, as the case may be, the Bus Company, and such other persons, if any, as the Minister may think fit, and lay a draft of the proposed order before each House of Parliament; and the order shall not be made unless that draft has been approved by resolution of each House of Parliament.

PART IV

PUBLIC SERVICE VEHICLES, RAILWAY CLOSURES AND PASSENGER TRANSPORT CHARGES

Regulation of services by public service vehicles in and around London.

23.—(1) As from the vesting date, any enactment passed before this Act which makes special provision as to the regulation of services by public service vehicles in the London Passenger Transport Area or the London Special Area shall cease to have effect; and, subject to the provisions of this section and Schedule 4 to this Act, Part III of the Act of 1960 shall have effect accordingly within as well as outside the limits of those areas.

(2) As from the vesting date, no person other than the Executive or a subsidiary of theirs shall provide a London bus service except in pursuance of an agreement with the Executive or under a consent continued in force or granted under Schedule 4 to this Act, and notwithstanding anything in Part III of the Act of 1960—

(*a*) no road service licence shall be required for the provision of any bus service operated wholly as a London bus service; and

(*b*) where such a licence is granted in respect of a bus service operated in part only as a London bus service, no condition shall be attached to the licence with respect to the carriage of passengers who are both taken up and set down in Greater London ; **Part IV**

and any such licence in force immediately before the vesting date, if or so far as that licence relates to the operation of a London bus service, and any condition attached to such a licence, if or so far as that condition relates to the carriage of passengers who are both taken up and set down in Greater London, shall cease to have effect.

(3) Where it is proposed—

(*a*) to provide a bus service which is to be operated wholly or in part as a London bus service and which has not been provided continuously since immediately before the vesting date, whether the proposed service is to be provided by, or by a subsidiary of, the Executive or by some other person in pursuance of an agreement under subsection (2) of this section ; or

(*b*) to vary a bus service which is being, and has at all times since before the vesting date been, operated as aforesaid,

then, before deciding on, or on the provisions to be contained in such an agreement with respect to, or on any variation affecting, the route of that service or a terminal point, point at which passengers may or may not be taken up or set down, or place at which, or street by the use of which, vehicles used for that service may turn at a terminal point, the Executive shall, so far as the service is or is to be provided in Greater London, consult with the Council, with the commissioner or commissioners of police concerned, with any of the councils of the London boroughs or the Common Council within whose area that route, point, place or street is situated, and with any other person whom it appears proper to the Executive for them to consult.

(4) Where any agreement under subsection (2) of this section relates to a bus service part only of which is operated as a London bus service, any provision contained in that agreement with respect to the carriage of passengers other than those who are both taken up and set down in Greater London shall be of no effect if or so far as it is inconsistent with any condition for the time being attached to any road service licence under which the bus service is provided.

(5) If any person provides a bus service in contravention of subsection (2) of this section, he shall be liable on summary conviction to a fine not exceeding £200 ; but proceedings for an offence under this subsection shall not be instituted except by or on behalf of the Director of Public Prosecutions, or by or with the authority of the Executive or a commissioner of police.

Part IV

(6) Section 21 of the Act of 1968 (which contains provisions as to the functions of traffic commissioners in connection with designated areas within the meaning of section 9(1) of that Act) shall have effect as if, except for the purposes of subsection (1)(*b*) of that section, Greater London were such a designated area and the Executive were the Executive for that designated area and as if—

(*a*) the reference in subsection (4) of the said section 21 to an agreement made for the purposes of section 19(2) of that Act included a reference to an agreement under subsection (2) of this section ; and

(*b*) the reference in subsection (5)(*a*)(iii) of the said section 21 to Schedule 6 to that Act included a reference to Schedule 4 to this Act ;

and subsections (2) and (3) of the said section 21 (which relate to disputes as to whether a service is or is not an excursion or tour) shall have effect for the purposes of this section as if references therein to an excursion or tour included references to an express feeder service.

(7) In this section and Schedule 4 to this Act—

" bus service " means a service for the carriage of passengers by road for which a road service licence is required, or would but for subsection (2)(*a*) of this section be required, other than an excursion or tour within the meaning of the Act of 1968 ;

" commissioner of police " means, in relation to the metropolitan police district, the Commissioner of Police of the Metropolis and, in relation to the City of London, the Commissioner of Police for the City of London ;

" express feeder service " means, subject to section 21(2) and (3) of the Act of 1968 as applied by subsection (6) of this section, a bus service—

(*a*) for the carriage of passengers to a terminal point in Greater London for the purpose of enabling those passengers to transfer to another vehicle forming part of a service of express carriages proceeding from that terminal point to a place outside Greater London, or for the carriage from a terminal point in Greater London of passengers who have transferred at that terminal point from another vehicle forming part of a service of express carriages proceeding to that terminal point from a place outside Greater London, and in either case whether or not the terminal point, other vehicle or service of express carriages in question is the same in the case of all those passengers ; and

PART IV

(*b*) in the case of which the following conditions are satisfied, that is to say—

(i) that no separate fare is charged for the conveyance to or from the terminal point; and

(ii) that the vehicle in which the passengers are carried is operated by or in association with the person providing the service of express carriages and is being used solely for the purpose of carrying passengers to and from the terminal point of that service;

" London bus service " means a bus service which is, or so far as it is, a service on which passengers may be taken up and set down at different places within Greater London, whether or not any passengers on that service may also be taken up or set down outside Greater London, but does not include an express feeder service;

" road service licence " has the same meaning as for the purposes of the Act of 1960 and includes a permit granted under section 30 of the Act of 1968.

Amendments as to functions of traffic commissioners in Metropolitan Traffic Area.

24.—(1) The provisions of the Act of 1960 with respect to traffic commissioners for traffic areas other than the Metropolitan Traffic Area shall apply also to the Metropolitan Traffic Area; and accordingly section 122 of that Act (which provides for a single traffic commissioner for the Metropolitan Traffic Area) shall cease to have effect.

(2) Without prejudice to section 163 of the Act of 1960, section 120(1) of that Act shall not by reason of subsection (1) of this section operate to confer on the traffic commissioners for the Metropolitan Traffic Area powers and duties as regards licences to drive, or act as conductor of, public service vehicles.

(3) In its application to the traffic commissioners for the Metropolitan Traffic Area, section 121(4) of the Act of 1960 shall have effect as if—

(*a*) Greater London were a county and the Council were the council of that county; and

(*b*) the City of London were a borough and the Common Council were the council of that borough.

(4) In the Act of 1960—

(*a*) in section 135(2) (which relates to the councils whose representations must be taken into consideration by traffic commissioners in granting or refusing a road service licence) after the word " by " in the last place where it occurs there shall be inserted the words " any of the following councils, namely, the Greater London

PART IV

Council, the council of any London borough, the Common Council of the City of London";

(*b*) in section 135(7) (which relates to the persons to whom notice of a grant of a road service licence must be sent) for the words " the council of every " there shall be substituted the words " each of the following councils, namely, the Greater London Council, the council of any London borough, the Common Council of the City of London, the council of any " and for the word " every " in the last place where it occurs there shall be substituted the word " any ";

(*c*) in sections 135(8) and 163(1), for the words " traffic commissioner " wherever they occur there shall be substituted the words " traffic commissioners ";

(*d*) in section 143(2)(*a*) (which relates to the persons who may appeal against a refusal of the traffic commissioners to vary the conditions attached to a road service licence) at the beginning there shall be inserted the words " the Greater London Council, the council of any London borough, the Common Council of the City of London ".

(5) Any reference in any statutory provision passed or made before the coming into force of this section to the traffic commissioner for the Metropolitan Traffic Area shall be construed as a reference to the traffic commissioners for that area, or to the chairman of those commissioners, as the context may require.

(6) The person who on the appointed day for the purposes of this section is the traffic commissioner for the Metropolitan Traffic Area shall be deemed to have been appointed on that day under section 121 of the Act of 1960 as chairman of the traffic commissioners for that area and until the other two traffic commissioners for that area have been appointed under subsection (4) of that section may act alone for the purposes of the discharge of any functions of the traffic commissioners for that area.

Railway closures in and around Greater London.

25.—(1) In subsections (7) to (9) and (13) of section 56 of the Act of 1962 and subsection (1) of section 54 of the Act of 1968 (being provisions relating to proposals by the Railways Board or the London Board for a closure, that is to say, the discontinuance of all railway passenger services from any station or on any line), references to the London Board shall be construed as references to the Executive.

(2) Where the Railways Board propose the closure of a station in Greater London or of a line the whole or part of which lies in Greater London, the Board shall send a copy of the notice of the closure published by the Board in pursuance

of subsection (7) of the said section 56 to the Council, and the Council may, within the period specified in the notice for objecting to the closure, lodge with the Minister a statement in writing that they oppose the closure and of their reasons for doing so; and where the Council lodge such a statement with the Minister they shall send a copy of that statement to the Board and, notwithstanding that no objection is lodged in accordance with subsection (8) of the said section 56, the closure shall not be proceeded with until the Minister has given his consent. PART IV

(3) Where under the said subsection (8) or under subsection (2) of this section any closure proposed by the Railways Board or by the Executive of a station in Greater London or of a line the whole or part of which lies in Greater London requires the consent of the Minister, the Minister shall before deciding whether or not to give his consent consult with the Council.

Grants on refusal of Minister's consent to closure by Executive.

26.—(1) Where under section 56(8) of the Act of 1962 the consent of the Minister is required to a proposed closure by the Executive, and the Minister refuses his consent to that closure, and the Minister is satisfied—

(*a*) that the railway passenger services for the time being provided by the Executive from the station or on the line in question are unremunerative; and

(*b*) that it is desirable for social or economic reasons that railway passenger services from that station or on that line should for the time being continue to be provided by the Executive either in the same or in some different form or manner; and

(*c*) that because of the unremunerative nature of the services which the Minister is satisfied are desirable for those reasons (hereafter in this section referred to as "the required services") the Executive cannot reasonably be expected to provide them without assistance under this section,

then, subject to the provisions of this section, the Minister may from time to time with the consent of the Treasury undertake to make grants to the Executive in respect of the provision of the required services for such period not exceeding three years at a time as the Minister may think fit.

(2) The Minister may on giving an undertaking under subsection (1) of this section as respects any period attach to that undertaking such conditions in connection with the provision of the required services during that period, and such other conditions in connection with the grants to be made in pursuance of the undertaking, as he thinks fit.

(3) The aggregate amount payable by way of grants in pursuance of an undertaking under subsection (1) of this section

PART IV

in respect of the period to which the undertaking relates shall, subject to any conditions attached to the undertaking, be the amount by which it is estimated, on such basis and in such manner as the Minister, with the approval of the Treasury and after consultation with the Executive, may determine, that the expenditure properly attributable to the provision during that period of the required services will exceed the revenue properly so attributable; and payments in pursuance of the undertaking shall be made in such manner and at such times as the Minister may with the approval of the Treasury determine.

Removal of control of Transport Tribunal over passenger fares in London.

27.—(1) Sections 44 to 49 of the Act of 1962 (which relate to the control of passenger fares in London by the Transport Tribunal) shall cease to have effect and, subject to the provisions of this Act, the powers conferred by section 43 of that Act shall be exercisable accordingly.

(2) During the period between the appointed day for the purposes of subsection (1) of this section and the vesting date, the London Board shall not make any alteration in the general level or structure of the fares to be charged for the time being for the carriage of passengers by the Board or any subsidiary of theirs unless their proposals for that alteration have been submitted to and approved by the Minister; and the Minister may direct the Board to cause any such alteration approved by him to be published in such manner as he may determine; and for the purposes of section 11(2)(*d*) and (3) of this Act the general level and structure of the fares aforesaid in force at the vesting date shall be deemed as from that date to have been submitted by the Executive to and approved by the Council.

(3) Any approval of the Minister under subsection (2) of this section shall be given in writing and may be given for any case or description of cases specified in the approval, or may be general, and may be given subject to conditions.

(4) For the purposes of subsection (2) of this section, subsection (2) of section 41 of this Act shall have effect as if there were substituted—

(*a*) for any reference to the Executive a reference to the London Board; and

(*b*) for any reference to the Council a reference to the Minister;

and subsection (3) of that section shall apply to any direction given to the London Board by the Minister under subsection (2) of this section or under subsection (2) of that section as applied by this subsection as it applies to a direction given to the Executive by the Council and accordingly as if for the relevant references in the said subsection (3) to the Council and the Executive

PART IV

there were substituted references respectively to the Minister and the London Board.

(5) As from the appointed day for the purposes of subsection (1) of this section, the division of the Transport Tribunal which under section 57(2) of the Act of 1962 is to be known as the London Fares and Miscellaneous Charges Division shall be known as the Railway Rates Division.

Fixing of certain charges by Railways Board.

28. As from the appointed day for the purposes of section 27(1) of this Act, in fixing in the exercise of their powers under section 43 of the Act of 1962 the charges to be made for the carriage of passengers by their railways on services determined in accordance with principles from time to time laid down by the Council to be required to meet the needs of Greater London, the Railways Board shall have regard to such financial objectives for those services as the Minister (after consultation with the Council) and the Board may from time to time agree; and the Board shall in each year consult with the Council as to the general level and structure of the fares to be charged for the carriage of passengers by the Board's railways on journeys wholly within Greater London and as to the general level of the provision to be made for such journeys and shall inform the Council in advance of any proposals for changes of substance in any such fares or in the level of the provision so to be made.

PART V

PROVISIONS AS TO HIGHWAYS AND TRAFFIC

Amendments as to metropolitan roads.

1963 c. 33.

29.—(1) Subsections (1) to (3) of section 17 of the London Government Act 1963 (which specify the highways which are to be metropolitan roads, that is to say, the highways for which the Council are the highway authority) shall cease to have effect, and references in any enactment to metropolitan roads shall be construed as references to—

(*a*) any highway or proposed highway in Greater London which is for the time being classified under section 27(2) of the Local Government Act 1966 as a principal road for the purposes of advances under section 235 of the Highways Act 1959; and

1966 c. 42.

1959 c. 25

(*b*) any other highway or proposed highway in Greater London which is for the time being designated as a metropolitan road by an order under section 7 of the said Act of 1959 directing that the highway shall cease to be a trunk road.

(2) A certificate by or on behalf of the Minister that any highway or proposed highway in Greater London is, or is not, for the time being classified as aforesaid shall be evidence of

PART V

the fact stated and any such certificate may describe the highway or proposed highway in question by reference to a map.

(3) The Council shall prepare and maintain a list of, and a map showing, the highways and proposed highways which are for the time being metropolitan roads and shall deposit a copy of that list and of that map with each of the councils of the London boroughs and the Common Council, and the Council and each of those other authorities shall make that list and map, or as the case may be the copies thereof so deposited with them, available for inspection by the public at all reasonable hours.

1963 c. 33. (4) In section 18 of the London Government Act 1963 (which relates to the delegation of functions of the Council with respect to a metropolitan road to the council of a London borough or the Common Council), after subsection (1) there shall be inserted the following subsection:—

"(1A) For the avoidance of doubt it is hereby declared that the functions of the Greater London Council which may be delegated by virtue of subsection (1) of this section include, and shall be deemed always to have included, the functions of that Council under the provisions of section 12
1967 c. 76. of the Road Traffic Regulation Act 1967 (being provisions relating to the temporary prohibition or restriction of traffic on roads), or, as respects any period before the coming into operation of the said section 12, under the corresponding
1960 c. 16. provisions contained in section 36 of the Road Traffic Act 1960, with respect to any metropolitan road in the case of which that Council have so delegated their functions with respect to the maintenance of that road."

(5) In this section, any expression (other than "metropolitan
1959 c. 25. road") which is also used in the Highways Act 1959 has the same meaning as in that Act.

(6) The provisions of this section other than subsection (4) thereof shall be deemed for the purposes of section 84 of the London Government Act 1963 (which relates to the making of supplementary and transitional provision by order) to be included in that Act.

Planning permission for development affecting metropolitan road.

30.—(1) The Minister may from time to time, after consultation with the Council, with the councils of the London boroughs and with the Common Council, direct that, for the purposes of regulations made by the Minister of Housing and Local Government under section 24(6) of the London Government Act 1963 (which enables that Minister by regulations to require particular applications, or applications of a particular class, for planning permission for development in Greater London to be referred in certain cases to that Minister or to the Council before they are

PART V

dealt with by the local planning authority), metropolitan roads and proposed metropolitan roads shall be divided into categories specified in the direction; and any such regulations—

(*a*) may designate a class of development, or a class of applications for planning permission for development, by reference to a particular category or categories only of those so specified; and

(*b*) may designate a class of such applications by reference to those only of the said roads included in a particular category or categories so specified in the case of which the Council have given to the local planning authority written notice containing such particulars as may be prescribed by the regulations of proposals by the Council with respect to the roads in question of such class as may be so prescribed, being proposals for the construction, improvement or alteration of those roads or for the regulation of means of access between premises and those roads.

(2) The Council shall prepare and maintain a list of, and a map showing, the metropolitan roads and the proposed metropolitan roads included in each respectively of the categories for the time being provided for by directions under subsection (1) of this section and shall deposit a copy of that list and of that map with each of the councils of the London boroughs and the Common Council, and the Council and each of those other authorities shall make that list and map, or as the case may be the copies thereof so deposited with them, available for inspection by the public at all reasonable hours.

(3) In this section the expression "proposed metropolitan road" means land which is not a proposed highway as defined by section 295(1) of the Highways Act 1959, but in the case of which— 1959 c. 25.

(*a*) the Council have applied to the Minister for the classification as a principal road of the highway proposed to be constructed on it; or

(*b*) the Council have given written notice to the local planning authority that the Council consider that it should be used for the provision of a metropolitan road.

Powers of Council where obstruction of highway is greater or longer than necessary.

31.—(1) If, in the case of any highway in Greater London which is not a trunk road, it appears to the Council that any of the following persons (hereafter in this section referred to as an "authorised person"), namely—

(*a*) any undertakers acting in the exercise of a statutory power to break up or open that highway; or

PART V

(*b*) where that highway is not a metropolitan road, the highway authority acting as aforesaid ; or

(*c*) any person acting in the exercise of the power conferred by section 15(1) of the Pipe-lines Act 1962 ; or

1962 c. 58.

(*d*) any person acting in the exercise of the power conferred by section 34(2) of the Public Health Act 1936,

1936 c. 49.

has by the deposit of excavated matter or other material, or by means of the erection of barriers, or otherwise, created an obstruction in the highway to a greater extent or for a longer period than is reasonably necessary, the Council may by notice require that authorised person to take such steps as may appear to the Council to be necessary and as are specified in the notice to mitigate or discontinue the obstruction ; and, subject to subsection (2) of this section, if that authorised person fails to comply with any such requirement within twenty-four hours of the receipt of the notice, the Council may take the necessary steps and may recover any expenses reasonably incurred by them in connection therewith from that authorised person.

(2) If, within twenty-four hours of receiving a notice under subsection (1) of this section, the authorised person in question makes representations to the Minister that the obstruction to which the notice relates is not greater, or has not been continued for a longer period, than is reasonably necessary, and sends to the Council a copy of the representations so made, the Council shall not take any such steps as aforesaid without the consent of the Minister.

(3) The Council may, if they think fit, delegate to an officer of the Council the power of making requirements conferred on the Council by this section.

(4) In this section, the expression " undertakers " means persons (other than persons acting on behalf of the Crown) having powers to break up or open highways in Greater London for the purposes of any sewerage system, or any water, gas, electricity, tramway or other undertaking, and any other expression (other than " metropolitan road ") which is also used in the Highways Act 1959 has the same meaning as in that Act.

1959 c. 25.

(5) The provisions of section 139 of the Highways Act 1959 as to the powers of highway authorities in the case of such obstruction as aforesaid shall cease to apply in relation to any metropolitan road, but save as provided in the foregoing provisions of this subsection or by subsection (6) of this section nothing in this section shall affect the operation of the said section 139.

(6) In subsection (1) of the said section 139 as amended by section 19 of the Pipe-lines Act 1962, after the words "Pipe-lines Act 1962" there shall be inserted the words "or by section 34(2) of the Public Health Act 1936". **Part V** 1962 c. 58. 1936 c. 49.

Amendments as to pedestrian crossings.

32.—(1) The Council shall be the local authority as respects Greater London for the purposes of section 21 of the Act of 1967 (which empowers a local authority to make schemes for the establishment on roads in their district other than trunk roads of crossings for foot passengers); and accordingly—

(*a*) in subsection (6) of that section (which defines the expression "local authority" as respects England and Wales other than Greater London and as respects Scotland) after paragraph (*b*) there shall be added the following paragraph:—

"(*c*) as respects Greater London, the Greater London Council"; and

(*b*) for subsection (8) of that section (which defines that expression in relation to Greater London and requires the Council to consult other authorities in Greater London before submitting certain schemes under that section) there shall be substituted the following:—

"(8) Before the Greater London Council submit any scheme under this section with respect to any road they shall consult with any other council, being the council of a London borough or the Common Council of the City of London, within whose area that road is situated."

(2) Any scheme with respect to a road in Greater London made, or having effect as if made, under the said section 21 by an authority other than the Council and in force immediately before the appointed day for the purposes of subsection (1) of this section shall be deemed to have been made by the Council and shall continue in force accordingly until varied or revoked by the Council or the Minister in accordance with subsection (4) of that section.

(3) On the appointed day aforesaid there shall be transferred to the Council—

(*a*) all traffic signs within the meaning of section 54(1) of the Act of 1967 placed in connection with any such scheme as aforesaid made in relation to a road in Greater London by any authority other than the Council; and

(*b*) subject to subsections (4) and (5) of this section, all other property or rights which, immediately before that day, were vested in that other authority for the pur-

PART V

poses of that scheme, and all liabilities incurred by that other authority for those purposes and not discharged before that day.

(4) There shall not be transferred to the Council by virtue of subsection (3) of this section any right or liability in respect of work done, services rendered, goods (including gas and electricity) supplied or money due for payment before the appointed day aforesaid.

(5) The Council and the other authority concerned may make agreements with respect to the transfer of property, rights and liabilities under subsection (3) of this section, including agreements for defining the property, rights and liabilities transferred, and for the transfer or retention of property, rights or liabilities held or incurred partly for the purposes of such a scheme as aforesaid and partly for other purposes ; and any dispute between the Council and that other authority as to the property, rights or liabilities transferred shall be determined by the Minister.

Expenditure on arrangements for patrolling school crossings.

33. In section 24 of the Act of 1967 (under which the appropriate authority for making arrangements for patrolling school crossings is, as respects places in England and Wales which are not in the metropolitan police district, other than places in the City of London, the council of the county or borough in which the places in question are and, as respects places in the metropolitan police district, the commissioner of police of the metropolis), after subsection (6) there shall be inserted the following subsection:—

" (6A) The expenses incurred for the purposes of this section by the council of a county any part of which is for the time being comprised in the metropolitan police district shall not be chargeable on that part."

Traffic signs. 1959 c. 25.

34.—(1) In section 64 of the Highways Act 1959 (which confers on a highway authority a general power to improve a highway maintainable at the public expense by them) at the end there shall be added the following subsection:—

" (4) In relation to any highway in Greater London maintainable at the public expense which is neither a trunk road nor a metropolitan road, subsections (2) and (3) of this section shall have effect for the purposes of, and of the provision of equipment for, the erection, maintenance, alteration or removal of traffic signs which are light signals for controlling the movement of vehicular traffic or of pedestrians, but for those purposes only, as if that highway were maintainable by the Greater London Council and not by the London borough council concerned or, as the case may be, by the Common Council."

(2) In section 55 of the Act of 1967 (which relates to the powers and duties of highway authorities as to the placing of traffic signs) at the end there shall be added the following subsection:— PART V

" (4) For the purposes of the provisions of this section and any other provisions of this Act relating to traffic signs—

(*a*) in the application of those provisions to traffic signs in Greater London which are light signals for controlling the movement of vehicular traffic or of pedestrians, but not in their application to any other matter, the Greater London Council shall at all times be deemed to be the highway authority for all roads in Greater London other than trunk roads ;

(*b*) without prejudice to the powers of the highway authority for the road in question, the Greater London Council shall also be deemed to be the highway authority for any road in Greater London for which they are not in fact the highway authority for the purposes, but for the purposes only, of the exercise by them as respects that road under section 56(1) of this Act of any powers exercisable by the highway authority for that road " ;

and accordingly subsection (2) of section 56 of that Act (which enables the Council to give directions to other highway authorities with respect to such light signals as aforesaid) shall cease to have effect.

(3) In subsection (1) of the said section 56 (under which the Council may, to such extent as the Council may consider necessary in connection with any order under section 6 or 9 of the Act of 1967 made or proposed to be made by the Council, exercise, as respects any road in Greater London which is not a trunk road, any powers exercisable by the highway authority for that road in connection with the placing of traffic signs on or near that road)—

(*a*) the provisions of that subsection shall be divided so that the words from " may " in the first place where it occurs to the words " the Council " in the third place where those words occur form paragraph (*a*) of that subsection ;

(*b*) after that paragraph (*a*) there shall be inserted the words " and

(*b*) may in any other circumstances after consultation with the highway authority concerned " ;

PART V

(*c*) for the words " not a trunk road " there shall be substituted the words " neither a trunk road nor a metropolitan road ".

(4) At the end of the said section 56 there shall be inserted the following subsection:—

" (4) The powers of the Council by virtue of paragraph (*b*) of subsection (1) above shall extend to the removal or repositioning of any traffic sign on or near the road in question whether or not placed by the Council, and on the removal or repositioning by the Council of any such sign placed by an authority other than the Council that sign shall vest in the Council; and, except with the consent of the Council or in pursuance of a direction under section 55(2) of this Act, the highway authority for that road shall not remove, alter or in any way interfere with any traffic sign placed or repositioned on or near that road by the Council by virtue of that paragraph."

(5) In section 104(1) of the Act of 1967, in the definition of " highway authority ", after the words " trunk road " in the first place where those words occur there shall be inserted the words " and subject to the provisions of section 55(4) of this Act ".

(6) On the appointed day for the purposes of subsection (2) of this section, there shall be transferred to the Council—

(*a*) all traffic signs which are such light signals as are mentioned in the subsection added by the said subsection (2) to section 55 of the Act of 1967 and which immediately before that date were vested in the council of any London borough or in the Common Council; and

(*b*) subject to subsections (7) and (8) of this section, all other property or rights which, immediately before that day, were vested in the council of a London borough or in the Common Council for the purposes of such light signals, and all liabilities incurred by the council of any London borough or the Common Council for such purposes and not discharged before that date.

(7) There shall not be transferred to the Council by virtue of subsection (6) of this section any right or liability in respect of work done, services rendered, goods (including gas and electricity) supplied or money due for payment before the appointed day aforesaid.

(8) The Council and the other authority concerned may make agreements with respect to the transfer of property, rights and liabilities under subsection (6) of this section, including agreements for defining the property, rights and liabilities transferred,

PART V

and for the transfer or retention of property, rights or liabilities, held or incurred partly for the purposes of such light signals as are mentioned in that subsection and partly for other purposes; and any dispute between the Council and that other authority as to the property, rights or liabilities transferred shall be determined by the Minister.

(9) Nothing in this section shall cause the Council to be treated for the purposes of the Public Utilities Street Works Act 1950 as the highway authority for any highway for which they would not be the highway authority apart from this section.

1950 c. 39.

Operation of parking places on highways where charges are made.

35. In section 35 of the Act of 1967, after subsection (5) (which enables the Council, without any application being made by the local authority, that is to say, the council of a London borough or the Common Council, to designate parking places on highways in the local authority's area where charges may be made for vehicles left therein, and by paragraph (*b*) empowers the Council to enter into an agreement with the local authority for the transfer to the local authority of the operation of any parking place so designated and of property, rights and liabilities of the Council in connection with that parking place) there shall be inserted the following subsection:—

"(5A) Where in the case of a parking place designated by an order made, or having effect as if made, by virtue of subsection (5) above, the Greater London Council have offered to enter into such an agreement with the local authority as is mentioned in paragraph (*b*) of that subsection but are satisfied that such an agreement cannot be reached, then, subject to sections 84A, 84B and 84C of this Act, the Council may by order provide that the operation of that parking place, and such apparatus or other things held by, and rights or liabilities of, the Council in connection with the parking place as may be specified in the order, shall be transferred to the local authority as from such date and on such terms (including terms as to the making of payments to or by the Greater London Council by or to the local authority) as may be so specified; and—

(*a*) paragraph (*c*) of subsection (5) above shall apply to the transfer of the operation of the parking place under the order as if it were a transfer in pursuance of an agreement under paragraph (*b*) of that subsection; and

(*b*) if the local authority fail to discharge any of their functions by virtue of the order the Greater London Council may themselves discharge those

PART V

functions and recover from the local authority summarily as a civil debt—

(i) any expenses incurred by the Council in discharging those functions; and

(ii) the amount of any payments falling to be made to the Council by the local authority under the order."

Control of off-street parking.

36.—(1) The provisions of this section shall apply to any area in Greater London which the Council may by regulations designate as a controlled area for the purposes of this section; and any such regulations—

(*a*) in addition to including any such provision as is authorised by subsection (6) of this section, may prescribe forms to be used for the purposes of this section and any other matters which under this section or Schedule 5 to this Act are to be prescribed;

(*b*) may include such supplementary, incidental and consequential provision as appears to the Council to be necessary or expedient for the purposes of this section; and

(*c*) may make different provision as respects like matters in different circumstances;

but the provisions of Part I of the said Schedule 5 shall apply to the making of any such regulations and no such regulations shall designate as aforesaid any area which for the purposes of the Airports Authority Act 1965 forms part of the British Airports Authority's aerodrome at Heathrow.

1965 c. 16.

(2) Subject to subsection (15) of this section, in a controlled area no person other than the local authority shall operate a public off-street parking place of a prescribed description except under and in accordance with the terms and conditions of a licence granted to that person by the local authority.

(3) An applicant for a licence in respect of any premises may apply either for a permanent licence or for a licence for such limited period not exceeding five years as the applicant may specify, and any application to the local authority for a licence shall be accompanied by the prescribed fee appropriate to the type of licence applied for towards the administrative expenses of the local authority under this section; and, subject to subsection (6) of this section, on any such application the local authority may at their discretion either grant the applicant a licence of the type applied for or refuse the application.

(4) Subject to subsection (6) of this section, every licence shall specify—

(*a*) the period of its duration, that is to say, whether it is a permanent licence or a licence for a limited period and, if for a limited period, the period for which it is granted;

(*b*) the maximum number of parking spaces to be provided at the licensed parking place for all, and, if the local authority think fit, for any respectively, of the following descriptions of parking, namely, short-term parking, long-term parking, casual parking and regular parking or any particular category of regular parking;

(*c*) any conditions in addition to those specified in subsection (5) of this section subject to which the licence is granted, being such conditions, if any, as the local authority may think fit with respect to all or any of the following matters, namely—

(i) the scale of charges, or the minimum charges, or the maximum and minimum charges, to be made for the use of parking spaces at the licensed parking place for all, or for any respectively, of the descriptions of parking referred to in paragraph (*b*) of this subsection;

(ii) the proportion of parking spaces to be available respectively for casual parking and for, or for any specified category of, regular parking;

(iii) the times of opening and closing of the licensed parking place for the reception of vehicles;

(iv) the manner in which users of the licensed parking place are to be informed of the effect of the terms and conditions of the licence;

(v) the keeping by the operator of the licensed parking place as respects all, or as respects any respectively, of the descriptions of parking referred to in the said paragraph (*b*) of records showing for each day the number of vehicles using parking spaces at the licensed parking place and the sums received by way of charges for the use of those parking spaces.

(5) It shall be a condition of every licence—

(*a*) that any person authorised in that behalf in writing by the local authority or by the Council may, subject to production if requested of his authority, at all reasonable hours enter upon and inspect the licensed parking place; and

Part V

(*b*) that the holder of the licence shall, on being given reasonable notice for the purpose by any such person, produce to that person and permit him to examine and make copies of, or take extracts from, any records required by virtue of subsection (4)(*c*)(v) of this section to be kept in connection with the operation of that parking place;

but if any such person discloses to any other person otherwise than in the performance of his duty any information with regard to the operation of that parking place or to any trade secret obtained by him at that parking place or from any such examination, or if any member or officer of the local authority to whom any such information is disclosed by reason of his official position discloses that information to any other person otherwise than in the performance of his duty, that person or, as the case may be, that member or officer shall be liable on summary conviction to a fine not exceeding £100.

(6) Regulations made by the Council under subsection (1) of this section may include provision—

(*a*) as to the maximum number of parking spaces to be made available at licensed parking places for all, or for any respectively, of the descriptions of parking referred to in subsection (4)(*b*) of this section in, or in any specified part of, any controlled area comprised within the area of a particular local authority;

(*b*) requiring that, in the case of licensed parking places in a particular controlled area or part of a controlled area, all or any of the matters referred to in subsection (4)(*c*) of this section shall or as the case may be shall not be the subject of conditions specified in the licence;

(*c*) regulating the conditions which may be imposed with respect to any of the matters aforesaid;

and every local authority shall exercise their functions under subsections (3) and (4) of this section in conformity with any regulations for the time being in force by virtue of this subsection.

(7) Where the local authority decide in pursuance of subsection (3) of this section—

(*a*) to refuse an application for a licence; or

(*b*) to grant a licence subject to any conditions which they are not required by regulations under subsection (6) of this section to impose with respect to any of the matters referred to in subsection (4)(*c*)(i) to (v) of this section, they shall inform the applicant in writing of the reasons for their decision at the same time as they inform him of that decision.

(8) Where a licence has been granted—

(*a*) the local authority shall, if so requested by a successor in title to the business (so far as it consists of the operation of the licensed parking place) of the person to whom the licence was granted, transfer the licence to that successor in title, but a licence shall not otherwise be transferable ;

(*b*) the holder of the licence may at any time surrender it by giving notice in writing for the purpose to the local authority which shall include a statement certifying either that the holder is the only person entitled to any interest in the licensed premises or that not less than twenty-one days before the date of the notice the holder has notified all other persons known to him to be so entitled of his intention to serve the notice ;

(*c*) the local authority may at any time on the application or with the agreement of the holder of the licence vary any of the terms and conditions specified in the licence under subsection (4)(*b*) and (*c*) of this section ;

(*d*) in the case of a permanent licence, the local authority shall have the powers of revocation or variation of the licence conferred by Part II of Schedule 5 to this Act.

(9) The provisions of Parts III and IV of Schedule 5 to this Act shall have effect with respect to appeals and compensation in connection with certain decisions of a local authority under this section ; and the local authority shall comply with the prescribed requirements as to the giving to an applicant for a licence of information as to the rights conferred by the said Parts III and IV ; and every person who applies for or is the holder of a licence in respect of any premises shall give to any other person known to him to be entitled to any interest in those premises information as soon as may be—

(*a*) of the making of the application ; and

(*b*) of any decision of the local authority relating to the premises of which he is, or is deemed under paragraph 14(2) of the said Schedule to have been, notified by the local authority ; and

(*c*) of the bringing, and of the determination or abandonment, of any appeal from any such decision brought by that person under the said Part III.

(10) Subject to subsection (15) of this section and to the provisions of Part V of Schedule 5 to this Act, any holder of a licence who contravenes or fails to comply with any of the

Part V

terms and conditions of the licence and who does not show that the contravention or failure was due to an act or omission of a person not connected with the operation of the licensed parking place which the persons so connected could not reasonably have been expected to prevent shall be liable on summary conviction—

(*a*) in the case of a term imposed under subsection (4)(*b*) or a condition with respect to any of the matters referred to in subsection (4)(*c*)(i), (ii), (iii) or (v) of this section, to a fine not exceeding £100 ;

(*b*) in any other case to a fine not exceeding £50 ;

and on the conviction of the holder of a licence of an offence under this subsection the court before whom he is convicted may, if on an application made for the purpose by the local authority the court is satisfied that it is proper so to do by reason of the extent to which, or the period over which, or the frequency with which, the holder of the licence has contravened or failed to comply with the terms and conditions of the licence or by reason of the wilfulness of the offence, make an order for the revocation of the licence.

(11) Save as provided by subsection (10) of this section or Part II of Schedule 5 to this Act, a licence shall not be revoked ; and the revocation of a licence in pursuance of an order under that subsection or the revocation or variation of a licence under the said Part II shall not take effect—

(*a*) before the expiration of the period for giving notice of appeal from the order or, as the case may be, notice of appeal under Part III of that Schedule from the local authority's decision to revoke or, as the case may be, vary the licence ; or

(*b*) if such a notice of appeal is duly given, until the effectiveness or otherwise of the order or, as the case may be, the local authority's decision is finally determined in accordance with the relevant procedure.

(12) Subject to subsection (15) of this section and to the provisions of Part V of Schedule 5 to this Act, any person who, in contravention of subsection (2) of this section, operates a public off-street parking place without holding a licence for the purpose shall be liable on summary conviction—

(*a*) to a fine not exceeding £200 ; or

(*b*) in the case of a second or subsequent conviction of an offence under this subsection, to a fine not exceeding £400.

(13) The local authority for a controlled area shall have regard to any regulations for the time being in force under this section when exercising in that area any of their functions

Part V

under sections 28 to 32 of the Act of 1967; and where a public off-street parking place is provided in a controlled area by the local authority under the said section 28, any such regulations shall apply to the operation of that parking place with such modifications as may be prescribed for the purpose, being modifications appearing to the Council to be necessary to ensure that the parking place is operated by or on behalf of the local authority with suitable provision as to the matters referred to in subsection (4)(*b*) and (*c*)(i) to (iv) of this section in like manner as if it were being operated under a licence granted by the local authority.

(14) In this section and in Schedule 5 to this Act—

"licence" means a licence under this section;

"local authority", in relation to a parking place, means, where the parking place is situated in a London borough, the council of that borough or, where the parking place is situated in the City of London, the Common Council;

"long-term parking" and "short-term parking" mean parking for a continuous period exceeding, or, as the case may be, not exceeding, four hours or such longer period as may be prescribed;

"public off-street parking place" means a place, whether above or below ground and whether or not consisting of or including buildings, where parking space for motor vehicles off the highway is made available by any person to the public for payment; and references to operating, or to the operator of, such a parking place shall be construed as references to making, or as the case may be to the person making, such parking space at the parking place so available.

(15) The Minister, after consultation with the Council, may at any time, if it appears to him expedient so to do by reason of any emergency which appears to him to have arisen or to be likely to arise, by order, which shall be laid before Parliament after being made, provide that this subsection shall apply either in relation to all areas for the time being designated as controlled areas or in relation to such part or parts of any of those areas as may be specified in the order; and—

(*a*) during the period while any such order is in force in relation to any controlled area or part thereof, any public off-street parking place in that area or part may be operated as if that area or part were not, or, as the case may be, were not comprised in, a controlled area; and

Part V

(*b*) nothing in subsection (10) or (12) of this section shall apply to anything done at any such parking place during that period.

Part VI

Miscellaneous and General

Compensation for loss of employment, etc.

37.—(1) The Minister shall by regulations require the payment by the Executive, the Railways Board or the Bus Company, as may be determined by or under the regulations, in such cases and to such extent as may be so determined, of compensation to or in respect of any person who is on the date of the happening of any of the following events, namely—

(*a*) a transfer of any property, rights or liabilities under section 16, 21 or 22 of, or Schedule 2 to, this Act, or in pursuance of a direction given under section 20(1) of this Act ; or

(*b*) any change in the manner in which the Executive's undertaking is organised made in accordance with section 11(6) of this Act in pursuance of a direction by, or with the approval of, the Council ; or

(*c*) the making of any adaptations such as are mentioned in paragraph 5(4) of Schedule 16 to the Act of 1968 as applied by paragraph 7(1) of Schedule 3 to this Act,

or who has before that date been, in any employment so determined and who suffers any loss of employment, or loss or diminution of emoluments or pension rights, or worsening of his position, which is properly attributable to the happening of that event.

(2) Any such regulations may apply in relation to any such person whether or not he continues in the employment determined as aforesaid until the date of the happening of the relevant event aforesaid, and whether or not he is a party to an agreement for the rendering of personal services which is affected by the happening of that event.

(3) Different regulations may be made under this section in relation to different classes of persons, and any such regulations may be so framed as to have effect from a date prior to the making thereof, so, however, that so much of any such regulations as provides that any provision thereof is to have effect as from a date earlier than the making thereof shall not place any person other than the person required to pay the compensation in a worse position than he would have been in if the regulations had been made to have effect only as from the making thereof.

(4) Regulations under this section—

(a) may prescribe the procedure to be followed in making claims for compensation, and the manner in which and the person by whom the question whether any or what compensation is payable is to be determined; and

(b) may in particular contain provisions enabling appeals from any determination as to any or what compensation is payable to be brought, in such cases and subject to such conditions as may be prescribed by the regulations, before a tribunal established under section 12 of the Industrial Training Act 1964. 1964 c. 16.

(5) No regulations shall be made under this section unless a draft thereof has been approved by a resolution of each House of Parliament.

(6) Where the Executive, the Railways Board or the Bus Company are required by any such regulations to pay compensation thereunder, the others of those authorities may arrange to make to the compensating authority payments by way of contributions towards the liability of the compensating authority under the regulations; and if the compensating authority satisfy the Minister that either of the other authorities have not made a proper contribution towards that liability, whether by payment of money or by finding employment for persons to or in respect of whom the compensation has become payable, the Minister may require that other authority to make such payment to the compensating authority as appears to the Minister to be just.

Payments on termination of appointment of members of London Board.

38.—(1) If a person ceases to be a member of the London Board, otherwise than on the expiration of his term of office, and it appears to the Minister that there are special circumstances which make it right that that person should receive compensation, then, if the Minister has not before the vesting date exercised his power under paragraph 8(1) of Schedule 1 to the Act of 1962 to require the London Board to make a payment for that purpose to that person, the Minister may with the approval of the Minister for the Civil Service require the Executive to make to that person a payment of such amount as the Minister may with the like approval determine.

(2) This section shall apply whether or not any pension is payable to the person in question under sub-paragraph (b) of the said paragraph 8(1), and shall apply to persons who ceased to be members of the London Board before the passing of this Act as well as to persons who cease to be members at a later time.

PART VI

Dissolution of London Board.

39.—(1) The London Board shall cease to exist on the vesting date.

(2) The Executive shall prepare a statement, in such form, and containing such particulars, compiled in such manner, as the Minister may with the approval of the Treasury direct, of the London Board's accounts for the period from the end of that dealt with in the last annual statement of accounts published by the London Board down to the vesting date.

(3) The Minister shall arrange that an auditor or auditors of the accounts aforesaid are appointed under section 24(2) of the Act of 1962 and the auditor or auditors so appointed shall, if the audit is not completed on the vesting date, continue and complete the audit after the vesting date; and any liability to pay the remuneration of the auditor or auditors so appointed outstanding on the vesting date shall be transferred to the Executive.

(4) The Executive shall as soon as may be after the vesting date make to the Minister a report on the exercise and performance by the London Board of their functions during any period since that dealt with in the last report made by the London Board under section 27(8) of the Act of 1962, and that report by the Executive—

(*a*) shall include a copy of the statement of accounts prepared under subsection (2) of this section and of the report on that statement made by the auditor or auditors appointed in pursuance of subsection (3) of this section; and

(*b*) shall set out any directions given by the Minister to the London Board during that period, unless the Minister has notified to the London Board or the Executive his opinion that it is against the interests of national security to do so; and

(*c*) shall include a statement of the salary or fees and emoluments of each of the members of the London Board during that period;

and the Minister shall lay a copy of that report before each House of Parliament.

(5) Any liability of the London Board in respect of payments by way of interest on, or the repayment of, the commencing capital debt of the Board under section 39 of the Act of 1962 or any sums lent to that Board by the Minister under section 20 of that Act, being payments in respect of a period before the vesting date which are outstanding at that date, shall be transferred to the Executive.

(6) As from the vesting date, the Minister may make to the Executive any payment under section 3 of the Selective Employment Payments Act 1966 which, as the designated Minister for the purposes of that section, he was authorised to make to the London Board and which had not been so made at that date.

PART VI
1966 c. 32.

40. Section 138 of the Act of 1968 (which relates to travel concessions) shall have effect—

Travel concessions.

(*a*) as if the expression " local authority " included the council of a London borough and the Common Council;

(*b*) as if the Executive were the Executive for a designated area within the meaning of section 9(1) of that Act and Greater London were that designated area; and

(*c*) as if the journeys referred to in subsection (1)(*a*) of the said section 138 included in the case of the Executive journeys between places outside but in the vicinity of Greater London;

and, in the application to the Executive of subsection (1) of the said section 138, the reference to the approval mentioned in that subsection as not required for any travel concessions granted under that subsection shall be construed as a reference to the approval of the Council under section 11(2)(*d*) of this Act.

41.—(1) Any approval or consent of the Council under any provision of, or applied by, this Act shall be given in writing; and any such approval or consent may be given for any case or description of cases specified in the approval or consent, or may be general, and may be given subject to conditions.

Provisions as to approvals, consents and directions.

(2) Nothing done by the Executive shall be held to be unlawful on the ground that the approval or consent of the Council to the doing of that thing was required by any provision of, or applied by, this Act and that it was done without obtaining that approval or consent; but if it appears to the Council that the Executive propose to do anything, or have done anything, without the approval or consent of the Council which in the opinion of the Council requires their approval or consent, the Council may give to the Executive such directions as appear to the Council to be appropriate to secure so far as practicable the observance of the rights of the Council in relation to the doing of that thing, and those directions may include directions to discontinue any specified activity or dispose of any specified assets.

(3) Any direction under this Act by the Council to the Executive or by the Minister to the Executive or to the Council shall be in writing, and the Executive or, as the case may be, the Council shall comply with any such direction given to them notwithstanding, in the case of a direction under subsection (2)

PART VI

of this section, that it may result in the Executive having to dispose of any assets at a loss or incurring liability to other persons; but before the Council give any direction to the Executive under this Act they shall consult with the Executive.

Power to modify Act by order.

42. In the event of any alteration in the boundaries of Greater London, the Minister may by order, which shall be subject to annulment in pursuance of a resolution of either House of Parliament, make any modifications to any of the provisions of this Act which appear to him to be necessary or expedient in consequence of that alteration.

Orders and regulations.

43. Any power to make orders or regulations conferred on a Minister by any provision of this Act shall be exercisable by statutory instrument; and any power to make an order conferred on a Minister by any provision of this Act shall include power to make an order under that provision varying or revoking any previous order thereunder.

Stamp duty.

1895 c. 16.

44.—(1) Nothing in section 12 of the Finance Act 1895 (which requires Acts to be stamped as conveyances on sale in certain cases) shall be taken as applying to this Act.

(2) Stamp duty shall not be chargeable—

1891 c. 39.

(*a*) under section 112 of the Stamp Act 1891 in respect of the amount which is to form the nominal share capital of the designated company, or in respect of any increase in the nominal share capital of that company which the Commissioners of Inland Revenue are satisfied is to take place before the vesting date; or

1899 c. 9.

(*b*) under section 8 of the Finance Act 1899 in respect of the amount proposed to be secured by an issue of loan capital by the designated company which those Commissioners are satisfied is to take place before that date,

if or to the extent that those Commissioners are also satisfied that the total capital of that company, whether nominal share capital or loan capital, on the vesting date will not exceed the total value of the assets less liabilities transferred to that company under section 16 of this Act.

(3) Stamp duty shall not be chargeable on any instrument which is certified to the Commissioners of Inland Revenue by the Executive or the Bus Company as having been made or executed in pursuance of Schedule 2 to this Act or in pursuance of Schedule 4 to the Act of 1968 as applied by section 22(3) of this Act; but no such instrument shall be deemed to be duly stamped unless it is stamped with the duty to which it would but for this subsection be liable or it has, in accordance with

the provisions of section 12 of the Stamp Act 1891, been stamped with a particular stamp denoting that it is not chargeable with any duty or that it is duly stamped. PART VI 1891 c. 39.

45.—(1) In this Act, except where the context otherwise requires, the following expressions have the following meanings respectively, that is to say— Interpretation.

" the Act of 1960 " means the Road Traffic Act 1960; 1960 c. 16.

" the Act of 1962 " means the Transport Act 1962; 1962 c. 46.

" the Act of 1967 " means the Road Traffic Regulation Act 1967; 1967 c. 76.

" the Act of 1968 " means the Transport Act 1968; 1968 c. 73.

" appointed day " means the relevant day appointed under section 47(5) of this Act;

" the Boards " means the Boards established under section 1 of the Act of 1962 other than the London Board, and references to a Board shall be construed accordingly;

" the Bus Company " means the National Bus Company established under section 24 of the Act of 1968;

" charges " includes fares, rates, tolls and dues of every description;

" the Commission " means the British Transport Commission dissolved in pursuance of section 80 of the Act of 1962;

" the Common Council " means the Common Council of the City of London;

" the Council " means the Greater London Council;

" the designated company " means the company designated under section 16(2) of this Act;

" the Executive " means the London Transport Executive established under section 4 of this Act;

" functions " includes powers, duties and obligations;

" goods " includes animals, parcels and mails;

" Greater London " means the administrative area of Greater London as for the time being constituted;

" hovercraft " has the same meaning as in the Hovercraft Act 1968; 1968 c. 59.

" land " includes land covered by water and any interest or right in, over or under land;

" lease " includes an agreement for a lease;

" liability " includes an obligation;

" the London Board " means the London Transport Board established under section 1 of the Act of 1962;

Part VI

"London bus service" has the meaning assigned by section 23(7) of this Act;

"the Minister" means the Minister of Transport;

"the national transport authorities" means the Boards, the Bus Company, the National Freight Corporation established under section 1 of the Act of 1968, the Scottish Transport Group established under section 24 of the Act of 1968 and the Transport Holding Company established under section 29 of the Act of 1962;

"participant", in relation to a pension scheme, means a person who (whether he is referred to in the scheme as a member, as a contributor or otherwise) contributes or has contributed under the scheme and has pension rights thereunder and "participate" shall be construed accordingly;

"pension", in relation to a person, means a pension, whether contributory or not, of any kind whatsoever payable to or in respect of him, and includes a gratuity so payable and a return of contributions to a pension fund, with or without interest thereon or any other addition thereto, and any sums payable on or in respect of the death of that person;

"pension fund" means a fund established for the purposes of paying pensions;

"pension rights" includes, in relation to any person, all forms of right to or liability for the present or future payment of a pension, and any expectation of the accruer of a pension under any customary practice, and includes a right of allocation in respect of present or future payment of a pension;

"pension scheme" includes any form of arrangement for the payment of pensions, whether subsisting by virtue of an Act of Parliament, trust, contract or otherwise;

"the Railways Board" means the British Railways Board established under section 1 of the Act of 1962;

"securities", in relation to a body corporate, means any shares, stock, debentures, debenture stock, and any other security of a like nature of the body corporate;

"statutory provision" means a provision, whether of a general or of a special nature, contained in, or in any document made or issued under, any Act, whether of a general or special nature;

"subsidiary" and "wholly-owned subsidiary" have the same meanings respectively as for the purposes of the Act of 1968;

PART VI

" vehicle " includes a hovercraft;

" the vesting date " means the appointed day for the purposes of section 16 of this Act.

(2) Except where the context otherwise requires, any reference in this Act to any enactment shall be construed as a reference to that enactment as amended, extended or applied by or under any other enactment, including this Act.

Expenses.

46. There shall be paid out of moneys provided by Parliament—

(*a*) any expenses incurred by any Minister under or in consequence of the provisions of this Act;

(*b*) any increase attributable to any of the provisions of this Act in the sums so payable under any other Act.

Short title, repeals, extent and commencement.

47.—(1) This Act may be cited as the Transport (London) Act 1969.

(2) The enactments specified in Schedule 6 to this Act are hereby repealed to the extent specified in the third column of that Schedule.

(3) The provisions of this Act other than—

(*a*) sections 8(8) and 9(2);

(*b*) section 27(5) and the repeal of section 57(3)(*a*) of the Transport Act 1962; and 1962 c. 46

(*c*) the repeals made in the House of Commons Disqualification Act 1957, 1957 c. 20.

shall not extend to Scotland.

(4) Except for the repeals made in the House of Commons Disqualification Act 1957, the provisions of this Act shall not extend to Northern Ireland.

(5) This Act shall come into force on such day as the Minister may by order appoint, and different days may be appointed for different purposes and different provisions of this Act.

SCHEDULES

Section 4.

SCHEDULE 1

THE LONDON TRANSPORT EXECUTIVE

1. The Executive may act notwithstanding a vacancy among their members.

2. The quorum of the Executive shall be three and, subject as aforesaid, the Executive may regulate their own procedure.

3. The application of the seal of the Executive shall be authenticated by the signature of the secretary of the Executive or some other person authorised by the Executive, either generally or specially, to act for that purpose.

4. Every document purporting to be an instrument issued by the Executive and to be sealed as aforesaid, or to be signed on behalf of the Executive, shall be received in evidence and be deemed to be such an instrument without further proof unless the contrary is shown.

5.—(1) A member of the Executive shall hold and vacate his office in accordance with the terms of his appointment and shall, on ceasing to be a member, be eligible for reappointment.

(2) Any member of the Executive may at any time by notice in writing to the Council resign his office.

6.—(1) A member of the Executive who is in any way directly or indirectly interested in a contract made or proposed to be made by the Executive shall disclose the nature of his interest at a meeting of the Executive; and the disclosure shall be recorded in the minutes of the Executive, and the member shall not take any part in any deliberation or decision of the Executive with respect to that contract.

(2) For the purposes of the foregoing sub-paragraph, a general notice given at a meeting of the Executive by a member of the Executive to the effect that he is a member of a specified company or firm and is to be regarded as interested in any contract which may, after the date of the notice, be made with that company or firm, shall be regarded as a sufficient disclosure of his interest in relation to any contract so made.

(3) A member of the Executive need not attend in person at a meeting of the Executive in order to make any disclosure which he is required to make under this paragraph if he takes reasonable steps to secure that the disclosure is made by a notice which is brought up and read at the meeting.

SCHEDULE 2

Section 16.

PROVISIONS AS TO TRANSFERS UNDER SECTION 16

Division or apportionment of certain property, etc.

1. It shall be the duty of the Executive, the Bus Company and the designated company to arrive, whether before or after the vesting date, and so far as practicable, at such written agreements with respect to any property, rights and liabilities transferred under section 16 of this Act, not being rights and liabilities under an agreement for the rendering of personal services, and to execute such other instruments, as are necessary or expedient—

(*a*) to make, as from the vesting date or as from such later date as may be specified in the relevant agreement, any clarifications or modifications of the division of the London Board's undertaking effected by the said section 16 which they consider will best serve the proper discharge of their respective functions ; or

(*b*) to divide or apportion between the Executive and the designated company in such proportions as may be appropriate any such property, rights and liabilities so transferred to one of them which immediately before the vesting date was property held, or a right or liability subsisting, partly for the purposes of the activities of the part of the London Board's undertaking referred to in subsection (2) of the said section 16 and partly for other purposes of the London Board ; or

(*c*) in the case of any such property, rights and liabilities as are mentioned in sub-paragraph (*b*) of this paragraph the nature of which does not permit such division or apportionment, to afford to the Executive, the designated company and the Bus Company as against one another such rights and safeguards as they may require for the proper discharge of their respective functions.

2. Any such agreement as is referred to in paragraph 1 of this Schedule shall make provision so far as it is expedient—

(*a*) for the granting of leases or the creation of other rights and liabilities over land whether amounting in law to interests in land or not, and whether involving the surrender of any existing interest or the creation of a new interest or not ;

(*b*) for the granting of indemnities in connection with the severance of leases and other matters ;

(*c*) for responsibility for registration of any matter in any description of statutory register.

3. If the Executive or the Bus Company represent to the Minister, or if it appears to the Minister without such a representation, that it is unlikely in the case of any matter on which agreement is required under paragraph 1 of this Schedule that such agreement will be reached, the Minister may, whether before or after the vesting date, give a direction determining the manner in which the property, rights or liabilities in question are to be divided or apportioned

SCH. 2 between the Executive and the designated company, and may include in the direction any provision which might have been included in an agreement under the said paragraph 1; and any property rights or liabilities required by the direction to be transferred from one to another of the Executive and the designated company shall be regarded as having been transferred to, and by virtue of this Act vested in, the transferee accordingly.

Rights and liabilities under agreement for rendering of personal services

4. The rights and liabilities transferred under subsection (2) of section 16 of this Act to the designated company shall include rights and liabilities under an agreement for the rendering of personal services by any person (hereafter in this Schedule referred to as an "employee") only if immediately before the vesting date the employee is employed wholly for the purposes of the part of the London Board's undertaking referred to in paragraph (*a*) of the said subsection (2).

5. Any right to services transferred under the said section 16 shall have effect on and after the vesting date as a right not only to the services to which the agreement relates but also to any reasonably comparable services under the transferee to be selected by the transferee; and any dispute between the transferee and the employee as to what are reasonably comparable services for the purposes of this paragraph may be reported to the Secretary of State for Employment and Productivity by the transferee and, if a dispute so reported is not otherwise disposed of, that Secretary of State shall refer it for determination by the industrial court.

6. The Executive and the Bus Company may before the vesting date enter into any arrangements with the London Board and any employee of the London Board for the determination of the employee's agreement on or before that date and for the conclusion of a new agreement between the Executive or the designated company and the employee for the rendering of services to the Executive or, as the case may be, that company, and the London Board may become a party to any arrangements between the Executive, the Bus Company, the designated company or any other employer and any of the London Board's employees for the transfer of those employees from the London Board to the new employer on or before the vesting date; and, without prejudice to paragraph 10(3)
1963 c. 49. of Schedule 1 to the Contracts of Employment Act 1963 and section
1965 c. 62. 8(2) of the Redundancy Payments Act 1965, for the purposes of those Acts the employee's period of employment at the time when the arrangements take effect shall count as a period of employment with the new employer, and the change of employer shall not break the continuity of the period of employment.

7. The Executive, the Bus Company, the designated company, or any employee may apply to the Minister to determine whether or not, or to whom, rights and liabilities in respect of the employee's services under any particular agreement are transferred by virtue of this Act, and the Minister's decision on the application shall be final.

Construction of agreements, statutory provisions and documents Sch. 2

8.—(1) Paragraph 7 (except sub-paragraph (*d*) thereof) and paragraphs 8 to 12 of Schedule 4 to the Act of 1968 (which relate to the construction of agreements, statutory provisions and documents after certain transfers) shall apply where any property, rights or liabilities of the London Board are transferred from that Board to the Executive or to the designated company under section 16 of this Act, including any case where they are so transferred by virtue of an agreement under paragraph 1 or a direction under paragraph 3 of this Schedule, as if for any reference in the said paragraphs of that Schedule to that Act there were substituted a reference to this Act.

(2) Where any agreement such as is mentioned in the said paragraph 7 refers to property, rights and liabilities which, under paragraph 1 or 3 of this Schedule, are divided or apportioned between the Executive and the designated company, the agreement shall have effect on and after the date from which the division or apportionment has effect as if it constituted two separate agreements separately enforceable by and against each of those bodies respectively as regards the part of the property, rights and liabilities vesting in that body and not as regards the other part; and this sub-paragraph shall apply in particular to the covenants, stipulations and conditions of any lease by or to the London Board.

(3) For the purposes of the said paragraphs 8 to 12 as applied by sub-paragraph (1) of this paragraph, sub-paragraph (2) of this paragraph shall be deemed to form part of the said paragraph 7.

Third parties affected by vesting provisions

9.—(1) Without prejudice to paragraph 8 of this Schedule, any division, apportionment or other transaction between the Executive and the designated company in pursuance of an agreement under paragraph 1 or a direction under paragraph 3 of this Schedule shall be binding on all other persons, and notwithstanding that it would, apart from this sub-paragraph, have required the consent or concurrence of some other person.

(2) It shall be the duty of the Executive and the designated company, if any such transaction is effected, to notify any person who has rights or liabilities which thereby become enforceable as to part by or against one, and as to part by or against the other, of those bodies, and if such a person applies to the Minister and satisfies him that the transaction operated unfairly against him the Minister may give such directions to those bodies as appear to him appropriate for varying the transaction.

10. If in consequence of any such transfer as is referred to in paragraph 8(1) of this Schedule the rights or liabilities of any person other than the Executive or the designated company which were enforceable against or by the London Board become enforceable in part against or by one, and in part against or by the other, of the Executive and the designated company, and the value of any property or interest of that person is thereby diminished, the Executive and the designated company shall pay to that person such compensation as may be just, and any dispute as to whether and if so how much compensation is so payable, or as to the

SCH. 2 person to whom it shall be paid, shall be referred to and determined by an arbitrator appointed by the Lord Chancellor.

11. Any instrument whereby the Executive or the designated company purport to make a disposal for consideration to some person other than the Executive, the Bus Company or a wholly-owned subsidiary of the Executive or the Bus Company of any land or other property which belonged to the London Board, or which is an interest in property which belonged to the London Board, whether that disposal is absolute or for a term of years, shall be as effective as if both the Executive and the designated company had been parties to that instrument and had thereby made the like disposal of any interest of theirs in the property in question.

12. If at any stage of any court proceedings to which the Executive or the designated company and a person other than the Executive, the Bus Company or a wholly-owned subsidiary of the Executive or the Bus Company are parties, it appears to the court that the issues in the proceedings depend on the identification or definition of any of the property, rights or liabilities transferred under section 16 of this Act which the Executive and the designated company have not yet effected, or raise a question of construction on that section or this Schedule which would not arise if the Executive and the designated company constituted a single person, the court may, if it thinks fit on the application of a person other than as aforesaid who is a party to the proceedings, hear and determine the proceedings on the footing that such one of the Executive and the designated company as is a party to the proceedings represents and is answerable for the other of them, and that they constitute a single person, and any judgment or order given by the court shall bind both the Executive and the designated company accordingly.

13. It shall be the duty of the Executive and designated company to keep one another informed of any case where either of them may be prejudiced by paragraph 11 or 12 of this Schedule, and if either of them claims that they have been so prejudiced and that the other of them ought to indemnify or make a payment to them on that account and has unreasonably failed to meet that claim, the body so claiming may refer the matter to the Minister for determination by the Minister.

Right to production of documents of title

14. Where in the case of any land or other property transferred from the London Board under this Act the Executive or the designated company are entitled to retain possession of any document relating in part to the title to, or to the management of, property so transferred to the other of those bodies, the retaining body shall be deemed to have given to the other an acknowledgment in writing of the right of the other body to production of that document and to
1925 c. 20. delivery of copies thereof; and section 64 of the Law of Property Act 1925 shall have effect accordingly, and on the basis that the acknowledgment did not contain any such expression of contrary intention as is mentioned in that section.

Proof of title by certificate

15. A joint certificate by or on behalf of the Executive and the Bus Company that any property specified in the certificate, or any

such interest in or right over any such property as may be so specified, or any right or liability so specified, is by virtue of this Act for the time being vested in, or in such wholly-owned subsidiary of, that one of the certifying authorities so specified shall be conclusive evidence for all purposes of that fact; and if on the expiration of one month after a request from one to the other of them for the preparation of such a joint certificate as respects any property, interest, right or liability, the Executive and the Bus Company have failed to agree on the terms of the certificate, they shall refer the matter to the Minister and issue the certificate in such terms as the Minister may direct. SCH. 2

SCHEDULE 3

Section 17.

DISPOSAL OF CERTAIN STATUTORY FUNCTIONS OF LONDON BOARD

1.—(1) The provisions specified in sub-paragraph (2) of this paragraph shall have effect as if for any reference therein to, or falling to be construed as a reference to, the London Board there were substituted a reference to the Executive and as if the expression " the Boards " included the Executive.

(2) The provisions referred to in sub-paragraph (1) of this paragraph are—

(*a*) section 4(2) of the Road Haulage Wages Act 1938; 1938 c. 44.

(*b*) sections 52(4) and 83(7) of the Act of 1962 (which exclude the Boards from the definition of independent railway undertakings);

(*c*) section 54(1) of the Act of 1962 (which relates to advance information about railway closures);

(*d*) section 60 of the Act of 1962 (which relates to carriers' licences for vehicles operated by subsidiaries of the Boards);

(*e*) section 82 of the Act of 1962 (which makes modifications of the enactments relating to Wages Councils);

(*f*) section 86 of the Act of 1962 and section 141 of the Act of 1968 (which relate to the application of the Town and Country Planning Acts);

(*g*) Schedule 2 to the Act of 1962 and paragraph 7(1) of Schedule 16 to the Act of 1968 (which relate to the transfer of certain statutory functions);

(*h*) Schedule 6 to the Act of 1962 (which relates to the distribution of the Commission's undertaking) other than paragraph 2(3) thereof;

(*i*) section 13(3)(*c*) of the Lee Valley Regional Park Act 1966 (which relates to the provision or operation of passenger transport services by the Regional Park Authority); 1966 c. xli.

(*j*) section 32 of the General Rate Act 1967 and section 162 of the Act of 1968 (which relate to the rating of railway or canal premises); 1967 c. 9.

(*k*) section 3(3) of the London Cab Act 1968 (which relates to restrictions on the parking of cabs); 1968 c. 7.

(*l*) sections 116 to 119 and 120 of the Act of 1968 (which relate to certain bridges);

Sch. 3

(*m*) section 125 of the Act of 1968 (which relates to the powers of inspectors of railways);

(*n*) section 144 of the Act of 1968 (which relates to the transfer and disposal of historical records and relics).

(3) In addition to the application to the Executive by virtue of sub-paragraph (2)(*f*) of this paragraph of the enactments there mentioned, section 69 of the Town and Country Planning Act 1968 (which relates to the determination of what is operational land for the purposes of the Town and Country Planning Act 1962) shall have effect as if in subsection (2)(*b*) thereof after the words "the Transport Act 1968", there were inserted the words "or the Transport (London) Act 1969".

1968 c. 72.
1962 c. 38.
1968 c. 73.

2.—(1) In the case of the provisions specified in sub-paragraph (2) of this paragraph, the functions thereunder of the London Board shall be transferred to the designated company as well as to the Executive; but those provisions shall not have effect, whether in relation to the Executive or to the designated company, with respect to any area with respect to which they did not have effect before the vesting date.

(2) The provisions referred to in sub-paragraph (1) of this paragraph are—

1934 c. xcvi. (*a*) in the London Passenger Transport Act 1934, sections 104 and 109;

1937 c. xc. (*b*) in the London Passenger Transport Act 1937, sections 64 and 68;

1938 c. xcii. (*c*) in the London Passenger Transport Act 1938, section 65;

1949 c. xxix. (*d*) in the British Transport Commission Act 1949, section 57;

1951 c. xxxix. (*e*) in the British Transport Commission Act 1951, section 15.

(3) The functions of the London Board under section 69 of the said Act of 1937, under section 61 of the said Act of 1938 and under section 25 of the London Transport Act 1969 shall be transferred to the Executive, but those sections shall not have effect with respect to any area outside the London Passenger Transport Area within the meaning of the London Passenger Transport Act 1933.

1969 c. l.
1933 c. 14.

3. In relation to the savings bank established under section 23 of the Metropolitan Railway Act 1873, references in section 65 of the Act of 1962 to the appropriate Board shall be construed as references to the Executive; and the persons entitled to deposit money in that savings bank shall, in addition to the persons specified in subsection (5) of the said section 65, include—

1873 c. lxxx.

(*a*) persons employed by the Executive or any subsidiary of the Executive;

(*b*) persons who owing to incapacity arising from ill-health or on reaching retirement age have retired from service with the Executive or any subsidiary of the Executive or with the London Board, the Commission, the London Passenger Transport Board or the Metropolitan Railway Company;

(*c*) the wife, widow (during the period of her widowhood), or children under twenty-one years of age, of such persons as are mentioned in sub-paragraph (*a*) or (*b*) of this paragraph ; SCH. 3

(*d*) any group, society or association the members of which consist, or mainly consist, of such persons as are mentioned in sub-paragraphs (*a*) to (*c*) of this paragraph or the said subsection (5).

4. In its application to the Executive by virtue of section 6(2)(*g*) of this Act, section 43(1)(*b*) of the Act of 1962 shall have effect as if any reference therein to a ship or boat included a reference to a hovercraft.

5.—(1) Section 67 of the Act of 1962 and paragraph 4(5) of Schedule 16 to the Act of 1968 (which relate to the power to make bylaws for railways) shall have effect as if for any reference to the London Board there were substituted a reference to the Executive; and any bylaws made by the London Board under subsection (1) of the said section 67 and in force immediately before the vesting date shall continue in force until varied or revoked by the Executive by virtue of subsection (12) of that section and have effect as aforesaid.

(2) Subsection (2) of the said section 67 (which empowers the Railways Board to make bylaws in relation to passengers and goods conveyed in or on ships operated by the Board, and as to their embarkation and disembarkation) shall apply to the Executive as if for references therein to that Board there were substituted references to the Executive and as if the expression " ships " included hovercraft.

6.—(1) In section 68 of the Act of 1962 (which relates to the custody of lost property), and in any regulations made, or having effect as if made, under section 160(1)(*i*) of the Act of 1960 (which relates to the like matters), any reference to, or falling to be construed as a reference to, the London Board shall be construed as a reference to the Executive.

(2) The Executive shall, not later than one year after the vesting date, and after consulting the Bus Company and the designated company, prepare and submit to the Minister a scheme for the allocation of any moneys arising from the sale, or from fees charged on the redelivery, of any property accidentally left before the vesting date on or in any premises or vehicles belonging to the London Board which was taken into the custody of that Board under regulations made, or having effect as if made, under section 106 of the London Passenger Transport Act 1933; and the Minister may 1933 c. 14. approve that scheme with or without modifications, and it shall be the duty of the Executive, the Bus Company and the designated company to give effect to the scheme as so approved.

7.—(1) Paragraph 5 of Schedule 16 to the Act of 1968 (which relates to transport police) shall apply to the Executive and, for the purposes only of any premises transferred under section 16(2) of this Act, to the Bus Company as it applies to the National Freight Corporation and the Scottish Transport Group.

(2) For the purpose only of applying section 54 of the British 1949 c. xxix. Transport Commission Act 1949 (which relates to powers of search and arrest) to premises transferred as aforesaid, the Bus Company

SCH. 3 shall be deemed to be one of the Boards; and in section 23 of the
1964 c. xxvi. London Transport Act 1964 (under which the said section 54 in its application to the London Board continues in force in relation to the Executive), and in any enactment passed after this Act which provides for the said section 54 to continue in force for a further period in its application to the Executive, any reference to, or falling to be construed as a reference to, the Executive shall be construed as a reference to the Executive, any wholly-owned subsidiary of the Executive and, for the purpose aforesaid but for that purpose only, the Bus Company and any wholly-owned subsidiary of the Bus Company.

(3) Subject to any agreement made by virtue of sub-paragraph (1) of this paragraph and to any adaptations made under sub-paragraph (4) of the said paragraph 5—

(*a*) the functions of the London Board under the scheme set
S.I. 1964/1456. out in the Schedule to the British Transport Police Force Scheme 1963 (Approval) Order 1964 made under section 69 of the Act of 1962 shall be transferred both to the Executive and, for the purposes only of any premises transferred under section 16(2) of this Act, to the Bus Company; and

(*b*) section 70 of the Act of 1962 shall have effect as if the expression "the Boards" included the Executive and, for the purposes aforesaid, the Bus Company and as if premises belonging to, leased to or worked by a wholly-owned subsidiary of the Executive or the Bus Company were premises belonging to, leased to or worked by the Executive or, as the case may be, the Bus Company.

1965 c. 25. 8. In section 92 of the Finance Act 1965 (which relates to the making of grants to operators of bus services towards duty charged on bus fuel) for subsection (8) there shall be substituted the following subsection:—

'(8) In this section—

"bus service" means a service of stage carriages as defined by
1960 c. 16. section 117 of the Road Traffic Act 1960;

"operator", in relation to a bus service, means—

(*a*) the holder of the road service licence under which the service is provided; or

(*b*) if the service is provided otherwise than under a road service licence by, or by a subsidiary of—

(i) the London Transport Executive; or

(ii) the Executive for a designated area within the
1968 c. 73. meaning of section 9(1) of the Transport Act 1968,

that Executive or subsidiary;

(*c*) if the service is provided otherwise than under a road service licence by a person—

(i) in pursuance of an agreement under section 23(2) of the Transport (London) Act 1969 or under a consent continued in force or granted under Schedule 4 to that Act; or

(ii) in pursuance of an agreement under section 19(2) of the Transport Act 1968 or under a consent granted under Schedule 6 to that Act, SCH. 3 1968 c. 73.

that person;

" road service licence " includes a permit under section 30 of the Transport Act 1968;

" subsidiary " has the same meaning as for the purposes of the Transport Act 1968.'

9.—(1) The provisions specified in sub-paragraph (2) of this paragraph shall each have effect as if the reference to the London Board were omitted.

(2) The provisions referred to in the foregoing sub-paragraph are—

(*a*) the Schedule to the Building Control Act 1966 (which specifies bodies to be exempted from the requirements of that Act); 1966 c. 27.

(*b*) Schedule 2 to the Industrial Development Act 1966 (which specifies bodies not eligible for certain grants); 1966 c. 34.

(*c*) Schedule 1 to the Industrial Expansion Act 1968 (which specifies bodies not eligible for financial support under industrial investment schemes). 1968 c. 32.

10. In the Dartford Tunnel Act 1967, section 71 shall have effect as if the proviso to subsection (1) and the proviso to subsection (3)(*a*) (which require the consent of the London Board to certain matters) were omitted. 1967 c. xxxvii.

11. In section 12(1) of the Education (Miscellaneous Provisions) Act 1953, in paragraph (*a*) of the proviso, for any reference to the special area there shall be substituted a reference to Greater London. 1953 c. 33.

SCHEDULE 4

Section 23.

LICENCES OR CONSENTS FOR CERTAIN EXISTING SERVICES

Right to grant of road service licence or consent for certain existing services

1. Where at any time within the period of twelve months ending with the vesting date the London Board were providing any service by means of public service vehicles, being a service—

(*a*) the whole of which was provided under a road service licence; or

(*b*) for the whole or part of which a road service licence was not then, but after that date is, required,

the appropriate traffic commissioners, on an application made before the vesting date by the Executive or, where that service was provided by that part of the Board's undertaking referred to in subsection (2) of section 16 of this Act, by the designated company, shall, subject to the provision by the applicant of any information the commissioners may require for the purpose, forthwith as the case may require either grant or back a road service licence or vary the existing road service licence so as to authorise the continuation of that service for a period of three years after the vesting date by

Sch. 4 the Executive or, as the case may be, by that company in the same form as before that date ; and nothing in sections 135 to 143 of the Act of 1960 shall apply in relation to any application under this paragraph.

2. Where at any time within the period of twelve months aforesaid the part aforesaid of the London Board's undertaking was providing a London bus service, the Executive, on an application made before the vesting date by the designated company, shall forthwith grant that company a consent to the provision of that service by that company on such terms as to permit the continuation of that service for a period of three years after the vesting date in the same form as before the vesting date.

Continuation of certain consents

3.—(1) Where at any time within the period of twelve months aforesaid a London bus service was provided by a person other than the London Board under a consent granted under the London Passenger Transport Act 1933 or under section 58(2) of the Act of 1962, then, subject to sub-paragraph (2) of this paragraph and to paragraph 11 of this Schedule, that consent, so far as it relates to the provision of that service, shall continue in force after the vesting date as if granted by the Executive under this Schedule, but with the omission of any requirement as to the obtaining of a road service licence and as if any conditions attached to the road service licence in respect of that service in force immediately before the vesting date, so far as those conditions relate to the provision of that London bus service, had been attached by the Executive to the consent.

1933 c. 14.

(2) Where the consent under the said Act of 1933 or the said section 58(2) relates to a bus service part only of which is operated as a London bus service, any term or condition with respect to the carriage of passengers other than those who are both taken up and set down in Greater London subject to which that consent was granted shall be of no effect if or so far as it is inconsistent with any condition for the time being attached to the road service licence under which the service is provided.

Right of certain successors in title to grant of consent

4. Subject to paragraph 11 of this Schedule, where such a consent as is referred to in paragraph 3 of this Schedule granted to any person is continued in force in respect of a London bus service by the said paragraph 3, the Executive shall, on the application of a successor in title to the undertaking of that person so far as it consists of the provision of that service, grant to that successor in title—

(*a*) except where the consent so continued was permanent, a consent on the like terms ; or

(*b*) where the consent so continued was permanent, a consent such as to permit the continuation of that service by that successor in title in the same form for a period of one year.

5. Subject to paragraph 11 of this Schedule, while a consent granted by the Executive to any person in respect of a London bus service under paragraph 4 of this Schedule remains in force, the Executive

shall on the application of any successor in title to the undertaking of that person so far as it consists of the provision of that service grant a consent on the same terms to that successor in title. SCH. 4

Rights pending grant of road service licence or consent in certain cases

6. Subject to paragraph 11 of this Schedule, as respects any period between the date when an application is duly made under paragraph 1, 2, 4 or 5 of this Schedule and the date of the grant of a licence or consent in pursuance of the application, a licence or consent in the form applied for shall be deemed to have been granted to the applicant on the date of the making of the application.

Right of appeal in connection with consent

7. The person to whom a consent is granted under paragraph 2, 4 or 5 of this Schedule may appeal to the metropolitan traffic commissioners within the prescribed period and in the prescribed manner on the ground that the terms on which the consent is granted do not comply with the requirements of the paragraph in question ; and, on such an appeal being made, the commissioners may make such order as they think fit and the Executive shall comply with that order.

Renewal of consent

8.—(1) The Executive may, if they think fit, on the application of the holder of any consent continued in force or granted under this Schedule, from time to time renew that consent for a period of one year.

(2) The person by whom an application for the renewal of a consent is made under this paragraph may appeal to the metropolitan traffic commissioners within the prescribed period and in the prescribed manner against any refusal or failure by the Executive to renew that consent ; and if on such an appeal being made the commissioners are of the opinion that it would be unreasonable to refuse the application, they may order the Executive to renew the consent either on the same terms or on such other terms as appear to the commissioners to be appropriate and the Executive shall comply with that order.

(3) Where an application is made under this paragraph before the expiry of the consent to which it relates, that consent shall not cease to be in force before the expiration of the period for appealing against a refusal of or failure to grant that renewal or, if such an appeal is duly made, until the appeal is determined or withdrawn.

Variation of terms or conditions of consent

9.—(1) The Executive—

(*a*) may on the application of the holder of any consent continued in force or granted under this Schedule vary any of the terms of, or any condition attached or deemed to be attached to, that consent ; and

(*b*) may at any time without any such application by notice in writing to the holder of such a consent make any reasonable variation of any such term or condition ;

SCH. 4 and the Executive shall not unreasonably refuse any application under paragraph (*a*) of this sub-paragraph ; but no such variation shall be made which affects the carriage of persons other than persons who are both taken up and set down in Greater London.

(2) The holder of any such consent as aforesaid may appeal to the metropolitan traffic commissioners within the prescribed period and in the prescribed manner against any refusal or failure by the Executive to make a variation of a term or condition applied for under sub-paragraph (1)(*a*), or against any such variation made under sub-paragraph (1)(*b*), of this paragraph ; and, on such an appeal being made, the commissioners may make such order as they think fit and the Executive shall comply with that order.

(3) A variation of which notice is given under sub-paragraph (1)(*b*) of this paragraph shall not take effect until the expiration of the period for appealing against that variation or, if such an appeal is duly made, until the appeal is determined or withdrawn.

Variation of route of service to which consent relates

10. Where, in the case of any bus service in respect of which a consent continued in force or granted under this Schedule is in force, the authorised route for that service becomes impracticable but a variation of a minor nature only in that route would enable that service to be continued in substantially the same form, paragraph 9 of this Schedule shall apply to that variation of that route, so far as it lies in Greater London, as it applies to the variation of such a term or condition as is mentioned in that paragraph, but as if sub-paragraph (3) of that paragraph were omitted.

Loss of right to, or cancellation of, consent in certain cases

11. A person shall not be entitled to the grant by the Executive of a consent under this Schedule with respect to any London bus service if that person has entered into an agreement with the Executive with respect to that service under section 23(2) of this Act ; and where a person has entered into such an agreement with the Executive with respect to any London bus service, any consent with respect to that service continued in force or granted under this Schedule shall be regarded as cancelled.

Power to cancel consent in certain circumstances

12.—(1) A consent continued in force or granted under this Schedule may be cancelled at any time by the Executive on the ground that any of the terms of, or any condition attached or deemed to be attached to, that consent has been contravened ; but, save in accordance with paragraph 11 of this Schedule, such a consent shall not be cancelled on any other ground ; and the Executive shall not cancel a consent under this paragraph unless owing to the frequency of the breach of the term or condition in question, or to the breach having been committed wilfully, or to the danger to the public involved in the breach, the Executive are satisfied that the consent should be cancelled.

(2) The holder of such a consent as aforesaid which is cancelled under this paragraph may appeal against the cancellation within

the prescribed period and in the prescribed manner to the metropolitan traffic commissioners, and on any such appeal the commissioners may make such order as they think fit and the Executive shall comply with that order. SCH. 4

(3) A cancellation of a consent under this paragraph shall not take effect until the expiration of the period prescribed for appealing against the cancellation or, if such an appeal is duly made, until the appeal is determined or withdrawn.

Interpretation

13. In this Schedule—

"metropolitan traffic commissioners" means the traffic commissioners for the Metropolitan Traffic Area;

"prescribed" means prescribed by regulations made by the Minister.

SCHEDULE 5

Section 36.

CONTROL OF OFF-STREET PARKING

PART I

Provisions as to making of regulations under section 36

1. Before deciding to propose the making of regulations under section 36 of this Act with respect to any matter, the Council shall consult with such representative organisations as they think fit and, if after such consultation they decide to make such a proposal, they shall cause to be published in the London Gazette and in one or more daily newspapers circulating throughout Greater London a notice stating that they propose to make such regulations, giving a summary of their effect, and specifying—

(*a*) a place at which provisional draft regulations may be inspected at all reasonable hours and from which a copy of those draft regulations may be obtained on request; and

(*b*) a date (not being earlier than six weeks after the date of publication of the notice) by which representations with respect to the draft regulations, which should include the grounds for any objection thereto, must be sent in writing to the Council;

and on causing such a notice to be published the Council shall send a copy of the notice and of the draft regulations to the Minister and to each local authority the whole or part of whose area is for the time being, or would under the draft regulations become, a controlled area; and the Council shall not make any regulations in pursuance of the proposal to which the notice relates before the expiration of the period of twelve weeks beginning with the date when the notice is published.

2. As soon as may be after the date specified by the notice aforesaid for the making of representations with respect to the draft regulations, the Council shall send to the Minister copies of all representations received by them by that date or, if no representations have been so received, shall inform the Minister in writing of that fact.

SCH. 5

3. In the case of any such proposal as aforesaid, the Minister may at any time before the expiration of the period of twelve weeks aforesaid give to the Council a direction in writing that, except with the consent of the Minister, regulations shall not be made in pursuance of that proposal—

(*a*) with respect to all, or with respect to such as may be specified, of the matters to which the proposal relates ; or

(*b*) in relation to, or to a specified part of, any specified area which has been or is proposed to be designated as a controlled area ;

and on any such direction being given the Minister shall cause notice thereof to be published in the London Gazette and the Council shall comply with that direction.

4.—(1) Where in the case of any such proposal as aforesaid the Minister has given such a direction as aforesaid, he shall as soon thereafter as he is in a position to do so notify the Council in writing with respect to each of the matters or areas to which the direction relates either—

(*a*) that he consents to the making of regulations with respect to that matter or in relation to that area in pursuance of that proposal ; or

(*b*) that he is not prepared in any circumstances to consent to the making of such regulations in pursuance of that proposal ; or

(*c*) that subject to sub-paragraph (2) of this paragraph he is prepared to consider consenting to the making of such regulations in pursuance of that proposal if a revised draft is submitted to him for the purpose incorporating modifications of a specified nature or in other specified circumstances ;

and before deciding the notification to be given to the Council under this paragraph with respect to any matter or in relation to any area the Minister may if he thinks fit appoint a person to hold an inquiry in connection with that matter or area, and subsections (2)
1933 c. 51. to (5) of section 290 of the Local Government Act 1933 shall apply to any such inquiry as they apply to such an inquiry as is referred to in subsection (1) of that section, with the substitution for any reference to a department of a reference to the Minister.

(2) The Minister shall not consider any such revised draft as is referred to in sub-paragraph (1)(*c*) of this paragraph unless he is satisfied that the Council—

(*a*) have taken appropriate steps to inform any persons affected by the modifications incorporated in the revised draft of the nature of those modifications and have afforded those persons a reasonable opportunity to make representations with respect to the revised draft regulations ; and

(*b*) have supplied the Minister with copies of any such representations made.

5.—(1) In the case of any such proposal as aforesaid, the Council may if they think fit at any time after the expiration of the period of twelve weeks aforesaid make regulations in pursuance of that proposal with respect to any matter or in relation to any area which is not the subject of a direction under paragraph 3, or which is the subject of a consent under paragraph 4(1)(*a*), of this Schedule, being regulations either— Sch. 5

(*a*) in the form of the provisional draft with any modifications necessary in consequence of any such direction with respect to any other matter or area ; or

(*b*) subject to sub-paragraph (2) of this paragraph, in the form of that draft modified in such manner as the Council think fit, whether as a result of any representations to which paragraph 2 of this Schedule applies or otherwise.

(2) The Council shall not make any regulations by virtue of sub-paragraph (1)(*b*) of this paragraph unless a draft of the regulations in the form in which they are to be made has been submitted to the Minister and the Minister has given his consent to their being made.

6. In deciding in the case of any such proposal as aforesaid whether or not to make any regulations in pursuance thereof by virtue of paragraph 5 of this Schedule the Council shall have regard to any representations to which paragraph 2 of this Schedule applies ; and in deciding whether or not to give any consent under this Part of this Schedule to the making of regulations by the Council in pursuance of any such proposal, the Minister shall have regard to any such representations, to the report of any person appointed to hold an inquiry under paragraph 4 of this Schedule in connection with the proposal in question, and to any such representations as are referred to in sub-paragraph (2) of the said paragraph 4 ; and the Minister shall cause notice of the giving by him of any consent under this Part of this Schedule to be published in the London Gazette.

Part II

Revocation or variation of permanent licence

7. Subject to the provisions of Parts III and IV of this Schedule with respect to appeals and compensation, the provisions of this Part of this Schedule shall apply in relation to any permanent licence granted by the local authority.

8. If at any time it appears to the local authority expedient to do so in the interests of the proper planning of transport in Greater London, they may by not less than twelve months notice in writing to the holder of the licence either—

(*a*) revoke the licence ; or

(*b*) vary the terms and conditions thereof specified under section 36(4)(*b*) and (*c*) of this Act.

SCH. 5

9. If at any time it appears to the local authority that the holder of a licence (whether the person for the time being holding that licence or a previous holder thereof) has discontinued making parking spaces available to the public at the licensed parking place and that the discontinuance has lasted for a period of not less than two years, then, subject to paragraph 13 of this Schedule, they may by notice in writing to the holder of the licence revoke it.

10. If at any time it appears to the local authority that for a period of not less than two years the person, or each of the persons, who was for the time being during that period the holder of a licence in respect of a licensed parking place has made available to the public at that parking place a substantially lower number of parking spaces than that authorised by the licence, then, subject to paragraph 13 of this Schedule, they may by notice in writing to the holder of the licence vary the terms and conditions of the licence specified under the said section 36(4)(*b*) and (*c*) so as to authorise the provision at the licensed parking place of only that number of parking spaces which it appears to the local authority was being provided at the date of the notice.

11. If in the case of a licensed parking place which was ready for operation at the date of the grant of the licence the local authority are satisfied at any time that for a period of not less than two years beginning with that date the person, or each of the persons, who was for the time being during that period the holder of the licence has not made any significant number of parking spaces available to the public at the licensed parking place, then, subject to paragraph 13 of this Schedule, they may by notice in writing to the holder of the licence revoke it.

12.—(1) Where at the date when the licence was granted the development as a public off-street parking place of the premises in respect of which the licence was granted had not been begun or had not been completed then, subject to paragraph 13 of this Schedule—

(*a*) if there has been a period of not less than three years since that date without that development being begun, or

(*b*) if there has been a period of not less than seven years since that date without that development being completed, or

(*c*) if for a period of not less than two years beginning with the date of the completion of that development the person, or each of the persons, who was for the time being during that period the holder of the licence has not made any significant number of parking spaces available to the public at the licensed parking place,

the local authority may by notice in writing to the holder of the licence revoke it.

(2) For the purposes of the foregoing sub-paragraph, the development there referred to shall be taken to begin at the earliest date on which any specified operation within the meaning of section 64(3) of the Land Commission Act 1967 comprised in that development begins to be carried out.

1967 c. 1.

13. Where notice under paragraph 9, 10, 11 or 12(1) of this Schedule is given after the expiration of the relevant period referred to in the paragraph in question the notice shall be of no effect if it is given more than three months after the expiration of that period. SCH. 5

PART III

Rights of appeal

14.—(1) If a person who is, or who proposes to become, the operator of a public off-street parking place in a controlled area or any other person entitled to an interest in the premises used or proposed to be used for the purposes of that parking place is aggrieved by a decision of the local authority—

(*a*) to refuse an application for the grant of a licence in respect of those premises ; or

(*b*) as to the terms and conditions to be specified under section 36(4)(*b*) and (*c*) of this Act in a licence granted in respect of those premises ; or

(*c*) to refuse an application for a variation of the terms and conditions so specified in a permanent licence granted in respect of those premises ; or

(*d*) to revoke a licence granted in respect of those premises ; or

(*e*) to vary under Part II of this Schedule any of the terms and conditions specified under the said section 36(4)(*b*) and (*c*) in a permanent licence granted in respect of those premises,

he may by notice served within such time (not being less than twenty-eight days from the date of notification of the decision to which it relates) and in such manner as the Minister may by regulations under paragraph 17 of this Schedule direct, appeal to the Minister from that decision.

(2) If in a case where—

(*a*) a person makes an application to the local authority for a licence in respect of premises in respect of which a licence is not for the time being in force ; or

(*b*) the person who is the holder of a permanent licence in respect of any premises duly makes an application to the local authority for a specified variation of the terms and conditions of the licence specified under the said section 36(4)(*b*) and (*c*),

the local authority have not notified that person of their decision on his application by the expiration of the period of two months beginning with the date when they received the application or such longer period beginning with that date as may have been agreed for the purpose between that person and the local authority, the local authority shall be deemed for the purposes of this Schedule to have notified that person at the date of the expiration of that period that they have decided to refuse the application.

15. The Minister shall not be required to entertain an appeal under this Part of this Schedule from any decision of a local authority if or to the extent that it appears to him that the decision was necessary in order to comply with the requirements of section

SCH. 5 36 of this Act or with any regulations made by the Council by virtue of subsection (6) of that section which are for the time being in force.

16.—(1) Subject to sub-paragraph (2) of this paragraph, before determining an appeal under this Part of this Schedule the Minister shall, if either the appellant or the local authority so request, afford to each of them an opportunity of appearing before, and being heard by, a person appointed by the Minister for the purpose.

(2) If the Minister thinks fit in any case where such a request as aforesaid is made, he may, instead of complying with that request, appoint a person to hold an inquiry in connection with the appeal, and subsections (2) to (5) of section 290 of the Local Government Act 1933 shall apply to any such inquiry as they apply to such an inquiry as is referred to in subsection (1) of that section, with the substitution for any reference to a department of a reference to the Minister.

1933 c. 51.

17.—(1) The Minister may by regulations make provision as to the procedure to be followed in connection with appeals under this Part of this Schedule, including the procedure in connection with matters preparatory to, or subsequent to, the consideration of the appeal.

(2) Any such regulations shall include provision for the giving of notice to the Council of any appeal under this Part of this Schedule and of any request made under paragraph 16(1) thereof, and for enabling the Council to make representations with respect to the matter in question and to appear before and be heard by any person appointed by the Minister for the purposes of sub-paragraph (1) or (2) of the said paragraph 16.

(3) Any regulations under this paragraph shall be made by statutory instrument and be subject to annulment in pursuance of a resolution of either House of Parliament.

18.—(1) On an appeal being brought under this part of this Schedule from a decision of the local authority, the Minister may either dismiss the appeal or substitute for that decision such other decision, as he thinks fit ; and, subject to sub-paragraph (2) of this paragraph, the decision of the Minister on the appeal shall be final and shall be binding both on the appellant and on the local authority, and the local authority shall take such steps as may be necessary to give effect to any such substituted decision.

1958 c. 66. (2) Subsection (1) of section 9 of the Tribunals and Inquiries Act 1958 (which relates to appeals on points of law from decisions of certain tribunals) shall apply to a decision of the Minister on an appeal under this Part of this Schedule as it applies to a decision of any of the tribunals mentioned in that subsection, but as if the reference to any party to proceedings before such a tribunal were a reference to the local authority or any person who had, or if aggrieved would have had, a right to appeal to the Minister under this Part of this Schedule, whether or not he has exercised that right ; and accordingly references in subsections (1) and (3) of that section to a tribunal shall be construed in relation to such an appeal as references to the Minister.

PART IV

SCH. 5

Right to compensation in certain circumstances

19. Where a person who, at the date when an area is first designated as a controlled area by regulations of the Council under section 36 of this Act, is the operator of a public off-street parking place at premises in that area which have at that date been used as such a parking place for a continuous period of not less than six months duly makes an application to the local authority for a licence in respect of those premises before the expiration of the period prescribed for such applications in respect of parking places in operation at that date, and the local authority decide either—

(*a*) to refuse the application ; or

(*b*) to grant the applicant a licence on terms and conditions specified under subsection (4)(*b*) and (*c*) of the said section 36 such that under the licence the applicant will not be able to operate the premises as a parking place to such advantage or potential advantage as immediately before he made his application,

paragraph 22 of this Schedule shall apply to that decision of the local authority.

20. Where—

(*a*) at the date when notice of a proposal to make regulations under the said section 36 designating an area as a controlled area for the purposes of that section is published by the Council under paragraph 1 of this Schedule—

(i) planning permission has been granted for a development which consists of or includes the provision at any premises in that area of a public off-street parking place ; and

(ii) that development involves substantial building or engineering operations within the meaning of section 221(1) of the Town and Country Planning Act 1962 ; and 1962 c. 38.

(iii) either one or more specified operations within the meaning of section 64(3) of the Land Commission Act 1967 comprised in that development have begun to be carried out or a contract (other than a lease) has been entered into with a person carrying on a business consisting wholly or mainly of the execution of building operations or of building operations and engineering operations whereby that person has undertaken to erect in the course of that business at the said premises a building or structure as a place for the provision of parking spaces for motor vehicles ; and 1967 c. 1.

(*b*) at the date when the area is designated as a controlled area in pursuance of that proposal those premises have not been in use as such a parking place to the full extent provided for by the planning permission for a continuous period of not less than six months ; and

SCH. 5

(*c*) the person operating or proposing to operate those premises as such a parking place duly makes application to the local authority for a licence in respect of those premises before the expiration of the period prescribed for such applications in respect of parking places in operation at the date referred to in sub-paragraph (*b*) of this paragraph ; and

(*d*) the local authority decide either—

(i) to refuse the application ; or

(ii) to grant the applicant a licence on terms and conditions specified under subsection (4)(*b*) and (*c*) of the said section 36 such that under the licence the applicant will not be able to operate the premises as such a parking place to such advantage or potential advantage as if the area had not been designated as a controlled area,

paragraph 22 of this Schedule shall apply to that decision of the local authority.

21. Paragraph 22 of this Schedule shall apply to any decision of the local authority—

(*a*) to revoke a permanent licence under paragraph 8 of this Schedule ; or

(*b*) to vary under the said paragraph 8 any of the terms and conditions specified in a permanent licence under the said section 36(4)(*b*) and (*c*) in such manner that the holder of the licence will not be able to operate the licensed parking place to such advantage or potential advantage as if the variation had not been made ; or

(*c*) to refuse an application by the holder of a permanent licence for a specified variation of the terms and conditions specified under the said section 36(4)(*b*) and (*c*) in a case where—

(i) by reason of a happening beyond the control of the holder of the licence he cannot continue to operate the licensed parking place in accordance with the licence as for the time being in force to such advantage or potential advantage as before that happening ; and

(ii) the making of that variation would wholly or partly mitigate the adverse effects of that happening without enabling the holder of the licence to operate the licensed parking place to greater advantage or potential advantage than before that happening.

22.—(1) If, on a claim made to the local authority in writing within the period of six months or such longer period as may be allowed under sub-paragraph (2) of this paragraph beginning with the date when the person who is, or who proposes to become, the operator of a public off-street parking place is, or is deemed under paragraph 14(2) of this Schedule to have been, notified of a decision of the local authority under section 36 of this Act or Part II of this Schedule relating to that parking place, that person or any other person entitled to an interest in the premises used or proposed to be used for the purposes of that parking place shows that the decision is one to which, under paragraph 19, 20 or 21 of this Schedule, this paragraph is to apply and that the claimant has suffered damage in consequence of that decision by depreciation of the value of his interest in those premises, or by being disturbed in his enjoyment of those premises, the local authority shall pay the claimant compensation in respect of that damage.

(2) If within the period of six months referred to in sub-paragraph (1) of this paragraph any such person as is referred to in that sub-paragraph has made an application to the Minister for that purpose and has given notice to the local authority of the making of that application, the Minister may, if he thinks fit in the circumstances of the case, direct that the said sub-paragraph (1) shall apply in relation to the decision in question as if for the reference in that sub-paragraph to six months there were substituted a reference to such longer period as the Minister thinks fit.

(3) For the purpose of determining whether or not a claimant has suffered such damage as aforesaid, there shall be taken into account any alternative use to which the premises aforesaid could reasonably be put, being a use in the case of which the local authority show either—

(*a*) that any necessary planning permission, whether conditional or unconditional, for that use has already been granted; or

(*b*) that the local planning authority have given an undertaking that if planning permission for that use is applied for it will be granted either unconditionally or subject to specified conditions;

and in a case where this paragraph applies by virtue of paragraph 21(*c*) of this Schedule there shall also be taken into account any alternative variation to that applied for by the holder of the licence in question which the local authority have undertaken to grant on an application being made for that purpose.

(4) Section 127 of the Town and Country Planning Act 1962 shall apply to any compensation payable under sub-paragraph (1) of this paragraph in respect of depreciation of the value of a claimant's interest in the premises aforesaid; and any question as to the right to, or the amount of, compensation under the said sub-paragraph (1) shall be referred to and determined by the Lands Tribunal, and in relation to the determination of any such question the provisions of sections 2 and 4 of the Land Compensation Act 1961 shall apply subject to any necessary modifications.

1962 c. 38.

1961 c. 33.

(5) Where compensation has become payable under sub-paragraph (1) of this paragraph in respect of an interest in any premises and subsequently an order with respect to the use of those premises as a parking place is made under section 27 or section 28 of the said Act of 1962, the amount of that compensation shall be taken into account in assessing any compensation on a claim by reason of expenditure, loss or damage in consequence of that order made in respect of that interest under section 118 or, as the case may be, section 124 of that Act.

SCH. 5

(6) Where any expenses are incurred by a local authority in the payment of compensation under sub-paragraph (1) of this paragraph in consequence of a decision of theirs, then, if or to any extent to which it appears to the Minister that the decision was attributable to regulations made by the Council under subsection (6) of the said section 36, the Minister may, if it appears to him to be expedient to do so, require the Council to contribute towards those expenses such sum as appears to him to be reasonable.

23. Where notice of appeal from any such decision of the local authority as is referred to in paragraph 19, 20 or 21 of this Schedule has been duly given under Part III of this Schedule—

(*a*) paragraph 22 of this Schedule shall not have effect in relation to that decision until that appeal is determined or abandoned ;

(*b*) the person who is, or who proposes to become, the operator of a public off-street parking place at the premises to which the decision relates shall be deemed for the purposes of the said paragraph 22 to have been notified of the local authority's decision on the date when the appeal is determined or abandoned ; and

(*c*) if on that appeal the Minister substitutes a different decision for that of the local authority, the local authority shall be deemed for the purposes of the said paragraph 22 to have made that substituted decision and not their original decision.

24. Where, in the case of a decision of the local authority relating to any premises, paragraph 22 of this Schedule applies to that decision both by virtue of paragraph 19 and by virtue of paragraph 20 of this Schedule, then—

(*a*) upon the person who is, or who proposes to become, the operator of a public off-street parking place at those premises making a claim in respect of that decision under the said paragraph 22 by virtue of either of the said paragraphs 19 and 20, any subsequent claim in respect thereof by that person by virtue of the other of those paragraphs, and any claim in respect thereof made whether before or after that person's claim by any other person by virtue of the other of those paragraphs, shall be of no effect ; and

(*b*) subject to the foregoing sub-paragraph, if a claim in respect of that decision is made under the said paragraph 22 by any person by virtue of either of the said paragraphs 19 and 20 any subsequent claim in respect thereof by virtue of the other of those paragraphs shall be of no effect.

PART V

SCH. 5

Permissible periods of unlicensed operation of parking place

25. Where, at the date when any area first becomes a controlled area, a person is operating a public off-street parking place in that area, he shall not be guilty of an offence under section 36(12) of this Act by reason of continuing to operate the parking place after that date without a licence—

(*a*) at any time before the expiration of the period prescribed for the making of applications for licences in respect of parking places in operation at that date ; or

(*b*) if during that period he duly makes an application for a licence in respect of the parking place, at any time after the expiration of that period but before the local authority notify him either that he has been granted a licence or that his application is refused ; or

(*c*) if the local authority notify him that his application is refused, at any time thereafter before the expiration of the time for giving notice of appeal from that decision under Part III of this Schedule ; or

(*d*) if such a notice of appeal is duly given, at any time thereafter until either the local authority's decision becomes finally effective under the procedure provided for by the said Part III or the licence is granted.

26. Where in pursuance of the application referred to in sub-paragraph (*b*) of paragraph 25 of this Schedule the person referred to in that paragraph is granted a licence, he shall not be guilty of an offence under subsection (10) of the said section 36 by reason of contravening or failing to comply with any of the terms and conditions specified in the licence under subsection (4)(*b*) and (*c*) of that section—

(*a*) at any time before the expiration of the time for giving notice of appeal under Part III of this Schedule from the decision of the local authority as to those terms and conditions ; or

(*b*) if such a notice of appeal is duly given, at any time thereafter until either the local authority's decision becomes finally effective under the procedure provided for by the said Part III or the terms and conditions specified as aforesaid in the licence are varied as a result of that procedure.

27. Where the operator of a public off-street parking place who is the holder of a licence in respect of that parking place granted for a limited period duly makes an application to the local authority before the date of expiry of that licence for a new licence (whether permanent or for a limited period) authorising the operation of that parking place for a further period after that date, then, if and for so long as he continues to operate that parking place after that date in accordance with the terms and conditions of the expired licence (other than the provision as to its date of expiry)—

(*a*) he shall not be guilty of an offence under the said section 36(12) by reason of operating the parking place after the date aforesaid without a licence—

SCH. 5

(i) at any time before the local authority notify him either that he has been granted a new licence in respect of the parking place or that his application is refused ; or

(ii) if the local authority notify him that his application is refused, at any time thereafter before the expiration of the period for giving notice of appeal from that decision under Part III of this Schedule ; or

(iii) if such a notice of appeal is duly given, at any time thereafter until either the local authority's decision becomes finally effective under the procedure provided for by the said Part III or a new licence is granted ;

(*b*) where he is granted a new licence in pursuance of the application aforesaid, he shall not be guilty of an offence under subsection (10) of the said section 36 by reason or contravening or failing to comply with any of the terms and conditions specified in that new licence under subsection (4)(*b*) and (*c*) of that section—

(i) at any time before the expiration of the time for giving notice of appeal under Part III of this Schedule from the decision of the local authority as to those terms and conditions ; or

(ii) if such a notice of appeal is duly given, at any time thereafter until either the local authority's decision becomes finally effective under the procedure provided for by the said Part III or the terms and conditions specified as aforesaid in the new licence are varied as a result of that procedure.

Section 47.

SCHEDULE 6

REPEALS

Chapter	Short Title	Extent of Repeal
23 & 24 Geo. 5. c. 14.	The London Passenger Transport Act 1933.	Sections 16, 17, 25 and 26. In section 107(1), the definition of " Special Area ". Parts II to IV of Schedule 7.
1 & 2 Geo. 6. c. xcii.	The London Passenger Transport Act 1938.	Section 66.
1 & 2 Eliz. 2. c. 33.	The Education (Miscellaneous Provisions) Act 1953.	Section 12(3).
5 & 6 Eliz. 2. c. 20.	The House of Commons Disqualification Act 1957.	In Part II of Schedule 1, and in the Part substituted therefor by Schedule III, the entry " The London Transport Board ".
7 & 8 Eliz. 2. c. 25.	The Highways Act 1959.	In section 295(1), the definition of " metropolitan road ".

Chapter	Short Title	Extent of Repeal
8 & 9 Eliz. 2. c. 16.	The Road Traffic Act 1960.	In section 120, in subsection (1), the words " other than the Metropolitan Traffic Area ", subsection (2), and in subsection (4) the words from " and references " onwards. In section 121(1), the words " other than the Metropolitan Traffic Area ". Section 122. In section 123(2), the words " the traffic commissioner for the Metropolitan Traffic Area ", the word " other ", the words " the said commissioner or " in the first place where they occur, and the words " said commissioner or " in the second place where they occur. In section 123(3), the words " traffic commissioner or " wherever they occur, and the words " traffic commissioner's or ". In section 125(1), the words " to the traffic commissioner for the Metropolitan Traffic Area " and the word " other ". In section 125(2), the words " or to the traffic commissioner for the Metropolitan Traffic Area ". In section 126, the words from " (other than the Metropolitan Traffic Area) " onwards. In section 135(2), the words from " except " to " Area " where next occurring. In section 135(7), the words from " except " to " Area " where next occurring. In section 136(2), the words from " except " to " Area" where next occurring. Sections 141, 142, 153(5), 161(2) and 165(3). In section 193(1), the words from " or is " to " so constituted " and the words " or commissioner ".

SCH. 6

Chapter	Short Title	Extent of Repeal
8 & 9 Eliz. 2. c. 16.—*cont.*	The Road Traffic Act 1960. —*cont.*	In section 252(1), the words from " and references " onwards. In section 252(2), the words from the beginning to " special area ". So much of Schedule 17 as amends section 16 or 17 of the London Passenger Transport Act 1933.
10 & 11 Eliz. 2. c. 46.	The Transport Act 1962.	In section 1(1), the word " four " and the words from " the London Transport " to " London Board ". Sections 1(4), 3(2), 7 and 8. In section 13(3) the words from " or section " onwards. Sections 19(3)(ii), 44 to 49, 57(3)(*a*), 58 and 59. In section 85(1) the words from " Before " where first occurring onwards. In section 92(1) the definitions of " the London Passenger Transport Area " and " the London Special Area ". In Schedule 2, so much of Part I as relates to section 141 or 142 of the Road Traffic Act 1960. Part II of Schedule 7. In Schedule 10, in paragraph 9, the words from " but " onwards.
10 & 11 Eliz. 2. c. 59.	The Road Traffic Act 1962.	In Schedule 4, so much of Part I as relates to section 135, 136 or 142 of the Road Traffic Act 1960.
1963 c. 33.	The London Government Act 1963.	In section 14(6)(*d*), the words " and 141(2) to (6) ", the word " respectively ", and the words from " and to " to " area ". In section 17, subsections (1) to (3), in subsection (4) the words from " (otherwise " to " section) ", and subsection (6). In section 89(1), the definition of " metropolitan road ". In Part I of Schedule 5, paragraph 26.

SCH. 6

Chapter	Short Title	Extent of Repeal
1963 c. 33.—*cont.*	The London Government Act 1963.—*cont.*	In Schedule 6, paragraph 68(*d*). Schedule 7. In Schedule 17, paragraphs 7 and 26(*a*) and (*c*).
1966 c. 17.	The Transport Finances Act 1966.	Section 1(3).
1966 c. 27.	The Building Control Act 1966.	In the Schedule, the entry " The London Transport Board ".
1966 c. 32.	The Selective Employment Payments Act 1966.	In Part I of Schedule 1, paragraph 10. In Part III of Schedule 1, the entry beginning " The London ".
1966 c. 33.	The Prices and Incomes Act 1966.	In Schedule 3, paragraph 2(1)(*g*).
1966 c. 34.	The Industrial Development Act 1966.	In Schedule 2, the entry " The London Transport Board ".
1967 c. 76.	The Road Traffic Regulation Act 1967.	Section 6(8)(*b*). In section 6(12), the words " the London special area and ". Section 9(8)(*b*). Section 56(2). In section 104(1) the definition of " metropolitan road ".
1967 c. xxxvii.	The Dartford Tunnel Act 1967.	In section 71, in subsection (1) the words from the beginning to " 1960 " and the proviso, and in subsection (3)(*a*) the proviso.
1968 c. 32.	The Industrial Expansion Act 1968.	In Schedule 1, the entry " The London Transport Board ".
1968 c. 73.	The Transport Act 1968.	Sections 24(3)(*a*), 33(2) and 41(6). In section 54(5)(*d*), the words " as the case may be the London Board and ". Section 59(4). In section 138(3), the words " or the London Board ". In section 145(2), the words " the traffic commissioner for the Metropolitan Traffic Area or ", the word " other ", and the words " any of ". In section 159(1), in the definition of " the Boards ", the words " the London Transport Board ", and the definition of " the London Board ".

Overseas Resources Development Act 1969

1969 CHAPTER 36

An Act to raise the limits imposed by the Overseas Resources Development Act 1959 on borrowings by the Commonwealth Development Corporation and on advances to the Corporation by the Minister of Overseas Development; to extend the area of operation of the Corporation; and for purposes connected with those matters. [25th July 1969]

BE IT ENACTED by the Queen's most Excellent Majesty, by and with the advice and consent of the Lords Spiritual and Temporal, and Commons, in this present Parliament assembled, and by the authority of the same, as follows:—

Raising of limits on borrowings and advances.
1959 c. 23.

1.—(1) The Overseas Resources Development Act 1959 (hereafter in this Act referred to as " the principal Act ") shall have effect with the following amendments, that is to say—

(*a*) in section 12(3) (which provides that apart from temporary borrowings the amount outstanding of the sums borrowed by the Commonwealth Development Corporation shall not at any time exceed one hundred and fifty million pounds) for the words " one hundred and fifty million pounds " there shall be substituted the words " two hundred and twenty-five million pounds or such larger sum, not exceeding two hundred and sixty million pounds, as the Minister with the consent of the Treasury may from time to time by order specify "; and

(*b*) in section 13(1) (which enables the Minister with the consent of the Treasury to make advances to the

Corporation, in respect of its capital expenditure, subject to a limit of one hundred and thirty million pounds outstanding at any time) for the words " one hundred and thirty million pounds " there shall be substituted the words " two hundred and five million pounds or such larger sum, not exceeding two hundred and forty million pounds, as the Minister with the consent of the Treasury may from time to time by order specify ".

(2) The power to make an order under the said section 12(3) or 13(1) as amended by the preceding subsection shall be exercisable by statutory instrument, but no such order shall be made unless a draft of it has been approved by a resolution of the House of Commons.

2.—(1) Subject to the following provisions of this Act, the principal Act shall apply in relation to any country or territory outside the United Kingdom which is not a colonial territory as defined by that Act as it applies in relation to a colonial territory as so defined; and references to a colonial territory or colonial territories in that Act, except in section 20, shall be construed accordingly. Extension of area of operation of Corporation.

(2) The Minister may give directions to the Corporation requiring it to obtain his approval, in such cases as may be specified in the directions, before performing functions in or in relation to any country or territory to which the principal Act applies by virtue of the preceding subsection and may give his approval subject to such conditions as he thinks fit; and any directions, approval or conditions having effect immediately before the commencement of this Act by virtue of section 1(3) of the Commonwealth Development Act 1963 (which contained provisions corresponding to the provisions of this subsection with respect to certain Commonwealth countries) shall continue to have effect as if given or specified in pursuance of this subsection. 1963 c. 40.

(3) Sections 1(3), 4 and 6 of the principal Act (which relate respectively to the qualifications of members of the Corporation, the removal of doubts as to the original purposes of the Corporation, and the continuation of its activities in territories which change their statuses) shall continue to have effect as if this Act had not been passed; and sections 8 and 9(2)(*b*) of that Act (which provide for consultation with local interests and governments) shall not apply in relation to the performance of functions in any country or territory to which that Act applies by virtue of subsection (1) of this section.

(4) In section 2(4) of the principal Act (which relates to the provision of means of communication situated outside the territory

with which they are designed to provide communication) for paragraph (*a*) there shall be substituted the following paragraph—

"(*a*) that territory is one in or in relation to which the Corporation is entitled to perform functions without or in consequence of the Minister's approval and the facilities or services are or will be wholly for communication between that territory and one or more other countries or territories in or in relation to which the Corporation is so entitled, or ".

Citation, interpretation and repeals.

3.—(1) This Act may be cited as the Overseas Resources Development Act 1969 and the Overseas Resources Development Acts 1959 and 1963 and this Act may be cited together as the Overseas Resources Development Acts 1959 to 1969.

(2) In this Act (including any amendment made by this Act in the principal Act) " the Corporation " means the Commonwealth Development Corporation and " the Minister " means the Minister of Overseas Development; and references in this Act to any enactment are to that enactment as amended by or under any other enactment.

(3) The following enactments are hereby repealed, that is to say—

(*a*) in the principal Act, section 7 and in section 8(3) the words " or seven ";

1963 c. 40.

(*b*) in the Commonwealth Development Act 1963, section 1(1), (3) and (5).

Employer's Liability (Defective Equipment) Act 1969

1969 CHAPTER 37

An Act to make further provision with respect to the liability of an employer for injury to his employee which is attributable to any defect in equipment provided by the employer for the purposes of the employer's business; and for purposes connected with the matter aforesaid. [25th July 1969]

BE IT ENACTED by the Queen's most Excellent Majesty, by and with the advice and consent of the Lords Spiritual and Temporal, and Commons, in this present Parliament assembled, and by the authority of the same, as follows:—

Extension of employer's liability for defective equipment.

1.—(1) Where after the commencement of this Act—

(*a*) an employee suffers personal injury in the course of his employment in consequence of a defect in equipment provided by his employer for the purposes of the employer's business; and

(*b*) the defect is attributable wholly or partly to the fault of a third party (whether identified or not),

the injury shall be deemed to be also attributable to negligence on the part of the employer (whether or not he is liable in respect of the injury apart from this subsection), but without prejudice to the law relating to contributory negligence and to any remedy by way of contribution or in contract or otherwise which is available to the employer in respect of the injury.

(2) In so far as any agreement purports to exclude or limit any liability of an employer arising under subsection (1) of this section, the agreement shall be void.

(3) In this section—

" business " includes the activities carried on by any public body;

"employee" means a person who is employed by another person under a contract of service or apprenticeship and is so employed for the purposes of a business carried on by that other person, and "employer" shall be construed accordingly;

"equipment" includes any plant and machinery, vehicle, aircraft and clothing;

"fault" means negligence, breach of statutory duty or other act or omission which gives rise to liability in tort in England and Wales or which is wrongful and gives rise to liability in damages in Scotland; and

"personal injury" includes loss of life, any impairment of a person's physical or mental condition and any disease.

(4) This section binds the Crown, and persons in the service of the Crown shall accordingly be treated for the purposes of this section as employees of the Crown if they would not be so treated apart from this subsection.

Short title, commencement and extent.

2.—(1) This Act may be cited as the Employer's Liability (Defective Equipment) Act 1969.

(2) This Act shall come into force on the expiration of the period of three months beginning with the date on which it is passed.

1920 c. 67.

(3) Nothing in the Government of Ireland Act 1920 shall prevent the Parliament of Northern Ireland from making laws for purposes similar to the purposes of section 1 of this Act.

(4) This Act, except the foregoing subsection, does not extend to Northern Ireland.

Sharing of Church Buildings Act 1969

1969 CHAPTER 38

An Act to provide for the sharing and using of church buildings by different Churches and for matters connected therewith. [25th July 1969]

BE IT ENACTED by the Queen's most Excellent Majesty, by and with the advice and consent of the Lords Spiritual and Temporal, and Commons, in this present Parliament assembled, and by the authority of the same, as follows:—

Agreements for sharing church buildings.

1.—(1) It shall be lawful, notwithstanding any statutory or other legal provision, for any two or more Churches to which this Act applies to make agreements, through the parties mentioned in this section and in accordance with the provisions thereof, for the sharing by them of church buildings, and to carry such agreements into effect, and such agreements are in this Act referred to as " sharing agreements ".

(2) A sharing agreement may be made in respect of a single church building or two or more church buildings in the same locality, and in respect of any existing or proposed church building, and, subject to the following provisions of this Act relating to consecrated churches of the Church of England and the sharing of residential buildings, may provide for the shared building or any of the shared buildings to be owned or continue to be owned by one only of the sharing Churches or to be jointly owned by all or some of the sharing Churches.

(3) The parties to a sharing agreement shall—

(*a*) as respects the Church of England, be the Diocesan Board of Finance of the diocese and the incumbent and parochial church council of the parish in which the building or buildings is or are or will be situated;

(*b*) as respects any other Church, be such persons as may be determined by the appropriate authority of that Church;

and shall also include, in the case of an existing building, the person (if not otherwise a party) in whom the building is vested and any managing trustees thereof, and may also include, in the case of a proposed building, any person in whom it is to be vested or who is to be a managing trustee thereof.

(4) A sharing agreement shall not be made on behalf of the Church of England without the consent of the bishop and the Pastoral Committee of the diocese concerned, and the appropriate authority of any other Church to which this Act applies may require the consent of any body or person specified by the authority to be given to sharing agreements made on behalf of that Church.

(5) Where a church building is held on trust for educational purposes which include instruction in religious knowledge according to the faith and practice of the Church of England, the consent of the Diocesan Education Committee of the diocese concerned to a sharing agreement in respect of that building shall be required in lieu of the consent of the Pastoral Committee thereof, and the agreement shall be subject to the approval of the Secretary of State.

(6) Where a benefice is vacant and a suspension period is current under section 67 of the Pastoral Measure 1968, subsection (3)(*a*) of this section shall have effect with the substitution for the reference to the incumbent of a reference to the minister in charge of the parish, but otherwise a sharing agreement shall not be made on behalf of the Church of England during a vacancy in the benefice concerned.

1968 No. 1.

(7) Where a see is vacant, or the bishop of the diocese is unable because of illness or absence to give his consent under subsection (4) of this section, the archbishop of the province may appoint by an instrument under his hand a suffragan or assistant bishop or an archdeacon of the diocese to act in place of the bishop under the said subsection for a period specified in the instrument; and in the event of a vacancy in the see of an archbishop or his illness or absence, an appointment under this subsection, either in respect of the see of the archbishop or another see in the province, may be made by the other archbishop.

(8) A sharing agreement shall be under seal and shall be registered, in the case of the Church of England, in the registries of the province and diocese, and, in the case of other Churches, in the registry or office of the appropriate authority, and the consents

required as aforesaid shall be signified in writing by the secretary or clerk of the body concerned or by the person concerned and shall be registered with the deed.

(9) A sharing agreement shall be binding on the successors to the parties thereto, that is to say, on the persons who would at any subsequent time be required to be parties if the agreement were then being made, and any reference in this Act to the parties to a sharing agreement shall be construed, as respects anything done at a subsequent time, as referring to the said persons.

(10) A sharing agreement may be amended by agreement of the parties thereto and with the consents that would then be required to a new sharing agreement.

Trusts of shared church buildings.

2.—(1) Where a sharing agreement is made with respect to an existing or proposed church building which is to be owned or continue to be owned by one only of the sharing Churches, the trusts or purposes on or for which the building is held or to be held shall include the purposes and provisions of the agreement, as for the time being in force, and any instrument declaring those trusts and purposes shall be deemed to have effect, or (in the case of a proposed building) shall provide, accordingly.

(2) Where a sharing agreement is made with respect to an existing or proposed church building which is to be owned jointly by all or some of the sharing Churches, that ownership shall be effected by vesting the building in trustees representing those Churches, or in a custodian trustee with managing trustees representing those Churches, to be held on trust to be used for the purposes of the sharing agreement and in accordance with its terms and, subject thereto, for such other charitable purposes of the sharing Churches as may be appropriate, and the trust instrument relating to the building shall provide accordingly.

(3) The body or person in whom an existing church building is vested shall have power, notwithstanding any statutory or other legal provision, to convey the building to the managing trustees or custodian trustee aforesaid, for such consideration (if any) as may be provided in the sharing agreement or determined thereunder.

(4) The references in this section to a custodian trustee shall, subject to the making of such an order as is required by the Charities Act 1960 for the vesting of property in the official custodian for charities, include references to the said custodian. 1960 c. 58.

(5) The purposes of a sharing agreement shall be limited to purposes which are exclusively charitable according to the law of England and Wales.

Financial and management provisions.

3.—(1) A sharing agreement shall make provision with respect to the financial and other obligations of the parties thereto in respect of the provision, improvement and management of the church building or buildings shared or to be shared under the agreement, and the powers of any body or person under any statutory or other legal provision to apply money, whether by grant or loan, in respect of the provision, improvement or management of church buildings of a Church to which this Act applies shall be applicable in like manner in respect of any church building shared or to be shared by that Church under a sharing agreement.

(2) The powers of any body or person under any statutory or other legal provision—

(*a*) to acquire, hold, improve or manage church buildings of a Church to which this Act applies, or any property to be used for or in connection with the provision of such church buildings, or

(*b*) to grant property for or in connection with the provision of such church buildings, whether for a full consideration or for less than a full consideration,

shall be applicable in like manner in respect of any church building to which a sharing agreement relates and which, under the agreement, is or is to be owned by that Church or jointly owned by that Church and any other Church or Churches, and any such power to hold church buildings shall include a power to be a trustee (representing that Church) of such a jointly owned church building or, in the case of a corporation aggregate, to be the custodian trustee thereof.

1954 No. 1. (3) The powers of the Church Commissioners under the New Housing Areas (Church Buildings) Measure 1954, and the powers of the said Commissioners and certain other bodies and persons
1943 No. 1. under sections 13 and 14 of the New Parishes Measure 1943 (which relate to the provision and improvement of church buildings), shall not be applicable for the purposes mentioned in the foregoing provisions of this section except as may be provided by a Measure of the Church Assembly extending the said Measures.

(4) The responsibility for the management of a church building owned by one only of the sharing Churches under a sharing agreement and of its contents shall remain with the authorities of or trustees representing that Church, but that responsibility shall be discharged in accordance with the provisions of the agreement and any arrangements made thereunder, including provisions or arrangements for consultation with any other sharing Church and for the payment of contributions by any other sharing Church towards the expenses of management.

(5) Where a sharing agreement provides for the joint ownership of the shared building by all or some of the sharing Churches, the responsibility of the trustees for the management of the building shall be in place of any responsibility of the authorities of the sharing Churches as respects that building, including responsibility under any statutory or other legal provision:

Provided that—

(*a*) the trustees shall discharge that responsibility in accordance with the provisions of the sharing agreement and any arrangements made thereunder, including provisions or arrangements for consultation with any sharing Church which is not a joint owner and for the payment of contributions by the sharing Churches towards the expenses of management;

(*b*) the agreement may provide that any moveables required for the worship of any sharing Church shall be the responsibility of the authorities of that Church.

(6) In this section " management ", in relation to a church building, includes the repair and furnishing of the building.

Sharing of church buildings for purposes of worship.

4.—(1) A sharing agreement shall make provision, in the case of a building used as a place of worship, for determining the extent to which it is to be available for worship in accordance with the forms of service and practice of the sharing Churches respectively, and may provide for the holding of such joint services on such occasions as may be approved by those Churches, and may dispense, to such extent as may be necessary, with the requirement to hold certain services of the Church of England on Sundays and other days.

(2) Notwithstanding any statutory or other legal provision, a minister, reader or lay preacher of one of the Churches sharing a church building under a sharing agreement may, by invitation of a minister, reader or lay preacher of another such Church, take part in conducting worship in that building in accordance with the forms of service and practice of that other Church; but the rights given by this subsection shall be exercised in accordance with any rules or directions given by either Church and to any limitation imposed by or under the sharing agreement.

(3) Subject to the foregoing provisions of this section, the participation of the communities of the sharing Churches in each other's worship shall be governed by the practices and disciplines of those Churches in like manner as if they worshipped in separate buildings.

Consecrated churches and parish churches of Church of England.

5.—(1) A sharing agreement shall not be made with respect to an existing consecrated church of the Church of England unless—

(*a*) the church will under the agreement remain in the sole ownership of the Church of England; or

(*b*) authority to make the agreement on behalf of the Church of England is given by a pastoral scheme under the Pastoral Measure 1968 as extended for the purpose by a subsequent Measure of the Church Assembly, and the church will under the agreement be in the joint ownership of the Church of England and another Church or Churches.

1968 No. 1.

(2) Where a sharing agreement is made on behalf of the Church of England with respect to a church building used or to be used as a place of worship, but not an existing consecrated church, the building shall not be consecrated unless it will under the agreement be in the sole ownership of the Church of England.

(3) Where a sharing agreement relates to a consecrated church, the faculty jurisdiction shall not apply in respect of movables required for the worship of any sharing Church other than the Church of England.

(4) Where a church building being a place of worship is shared by the Church of England under a sharing agreement:—

(*a*) if the agreement provides for the sole ownership of the building by the Church of England, but not otherwise, the building may become or remain a parish church;

(*b*) in any case the agreement shall not prevent or affect the designation of the building as a parish centre of worship under section 29 of the Pastoral Measure 1968.

Solemnization of marriages in shared or other inter-denominational buildings.

1855 c. 81.

1949 c. 76.

6.—(1) A church building to which a sharing agreement relates (including a building in the sole ownership of the Church of England) may be certified under the Places of Worship Registration Act 1855 as a place of religious worship of any Church sharing the building other than the Church of England, and the provisions of the Marriage Act 1949 relating to the registration of buildings shall apply for and in relation to the registration of any such church building certified as aforesaid, subject to the modifications specified in Schedule 1 to this Act.

(2) The provisions of the Marriage Act 1949 relating to the publication of banns and the solemnization of marriages according to the rites of the Church of England shall apply to a church building shared by the Church of England under a sharing agreement, and shall so apply notwithstanding that the building is registered under Part III of the Act, and accordingly—

(*a*) if the building is a parish church or parish centre of worship, the said provisions shall apply as they apply to other parish churches and parish centres of worship; and

(*b*) in any other case, section 20 of the said Act (which provides for the licensing of chapels for such publication and solemnization) shall apply.

(3) The proviso to section 26(2) of the said Act shall not apply to a church building to which a sharing agreement relates, except in respect of marriages to be solemnized according to the rites of the Church of England.

(4) Where a chapel of any university, college, school, hospital or other public or charitable institution, or a building held on trust for purposes of public worship but not a church building to which a sharing agreement relates, is used for the purposes of public worship in accordance with the forms of service and practice of two or more Churches to which this Act applies, the foregoing provisions of this section shall apply thereto in like manner as they apply to church buildings to which a sharing agreement relates, except that—

(*a*) the provisions of Schedule 1 other than paragraph 1 thereof shall not apply;

(*b*) in subsection (2)(*b*) of this section the reference to section 20 of the Marriage Act 1949 shall include a reference to section 21 of that Act. 1949 c. 76.

(5) This section (except where it refers to parish centres of worship) shall apply to the Church in Wales in like manner as it applies to the Church of England.

Sharing of residential buildings.

7.—(1) Where a sharing agreement is made with respect to a church building or buildings proposed to be used under the agreement as a residence or residences for ministers or lay workers, the purpose of the agreement shall be to provide residential accommodation, whether in the form of separate residences or otherwise, available for occupation by the ministers or lay workers of the sharing Churches in accordance with arrangements made under the agreement.

(2) Where under any such agreement a separate residence is let to an incumbent of the Church of England in his corporate capacity, it shall be the residence house of the benefice during the term of the lease.

(3) A sharing agreement shall not be made with respect to an existing residence house of a benefice of the Church of England, unless authority to make the agreement on behalf of that Church is given by a pastoral scheme under the Pastoral Measure 1968 as extended for the purpose by a subsequent Measure of the Church Assembly. 1968 No. 1.

(4) No right of pre-emption, or provision for the property to revert to previous ownership, shall be exercisable or operate on the conveyance, vesting or disposal of such an existing residence house under section 2 or section 9 of this Act (except section 9(4)).

Application to shared buildings of certain provisions of Charities Act 1960.
1960 c. 58.

8.—(1) A sharing agreement with respect to any church building shall not affect any exception or exemption for the building from any provisions of the Charities Act 1960.

(2) A sharing agreement with respect to any church building which under the agreement is owned by the Church of England shall not affect the application to the building of section 45(2) of the Charities Act 1960 (which excludes from the definition of " charity " certain corporations of the Church of England in respect of their corporate property and certain trusts of consecrated property).

(3) Section 29 of the Charities Act 1960 (which requires dealings with charity property to be authorised by an order of the court or the Charity Commissioners) shall not apply to the conveyance, vesting or disposal of church buildings under section 2 or section 9 of this Act.

Termination of sharing.

9.—(1) A sharing agreement shall contain provisions for terminating the sharing of the church building or buildings, and such provisions may—

(*a*) if the agreement relates to two or more buildings, provide for terminating the sharing of any building before the others; and

(*b*) if there are two or more sharing Churches, provide for the withdrawal of any Church from the sharing of any church building, not being a Church which is the sole owner or previous owner of the building;

and the sharing agreement may make provision for financial adjustments as between the Churches, on such termination or withdrawal, by payments out of moneys held for the purposes of the sharing agreement or of any shared building or by other payments by one Church to another.

(2) On the termination of the sharing of a church building owned by one only of the sharing Churches, the building shall be held on the trusts or for the purposes on or for which it was held before the sharing agreement or would be held but for the sharing agreement.

(3) On the termination of the sharing of a church building jointly owned by all or some of the sharing Churches, being a building which before the sharing agreement was owned by one

only of those Churches, the building shall, without any conveyance or other assurance, vest as follows:—

(*a*) if the building was previously a consecrated church of the Church of England or a building (other than a consecrated church) vested in the incumbent of a Church of England parish, it shall vest in the incumbent of the parish in which the building is then situated, for the same purposes as before, as nearly as may be;

(*b*) in any other case, it shall vest in such of the trustees in whom the building is vested as represent the Church who previously owned the building or, if the building is vested in a custodian trustee, it shall remain so vested but be managed by such of the managing trustees as represent that Church, and it shall be held and managed on the trusts or for the same purposes as before, as nearly as may be.

(4) Where the sharing of a church building jointly owned as aforesaid but not previously owned by one only of the sharing Churches is terminated, the sharing agreement and the trust instrument may provide for the disposal of the building (including disposal to one of the sharing Churches) and for the application of the proceeds to charitable purposes of the sharing Churches.

Cathedrals, peculiars, extra-diocesan and extra-parochial churches of the Church of England.

10.—(1) No sharing agreement shall be made with respect to a cathedral church or peculiar of the Church of England or any church building of that Church situated in an extra-diocesan or extra-parochial place.

(2) The dean or provost and chapter of such a cathedral church may, notwithstanding any statutory or other legal provision, authorise a chapel or other part of the cathedral church to be used for the purposes of public worship in accordance with the forms of service and practice of two or more Churches to which this Act applies, and section 6 of this Act shall apply to any such chapel or part of a cathedral church in like manner as it applies to a chapel of any such institution as is mentioned in subsection (4) of that section.

(3) Nothing in this section shall be taken as preventing a church building in an extra-diocesan or extra-parochial place being used, otherwise than in pursuance of a sharing agreement, by two or more Churches to which this Act applies, or as preventing the application of section 6(4) of this Act to such a church building.

Churches to which this Act applies, and appropriate authorities thereof.

11.—(1) The Churches to which this Act applies are the Churches specified in the first column of Schedule 2 to this Act, the Church of England and all other Churches who give notice under subsection (3) of this section.

(2) The expression " appropriate authority ", in relation to each of the Churches specified in the first column of Schedule 2

to this Act, means the authority specified in the second column of the Schedule in respect of that Church, and if different authorities are specified in relation to different provisions of this Act, means in each such provision the authority specified in relation thereto.

(3) Any Church for the time being represented on the General Council of the British Council of Churches or on the governing body of the Evangelical Alliance or the British Evangelical Council may give notice in writing to the General Secretary of the British Council of Churches or as the case may be of the governing body concerned, that it desires that this Act should apply to that Church, and the notice shall specify the appropriate authority or authorities of that Church for the purposes of this Act, and the General Secretary concerned shall publish in the London Gazette a notice signed by him—

(*a*) stating that the Church concerned is represented on the said General Council or governing body and has expressed its desire that this Act should apply to that Church;

(*b*) stating that this Act will apply to that Church as from the date of publication of the notice; and

(*c*) specifying the appropriate authority or authorities of that Church for the purposes of this Act;

and thereupon this Act shall apply to that Church as from that date and shall have effect as if an entry in respect of that Church and the appropriate authority or authorities so specified were made in Schedule 2 thereto.

Interpretation.

12.—(1) In this Act, unless the context otherwise requires,—

" building " includes a part of a building;

" church building " means a building used or proposed to be used by a Church or Churches to which this Act applies—

(*a*) as a place of worship;

(*b*) as a church hall or centre available wholly or mainly for activities other than worship;

(*c*) as a youth club or centre or youth hostel;

(*d*) as a residence or residences for ministers or lay workers:

Provided that—

(i) a sharing agreement may provide for including any land (other than land used or appropriated for use for burials) or outbuildings held or to be held with a church building, and any easements or rights enjoyed or to be enjoyed with a church building, and references to a church building shall in relation to that agreement, be construed accordingly;

(ii) the said expression shall not include any school;

" consecrated " means consecrated for the purpose of public worship according to the rites and ceremonies of the Church of England;

" Diocesan Board of Finance " means the Board of that name constituted under the Diocesan Board of Finance Measure 1925 for that diocese: 1925 No. 3.

Provided that, if the bishop certifies that a board of finance not so constituted or a body constituted for the holding on trust of diocesan property is to be treated for the purposes of this Measure as the Diocesan Board of Finance for that diocese, the board or body so certified shall be so treated;

" Diocesan Education Committee " means a committee constituted in accordance with the Schedule to the Diocesan Education Committees Measure 1955 or in accordance with an order made by the Secretary of State under that Measure; 1955 No. 1 (4 & 5 Eliz. 2).

" statutory or other legal provision " means any Act or Measure, any instrument or document made or having effect under or by virtue of any Act or Measure, any other instrument or document affecting legal rights or obligations, any trust (whether arising under a trust instrument or otherwise), and any rule of law, being an Act, Measure, instrument, document, trust, or rule in force at the passing of this Act:

Provided that the said expression shall not include a lease or tenancy of a church building or any mortgage, charge, covenant or rights affecting a church building and operating for the benefit of persons other than a Church to which this Act applies, or any general Act of Parliament regulating or affecting the use of land.

(2) For the purposes of this Act, a church building shall be deemed to be owned by a Church if the building is held by any body or person, whether for a freehold or leasehold estate, for purposes of that Church or on behalf of that Church, and, in the case of a leasehold building, any reference to the conveyance or vesting of the building shall be construed as a reference to the conveyance or vesting of the leasehold estate.

(3) If it is certified by the Church Commissioners that the ownership of a consecrated church of the Church of England

cannot be ascertained with certainty, and that the church ought to be treated as vested in the incumbent of the parish in which it is situated, the church shall be deemed for the purposes of this Act to be so vested.

(4) Any reference in this Act to any Act or Measure shall be construed as a reference to that Act or Measure as amended by any subsequent Act or Measure.

Saving for temporary loans of church buildings.

13. Nothing in this Act shall be taken as affecting any practice of a Church to which this Act applies of lending church buildings temporarily for particular occasions to other religious bodies.

Extent.

14.—(1) This Act shall extend to church buildings in England and Wales.

(2) This Act may be extended to church buildings in the Isle of Man by an Act of Tynwald, and shall then have effect, in relation to such buildings, subject to such exemptions, adaptations or modifications as may be specified in that or a subsequent Act of Tynwald.

Short title.

15. This Act may be cited as the Sharing of Church Buildings Act 1969.

SCHEDULES

SCHEDULE 1

Section 6.

MODIFICATIONS OF PROVISIONS OF THE MARRIAGE ACT 1949 RELATING TO THE REGISTRATION OF BUILDINGS, IN THEIR APPLICATION TO SHARED CHURCH BUILDINGS

1. A church building to which a sharing agreement relates may be registered under section 41 of the Marriage Act 1949 (hereinafter referred to as " the Act ") notwithstanding that it is not a separate building or deemed to be a separate building within the meaning of that section. 1949 c. 76.

2. An application under the said section 41 shall be made by a representative (as hereinafter defined) of a sharing Church other than the Church of England, and, if there are two or more such Churches, the registration shall be deemed to have been made on behalf of the congregations of all those Churches, whether or not their representatives joined in the application.

3. Where a sharing Church other than the Church of England withdraws from the sharing of a registered church building, which continues to be used by another such Church, the registration shall not be cancelled.

4. An authorisation and certification of a person under section 43(1) of the Act to be present at the solemnization of marriages in a church building to which a sharing agreement relates shall be effected by a representative of a sharing Church other than the Church of England, and, if there are two or more such sharing Churches, different persons may be so authorised and certified on behalf of those Churches, but each such person shall be an authorised person for the purposes of the Act in respect of the solemnization of any marriage in that building; and references in the Act to authorised persons and their certification shall be construed accordingly.

5. The proviso added to the said section 43(1) by the Marriage Acts Amendment Act 1958, which prescribes a period of twelve months before a person may be authorised as aforesaid, shall not apply to any authorisation under this Schedule, and, if a sharing Church withdraws, in the circumstances mentioned in paragraph 3 above, from the sharing of a registered church building, the registration shall, for the purpose of the application of the said proviso to another building registered on behalf of the congregation of the withdrawing Church, be deemed to have been cancelled at the time of the withdrawal. 1958 c. 29.

6. The consent required under the proviso to section 44(1) of the Act shall, if the marriage is to be solemnized according to the rites of a sharing Church, be given by the minister ordinarily responsible for the conduct of worship by the congregation of that Church or, if the sharing Church is not the Roman Catholic Church, by a representative of that sharing Church, and in the case of other marriages shall be given by one of the trustees, owners or managers of the building.

7. The appointment of two or more authorised persons in respect of the same building shall not require any additional set or sets of

SCH. 1

duplicate marriage register books to be supplied for that building, and regulations made under section 74 of the Act may make provision with respect to the custody and use of the register books and the returns to be made by the authorised persons of the entries therein and may make any necessary modifications of the provisions of the Act relating to those matters.

8. Nothing in this Schedule shall affect any registration or authorisation which is in force when a sharing agreement takes effect in respect of the building concerned, and any such registration or authorisation shall continue in force and have effect as if it had been made under this Schedule.

9. In this Schedule "representative", in relation to a Church sharing a church building, means—

(*a*) if the building is jointly owned, a trustee representing that Church;

(*b*) in any other case, a party to the agreement on behalf of that Church.

Section 11.

SCHEDULE 2

CHURCHES AND THEIR APPROPRIATE AUTHORITIES

Name of Church	*Appropriate Authority or Authorities*
Any Church of the Baptist Denomination.	As respects section 1(3) and (4), the Baptist Trust Corporation as hereinafter defined, acting with the concurrence of the Church meeting. As respects section 1(8), the Baptist Trust Corporation.
Any Church of the Congregational Denomination.	As respects section 1(3) and (4), the Congregational Trust Corporation as hereinafter defined, acting with the concurrence of the Church meeting. As respects section 1(8), the Congregational Trust Corporation.
Any Congregation of the Association of Churches of Christ in Great Britain and Ireland.	As respects section 1(3) and (4), the Annual Conference of the Association of Churches of Christ acting with the concurrence of the duly constituted Church meeting. As respects section 1(8), the Annual Conference of the Association of Churches of Christ.
The Methodist Church	The Annual Conference of the Methodist Church.
The Presbyterian Church of England.	The Presbytery in whose bounds the church building or buildings is or are or will be situated.
The Roman Catholic Church.	The Bishop of the diocese in which the church building or buildings is or are or will be situated.

Sch. 2

The Church in Wales ...	The Governing Body of the Church in Wales.

For the purposes of this Schedule, " the Baptist Trust Corporation " and " the Congregational Trust Corporation " have the following meanings:—

(*a*) if the church building or buildings to which the sharing agreement concerned relates is or are or will be vested in a Baptist or Congregational Trust Corporation within the meaning of the Baptist and Congregational Trusts Act 1951, it means that Corporation; 1951 c. xvii.

(*b*) otherwise it means the Baptist or Congregational Trust Corporation (within the meaning of the said Act) in whose area of operations the church building or buildings is or are or will be situated, or if there is more than one such Corporation, the one determined by the Church meeting.

Age of Majority (Scotland) Act 1969

1969 CHAPTER 39

An Act to amend the law of Scotland relating to the age of majority; and for connected purposes.
[25th July 1969]

BE IT ENACTED by the Queen's most Excellent Majesty, by and with the advice and consent of the Lords Spiritual and Temporal, and Commons, in this present Parliament assembled, and by the authority of the same, as follows:—

Reduction of age of majority to 18.

1.—(1) As from the date on which this Act comes into force a person shall attain majority on attaining the age of eighteen instead of on attaining the age of twenty-one; and a person shall attain majority on that date if he has then already attained the age of eighteen but not the age of twenty-one.

(2) The foregoing subsection applies for the purposes of any rule of law, and, in the absence of a definition or of any indication of a contrary intention, for the construction of " major ", " majority ", " full age ", " perfect age ", " complete age ", " lawful age ", " minor ", " minority ", " under age ", " less age " and similar expressions in—

(*a*) any statutory provision, whether passed or made before, on or after the date on which this Act comes into force; and

(*b*) any deed executed on or after that date other than a deed made in the exercise of a special power of appointment where the deed creating the power was executed before that date.

(3) In the statutory provisions specified in Schedule 1 to this Act, for any reference to the age of twenty-one years or twenty-five years there shall be substituted a reference to the age of eighteen years.

(4) This section does not affect the construction of any suc expression as is referred to in subsection (2) of this section i any of the statutory provisions described in Schedule 2 to th Act.

(5) The Secretary of State may, by order made by statutor instrument, amend any provision in any local enactment passe on or before the date on which this Act comes into force b substituting a reference to the age of eighteen years for an reference therein to the age of twenty-one years; and any statutor instrument containing an order under this subsection shall b subject to annulment in pursuance of a resolution of either Hous of Parliament.

(6) Notwithstanding any rule of law, a testamentary instrument or codicil executed before the date on which this Act comes into force shall not be treated for the purposes of this section as made on or after that date by reason only that the instrument or codicil is confirmed by a codicil executed on or after that date.

(7) This section shall not affect the construction of any statutory provision where it is incorporated in and has effect as part of any deed the construction of which is not affected by this section.

1958 c. 5 (7 & 8 Eliz. 2.).

(8) This section shall not prevent the making of an adoption order or provisional adoption order under the Adoption Act 1958 in respect of a person who has attained the age of eighteen if the application for the order was made before this Act comes into force, and in relation to any such case that Act shall have effect as if this section had not been enacted.

1875 c. 61.

(9) Section 4 of the Entail Amendment (Scotland) Act 1875 (consent to disentail may be given at 21) is hereby repealed.

(10) In this section—

" statutory provision " means any enactment and any order, rule, regulation, byelaw or other instrument made in the exercise of a power conferred by any enactment; and

" deed " includes any disposition, contract, instrument or writing (not being a statutory provision), whether *inter vivos* or *mortis causa*.

Short title, interpretation, commencement and extent.

2.—(1) This Act may be cited as the Age of Majority (Scotland) Act 1969.

(2) Except where the context otherwise requires, any reference in this Act to any enactment shall be construed as a reference to that enactment as amended, extended or applied by or under any other enactment.

(3) This Act shall come into force on such date as the Secretary of State may appoint by order made by statutory instrument.

(4) This Act shall extend to Scotland only.

SCHEDULES

SCHEDULE 1

Section 1(3).

Statutory Provisions amended by substituting 18 for 21 or 25 Years

Part I

Enactments

	Short title	*Section*	*Subject matter*
. 6.	The Tutors Act 1474.		Nearest agnate over 25 to be tutor.
. 12.	The Prescription Act 1617.		Prescription not to run during minority.
. 6.	The Diligence Act 1621.		Right of person under 25 and of his successor to redeem comprised lands.
c. 4.	The Minority Act 1663.		Right of person under 21 to surplus of maills and duties from comprised lands.
c. 85.	The Oaths of Minors Act 1681.		Ratification of writ by oath of minor not to deprive him of right of reduction.
c. 120.	The Court of Session Act 1825.	Section 25.	Limitation of time for appeal to House of Lords.
c. 36.	The Entail Amendment Act 1848.	Sections 1, 2 and 3.	Power to disentail.
c. 22.	The Trade Union Act Amendment Act 1876.	Section 9.	Person under 21 but above 16 eligible as member of trade union but not of committee of management etc.
c. 25.	The Friendly Societies Act 1896.	Section 36.	Person under 21 eligible as member of society and branches but not of committee etc.
c. 44.	The Customs and Excise Act 1952.	Section 244(2)(*a*).	Entry invalid unless made by person over 21.
c. 46.	The Hypnotism Act 1952.	Section 3.	Persons under 21 not to be hypnotised at public entertainment.
c. 63.	The Trustee Savings Banks Act 1954.	Section 23.	Payments to persons under 21.
c. 5.	The Adoption Act 1958.	Section 57(1).	Definition of " infant " by reference to age of 21.
c. 61.	The Mental Health (Scotland) Act 1960.	Section 45(4)(*c*).	Provision where nearest relative of patient is under 21.
		Section 47(1)	Meaning of " nearest relative " of patient who has not attained the age of 21.
c. 57.	The Trusts (Scotland) Act 1961.	Section 1(2).	Person over age of pupillarity but under 21 incapable of assenting to variation of trust purposes etc.

Sch. 1

Short Title	Section	Subject matter
c. 37. The Building Societies Act 1962.	Section 9.	Person under 21 eligible a member of building socie but cannot vote or hold offic
	Section 47.	Receipt given to building societ by person under 21 to be vali
c. 2. The Betting, Gaming and Lotteries Act 1963.	Section 22(1) and (3).	Offence of sending betting adve tisements to persons under 21
c. 12. The Industrial and Provident Societies Act 1965.	Section 20.	Person under 21 but above 1 eligible as member of societ but not of committee etc.
c. 49. The Registration of Births, Deaths and Marriages (Scotland) Act 1965.	Section 43(5), (6) and (7).	Application for change of nam etc. by person over 16 and under 21.

Part II

Regulations and Rules

Title	Provision	Subject matter
1929 S.R. & O. 1048. The Trustee Savings Banks Regulations 1929.	Regulation 28(2).	Payments to persons under 21.
1933 S.R. & O. 1149. The Savings Certificates Regulations 1933.	Regulation 2(1)(*a*).	Persons entitled to purchase and hold certificates.
	Regulation 21(2).	Persons under disability.
1946 S.R. & O. 1156. The North of Scotland Hydro-Electric Board (Borrowing and Stock) Regulations 1946.	Regulation 36(1) and (2).	Stock held by persons under 21.
1949 S.I. 751. The Gas (Stock) Regulations 1949.	Regulation 19(1) and (2).	Stock held by persons under 21.
1953 S.I. 42. The Local and Other Authorities (Scotland) (Transfer of Stock) Regulations 1953.	Regulation 12(1) and (2).	Stock held by persons under 21.
1955 S.I. 1752. The South of Scotland Electricity Board (Borrowing and Stock) Regulations 1955.	Regulation 30(1) and (2).	Stock held by persons under 21.
1956 S.I. 1657. The Premium Savings Bonds Regulations 1956.	Regulation 2(1).	Persons entitled to purchase and hold bonds.
	Regulation 12(2).	Persons under disability.
1957 S.I. 2228. The Electricity (Stock) Regulations 1957.	Regulation 22(1) and (2).	Stock held by persons under 21.
1963 S.I. 935. The Exchange of Securities (General) Rules 1963.	Rule 1(1).	Definition of " minor ".
1965 S.I. 1420. The Government Stock Regulations 1965.	Regulation 14(1), (2), (3) and (5).	Stock held by persons under 21.
1965 S.I. 1839 The Registration of Births, Still-births, Deaths and Marriages (Prescription of Forms) (Scotland) Regulations 1965.	Schedule 24.	Recording of change of name or surname.

SCHEDULE 2

Section 1(4).

STATUTORY PROVISIONS UNAFFECTED BY SECTION 1

1. The Regency Acts 1937 to 1953.

2. The Representation of the People Acts (and any regulations, rules or other instruments thereunder) and section 50 of the Local Government (Scotland) Act 1947. 1947 c. 43.

3. Any statutory provision relating to income tax (including surtax), capital gains tax, corporation tax or estate duty.

Medical Act 1969

1969 CHAPTER 40

An Act to amend the Medical Act 1956, and for connected purposes. [25th July 1969]

BE IT ENACTED by the Queen's most Excellent Majesty, by and with the advice and consent of the Lords Spiritual and Temporal, and Commons, in this present Parliament assembled, and by the authority of the same, as follows:—

The registers and procedure for registration

Abolition of local registers and re-naming of general register.

1.—(1) The local registers provided for by section 41(1) of the Act of 1956 are hereby abolished.

(2) In consequence of the abolition of those registers—

(*a*) the general register kept for the purposes of that Act by the registrar of the General Council (hereafter in this Act referred to as " the Registrar ") shall as from the commencement of this section be known as the register of medical practitioners ; and

(*b*) references (however worded) to the general register so kept in any enactment or instrument passed or made before the commencement of this section shall as from the commencement of this section be construed as references to the register or, as regards persons temporarily registered under section 25 of the Act of 1956, as references to the register of temporarily registered medical practitioners mentioned in section 3(3) of this Act.

(3) In this Act " the register ", unless the context otherwise requires, means the register of medical practitioners.

Replacement of ss. 41 to 46 of Act of 1956.

2. Sections 3 to 9 of this Act shall have effect instead of sections 41 to 46 of the Act of 1956 with respect to registers and the procedure for registration under that Act.

The registers.

3.—(1) The register shall continue to be kept by the Registrar, and shall contain, in addition to names and qualifications, the addresses and dates of registration of the persons registered therein and such other particulars (if any) of those persons as may be prescribed.

(2) The register shall consist of two lists—

(*a*) one, to be called the principal list, of persons entitled to be registered under section 7, 17, 18, or 23 of the Act of 1956 but not entitled to be included in the overseas list mentioned in paragraph (*b*) below; and

(*b*) one, to be called the overseas list, of persons entitled to be so registered who by virtue of regulations made under section 4 of this Act are for the time being entitled to be included in that list by reason of residence overseas.

(3) Temporary registration under section 25 of the Act of 1956 shall be effected in a separate register, to be known as the register of temporarily registered medical practitioners, which shall be prepared and kept by the Registrar and shall contain the names, and such other particulars as may be prescribed, of the persons registered therein.

(4) It shall be the duty of the Registrar to keep the register correct in accordance with the provisions of the Act of 1956, this Act and regulations made by the General Council, to erase the names of persons who have died, and from time to time to make the necessary alterations in the addresses, qualifications and other registered particulars of registered persons.

(5) The Registrar may, by letter addressed to any registered person at his address on the register, inquire whether he has changed his address and, if no answer is received to the inquiry within six months from the posting of the letter, may erase from the register the entry relating to that person.

(6) On registering the death of a medical practitioner a registrar of births and deaths shall, without charge to the Registrar, send forthwith by post to the Registrar a copy certified under his hand of the entry in the register of deaths relating to the death.

(7) So far as applicable, subsection (4) above shall apply in relation to the register of temporarily registered medical practitioners and to persons and matters registered therein as it applies in relation to the register and to persons and matters registered in the register.

(8) In this section " prescribed " means prescribed by regulations under section 4 of this Act.

4.—(1) Subject to the provisions of this Act, the General Council may make regulations with respect to the form and keeping of the register and the making of entries, alterations and corrections therein.

Power to make regulations with respect to the registers.

(2) Regulations under this section may provide for the register to be kept either by making entries in bound books or by recording the matters in question in any other manner; and if the register is not kept by making entries in bound books, adequate precautions shall be taken for guarding against, and facilitating the discovery of, falsification.

(3) Regulations under this section shall provide for the marking of the register so as to distinguish those provisionally registered under section 17 or 23 of the Act of 1956, those registered as Commonwealth practitioners under section 18 or 23 of that Act and those registered as foreign practitioners under the said section 18 or 23.

(4) Regulations under this section shall prescribe—

(*a*) the circumstances in which persons are to be treated for the purposes of this Act and of any regulations made by the General Council as residing overseas;

(*b*) the conditions (which may include the making of an application in the prescribed manner) subject to which persons are to be entitled to be included in the overseas list by reason of residence overseas; and

(*c*) the circumstances in which persons are to cease to be entitled to be included in that list;

but regulations made in pursuance of this subsection shall not provide for a person to be treated for the said purposes as residing overseas unless he resides outside the United Kingdom, the Republic of Ireland, the Channel Islands and the Isle of Man.

(5) Regulations under this section may authorise the Registrar to erase from the overseas list the name of any person who has ceased to be entitled to be included therein, but any regulations made in pursuance of this subsection shall include provision for entitling a person whose name is erased from that list by virtue of this subsection otherwise than on his own application to appeal within a prescribed period to such committee of the General Council as may be prescribed; and on any such appeal the committee in question, after making such investigation (if any) of the appellant's conduct as they think fit, may if they think fit direct his name to be restored to that list.

(6) Regulations under this section may make provision with respect to the restoration to the register or a particular list

therein of the name of any person whose name has been erased therefrom by virtue of section 3(5) of this Act or of any regulations made in pursuance of subsection (5) above or section 5(2) of this Act, including provision—

(*a*) for authorising the Registrar, notwithstanding anything in the Act of 1956 or this Act, to refuse to restore as aforesaid the name of any such person unless he furnishes to the Registrar such evidence of his identity and good character as may be prescribed ; and

(*b*) for securing that, in such circumstances as may be prescribed, such a person's name is not so restored unless the General Council or a committee thereof so direct after making such investigation of his conduct as they think fit:

Provided that nothing in any regulation made in pursuance of paragraph (*a*) or (*b*) above shall apply to the restoration of a person's name to the overseas list in pursuance of a direction under subsection (5) above.

(7) Subsections (1) and (2) above shall apply in relation to the register of temporarily registered medical practitioners as they apply in relation to the register ; but any regulations under this section made by virtue of those subsections may make different provision in relation to the two registers.

(8) Regulations made in pursuance of subsection (4), (5) or (6) above shall not have effect until approved by order of the Privy Council, and the power to make any such order shall be exercisable by statutory instrument and shall include power to vary or revoke any such order.

(9) In this section " prescribed " means prescribed by regulations under this section.

Power to make regulations with respect to registration fees.

5.—(1) Subject to the provisions of this Act, the General Council may make regulations with respect to the charging of fees in connection with the making of entries in the register, and in particular—

(*a*) prescribing a fee to be charged on the entry of a name or qualification in the register or on the restoration of any entry to the register ;

(*b*) prescribing a fee to be charged in respect of the retention in the register of the name of a person in any year subsequent to the year beginning with the date on which he was first registered ;

(*c*) authorising the Registrar, notwithstanding anything in the Act of 1956 or this Act, to refuse to make any entry in, or restore any entry to, the register or a particular list therein until a fee prescribed by regulations under this section has been paid.

(2) Regulations under this section may authorise the Registrar to erase from the register the name of—

(*a*) any person who, after such notices and warnings as may be prescribed by the regulations, fails to pay a fee prescribed in pursuance of subsection (1)(*b*) above; or

(*b*) any person who in the manner prescribed by the regulations applies for his name to be erased from the register on the ground that he does not wish to pay or continue to pay fees prescribed in pursuance of the said subsection (1)(*b*).

(3) If a person whose name has been erased from the register in accordance with regulations made in pursuance of subsection (2) above at any time pays—

(*a*) such sum (if any) as may be prescribed for the purposes of this subsection by regulations under this section; and

(*b*) the fee (if any) which, if his name had not been so erased, would be due from him in respect of the current year,

his name shall be restored to the register.

(4) Regulations under this section prescribing fees may provide for the charging of different fees in different cases and may provide that fees shall not be chargeable in cases prescribed by the regulations.

(5) Regulations under this section shall not have effect until approved by order of the Privy Council, and the power to make any such order shall be exercisable by statutory instrument and shall include power to vary or revoke any such order.

(6) For the avoidance of doubt it is hereby declared that in this section " entry " includes an entry by way of alteration of a previous entry.

Special provisions with respect to registration fees.

6.—(1) In the case of a person who is or has at any time been registered by virtue of any provision of the law of the Republic of Ireland made for purposes similar to those of section 17 of the Act of 1956 (provisional registration)—

(*a*) no fee shall be chargeable on provisional registration under the said section 17; and

(*b*) the fee payable on registration under section 7 of that Act shall not exceed the fee which is payable on registration thereunder in the case of a person provisionally registered under the said section 17.

(2) Regulations under section 5 of this Act shall not provide for any fee to be chargeable in respect of anything done in pursuance of a direction under section 34 of the Act of 1956 (restoration to register of names erased for conviction of crime or for professional misconduct).

(3) Where a direction for temporary registration in pursuance of section 25 of the Act of 1956 is given, the General Council may include therein a direction that the right to registration conferred thereby shall be subject to payment by the person to whom the direction relates of such fee as may be specified in the direction.

Applications for registration.

7.—(1) Subject to the provisions of this section, any right to registration conferred by the Act of 1956 shall be conditional on the making of such an application, supported by such evidence, as is required by the provisions of this section.

(2) An application for registration under Part II of the Act of 1956, whether fully or provisionally and whether of persons, qualifications or other matters, shall be made to the registrar of one of the branch councils.

(3) Any other application for registration under the Act of 1956, and any application relating to inclusion in the overseas list, shall be made to the Registrar.

(4) Subject to subsection (5) below, a person making an application for registration under section 7, 17, 18 or 23 of the Act of 1956 shall produce or send to the registrar to whom in accordance with subsection (2) or (3) above the application is made the document conferring or evidencing the qualification by virtue of which the application is made together with a statement of his name and address and such other particulars, if any, as may be required for registration.

(5) Any university or other body specified in Schedule 3 to the Act of 1956 may from time to time send to the Registrar or the registrar of a branch council lists certified under the body's seal of the persons who have been granted qualifications by the body, stating the qualifications and addresses of the persons included in the list, and a registrar—

(*a*) may for the purposes of that Act and this Act treat any such list sent to that registrar as sufficient evidence of the entitlement of any person mentioned therein to the qualification or qualifications which he is stated therein to have been granted; and

(*b*) on an application for registration under section 7 or 17 of that Act may issue a certificate of registration under the next following section to a person mentioned in any such list sent to that registrar as having been granted a primary qualification without the document mentioned in subsection (4) above being produced or sent to him.

(6) A registrar shall not register any qualification, whether on first registration of a person or by way of addition, unless he is satisfied that the person claiming the qualification is entitled to it; but if a registrar to whom an application for registration of a qualification is made determines that he is not satisfied as aforesaid, the applicant may appeal to the General Council.

(7) This section shall not apply to temporary registration under section 25 of the Act of 1956 or to anything done in pursuance of a direction under section 34 of that Act (restoration of names erased for crime or misconduct).

Certificates of full or provisional registration.

8.—(1) Subject to section 7 of this Act, if the registrar to whom in accordance with subsection (2) or (3) of that section there is made any application for—

(*a*) the registration of a person under Part II of the Act of 1956, whether fully or provisionally; or

(*b*) the registration of a person under Part III of that Act (otherwise than under section 25), whether fully or provisionally; or

(*c*) the registration of a qualification under section 8 or 21 of that Act,

is satisfied that the applicant is entitled to be registered or to have the qualification registered in accordance with the application, he shall issue to the applicant an appropriate certificate of registration stating, in the form prescribed by regulations under section 4 of this Act for entries in the register, the name of the applicant and such other particulars as may be so prescribed.

(2) Without prejudice to subsection (3) below, the particulars stated in any certificate of registration issued under this section shall be deemed for all purposes to have been duly registered on the date of issue of the certificate except in so far as they were actually registered before that date, and references in the Act of 1956 or this Act to registration shall be construed accordingly.

(3) On issuing a certificate of registration under this section a registrar shall—

(*a*) if he is the registrar of the branch council for Scotland or Ireland, with all convenient speed send a copy thereof, certified under his hand, to the Registrar, who shall forthwith cause an appropriate entry or alteration to be made in the register; or (*b*) if he is the Registrar or the registrar of the branch council for England and Wales, forthwith cause an appropriate entry or alteration to be made in the register.

(4) An entry or alteration made in the register in pursuance of subsection (3) above shall bear the same date as the certificate of registration by virtue of which it is made.

(5) This section shall not apply to anything done in pursuance of a direction under section 34 of the Act of 1956 (restoration of names erased for crime or misconduct).

The Medical Register and the Overseas Medical Register.

9.—(1) The Registrar shall in every year cause to be printed, published and sold, under the direction of the General Council, a publication, to be called " the Medical Register ", being a correct register of the names in alphabetical order of surnames, with the addresses and registered qualifications and such other particulars (if any) as the General Council may direct, of all persons appearing in the principal list in the register, as existing on the 1st January in that year, excluding those whose registration therein is for the time being suspended.

(2) The General Council may if they think fit direct in respect of any year that, in addition to the publication of the Medical Register in that year, the Registrar shall, at such time during that year as the Council may determine, cause to be printed, published and sold, under the direction of the Council, a publication, to be called " the Overseas Medical Register ", being a correct register of the names in alphabetical order of surnames, with the addresses and registered qualifications and such other particulars (if any) as the General Council may direct, of all persons appearing in the overseas list in the register, as existing on such date in that year as the Council may direct, excluding those whose registration therein is for the time being suspended.

(3) A copy of either of the said publications purporting to be printed and published as aforesaid shall be evidence (and in Scotland sufficient evidence) that the persons specified therein are registered fully or provisionally in the principal list or the overseas list in the register as appears from the publication; and the absence of the name of any person both from such a copy of the Medical Register and from such a copy of the Overseas Medical Register shall be evidence (and in Scotland sufficient evidence) that he is not registered under section 7, 17, 18 or 23 of the Act of 1956.

(4) In the case of a person whose name does not appear in either of the said publications—

(*a*) a certified copy, under the hand of the Registrar, of an entry relating to that person in the register or the register of temporarily registered medical practitioners shall be evidence (and in Scotland sufficient evidence) of that entry; and

(b) a certificate of registration issued under section 8 of this Act or section 25 of the Act of 1956 in respect of that person shall be evidence (and in Scotland sufficient evidence) that he is registered fully or provisionally in the register, or temporarily under the said section 25, as appears from the certificate.

Expenses and accounts

10.—(1) The following provisions of this section shall have effect instead of paragraphs 12 and 13 of Schedule 1 to the Act of 1956 with respect to the expenses of the General Council and branch councils, and accounts.

Expenses and accounts.

(2) Any fees or other sums payable by virtue of this Act in connection with registration thereunder shall be paid to the General Council, and any expenses of the Council shall be defrayed out of the sums received by the Council either on account of those fees and sums, or from the sale of registers, or otherwise.

(3) The General Council shall furnish each branch council with such sums as the branch council may require for defraying—

(a) any salaries, fees, expenses or allowances which the branch council is authorised by the Act of 1956 or this Act to pay; and

(b) any other expenses incurred by the branch council with the approval of the General Council;

and each branch council shall furnish the General Council with such evidence as the Council may reasonably require of all payments made by the branch council out of sums furnished by the Council.

(4) The General Council shall keep proper accounts of all sums received or paid by them, and proper records in relation to those accounts (including records of the evidence furnished as aforesaid), and their accounts for each financial year of the Council shall be audited by auditors appointed by the Council.

(5) No person shall be qualified to be appointed auditor under this section unless he is a member of one or more of the following bodies:—

the Institute of Chartered Accountants in England and Wales;

the Institute of Chartered Accountants of Scotland;

the Association of Certified and Corporate Accountants;

the Institute of Chartered Accountants in Ireland;

any other body of accountants established in the United Kingdom and for the time being recognised by the Board of Trade for the purposes of section 161(1)(*a*)

1948 c. 38. of the Companies Act 1948;

but a Scottish firm may be so appointed if each of the partners thereof is qualified to be so appointed.

(6) As soon as may be after the accounts of the General Council have been audited, the Council shall cause them to be published and shall send a copy of them to the Privy Council together with a copy of any report of the auditors thereon, and the Privy Council shall lay a copy of the accounts and of any report of the auditors thereon before each House of Parliament.

(7) As soon as may be after the date of commencement of this section each branch council shall cause to be paid or transferred to the General Council all money and investments held by the branch council on that date other than such sum as they may be authorised by the Council to retain for defraying the expenses of the branch council; and for the purposes of this section any sum retained by a branch council by virtue of this subsection shall be treated as having been furnished to them by the Council.

Registration of qualifications, and temporary registration

Registration of qualifications.

11.—(1) For subsections (1) to (3) of section 8 of the Act of 1956 (right to registration by virtue of additional qualifications specified in column 3 of Schedule 3 to that Act, and right to have those and certain other qualifications registered) there shall be substituted—

"(1) A person holding any additional qualification which the General Council determine ought to be registrable by virtue of this subsection shall, if registered under section 7 or 17 of this Act or on becoming so registered, be entitled to have the qualification registered:

Provided that if, in the case of any such qualification, the Council determine that it ought not to be registrable by virtue of this subsection if granted before or after a particular date, a person holding that qualification shall not be entitled to have it registered if it was granted to him before or, as the case may be, after that date.

(2) In this Act 'additional qualification' means any qualification granted in the United Kingdom or the Republic of Ireland other than a primary qualification.

(3) A person registered under section 7 or 17 of this Act who obtains any primary qualification in addition to the primary qualification or qualifications by virtue of which he was so registered shall be entitled to have it registered in addition thereto."

(2) Subsections (2) and (3) of section 21 of the Act of 1956 (registration of further qualifications held by Commonwealth or foreign practitioners) shall apply to persons registered or becoming registered provisionally under section 23 of that Act as they apply to persons registered or becoming registered under section 18 thereof, and accordingly after the word " eighteen " in those subsections there shall be inserted the words " or twenty-three ".

(3) In section 10(2) and (4) of the Act of 1956 the references to an additional qualification shall be construed as references to an additional qualification for the time being registrable under Part II of that Act; in sections 11(1), 16(4) and 17(4) of that Act the references to qualifications registrable under Part II of that Act shall be construed as references to primary qualifications so registrable; and in section 33(3) of that Act the reference to a qualification registrable under that Act shall include a reference to a qualification which has at any time been registrable under that Act.

(4) In the Act of 1956 and this Act, unless the context otherwise requires, the expression " qualification " means any diploma, degree, fellowship, membership, licence, authority to practice, letters testimonial, certificate or other status or document granted in respect of medicine, surgery and midwifery or any of them, or any branch of medicine or surgery, and so granted by any university, corporation, college or other body or by any department of, or persons acting under the authority of, the government of any country or place.

Temporary registration for purposes of employment in hospitals in United Kingdom or Isle of Man.

12. The following section shall be substituted for section 25 of the Act of 1956—

" 25.—(1) Where a person satisfies the General Council—

(*a*) that he has been selected for employment in the United Kingdom or the Isle of Man as a medical practitioner in one or more hospitals or other institutions approved by the Council for the purposes of this section ; and

(*b*) that he holds, has held, or has passed the examinations necessary for obtaining, some Commonwealth or foreign qualification or qualifications recognised for the time being by the Council for the purposes of this section as furnishing a sufficient guarantee of the possession of the requisite knowledge and skill for the efficient practice of medicine, surgery and midwifery, the Council may if they think fit give a direction that for the purposes of his employment as a medical practitioner in that institution, or such of those institutions as may be specified in the direction, and in such post or grade (or both) there as may be so specified he shall be registered under this section for a period so specified.

(2) Registration of a person under this section shall continue only while he is in the employment to which the direction by virtue of which he is so registered relates, and accordingly, subject to subsection (5) below, a person registered under this section shall cease to be so registered at the end of the period specified in the direction by virtue of which he is so registered or, if the employment to which that direction relates terminates before the end of that period, on the termination of that employment.

(3) In case of doubt, the decision of the General Council as to the termination of the employment to which a direction for a person's registration under this section relates shall be conclusive for the purposes of subsection (2) above.

(4) A person registered under this section shall, in relation to the employment to which the direction by virtue of which he is so registered relates, and to things done and omitted in the course thereof, be treated as registered under section 18 of this Act as a fully registered medical practitioner, but in relation to other matters shall be treated as not so registered.

(5) Nothing in subsection (2) above shall preclude the General Council from specifying in a direction for a person's registration under this section a period immediately following the period specified in a previous direction for his registration thereunder.

(6) On registering a person under this section the Registrar shall issue to him an appropriate certificate of registration stating, in the form prescribed by regulations under section 4 of the Medical Act 1969 for entries in the register of temporarily registered medical practitioners, the person's name and such other particulars as may be so prescribed."

Disciplinary proceedings

Powers of Disciplinary Committee.

13.—(1) For subsection (1) of section 33 of the Act of 1956 (erasure from register for conviction of crime or for infamous conduct in any professional respect) there shall be substituted the following subsections—

"(1) Where a fully registered person—

(*a*) is found by the Disciplinary Committee to have been convicted (whether while so registered or not) in the United Kingdom or the Republic of Ireland or any of the Channel Islands or the Isle of Man of a criminal offence; or

(b) is judged by the Disciplinary Committee to have been (whether while so registered or not) guilty of serious professional misconduct,

the Committee may, if they think fit, direct that his name shall be erased from the register or that his registration therein shall be suspended (that is to say, shall not have effect) during such period not exceeding twelve months as may be specified in the direction.

(1A) Where a direction for the suspension of a person's registration in the register has been given under this section the Disciplinary Committee may—

(a) from time to time direct that the period of suspension specified in the original direction shall be extended or further extended for such further period from the time when it would otherwise expire as may be specified in the direction; or

(b) at any time while the suspension continues to have effect direct that the person's name shall be erased from the register;

but the Committee shall not extend any period of suspension under this section for more than twelve months at a time.

(1B) Where a direction under this section for the suspension or suspension for an extended period of a person's registration in the register takes effect, the Registrar shall make a note of the fact in the register; and while a person's registration in the register is suspended by virtue of this section he shall be treated as not being registered therein notwithstanding that his name still appears therein."

(2) Accordingly—

(a) for the words "infamous conduct in any professional respect", wherever they occur in the Act of 1956, there shall be substituted the words "serious professional misconduct";

(b) in section 37(1)(f) of that Act, for the words "such conduct" there shall be substituted the words "such misconduct"; and

(c) any reference to infamous conduct in any professional respect in any other enactment passed, or in any instrument made, before the commencement of this section shall, in so far as it relates to the conduct of medical practitioners, be construed as, or as including, a reference to serious professional misconduct.

(3) If, while a person's registration in the register is suspended under section 33 of the Act of 1956, a direction under that section is given by virtue of subsection (1A) thereof, the suspension of his registration in the register shall continue to have effect throughout any period which may intervene between the time when, but for this subsection, the suspension of his registration would end and the time when the direction takes effect in accordance with section 36 of the Act of 1956 or an appeal against it under that section is (in whatever manner) determined; but if on the determination of such an appeal a direction extending the suspension of the appellant's registration for a further period takes effect after the time when, but for this subsection, that suspension would have ended, that further period shall be treated as having started to run from that time.

(4) In section 39(2) of the Act of 1956 (General Council's duty to report disciplinary action against persons registered in medical register of the Republic of Ireland), after the words "the register" there shall be inserted the words "or suspension of registration therein".

Appeal against erasure or suspension.

14.—(1) In section 36 of the Act of 1956 (appeal against erasure from register), for subsections (1) and (2) (notification of Disciplinary Committee's determinations) there shall be substituted—

"(1) Where the Disciplinary Committee give or make a direction under section 33 or an order under section 35 of this Act for the erasure of a person's name from the register or a direction under the said section 33 for the suspension or suspension for an extended period of a person's registration in the register, the Registrar shall forthwith serve on him a notification of the direction or order.

(2) Any notification required to be served on a person by the foregoing subsection may be served on him either by delivering it to him or by leaving it at his proper address or by sending it by registered post or by the recorded delivery service; and

(*a*) for the purposes of this subsection and of section 26 of the Interpretation Act 1889 in its application to this subsection, a person's proper address shall be his address on the register or, if his last known address differs from his address on the register and it appears to the Registrar that a letter sent to him there is more likely to reach him, his last known address; and

1889 c. 63.

(*b*) where such a notification is served by sending it by post, service thereof shall be deemed to have been effected at the time when the letter containing it would be delivered in the ordinary course of post;

and so much of the said section 26 as relates to the time when service is deemed to have been effected shall not apply to such a notification."

(2) In the said section 36 of the Act of 1956, for subsections (5) and (6) (time when a determination of the Disciplinary Committee takes effect) there shall be substituted the following subsections—

" (5) A direction or order such as is mentioned in subsection (1) of this section shall take effect—

(*a*) where no appeal under this section is brought against the direction or order within the time mentioned in subsection (3) of this section, on the expiration of that time;

(*b*) where such an appeal is so brought but is withdrawn or dismissed for want of prosecution, on the withdrawal or dismissal of the appeal;

(*c*) where such an appeal is so brought and is not withdrawn or dismissed as aforesaid, if and when the appeal is determined by the upholding of the direction or order, and not otherwise (but, in the case of a direction under section 33 of this Act, without prejudice to the power of the Judicial Committee to substitute for it any other direction which the Disciplinary Committee would have had power to make under that section).

(6) Where any notification required to be served on a person by subsection (1) of this section is served on him by sending it by post then, on an application made at any time by that person, the President of the General Council or any other member of the Council authorised by the President to act for the purposes of this subsection, if satisfied that the notification was not received by that person within fourteen days of the giving or making of the direction or order to which the notification relates, may if he thinks fit by authorisation in writing extend the time within which an appeal under this section may be brought against the direction or order.

(7) Where the time for appealing against a direction or order such as is mentioned in subsection (1) of this section is extended by an authorisation under subsection (6) of this section, subsection (5) of this section shall apply to the direction or order as if the reference in paragraph (*a*) to the time mentioned in subsection (3) of this section

were a reference to that time as so extended; and if the authorisation is given after the expiration of the time mentioned in the said subsection (3), the direction or order shall be deemed not to have taken effect on the expiration of that time, and any reference in the Act of 1956 or this Act to the time when such a direction or order takes effect in accordance with this section shall be construed accordingly."

Power to order immediate suspension.

15.—(1) On giving a direction for erasure or a direction for suspension in respect of any person the Disciplinary Committee, if satisfied that to do so is necessary for the protection of members of the public or would be in the best interests of that person, may order that his registration in the register shall be suspended forthwith in accordance with this section.

(2) Where an order under subsection (1) above is made in respect of a person, his registration in the register shall be suspended (that is to say, shall not have effect) from the time when the order is made until the time when the relevant direction takes effect in accordance with section 36 of the Act of 1956 or an appeal against it under that section is (in whatever manner) determined:

Provided that if, when the order is made, the person in question is neither present nor represented at the proceedings, this subsection shall have effect as if for the reference to the time when the order is made there were substituted a reference to the time of service of a notification of the order under the provisions applied by subsection (3) below.

(3) Subsections (1) and (2) of section 36 of the Act of 1956 (service of notification of Disciplinary Committee's directions) shall apply in relation to an order under this section as they apply in relation to a direction for erasure or suspension.

(4) The court may terminate any suspension of a person's registration in the register which has effect by virtue of subsection (2) above, and the decision of the court on any application under this subsection shall be final.

In this subsection "the court", in the case of a person whose address on the register is in Scotland, means the Court of Session, in the case of a person whose address on the register is in Northern Ireland, means Her Majesty's High Court of Justice in Northern Ireland, and in the case of any other person means Her Majesty's High Court of Justice in England.

(5) In this section "direction for erasure" means a direction under subsection (1) of section 33 of the Act of 1956 for the erasure of a person's name from the register, and "direction for suspension" means a direction under that subsection for the

suspension of a person's registration in the register; and "the relevant direction", in relation to an order under subsection (1) above, means the direction for erasure or suspension on the giving of which the order was made.

16.—(1) Subsections (2) and (3) of section 33 of the Act of 1956 and, so far as it confers on the Disciplinary Committee power to direct that a person's name shall be erased from the register, subsection (1) of that section shall apply to a temporarily registered person, and shall so apply whether or not the circumstances are such that he falls within the meaning in that Act of the expression "fully registered person". Application of disciplinary provisions to temporarily registered persons.

(2) Except as provided in subsection (1) above as regards section 33 of the Act of 1956, that section, section 34 of that Act (restoration of names to register) and section 15 of this Act shall not apply to temporarily registered persons.

(3) For the purposes of the application of any provision of the Act of 1956 or this Act to a temporarily registered person by virtue of subsection (1) above, "the register" means the register of temporarily registered medical practitioners.

(4) In this section "temporarily registered" means temporarily registered under section 25 of the Act of 1956.

Miscellaneous and general

17.—(1) Elections of elected members of the General Council shall be conducted in accordance with a scheme made by the Council and approved by the Privy Council instead of as provided in Schedule 2 to the Act of 1956, and the provisions of that Schedule shall cease to have effect. Election of elected members of General Council.

(2) A scheme under this section may make special provision with respect to the election (in pursuance of section 4(1)(*a*) of the Act of 1956) of persons as resident in Wales, and generally may make different provision for elections falling to be held in different circumstances.

(3) A scheme under this section may be amended by the General Council, but no amendment of the scheme shall have effect unless approved by the Privy Council.

(4) The time for coming into office of a person elected in pursuance of a scheme under this section shall be—

(*a*) if his predecessor retired at the end of his term of office or vacated office in the last twelve months of that term, whether by death or resignation, the expiration of that term;

(*b*) in any other case, such time as may be specified for the purposes of this paragraph in the scheme.

Power to make certain examinations qualifying ones.

18.—(1) If it appears to the General Council that the standard of proficiency in medicine, surgery and midwifery required from candidates at examinations held or to be held by any university or combination of universities in the United Kingdom for the purpose of granting one or more primary qualifications is or will be such as is required in the case of a qualifying examination by section 10(1) of the Act of 1956, the General Council may represent to the Privy Council that it is expedient that those examinations should become qualifying examinations for the purposes of Part II of that Act.

(2) Her Majesty may by Order in Council give effect to any representation made to the Privy Council under this section, and any such Order may make such amendments in section 11 of the Act of 1956 as are necessary for giving effect to the Order.

(3) The power to make representations under this section shall not be capable of delegation; and, accordingly, in section 6(3) of the Act of 1956 and in paragraph 6(1) of Schedule 1 to that Act, after the word " Act " there shall in each case be added the words " or under section 18 of the Medical Act 1969 ".

Power to request information from registered persons for statistical purposes.

19. For the purpose of enabling the General Council to compile or assist in the compilation of statistics relating to medical practice and practitioners the Council may from time to time issue to persons registered under the Act of 1956 (including those temporarily registered under section 25) requests for information on matters which in the opinion of the Council are relevant for that purpose.

Amendment of Act of 1956.

20. The Act of 1956 shall have effect subject to the amendments set out in Schedule 1 to this Act.

Interpretation and construction.

21.—(1) In this Act, unless the context otherwise requires, the following expressions have the meanings hereby assigned to them respectively, that is to say—

1956 c. 76.

" the Act of 1956 " means the Medical Act 1956 ;

" qualification " has the meaning assigned by section 11(4) of this Act ;

" the register " means the register of medical practitioners, and " registered " means registered in that register ;

" the Registrar " means the registrar of the General Council.

(2) References in this Act to any other enactment shall, unless the context otherwise requires, be construed as references to that enactment as amended by or under any other enactment, including this Act.

(3) This Act shall be construed as one with the Act of 1956.

(4) Notwithstanding subsection (3) above, references to the Act of 1956 in section 57 of that Act shall not be construed as including references to this Act.

22. This Act extends to Northern Ireland; and without prejudice to section 21(3) of this Act, section 56(2) of the Act of 1956 (powers of Parliament of Northern Ireland) shall have effect as if the references to that Act included references to this Act.

Application to Northern Ireland.

23.—(1) The enactments mentioned in Schedule 2 to this Act are hereby repealed to the extent specified in column 3 of that Schedule.

Repeals and transitional provisions.

(2) Schedule 3 to this Act shall have effect for the purpose of the transition to the provisions of this Act from the law in force before the commencement of those provisions.

24.—(1) This Act may be cited as the Medical Act 1969, and the Act of 1956, the Medical Act 1956 (Amendment) Act 1958 and this Act may be cited together as the Medical Acts 1956 to 1969.

Short title, citation and commencement.

1958 c. 58.

(2) This Act shall come into operation on such day as Her Majesty may by Order in Council appoint, and different days may be appointed under this subsection for different purposes; and any reference in this Act to the commencement of any provision thereof shall be construed as a reference to the day appointed under this subsection for the coming into operation of that provision.

(3) An Order under this section may make such transitional provision as appears to Her Majesty to be necessary or expedient in connection with the provisions thereby brought into force, including such adaptations of those provisions or any provision of this Act then in force as appear to Her to be necessary or expedient in consequence of the partial operation of this Act (whether before or after the day appointed by the Order).

SCHEDULES

Section 20.

SCHEDULE 1

Amendments of Act of 1956

Abolition of need for approval by Privy Council of remuneration payable to certain persons

1. In the following provisions authorising the payment of remuneration by the General Council, namely section 9(5) (visitors of medical schools), section 10(7) (inspectors of qualifying examinations) and section 38(4) (assessors to Disciplinary Committee), the words " with the approval of the Privy Council " or " with the sanction of the Privy Council ", as the case may be, shall be omitted.

Power of Privy Council to approve regulations made under section 15(2) subject to modifications

2. In section 15(9), at the end there shall be added the words " and the Privy Council may approve such regulations either as submitted to them or subject to such modifications as appear to them requisite:

Provided that where the Privy Council propose to approve any such regulations subject to modifications they shall notify to the General Council the modifications they propose to make and consider any observations of the General Council thereon."

Removal of certain restrictions on right to registration as Commonwealth or foreign practitioner

3. The following provisions of section 18 (registration of Commonwealth and foreign practitioners) shall cease to have effect, namely—

(*a*) subsection (1) (*c*) (applicant required to show that he is entitled to practise in country where his qualifications were granted) ;

(*b*) subsections (3) and (4) (applicant required to prove one or more of certain matters relating to domicile, residence, nationality etc.).

Power to limit registrability of further qualifications under section 21(2)

4. In section 21(2), at the end there shall be added as a proviso—

" Provided that if, in the case of any such qualification, the Council determine that it ought not to be registrable by virtue of this subsection if granted before or after a particular date, a person holding that qualification shall not be entitled to have it registered if it was granted to him before or, as the case may be, after that date."

Reduction of period which must elapse before application for restoration to register can be made after erasure

5. In section 34(1), for the words " eleven months ", in both places where they occur, there shall be substituted the words " ten months ".

Matters not subject to default powers of Privy Council

6. In section 49(1), at the end there shall be added the words " or section 5 or 9(2) of the Medical Act 1969 ".

Proof of regulations and orders

7. Section 51 (proof of certain instruments mentioned therein) shall apply to a copy of any regulations made by the General Council under section 4 or 5 of this Act or of any order made by the Disciplinary Committee under section 15 of this Act as it applies to a copy of any such instrument.

Interpretation of certain expressions in Act of 1956

8. Without prejudice to section 21(3) of this Act, expressions to which a meaning is assigned by section 21(1) of this Act shall, unless the context otherwise requires, have the same meaning in the Act of 1956.

Capacity of General Council

9. Schedule 1 shall have effect and be deemed always to have had effect as if after paragraph 1 there were inserted as paragraph (1A)—

> " (1A) It shall be within the capacity of the General Council as a corporation to do such things and enter into such transactions as are in their opinion incidental or conducive to the performance of their functions under this Act, including the borrowing of money."

Payment of fees and allowances to members of General Council and branch councils otherwise than for attendance

10. In paragraph 7(1) of Schedule 1, for the words from " for " (where it first occurs) to " subsistence " there shall be substituted the words " and such travelling, subsistence or other ", and in the proviso the words " for attendance " shall be omitted.

Repeal of requirements as to treasurers

11. Paragraph 9 of Schedule 1 (under which the General Council and each of the branch councils must have a treasurer) shall cease to have effect.

Honorary officers

12. In paragraph 11 of Schedule 1 (payment of salaries to officers and servants of councils), after the words " branch council shall " there shall be inserted the words " (except in the case of any honorary treasurer or other honorary officer) ".

Amendment of reference to Royal Faculty of Physicians and Surgeons of Glasgow

13. In column 1 of Schedule 3, for the words " Royal Faculty of Physicians and Surgeons of Glasgow " there shall be substituted the words " Royal College (formerly Royal Faculty) of Physicians and Surgeons of Glasgow ".

Section 23(1).

SCHEDULE 2

ENACTMENTS REPEALED

Chapter	Short Title	Extent of Repeal
4 & 5 Eliz. 2. c. 76.	The Medical Act 1956.	Section 4(8). In section 6(4), the words " and the expenses and accounts of those councils ". In section 9(5), the words " with the approval of the Privy Council ". In section 10(7), the words " with the sanction of the Privy Council ". In section 11(4)(*a*), the words " or additional ". In section 12(1), the words " or additional ". In section 13(1), the words " or additional ". In section 18, in subsection (1), paragraph (*c*) and the word " and " preceding it, and subsections (3) to (6). In section 24(1)(*b*) the words from " or that " to the end of the paragraph. In section 28(3), the words " (within the meaning of Part III of this Act) ". In section 38(4), the words " with the approval of the Privy Council ". Sections 41 to 46. Section 48(2). In section 49(1) proviso, the words from " or forty-five " to " forty-six ". In section 51, the words " or under section forty-one ". In section 54(1), the definitions of " registered " and " the register " and, in the definition of " additional qualification ", the words " subsection (1) of ". Section 57(7) and (8). In Schedule 1, in paragraph 7(1) proviso, the words " for attendance "; paragraph 9; in paragraph 11, the word " treasurer "; and paragraphs 12 and 13. Schedule 2. In Schedule 3, column 3.

SCHEDULE 3

Section 23(2).

TRANSITIONAL PROVISIONS

1. Until the commencement of section 1 of this Act references in this Act to the register shall be construed as references to the general register kept for the purposes of the Act of 1956 by the Registrar.

2. Without prejudice to his general duty to keep the register correct, the Registrar shall secure that as from the commencement of section 3 of this Act the names of persons temporarily registered under section 25 of the Act of 1956 and not otherwise registered under that Act do not appear in the register.

3. The Registrar shall so prepare the register of temporarily registered medical practitioners mentioned in subsection (3) of section 3 of this Act as to secure that at the commencement of that section it contains the names of all persons who immediately before the commencement of that section were temporarily registered under section 25 of the Act of 1956.

4. If at any time after the repeal of section 44 of the Act of 1956 (co-ordination of central and local registers) the Registrar receives particulars of any alteration (within the meaning of that section) made in the local register for Scotland or Ireland before the repeal of that section, he shall forthwith cause the like alteration to be made in the register; and any alteration made in pursuance of this paragraph shall bear the same date as it would have borne if that section had remained in force, and be deemed to have been made on that date.

5. References in section 4(6) of this Act to a person whose name has been erased from the register by virtue of section 3(5) of this Act shall include references to a person whose name has been erased therefrom by virtue of section 41(7) of the Act of 1956 or the corresponding enactment repealed by that Act.

6. Section 7 of this Act shall not apply to registration in pursuance of a direction of the General Council under the Medical Practitioners and Pharmacists Act 1947.

1947 c. 11 (11 & 12 Geo. 6.).

7. In section 9(3) of this Act the references to sections 7, 17, 18 and 23 of the Act of 1956 include references to the corresponding provisions of the enactments repealed by that Act and the reference to the said section 18 includes also a reference to section 1 of the Medical Practitioners and Pharmacists Act 1947.

8. A person who immediately before the commencement of section 11 of this Act holds an additional qualification within the meaning of section 8 of the Act of 1956 as originally enacted shall, if registered under section 7 of that Act or on becoming so registered, be entitled to have the qualification registered; and if he is not registered under the said section 7, that qualification shall confer on him the same right to registration under the said section 7 as a primary qualification.

SCH. 3
1889 c. 63.

9. Without prejudice to section 37 of the Interpretation Act 1889 (which authorises the exercise of statutory powers between the passing and the commencement of an Act conferring them), regulations made under section 4 of this Act before the commencement of section 3 of this Act may include provision for enabling applications for inclusion in the overseas list mentioned in section 3(2)(*b*) of this Act to be made before the commencement of the said section 3.

10. In the case of a person who immediately before the commencement of section 12 of this Act is registered under section 25 of the Act of 1956 by virtue of a direction thereunder, subsections (2) to (4) of the said section 25 shall, as regards his registration thereunder by virtue of that direction, continue to have effect in relation to him as if the said section 12 had not been passed, but without prejudice to the operation of the said section 12 for the purposes of any subsequent direction under the said section 25.

11. For the purposes of any case referred to the Disciplinary Committee for inquiry before the commencement of section 13 of this Act and of any appeal or other proceedings arising out of any such case—

(*a*) the Act of 1956 and, so far as still in force, any rules made thereunder before the commencement of that section shall have effect as if section 13(2) of this Act had not been passed ; and

(*b*) this Act (except the said section 13(2)) and any rules made under the Act of 1956 after the passing of this Act shall have effect as if for references to serious professional misconduct there were substituted references to infamous conduct in any professional respect.

National Mod (Scotland) Act 1969

1969 CHAPTER 41

An Act to make further provision for contributions by local authorities in Scotland towards the expenses of the National Mod. [25th July 1969]

BE IT ENACTED by the Queen's most Excellent Majesty, by and with the advice and consent of the Lords Spiritual and Temporal, and Commons, in this present Parliament assembled, and by the authority of the same, as follows:—

Contributions towards expenses of the National Mod. 1948 c. 26.

1. The power conferred on a local authority by section 132 of the Local Government Act 1948 to contribute towards the expenses of an entertainment held in the area of another authority shall, in relation to the National Mod held under the auspices of An Comunn Gaidhealach, be exercisable by any local authority in Scotland, whether or not the place in which it is held is convenient for residents in their area, and whether or not the other authority consent.

Consequential increase in rate support grant.

2. Any increase attributable to this Act in the sums payable by way of rate support grant under the enactments relating to local government in Scotland shall be defrayed out of moneys provided by Parliament.

Short title.

3. This Act may be cited as the National Mod (Scotland) Act 1969.

Architects Registration (Amendment) Act 1969

1969 CHAPTER 42

An Act to amend section 14 of the Architects (Registration) Act 1931; to vary from time to time the proportion of the income of the Architects' Registration Council of the United Kingdom which has to be put into the fund maintained by the Council for the support of needy students of architecture; to widen the purposes of the fund; and for purposes connected therewith.

[25th July 1969]

BE IT ENACTED by the Queen's most Excellent Majesty, by and with the advice and consent of the Lords Spiritual and Temporal, and Commons, in this present Parliament assembled, and by the authority of the same, as follows:—

Establishment of Architects' Registration Council Education Fund.

1.—(1) There shall be constituted a fund, to be known as the Architects' Registration Council Education Fund, which, together with its income, shall be applied for the purposes authorised in subsection (4) of this section in such manner and upon such conditions and at such times as the Council may from time to time determine and pending such application may be invested in any manner authorised by the law of any part of the United Kingdom for the investment of trust property.

(2) The Architects' Registration Council Education Fund shall consist of—

(*a*) such monies as at the passing of this Act shall remain in the hands of the Council pursuant to the provisions of section 14 of the Act of 1931; and

(*b*) such proportion of the total amount of the fees received after the passing of this Act in each calendar year or part thereof by the Council under the Act of 1931 as shall be determined from time to time by the Council with the approval of the Privy Council.

(3) Section 13(3) and (4) of the Act of 1931 shall apply to the giving by the Privy Council of the approval mentioned in subsection (2) of this section.

(4) The purposes authorised for the application of th Architects' Registration Council Education Fund and its incom are:—

(*a*) the provision of scholarships and grants for the assistanc of students in architecture whose means appear to th Council to be insufficient to enable them to pursue thei studies and the provision for the purpose of advancin education in architecture of grants for architects anc other persons;

(*b*) the support and furtherance of education and researcl in architecture:

Provided that such research shall consist of work designed to improve the general practice of architecture or of historical research designed to improve the educa-tion of architects;

(*c*) the dissemination of teaching or the results of research concerning architecture.

(5) In making grants under paragraph (*a*) of subsection (4) of this section to persons other than students in architecture regard may be had to their means as well as in making grants to students.

(6) In this section " architecture " includes all subjects related to architecture or affecting the practice thereof.

Repeals.

2. Section 14 of the Act of 1931 (which provides that at least half of the fees received under that Act shall be used for scholarships and maintenance grants for students in architecture) and the Architects (Registration) Act 1934 (which amends section 14 so as to defer its commencement) are hereby repealed.

1934 c. 38.

Interpretation.

3. In this Act—

" the Act of 1931 " means the Architects (Registration) Act 1931 as amended by the Architects Registration Act 1938;

1931 c. 33.
1938 c. 54.

" the Council " has the same meaning as in the Act of 1931.

Short title, citation and extent.

4.—(1) This Act may be cited as the Architects Registration (Amendment) Act 1969, and the Act of 1931 and the Architects Registration Act 1938 and this Act may be cited together as the Architects Registration Acts 1931 to 1969.

(2) It is hereby declared that this Act extends to Northern Ireland, but, for the purposes of section 6 of the Government of Ireland Act 1920 (which precludes the Parliament of Northern Ireland from amending Acts of the Parliament of the United Kingdom passed after the day appointed under that Act) this Act shall be deemed to have been passed before that day.

1920 c. 67.

Air Corporations Act 1969

1969 CHAPTER 43

n Act to make new provision in relation to the finances of the British European Airways Corporation; and to amend the provisions of the Air Corporations Act 1967 relating to members of the corporations in order to prevent conflicts of interest. [25th July 1969]

3E IT ENACTED by the Queen's most Excellent Majesty, by and with the advice and consent of the Lords Spiritual and Temporal, and Commons, in this present Parliament sembled, and by the authority of the same, as follows:—

Financial assistance for B.E.A. by reduction of indebtedness and transfer of stock.

1.—(1) As from 1st April 1968—

(*a*) all outstanding liabilities of the British European Airways Corporation in respect of advances made before that date under section 42 of the Finance Act 1956 or section 8 of the Air Corporations Act 1967 (or any enactment repealed by that Act) shall be extinguished; and 1956 c. 54. 1967 c. 33.

(*b*) all rights and liabilities which under the terms of issue of any stock issued under section 9 of the Air Corporations Act 1949 (or any enactment repealed by that Act) were immediately before that date rights and liabilities of the Corporation shall be rights and liabilities of the Treasury. 1949 c. 91.

(2) As from the said 1st April, the Corporation shall assume debt due to the Board of Trade of £91,585,714 4s. 0d. (which £25 million less than the total of the advances and stock in espect of which the Corporation are relieved of liability by subection (1) of this section); and the debt so assumed by the Corporation shall be paid off at such times and by such methods, nd interest thereon shall be paid at such rates and at such times, s the Board may with the approval of the Treasury from time o time direct.

(3) The sum of £25 million (representing the amount by whi the indebtedness of the Corporation is reduced as aforesa shall be carried to a special account of the Corporation a transferred from it, by instalments specified in directions giv by the Board, to the credit of the Corporation's revenue accou for the four years ending with 31st March 1972.

(4) The Board may by order made by statutory instrume extinguish the liabilities of the Corporation which are o standing on 1st April 1972 in respect of such amount (n exceeding £12½ million) of the debt assumed by the Corporati under subsection (2) of this section as may be specified in t order; and, if such an order is made, subsection (3) of th section shall apply to the amount specified in the order and the three years ending with 31st March 1975 as it applies the sum specified in that subsection and to the four years the mentioned.

1967 c. 33. (5) Subsections (5) and (6) of section 8 of the Air Corpor tions Act 1967 (ancillary provisions relating to sums receive as repayment of and interest on advances under that sectio shall apply to sums received by the Board under subsection (of this section as they apply to sums received by them und that section; and subsection (7) of that section (which relat to advances in respect of which liability is extinguished b subsection (1) of this section) is hereby repealed.

(6) No directions shall be given under subsection (3) of th section except after consultation with the Corporation and wit the approval of the Treasury; and any directions specifying th sum to be transferred under that subsection in respect of an year may (after the like consultation and with the like approva be revoked or varied at any time before the beginning of tha year.

(7) An order may be made under subsection (4) of this sectio before, on or after 1st April 1972, but no such order shall b made except with the approval of the Treasury and unless draft of it has been laid before the Commons House of Parlia ment on or before 31st March 1973 and has been approved by resolution of that House.

(8) The transitional provisions contained in Schedule 1 t this Act shall have effect in relation to subsection (1) of thi section.

Power to provide for investment of public dividend capital in B.E.A.

2.—(1) The Board of Trade may by order made by statutor instrument direct that as from such date, not being earlier tha 1st April 1972, as may be specified in the order, the followin provisions of the Air Corporations Act 1967, that is to say—

(*a*) section 14 (which provides for the investment of publi dividend capital in B.O.A.C.); and

(b) section 17 (which imposes on B.O.A.C. a financial duty related to the said section 14),

ll have effect as if any reference in those provisions to the tish Overseas Airways Corporation included a reference to British European Airways Corporation.

2) On the date on which an order under this section comes ɔ force—

(a) section 20 of the said Act of 1967 (which lays down the existing financial duty of B.E.A.); and

(b) section 21 of that Act (which enables the Board to give directions as to the application of any revenue surplus of B.E.A.),

ıll cease to apply to the British European Airways Corporation cept as respects any direction already given under the said ction 21; and as from that date section 22 of that Act (which ys down the borrowing limits for B.E.A.) shall have effect as the amount to which the limit under that section applies cluded the aggregate amount of any sums paid to the Corpora-n under section 14 of that Act (but not any sum treated as paid by virtue of subsection (3)(b) of the said section 14).

(3) In the application of section 14 of the said Act of 1967 the British European Airways Corporation by virtue of an der under this section—

(a) subsection (1) shall have effect as if the reference therein to section 16 of that Act were a reference to section 22 of that Act; and

(b) subsection (3)(a) shall have effect as if the reference therein to the financial year ending on 31st March 1966 were a reference to the financial year in which the order comes into force.

(4) No order shall be made under this section—

(a) except after consultation with the Corporation and with the approval of the Treasury; and

(b) unless a draft of it has been laid before, and approved by a resolution of, the Commons House of Parliament.

Consequential financial provisions.
1967 c. 33.

3.—(1) In section 18 of the Air Corporations Act 1967 (power f Board of Trade to require sums in reserve fund of B.O.A.C. ɔ be paid into the Consolidated Fund if surplus to the require-nents of the Corporation) the reference to the British Overseas Airways Corporation shall include a reference to the British European Airways Corporation but in relation to that Corpora-ion the powers conferred by that section shall be exercisable only as from 1st April 1972.

(2) The Board may, after consultation with the British Eu pean Airways Corporation and with the approval of the Treasu direct that any sum in respect of which the Board have po to give a direction under section 18 of the said Act of 1967 applied to that Corporation by the foregoing subsection shall treated as if it had been borrowed by the Corporation and w an advance to them by the Board under section 8 of that A

(3) The expiry of the provisions of sections 14, 17 and 18 the said Act of 1967 by virtue of section 19 of that Act (wh provides for the temporary duration of those provisions) sh not affect their application to the British European Airw Corporation by virtue of section 2 of this Act or of subsect (1) of this section; and accordingly in the said section references to the expiry of those provisions shall be co strued as references to their expiry in relation to the Brit Overseas Airways Corporation only.

(4) The fact that sections 20 and 21 of the said Act of 19 cease to apply to the British European Airways Corporation consequence of section 2(2) of this Act shall not affect t application of those sections to the British Overseas Airwa Corporation by virtue of section 19(3)(*b*) of that Act.

1968 c. 30.

(5) In section 22(1) of the said Act of 1967 (which, as amend by section 1(1) of the Air Corporations Act 1968, restricts bo rowing by B.E.A. to a limit of £210 million or such greater su not exceeding £240 million as the Board of Trade may fro time to time by order specify) for the references to £210 millic and £240 million there shall be substituted respectively referenc to £200 million and £230 million; and the amount to which th limit imposed by the said section 22(1) applies—

(*a*) shall include the amount for the time being outstandi in respect of the principal of the debt assumed by th Corporation under section 1(2) of this Act; but

(*b*) shall not include the amount for the time being outstan ing in respect of the principal of any sum which b virtue of a direction under subsection (2) of this sectio is treated as if it had been borrowed by the Corpora tion.

(6) The Air Corporations Act 1968 (which amends the sai section 22(1) as aforesaid and also enables B.E.A. to borro from the Board of Trade for the purpose of financing accumu lated deficits on revenue account) is hereby repealed.

Conflicts of interest in case of members of air corporations. 1967 c. 33.

4. Schedule 1 to the Air Corporations Act 1967 (which con tains provisions relating to the members of B.E.A. and B.O.A.C and with respect to certain other matters affecting those Corpora tions) shall be amended by the insertion, after paragraph 6, o the paragraph set out in Schedule 2 to this Act.

5.—(1) This Act may be cited as the Air Corporations Act 1969. Short title, citation and interpretation.

(2) The Air Corporations Act 1967 and this Act may be cited together as the Air Corporations Acts 1967 and 1969. 1967 c. 33.

(3) Except where the context otherwise requires, any reference in this Act to any enactment is a reference to that enactment as amended by any other enactment, including this Act.

SCHEDULES

Section 1.

SCHEDULE 1

TRANSITIONAL PROVISIONS

PART I

EXTINGUISHMENT OF LIABILITIES IN RESPECT OF ADVANCES

1. As soon as may be after the commencement of this Act the shall be made between the Treasury and the Corporation all su adjustments in respect of the period beginning with 1st April 19 and ending with the commencement of this Act as may be requir for carrying section 1(1)(*a*) of this Act into effect, including in pa ticular provisions for dealing with sums paid by the Corporatic during that period in discharge of liabilities which are retrospective extinguished by the said section 1(1)(*a*), whether by repayment the sums out of the National Loans Fund, by crediting them again other liabilities of the Corporation to the Board of Trade or part one and partly the other.

PART II

TRANSFERRED STOCK

Renaming of stock

2. As from 1st April 1968 (in this Part of this Schedule referre to as "the date of transfer") the following stock, that is to say—

(*a*) the 4½ per cent. British European Airways Guarantee Stock 1972-1977; and

(*b*) the 3 per cent. British European Airways Guarantee Stock 1980-1983,

(being the issues comprised in the stock to which section 1(1)(*b*) o this Act applies) shall each be renamed by omitting the wor "Guaranteed".

Application of provisions applicable to government stock

3. As from the date of transfer, the stock to which section 1(1)(*b*) of this Act applies (in this Part of this Schedule referred to as "the stock") shall be deemed for all purposes, but subject to the rights and liabilities mentioned in the said section 1(1)(*b*), to have been created and issued under the National Loans Act 1968, and that Act and any other enactment, regulation or rule relating to securities issued under that Act shall apply accordingly to the stock.

1968 c. 13.

4. As from the date of transfer, the Airways Corporations Stock Regulations 1947 and the Airways Corporations Stock Regulations 1948 shall be deemed not to have applied to the stock, but this paragraph shall not affect the validity of any thing done under or for the purposes of any provision of those regulations before the commencement of this Act, and any such thing shall continue to have effect after the commencement of this Act in relation to the

S.I. 1947/99. S.I. 1948/2858.

ck and shall be deemed to have been done under or for the rposes of the corresponding enactment, regulation or rule for the ie being applicable to the stock. SCH. 1

Payments of interest

5. In relation to the person entitled to any payment of interest respect of the stock before the commencement of this Act, any yment of such interest made by the British European Airways rporation on or after the date of transfer shall have effect as if ade by the Treasury.

Transitional adjustments

6. As soon as may be after the commencement of this Act there all be made between the Treasury and the said Corporation all ch adjustments in respect of the period beginning with the date transfer and ending with the commencement of this Act as may required for carrying section 1(1)(*b*) of this Act into effect, cluding in particular payments by the Treasury out of the National oans Fund for reimbursing to the Corporation interest paid by em in respect of the stock during that period.

SCHEDULE 2

Section 4.

PARAGRAPH INSERTED IN SCHEDULE 1 TO AIR CORPORATIONS ACT 1967

1967 c. 33.

6A.—(1) Before appointing a person to be a member of the orporation the Board shall satisfy themselves that that person will ave no such financial or other interest as is likely to affect preudicially the discharge by him of his functions as a member of ie corporation, and the Board shall also satisfy themselves from me to time with respect to every member of the corporation that e has no such interest; and any person who is, or whom the Board ropose to appoint to be, a member of the corporation shall, whenver requested by the Board so to do, furnish to the Board such nformation as the Board consider necessary for the performance y the Board of their duties under this paragraph.

(2) A member of the corporation who is in any way directly r indirectly interested in a contract made or proposed to be made y the corporation shall disclose the nature of his interest at a neeting of the corporation; and the disclosure shall be recorded in he minutes of the corporation, and the member shall not take any art in any deliberation or decision of the corporation with respect o that contract.

(3) For the purposes of the last foregoing sub-paragraph a general notice given at a meeting of the corporation by a member of the corporation to the effect that he is a member of a specified company or firm and is to be regarded as interested in any contract which may, after the date of the notice, be made with the company or firm, shall be regarded as a sufficient disclosure of his interest in relation to any contract so made.

SCH. 2

(4) A member of the corporation need not attend in person at meeting of the corporation in order to make any disclosure whi he is required to make under this paragraph if he takes reasonat steps to secure that the disclosure is made by a notice which brought up and read at the meeting.

National Insurance Act 1969

1969 CHAPTER 44

An Act to amend the provisions of the National Insurance Act 1965, the National Insurance (Industrial Injuries) Act 1965 and the Industrial Injuries and Diseases (Old Cases) Act 1967 as to the rate or amount of contributions and benefit; to make further provision as to death grant under the National Insurance Act 1965, as to the assessment of disablement under the National Insurance (Industrial Injuries) Act 1965 and, for purposes of those and certain other Acts, as to the introduction of a decimal currency; to make temporary provision consequential on or related to the matters aforesaid; and for other purposes connected therewith.
[25th July 1969]

BE IT ENACTED by the Queen's most Excellent Majesty, by and with the advice and consent of the Lords Spiritual and Temporal, and Commons, in this present Parliament assembled, and by the authority of the same, as follows:—

Contributions and benefits under National Insurance Act 1965

Increased contributions under National Insurance Act 1965. 1965 c. 51. 1968 c. 14.

1.—(1) In the National Insurance Act 1965 for the provisions of Schedule 1 there shall be substituted the provisions set out in Schedule 1 to this Act (in place of the provisions previously substituted by section 1 of the Public Expenditure and Receipts Act 1968); and there shall be paid out of moneys provided by Parliament any resulting increase in the sums so payable by way of Exchequer supplement under section 7 of the National Insurance Act 1965.

1965 c. 51. (2) In section 4(1) of the National Insurance Act 1965 for th paragraphs (*c*) and (*d*) substituted for paragraph (*c*) by sectic
1966 c. 6. 1 of the National Insurance Act 1966 there shall be substitute the following paragraph (*c*):—

"(*c*) the amount of the graduated contribution payable b each of them shall be the aggregate of—

(i) where the employment is not at the time of th payment a non-participating employment, 4¾ pe cent. of any amount, up to £9, by which that pay ment exceeds £9 (or of the equivalent amount fo remuneration not paid weekly); or

(ii) where the employment is at the time of th payment a non-participating employment, ½ per cent of that amount;

and, whether the employment is or is not a non-partici pating employment, 3¼ per cent. of any amount, up to £12, by which the payment exceeds £18 (or of the equivalent amount for remuneration not paid weekly)".

Accordingly in section 58 of the National Insurance Act 1965 as amended by paragraph 8 of Schedule 1 to the National Insurance Act 1966, for the words "under section 4(1)(*d*) of this Act" there shall be substituted the words "as a non-participating employment".

(3) No increase in contributions shall be made under section 5 of the National Insurance Act 1965 in the year 1970; and accordingly—

(*a*) in section 5(1) there shall be omitted the word "three", where first occurring, and the words "1970"; and

(*b*) in section 5(2) for the words "any of the three years" there shall be substituted the words "either of the two years".

(4) The contributions to be paid under the National Insurance Act 1965 out of moneys provided by Parliament shall include, in addition to the Exchequer supplements,—

(*a*) in respect of the financial year 1969-70, the sum of £10 million;

(*b*) in respect of each subsequent financial year, the sum of £45 million;

and those contributions shall be paid in such manner and at such times as the Treasury may determine.

2.—(1) The rates of benefit provided by Schedule 3 to the ational Insurance Act 1965, as amended by the Family Allowces and National Insurance Act 1968, shall be modified as llows:— Increased benefit under National Insurance Act 1965. 1965 c. 51. 1968 c. 40.

(*a*) except in the cases dealt with by paragraphs (*b*) to (*d*) below, the rates specified in column 2 (weekly rate without increases) shall each be increased by 10s., the rates specified in columns 3, 4 and 5 (increases for children) shall each be increased by 3s., and the rates specified in column 6 (increases for adult dependants) shall each be increased by 6s.;

(*b*) the rate (in column 2) of widow's allowance shall be increased by 13s., the rates in columns 3, 4 and 5 of increases for children in the case of widow's allowance, widowed mother's allowance and child's special allowance shall each be increased by 3s. 6d., and the rates in column 2 of guardian's allowance and child's special allowance shall each be increased by 3s. 6d.;

(*c*) in the case of unemployment benefit and sickness benefit, the rates in column 2 of £3 2s. and £2 10s. (being the rates for certain married women or persons under 18) shall be increased respectively by 8s. and 5s.;

(*d*) in the case of retirement pensions the rate in column 2 of £2 16s. (being the rate applicable where the pension is payable to a woman by virtue of her husband's insurance and he is alive) shall be increased by 6s.;

nd accordingly for the provisions of that Schedule there shall be ubstituted the provisions set out in Schedule 2 to this Act (in lace of the provisions previously substituted by section 1 of he Family Allowances and National Insurance Act 1968).

(2) The amount of maternity grant provided for by Schedule 4 to the National Insurance Act 1965, as amended by the National Insurance Act 1967, shall be increased by £3; and accordingly for the provisions of that Schedule there shall be substituted the provisions set out in Schedule 3 to this Act (in place of the provisions previously substituted by section 1 of the National Insurance Act 1967). 1967 c. 73.

3.—(1) The weekly amount of earnings above which, under section 30(7) of the National Insurance Act 1965, earnings affect the rate of retirement pension, and the weekly amount above which they result in an increased reduction in the rate of pension, shall each be increased by one pound above the amounts provided for by the National Insurance (Earnings) Regulations 1967; and accordingly in section 30(7) there shall Earnings rule for retirement pensions.

be made the following amendments, in place of those ma by the regulations, that is to say,—

(*a*) for the words " five pounds " there shall be substitut the words " seven pounds ten shillings " ; and

(*b*) subject to subsection (2) below, for the words " s pounds " there shall be substituted the words " ni pounds ten shillings ".

(2) As from the 14th February 1971 (being the day before th
1967 c. 47. appointed day under section 1 of the Decimal Currency A
1965 c. 51. 1967), section 30(7) of the National Insurance Act 1965 sha have effect as if for the words " by sixpence for each comple shilling of the excess and a further sixpence for each comple shilling by which the earnings exceed six pounds " there ha been substituted the words " by a shilling for each complete tw shillings of the excess or, if the excess is more than two pound then by one pound in respect of the first two pounds of th excess and by a shilling for each further complete shilling c the excess ; " and section 44 of the National Insurance Act 196 (which confers power to vary section 30(7) by regulations) sha have effect as if in paragraph (*a*)(ii) for the words " for eac shilling of the excess " there had been substituted the word " in respect of the excess ".

Death grant. **4.**—(1) The deaths in respect of which a death grant is pay able in accordance with section 39(1) of the National Insuranc Act 1965 shall, subject to the other provisions of that Act apply ing to death grants, include the death after the coming into forc of this section of a person who at death—

(*a*) is over the age of nineteen but is, and ever since he became nineteen has been, by reason of illness o disability of mind or body incapacitated for regula employment ; and

(*b*) is residing, or would, if not living in a school, hospita or recognised home, have been residing, with a relative mentioned in subsection (2) below, that relative being a person satisfying the contribution conditions referred to in section 39(1) or the wife or widow of such a person.

(2) The deceased's relative referred to in subsection (1)(*b*) above must be a person of whom the deceased was the child or remoter issue, or who was the deceased's child or remoter issue, or the deceased's step-father, step-mother or step-child, or the deceased's brother, sister, half-brother, half-sister, step-brother or step-sister ; but a person shall be treated as such a relative if he was such a relative by adoption or would have been such a relative if some person born illegitimate had been born legitimate.

(3) For purposes of this section "recognised home" means ı establishment which is for those purposes accepted by the :cretary of State as providing residential accommodation for sabled persons.

Industrial injuries and diseases

Increased contributions under National Insurance (Industrial Injuries) Act 1965.

5.—(1) In the National Insurance (Industrial Injuries) Act 965, for the Table set out in Part I of Schedule 2 (weekly ıtes of contribution payable by insured persons and employers) ıere shall be substituted the Table set out in Schedule 4 to ıis Act (in place of the Table previously substituted by section 2 f the National Insurance Act 1967).

1965 c. 52.
1967 c. 73.

(2) There shall be paid out of moneys provided by Parliament ny increase resulting from this section in the contributions so ayable under section 2(1)(*b*) of the National Insurance (Industrial Injuries) Act 1965.

Increased benefit for industrial injuries and diseases.

6.—(1) In the National Insurance (Industrial Injuries) Act 965, for the provisions of Schedule 3 (rate or amount of benefit :tc.) there shall be substituted the provisions set out in Schedule 5 o this Act (in place of the provisions previously substituted by ection 2 of the National Insurance Act 1967 and amended by ection 1 of the Family Allowances and National Insurance Act 1967 and section 1 of the Family Allowances and National nsurance Act 1968). 1968 c. 40.

(2) The following rates of allowance provided for by the Industrial Injuries and Diseases (Old Cases) Act 1967 shall be increased to three pounds one shilling, that is to say,— 1967 c. 34.

(*a*) the maximum weekly rate of a lesser incapacity allowance payable by virtue of section 2 of the Act (supplementation of workmen's compensation); and

(*b*) the weekly rate of an allowance payable by virtue of section 5(1)(*a*) (industrial diseases benefit schemes) in respect of disablement which is not total;

and accordingly the words "three pounds one shilling" shall be substituted in section 2(6)(*c*) of the Act for the words "two pounds seven shillings and sixpence" and in section 7(2)(*b*) for the words "two pounds ten shillings" (in place of the words "two pounds fifteen shillings" previously substituted in both places by section 3(1) of the National Insurance Act 1967).

Assessment of extent of disablement.

7. In Schedule 4 (assessment of extent of disablement) to the National Insurance (Industrial Injuries) Act 1965 there shall be omitted paragraph 1(*b*) (which makes provision for determining when a claimant's disabilities are to be treated as incurred as a result of the relevant loss of faculty), and accordingly in paragraph 1(*a*) after the words "all disabilities" there shall be inserted the words "so incurred"; but after paragraph 1(there shall be inserted as a new paragraph 1(*aa*)—

"(*aa*) regulations may make provision as to the extent (any) to which any disabilities are to be taken int account where they are disabilities which, thoug resulting from the relevant loss of faculty, also resul or without the relevant accident might have been ex pected to result, from a cause other than the relevar accident."

General

Decimalisation.

8.—(1) The Secretary of State may by regulations—

1967 c. 47.

(*a*) modify, so as to take account of the introduction of th new currency provided for by the Decimal Currency Act 1967, provisions which operate by reference to sums expressed in terms of the previous currency and are contained in or have effect under the enactments listed in subsection (2) below;

(*b*) provide for adjusting the amount of any payment by way of benefit or allowance under those enactments so as to eliminate fractions of a new penny;

(*c*) make such further consequential, supplementary or transitional provision as appears to the Secretary of State expedient for the purpose of those enactments in connection with the introduction of the new currency.

(2) The enactments referred to in subsection (1) above are—

1965 c. 51. (*a*) the National Insurance Act 1965;

1965 c. 52. (*b*) the National Insurance (Industrial Injuries) Act 1965;

1965 c. 53. (*c*) the Family Allowances Act 1965;

1965 c. 54. (*d*) section 1 of the National Health Service Contributions Act 1965;

1965 c. 62. (*e*) section 27 of the Redundancy Payments Act 1965;

1966 c. 20. (*f*) Part II of the Ministry of Social Security Act 1966 (including that Part as modified for certain cases by paragraph 4 of Schedule 7 to the Act);

1967 c. 34. (*g*) the Industrial Injuries and Diseases (Old Cases) Act 1967;

(*h*) any enactment amending an enactment included in paragraphs (*a*) to (*g*) above.

(3) Regulations shall not be made under this section so as to take effect from a date earlier than the 15th February 1971, except that regulations made by virtue of subsection (1)(*c*) may

ıake provision taking effect before that date for the keeping f records or other incidental matters relevant for the period fter that date.

(4) Regulations made under this section shall have effect otwithstanding anything in section 10 of the Decimal Currency .ct 1969.

1969 c. 19.

(5) Regulations under this section shall be made by statutory ıstrument, which shall be subject to annulment in pursuance f a resolution of either House of Parliament.

Administrative expenses.

1965 c. 51.
1965 c. 52.

9. Subject to the provision made by section 85 of the National nsurance Act 1965 for reimbursement out of the National nsurance Fund, or by section 61 of the National Insurance Industrial Injuries) Act 1965 for reimbursement out of the ndustrial Injuries Fund, there shall be paid out of moneys rovided by Parliament any increase attributable to this Act n the expenses of the Secretary of State for Social Services or ny other government department which are so payable under ither of those sections; and any reference in this section to ection 61 of the National Insurance (Industrial Injuries) Act 965 shall include that section as applied by section 13 of the ndustrial Injuries and Diseases (Old Cases) Act 1967.

1967 c. 34.

Temporary exclusion of certain requirements as to regulations and schemes, and omission of quinquennial review.

10.—(1) Section 108 of the National Insurance Act 1965 which requires a preliminary draft of regulations to be submitted to the National Insurance Advisory Committee before the regulations are made or, in certain cases, before a draft is laid efore Parliament) and section 62(2) of the National Insurance (Industrial Injuries) Act 1965 (which requires a proposal to make regulations to be referred to the Industrial Injuries Advisory Council for consideration and advice) shall not apply—

(*a*) to regulations made, or to a draft of regulations laid, before the expiration of six months beginning with the date of the passing of this Act if the instrument containing the regulations or, as the case may be, the draft states that the regulations contain no provisions other than such as—

(i) are made in consequence of this Act; or

(ii) operate with reference to the amount of a person's earnings, and are made under one or more of the following provisions (which relate to the classification of insured persons or the liability to contributions), that is to say, sections 1(3) and 8(5) of the National Insurance Act 1965 and section 3(3)(*b*) of the National Insurance (Industrial Injuries) Act 1965, or made for the purpose of any of those

1965 c. 51. provisions under section 114(5) of the Nationa Insurance Act 1965;

(*b*) to regulations made before the 15th February 197 and containing no provisions other than such as ar made under section 8 of this Act.

(2) The following enactments, that is to say—

(*a*) section 107(1) of the National Insurance Act 1965;

(*b*) section 4(8)(*a*) of the Industrial Injuries and Disease
1967 c. 34. (Old Cases) Act 1967;

1948 c. 24. (*c*) section 1(7) of the Police Pensions Act 1948;

shall not require a draft of any regulations or scheme to be lai before Parliament or approved by resolution of either Hous before the making of the regulations or scheme, if the regula tions or scheme are or is made before the expiration of si months beginning with the date of the passing of this Act and if the instrument containing the regulations or scheme state that they or it are or is made in consequence of this Act; bu where any of those enactments would otherwise so require, th instrument containing the regulations or scheme shall instead be subject to annulment in pursuance of a resolution of either House of Parliament.

(3) Section 86 of the National Insurance Act 1965 and section
1965 c. 52. 60 of the National Insurance (Industrial Injuries) Act 1965 (which by subsection (1)(*a*) provide in each case for the Government Actuary to review the operation of the Act during the period of five years ending with 31st March in 1969 and in every fifth year thereafter) shall each be amended by substituting " 1974 " for " 1969 " in subsection (1)(*a*).

Citation, construction, commencement etc., repeal and extent.

11.—(1) This Act may be cited as the National Insurance Act 1969, and—

(*a*) shall be included among the Acts which may be cited together as the National Insurance Acts 1965 to 1969 and, so far as it relates to the subject-matter of those Acts, shall be construed as one with the National Insurance Act 1965; and

(*b*) shall be included among the Acts which may be cited together as the National Insurance (Industrial Injuries) Acts 1965 to 1969 and, so far as it relates to the subject-matter of those Acts, shall be construed as one with the National Insurance (Industrial Injuries) Act 1965; and

(*c*) may be cited together with the Industrial Injuries and Diseases (Old Cases) Acts 1967 as the Industrial Injuries and Diseases (Old Cases) Acts 1967 and 1969

and, so far as it relates to the subject-matter of those Acts, shall be construed as one with the Industrial 1967 c. 34
Injuries and Diseases (Old Cases) Act 1967.

(2) Schedule 6 to this Act shall have effect with respect to the commencement of this Act and with respect to the transitory matters dealt with in that Schedule; and, subject to any transitional provisions in Schedule 6, the enactments mentioned in Schedule 7 to this Act are hereby repealed to the extent specified in column 3 of the Schedule.

(3) Without prejudice to subsection (1)(*a*) to (*c*) above, and without prejudice to the operation by virtue of any of those paragraphs, in relation to matters arising out of this Act, of any provisions relating to Northern Ireland of the Acts referred to in the paragraph, this Act shall not extend to Northern Ireland.

SCHEDULES

Section 1.

SCHEDULE 1

1965 c. 51.

PROVISIONS TO BE SUBSTITUTED IN SCHEDULE 1 TO NATIONAL INSURANCE ACT 1965

RATES OF FLAT-RATE CONTRIBUTIONS

PART I

Employed persons

Description of employed person	Weekly Rate of Contribution	
	Unless by virtue of a non-participating employment	If by virtue of a non-participating employment
1	2	3
	s. d.	s. d.
Men between the ages of 18 and 70 (other than men over the age of 65 who have retired from regular employment)—		
Earning remuneration at a weekly rate exceeding £6	13 7	16 0
Earning remuneration at a weekly rate of £6 or less	8 2	9 5
Women between the ages of 18 and 65 (other than women over the age of 60 who have retired from regular employment)—		
Earning remuneration at a weekly rate exceeding £6	11 10	13 4
Earning remuneration at a weekly rate of £6 or less	7 0	7 9
Boys under the age of 18	9 5	—
Girls under the age of 18	7 9	—

For the purposes of this Part and Part II of this Schedule a person shall be deemed to be earning remuneration at a weekly rate of £6 or less if, but only if, his remuneration does not include the provision of board and lodging by the employer and the rate of the remuneration neither exceeds, nor is deemed in accordance with regulations made under section 114(5) of this Act to exceed, £6 a week, and to be earning remuneration at a weekly rate exceeding £6 in any other case.

SCH. 1

PART II

Employers

Description of employed person 1	Weekly Rate of Contribution Unless by virtue of a non-participating employment 2	If by virtue of a non-participating employment 3
	s. d.	s. d.
Men over the age of 18—		
Earning remuneration at a weekly rate exceeding £6 or not being liable to pay a contribution as an employed person ...	15 0	17 5
Earning remuneration at a weekly rate of £6 or less and being liable to pay a contribution as an employed person ...	20 5	24 0
Women over the age of 18—		
Earning remuneration at a weekly rate exceeding £6 or not being liable to pay a contribution as an employed person	13 1	14 7
Earning remuneration at a weekly rate of £6 or less and being liable to pay a contribution as an employed person ...	17 11	20 2
Boys under the age of 18	10 3	—
Girls under the age of 18	8 6	—

For the purposes of this Part of this Schedule a person over pensionable age, not being an insured person, shall be treated as an employed person if he would be an insured person were he under pensionable age and would be an employed person were he an insured person.

PART III

Self-Employed Persons

Description of self-employed person 1	Weekly Rate of Contribution 2
	s. d.
Men between the ages of 18 and 70 (other than men over the age of 65 who have retired from regular employment)	21 6
Women between the ages of 18 and 65 (other than women over the age of 60 who have retired from regular employment)	18 0
Boys under the age of 18	12 3
Girls under the age of 18	10 3

SCH. 1

PART IV

Non-Employed Persons

Description of non-employed person 1	Weekly Rate of Contribution 2
	s. d.
Men between the ages of 18 and 65...	16 5
Women between the ages of 18 and 60	13 0
Boys under the age of 18	9 5
Girls under the age of 18	7 5

SCHEDULE 2

Section 2(1).

PROVISIONS TO BE SUBSTITUTED IN SCHEDULE 3 TO NATIONAL INSURANCE ACT 1965

1965 c. 51.

RATES OF PERIODICAL BENEFITS AND OF INCREASES FOR DEPENDANTS

1 Description of Benefit	2 Weekly rate	3 Increase for only, elder or eldest qualifying child	4 Increase for second qualifying child	5 Increase for each additional qualifying child	6 Increase for adult dependant (where payable)
	£ s. d.	£ s. d.	£ s. d.	£ s. d.	£ s. d.
1. Unemployment or sickness benefit under s. 19(2)—					
(a) in the case of a person over the age of 18, not being a married woman	5 0 0	1 11 0	13 0	11 0	3 2 0
(b) in the case of a person under the age of 18, not being a married woman—					
(i) during any period during which that person is entitled to an increase of benefit in respect of a child or adult dependant ...	5 0 0	1 11 0	13 0	11 0	3 2 0
(ii) during any other period	2 15 0	—	—	—	—
(c) in the case of a married woman over the age of 18—					
(i) during any period during which she is entitled to an increase of benefit in respect of her husband, or during which she is not residing with her husband nor is he contributing to her maintenance at not less than the relevant rate	5 0 0	1 11 0	13 0	11 0	3 2 0
(ii) during any other period	3 10 0	1 11 0	13 0	11 0	3 2 0
(d) in the case of a married woman under the age of 18—					
(i) during any period during					

SCH. 2

1 Description of Benefit	2 Weekly rate	3 Increase for only, elder or eldest qualifying child	4 Increase for second qualifying child	5 Increase for each additional qualifying child	6 Increase for adult dependant (where payable)
	£ s. d.	£ s. d.	£ s. d.	£ s. d.	£ s. d.
1. Unemployment or sickness benefit under s. 19(2) —*cont.*					
which she is entitled to an increase of benefit in respect of her husband, or during which she is entitled to an increase of benefit in respect of a child or an adult dependant other than her husband and she is not residing with her husband nor is he contributing to her maintenance at not less than the relevant rate	5 0 0	1 11 0	13 0	11 0	3 2 0
(ii) during any other period during which she is entitled to an increase of benefit in respect of a child or adult dependant ...	3 10 0	1 11 0	13 0	11 0	3 2 0
(iii) during any other period ...	2 15 0	—	—	—	—
2. Unemployment or sickness benefit at a weekly rate determined under s. 19(3)	—	1 11 0	13 0	11 0	3 2 0
3. Maternity allowance ...	5 0 0	1 11 0	13 0	11 0	3 2 0
4. Widow's allowance ...	7 0 0	2 9 0	1 11 0	1 9 0	—
5. Widowed mother's allowance	5 0 0	2 9 0	1 11 0	1 9 0	—
6. Widow's pension ...	5 0 0	—	—	—	—
7. Guardian's allowance ...	2 9 0	—	—	—	—
8. Retirement pension—					
(*a*) where the pension is payable to a woman by virtue of her husband's insurance and he is alive	3 2 0	1 11 0	13 0	11 0	—
(*b*) in any other case ...	5 0 0	1 11 0	13 0	11 0	3 2 0
9. Child's special allowance	2 9 0	—	1 11 0	1 9 0	—

1. In paragraphs 1(*c*)(i) and 1(*d*)(i) of this Schedule " the relevant ate " means a weekly rate equal to the difference under this Schedule etween the rates of benefit applying if the husband is, and if he is ot, contributing to the wife's maintenance at not less than the relevant ate. SCH. 2

2. In paragraph 2 of this Schedule, column 6 shall have effect ubject to section 43(3)(*b*) of this Act.

SCHEDULE 3

Section 2(2).

PROVISIONS TO BE SUBSTITUTED IN SCHEDULE 4 TO NATIONAL INSURANCE ACT 1965

1965 c. 51.

AMOUNTS OF GRANTS

Description of Grant	Amount
	£ s. d.
. Maternity grant	25 0 0
. Death grant, where the person in respect of whose death the grant is paid was at his death—	
(*a*) under the age of 3...	9 0 0
(*b*) between the ages of 3 and 6	15 0 0
(*c*) between the ages of 6 and 18	22 10 0
(*d*) over the age of 18—	
(i) if on 5th July 1948 that person had attained the age of 55 in the case of a man or 50 in the case of a woman	15 0 0
(ii) in any other case	30 0 0

SCHEDULE 4

Section 5.

PROVISIONS TO BE SUBSTITUTED IN PART I OF SCHEDULE 2 TO NATIONAL INSURANCE (INDUSTRIAL INJURIES) ACT 1965

1965 c. 52.

WEEKLY RATES OF CONTRIBUTIONS PAYABLE BY INSURED PERSONS AND EMPLOYERS

Class of insured person to which rate applies	Weekly rate of contribution	
	By the insured person	By the employer
1	2	3
	s. d.	s. d.
Men over the age of 18	11	1 0
Women over the age of 18	8	9
Boys under the age of 18	5	5
Girls under the age of 18	3	4

Section 6.

SCHEDULE 5

1965 c. 52.

PROVISIONS TO BE SUBSTITUTED IN SCHEDULE 3 TO NATIONAL INSURANCE (INDUSTRIAL INJURIES) ACT 1965
RATE OR AMOUNT OF BENEFIT, ETC.

Description of benefit, etc.	Amount
1. Injury benefit under s. 11 (weekly rate).	(*a*) for any period during which the beneficiary is over the age of 18 or is entitled to an increase of benefit in respect of a child or adult dependant ... £7 15s. (*b*) for any period during which the beneficiary is between the ages of 17 and 18 and not entitled as aforesaid ... ... £5 5s. (*c*) for any period during which the beneficiary is under the age of 17 and not entitled as aforesaid ... ... £4 10s.
2. Maximum disablement gratuity under s. 12(3).	£550.
3. Disablement pension under s. 12(5) (weekly rate).	For the several degrees of disablement set out in column 1 of the following Table, for the following periods respectively the respective amounts set out in the following columns respectively of that Table, namely: (*a*) for any period such as is mentioned in paragraph 1(*a*) of this Schedule, column 2; (*b*) for any period such as is mentioned in paragraph 1(*b*) of this Schedule, column 3; (*c*) for any period such as is mentioned in paragraph 1(*c*) of this Schedule, column 4.

TABLE

Degree of disablement	*Amount*								
1	2			3			4		
per cent.	£	s.	d.	£	s.	d.	£	s.	d.
100	8	8	0	5	10	0	5	0	0
90	7	11	0	4	19	0	4	10	0
80	6	14	0	4	8	0	4	0	0
70	5	18	0	3	17	0	3	10	0
60	5	1	0	3	6	0	3	0	0
50	4	4	0	2	15	0	2	10	0
40	3	7	0	2	4	0	2	0	0
30	2	10	0	1	13	0	1	10	0
20	1	14	0	1	2	0	1	0	0

Description of benefit, etc.	Amount
. Unemployability supplement under s. 13 (increase of weekly rate of disablement pension).	(*a*) for any period such as is mentioned in paragraph 1(*a*) of this Schedule ... ... £5 0s. (*b*) for any period such as is mentioned in paragraph 1(*b*) or (*c*) of this Schedule ... ... £2 15s.
5. Maximum increase under s. 14 of weekly rate of disablement pension in cases of special hardship.	£3 7s., or the amount (if any) by which the weekly rate of the pension, apart from any increase under s. 15, 17 or 18 of this Act or under section 6 of the National Insurance Act 1966, falls short of £8 8s., whichever is the less.
6. Maximum increase under s. 15 of weekly rate of disablement pension where constant attendance needed.	(*a*) except in cases of exceptionally severe disablement ... £3 6s. (*b*) in any case ... ... £6 12s.
7. Increase under s. 17 of weekly rate of injury benefit or disablement pension in respect of children.	(*a*) in respect of only, elder or eldest child of beneficiary's family £1 11s. (*b*) in respect of second child of beneficiary's family ... 13s. (*c*) in respect of each additional child of beneficiary's family 11s.
8. Increase under s. 18 of weekly rate of injury benefit or disablement pension in respect of adult dependant.	£3 2s.
9. Widow's pension under s. 19—	
(*a*) weekly rate where payable by virtue of s. 19(3) (*a*)–(*e*).	£5 11s.
(*b*) maximum higher weekly rate for prescribed period after deceased's death.	£7.
10. Widower's pension under s. 20 (weekly rate).	£5 11s.
11. Allowance under s. 21 in respect of children of deceased's family—	
(*a*) weekly rate of allowance under s. 21(1).	(i) in respect of only, elder or eldest qualifying child ... £1 11s. (ii) in respect of second qualifying child ... 13s. (iii) in respect of each additional qualifying child ... 11s.
(*b*) increase under s. 21(2)	18s.
12. Maximum under s. 29(1)(*a*) of aggregate of weekly benefits payable for successive accidents.	(*a*) for any period such as is mentioned in paragraph 1(*a*) of this Schedule ... ... £8 8s.

SCH. 5

Description of benefit, etc.	Amount
	(*b*) for any period such as is mentioned in paragraph 1(*b*) of this Schedule— (i) apart from any increase under s. 14 ... £5 10s. (ii) including any such increase £8 8s. (*c*) for any period such as is mentioned in paragraph 1(*c*) of this Schedule ... ... £5 0s.

Section 11.

SCHEDULE 6

COMMENCEMENT AND TRANSITORY PROVISIONS

PART I

COMMENCEMENT OF THIS ACT

1.—(1) The provisions of this Act, except section 8 (and sections 9 to 11 so far as they have effect for purposes of section 8), shall not come into force until such date or dates as the Secretary of State may by order appoint for those provisions or any of them.

(2) Different days may be appointed under this paragraph for different purposes of the relevant provisions (that is to say, the provisions to which sub-paragraph (1) above applies) or for the same purposes in relation to different cases or classes of case; and if that is done, or if different days are appointed for different provisions, then—

(*a*) an order under this paragraph may contain such incidental or supplemental provisions as appear to the Secretary of State to be necessary or expedient as respects the period or any part of the period when the relevant provisions are to have a partial operation only, and, in particular, may contain provisions modifying and supplementing, in relation to the period to which the order is to apply, the relevant provisions or the provisions of any Act amended by this Act; and

(*b*) any provision made in pursuance of paragraph (*a*) above may be varied or revoked by a subsequent order of the Secretary of State.

1965 c. 51. (3) Section 107(4) of the National Insurance Act 1965 (which provides for orders under that Act to be subject to annulment in pursuance of a resolution of either House of Parliament) shall not apply to any order under this paragraph, but a statutory instrument containing any such order shall be laid before Parliament after being made.

Part II

Sch. 6

Provisions to Apply Generally on Changes in Rates of Benefit

Preliminary

2.—(1) The provisions of this Part of this Schedule shall have effect
ith respect to benefit under the National Insurance Act 1965, the 1965 c. 51.
ational Insurance (Industrial Injuries) Act 1965 or the Industrial 1965 c. 52.
njuries and Diseases (Old Cases) Act 1967, where rates of benefit are 1967 c. 34.
ltered by this or any subsequent Act, or are altered in consequence
f the passing of this Act or of any subsequent Act altering any
naximum rate of benefit.

(2) In this Part of this Schedule "commencing date" means the ate fixed for payment of benefit at an altered rate to commence.

Awards made before commencing date

3.—(1) Where the weekly rate of any benefit is altered to a fixed mount higher or lower than the previous amount, and before the ommencing date an award of that benefit has been made (whether efore or after the passing of the relevant Act), then subject to such xceptions or conditions as may be prescribed by regulations made by he Secretary of State the benefit shall, except as respects any period alling before the commencing date, become payable at the altered ate without any claim being made therefor in the case of an increase n the rate of benefit or any review of the award in the case of a lecrease, and the award shall have effect accordingly.

(2) Where the weekly rate of any benefit is altered, and before the ommencing date (but after that date is fixed) an award is made of he benefit, the award either may provide for the benefit to be paid s from the commencing date at the altered rate or may be expressed n terms of the rates appropriate at the date of the award.

Variation of disablement gratuities

4. Where, in consequence of the passing of this Act or another Act altering the rate of disablement pension under section 12 of the National Insurance (Industrial Injuries) Act 1965, regulations are made varying the scale of disablement gratuities under section 12(3), the regulations may provide that the scale as varied shall apply only in cases where the period taken into account by the assessment of the extent of the disablement in respect of which the gratuity is awarded begins or began after such day as may be prescribed.

Benefit in respect of children or adult dependants

5.—(1) Where for any purpose of the provisions referred to in sub-paragraph (2) below the weekly rate at which a person contributes to the cost of providing for a child, or to the maintenance of an adult dependant, is to be calculated for a period beginning on or after the commencing date for an increase in the weekly rate of benefit, but account is to be taken of amounts referable to the period before the commencing date, then those amounts shall be treated as increased in proportion to the increase in the weekly rate of benefit.

SCH. 6

(2) The provisions for which this paragraph has effect are—

1965 c. 51. (*a*) section 42(1)(*b*) and section 43(1)(*a*)(ii) of the National Insurance Act 1965, and any regulations made by virtue of sectio 43(2)(*c*); and

1965 c. 52. (*b*) section 17(4)(*b*) and section 18(1)(*a*)(ii) of the Nationa Insurance (Industrial Injuries) Act 1965, and any regulation made by virtue of section 18(1)(*d*), both as those sections o regulations apply for purposes of that Act and as they appl
1967 c. 34. for purposes of section 7 of the Industrial Injuries an Diseases (Old Cases) Act 1967.

Section 11.

SCHEDULE 7

REPEALS

Chapter or Number	Short Title	Extent of Repeal
1965 c. 51.	The National Insurance Act 1965.	Section 7(1) from " so however " onwards.
1965 c. 52.	The National Insurance (Industrial Injuries) Act 1965.	In Schedule 4, paragraph 1(*b*).
1966 c. 6.	The National Insurance Act 1966.	Section 1(2).
1967 c. 73.	The National Insurance Act 1967.	Section 1(1)(*c*). Section 2(1)(*a*) and (*b*). Section 3(1). Schedules 3, 5 and 6.
1968 c. 14.	The Public Expenditure and Receipts Act 1968.	Section 1(1) and (5). In section 7(2) the words " in the National Insurance Acts 1965 to 1967 or ". Schedule 1.
1968 c. 40.	The Family Allowances and National Insurance Act 1968.	Section 1(2) and (3). Section 2(2). Schedules 1 and 2.
S.I. 1967/756.	The National Insurance (Earnings) Regulations 1967.	The whole regulations.

Iron and Steel Act 1969

1969 CHAPTER 45

An Act to make new provision in relation to the finances of the British Steel Corporation and certain of their subsidiaries; to empower the Minister of Power to vest property, rights, liabilities or obligations of certain of that Corporation's subsidiaries in them and dissolve certain of their subsidiaries and, in that connection, to amend section 41 of the Iron and Steel Act 1949; to amend the enactments relating to corporation tax in their application, in certain circumstances, to that Corporation; to empower the Board of Trade to make to that Corporation grants comparable to certain of those that may be made under the Industrial Development Act 1966 and the Ministry of Commerce for Northern Ireland to make to them grants comparable to certain of those that may be made under the Industrial Investment (General Assistance) Act (Northern Ireland) 1966; to alter that Corporation's financial year; and to make new provision with respect to the authentication of the fixing of their seal.

[25th July 1969]

BE IT ENACTED by the Queen's most Excellent Majesty, by and with the advice and consent of the Lords Spiritual and Temporal, and Commons, in this present Parliament assembled, and by the authority of the same, as follows:—

Alteration of the British Steel Corporation's financial Structure, and Provisions consequential thereon

1. Section 18 of the principal Act shall have effect, and be deemed always to have had effect, with the substitution, for subsection (1) thereof (by virtue of which the Corporation

Reduction of the Corporation's commencing capital debt.

assumed, on the vesting date, a debt due to the Minister of £833,988,359 4s. 1d.), of the following subsection:—

"(1) The Corporation shall, on the vesting date, assume a debt due to the Minister of £133,988,359 4s. 1d.".

Public investment in the Corporation otherwise than by way of loan.

2.—(1) Subject to the limit imposed by the next following section, the Minister may, with the approval of the Treasury pay to the Corporation such sums as he thinks fit; and for the purposes of this subsection, £700,000,000 shall be deemed to have been paid thereunder by the Minister to the Corporation on the vesting date.

(2) The Corporation shall, as respects each of their financial years, be under obligation either—

(*a*) to make to the Minister, within such reasonable period as he may determine (beginning with the day on which a copy of the statement of the Corporation's accounts in respect of the year is sent to him in compliance with section 24(4) of the principal Act), a proposal for the payment by them to him of a dividend, in respect of that year, on the aggregate of the sums which have been paid under the foregoing subsection by him to them or are deemed, by virtue of that subsection or the following provisions of this Act, to have been so paid, being a dividend at a specified rate per cent.; or

(*b*) to satisfy him, within that period, that no dividend in respect of that year ought to be paid on that aggregate;

and, if they neither so make such a proposal, nor so make one acceptable to the Minister and the Treasury nor satisfy the Minister within that period that no dividend in respect of that year ought to be paid on that aggregate, he may, with the approval of the Treasury and after consultation with the Corporation, direct them to pay to him such a dividend as aforesaid at such rate per cent. as he specifies.

(3) Where a proposal made in satisfaction of the obligation imposed by the last foregoing subsection is accepted by the Minister or a direction is given under that subsection by him, a dividend on the aggregate to which the proposal or direction relates at the rate proposed or directed shall become payable by the Corporation to the Minister on the expiration of the period of seven days beginning with the day next following that on which, as the case may be, written notice of acceptance of the proposal is given to the Corporation or the direction is communicated to them in writing.

(4) Any sums required by the Minister for making payments under this section shall be defrayed out of moneys provided by

Parliament; and any sums received under this section by him shall be paid into the Consolidated Fund.

(5) The account required by section 21 of the principal Act to be prepared by the Minister in respect of each financial year shall include sums paid under this section by him and sums received under this section by him.

(6) In relation to the Corporation's first financial year, subsection (2) above shall have effect with the substitution, for the reference to the day on which a copy of the statement of the Corporation's accounts is sent to the Minister in compliance with section 24(4) of the principal Act, of a reference to the day on which this Act is passed.

Limit on borrowing by, and investment in, the Corporation.

3.—(1) The aggregate of the following, namely,—

(*a*) the amount outstanding in respect of the principal of any money borrowed under section 19 of the principal Act by the Corporation (other than money borrowed for the payment off of any part of the debt assumed by them under section 18 of that Act);

(*b*) any sums paid under section 2(1) of this Act by the Minister to the Corporation; and

(*c*) the amount outstanding in respect of the principal of any money borrowed under section 19 of the principal Act by the publicly-owned companies otherwise than from the Corporation;

shall not at any time exceed £500,000,000, or such greater sum, not exceeding £650,000,000, as the Minister may from time to time by order (made by statutory instrument) specify.

(2) No order shall be made under this section unless a draft of the order has been approved by a resolution of the Commons House of Parliament.

Power of the Minister to effect, for purposes of section 2(1), notional capitalisation of reserves of the Corporation and the publicly-owned companies.

4. Once in each of the Corporation's financial years the Minister may, after consultation with the Corporation and with the approval of the Treasury, direct that a specified sum (not exceeding the aggregate of the reserves, at the end of the Corporation's last preceding financial year, of the Corporation and the companies that were then in public ownership) shall, for the purposes of section 2(1) of this Act, be deemed to have been paid thereunder by him to the Corporation.

The Corporation's financial duty.

5.—(1) The Minister may from time to time determine, with the approval of the Treasury and after consultation with the Corporation, as respects such period as the Minister may so determine, the rate of return on net assets (as for the time being defined for the purposes of this subsection by the Minister) which the Minister considers it is reasonable for the Corporation to achieve in that period; and the Minister may, with the like approval and after such consultation as aforesaid, vary a determination under this subsection as respects any period by a further determination.

(2) The Minister shall give notice to the Corporation of any determination under the foregoing subsection.

(3) The Corporation shall conduct their affairs during any period as respects which a determination has been made under subsection (1) above with a view to achieving in that period a rate of return on net assets not less than that specified by the determination as for the time being in force, and the operation of section 16(1) of the principal Act (which requires the Corporation so to exercise their functions under that Act and the Iron and Steel Act 1949 as to secure that the combined revenues of the Corporation and the publicly-owned companies are not less than sufficient to meet their combined charges properly chargeable to revenue account, taking one year with another) shall be suspended during any such period.

(4) The Minister may by order (made by statutory instrument)—

(*a*) substitute, for the duty imposed by the last foregoing subsection, a financial duty expressed otherwise than by reference to a rate of return on net assets; and

(*b*) for that purpose direct that the foregoing provisions of this section shall have effect subject to such modifications as may be specified in the order and make such other incidental and transitional provisions as appear to the Minister to be necessary or expedient;

but no such order shall be made unless a draft of the order has been approved by a resolution of each House of Parliament.

Duration of certain of the foregoing provisions.

6.—(1) Subject to the next following subsection, sections 2(1), 4 and 5 of this Act shall continue in force until the end of the financial year of the Corporation's that first ends after 1973 and shall then expire; but their previous operation shall not be affected by their expiry.

(2) The Minister may by order (made by statutory instrument) direct that the said sections—

(*a*) shall continue in force permanently after the time at which they would otherwise expire; or

(*b*) shall continue in force after that time until the expiration of such of the Corporation's financial years as may be specified in the order;

but no order shall be made under this subsection unless a draft of the order has been approved by a resolution of each House of Parliament.

(3) If section 2(1) of this Act expires, the following provisions shall have effect:—

(*a*) section 2(2) thereof shall not have effect as respects a financial year of the Corporation's subsequent to that at the end of which section 2(1) expires;

(*b*) the Corporation shall, on the expiry, assume a debt to the Minister of £700,000,000, and subsections (2) and (3) of section 18 of the principal Act and section 3(1)(*a*) of this Act shall have effect as if references therein to the debt assumed by the Corporation by virtue of subsection (1) of the first-mentioned section included references to the debt assumed by them by virtue of this paragraph;

(*c*) any sums paid under section 2(1) of this Act by the Minister to the Corporation shall be deemed to have been borrowed under section 19 of the principal Act by the Corporation from the Minister on the expiry and to have been then lent under section 20(1) of that Act by the Minister to the Corporation; and

(*d*) section 3(1) of this Act shall have effect as if paragraph (*b*) thereof were omitted.

Miscellaneous Provisions relating to the British Steel Corporation and the publicly-owned Companies

Power of the Corporation and the publicly-owned companies to borrow money in foreign currency.

7.—(1) In subsections (1) and (2) of section 19 of the principal Act (which respectively empower the Corporation to borrow temporarily and empower them to borrow otherwise than by way of temporary loan) after the words " such sums " there shall be inserted the words " in sterling ", and after subsection (2), there shall be inserted the following subsection:—

" (2A) The Corporation, with the consent of the Minister, may, from such person and on such terms as he may, with the approval of the Treasury, specify, borrow, in a currency other than sterling, any sum which they have power to borrow in sterling from the Minister ",

and, accordingly, in section 20(1) of that Act (which empowers the Minister to lend to the Corporation any sums which the Corporation have power to borrow under section 19), for the words " under the last foregoing section " there shall be substituted the words " under subsection (1) or (2) of the last foregoing section ".

(2) For subsection (3) of the said section 19 (borrowing powers of the publicly-owned companies) there shall be substituted the following subsection:—

" (3) A publicly-owned company may borrow from the Corporation such sums (whether in sterling or in any other currency) as the company may require for the purposes of their undertaking ; and they may—

(*a*) with the consent of the Minister and the Corporation borrow, by way of temporary loan from any other person, any such sum in sterling as they may so require ; and

(*b*) with the like consent, from such person and on such terms as the Minister may, with the approval of the Treasury specify, borrow by way of temporary loan, in a currency other than sterling any such sum as they may so require ".

Power of the Minister to vest in the Corporation property, rights, liabilities and obligations of certain publicly-owned companies and to dissolve certain such companies.

8.—(1) The Minister may, with respect to a publicly-owned company which was in public ownership on 30th April 1969, by order (made by statutory instrument whereof a draft shall be laid before Parliament) vest all or any of its property, rights, liabilities and obligations in the Corporation ; and an order under this section may contain provision for any matter for which it appears to the Minister requisite or expedient to make provision in connection with, or in consequence of, the vesting.

(2) If, at any time, it appears to the Minister that a publicly-owned company which was in public ownership on 30th April 1969 is void of property, rights, liabilities and obligations, he may by order (made by statutory instrument whereof a draft shall be laid before Parliament) dissolve it.

1949 c. 72.

(3) Section 41 of the Iron and Steel Act 1949 (compensation to officers in connection with transfers) shall have effect as if, at the end of subsection (1), there were added the words " and compensation to officers of the Corporation or a publicly-owned company who suffer loss of employment or loss or diminution of emoluments or pension rights in consequence of the making of an order under section 8 of the Iron and Steel Act 1969 ".

Modification of provisions of the Finance Act 1965 as to company reconstructions without change of ownership in their application, in certain circumstances, to the Corporation. 1965 c. 25.

9. Where, in accordance with arrangements approved for the purposes of this section by the Minister, a publicly-owned company which was in public ownership on 30th April 1969 ceases to carry on a trade and the Corporation begin to carry on activities of that trade as part of its trade, subsection (3) of section 61 of the Finance Act 1965 (company reconstructions without change of ownership) shall, in its application to the company and the Corporation, have effect as if, after the words " carrying on the trade ", there were inserted the words " or any trade of which it has come to form part ".

10. In the event of the dissolution of a company which was in ublic ownership both on 30th April 1969 and immediately efore its dissolution, the Corporation shall be entitled to relief rom corporation tax under section 55(1) of the Finance Act 965 for any amount for which the company, had it not been issolved, would have been entitled to claim relief in respect f allowable losses.

On dissolution of certain publicly-owned companies, their losses that can be set against chargeable gains to enure for the Corporation's benefit.

1965 c. 25.

11.—(1) In the event of the vesting in the Corporation, by virtue of section 8(1) of this Act or in pursuance of arrangements approved for the purposes of this section by the Minister, of an asset of a company which, on 30th April 1969, was in public ownership, being an asset in respect of which a grant might have been made under section 1, 2 or 6 of the Industrial Development Act 1966 to the company had the asset not vested in the Corporation and, in a case in which capital expenditure is incurred with reference to the asset by the Corporation, had it been incurred by the company, the Board of Trade may, out of moneys provided by Parliament, make to the Corporation a grant of the like amount as they might have made to the company in those circumstances.

Power of the Board of Trade, in certain cases of transfer of assets of publicly-owned companies to the Corporation, to make grants to them comparable to those under the Industrial Development Act 1966.

(2) Section 8 (conditions) of the said Act of 1966 shall have effect as if references therein to Part I of that Act included references to the foregoing subsection.

1966 c. 34.

12.—(1) In the event of the vesting in the Corporation, by virtue of section 8 of this Act or in pursuance of arrangements approved for the purposes of this section by the Minister, of an asset of a company which, on 30th April 1969, was in public ownership, being an asset in respect of which a grant might have been made under section 1, 2, 5 or 7 of the Industrial Investment (General Assistance) Act (Northern Ireland) 1966 to the company had the asset not vested in the Corporation and, in a case in which capital expenditure is incurred with reference to the asset by the Corporation, had it been incurred by the company, the Ministry of Commerce for Northern Ireland may, if the Parliament of Northern Ireland makes provision for the defrayal out of moneys provided by that Parliament of any expenses which may be incurred by that Ministry under this section, make to the Corporation a grant of the like amount as it might have made to the company in those circumstances.

Power of the Ministry of Commerce, in certain cases of transfer of assets of publicly-owned companies to the Corporation, to make grants to them comparable to those under the Industrial Investment (General Assistance) Act (Northern Ireland) 1966.

1966 c. 41 (N.I.).

(2) Sections 10 and 11 (conditions and fraudulent applications) of the said Act of 1966 shall have effect as if references therein to that Act include references to the foregoing subsection.

Alteration of the Corporation's financial year.

13.—(1) Each of the Corporation's financial years after the first shall (unless a different period is prescribed by order of the Minister made by statutory instrument) be a period beginning with the end of the preceding financial year and ending,—

(*a*) if the last day of September next following is a Saturday, with that day; or

(*b*) if not, with the Saturday which (whether falling in September or October) falls nearest to the last day of September next following.

(2) The power conferred by the foregoing subsection on the Minister to make an order shall include power exercisable in the like manner to vary or revoke it by a subsequent order; and a statutory instrument containing an order under that subsection shall be subject to annulment in pursuance of a resolution of either House of Parliament.

Authentication of application of the Corporation's seal.
1949 c. 72.

14. For paragraph 5 of Schedule 1 to the Iron and Steel Act 1949 (which requires the fixing of the Corporation's seal to be authenticated jointly by a member of the Corporation and the secretary of the Corporation or a person acting in his stead), there shall be substituted the following paragraph:—

"5. The fixing of the seal of the Corporation shall be authenticated by the signature of the secretary of the Corporation or of some other person authorised, either generally or specially, by the Corporation to act for that purpose".

Interpretation, Short Title, Extent and Repeal

Interpretation.

15.—(1) In this Act, "the principal Act" means the Iron and Steel Act 1967; and a reference in this Act to a provision of that Act which is amended by this Act shall be taken to refer to that provision as so amended.

(2) In this Act "the Corporation" means the British Steel Corporation and "the Minister" means the Minister of Power, and other expressions used in this Act to which meanings are assigned by, or by virtue of, the principal Act for the purposes thereof have those meanings also for the purposes of this Act.

Short title, extent and repeal.

16.—(1) This Act may be cited as the Iron and Steel Act 1969.

(2) None of the provisions of this Act, apart from those of sections 8(1), 9, 10 and 12 shall extend to Northern Ireland.

(3) The enactments specified in columns 1 and 2 of the Schedule to this Act are hereby repealed to the extent specified in column 3 of that Schedule.

SCHEDULE

Section 16.

Enactments repealed

Chapter	Short Title	Extent of Repeal
12, 13 & 14 Geo. 6. c. 72.	The Iron and Steel Act 1949.	In section 59(1), in the definition of " financial year ", paragraph (*a*).
1967 c. 17.	The Iron and Steel Act 1967.	Section 19(4) and (5). In Schedule 3, in the entry relating to section 59 of the Iron and Steel Act 1949, the words from " in the definition " to " shall be omitted " (where first occurring).

Family Law Reform Act 1969

1969 CHAPTER 46

An Act to amend the law relating to the age of majority, to persons who have not attained that age and to the time when a particular age is attained; to amend the law relating to the property rights of illegitimate children and of other persons whose relationship is traced through an illegitimate link; to make provision for the use of blood tests for the purpose of determining the paternity of any person in civil proceedings; to make provision with respect to the evidence required to rebut a presumption of legitimacy and illegitimacy; to make further provision, in connection with the registration of the birth of an illegitimate child, for entering the name of the father; and for connected purposes. [25th July 1969]

BE IT ENACTED by the Queen's most Excellent Majesty, by and with the advice and consent of the Lords Spiritual and Temporal, and Commons, in this present Parliament assembled, and by the authority of the same, as follows:—

PART I

REDUCTION OF AGE OF MAJORITY AND RELATED PROVISIONS

Reduction of age of majority from 21 to 18.

1.—(1) As from the date on which this section comes into force a person shall attain full age on attaining the age of eighteen instead of on attaining the age of twenty-one; and a person shall attain full age on that date if he has then already attained the age of eighteen but not the age of twenty-one.

PART I

(2) The foregoing subsection applies for the purposes of ar rule of law, and, in the absence of a definition or of an indication of a contrary intention, for the construction c "full age", "infant", "infancy", "minor", "minority" an similar expressions in—

(*a*) any statutory provision, whether passed or made befor on or after the date on which this section comes int force; and

(*b*) any deed, will or other instrument of whatever natur (not being a statutory provision) made on or afte that date.

(3) In the statutory provisions specified in Schedule 1 to thi Act for any reference to the age of twenty-one years there shal be substituted a reference to the age of eighteen years; but th amendment by this subsection of the provisions specified in Par II of that Schedule shall be without prejudice to any power o amending or revoking those provisions.

(4) This section does not affect the construction of any suct expression as is referred to in subsection (2) of this section ir any of the statutory provisions described in Schedule 2 to thi Act, and the transitional provisions and savings contained ir Schedule 3 to this Act shall have effect in relation to thi section.

(5) The Lord Chancellor may by order made by statutory instrument amend any provision in any local enactment passed on or before the date on which this section comes into force (not being a provision described in paragraph 2 of Schedule 2 to this Act) by substituting a reference to the age of eighteen years for any reference therein to the age of twenty-one years; and any statutory instrument containing an order under this subsection shall be subject to annulment in pursuance of a resolution of either House of Parliament.

(6) In this section "statutory provision" means any enactment (including, except where the context otherwise requires, this Act) and any order, rule, regulation, byelaw or other instrument made in the exercise of a power conferred by any enactment.

(7) Notwithstanding any rule of law, a will or codicil executed before the date on which this section comes into force shall not be treated for the purposes of this section as made on or after that date by reason only that the will or codicil is confirmed by a codicil executed on or after that date.

Provisions relating to marriage.

1892 c. 23.

2.—(1) In the following enactments, that is to say—

(*a*) section 7(*c*) of the Foreign Marriage Act 1892 (persons under 21 intending to be married by a marriage officer to swear that necessary consents have been obtained);

PART I

(*b*) paragraph 2(*c*) of Part I of the Schedule to the Marriage with Foreigners Act 1906 (persons under 21 seeking certificate to swear that necessary consents have been obtained) ; 1906 c. 40.

(*c*) section 78(1) of the Marriage Act 1949 (definition of " infant " as person under the age of 21), 1949 c. 76.

or the words " twenty-one years " there shall be substituted the words " eighteen years ".

(2) In subsection (5) of section 3 of the said Act of 1949 which defines the courts having jurisdiction to consent to the marriage of an infant)—

(*a*) for the words " the county court of the district in which any respondent resides " there shall be substituted the words " the county court of the district in which any applicant or respondent resides " ; and

(*b*) after the words " or a court of summary jurisdiction " there shall be inserted the words " having jurisdiction in the place in which any applicant or respondent resides ".

(3) Where for the purpose of obtaining a certificate or licence for marriage under Part III of the said Act of 1949 a person declares that the consent of any person or persons whose consent to the marriage is required under the said section 3 has been obtained, the superintendent registrar may refuse to issue the certificate or licence for marriage unless satisfied by the production of written evidence that the consent of that person or of those persons has in fact been obtained.

(4) In this section any expression which is also used in the said Act of 1949 has the same meaning as in that Act.

Provisions relating to wills and intestacy.

3.—(1) In the following enactments, that is to say—

(*a*) section 7 of the Wills Act 1837 (invalidity of wills made by persons under 21) ;

(*b*) sections 1 and 3(1) of the Wills (Soldiers and Sailors) Act 1918 (soldier etc. eligible to make will and dispose of real property although under 21), 1837 c. 26. 1918 c. 58 (7 & 8 Geo. V).

in their application to wills made after the coming into force of this section, for the words " twenty-one years " there shall be substituted the words " eighteen years ".

(2) In section 47(1)(i) of the Administration of Estates Act 1925 (statutory trusts on intestacy), in its application to the estate of an intestate dying after the coming into force of this section, for the words " twenty-one years " in both places where they occur there shall be substituted the words " eighteen years ". 1925 c. 23.

PART I

(3) Any will which—

(*a*) has been made, whether before or after the comin into force of this section, by a person under the ag of eighteen ; and

(*b*) is valid by virtue of the provisions of section 11 of th said Act of 1837 and the said Act of 1918,

may be revoked by that person notwithstanding that he is sti under that age whether or not the circumstances are then suc that he would be entitled to make a valid will under thos provisions.

(4) In this section " will " has the same meaning as in th said Act of 1837 and " intestate " has the same meaning as i the said Act of 1925.

Maintenance for children under Guardianship of Infants Acts to continue to age of 21.
1925 c. 45.

4.—(1) An order under section 3(2), 5(4) or 6 of th Guardianship of Infants Act 1925 for the payment of sum towards the maintenance or education of a minor may requir such sums to continue to be paid in respect of any period afte the date on which he ceases to be a minor but not extending beyond the date on which he attains the age of twenty-one ; and any order which is made as aforesaid may provide that any sum which is payable thereunder for the benefit of a person who has ceased to be a minor shall be paid to that person himself.

(2) Subject to subsections (3) and (4) of this section, where a person who has ceased to be a minor but has not attained the age of twenty-one has, while a minor, been the subject of an order under any of the provisions of the Guardianship of Infants Acts 1886 and 1925, the court may, on the application of either parent of that person or of that person himself, make an order requiring either parent to pay to the other parent, to anyone else for the benefit of that person or to that person himself, in respect of any period not extending beyond the date when he attains the said age, such weekly or other periodical sums towards his maintenance or education as the court thinks reasonable having regard to the means of the person on whom the requirement is imposed.

(3) No order shall be made under subsection (2) of this section, and no liability under such an order shall accrue, at a time when the parents of the person in question are residing together, and if they so reside for a period of three months after such an order has been made it shall cease to have effect.

(4) No order shall be made under subsection (2) of this section requiring any person to pay any sum towards the maintenance or education of an illegitimate child of that person.

PART I

(5) Subsection (2) of this section shall be construed as one with the said Acts of 1886 and 1925, and—

(*a*) any order under that subsection, or under any corresponding enactment of the Parliament of Northern Ireland, shall be included among the orders to which section 16 of the Maintenance Orders Act 1950 applies; 1950 c. 37.

(*b*) any order under that subsection shall be included among the orders mentioned in section 2(1)(*d*) of the Reserve 1951 c. 65. and Auxiliary Forces (Protection of Civil Interests) Act 1951 and be deemed to be a maintenance order within the meaning of the Maintenance Orders Act 1958 c. 39. 1958.

Modification of other enactments relating to maintenance of children so as to preserve benefits up to age of 21.

5.—(1) For the purposes of the Inheritance (Family Provision) Act 1938, the dependants of a deceased person shall continue to include any son who has not attained the age of twenty-one; and accordingly—

(*a*) in subsection (1)(*c*) of that Act for the words " infant son " there shall be substituted the words " a son who has not attained the age of twenty-one years ";

(*b*) in subsection (2)(*c*) of that Act for the words " in the case of an infant son, his attaining the age of twenty- 1938 c. 45. one years " there shall be substituted the words " in the case of a son who has not attained the age of twenty-one years, his attaining that age ".

(2) Where a child in respect of whom an affiliation order has been made under the Affiliation Proceedings Act 1957 has 1957 c. 55. attained the age of eighteen and his mother is dead, of unsound mind or in prison—

(*a*) any application for an order under subsection (2) or (3) of section 7 of that Act directing that payments shall be made under the affiliation order for any period after he has attained that age may be made by the child himself; and

(*b*) the child himself shall be the person entitled to any payments directed by an order under that section to be so made for any such period as aforesaid.

(3) Section 22 of the Matrimonial Causes Act 1965 (power 1965 c. 72. to order maintenance for infant children in cases of wilful neglect) shall continue to apply to children up to the age of twenty-one, but not so as to enable an order for custody to be made under section 35(1) of that Act (custody of children where maintenance is ordered under section 22) in respect of any child who has attained the age of eighteen; and accordingly—

(*a*) in subsection (2) of the said section 22 for the words " any infant child of the marriage in question and any infant illegitimate child of both parties to the marriage "

PART I

there shall be substituted the words " any child of the marriage who is under twenty-one and any illegitimate child of both parties to the marriage who is under that age ";

(*b*) in the said section 35(1) after the words " any child to whom that subsection applies " there shall be inserted the words " who is under eighteen ", and at the end there shall be added the words " and the child is under that age ".

Maintenance for wards of court.

6.—(1) In this section " the court " means any of the following courts in the exercise of its jurisdiction relating to the wardship of children, that is to say, the High Court, the Court of Chancery of the County Palatine of Lancaster and the Court of Chancery of the County Palatine of Durham, and " ward of court " means a ward of the court in question.

(2) Subject to the provisions of this section, the court may make an order—

(*a*) requiring either parent of a ward of court to pay to the other parent; or

(*b*) requiring either parent or both parents of a ward of court to pay to any other person having the care and control of the ward,

such weekly or other periodical sums towards the maintenance and education of the ward as the court thinks reasonable having regard to the means of the person or persons on whom the requirement is imposed.

(3) An order under subsection (2) of this section may require such sums as are mentioned in that subsection to continue to be paid in respect of any period after the date on which the person for whose benefit the payments are to be made ceases to be a minor but not beyond the date on which he attains the age of twenty-one, and any order made as aforesaid may provide that any sum which is payable thereunder for the benefit of that person after he has ceased to be a minor shall be paid to that person himself.

(4) Subject to the provisions of this section, where a person who has ceased to be a minor but has not attained the age of twenty-one has at any time been the subject of an order making him a ward of court, the court may, on the application of either parent of that person or of that person himself, make an order requiring either parent to pay to the other parent, to anyone else for the benefit of that person or to that person himself, in respect of any period not extending beyond the date when he attains the said age, such weekly or other periodical

PART I

sums towards his maintenance or education as the court thinks reasonable having regard to the means of the person on whom the requirement in question is imposed.

(5) No order shall be made under this section, and no liability under such an order shall accrue, at a time when the parents of the ward or former ward, as the case may be, are residing together, and if they so reside for a period of three months after such an order has been made it shall cease to have effect; but the foregoing provisions of this subsection shall not apply to any order made by virtue of subsection (2)(*b*) of this section.

(6) No order shall be made under this section requiring any person to pay any sum towards the maintenance or education of an illegitimate child of that person.

(7) Any order under this section, or under any corresponding enactment of the Parliament of Northern Ireland, shall be included among the orders to which section 16 of the Maintenance Orders Act 1950 applies; and any order under this section shall be included among the orders mentioned in section 2(1)(*d*) of the Reserve and Auxiliary Forces (Protection of Civil Interests) Act 1951 and be deemed to be a maintenance order within the meaning of the Maintenance Orders Act 1958.

1950 c. 37.
1951 c. 65.
1958 c. 39.

(8) The court shall have power from time to time by an order under this section to vary or discharge any previous order thereunder.

Committal of wards of court to care of local authority and supervision of wards of court.

7.—(1) In this section " the court " means any of the following courts in the exercise of its jurisdiction relating to the wardship of children, that is to say, the High Court, the Court of Chancery of the County Palatine of Lancaster and the Court of Chancery of the County Palatine of Durham, and " ward of court " means a ward of the court in question.

(2) Where it appears to the court that there are exceptional circumstances making it impracticable or undesirable for a ward of court to be, or to continue to be, under the care of either of his parents or of any other individual the court may, if it thinks fit, make an order committing the care of the ward to a local authority; and thereupon Part II of the Children Act 1948 (which relates to the treatment of children in the care of a local authority) shall, subject to the next following subsection, apply as if the child had been received by the local authority into their care under section 1 of that Act.

1948 c. 43.

(3) In subsection (2) of this section " local authority " means one of the local authorities referred to in subsection (1) of section 36 of the Matrimonial Causes Act 1965 (under which a child may be committed to the care of a local authority by a

1965 c. 72.

Part I

court having jurisdiction to make an order for its custody) and subsections (2) to (6) of that section (ancillary provisions) shall have effect as if any reference therein to that section included a reference to subsection (2) of this section.

(4) Where it appears to the court that there are exceptional circumstances making it desirable that a ward of court (not being a ward who in pursuance of an order under subsection (2) of this section is in the care of a local authority) should be under the supervision of an independent person, the court may, as respects such period as the court thinks fit, order that the ward be under the supervision of a welfare officer or of a local authority; and subsections (2) and (3) of section 37 of the said Act of 1965 (ancillary provisions where a child is placed under supervision by a court having jurisdiction to make an order for its custody) shall have effect as if any reference therein to that section included a reference to this subsection.

(5) The court shall have power from time to time by an order under this section to vary or discharge any previous order thereunder.

Consent by persons over 16 to surgical, medical and dental treatment.

8.—(1) The consent of a minor who has attained the age of sixteen years to any surgical, medical or dental treatment which, in the absence of consent, would constitute a trespass to his person, shall be as effective as it would be if he were of full age; and where a minor has by virtue of this section given an effective consent to any treatment it shall not be necessary to obtain any consent for it from his parent or guardian.

(2) In this section "surgical, medical or dental treatment" includes any procedure undertaken for the purposes of diagnosis, and this section applies to any procedure (including, in particular, the administration of an anaesthetic) which is ancillary to any treatment as it applies to that treatment.

(3) Nothing in this section shall be construed as making ineffective any consent which would have been effective if this section had not been enacted.

Time at which a person attains a particular age.

9.—(1) The time at which a person attains a particular age expressed in years shall be the commencement of the relevant anniversary of the date of his birth.

(2) This section applies only where the relevant anniversary falls on a date after that on which this section comes into force, and, in relation to any enactment, deed, will or other instrument, has effect subject to any provision therein.

PART I

Modification of enactments relating to Duke of Cornwall and other children of Her Majesty.

1952 c. 37.

10.—(1) Section 1(1) of this Act shall apply for the construction of the expression "minor" in section 2(2) of the Civil List Act 1952 (which relates to the amount payable for the Queen's Civil List while the Duke of Cornwall is for the time being a minor) and accordingly—

(*a*) section 2(2)(*b*) of that Act (which relates to the three years during which the Duke is over 18 but under 21); and

(*b*) in section 2(2)(*a*) of that Act the words "for each year whilst he is under the age of eighteen years",

are hereby repealed except in relation to any period falling before section 1 of this Act comes into force.

(2) In section 4(1)(*a*) of the said Act of 1952 (under which benefits are provided for the children of Her Majesty, other than the Duke of Cornwall, who attain the age of 21 or marry) for the words "twenty-one years" there shall be substituted the words "eighteen years" but no sum shall be payable by virtue of this subsection in respect of any period falling before section 1 of this Act comes into force.

1863 c. 49.

(3) In section 38 of the Duchy of Cornwall Management Act 1863 (under which certain rights and powers of the Duke of Cornwall may, while he is under 21, be exercised on his behalf by the Sovereign or persons acting under Her authority) for the words "twenty-one years" wherever they occur there shall be substituted the words "eighteen years".

Repeal of certain enactments relating to minors.

11. The following enactments are hereby repealed—

1855 c. 43.
1925 c. 18.

(*a*) the Infant Settlements Act 1855 (which enables a male infant over 20 and a female infant over 17 to make a marriage settlement), together with section 27(3) of the Settled Land Act 1925, except in relation to anything done before the coming into force of this section;

1875 c. 90.

(*b*) in section 6 of the Employers and Workmen Act 1875 (powers of justices in respect of apprentices)—

(i) the paragraph numbered (1) (power to direct apprentice to perform his duties), and

(ii) the sentence following the paragraph numbered (2) (power to order imprisonment of an apprentice who fails to comply with direction);

1956 c. 69.

(*c*) in the Sexual Offences Act 1956, section 18 and paragraph 5 of Schedule 2 (fraudulent abduction of heiress).

Persons under full age may be described as minors instead of infants.

12. A person who is not of full age may be described as a minor instead of as an infant, and accordingly in this Act "minor" means such a person as aforesaid.

Part I

Powers of Parliament of Northern Ireland.

1920 c. 67.

13. Notwithstanding anything in the Government of Ireland Act 1920 the Parliament of Northern Ireland shall have power to make laws for purposes similar to any of the purposes of this Part of this Act.

Part II

Property Rights of Illegitimate Children

Right of illegitimate child to succeed on intestacy of parents, and of parents to succeed on intestacy of illegitimate child.

14.—(1) Where either parent of an illegitimate child dies intestate as respects all or any of his or her real or personal property, the illegitimate child or, if he is dead, his issue, shall be entitled to take any interest therein to which he or such issue would have been entitled if he had been born legitimate.

(2) Where an illegitimate child dies intestate in respect of all or any of his real or personal property, each of his parents, if surviving, shall be entitled to take any interest therein to which that parent would have been entitled if the child had been born legitimate.

1925 c. 23.

(3) In accordance with the foregoing provisions of this section, Part IV of the Administration of Estates Act 1925 (which deals with the distribution of the estate of an intestate) shall have effect as if—

(*a*) any reference to the issue of the intestate included a reference to any illegitimate child of his and to the issue of any such child;

(*b*) any reference to the child or children of the intestate included a reference to any illegitimate child or children of his; and

(*c*) in relation to an intestate who is an illegitimate child, any reference to the parent, parents, father or mother of the intestate were a reference to his natural parent, parents, father or mother.

(4) For the purposes of subsection (2) of this section and of the provisions amended by subsection (3)(*c*) thereof, an illegitimate child shall be presumed not to have been survived by his father unless the contrary is shown.

(5) This section does not apply to or affect the right of any person to take any entailed interest in real or personal property.

(6) The reference in section 50(1) of the said Act of 1925 (which relates to the construction of documents) to Part IV of that Act, or to the foregoing provisions of that Part, shall in relation to an instrument inter vivos made, or a will or codicil

PART II

oming into operation, after the coming into force of this ection (but not in relation to instruments inter vivos made r wills or codicils coming into operation earlier) be construed s including references to this section.

(7) Section 9 of the Legitimacy Act 1926 (under which an llegitimate child and his issue are entitled to succeed on the ntestacy of his mother if she leaves no legitimate issue, and the nother of an illegitimate child is entitled to succeed on his ntestacy as if she were the only surviving parent) is hereby epealed. 1926 c. 60.

(8) In this section " illegitimate child " does not include an llegitimate child who is—

(*a*) a legitimated person within the meaning of the said Act of 1926 or a person recognised by virtue of that Act or at common law as having been legitimated ; or

(*b*) an adopted person under an adoption order made in any part of the United Kingdom, the Isle of Man or the Channel Islands or under an overseas adoption as defined in section 4(3) of the Adoption Act 1968. 1968 c. 53.

(9) This section does not affect any rights under the intestacy of a person dying before the coming into force of this section.

Presumption that in dispositions of property references to children and other relatives include references to, and to persons related through, illegitimate children.

15.—(1) In any disposition made after the coming into force of this section—

(*a*) any reference (whether express or implied) to the child or children of any person shall, unless the contrary intention appears, be construed as, or as including, a reference to any illegitimate child of that person ; and

(*b*) any reference (whether express or implied) to a person or persons related in some other manner to any person shall, unless the contrary intention appears, be construed as, or as including, a reference to anyone who would be so related if he, or some other person through whom the relationship is deduced, had been born legitimate.

(2) The foregoing subsection applies only where the reference in question is to a person who is to benefit or to be capable of benefiting under the disposition or, for the purpose of designating such a person, to someone else to or through whom that person is related ; but that subsection does not affect the construction of the word " heir " or " heirs " or of any expression which is used to create an entailed interest in real or personal property.

(3) In relation to any disposition made after the coming into force of this section, section 33 of the Trustee Act 1925 (which specifies the trusts implied by a direction that income 1925 c. 19.

Part II is to be held on protective trusts for the benefit of any person shall have effect as if—

(*a*) the reference to the children or more remote issue of the principal beneficiary included a reference to any illegitimate child of the principal beneficiary and to anyone who would rank as such issue if he, or some other person through whom he is descended from the principal beneficiary, had been born legitimate; and

(*b*) the reference to the issue of the principal beneficiary included a reference to anyone who would rank as such issue if he, or some other person through whom he is descended from the principal beneficiary, had been born legitimate.

(4) In this section references to an illegitimate child include references to an illegitimate child who is or becomes a legitimated

1926 c. 60. person within the meaning of the Legitimacy Act 1926 or a person recognised by virtue of that Act or at common law as having been legitimated; and in section 3 of that Act—

(*a*) subsection (1)(*b*) (which relates to the effect of dispositions where a person has been legitimated) shall not apply to a disposition made after the coming into force of this section except as respects any interest in relation to which the disposition refers only to persons who are, or whose relationship is deduced through, legitimate persons; and

(*b*) subsection (2) (which provides that, where the right to any property depends on the relative seniority of the children of any person, legitimated persons shall rank as if born on the date of legitimation) shall not apply in relation to any right conferred by a disposition made after the coming into force of this section unless the terms of the disposition are such that the children whose relative seniority is in question cannot include any illegitimate children who are not either legitimated persons within the meaning of that Act or persons recognised by virtue of that Act as having been legitimated.

(5) Where under any disposition any real or personal property or any interest in such property is limited (whether subject to any preceding limitation or charge or not) in such a way that it would, apart from this section, devolve (as nearly as the law permits) along with a dignity or title of honour, then, whether or not the disposition contains an express reference to the dignity or title of honour, and whether or not the property or some interest in the property may in some event become severed therefrom, nothing in this section shall operate to sever the property or any interest therein from the dignity or title,

PART II

but the property or interest shall devolve in all respects as if this section had not been enacted.

(6) This section is without prejudice to sections 16 and 17 of the Adoption Act 1958 (which relate to the construction of dispositions in cases of adoption). 1958 c. 5 (7 & 8 Eliz. 2).

(7) There is hereby abolished, as respects dispositions made after the coming into force of this section, any rule of law that a disposition in favour of illegitimate children not in being when the disposition takes effect is void as contrary to public policy.

(8) In this section " disposition " means a disposition, including an oral disposition, of real or personal property whether inter vivos or by will or codicil ; and, notwithstanding any rule of law, a disposition made by will or codicil executed before the date on which this section comes into force shall not be treated for the purposes of this section as made on or after that date by reason only that the will or codicil is confirmed by a codicil executed on or after that date.

Meaning of " child " and " issue " in s. 33 of Wills Act 1837.

16.—(1) In relation to a testator who dies after the coming into force of this section, section 33 of the Wills Act 1837 (gift to children or other issue of testator not to lapse if they predecease him but themselves leave issue) shall have effect as if— 1837 c. 26.

(*a*) the reference to a child or other issue of the testator (that is, the intended beneficiary) included a reference to any illegitimate child of the testator and to anyone who would rank as such issue if he, or some other person through whom he is descended from the testator, had been born legitimate ; and

(*b*) the reference to the issue of the intended beneficiary included a reference to anyone who would rank as such issue if he, or some other person through whom he is descended from the intended beneficiary, had been born legitimate.

(2) In this section " illegitimate child " includes an illegitimate child who is a legitimated person within the meaning of the Legitimacy Act 1926 or a person recognised by virtue of that Act or at common law as having been legitimated. 1926 c. 60.

Protection of trustees and personal representatives.

17. Notwithstanding the foregoing provisions of this Part of this Act, trustees or personal representatives may convey or distribute any real or personal property to or among the persons entitled thereto without having ascertained that there is no person who is or may be entitled to any interest therein by virtue of—

(*a*) section 14 of this Act so far as it confers any interest on illegitimate children or their issue or on the father of an illegitimate child ; or

Part II

(*b*) section 15 or 16 of this Act,

and shall not be liable to any such person of whose claim they have not had notice at the time of the conveyance or distribution but nothing in this section shall prejudice the right of any such person to follow the property, or any property representing it, into the hands of any person, other than a purchaser, who may have received it.

Illegitimate children to count as dependants under Inheritance (Family Provision) Act 1938.
1938 c. 45.
1966 c. 35.
1965 c. 72.

18.—(1) For the purposes of the Inheritance (Family Provision) Act 1938, a person's illegitimate son or daughter shall be treated as his dependant in any case in which a legitimate son or daughter of that person would be so treated, and accordingly in the definition of the expressions " son " and " daughter " in section 5(1) of that Act, as amended by the Family Provision Act 1966, after the words " respectively include " there shall be inserted the words " an illegitimate son or daughter of the deceased ".

(2) In section 26(6) of the Matrimonial Causes Act 1965 (which provides, among other things, for the word " dependant " to have the same meaning as in the said Act of 1938 as amended by the said Act of 1966), after the words " as amended by the Family Provision Act 1966 " there shall be inserted the words " and the Family Law Reform Act 1969 ".

(3) This section does not affect the operation of the said Acts of 1938 and 1965 in relation to a person dying before the coming into force of this section.

Policies of assurance and property in industrial and provident societies.
1882 c. 75.
1880 c. 26.
1965 c. 12.

19.—(1) In section 11 of the Married Women's Property Act 1882 and section 2 of the Married Women's Policies of Assurance (Scotland) Act 1880 (policies of assurance effected for the benefit of children) the expression " children " shall include illegitimate children.

(2) In section 25(2) of the Industrial and Provident Societies Act 1965 (application of property in registered society where member was illegitimate and is not survived by certain specified relatives) for the words " and leaves no widow, widower or issue, and his mother does not survive him " there shall be substituted the words " and leaves no widow, widower or issue (including any illegitimate child of the member) and neither of his parents survives him ".

(3) Subsection (1) of this section does not affect the operation of the said Acts of 1882 and 1880 in relation to a policy effected before the coming into force of that subsection ; and subsection (2) of this section does not affect the operation of the said Act of 1965 in relation to a member of a registered society who dies before the coming into force of the said subsection (2).

PART III

PROVISIONS FOR USE OF BLOOD TESTS IN DETERMINING PATERNITY

Power of court to require use of blood tests.

20.—(1) In any civil proceedings in which the paternity of ny person falls to be determined by the court hearing the roceedings, the court may, on an application by any party to ıe proceedings, give a direction for the use of blood tests to scertain whether such tests show that a party to the proceedings or is not thereby excluded from being the father of that person nd for the taking, within a period to be specified in the irection, of blood samples from that person, the mother of hat person and any party alleged to be the father of that person r from any, or any two, of those persons.

A court may at any time revoke or vary a direction previously given by it under this section.

(2) The person responsible for carrying out blood tests taken or the purpose of giving effect to a direction under this section hall make to the court by which the direction was given a report n which he shall state—

(*a*) the results of the tests ;

(*b*) whether the party to whom the report relates is or is not excluded by the results from being the father of the person whose paternity is to be determined ; and

(*c*) if that party is not so excluded, the value, if any, of the results in determining whether that party is that person's father ;

and the report shall be received by the court as evidence in the proceedings of the matters stated therein.

(3) A report under subsection (2) of this section shall be in the form prescribed by regulations made under section 22 of this Act.

(4) Where a report has been made to a court under subsection (2) of this section, any party may, with the leave of the court, or shall, if the court so directs, obtain from the person who made the report a written statement explaining or amplifying any statement made in the report, and that statement shall be deemed for the purposes of this section (except subsection (3) thereof) to form part of the report made to the court.

(5) Where a direction is given under this section in any proceedings, a party to the proceedings, unless the court otherwise directs, shall not be entitled to call as a witness the person responsible for carrying out the tests taken for the purpose of giving effect to the direction, or any person by whom any thing necessary for the purpose of enabling those tests to be carried out was done, unless within fourteen days after receiving a copy

PART III

of the report he serves notice on the other parties to the pr ceedings, or on such of them as the court may direct, of h intention to call that person; and where any such person called as a witness the party who called him shall be entitle to cross-examine him.

(6) Where a direction is given under this section the party c whose application the direction is given shall pay the cost taking and testing blood samples for the purpose of giving effe to the direction (including any expenses reasonably incurre by any person in taking any steps required of him for th purpose), and of making a report to the court under this sectio but the amount paid shall be treated as costs incurred by hi in the proceedings.

Consents, etc., required for taking of blood samples.

21.—(1) Subject to the provisions of subsections (3) and (4 of this section, a blood sample which is required to be take from any person for the purpose of giving effect to a directio under section 20 of this Act shall not be taken from that perso except with his consent.

(2) The consent of a minor who has attained the age of sixtee years to the taking from himself of a blood sample shall be a effective as it would be if he were of full age; and where a minor has by virtue of this subsection given an effective consen to the taking of a blood sample it shall not be necessary to obtain any consent for it from any other person.

(3) A blood sample may be taken from a person under the age of sixteen years, not being such a person as is referred to in subsection (4) of this section, if the person who has the care and control of him consents.

1959 c. 72.

(4) A blood sample may be taken from a person who is suffering from mental disorder within the meaning of the Mental Health Act 1959 and is incapable of understanding the nature and purpose of blood tests if the person who has the care and control of him consents and the medical practitioner in whose care he is has certified that the taking of a blood sample from him will not be prejudicial to his proper care and treatment.

(5) The foregoing provisions of this section are without prejudice to the provisions of section 23 of this Act.

Power to provide for manner of giving effect to direction for use of blood tests.

22.—(1) The Secretary of State may by regulations make provision as to the manner of giving effect to directions under section 20 of this Act and, in particular, any such regulations may—

(*a*) provide that blood samples shall not be taken except by such medical practitioners as may be appointed by the Secretary of State;

PART III

(b) regulate the taking, identification and transport of blood samples;

(c) require the production at the time when a blood sample is to be taken of such evidence of the identity of the person from whom it is to be taken as may be prescribed by the regulations;

(d) require any person from whom a blood sample is to be taken, or, in such cases as may be prescribed by the regulations, such other person as may be so prescribed, to state in writing whether he or the person from whom the sample is to be taken, as the case may be, has during such period as may be specified in the regulations suffered from any such illness as may be so specified or received a transfusion of blood;

(e) provide that blood tests shall not be carried out except by such persons, and at such places, as may be appointed by the Secretary of State;

(f) prescribe the blood tests to be carried out and the manner in which they are to be carried out;

(g) regulate the charges that may be made for the taking and testing of blood samples and for the making of a report to a court under section 20 of this Act;

(h) make provision for securing that so far as practicable the blood samples to be tested for the purpose of giving effect to a direction under section 20 of this Act are tested by the same person;

(i) prescribe the form of the report to be made to a court under section 20 of this Act.

(2) The power to make regulations under this section shall be exercisable by statutory instrument which shall be subject to annulment in pursuance of a resolution of either House of Parliament.

Failure to comply with direction for taking blood tests.

23.—(1) Where a court gives a direction under section 20 of this Act and any person fails to take any step required of him for the purpose of giving effect to the direction, the court may draw such inferences, if any, from that fact as appear proper in the circumstances.

(2) Where in any proceedings in which the paternity of any person falls to be determined by the court hearing the proceedings there is a presumption of law that that person is legitimate, then if—

(a) a direction is given under section 20 of this Act in those proceedings, and

(b) any party who is claiming any relief in the proceedings and who for the purpose of obtaining that relief is

Part III

entitled to rely on the presumption fails to take ar step required of him for the purpose of giving effe to the direction,

the court may adjourn the hearing for such period as it thin fit to enable that party to take that step, and if at the en of that period he has failed without reasonable cause to tak it the court may, without prejudice to subsection (1) of th section, dismiss his claim for relief notwithstanding the absenc of evidence to rebut the presumption.

(3) Where any person named in a direction under section 2 of this Act fails to consent to the taking of a blood sample fror himself or from any person named in the direction of whom h has the care and control, he shall be deemed for the purpose of this section to have failed to take a step required of him fo the purpose of giving effect to the direction.

Penalty for personating another, etc., for purpose of providing blood sample.

24. If for the purpose of providing a blood sample for a tes required to give effect to a direction under section 20 of thi Act any person personates another, or proffers a child knowin that it is not the child named in the direction, he shall be liable—

(*a*) on conviction on indictment, to imprisonment for a term not exceeding two years, or

(*b*) on summary conviction, to a fine not exceeding £400.

Interpretation of Part III.

25. In this Part of this Act the following expressions have the meanings hereby respectively assigned to them, that is to say—

" blood samples " means blood taken for the purpose of blood tests;

" blood tests " means blood tests carried out under this Part of this Act and includes any test made with the object of ascertaining the inheritable characteristics of blood;

" excluded " means excluded subject to the occurrence of mutation.

Part IV

Miscellaneous and General

Rebuttal of presumption as to legitimacy and illegitimacy.

26. Any presumption of law as to the legitimacy or illegitimacy of any person may in any civil proceedings be rebutted by evidence which shows that it is more probable than not that that person is illegitimate or legitimate, as the case may be, and it shall not be necessary to prove that fact beyond reasonable doubt in order to rebut the presumption.

PART IV

Entry of father's name on registration of birth of illegitimate child.

1953 c. 20.

27.—(1) In section 10 of the Births and Deaths Registration ct 1953 (which provides that the registrar shall not enter the me of any person as the father of an illegitimate child except the joint request of the mother and the person acknowledging mself to be the father and requires that person to sign the gister together with the mother) for the words from " except " wards there shall be substituted the words " except—

(*a*) at the joint request of the mother and the person acknowledging himself to be the father of the child (in which case that person shall sign the register together with the mother) ; or

(*b*) at the request of the mother on production of—

(i) a declaration in the prescribed form made by the mother stating that the said person is the father of the child ; and

(ii) a statutory declaration made by that person acknowledging himself to be the father of the child."

(2) If on the registration under Part I of the said Act of 1953 f the birth of an illegitimate child no person has been entered 1 the register as the father, the registrar may re-register the irth so as to show a person as the father—

(*a*) at the joint request of the mother and of that person (in which case the mother and that person shall both sign the register in the presence of the registrar) ; or

(*b*) at the request of the mother on production of—

(i) a declaration in the prescribed form made by the mother stating that the person in question is the father of the child ; and

(ii) a statutory declaration made by that person acknowledging himself to be the father of the child ;

ut no birth shall be re-registered as aforesaid except with the uthority of the Registrar General and any such re-registration hall be effected in such manner as may be prescribed.

(3) A request under paragraph (*a*) or (*b*) of section 10 of the aid Act of 1953 as amended by subsection (1) of this section may be included in a declaration under section 9 of that Act registration of birth pursuant to a declaration made in another listrict) and, if a request under the said paragraph (*b*) is included n such a declaration, the documents mentioned in that paragraph shall be produced to the officer in whose presence the declaration is made and sent by him, together with the declaration, to the registrar.

(4) A request under paragraph (*a*) or (*b*) of subsection (2) of this section may, instead of being made to the registrar, be made by making and signing in the presence of and delivering to such

PART IV

officer as may be prescribed a written statement in the prescrib form and, in the case of a request under the said paragraph (producing to that officer the documents mentioned in that par graph, and the officer shall send the statement together with th documents, if any, to the registrar; and thereupon that su section shall have effect as if the request had been made to th registrar and, if the birth is re-registered pursuant to the reques the person or persons who signed the statement shall be treate as having signed the register as required by that subsection.

(5) This section shall be construed as one with the said A of 1953; and in section 14(1)(*a*) of that Act (re-registration birth of legitimated person) the reference to section 10 of th Act shall include a reference to subsection (2) of this section.

Short title, interpretation, commencement and extent.

28.—(1) This Act may be cited as the Family Law Reform Act 1969.

(2) Except where the context otherwise requires, any referenc in this Act to any enactment shall be construed as a referenc to that enactment as amended, extended or applied by o under any other enactment, including this Act.

(3) This Act shall come into force on such date as the Lor Chancellor may appoint by order made by statutory instrumen and different dates may be appointed for the coming into forc of different provisions.

(4) In this Act—

(*a*) section 1 and Schedule 1, so far as they amend th
1948 c. 56. British Nationality Act 1948, have the same extent a that Act and are hereby declared for the purposes o
1967 c. 4. section 3(3) of the West Indies Act 1967 to extend t all the associated states;

(*b*) section 2, so far as it amends any provision of the
1892 c. 23. Foreign Marriage Act 1892 or the Marriage wit
1906 c. 40. Foreigners Act 1906, has the same extent as tha provision;

(*c*) sections 4(5) and 6(7), so far as they affect Part II of the
1950 c. 37. Maintenance Orders Act 1950, extend to Scotland and Northern Ireland;

1952 c. 37. (*d*) section 10, so far as it relates to the Civil List Act 1952, extends to Scotland and Northern Ireland;

1875 c. 90. (*e*) section 11, so far as it relates to the Employers and Workmen Act 1875, extends to Scotland;

(*f*) section 13 extends to Northern Ireland;

(*g*) section 19 extends to Scotland;

but, save as aforesaid, this Act shall extend to England and Wales only.

SCHEDULES

SCHEDULE 1

Section 1(3).

TATUTORY PROVISIONS AMENDED BY SUBSTITUTING 18 FOR 21 YEARS

PART I

ENACTMENTS

	Short title	*Section*	*Subject matter*
. 24.	The Tenures Abolition Act 1660.	Sections 8 and 9.	Custody of children under 21.
c. 22.	The Trade Union Act Amendment Act 1876.	Section 9.	Persons under 21 but above 16 eligible as members of trade union but not of committee of management etc.
c. 25.	The Friendly Societies Act 1896.	Section 36.	Persons under 21 eligible as members of society and branches but not of committee etc.
c. 18.	The Settled Land Act 1925.	Section 102(5).	Management of land during minority.
c. 19.	The Trustee Act 1925.	Section 31(1)(ii), (2)(i)(*a*)and(*b*).	Power to apply income for maintenance and to accumulate surplus income during a minority.
c. 20.	The Law of Property Act 1925.	Section 134(1).	Restriction on executory limitations.
c. 49.	The Supreme Court of Judicature (Consolidation) Act 1925.	Section 165(1).	Probate not to be granted to infant if appointed sole executor until he attains the age of 21 years.
c. 56.	The British Nationality Act 1948.	Section 32(1) and (9).	Definition of " minor " and " full age " by reference to age of 21.
c. 44.	The Customs and Excise Act 1952.	Section 244(2)(*a*)	Entry invalid unless made by person over 21.
c. 46.	The Hypnotism Act 1952.	Section 3.	Persons under 21 not to be hypnotised at public entertainment.
c. 63.	The Trustee Savings Banks Act 1954.	Section 23.	Payments to persons under 21.
c. 69.	The Sexual Offences Act 1956.	Section 38.	Power of court where person convicted of incest with girl under 21.
c. 5.	The Adoption Act 1958.	Section 57(1).	Definition of " infant " by reference to age of 21.
c. 22.	The County Courts Act 1959.	Section 80.	Persons under 21 may sue for wages in same manner as if of full age.
c. 72.	The Mental Health Act 1959.	Section 49(4)(*c*).	Provision where nearest relative of patient is under 21.
		Section 51(1).	Meaning of " nearest relative " of patient who has not attained the age of 21.

SCH. 1

	Short title	*Section*	*Subject matter*
c. 72.	The Mental Health Act 1959—*cont.*	Section 127(2).	Rescinding order under s. 38 o Sexual Offences Act 1956 i case of girl under 21 who a defective.
c. 37.	The Building Societies Act 1962.	Section 9.	Persons under 21 eligible a members of building societ but cannot vote or hol office.
		Section 47.	Receipts given to buildin society by persons under 2 to be valid.
c. 2.	The Betting, Gaming and Lotteries Act 1963.	Section 22(1) and (3).	Offence of sending bettin advertisements to person under 21.
c. 12.	The Industrial and Provident Societies Act 1965.	Section 20.	Persons under 21 but above 1 eligible as members of societ but not of committee etc.

PART II

RULES, REGULATIONS ETC.

	Title	*Provision*	*Subject matter*
1927 S.R. & O. 1184; 1953 S.I 264.	The Supreme Court Funds Rules 1927 as amended by the Supreme Court Funds Rules 1953.	Rule 97(1)(i).	Unclaimed moneys in court.
1929 S.R. & O. 1048.	The Trustee Savings Banks Regulations 1929.	Regulation 28(2).	Payments to persons under 21.
1933 S.R. & O. 1149.	The Savings Certificates Regulations 1933.	Regulation 2(1) (*a*).	Persons entitled to purchase and hold certificates.
		Regulation 21(2).	Persons under disability.
1946 S.R. & O. 1156.	The North of Scotland Hydro-Electric Board (Borrowing and Stock) Regulations 1946.	Regulation 36(1) and (2).	Stock held by persons under 21.
1949 S.I. 751.	The Gas (Stock) Regulations 1949.	Regulation 19(1) and (2).	Stock held by persons under 21.
1954 S.I. 796.	The Non-Contentious Probate Rules 1954.	Rules 31 and 32.	Grants of probate on behalf of infant and where infant is co-executor.
1955 S.I. 1752.	The South of Scotland Electricity Board (Borrowing and Stock) Regulations 1955.	Regulation 30(1) and (2).	Stock held by persons under 21.

SCH. 1

	Title	Provision	Subject matter
956 S.I. 1657.	The Premium Savings Bonds Regulations 1956.	Regulation 2(1).	Persons entitled to purchase and hold bonds.
		Regulation 12(2).	Persons under disability.
957 S.I. 2228.	The Electricity (Stock) Regulations 1957.	Regulation 22(1) and (2).	Stock held by persons under 21.
963 S.I. 935.	The Exchange of Securities (General) Rules 1963.	Rule 1(1).	Definition of "minor".
965 S.I. 1420.	The Government Stock Regulations 1965.	Regulation 14(1), (2), (3) and (5).	Stock held by persons under 21.
965 S.I. 1500.	The County Court Funds Rules 1965.	Rule 36(1)(*b*).	Unclaimed moneys in court.
1965 S.I. 1707.	The Mayor's and City of London Court Funds Rules 1965.	Rule 25(1)(*b*).	Unclaimed moneys in court.
1968 S.I. 2049.	The Registration of Births, Deaths and Marriages Regulations 1968.	Regulation 63 and, in Schedule 1, Forms 15 to 18.	Forms of notice of marriage.

SCHEDULE 2

Section 1(4).

STATUTORY PROVISIONS UNAFFECTED BY SECTION 1

1. The Regency Acts 1937 to 1953.

2. The Representation of the People Acts (and any regulations, rules or other instruments thereunder), section 7 of the Parliamentary 1695 c. 25.
Elections Act 1695, section 57 of the Local Government Act 1933 1933 c. 51.
and any statutory provision relating to municipal elections in the City of London within the meaning of section 167(1)(*a*) of the Representation of the People Act 1949. 1949 c. 68.

3. Any statutory provision relating to income tax (including surtax) capital gains tax, corporation tax or estate duty.

SCHEDULE 3

Section 1(4).

TRANSITIONAL PROVISIONS AND SAVINGS

Interpretation

1.—(1) In this Schedule " the principal section " means section 1 of this Act and " the commencement date " means the date on which that section comes into force.

(2) Subsection (7) of the principal section shall apply for the purposes of this Schedule as it applies for the purposes of that section.

SCH. 3

Funds in court

2. Any order or directions in force immediately before the com
mencement date by virtue of—

(*a*) any rules of court or other statutory provision (including, i
1959 c. 22. particular, section 174 of the County Courts Act 195
relating to the control of money recovered by or otherwis
payable to an infant in any proceedings ; or

1965 c. 2. (*b*) section 19 of the Administration of Justice Act 1965 (contr
of money recovered by widow in fatal accident proceedin
which are also brought for the benefit of an infant),

shall have effect as if any reference therein to the infant's attainin
the age of twenty-one were a reference to his attaining the age o
eighteen or, in relation to a person who by virtue of the princip
section attains full age on the commencement date, to that date.

Wardship and custody orders

3.—(1) Any order in force immediately before the commencemen
date—

(*a*) making a person a ward of court ; or

(*b*) under the Guardianship of Infants Acts 1886 and 1925, o
1965 c. 72. under the Matrimonial Causes Act 1965 or any enactmen
repealed by that Act, for the custody of, or access to, an
person,

which is expressed to continue in force until the person who is th
subject of the order attains the age of twenty-one, or any age betwee
eighteen and twenty-one, shall have effect as if the reference to hi
attaining that age were a reference to his attaining the age of eightee
or, in relation to a person who by virtue of the principal sectio
attains full age on the commencement date, to that date.

(2) This paragraph is without prejudice to so much of any
order as makes provision for the maintenance or education of a
person after he has attained the age of eighteen.

Adoption orders

4. The principal section shall not prevent the making of an
1958 c. 5. adoption order or provisional adoption order under the Adoption
(7 & 8 Eliz. 2) Act 1958 in respect of a person who has attained the age of eighteen
if the application for the order was made before the commencement
date, and in relation to any such case that Act shall have effect as
if the principal section had not been enacted.

Power of trustees to apply income for maintenance of minor

5.—(1) The principal section shall not affect section 31 of the
1925 c. 19. Trustee Act 1925—

(*a*) in its application to any interest under an instrument made
before the commencement date ; or

(*b*) in its application, by virtue of section 47(1)(ii) of the Administration of Estates Act 1925, to the estate of an intestate (within the meaning of that Act) dying before that date. SCH. 3 1925 c. 23.

(2) In any case in which (whether by virtue of this paragraph or aragraph 9 of this Schedule) trustees have power under subsection)(i) of the said section 31 to pay income to the parent or guardian any person who has attained the age of eighteen, or to apply it or or towards the maintenance, education or benefit of any such erson, they shall also have power to pay it to that person himself.

Personal representatives' powers during minority of beneficiary

6. The principal section shall not affect the meaning of minority" in sections 33(3) and 39(1) of the Administration of states Act 1925 in the case of a beneficiary whose interest arises nder a will or codicil made before the commencement date or on he death before that date of an intestate (within the meaning of hat Act).

Accumulation periods

7. The change, by virtue of the principal section, in the construcion of—

(*a*) sections 164 to 166 of the Law of Property Act 1925; 1925 c. 20.

(*b*) section 13(1) of the Perpetuities and Accumulations Act 1964, 1964 c. 55.

which lay down permissible periods for the accumulation of income nder settlements and other dispositions) shall not invalidate any direction for accumulation in a settlement or other disposition made by a deed, will or other instrument which was made before the commencement date.

Limitation of actions

8. The change, by virtue of the principal section, in the construction of section 31(2) of the Limitation Act 1939 (limitation in case of person under disability) shall not affect the time for bringing proceedings in respect of a cause of action which arose before the commencement date. 1939 c. 21.

Statutory provisions incorporated in deeds, wills, etc.

9. The principal section shall not affect the construction of any statutory provision where it is incorporated in and has effect as part of any deed, will or other instrument the construction of which is not affected by that section.

TABLE VI

Effect of Legislation

See Part II

INDEX

TO THE

Public General Acts

AND

CHURCH ASSEMBLY MEASURES, 1969

A

E

F

FINANCE ACT—*continued*

PART II—*continued*

Children

Disallowance of interest as a deduction

Companies

Avoidance of tax

Case VIII of Schedule D

PART III.—ESTATE DUTY

PART IV.—CAPITAL GAINS AND BETTERMENT LEVY

Capital gains

Betterment Levy

PART V.—SELECTIVE EMPLOYMENT TAX

VI.—MISCELLANEOUS

G

H

HOUSING (SCOTLAND) ACT—*continued*

PART I—*continued*

Housing Treatment Areas

Application of tolerable standard for certain purposes of Part II of principal Act

Payments to certain owner-occupiers and others in respect of houses not meeting tolerable standard which are purchased or demolished

Payments for well maintained houses

Transitional provisions for the purposes of ss. 18 *to* 21

Repayment of certain payments

PART II.—HOUSES IN DISREPAIR

PART III.—FINANCIAL ASSISTANCE TOWARDS COST OF IMPROVEMENTS AND CONVERSIONS

Exchequer contributions towards improvement of housing accommodation

O

P

Q

R

ENANCY.
Restriction on termination of, by agreement (c. 59, s. 4) ... II, p. 1647
Restrictions on increases in rents under regulated (c. 62, Pt. II) II, p. 1690

ITLE. Reduction of statutory period of, in application to contracts (c. 59, s. 23) II, p. 1658

OBACCO. Customs and Excise (c. 32, sch. 5).

OLLS. Abolition of exemption from (c. 48 s. 68) ... ... II, p. 1094

ORT.
Exclusion of liability of the Post Office, officers and servants (c. 48, s. 29) II, p. 1067
Increase jurisdiction of county court (c. 58, s. 1) ... ... II, p. 1620

TOURIST BOARDS. Establishment of (c. 51, s. 1) ... ... II, p. 1421

TOWN AND COUNTRY PLANNING (SCOTLAND) ACT: c. 30 ... ... I, p. 275

PART I.—NEW PROVISIONS AS TO DEVELOPMENT PLANS

Survey and structure plan

§ 1. Survey of planning districts, I, p. 275.
2. Preparation of structure plans, I, p. 276.
3. Publicity in connection with preparation of structure plan, I, p. 278.
4. Approval or rejection of structure plan by Secretary of State, I, p. 279.
5. Alteration of structure plans, I, p. 280.

Local plans

6. Preparation of local plans, I, p. 280.
7. Publicity for preparation of local plans, I, p. 282.
8. Inquiries, etc. with respect to local plans, I, p. 283.
9. Adoption and approval of local plans, I, p. 284.
10. Alteration to local plans, I, p. 284.

Supplementary provisions

11. Disregarding of representations with respect to development authorised by or under other enactments, I, p. 285.
12. Default powers of Secretary of State, I, p. 285.
13. Supplementary provisions as to structure and local plans, I, p. 286.
14. Proceedings for questioning validity of structure plans, etc., I, p. 288.

PART II.—ENFORCEMENT OF PLANNING CONTROL

Enforcement notices

15. New provision as to enforcement notices, I, p. 288.
16. Appeal against enforcement notice, I, p. 290.
17. Enforcement notice to have effect against subsequent development, I, p. 292.

Established use

18, and schedule 1. Certification of established use, I, pp. 293, 364.
19. Grant of certificate by Secretary of State on referred application or appeal against refusal, I, p. 295.

Stop notices

20. Power to stop further development pending proceedings on enforcement notice I, p. 296.
21. Compensation for loss due to stop notice, I, p. 297.

TOWN AND COUNTRY PLANNING (SCOTLAND) ACT—*continued*

PART III.—APPEALS

PART IV.—ACQUISITION AND DISPOSAL OF LAND

Land acquisition by government departments and local authorities

Planning blight

Disposal of land by public authorities

PART V.—BUILDINGS OF ARCHITECTURAL OR HISTORIC INTEREST

Restrictions on demolition and other works

Owner's and lessee's rights on refusal of consent to works

Enforcement

Other measures open to local planning authority and the Secretary of State

U

V